Routledge International Encyclopedia of Women

Global Women's Issues and Knowledge

Volume 1   Ability—Education: Globalization

Routledge International Encyclopedia of Women

Global Women's Issues and Knowledge

Volume 1   Ability—Education: Globalization

Cheris Kramarae and Dale Spender

General Editors

Routledge

New York • London

Published in 2000 by
Routledge
29 West 35 Street
New York, NY 10001

Routledge is an imprint of the Taylor & Francis Group

Published in Great Britain by
Routledge
11 New Fetter Lane
London EC4P 4EE

Library of Congress Cataloging-in-Publication Data
Routledge international encyclopedia of women: global women's issues and knowledge / general editors, Cheris Kramarae, Dale Spender.
    p. cm.
    Includes bibliographical references and index.
    ISBN 0-415-92088-4 (set) — ISBN 0-415-92089-2 (v.1) —
    ISBN 0-415-92090-6 (v.2) — ISBN 0-415-92091-4 (v.3) —
    ISBN 0-415-92092-2 (v.4)
    1. Women—Encyclopedias. 2. Feminism—Encyclopedias.
I. Title: International encyclopedia of women. II. Kramarea, Cheris. III. Spender, Dale.
HQ1115 .R69 2000
305.4'03—dc21   00-045792

10 9 8 7 6 5 4 3 2 1

ISBN 0-415-92088-4 (4-volume set)
ISBN 0-415-92089-2 (volume 1)
ISBN 0-415-92090-6 (volume 2)
ISBN 0-415-92091-4 (volume 3)
ISBN 0-415-92092-2 (volume 4)

Contents

Alphabetical List of Articles

Topical List of Articles

Note: An article may be listed in more than one topic area.

POLITICS AND THE STATE

Contributors

Pamela Abbott
Glasgow Caledonian University
Scotland
*Androcentrism; Consciousness-raising;
    Essentialism; Feminine mystique;
    Femininity; Gender; Masculinity;
    Other; Sisterhood*

Yaa Abofraa and Ibigail Reid
Atlanta, Georgia
United States
*Health of the women of Rastafari: Case
    study*

Keshia Abraham
Florida International University
United States
Literature: Southern Africa

Margaret Abraham
Hofstra University
United States
Femicide; Infanticide

Evelyne Accad
University of Illinois
United States
*Literature: Arabic; Violence and peace:
    Overview*

Martha Ackelsberg
Smith College
United States
Community politics; Liberalism

Carolina Acosta-Alzuru
University of Georgia
United States
*Images of women: Central and South
    America*

Carol Adams
Writer and activist, Richardson, Texas
United States
Animal rights; Vegetarianism

Bina Agarwal
University of Delhi
India
Environment: South Asia

Amy Agigian
Suffolk University
United States
Infertility

Delia Aguilar
Washington State University
United States
Womanculture

Joanne Ailwood
University of Queensland
Australia
Educators: Preschool

Olabisi Aina
Obafemi Awolowo University
Nigeria
Technology: Women and development

Eileen Aird
Women's Therapy Centre, London
England
Education: Political

Saminaz Akhter
Boston Women's Health Book
    Collective
United States
Health: Overview

Irina Akimushkina
George Washington University
United States
*Women's studies: Commonwealth of
    Independent States*

Salma Al-Khudairi
Planning and development
    consultant, Riyadh
Saudi Arabia
*Development: Middle East and the
    Arab region*

Priscilla Alexander
North American Task Force on
    Prostitution
United States
Sex work

Beverly Allen
Syracuse University
United States
Ethnic cleansing

Edith Almhofer
University of Vienna
Austria
Performance art; Photography

Andaiye
Educator and political activist
Guyana
Cancer

Barbara Watson Andaya
University of Hawaii
United States
Politics and the state: Southeast Asia

Sonya Andermahr
University College Northhampton
England
Science fiction

Bonnie S. Anderson
Brooklyn College and Graduate
    Center, City University of New
    York
United States
*Women's movement: Early
    international movement; Women's
    movement: Modern international
    movement*

Linda Anderson
University of Newcastle upon Tyne
England
Autobiography

Wendy Annecke
University of Cape Town
South Africa
*Alternative energy; Education:
    Southern Africa; Energy*

Paula Arai
Vanderbilt University
United States
Zen

Pat Armstrong
Carleton University
Canada
*Family wage; Maternity leave; Work:
    Equal pay and conditions*

Charon Asetoya
Native American Community Board,
    Lake Andes, South Dakota
United States
Sterilization

Minna Aslama
Finnish Broadcasting Company
Finland
Media and politics

Barbara Aswad
Wayne State University
United States
Polygyny and polyandry

Elyn Aviva
Independent anthropologist and
    writer, Boulder, Colorado
United States
*Music: North Africa and Islamic
    Middle East; Music: Sub-Saharan
    and southern Africa; Tourism*

Pauline Ogho Aweto
African Migrant Women Association,
    Rome
Italy
Feminism: North Africa

Yamila Azize-Vargas
University of Puerto Rico, Cayey
Puerto Rico
Women's studies: Caribbean

Margaret Hope Bacon
Independent scholar, lecturer, and
    author, Kennett Square,
    Pennsylvania
United States
Quakers

Ruth Bailey
Disability researcher, London
England
Disability: Quality of life

Susan Baker
Cardiff University
Wales
Green movement

Cora V. Baldock
Murdoch University
Australia
*Altruism; Charity; Determinism:
    Economic; Economy: Overview;
    Third world; Volunteerism*

Ellen Balka
Simon Fraser University
Canada
Professional societies

Anne Balsamo
Xerox Palo Alto Research Center
United States
Cultural studies; Culture: Overview

Asoka Bandarage
Mount Holyoke College
United States
Multinational corporations

Sarah Banet-Weiser
University of Southern California
United States
Beauty contests and pageants

Adele M. Barker
University of Arizona
United States
Literature: Russia

Paula C. Barnes
Auburn University
United States
Peace movements: North America

D. Rae Barnhisel
Antioch New England Graduate
    School
United States
Plagiarism in science

Caroline Bassett
Sussex University
England
Cyberspace and virtual reality

Susan Bassnett
University of Warwick
England
*Feminism: Second-wave European;
    Literature: Central and South
    America*

Alaka Basu
Cornell University
United States
Health care: South Asia

Martha Bayne
Founding editor, Maxine, Chicago
United States
Zines

Gerlin Bean
3-D Projects, Saint Catherine
Jamaica
Politics and the state: Caribbean

Nasa Begum
University of East London
England
Simultaneous oppressions

Ann Belford Ulanov
Union Theological Seminary
United States
Archetype

Barbara Belmont
National Organization of Gay and
    Lesbian Scientists and Technical
    Professionals (NOGLSTP)
United States
Lesbians in science

Miriam Ben-Yoseph
De Paul University
United States
Entrepreneurship

Susan J. Bender
Skidmore College
United States
Anthropology

Dalida Maria Benfield
School of the Art Institute of Chicago
United States
Video

Joyce Berkman
University of Massachusetts
United States
Feminism: First-wave North American

Elaine Bernard
Harvard Trade Union Program
United States
Union movements

Lorraine Bernotsky
West Chester University
United States
Conservatism

Alison Bernstein
Ford Foundation
United States
Women's studies: Funding

Rosalie Bertell
Concern for Public Health, Toronto
Canada
Radiation

Vicki Bertram
Oxford Brookes University
England
Poetry: Feminist theory and criticism

Jacqueline Bhabha
University of Chicago
United States
Political asylum

Delys Margaret Bird
University of Western Australia
Australia
Detective fiction

Gene Bishop
University of Pennsylvania School of
    Medicine
United States
Medicine: Internal II

Prudence Black
University of Technology, Sydney
Australia
Fashion

Maud Blair
Open University
England
Education: Antiracist

Lori Blewett
Pacific Lutheran University
United States
Blackness and whiteness; Eugenics

Christine Bolt
University of Kent at Canterbury
England
Liberation movements

Barbara I. Bond
Freelance writer, Portland, Oregon
United States
*Biological determinism; Lesbians in
    science*

Gloria Bonder
Centro de Estudios de la Mujer,
    Ministerio de Cultura y Educación
Argentina
*Women's studies: Central and South
    America*

Peg Bortner
Arizona State University
United States
Crime and punishment

Sylvia Bowerbank
McMaster University
Canada
*Science: Early modern to late eighteenth
    century*

Cynthia Bowman
Northwestern University
United States
Law: Feminist critiques

Charlotte Boyle
British Foundation / University of
    Bahrain
England
*Education: Middle East and North
    Africa*

Tone Bratteteig
Universitetet I Oslo
Norway
*Computing: Participatory and feminist
    design*

Virginia Lieson Brereton
Tufts University
United States
*Family: Religious and legal systems—
    Protestant*

Diane Bretherton
University of Melbourne
Australia
*Peace movements: Australia, New
    Zealand, and the Pacific Islands*

Sherry Breyette
City University of New York
United States
Butch/femme

Lyndie Brimstone
University of Surrey Roehampton
England
Feminism: Lesbian

Birgit Brock-Utne
Institute for Educational Research
Norway
Peace education

Somer Brodribb
University of Victoria
Canada
Postmodernism: Feminist critiques

Barbara Brook
Victoria University, St. Albans
Australia
Gender studies

Mikita Brottman
Indiana University
United States
*Cultural criticism; Postcolonialism:
    Theory and criticism*

Mary Ellen Brown
Mars Hill College
United States
*Culture: Women as consumers of
    culture; Culture: Women as
    producers of culture; Oral tradition*

Sam Brown
Journalist, Bangkok
Thailand
Environment: Southeast Asia

Naima Browne
Goldsmith's College, University of
    London
England
Education: Preschool

Lois Bryson
University of Newcastle
Australia
*Economy: Welfare and the economy;
    Political economy; Privatization*

Valerie Bryson
University of Huddersfield
England
Feminism: Marxist

Chilla Bulbeck
University of Adelaide
Australia
Women's studies: Australia

Charlotte Bunch
Rutgers University
United States
Empowerment; Human rights

Leone Burton
University of Birmingham
England
Education: Mathematics

Urvashi Butalia
Kali for Women, New Delhi
India
*Literature: South Asia; Publishing:
    Feminist publishing in the third
    world*

Johnnella Butler
University of Washington
United States
Ethnic studies I

Carolyn Byerly
Ithaca College
United States
Press: Feminist alternatives

Naomi Cahn
George Washington University
United States
Adoption

Kristina Canizares
Food First/ Institute for Food and
    Development Policy
United States
Food, hunger, and famine

Mary Ellen Capek
National Council for Research on
    Women
United States
*Philanthropy; Women's studies: Research
    centers and institutes*

Jane E. Caputi
Florida Atlantic University
United States
Pornography in art and literature

Vicki Carrington
University of Tasmania
Australia
Globalization of education

Alexandra Carter
Middlesex University
England
Dance: Classical

April Carter
University of Queensland
Australia
*Emancipation and liberation
    movements; Feminism: Liberal
    British and European*

Jennifer Casey
Colombus, Ohio
United States
Chastity

Monica Casper
University of California, Santa Cruz
United States
Fetus; Space

Catherine A. Cerny
Virginia Polytechnic Institute
United States
Quilting

Uma Chakravarti
Delhi University
India
Suttee (Sati)

Mariam Chamberlain
National Council for Research on
   Women
United States
*Women's studies: Funding; Women's
   studies: Research centers and
   institutes*

Elsa Chaney
University of Iowa
United States
Household workers; Migration

Rita Charon
Columbia University
United States
Medicine: Internal I

Annie Cheng Jinglan
Jiangmen TV University
China
Violence: East Asia (China) I

Phyllis Chesler
Writer and editor; research scholar,
   Brandeis University
United States
Mental health II

Fanny Mui Ching Cheung
Chinese University of Hong Kong
Hong Kong
Psychology: Social

Julia Ching
University of Toronto
Canada
Confucianism

Jane Cholmeley
Silver Moon Women's Bookshop,
   London
England
Bookshops

Esther Ngan-ling Chow
American University
United States
Feminism: Asian-American

Carol Christ
Ariadne Institute for the Study of
   Myth and Ritual
Greece
Womanspirit

Linda Christian-Smith
University of Wisconsin, Oshkosh
United States
Romantic fiction

Loren Chuse
University of California, Davis
United States
Music: Latin America

M. Kathryn Cirksena
Communications Research
   Consulting, Albany
United States
Gatekeeping

Adele E. Clarke
University of California, San
   Francisco
United States
Reproductive physiology

Sally Cline
Independent research consultant,
   Cambridge
England
Celibacy: Secular

Mary T. Condren
Institute for Feminism and Religion
Ireland
Myth

Sandra Coney
Women's Health Action, Auckland
New Zealand
Hormone replacement therapy

Maryanne Confoy
Jesuit Theological College
Australia
Spirituality: Sexuality

Sara Connell
University of Illinois, Urbana-
   Champaign
United States
Journalism

Kate Connelly
Deakin University
Australia
Exercise and fitness

Patricia Connelly
St. Mary's University
Canada
Development: North America

Maeve Conrick
University College Cork
Ireland
Linguistics

Diana Coole
Queen Mary and Westfield College,
   University of London
England
Critical and cultural theory

Ann Cooper
Putney Inn, Vermont
United States
Cooking

Yvonne Corcoran-Nantes
Flinders University of South Australia
Australia
*Environment: Commonwealth of
   Independent States*

Chris Corrin
University of Glasgow
Scotland
Marxism; Socialism

Carole Counihan
Millersville University
United States
Food and culture

Krista Cowman
University of York
England
Suffrage

Sarah Cox
Writer, Roanoke, Virginia
United States
Education: Southeast Asia

Erin Ryan Croddick
Black Friars Hall, St. Giles, Oxford
 University
England
*Family: Religious and legal systems—
 Catholic and Orthodox*

Barbara Crosby
University of Minnesota
United States
Leadership

Lisa Cuklanz
Boston College
United States
*Communications: Content and
 discourse analysis*

Jan Currie
Murdoch University
Australia
*Development: North America;
 Modernization*

Barbara K. Curry
University of Delaware
United States
*Literature: North America—Note on
 African-American, Latina, and
 Native American Poets; Women's
 centers*

Ramona Curry
University of Illinois
United States
Film theory

Liane Curtis
Brandeis University
United States
Music: Western classical

Susan Cutter
University of South Carolina
United States
Environmental disasters

Sr. Irene Dabalus
Missionary Benedictine Sisters of
 Tutzing
Italy
Celibacy: Religious; Veiling; Virginity

Laura Daly
Editor and writer, Maywood, New
 Jersey
United States
*Nuclear weapons; Pacifism and peace
 activism; Peace movements: Europe*

Susan Danby
Queensland University of Technology
Australia
Gendered play

Eliza Darling
Graduate School, City University of
 New York
United States
Class

Robbie Davis-Floyd
University of Texas at Austin
United States
*Cyborg anthropology; Reproductive
 technologies*

Gaynor Dawson
Murdoch University
Australia
*Child labor; Economy: History of
 women's participation;
 Industrialization*

Jane de Gay
Open University
England
Theater: 1500–1900

Erica De'Ath
National Stepfamily Association,
 London
England
Stepfamilies

Katy Deepwell
University of Ulster, Belfast; Editor,
 n. paradoxa, London
England and Northern Ireland
Art practice: Feminist

Victoria DeFrancisco
University of Northern Iowa
United States
Domestic technology

Anna Lou Dehavenon
Mount Sinai Medical Center, New
 York
United States
*Homelessness; Households and families:
 North America*

Amelia DeLoach
Mobius Group, North Carolina
United States
Grrls

Brenda Dervin
Ohio State University
United States
Communications: Overview

Irene Diamond
University of Oregon
United States
Ecofeminism

Rochelle Diamond
California Institute of Technology
United States
Lesbians in science

Amal Dibo
American University of Beirut
Lebanon
*Peace movements: Middle East and the
 Arab world*

Beth Dingman
New Victoria Publishers, Norwich,
 Vermont
United States
*Publishing: Feminist publishing in the
 western world*

Jennifer Disney
Graduate Center, City University of
   New York
United States
Democracy

Molly Doane
Graduate Center, City University of
   New York
United States
*Environment: Central and South
   America*

Betty Dodson
Independent sex educator, New York
   City
United States
Masturbation

Anne Donchin
Indiana University
United States
Bioethics: Feminist

Wendy Dossett
Trinity College
Wales
Education: Religious studies

Elaine Douglas-Noel
Graduate Center, City University of
   New York
United States
Girl child

Kirstin Dow
University of South Carolina
United States
Environment: North America

Lesley Doyal
University of the West of England,
   Bristol
England
Health challenges

Rosemary Du Plessis
University of Canterbury
New Zealand
Work: Feminist theories

Juliette Dworzak
University of Sierra Leone
Sierra Leone
Education: Sub-Saharan Africa

Susan Dyer-Bennem
Independent scholar, Braintree,
   Massachusetts
United States
Culture: Women as producers of culture

Robin Eagle
Community educator, writer, and
   editor
Australia
Lesbian popular music

Maureen Ebben
St. Mary's University
United States
Networks, electronic

Joanne Eicher
University of Minnesota
United States
Dress

Tatiana Lvovna Eidinova
Journalist and cultural consultant,
   Moscow
Russia
*Households and families:
   Commonwealth of Independent
   States*

Ellen A. F. Eland
George Mason University
United States
Management

Laura Eldridge
Barnard College
United States
The Pill

Mona Lisbet Eliasson
Uppsala University
Sweden
Rape

Gillian Elinor
University of East London
England
Crafts

Jean Bethke Elshtain
University of Chicago
United States
War

Julia V. Emberley
University of Northern British
   Columbia
Canada
Furs

Gloria Emeagwali
Central Connecticut State University
United States
Feminism: Sub-Saharan Africa

Margorie L. Engel
Hamilton Forbes Association, Boston
United States
Divorce

Cynthia Enloe
Clark University
United States
Military

Inger V. Eriksson
University of Türku
Finland
Computer science

Philomena Essed
University of Amsterdam
Netherlands
Political leadership

Eka Esu-Williams
Population Council/Horizons,
   Washington D.C.
United States
AIDS and HIV: Case study—Africa

Judith Evans
University of York
England
Feminism: Second-wave British

Mary Evans
University of Kent
England
Feminism: Existential

Lillian Faderman
California State University, Fresno
United States
Romantic friendship

Jo Ellen Fair
University of Wisconsin, Madison
United States
Images of women: Africa

Karlene Faith
Simon Fraser University
Canada
Criminology

Susan Faludi
Journalist, Los Angeles
United States
Postfeminism

Jennie Farley
Cornell University
United States
Affirmative action

Elizabeth Fay
University of Massachusetts, Boston
United States
Bluestockings

Linda Marie Fedigan
University of Alberta
Canada
Primatology

Elizabeth Fee
National Library of Medicine,
  Baltimore
United States
*Experiments on women; Science:
  Feminist critiques*

Liu Fengquin
China Agricultural University
China
*Development: Chinese case study—
  Rural women*

Albina Peczon Fernandez
University of the Philippines
Philippines
Feminism: Southeast Asia

Myra Marx Ferree
University of Wisconsin
United States
Activism

Lesley Ferris
Ohio State University
United States
*Theater: Overview; Theater: Women in
  theater*

Lynne Fessenden
University of Oregon
United States
Water

Terri Field
University of Queensland
Australia
Global feminism

Margaret J. Finders
Purdue University
United States
Education: North America

Byrgen Finkelman
Freelance Writer and Editor, Tulsa,
  Oklahoma
United States
*Terrorism; Violence: Caribbean;
  Violence: Southeast Asia*

Berenice Fisher
New York University
United States
Caregivers

Pamela Fletcher
Ohio State University
United States
*Fine arts: Painting; Fine arts: Politics of
  representation*

Anne Flintoff
Leeds Metropolitan University
England
Education: Physical

Pamela A. Foresman
University of Virginia
United States
Healers

Dianne Forte
Boston Women's Health Book
  Collective
United States
Health: Overview

Marie Fortune
Center for the Prevention of Sexual
  and Domestic Violence, Seattle,
  Washington
United States
Domestic violence

Mary Frank Fox
Georgia Institute of Technology
United States
Science: Feminism and science studies

Mary Jo Tippeconnic Fox
University of Arizona
United States
*Ancient indigenous cultures: Women's
  roles*

Anne Francis-Okongwu
Queens College, City University of
  New York
United States
Households and families: Overview

Sarah Franklin
Lancaster University
England
Reproductive technologies

Diane Freedman
University of New Hampshire
United States
Autobiographical criticism

Marsha A. Freeman
University of Minnesota
United States
*Nongovernmental organizations
(NGOs)*

Karen Frojen Herrera
Graduate Center, City University of
New York
United States
*Adultery; Initiation rites; Marriage:
Lesbian; Mistress; Motherhood:
Lesbian*

Samantha Frost
University of California at Santa Cruz
United States
Empowerment; Human rights

Adriane Fugh-Berman
National Women's Health Network,
Washington, D.C.
United States
Disease

Kuniko Fujita
Hiroshima University
Japan
Development: Japan

Rudo Gaidzanwa
University of Zimbabwe
Zimbabwe
Politics and the state: Southern Africa

Margaret Gallagher
Media consultant
Ireland
Images of women: Europe

Mary Gallet
Technology, diversity, and synergy
consultant, Oviedo, Florida
United States
Assertiveness training

Kamala Ganesh
University of Mumbai
India
Households and families: South Asia

Viv Gardner
University of Manchester
England
Theater: Modern and contemporary

Jane Gaskell
University of British Columbia
Canada
Education: Gendered subject choice

Ina Mae Gaskin
Farm Midwifery Center,
Summertown, Tennessee
United States
Midwives

Rochelle Gatlin
City College of San Francisco
United States
*Feminism: Second-wave North
American*

Ivone Gebara
Writer, feminist philosopher, and
theologian, Camaragibe
Brazil
Curse; Martyrs; Nuns; Saints

Irene Gedalof
University of North London
England
Hybridity and miscegenation

V. Geetha
Tara Publishing, Chennai
India
Women's studies: South Asia

Suja George
University of Illinois
United States
Violence: North America

Ratna Ghosh
McGill University
Canada
Development: Overview

Mai Ghoussoub
Al Saqi Books, London
England
Feminism: Middle East

Diane Gibson
Australian Institute of Health and
Welfare, Canberra
Australia
Work: Occupational experiences

Ilsa M. Glazer
Kingsborough Community College,
City University of New York
United States
*Family: Religious and legal systems—
Judaic traditions*

Kristina E. Gleeson
Sakkara Language School, Cairo
Egypt
Trafficking

Ivy Glennon
Eastern Illinois University
United States
Knowledge; Naming

Aruna Gnanadason
World Council of Churches, Geneva
Switzerland
*Christianity: Status of women in the
church*

Rashmi Goel
University of Tulsa
United States
Indigenous women's rights

Suzanne Goh
Harvard Medical School
United States
Elderly care: Western world

Vesna Goldsworthy
Birkbeck College, University of
London
England
Literature: Eastern Europe

Sharon Golub
College of New Rochelle
United States
Menarche

Savitri Goonesekere
Open University of Sri Lanka
Sri Lanka
Family: Religious and legal systems—
Buddhist traditions

Tuula Gordon
University of Tampere
Finland
Single people; Spinster

Jennifer L. Gossett
University of Cincinnati
United States
Education: Adult and continuing;
Education: Single-sex and
coeducation; Education: Vocational

Laurel Graham
University of South Florida
United States
Nutrition and home economics

Eileen Green
Sheffield Hallam University
England
Leisure

Judy Green
Marymount University
United States
Mathematics

Lucy Green
University of London
England
Music: Education

Judy Greenway
University of East London
England
Feminism: Anarchist

Jeanne Gregory
Middlesex University
England
Legal systems

Mary Grey
Sarum College
England
Misogyny

Gabriele Griffin
Kingston University
England
Lesbian writing: Overview; Modernism

Natalia Grigorieva
Moscow School of Social and
    Economic Studies
Russia
Health care: Commonwealth of
Independent States

Jean Grimshaw
University of the West of England
England
Epistemology; Philosophy

Isobel Grundy
University of Alberta
Canada
Feminism: Eighteenth century

Zoubida Guernina
Thames Valley University
England
Sexuality: Adolescent sexuality;
Sexuality: Psychology of sexuality in
cross-cultural perspectives

Ma Guihua
China Features, Beijing
China
Elderly care: Case study—China

Leela Gulati
Centre for Development Studies,
    Kerala
India
Elderly care: Case study—India

Kirstin Gulling
Attorney, Johnson and Gulling,
    Minneapolis
United States
Law and sex

Lisa Gundry
De Paul University
United States
Entrepreneurship

Sneja Gunew
University of British Columbia
Canada
Multiculturalism

Jayoti Gupta
Independent research scholar, New
    Delhi
India
Dowry and brideprice

Solveig Hagglund
Göteborg University
Sweden
Gender constructions in the family

Melanie Hahn
Journalist and medical writer, New
    York
United States
RU 486; Traditional healing: Africa I;
Traditional healing: Central and
South America and the Caribbean;
Traditional healing: East and
southeast Asia

Ilse Hakvoort
Göteborg University
Sweden
Gender construction in the family

Laura Hanish
Arizona State University
United States
Child development

Jalna Hanmer
University of Sunderland
England
Abuse; Violence: Western Europe

Gillian Hanscombe
University of Exeter
England
Lesbian writing: Contemporary poetry;
Poetry: Overview

Jarice Hanson
University of Massachusetts
United States
Information technology

Pamela Harris
Griffith University
Australia
Environment: Pacific Islands

Patricia Harris
Murdoch University
Australia
Poverty

Jane Harrison
Murdoch University
Australia
Finance

Delia Hart
Queensland University of Technology
Australia
Discipline in schools

Maria Ramona Hart
Graduate Center, City University of
    New York
United States
*Daughter; Division of labor;
    Grandmother; Mother; Sister; Wife*

Vivien Hart
University of Sussex
England
Constitutions

Betsy Hartmann
Hampshire College
United States
Population control

Evelyn Hartogh
University of Queensland
Australia
Heterophobia and homophobia

Mary Hawkesworth
Rutgers University
United States
Government

Susan Hawthorne
Victoria University of Technology
Australia
Fiction

Debbie Heck
Griffith University
Australia
Natural resources

Frances Heidensohn
Goldsmiths College, University of
    London
England
Law enforcement

Renee Heller
Ecofys Energy and Environment
Netherlands
Physical sciences

Laura Hershey
Writer, editor, and activist, Denver,
    Colorado
United States
Disability: Health and sexuality

Kristin Herzog
Independent Scholars' Association of
    the North Carolina Triangle
United States
*Peace movements: Central and South
    America*

Leslie Heywood
State University of New York,
    Binghamton
United States
Girl studies

Carrie Hintz
Queen's College, City University of
    New York
United States
Utopian writing

Nancy J. Hirschmann
Cornell University
United States
*Equality; Feminism: Liberal North
    American*

Janet Holland
Open University
England
Equal Opportunities: Education

Phyllis Holman Weisbard
University of Wisconsin
United States
Reference sources

Renee C. Hoogland
University of Nijmegen
Netherlands
Lesbian cultural criticism

Jude Howell
University of Sussex
England
Politics and the state: East Asia

Jolan Hsieh
Arizona State University
United States
Crime and punishment

Julie Hucke
Miami University
United States
Girls' subcultures; Magazines

Tori Hudson
Natural College of Naturopathic
    Medicine
United States
Breast

Joan E. Huebl
Catalyst Consulting Group,
    La Crescenta, California
United States
*Adolescence; Depression; Drug and
    alcohol abuse; Psychology:
    Developmental; Psychology:
    Neuroscience and brain research;
    Suicide*

Maggie Humm
University of East London
England
Feminism: Overview

Mary Elizabeth Hunt
Women's Alliance for Theology,
    Ethics, and Ritual (WATER),
    Silver Spring, Maryland
United States
Women-church

Geraldine Hutchinson
CfBT Education Services
England
Education: Domestic science and home economics

Janet Shibley Hyde
University of Wisconsin
United States
Contraception

Prue Hyman
Victoria University of Wellington
New Zealand
Development: Australia and New Zealand

Lici Inge
University of Sydney
Australia
Education: Higher education

Chrys Ingraham
Russell Sage College
United States
Weddings

Sherrie A. Inness
Miami University
United States
Girls' subcultures; Magazines

Merete Ipsen
Women's Museum
Denmark
Archaeology: Northern European case study

Lisa Isherwood
University College of St. Mark and St. John
England
Heresy

Radha Iyer
University of Queensland
Australia
Education: South Asia

Tamara Jacka
Murdoch University
Australia
Development: China

Lynnette Jackson
Barnard College
United States
Violence: Sub-Saharan and southern Africa

Stevi Jackson
University of York
England
Households: Domestic consumption; Romance

Sue Jackson
University of Surrey, Roehampton
England
Women's studies: Western Europe

Devaki Jain
Development Alternatives with Women for a New Era (DAWN)
India
DAWN movement

Joy James
Brown University
United States
Feminism: African-American

Sue Curry Jansen
Muhlenberg College
United States
Censorship

Sheila Jeffreys
University of Melbourne
Australia
Sexual slavery

Ma Jiang
Center for Science and Technology, Beijing
China
Environment: East Asia (China)

Jane Juffer
University of Illinois at Urbana-Champaign
United States
Erotica

Chatsumarn Kabilsingh
Thammasat University
Thailand
Buddhism

Agnieszka Kajrukszto
Graduate Center, City University of New York
United States
Households and families: Central and eastern Europe

Kalpana Kannabiran
Asmita Resource Centre for Women, Secunderabad
India
Caste

Musimbi R.A. Kanyoro
World Young Women's Christian Association
Switzerland
Matriarchy

Rehana Kapadia
London
England
Feminism: British Asian

Gisela Kaplan
University of New England
Australia
Development: Western Europe; Ethnicity

Naina Kapur
Sakshi Violence Intervention Centre, New Delhi
India
Family law: Case study—India

Azza Karam
Queens University of Belfast
Northern Ireland
Politics and the state: Middle East and North Africa

Ellyn Kaschak
San Jose State University
United States
*Psychology: Psychopathology and
    psychotherapy*

Judit Katona-Apte
United Nations World Food
    Programme, Rome
Italy
Refugees

Gloria Kaufman
Indiana University, South Bend
United States
Humor

Yasuko Kawashima
National Institute for Environmental
    Studies
Japan
Environment: East Asia (Japan)

Govind Kelkar
Asian Institute of Technology
Thailand
Witches: Asia

Mona Khalaf
Lebanese American University
Lebanon
*Women's studies: Middle East and
    North Africa*

Natalia V. Khodyreva
St. Petersburg State University
Russia
*Violence: Commonwealth of
    Independent States*

Tseen-Ling Khoo
University of Queensland
Australia
*Multiculturalism: Arts, literature, and
    popular culture*

Catherine King
Open University
England
Genres: Gendered; Representation

Jean King
University of Massachusetts Medical
    Center
United States
Health careers; Stress

Ros King
University of London
England
Drama

Gill Kirkup
Open University
England
Education: Distance education

Elizabeth Arveda Kissling
Eastern Washington University
United States
Sexual harassment; Street harassment

Gunilla Kleiverda
Netwerk Vrouwelijke Gynaecologen,
    Amsterdam
Netherlands
Gynecology

Mary Knighton
University of California at Berkeley
United States
Literature: Japan

Fukuko Kobayashi
Waseda University
Japan
Literature: Japan

Wendy Kolmar
Drew University
United States
Feminism: Nineteenth century

Leslie Korn
Center for World Indigenous Studies,
    Olympia, Washington
United States
*Science: Traditional and indigenous
    knowledge; Traditional healing:
    Aboriginal Australia; Traditional
    healing: Africa II*

Georgia Kornbluth
Writer and editor, New York
United States
*Aesthetics: Black feminist—A debate;
    Literature: Australia, New Zealand,
    and the Pacific Islands; Literature:
    Sub-Saharan Africa*

Natalya Kosmarskaya
Moscow Center for Gender Studies
Russia
*Politics and the state: Commonwealth
    of Independent States*

Cheris Kramarae
University of Oregon
United States
*Ability; Education: On-line;
    Information revolution; Shakers*

Brinlee Kramer
Naturopathic Physician, Beaverton,
    Oregon
United States
*Breast feeding; Cosmetics; Holistic
    health II; Nutrition II*

Nancy Krieger
Harvard School of Public Health
United States
*Hypertension: Case Study—Class, race,
    and gender*

P. Pratap Kumar
University of Durban-Westville
South Africa
Hinduism

Junko Kuninobu
Aichi Shukutoku University
Japan
Women's studies: East Asia

Insook Kwon
Harvard University
United States
Feminism: Korea

Michele LaBella
Catalyst, New York
United States
Engineering

Sue A. Lafky
University of Iowa
United States
Journalists

Marilyn Lake
La Trobe University
Australia
Feminism: Australia and New Zealand

Sue Lambert
Murdoch University
Australia
Development: Australia and New Zealand

Kyra Marie Landzelius
Gothenburg University
Sweden
Medical control of women

Barbara Larson
University of New Hampshire
United States
Households and families: Middle East and North Africa

Maria Lauret
University of Sussex
England
Literature: North America

Galina Laurie
University of Sydney
Australia
Pedagogy: Feminist II

Jacqueline Leavitt
University of California, Los Angeles
United States
Housing

Ruth E. Lechte
Energy and Environment/
    Appropriate Technology
Fiji
Violence: Australia, New Zealand, and the Pacific Islands

Judy Ledgerwood
Northern Illinois University
United States
Households and families: Southeast Asia

Anru Lee
California State University, Sacramento
United States
Households and families: East Asia; Patriarchy: Development

Elaine Leeder
Ithaca College
United States
Anarchism

Sue Lees
University of North London
England
Sexual violence

Beverly Leipert
University of Northern British Columbia
Canada
Health care: Canada

Winnie Lem
Trent University
Canada
Households and families: Western Europe

Jennifer Lemon
University of South Africa
South Africa
Feminism: South Africa

Ronit Lentin
Trinity College
Ireland
Genocide

Debbie Lerman
Coalition of Women and Peace, Tel Aviv
Israel
Peace movements: Israel

Tobe Levin
University of Maryland, European Division
Germany
Feminism: Jewish

Ruth Levitas
University of Bristol
England
Utopianism

Sheila Lewenhak
University of London
England
Economic status: Comparative analysis

Reina Lewis
University of East London
England
Queer theory

Angela Liberatore
European Commission DG XII
Belgium
Environment: Western Europe

Hilary Lim
University of East London
England
Justice and rights

Karin E. Limburg
College of Environmental Science and Forestry, State University of New York
United States
Ecosystem

L. H. M. Ling
Institute of Social Studies
Netherlands
Hypermasculinity

Catherine Lloyd
University of Oxford
England
Antiracist and civil rights movements

Ann Loades
University of Durham
England
Creed

Barbara Logue
Mississippi Institutions of Higher
 Learning
United States
Ethics: Medical; Euthanasia

Asphodel Long
University College of St. Mark and
 St. John
England
Goddess

Erica Longfellow
Lincoln College, Oxford University
England
Literature: Overview

Antoinette Sedillo Lopez
University of New Mexico
United States
*Education: Central and South America
 and the Caribbean; Health care:
 Central and South America and the
 Caribbean*

Maria Lord
Independent scholar and writer,
 London
England
Music: South Asia

JoAnn Loulan
Marriage family counselor, writer,
 and political activist, Portola
 Valley, California
United States
Lesbian sexuality

Joni Lovenduski
Birkbeck College, University of
 London
England
Political parties

Christine Lucia
Rhodes University, Grahamstown
South Africa
Musicians

Rashmi Luthra
University of Michigan at Dearborn
United States
Images of women: Asia

Helma Lutz
University of Münster
Germany
Eurocentrism

Carol MacCormack
Bryn Mawr College
United States
Nature

Martha MacDonald
Saint Mary's University
Canada
Abortion; Economics: Feminist critiques

Mia MacDonald
International Women's Health
 Coalition, New York
United States
Reproductive health

Martha MacIntyre
University of Melbourne
Australia
*Health care: Australia, New Zealand,
 and the Pacific Islands*

Alison Mackinnon
University of South Australia
Australia
Computing: Overview; Demography

Frinde Maher
Wheaton College
United States
Pedagogy: Feminist I

Veronique Maingi-Dozier
Georgetown University
United States
Digital divide

Helen Malson
University of Western Sydney,
 Nepean
Australia
Eating disorders

Amina Mama
University of Cape Town
South Africa
Women's studies: Sub-Saharan Africa

Sr. Mary John Mananzan
St. Scholastica's College
Philippines
Spirituality: Overview

Chris Mann
Cambridge University
England
*Education: Achievement; Research:
 On-line*

Christel Manning
Sacred Heart University
United States
Fundamentalism: Religious

Takyiwaa Manuh
University of Ghana
Ghana
*Family: Religious and legal systems—
 West Africa*

Sylvia Marcos
Centro de Investigaciones
 Psicoetnologicas
Mexico
Sex: Beliefs and customs

Carine M. Mardorossian
University of Illinois at Urbana-
 Champaign
United States
Sexual difference

Miriam E. Martin
Goshen College
United States
Nursing

Rosy Martin
Phototherapist, artist, writer, and
 lecturer, London
England
Phototherapy

Maria Mastronardi
University of Illinois at Chicago
United States
Youth culture

**Yelena Vladimirovna Mayakovska
(Patricia J. Thompson)**
Lehman College, City University of
New York
United States
*Households and families:
Commonwealth of Independent
States*

Shoshanna Mayer-Young
University of Haifa
Israel
Education: Nonsexist

Katherine McCaffrey
John Jay College of Criminal Justice,
City University of New York
United States
Bigamy; Households: Resources

Mary McCullough
West Chester University
United States
Friendship

Judith McDaniel
University of Arizona
United States
*Lesbianism; Lesbians: HIV prevalence
and transmission; Sexual orientation*

Dorothea McEwan
University of London
England
Death

Jane McGary
Freelance editor, Estacada, Oregon
United States
*Agriculture; Environment: Australia
and New Zealand; Heroine; Interior
design and decoration*

Patrice McMahon
LeHigh University
United States
*Development: Commonwealth of
Independent States*

Pearlie McNeill
Writer, Woonona, New South Wales
Australia
Short story

Beatrice Medicine
California State University,
Northridge
United States
*Family: Religious and legal systems—
Native North America; Households
and families: Native North
America; Socialization for
complementarity; Traditional
healing: Native North America*

Eileen Meehan
University of Arizona
United States
Advertising industry

Joan Mencher
Lehman College, City University of
New York
United States
*Households: Female-headed and
female-supported*

Cecilia Menjivar
Arizona State University
United States
Immigration

Padma Menon
Mudra Dance, The Hague
Netherlands
Dance: South Asia

Susan V. Meschel
University of Chicago
United States
Science: Ancient and medieval

Andrée Michel
National Center of Scientific
Research, Paris
France
Disarmament

Magda Michielsens
University of Antwerp
Belgium
Violence: Media

Maria Mies
Fachschule Köln
Germany
Economy: Global restructuring

Angela Miles
University of Toronto
Canada
Feminism: Cultural

Jennifer Milioto
University of Chicago
United States
Music: East Asia

Sara Mills
Sheffield Hallam University
England
Language; Travel writing

Ivana Milojevic
University of Queensland
Australia
Future studies

Barbara Mintzes
Health Action International, Europe
Netherlands
Pharmaceuticals

Kalpana Misra
University of Tulsa
United States
Politics and the state: South Asia II

Mori Mizue
International Institute for the Study
of Religions
Japan
Shinto

Valentine M. Moghadam
Illinois State University
United States
Fundamentalism and public policy;
Revolutions

Patricia Mohammed
University of the West Indies
Jamaica
Feminism: Caribbean

Isabel Molina Guzman
University of Pennsylvania
United States
Images of women: Caribbean

Maxine Molyneux
University of London
England
Interests: Strategic and practical

Janet Henshall Momsen
University of California
United States
Environment: Caribbean

Kathleen Montgomery
Illinois Wesleyan University
United States
Politics and the state: Eastern Europe

Lisa Jean Moore
College of Staten Island, City
University of New York
United States
Safer sex; Space

Barbara Mor
Writer and independent scholar,
Portland, Oregon
United States
Androgyny

Regina Markell Morantz-Sanchez
University of Michigan
United States
Surgery

Sandra Morgen
University of Oregon
United States
Scientific sexism and racism

Jenny Morris
Freelance researcher and writer,
London
England
Disability and feminism

Joy Florence Morrison
University of Alaska at Fairbanks
United States
Radio

Mairi Morrison
New College, Oxford University
England
Family law

Deborah Moskowitz
McGill University
Canada
Psychology: Personality research

Gemma Moss
University of Southampton
England
Literacy

Negar Mottahedeh
University of Minnesota
United States
Images of women: Middle East

Marie Mulvey-Roberts
St. Matthias University of West
England
England
Feminism: First-wave British

Margie Mulela Munalula
University of Zambia
Zambia
Family: Religious and legal systems—
Southern Africa

Sally Munt
University of Brighton
England
Lesbian writing: Crime fiction

M. Lynne Murphy
Baylor University
United States
Race

Patricia Murphy
Open University
England
Examinations and assessment

Caryn McTighe Musil
Association of American Colleges and
Universities
United States
Women's studies: Overview; Women's
studies: United States

Meredith Nachman
New York University
United States
Anorexia nervosa

Vahida Nainar
Women's Caucus for Gender Justice
United States
Torture

Suniti Namjoshi
University of Exeter
England
Lesbian writing: Contemporary poetry;
Poetry: Overview

Sarah Neal
Filmmaker and writer, Melbourne
Australia
Film

Retha R. Newbold
National Institute of Environmental
Health Sciences
United States
Toxicology

Celeste Newbrough
San Francisco College
United States
Cloning

Janice Newton
University of Ballarat
Australia
Households and families: Melanesia
and aboriginal Australia

Irene Nørlund
Copenhagen University
Denmark
Economy: Informal

Mary W. Norris
Philadelphia
United States
Health: Overview

Lucy O'Brien
Writer and journalist, London
England
Music: Anglo-American folk; Music: Rock and pop; Music: Soul, jazz, rap, blues, and gospel

Mary O'Brien
Environmental Research Foundation
United States
Pollution: Chemical

Marjorie Och
Mary Washington College
United States
Fine arts: Overview

Gina Ogden
Harvard University
United States
Sexuality: Overview

Miho Ogino
Osaka University
Japan
Aging: Japanese case study

Mary Okumu
Feed the Children, Kenya
Kenya
Sexuality in Africa

Gerda Johanna Olafsen
Inala Uniting Church, Queensland
Australia
Guilt

Gail Omvedt
University of Pune
India
Households: Political economy

Gloria Feman Orenstein
University of Southern California
United States
Gyn/Ecology

Collette Oseen
Athabasca University
Canada
Organizational theory

Sanàa Osseiran
IPRA Representative to UNESCO
France
Conflict resolution: Mediation and negotiation

Norani Othman
Universiti Kebangsaan Malaysia
Malaysia
Islam

Nelly Oudshoorn
University Twente
Netherlands
Hormones

Jenny Owen
University of Sheffield
England
Automation

Ingar Palmlund
Tufts University
United States
Endocrine disruption; Environment: Overview; Estrogen; Population: Overview

Rajni Palriwala
University of Delhi
India
Family: Power relations and power structures; Family: Property relations

Hanna Papanek
Harvard University
United States
Socialization for inequality

Zarana Papic
University of Belgrade
Yugoslavia
Violence: Central and Eastern Europe

Sharon Parker
Union Institute, Washington D.C.
United States
Community

Mary Brown Parlee
Massachusetts Institute of Technology
United States
Psychology: Overview

Pratibha Parmar
Independent filmmaker, London
England
Feminism: British Asian

Jane Parpart
Dalhousie University
Canada
Postmodernism and development

Reena Patel
Warwick University
England
Politics and the state: South Asia I

Vibhuti Patel
Centre for Enquiry into Health and Allied Themes (CEHAT)
India
Sex selection; Violence: South Asia

Gloria Pedroza
Calabasas, California
United States
Psychology: Cognitive

Cathy Peppers
Idaho State University
United States
Curse; Martyrs; Nuns; Saints; Vodou

Charmaine Pereira
Center for Research and
    Documentation, Kano
Nigeria
*Politics and the state: Sub-Saharan
    Africa*

Beverley Perel
Consultant, Barden, Queensland
Australia
International Women's Day

Rosalind Petchesky
Hunter College, City University of
    New York
United States
Reproductive rights

Jan Jindy Pettman
Australian National University
Australia
Femocrat; International relations

Ann Phoenix
Open University
England
Identity politics

Jane Pincus
Boston Women's Health Book
    Collective
United States
Childbirth

Renee Pittin
Institute of Social Studies
Netherlands
*Households and families: Sub-Saharan
    Africa*

Sara Poggio
University of Maryland, Baltimore
    County
United States
Feminism: Central and South America

Teresa L. Polowy
University of Arizona
United States
Literature: Ukraine

Iva Popovicova
Rutgers University
United States
*Women's studies: Central and eastern
    Europe*

Ros Posel
University of Natal
South Africa
Reproduction: Overview

Cheryl-Ann Potgieter
University of the Western Cape
South Africa
Women's studies: Southern Africa

Andrea Press
University of Illinois
United States
Communications: Audience analysis

Rosemary Pringle
Griffith University
Australia
Power

Priscilla Qolisaya Puamau
Fiji College of Advanced Education
Fiji
*Education: Central Pacific and South
    Pacific Islands*

Marilyn Pukkila
Colby College
United States
Wicca

Jasjit Purewal
Sakshi Violence Intervention Centre,
    New Delhi
India
Family law: Case study—India

June Purvis
University of Portsmouth
England
Feminism: Militant

Kathryn Pyne Addelson
Smith College
United States
Ethics: Scientific

Carolyn Quadrio
Caroline Quadrio Pty/Ltd, New
    South Wales
Australia
Psychiatry

Robyn Quin
Edith Cowan University
Australia
*Images of women: Australia and New
    Zealand*

Sarah A. Radcliffe
University of Cambridge
England
*Politics and the state: Central and
    South America*

Shirin M. Rai
University of Warwick
England
*Colonialism and postcolonialism;
    Communism; Politics and the state:
    Overview*

Caroline Ramazanoglu
Goldsmiths College, University of
    London
England
Liberation

Annette B. Ramirez de Arellano
National Medical Fellowships
United States
Ageism; Aging

Vicky Randall
University of Bergen
Norway
Politics and the state: Western Europe

Viviana Rangil
Skidmore College
United States
Feminism: Chicana

Matshediso Rankoe
Trauma Centre for Survivors of
    Violence and Torture, Cape Town
South Africa
Health care: Southern Africa

Elayne Rapping
State University of New York, Buffalo
United States
Media: Mainstream

Nora Rathzel
University of Umea
Sweden
Racism and xenophobia

Sundari Ravindran
Achutha Menon Centre for Health
     Science Studies
India
Family planning

Nancy Reame
University of Michigan
United States
*Life cycle; Menstruation; Premenstrual
     syndrome (PMS)*

Audrey Rebera
SCM Office
Sri Lanka
Taboo

Rhoda Reddock
University of the West Indies
Trinidad and Tobago
Households and families: Caribbean

Layne Redmond
Independent scholar and musician,
     Chiefland, Florida
United States
Drumming

Lori Reed
University of Rhode Island
United States
Silence

Gail Reekie
Australian National University
Australia
Commodity culture

Jo Reger
Skidmore College
United States
Women's movement: United States

Shulamit Reinharz
Brandeis University
United States
Social sciences: Feminist methods

Barbara Reskin
Harvard University
United States
Stereotypes

Mary Judith Ress
Colectivo Con-spirando, Santiago
Chile
Witches: Western world

Kimberly Reynolds
University of Surrey
England
Children's literature

Pilar Riano
University of British Columbia
Canada
Media: Grassroots

Esther Mary Rice
University of Sydney
Australia
Education: Higher education

Evelleen Richards
University of Sydney
Australia
Evolution

Darlene S. Richardson
Indiana University of Pennsylvania
United States
*Science: Nineteenth century; Science:
     Twentieth century*

Judith Richter
Health professional, sociologist, and
     activist, Tübingen
Germany
Contraceptives: Development

Sheila Riddell
University of Glasgow
Scotland
Education: Special needs

Eva Rieger
University of Bremen
Germany
Music: Opera

Carla Risseeuw
University of Leiden
Netherlands
Kinship

Hilary Robinson
University of Ulster
Northern Ireland
*Fine arts: Criticism and art history;
     Fine arts: Sculpture and installation*

Victoria Robinson
University of Sheffield
England
Men's studies

Belinda Robson
University of Melbourne
Australia
Biography

Esther Rome
Boston Women's Health Book
     Collective
United States
Cosmetic surgery

Birgit Rommelspacher
Alice-Salomon-Fachhochschule für
     Sozialarbeit und Sozialpädagogi
Germany
Anti-Semitism; Fascism and Nazism

Melody Rose
Portland State University
United States
Pro-choice movement

Loretta Ross
National Center for Human Rights
 Education, Atlanta, Georgia
United States
*Eugenics: African-American case
 study—Eugenics and family
 planning*

Sue V. Rosser
Georgia Institute of Technology
United States
Science: Feminist philosophy

Margot Roth
Wellington
New Zealand
Women's studies: New Zealand

Alice Rothchild
Harvard Vanguard Medical
 Association
United States
Obstetrics

Paula Rothenberg
William Paterson College of New
 Jersey
United States
Curriculum transformation movement

Joyce Rothschild
Virginia Tech
United States
Hierarchy and bureaucracy

Robin Rowland
Deakin University
Australia
Surrogacy

Erica Royston
World Health Organization
Switzerland
Maternal health and morbidity

Jill Rubery
University of Manchester Institute of
 Science and Technology
England
Underemployment; Unemployment

Rosemary Ruether
Garrett Evangelical Theological
 Seminary
United States
Creation stories; Deity

Karen Ruhleder
University of Illinois
United States
Networks, electronic

Ramona Rush
University of Kentucky
United States
Networking

Letty Russell
Yale Divinity School
United States
Theologies: Feminist

Ann Russo
De Paul University
United States
Pornography and violence

Susan Rutherford
University of Manchester
England
Theater: Modern and contemporary

Vickie Rutledge Shields
Bowling Green State University
United States
Advertising

Sheryl Burt Ruzek
Temple University
United States
Health care: United States

Katherine Ryan
University of Illinois
United States
Psychology: Psychometrics

Marilyn P. Safir
University of Haifa
Israel
Kibbutz

Khadiga M. Safwat
Middle Eastern and African Research
 Centre/Wales
Wales
Environment: North Africa

Diane Sainsbury
University of Stockholm
Sweden
Welfare

Sara Salih
Wadham College, Oxford University
England
Postmodernism: Literary theory

JoAn A. Saltzen
Writer and researcher, Pollock Pines,
 California
United States
Armament and militarization

Rhian Samuel
University of Reading
England
Music: Composers

Nelia Sancho
Asian Women's Human Rights
 Council, Manila Office
Philippines
Peace movements: Asia

Bernice R. Sandler
National Association for Women in
 Education
United States
*Education: Chilly climate in the
 classroom*

Lisa Sanmiguel
University of Illinois at Urbana-
 Champaign
United States
*Communications: Speech; Images of
 women: North America*

Jo Sanson
Graduate Center, City University of
 New York
United States
Citizenship; Heterosexuality

N. B. Sarojini
Jagori Women's Documentation,
    Training, and Communication
    Centre, New Delhi
India
Traditional healing: India

Irma Saucedo Gonzalez
Colegio de México
Mexico
Body

Mira Savara
SHAKTI, Mumbai
India
Sexuality in Hindu culture

Marian Sawer
Australian National University
Australia
*Antidiscrimination; Discrimination;
    Equal opportunities; Equity;
    Nepotism; Politics and the state:
    Australia, New Zealand, and the
    Pacific Islands*

Elizabeth Schafer
Independent scholar, Loachapoka,
    Alabama
United States
Ethnic studies II

Londa Schiebinger
Penn State University
United States
Nature-nurture debate

Ana Maria Schluter Rodes
Zen master, Community of Bethany
Spain
Mysticism

Frauke Schnell
West Chester University
United States
Conservatism

Rosa Schnyer
University of Arizona
United States
*Depression: Case study—Chinese
    medicine*

Debra Schultz
Open Society Institute
United States
Women's studies: Backlash

Muriel Schulz
California State University at
    Fullerton
United States
Women: Terms for women

Karla D. Scott
Saint Louis University
United States
Womanism

Sheila Scraton
Leeds Metropolitan University
England
Education: Physical

Joni Seager
University of Vermont
United States
Census; Geography; Pollution

Karen Seago
University of North London
England
Literature: Western Europe

Barbara Seaman
National Women's Health Network;
    contributing editor, MS. Magazine
United States
Norplant; The Pill

Lynne Segal
Feminist Review
England
Feminism: Socialist

Ellen Seiter
University of California, San Diego
United States
Television

Susan Sellers
University of St. Andrews
Scotland
Difference I; Écriture féminine

Thalatha Seneviratne
Australian Agency for International
    Development
Australia
Development: South Asia

Aysan Sev'er
University of Toronto
Canada
Incest

A. M. Shah
University of Delhi
India
Family structures

Sr. Margaret Shanthi Stephens
St. Joseph Hospital Community,
    Tamilnadu
India
Holy Spirit; Shakti

Renuka Sharma
University of Melbourne
Australia
Feminism: South Asia

Simona Sharoni
American University
United States
Zionism

Rose Shayo
University of Dar es Salaam
Tanzania
*Alternative technology: Case study—
    Africa*

Joanne Sheehan
War Resisters League, Norwich,
    Connecticut
United States
Nonviolence

Susan Sheridan
Flinders University
Australia
Popular culture

Joyce Sherlock
De Montfort University Bedford
England
Sport

Vandana Shiva
Research Foundation for Science,
	Technology, and Ecology, New
	Delhi
India
*Environment: South Asian case study—
	Forests in India; Nature: Philosophy
	and spirituality*

Diana Laskin Siegal
Massachusetts Department of Public
	Health
United States
Long-term care services

Cathy Silber
Williams College
United States
Literature: China

Felly Nkweto Simmonds
University of Northumbria
England
Film criticism

Jen Skattebol
University of Western Sydney
Australia
Pedagogy: Feminist

Jirina Smejkalova
Central European University
Hungary
Feminism: Eastern Europe

Laurajane Smith
University of York
England
Archaeology

Beatrice Smulders
Birth Center, Amsterdam
Netherlands
Pregnancy and birth

Katherine Snyder
Queens College, City University of
	New York
United States
*Family: Religious and legal systems—
	East Africa*

Zoann Snyder
Western Michigan University
United States
*Crime and punishment: Case study—
	Women in prisons in the United
	States*

Izabel Soliman
University of New England
Australia
Educators: Higher education

Carron Somerset
End Child Prostitution, Pornography,
	and Trafficking (ECPAT, UK)
England
Slavery

Tamsin Spargo
Liverpool John Moores University
England
Literary theory and criticism

Dale Spender
Australian Interactive Multimedia
	Industry Association, Sydney
Australia
Ability; Diaries and journals; Novel

Lynne Spender
Australian Interactive Multimedia
	Industry Association, Sydney
Australia
Money

Wendy A. Spinks
Science University of Tokyo
Japan
Teleworking

Charlene Spretnak
California Institute of Integral
	Studies in San Francisco
United States
Gaia hypothesis

Judith Squires
University of Bristol
England
*Political participation; Political
	representation*

Annabelle Sreberny
University of Leicester
England
Globalization

Beth Stafford
University of Illinois at Urbana-
	Champaign
United States
*Libraries; Third world women: Selected
	resources*

Patricia Stamp
York University
Canada
Sexism

Mary Zeiss Stange
Skidmore College
United States
Christianity; Hunting; Mormons

Autumn Stanley
Independent scholar, Portola Valley,
	California
United States
Inventors

Liz Stanley
University of Manchester
England
*Anger; Feminism: Radical; Gay pride;
	Heterosexism; Phallocentrism;
	Slogans: "The personal is the
	political"; Sociology; Universalism;
	Woman-centeredness*

Susan Leigh Star
University of California, San Diego
United States
Science: Overview; Technology

Anna Starzewska-Sikorska
Institute for Ecology of Industrial
    Areas
Poland
*Environment: Central and eastern
    Europe*

Daiva Stasiulis
Carleton University
Canada
Settler societies

Kathleen Staudt
University of Texas at El Paso
United States
Borders

Jennifer Steinberg
National Geographic Magazine
United States
*Environment: Sub-Saharan and
    southern Africa*

Linda Steiner
Rutgers University
United States
Media: Alternative

Jeanne Mager Stellman
Columbia University
United States
Occupational health and safety

Ann Stewart
University of Warwick
England
Personal and customary laws

Fiona Stewart
Real World Research and
    Communications, Melbourne
Australia
*Feminism: Third-wave; Humanities
    and social sciences: Feminist
    critiques; Life expectancy; Research:
    Online*

Deborah Stienstra
University of Winnipeg
Canada
Social movements

Maila Stivens
University of Melbourne
Australia
Women's studies: Southeast Asia

Sandy Stone
University of Texas at Austin
United States
Transgender

Merl Storr
University of East London
England
Bisexuality

Doris Strahm
Feminist theologian, Basel
Switzerland
Christianity: Feminist Christology

Jean A. S. Strauss
Writer, Silver Spring, Maryland
United States
Adoption: Mental health issues

Nelly Stromquist
University of Southern California
United States
*Development: Central and South
    America and the Caribbean*

Banu Subramaniam
University of Arizona
United States
Biology

Mangala Subramaniam
University of Connecticut
United States
Activism

Julia Sudbury
Mills College
United States
Feminism: Black British

Shehnaaz Suliman
Medical doctor
South Africa and United States
*Households and families: Southern
    Africa*

Yifat Susskind
MADRE, New York
United States
Violence: Central and South America

Mina Swaminathan
M. S. Swaminathan Research
    Foundation, Chennai
India
Child care

Marja-Liisa Swantz
University of Helsinki
Finland
*Development: Sub-Saharan and
    southern Africa*

Catherine Swender
Alma College
United States
Soap operas

Norma Swenson
Boston Women's Health Book
    Collective
United States
*Global health movement; Global health
    movement: Resources*

Koh Tai Ann
Nanyang Technological University
Singapore
Literature: Southeast Asia

Peta Tait
La Trobe University
Australia
Lesbian drama; Performance texts

Ghada Talhami
Lake Forest College
United States
*Peace movements: Middle East and the
    Arab world*

Elizabeth Tapia
Union Theological Seminary
Philippines
Prayer

Ann Gill Taylor
University of Virginia
United States
Healers; Holistic health I

Lee Taylor
Open University
England
Equal opportunities: Education

Sandra Taylor
Queensland University of Technology
Australia
Education: Gender equity

Vana Tentokali
Aristotle University of Thessalonik
Greece
Built environment

Tove Thagaard
University of Oslo
Norway
*Science: Technological and scientific
    research*

Beverly Thiele
Murdoch University
Australia
*Family life cycle and work; Part-time
    and casual work; Work: Patterns*

Helen Thomas
Goldsmiths College
England
Dance: Overview; Dance: Modern

Linda Thomas
Lutheran School of Theology at
    Chicago
United States
Womanist theology

Rachel Thomson
South Bank University
England
Sex education

Leonore Tiefer
New York University
United States
Sexology and sex research

Rosemarie Tong
University of North Carolina
United States
Ethics: Feminist

Nahid Toubia
RAINBO, New York
United States
*Female circumcision and genital
    mutilation*

Patricia Tovar
Instituto Colombiano de
    Antropología
Colombia
*Marriage: Overview; Marriage:
    Interracial and interreligious;
    Marriage: Regional traditions and
    practices; Marriage: Remarriage;
    Widowhood*

Reinhild Traitler-Espiritu
European Women's College
Switzerland
Mother Earth

Thanh-Dam Truong
Institute of Social Studies
Netherlands
Prostitution

Azumi Tsuge
Health Science University Hokkaido
Japan
Fertility and fertility treatment

Nancy Tuana
University of Oregon
United States
Physiology

Vappu Tyyskä
Ryerson Polytechnic University
Canada
*Cohabitation; Courtship; Housework;
    Motherhood; Parenthood*

Valerie Ubbes
Miami University, Oxford Ohio
United States
Health education

Elaine Unterhalter
University of London
England
Apartheid, segregation, and ghettoization

Kimberley Updegraff
Arizona State University
United States
Child development

Jane Ussher
University of Western Sydney, Nepean
Australia
Mental health I; Physical strength

Angharad N. Valdivia
University of Illinois
United States
*Images of women: Overview; Media:
    Overview*

Irma van der Ploeg
Erasmus University Rotterdam
Netherlands
Anatomy

Jan van Dyke
University of North Carolina
United States
Dance: Choreography

Shouleh Vatanabadi
New York University
United States
Literature: Persian

Bella Vivante
University of Arizona
United States
Ancient nation-states: Women's roles

Olga Voronina
Institute of Philosophy
Russia
*Feminism: Commonwealth of
    Independent States*

Ariella Vraneski
Technion-Israel Institute of
    Technology
Israel
Environment: Middle East

Amina Wadud
Virginia Commonwealth University
United States
Faith

Jennifer Waelti-Walters
University of Victoria
Canada
Fairy tales

Val Walsh
University of Central Lancashire
England
Creativity; Disability: Elite body

Carol Warren
Murdoch University
Australia
*Economy: History of women's
    participation*

Roz Warren
Humorist, Bala Cynwyd,
    Pennsylvania
United States
*Cartoons and comics; Humor: Case
    study—Comedy, United States*

Eva Warth
Universiteit Utrecht
Netherlands
Gaze

Kazuko Watanabe
Kyoto Sangyo University
Japan
Feminism: Japan

Mary Ann Watson
Metropolitan State College of Denver
United States
*Sexuality: Psychology of sexuality in the
    United States*

Peggy Watson
University of Cambridge
England
*Education: Commonwealth of
    Independent States; Education:
    Eastern Europe*

Maria-Barbara Watson-Franke
San Diego State University
United States
Matrilineal systems

Patricia Waugh
University of Durham
England
Feminism: Postmodern

Georgina Waylen
University of Sheffield
England
Democratization; Imperialism

Susun S. Weed
Wise Women Center/Ash Tree
    Publishing, Woodstock, New York
United States
*Menopause; Nutrition I; Traditional
    healing: Herbalists*

Judith Romney Wegner
Brown University
United States
Judaism

Zhang Wei
Peking University
China
Education: East Asia

Lynne Weikart
Baruch College, City University of
    New York
United States
Politics and the state: North America

Gaby Weiner
Umea University
Sweden
Education: Curriculum in schools

Leslie Kanes Weisman
New Jersey Institute of Technology
United States
Architecture

Giselle Weiss
Writer, Basel
Switzerland
*Health care: Eastern Europe; Health
    care: North Africa and the Middle
    East; Health care: Southeast Asia;
    Health care: Sub-Saharan Africa;
    Health care: Western Europe*

Catherine Wessinger
Loyola University, New Orleans
United States
Sects and cults

Jackie West
University of Bristol
England
Work: Occupational segregation

Louise Westling
University of Oregon
United States
Earth

Melissa White
University of Sydney
Australia
Class and feminism; Difference II

Elizabeth L. Whitelegg
Open University
England
Education: Science

Margaret Whitford
Queen Mary and Westfield College,
    University of London
England
Psychoanalysis

Sandra Whitworth
York University
Canada
*International organizations and
    agencies; Peacekeeping*

Saskia Wieringa
Institute of Social Studies
Netherlands
Sex and culture

Anne Wigglesworth
Medical doctor and writer, Lawrence,
    Kansas
United States
*Surgery: Case study—Contemporary
    issues in the United States*

Lynette Willoughby
Women's Engineering Society, Leeds
England
Education: Technology

Ara Wilson
Ohio State University
United States
Patriarchy: Feminist theory

Maggie Wilson
Oxford Brookes University
England
Education: Western Europe

Tamsin Wilton
University of the West of England
England
Film: Lesbian

Jan Windebank
University of Sheffield
England
Domestic labor

Sue Wise
University of Lancaster
England
Sexism

Sharon L. Wolchik
George Washington University
United States
*Development: Central and Eastern
    Europe*

Carol Wolkowitz
University of Warwick
England
Capitalism

Julia T. Wood
University of North Carolina
United States
Conversation

Sarah Worth
Furman University
United States
Aesthetics: Feminist

Katharine Wright
Liverpool University
England
*Households and families: Central and
    South America*

Lee Wright
University of Ulster, Belfast
Northern Ireland
Textiles

Susan J. Wurtzburg
Lincoln University
New Zealand
*Battery; Households and families:
    Micronesia and Polynesia*

Xiong Lei
China Features and Information
    Services, Beijing
China
Media: Chinese case study

Ryoko Yanagibori
Aichi Prefectural College of Nursing
Japan
Health care: East Asia

Nazik Yared
Lebanese American University
Lebanon
*Violence: Middle East and the Arab
    world (Lebanon)*

Anna Yeatman
Macquarie University
Australia
Bureaucracy

Barbara Yost
Arizona Republic, Phoenix
United States
History; Sports and discrimination

Serinity Young
Columbia University
United States
Religion: Overview; Sacred texts

Heather Young Leslie
University of Alberta
Canada
Fostering: Case study—Oceania

Gillian Youngs
University of Leicester
England
Internet politics and states

Nira Yuval-Davis
University of Greenwich
England
Citizenship; Nation and nationalism

Weisi Zhao
International College at Beijing of
    China Agricultural University
China
Population: Chinese case study

Wang Zheng
Stanford University
United States
Feminism: China

Shahla Zia
Aurat Publication and Information
    Service Foundation, Islamabad
Pakistan
*Family: Religious and legal systems—
    Islamic traditions*

Bonnie Zimmerman
San Diego State University
United States
Lesbian studies

Faye Zucker
Faye Zucker Editorial Services, New
    York
United States
*AIDS and HIV; Bulimia nervosa;
    Demonization; Genetic screening;
    Genetics and genetic technologies;
    Nursing homes; Publishing*

Project Staff

Introduction

The preservation of women's knowledge and experience—in terms of the body, the community, work, the environment, and history—is vital to women's visibility and empowerment in the future. This international encyclopedia of women began when Phyllis Hall at Pergamon Press, our original publisher, recognized the importance of recording such knowledge and experience.

When Phyllis invited us to serve as general editors of the encyclopedia, we knew that we were being offered a significant opportunity. We shared her vision of an encyclopedia that would address the concerns of women and the theory and practice of feminism around the world, and we decided to develop a reference work that would be an accessible, trustworthy resource not only for scholars, professionals, and activists but for the general reader everywhere.

The Development Process

To understand what the *Routledge International Encyclopedia of Women* is, and how it works, our readers may find it helpful to know something about how it was planned and put together.

In preparing a women's encyclopedia, we did not have many guides or precedents. We began to plan the framework in February 1990, with a small meeting of academics and activists at the University of Oregon, where Cheris Kramarae was acting director of the Center for the Study of Women in Society. These initial planners—from England, the Philippines, India, Canada, Australia, and the United States—had an abundance of ideas, and Charlotte Bunch of our editorial board helped us schematize them so that we could visualize various possibilities for content and organization.

Of course, there were limits to the scope of the project. The encyclopedia would be published in English in four volumes. In addition to the two general editors, it would have about a dozen topic editors who would consider what specific articles to include. At the outset, we decided—though not without regrets—that a work of this size could not include essays on individual women: such entries would have required something combining the features of an encyclopedia and a dictionary of biography, and would have filled many more volumes. Accordingly, we agreed to focus on ideas and actions, a format that still allowed us to include information about numerous individuals. We also agreed

not to have overall entries on specific countries, but rather to cover certain topic areas region by region.

Determining the categories of topics was a considerable challenge, since any such division is difficult and to some extent arbitrary. We realized that, whatever scheme we chose, we would need to watch for ideas and issues that might fall into the cracks—we needed to ensure that subjects such as psychology, psychoanalysis, sociology, sports, and anthropology, along with new and expanding areas of study, would be adequately presented. Eventually, we decided on thirteen thematic categories; they are not exhaustive, and some overlapping has been inevitable, but we feel that they represent the broad coverage we wanted:

1. Arts and literature
2. Culture and communication
3. Ecology and the environment
4. Economy and development
5. Education
6. Health, reproduction, and sexuality
7. History and philosophy of feminism
8. Households and families
9. Politics and the state
10. Religion and spirituality
11. Science and technology
12. Violence and peace
13. Women's studies

These topic areas were created only for developmental purposes; in the final encyclopedia, the articles would be in alphabetical order across topics.

We then found our specialist topic editors to oversee each category. The topic editors were invited to a second meeting, in November 1990, at the University of Illinois, where Cheris was teaching in the Speech Communication Department and Women's Studies Program. They brought outlines for their sections, which were discussed and revised through collective efforts. As early as this meeting, we began to consider the relationships between specific topics—an important aspect of a truly integrated multidisciplinary reference work. Throughout the production of the encyclopedia, special care has been taken to highlight the links between topics through cross-references that will lead users to comparative articles, such as entries about different regions and related topics of interest.

The Publishing Process

In the years since those first two meetings, our encyclopedia project has had a long publishing history. Before it arrived at Routledge in New York, not only its publishing house but also its in-house editorial staff had changed more than once, with the files moving from the United States to the United Kingdom and back again. Throughout the project, however, we have always been fortunate in working with staff members who had a passion for the encyclopedia and were determined to see it through to publication.

We have also—not surprisingly, considering the long-term nature of the project—seen some changes in topic editors, and among the individual contributors. Yet the initial plan, devised in our early conferences and meetings, has remained basically intact. The perseverance and dedication of the topic editors and contributors have been amazing—a testament, we hope, to the worth of the project.

The Articles and Contributors

The articles in the *Routledge International Encyclopedia of Women* were written by authors from many disciplines, languages, and cultures. All the contributors were asked to keep in mind the needs of users. Most readers, we assumed, would look for an introduction to the issues involved in any topic, a basic understanding as well as directions to further and more specialized sources of information. In general, each author was asked to survey the topic rather than adopt a specialist's position, although some exceptions were made when a brief article could not, as a practical matter, discuss a multiplicity of views, and when, occasionally, a specific view was the point of an article. Overall, the articles are designed to be accessible and useful for a wide range of readers, including advanced high school students, undergraduate and graduate students, scholars from many disciplines (such as women's studies and related fields), and professionals working on women's issues at the local or international level.

While our goal was to focus on real issues and ideas rather than on academic theories, we have included some theoretical articles. Some of these, necessarily, are written at a higher level, but we believe that they will still be of interest, and use, to most if not all readers. Our authors were also reminded that the readers would come from many different countries and cultural backgrounds, and that the language and examples in each article should therefore be broadly accessible.

The International Focus

We offer an international perspective in at least three ways. First, the authors themselves are international—writers from around the world have contributed articles in every topic area. Networks of women scholars and activists around the globe have enabled us to find expert writers from as many as 70 countries; in particular, international conferences such as the International Interdisciplinary Congress on Women were excellent settings for finding extraordinary writers, many of whom had never before been published in English. Second, as noted above, we cover many subjects region by region, encompassing diverse cultural traditions. Third, we have included numerous "case studies," articles that focus on a specific aspect of a larger topic; and typically, this specific focus is regional.

We would have liked to work with even more international writers and to include even more international topics, but there were, understandably, practical constraints: we encountered some problems related to communication channels, political conflicts, migration, censorship, or economics. For some topics, data and expert writers seemed to be unavailable; occasionally, too, we simply lost touch with a writer. We believe, however, that the international coverage here is more far-reaching than in any other single reference work focusing on women's issues.

The Updating Process

Because any encyclopedia takes a long time to publish, updating becomes an important issue. In our case, social and political developments have affected women around the world; women's movements have evolved, becoming stronger in some places and being threatened in others; ongoing scholarship and research have cast new light on some ideas; new debates have taken center stage; new trends have emerged. To take just two examples, radical feminism has, for many women, given way to postmodern feminism and beyond; and women's studies as a discipline has seen significant changes (in some ways, the development of the encyclopedia has mirrored the development of women's studies). As a result, many of the original articles in the encyclopedia have been revised or rewritten, and many new articles have been added. Throughout the production process, we have tried to ensure that topics of current interest were represented. In this effort, we drew on the expertise of younger feminists, scholars in emerging fields, and librarians—particularly those from the Women's Studies Section of the American Library Association's Association of College and Research Libraries. We invited authors to write new articles about technology, cyberculture, sexuality, lesbian studies, transgender, queer theory, postmodernism, postcolonialism, girl studies, and ethics, to name a few subjects; and we have integrated older and newer material through cross-referencing. The encyclopedia now represents more than three decades of worldwide scholarship—especially, though not exclusively, feminist scholarship—in numerous fields of knowledge.

The Representation of Values

As we worked on this encyclopedia, we have been very much aware of what has been called the politics of legitimacy. At any time, in a given society or culture, certain groups are privileged, and it is such groups that often decide what is valid and what knowledge counts. Systems of values change over time, but in the last few centuries, at least, women have seldom been included among the "knowledge makers." This exclusion of women has been increasingly challenged in recent decades: we have witnessed the emergence of a plurality of truths, partly as a result of feminist interventions. Traditionally, encyclopedia articles have tended to be—or to be presented as—"value-free"; but feminist scholarship often acknowledges the "politics of the personal," or the political importance of women's personal experience, and takes an interest in transforming the theory, practice, and purpose of social institutions. Many of the entries in this encyclopedia of women offer "values" in this sense, and we believe the reader will enjoy and learn from the cultural exchange that they represent.

We realize that the *Routledge International Encyclopedia of Women* does not, and could not, contain everything that might have been included, but we also believe that the encyclopedia contains much more about women's scholarship—and a wider exploration of its variety, richness, and range—than can be found in any other international reference work. We wish our readers well, and we hope that what we have accomplished here may inspire some to make their own contributions to the field of global women's issues and knowledge.

Acknowledgments

The *Routledge International Encyclopedia of Women* has been a major task involving more than a thousand people: authors, editors, advisers, and others. We thank everyone involved, beginning with the members of our editorial board (listed on page ii), our contributors (pages xxv–li), and the project staff (page liii).

A number of people worked with the editorial board in important supporting roles. Our special thanks to Cheris Kramarae's project assistants, Elizabeth A. Kissling and Aki Uchida; and to Dale Spender's project assistant, Georgina Hampson. Anna Hodson and Robin Mann of Wisbech, England, served as acting topic editors for arts and literature. Robert Sloane and Diane Tipps worked with Angharad Valdiva on culture and communications—Robert as editorial assisant and Diane as secretary. Sharon McDuell of London, England, was an acting topic editor for ecology and the environment. Cora Baldock, the topic editor for economy and development, worked continually and closely with the Murdoch Encyclopedia Collective. Susie O'Brien was the second topic editor for education. Jo Sanson was an assistant to Joan Mencher, the topic editor for households and families.

We have also received help from hundreds of others—including people in universities, women's organizations, and libraries—in many countries. Here, we mention a few of those who contributed time and knowledge to the process of creating this encyclopedia.

During the earlier stages of the project, several people were involved in planning and editorial work, including Joan Burks, Clair Chaventré, Caroline Cornish, Bonnie Thornton Dill, Clare Grist, Elise Hansen, Sue Henley, Jackie Jones, Candida Lacey, Robert Miranda, Cathy Peppers, Marilyn Plowman, Wei Chi Poon, Susan Richards, Ann Russo, Carolyn Royston, Sari Schnitzlein, Lynne Spender, and Mary Walstrom.

Cheris Kramarae acknowledges particularly the help received from the Center for the Study of Women in Society at the University of Oregon, the Speech Communication Department at the University of Illinois at Urbana-Champaign, and the Women's Studies Program at the University of Illinois at Urbana-Champaign.

The Boston Women's Health Book Collective (BWHBC) reviewed nearly every article related to health, reproduction, and sexuality and provided much valuable advice about this topic area. In particular, our thanks to Claudine Mussuto and Judy Norsigian at BWHBC.

When we were seeking writers, many people very kindly recommended colleagues and helped in other ways. We would especially like to thank Madeleine Wing Adler, Douglas Anderson, Joan Jacobs Brumberg, Sheila ffoliot, Ada Finifter, Paul Finkelman, Vernon M. Goetcheus, Sondra Hale, Ellen Herman, Bruce Itule, Natalie B. Kampen, Robert P. Lamm, Frederick Lane, Laura Macdonald, Anthony Marcus, Thomas McCarthy, Jean O'Barr, Elsa Peterson, Judith Raiskin, Sheila M. Rothman, Scott Slovic, David Vintinner, and Delese Wear.

There are also our own personal acknowledgments. Cheris Kramarae would like to give special thanks for long-term friendly advice and support from Mary Ellen Capek, Victoria DeFrancisco, Irene Diamond, Sonja Foss, Nancy Henley, Lorraine Ironplow, Sandra Morgan, Mary Ellen

O'Shaughnessey, Barbara Reskin, Diana Sheridan, Verna Smith, Leslie Steeves, Jeanie Taylor, and Barrie Thorne; to the many feminist friends in several countries who offered their homes for meetings as well as advice, assistance, and encouragment; and to her family—Jana, Brinlee, and Dale Kramer—who shared space and time with this complex project.

Dale Spender would especially like to thank the following people for their advice, help, and support: Quentin Bryce, principal, Women's College, University of Syndey; David Doughan, librarian, Fawcett Library, for invaluable assistance in finding people; Rick Ernst for ongoing IT support; Kirsten Lees for research, and for her insights; Sheryle Moon; Sarah Neal for research; Janine Schmdt, university librarian, University of Queensland, particularly for her help with on-line strategies; Joni Seegar; Fiona Stewart for dealing with emergencies; and Leslie Weisman.

Both general editors are grateful to the publishers who have participated in this project, providing resources and expertise; and, finally and fully, to Phyllis Hall, who initiated and guided it.

Cheris Kramarae
Dale Spender

Routledge International Encyclopedia of Women

Global Women's Issues and Knowledge

Volume 1   Ability—Education: Globalization

ABILITY

Ability is a broad concept but has been associated mainly with intellectual ability in the western world. (As *dis*ability, it has been linked with physical as well as intellectual handicap.) According to a feminist analysis, because of the traditional need for males to be seen as leaders—and for their achievement to be justified, or based on merit—the management of intellectual ability has played a critical role in the relationship between the sexes.

In most societies, it has been necessary for men to be seen as smarter than women, and this has required specific forms of social organization. Assertions that women should not be as able as men have led to the construction of systems and beliefs implying that women could not be as competent as their male counterparts. This has been particularly the case for women of color (Robinson, 1998).

For example, by denying females access to education, it has been possible to portray women as silly and thereby to explain the supposedly superior ability of males (Mackinnon, 1997). Basically all societies have at some stage restricted women's education (women account for two-thirds of the world's illiterate, according to the United Nations' statistics for the year 2000), but the Taliban in Afghanistan appear to be the only current regime that expressly forbids both education and occupations to women.

Throughout history, various explanations have been put forward for women's supposed inability: some had a religious basis; others have been associated with physical attributes, such as reproductive issues or brain size. In the nineteenth century, there were those who insisted that women should not be allowed to exercise their intellectual ability because it would interfere with their reproductive health. Arguments that women had less ability because their brains were smaller were soon discredited when it was established that, in relation to body size, the female brain is bigger than that of the male (Kern, 1996; Schiebinger, 1989). But theories about reproductive influences, brain size, and hormones are still sometimes used.

In western societies where the campaign for equal rights has been under way for more than a century, girls are now better able to demonstrate their ability; they are generally staying on longer at school, and more girls than boys are entering colleges and universities. However, this comes at a time when the credentials of formal education are increasingly being challenged, and women remain underrepresented at the higher levels as students, school principals, and academics.

Where girls have been able to enter educational institutions, their performance often has been systematically distorted so that it would not pose a challenge to males. This has been the case where girls have been restricted to a specific sphere, such as domestic training. Mary Wollstonecraft (1759–1797), one of the early champions of equal educational opportunity, criticized the system that educated boys for the world, and girls to please men (1978).

Other examples include particularly prestigious academic areas in which the ability of girls is held to be inferior, such as mathematics, engineering, or computer science. Although women were considered numerically able in the eighteenth century (Schiebinger, 1989), when mathematics was not held to be centrally important, the belief that women were unable to do mathematics took hold in many minds during the twentieth century. In some societies

(Singapore, Malaysia, and India), women are seen as able in relation to computer science and information technology, whereas in the western world the number of women in these fields is decreasing.

Tests, too, have been weighted in favor of males. IQ tests, Scholastic Aptitude Tests in the United States, the English "Eleven Plus" exams, and other forms of public examination have been exposed as biased (Castro and Garcia, 1975; Mensh and Mensh, 1991).

Outside the educational sphere, social organization also has decreed—across many cultures—that "strong-minded women" are unattractive to males. For this reason, women themselves have been urged to "hide their brains" and to disguise their ability. In more subtle ways, women's codes of behavior and conversation often construct men as being smarter and better informed. Women may be advised to ask questions (so that males will look knowledgeable), to defer to men's opinions, and to refrain from criticizing men in public (Spender, 1980).

It was this phenomenon that the English writer Virginia Woolf was describing when she wrote of women serving "all these centuries as looking glasses, possessing the magic and delicious power of reflecting the figure of men at twice their natural size" (Woolf, 1928). This practice has sometimes been regarded as collusion by those who insist on the right of women to exercise their full ability and to be given credit for their achievements (Jeffrey and Basu, 1996).

With the advent of the information revolution, there are signs in some countries that women might be freer to realize their full potential, as creative and intellectual ability is increasingly valued because it is a source of wealth (Spender, 2001).

Disability

The term *disability* has been used to indicate physical as well as intellectual handicaps. It is often considered a limiting term that needs to be challenged. Disability can suggest deficiency and can be used to justify many forms of discrimination. To counter the negative meanings of disability, the term "ableism" has been suggested, with the term "differently abled" indicating that there is a wide range of abilities among human beings.

An equitable social policy would encourage the full development of the ability of every individual, including the use of practices and devices ranging from large-print books and voice-activated software to physical facilities that allow access for all to the built environment.

The information revolution also continues to provide new opportunities for the differently abled to engage in learning and working on computers.

See Also

DISABILITY AND FEMINISM; DISABILITY: ELITE BODY; EDUCATION: ACHIEVEMENT; EDUCATION: GENDER EQUITY; EXAMINATIONS AND ASSESSMENT

References and Further Reading

Castro, R., and Garcia, J. 1975. Admissions: Who shall occupy the seats of privilege? *Aztlan* 6(3): 363–377.

Kern, K. 1996. Gray matters: Brains, identities, and natural rights. In T. R. Schatzki and W. Natter, eds., *The social and political body*, 103–121. New York: Guilford.

Jeffrey, R., and Basu, A. 1996. *Girls schooling, women's autonomy and fertility change in South Asia.* Thousand Oaks, Calif.: Sage.

Mackinnon, A. 1997. *Love and freedom: Professional women and the reshaping of personal life.* Cambridge: Cambridge University Press.

Mensh, Elaine, and Harry Mensh. 1991. *The IQ mythology.* Edwardsville: Southern Illinois University Press.

Robinson, C. 1998. Blaxploitation and the misrepresentation of liberation. *Race-and-Class* 40(1): 1–12.

Schiebinger, Londa. 1989. *The mind has no sex.* Cambridge, Mass.: Harvard University Press.

Spender, Dale. 2001. Brains and beauty. *Transworld.*

———. 1980. *Man made language.* London: Routledge and Kegan Paul.

Wollstonecraft, Mary. 1978. *A vindication of the rights of women.* Penguin.

Woolf, Virginia. 1928. *A room of one's own.* Penguin.

Dale Spender
Cheris Kramarae

ABORTION

Globally, an estimated forty to fifty million induced abortions are performed each year. Additionally, unknown numbers of women attempt to abort but are unsuccessful. Although most abortions are performed under safe conditions, about fifteen million clandestine abortions take place annually in countries where the procedure is highly restricted or prohibited; this adds greatly to the physical dangers to women, and to the social costs (Alan Guttmacher Institute, 1994).

Throughout history, women have resorted to abortion to terminate unwanted or mistimed pregnancies. Anthropologists have documented a variety of abortion methods, including heavy massage of the uterus, insertion of a stick or another object into the vagina, and ingestion of herbs (Devereux, 1975). These methods are still practiced in both developed (or "northern") countries and developing ("southern" or third world) countries, most often where safe abortions performed by health professionals are either illegal or inaccessible.

World Abortion Politics

All governments place some legal restrictions on access to abortions. In 1994, abortion was outlawed in sixteen countries, including Chile, Ireland, the Philippines, Egypt, Mauritius, Honduras, and the Dominican Republic. (Of these sixteen, however, only Chile forbade abortion under all circumstances. In the other fifteen, in theory a woman could be granted permission to have an abortion to save her own life.) Most countries—173 in 1994—permit abortions at least in cases where the woman's life is in danger. Forty-one countries, representing 38 percent of the world's population, permit abortion "on request," although all still place some restrictions on the procedure, such as length of pregnancy or ability to pay (United Nations, 1994).

In the 1950s, abortion was severely restricted in most regions of the world, except for some European countries, the Soviet Union, and Japan. After independence, many former colonies retained strict antiabortion laws that had been imposed by their colonizers. Laws permitting abortion only to save a woman's life still prevail in most of Latin America, sub-Saharan Africa, and the Arab world (Cook, 1989; Dixon-Mueller, 1990).

In the 1980s and 1990s, abortion laws in both developed and developing nations were liberalized, in recognition of the impact on women's health of abortions carried out under unsafe conditions. Since 1988, five European countries, six countries of the former Eastern bloc, and five developing countries have made their abortion laws less restrictive (Henshaw, 1994). Countries with the least restrictive abortion laws include Cuba, Canada, the United States, many republics of the former Soviet Union, Russia, Singapore, South Korea, Tunisia, and Turkey.

Concurrent with the trend toward legalization, however, a number of powerful religious groups, together with an increasingly vocal right-to-life movement, originating in the United States and spreading to the former Soviet Union and eastern bloc, Australia, and many developing countries, seeks to outlaw all abortions. Some are also opposed to the use of contraception.

Abortion Procedures

First-trimester abortions are typically carried out through vacuum aspiration, a five- to ten-minute procedure in which the cervix is dilated and the product of conception (the conceptus), along with the material lining the uterus, is extracted by suction. During the 1970s and 1980s, methods of nonsurgical medical abortion were developed, among them RU 486 (mifepristone, followed by one dose of a prostaglandin) and quinacrine (a more controversial method, the safety of which has not been fully established, despite its use in some developing countries). Administered orally, vaginally, or intramuscularly, these drugs cause the uterus to contract and expel its contents, in a manner similar to miscarriage.

Abortions after the first trimester often require dilation and evacuation of the uterus with the use of a sharp instrument (a curette) for scraping the uterine lining. Late-term abortions often involve inducing labor. The amniotic fluid is removed from the uterus through a needle, after which a medication (prostaglandin, urea, saline solution, or a combination) is injected into the uterus to induce contractions; a few hours later, labor occurs and the fetus is expelled.

For early procedures—pregnancies up to six or eight weeks—manual vacuum aspirations (MVA) can be used safely in health clinics and in primary health centers, when administered by trained health workers such as nurses with obstetric-gynecological training, midwives, paramedics, or physicians. MVA can also be provided on an outpatient basis at very low cost (Rosenfield, 1992).

Many women turn to abortion as a method of family planning because they do not have access to reliable methods of contraception; they find the available methods inconvenient or suffer from side effects or contraceptive failure; or they feel powerless to use a contraceptive method in their sexual relationships. For a variety of reasons, abortion also may be the method that best meets a woman's needs at a particular time in her life. Many women's health advocates suggest that the ideological division between "family planning" and "abortion" no longer makes sense. Seeking to build holistic systems for reproductive health care, women's health advocates call for safe abortion to be a part of a comprehensive program of sexual and reproductive health services accessible to all women (Dixon-Mueller, 1993).

The Toll of Unsafe Abortions

Unsafe abortion is recognized as a global problem with enormous impact on women's health and lives, particularly in poorer, less developed countries where abortion is also the most legally restricted. Mortality rates for unsafe abortions—those that are self-induced or clandestine because laws and politics restrict women's access to safe, legal services—are far higher than for legal abortions carried out by trained health professionals in sanitary conditions. Under unsafe conditions, mortality rates range between 15 and 300 deaths per 100,000 abortions performed (Royston and Armstrong, 1989), as opposed to the mortality rate of 1.4 deaths per 100,000 abortions carried out under safe conditions. The World Health Organization (WHO) estimates that more than 100,000 women die each year from unsafe abortions. Because these deaths are generally underreported, the true figure may be much higher.

As a result of unsafe abortions, even higher numbers of women experience chronic or severe health problems, infections of the reproductive tract, infertility, and severe physical or emotional trauma. Women also may feel depressed, powerless, and alone after the procedure, especially if denied compassionate counseling, legal sanction, and—in most cases—any form of postprocedure pain management. Poor, young, and less-educated women suffer the most from restrictive abortion laws, and they suffer the most in poor countries.

The United Nations International Conference on Population and Development, held in Cairo in September 1994, defined unsafe abortion as "a major public health concern" in an agreement signed by 184 nations. Although no specific recommendations were made for removing legal restrictions against abortion, the Programme of Action urged governments and nongovernmental organizations to "strengthen their commitment to women's health" and "to deal with the health impact of unsafe abortion."

Of additional concern to health officials are the costs of treating women who have incomplete or botched abortions. Such treatment is an overwhelming and often unsuccessful task, as well as a significant drain on the medical resources of already overburdened health systems (Germain, 1989).

Women's Health in the Balance

Despite the increasing legality of abortion, women's health and lives are still threatened. Many governments install, as gatekeeping mechanisms, requirements that impede women seeking abortions, such as a mandatory waiting period; filing of police reports or other legal documents; proof of rape, incest, physical disability, or mental distress; or evidence of fetal impairment. Disparities exist in access to abortion, with poor and rural populations having greatly reduced access to services. In the United States, for example, 83 percent of counties have no abortion provider (National Abortion Federation, 1991), and the federal government does not pay for abortion for poor women. In India and Zambia, abortion is legal, but millions of women each year still resort to clandestine abortions when and where services are not available (McLaurin et al., 1991). China and India, the

world's two most populous nations, have fairly liberal abortion laws. The cultural preference for sons is so great in these countries, however, that many women seek abortions following amniocentesis if they learn that the fetus is female.

Feminists and the international women's health movement have, since the 1970s, made access to safe abortion services a central issue of rights, equity, and reproductive health, and support a woman's right to choose an abortion on medical, moral, or ethical grounds.

See Also

CONTRACEPTION; FAMILY PLANNING; FETUS; MATERNAL HEALTH AND MORBIDITY; THE PILL; PRO-CHOICE MOVEMENT; REPRODUCTION: OVERVIEW; REPRODUCTIVE HEALTH; REPRODUCTIVE RIGHTS; REPRODUCTIVE TECHNOLOGIES

References and Further Reading

Alan Guttmacher Institute. 1994. *Clandestine abortion: A Latin American reality.* New York: Alan Guttmacher Institute.

Cook, Rebecca J. 1989. Abortion laws and politics: Challenges and opportunities. *International Journal of Gynecology and Obstetrics* 3 (Supplement): 61–87.

Devereux, George. 1975. *Study of abortion in primitive culture.* Madison, Conn.: International Universities Press.

Dixon-Mueller, Ruth. 1990. Abortion policy and women's health in developing countries. *International Journal of Health Services* 20: 297–314.

———. 1993. Abortion is a method of family planning. In *Four essays on birth control needs and risks.* New York: International Women's Health Coalition.

Germain, Adrienne. 1989. The Christopher Tietze International Symposium: An overview. *International Journal of Gynecology and Obstetrics* 3 (Supplement): 1–8.

———, and Jane Ordway. 1989. *Population control and women's health: Balancing the scales.* New York: International Women's Health Coalition (in cooperation with the Overseas Development Council).

Henshaw, Stanley K. 1994. Recent trends in the legal status of induced abortions. *Journal of Public Health Policy* 15(2): 165–172.

McLaurin, Kate E., Charlotte E. Hord, and Merrill Wolf. 1991. Health systems' role in abortion care: The need for a proactive approach. *Issues in Abortion Care 1. IPAS: International Projects Assistance Services* 1: 1–34.

National Abortion Federation. 1991. *The truth about abortion.* Washington, D.C.: National Abortion Federation.

Rosenfield, Allan. 1992. Maternal mortality: Community-based interventions. *International Journal of Gynecology and Obstetrics* 38 (Supplement): 17–22.

Royston, Erica, and Sue Armstrong. 1989. *Preventing maternal deaths.* Geneva: World Health Organization.

United Nations. 1994. *Programme of Action of the International Conference on Population and Development.*

United Nations, Department for Economic and Social Information and Policy Analysis. 1994. *World Abortion Policies.*

World Health Organization. 1997. *Maternal mortality, ratios and rates: A tabulation of available information.* Geneva: World Health Organization.

Martha MacDonald

ABSTINENCE, SEXUAL

See CELIBACY: RELIGIOUS; CELIBACY: SECULAR; and VIRGINITY.

ABUSE

Abuse—a term often linked with violence against women or children—is one of several terms, along with *violence* and *battering,* that gained widespread use in the latter half of the twentieth century. These terms can be used interchangeably. They may be linked with other words, such as *syndrome, family,* and *marital,* to develop conceptual meaning, or they may be defined differently.

Recognizing an Issue

The term *abuse* may be restricted to children and *violence* to adults in order to make theoretical distinctions useful to professional responses (Stark and Flitcraft, 1996). Using different terms can be helpful in differentiating the relevance of coercion and control; for children, these are an aspect of childhood development, whereas for adults they are the antithesis of independence and autonomy. These differences are reflected in interventions for adults and those for children—protective services for children, contrasted with support, advocacy, and empowerment for independent adults. Battering can be seen as a process, the "dynamics of partner assaults as a pattern of coercive control" encompassing a range of behaviors to "hurt, intimidate, coerce, isolate, control, or humiliate a partner" (Stark and Flitcraft, 1996: 161).

Using different terms can also be a way of confirming differential responses based on a distinction between appropriate interventions in the private and the public domain. For example, *domestic violence* is a policing term for violence against women from men known to them, usually husbands, cohabitees, or boyfriends. It defines the location of a call for assistance and implies a lesser response than would result from public violence. In policing, the term *domestic violence* can be used to distinguish between criminal (that is, violent) and noncriminal behavior. Another term used to describe the location of a type of abuse is *harassment,* which began as a descriptor for workplace abuse encompassing both violent crime and noncriminal acts.

However defined, abusive experiences challenge theory, policy, and practice in relation to the family and social life more generally. The recognition of abuse calls into question the view of the heterosexual family as a haven of warmth and caring and as invariably a social good. Abuse also raises issues about the separation between public and private life and, most important, about gender and gender relations. Gender differences are a factor not only in who does what to whom, but also in how abusive acts are interpreted and understood by women, men, and children of both sexes.

In this article, in keeping with much of the literature, *abuse, violence, battering,* and *harassment* will be used interchangeably in relation to a wide range of behaviors. These varying forms of abuse take place in families consisting of adult partners with and without dependent children and between acquaintances, friends, workplace colleagues, and strangers. This discussion will include the issues of the abuse of men and of women as abusers.

Rediscovering Child Abuse

The rediscovery of the extent of violence against children began in the early 1960s, when unexplained injury to children was identified through radiology (Kempe et al., 1962). Although forms of harm to infants and children, such as serious physical neglect and infanticide, were part of the knowledge of professional practice, X rays found multiple fractures, both old and new, in children from birth onward that could not be explained away as accidental. The recognition of extreme physical violence, initially called battering, deliberately inflicted by adults responsible for the care of infants and older children spread quickly and began to have an influence on medical and other services. Because this abuse was taking place primarily within families, new ways of understanding family dynamics and life had to be developed. But the recognition of physical abuse was only the beginning.

Sexual abuse of children, along with physical abuse and neglect, was understood to be a social problem in the nineteenth century, but this knowledge was contested, particularly by theoretical developments in psychoanalysis. Over the early years of the twentieth century, knowledge of child sexual abuse as a major social problem became so restricted that, as with physical abuse, we can speak of its subsequent rediscovery. In 1980 the publication of *The Best Kept Secret* by Florence Rush launched an attack on Freud for his belief that claims by women in therapy that they had been sexually abused as children were fantasies, not reality. At the same time, women began to publish experiential accounts challenging this view (for example, Armstrong, 1978) along with exposures of the sexual abuse of women patients by male therapists.

Initially Freud thought that childhood experiences of rape and other sexual acts by fathers were reality, but his medical colleagues disagreed. Male therapists, comfortable with the belief that women fantasize sexual experiences with their fathers, developed a theory that such fantasies were merely an aspect of child development. This type of theoretical battle continues today through the debate over "false memory syndrome," the view that women falsely recall experiences of abuse by their fathers. Further, false memories are said to be encouraged by the therapeutic process, a view that challenges psychoanalysis and related therapies in a new way. These views serve to deny not only the reality of sexual abuse of girls by adult males but also the long-term detrimental emotional harm that can follow children of both sexes into adulthood.

Prevalence of Child Abuse

Both professionals and society in general resisted the recognition of sexual abuse of girls by fathers and other male relatives more strongly than that of the extreme physical abuse of boys and girls. Once such abuse could no longer be denied, the sexual abuse of boys was raised as an issue. (Similarly, when resistance to recognition of the abuse of women by their male partners ceased to be tenable, men were said to be physically victimized as well.) The scale of the problems, the gender of abusers and victims, and other characteristics increasingly came to be recognized as areas for study.

As with all forms of violence, the precise number of abusers and victims cannot be known with absolute certainty, but surveys and studies of varying sizes have established that both physical abuse and sexual abuse of girls and boys are substantial problems. Even adjusting for methodologies, the general finding is that girls are more likely to be sexually abused than boys. Men in and around the family, such as uncles or grandfathers, may abuse only girls, although in some families men sexually abuse children of both sexes. Studies suggest that approximately three times as many girls as boys are sexually abused. Children are also abused in residential and other institutions, such as day schools and youth groups, in which adults occupy a position of leadership and trust. Abuse by strangers is comparatively rare.

Sexual abuse can happen at any age from birth onward but is likely to begin before and cease at adolescence. Research with sex offenders has increased understanding of the ways in which men approach and use children and how they keep children from telling others about the abuse. Some children may be physically injured through adult male penetration, but a child may be required to engage in activities that leave no physical damage, such as masturbation and oral sex. Children are silenced through various strategies, such as threats of harm and even death, or warnings that no one will believe them, that they will be severely punished, or that their mothers will die if they are told.

Women also may abuse children, but sexual abuse is almost entirely undertaken by men. In the United Kingdom, for example, 98 percent of the prosecutions for sexual abuse are of men. Although criminal prosecution, given its rarity, is not a complete measure of the proportion of male or female abusers of children, it is a major indicator. There are also qualitative differences. Women who sexually abuse may do so alone, or they may be in a couple or part of a group with male members and may be abused themselves by these men. Because the number of women who sexually abuse children is so small relative to men, these women are truly deviant. With men, deviance is a more difficult argument to make.

The term *pedophile* could be applied to any man who seeks sexual encounters with children, but it is used primarily to refer to strangers—that is, to men who operate in same-sex groups to abuse children, particularly boys, or who operate alone seeking out single mothers with children of the "right" age. Abusive rings can be established through the Internet, can involve men from different nations, and can include child pornography. On rare occasions a very limited number of these may be apprehended and prosecuted and the images seized, but the children whose bodies were used to make them are unlikely to be found. An extreme case of police, judicial, and governmental incompetence and corruption took place in the 1990s in Belgium, when four abducted and sexually abused young girls died of starvation in locked cellars. Public outrage is not sufficient to curtail widespread child abuse within or around or outside the family; abusers are often socially well connected and highly manipulative men rather than loners or similar outsiders.

With physical and emotional abuse, the proportion of male abusers decreases to approximately 50 percent of all cases. This percentage increases, however, when the proportion of men who abuse is compared only with women abusers living with men. Men are more likely to commit major assaults and homicide. As with sexual abuse, women's abuse of both boy and girl children may be undertaken alone or in conjunction with a male partner and, more rarely, with other relatives or people. Here too, the abuser may be abused herself.

How Agencies Respond to Child Abuse

Definitions of child abuse change over time. Is physical chastisement with whips and other instruments necessary to achieve an obedient, well-brought-up child? Does sexual abuse harm girls? The answers to these questions determine how society responds. Since the turn of the twentieth century, a growing social consensus that extreme physical abuse is unacceptable has emerged, and the forensic evidence produced by radiology began to give child abuse a greater profile in policing and the criminal justice system as well as with regard to health. The acknowledgment of sexual abuse of children as social problem came later and is now an integral part of police work in the western world.

Police forces may have specialist units to investigate child abuse, including taking video statements from children old enough to speak about their experiences. Court procedures may be altered so that children can give evidence behind a screen or by video or be located in another room while giving evidence and during cross-examination. These strategies are adopted to ensure that children do not have to see their abuser and receive nonverbal messages from an intimately known abuser or experience the terror of their abuser's being in such close proximity. However, even with these protective measures, successful prosecutions are far from easy to obtain. Another strategy adopted by women and men is to seek the prosecution of their abusers once they are adults. In some cases police will interview accused men, and if they admit guilt, they will be prosecuted. If they do not, it is likely that collaborative evidence will no longer be available; the exception is when the abuse took place in a residential establishment, where hundreds of former pupils or children's home residents may be interviewed and successful prosecutions ensue.

Other agencies also are involved. Social work, with its statutory responsibility for child protection, may maintain child-abuse registers. Because this area of work is multidisciplinary, formal procedures for working together may be in place. Many agencies may be involved, but key players are the police and the health and social service systems. Schools, too, may have an information-gathering and -reporting system, which may be formally organized so that the suspicions of a classroom teacher are reported to the appropriate supervisor and thence to other agencies as required. (An example of how agencies collaborate on child protection cases is provided by the U.K. Department of Health and Social Service document *Working Together.*) Compliance with mandatory reporting systems may vary, as may the quality of the work that flows from it.

Only in the 1990s did the connections between abuse of children and abuse of women begin to be widely recognized. It is estimated that when mothers are abused, at least 50 percent of the children may be as well. This abuse can be both physical and sexual. If witnessing and knowing about the abuse of one's mother is understood as psychologically abusive, then almost all children in these families are being adversely affected. However, translating this recognition into professional practice in civil law, criminal justice, and social and welfare work is just beginning. For example, civil court proceedings to decide on custody or residence of children or access to them often present a major problem for abused mothers and children. Access to children by abusive male partners can be granted not only when women deem it to be unsafe for themselves and the children, but even when the children express the wish not to see their father again. These decisions have led to repeated abuse and even homicide.

Rediscovering the Abuse of Women

The rediscovery of violence against women by men known to them was separate from the recognition of child abuse. It was initiated independently in the United Kingdom and in the Netherlands by politically active women and led to the setting up of the first shelters for abused women and their children in 1971. The experiences of women, though varied, had commonalities (Dobash and Dobash, 1979). Women described physical, sexual, emotional, and financial abuses and social isolation from family and friends. The major focus continues to be on physical violence, while the least visible form of harm is sexual abuse. Marital rape is recognized as a crime in some countries, but prosecutions are very rare and usually involve some additional form of abuse. Controlling behavior and the exercise of power characterize the experiences of women with abusive male partners.

As with child abuse, these behaviors were well known in the nineteenth century, but by the mid–twentieth century they were no longer common knowledge. The nineteenth- and early-twentieth-century advocates of civil rights for women—including the right to property and earnings; the right to divorce; the right to access, care, control, and guardianship of their children; and the right to vote—argued that these rights would ensure better treatment of women by their husbands, as the latter would have more respect for their wives. Although the extension of civil rights has not eliminated the abuse of wives or even reduced it to an insignificant problem, it has broadened the legal protection offered to women, even if this protection is not always enforced.

All forms of violence can be devastating, but many women say that emotional or psychological abuse—which can reduce and destroy self-esteem and a sense of self-worth, thereby restricting personal independence and autonomy—is the worst. Abused women are often severely depressed, overwhelmed by feelings of hopelessness that greatly reduce their ability to cope with everyday tasks. They may begin to believe that they are totally incompetent and even feel grateful to have an abusive partner. Extreme abuse over a long period of time can be described as a form of torture or brainwashing that reduces the individual to full compliance with her torturer.

Abusive men are likely to minimize and deny the harm caused by their behavior. Men often deny that they are violent, even when they have killed. They also excuse and justify their abuse, partly because their social position is superior and the exercise of power and control over women and children is a "right" emanating from being a man. As Jeff Hearn explains, violence both demonstrates that one is a man and symbolically shows that one is a man (1998). Not all men are equally violent, or even violent at all, but the connection between violence and masculinity is everywhere. When interviewed, men usually describe their violence in terms of specific incidents, mirroring the approach taken by the criminal justice system.

These responses suggest a complex relationship between heterosexuality as a system of social relations and abusive behavior by men. Heterosexuality is the major social context in which gender-differentiated and sexually violent relationships involving women and children occur. The dominance of men can be eroticized both in behavior and in representations, such as pornography, but in men's accounts of their violence, sexual abuse is rarely mentioned. Individual negotiation and resistance to eroticized violence are possible but difficult for both men and women, given the connections between violence, the erotic, and masculine and feminine ideals and expectations.

Prevalence

Abusive behavior by men known to them is a common feature of family life for many women. The number of attacks (incidence) always exceeds the number of those who are victimized (prevalence). In terms of abuse or assault, the home is the least safe place for women. For both women and children the conclusion is this: the closer the relationship, the greater the danger. Family-based violence or abuse is characterized by repetition, and over time it may increase in severity and frequency. Studies in western countries show that one-quarter to one-third of women will experience domestic violence at some time in their lives, and some women will be abused over many years (for example, see Haskell and Randall, 1993). In the United States each year, 1.5 million women seek medical attention for injuries related to abuse, but only 27 out of every 1,000 women are new cases previously unknown to the medical facility (Stark and Flitcraft, 1996). In approximately 50 percent of homicides of women, the perpetrators are husbands or cohabitees. Men, too, suffer injury from women, even death, but death is relatively rare and often occurs as male violence escalates. Men are more likely to experience violent abuse from male strangers and acquaintances.

The group of women who suffer the most domestic abuse are those in prostitution. Studies suggest that prostitution, at a minimum, doubles the risk of domestic violence. A prostitute's boyfriend or partner is often a pimp who may use coercion to ensure that women and girls continue to bring in the money he wants. Increases in heroin and crack addiction have made it even harder for women to abandon prostitution and hence even more difficult for them to end the violence by leaving abusive men. Other forms of violence, from acquaintances and strangers, are also greatly increased for women in prostitution.

Prostitution also entails abuse of children, as both girls and boys frequently enter prostitution before the age of 18. Children may flee sexual abuse at home or at group care facilities only to be quickly picked up by men who, in exchange for sex, offer accommodation, food, and sometimes money. Pimps not only are able to recognize vulnerable children but are on the lookout for them, and they also can be successful in recruiting girls from stable homes. Prosecution of pimps is infrequent, although an awareness of the need to prosecute is increasing.

This form of sexual exploitation of vulnerable girls and women is greatly extended with war, civil unrest, and economic disintegration, when criminal gangs of men move women, children, and anything that sellers and buyers want—such as illegal weapons, nuclear materials, and drugs—between one country and another. Women who arrive as illegal immigrants may be forced to surrender their passports and other documents, their earnings, and their personal freedom. Women and girls who do not speak the language of the receiving country find it even more difficult to escape conditions of bondage. Women have been seized from refugee camps and exported against their will. Europe has many examples of such abuse of women and children since the economic collapse of the Soviet Union and the wars in the former Yugoslavia. Other parts of the world experience similar forms of sexual exploitation and violations of human rights.

How Agencies Respond to the Abuse of Women

Recognition of and initial responses to the abuse of women came from nongovernmental agencies, through services organized by women for women. The aim was to offer women and their children a safe place to live with other women who shared similar experiences. In these safe havens, women were empowered by a decrease in self-blame through new knowledge that came from living with other women with similar experiences. Volunteers and paid staffs assisted women with legal, housing, income maintenance, and other problems, and, as funds increased, so did play groups and other services for children.

Statutory agencies, such as criminal justice, health, social, and welfare services, have been slow to respond to violence against women; as a result, men have continued to receive social and institutional support for their violent, abusive behaviors. But actions at a local level have focused on the development of agency policy to provide guidelines for intervention. In the United Kingdom, for example, central government policy statements and good-practice guidelines promoted the extension of these developments. Proactive responses that assist women and convey to men the message that their abusive behavior toward women is unacceptable are beginning to develop in an uneven way within and between agencies. For example, an operational model of policing that responds to repeat victimization with increasing interventions is a new crime-prevention approach that could be adapted by other statutory agencies (Hanmer, Griffiths, and Jerwood, 1999).

Multiagency or partnership work in response to the abuse of women is at an earlier stage of development than that adopted for child abuse. Domestic violence forums offer a meeting point for all agencies and the possibility of joint work. Internationally recognized approaches combine prosecutions of other mandated outcomes for the perpetrators.

Although the response from government varies in different western countries, funding for refuges or shelters is increasingly seen as a state responsibility, whether organized at local or higher levels. Within nation-states, statutory agencies differ in the extent of their proactive responses, but progress is gathering pace.

From National to International Responses

Recognition of the problem includes activities undertaken by multinational groups, such as the European Union and the Council of Europe, the Commonwealth Secretariat, and the United Nations. For example, the UN Convention on the Elimination of All Forms of Discrimination against Women, the UN Convention on the Rights of the Child, and the Beijing Platform of Action, as well as the appointment of a UN Rapporteur on Violence, have the potential to increase visibility and interventions in nation-states where the abuse of women and children continues to have a low profile. The aim is to establish policy and practice to protect and empower women and children.

These international responses are the result of an understanding of violence and abuse as a violation of human rights. Abuse of women and children now incorporates war; the sexual exploitation, trafficking, and forced migration of refugees; rape as a militarized political policy; forced pregnancy; slavery; and cultural and literal genocide through the use of mass weapons of destruction such as nuclear testing, as well as through famine and disease that are consequences of war (Lentin, 1997). These human rights abuses occur throughout the world, often aided and abetted by the actions of the West in supplying weapons, military training, and active support for military dictators. Women and children are always the losers; in a war, the safest place to be is usually in the armed forces, even when they are engaged in combat.

In conclusion, *abuse* can be seen as an overworked term or as a word to open a door to a new understanding of gender dynamics and, beyond that, to a new understanding of what needs to change to render the widespread use of *abuse* obsolete.

See Also

BATTERY; DOMESTIC VIOLENCE; INCEST; PORNOGRAPHY AND VIOLENCE; PROSTITUTION; RAPE; SEXUAL VIOLENCE; TRAFFICKING; VIOLENCE, *all entries*

References and Further Reading

Armstrong, Louise. 1978. *Kiss Daddy goodnight: A speak-out on incest.* New York: Pocket Books.

Dobash, Rebecca Emerson, and Russell Dobash. 1979. *Violence against wives: The case against the patriarchy.* New York: Free Press.

Hanmer, Jalna, Sue Griffiths, and Dave Jerwood. 1999. *Arresting evidence: Domestic violence and repeat victimisation.* Paper no. 104, Policing and Reducing Crime Unit. London: Home Office.

Haskell, Lori, and Melanie Randall. 1993. *Women's safety project: A summary of key statistical findings.* Ottawa: Panel on Violence against Women.

Hearn, Jeff. 1998. *The violences of men.* London: Sage.

Kempe, C. H., F. Silverman, W. Droegmueller, and H. Silver. 1962. The battered child syndrome. *Journal of the American Medical Association,* 181: 17–24.

Lentin, Ronit, ed. 1997. *Gender and catastrophe.* London and New York: Zed.

Mullender, Audrey. 1996. *rethinking domestic violence: The social work and probation response.* London and New York: Routledge.

Rush, Florence. 1980. *The best kept secret: Sexual abuse of children.* Englewood Cliffs, N.J.: Prentice-Hall.

Stark, Evan, and Anne Flitcraft. 1996. *Women at risk: Domestic violence and women's health.* Thousand Oaks, Calif.: Sage.

Jalna Hanmer

ACHIEVEMENT

See ABILITY and EDUCATION: ACHIEVEMENT.

ACQUIRED IMMUNE DEFICIENCY SYNDROME

See AIDS AND HIV.

ACTIVISM

Activism is a broad concept. Whereas *activism* refers primarily to political actions, the boundaries of what counts as political cannot be narrowly drawn, because, in a feminist view, the personal is also political. Thus, activism as we define it encompasses all collective efforts to change power relations at all levels, from the interpersonal to the international.

Women's activism is not new. The Greek play *Lysistrata* portrayed women collectively attempting to change the balance of power in their relationships with men several millennia ago. At the beginning of the twentieth century, there was already a strongly developed international women's movement challenging the subordination of women (Rupp, 1998). Women's current activism takes place within a context of struggles for gender equality and other political and economic goals, across a range of international and nationally based organizations, and includes ongoing efforts to establish constructive discussions between privileged and disadvantaged women about the nature of women's needs (see, for example, Booth, 1998; Moghadam, 2000).

Within activism, we differentiate between women's movements and feminism (see also Ferree et al., 1999). By *women's movements* we mean the work of women who are motivated *as women* to work on issues that they view as particularly important, such as environmental protection, health, deindustrialization, poverty, gender equality, or peace. By definition, women's movements involve a collective mobilization of women as social and political actors. These movements address women as women or sometimes as mothers, and organizations are typically by and for women alone.

We define *feminism* by its focus on changes in women's social status in three critical dimensions: access to economic resources, power to affect decisions in the community as a whole, and autonomy in relation to personal life choices. Feminist movements have changing gender relationships as their goal; they specifically aim to empower women and to change social arrangements that unequally benefit men. Feminist groups—that is, those that are concerned with gender relations as a target of social and political change—are but one part of the women's movement.

Women's activism encompasses both women's movements and feminism but also can be found in other mobilizations for political change that neither specifically appeal to gender as a basis for mobilization nor set out to challenge gender relations as a goal. Labor movements, movements of national liberation, and environmental movements are examples of such other contexts.

Within women's movements there are multiple types of activist organizations. We classify these into three broad categories. First, *autonomous women's organizations* are groups that exist independent of state support and play no official role in state decision making. These may or may not be feminist. Many autonomous activist groups are small, local, informal, and nonhierarchical in structure, but this is not necessarily the case (Miles, 1996). Among the autonomous feminist organizations active at the turn of the twenty-first century are an increasing number that are international in scope—that is, nongovernmental organizations (NGOs) that draw their membership and define their goals beyond the boundaries of individual nation-states. Autonomous women's NGOs such as Developmental Alternatives for Women in a New Era (DAWN) and the International Women's Tribune Center focus on developing and supporting grassroots activism.

Second, *state feminism* refers to mobilization within and through formal government organizations charged with attending to women's interests, such as the Women's

Bureau of the U.S. Department of Labor (Stetson and Mazur, 1995). State feminism includes mobilization within international quasi-governmental organizations such as the United Nations and the European Union. State feminists also are sometimes called "femocrats," a term coined to describe the Australian experience but widely picked up because it so appropriately describes the situation around the world (Eisenstein, 1996). Femocrats are women in official positions within the state whose formal responsibilities include representing women as a distinctive constituency and responding to women's particular needs. They often head women's ministries in parliamentary systems, such as in Germany or France, and administer a variety of programs specifically designed for women.

Third, *unobtrusive mobilization within institutions* refers to the process through which women have come together inside other associations, organizations, and social movements. Katzenstein (1998) describes how activists working with the U.S. military and within the Catholic church challenged the practices and discourses of these powerful hierarchical institutions, using a variety of strategies from lawsuits to conferences. Unobtrusive mobilization also can happen in less well institutionalized groups, such as social movements. Activists challenge gender relations within the movement's organizations and struggle to put gender equality on the agenda of the movement's concerns. In nationalist movements, unobtrusive mobilization by feminists can lead to activists' becoming state feminists if the movement succeeds in coming to power.

Organizational Issues for Activists

Although social movements are more than the organizations to which they give rise, organizations are among the most enduring and powerful resources that activists have to produce long-term change. Organizations allow the transmission of information and material resources across generations, and allow the movement to institutionalize its ideas in practices that can financed and taught in larger numbers than could be done by individuals working separately. Organizational structure has long been a concern for activists, who debate the merits of more bureaucratic or collectivist forms, consider the risks of co-optation that come from working inside larger groups, and deal with problems of authority and hierarchy (Ferree and Martin, 1995). New issues for women activists are emerging as women's movements generally, and feminist organizations in particular, grow in number and scope around the world (Alvarez, 1997).

First, the wide networks of women activists that are being built are bringing feminist perspectives to a great variety of issues, hence diffusing the movement. As women activists become unobtrusively mobilized in a variety of associations and movements, feminist perspectives and gender interests come to be seen as relevant to more and more issues. This diffused activism has the potential to challenge gender relations very broadly, but activists on specific issues run the risk of losing sight of the connections between specific issues. Building and maintaining cross-issue networks in their particular countries and regions is one strategy that women activists have used to integrate diverse concerns. The development of issue-specific activist groups in a variety of countries and regions has been accompanied by efforts to link them into *international issue advocacy networks* (Keck and Sikkink, 1998).

Second, the expansion of networking and diffusion into state institutions has contributed to making activism more professionalized. Women's activism often takes the form of building or working in formal NGOs rather than in informal, fact-to-face groups. As they have become more professional in form, activist organizations also have acquired more resources and expertise and are more likely to be consulted by authorities and officials. Activists with specialized expertise also have built up alternative institutions for providing services, from rape counseling to job training. The risk of co-optation into the welfare state, however, is not trivial when activists affiliated with women's organizations lobby to influence state policy making and compete for resources.

Third, the expansion and professionalization of activist networks has increased feminist influence on where and how resources are channeled. In postcolonial nations, international aid has particularly gone under the rubric of "capacity building" (Grindle, 1997). Capacity-building initiatives have brought substantial new funding for women's activism, but there are also costs associated with such sponsored growth. Rivalries over who will be funded, implicit pressure to accept western priorities, and a tendency to favor organizations that are more formalized and can be held more accountable to the donors are all likely results.

Feminists worry that these developments may change grassroots women into recipients of services from the movement rather than active participants in its ongoing development. This transformation of grassroots women into mere beneficiaries of services is sometimes called *clientelism*, because it defines the service providers rather than the recipients as those who best understand the clients' needs and interests. By contrast, feminists generally believe that grassroots women should be defining their own needs and speaking out in their own cause. Such *empowerment* means much more than access to the formal institutions of politics, because self-determination is significant in many aspects of civil society (Kabeer, 1999; Karl, 1995).

In sum, activist organizations have grown in number and scope, and feminists have unobtrusively mobilized in governments, foundations, and community organizations worldwide. More diverse in activities, more professionalized in form, and more targeted to international decision-making bodies, women activists have had a discernible influence on the discourses used and policies adopted regarding gender issues around the world. Activists strive to channel resources from non-gender-specific sources to women, and they insist on empowerment through local initiative and grassroots consciousness raising to avoid reducing women to mere recipients of benefits.

For all these successes, there are still multiple challenges ahead. Informal networks are less easily institutionalized, less permanent, and lacking in any structure for ensuring democratic accountability to those whom they claim to represent. In addition, the "NGO-ized" form of organization, directed at lobbying a national or international decision makers, tends to marginalize the less skilled and less affluent. Women's activism is not only about gaining access and influence in political structures (that is, femocracy). It is also about reenvisioning civil society and changing gender relations in ways that will challenge the division between state and society, public and private, politics and personal life.

See Also

FEMINISM: OVERVIEW; FEMOCRAT; NONGOVERNMENTAL ORGANIZATIONS (NGOS); POLITICAL PARTICIPATION; POLITICS AND THE STATE: OVERVIEW; WOMEN'S MOVEMENT: MODERN INTERNATIONAL MOVEMENT

References and Further Reading

Alvarez, Sonia. 1997. Dilemmas of gendered citizenship in post authoritarian Latin America. Paper presented at the Conference on Gendered Citizenships: European and Latin American Perspectives, Minda de Gunzburg Center for European Studies, Harvard University, 14–17 March.

Booth, Karen M. 1998. National mother, global whore, and transnational femocrats: The politics of AIDS and the construction of women at the World Health Organization. *Feminist Studies* 24(1): 115–139.

Connelly, Patricia M. 1996. Gender matters: Global restructuring and adjustment. *Social Politics* 3(1): 12–31.

Eisenstein, Hester. 1996. *Inside agitators: Australian femocrats and the state.* Philadelphia: Temple University Press.

Ferree, Myra Marx, and Martin, Patricia Yancey. 1995. *Feminist organizations: Harvest of the new women's movement.* Philadelphia: Temple University Press.

Ferree, Myra Marx, Barbara Risman, Valerie Sperling, Tatiana Gurikova, and Katherine Hyde. 1999. The Russian women's movement: Activists' strategies and identities. *Women and Politics* 20(3): 83–109.

Grindle, Merilee. 1997. The good government imperative: Human resources, organizations, and institutions. In Merilee S. Grindle, ed., *Getting good government: Capacity building in the public sectors of developing countries.* Cambridge, Mass.: Harvard Institute for International Development.

Kabeer, Naila. 1999. Resources, agency, achievement: Reflections on the measurement of women's empowerment. *Development and Change* 30: 435–464.

Karl, Marilee. 1995. *Women and empowerment: Participation and decision-making.* London: Zed.

Katzenstein, Mary F. 1990. Feminism within American institutions: Unobtrusive mobilizations in the 1980s. *Signs* 16(1): 27–54.

———. 1998. *Faithful and fearless: Moving feminist protest inside the church and military.* Princeton, N.J.: Princeton University Press.

Keck, Margaret E., and Sikkink, Kathryn. 1998. *Activists beyond border: Advocacy networks in international politics.* Ithaca, N.Y.: Cornell University Press.

Miles, Angela. 1996. *Integrative feminisms: Building global visions, 1960s–1990s.* New York: Routledge.

Moghadam, Valentine M. 2000. Transnational feminist networks: Collective action in an era of globalization. *International Sociology* 15(1): 57–85.

Rupp, Leila J. 1998. *Worlds of women: The making of an international women's movement.* Princeton, N.J.: Princeton University Press.

Stetson, Dorothy McBride, and Amy G. Mazur. 1995. *Comparative state feminism.* Thousand Oaks, Calif.: Sage.

Myra Marx Ferree
Mangala Subramaniam

ADDICTION

See DRUG AND ALCOHOL ABUSE.

ADOLESCENCE

Adolescence—which is largely a twentieth-century western "invention" that originated mainly in the United States and the United Kingdom—is now considered a chronological period of accelerated cognitive, emotional, and physical growth. The outcome of these changes is sexual and psychological maturity. This period is thought to begin around age 12 and end when the individual gains independence, usually between ages 18 and 20. The actual end of this period depends on many factors, including cultural expectations, individual physical maturation, and emotional development. The changes that occur during adolescence can be difficult and confusing for the adolescent as well as the family and society.

The most visible change for the adolescent is puberty. This is the period during which there is rapid physical growth as well as sexual maturation. Young women will experience menarche—first menstruation—during early puberty. In the United States the average age of menarche is about 12.45 years; in Europe it is about 13 years. The onset of menses may occur as early as 10 years or as late as 15.5 years and still be considered normal. Menarche, however, is only part of the gradual process of puberty. Both boys and girls experience a powerful rush of hormones from the endocrine glands—testosterone for boys and estradiol for girls. Estradiol is necessary for breast, uterine, and skeletal development. The concentration of this hormone increases eightfold during puberty (Lerner and Foch, 1987).

This is the period during which young people see their bodies change virtually overnight. Many young women develop a new and heightened awareness of their bodies during adolescence. Many also may begin to experience problems such as eating disorders, depression, alcohol and drug use, and sexual experimentation during this time (Santrock, 1997). These issues have been thought to be more common among earlier-maturing girls. However, early maturation is thought to benefit girls in some ways, in that they demonstrate more independence and greater popularity. Young women experience the rapid physical changes and growth spurts of puberty, on average, two years before young men; in fact, many young women have completed this portion of puberty before their male peers have even begun.

Cognitive changes also occur during adolescence. Adolescents begin to display "formal operational" thought, a developmental phase suggested by Jean Piaget, which occurs around age 12. This type of thinking is more logical, organized, abstract, and idealistic than younger children's thinking. Adolescents also become more interested in and capable of introspection and social cognition. Given these changes, many adolescents appear to become self-absorbed as they begin to engage in hypothetical and abstract reasoning about themselves and their lives. They may perceive the world around them subjectively, which can cause problems with

others for adolescents who harbor a belief that "no one"—certainly not a parent—could understand them. This tendency is often referred to as adolescent egocentrism. Some theorists attribute many of the reckless behaviors of adolescents, including drug and alcohol use, excessive speed while driving, and in some cases suicidal thoughts, to their egocentrism (Elkind, 1978). Unfortunately, adolescents often act on their own feelings in harmful ways. Suicide accounts for about 12 percent of the mortality rate among adolescents and young adults, and in the United States the incidence of suicide in this age group tripled between 1952 and 1992 (Center for Disease Control, 1995). The changes in adolescent cognition also necessitate changes in the manner in which adolescents are educated. Young women, at this time, may respond better to more abstract than to concrete methods of instruction.

Conflict, conformity, and changes in identity can mark the social and emotional development of adolescence, and the young person addresses two critical questions: what one does in the face of conflict and how one can live with others.

The conflict between a young woman and her family that often occurs in early adolescence may play an important role in her continuing individual development, as well as in her understanding of who she is in relation to others. These conflicts and their resolutions allow the young woman to separate her unfolding sense of *self* from her sense of *herself in relation to her family.* Sometimes the conflict is particularly intense and stressful. This type of prolonged conflict has been shown to be associated with a number of problems of adolescence, such as juvenile delinquency, dropping out of school, drug abuse, running away, and cult membership (Brook et al., 1990). Peer group conformity (peer pressure) also occurs during the early stages of adolescence. For young women, "being in relationship to others" is a crucial part of their development. This interest in identifying with others allows for the development of social consciousness, social skills, and feelings of inclusion. The developmental theorist Erik Erikson has noted that adolescence is in the fifth stage of the life cycle, "identity versus identity confusion." Together with the development of formal operational thinking, this period is marked by experimentation with a number of roles and identities from adolescents' own imagination or the world around them. As the adolescent girl successfully integrates these identities and manages the stress surrounding conflicting identities, she is able to develop a new and unique core sense of self, involving awareness of such things as career direction, basic values, and sexual orientation. Although this sense of self will change over the life span, at this stage it allows the adolescent to begin her movement toward adult maturity.

See Also

EATING DISORDERS; GIRL STUDIES; GIRLS' SUBCULTURES; INITIATION RITES; MENARCHE; MENSTRUATION; SEXUALITY: ADOLESCENT SEXUALITY; SUICIDE

References and Further Reading

Brook, J. S., D. W. Brook, A. S. Gordon, M. Whiteman, and P. Cohen. 1990. The psychological etiology of adolescent drug use: A family interactional approach. *Genetic, Social and General Psychology Monographs* 116: 110–267.

Center for Disease Control. 1995. Suicide among children, adolescents, and young adults—United States, 1980–1992. *Morbidity Mortality Weekly Report* 44: 289–291.

Elkind, D. 1978. Understanding the young adolescent. *Adolescence* 13: 127–134.

Lerner, R. M., and T. T. Foch, eds. 1987. *Biological–psychological interactions in early adolescence.* Hillsdale, N.J.: Erlbaum.

Santrock, J. W. 1997. *Life-span development.* Madison, Wis.: Brown and Benchmark.

Joan E. Huebl

ADOPTION

Adoption establishes a permanent legal relationship between a parent and a non–biologically related child. The adoptive parent or parents assume all the responsibilities associated with parenthood, and the child has no remaining legal link with the biological mother or father. Adoption may occur between a child and a family member (such as a grandmother or a stepfather) or between a child and a completely unrelated adult. In the United States, for example, adoption is more likely to occur between a child and a family member than between a child and a stranger (Hollinger, 1999). Although typically there are age limits on who can be adopted, these age limits are not universal.

Adoption has a long history. It is mentioned in the Code of Hammurabi and in Hindu Sanskrit texts, and it was practiced in ancient Rome, where it was generally used to perpetuate a male familial line. Adoption was also traditional in many societies in Africa and Oceania, and in indigenous American Indian societies. The Muslim personal law Shariyat does not mention adoption, although it occurs among Muslims in many countries.

Adoption of an unrelated child is of fairly recent origin under common law (legal systems based on English law). England did not enact a general adoption law until 1926; in the United States, adoption in its modern form dates back only to the mid-nineteenth century (Hollinger, 1999). Nineteenth-century adoption statutes often specified that courts must consider the suitability of the adoptive parents as well as whether the adoption was suitable for the child; they were also designed to ensure that the biological parents would be involved in the adoption process. Although these early statutes provided that the adoptive family would substitute for the biological family, they still frequently expressed a preference for blood relationships. For example, a child was allowed to inherit from the biological parents but was precluded from inheriting from relatives of the adoptive parents because they were "strangers to the adoption."

Today, adoption laws vary somewhat between countries. In the United States, for instance, contemporary law emphasizes the complete substitution of the adoptive family for the biological family. A child becomes available for adoption when the biological parents voluntarily decide to give up their parental rights or when those rights are terminated involuntarily. The adoption may occur through an agency, or it may be a private adoption arranged directly between the biological and adoptive parents, frequently with the help of a lawyer. The adoptive parents must receive a court order that confers on them the status of parenthood. In the United States, the adoptee receives a new birth certificate that lists the adoptive parents as the parents and also lists the child's new name. In other countries, adoption does not necessarily lead to a new birth certificate.

Traditionally, adoption has meant that the adoptee and the biological parents have no further contact, but under some contemporary adoption laws—as in the United States—the biological parents may continue to see their child pursuant to an open adoption, or adoption-with-contact, arrangement. This change in adoption practice is a response both to the needs of adopted children and to requests by birth mothers (Appell, 1998; Carp, 1999). Moreover, although adoption records have typically been sealed and unavailable for review, this too is changing. In New South Wales (Australia), England, Wales, and some parts of the United States, adoptees now have access to their original birth certificates.

In addition to legally recognized adoption, numerous informal adoptions occur outside the legal system, without formal recognition of the new relationship. In the African-American community, for instance, informal adoption has a long history (Perry, 1998). The practice of fostering in Oceania is another example. In the United States, foster care refers to the temporary placement of children in a substitute family; although the foster family may ultimately seek to adopt the child, the child also may be returned to the biological family.

Given that the adoptive family was supposed to look like a typical family, it has been difficult for single women or lesbian couples to adopt children. The traditionally preferred adoptive placement has been with a married heterosexual couple (Hollinger, 1999). This is beginning to change. Single parents are becoming eligible for adoption, and practices that prevented lesbians from becoming adoptive parents are changing as well. Even the partners of lesbian women are becoming increasingly able to adopt through several different strategies. Where one partner has adopted a child, the other partner may seek a "second-parent" adoption to enable her to exercise parental rights (Goldenberg, 2000). Such adoptions have been recognized in several countries, including the United States and Israel. Another alternative is available to relatively few couples: where one partner is pregnant with an egg from the other parent, the other partner can seek a prebirth ruling that she will also be the child's legal parent.

Some parents adopt children from other countries, leading to adoptive relationships that are interracial, intercultural, and interreligious. A number of international treaties and conventions, such as the Hague Convention on Intercountry Adoption, govern various substantive and procedural aspects of international adoptions. Nonetheless, each country develops its own adoption policies.

Some feminists have claimed that international adoption allows more privileged adopting women to exploit less advantaged birth mothers from other countries by removing the children without giving the mothers any help (Perry, 1998). On the other hand, adoptive mothers are providing a home for children who might otherwise grow up under marginal conditions in an institution. Adoptive mothers have also spoken of their overwhelming love for their adopted children and their construction as mothers (Bartholet, 1992; Lacey, 1998). Moreover, adoptive parents have stressed that they will attempt to respect their children's original backgrounds.

During the mid-twentieth century in the United States, a birth mother was frequently told that adoption would be best for the child and that she herself would be able to forget the child completely and go on with her life (Cahn and Singer, 1999; Solinger, 1992). Increasingly, however, birth mothers have begun to speak out about their pain in not knowing their children and about the connection that they continue to feel to these children (Cahn and Singer, 1999). Although a few birth mothers, particularly victims of rape, have spoken about the significance of keeping the past private, the overwhelming majority of birth mothers have welcomed the opportunity to have contact with their children.

Adoptees have become increasingly vocal about their need to know about their biological origins (Lifton, 1994). Adoptees' desire to search for their biological relatives develops from many different sources and may include both physical and psychological motives.

Public attitudes toward adoption vary. In a recent study in the United States, most of the participants were extremely accepting of adoption. On the other hand, only two-thirds of the respondents believed that it was highly likely that an adoptee would love the adoptive parents as much as the biological parents (Princeton Survey Research Associates, 1997).

Ultimately, adoption is one of several methods for creating a new family. Adoption practices have changed significantly over the past several decades as we gain improved understanding of how adoption affects birth parents, adoptive parents, and adoptees.

See Also

ADOPTION: MENTAL HEALTH ISSUES; FOSTERING: CASE STUDY—OCEANIA; STEPFAMILIES

References and Further Reading

Appell, Annette R. 1998. Increasing options to improve permanency: Considerations in drafting an adoption with contact statute. *Children's Legal Rights Journal* 18: 24.

Bartholet, Elizabeth. 1992. *Family bonds.* Boston: Beacon.

Cahn, Naomi, and Jana Singer. 1999. Adoption, identity, and the Constitution. *University of Pennsylvania Journal of Constitutional Law* 2: 150.

Carp, E. Wayne. 1999. *Family matters: Secrecy and disclosure in the history of adoption.* Cambridge, Mass.: Harvard University Press.

Goldenberg, Suzanne. 2000. Israel grants rights to lesbian mothers. *Guardian* (London), 30 May: 14.

Hollinger, Joan Heifetz. 1999. *Adoption law and practice.* New York: Matthew Bender.

Lacey, Linda. 1998. O wind, remind him that I have no child: Infertility and feminist jurisprudence. *Michigan Journal of Gender and Law* 5: 163.

Lifton, Betty Jean. 1994. *Journey of the adopted self.* Boston: Beacon.

Perry, Twila. 1998. Transracial and international adoption: Mothers, hierarchy, race, and feminist theory. *Yale Journal of Law and Feminism* 10: 101.

Princeton Survey Research Associates. 1997. *Benchmark adoption study.*

Solinger, Ricki. 1992. *Wake up little Susie: Single pregnancy and race before Roe v. Wade.* New York: Routledge.

Naomi Cahn

ADOPTION: Mental Health Issues

As a legal process confirming an adult as the parent of a child, adoption is routine in western nations. It provides homes for children who might otherwise be raised in foster care or in group homes. It is seen as a way of handling unwanted pregnancy and as a way of creating a family for others: both infertile and fertile couples, including gay and lesbian couples, as well as individuals who opt to become single parents. In developing countries, adoption may be a formal legal process, though this is rare. It is more commonly an informal obligation, often assumed by a relative or community member, to care for a child whose parents have died or are unable or unwilling to raise the child themselves.

Defining adoption by these parameters alone, however, trivializes and ignores the psychological impact that separating a child from his or her birth mother will have on all members of the "adoption triad"—a term used to refer to adoptees, birth parents, and adoptive parents. Adoption can have a profound effect on all three members of the triad: the adopted child, the adoptive mother, and the birth mother.

Adoption is not merely a social and legal reaction to a problem that then disappears when papers are signed and the adoption is finalized. It raises issues of mental health that have particularly strong consequences for the women of the adoption triad. It is not only a formal procedure but a delicate, long-term process that will have lifelong effects on the well-being of the child, the birth mother, and the adopting family.

Many factors positively influence the integration of an adopted child into a family: early adoption, a stable adopting family, the readiness of parent and child to create an enduring and trusting attachment, a sense of a "good fit" between parent and child, and an openness in the family toward the issue of adoption itself. When adopted children have special needs, the families often require additional support. Financial and medical assistance may be critical to ensuring a stable family environment, and supportive group networks may also help adopting parents work with the needs of their child. Interracial and international adoptions require creating an environment in which a child's dual heritage can flourish and a healthy sense of identity is maximized.

In regions of the world where legal adoption is rare, the role of the adopting family is often filled by siblings, cousins, aunts, uncles, or grandparents of the birth mother. When possible, adoption is a family and community responsibility. In countries where adoption is considered primarily a legal bond between parent and child, the adopting family usually does not know the birth mother. The psychological effects of legal adoption can be serious and are often overlooked. When close kinship adoptions are not possible, many complex issues arise.

As Brodzinsky, Schechter, and Henig (1990) state, "Professionals and lay people have had trouble accepting the possibility that the solution itself could at times be a problem." This may explain the dearth of research on the psychological ramifications of formal adoption for the adoption triad. Little empirical work has been done to evaluate the impact of adoption on the development of adopted children, the effect of relinquishment on birth mothers, or the difficult issues faced by adoptive parents. However, those studies that have been done, based on casework and clinical observations, suggest that the severance inherent in adoption can create long-term complications and difficulties for the triad.

Much is at stake. There is a birth mother who may have opted to relinquish a child; there is an adoptive mother who may be childless; and there is an adoptee who has lost a connection to his or her roots and birth mother.

The psychological effect is perhaps most easily identifiable, and most profound, on adoptees cut off from their original family and relatives. With little knowledge of their origins, adoptees are encouraged to deny a significant aspect of themselves and to resign themselves to a sense of permanent loss. This can ultimately lead to low self-esteem, academic difficulties, and a range of rebellious activities known as "acting-out" behaviors, such as aggression, stealing, lying, hyperactivity, oppositional behavior, and truancy. Where legal adoption is common, studies suggest that these behaviors account for the high ratio of adoptees in counseling as teenagers—which, for instance, some professionals say is as much as 40 percent in the United States, although adoptees represent only 2 percent of the American population. Only recently has legal adoption been seriously considered a causal agent for the difficulties these adolescents experience.

To consider legal adoption itself as a contributor to the behavioral problems of an adopted child is difficult, because pointing an accusatory finger at legal adoption would seem to blame the adoptive mother. This places her in an especially difficult position because, as a mother, she is expected to be a parent to her child in a supportive and responsive home, yet she is blamed for the child's behavior. One study suggests that adoptive parents may create relationships and expectations that can affect adopted children and increase their likelihood of exhibiting problem behavior (Verhulst, 1992). Yet questions remain whether adoptive parents can truly be at fault for the myriad behavioral problems that seem prevalent among some adolescent adoptees. One must still ask whether the original severance and subsequent avoidance of adoption issues may be powerful enough in themselves to generate mental health problems for adoptees. Also, in many parts of the world girls, being less valued, are more likely than boys to be relinquished for adoption—a unique and formidable rejection whose ramifications will continue into adulthood. Certainly, numerous contributing factors may exist in any given case. To ignore the effect of relinquishment on the adoptee, however, is to exclude examination of the most profound event of adoptees' lives: their mothers' having given them away.

This severance of a child from the birth mother affects the adoptive mother as well. Frequently, adoption laws allow for little or no information to be shared with the adoptive family other than vague physical descriptions. Hence, an adoptive mother is often parenting "blind." Cut off from any contact with the biological family, and uninformed about her adoptive child's background, including the health of the birth mother and her condition during pregnancy, the adoptive mother can face enormous uncertainty and confusion. Responsible yet uninformed, she often blames herself for issues beyond her control.

The birth mother is, in many ways, the most vulnerable member of the adoption triad. The psychological consequences of relinquishing her child may not be evident for many years. The vast majority of birth mothers are encouraged to "bury" forever the events of pregnancy and birth and the subsequent loss of their children, to ignore their grief, and to keep these events secret from others, even spouses and children. In many cases, birth mothers put a child up for adoption under stressful circumstances or because they are told to do so. Only decades later may the effects of the denial and avoidance of this loss begin to surface. Again, little empirical research has been performed on the psychological impact of adoption on birth mothers. What data do exist are anecdotal, from clinical observation and casework.

Adoption is an important institution and will always be necessary and often desirable. Equally necessary, however, to allow healthier lives for all, is evaluation of the circumstances in which adoption takes place.

See Also

ADOPTION; FAMILY PLANNING; FAMILY STRUCTURES; MOTHERHOOD; PARENTHOOD; STEPFAMILIES

References and Selected Reading

Baran, Annette, Reuben Pannor, and Arthur Sorosky. 1978, 1984. *The adoption triangle.* San Antonio, Tex.: Corona.

Brodzinsky, David M. 1990. *The psychology of adoption.* New York: Oxford University Press.

———, Marshall Schechter, and Robin Marantz Henig. 1992. *Being adopted: The lifelong search for self.* New York: Doubleday.

Kirk, David. 1984. *Shared fate.* New York: Free Press.

Shannon, Thomas. 1988. *Surrogate motherhood.* New York: Crossroad.

Verhulst, Frank C. 1992. Damaging backgrounds: Later adjustment of international adoptees. *Journal of the American Academy of Child and Adolescent Psychiatry* 31(3 May): 518–524.

Jean A. S. Strauss

ADULT EDUCATION

See EDUCATION: ADULT AND CONTINUING.

ADULTERY

Adultery refers to sexual relations outside a union of marriage, although legal and cultural definitions of what constitutes an act of adultery are as varied as legal and cultural definitions of marriage itself. Any definition of adultery must be sensitive to cross-cultural variation in rights of access to sexual reproduction, including rights to children, as well as to variation in rights of access to sexuality. Theories of adultery contend with the fact of its common practice even in the face of widespread cultural norms and social sanctions against it.

Fisher (1992) argues that although cross-cultural rates of adultery are high for both sexes, the evolutionary benefits of adultery differ for men and women. For men, adultery increases the likelihood of passing on their genetic material to future generations. For women, adultery is less a reproductive than an economic strategy for guaranteeing multiple sources of aid and protection for themselves and their children. But for both sexes, she claims, "it is the millennia of sneaking off with lovers—and the genetic payoffs these dalliances accrued—that have produced the propensity for adultery around the world today" (1992: 97). Fisher also claims that intense feelings of guilt and jealousy concerning extramarital affairs are another universal experience related to genetic inheritance, although Leacock's quotations from the Montagnais-Naskapi seem to refute this (see her contribution in Etienne and Leacock, 1980: 28). Atkinson and Errington's discussion of adultery among the Wana shows how discourse on jealousy can vary considerably cross-culturally:

> In explaining why a wife would be jealous of her husband's lover, one woman explained that to seduce an unmarried woman, a married man disparages his own wife. He tells his lover that his wife is lazy, weak, and will not work for his mother. He proceeds to praise his would-be lover for her strength and industry.... Similarly, women will divorce men who are shiftless workers. Wana talk about marriage brings out the point that both spouses are expected to be hard-working contributors to their productive unit. (Atkinson and Errington, 1990: 68)

Although adultery may be a human universal, it has often been stigmatized and subject to legal sanctions, but the degree of stigmatization and sanctions varies historically and cross-culturally. Suzanne Frayser's (1985) cross-cultural survey found that 74 percent of 58 cultures punished adultery to some degree:

> In 83 percent of 48 societies, both partners receive penalties for adultery; in 40 percent of them men and women get the same degree of chastisement; in 31 percent of them the man's punishment is more severe than that of his female lover. No society tolerates a female's dalliances while punishing males; and significantly more cultures have restrictions on women than on men. (Cited in Fisher, 1992: 321)

Strong sanctions against adultery, where they occur, tend to be more dire for women than for men and extend to differing definitions of adultery for men and women. A married woman's pursuit of sexual relations outside her marriage is automatically considered adultery, whereas a married man is defined as adulterous only if he has sex with another man's wife. Vogel's study (1992) of European legislation against adultery in the nineteenth century locates the source of this double standard in notions of wives and children as the property of males—notions that underlie legal and religious codes regarding marriage. Islamic law is an extreme example of a legal code with such a double standard based on patriarchal notions of family and property. In countries where civil legal codes rely on Islamic law, women who commit adultery are subject to public beatings or stoning, whereas sanctions against men are serious only if a man has "violated" another man's wife (see Sahebjam, 1994, for a recent case study in Iran).

Cross-culturally, the degree of differentiation in sanctions against acts of adultery for men and women is an indicator of the degree of sexual inequality in a particular society. Where women have access to political decision making and control important economic resources, women's status is higher, divorce is easier for women to obtain, and sanctions against women's adultery are relatively mild. The studies in Etienne and Leacock (1980) collectively argue that a concomitant of western imperialism and colonization has been a global decline in women's status in most societies, including increased regulation of women's sexuality and increased sanctions against women's adultery.

Perhaps ironically, the adulterous affair as symbolic of autonomy and freedom from harsh societal mores is an important trope in western literature. An early example is a novel by Kate Chopin (1851–1904), *The Awakening*, which explores the notion of adultery for a married woman as a path to freedom and self-discovery. But her heroine's ultimately self-destructive fate reminds us of Foucault's point (1978: 41) about western psychological interpretations of social sanctions against adultery beginning in the nineteenth century. In the West, the act of adultery may now more often be viewed as pathological rather than illegal or sinful, but it is still heavily stigmatized, especially for women.

See Also

DIVORCE; FAMILY: RELIGIOUS AND LEGAL SYSTEMS, *specific regions;* MARRIAGE: REGIONAL TRADITIONS AND PRACTICES; MISTRESS; SEX AND CULTURE; SPIRITUALITY: SEXUALITY

References and Further Reading

Atkinson, Jane Monnig, and Shelly Errington, eds. 1990. *Power and difference: Gender in island Southeast Asia.* Stanford, Calif.: Stanford University Press.

Chopin, Kate. 1994. *The awakening: An authoritative text, biographical and historical contexts, and criticism,* 2nd ed. Margo Culley, ed. New York: Norton.

Etienne, Mona, and Eleanor Leacock, eds. 1980. *Women and colonization: Anthropological perspectives.* New York: Bergin and Garvey.

Fisher, Helen E. 1992. *Anatomy of love: The natural history of monogamy, adultery, and divorce.* New York: Norton.

Foucault, Michel. 1978. *The history of sexuality.* Vol. 1, *An intro-duction.* New York: Vintage.

Frayser, Suzanne. 1985. *Varieties of sexual experience: An anthro-pological perspective.* New Haven, Conn.: HRAF.

Sahebjam, Freidoune. 1994. *The stoning of Soraya M.* Trans. Richard Seaver. New York: Arcade.

Vogel, Ursula. 1992. Whose property? The double standard of adultery in nineteenth-century law. In Carol Smart, ed., *Regulating womanhood: Historical essays on marriage, moth-erhood, and sexuality,* 147–165. London: Routledge.

Karen Frojen Herrera

ADVERTISING

Advertising, a ubiquitous feature of the mass media, is a key institution of socialization in advanced and emerging indus-trialized societies. Fueled by the perennial struggle to mar-ket goods and services in a multimedia environment, advertising images increasingly pervade everyday life in these societies, bombarding individuals with snapshots of what they supposedly lack and what they need to acquire to fill the void. This "lack" typically has more to do with lifestyles, looks, and aspirations associated with products by advertis-ers than with the inherent qualities of the products them-selves. The ability of advertising not only to reflect but also to mold social meanings is central to the study of gender and advertising.

According to this study, almost from its inception mass advertising has played a role in perpetuating partic-ular definitions—often stereotypes—of gender roles and gender relationships. Throughout the history of advertis-ing, detailed definitions of the perfect female—her beauty, her societal roles, and her sexuality—have occupied a cen-tral place. These messages, selling everything from cos-metics to cars to beverages, prescribe how women should look and be looked at, how they should feel, and how they should act. In short, these messages prescribe particular gender identities for women. They also prescribe how men should relate to women. Advertising has been criticized for appropriating hard-fought gains of the women's move-ment (and of other marginalized groups) and assigning them to products. In the process of appropriation, the political gains are depoliticized and divorced from the contexts within which they were produced. An often-cited example is the ad campaign for Virginia Slims cigarettes, which associated women's liberation with addiction and ideals of thinness.

Perspectives

An interdisciplinary interest in gender and advertising has emerged rapidly over the past 25 to 30 years. Academic fields such as communication, journalism, sociology, anthropol-ogy, literature, film studies, and women's studies have offered analyses of the relationship between gender and advertising in various cultural contexts. This body of research includes a wide variety of perspectives, theoretical assumptions, and methodologies from both the humanities and the social sci-ences.

Serious scholarship on gender and advertising flour-ished in the 1970s—though some influential work, such as Betty Friedan's *The Feminine Mystique* (1963) came ear-lier—as a response to the women's movement and to the increased numbers of female researchers in higher educa-tion. Scholars in departments of journalism, mass com-munication, and marketing produced content analyses of sex-role stereotyping found in print advertising and on tele-vision. "Sex-roles research," which remains popular today, uncovered major inequalities in the representations of males and females in advertising. Often, women's roles are stereotyped in ads—either women's place is in the home or women are decorative sex objects; women do not make "important" decisions or do important things; women are dependent on men's protection; advertising gives a false pic-ture of women's real lives. More recent sex-roles research has found that the status of women, especially in the work-force, has increased dramatically in ads, although it is still lower than men's. But as images of working women have become more prevalent, so too have images of women in decorative capacities.

The early flourishing of sex-roles research coincided with the publication of Erving Goffman's influential work *Gender Advertisements* (1976). Guided by his symbolic interactionist orientation toward human communication, Goffman's approach differed from sex-roles research primarily in the questions asked. Goffman was less concerned with the accu-racy of the representation of larger society in advertising than with its function in society, its social effects, and its ability to communicate to people. Goffman found that advertising pre-sents us with consistent and familiar "gender displays" such as male and female adults in parent–child interaction pat-terns; women positioned spatially lower than males in adver-tising photographs; men executing or overseeing action or giving instruction; women as the passive objects of action by males; and women in positions of body canting (the bend-ing of body parts).

Since *Gender Advertisements,* many scholars have expanded on the concept of gender display, examining how and what these rituals communicate to viewers when seen repeatedly. Two additional gender displays have been identified and are central to this body of work. The first is "body cropping," the photographic technique of the "dismemberment" of the female body in ads. Women's bodies are often dismembered and treated as separate parts, perpetuating the notion that a woman's body is not connected to her mind or emotions. Feminist scholars suggest that this type of objectification dehumanizes women for the viewer. When body parts are presented as objects among the other products being advertised, women viewers are positioned to see the female body as a collection of individual parts in need of change or improvement. Male viewers are encouraged to focus on female body parts as fetishes, assessing a woman's worth by breast size, hip curvature, thigh firmness, and so on. Feminist scholars have linked this type of objectification to a general climate of violence against women. They argue that seeing a person as an object helps legitimize committing violence against her.

The second gender display relates to a dichotomy between "male as society" and "female as nature." In ads, men are presented as the active participants in the public domain of work and culture, while women occupy a presence outside the public sphere, in either the domestic world of home and children or the sphere of leisure. Men are often positioned in culturally specific and purposive poses and attire—working, conversing on the telephone, or conveying a commanding stare. Men are shown as the consumers of the objects being advertised. Women are often positioned in decorative poses lacking any sense of action or purpose. In ads, women are shown not as the consumer but as the passive object of consumption.

Throughout the 1980s and 1990s, research on gender and advertising grew in volume and in sophistication. Key to this process has been the application of more critical theoretical approaches. Drawing on semiotics, structuralism, poststructuralism, and psychoanalysis, many feminist scholars examine advertisements as texts, inscribed with the dominant codes and ideologies shared by viewers in the larger culture. The concern here is less with analyzing the content of advertising than it is with the *meanings* people make of advertising as a "system of cultural messages."

A primary focus of this work has been to "deconstruct" the seemingly natural attachment of female sexuality to commodities in advertising. John Berger (1972) suggests that this naturalized relationship between female sexuality and commodities has become a "cultural way of seeing," at least in western societies. He explains that the rise to prominence of the female nude in European oil painting depicts a turning point whereby women's bodies became the object of the

"male gaze." Although gazing on nakedness was taboo, gazing on "the nude" became a respectable practice, belonging to high-art aesthetics. The painters and spectators of nudes were almost always men, and the persons treated as the objects of the gaze were almost always women. The acceptable way of viewing women today has its roots in this historical arrangement. Women and men are depicted differently in advertising and across media. The "ideal spectator" is assumed to be male, and the image of the woman is designed to flatter *him*. Women as well as men are trained in this cultural way of seeing. This perspective contends that women grow up watching themselves being looked at. A woman assesses her appearance, and consequently her worth, through prescriptions defined by men as the producers of art, ads, television programs, films, music, videos, and so on. Advertising encourages women to view themselves as objects to be improved on for the male "other," rather than viewing themselves as the subjects of their own femaleness.

Many feminist writers have expressed a growing discomfort with the limiting nature of the male gaze and concepts of split consciousness, especially when examining female "pleasures" in looking. These scholars contend that although the conventions of the male gaze in visual images *are* dominant ways of seeing, it is wrong to theorize that female viewing is an activity dictated solely by the male gaze. Instead, women have developed their own ways of looking that should not always be reduced to these strict categories.

Theories about the conspiratorial partnership of "beauty culture," promoted through advertising, and the codes of the male gaze are under scrutiny as closed theoretical systems. Recent scholarship has brought into question feminism's ongoing attack on "beauty culture" as a major source of women's oppression. This critique is based on the following assertions. First, advertising images, especially viewed in a global context, do not present one standard of beauty at any one time. Second, women are active, not passive, audience members, who produce meaning when viewing advertising images. Therefore, they bring their own experiences of age, class, ethnicity, social status, sexual preference, and so on to every reading.

Also brought into question is the traditional feminist stance that women should be allowed the freedom to experience their "natural" selves as beautiful without artificial beauty products or adornments. This begs the question, What is natural? In many different cultures and at all times (most of them preceding the age of advertising), women have decorated and groomed themselves. This type of decoration and adornment historically has signaled the sociability of human beings and the placement of individuals in a social hierarchy. This critique suggests that advertising and beauty culture should not be blamed for women's oppression but should instead be seen as one ground where the issues of what is beautiful, natural, and appropriate are played out—through either adherence, negotiation, or opposition/subversion by women.

Societal Influences

Feminist scholars in particular have addressed how the consistent objectification of the female body in advertising and across media produces harmful effects in the everyday lives of women and in female–male relationships. According to Rosalind Coward (1985), females' obsession with outward appearance and body shape has traditionally been attributed to innate female narcissism. However, Coward contends it is not a sense of "self-love" that drives women to obsess over their appearance but a kind of "self-hate," continually perpetuated by images of idealized femininity produced by advertisers. This self-hate manifests itself in a sense of anxiety and urgency stemming from the knowledge that appearance is probably the most crucial way in which men form opinions about the worth of women. Therefore, feelings about appearance and self-image easily mingle with feelings about security and comfort. Absorption into the world of one's own image can be seen as a means of cultural survival, a bid for acceptance.

Conforming to ideal femininity in this culture involves constantly focusing on the body as a site of improvement and as an object of judgment—preparing it, painting it, trimming it, exercising it, feeding it, and even starving it. All this can be seen as self-imposed "discipline." The feminist communication scholar Carole Spitzack (1990) explored the roots of this willingness to impose discipline on the body. As long as women are the objects of the inspecting gaze of male power, men are imbued with the power to gather information about a woman through inspection (as in the assessing stare or whistle) without any obligation to communicate with her. Further, in many western cultures, discourses of "women's health" are directly associated with a thin body, and discourses of "disease" are often associated with "weight" or fat. These complementary discourses work with other institutions and practices to encourage self-correction and therefore "liberation" for women—liberation from the "disease" of fat and "control" over one's health and beauty.

The anxiety that women feel over the difference between the body they see promoted in advertising (and throughout media) and the body they live in can often lead to types of self-surveillance and extreme discipline that fall outside societal parameters of health or even beauty. In the United States, among particular segments of the population, these pressures are considered prominent contributors to the onset of eating disorders such as anorexia nervosa (self-starvation) and bulimia (bingeing and purging). Reports by anorexics have revealed that, for many, their illness is the logical conclusion of the unreasonable expectation suggested by the fashion, cosmetics, and fitness industries that one can never be too thin and that fat equals failure.

The preceding points deal directly with women's encounters with messages that prescribe an often oppressive ideal female beauty, as well as women's attempts to emulate that ideal. Women of color and members of other "marginalized" groups face more complex issues. In advanced and emerging industrialized societies, the cultural "gaze" is not only male but also white. Most women of color grow up not seeing themselves reflected in mainstream advertising, which has deemed them unworthy of representation. In media theory, this type of underrepresentation has been called "symbolic annihilation." Until recently, women of color appeared in advertising only if they were "fine-featured" and light-skinned, resembling the European standard of beauty. For women of color who are viewers, striving to achieve idealized femininity entails not only adjusting or refining one's body but also rejecting one's identity and certain physical characteristics altogether. To resist this artificial standard is always to "stand apart" from beauty as defined by society.

Therefore, although women of color are sometimes represented in advertising, there is still little diversity within the "acceptable" stereotypes of women of color in mainstream ads. However, in the United States, at least, some innovators are improving the representation of black women in advertising. These include *Essence* magazine and the Burrell advertising agency. *Essence,* now considered a standard newsstand publication, has broadened the spectrum of beauty prescriptions for its readers, depicting many skin colors, body shapes, and ethnic fashions and hairstyles, and offering articles and editorials that address black women's experiences. The Burrell advertising agency is credited with bringing positive minority images to mainstream commercial advertising for products such as Crest toothpaste and McDonald's.

On the other hand, the same kinds of breakthroughs in representation have not occurred for Hispanics, Native Americans, or other minority groups, especially in advertising originating in the United States. Moreover, although gay men and lesbians are prominent in the fashion and entertainment industries, representation of homosexual relationships is rarely made explicit in mainstream advertising, where these minorities suffer from "symbolic invisibility."

Empirical research has found that two groups—children and adolescents—are particularly vulnerable to the messages in advertising, including sex-role stereotyping, symbolic invisibility, and cultural ways of seeing. Research on children and television shows that children under age 6 are less likely than older children to be able to distinguish commercials from programs or to distinguish fantasy from reality. This is also the age at which some of the most fundamental learning of social roles and rules takes place. Advertising presents children with conventionalized and often stereotyped views of gender roles and relationships. The effects these messages have on children depend on their exposure to other institutions of socialization (for example, the family, preschool, or books). Adolescents are vulnerable to advertising messages for several reasons: they are prime targets of many advertisements in magazines and on television; they are new and inexperienced consumers; and they are developing their self-concept and self-esteem.

Adolescence is a time when individuals try to gain independence from the institutions that have guided their behavior up to that point, such as family, teachers, and religious leaders. Peer pressure is heightened during this time as teens take their cues on fashion, language, and behaviors, including purchasing behaviors, from same-aged opinion leaders and from the media. Advertising produces a type of mass-mediated peer pressure, giving teens prescriptions for what to buy and how to behave.

Advertising mediates the relationship between people and goods in advanced and emerging industrialized societies. For women, this process of mediation involves a complex set of issues, often pitting women against ideal images of themselves. Advertising is fertile ground for the study of gender relationships in these cultures because it is the precise point where patriarchy, capitalism, and consumerism converge. It is also the point where women are confronted daily with idealized images of who and what they should be.

See Also

ADVERTISING INDUSTRY; IMAGES OF WOMEN: OVERVIEW; MEDIA: OVERVIEW.

References and Further Readings

Berger, John. 1972. *Ways of seeing.* London: British Film Institute.

Cortese, A. J. 1999. *Provocateur: Images of women and minorities in advertising.* Lanham, Md.: Rowman and Littlefield.

Courtney, Alice E. 1983. *Sex stereotyping in advertising.* Lexington, Mass.: Lexington.

Coward, Rosalind. 1985. *Female desires: How they are sought, bought and packaged.* New York: Grove.

Friedan, Betty. 1963. *The feminine mystique.* New York: Norton.

Frith, K., ed. 1997. *Undressing the ad: Reading culture in advertising.* New York: Peter Lang.

Goffman, Erving. 1976. *Gender advertisements.* New York: Harper and Row.

Goldman, Robert. 1992. *Reading ads socially.* London: Routledge.

Jhally, Sut. 1990. *Codes of advertising.* London: Frances Pinter.

Kilbourne, Jean. 1978. *Still killing us softly: Advertising images of women.* Cambridge Documentary Films.

Lazier, L., and Kendrick, A. G. 1993. Women in advertisements: Sizing up the images, roles, and functions. In P. J. Creedon, ed., *Women in mass communication,* 2nd ed., 199–219. Newbury Park, Calif.: Sage.

McCracken, E. 1993. *Decoding women's magazines: From Mademoiselle to Ms.* London: Macmillan.

Pribram, E. Diedre, ed. 1988. *Female spectators: Looking at film and television.* London: Verso.

Spitzack, Carole. 1990. *Confessing excess: Women and the politics of body reduction.* Albany: State University of New York Press.

Williamson, Judith. 1978. *Decoding advertisements.* London: Methuen.

Vickie Rutledge Shields

ADVERTISING INDUSTRY

In Adam Smith's market model, advertising played a minor and strictly informational role in capitalist economies, whether within the economy of the nation-state or the global economy, integrating nations and guaranteeing their wealth. Smith's focus on buyers and sellers elided power differentials based on gender, class, and imperialism. Whereas male capitalists paid low wages to workers in England, capitalists structured wages so that English men made more than women, women more than children, and children more than male workers in India. For Karl Marx, the power differential was crucial; for Smith, the power of buyers was such that their demands would drive markets to create so much wealth that everyone would eventually benefit. Modern appropriations of Smith's model prefer to examine consumer-based markets, avoiding the power differential between capitalist and consumer and erasing the domestic division of labor that makes women into household purchasing agents. When modern advertisers buy consumers—that is, audiences—from commercial media, the highest price is paid for young males regardless of the woman's role as her household's primary buyer.

Smith assumed that advertising was insignificant, in the belief that buyers' demands drove markets; therefore, buyers needed no images to create desires for products they demanded. Historically, the volatility of demand-driven markets encouraged capitalists to rebuild them as more controllable supply-driven markets. In those markets, a few sellers (oligopolists) set the range of products to be offered to buyers. Because products were substantively similar, each oligopolist needed to differentiate its product from its rivals' and to motivate buyers to purchase its product. Noninformational advertising solved both problems by creating an image that differentiated the product and associated it with powerful emotions.

Particularly interesting are associations with love or lust—emotions that capitalism treats as irrational, irresistible, and heterosexual. By evoking such themess, advertising symbolizes a dominant ideology regarding gender and sexuality. When ads rely on nonsexual love, they tap a yearning for social harmony and make products the key to bringing us together. Togetherness ranges from the dyadic (AT&T's "reach out and touch someone") to the universal (Coca-Cola's "I'd like to teach the world to sing in perfect harmony"), but the associative logic remains: buy this and belong. Such advertising locates social problems in individual failures and then resolves those problems through consumption. Loneliness is eradicated by AT&T; world peace means Coca-Cola. This overlooks economic structures that foster sociopolitical conflicts—including westernized economies' overconsumption of raw materials and manufactured goods—and reinforce inequities between developing, westernizing, and westernized nations. Such ads present consumption and capitalism as solutions for global problems fostered by capitalism.

Other ads trade on lust, offering the product as a means to sexual fulfillment and desirability. Advertisements' representations of lust typically objectify women in two ways. To male viewers, the ads associate the acquisition of the product with acquisition of a woman. To female viewers, the ads identify a specific body type and associate it with the product as the key to desirability. Although this symbolism may seem to exploit females and males equally, advertisers' willingness to pay more for male audiences than female audiences means that such ads are primarily aimed at men. Because advertisers pay more for male audiences, commercial media define the audience as male. While women constitute 52 percent of the population and purchase most goods regardless of ultimate user, advertisers and commercial media treat the female audience as a niche mar-

ket. International advertising repeats this process through the "new" global economy, in which the collapse of the so-called second world (including the nations of the former Soviet bloc, the former Yugoslavia, and Albania) has been interpreted by commercial media as the triumph of consumer-based capitalism.

In that global economy, the corporate division of international labor sharpens class divisions within the developing, westernizing, and western economies. For advertisers, this has meant intensifying the circulation of emotionally loaded ads, expanding operations, and aiming those operations at households whose disposable income, consumerist outlook, and proximity to global retailing make them part of a global consumerist caste.

The emergence of that subpopulation internationalized but also narrowed the focus of advertisers, retailers, and media conglomerates. The narrowing is reflected by advertisers' willingness to pay more for "upscale" than "downscale" consumers, even when class status and income are irrelevant to affording the product. As advertisers pay more for upscale audiences, the media shift their focus from mass audiences to "class" audiences. Although the raison d'être of commercial media remains the delivery of millions of potential buyers to advertisers, media outlets now target households that are above a nation's average income, and they target those households around the globe. This shift results from economic and social changes beginning in the 1970s and continuing today.

One significant source of change was a conjunction of second-wave feminism and economic recessions in the 1970s. In western economies, feminists struggled for and secured greater access to education and professional employment. Recessions in those economies, starting in 1975, pushed more middle-class women into the workforce, even as feminists won legal battles for greater opportunities. In the 1980s, monetarism stabilized the recessionary cycle by refocusing industrial economies on international finance, transferring revenues from working people to financial elites, and exporting industrial operations to developing nations, particularly those in southeast Asia. The upsurge of neoconservative ideology in western nations further sharpened internal class divisions by dissolving welfare states and also concentrating economic control in transnational corporations.

By the 1990s, advertisers no longer assumed that the consumerist caste resided primarily in western nations or that impoverished populations lived mainly in developing nations. Advertisers focused on global subpopulations able to sustain ritualized brand loyalty, and made impulse buying routine. This shifted their interest to media charging access fees (cable, film, Internet, and so on). Advertisers still differentiated consumers by gender and class—paying more for "upscale" men than "upscale" women—but now hunted for them globally. With capitalist power differentials based on sex, class, and imperialism entrenched across the entire world, advertisers perpetuated the associative logic that naturalizes capitalism and objectifies women on a truly global basis. Dependent on advertisers for revenue, media distributed advertisers' symbolism internationally, defining women as second-class consumers.

At the turn of the twenty-first century, advertising agencies, media corporations, and advertisers undertook another round of conglomeration and acquisition. This has concentrated industrial control in a steadily diminishing number of increasingly powerful companies. Conglomerates like AOL–Time Warner and Disney integrate Internet, film, television, print, and other media to provide advertisers with "one-stop shopping." For advertising agencies, this has left global and national markets dominated by three "mega-agencies": Omnicom Group (U.S.), Interpublic Group (U.S.), and WPP Group (U.K.). As media conglomerations and vertically integrated advertising agencies buy and sell audiences, they remain focused on middle-class men as the global audience for media.

In first-world nations, twenty-first-century economic conditions continue to make paid employment necessary for most middle-class women and crucial for most working-class women. As a result, more college-educated women work in media corporations and advertising agencies than in the past. Institutional sexism nevertheless persists in these companies, where few women rise above the "glass ceiling" and those few who do rarely shed the corporate socialization that makes them exceptions to the rule of second-class status for women as employees, audiences, and buyers. Where cable channels and Web sites for men are characterized as targeting "the audience," similar services for women are treated as niche media cable channels. All this suggests that objectified representations of women in advertisements, news, and entertainment will remain the norm.

See Also

ADVERTISING; CAPITALISM; COMMUNICATIONS: OVERVIEW; CULTURE: WOMEN AS CONSUMERS OF CULTURE; FASHION; GLOBALIZATION; HOUSEHOLDS: DOMESTIC CONSUMPTION; MEDIA: OVERVIEW

References and Further Reading

Andersen, Robin. 1995. *Consumer culture and TV programming.* Boulder, Col.: Westview.

Ewen, Stuart. 1976. *Captains of consciousness: Advertising and the social roots of the consumer culture.* New York: McGraw-Hill.

———, and Elizabeth Ewen. 1982. *Channels of desire: Mass images and the shaping of American consciousness.* New York: McGraw-Hill.

Jhally, Sut. 1989. Advertising as religion: The dialectic of technology and magic. In Ian Angus and Sut Jhally, eds., *Cultural politics in contemporary America.* New York: Routledge.

McAlister, Matthew P. 1996. *The commoditization of American culture.* Thousand Oaks, Calif.: Sage.

Schudson, Michael. 1984. *Advertising, the uneasy persuasion.* New York: Basic Books.

Williamson, Judith. 1978. *Decoding advertisements.* London: Marion Boyars.

Eileen Meehan

AESTHETICS: Feminist

The making of art and the experience of art are often held to be gendered in a significant way. This must be taken into account, it is argued, if we are to understand art fully. Feminist aesthetics is not a way of evaluating art or our experience of art; rather, it examines and questions aesthetic theory and attitudes concerning gender.

Although feminist work in literary criticism, film theory, and art history is well established, feminist aesthetics is a relatively young discipline, dating from the early 1990s. Because of its relatively recent beginnings, feminist aesthetics is still a discipline without a canon. In fact, several writers resist the idea that feminist aesthetics should have a canon at all, since they believe that work in this field necessarily needs to develop as women artists and theorists do themselves. Moreover, since it draws upon several brands of feminism and feminist work in other disciplines, feminist aesthetics is rarely concerned to respect disciplinary boundaries. Further, one of its primary tasks is to broaden our concept of what counts as art—and enable the discipline to include more varied perspectives of artists, art appreciators, and the wider contexts in which art develops.

It is important to keep in mind, however, that feminist aesthetics does not claim that women necessarily produce different kinds of art from men, or that women necessarily have different experiences of art from men. Not only is there no clear distinction between women's art and men's art; there is also no clear similarity among all women's art.

Again, the *experience* is what feminist aesthetics is concerned with. That is, the different kinds of art men and women produce are less significant than the recognition that they will have fundamentally different kinds of experiences in response to art because of the way society influences gender. By starting with the assumption that art and the way we experience it are fundamentally gendered, feminist aesthetics acknowledges the different kinds of experiences art can produce, and hence can take more varied kinds of experiences into account. There is no assumption that the differences are necessarily essential; but because of the way in which society influences gender and our resulting experiences seen through gender, the experience of art, be it made by males or by females, is likely to influence men and women in different ways.

Almost all feminist scholarship challenges the view that there can be a generic perceiver. Awareness of gender informs the content of perception itself so that what is perceived and how it is perceived depend on whether the perceiver occupies a more or less privileged social and political position. Feminist aesthetics assumes that art is not and should not be gender-neutral, and it begins by recognizing how art and artists are privileged and affected by gender. Since art and art history are gendered, there is no universal, ideal, disinterested spectator. Standard aesthetic theory oppresses women by assuming a gender-neutral, disinterested ideal spectator who in fact embodies a privileged, white male perspective. Understanding that gender influences the viewer and accounting for the varied spectators that we do have are not the same. Understanding the varied perspectives and experiences is one of the main objectives of feminist aesthetics. Thus it goes beyond the acknowledgment that gender matters to show *how* it matters and to show how different women create and experience art.

Feminist aesthetics offers not merely a critique of traditional aesthetics but alternatives to the critique as well. First, traditional formalist theory defines art in terms of formal characteristics and formal principles. It strives to be able to define art exclusively in these terms. According to this view, aesthetics is always moving toward a definition that will ultimately, always, come up short. Feminist theory, on the other hand, seeks to describe rather than define art and thus is able to take account of its changing nature and can incorporate different contexts and meanings.

Second, formalism gives priority to products of artistic endeavors that are viewed disinterestedly—and gives priority to the view that art objects should be viewed disinterestedly. Conversely, feminist aesthetics emphasizes the connection between art and life. Feminist aesthetics consists not only of objects in their contexts but also of performances (perfor-

mance art), environments (gardens or architecture), and other interactive productions viewed within their contexts.

Although feminist aesthetics begins with the recognition that gender matters in art, the study of feminist aesthetics should not be confused with the study of feminist art history or feminist art criticism, each of which also begins with the same assumption. The fact that women are oppressed as subjects of art does play a part in the acknowledgment that gender is influential, but it is not necessarily all that matters. There is a bias in painting (and print media) toward female subjects (often nude women perceived as passive and wanting to be looked at) and male artists (always in control, always doing the looking). What this feminist view of art history produces is our recognition of the "male gaze," which is a significant part of feminist aesthetics. In this case, feminist aesthetics has contributed something that traditional aesthetics has not so much gotten wrong as overlooked entirely.

Both feminist aesthetics and feminist art criticism have focused on the unbalanced relationship between the subject and object of aesthetic contemplation—and both want to initiate an important blurring of distinctions between them. Further, there is an emphasis on the aesthetic dimensions of everyday life and the importance of seeing art as a process or activity rather than a product. Feminist analyses attempt to link aesthetic judgment and the resultant implied meaning and value of works of art to beliefs and desires in everyday life. That is, we need to consider art and the aesthetic within their own context. It is only here, in this complicated nexus of circumstances, that we can fully understand the significance of art.

See Also

AESTHETICS: BLACK FEMINIST; ART PRACTICE: FEMINIST; CREATIVITY; FINE ARTS: CRITICISM AND ART HISTORY; GAZE; PHILOSOPHY

References and Further Readings

Battersby, C. 1989. *Gender and genius: Towards a feminist aesthetics.* Bloomington: Indiana University Press.

Berger, J. 1972. *Ways of seeing.* London: Penguin.

Brand, P. 1998. Disinterestedness and political art. In C. Korsmeyer, ed., *Aesthetics: The big questions.* Oxford: Blackwell.

———,. and C. Korsmeyer, eds. 1995. *Feminism and tradition in aesthetics.* University Park: Pennsylvania State University Press.

Felski, R. 1989. *Beyond feminist aesthetics: Feminist literature and social change.* Cambridge, Mass.: Harvard University Press.

Hein, H., and C. Korsmeyer, eds. 1993. *Aesthetics in feminist perspective*. Bloomington: Indiana University Press.

Korsmeyer, C. 1998. Perceptions, pleasures, arts: Considering aesthetics. In Janet Kourany, ed., *Philosophy in a feminist voice: Critiques and reconstructions*. Princeton: Princeton University Press.

Mulvey, L. 1989. *Visual and other pleasures*. Bloomington: Indiana University Press.

Nochlin, L. 1971. Why are there no great women artists? In V. Gornick and B. K. Moran, eds., *Woman in sexist society*. New York: Basic Books.

Sarah Worth

AESTHETICS: Black Feminist—A Debate

The black feminist in the United States may exist in a state of heightened aesthetic awareness, living daily not only with the black person's double consciousness of being both object and subject in a racist society but also with the feminist awareness of woman as both object and subject in a gendered world. It is precisely the sense of doubleness that differentiates feminist aesthetics from standard aesthetic theory, and it is the duplication of this sense, as experienced by black feminists, that further differentiates black feminist aesthetics from white feminist aesthetics.

Some African-American feminists further distance themselves from white feminism, and, thus, from white feminist aesthetics, by claiming that white feminism deals with middle-class white women's issues, and with those issues alone, offering nothing to poor and black women. Other black women refuse the label "feminist" altogether, pointing out that, whereas white women may want to be equal to white men, black women have no similar incentive to resemble black men. Many black women prefer "womanist," a folk term used by Alice Walker. The Afrocentric scholar Clenora Hudson Weems has proposed still another term, "Africana womanism."

Besides its differences with white feminist aesthetics in the United States, black feminist aesthetics is beset with internal controversies. In such a climate, black critics have no stable, agreed-on guidelines for their work, and each feminist writer propounds her own theory. At worst, this state of uncertainty can lead to polarization and recrimination, even as the protagonists attempt on higher levels to create a workable consensus on issues important to all black feminist aestheticians.

The writer and professor Michelle Wallace, for instance, contends that black women writers present critical work that is not of high quality. She has a reputation for writing scathing reviews of her contemporaries' work ("bell hooks Reads between the Lines," 1999). Her colleague bell hooks, who uses lowercase for her pen name to indicate an absence of authorial ego and is one of the best-known black feminists in the United States, is concerned about the divisiveness she believes Wallace causes. In addition, hooks argues, Wallace's unfavorable reviews downgrade black feminist writers in the eyes of the mainstream, making it more difficult for these writers to publish and to achieve the respect they deserve ("bell hooks Reads between the Lines," 1999). Wallace's motives for publicly expressing harsh opinions about the works of hooks and other contemporaries may sometimes be misunderstood. Her goal is to inspire black feminist writers to adhere to the highest standards, and she has never shrunk from controversy but, rather, has been outspoken on controversial matters.

bell hooks writes in a poetic and persuasive style. She and her work have become popular in white as well as black feminist circles, but some critics see her work as marred by a casual approach to documentation (see, for instance, Farris, 1999: 91). hooks's goals are to spur development of criticism, and of a feminist aesthetic, that will transcend boundaries of gender, race, and class, and to persuade the literary world that African-American women aestheticians and critics are serious thinkers and writers.

One cause of the differences between Wallace and hooks may be that they do not use the same definition of quality. Perhaps Wallace considers use of standard English and accurate documentation a requisite for high quality, whereas for hooks the presentation of ideas in an imaginative and accomplished literary style may simply *be* high quality. Another cause may be their opposed personal styles: whereas Wallace sparks controversy and seeks to spur change through her confrontational style, hooks uses her persuasive and harmonizing style to create mutual benefit and acceptance.

Despite, or perhaps in part because of, these controversies, black feminist aesthetics in the United States exists in a state of lively ferment. Debate is fueled by the aesthetic and critical writings of Wallace and hooks as well as many others. Some questions at the heart of black feminist aesthetics may remain to be formulated, and some answers do not yet seem to be in sight. Possibly, one topic of general agreement is the need for African-American women aestheticians to take their work even more seriously and to gain the increased respect of other critics and writers, both in the so-called white feminist world and in the mainstream culture.

See Also

AESTHETICS; CREATIVITY; FEMINISM: AFRICAN-AMERICAN; LITERARY THEORY AND CRITICISM; LITERATURE: NORTH AMERICA

References and Further Reading

"bell hooks reads between the lines in new book" (book review). *New York Amsterdam News,* 27 January 1999, p. 20.

Bordo, Susan. 1998. *Twilight zones: Feminism and Film; Feminism, media and the law* (book review). *Contemporary Women's Issues Database,* 10 (1 June): 148–153.

Bordo, Susan. 1997. *Twilight zones: The hidden life of cultural images from Plato to O.J.* Berkeley: University of California Press.

Farris, Phoebe. 1999. *English is broken here: Notes on cultural fusion in the Americas* (book review), *Art Journal* 55(3): 91.

Gentile, Mary C. 1985. *Film feminisms: Theory and practice.* Westport, Conn.: Greenwood.

hooks, bell. 1981. *Ain't I a woman: Black women and feminism.* Boston: South End.

Humm, Maggie. 1995. *The dictionary of feminist theory.* Ohio State University.

Lorde, Audrey. 1984. *Sister outsider: Essays and speeches.* Trumansburg, N.Y.: Crossing.

McCluskey, Audrey Thomas. 1994. Am I not a woman and a sister? Reflections on the role of black women's studies in the academy. *Contemporary Women's Issues Database* 8: 105–111.

Morrison, Toni. 1992. *Playing in the dark: Whiteness and the literary imagination.* Cambridge, Mass.: Harvard University Press.

Wallace, Michele. 1999. *Black macho and the myth of the superwoman.* London: Verso.

Weems, Clenora Hudson. 1995. *Africana womanism: Reclaiming ourselves.* Bedford.

Georgia Kornbluth

AFFIRMATIVE ACTION

"Affirmative action" did not become part of the general vocabulary in the United States until President John F. Kennedy issued an executive order that required federal contractors to take "affirmative action to recruit, hire, and promote minorities." In an executive order of 1967, President Lyndon Johnson added women to the protected group (Stewart, 1998). These orders ban discrimination against applicants and employees on the basis of race, color, religion, sex, or national origin, but they also require that employers take affirmative action or positive steps to ensure equal opportunity. Furthermore, employers must state in all advertising that they are indeed affirmative action–equal opportunity employers. According to Revised Order 4, employers with over $50,000 in federal contracts and 50 or more workers had to file affirmative action plans, including goals and timetables, with the Office of Federal Contract Compliance.

In March 1972, the Equal Employment Opportunity Commission (EEOC) issued a report ("Guidelines on Discrimination Because of Sex"), which set forth general principles to assist employers in complying with Title VII of the Civil Rights Act of 1964, as amended in 1972. Employers could not refuse to hire a woman because they believed women in general have a higher turnover rate than men do. Nor could they refuse to hire a woman because of the assumption that women as a group are less capable of performing certain tasks than men are. Nor could employers cite the preferences of coworkers or customers in excluding women (or men) from consideration for employment. The guidelines also provided the useful information that title VII supersedes state laws which treat women differently from men. And the guidelines provide clarification as to the illegality of separate seniority systems by sex, discrimination against married women, sex-separated advertising, discriminatory practices by employment agencies, pre-employment inquiries by sex, provision of unequal fringe benefits, and provision of discriminatory benefits for temporary disabilities such as those related to pregnancy and childbirth.

The requirements for "acting affirmatively" stipulated not only that employers cease taking the discriminatory actions described above but that they take positive steps to ensure the provision of equal opportunity to women of all races and minority men. In other words, employers cannot simply say that they would welcome applicants of underrepresented groups; they must take affirmative action in three areas: (1) recruitment, (2) selection, and (3) training.

In the area of recruitment, for example, the employer could show good faith by making certain that advertisements for job openings were sent not only to traditional outlets but also to agencies and publications that might reach groups unreached before. If the employer was fair in using only job-related criteria in selecting among the applicants, then he or she would be deemed to have satisfied the standards for fair selection. And in the area of training, employees who are women of any race (or minority men) must be offered opportunities for training on the same basis as majority employees.

These requirements—indeed, the whole concept of affirmative action—had critics in the decades that followed. In 1976, researchers compared the sex and race composition of companies that were visited by compliance officers with companies that were not. Their study suggested strongly that affirmative action programs were helping men—especially white men—but having an adverse effect on women (Goldstein and Smith, 1976).

A review of the status of women and minorities in administrative posts in institutions of higher education showed that, despite professed commitment, little progress had been made (Van Alstyne et al., 1977).

Other researchers have suggested that the excess of government regulations applying to academic institutions acted as a damper to change rather than encouraging it (Spriestersbach and Farrell, 1977).

Members of protected groups sometimes argued, in the 1980s, that antibias laws in general and affirmative action in particular were not working. They pointed to the paucity of women leaders in corporations and in the professions as evidence that majority men were not practicing affirmative action. Others argued that, while affirmative action was helping elite managerial women to some extent, it was not helping large numbers of low-paid women (Blum, 1997). Many felt that it was inherently unfair to make special efforts to ensure fairness in recruitment, selection, and training. Many seemed to believe that affirmative action was equal to preferential hiring, to hiring and promoting unqualified women and minorities, and to granting special privileges to protected groups. Proponents of affirmative action defended the concept by pointing out that it is illegal under Title VII to hire an unqualified person because he or she is a member of an underrepresented group. In some other countries, it is legal to specify that one seeks a woman or a member of a minority group for a specified job: "No white males need apply." This is illegal in the United States.

In the 1980s, there was considerable pressure to declare that hiring and admissions would be best left color-blind. Proponents of race-conscious hiring countered by acknowledging that places at universities, in industrial organizations, and in the professions should ideally be awarded on merit and merit only. Ideally:

> …colorblind policies often put racial minorities at a disadvantage. For instance, all else being equal, colorblind seniority systems tend to protect white workers against job layoffs, because senior employees are usually white. Likewise, colorblind college admissions favor white students because of their earlier educa-

tional advantages. Unless pre-existing inequities are corrected or otherwise taken into account, colorblind policies do not eliminate racial injustice—they reinforce it. (Plous, 2000)

At Cornell University in Ithaca, New York, the Office of Affirmative Action changed its name in the 1980s to the Office of Equal Opportunity. In 2000, the name was changed once again, this time to Workforce Diversity, Equity, and Life Quality. In the spring 2000 issue of the university publication on benefits, the change was explained as follows:

> Diversity is related to equal opportunity and affirmative action in that those who promote diversity recognize that there are differences among us that do not affect the quality of our work, teaching, or research. But, in addition to those differences covered by affirmative action or local equal employment law and regulations—race, gender, disability status, veteran status, age, marital status, national origin, religion, and sexual orientation—diversity includes differences that are not specifically protected by law, such as educational background, socioeconomic class, job title/responsibilities, or a person's status (whether a person is faculty or staff, supervisor or non-supervisor, exempt or nonexempt, for instance.) To recognize the importance of diversity is to recognize that having a diverse population in an organization is good both for the organization as a whole and the people within it. (Chappell-Williams, 2000)

Concern with affirmative action has mutated into a focus on equal opportunity, which has in turn given way to a larger concern with diversity. Whether this moves the society as a whole toward a merit-based ideal or a continuation of current injustice is a matter on which good people differ. The news of Microsoft Chairman Bill Gate's $1 billion Millennium Scholarship Program was no sooner announced than criticized:

> Bill Gates's $1 billion Millennium Scholarship Program may do more harm than good unless its criteria for awarding college scholarships are altered. Based strictly on "minority" preference rather than need, it is bound to exacerbate racial resentment. (LeFever, 2000)

> Critics of Gates's aid to the United Negro College Fund are more than a little off base in assuming that any type of educational aid to minority groups

is about some form of affirmative action. Many minority students, myself included, who are accepted into. Ivy League schools (which typically serve as springboards to a brighter future) simply cannot afford to go. There are few scholarships that cover four-year tuitions in excess of $25,000 [per year]. (Clark, 2000)

Some criticized affirmative action because it did not work; others, because they felt it was working too well. A merit-based hiring and promotion system is one most Americans want. How to achieve a diverse, fair one is the point of disagreement.

See Also

ANTIDISCRIMINATION; DISCRIMINATION; EDUCATION: GENDER EQUITY; WORK: EQUAL PAY AND CONDITIONS; WORK: OCCUPATIONAL SEGREGATION

References and Further Reading

Blum, Linda M. 1997. Possibilities and limitations of the comparable worth movement. In Dana Dunn, ed., *Workplace, women's place: An anthology*. Los Angeles: Roxbury.

Chappell-Williams, Lynne, Director, Office of Workforce Diversity, Equity, and Life Quality, interviewed in *For your benefit: Official information on Cornell's benefits, policies, and work-related developments*. Spring 2000, Special Edition on Diversity, A.

Clarke, T. A. 2000. Letter to the editor. *The New York Times Magazine* (Sunday, May 14): 14.

Goldstein, Morris, and Robert S. Smith. 1976. The estimated impact of the antidiscrimination program aimed at federal contractors. *Industrial and Labor Relations Review* 29. (4): 523–543.

LeFever, Ernest W. 2000. Letter to the editor. *New York Times Magazine* (Sunday, May 14): 14.

Plous, Sarah. 2000. *Journal of social issues*, excerpted in Some myths about affirmative action: Why too many "con" cases are weak. *Ithaca* (N.Y.) *Journal* (Thursday, May 4): 11 A.

Spriestersbach, D. C., and William J. Farrell. 1977. Impact of federal regulations at a university. *Science* (4312): 27–30.

Stewart, Karn. 1998. Women in business: The experiences of women in the U.S. workforce. In Donna M. Ashcraft, ed., *Women's work: A survey of scholarship by and about women*, 205. New York: Harrington Park.

Van Alstyne, Carol, et al. 1977. Affirmative inaction: The bottom line tells the tale. *Change* 39–41.

Jennie Farley

AGEISM

Ageism is prejudice against the elderly. Coined by Robert Butler in 1968, the word *ageism* is more precisely defined as "a process of systematic stereotyping of and discrimination against people because they are old, just as racism and sexism accomplish this with skin color and gender" (Butler, 1975). This tendency to homogenize the old and classify them as "the other" in turn leads to their being marginalized as a discrete population, separate from the mainstream.

At the individual level, ageism is rooted in a personal revulsion toward growing old and experiencing disease and disability, and to a fear of uselessness and death (Butler, 1969). Collectively, at the social level, ageism stems from the apprehension that the needs of the aged may burden a nation's resources and siphon off resources from younger segments of the population.

Probably the most blatant form of ageism occurs in the job market in western industrial societies, where chronological age has served as a marker for retirement. Although there is no rationale for specifying a given retirement age, many bureaucracies, both public and private, have established a certain age (usually between 65 and 70) as the age of pension eligibility and retirement. Ageism also plays a role in hiring; for instance, employers may be biased against older workers, who are perceived as less adaptable and less willing to learn. Moreover, an employer may be reluctant to invest in the training of workers whose tenure with the company is uncertain. Economic recession, automation, and corporate restructuring also result in the replacement of company "veterans," or long-standing employees, by younger, lower-paid workers. Although the United States and other countries have enacted legislation banning the arbitrary dismissal of workers on the basis of age, corporate mergers and the accelerating pace of technology have led companies to streamline their staffs. In the process, long-tenured and higher paid employees are often targeted and older workers are disproportionately affected.

In youth-oriented cultures, where beauty and physical prowess are held in great esteem, individual and institutional ageism may take more subtle forms. There is, for example, an entire vocabulary that describes and stigmatizes persons on the basis of age. The elderly are also depicted as comical figures, the butt of jokes. In addition, the aged are excluded from public images, as if this segment of the population did not count. Some of these stereotypes are self-reinforcing: the elderly may tend to adopt negative views of themselves and thus either conform to these stereotypes or make special efforts to counteract them.

Ageism often represents a more formidable barrier for women than for men. Because many cultures regard childbearing and childrearing as women's central, if not exclusive, mission, menopause represents the beginning of women's loss of status. Thus as women age and are no longer considered indispensable to the family, they may feel increasingly useless—and this effect, too, reinforces negative ageist stereotypes. The premium placed on good looks may also have a greater negative impact on women, many of whom have internalized the prevailing social value placed on beauty, and particularly the association of beauty with a youthful appearance.

In the workplace, women also are differentially affected. In rural societies, where women have traditionally participated in agricultural labor, loss of physical strength may signal loss of a woman's income-producing capacity. In industrial and service societies, where women often enter the labor market only after their child-rearing obligations have decreased or ended, women may find themselves at a disadvantage in competing against younger workers of both genders. And because women leave and enter the labor market with greater frequency than men, they are less likely to have attained seniority and are therefore more vulnerable to employment shifts than males of the same age group.

Laws as well as the roles that society decrees for the elderly determine the extent to which ageism is allowed to prevail. Where age is equated with wisdom, the elderly are seen as a repository of tradition and as nurturers of family unity. The status of the aged is also enhanced in societies in which older people command resources (including skills, money, and time), which give them power over others. By contrast, societies that prize youth and perceive old age as obsolescence rather than experience—and as the approach of death rather than as the culmination of life—will find that ageism persists regardless of laws to protect the rights of the aged.

See Also

AGING; AGING: JAPANESE CASE STUDY; ANTIDISCRIMINATION; BODY; DISCRIMINATION; ELDERLY CARE, *specific topics;* FAMILY STRUCTURES; LONG-TERM CARE SERVICES; NURSING HOMES; YOUTH CULTURE

References and Further Reading

Butler, Robert N. 1969. Age-ism: Another form of bigotry. *Gerontologist* 9(4): 243–246.

———. 1975. *Why survive? Being old in America.* New York: Harper and Row.

Bytheway, Bill. 1995. *Ageism.* Buckingham, U.K.: Open University Press.

Holmes, Ellen Rhoads, and Lowell D. Holmes. 1995. *Other cultures, elder years.* Thousand Oaks, Calif.: Sage.

Williamson, John B., Linda Evans, and Anne Munley. 1980. *Aging and society.* New York: Holt, Rinehart and Winston.

Annette B. Ramírez de Arellano

AGING

Aging is a lifelong process, but the term *aging* itself usually refers to "patterns of late-life changes which are eventually seen in all persons but which vary in rate and degree" (Butler, 1975) from one individual to another.

Aging As a Time of Biological Change

Biological aging, called *senescence,* involves cellular changes that may affect physical appearance and functional capacities. This process is associated with a decline in the immunological system and with a reduction in the effectiveness of the hormonal system leading, in turn, to a deterioration in the ability to adapt and a gradual increase in vulnerability to disease. Physiological changes include the decline or atrophy of certain systems and a decrease in sensory functions. Some of the more overt signs of aging include wrinkled skin, graying hair, and stiffened joints. The pace at which aging occurs varies not only among individuals, but also from one organ to another. Faculties peak at different ages, and their loss occurs at different rates. Thus, for example, hearing peaks at infancy, while muscular strength peaks in the twenties (Williamson et al., 1980).

Many biological changes associated with aging, however, are effects more of disease than of aging per se. Moreover, biology may be tempered or offset by social, emotional, economic, and environmental factors. Certain cultures have been more successful than others in ensuring that the losses of old age are cushioned by adequate income, supportive networks, access to care, and the recognition that the aged have a valuable role in society.

In women, menopause is often seen as a biological milestone that marks the onset of middle age, with loss of the capacity for childbearing seen as the end of a biological stage. Although twentieth-century health practitioners tended to consider menopause a pathological condition requiring medical treatment, by the end of the century there was increased recognition that it is neither an illness nor a deficiency (Porcino, 1991). Furthermore, the prolongation of postmenopausal fertility made possible by medical technology is making this stage less of a clear-cut transition.

Aging As a Time of Psychological Change

At the time of menopause, however, women may be experiencing other changes that affect their self-image and relationships. These changes may include children's departure from the home (a process termed the "empty nest syndrome"), new responsibilities involving caring for elderly parents, and entry or reentry into the workforce. Women may thus be confronted with the need to make numerous adaptations at this time in their lives.

For most women, therefore, aging is associated with role changes and the probability of coping with loss. Because women tend to outlive men in nearly all countries and age groups, the proportion of women who are heads of households tends to increase with age. As a result, many of the health, social, and economic problems of the aging population are largely the problems of women.

Old age may involve separation from relatives, friends, and familiar surroundings; loss of work; a reduction in income; and the death of a spouse and peers. For women, the situation may be exacerbated by financial insecurity. Because women's work is often unpaid, unreported, unrecognized, and unstable, women tend to lack pensions and other benefits that would allow them a measure of financial independence.

Some of these changes may produce feelings of isolation, dependence, and powerlessness, which in turn produce depression. The psychological effects of aging are therefore receiving increasing attention. In the elderly, mental and physical problems often go together, with symptoms in one sphere masking those in another.

Rethinking Images of Old Age

Various studies have attempted to disentangle the effects of aging from those of disease. These have tended to find that, despite the prevailing myths, both serious memory loss and intellectual decline are quite gradual in healthy individuals as they age. In addition, aging women tend to maintain a higher level of intellectual functioning than their male counterparts, who show earlier and faster declines (Williamson et al., 1980).

The available evidence also indicates that learning continues into old age and that those who continue to exercise their learning skills throughout their lives are better able to adapt and learn new things. "Use it or lose it" has therefore become a popular slogan for successful aging and the maintenance of both physical and intellectual abilities. Resiliency and optimism are also associated with a fulfilling old age.

The social aspects of aging have been encoded in employment practices and legislation. The ages between 60 or 65 and 70 have been selected for determining retirement and eligibility for financial entitlements. This social definition of old age, while essentially arbitrary, has nonetheless shaped the images and expectations of the elderly, and society's attitudes toward the aged.

As the population pyramid in many countries becomes more top-heavy, with the aged constituting a larger proportion of the population, the political power of the elderly and hence the importance given to the biological, psychological, and social aspects of aging are likely to increase. This shift has been recognized by the United Nations Action Program on Aging, which culminated in 1999 with the International Year of Older Persons.

See Also

AGEISM, AGING: JAPANESE CASE STUDY; DISEASE; ELDERLY CARE, *specific topics;* FAMILY STRUCTURES; GRANDMOTHER; HORMONES; LIFE EXPECTANCY; MENOPAUSE; WIDOWHOOD

References and Further Reading

Butler, Robert N. 1975. *Why survive? Being old in America.* New York: Harper and Row.

Holmes, Ellen Rhoads, and Lowell D. Holmes. 1995. *Other cultures, elder years* (2nd ed.). Thousand Oaks, Calif.: Sage.

Porcino, Jane. 1991. *Growing older, getting better.* New York: Continuum.

Shenk, Dena, and W. Andrew Achenbaum, eds. 1994. *Changing perceptions of aging and the aged.* New York: Springer.

Williamson, John B., Linda Evans, and Anne Munley. 1980. *Aging and society.* New York: Holt, Rinehart and Winston.

Annette B. Ramírez de Arellano

AGING: Japanese Case Study

In the half century after the end of World War II, women in Japan experienced drastic changes in their life cycle. While the average life span reached 83.82 years by 1997, the total fertility rate declined from 4.32 in 1949 to 1.39 in 1997 as a result of changes in the state's population policy, which shifted from pronatalist to antinatalist in the postwar era. The legalization of abortion in 1948 played an important role in this process. By the end of the twentieth century, however, Japan's declining birthrate and its rapidly aging society were causing anxiety among political and economic leaders, who began encouraging women to bear more children in order to rejuvenate the population. Many women retorted that they could not and did not want to have bigger families because modern Japanese society does not provide them with a favorable environment for bearing and raising many children.

One of the major problems of the aging society, especially for women, is the care of bedridden or senile people at home. In Japan, more than 50 percent of the aged live with their adult children. Although the eldest son is traditionally expected to live with his parents, in fact it is his wife who is responsible for care of parents-in-law when they become bedridden or senile. Also, with the decrease in number of children per family, the rate of parents living with a single or married daughter is increasing rapidly. The Japanese assume, in general, that it is natural for family members to take care of the aged at home, and public and private services to help old people or caregivers are far from adequate.

Accordingly, the burden of caregiving rests heavily on women. In 1995 more than 2 million old people were estimated to be in need of care, of which about 860,000 were cared for at home. Most of the caregivers at home were women, including wives (31.6 percent), wives of eldest sons (27.6 percent), eldest daughters (15.5 percent), and other daughters (4.5 percent). It is not uncommon for a woman to spend many years taking care of one or both parents of parents-in-law, and later her husband. Working women are frequently forced to quit their jobs because of this highly demanding caregiving labor.

The situation is also critical for women who are themselves in need of care. Because women, on average, live longer than men, the rate of bedridden or senile women increases with age. It is reported that old women are twice as liable as old men to be abused by caregivers, and the number of old women killed by exhausted caregivers is six times greater than that of old men. Although sons and husbands are a minority among caregivers, the incidence of abuse and murder increases when the caregiver is a man, sometimes taking the ultimate form of double suicide in which a desperate male caregiver kills both the old woman and himself.

There have been recent efforts to remedy such gender imbalance in the care of the old. For example, newspapers and television programs have included positive coverage of men who willingly resigned from high-status jobs, such as bank president or mayor, in order to care for their elderly and ill wives. Books written by sons and husbands about their caregiving experiences are published and received favorably. Also, in April 2000, a new national insurance system for the care of the aged was implemented with the purpose of facilitating social support for caregiving labor. However, it is unclear whether such new phenomena signal any substantive change in the conditions surrounding Japanese women and aging.

See Also

AGEISM; AGING; CAREGIVERS; ELDERLY CARE: CASE STUDY—CHINA; ELDERLY CARE: WESTERN WORLD; FAMILY STRUCTURES; LONG-TERM CARE SERVICES; NURSING HOMES; POPULATION CONTROL

References and Further Reading

Amano, Masako. 1999. *Oino kindai* (Aging in the modern period). Tokyo: Iwanami Shoten.

Lock, Margaret. 1993. *Encounters with aging: Mythologies of midlife and menopause in Japan and North America.* Berkeley: University of California Press.

———. 1999. The cultural politics of female aging in Japan and North America. In Wakita Haruko, Anne Bouchy, and Ueno Chizuko, eds., *Gender and Japanese history,* Vol. 1. Osaka: Osaka University Press.

Takeda, Kyoko. 1994. *Rojowa naze kaxokuni korosarerunoka.* (Why are old women killed by their families?) Kyoto: Minerva.

Tanaka, Kazuko. 1989. *Women, work and family in Japan: A life cycle perspective.* Iowa City: University of Iowa.

Miho Ogino

AGRICULTURE

Women around the world contribute a significant proportion of the labor and expertise required to feed human populations. Their roles have varied through times and regions, but even in modern industrialized societies, there are many opportunities for women in food production. "Agriculture" is narrowly defined as the cultivation of domesticated plants ("cultigens") for food and fiber; more broadly, "farming" also includes the management of domestic animals for meat, milk, eggs, and other uses such as fiber. The term "horticulture" is used to distinguish the production of edible and ornamental plants, usually for eventual transplanting.

Agriculture arose independently in different parts of the ancient world at different times. The wheat-based system that characterizes Europe, western Asia, and the Middle East probably began in present-day Turkey between 9,000 and 10,000 years ago; rice was farmed in China as early as 8,500 years ago, sorghum in western and central Africa 5,000 years ago, and maize (corn) in Mesoamerica by 4,000 years ago. Before these innovations, people subsisted by hunting game and gathering wild plant foods. In recent hunting-and-gathering societies, men specialize in hunting large game, while women forage for plants and small game, an activity that can be combined with the physical restrictions of pregnancy and child care. Possibly, therefore, it was women who learned the life cycles of plants and their response to environmental conditions. When they observed food plants growing from discarded seeds near dwelling sites, they probably encouraged plant growth by manipulating soil disturbance and irrigation, and selected particularly productive individual plants. Thus, they created the first farms.

The increased food security granted by agriculture brought fundamental changes to human society. Women, no longer required to travel so much, could bear, nourish, and tend more children—who were needed to labor in the fields and defend the territory. In their permanent dwellings, they could keep nonportable tools and store heavy foods. Early agricultural societies exploited these advantages to move their increasing populations into new territories, where they eventually displaced hunter-gatherer groups. The spread of Indo-Europeans in Eurasia and that of Bantu-speaking peoples in sub-Saharan Africa, for example, are attributed in large part to their management of agriculture.

Despite women's fundamental role in the creation and maintenance of agriculture, they are often said to be "invisible farmers." In most parts of the world—especially in western cultures—the stereotypical farmer is male. Many factors combine to make rural women less visible than men, including male ownership of land, male domination of the credit system, and the submersion of women's farm labor in the sphere of domestic work. Even in Africa, where women dominate farm production, they tend to work on land owned by their husbands or other male relatives. They usually concentrate on producing food for domestic or local market consumption, whereas men are more likely to raise crops for external sale. Throughout the world, large agricultural enterprises tend to be male-operated. The actual extent of women's contribution to farm production can be difficult for researchers to determine because government databases tend not to identify it separately; however, there is increasing recognition of the need for "gender disaggregated" data for use in development planning.

Women's work on farms is likely to be considered a natural extension of their work in the home, and both are often undervalued in economic treatments and more general views. In fact, farm women in developed countries have been found to work longer hours, on average, than women in other types of employment. Moreover, most farm women contribute agricultural labor at peak periods, but farm men typically contribute little domestic labor (housework, cooking, or child care).

Physiological differences affect women's role in agriculture in several ways. Worldwide, they reduce their farm activity while pregnant and lactating. Caring for small children limits the time a woman can devote to field labor, although older children can help with the work. There is rising concern about women's exposure to agricultural chemicals, which—especially in developing countries—are often applied without adequate safeguards; some of these substances are especially dangerous to pregnant women and children.

The economic constraints on women's successful participation in agriculture fall under two broad headings: land tenure and access to credit. In many parts of the world, legal ownership of land is still restricted by law or custom to males; thus, it is difficult for women to secure land for their own use or to use it as collateral for loans in their own names. Land and other agricultural resources tend to be inherited by male rather than female children, and a widow or divorced woman may lose the use of her family's land.

There are several kinds of land tenure among rural households, ranging in level of security from landless squatters through various lease and sharecropping arrangements to actual ownership. Landless women tend to work for wages as unskilled agricultural laborers, but men are more in demand for this kind of work, which is often migratory; as a result, these women are more likely to head households (at least periodically), to be poor, and to have a high birthrate. Women in landowning households, by contrast, devote less time to cultivation (though sometimes more time to animal husbandry) and enjoy more leisure and economic independence. They may be able to hire domestic help, and they often manage small nonfarm businesses.

Poor rural people, especially those who own no land, have little access to the credit that would enable them to invest in income-producing ventures. Unequal access to credit has restricted women's success and autonomy in all regions and economic spheres, and nowhere more than on the farm. Legislation is now making farm credit more accessible to women in western nations, although entrenched attitudes may still impede their equal participation. In developing nations, women farmers may depend on loans from government and international aid programs to fund their ventures. They tend to have a better record of repayment in rural small loan programs than do male borrowers; in India in the 1980s, for example, the Working Women's Forum's rural credit society reported a repayment rate of 90 to 95 percent, compared with a national average of 30 to 40 percent for similar loans from commercial banks. An exciting development is the Grameen Bank, started in Bangladesh, which lends small amounts to help poor people start businesses. In 1990, 80 percent of Grameen's borrowers were women. These loans do not support the purchase of land, but they are often extended to help women buy small livestock, poultry, or fish for pisciculture, or to develop business that utilize local agricultural products to make processed foodstuffs, textiles, and other craft items. Grameen Bank programs now exist in many countries, including the United states.

Women farmers tend to concentrate on certain types of production. In developing countries, they produce food for their own households and sell the surplus in local markets. Among low- to moderate-income groups, female-specialized cultivation often supports expenditures for women's and children's needs: the African vegetable grower may pay her daughter's school fees by selling extra squash, and many pioneer American farm women bought pianos and books with the "egg money." Other typically female agricultural specialties include culinary and medicinal herbs, dye plants, cut flowers, and ornamental potted plants. Small livestock (for example, goats) and poultry are often managed by women, whereas men tend cattle and other large animals. This division of labor reflects women's need to remain close to home to care for children and elders, as well as differential physical strength and cultural restrictions on mobility.

A little-recognized dimension of women's agriculture is urban farming. Especially in developing countries, people living in cities often have small plots where they produce vegetables, fruits, and small livestock for home consumption, market sale, or barter. Especially where cultural patterns limit women's employment outside the home (for example, in some Islamic societies), they often can make more money market gardening than in any other work. Women's urban farming, however, is rarely reflected in official statistics or made the object of development programs. An exception is Peru Mujer, a Peruvian nongovernmental organization, which established a community gardening project that eventually reached 5,000 households in Lima; women received training and extension visits as well as support in marketing and food processing ventures. In the United States, women are likely to participate in community garden programs in low-income urban neighborhoods.

In the early 1990s, according to a World Bank report, approximately 40 percent of agricultural holdings in developing countries were managed by women. Women's direct involvement in farm production is highest in sub-Saharan Africa, eastern Asia, and the Indian subcontinent, and lowest in highly industrialized nations and Latin America. Complex interactions of historical, religious, and economic factors have created the differing regional patterns.

Sub-Saharan Africa is the focus of many studies and development programs in the field of women's agriculture. women here have been estimated to constitute between 60 and 80 percent of the agricultural labor force; there are more females than males engaged in the subsectors of homestead production (small farms), urban agriculture, pisciculture (raising food fish), small animal production (including poultry), and tree culture. Household economy in this region tends to be dual: women are responsible for obtaining food, while men perform outside wage labor for other needs; men's and women's earnings are not typically pooled; and budgets are separate.

Food production by African smallholders has declined in recent decades for several reasons. National governments, often at the urging of international lenders, encouraged increased production of export crops, which are owned and worked mostly by men. Collapsing prices for these commodities have thrown many men back into food production, where they may displace women from their traditional source of income. Moreover, export crops are typically grown on large holdings constituted by combining former small farms; this disappearance of smallholdings increases the gap between economically secure landowners and the landless poor, and exacerbates malnutrition. As land for food production becomes scarcer, the remaining available land is overexploited and soil fertility drops; only additional labor—from exhausted farmers and their increasingly numerous children—and the fertilizer and technology they cannot afford can wring more food from the land. Warfare adds to the woes of rural Africans; as men die or become disabled, the burden of providing food falls ever more heavily on women.

Aid organizations in Africa, especially those associated with the United Nations, have made special efforts in the past two decades to assist African rural women, but many obstacles persist. In most areas, men have ultimate control over land tenure, and inheritance is patrilineal (although matrilineal systems also exist). National authority structures tend to reinforce the subordinate status of women in the interest of conserving male dominance. Credit associations and export marketing groups may restrict membership to heads of households, who are rarely female (at least officially), even though pilot projects have demonstrated that women borrowers tend to have higher repayment rates. Infrastructure improvements are concentrated on serving the industrial sector rather than the rural areas, where women's food production is known to increase with road access to markets.

Women are also prominent in Asian agriculture—especially in less developed nations—but here the sexes tend to cooperate in a single cultivation process, performing complementary tasks. In rice farming, for example, men do the heavier work, while women perform repetitive tasks such as planting and weeding. Men, however, usually control land tenure and make decisions about crops. In a pattern similar to early European peasant farming, women contribute field labor at peak times and otherwise specialize in raising small livestock and poultry. As in Africa, men are more likely to migrate for wage labor, while women assume an increasing share of farmwork; for example, the 1990 Chinese census found that women constituted 48 percent of farmworkers nationally, but more than 50 percent in industrially developed areas of the country. By 1997, a survey by the Chinese Women's Federation reported that women constituted more than half the nation's agricultural workforce; at the same time, the proportion of women managing or owning farm enterprises fell from 26 percent in 1988 to only 8 percent in 1995, indicating that men have been more successful in taking advantage of Chinese economic reforms (Riskin, 2000). In difficult economic conditions in Malawi, young male entrepreneurs have taken over the formerly female niche of operating vegetable market stalls; in addition to depriving market women of employment, they are reported to steal crops from the farms of women, especially single women.

Two cultural areas in which women are less prominent in agriculture are the Islamic world and Latin America. In the former, religious restrictions on the activities of women of reproductive age tend to keep them near home, where they often engage in domestic food gardening and especially in food processing; young girls and old women, however, may work more in the fields. In colonial Latin America, men were withdrawn from subsistence farming to provide labor on cash crops, and women took up the responsibility of feeding the family; but recent consolidation of landholdings, industrialization, and emphasis on export crops have reduced the presence of women in the farm workforce. Land available for leasing by subsistence farmers has greatly diminished, further excluding women. Many rural women here migrate to cities for domestic or industrial jobs, in the reverse of the pattern in other parts of the developing world.

In western Europe and North America, social, religious, and legal constraints on women's farming are less salient, but women are a minority presence among farmers. In Canada, for example, they constitute about one-third of the half million people who derive their income from agriculture. Married farm women often manage the financial side of the enterprise, contribute labor to main crops at peak periods, and engage in specialized production such as ornamental horticulture. They are more likely than rural women in less developed areas to take part-time or seasonal wage employment.

Professions ancillary to farming attract many women, especially in the West. In 1997, women received 46.8 percent of agriculture-related baccalaureate degrees granted by U.S. universities, but only about 10 percent of these graduates are likely to become farmers. Instead, they find employment as farm credit managers, laboratory researchers, extension agents, or development specialists, and in other professions. Historically, women have been especially numerous in animal science, horticulture, food science and technology, nutrition, plant pathology, and entomology. Agricultural colleges actively recruit women students, and a few, such as Wageningen Agricultural University in the Netherlands have specialized programs focusing on gender issues. In most African countries, however, national committees on crop resources and biotechnology are largely or even exclusively staffed by men, and none of these bodies include women farmers.

Since 1950, world agriculture has been transformed by three related movements: cash or export cropping has increased at the expense of varied domestic food production; landholdings have become larger, on average, eating up small farms; and the so-called green revolution, while increasing productivity through the introduction of industrial chemicals, improved plant varieties, and mechanization, has also increased reliance on capital-intensive activities. All these changes have altered the position of women in agriculture in fundamental ways. Large cash-crop operations are primarily male enterprises, so women's food-producing property may be marginalized as the best land is taken up for export production. When men migrate for wage labor, women assume added burdens at home—and they often have to support temporarily unemployed, sick, and elderly men. Differential access to credit may make technological improvements less available to women smallholders, who thus cannot compete effectively. Overall improvements in total farm production, average income, and world food supply can thus mask a deteriorating situation for women farmers.

To ameliorate this problem, international development agencies and national support organizations are increasingly offering programs aimed at women food farmers. Most prominent among these are the Food and Agriculture Organization and UNICEF, branches of the United Nations, and the U.S. Agency for International Development and Peace Corps. Most developed countries have farm women's organizations that now address such issues as access to credit. There is hope that the drive for gender equality will extend to the women who work the land, as women have for millennia.

See Also

ANCIENT INDIGENOUS CULTURES: WOMEN'S ROLES; DEVELOPMENT: OVERVIEW; DEVELOPMENT: CHINESE CASE STUDY—RURAL WOMEN; ECOSYSTEM; ENVIRONMENT: OVERVIEW; FOOD, HUNGER, AND FAMINE; WORK: EQUAL PAY AND CONDITIONS; WORK: OCCUPATIONAL SEGREGATION

References and Further Reading

Folbre, Nancy, Barbara Bergmann, Bina Agarwal, and Maria Floro, eds. 1992. *Women's work in the world economy.* New York: New York University Press.

Henderson, Helen Kreider. 1995. *Gender and agricultural development: Surveying the field.* Tucson: University of Arizona Press.

Joekes, Susan P. 1987. *Women in the world economy: An INSTRAW study.* New York and Oxford: Oxford University Press.

Riskin, Jerome. 2000. *Poverty and nequality in China.* New York: Oxford University Press.

Sachs, Carolyn E. 1995. *Gendered fields: Rural women, agriculture, and environment.* Boulder, Colo.: Westview. 1999.

Shortall, Sally. 1999. *Women and farming: Property and power.* New York: St. Martin's.

Young, Kate. 1993. *Planning development with women: Making a world of difference.* New York: St. Martin's.

Jane McGary

AIDS AND HIV

Acquired immunodeficiency syndrome (AIDS) is a serious disease resulting from infection by the human immunodeficiency virus (HIV). AIDS and HIV infections have reached pandemic levels in many parts of the world (Mann and Tarantola, 1996; World Health Organization).

Retroviruses, Infections, and the Immune System

HIV is a retrovirus that can be transmitted through infected blood, semen, or other body fluids and tissues; and from mother to child during pregnancy, childbirth, or breastfeeding. After HIV enters the body, it targets CD4 lymphocytes (also called T-helper cells), which are white blood cells that function as an essential part of the body's immune system. By penetrating the nucleus of a CD4 cells, HIV can use the cell's genetic machinery to replicate itself, with the enzymes reverse transcriptase and protease playing impor-

tant roles in the replication process. HIV replicates each time the lymphocyte replicates. A nonsymptomatic latency period usually follows, often lasting for years. Eventually, however, HIV destroys its host lymphocytes, releasing new viral particles into the body. As the immune system loses its CD4 lymphocytes, it loses its ability to protect the body against other infectious viruses, bacteria, and fungi. Seroconversion from HIV-negative (HIV–) status to HIV-positive (HIV+) status occurs when an enzyme-linked immunosorbent assay (ELISA test) detects measurable levels of antibodies to HIV in the bloodstream. The ongoing impact of HIV on the immune system is commonly measured by CD4 cell counts, which decline as the disease progresses and improve when medications work effectively.

Medications to control and treat HIV infection usually target the replication enzymes reverse transcriptase and protease. Drug "cocktails" that combine multiple reverse transcriptase and protease inhibitors have been the most effective treatment to date and are classified as "highly active antiretroviral therapy" (HAART). Important medications approved for treatment of AIDS in women in the United States include the reverse transcriptase inhibitors zidovudine (AZT or Retrovir), stavudine (d4T or Zerit), lamivudine (3TC or Epivir), zalcitibine (ddC or Hivid), and didanosine (ddI or Videx), and the protease inhibitors saquinavir (Invirase), ritonavir (Norvir), indinavi (Crixivan), and efavirenz (Sustiva) (US Food and Drug Administration, 1997).

During the 1980s and early 1990s, AIDS was considered a terminal illness (except for a few anomalous cases) and HIV+ status was considered a death sentence. Current treatments have changed AIDS to a chronic condition amenable to long-term management if (an important qualification) people with AIDS have access to early diagnosis, if they can pay for treatment, and if they can adhere to the complexities of treatment and tolerate its side effects. As of this writing, a vaccine to immunize people against HIV infection had not yet been developed.

The AIDS Epidemic

There are multiple strains of human immunodeficiency virus (HIV). The earliest strain is believed to have developed from a simian immunodeficiency virus (SIV) that crossed the species barrier in Africa from chimpanzees to people during the early years of the twentieth century, HIV-1 is the viral strain that has spread worldwide; HIV-2 has been mostly localized in west Africa.

In 1980, the scholarly *Journal of Homosexuality* (volume 5) published reports from several physicians in San Francisco, New York, and Chicago whose medical practices included sexually active homosexual men with sexually transmitted diseases (STDs). These physicians were seeing an unusual form of pneumonia (*Pneumocystis carinii*) and an unusual cancer (Kaposi's sarcoma) in that patient population. On 5 June 1981, the U.S. Centers for Disease Control and Prevention (CDC) issued the first in a series of similar alerts as part of the epidemiologic *Morbidity and Mortality Weekly Report*. In 1983, the virus itself was identified, allowing the field of AIDS medicine to expand (Merigan, 1999).

In addition to *Pneumocystis* pneumonia and Kaposi's sarcoma, researchers designated a list of infections that "opportunistically" targeted the HIV+ population: cytomegalovirus, toxoplasmosis, thrush (oral candidiasis), cryptosporidiosis, amoebiasis, giardiasis, histoplasmosis, *Mycobacterium avium* infections, and others. These infections were considered indicators of HIV+ status and their presence became part of the diagnostic protocol for AIDS that determined eligibility for treatment.

Conspicuously missing from the diagnostic lists of AIDS indicators until 1993 were gynecologic disorders: vaginal yeast infections (candidiasis), pelvic inflammatory disease, genital warts (human papillomavirus infection), cervical dysplasia, and cervical cancer. Women, particularly women of childbearing age, were explicitly excluded from participation in research and clinical trials of medications. The results of those early failures to diagnose and treat women are still evident.

During the the first decade of the epidemic (the 1980s), the patient population was primarily male and usually white: sexually active homosexual and bisexual men, users of heroin and other injectable street drugs who shared needles; prison inmates; surgical patients and people with hemophilia who received blood transfusions; and transplant patients who received donor organs, immunosuppresant medications, or both. Women who were diagnosed with AIDS had to meet the diagnostic criteria established for men, and most HIV+ women were linked to the at-risk male population: women whose husbands were bisexual men or users of injected drugs, women who injected drugs themselves, women who were sex workers or prison inmates, and women who gave birth to children with HIV. However, by the second decade of the epidemic (the 1990s) the patient population had shifted toward people of color, with young pregnant women at particularly high risk (U.S. Centers for Disease Control and Prevention, 1999).

Public health efforts during these first two decades were aimed at educating at-risk populations never to share needles, always to use condoms during sex ("safer sex") so as to reduce viral transmission, and to seek early diagnosis and treatment. Several gay organizations (including Project Inform in San Francisco and Gay Men's Health Crisis in New York) helped to set the original public health agendas (an unusual pattern, given the homophobia of most cultures). Those agendas still have not shifted their primary focus from sexually active men in developed countries to young women of color and mother-to-child transmission among poorer populations (Center for AIDS Prevention Studies). The research agenda continues to be androcentric as well.

Special Problems for Women with HIV and AIDS

Although women are no longer invisible in the AIDS patient population, problems continue for HIV+ women as a result of women's subordination to men, their exploitation by men, and their disadvantaged socioeconomic and legal status (UNAIDS, 1996):

- Women are no longer explicitly excluded from research and clinical trials of new medications, but barriers to women's equitable participation in clinical trials still exist (Lucey and Zangeneh, 1999).
- Women receive HIV screening tests less often than men, even when HIV tests are supposed to be mandatory (Link, 1999).
- Women must negotiate with men for safe sexual behaviors (use of condoms and caution regarding multiple partners). Rates of male-to-female transmission continue to rise, however, indicating that women are unlikely ever to achieve parity in heterosexual dyads.
- Prostitution and pornography put sex workers (primarily women and children) at greater risk of HIV infection, and this population is less likely to have access to health care.
- AIDS and other sexually transmitted diseases (STDs) carry considerable social stigma along with their physiological complications. Women who report STDs or HIV+ status to male sexual partners are at greater risk of domestic violence and of discrimination (Roth and Fuller, 1998; UNAIDS, 1996). There is also some evidence that this stigma interfered with how energetically feminist media and feminist activists have reacted to the AIDS epidemic (Treichler and Warren, 1998).
- Mother-to-child transmission of HIV usually occurs during late pregnancy, during childbirth, or during breastfeeding. Unless pregnant women can improve their access to HIV testing, counseling, treatment, and safe substitutes for breast milk, this problem cannot be solved (UNAIDS, undated).

Researchers hope that, in the future, HIV and AIDS can be limited to occasional outbreaks in isolated areas (as happened with the *Yersinia pestis* bacterium that caused bubonic plague in Europe during the "black death" of the 1300s) or to a research vault (as happened with the variola virus that caused smallpox), or that HIV/AIDS will be added to the list of diseases that can be prevented through childhood immunization. Until any of these things happen, however, the Joint United Nations Programs on HIV/AIDS (UNAIDS) have identified public health goals for 1999–2004 as: (1) to reduce incidence of HIV in people 15 to 24 years old by 25 percent in the 25 most affected countries; (2) to give at least 50 percent of all HIV+ pregnant women access to HIV-related health services; (3) to give at least 75 percent of all HIV+ people access to medications for AIDS-related infections; and (4) to give all AIDS orphans in Africa access to food and education on an equal basis with their nonorphan peers. Although these public health goals for children and pregnant women are ambitious, one might suspect that if wealthy white men in developed nations were the primary patient population, prevention and treatment goals would be 100 percent and immediate.

See Also

References and Further Reading

Center for AIDS Prevention Studies, AIDS Research Institute, University of California, San Francisco. *HIV Prevention Fact Sheets.*

Link, Derek. 1999. HIV treatment and diagnosis in the United States. *GMHC treatment issues: Newsletter of experimental AIDS therapies* 13 (5/6 May–June).

Lucey, Mary, and Tardad Zangeneh. 1999. Gender agenda: Science *not* psychology; biology *not* behavior. *Women Alive* (Summer).

Mann, Jonathan, and Daniel Tarantola, eds. 1996. *AIDS in the world II.* New York: Oxford University Press.

Merigan, Thomas C., ed. 1999. *Textbook of AIDS medicine* (2nd ed.). Baltimore, Md.: Williams and Wilkins.

Roth, Nancy L., and Linda K. Fuller, eds. 1998. *Women and AIDS: Negotiating safer practices, care, and representation.* Binghamton, N.Y.: Harrington Park.

Treichler, Paula, and Catherine Warren. 1998. Maybe next year: Feminist silence and the AIDS epidemic. In Nancy L.

Roth and Katie Hogan, eds., *Gendered epidemic: Representations of women in the age of AIDS.* New York: Routledge.

UNAIDS (Joint United Nations Programs on HIV/AIDS) (undated). *HIV and infant feeding.*

UNAIDS (Joint United Nations Programs on HIV/AIDS). 1996. *Discrimination in the context of human immunodeficiency virus (HIV) or acquired immune deficiency syndrome (AIDS).*

U.S. Centers for Disease Control and Prevention, National Center for HIV, STD and TB Prevention. 1999. *HIV/AIDS among U.S. women: Minority and young women at continuing risk.*

U.S. Food and Drug Administration (1997). *Women and AIDS.*

World Health Organization. *WHO Initiative on HIV/AIDS and Sexually Transmitted Infections (HIS). Global surveillance on HIV/AIDS/STI.*

Faye Zucker

AIDS AND HIV: Case Study—Africa

In the year 2000, about 70 percent of all those infected with AIDS lived in sub-Saharan and southern Africa. Worldwide, about 34 million people carried HIV, and 23 million of these were in Africa. Of the 5.6 million people who were newly infected, 3.8 million were in Africa.

Background

The AIDS/HIV epidemic in the developing world—as of the year 2000—is a complex problem, medically and socially. AIDS/HIV is often seen as a gay disease, and this has been a potent reason for denial. Also, the biological characteristics of the virus, and the mechanisms of infection, which took many years to elucidate, remain difficult to understand. Moreover, the long incubation period makes AIDS/HIV hard to describe in practical terms to people accustomed to infections like malaria, which have more immediate manifestations. And although drug therapy has continued to evolve, it is inaccessible in regions where the epidemic is most prevalent. Strategies for prevention have relied on motivating people to make changes in their sexual behavior: abstinence, monogamy, fewer sexual partners, and the use of condoms.

The challenges of this epidemic have become most evident in sub-Saharan and southern Africa, especially in women. There, AIDS/HIV is primarily transmitted sexually between men and women, or transmitted from mother to child; to a lesser extent it is transmitted through contaminated blood. Women are implicated in each mode of transmission and become diseased as a result of their own infection or that of their children, spouses, families, or communities. They suffer enormously and variously: they are predisposed to infection because of biological and social factors, blamed and stigmatized for the spread of the virus, perceived as responsible for infecting their children, burdened with caring for the sick and orphans, and denied their rights or violated as a consequence of their perceived guilt or complicity.

In 1999 UNAIDS reported that in Africa 2 million more women than men were infected, and that girls were most vulnerable: girls aged 15 to 19 were five to six times more likely to be infected with HIV than boys of the same age. At that time, 12.2 million African women and 10.1 million men carried HIV, a ratio of 6 women to 5 men.

Factors such as poverty and foreign debt prevent countries in this region from responding adequately to the crisis: of the world's 50 poorest countries, 33 are African. In Africa, AIDS was expected to reduce life expectancy to 45 years by 2005. More than 7 million children in Africa have already been orphaned by AIDS/HIV, and often the people who should care for children are themselves dead, ill, old, or desperately poor.

The rate of increase in HIV is greatest in southern Africa, as compared with east and central Africa; the highest rates of infection are in Namibia, Botswana, Zimbabwe, Zambia, and South Africa, where as many as 1 in 7 people are infected. The spread of HIV in Africa is affected by cultural and socioeconomic factors such as sexual behavior, stigma, tradition, access to services, women's social status, and migration. Some occupations are associated with higher risk, including long-distance driving, migrant labor, and military service. Another factor is male circumcision: in one study, the two cities with the highest rates of HIV and ulcerative sexually transmitted diseases (Kisumu, Kenya; and Ndola, Zambia) also had the lowest percentage of circumcised males.

Transmission of HIV from mother to child has become a significant problem, in part because most infected women have contracted the virus at an early age, before marrying or bearing children. (In the University Teaching Hospital in Lusaka, Zambia, for example, many pediatric AIDS cases are firstborn children of young, recently married couples.) About 570,000 African children are infected, 90 percent by their mothers, and according to estimates, 1 million more HIV-positive infants will be born to infected mothers by 2003.

A joint study by Uganda and the United States (HIVNET 012) found that a single dose of an inexpensive antiretroviral drug, nevirapine (NVP), given to mother and infant, reduced HIV transmission by 47 percent; thus, annually, NVP could prevent infection in about 300,000 to 400,000 newborns. However, successful use of NVP—and of the earlier drug AZT—requires not only access to the drug but also testing, counseling, and community support. Another strategy involves preventing transmission of HIV through breast milk; a study in Kenya compared breastfed and formula-fed babies and found that an additional 16.2 percent of breastfed babies, uninfected at birth, became HIV-positive during the first six months of life (Nduati, 2000).

There are two forms of HIV in Africa. The more virulent, HIV-1, has perhaps ten subtypes. Subtype B predominates in the developed world, but many subtypes are common in Africa (and in Asia). The major cause of death is disease induced by subtypes A, C, D, and E. The Harvard AIDS Institute believes that of the subtypes, C is most transmissible through sexual intercourse, and this is thought to have contributed to the spread of HIV in Africa, especially southern Africa. HIV-2, a weaker virus, was first described in the mid-1980s in west Africa and has remained mostly confined to this area, and to sex workers.

Women's Risk of HIV

For African women, the risk of HIV is determined more by cultural, social, and economic context than by individual behavior. Women are valued for marrying and remaining married, bearing children, caring for their families, placing men's and children's interests above their own, and deferring to men's authority. Thus women have little say in decisions regarding sex and reproductive health—for example, whether or not to have children or whether to breastfeed or bottle-feed a child. Women in situations where it is difficult to claim any rights—refugee camps, prisons, and forced prostitution—are especially at risk of sexual abuse and rape, and therefore also of HIV.

Studies in Kenya have found that nearly one girl in four between ages 15 and 19 is HIV-infected. Among females, the peak age for infection is between 15 and 24 (compared with 25 to 34 for males). Even women in stable relationships are highly vulnerable. For young women, societal norms increase the risk of infection: they are not expected to learn about sex, and others decide when and whom a woman will marry. Reproductive health services, preventive or curative, are often inaccessible to young people. Child marriages, often between teenage girls and much older men, and female circumcision are still common; both practices increase the risk of HIV. Poverty also has an effect: poor parents are unable to meet their children's basic needs, and many young girls turn to commercial sex to support themselves—often with men who refuse to use condoms.

Addressing AIDS/HIV

Strategies for combating AIDS/HIV in Africa have tended not to confront men's sexual behavior directly but rather to focus on women. The message has been that women should empower themselves to prevent infection by changing their own behavior or negotiating with their male partners for safer sex. Given women's lack of power and their economic dependence on men, this approach has been largely ineffective.

Moreover, prevention has stressed individual actions, whereas traditionally African women's strength has been in working together, teaching and supporting one another, and sharing experiences. More effective strategies would build on this strength by identifying and overcoming gender-based and sociocultural problems: women would develop solidarity to eliminate risky behaviors by men, and to impart new values to their sons and daughters. Realistically, however, this would require a social revolution.

As of the year 2000, the most important preventive measure remains the condom. But although condoms are used effectively in the western world, this is not true in Africa, where the condom is considered appropriate only for promiscuous people and for sex workers. Condoms (male and female) could be used more successfully in Africa if greater efforts were directed toward building skills, improving access, and making condoms respectable. A promising development for the future is microbicides, chemical agents that would improve women's ability to protect themselves.

A simple, basic strategy is improving communication within couples. To enhance communication about sex, general communication skills, such as problem solving, should be promoted. This would make couples better able to deal with sensitive issues such as HIV testing, disclosing test results, monogamy, condoms, treatment of sexually transmitted diseases (STDs), childbearing, and breastfeeding.

Testing has been a problematic strategy. Many women who are offered an HIV test in order to participate in programs providing antiretroviral drugs and free formula refuse because of the difficulties they would face if they tested positive: rejection by their partners, loss of rights and social support, stigma, and psychological stress. Widows of men who died of AIDS are not an encouraging example: they have been dispossessed of their farms, household property, and money, although they are still held responsible for caring for their children.

In fact, women in Africa are the chief caregivers for victims of AIDS, often without support and despite their other responsibilities. When a woman herself has AIDS, she is commonly her own caregiver. Further, women are disadvantaged regarding access to paid care and treatment such as drugs and hospitals; they tend to lack money, and in some cultures they need their husband's permission to go to a hospital. In many African countries, the health care system thinks of women's health in terms of fetal health during pregnancy and infants' health after delivery. Changes are needed so that African women will value their health and seek care.

Responding to the Challenges of AIDS/HIV

Interventions to reduce women's risk and to enable them to cope with AIDS/HIV should span the life cycle. Many groups have mobilized African women to address this challenge. The Society for Women and AIDS in Africa (SWAA), founded in the 1980s, is a grassroots organization working with women in more than twenty-five countries. The International Community of Women Living with HIV/AIDS in Africa (ICW), working closely with SWAA, has promoted women's rights. In Senegal, women's associations such as Dimba (which offers advice about reproductive health) and Laobe (which offers erotic products) have used traditional methods of communication and social mobilization (Cheikh Niang, 1995).

See Also

AIDS AND HIV; HEALTH CARE: SOUTHERN AFRICA; HEALTH CARE: SUB-SAHARAN AFRICA

References and Further Reading

Chiekh Niang. 1995. Sociocultural factors favoring HIV infection and integration of traditional women's association in AIDS prevention in Kolda, Senegal.

International Center for Research on Women. *Women and AIDS research report*, Series No. 8. Washington, D.C.: International Center for Research on Women.

Elias, C., and C. Coggins. 2000. Female-controlled methods to prevent sexual transmission of HIV. Unpublished paper presented by ACT-UP, Philadelphia, Pennsylvania, April.

Foreman, Martin, ed. 1999. *AIDS and men: Taking risks or taking responsibility?* London: Panos/Zed.

Ndauti, Ruth. 2000. In *Journal of the American Medical Association*, March.

Piot, Peter, Executive Director, UNAIDS. 1999. AIDS and violence against women. Panel on Women and Health, Commission on the Status of Women, 43rd session, March.

Rethinking the African AIDS epidemic. 2000. *Population and Development Report Review* 26(1; March): 117–135.

UNICEF. 1999. *Children orphaned by AIDS: Frontline responses from Eastern and Southern Africa.* UNICEF Publication, December.

World Health Organization. 2000. *Women and AIDS fact sheet.* March.

Eka Esu-Williams

ALCOHOLISM
See DRUG AND ALCOHOL ABUSE.

ALTERNATIVE ENERGY

From time immemorial the power of the sun, forests, wind, tides, and water has been harnessed for such diverse activities as lighting fires, drying clothes, sailing ships, and turning windmills. Only since the industrial revolution have the energy-hungry nations of the world used large quantities of coal and oil in their raw states to generate the quintessential modern fuel: electricity. Electricity is transmitted through power lines and grid systems that traverse countries. Coal and oil are now considered the mainstream sources of energy and are used to power the economies of the industrialized world, often male-initiated and which marginalize women.

A broad definition of alternative energy refers to systems such as mini-hydro power plants, wind generators, solar heating panels, and photo voltaic (PV) systems, water, wind, and the sun's energy (respectively) to generate and store electricity away from the major grid networks. Apart from off-grid systems, other renewables such as biogas and, arguably, biomass (in the form of wood fuel, crop waste, and dung), may be included in the definition of alternative energy. In developing countries wood fuel resources are being depleted, and supplies of fossil fuels (oil, gas, and coal) and grid-electricity are either erratic or beyond the reach of the poor, particularly poor women. Under these circumstances, renewable resources and alternative forms of energy are consistently suggested as the solution to energy scarcity.

Proponents of alternative energy use suggest that poor and rural people, in particular rural women, could have better lighting and communications through solar-powered telephones, computers, and online microcredit systems. Access to global communication systems would also raise the profiles of these communities. Skeptics point out the limited success over the past thirty years in improv-ing the lives of women through low-key technology such as improved woodstoves, biogas digesters, and solar cookers. PV systems are limited because they do not supply sufficient electricity to cook by and thus do not address the primary energy-consuming task.

Some critics of alternative electricity supplies argue further that affordable, safe, and secure supplies of multiple energy sources are a more important consideration than computer networks or on-line credit systems, although these are not necessarily mutually exclusive. They also point out that large users of coal-fired or nuclear-generated electricity are generally found among the wealthy classes in cities, and this is where alternative energy should be most used and mainstreamed. Instead it is often poor and rural people, especially women, who are small consumers of energy that are expected to use energy efficiently. Without the benefit of technical expertise and support available in cities, they are expected to experiment with alternative systems. Attempts to reduce energy consumption in wealthy countries and introduce more sustainable systems such as using PV systems in new buildings, harvesting methane from land fill sites, and developing electric cars are underway. However, a great deal remains to be done. Concerned research and development activists are working on these challenges.

See Also
ENERGY; TECHNOLOGY: WOMEN AND DEVELOPMENT

References and Further Reading
ENERGIA: Women and Energy Newsletter. ETC Energy, P.O. Box 64, 3830 AB Leusden, Netherlands.

The Challenge of rural energy poverty in developing countries. 1999. World Energy Council (Conseil Mondial de l'Energie) and the Food and Agriculture Organization of the United Nations.

World energy assessment. 2000. New York: United Nations Development Program and World Energy Council.

Wendy Annecke

ALTERNATIVE MEDIA
See MEDIA: ALTERNATIVE and PRESS: FEMINIST ALTERNATIVES.

ALTERNATIVE MEDICINE
See HOLISTIC HEALTH I; HOLISTIC HEALTH II; and TRADITIONAL HEALING.

ALTERNATIVE TECHNOLOGY:
Case Study—Africa

Technology may be defined as the totality of knowledge applied to improve productivity. Some technology—though of course not all—causes environmental problems such as pollution. Alternative technology is any technology that is environmentally friendly and differs from an environmentally hostile conventional technology. Examples of alternative technologies are:

- Harnessing solar energy or wind energy to generate electricity or heat for domestic uses such as heating water.
- Practicing sustainable agriculture (such as organic farming and avoiding chemicals and pesticides) that preserves soil fertility without endangering life or polluting the environment.
- Using biogas technology to supply domestic heating and lighting energy by converting biomass into gas.
- Developing fuel-efficient engines.
- Recycling industrial and agricultural wastes to produce economically usable products.

Agrochemicals are one area in which alternative technology may be needed, especially in developing countries where poor education and poverty make them a dangerous undertaking: there is a risk of overdosing the soil, and there are also issues of the availability and affordability of the appropriate agrochemicals. In many developing countries, small-scale farming has become economically unreliable because of the rising cost of agrochemicals.

Much alternative technology has to do with alternative energy sources, because conventional fossil fuels—on the scale on which they are used today—are dangerous to the environment. Burning fossil fuels creates carbon dioxide, which has accumulated in the atmosphere and is contributing to problems such as global warming and depletion of the ozone layer. Gasoline is an an obvious example, but the indiscriminate use of wood as a source of energy is also a serious environmental problem that has led (directly and indirectly) to deforestation and thus has reduced biodiversity.

The need for global action on alternative technologies was set forth in 1992 by the United Nations Earth Summit in Rio de Janeiro. Agenda 21, signed by all the countries that were represented, is a program of sustainable development at the international, national, and local level.

Problems of Alternative Technology in Africa

Many African countries have yet to industrialize and therefore can choose between several alternatives with regard to industrialization. Thus Africa is in an advantageous position: it has an opportunity to avoid repeating the mistake of adopting environmentally unfriendly technologies. On the other hand, it has problems that must be resolved if it is to benefit from the experience of developed countries.

Cost: First is the problem of costs. Although alternative technologies, like many other technologies imported to Africa from developed coutries, may be useful in settings such as hospitals, hotels, schools, large businesses, and affluent homes, they are often prohibitively expensive in contexts where most African women would use them.

Even in the developed world, the large-scale use of alternative technologies has been hampered by the cost of installation. Solar energy is a clear example. In rural Africa, as elsewhere, the sun has always been a direct source of energy—laundry and agricultural harvests, such as maize and millet, are dried in the sun—but solar energy as a modern technology can be very costly.

Solar energy is harnessed by three methods: passive, thermal, and photovoltaic. Passive methodology involves deliberate building design: up to 70 percent of a building's energy needs can be provided by sensible design and solar orientation. Today, this is the most commercially mature of all the solar technologies, competing very well with conventional energy sources. However, the building design requirements are far beyond the reach of poor families such as those in most of rural Africa.

Thermal methodology uses solar energy to heat water. It is quite basic—a solar water heater is simply water pipes painted black to improve heat absorption. But here too, the technology is not yet in significant use by the majority of poor communities in rural Africa, because these communities have yet to be provided with clean pipe water. In some places people, especially women, must still walk more than 5 miles to fetch water, and in such a setting it is unrealistic to talk about solar water heaters. Moreover, despite its simplicity, this alternative technology is not cheap, even by the economic standards prevailing in most urban areas in Africa. Around the year 2000, typical installation costs (in United States dollars) varied from perhaps $1,000 to $1,500 for a "do it yourself" home system to $5,000 for a commercial system. These figures are by far too high for an average African family or small business; in Tanzania, for instance, per capita income at that time was less than $200.

Photovoltaic methodology, which is the most expensive, involves generating electricity from sunlight. A photovoltaic power supply system capable of meeting the demands of a typical energy-efficient house costs the equivalent of $30,000 to $35,000. Even in the developed world, grid-linked photovoltaic electricity is appealing because it is clean, not because it is cheap; it is far more expensive than conventional electricity. This form of photovoltaic electricity is obviously of little practical use for poor communities. However, photovoltaic generators—solar panels in the design of roofs of buildings—are becoming cost-effective. These generators operate with no moving parts and create no noise or pollution; they are the most appropriate renewable energy source for domestic and public settings. In a few countries in sub-Saharan and southern Africa, solar pumps are widespread in rural areas. Mali, for instance, had more than 100 solar pumps as of about the year 2000.

Foreign influences: A second problem confronting Africa is foreign influence. This problem is related to costs because it often takes the form of demands that are beyond Africa's economic means. What technology to acquire and what products of technology to import are often dictated by the interests of a minute affluent part of the population with foreign consumption values. In Tanzania, for example, the number and types of motor vehicles imported annually are characteristic of an affluent society in the developed world—not a poor society (which Tanzania is) or a society conscious of the environment (which Tanzania, like every other nation, should be). Although some well-off families in the developed world choose smaller fuel-efficient cars, wealthy Tanzanians choose cars that are large, luxurious, and fuel-inefficient.

Foreign influence also has an effect on technological research, most of which is foreign-funded. Given the poverty of Africa, this might seem to be a benefit—and so it could be, if the researchers were left alone to choose their studies. On the contrary, most research is done collaboratively with peers in the developed world who are often ignorant of the needs of developing regions. As a result, to take just one example, most of the research on alternative energy conducted by the only university department of physics in Tanzania—at the University of Dar es Salaam—is high-level research remote from the realities of the country.

Lack of researchers: The problem of foreign influence is made worse because there is often no critical mass of African researchers. In the whole of Tanzania, for instance, there was only one professor of solar energy as of about the year 2000, and there were no woman in this field—a significant lack, since women researchers could be more sympathetic to the needs and interests of African women.

Lack of policy: Another problem confronting Africa is a lack of legislative policies to promote the development and use of alternative technologies. African nations that are serious about alternative technology need the kind of legislation that exists in the developed world. In the Netherlands, for instance, the government, power companies, architects, planners, financial institutions, local authorities, scientists,

and manufacturers have cooperated to develop solar energy; Great Britain has a legislative program called the Non-Fossil Fuel Obligation (NFFO).

Better legislative policy is also needed to increase public concern for the environment. In countries such as Tanzania—probably because educational levels are low—the majority if people seem unaware of industrial pollution and other environmental threats.

African Women and Alternative Technology

In Africa, urban and rural communities differ in their need for energy and their capability for capturing it. The energy needs and the "capture potential" of urban African women are not significantly different from those of their counterparts in the developed world. Thus alternative technologies such as biogas, solar panels, and passive solar heating (building design) are all within the reach of many urban African households. However, the use of such technologies is limited by the availability of cheaper energy. In most cases, for instance, hydroelectric power is available; but when it is deemed expensive, charcoal, firewood, and kerosene are used instead, in complete disregard of any environmental hazards. Three-quarters of the energy in sub-Saharan and southern Africa is still derived from biomass in the form of wood, charcoal, crop and wood residues, and cow dung (Hall, 1991).

In rural areas, where there are no industrial sources of energy, life is very traditional. The main problems confronting rural African woman are the fundamental ones: producing, preserving, and cooking food with primitive technologies; walking long distances to get water; procuring clothing; constructing shelter (family houses); and gathering firewood. The hand hoe is the main technology in agriculture; since modern agrochemicals are not affordable, animal manure is the only fertilizer. "Alternative technology" may have no meaning for a rural society that has been exposed to little if any conventional technology.

There are alternative technologies appropriate for rural Africa—environmentally friendly technologies that are affordable and sustainable and address the problems and needs of both rural and urban communities. The development and marketing of fuel-efficient stoves have received considerable attention from researchers in universities and other institutions in Africa, as a response to political calls to address the energy problem. Other technologies that have received attention include solar energy, windmills (especially for pumping underground water), animal manure, and biogas (Sadhu and Sandler, 1986). However, progress in these areas has been impeded by several factors, including costs, conservative attitudes, and cultural taboos.

In addition to the costs noted above, prototypes of energy-efficient utilities are expensive because they cannot achieve economies of scale. Too many families cannot afford to become customers, and governments have not created the necessary links between researchers, industrialists, and entrepreneurs.

Conservatism is characteristic of many African societies: people are suspicious of new technologies and reluctant to discard methods they have been using for centuries. New marketing techniques and strategies are needed to educate the end user about the advantages of innovations. In Europe, the Center for Alternative Technology (CAT) explores and demonstrates a wide range of practical alternative technologies regarding land use, shelter, energy, diet, health, and waste management. African researchers have nothing analogous, and they also confront low standards of education and sparsely populated regions in which the communication infrastructure is so poor that many villages are not easily reachable.

Cultural taboos are also a hindrance. For instance, in the Masai culture (Kenya and Tanzania), housing construction is a woman's occupation. It may be difficult for such a culture to adopt the construction and design methods needed for solar energy or biogas technology.

Nevertheless, some methods that are usually not thought of as "alternative technologies" in the developed world are very important in terms of liberating rural African women. Examples include weaving and food preparation. In areas where cotton is grown, household weaving can provide all of a family's clothing, so that the family income can be used for other needs. Rural women could also be taught about nutrition; too often, lack of knowledge about healthful food combinations has resulted in malnutrition existing along with an abundant variety of foods. There is no reason why these simple technologies should not be spread widely in African rural communities.

The Way Ahead

Several avenues could improve the situation in Africa. First and foremost is the need to train a critical mass of African men and women who can adequately address issues of alternative technology.

Second, African governments should translate their political pronouncements into action. such as setting aside funds specifically for research on alternative technology and for training, especially of women.

Third, African governments should pass legislation to preserve the environment, discouraging utilities that waste enegy or create pollution and encouraging environmentally friendly technology. Examples include using animal manure instead of agrochemicals; reviving healthful traditional methods of preserving and storing food, especially in rural areas; constructing houses that use renewable energy sources, such as sunlight and rainwater; using windmills to harvest groundwater; and using biomass to provide biogas for domestic heating and lighting to reduce overdependence on firewood and charcoal and diminish deforestation.

African governments should also raise the general level of education. Primary school education is inadequate in the modern world; a secondary school education (at least) should be provided for the majority of the population.

Finally, African nations should modernize agriculture; in particular, they should say good-bye to the hand hoe. Food shortages have persisted in almost all African countries for several decades despite the existence of numerous technologies that could solve this problem once and for all. Even the ox-drawn plow in place of the hand hoe would constitute an alternative technology.

Conclusion

African women are still struggling with poverty characterized by primitive agriculture and shortages of food and water. In some cases, alternative technology is meaningless because there is really no technology in use that can be said to require an alternative. What is often required is to relieve African woman of some primitive technology and provide environmentally friendly technology—while avoiding, as far as possible, the mistakes made by developed nations. Agrochemicals, for example, should be discouraged in favor of more natural and sustainable alternatives.

Many African women—particularly rural women—want access to better education. They may need to learn about the dangers of some traditional technologies of food production, preparation, preservation, and storage, and about alternative sources of energy; and whatever alternatives are adapted must be less troublesome than the old metnods. The communication infrastructure must be improved; it is crucial for survival. Research is needed to clarify the status quo in a given community, identify the best alternatives available and affordable, and only then design the mechanisms for bringing about change. Opportunities for technological training must be provided to African women, so that they can participate more fully in the development and promotion of alternative technology.

References and Further Reading

Bhagavan, M. R., and S. Karekazi. 1992. *Energy management in Africa*. London: Zed.

Bradley, P. N. 1991. *Wood-fuel, women, and woodlots,* Vol. 1, *The foundation of a wood-fuel development strategy for East Africa.* Hong Kong: Macmillan.

Bryceson, D. F. 1993. *Liberalizing Tanzania food trader.* London: James Curry Books, Heinemann, Zed.

Foley, G. 1987. Exaggerating the Sahelian wood-fuel problem. *Ambi* 16(6).

Hall, D. O. 1991. Biomass energy. *Energy Policy* 19(8): 711–737.

———, and Y. S. Mao. 1980. *African Energy Policy Research Network (AFRE PREN).* London: Zed.

Leach, G., and R. Mearns. 1988. *Beyond the wood-fuel crisis: People, land, and trees in Africa.* London: Earth Scan.

Mackintosh, M. 1987. *Gender, class, and rural transition: Agribusiness and the food crises in Senegal.* London: Zed.

O' Keefe, P., and B. Musislow. 1984. *Energy and development in southern Africa.* Uppsala, Sweden: SADCC Countries Studies, part by SIAS.

Pohjonein, V. 1989. Establishment of fuel-wood plantations in Ethiopia. *Silva Carfelica* (14).

Ranganathan, V. 1992. *Rural electrification in Africa.* London: Zed.

Sadhu, R., and J. Sandler. 1986. *The technology and tools book: A guide to technologies women are using worldwide.* Nairobi: Report of the Third International Conference on Women.

Soussan, J. 1990. Formulating Africa energy policy: A discussion document. E.T.C. Foundation.

Rose Shayo

ALTRUISM

It has been common in the literature for connections to be made between *volunteerism* and *altruism*. In other words, writers attempting to understand why people give their time freely, without expecting to be paid, have assumed that this is due to altruism. Altruism in this context is defined as an act that is not directed at gain, is given voluntarily, and is for the benefit of others. Feminists have pointed out that in the tradition of liberal economic thought, altruism tends to be seen as part of the *private sphere,* the family and the world of women. Thus although altruism is cherished as a human trait, it has no place in the *public sphere*—the competitive world of men. It is women who are seen to be the embodiment of the altruistic spirit and of the caring and helping mentality needed for the charitable activities of the voluntary sector (Blum et al., 1976). The central argument of feminist writers, then, is the existence of an *"ideology of altruism"* that compels women to provide their

services without receiving anything in return. Land and Rose (1985) coined the term *compulsory altruism* to describe this situation.

See Also

VOLUNTEERISM

References and Further Reading

Blum, L., M. Homiak, J. Housman and N. Scheman. 1976. Altruism and women's oppression. In Carol C. Gould and M. W. Wartofsky, eds., *Women and philosophy,* 222–247.

Land, Hilary, and Hilary Rose. 1985. Compulsory altruism for some or an altruistic society for all? In P. Bean, J. Ferris, and D. Whynes, eds., *In defense of welfare,* 74–99. London: Tavistock.

Cora V. Baldock

AMENORRHEA

See MENSTRUATION.

ANARCHISM

The term *anarchism* has, unfortunately, long been associated with violence and mayhem. Its connotation is often chaos and complete destruction of the social order. In fact, however, the literal definition of *anarchism,* "without government," actually means a social, political, and economic system in which there is no hierarchy and no domination from above. It is a structure in which no one person or group of people has any power over other. Those who espouse this ideology believe that individuals can best decide how to live their own lives, without the intervention of government. Anarchists are opposed to domination in any form—governmental, religious, economic, societal, or interpersonal.

Anarchism is similar to other socialist ideologies in its analysis and critique of economic domination, but it goes further than Marxism in its thinking about the state, hierarchy, and all authority relations. Anarchists want to abolish all structured relations of dominance and powerlessness in society. They aim to create a society based on equality, mutuality, and reciprocity, in which each person is valued and respected as an individual (Ackelsberg, 1991). Anarchists believe that "the means are the ends" and that people must create the new society themselves, in a leaderless and self-directed manner.

Ideology

Anarchists believe in the use of direct action, such as general strikes and boycotts, as well as the use of political propaganda. Generally, anarchists believe that the poor and powerless will bring about dramatic social transformation by revolutionary means rather than reformist measures such as the ballot. For the most part, anarchists are atheists and believe that the idea of God is used by the church to maintain its own authority. Religion is seen as a tool for containing social change. Some anarchists believe that revolution will come through the establishment of small, leaderless communes and work groups that have the power to determine for themselves how they will operate. This is called *anarchist-communism*. Others, more individualist in their thinking, believe that a person is best left alone and unencumbered by forced social arrangements. This is called *anarcho-individualism*. People who believe in this ideology are more interested in social contracts between people as the basis for an economic system (Leeder, 1993). Another important thread in anarchist history is the *anarcho-syndicalist* movement, which was primarily based in Europe—particularly Spain—but also spread to Mexico, Brazil, and Argentina. This movement believed that revolution would come through labor activities and that the basis of the new society would be found in the workplace and through unions. In some countries, anarchists also have been involved in violent attacks on people in positions of power and authority. Additionally, there have always been anarchists involved in terrorism and attempts to overthrow governments.

The origins of the concept go far back, to the writings of Lao-Tse, Zeno, the apostles of Jesus Christ, Diderot, William Godwin, Sir Thomas More, and the Anabaptists, to name a few. The ideology seems to have evolved into a full-blown articulation in the works of Pierre Proudhon, Mikael Bakunin, and Peter Kropotkin, who developed the ideas of federalism, mutual aid, and inevitability of revolution by peasants, not just workers. Out of a long evolution of the ideology came the organizations in which women played an important role. It also might be postulated that anarchist-feminist ideology, particularly the belief in the harmony of humankind working together, has its roots in the Babylonian myth of Tiamat. In this myth, Tiamat created the world whole and without division so that life flowed spontaneously between light and dark, season and season, birth and death. Humans were not owned, separated, or put into categories. But Tiamat's son grew in power, overthrew his mother, cut her into pieces, created his own world, and was called creator. She became the goddess of destruction, of chaos, and was feared. This concept—the overthrow of woman as creator—also provides insight into the evolution of the idea of anarchism from a feminist perspective.

Politically, anarchism has been a useful ideology in understanding women in the context of domination and oppression. Anarchists believe that all people have the right to complete liberty as long as one person's actions do not interfere with the rights of other individuals. Although it is not an explicitly feminist doctrine, the seeds of women's liberation exist within this school of thought. For that reason, the anarchist movement has long attracted and has had at its center noteworthy women who have influenced the development of the movement worldwide. These women have challenged male assumptions and have transcended conventional moral dictates on personal and political levels. They urged economic and psychological independence from men in the belief that personal autonomy was an essential component of sexual equality. It was their belief that sexual and personal liberation was a political goal and led to ultimate freedom for women, which also would be good for the greater society.

History

As early as the 1870s in the United States and Europe, anarchist writings declared that women ought to be fully the equals of men in the home and the workplace (Ackelsberg, 1991). A number of noted anarchist theoreticians, however, maintained fairly traditional ideas about the roles of women. Kropotkin (Russia), Bakunin (Russia), and Proudhon (France) all espoused a belief in certain "natural" behavior patterns for each sex and all maintained fairly conventional families. These same women, however, often challenged the dominant assumptions and sexism of anarchist men.

Anarchist Women in Europe and Asia

In Europe, the anarchist impulse has long been alive and well, manifesting itself in Russia, Ukraine, Spain, France, Germany, England, and Italy, to name but a few countries. Women have long been influenced by anarchist ideology and activism in those places.

In France during the Paris Commune (March–May 1871) a significantly important anarchist woman emerged. Louise Michel was a teacher whose devotion to the anarchist cause led her to be called the "anarchist saint" (March, 1981). In fact, because of her love of humankind, when she was almost assassinated she refused to press charges against her assailant. During the Commune, she served as an ambulance nurse and soldier. When the Commune was over and her mother had been arrested, Michel cajoled the military into arresting her instead and freeing her mother. She was charged with trying to overthrow the government, inciting civil war, having borne arms and worn a uniform in an insurrectional movement, and being complicit in assassinations (Thomas, 1980). As a result, she was banished to New Caledonia near Australia from 1873 to 1880, when complete amnesty was granted to all Communard deportees.

On her return to France, Michel became a charismatic and magical figure in politics. She spoke on the rights of women and took an anarchist perspective. She urged totally free education for women, and free marriages in which men held no proprietary rights over women. Her speeches drew thousands to the streets to hear her. Being imprisoned became a way of life for Michel because of her radical activities and her challenges to the French authorities. When she died, at the age of 75, as many as 100,000 people marched in her funeral procession. All were there to honor the memory of this valiant poet and revolutionary.

Anarchist women have long been important characters in Russian revolutionary activities. Many of these women later emigrated to the United States, and their influence was felt by contemporary radical women. During the Russian Revolution, anarchist women played important roles in the early stages of the rebellion and were instrumental in establishing anarchist federations in Petrograd (now St. Petersburg) and Moscow. Women played important roles as propagandists, theorists, and agitators. Vera Figner, Sophia Perovskaya, and Sophia Bardina were particularly known for their revolutionary zeal and contribution to the Russian revolution through the group V Narod ("to the populace"). Later, the Krontstadt rebellion—in which sailors fought against the authoritarian practices of the Bolsheviks—was put down and the anarchist impulse was thwarted by repression that became the norm of the Bolshevik government's political policies. Many women were arrested, imprisoned, and tortured as anarchist leaders.

In Spain, an equally important anarchist female presence, the Free Women of Spain (Mujeres Libres), was founded in 1936. This was a movement of over 20,000 women from Madrid and Barcelona, mobilized to develop a network of activities designed to empower individual women while building a sense of community (Ackelsberg, 1991). It grew out of the activities of antifascists who were active in the first months of the Spanish Civil War. The movement was rooted in anarcho-syndicalism, which envisioned a society with unions as its base, in which each union would send a delegate to coordinate local and industrial federations to run the social and economic order. This left out many women, children, and other nonworkers, however, and did not include an analysis of the subordination of women.

Mujeres Libres provided such an analysis and established storefront cultural centers, schools based on an anarchist model of education, and other community-based organizations offering theater, recreation, and education for women and young people. The movement was based on the concept of direct action and "propaganda by the dead," which consists of engaging in activities that are exemplary and that attract adherents by the power of the positive example they set (Ackelsberg, 1991: 33). In this way, self-generated, spontaneous organizations were encouraged, in which people who participate eventually learn how to gain and use power. These organizations were then federated and networked, rather than dictated from above, following the basic tenets of anarchist theory. Groups were organized to publish, to provide jobs and apprenticeships, and to discuss and challenge assumptions about the role of women as mothers and other traditional expectations. Their dual goals were education and activism.

A number of important women emerged from Mujeres Libres, including Frederica Montseny, Mercedes Comaposada, Lucia Sanchez Saornil, and Amparo Poch y Gascon. These women influenced others through their writing, and insisted on women's separate and autonomous status. They argued that women were oppressed as a group and that women's grievances could be addressed only through collective action. They challenged the dominant society and their anarchist comrades to recognize and respect their presence. For three important years, Mujeres Libres made a difference and a statement about the role of women in Spanish society.

In Asia, anarchism had a presence for quite a while as well. In China in the early 1900s, the thinkers Liu Khipei and Wu Zhihu began articulating anarchist ideas and tapped the indigenous sources of the anarchist vision. In the 1930s, a labor college (Laoda in Shanghai) was established, in which a number of women were recruited to participate in this showpiece of higher education for manual labor. Later Chinese anarchists studied in Paris and Tokyo and brought the concepts home to influence aspects of the Chinese revolution. Anarchism, though not a prime ideology in China, has served as a counterpoint to the authoritarian aspects of that revolution and serves as a critical perspective on the course of Chinese history.

In India, anarchism also played an important role in the thinking of Gandhi, who called himself a "kind of anarchist." He planned a decentralized society based on autonomous village communes. This did not come about because the political vagaries led to the formation of an Indian state modeled on the British system.

Anarchist Women in the United States and Latin America

Anarchist women have questioned the subjugation of women and have urged economic, psychological independence from men, often believing that personal autonomy is an essential component of sexual equality (Marsh, 1981). They were very important in influencing anarchist thought by their challenges to men and by their contributions to public awareness. Anarchist women who were active from 1870 to 1920 in the United States argued for the abolition of the institution of marriage and the nuclear family. They advocated "sexual varietism," that is, nonexclusive sexual relationships. They also wanted women to be self-supporting and often urged communal child rearing and large cooperative houses. Some believed that heterosexual lovers should never live together because of the treatment of females by males. Some women of this era even argued that homosexuality was part of the fight to free sexuality and saw it as a legitimate sexual alternative.

Emma Goldman, Voltairine deCleyre, Florence Finch Kelly, Lucy Parsons, Mollie Steimer, and Rose Pesotta are among the famous—and obscure—who were part of the early development of anarchism in the United States. Emma Goldman, long known in radical feminist circles as "Red Emma," is probably the best-known anarchist woman of that era. Goldman, a Russian Jewish immigrant, became known for her early advocacy of birth control, her propaganda activities against World War I, her famous lectures around the United States on theater and literature, and her long association with her anarchist comrade, Alexander Berkman. Goldman's activities, in her public espousal of free speech, led to the development of the American Civil Liberties Union (ACLU). Her refusal to adhere to conventional expectations for women in social and sexual behavior led to her being adored by many and reviled by the government. She was incarcerated for her activities and, eventually, deported in 1919 as a result of the "Red scare," in which hundreds of anarchists were sent back to Russia because of their politics. To this day, Emma Goldman's name is used to evoke the image of the revolutionary woman. Her ideology was rooted in an anarchist analysis of the world, and she lived her ideology fully, even unto her death.

Voltairine deCleyre—less well known but equally important in the development of anarchist theory and action—is noteworthy for organizing women's groups for education and consciousness raising. She was a Catholic anarchist intellectual from Michigan, who espoused women's taking their own liberty, "being what we teach," and expecting nothing from men, and generally advocating a leaderless general strike against marriage and motherhood (Marsh, 1981). She became somewhat of a myth in anarchist circles because of her passion and revolutionary zeal. She was called the "revolutionary vestal" and the "priestess of pity and vengance."

Neither Goldman nor deCleyre believed that women should participate in the "women's suffrage question," because neither had respect for the political arena of legislation and voting. Both argued, as did other anarchists, that freedom would mainly come through self-assertion, by refusing to be a sexual commodity, by refusing to be a servant to God or the state or any domination. Goldman argued that women needed internal emancipation to know their own value, respect themselves, and refuse to become psychic or economic slaves to their husbands.

Other anarchist women, such as Kelly, Steimer, and Pesotta, chose to be involved in progressive political causes of their times. Florence Finch Kelly, for example, was a well-educated, middle-class woman who defied traditional roles by becoming a journalist and novelist. She never chose conventional solutions to problems and held a healthy skepticism regarding tradition.

Another important thread in anarchist women's history is the Modern School. This educational movement, which was founded by Francisco Ferrer in Spain, held that children needed a healthy physical environment in which to learn as well as short and interesting instructional periods. Through nonimposition of ideas and lack of restraints on a child's natural inclination to learn, educators in the Modern School emphasized the process of learning and learning by example, rather than learning by rote. Children were taught to be self-reliant and were not viewed as their parents' property (Avrich, 1980). Anarchist women participated in the Modern School movement from the outset. They understood that politics occurred in the home and private arena as well as in the public domain. As a result, women emphasized the need for egalitarian relationships with one's children and saw the importance of education in attaining that equality. Many women took their children to live in rural areas where Modern School programs were established. Some of those settings—Stelton in New Jersey and Mohegan in New York—thrived well into the 1960s. The threads of libertarian education can be found even today in "free schools" and in writings about open classrooms and the active involvement of students in decision making and in their own learning.

Anarchism has thrived in lands of the sun, and Spanish immigrants brought the ideology to Argentina, Mexico, Cuba, Uruguay, and Brazil in the 1800s. Anarchists were active in setting up anarcho-syndicalist organizations; and in Mexico an anarchist, Ricardo Flores Magnon, is considered a father of the Mexican revolution. Women were integrated early into the Mexican labor movement as a result of anarchist advocacy. Carmen Huerta became the president of the labor congress as early as 1879, and labor policies always reflected women's concerns as a result of anarchist demands.

The anarchist impulse remains alive in many of the countries discussed around the world. Invariably, wherever one travels, one finds anarchists and anarchist feminists active in grassroots and decentralized activities, espousing the ideology that has been around for hundreds of years.

Contemporary Anarchist Feminism

The legacy of the anarchist foremothers has not been lost on a new generation of women. Since the 1960s, anarchist feminism has seen a resurgence of interest. With the emergence of third-wave feminism, there is an anarchist impulse alive and well in the women's movement. Often these women might not even call themselves anarchists; more often, they identify themselves as radical feminists. Emma Goldman became an early role model for radical feminists, and her name is conjured up when one thinks of strong-minded and revolutionary women who will not kowtow to domination and oppression by men. Radical feminists—some of whom have the anarchist ideology but not the anarchist name—believe that "the personal is political" and that it is necessary to "build the new society in the vacant lots of the old." The writings of Carol Ehrlich, Peggy Komegger, Elaine Leeder, and Martha Ackelsberg were early manifestations of the anarchist presence in the contemporary feminist movement.

Anarchist feminism and other forms of radical feminism exist worldwide in new, contemporary forms of direct action. Food co-ops, self-help collectives, squats, equity housing programs, rape crisis centers, and battered women's shelters are all examples of decentralized, nonhierarchical structures that reflect the anarchist impulse. Women's peace encampments in the United States, Scandinavia, and England were all anarchistic in orientation. These groups are run in ways that empower the women who participate and present daily direct challenges to the local and national authorities they confront. Anarchism and anarchist women remain active, demanding equal rights for women but insisting that change will not come through reformist means such as the ballot. Instead, the emphasis remains on direct action, propaganda by deed, and involvement in voluntary, nonhierarchical organizations. Anarchist women continue to influence the thinking of the contemporary anarchist movement. This includes informing the ecological orientation of current anarchist thinking with a feminist analysis and demanding a "politics of diversity" (Ackelsberg, 1991), in which a gender perspective is valued equally to that of race, class, and ethnicity. Anarchism, although now old in its traditions and analysis, is surprisingly relevant to today's issues and the concerns of modern women.

See Also

ACTIVISM; COMMUNISM; COMMUNITY POLITICS; FEMINISM: ANARCHIST

References and Further Reading

Ackelsberg, Martha. 1991. *Free women of Spain: Anarchism and the struggle for the emancipation of women.* Bloomington: Indiana University Press.

Avrich, Paul. 1978. *An American anarchist: The life of Voltairine deCleyre.* Princeton, N.J.: Princeton University Press.

———. 1980. *The modern school movement: Anarchism and education in the United States.* Princeton, N.J.: Princeton University Press.

Chan, Ming, and Arif Dirlik. 1991. *Schools into fields and factories: Anarchists, the Guomindang, and National Labor University in Shanghai, 1927–1932.* Durham, N.C.: Duke University Press.

Dirlik, Arif. 1991. *China and Inner Asia: Anarchism in the Chinese Revolution.* Berkeley: University of California Press.

Doctor, Adi. 1964. *Anarchist thought in India.* Bombay: Asia Publishing House.

Ehrlich, Howard J., ed. 1995. *Reinventing anarchy, again.* Edinburgh: AK.

Hart, John. 1978. *Anarchism and the Mexican working class, 1860–1931.* Austin: University of Texas Press.

Leeder, Elaine. 1993. *The gentle general: Rose Pesotta, anarchist and labor organizer.* Albany: State University of New York Press.

Marsh, Margaret. 1981. *Anarchist women: 1870–1920.* Philadelphia, Pa.: Temple University Press.

Polenberg, Richard. 1987. *Fighting faiths: The Abrams case, the Supreme Court and free speech.* New York: Viking.

Thomas, Edith. 1980. *Louise Michel.* Montreal: Black Rose.

Wexler, Alice. 1984. *Emma Goldman: An intimate life.* New York: Pantheon.

Zarrow, Peter. 1990. *Anarchism and Chinese political culture.* New York: Columbia University Press.

Elaine Leeder

ANATOMY

Anatomy—(From Greek ana-temnein, to cut open.) (1) Science of the build, shape, and composition of the body, in terms of internal organs and glandular, skeletal, muscular, arterial, and neural structures. Study of these structures by cutting up the body. (2) The build, shape, and composition of the body.

Introduction

The significance of "anatomy" for feminism and women's studies stems from a historical blurring of the difference between these two meanings. This was made possible by seventeenth- and eighteenth-century developments underlying the rise of the empirical sciences, among which anatomy was prominent. Anatomy came into being as a practice in the historical period in which the separation of "nature" from "politics" and "culture" originates. This separation was designed and invoked to argue the possibility and necessity of the objective scientific study of nature and to endow its results with the status of universal truth outside the scope of human authority, politics, or prejudice. In the definition here, the first meaning, "anatomy" as a science, refers to a human practice, but the second refers to the product of that practice, anatomical knowledge. In this second meaning, *anatomy* has acquired a material referent outside human history, culture, and practices and has come to stand for the body itself.

In this latter guise, anatomy has long been perceived within feminism as a problem to get around rather than to confront (as has "biology" in general). As "the body itself," anatomy stood for the eternal, natural, and therefore unalterable and apolitical differences between the sexes, setting the limits for all arguments for social equality. In this way, anatomy figured in many biological-deterministic arguments about "women's role," as epitomized in the Freudian dictum, "Anatomy is destiny." Consequently, feminists contested the relevance of the "facts about the body" for social order and shifted the boundary between the "social" and the "biological" to diminish anatomy as an explanation of existing sex differences. In its most powerful form, this strategy generated the distinction between sex and gender, which separates the biological (including the anatomical) realm from a cultural and historical realm of "gender." Feminists have tried to expand the domain of gender to leave as little as possible accounted for by biology and anatomy.

Useful as this strategy has been in countering biological determinism, it left essentially untouched the status of anatomy as the ahistorical limit to any argument for change. Because it still equated "anatomy" as a set of representations produced by historically located human practices with anatomy as "the body itself," it remained an Achilles' heel for biological determinism. For instance, if feminists, in arguing against an appeal to "maternal instincts" in explaining why women (should) take care of children more than men do, pointed to sociocultural ideas about femininity and mothering, to tradition, or to psychodynamics within families, then any newly found correspondence between women's postpartum emotions toward newborns and hormonal levels seemed to pose a "problem."

Two connotations of the biological, and consequently the anatomical, body that motivated the feminist gender strategy to a great extent have been effectively criticized: (1) that biology and anatomy are outside culture and history and (2) that with regard to the duality of "the social" and "the natural," it is (only) in the sphere of the social that political change can be achieved.

Anatomy As Historical Cultural Practice

A rapidly growing body of historical research suggests that the science of anatomy has been intrinsically guided by agendas reflecting contemporary political struggles. Thus, at the time of the Enlightenment, when formulations of "equality among all men" generated claims for political equality from women and from people of color, anatomists set out to investigate and locate sexual and racial differences in the body in unprecedented ways. Until then, the male body and the female body were seen as essentially the same, with female reproductive organs an inverse version of the male organs. Sexual differences, in this model, were differential positionings of women and men on one scale of metaphysical being, with the male as the perfect form. Women were a less perfect version of men; this imperfection was caused by women's lack of "heat," a characteristic that, among other things, prevented their reproductive organs from extruding as male organs extrude. Thus, women were seen as producing seed, as men do, in their internal "testes," with their vagina, cervix, and uterus pictured as inverse versions of the penis and scrotum. This account, especially in its formulation by Galen (second century after Christ), was passed on to the medieval West through the writings of the Arab Ibn Sina (Avicenna) and remained authoritative and influential all through the Renaissance, as is still discernible in the first anatomical drawings (by Leonardo Da Vinci and Vesalius) of dissected corpses. It was then gradually replaced by a fundamentally new account that saw the sexes as essentially and incompatibly different, instead of as a perfect and imperfect version of the same ideal. At the moment in history when human inequality was contested by an appeal to "universal man," anatomical, natural differences were produced that presented women not as "less" than men but as altogether incomparable: the naturalists' complementarity model of the sexes came into being.

Significantly, the shift from "a lesser version of the same" to "not less but essentially different" did not coincide with the turn toward empirical study of the human body by actual dissection and graphical description. Corpses had been dissected occasionally for centuries, and the graphic renderings of female and male organs by Leonardo da Vinci and Vesalius show how they actually saw what they dissected as inverse versions. This implies that it took "something else" besides just opening the body and merely "looking at how things really were," as the standard story about the "discovery" of the modern anatomical body goes.

The complementarity model of sex differences gained ground when women's claim to equality and access to the public sphere could no longer be countered by an appeal to a metaphysically grounded cosmology, in which everyone had his or her ordained place in accordance with a natural hierarchical order of being that did not distinguish between the natural and the social. That very distinction, in fact, was produced in the process of overthrowing this old cosmology and its claim to "natural," God-given authority for some over everyone else, and in the creation of a separate domain called "nature" over which neither church nor king would have any authority. The newly articulated basis from which to proclaim equality among all men, however, provided no reason to exclude groups that were never meant to be included in the brotherhood of men, such as women and people of color. Therefore, it became important, in a way it had not been before, to ground empirically essential differences between white males and everybody else.

Within this project, the anatomical search for sexual difference concentrated on female reproductive organs and skeletons (in particular, pelvises and skulls). With the rise of evolutionary models of human origins, difference as "race"

became conceptualized as relative proximity to animals, most notably apes. White women, because their skulls were relatively larger than men's, were described as being less developed in the sense of being closer to children. The anatomical racial and gender characteristics produced were without exception conceptualized as differences from the white, male body, the norm against which all difference became essential otherness. Then, after their transformation into "scientific fact," such naturalized differences were reintroduced into political debates to contest claims to political equality and representation, access to scientific education, and so forth. This type of historical work has provided a basis for reversing the biological-deterministic premise: "Destiny is anatomy," rather than the other way around.

The fact that the model of antiquity, with women's bodies as inverse, imperfect versions of men's bodies, remained in place for a long time, even after the first anatomists set out to dissect and study corpses, not only points to the role of preconceived ideas and political agendas in the making of the modern anatomical body but also challenges the notion of objectivity—unmediated vision and pure observation—as the distinguishing methodological novelty of modern empirical anatomy. Besides the broader political changes mentioned here, and their role in defining research questions and conceptualizing difference, there are other factors determining what the eye can see at any particular historical moment. The "anatomical gaze" was shaped to a large extent by the development of specific tools and techniques as well. One cannot "see" the anatomical body as it developed from the seventeenth century onward, in messy and bloody bowels lying on a dissection table, with a naked, untrained, and unaided eye; it took the later development of techniques of preservation for the corpses, and specifically drawings and etchings of the body, to guide and train the hand how to cut and the eye what to see. In this sense, even the anatomical body was never the product of enlightened and pure empirical observation but very much a body crafted by a broad variety of factors.

Changeable Anatomy

The second connotation of the anatomical (biological) body, underlying feminist strategies of explaining existing sex differences as much as possible in terms of the social, is that "anatomy" stands for the unchangeable, and therefore the apolitical. Connected to this was the idea that whenever one could prove a particular inequality "social" in origin, this in itself would render it amenable to change. Neither idea is still considered self-evident. Twentieth-century western biomedical sciences and technologies created unprecedented and seemingly infinite possibilities of manipulation and reshaping of the body, while at the same time belief in the malleability of social structures has been diminished by their unforeseen persistence in the face of emancipatory social policies.

For instance, the latter decades of the twentieth century proved that the manipulation of women's reproductive anatomy and physiology—with hormonal treatments, in vitro fertilization (IVF), gamete intrafallopian transfer (GIFT), and so on—was far easier to accomplish than changing attitudes toward the necessity of genetically related children for a fulfilled life. Similarly, the statistics on cosmetic surgery show that psychosocial pressures to conform to ideals of beauty, despite many analyses and criticisms of the female role in heterosexual relationships, are still far stronger for many women than the fear of pain and health hazards. Far from being outside history and politics, the body in general, and the female body in particular, has been a site of "materialized politics" and remains so in an relentlessly intense way.

Consequently, anatomy, like biology and the biomedical sciences in general, is no longer considered a realm closed to feminist scrutiny but is regarded instead as a domain where critical analysis is urgent. This urgency is produced by a growing awareness that current medical practices, combined with the growing transformative powers generated by rapidly proliferating biomedical technologies, may affect women's lives profoundly. Since these practices and technologies are building on scientific traditions, such as anatomy, that are increasingly proved to carry historically and culturally determined accounts of femininity, it has become a prime task for women's studies to investigate how these accounts are currently shaping our medical sciences, practices, and technologies. Many areas within medicine are currently being investigated, providing new insights into the relationships between cultural and historical definitions and structures of gender inscribed in the "natural body" and current reproductions of gender assymmetries within medical practices.

Traces of History in Contemporary Medical Practices

The focus on female sexual and reproductive organs in the search for sexual difference, the fascination with the *secreta mulierum,* has found historical continuity in a persistent relative overexposure of women's reproductive biology compared with men's. This overexposure has produced a female reproductive body that is known and subject to medical interventions to a much greater extent than its male counterpart. There is no medical specialty for men's reproductive functions comparable in history, scale, or scope to gynecol-

ogy. Men's reproductive parts have never been studied or manipulated with respect to as wide a variety of hypotheses concerning physical and mental pathologies. As a consequence, great asymmetries in the medical treatment of males and females as reproducers persist in ways not attributable to nature or necessity. For instance, in the domain of contraception, large asymmetries between women and men with respect to contraceptive methods, in terms of availability, invasiveness, effectiveness, risk, side effects, and necessity for medical surveillance, still leave the female body as the primary site of birth control. Similar asymmetries in the area of infertility treatment are so large that today both female and male fertility problems are increasingly solved by medical interventions such as in vitro fertilization and gamete intrafallopian transfer; these take the female body as their object of intervention.

Where "difference" was also practically equated with inferiority and imperfection, it has historically proved to be easily translatable into "prone to pathology," thus producing anatomical and physiological accounts of female reproductive bodies as "naturally" in need of intervention. Today, pregnancy, childbirth, menstruation, and menopause have come to be perceived as diseaselike, high-risk events requiring medical surveillance and, more often than not, pharmaceutical, hormonal, surgical, or other types of intervention.

The mirror image of this is that the male body often functioned (and still sometimes does function) as the model for the human body in areas related to parts less deeply inscribed by struggles over cultural definitions of masculinity and femininity than the reproductive organs, the skull, the brain, and so on. This overexposure of the genital-reproductive female body is reflected, for instance, in contemporary cancer research, where the percentage of women studied for genital and breast cancers is larger than the relative incidence of these types of cancer in women, whereas, conversely, the same types of cancer in men are studied less in relation to incidence. Mirroring this is the fact that when women and men share a certain body part—for example, the lung—researchers tend to study the related form of cancer in the male. Thus, nonsexual parts are studied in males as the model for women and men alike. Women were often excluded from clinical trials (as were female animals in animal models) because the particularities of female bodies were thought to interfere with the results—results that, once established, were nevertheless thought generalizable to women. This practice results in therapies that are designed on the basis of male bodies but may work differently in women in terms of effectiveness or side effects.

See Also

BIOLOGICAL DETERMINISM; BIOLOGY; BODY; CANCER; CHILDBIRTH; CONTRACEPTION; COSMETIC SURGERY; DIFFERENCE; FEMINISM: EIGHTEENTH-CENTURY; FERTILITY AND FERTILITY TREATMENT; GENDER; MEDICAL CONTROL OF WOMEN; PHYSIOLOGY; PREGNANCY AND BIRTH; PREMENSTRUAL SYNDROME (PMS); PRIMATOLOGY; REPRESENTATION; REPRODUCTION: OVERVIEW; REPRODUCTIVE PHYSIOLOGY; REPRODUCTIVE TECHNOLOGIES; SCIENTIFIC SEXISM AND RACISM; SEXUAL DIFFERENCE

References and Further Reading

Balsamo, Anne. 1992. On the cutting edge: Cosmetic surgery and the technological production of the gendered body. *Camera Obscura* 28: 207–38.

Bordo, Susan. 1993. *Unbearable weight: Feminism, Western culture and the body.* Berkeley: University of California Press.

Duden, Barbara. 1991. *The woman beneath the skin: A doctor's patients in eighteenth-century Germany.* Cambridge, Mass.: Harvard University Press.

Gallagher, Catherine, and Thomas Lacqueur, eds. 1987. *The making of the modern body: Sexuality and society in the nineteenth century.* Berkeley: University of California Press.

Hubbard, Ruth, Mary Sue Henifin, and Barbara Fried, eds. 1979. *Biological woman—The convenient myth: A collection of essays and a comprehensive bibliography.* Cambridge, Mass.: Schenkman.

Jacobus, Mary, Evelyn Fox Keller, and Sally Shuttleworth, eds. 1990. *Body politics: Women and the discourses of science.* New York: Routledge.

Kammen, Jessika van. 2000. *Conceiving contraceptives: The involvement of users in anti-fertility vaccines development.* Thesis, University of Amsterdam.

Lacqueur, Thomas. 1991. *Making sex: Gender and body from the Greeks to Freud.* Cambridge, Mass.: Harvard University Press.

Martin, Emily. 1987. *The woman in the body: A cultural analysis of reproduction.* Boston: Beacon.

van der Ploeg, Irma. 2000. *Prosthetic bodies: Female embodiment in reproductive technologies.* Dordrecht: Kluwer Academic.

Schiebinger, Londa. 1994. *Nature's body: Gender in the making of modern science.* Boston: Beacon.

———. 1999. *Has feminism changed science?* Cambridge, Mass.: Harvard University Press.

Sloane, Ethel. 1980. *Biology of women.* New York: Wiley.

Irma van der Ploeg

ANCIENT INDIGENOUS CULTURES:
Women's Roles

The original inhabitants of a geographic region are often referred to as indigenous cultures. The indigenous peoples who originated and lived in specific territories have a historical continuity with preinvasion and precolonial societies, which consider themselves distinct from those that now prevail on the land. Most continents in the world had indigenous populations and cultures—for example, the Aboriginal and Torres Strait Landers of Australia, the Igbo-Ukwu and Nok of Africa; the Maori of New Zealand; the Aztec, Mayan, Ojibway, and Iroquois of the Americas; and the peoples of ancient Mesopotamia, Levant, China, India, Japan, the Mediterranean, Caribbean, and South Pacific. These are all peoples, communities, and nations with their own culture and society based on their own values and traditions. Today, many indigenous peoples and nations are nondominant sectors of society, but they are determined to preserve and maintain their identity, culture, and ancestral territories for future generations (Aboriginal and Torres Strait Islander Commission, 1999: 61).

Colonization had a destructive effect on the gender relationships of indigenous people and an impact on all spheres of the society, including family organization, childbearing, child rearing, politics, spiritual life, work, and social activities (Smith, 1999). Ancient indigenous women's roles were unique to their specific society. Although commonalities existed, there was no universal role other than bearing children. No "universal ancient indigenous woman" exists. It is important not to generalize and to be as specific as possible when speaking of indigenous women. Their specific physical environment, culture (values and traditions), subsistence patterns, and resources influenced their roles, identity, and lifestyle. Some were nomadic hunters and gatherers, others agrarian, more sedentary, and more socially complex. Many were matrilineal, others male-centered or a combination.

Ancient indigenous women had many roles, including but not limited to roles in religion, the economy, leadership, and domestic life. Selected roles and cultures will be highlighted to illustrate the diversity of the indigenous women around the world (Vivante, 1999).

Domestic Roles

Many ancient indigenous cultures embraced women as nurturers: care providers as well as leaders. A key role for most indigenous women was motherhood, and childbearing was highly valued and honored. This was true for most indigenous women, including those of Native North America and Mesoamerica. Women's work was recognized as being as essential as men's for tribal survival. Men's and women's roles were complementary, with neither more important than the other. In Aztec and Mayan cultures, the home was the domain of the woman, where most of her work was performed, and the women were responsible for childbearing, child rearing, and processing of maize. This was also true for women in indigenous west African societies. Although the man was the formal head, the woman controlled the family and domestic issues and was responsible for the education of the children. Transmission of culture, values, and traditions to their children was also the responsibility of Iroquois women of North America. In the Jomon society of Japan, women enjoyed freedom and high status in matrilineal households, where they often continued to live after marriage. Women's primary responsibility was childbearing. Ancient Mesopotamia is an example of a patriarchal family system in which the women were not independent of male influence throughout their lives. The father was head of the family and had this authority until his death. The women were to bear children, especially sons, to ensure continuation of the male line, and they were generally subordinate to men.

Leadership Roles

The degree of involvement of ancient indigenous women in leadership of their societies varied greatly. For instance, the Iroquois women of North America were the heads of their clans and villages, and it was their responsibility to fill leadership positions. The women not only selected the men who represented the village but could depose or "dehorn" a chief who did not do the will of the people. In ancient Egypt, kingship was essentially a male institution; Hatshepsut was one of the few women ever to hold this position. Women's influence on government was indirect, through their husbands, but they did exercise authority over their households and children. In west Africa, women influenced the building and maintenance of their nations in matters of governance and structure, and succession to leadership positions was often based on matrilineal descent. The ancient tribal group of Yamato in Japan was jointly ruled. A male was responsible for military and civil affairs, and a woman priestess was in charge of spiritual matters.

Economics

Most ancient indigenous women contributed to the economy of their societies. Indigenous Iroquois women had a significant impact on the tribal economy. They were responsible for planting, cultivating, harvesting, storing, and trading crops and foodstuffs, and they also managed the distribution and trading of agricultural and hunting resources. In Japan, Jomon women were the principal contributors to a domestic economy based on household goods gathered from their coastlines and forest environments and were instrumental in bartering the goods. In Mayan society, the men did most of the agricultural work, although women tended gardens and orchards and raised animals. Mayan and Aztec women were both involved in commerce and in trading foodstuffs and woven goods. Textiles were essential for daily and ritual use in Mesoamerica; in ancient Japan, the women processed food and excelled in basketry, pottery, and weaving, producing many items for ceremonial use.

Property Rights

Ancient indigenous women owned or used property in their societies to various degrees. In fact, a man's association with a woman often brought benefits to the husband. In Aztec society, a man could not acquire land without being married. Women were also free to divorce and remarry, and the property a woman brought into a marriage remained with her. In indigenous North America, Iroquois women owned houses and stores, and the use of property was passed through the matrilineal line without actual ownership; property was owned by those who used it. The longhouse and the village were women's domains. Men owned their own personal property, and other property remained separate during the marriage. In Japan, Jomon property (usually land) jointly owned by households was inherited matrilineally and entrusted to a matriarch. In Mesopotamia, inheritance generally was divided among the sons or survivors in the male line.

Religious and Spiritual Roles

Women in ancient indigenous cultures had an influence on religious and spiritual practices. Many creation stories involved women, and there were female deities. Aztec culture had female deities, and women participated extensively in the cycle of religious activities and festivities. They danced, impersonated goddesses, and were sacrificed in ritual human sacrifices. Women's role was not straightforward but penetrated many levels of symbolism, including male activities. In ancient Japan, women (usually the daughters of a male or female chieftain) were priestesses of their tribes or kinship groups and acted as protectors and healers. They were sought to cure injuries and illnesses and to make predictions with their magic and prayers.

Conclusion

Ancient indigenous women's roles were as diverse as the environments in which they lived and the cultures they represented. To get a complete picture, one must research a specific culture thoroughly. Commonalities do exist, but generalizing is problematic, and information on indigenous women is often lacking and inadequate. Directly or indirectly, indigenous women influenced the daily life of their societies, and their roles were essential to me survival and continuance of their people.

See Also

ANCIENT NATION STATES, WOMEN'S ROLES; FAMILY: PROPERTY RELATIONS; FAMILY: RELIGIOUS AND LEGAL SYSTEMS; GODDESS; HOUSEHOLDS: FEMALE-HEADED AND FEMALE-SUPPORTED; INDIGENOUS WOMEN'S RIGHTS; MATRIARCHY; MATRILINEAL SYSTEMS; TRADITIONAL HEALING, *various topics*

References and Further Reading

Aboriginal and Torres Strait Islander Commission. 1999. *As a matter of fact: answering the myths and misconceptions about indigenous Australians* (2nd ed.).

Berndt, Catherine H. 1983. Mythical women, past and present. In Fay Gale, ed., *We are bosses ourselves: The status and role of aboriginal women today*, 13–23. Canberra: Australian Institute of Aboriginal Studies.

Smith, Linda Tuhiwai. 1991. *Decolorizing methodologies research and indigenous peoples*. Dunedin, Scotland: University of Otago Press.

Vivante, Bella, ed. 1999. *Women's roles in ancient civilizations: A reference guide*. Westport, Conn: Greenwood. See articles by: Michiko Y. Aoki (on ancient Japan), Mary Jo Tippeconnic Fox (on Ojibway and Iroquois women in ancient North America), Karen Rhea Nemet-Nejat (on Mesopotamia), Tolagbe Ogunleye (on ancient west Africa), Gay Robins (on ancient Egypt), and Andrea J. Stone (on ancient Mesoamerica).

Mary Jo Tippeconnic Fox

ANCIENT NATION-STATES:
Women's Roles

Women's roles in ancient nation-states display numerous similarities, beginning with childbearing and child rearing, and including the harvesting, gathering, and preparation of food; weaving and textile manufacture; midwifery; nursing and healing; various creative, economic, and ritual activities; and—not infrequently—political and even military leadership. The values accorded to these roles differ markedly: generally the roles were highly valued in indigenous and developing state societies, but value eroded as nation-states evolved.

The Development of Nation-States

The development of nation-states also displays similarities. Shifting from family- or clan-based social organizations, which value all members for their contributions, state societies develop to administer larger population groups. They show increasing centralization of governing and religious functions, with increasingly structured and hierarchical administrative systems, frequently accompanied by shifts to male domination. Although many indigenous societies highly value women's roles, often calling themselves matriarchal (not, however, in the sense of being simply a reversal of modern concepts of patriarchy), many nation-states show increasing male domination in realms deemed authoritative: political, legal, economic, and, ultimately, religious and artistic. Realms deemed characteristically female, notably the home and domestic occupations, then become undervalued. Archaeological and historical evidence from civilizations worldwide documents this progressive devaluing of women's activities as nation-states developed. Some state societies, however, still valued women's roles: Minoan Crete, Sparta, and the various states of Mesoamerica and pre-Islamic west Africa.

The criterion for a nation-state, then, is not size but rather this shift to a centralized, hierarchical social organization. Hence, this article considers women's roles from the relatively small "city-states" of ancient Greece, Japan, and Mesoamerica to the larger empires of Mesopotamia (Sumer and Babylon), China, Egypt, India, Rome, and west Africa. In the time periods considered here—mostly the third to the first millennium B.C.E., but the third to the seventeenth centuries C.E. for Japan, Mesoamerica, and west Africa—patriarchal customs were developing but were hardly uniform or fixed. Most evidence refers to the lives of elite women; women of lower classes were generally acknowledged only through their various roles of support and work for the elite.

Principal Roles for Women

Women's principal roles in all these nation-states centered on the home on activities of childbearing and child rearing. Women's rights in marriage, divorce, and controlling their own sexuality suggest the power and status women held. Although the husband might nominally be head of the household, women often were recognized to be in charge of domestic affairs—this was explicitly so in

Egypt, India, Sparta, Mesoamerica, and west Africa. Texts from India, Sparta, and west Africa indicate that women's control of household affairs included—to a greater or lesser degree—control over their husbands' activities as well. Many societies favored monogamous marriages. In one type of Indian marriage, women could freely choose their partners, and, although this was not a frequent option, Indian women could choose the life of a religious ascetic—affording greater individual independence—instead of marriage. In Sumer, Egypt, and west Africa, married women had legal parity with men. A Chinese woman's right to defy her husband in the Qin dynasty (221–207 B.C.E.) suggests her autonomy in the home and equal status with her husband. In many cultures, women could divorce without stigma or penalty and had the right to remarry; widows often gained greater independence than they had while married. In Mesopotamia, a man could be heavily penalized for divorcing his wife, especially if she had borne sons. In Athens and Rome, women required legal guardians their entire lives and could not independently choose marriage partners or decide to divorce or remarry. Nevertheless, elite Roman women often circumvented their legal restrictions.

Hierarchical polygyny—ranking first and subsequent legal wives and concubines—was practiced in China and sometimes India, but multiple wives in Japan were not ranked; the Dravids in southern India practiced polyandry. In Japan and west Africa, women could choose their husbands, residence was matrilocal, households were registered under the mother's name, inheritance was matrilineal, and children were not marked as legitimate or illegitimate. Laws in Mesopotamia, Egypt, and India stressed the husband's role in providing for his wife's security and sexual pleasure; art and literature portrayed the loving couples. A recognized benefit of marriage was sexual pleasure. In India, Japan, and Sparta, female adultery was not taboo; in some cases, women were encouraged to have extramarital sexual partners both to produce healthy children and to enhance the married couple's sexual pleasure. Roman poetry extolled the adulterous liaisons of elite women.

In Athens, China, India, and Mesoamerica, a man had to be married in order to fulfill his public and ritual obligations—these dual-gender obligations were incorporated into Chinese marriage vows—and in Mesoamerica men had to be married in order to own land as well. Chinese and Greek female philosophers and Mesoamerican art and hieroglyphics make explicit the concept of complementarity underlying women's and men's spheres in the home and public life, respectively. This complementarity, a key to gender relations in indigenous societies, suggests that, despite women's frequent legal and marital restrictions, early state societies valued women's domestic role, and mothers were highly honored. Although Confucianism led to women's devaluation in China, its emphasis on filial piety resulted in great deference to the elder matriarch of the household, even by the emperor to his mother.

Economic Roles for Women

Much of women's economic activities, primarily gathering, harvesting, and preparing food and textile production, also centered on the home. Women were not always economically rewarded for these essential activities, although they might gain status and esteem for excelling in them. In China, women's textile production released their male relatives from labor conscription. In Japan, women supported their households and the government from their cloth and food surpluses. Greek and Mayan women's weavings were important items in trade, gifts, dowries, bride wealth, tribute, and rituals—weavings were prized offerings made to Greek deities, as in the annual rites to Athena, portrayed in the central part of the frieze of the Parthenon, the temple to Athena in Athens. The attention to intricate detail of clothing design in the art of both cultures illustrates the cultural importance of Greek and Mayan women's weavings and the esteem accorded to this characteristically women's art.

Women also participated in the larger economy of their societies, including business, trade, owning and managing property, and manufacturing; and as doctors, midwives, nurses, and prostitutes. Some women's work was underpaid and undervalued, but where women controlled their economic activities, they had greater independence, status, and power. Women could often sell the surplus and control the income from household agricultural, textile, or craft production. Some women's activities were central to the economy, for example, in Japan, deep-sea diving and making salt (from sea water); in Mesopotamia, perfume manufacture, and brewing and selling beer; in west Africa, salt trade, soap manufacture, and gold mining and trade. In Sumer, Egypt, Sparta, Rome, and Japan, women owned, could bequeath, and could inherit large tracts of land, and they controlled the wealth from its production. In Mesopotamia, Egypt, Rome, and west Africa, women actively engaged in business. Prostitutes were generally not highly paid or esteemed, but courtesans were educated and gained great wealth: in India and Rome many were noted for their business acumen; in India some became wealthy patrons of religious orders; in Greece some achieved political prominence. In India, Rome, and imperial Greece, wealthy women underwrote public, religious, and artistic activities independent of their husbands.

Women and Positions of Authority

Rulers were frequently male, but royal women had several means of access to ruling power. In political marriages, women exercised influence on behalf of their natal families, thereby acquiring esteem. Queen mothers of minor sons too young to rule wielded significant power. Royal courts everywhere were notorious for political intrigues and murders by royal wives and mothers on behalf of their sons. In Japan, Palenque (sixth- to seventh-century classic Maya), and west Africa, many women ruled in their own right as queen, a role that often included military leadership. Japan, west African states, and, possibly, Sparta had traditions of dual rulership. In other countries, women occasionally ruled in extraordinary circumstances, such as the Egyptian "female-king" Hatshepsut (fifteenth century B.C.E.). Nonroyal women had varying access to authoritative decision making in their communities, depending on their class, legal, and economic standing; on cultural appreciation of women's authority; and frequently on their ritual roles. Such access tended to be considerable in Sumer, Crete, Sparta, Japan, Maya, and west Africa.

In most cultures, women held significant ritual roles, and many important deities were female. Goddesses were worshiped as deities associated with, for example, creation (Nü Wa—China, Aditi—India, Gaia—Greece, Amat-erasu—Japan, Atoapoma [Akan], Idemili [Igbo], Nana-Daho [Fon]—west Africa); the earth (Demeter—Greece, Bona Dea—Rome, Asase Ya [Asante], Oto [Binis], Tenga [Mossi]—west Africa); sky (Nut—Egypt); fertility, sexuality, erotic desire (Inanna/Ishtar—Sumer/Babylon, Hathor— Egypt, Aphrodite—Greece, Yemoja—Yoruba); marriage, motherhood (Isis—Egypt, Hera—Greece, Juno—Rome); childbirth (Hathor, Isis—Egypt, Aditi—India, Toci—Maya); crafts (Athena—Greece); learning (Saraswati—India); power and rulership (Queen mother of the West—China, Inanna/Ishtar—Sumer/Babylon, Athena—Greece, Shakti—India); and wealth (Lakshami—India). Goddesses also were associated with the sun, the moon, planets, stars, water, natural forces, weaving, justice, death (often in the sense of the earth or mother taking the dead back into her care), destruction, and numerous other qualities. Many of these roles overlapped, and in India, in west Africa, and among the Maya, these goddesses continue to be worshiped today. Worship of female deities reinforced on a divine level the respect accorded actual women. Women often held important roles as priestesses.

Many cultures held important rites marking significant stages in a woman's life: rites for puberty and adolescent transitions; entry into adulthood, marriage, birth, motherhood; and annual cycles of women's fertility and sexuality. These cycles often were celebrated in "sacred marriage" rites known throughout the ancient world. Many women's rites were for women only and were considered fundamental for promoting and maintaining the well-being of the society. Women gained crucial support for their identity, sense of self-worth, and esteem from these recurrent ritual practices. Moreover, because religious practices often were fundamental to much societal activity, the central and important roles women held in religious life, both as priestesses and often as ordinary female practitioners, gave them respected, public roles within their community.

In Greece, a woman's entire life from the age of 6 or 7 through adulthood was marked by frequent rituals. The numerous religious festivals in which women engaged afforded women opportunities to move about independently and, apparently, without restriction in the community. For 2,000 years (until their sanctuaries and rites were deliberately destroyed by Christian zealots in the fourth and fifth centuries), the Eleusinian mysteries for the two goddesses Demeter and Persephone were the most important form of religious expression for both women and men in Greece. A comparable centrality of worship of female deities and of women's ritual roles can be found in Mesopotamia, Japan, Mesoamerica, and west Africa; however, they were later eclipsed by male-dominated religious and philosophical beliefs.

Although in many nation-states women's lives were restricted politically and legally, the importance of other spheres of activity indicates that political or legal status does not adequately convey the full picture of women's roles. Frequently, women's importance in domestic, religious, economic, and creative activities substantially offsets legal and political restrictions. The esteem—and often direct economic and status rewards—women received for their activities testifies to the value accorded to women even in patriarchal societies where gender inequities were developing. Moreover, many state societies still maintained considerable respect for women ideologically as well as politically, legally, and economically. These various sources of esteem in ancient nation-states deteriorated in the face of increasing male supremacy advocated by religious and philosophical ideologies with their concomitant increasing male domination in the political, legal, economic, religious, and—ultimately—domestic spheres.

Awareness of the numerous ways women were fully participatory agents, or enjoyed arenas of esteem even in predominantly patriarchal systems, provides an important corrective to previous historical views of women as being completely subjected and subordinate in ancient cultures. It also challenges the commonly held notion that the position of women in modern, democratic, industrialized nations represents an advance over women's position in earlier societies—a linear view of social and historical development. Although this "advance" may be valid when compared with the position of women in recent histories of patriarchal nation-states, it does not hold up in the longer historical perspective when set against women's roles in most ancient societies. In contrast, there are great complexities in gender relations and in the roles women have held historically in civilizations around the world, which often have been roles of power and strength.

See Also

ANCIENT INDIGENOUS CULTURES: WOMEN'S ROLES; GODDESS; HISTORY; HOUSEHOLDS AND FAMILIES: OVERVIEW; POLITICS AND THE STATE: OVERVIEW

References and Further Reading

Bhattacharji, Sukumari. 1994. *Women and society in ancient India.* Calcutta: Basumati.

Bingham, Marjorie W., and Susan H. Gross. 1987. *Women in Japan: From ancient times to the present.* St. Louis Park, Minn.: Women's History Curriculum Central Community Center.

Gero, Joan M., and Margaret W. Conkey, eds. 1991. *Engendering archaeology: Women and prehistory.* Oxford: Blackwell.

Gruber, Mayer I. 1995. *Women in the biblical world.* American Theological Library Association Bibliography Series, no. 38. Lanham, Md.: Scarecrow.

Hallett, Judith P. 1984. *Fathers and daughters in Roman society: Women and the elite family.* Princeton, N.J.: Princeton University Press.

Henshaw, Richard A. 1994. *Female and male: The cultic personnel: The Bible and the rest of the ancient Near East.* Allison Park, Pa.: Pickwick.

Jackson, Guida M. 1999. *Women rulers throughout the ages: An illustrated guide.* Santa Barbara, Calif.: ABC-CLIO.

Jamison, Stephanie W. 1996. *Sacrificed wife/sacrificer's wife: Women, ritual and hospitality in ancient India.* New York: Oxford University Press.

Kraemer, Ross S. 1992. *Her share of the blessings: Women's religions among pagans, Jews, and Christians in the Greco-Roman world.* New York and Oxford: Oxford University Press.

Lefkowitz, Mary R., and Maureen B. Fant, eds. 1992. *Women's life in Greece and Rome: A source book in translation.* 2nd ed. Baltimore, Md.: Johns Hopkins University Press.

Lerner, Gerda. 1986. *The creation of patriarchy.* New York and Oxford: Oxford University Press.

Lesko, Barbara, ed. 1989. *Women's earliest records from ancient Egypt and western Asia.* Atlanta, Ga.: Scholars.

Murcott, Susan. 1991. *The first Buddhist women.* Berkeley, Calif.: Parallax.

Nemet-Nejat, Karen Rhea. 1998. *Daily life in the ancient Near East.* Westport, Conn.: Greenwood.

Oppong, Christine, ed. 1983. *Female and male in west Africa.* London: George Allen and Unwin.

Paul, Diana. 1979. *Women in Buddhism: Images of the feminine in Mahayana tradition.* Berkeley, Calif.: Asian Humanities.

Pintchman, Tracy. 1994. *The rise of the goddess in the Hindu tradition.* Albany: State University of New York Press.

Pomeroy, Sarah B. 1975. *Goddesses, whores, wives, and slaves: Women in classical antiquity.* New York: Schocken.

Rabinowitz, Nancy Sorkin, and Amy Richlin, eds. 1993. *Feminist theory and the classics.* New York and London: Routledge.

Raphals, Lisa. 1998. *Sharing the light: Representations of women and virtue in early China.* Albany: State University of New York.

Robins, Gay. 1993. *Women in Ancient Egypt.* Cambridge, Mass.: Harvard University.

———. 1995. *Reflections of women in the New Kingdom: Ancient Egyptian art from the British Museum.* San Antonio, Tex.: Van Siclen.

Sertima, Ivan Van, ed. 1988. *Black women of antiquity.* New Brunswick, N.J.: Transaction.

Sherer, Robert. 1996. *Daily life in Maya civilization.* Westport, Conn.: Greenwood.

Snyder, Jane McIntosh. 1989. *The woman and the lyre: Women writers in classical Greece and Rome.* Carbondale: Southern Illinois University.

Swann, Nancy Lee. 1968 (1932 reprint). *Pan Chao: Foremost woman scholar of China, first century A.D.* New York: Russell and Russell.

Sweetman, David. 1984. *Women leaders in African history.* London: Heinemann.

Tharu, Susie, and K. Lalita, eds. 1993. *Women writing in India: 600 B.C. to the present.* Delhi: Oxford University Press.

Toorn, Karel Van Der. 1994. *From her cradle to her grave: The role of religion in the life of the Israelite and the Babylonian woman.* Sheffield: JSOT.

Tsurumi, E. Patricia. 1981. Japan's early female emperors. *Historical Reflections* 8(1):

Vivante, Bella, ed. 1999. *Women's roles in ancient civilizations: A reference guide.* Westport, Conn.: Greenwood.

Watson, Rubie S., and Patricia Buckley Ebrey, eds. 1991. *Marriage and inequality in Chinese society.* Berkeley: University of California Press.

Watterson, Barbara. 1991. *Women in ancient Egypt.* New York: St. Martin's.

White, E. Frances. 1988. Women of western and western central Africa. In *Restoring women to history,* 57–113. Bloomington, Ind.: Organization of American Historians.

Zweig, Bella. 1993. The only women who give birth to men: A gynocentric, cross-cultural view of women in ancient Sparta. In Mary Deforest, ed., *Woman's power, man's game: Essays on classical antiquity in honor of Joy King,* 32–53. Wauconda, Ill.: Bolchazy-Carducci.

———. 1993. The primal mind: Using Native American models to approach the study of women in ancient Greece. In Nancy Sorkin Rabinowitz and Amy Richlin, eds., *Feminist theory and the classics,* 145–180. New York: Routledge.

Bella Vivante

ANDROCENTRISM

Androcentrism is the view that male behavior and characteristics are central—are the norm. This view so permeates society that female behavior is understood and seen as deviant, that is, deviating from the male norm.

Androcentric society values characteristics associated with men and maleness. Thus, competitiveness and aggressiveness are highly valued and rewarded, whereas characteristics associated with women—caring and cooperation—are devalued.

Androcentric societies are organized on the assumption that the male is the norm. This is clearly illustrated by the ways in which paid employment is organized in advanced industrial societies: full-time work with a lifelong and uninterrupted commitment to the labor market is assumed to be the norm. Women who have domestic responsibilities and cannot conform to this expectation are disadvantaged both in the jobs for which they are seen as eligible in the labor market and in their promotion prospects in employment.

Androcentric texts and scholarship present women as absent or silent or treat them in stereotyped ways. Hartmann (1978), for example, points out the inherent sexism in Marxist theory. Hoagland (1980) points to the way in which androcentric rhetoric is used in sociobiology. Forenza (1983) demonstrates that theological texts present women as absent or silent or in their traditional roles. In this way women have been "hidden from history."

See Also

HISTORY; OTHER; SEXISM; WORK: FEMINIST THEORIES

References and Further Readings

Fiorenza, Elizabeth. 1983. *In memory of her: A feminist theological reconstruction of Christian origins.* New York: Crossroad.

Hartmann, Heidi. 1978. The unhappy marriage of Marxism and feminism: Towards a more progressive union. *Capital and Class* 8: 1–33.

Hoagland, Sarah. 1980. Androcentric rhetoric in sociobiology. *Women's Studies International Forum,* 3(2–3): 285–294.

Pamela Abbott

ANDROGYNY

Androgyny, or gynandry, is the presence, within one body, of both female and male sex characteristics. The human species is gynandrous in several ways. The fetus is female up to six weeks; then, if sperm is present, the clitoris enlarges to become a penis, vaginal skin folds over to become the scrotum, and a male grows. Also, estrogen and testosterone are varyingly present in both sexes. Thus human genders branch from a female root, and from earlier kinds of reproduction—for billions of years on Earth, reproduction occurred by asexual, bisexual, or parthenogenic cloning.

Early human cultures often envisioned deities as female. Paleolithic cave art and icons, Megalithic and Neolithic archaeologic sites, and many rituals and myths worldwide indicate worship of a "great mother" who, as Earth, gave birth, sustained life, and after death recycled all life forms. Everything created, in both its "female" and its "male" aspects, expressed this gynandrous process of a living, sacred planet. Hunting-and-gathering peoples did not strictly differentiate sex roles. Among animistic cultures, to become "the other"—that is, to experience otherness in oneself—is a psychic moment of both integration and release. Tribal shamans, medicine women and men, the berdache, and the wiccan all enacted this participatory fusion, becoming not only other animals but the other sex: shamanic males wore ornamental breasts and acted as spirit mothers; shamanic females wrestled and hunted and, in later Neolithic depictions, wore beards. The androgynous "both-in-one" activated pragmatic and sacred powers of magic, healing, tribal integrity, and prophecy.

In historic eras, patriarchal cultures, which value fixed sex roles, have superseded most of the primal animistic beliefs. Yet androgyny as symbol of human balance and fusion, or psychic holism, is still found worldwide, for example in the Taoist yin and yang, tantra, the gnostic and alchemic hermaphrodite, African and Caribbean Voudoun, and Hindu devas. Catalytic powers of the androgyne are also popularly embodied in the artist: the poet, the dancer, the actor, and the rock star bear witness to the constant other who lives within us. In reaction to the commercial bombardment of global culture, with its extreme, sensational sexual stereotypes, many young people have adopted more androgynous or unisex styles and attitudes, both as a fashion statement and as a mode of conscious behavior.

In a sense, then, androgyny activates and celebrates the full spectrum of human possibilities. Few people fit a completely male or completely female norm—most range along a continuum of body types, talents, and concerns. Restriction of human work and human dreams to stringent sex roles could entail a real loss of evolutionary capacity. Twenty-first-century technology—such as space travel, computer networks, biospheres, and microsurgery—requires patient precision and bold decision making, that is, androgynous skills. The astronaut is not "male" or "female" but a heroic, though fragile, human being floating in space. The globe will be—in fact, it already is—crowded and beset by problems of scarce, polluted resources confronting burgeoning populations. Such a planet cannot sustain the continuous aggression, repression, forced breeding, and warfare that characterize, as Margaret Mead and other anthropologists have documented, those cultures that depend on fixed sex roles (that is, the denial of androgyny) as their rationale. Our species' survival might well require universal retraining in the ancient gynandrous art of experiencing the other as oneself.

See Also

ANDROCENTRISM; BUTCH/FEMME; GODDESS; HETEROSEXUALITY; HYPERMASCULINITY; LESBIANISM; MOTHER EARTH; OTHER; SEX AND CULTURE; SEXUAL ORIENTATION

References and Further Reading

Deren, Maya. 1953. *Divine horsemen: The living gods of Haiti.* Kingston, N.Y.: McPherson, Documentext (reprint 1970).
Feinberg, Leslie. 1998. *Transliberation: Beyond pink or blue.* Boston: Beacon.
Juno, Andrea, and V. Vale, eds. 1991. *Angry women.* San Francisco: Re/Search.
Mor, Barbara, and Monica Sjoo. 1987. The great cosmic mother: Rediscovering the religion of the earth. San Francisco: Harper (reprint with added Forewords and color plates, 1991).
Weise, Elizabeth Reba, ed. 1992. *Closer to home: Bisexuality and feminism.* Seattle: Seal.

Barbara Mor

ANGER

In *A Room of One's Own* (1929), Virginia Woolf argued that women should not dwell on their anger at male treatment of womankind, because anger consumes women's productive energies by "reflecting men at twice their natural size," in Woolf's own phrase. Her argument is that such anger "centers" men. More recent feminist analysis has taken an apparently very different stance, seeing anger as women's legitimate response to injustice and oppression and also, more important, as the dynamics of change, both individual and societal, because it motivates and propels feminist action. Slogans like "angry women," "take back the night," and more recently "zero tolerance" are public expressions of feminist anger at male violence that are designed to bring to public consciousness both male violence and women's knowledge of and active and organized opposition to this violence. Woolf's comments were directed toward anger experienced and understood as an uncontrollable and directionless force, one turned inward toward the self rather than outward toward the delineation of the sources and substance of power and evil; by contrast, Woolf had no reservations about writing in the white heat of rage against fascism in *Three Guineas* (1938). Woolf's position actually has much in common with feminist theorizing about emotions (for example, Jaggar, 1989; Lorde, 1981), which sees emotions as culturally proscribed in content and definition and as capable of rational expression, redirection, and use.

See Also

PSYCHOLOGY: OVERVIEW; SOCIALIZATION

References and Further Reading

Jaggar, Alison. 1989. Love and knowledge: Emotion in feminist epistemology. In Alison Jaggar and Susan Bordo, eds., *Gender/body/knowledge: Feminist reconstructions of being and knowing.* New Brunswick, N.J.: Rutgers University Press.

Lorde, Audre. 1981. The uses of anger. *Women's Studies Quarterly* 9(7–10). Reprinted in *Sister/outsider,* 124–133. New York: Crossing.

Woolf, Virginia. 1929. *A Room of One's Own.* London: Hogarth.

————. 1938. *Three guineas.* London: Hogarth.

Liz Stanley

ANIMAL RIGHTS

Animal rights is a specific philosophical argument—that animals possess rights, including the right not to be harmed—as a well as the general term for the movement to end the exploitation of animals by people. The animal rights movement targets the main forms of animal exploitation—eating, wearing, exhibiting, and experimenting on animals. Women have been prominent in this movement; there is a long tradition of women evidencing concern for the treatment of animals (see Donovan in Donovan and Adams, 1995), and attention to the issue continues to grow. However, animal rights has not been central to contemporary feminism, nor has the animal rights movement necessarily reflected feminist commitments.

Historical Background

Several feminist theorists associate women's oppression with animal exploitation. A few argue that matriarchy preceded patriarchy and that its overthrow—due in part to a change in humans' relationships with the other animals—enabled both women's and animals' oppression. Peggy Sanday correlates male domination with animal-based economies and concludes that gatherer societies were egalitarian. The feminist theologian Rosemary Radford Ruether establishes a connection between the domestication of animals, the development of urban centers, the creation of slavery, and the creation of the inequality of the sexes. One ecofeminist has speculated that patriarchal religion itself resulted from the guilt of killing animals for food. Others proposed that after the domestication of animals, it was the breeding of animals that suggested the idea of controlling women's reproductivity (see Mason, 1993). Feminists have noted that the first reproductive technologies, such as embryo transfer, were developed as part of the cattle industry and then transferred to women (see Corea, 1986). Theoretically, western cultures have equated women, children, animals, and "the natural" with one another and with the body—which was devalued, if not repudiated (see Adams, 1994).

Historically, animal rights arguments appeared as part of the revolutionary fervor in the United Kingdom during the 1790s, when support of the French Revolution, antislavery activism, and animal rights were seen to be interconnected. Again, in the 1890s and the following decade, in both Great Britain and the United States, connections were made among pacifist, temperance, suffragist, vegetarian, antivivisection, and trade union activists (see Adams, 2000; Lansbury, 1985). Contemporary feminists consider animal activism part of a progressive agenda. Feminist theoreticians are developing a cross-cultural ethics that identifies how sexism, racism, and specisim interact. They challenge the hyperrationalistic philosophical language of rights, arguing that it arises from a male-identified concept of an autonomous, separate individual.

Many women in the western tradition have an ethical history that is rooted in culturally prescribed practices of caring. Part of this history is an active concern about animals. Josephine Donovan suggests that the eighteenth-century emphasis on sentiment, associated with the appearance of numerous women writers, paved the intellectual ground for the appearance of animal rights, in the nineteenth century (Donovan in Donovan and Adams, 1995).

Women have composed the majority in many animal welfare groups. Animal advocacy has often been belittled because of this association with women: Spinoza argued that opposing animal exploitation was "womanish" (see Adams, 1994). During the nineteenth century, when most antivivisectionists were women, the movement was called "illogical" and "emotional." Meanwhile, women's claims on behalf of themselves were ridiculed by equating women with animals. For instance, the philosopher Mary Wollstonecraft's *A Vindication of the Rights of Woman* was dismissively parodied in *Vindication of the Rights of Brutes.*

Historically, the ideological justification for women's alleged inferiority was made by associating them with animals: women's bodies supposedly impaired their rationality. Since most western theorists construed rationality as the defining requirement for membership in the moral community, women—along with men of color and animals—who were seen as less able to transcend their bodies, were long excluded.

At least three responses to the historical alignment of women and animals have appeared in feminist theory. The first argues against identifying women with animals, asserting that women are rational—*like* men and *unlike* animals; the second argues that feminist theory has nothing to do with animals; and the third affirms the identification of women with animals, insisting that feminist theory must engage itself with the status and treatment of the other animals. Those who take this third position argue, for instance, that activism by women on behalf of animals arises: (1) from identification with victimized animals (see, for instance, the discussion by Lansbury, 1985, for early twentieth-century women's activism); (2) from empathy for the suffering of another being; and (3) as a part of an understanding of the interlocking systems of oppression that organize the world (and the oppressed) by gender, race, class, and species. Thus, some feminists argue that animal advocacy is a necessary extension of feminist insights, while simultaneously refusing to adopt the terminology of "rights."

The Feminist Animal Rights Argument

Since the 1970s feminists in the United States and the United Kingdom have articulated several central premises regarding the position of animals. (1) The oppression of women and animals is interconnected; women will not be free unless animals are free as well. (2) Violence against animals is one aspect of patriarchal culture—arising within and receiving legitimation from the way male sexual identity is constituted. For instance, eating animals enacts and symbolizes male dominance. (3) Feminism is a transformative philosophy that embraces the amelioration of life on Earth for all life-forms and challenges all forms of oppression; thus feminists must refuse to participate in or benefit from violence against animals. (4) Species, like gender, race, and class, is socially constructed and should not be the basis on which ethical decisions rest. These arguments constitute one aspect of ecofeminist thought, sometimes called "animal ecofeminism" (Gaard, 1998).

Insights into Feminist Issues from Animal Ecofeminism

Animal ecofeminism joins a variety of discussions in feminist theory, offering its own distinctive interpretation. For instance, while antipornography feminists in the United States must contend with the question of the encroachment on freedom of speech from legislation that addresses the harms of pornography, animal rights activists have had their speech curbed by "hunter harassment" laws passed by Congress and various states. (Thus pornography remains protected speech, but talking to hunters while they hunt or warning the animals is not protected speech.) Meanwhile, although sexual harassment has been a contested area, in part because of the question of defining harassment, hunter

harassment bills have not faced such scrutiny. Maria Comninou argues that "those in power make and interpret the laws to suit their purposes" (Adams and Donovan, 1995: 128), and that this can be seen when we analyze such laws with the interests of both animals and women in mind.

Animal ecofeminists argue that falsely generic words (such as *man* and *mankind*) that give men full human status must be analyzed in tandem with animal pejoratives for women (*catty, bitch, sow, shrew, dog, chick, cow*). Joan Dunayer observes that "Applying images of denigrated nonhuman species to women labels women inferior and available for abuse; attaching images of the aggrandized human species to men designates them superior and entitled to exploit" (Adams and Donovan, 1995: 11).

Feminist philosophers raise feminist questions in science; animal ecofeminist scholars raise questions about animals in feminism. Lynda Birke and Barbara Noske specifically argue that while feminist analyses of patriarchal science reject biological determinism for women, they do so by relying on overgeneralized and inaccurate ideas—fostered by patriarchal science—of "animals" as well as "humans," thus tacitly accepting biological determinism and female and male stereotypes for animals (see Birke, 1994; Noske, 1997).

Violence toward animals is a central aspect of much sexual violence against women and children, including incest, woman battering, and marital rape. Carol Adams explains that antiviolence interventions and theories will be inadequate if they ignore the control perpetrators gain by violence toward animals loved by the victims (see Adams, 1994: 144–61; and Adams and Donovan, 1995: 55–84).

Feminist Insights into the Status of Animals

Just as incorporating the status of animals into feminist analyses enhances these analyses, so, animal ecofeminist argue, a feminist analysis is required to understand the current treatment and maltreatment of animals. Basically, various analyses hold that a patriarchal culture feminizes animal victims. For instance, Karen Davis argues that the reason farm animals have been neglected by the environmental movement is that they are "creatures whose lives appear too slavishly, too boringly, too stupidly female, too 'cowlike'" (Adams and Donovan, 1995: 196). Marti Kheel, founder of Feminists for Animal Rights, argues that the reason hunting has been defended in some environmental writings is that it is associated with male self-identity (Adams and Donovan, 1995: 85–125). Carol Adams (2000) proposes that vegetarianism is opposed in patriarchal cultures because of the sexual politics of meat, in which meat eating is associated with virility and seen as symbolic of masculinity; vegetarianism, on the contrary, is seen as feminine.

Debates about the Status of Animals in the Feminist Movement

Feminist perspectives on the condition of animals are just beginning to emerge around the world. Until very recently, animal ecofeminists wrote mainly in the United States or the United Kingdom and clearly represented a western approach. International dialogue on the subject is beginning and includes, in part, German, Italian, and Japanese translations of some American works. In addition, with the proliferation of U.S.-based transnational corporations in other parts of the world (especially fast-food restaurants that specialize in hamburgers), many of the issues raised by western animal ecofeminists, especially issues concerning the health and environmental consequences of animal agriculture, increasingly apply to more cultures.

Animal ecofeminism is far from being a settled issue within feminist theory and activism; indeed it often provokes contention. This is due in part to the apparent sexism of the animal rights movement in both its leadership and its attitudes toward women. For instance, the antifur campaign, in its targeting of women as consumers, may be thought of as countenancing harassment of women on the street. Feminists may fear that successes with animal rights pave the way for human fetal rights. Some feminists worry about whether a pluralistic feminism should hold what appear to be absolute positions on animal-related issues. Arguments for vegetarianism, for instance, are sometimes viewed as restrictive or legislative. Animal ecofeminists, on the other hand, argue for a pluralistic feminism that includes concern for other animals and contend that animal advocacy, by exposing the anthropocentrism of the antiabortion movement, actually bolsters the arguments for reproductive choice (Adams, 1994: 55–70).

The unique perspective animal ecofeminism brings to the issue of environmental concerns and feminism is its focus on the contested idea of "animals." For instance, this article has followed conventional English usage in its discussion of animals; that is, accepting the idea that the word *animal* applies to all creatures except human beings. But animal ecofeminists argue that this language masks people's own animal status. They argue that until people confront their own animality, their "membership in animalkind" (Adams and Donovan, 1995: 23), they will endorse a strict— but false—boundary between animals and humans that upholds institutionalized and individual maltreatment of the other animals while providing a conceptual foundation for other forms of oppression.

See Also

ECOFEMINISM; ETHICS: FEMINIST; FURS; HUMAN RIGHTS; HUNTING; VEGETARIANISM

References and Further Reading

Adams, Carol J. 1994. *Neither man nor beast; Feminism and the defense of animals.* New York: Continuum.

———. 2000. *The sexual politics of meat: A feminist-vegetarian critical theory.* Tenth Anniversary Edition. New York: Continuum; Oxford: Polity.

———, and Josephine Donovan, eds. 1995. *Animals and women: Feminist theoretical explorations.* Durham, N.C.: Duke University Press.

Birke, Lynda. 1994. *Feminism, animals and science.* Buckingham, England and Philadelphia: Open University Press.

Collard, Andree, with Joyce Construcci. 1988. *Rape of the wild: Man's violence against animals and the earth.* London: Women's Press; Bloomington: Indiana University Press.

Corea, Gena. 1986. *The mother machine.* New York: Harper and Row.

Donovan, Josephine, and Carol J. Adams, eds. 1995. *Beyond animal rights: A feminist caring ethic for the treatment of animals.* New York: Continuum.

Gaard, Greta, ed. 1993. *Ecofeminism: Women, animals, nature.* Philadelphia: Temple University Press.

———. 1998. *Ecological politics: Ecofeminists and the greens.* Philadelphia: Temple University Press.

Lansbury, Coral. 1985. *The old brown dog: Women, workers and vivisection in Edwardian England.* Madison: University of Wisconsin Press.

Luke, Brian. 1998. Violent love: Hunting, heterosexuality, and the erotics of men's predation. *Feminist Studies* 24.3 (Fall): 627–655.

Mason, Jim. 1993. *An unnatural order.* New York: Continuum.

Noske, Barbara. 1997. London: Pluto. *Beyond Boundaries: Humans and Animals.* Montreal: Black Rose.

Carol J. Adams

ANOREXIA NERVOSA

There are well-documented instances of religious ascetics suffering from anorexia nervosa in the mid-thirteenth century, and the first medical description was written as early as 1694 by Richard Morton, a doctor in London. Morton had observed patients with symptoms of an unfamiliar disorder: they felt no hunger and had lost a great deal of weight but seemed unconcerned about this. Today, it is generally believed that anorexics do experience hunger but resist it; however, Morton made several astute observations that are still used to diagnose anorexia nervosa: emaciation, amenorrhea (cessation of menstruation), preoccupation with food, and observance of many rituals related to eating and food. Other fundamental characteristics of anorexics include a strong drive to be thin, with self-esteem being closely tied to weight and shape; preoccupation with weight, body image, and eating; severe weight loss or, in young girls, failure to gain weight at critical developmental stages; and, often, a skewed or unrealistic perception of one's own body, usually referred to as "distorted body image."

Before the 1960s there was not a great deal of interest in studying or writing about eating disorders, and until the 1980s the sociocultural analysis of these disorders—which is now the prevailing approach—hardly existed. During the 1980s, awareness of eating disorders heightened and researchers and others began to think of them more in terms of the societal milieu. Anorexia nervosa is now recognized as a significant problem and is the subject of much research and literature; this entry can provide only a brief introduction to what has become a vast, complex, and multifaceted topic.

Diagnostic criteria for anorexia nervosa have been specified by the American Psychiatric Association (APA) in its *Diagnostic and Statistical Manual of Mental Disorders,* indicating that this disorder is considered to be psychological. The criteria include percentage of body weight lost. It is interesting to note that between 1980, when the third edition of the manual (DSM-III) was published, and 1987, when it was revised as DSM-III-R, the weight loss necessary to make a diagnosis of anorexia nervosa was lowered from 25 percent to 15 percent of total body weight. A fourth edition of the *Diagnostic and Statistical Manual* was published in 1994. According to DSM-IV, anorexia nervosa is most prevalent in western and developed nations where food abounds and women feel pressure to be thin.

Anorexia nervosa was once seen as a white, upper-middle-class disorder, but today it appears to be on the rise in all racial groups and all social classes. A typical sequence begins with dieting and reasonable weight loss, which in the short run boosts self-esteem but then develops into more and more stringent dieting, eventually progressing to self-starvation, emaciation, and in some cases death.

Although the risk factors for anorexia nervosa are highly individualized, certain important factors are well known. The greatest risk factor is being female: 90 percent of anorectics are girls and women. The second-largest factor is being young: the average age of onset is 17. Studies have found that women in careers that emphasize thinness—such as dancing and modeling—are also at a high risk of anorexia nervosa. Female athletes in general are at risk, and those in sports where leanness is considered essential, such as gymnastics and figure skating, are particularly vulnerable. (In fact, a *female athlete triad* of three related disorders—anorexia and, as a result, amenorrhea and osteoporosis—has been identified.) Some studies have found evidence of a genetic predisposition to anorexia nervosa. It has also been found that there is a disproportionately high incidence of eating disorders in girls whose mothers are obese.

In western societies, a distorted body image is typically associated with anorexia nervosa: anorectics see themselves as fat even when they are alarmingly thin and wasted. However, anorexics in certain cultures may not have a distorted perception of their body shape and may report different reasons for not wishing to eat, such as stomachaches, indigestion, or dislike of food.

Treatment of anorexia nervosa usually combines medical, pscyhological, and nutritional interventions; these vary according to the seriousness of the patient's condition and range up to hospitalization and tube-feeding for those in imminent danger of death. At present, the outcome of treatment is by no means certain: probably only about half of those treated can be expected to recover fully; among the others there may be some or very little improvement, and relapse is common. Moreover, many anorectics never receive treatment at all, because denial is typical and help is not sought. Many people consider prevention a better approach, but there are as yet few systematic preventive programs—and many societies, meanwhile, continue to equate thinness with beauty, attractiveness, and even health, making preventive efforts very difficult.

See Also

ADVERTISING; BODY; BULIMIA NERVOSA; EATING DISORDERS; EXERCISE AND FITNESS; FOOD AND CULTURE; IMAGES OF WOMEN: OVERVIEW; PSYCHOLOGY: SOCIAL

References and Further Reading

Alexander-Mott, LeeAnn, and D. Barry Lumsden, eds. 1994. *Understanding eating disorders: Anorexia nervosa, bulimia nervosa, and obesity.* Washington, D.C.: Taylor and Francis.

American Psychiatric Association (APA). 1980, 1987, 1994. *Diagnostic and statistical manual of mental disorders.* 3rd ed., 3rd ed. rev., 4th ed. Washington, D.C.: APA.

Brown, Catrina, and Karin Jasper, eds. 1993. *Consuming passions: Feminist approaches to weight preoccupation and eating disorders.* New York: Second Story.

Bruch, Hilde. 1974. *Eating disorders: Obesity and anorexia nervosa and the person within.* London: Routledge.

Fallon, Patricia, Melanie A. Katzman, and Susan C. Wooley, eds. 1994. *Feminist perspectives on eating disorders.* New York: Guilford.

Garfinkel, Paul E., and David M. Garner, eds. 1997. *Handbook of treatment for eating disorders.* 2nd ed. New York: Guilford.

MacSween, Morag. 1996. *Anorexic bodies: A feminist and sociological perspective on anorexia nervosa.* New York: Routledge.

Zeman, Ellen J. Female athletes. In John Zumerchik, ed., *Encyclopedia of sports science.* Vol. 2. New York: Simon and Schuster Macmillan.

Meredith Nachman

ANTHROPOLOGY

Anthropology is the discipline that seeks to explain cross-cultural variation in human behavior, and it takes as its subject matter the span of human cultural behavior across time and space, focusing traditionally—although not exclusively—on social groups that do not or did not maintain written records. Variation among contemporary cultural forms is studied through methods and theory of sociocultural anthropology, while archaeology is used to reconstruct the prehistories of these traditions. In addition, biological anthropologists investigate the synergistic relationship between human cultural behavior and biology through the lens of evolutionary biology. Hence the temporal scope of anthropology ranges over at least 4 million years of evolutionary history, the time period in which the first direct human ancestors appear in the fossil record and the first evidence of cultural behavior is recorded in the systematic manufacture of stone tools (ca. 2.5 million years ago). Conforming to the challenges posed by its diverse subject matter, anthropology's methods and theories embrace modes of analysis that range freely among the humanistic, social scientific, and scientific. Feminist studies within anthropology similarly assume this wide range of intellectual positions, rendering anthropological work on gender relations unique in its ability to access and synthesize or juxtapose diverse intellectual standpoints. Under the heading of this one discipline is an array of subjects, methods, and explana-tions—including everything from analysis of gender relations in primate societies (used as models for early hominids' social life) through reconstruction of women's activities and roles in now extinct societies to the study of women as active agents in the construction of social relations of power within a specific cultural setting. Although there has been a good deal of cross-fertilization among feminist researchers working in the various subfields of anthropology, the timing and historical development of their work have been quite different.

In its aspiration to represent and explain the range of variation in human cultural behavior, anthropology has always made a place for accounts of women's activities. Indeed, the intellectual framework of anthropology's founding traditions as practiced through the 1950s required that descriptions of women's activities and roles be included in ethnographies. In the tradition of the British structural-functional school, which emphasized the complementary functioning of the structural components of a stable social whole, women's roles were consistently described in accounts of the kinship and marriage structures understood to be the primary structures of social integration in nonwestern societies. Women's work, however, was less uniformly considered in functionalist descriptions of subsistence or economic activity, and women were almost never incorporated into accounts of ritual and politics. Similarly, the culture historical approach espoused by Boasian anthropologists in the United States required documentation of women's roles within cultural wholes that were the object of description and reconstruction. Boas encouraged and sponsored a number of women fieldworkers among the native cultures of the southwestern United States, where their charge was to gather information on "women's affairs," a task for which Boas assumed they were uniquely suited. Margaret Mead—undoubtedly the most famous of Boas's students—set out to study "sex roles" specifically, and through her fieldwork in Samoa in the 1930s was the first scholar to document the role of culture in determining gender roles and personalities. Mead's work added weight to the early feminist argument that gender is culturally constructed rather than innate.

Anthropological theory of the 1960s grew out of and sought to deepen insights gained in these formative years. Three major schools of thought came to dominate investigation in this era, and these tended to split the explanation of human behavioral variability between either mentalist-idealist or materialist causality. The structuralism of Levi-Strauss and the symbolic anthropology of Clifford Geertz constituted the former approach. Structuralists centered their efforts on understanding variability in human behavior through the apprehension of underlying structuring cultural principles expressed as dualisms encoded in myth and ritual; symbolic anthropologists sought to penetrate the cultural meaning embodied in public symbols. Opposed to these two schools of thought was cultural ecology, representing the materialist school of thought that sought to explain variation in culture as a result of human cultural adaptation to specific environmental settings. Although strikingly different in method and underlying assumptions, all of these theoretical structures shared in the perspective that social actors were passively shaped by cultural forms. In this context the contributions of early "prefeminist" women anthropologists were overshadowed by theoretical positions that either ignored or made unwarranted assumptions about gender. That is, gender could be ignored because it was irrelevant to understanding either the public myth and ritual assumed to be the domain of men or the process of adaptation, again dominated by male subsistence activity. Alternatively, where gender demanded treatment, explanations were underwritten by assumptions about gender structures mirroring middle- and upper-class western culture that were supposedly based on "natural" differences between women and men and therefore common to all cultures. This context confronted emergent feminist anthropology of the 1970s.

Feminist anthropologists of the 1970s, drawing inspiration from the widespread intellectual and social ferment of the period, cast the male-biased assumptions underlying this knowledge structure into relief and began the process of challenging and replacing them. Resurrecting the work of Mead, these scholars first began documenting variability in women's experiences across cultures. Questioning earlier theoretical models that assumed a peripheral position for women in social relations, new ethnographies were written that put the female subject at the center of examination or action. At the same time that these data on women's lives in traditional societies began to accumulate, a coherent picture of gender asymmetry across cultures began to emerge, and this became the dominant issue for the feminist discourse of the 1970s: how to account for the nearly universal or historically developed subordination of women, even as it was apparent that women's roles and their individual power or autonomy varied considerably in different cultures.

Several lines of thought were developed to address this issue, and this body of work came to be identified as the "anthropology of women." One school of thought, taking its inspiration from newly revived Marxist thinking in anthropology, sought to explain women's status on the basis of transformations of the material conditions of life. Here the central arguments were mounted by Karen Sacks and Eleanor Leacock, who proposed that women in foraging and early horticultural societies enjoyed egalitarian relationships with men, based primarily on their relatively equal contribution to subsistence. Structures of male dominance, in turn, came into play with the social stratification and privatization of kinship associated with the rise of the state and the spread of capitalism through colonialism. Hence the universal subordination of women is more an artifact of world economic structures than a "natural" condition. Another formative position was mapped out at this time by Michelle Rosaldo, who argued that women's roles in childbearing and child rearing associated them with the domestic and private spheres in all societies. To the degree that the public and private may be separate spheres of influence in any given society, this separation provides the basis for hierarchical valuing and dominance of men over women's affairs in the public arena. While Rosaldo's formulation incorporated both symbolic and institutional factors, Sherry Ortner offered another key to understanding women's status that followed from the structuralist paradigm, suggesting that women are conceptualized worldwide as natural, while men are associated with culture. This dichotomous categorization then accounts for women's devalued position relative to men, who are the possessors and creators of the cultural phenomena that dominate and transcend nature. Here again the variability in arguments should not obscure a basic similarity in all of these approaches to the study of women; they search for key structures that allow systematic cross-cultural comparison and explain women's status within that framework.

Related issues were engaged within biological anthropology during this period, and these debates both crosscut and drew inspiration from work going on in sociocultural anthropology. Like their colleagues in sociocultural anthropology, feminists in biological anthropology began their critique with direct challenges to models of primate society and, by extension, reconstructions of early hominid society that rested on androcentric assumptions. Central to this critique was the issue of the accuracy of Sherwood Washburn and Irven DeVore's model of baboon behavior that featured the organizing axis of baboon society as a stable male dominance hierarchy. According to this model, baboon social groups consisted of a few powerful, central males that aggressively controlled the behavior (especially mating patterns) of a set of physically weaker females and their dependent offspring. From this form of organization, females were thought to gain protection for themselves and their young in a dangerous savannah environment, while the dominant males gained exclusive mating rights. Since human ancestors evolved in the savannah environment and this particular form of social organization was interpreted as an adaptation to this environment, it was a short step to conclude that early hominids were likely to have been organized on similar principles. Thus emerged the "man the hunter" model of early hominid social organization in which a core group of male hunters who provided meat and physical protection to a their female mates and dependent young were cast as the central and distinctive feature of hominid social life. All other features of hominid social life and indeed biology were then considered to be the result of various selective forces acting on this male-dominated base.

Feminist challenges to these models took two related forms. Within primatology, Washburn and Devore's model of baboon social organization was first called into question by the work of Thelma Rowell throughout the late 1960s and into the 1970s. Through her painstaking longitudinal studies that paid equal attention to the activities of females and males, Rowell was able to demonstrate that a stable male hierarchy was an artifact of short-term observation of more noticeable male behavior patterns. Her observations uncovered instead a primate society in which baboon mothers and their offspring (particularly daughters) constituted the stable core of a social group resident within a particular range, while adult males moved among these groups. By 1980, Jeanne Altman—following a similar field observation strategy—was able to demonstrate that the knowledge of range and social history possessed by females residing in a troop over relatively long periods of time could be translated into social power. Finally, Barbara Smuts, working into the 1980s, enhanced this alternative model by demonstrating a lack of correspondence between reproductive success and dominance among male baboons. She postulated instead that male "friends" (in other words, those individuals with learned social skills and maturity) were most frequently solicited as mates by females. In these alternative models of baboon society females were moved from subordination to being key social actors.

Even as these studies were being conducted, Adrienne Zihlman and Nancy Tanner offered their "woman the gatherer" challenge to the "man the hunter" model of human evolution. Specifically rejecting the traditional model of baboon social organization, Zihlman and Tanner turned to the then available data on chimpanzees that suggested the centrality of the mother-offspring relationship and female mate choice in the social organization of our closest primate relatives. Using this alternative primate model and data from the fossil record and contemporary foraging peoples, Zihlman and Tanner proposed that women's gathering activities and the tools associated with them, coupled with food sharing among related females and their offspring, formed the basis for human social life. Various selective forces acting upon this set of hominid behaviors were then keys to determining the human evolutionary path. Far from leaving women on the fringes of the human evolutionary process, the "woman the gatherer" model placed women at the center.

The body of work produced by feminist anthropologists up through the 1970s thus successfully integrated women into the study of human culture and demonstrated the necessity of documenting women's experiences in coming to a more accurate depiction of human cultural and biological variability. But it did so by simply inserting women or women's perspectives into anthropology's then-reigning theoretical constructs. It was soon discovered that this approach to studying women had two major drawbacks. First, it resulted in an anthropology where one simply did traditional anthropology but added women into the mix. This has been called the "add women and stir" approach to the study of gender, and it fostered the ghettoization of women's studies within anthropology. Second, by failing to question the constructs that we use to study gender, this approach ended up seeing the male-female matrix as the most important domain for understanding women's lives. Single or "key" variables were sought that might explain differences in, for example, women's status. This approach masked the variability among women, and it is the redress of these shortcomings that has absorbed the most recent feminist anthropology.

As sociocultural anthropology as moved into a self-reflective, postmodern critique of its underlying assumptions and operating principles, feminists moved in a parallel direction and, some would argue, even led the dialogue. Central to this movement has been the understanding that categories we use to describe other cultures are in themselves constructs of our own culture and knowledge system that enforce a potentially misleading categorization on cultural others. Thus when a scholar studying the anthropology of women makes an assertion about "women's status among the X," he or she assumes the unchanging reality of three variables: women, status, and population X. The feminist anthropology of the 1980s sought to address such categorization by emphasizing the historical contingency of all three variables. Thus gender was emphasized as an embedded construct sensitive to the historical trajectory of social, political, and economic contexts in any given society. So also did concepts like "status" and a historically unchanging and definable population come into question as each social group under study came to be understood as the momentary product of its own unique history. Within this reformulated structure, the meaning and implications of gender must be explored rather than presumed, and this exploration must take place in relation to other key cultural variables. Hence gender becomes intimately linked to other analytical concepts, such as the social relations of production, and constitutes a critical analytical concept for all cultural studies. It then becomes just as important to understand differences among women in their relation to other cultural features as it is to understand differences between males and females, and understanding gender constructs is another key for apprehending cultural difference.

Parallel understandings percolated through biological anthropology over the same time period. In primatology, the construct of dominance hierarchy has been increasingly eschewed for an understanding (derived primarily from the baboon work discussed above) that primates live in a complex web of social interactions in which varying contexts will lead to differential expressions of dominance as individuals predict and manipulate interactions to attain specific and shifting goals. So also has it become clear from rapidly accumulating primate studies of female activity patterns that there is a great deal of variability in behavior that cannot be neatly subsumed under simplistic gendered dichotomies. Hence among primates as well, a new call has been issued to study variability across individual life spans and troop histories. The field of evolutionary biology has also responded to such insights, and beginning from the proposition that human females should have evolved a reproductive biology attuned to protecting offspring, has begun to study specialized and varying female patterns of growth, development, and psychological and behavioral adjustment across the life span in response to reproductive status. In short, the category of "female" is no longer invariant and essential in biological anthropology, just as the construction of gender has been substituted for "women" in sociocultural anthropology.

Despite these advances in allied subdisciplines, it was not until the mid-1980s that archaeologists finally sought to incorporate systematically understandings of gender into their reconstructions of past human societies. As early work in this area pointed out, archaeology has not been silent on the gender issue in its traditional reconstructions; rather, unexamined androcentric models stemming from contemporary western ideals sneaked into the description of past human society. Thus there was a brief flurry of "remedial" work in which feminist archaeologists identified the ways in which male bias has colored our readings of the past and the female perspective might be inserted. Borrowing perspectives from colleagues in sociocultural anthropology, feminist archaeologists moved quickly beyond this type of work and sought to redefine how we write and think about the past so as to make gender part of an overall interpretive shift. Contextual archaeology, introduced in European archaeology of the 1980s, became an initial attractive home for feminist perspectives, emphasizing the necessity of tracking and describing the development of particular past cultural contexts and the worldview that informed them. Here gendered constructs could be construed as one of the key attributes of cultural traditions. The Americanist tradition experimented with alternative narrative form that eschewed the supposedly neutral voice of the male scientist and introduced the explicitly female voice of past cultural participants. Conceptual categories were also called into question, as feminist archaeologists have attempted to move beyond the gender essentialism inherent in reconstructions of origins of particular cultural practices or institutions such as plant domestication, female subordination, or the state. Thus, though late to the debate, archaeology has quickly adopted contemporary understandings of gender constructs from feminist research and stands to reshape the discipline in significant ways.

As feminist anthropology develops, it is likely that the pattern of increased dialogue across the subdisciplines will continue, and a disciplinary understanding may emerge so that it will no longer be possible to study the category of "woman" in isolation. Rather, gender constructs will be understood as a basic organizing principle of human experience that must be accommodated in any adequate account of human biological and cultural variability.

See Also

ARCHAEOLOGY; CULTURE: OVERVIEW; EVOLUTION

References and Further Reading

Barnard, Allen, and Jonathan Spencer, eds. 1996. *Encyclopedia of social and cultural anthropology*. New York: Routledge.

Ingold, Tim, ed. 1994. *Companion encyclopedia of anthropology*. London and New York: Routledge.

Levinson, David, and Melvin Ember. 1996. *Encyclopedia of cultural anthropology*. New York: Holt.

Moore, Henrietta L. *A passion for difference: Essays in anthropology and gender*. Cambridge: Polity.

Susan J. Bender

ANTIDISCRIMINATION

Discrimination may be defined as a denial of equal enjoyment of rights. From the 1960s the resurgent women's movement focused attention on the prevalence of discrimination based on sex and marital status. The women's movement demanded antidiscrimination measures similar to those already being introduced around the world as a result of the 1965 United Nations (UN) Convention on the Elimination of All Forms of Racial Discrimination.

Legislation forbidding sex discrimination was passed by many countries in the 1970s, particularly as a result of the momentum created by International Women's Year (IWY) in 1975 and the UN Decade for Women (1976–1985). The World Plan of Action adopted at the IWY Conference in Mexico City placed special emphasis both on government machinery to advance the status of women and on antidiscrimination legislation. Such legislation usually prohibited both direct discrimination (less favorable treatment or unfavorable treatment because of sex or marital status) and indirect discrimination (employment requirements such as continuity of service, which, although apparently neutral, have a disparate impact because women are more likely to have interrupted work histories).

As can be seen from the above description of indirect discrimination, sameness of treatment or "facial" neutrality does not necessarily mean the absence of discrimination. Nor is it necessary for discrimination to be intentional (this applies to direct as well as indirect discrimination). The concept of indirect discrimination as incorporated in much recent antidiscrimination legislation has its origin in a U.S. Supreme Court case of 1971, *Griggs* v. *Duke Power Co.* The Court found in this case that requiring a high school education or a certain minimum score on an intelligence quotient (IQ) test as a criterion for recruitment or promotion was discriminatory in effect against the black complainant and could not be defended as directly job-related. The court determined that the legal proscription of discrimination in the Civil Rights Act extended to "practices that are fair in form but discriminatory in operation."

Similarly, it is now widely recognized that apparently gender-neutral requirements may discriminate in effect against women. In 1984, in *Holmes* v. *the Home Office,* it was found under the U.K. Sex Discrimination Act that the refusal to make part-time work available to the complainant after return from maternity leave constituted indirect discrimination, and the Home Office had failed to justify its requirement for full-time hours. (Discriminatory requirements may be defended as a business necessity and therefore as reasonable in the circumstances.) The concept of indirect discrimination involves recognition that relevant "differences" such as women's reproductive role or their role as primary carers must be accommodated if equal opportunity is to be achieved—that is, women's full enjoyment of the right to paid work.

The concept of indirect discrimination has also been accepted in the interpretation of the guarantees of equality in the Canadian constitution. In 1989, in the pathbreaking *Andrews* case, the Supreme Court of Canada adopted a disadvantage test to establish whether discrimination had taken place. The test requires examining whether the claimant is a member of a group that has experienced persistent disadvantage on the basis of personal characteristics, and, if so, whether the measure in question continues or worsens that disadvantage. The Supreme Court of Canada was the first court in the world to use the test of social disadvantage when interpreting constitutional guarantees of equality (Mahoney, 1994).

A narrower test but one with a similar effect was applied by the High Court of Australia in 1989 in the *Australian Iron and Steel (AIS)* case. AIS had for many years discriminated against women, but thanks to an earlier case had started recruiting them. Soon after, during a recession, AIS began dismissing workers, according to the traditional "last on, first off" rule. The High Court found that the application of this rule, while facially neutral, had the effect of compounding and perpetuating the discrimination the women had experienced in the past at AIS.

In addition to prohibiting direct and indirect discrimination, antidiscrimination legislation characteristically has a "special measures" exemption, which excludes measures designed to promote equality or to overcome disadvantages arising from characteristics such as sex or marital status. Unfortunately, special measures exemptions have often been very narrowly interpreted by the courts when men have brought complaints of being discriminated against by "women-only" programs. Another exemption that routinely forms part of such legislation covers special measures for the protection of maternity. Other characteristic exemptions are for situations where sex is a "bona fide occupational qualification."

Later legislation often prohibited unwelcome sexual conduct, particularly in the workplace or in educational institutions, where the victim might reasonably feel offended, humiliated, or intimidated. The American feminist Catharine MacKinnon argued in *The Sexual Harassment of Working Women* (1979) that sexual harassment was a form of sex discrimination, an argument subsequently accepted by courts. She was largely responsible for "naming" this phenomenon, which earlier generations of women had thought was just called life. She later commented (1987) that the experience of providing legal remedies for sexual harassment suggested that legal initiatives designed from women's real experience of violations could make a difference. Her attempt (together with Andrea Dworkin) to construe pornography as a form of sex discrimination proved more controversial, both with civil libertarians and with many feminists.

Discrimination based on sexual orientation is not explicitly included in the international instruments relating to sex discrimination (or in domestic legislation closely tied to such international instruments), and same-sex relations are not protected by marital status provisions. Discrimination on the grounds of sexual orientation or sex of partner may, however, be proscribed in omnibus antidiscrimination or equal opportunity legislation. A considerable amount of antidiscrimination legislation is of this omnibus character—for example, prohibiting discrimination on a range of grounds such as sex, race, disability, age, and sexual preference. Complaints of discrimination on more than one ground (for example, sex and race or age and sex) may be handled under such legislation.

There has been debate over the relative merits of omnibus and specialized legislation regarding sex discrimination, but in both cases prohibition of sex-related forms of discrimination such as sexual harassment became more detailed and specific in the 1980s as a result of both accumulated case law and legislative amendments. One area that became important was discrimination based on "demeanor"—that is, discrimination resulting from stereotyped expectations of gender-appropriate behavior and double standards.

As we shall see below, discrimination on the grounds of family responsibilities (or parental or career status) was frequently added to antidiscrimination legislation. Other grounds made explicit in different Australian jurisdictions in the 1990s included potential pregnancy (in addition to pregnancy, breast feeding, the identity of a spouse, and occupation (the last to protect sex workers).

Antidiscrimination legislation is usually complaint-based and oriented toward providing remedies for discrimination that has already occurred. Critics have pointed out that the onus for reform is thus placed on the victims of discrimination, and little impact is made on forms of systemic discrimination such as the sex segregation of the labor market and the undervaluing of women's work (for example, Thornton, 1990). Class actions and government funding of public interest advocacy are two ways in which the disadvantages of complaint-based legislation can be mitigated. Class actions have been most common in the United States, where contingent fees are available as an incentive for lawyers to take on such litigation. The Canadian Legal Education and Action Fund (LEAF) was established by feminist lawyers in 1985 to help women exercise their constitutional equality rights. LEAF has received substantial public as well as private funding and has been involved in more than 100 test cases.

Nonetheless, complaint-based approaches have definite limitations as a means of achieving social reform. Recognition of these limitations led to increased emphasis on affirmative action—known as "positive action" in Europe and "employment equity" in Canada. Affirmative action places the onus on employers to identify sources of direct, indirect, or systemic discrimination within their organizations and to develop programs involving a series of steps to remove barriers and achieve measurable improvement. Typically such programs involve allocation of management responsibility; appointment of an action officer; consultation; the production of relevant statistics, strategies, timetables and targets; and monitoring, evaluation, and reporting mechanisms.

The term *equal employment opportunity* (EEO) is also used, as here, for such voluntary or legislated programs, although EEO is the hoped-for outcome rather than the means of achieving it. The term *affirmative action* has been associated with pioneering measures in the United States and, to a lesser extent, in Canada, and with the remedial imposition of numerical quotas by their courts—seen by critics as "reverse discrimination." Controversy over the nature and effectiveness of the EEO approach is examined later in this article.

EEO programs tackle issues such as the distribution of women in organizations and the training, staff development, and promotional opportunities available to them. Recruitment practices and promotion criteria as well as the criteria used in job classification and performance appraisal are examined for gender bias. EEO programs also try to tackle broader issues of organizational culture, including the accommodation of family responsibilities and forms of work-based harassment or exclusion. Mentoring systems are sometimes developed for women or members of other disadvantaged groups so that they can become familiar with the unwritten rules of the organization.

The need for affirmative action was confirmed by the UN Convention on the Elimination of All Forms of Discrimination against Women, adopted in 1979 after more than a decade's work by the Commission on the Status of

Women. The Convention does not prohibit differential treatment on the basis of sex, but only differential treatment adverse to women's equal enjoyment of human rights. In 1988 the Committee on the Elimination of Discrimination against Women (CEDAW), the body responsible for monitoring implementation of the Convention, recommended that "States Parties make more use of temporary special measures such as positive action, preferential treatment or quota systems to advance women's integration into education, the economy, politics and employment."

The Convention builds on the guarantees of equality and nondiscrimination in the UN Charter, the Universal Declaration of Human Rights, the International Covenant on civil and Political Rights, and the International Covenant on Social, Economic, and Cultural Rights. It extends the principle of equality into the private as well as the public sphere and deals with sexist attitudes as well as discriminatory actions. Topics covered include the elimination of stereotyped concepts of the roles of men and women from the education system; recognition of the common responsibility of men and women in the upbringing and development of their children; the inalienable right of all human beings to paid work; the right to equal remuneration for work of equal value; and equality of treatment in work evaluation (later spelled out as gender-neutral criteria for job evaluation). The Convention requires that the principle of the equality of men and women and their equal enjoyment of rights and freedoms be embodied in national constitutions as well as in antidiscrimination legislation.

The Convention was signed in 1980 by 53 countries at the opening ceremony of the Mid-Decade UN Women's Conference in Copenhagen, and by February 1994, 131 countries had ratified the Convention. Ratification signals acceptance of an obligation to eliminate discrimination against women by all appropriate means, from antidiscrimination legislation and affirmative action to community education. Reports on implementation of the Convention must be submitted on a four-year cycle.

Despite the apparent readiness to ratify the Convention, there has been controversy over sweeping reservations entered by some countries and debate over whether they are compatible with its object and purpose. The Convention has been subject to more substantive reservations than any other major human rights treaty. Islamic countries have entered reservations over even the general principle of nondiscrimination, on the basis of incompatibility with the Shari'a. Conversely, some countries have not entered reservations but continue to allow violations of women's rights. Despite the important role of CEDAW in setting international standards for women's rights, it has been the poor

cousin of the international human rights treaty bodies (Byrnes, 1989). It is the only such body with a limitation (two weeks) placed on its annual meeting time, causing a substantial backlog in consideration of reports. Moreover, the Convention does not provide for CEDAW to receive complaints from individuals, unlike the Racial Discrimination Convention or the International Covenant on Civil and Political Rights.

CEDAW has had fewer resources than the other (male-dominated) treaty bodies that have been serviced by the Human Rights Center in Geneva. CEDAW has been serviced by the UN Division for the Advancement of Women, based in Vienna, and now in New York, which may have contributed to its marginalization. The 1993 World Conference on Human Rights in Vienna called for the greater integration of women's rights into the international human rights system.

For a time there was one nongovernmental organization (NGO) focusing on CEDAW—International Women's Rights Action Watch, based at the University of Minnesota. Justice Elizabeth Evatt (1990), when Chair of CEDAW, called for greater involvement by NGOs in supporting the committee's work, in providing independent information to supplement government reports, and in querying government reservations. It is accepted wisdom that the effectiveness of human rights–monitoring bodies depends on such independent sources of information. Ideally, NGO representatives should be present when their country's report is being reviewed and ensure publicity at home for the issues raised.

One development during the 1980s was increased international recognition that violence against women underpins women's subordination, preventing equal participation in public and private life. In 1989 CEDAW issued a recommendation that gender-based violence be covered by the Convention (although not explicitly mentioned in it) and that governments should report on measures taken to prevent it: "Discrimination is most dramatically illustrated by toleration of violence and acceptance of it as a cultural norm." A UN Declaration on the Elimination of Violence against Women, instigated by Australia and Canada, was adopted by the General Assembly in 1993 and reiterated that "violence against women is one of the crucial social mechanisms by which women are forced into a subordinate position."

Another important development in the 1980s was a focus on the links between paid and unpaid work and the impact of the latter on equal opportunity. The International Labor Organization (ILO) in Geneva has a history of pioneering antidiscrimination measures, including ILO

Convention 100 on Equal Remuneration (1951) and ILO Convention 111 on Discrimination in Employment and Occupation (1958). The ILO claims that the global trend toward enactment of measures to prohibit sex discrimination may be attributed directly to the impact of these conventions (International Labor Conference, 1993).

The ILO has also led the way on the need for the redesign of paid work to enable men to take up a more equal share of family responsibilities. Convention 156 on Workers with Family Responsibilities was adopted in 1981 and together with its accompanying Recommendation superseded the 1965 Recommendation on Women with Family Responsibilities. The preamble refers to the statement in the UN Women's Convention that "a change in the traditional role of men as well as the role of women in society is needed to achieve full equality between men and women." It stressed the need for changes in the terms and conditions of paid work and of social security as well as the provision of community services such as child care to ensure equal opportunity for workers with family responsibilities. The Convention aimed to minimize the conflict between paid work and family responsibilities to exercise their right to paid employment.

Relatively few countries have ratified ILO 156 (20 by December 1993), perhaps because it requires policies enabling men as well as women to combine family responsibilities with paid work. However, a number of countries, including Canada, have adopted policies consonant with ratification (International Labor Conference, 1993). Countries ratifying the Convention, such as most of the Nordic countries and France, the Netherlands, and Australia, have passed legislation prohibiting discrimination in employment on the grounds of family or carer responsibilities and have encouraged employers to adopt "family friendly" policies, such as flexible working hours, reduced hours for parents of young children, career breaks, 48-week years, and help with child care, vacation care, and care for aged family members.

Educational programs undertaken by countries that have ratified ILO 156 have been directed toward raising employers' consciousness of the impact of family responsibilities on employees. They have also been directed toward raising community awareness of the disproportionate share of unpaid work carried by women (in part through time-use studies) and the need for a more equal sharing of the load if equal opportunities are to be achieved.

Another international pressure point for the adoption of antidiscrimination measures has been the European Economic Community (EEC)—now known as the European Union (ECI). Article 119 of the Treaty of Rome, establishing the EEC, required equal pay for men and women; subsequent Council Directives and judgments by the European Court of Justice have strengthened this requirement. Directives have covered areas such as equal treatment in employment, self-employment, and social security, and a minimum standard for paid maternity leave. Community members such as the United Kingdom have had to amend their legislation to conform to community standards. The EEC has also provided financial support to increase access by women to nontraditional jobs, to assist women in setting up small businesses, and to increase the provision of child care facilities and vocational training for child care workers.

There have been a series of Community Action Program to promote equal opportunities for men and women workers and a considerable amount of comparative research and dissemination of best-practice models, including models of positive action in public and private sectors. Current themes include discrimination in job assessment and classification, the concept of indirect discrimination, and the reconciliation of work and family responsibilities (see also the Community Charter of 1989). Community legislation and programs promoting equal opportunity for women have flowed (with a little help from European feminists) from the economic aim enshrined in the Treaty of Rome of preventing any distortion of competition stemming from a lower-paid female workforce.

There has been considerable debate over the introduction of affirmative action EEO programs, particularly in the private sector. These programs have been introduced at a time when the political climate in western countries has been increasingly unfavorable to regulation and government intervention in the economy. This may mean a reluctance on the part of governments to provide adequate sanctions for noncompliance or incentives for compliance. It may also mean depriving EEO agencies of resources, so they are unable to perform their role of ensuring that legislation is implemented.

Research has indicated that political will on the part of governments is an important element in the effectiveness of EEO programs, as is the existence of a political base for EEO personnel, whether provided by trade unions, women's caucuses, EEO practitioner organizations, or strong EEO agencies. Without a base that provides political support and social validation of equity principles, isolated EEO officers are likely to become assimilated to prevailing organizational values. This is in any case believed by some critics to be inevitable, given the management focus of EEO programs, and the need for organizations to "own" their programs and to be convinced that they will contribute to greater productivity or profitability.

EEO programs have also been criticized from other directions. Some equate affirmative action for women with violation of the merit principle. This assumes that the existing skewed distribution of the sexes in occupational hierarchies reflects greater merit on the part of men—or greater commitment to paid work, greater competitiveness, greater capacity for leadership, and so on. The way in which merit is constructed is indeed central to EEO, as is the removal of those elements that are more related to homosocial reproduction (like recruiting like) than to job performance (Burton, 1988).

Conservative elements have viewed EEO legislation as a threat to traditional gender roles and to the role of the male as the provider. Women who have chosen to be full-time homemakers have been described as disadvantaged by programs under which their breadwinner is exposed to greater competition from other women. Conservative parties have also fanned resentment at the level of taxation needed to provide community services, which they believe could be provided by women "for nothing" if they were not being encouraged to pursue careers in the paid workforce.

On the other hand, equal opportunity programs have also been criticized for their failure to grapple with issues of class and economic disadvantage and their complicity in maintaining structures of inequality. EEO programs seek not to narrow the gap between top and bottom but rather to remove forms of group closure that prevent individuals from entering nontraditional jobs or rising up the job hierarchy. Such programs do not tackle broader issues of social inequality and may indeed help to legitimize inequality by ensuring that ascriptive criteria such as sex and race do not preclude some individuals from rising to the top, even at the expense of solidarity. Hester Eisenstein (1991) has commented that letting women in has been found more palatable than letting women's values in.

In general, EEO programs are seen as directed more toward ensuring that women can compete for male jobs than toward improving the conditions and remuneration of female jobs. It is difficult to evaluate the effectiveness of EEO programs because of the number of other changes simultaneously occurring in the labor market. Greater equity in employment is described by advocates of EEO as contributing to greater productivity, but there is also a fear that employers will switch production—for example, in female process work—to unregulated free-trade zones in the third world.

The adverse impact of economic restructuring on women in both rich and poor countries has been an insistent theme of recent reports to CEDAW. The cutting of social budgets in the interest of more "productive invest-ment" has a disparate impact on women and adds to their burdens. So although there is increased sophistication regarding the nature of discrimination and in the provision of legal remedies, there is at the same time an adoption of economic policies that undermine the ability of governments to provide equal opportunity.

See Also

AFFIRMATIVE ACTION; DISCRIMINATION; ECONOMIC STATUS: COMPARATIVE ANALYSIS; EQUAL OPPORTUNITIES; EQUITY; NEPOTISM; SEXUAL HARASSMENT; VIOLENCE; WORK: OCCUPATIONAL SEGREGATION

References and Further Reading

Burton, Clare. 1988. *Redefining merit.* Canberra: Australian Government Publishing Service.

Byrnes, Andrew. 1989. The "other" human rights treaty body: The work of the Committee on the Elimination of Discrimination against Women. *Yale Journal of International Law* 14(F1): 1–67.

Eisenstein, Hester. 1991. *Gender shock: Practicing feminism on two continents.* Sydney: Allen and Unwin.

Evatt, Elizabeth. 1990. The next ten years. In *Ten years of the Convention on the Elimination of All Forms of Discrimination against Women.* Occasional paper no. 4 from the Sex Discrimination Commission. Sydney: Human Rights and Equal Opportunity Commission.

Hunter, Rosemary. 1992. *Indirect discrimination in the workplace.* Annandale, New South Wales, Australia: Federation.

International Labor Conference. 1993. *Workers with family responsibilities.* Geneva: International Labor Office.

International Women's Rights Action Watch. 1986–. *CEDAW.* University of Minnesota, Hubert H. Humphrey Institute of Public Affairs.

MacKinnon, Catharine. 1979. *The sexual harassment of working women.* New Haven, Conn.: Yale University Press.

———.1987. *Feminism unmodifid.* Cambridge: Harvard University Press.

Mahoney, Kathleen. 1994. A charter of rights: The Canadian experience. In *Papers on Parliament,* No. 23, Canberra, Australia: Department of the Senate, Parliament House.

Thornton, Margaret. 1990. *The liberal promise: Anti-discrimination legislation in Australia.* Melbourne: Oxford University Press.

Tomasevski, Katarina. 1993. *Women and human rights.* London: Zed.

Marian Sawer

ANTIQUITY

See ANCIENT INDIGENOUS CULTURES: WOMEN'S ROLES; and ANCIENT NATION-STATES: WOMEN'S ROLES.

ANTIRACIST AND CIVIL RIGHTS MOVEMENTS

Antiracist and civil rights movements are significant driving forces in contemporary civil society and are central components of the history of worldwide democratic actions. They are often the springboard for other humanitarian movements, connected by ideas, personnel, structures, and forms of activity.

One of the earliest uses of the term *antiracism* follows a world conference in France in the 1930s, which included anticolonial and antifascist mobilizing (Lloyd, 1998). Antiracist movements vary according to national political cultures. British antiracist organizations tend to identify with the responses to the discrimination faced by postwar migrants or with some of the solidarity organizations set up during the period of decolonization. The publications of the Mouvement Contre le Racisme (MRAP), one of the longest-established organizations in France, refer to the "antiracists" of the Enlightenment, such as the Abbé Grégoire. This poses the problem of how to understand an eighteenth-century mindset in terms of a twentieth-century concept.

Today we would not see Grégoire as an antiracist. He helped establish the Société des Amis des Noirs in the 1790s, which argued that slaves were unprepared for emancipation. They planned a gradual transition based on a paternalistic, European idea of civilization and progress, which the peoples of the rest of the world would have to learn. They distinguished between the present situation and the potential of human populations.

The actions of the African American–Caribbean antislavery campaigners were distinct from those of the white sympathizers. The black antislavery organizations were widespread, helping to provide refuge for runaway slaves. Sojourner Truth, who had spoken at the Women's Rights Convention in 1850, also insisted that black women should be allowed to address the convention in 1851:

> That man over there say that women needs to be helped into carriages, and lifted over ditches, and to have the best place everywhere. Nobody ever helps me into carriages, or over mud-puddles, or gives me any best place! And ain't I a woman? Look at me! Look at

my arm! I could work as much and eat as much as a man—when I could get it—and bear the lash as well! And ain't I a woman? I have borne thirteen children and seen them most all sold off into slavery, and when I cried out with my mother's grief, none but Jesus heard me! And ain't I a woman! (Stanton et al., 1889).

Many of the European and North American organizations for slave emancipation were motivated by evangelical beliefs. The Quakers were an important element, working within an international framework. There was an important link between antislavery and the development of first-wave feminism. When they began to engage in public campaigning, address public meetings, and boycott sugar, women found that men opposed their participation in public life.

In *Blues Legacies and Black Feminism,* Angela Davis shows how in the Reconstruction period that followed the ending of slavery in the United States, black women blues and jazz singers suggested new ways in which women could live. In their songs and lives they struggled to be free from racism and abusive marriages, to travel independently, to earn their own living, and to choose their sexual partners freely (Davis, 1999). Billie Holiday's song "Strange Fruit," a protest against lynching, was, argues Davis, one of the first of many antiracist songs.

Civil Rights and Anticolonialism

The civil rights movement in the United States and anticolonial movements overlap in a number of ways. Activists in the United States frequently referred to their situation as an "internal colony." The civil rights movement coincided with worldwide protests against the war in Vietnam, as well as other anticolonial movements. Mass media and rapid communications helped to produce a consciousness of a global movement.

Earlier gender dynamics continued in both movements. In the United States women played an important part in the mobilizations for black Americans to register to vote and to challenge racial segregation and discrimination. Rosa Parks, tired at the end of her day's work, refused to sit in the "blacks only" section of a bus, initiating a transit boycott in Alabama, the heart of the early civil rights movement. Although women played a significant part, many were relegated to supporting roles: typing, making tea, assisting their male colleagues, and sometimes being sexually exploited.

Similar dynamics operated in anticolonialism and national liberation. Many national liberation movements revived stories of heroic women who resisted colonialism: for example, the Asante queen mother Yaa Asante Waa, who led troops against the British in Ghana in the 1860s, and the

Kabyle heroine in Algeria Al Kahina (Ferrah, 1999). Women resisters took on a symbolic resonance as guardians of a people's integrity and traditions. In Algeria women moudjhadiates played an important role in the war for national liberation; women were also important in Kenya in the Land and Freedom movement, and more recently in Zimbabwe and South Africa. In these and other cases women were pushed aside at independence and were unable to take their place in national governments or other areas of public life.

Feminism and Antiracism

With post-1945 immigration to western Europe, discrimination, restrictive immigration regulations, and racist violence prompted antiracist mobilization. In the 1970s, important debates took place within the antiracist and women's movement in the United Kingdom, informed by earlier experiences. Second-wave feminism was part of a wave of social movements in the West inspired by movements for national liberation, protests against the Vietnam war, and the civil rights movement in the United States.

At the center of feminist arguments in the 1960s and 1970s was patriarchy: the universal system by which women were oppressed by men. This set the terms of debates between women about the priorities of their movement, which had a bearing on the feminist and the antiracist movements. Although the family was the core of white women's oppression, black women defended their families from racism. They argued that the most important problem for them was not patriarchy but racism.

Black women insisted that their specific experience had to be taken into account. Whereas the white women's movement was campaigning for the right to work, black women had always worked, often as domestic workers in the homes of white professional women. While the women's movement campaigned for abortion rights, black women were concerned about the racist effects of population policies which legitimized forced sterilization or the use of dangerous injectable contraceptives. They criticized international campaigns against female circumcision for augmenting sterotyping and at the same time ignoring violence against women closer to home. In France, only a handful of commentators stood back from the debate about Muslim women's appearance to ask more about the meaning of the head scarf for young immigrant women (Gaspard and Khosrokhavar, 1995).

Many black women argued that their oppression was inseparable from racism but could not be reduced to it, wanting to be able to express their grievances while still remaining rooted in their communities. Black women's organizations in the United Kingdom, such as the Organi-

sation of Women of African and Asian Descent, argued that they were subject to "triple oppression": gender, race, and class (Bryan et al., 1985). There were divisions within the black and ethnic minority communities in the United Kingdom over issues such as women's rights, domestic violence, and arranged marriages. Southall Black Sisters continues to campaign on these issues. Although not all black women's organizations would identify themselves as feminists, their priorities have had a great impact on contemporary feminism.

Defining Antiracism

Although antiracism can be seen as an oppositional discourse, it is important to focus on how antiracists organize, what they stand for, and what they do. At an institutional level antiracism is a constellation of organizations shifting between a series of linked pressure groups and a social movement (Heineman, 1972). It is deeply rooted in different political cultures. Antiracist organizations vary from relatively well-endowed statutory bodies such as the British Commission for Racial Equality to more informal organizations run by volunteers at the grassroots level, campaigns based on an individual or family, such as the Stephen Lawrence Family Campaign or politically based movements such as SOS Racisme in France. Broader social movements, such as those of undocumented people or people seeking asylum, have been significant in recent years. The main themes of antiracism are antidiscrimination, representation, solidarity, and the hegemonic establishment of an antiracist common sense indissociable from a wider agenda of social justice. Antiracism also affirms the need to develop different ways in which human beings can relate to one another, respecting human rights and civil liberties.

Another important aspect is the basis of membership within antiracist groups: this varies within and between different countries. Groups can be categorized by whether membership is based on ethnicity or support for a more universalist program (Neveu, 1994), although the same organization may articulate discourses based on different aspects at the same time or during different periods. Antiracists are caught between universalism and particularism: at one level they argue for human equality and the application of social justice. In opposing discrimination, representing and practising solidarity toward certain groups of people, they also work within a particularist agenda.

Globalization emphasizes an increased consciousness of the international, often accompanied by yearnings for the recognition of difference and identity. Politically this may involve an apparent loss of control of key aspects of sovereignty by the nation-state, leading to a focus on the control of its own population and its borders. Under these conditions, power leaves traditional political channels; the result is political demobilization, disillusion with mainstream politics, increasing social insecurity, and swings between universalizing and particularistic impulses. Economic globalization may increase insecurity among migrant and ethnic minority populations. If they have the resources, groups can exploit the enhanced opportunities for rapid communications by means of the Internet and E-mail. At the same time, there are problems of alliance building: structure, hierarchies, equality between well-resourced and impoverished groups. While creating uniformity, globalization also stimulates particularist agendas: racism and extreme forms of nationalism. Thus globalization has produced new problems for antiracists, but it has also opened up new opportunities for dialogues and intervention.

Antiracism is multifaceted and various and cannot be wholly separated from ethnic mobilization. At different levels of mobilization (international, national, civil society, grassroots) organizations vary in their distance from policy makers. Groups close to centers of power benefit from funding and may help to set the political agenda, but they may lose their credibility with the grassroots sections of the antiracist movement who fear their concerns may be diluted. Co-option is dangerous for antiracists because they claim to be representative. Despite cultural and generational differences, "transversal" ways of working, common aims, and respect for the positions of different participants are possible. As a system of "alliances" transversal collectives are unstable over the long term, but they also offer a more tolerant and pluralist way for pressure groups and social movement organizations to cooperate (Yuval-Davis, 1997). This may suggest future forms of international antiracism.

See Also

ACTIVISM; FEMINISM: AFRICAN-AMERICAN; FEMINISM: BLACK BRITISH; FEMINISM: BRITISH ASIAN; NONGOVERNMENTAL ORGANIZATIONS; QUAKERS; RACE; RACISM AND XENOPHOBIA

References and Further Reading

Bryan, B., S. Dadzie, and S. Scafe. 1985. *The heart of the race: Black women's lives in Britain.* London: Virago.

Davis, A. 1999. *Blues legacies and black feminism.* New York: Vintage.

Ferrah, A. 1999. *Kahina.* lger: Editions Marinoor.

Gaspard, F., and F. Khosrokhavar. 1995. *Le foulard et la république.* Paris: La Decouverte.

Heineman, B. 1972. *The politics of the powerless: A study of the campaign against racial discrimination.* Oxford: Oxford University Press.

Lloyd, C. 1998. *Discourses of antiracism in France.* Aldershot: Ashgate.

Neveu, C. 1994. Is "black" an exportable category to mainland Europe? Race and citizenship in a European context. In J. Rex and B. Drury, eds. *Ethnic mobilisation in a multicutural Europe,* 97–105. Aldershot: Avebury.

Stanton, E., S. Anthony, and M. Gage. 1889. *History of woman suffrage.* New York: Susan B. Anthony.

Yuval-Davis, N. 1997. *Gender and nation.* London: Sage.

Catherine Lloyd

ANTIRACIST EDUCATION

See EDUCATION: ANTIRACIST.

ANTI-SEMITISM

Anti-Semitism is a special form of racism, directed toward Jews and based mainly on Christian anti-Judaism. Of course anti-Jewish resentment had existed even before the rise of Christianity—for example, the mistrust and persecution which accompanied Jewish monotheism during the Roman Empire as well as the Jewish people's marginal though powerful position in classical Egypt. This, however, is not comparable to the endemic and enduring Christian persecution of the Jews. Christianity has a specific problematic relationship to Jews, since it has its origins in the Jewish religion and Christ was a Jew. The new religion denied the teachings of the Jewish religion in order to assert its own doctrines. The credibility of Christianity was therefore at stake. The resulting tension is responsible, for example, for the centuries-old reproach that the Jews had murdered Christ.

Christian persecution of the Jews—ubiquitous since the founding of Christianity—was pronounced throughout the late Middle Ages, especially during the Crusades in the eleventh and twelfth centuries and during plagues and epidemics. The Jews were expelled from England in 1290, from France in 1306, and from Spain in 1492. The expulsion from Spain marks the emergence of racist anti-Semitism from religious anti-Judaism.

At that time the Spaniards had reconquered Spain from the Muslims (the Reconquista). This marked the end of a "golden age" of tolerance during which the Jews had experienced a certain degree of acceptance. The Jews were then forced either to leave the country or to convert to Christianity. The "conversos," however, as the converts were called, were never fully accepted or trusted as authentic Christians. With time, this mistrust led to desperate attempts to "prove" Christian authenticity by referring to Christian ancestors. The "impiezza de sangre" (purity of blood) became all-important, and religion became a matter of ancestry, of blood, of race.

The Reconquista coincided with the Conquista, the Christian conquest of the Americas. Therefore—it is often held—the murderous missionaryism in the world outside of Europe's borders ran parallel to the murderous missionaryism within, persecuting all "others," all religious dissidents as well as real or alleged opponents—especially women, who were burned as witches. On this view, Christian missionaryism gave birth to the secular universalism formulated in a Eurocentric male science. Christian doctrine propagates universal equality under (a Christian) God, and secular universalism propagates a universal equality of reason. The criteria set for the equality of secular universalism, based on a Eurocentric male viewpoint, necessarily led to race hierarchy backed by science.

In the eighteenth century a "Semitic race" was constructed from common traits between Judeo-Arab languages. Language, however, was an unsuitable criterion even according to racist standards, so secular anti-Semitism fell back on religious sources. Even anti-Christian racist Nazi Germany was dependent on parochial registration lists for proof of Jewishness. Religious anti-Judaism therefore was a cornerstone for secular anti-Semitism. For example, the central Christian anti-Judaistic figure Judas, who betrayed Jesus for 36 pieces of silver, was represented in the secular anti-Semitic stereotype as the money-hungry, two-faced, underhanded Jew.

In western feminist discourse we also find anti-Semitic Christian traditions, especially in the research on matriarchy. Here Jewish monotheism is charged with killing the mother goddess in a symbolic sense. Feminist theologists attempting to emphasize the androgynity of Christ require a rigid, patriarichal Judaism as a contrast. The image of the lusty old Jew is frequently reactivated in discussions of incest, for example, the story of Lot and his daughters.

In anti-Semitism Jewish women are mostly ignored. The image of the male Jew is usually understood to represent Jewishness. There are, however, a few female stereotypes: for example, the image of the submissive Jewish woman bowing to Jewish patriarchy or, in contrast, the image of the castrating, vengeful Jewess as personified by the biblical figures Judith, Esther, and Salome. The contradic-

tions in anti-Semitic stereotypes are always striking. The anti-Semites had no difficulty declaring a Jewish capitalist conspiracy ("die goldene Internationale," or golden association), that is, a notion that Jews secretly govern the world through their financial superiority, and at the same time portraying Jews as communist revolutionaries and Bolshevists. This contradiction is inherent, for example, in the post-Soviet anti-Semitic Pamjat movement in Russia in the late 1990s. On the one hand, Jews are declared responsible for the disastrous and corrupt socialist system. On the other hand—a typical anti-Zionist attitude—the Jews were accused of being imperialists.

It is important, however, to distinguish between anti-Semitism and colonial racism. According to the racist view, blacks and people of color were considered to be less civilized, more "primitive," somehow subhuman, whereas the Jews in contrast were considered to be "too civilized," too rich, too intelligent, and so on. The Jews supposedly embodied modernity and the cosmopolitan lifestyle. Envy and feelings of inferiority seem to have played an important role in resentment toward Jews.

Another difference between colonial racism and anti-Semitism is that Jews were not strangers from another country but citizens who had lived with Christians side by side for centuries. Colonial racism is based on external economic and political expansion, whereas anti-Semitism is based on an ideal of cultural purity within. This ideal became an obsession that reached its terrible climax in Nazi fascism, when Jews became the ultimate scapegoats. Barely a few months in power, the Nazis had "legally" reduced the Jews to second-class citizens. They were gradually excluded from their professions, it was forbidden for them to marry an "Aryan," they were banned from cultural events, they were forced to wear a yellow star marking them as Jews, and so on. This process of delegitimization finally ended up in the planning of the complete extermination of European Jewry. From 1939 to 1945 about six million Jews were murdered: they were shot, were worked to death, died of disease and hunger, or were gassed in the concentration camps.

The most far-reaching Jewish reaction to the persistent European anti-Semitism was the immigration to Palestine initiated by Herzl in 1896 (der Judenstaat). They were backed by the English (Balfour Declaration, 1917) and founded the state of Israel in 1948. Israel's politics met with critiques and resistance. A campaign was launched against "the" Jews, leaning upon traditional anti-Semitic stereotypes, especially the stereotype depicting Jewry as a secret world power. It is argued that Jews should have learned from their own history as victims of the Holocaust and should—more than others—consequently turn away from violence. Their tragic loss is therefore used against them.

The conflicts over Jewish settlement in Israel have taken on many of the discursive and ideological elements of traditional European anti-Semitism. The Islamization of anti-Semitism is the most important recent change (Lewis, 1986).

See Also

FASCISM AND NAZISM

References and Further Reading

Adorno, Theodor, et al. 1993. *The authoritarian personality.* New York: Norton.

Heschel, Susannah. 1992. *From the Bible to Nazism: German feminists on the Jewish origins of patriarchy.* Tel Aviver Jahrbuch für deutsche Geschichte Tel Aviv.

Poliakov, Leon. 1977–1987. Geschichte des Antisemitismus 6 Bde. Worms.

Mosse, G. L. 1970. *Germans and Jews.* New York: Fertig.

Plaskow, Judith. 1978. Blaming the Jews for the birth of patriarchy. *Cross Currents.*

Birgit Rommelspacher

APARTHEID, SEGREGATION, AND GHETTOIZATION

Apartheid, segregation, and ghettoization all entail enforced separation of communities that are identified by ascribed differences of race, religion, caste, or nationality. The separation is generally between unequal groups. Thus, in such societies, greater access to political, economic, and social power is usually vested in certain groups and specifically forbidden to others. Under conditions of apartheid, segregation, or ghettoization, gender differences are often amplified, partly because of the need to control the membership of both dominant and subordinate groups through birth and marriage. Hence particular controls are exerted over women to maintain racial purity, for example, or to ensure that religious instruction is carried out appropriately in the home. Despite the powerful enforcement of identities in such societies, however, women often have been active in opposing the controls placed on them, and in creating bonds across the boundaries that separate them from women and men of different groups.

Apartheid, narrowly defined, was the political and economic system that prevailed in South Africa between 1948 and 1990. This system of laws decreed that all South Africans should be assigned membership in a racialized group. Different racialized groups had different levels of access to political power and economic and social resources. Thus, those defined as white—although a relatively small minority of the population—controlled all the major political institutions; owned most of the land, the mines, and the industrial wealth; and earned higher wages than the black majority. White South Africans had better education and health care, better housing, and better social welfare. Most white women, though owning less than white men and earning lower wages, generally had a much better standard of living than black men and women.

Apartheid was a form of *segregation*, the division of populations based on perceived racial, linguistic, religious, caste, or national differences. Segregation generally entails a separation of social activities (for example, housing or schooling) that reinforces and may be used to legitimate political and economic inequalities between groups. All societies that practice segregation value certain groups more highly than others. One purpose of segregation is to regulate political, economic, and social relations so that the power of the dominant group, which may be a majority or a minority, is not threatened. Examples of segregation are the different treatment accorded to African-Americans in many parts of the United States, enforced settlement of low-caste people on the outskirts of towns and villages in parts of India, and the division of some cities of Northern Ireland between Protestant and Catholic communities.

Although in segregated societies there are gender inequalities within racial or religious groups, these gender divisions may have different features from group to group. The different forms of gender inequity must be examined within the context of segregation. Women of dominant groups may not suffer the same gender discrimination as women form subordinate groups, and generally have better living conditions than both women and men from subordinate groups. Thus women from a subordinate group, although subject to strict controls within it, may in fact identify more with men from that group because of the shared conditions of hardship at the hands of the dominant group. Achieving a universal feminism across the boundaries of segregated societies is therefore problematic, despite the similar forms of oppression women suffer within racialized or nationally defined communities.

Apartheid no longer describes South African society, which has changed dramatically since its first democratic elections in 1994. The term is now used widely outside South

Africa, however, to describe segregation and the accompanying political, economic, and social inequality.

Ghettoization has many features similar to apartheid. The word *ghetto* was used from the twelfth century in Europe to identify parts of cities where Jews were compelled to live. Segregated in ghettos, they could work only in certain occupations. The dominant population was generally hostile and strictly limited its interaction with the ghetto. From the beginning of the nineteenth century, European Jews slowly gained some measure of acceptance and moved out of the ghetto. The term continues to be used, however, to signify any area where a group—generally noticeably different from and considered inferior to the majority of the population of a city—is forced to live. One of the clearest examples of ghettoization at the turn of the twenty-first century can be seen in the treatment of the Roma (Gypsies) in various postcommunist central and eastern European countries. Ghettoization, evident in cities of North America that have distinct communities of black and white, is now usually the result of discrimination in housing and employment and fear of violence. While the laws of a country such as the United States do not enforce ghettoization as it was applied in Europe against Jews, neither do the laws make it easy for African-Americans to overcome social discrimination. Thus, for example, the decentralization of schools means that unequal education resources are available for poor ghetto communities.

Because segregation, apartheid, and ghettoization all work by delimiting which groups can live in certain places and have access to certain resources, all rely on some form of biological or social marker for members of a particular group. Women, because they bear children, are important in this regard. Dominant groups go to great lengths to keep "their" women from living or working with subordinated groups, except in settings where appropriate relations between groups are established. For example, women from subordinated groups may be employed as domestic workers by dominant groups. Strict rules, however, often govern the kinds of domestic work they can do. They may be allowed to be nannies to young children, for example, but not to teach somewhat older children; they may be allowed to be cleaners or work outside, but not to cook or touch food. These rules vary considerably from society to society.

Often women who cross these socially imposed boundaries are vilified. For instance, the apartheid system imposed strict legal sanctions against sex or marriage across racial barriers. The South African writer Bessie Head was the child of a rich white South African woman and a black man who worked in her father's stables. Head was brought up in an orphanage after her mother was placed in a mental asylum for crossing the barrier.

Although gender discrimination is marked in segregated societies, gender cannot be understood in these societies outside of the additional forms of segregated social division maintained by the legal, economic, and social framework. In such societies women are generally not easily able to work together politically despite their common experience of gender discrimination. However, both women and men have joined opposition movements, which often unite people across imposed divisions of nationality, caste, or race. Thus, in South Africa, action against apartheid was undertaken by people of all races, often working together in nonracial organizations. Small numbers of white women were critics of apartheid and tried to work together with black women in organizations based on class (like the trade unions and the Communist Party) or in organizations based on liberal ideas about human rights, or in the national liberation movement of the African National Congress (ANC). In segregated societies such as South Africa under apartheid, or parts of the United States or Israel, alliances made by women across boundaries of race or religion have been very fragile and sometimes difficult to maintain. Nonetheless, in many segregated societies, the high degree of discrimination against women, even those of dominant groups, means they are often more receptive to ideas and political strategies that try to break down barriers. Women from dominant groups often differ in this way from men of those groups, who may have vested interests in maintaining the system. In South Africa, women's contribution to the resistance against apartheid is celebrated on Women's Day, a national holiday on August 9th, which commemorates a large and courageous protest, held mainly by black women with the support of a small number of white women.

See Also

FEMINISM: AFRICAN-AMERICAN; FEMINISM: SOUTH AFRICA; HOUSEHOLD WORKERS; RACE; RACISM AND XENOPHOBIA

References and Further Reading

Anthias, F., and N. Yuval-Davis. 1989. *Woman-nation-state.* London: Macmillan.

Cock, J., 1989. *Maids and madams.* London: Women's Press.

Cockburn, C., *1998. The space between us: Negotiating gender and national identities in conflict.* London: Zed.

Stasiulis, D., and N. Yuval-Davis. 1995. *Unsettling settler societies: Articulations of gender, race, ethnicity, and class.* London: Sage.

Young, G., and B. J. Dickerson. 1994. *Color, class, and country: Experiences of gender* London: Zed.

Unterhalte, E., 1987. *Forced removal: The division, segregation, and control of the people of South Africa.* London: International Defence and Aid Fund for Southern Africa.

Walker, C., 1982. *Women and resistance in South Africa.* London: Onyx.

Elaine Unterhalter

ARCHAEOLOGY

Archaeology is the study of the past; it aims to reconstruct the way people lived in the past and to explore and reconstruct past cultures. To this end, archaeologists study material culture—that is, things made and used by humans. The term *material culture* assumes that the manufacture and use of artifacts and other objects will in some way be influenced by and reflect the culture of the period or people that made and used the objects. Archaeologists also study remains of humans as well as plants and animals that were used as food or domesticated.

Archaeology and Its Masculine Image

Indiana Jones is a popular Hollywood character who portrays the archaeologist's professional life as one full of high adventure, treasure hunts, and danger. The masculine stereotype personified by Indiana Jones is one that has been widely held about archaeologists for a long time. For instance, in 1949 A. V. Kidder noted that two publicly held stereotypes existed: that of the "hairy chested" archaeologist seeking adventure and treasure and that of the "hairy chinned" archaeologist, a vague although highly intelligent type, capable of correctly interpreting the most puzzling aspects of the past (Ascher, 1960). These romantic images have little or no relevance in describing the actual nature of archaeological research and endeavor. However, a number of commentators have noted that these images do have some currency in archaeology because they are often used, particularly in western countries, to socialize students into the "culture" of the discipline (see Woodall and Perricone, 1981; Zarmati, 1995, for further details). Masculine images, particularly of "cowboys," are used to develop camaraderie on excavations and during other fieldwork. They are images that, in the view of many women archaeologists, work to marginalize both them and their research (see Nelson et al., 1994).

Feminist Archaeology

Feminist archaeology arose in part as a response to the existence of these stereotypes in the discipline, and in part as a response to assumptions made about the nature of gender relations in the past. Many researchers assumed that the western gender division of labor was "natural" and thus unworthy of critical scrutiny. Interpretations regarding the past often implicitly assumed that men made most artifacts, hunted, went to war, and were the main contributors to religious and intellectual life. On the other hand, it was assumed that women gathered food, cared for children, and were often invisible in the archaeological record because they were not primary actors in developing technologies and making tools. Early feminist researchers were able to show the fallacy of these assumptions by examining women's grave sites, such as those described by Merete Ipsen, which contained tools and weapons that, in other contexts, had been assumed to have been made and used by men.

The feminist response in archaeology developed during the 1980s with a number of aims and goals. One of the primary goals was to challenge many of the androcentric assumptions made by archaeologists and to illustrate the extent to which many researchers unwittingly extrapolate present-day values and assumptions about gender into the past. Another goal was to introduce "gender" as an active and critical factor in the interpretation of past material culture, and, by so doing, to bring archaeological theory up-to-date with a number of sister disciplines already studying gender issues. Another primary goal was to challenge the masculine stereotypes of the discipline and to provide women with a support network to better the working conditions and career prospects of women archaeologists. Organizations such as Kvindelige Arkaeologer i Norge (KAN) and Women in Archaeology (Australia) were developed to provide these networks of support.

Conferences were held to promote gender research, many of which have had significant impacts on archaeological theoretical debates and on research questions and interpretations. The earliest and most nationally or internationally influential conferences and resulting publications included one held in Norway in 1979 (Bertelsen et al., 1987); "Women and Production in Prehistory," 1988, South Carolina, United States (Gero and Conkey, 1991); 1989 Chacmool Conference, Canada (Walde and Willows, 1991); "Feminism and Archaeology?!" 1991, Germany (Kastner and Karlisch, 1991); Women in Archaeology, 1991, Australia (du Cros and Smith, 1993); and many more (e.g., Claassen, 1992, 1994). Some of these conferences, such as Women in Archaeology (Australia) are now held biannually (Balme and Beck, 1995; Casey et al., 1998), and many annual mainstream archaeological conferences now have sessions dedicated to gender and feminist research.

A further goal of feminist archaeology was to challenge the "naturalness" of present-day gender categories and roles. Archaeology as a study of the past is in a significant position, although an apparently paradoxical one, to question the way in which the present is understood. The past is used to validate what we do in the present and to help us understand ourselves and our culture. For instance, we may use the history and past of the country we live in to help us define our cultural or national identity. The fact that archaeology examines physical evidence further reinforces the role archaeological research can play in reinforcing the use of the past in understanding and validating the present. This thing we call "the past" is intangible and often difficult to conceptualize. However, the tangibility and physical reality of material culture help to give substance to the past and to the links we may make between the past and the present.

Feminist archaeologists have thus argued that interpretations of our past have a real ability to influence how we see the present. Studies of past material culture that question how gender categories and roles were organized in the past will have an impact on public debates about present-day gender roles. This goal of feminist archaeology has significant implications not only for archaeological research but also on how archaeologists manage archaeological sites and places for the future.

Cultural Heritage

Archaeologists in many countries not only research the past but may also be active players in the management of their country's heritage. Archaeological sites, artifacts, and places are often part of a country's or a people's cultural heritage. The process of looking after a cultural heritage is called "cultural heritage management" or "cultural resource management" or even "archaeological heritage management." Feminists involved in cultural heritage management are concerned to identify, save, and preserve places of value and significance to women. Feminist archaeologists argue that the preservation of women's heritage will ensure that women's history, culture, and past experiences will be made visible and that women will be acknowledged as having made important contributions to the present. If women's heritage and material culture are not saved and actively managed, then it is possible that the roles that women played in the past will remain or be regarded as invisible and intangible. Further, the multiplicity and complexity of women's experiences and cultures may also be explored and celebrated through the conservation and preservation of the range of material culture and heritage associated with past women's lives.

A significant part of cultural heritage management is the interpretation of heritage for the public. The physicality offered by material culture provides a significant resource through which critical interpretations that challenge androcentric notions about gender roles in the past and present can be made. Thus, it is through cultural heritage management that feminist archaeologists may have a direct and active impact on public perceptions about past and present gender roles and experiences.

Future Directions in Feminist Research

Although there have now been two decades of active feminist debate in archaeology, many androcentric assumptions and practices still remain. Initially, feminist archaeologists—in challenging archaeological androcentric preconceptions—attempted to identify individual women in the past, a practice that has left two legacies. The first concerns a tendency by many to equate "gender" issues with women; when this happens, the identification of gender in the past becomes simply a matter of "finding women." The concept that males are gendered and that masculinity may be a variable in the interpretation of the past is yet to be self-consciously taken up in archaeological discourse. The second legacy is the realization that in many cases archaeology cannot identify individual women or men in the past, and that the desire to identify individuals in fact limits the scope of archaeological interpretation and debate. Rather, the recognition of gender as a variable of interpretation has the exciting potential to extend the scope of archaeological endeavor to include an examination of dynamics, complexities, and developments in gender relations in the past.

See Also

ANDOCENTRISM; ANTHROPOLOGY; ARCHAEOLOGY: NORTHERN EUROPEAN CASE STUDY; HISTORY; HUNTING; PRIMATOLOGY; SCIENCE: FEMINIST CRITIQUES

References and Further Reading

Ascher, Robert. 1960. Archaeology and the public image. *American Antiquity* 25(3): 402–403.

Balme, Jane, and Wendy Beck, eds. 1995. *Gendered archaeology.* Canberra: ANH Publications, Research School of Pacific and Asian Studies, Australian National University.

Bertelsen, R., A. Lillehammer, and J. R. Naess, eds. 1987. *Were they all men?* Stavanger, Norway: Arkaeologish Museum i Stavanger.

Casey, Mary, Denise Donlan, Jeannette Hope, and Sharon Wellfare, eds. 1998. *Redefining archaeology: Feminist per-*

spectives. Canberra: ANH Publications, Research School of Pacific and Asian Studies, Australian National University.

Claassen, Cheryl, ed. 1992. *Exploring gender through archaeology: Selected papers from the 1991 Boone conference*. Madison, Wis.: Prehistory.

———, ed. 1994. *Women in archaeology*. Philadelphia: University of Pennsylvania Press.

Díaz-Andreu, Margarita, and Marie Louise Stig Sorensen, eds. 1998. *Women in European archaeology*. London: Routledge.

du Cros, Hilary, and Laurajane Smith, eds. 1993. *Women in archaeology: A feminist critique*. Canberra: ANH Publications, Research School of Pacific and Asian Studies, Australian National University.

Gero, Joan M., and Margaret W. Conkey, eds. 1991. *Engendering archaeology: Women and prehistory*. Oxford: Blackwell.

Kästner, Sibylle, and Sigrun M. Karlisch, eds. 1991. *Feminismus und Archäologie?!* Tübingen: Institut für Vor- und Frühgeschichte.

Nelson, Margaret C., Sarah M. Nelson, and Alison Wylie, eds. 1994. *Equity issues for women in archaeology*. Washington, D.C.: Archaeological Papers of the American Anthropological Association Number 5.

Smith, Laurajane. 1995. Cultural resource management and feminist expression in Australian archaeology. *Norwegian Archaeological Review* 28(1) 55–63.

Walde, Dale, and Noreen D. Willows, eds. 1991. *The archaeology of gender*. Calgary: University of Calgary Archaeological Association.

Woodall, J. Ned, and Phillip J. Perricone. 1981. The archaeologist as cowboy: The consequence of professional stereotype. *Journal of Field Archaeology* 8: 506–509.

Zarmati, Louise. 1995. Popular archaeology, and the archaeologist as hero. In Jane Balme and Wendy Beck, eds., *Gendered archaeology*. Canberra: ANH Publications, Research School of Pacific and Asian Studies, Australian National University.

Laurajane Smith

ARCHAEOLOGY:
Northern European Case Study

Archaeological findings are the physical remains of our past, and when we look at them they can change the way we see the past. Archaeologists find real things, and as a science archaeology presents us with concrete, tangible knowledge. But we need to be aware of the ways in which such knowledge is filtered through what we already know or think we know. The knowledge generated by archaeological findings is shaped and reshaped both by the period in which these discoveries are made and by what the people who seek and find information from the past tell us about it and how they interpret it.

For women anthropologists, archaeologists, historians, and psychologists it is important that we make our own discoveries, but even more important that we interpret the findings ourselves—that we trace the steps of prehistoric women and witness their actions through the interpretation of their bones, their tools, and their utensils.

The majority of excavation reports and museum exhibitions present the actions of men and women and the relationship between them in such a way that the man is seen as active, strong, and dominant, whereas the woman is seen as dependent and in need of protection.

This article presents a number of archaeological findings from Scandinavia that can be seen to challenge commonly held beliefs about the prehistoric relationship between the sexes.

Man, the Hunter

More often than not, our prehistoric forefathers are represented trough masculine metaphors. In western European culture it is the exception rather than the rule for these, the oldest remains of the human race, to be spoken of as belonging to our foremothers.

In most of the findings men have a larger physique than women, leading to theories claiming that the choice of a partner was primarily the initiative of males. Darwin's theory of evolution of the mid-1800s had a great impact on the interpretation of human—indeed all species'—development. In Darwin's theory, male strength and dominance are the motivating forces behind the reproduction of the species. Among humans, gender characteristics such as the strength of the male and the weakness of the female are amplified by the males' choice of curvaceous partners with little body hair and the females' preference for large and powerful suitors. The Darwinian theory of evolution perpetrates this gendered division of strength and weakness in much the same way as the Victorians did in Darwin's time.

Similarly, according to such theories, it was man who was the prehistoric inventor of tools—tools for hunting and battle. Women's tools as gatherers—which many anthropologists and archaeologists agree was their "natural" occupation—are largely ignored, as is the inventiveness involved in the development of tools like digging sticks and bags to carry the gathered roots, seeds, berries, and small animals.

Man, then, is the warrior. Some women like to pride themselves on their allegedly peaceful nature, but in the context of this discussion, to be the peaceful sex is to be the passive sex. Do the archaeological findings support this view of man as the initiator in the choice of partner, the protector, and the warrior, and of woman as the hesitant, passive pacifist?

When a grave containing swords and hunting tools is discovered, archaeologists see it as unambiguously male. On this issue there is widespread agreement. Women's graves contain household utensils such as pots, knives, sewing equipment, and jewelry.

Valkyries and Queens

A number of findings do, however, support an interpretation different from that of the weak, dependent woman. What follows is a discussion of three very different discoveries, all thought to be between 1,000 and 1,200 years old.

During the past 15 years an unusual discovery was made in Denmark: two skeletons buried alongside each other. One was small and slender, with stones on the chest to prevent the deceased from rising again. Buried with the body were a sword, a knife, and a needle case. The skeleton's dimensions—especially the width of the hips—together with the knife and needle case, all led to the same conclusion: the remains were those of a woman. But the sword was unusual in a woman's grave; thus this discovery was called the Valkyrie grave.

The second skeleton was that of a tall, well-built person—without doubt a man. The neck was broken as it would be after hanging. Possibly the body was that of a slave. He had neither a sword nor a knife to protect himself, and there were no stones to prevent him rising from the burial place. There are no conclusive theories as to why he was hanged and buried with the woman.

What is interesting in this context is that the woman has a sword. It did happen that women bore arms. Chronicles, such as those of Saxo, written 800 years ago, tell of women's participation in armed battle in much the same way as those that recount the battles of the Greek Amazons. These accounts are usually regarded as myths. Contrary to this interpretation, however, the discovery of the female skeleton provided concrete evidence that women might bear arms.

Three brooches from the same period have also been found, two in Denmark and one in Sweden. The motif that decorates them is a mounted woman bearing a sword. She is being offered a goblet of wine, is being saluted, and is obviously of high rank and a warrior.

This picture of independent women from the same period in prehistoric Scandinavia is strengthened by a very important discovery, made as early as 1904: the Oseberg grave in Norway. Two people were buried (A.D. 834) in a well-equipped ship containing coffers, household utensils, and many other artifacts, including a fascinating small tapestry depicting sword-bearing women in a funeral procession together with men. The remains are believed to be those of a queen and her female servant.

Such discoveries make any simple interpretation of the relative strength of men and women during this period impossible. Not all prehistoric women were dependent on strong, protective men. Some were independent and equal with men, while others were queens or rulers of both men and women. We do not know how many such women existed, but it seems feasible that there were more than the interpretations of archaeologists would lead us to believe.

Sexing the Remains

Just as there is today, in prehistoric times there was a wide range of body sizes for both men and women—tall women who were larger than short men, slender women who were tinier than large men. Perhaps graves containing swords belong to women more often than we are told. It is difficult to classify remains as male or female merely by looking at the skeleton. When asked, all archaeologists and paleoanthropologists admit that there are no absolute deciding factors; they have only body height and breadth and hip width to judge by—all of which are very much open to interpretation.

Today's DNA analysis would appear to make such uncertainties a thing of the past. But DNA analysis of remains is expensive and is itself plagued with uncertainty. The slightest contact with the remains during excavation or examination can result in the modern scientist's DNA code being taken instead of that of the excavated skeleton. Thus scientists can at best make only educated guesses about the sex of remains.

The findings discussed above raise important questions about the interpretation of gender and behavior in prehistoric times. But unfortunately this questioning has had very little impact on the way in which prehistoric life continues to be presented. Time and again museum exhibitions in Scandinavia present a child's skeleton with a knife, and viewers are told, without a trace of doubt, that the skeleton is that of a little boy who was buried with his knife. Why not a little girl? As mentioned above, knives are among the most common tools found in women's graves. Therefore, a little girl—who was presumably taught by her mother—might have a knife at her side when she was buried. Perhaps archaeology is as blinded by contemporary images and expectations as Darwin's theory of evolution and gender. Perhaps it is thought unsuitable for a little girl to use a knife. Perhaps knives are more immediately associated in the modern mind with bold boys than with girls. Until physical analyses can accurately identify the sex of all human remains, we can only speculate.

The discoveries described above all come from the latter years of the Viking period of Nordic history. This period also marked the end of a paganism in which Nordic mythology formed the basis of religious beliefs. Cults of fertility were at the core of Nordic paganism, which elevated the status of women, associating them with Mother Earth and the goddess of fertility.

Goddesses and Priestesses

The worship of personified gods was apparently not practiced at the time in the same way that it is in contemporary Christian culture. Since the mid-1500s Protestantism has been the predominant religion of northern Europe—a religion based on male figures: the Father, his Son, and the Holy Spirit, with all their masculine characteristics.

Around the turn of the twentieth century there were a number of interesting archaeological discoveries, which have formed the basis for theories of widespread goddess worship in our past. Throughout Europe at this time small, full-bodied Venus figures were discovered. These statues pay tribute to women and are an homage to the female form. No male figures were discovered at the same sites; this would seem to point strongly toward goddess worship in our distant past.

In pagan times in the Nordic region the asa (pre-Christian) beliefs were central to all aspects of life. Sacrifices and other religious rituals are believed to have been as significant as the work of the individual in sowing and reaping crops. With fertility rituals it seems most logical that the religious ceremonies of the farming communities would have been led by women.

In Denmark in 1891 a large ancient silver vessel was found in a swamp. It was decorated with fantastic patterns, including images of women. The vessel is thought to date from around 100 B.C., and the decorative motifs, together with the techniques used, indicate that it was probably brought to Denmark during a migration from the Celtic regions.

The vessel is decorated with many relief images of animals and people—or beings that resemble people. There is no direct narrative in the pictures, which show men fighting with wild animals and marching with swords and shields. But the base of the vessel is decorated with a picture of a wounded bull awaiting the final merciful blow. The killer, a woman, is shown with her sword drawn behind the bull's back. The vessel was probably used for blood offerings, and the seven upper panels all show different people. The missing eighth panel probably continued the motif of the upper torsos of men and women. They could be male or female gods or priests and are the same size, indicating that they are of equal importance. The men, shown in four of these panels, have their hands in the air as if they are surrendering, while the women in the remaining three panels all have contact with their own bodies. One touches her breasts, while a man fights with a wild animal near her; one bears a small man in her arm whom she is about to suckle, while a dog lies beside her other breast, and a small woman stands arranging her hair. The last woman is flanked by two men with the characteristic raised arms.

This vessel is evidence of the cross-cultural exchange of religious representations, and it functions in the same way as the goddess status to show the high, or at least the equal, status women had in prehistoric religious rituals.

Despite evidence such as this, we are still given our knowledge of the past through myths of fore*fathers* and concepts of heroism attached to men. Dominant scientific traditions focus on prehistoric man. These traditions either refuse to take alternative evidence into account or else represent it as aberrations without meaning or relevance to an understanding of the life of Nordic peoples in prehistoric times.

Almost 15 years ago a group of women archaeologists in Norway formed the association Kvindelige Arkaeologer i Norge, KAN (Women archaeologists in Norway; *kan* means *can* in English). This association has the dual goals of bringing gender analysis to archaeological findings and spreading knowledge of the alternative interpretations that an awareness of gender can bring to the field. Similar organizations have yet to be established in Denmark and Sweden, but informal networks and multidisciplinary forums create an environment for research, interpretation, and representation with an awareness how projections from our present—particularly our gender roles and rules—can affect our understanding of the past.

See Also

ANTHROPOLOGY; ARCHAEOLOGY; GODDESS; HUNTING; PRIMATOLOGY

References and Further Reading

Dahlberg, Frances, ed. 1981. *Woman the gatherer.* New Haven, Conn.: Yale University Press.

Darwin, Charles. 1871. *The descent of man and selection in relation to sex.* New York: Modern Library.

Müller, Sophus. 1892. *Det store Sölvkar fra Gundestrup.* Copenhagen: Nordiske Fortidsminder.

Saxos Danmarks Krönnike (Saxonis Grammatici Historia Danica). [ca. 1210] 1898. Copenhagen: A. Christiansen.

Merete Ipsen

ARCHETYPE

Archetype is a term occurring as early as Philo Judaeus (13 B.C. –A.D 45) and Irenaeus (c. A.D. 130–200), used by Plato (428–348 B.C.) and Augustine (d. 604 A.D.), and adopted by the twentieth-century psychiatrist and psychologist C. G. Jung to describe "universal images that have existed since the remotest times" (Jung, *Collected Works CW* 9:1, 4–5, para. 5). For Jung the archetype "is an irrepresentable unconscious, pre-existent form that seems to be part of the inherited structure of the psyche and can therefore manifest itself spontaneously anywhere, at any time" (1963: 380). Evidence for the existence of archetypes can be found in recurrent motifs in world myths, fairy tales, and religious texts, as well as in personal dreams, fantasies, hallucinations, and delusions at every time in history.

Archetypes symbolize the life of the nonindividual depths of the unconscious psyche that everyone experiences but that no one possesses. One feels the instinctual "drive-effects" of the archetype, its emotional patterns and images, but without experiencing the archetype per se, because "an archetypal content expresses itself, first and foremost, in metaphors." (*CW* 9:1, 157, para. 267). In order, then, to be in touch with the objective reality that archetypal symbols communicate, one must be wiling to work with the imagination and to trust it.

Archetypes have biological and psychological aspects, as well as form and content. The biological aspect denotes inherited modes of psychic functioning that are preformed, instinctual patterns of response, experienced psychologically in individual lives as goal-directedness of purposeful behavior, in patterns of emotional response and expectation, and in value systems. Jung describes this sort of primordial archetypal image as "the *instinct's perception of itself*" (*CW* 8, 136, para. 275). The archetypes, like the instincts, are part of the given structure of life, although their patterns may be modified over the centuries. Jung calls them "organs of the pre-rational psyche" (*CW* 11, 518, para. 845).

Archetypes are not determined as to content but are determined only in form. For example, one's experience of the mother archetype comprises one's actual relation to one's own specific mother and other maternal figures, both positive and negative, of one's culture's images of the mothering role, as well as the primordial images of the mother that arise in everyone spontaneously from the deep unconscious. Like instincts, archetypes underlie the feeling-toned complexes in individuals' psyches but are themselves purely formal, beginning only as a possibility of representation that is later to be filled in by one's actual living experience.

Important archetypal images of woman include mother, daughter, amazon, witch, wife, virgin, siren, spiritual partner, sister, hetira, and wise woman. In religion, such figures as Lilith, Eve, Kali, Kwan-Yin, the Virgin Mary, and Sophia personify archetypal images of feminine potency. The feminine modality of being makes itself known in human history in various archetypal forms, that is, in recurrent clusters of images and patterns of behavior associated with certain dominant types of the feminine. The fundamental archetypal forms of the feminine come from various combinations of one's basic instinctual traits, from the influence of environment and culture, and from one's adaptation to these factors.

These archetypal patterns are only a potential presence in individuals, never predetermined as to content. An individual woman must work out her personal relation to the conditioning images of her culture and the primordial images that address her from her own experience of the unconscious. Often a woman finds strength to defy and to influence cultural stereotypes of the female from the power that the primordial images in her own unconscious provide.

See Also

DAUGHTER; FAIRY TALES; FEMININITY; MOTHER; MYTH; WIFE; WITCHES: ASIA; WITCHES: WESTERN WORLD

References and Further Reading

Lauter, Estella, and Carol Schreier Rupprecht, eds. 1985. *Feminist archetypal theory: Interdisciplinary re-visions of Jungian thought.* Knoxville: University of Tennessee Press.

Jung, C. G., 1953–1975. *Collected works.* Trans. R. F. C. Hull. Published by the Bollingen Foundation (Bollingen Series XX) in the United States by Princeton University Press and in England by Routledge and Kegan Paul.

———. 1963. *Memories, dreams, reflections.* Recorded and ed. Aniela Jaffé. Trans. Richard and Clara Winston. New York: Pantheon.

Ulanov, Ann Belford. 1971. *The feminine in Jungian psychology and in Christian theology.* Evanston, Ill: Northwestern University Press.

Ann Belford Ulanov

ARCHITECTURE

Buildings, neighborhoods, and cities are cultural artifacts that symbolically declare to society the place held by each of their members. This is true among all cultures throughout time, from the spatial segregation of women from men in the domestic architecture of almost all Islamic societies, to the segregation of rich and poor in luxury housing and public housing in North American cities.

Even though built space shapes the experiences of people's daily lives and the cultural assumptions in which they are immersed, it is easy to accept the physical landscape unthinkingly as a neutral background. But the spatial arrangements of buildings and communities are neither value-free nor neutral; they reflect and reinforce the nature of each society's gender, race, and class relations. They are shaped by social, political, and economic forces and values embodied in the forms themselves, the processes through which they are built, and the manner in which they are used. The built environment contributes to the power of some groups over others and the maintenance of human inequality.

Architecture thus defined is a record of deeds by those who have the power to build. Professional architects, be they women or men, generally have little to say about what actually gets built, where, how, and for whom. Most of these decisions are made by men, who are the majority of industrialists, financiers, building developers, engineers, politicians, real estate investors, and corporate heads. Individual buildings designed by architects as technologically and aesthetically unified works of art represent only a small percentage of this larger anonymous landscape.

While it is possible to critique architectural history, education, and practice, as well as built architectural work, from a feminist perspective, it is within the cultural context of built space that feminist criticism and activism have an especially important role to play. Therefore, this article will introduce the former and focus on the latter.

Women, Feminism, and the Discipline of Architecture

A feminist analysis of the built environment as a form of social oppression, an expression of social power, and a part of women's struggle for equality is relatively recent. The reason is that such an evaluation would logically be initiated by women architects, and there are simply fewer of them worldwide than there are women in other fields and fewer still who are committed to feminism and directing their work accordingly.

Entry into the architectural profession was historically accomplished either by gaining practical experience as an apprentice in the atelier of a master architect or by obtaining a formal architectural education. Both routes presented formidable obstacles for women. Whereas the personal prejudice of individual males made it difficult for women to obtain professional training through apprenticeship, discriminatory policies in the academy made it equally difficult for women to obtain architectural degrees.

Although the percentage of women practicing architecture varies from country to country, it has been consistently low. In 1989 in Great Britain, the proportion was 10 percent, in Norway 19 percent, and in New South Wales, Australia, 3.2 percent. In the United States in 1988, 14.6 percent of architects were women; in 1983, the figure in Spain was 3 percent. While the percentage slowly increased worldwide throughout the 1980s and 1990s (although in some countries it actually decreased) today women remain dramatically underrepresented in the field. The same is true in architectural education. Among the total number of architecture faculty members teaching in accredited degree programs in North American universities in 1990, women represented only 15.7 percent, and of this total, only 2.8 percent were tenured. Moreover, although the enrollment of women students in schools of architecture in North America made up 30 percent of the bachelor's programs and 40 percent of the master's programs between 1993 and 1994, enrollment patterns are very uneven among schools; in some, women may number as high as 50 percent; in others, there are too few to count.

Throughout the 1950s, 1960s, and early 1970s, the education and employment experiences of women in architecture paralleled those of other professional women in male-dominated fields. In the schools students were not taken seriously; there was a paucity of women professors, and among them the design studio "master" was a rarity. In architectural practice women made less money than men and in the large firms were clustered in lower-status ancillary specialities and were promoted less. Few had achieved associate or partner status; fewer still had their own practices.

The New Feminism versus the Old Professionalism

Beginning in the late 1960s, the "new" lessons of feminism caused significant numbers of women architects and architectural educators to shift their energies from proving that they could work in a man's field to challenging architectural practice itself. Advocates of change within the established profession sought to identify and eliminate various forms of discrimination and to develop an affirmative action plan; to promote careers for women in architecture and to help prepare women for professional licensing exams; and to revise the traditional office work structure to incorporate flexible and part-time schedules helpful to women with families.

Advocates of change outside the established profession began to form women's design collectives in which all members participated equally in decision making. The inherent conflict between the profit motive and the social responsibility of the architect was resolved by paying members only for work done and using the profits to subsidize projects beneficial to women. The professional practitioner identified with nonprofessionals as clients and collaborators by accepting and respecting their values, life experiences, and aesthetic preferences, even when they violated the canon of "architects' architecture."

Women and Environments

Beginning in the late 1970s, feminist architects, sociologists, historians, planners, geographers, and environmental psychologists joined forces to create a new cross-disciplinary field of research known as *women and environments*. Four dominant directions emerged to guide this ongoing work.

The first direction emphasized gender-based *spatial dichotomies* produced by industrial capitalism: the segregation of workplace and dwelling, cities and suburbs, and private life from public existence. Academicians analyzed how proscriptive residential zoning prevents the establishment of neighborhood-based commercial services essential to women and prohibits home occupations that would make the combination of work and family roles easier. Architects and planners proposed designing new forms of congregate and cohousing in neighborhoods that would encourage personal support, companionship, and the sharing of domestic tasks.

The second direction, *environmental fit,* provided empirical research on the compatibility between the activities that characterize women's daily lives and the design of dwellings, neighborhoods, and cities. For example, in North America, inner-city neighborhoods that are often labeled as deteriorating and disorganized by professional urban planners frequently provide precisely the kinds of services that divorced mothers need: child care, schools, public transportation, shopping, apartment houses, welfare, and social services.

The third direction, *environmental equity,* analyzed how women are unfairly disadvantaged and rendered invisible by public policies and practices relating to housing, transportation, and social services. For example, subsidized public housing policy in most countries is evaluated relative to its impact on the poor, not on women. Yet the vast majority of the poor worldwide are women and children. As a result, in the United States, for example, public housing is virtually a female ghetto, with women heading more than 90 percent of households.

The fourth direction, *female principles in architecture,* articulated the special sensibilities, attributes, and priorities women bring to architecture. For some that meant searching for a woman's cultural heritage and archetypal female imagery in architecture derived from sources in the matrifocal Paleolithic and Neolithic cultures. Others developed hypotheses about "female" and "male" principles in architecture based on different socially constructed gender roles for women and men.

Gender socialization in most cultures has historically encouraged women to consider the needs, comfort, and well-being of others in their decisions, while encouraging men to be self-expressive and intellectually independent. Among women and men who practice architecture, the manifestation of these differences appears not so much in the use of different spatial forms and building technologies, but rather in the different social and ethical contexts in which women and men are likely to conceptualize and design buildings and spaces.

In 1941 Henry Atherton Frost, the man responsible for founding and running the first professional architecture school for women in the United States, the Cambridge School of Architecture and Landscape Architecture (1917–1942), wrote: "The woman architect is interested in housing rather than houses, in community centers for the masses rather than in neighborhood clubs for the elect.... Her interest in her profession embraces its social and human implications" (Stevens, 1977: 91–95).

In an interview in Paris in 1929 the English architect and designer Eileen Gray compared her work with the "new" modern architecture with which her male contemporaries—masters of the modern movement like Walter Gropius, Le Corbusier, and Ludwig Mies van der Rohe—were obsessed:

> This intellectual coldness which we have arrived at and which interprets only too well the hard laws of modern machinery can only be a temporary phenomenon.... I want to develop these formulas and push them to the point at which they are in contact with life.... The avant-garde is intoxicated by the machine aesthetic. Their intense intellectualism wants to suppress that which is marvelous in life... as their concern with a misunderstood hygiene makes hygiene unbearable. Their desire for rigid precision makes them neglect the beauty of all these

forms: discs, cylinders, lines which undulate and zigzag, elliptical lines which are like straight lines in movement. Their architecture is without soul. (1981: 71–72)

Gray was far ahead of her time in predicting the demise of the noncontextual, rational, and often sterile glass box buildings of the new international style. Her work, though designed with the same understated elegance as that of the modern movement and using the same materials and architectural forms, expresses an exceptional sensitivity to human comfort, the movement of the body, and the activities of daily life.

The Impact of Feminist Scholarship on Current Architectural Education and Practice

Convincing evidence now exists that women, to the extent that their roles differ from men's, use, perceive, and design environments differently and have different environmental needs. Yet there is little evidence that the fundamental challenge posed by feminist values and environmental design research has had any effect on the dominant mode of architectural thought. For the most part, architecture is still taught and practiced, and has its content determined and controlled, by men. The integration of feminist theory, content, and pedagogy within the standard architectural curriculum is entirely dependent on the feminist consciousness of those doing the teaching; and most architects, be they women or men, still practice in traditional ways, serving clients who commission projects that usually have little to do with social justice or benefiting women.

The obstacles women historically faced that hindered their careers as architectural practitioners have ensured that very few have achieved more than a modest reputation. Some notable exceptions include, from the United States, Julia Morgan (1872–1957), Marion Mahony Griffin (1891–1961, whose work is best known in Australia), Denise Scott Brown, Adel Naude Santos, Elizabeth Plater-Zyberk, and Jane Thompson. The Iraqi-born architect Zaha Hadid lives in London; Jane Drew and Christine Hawley are also in Britain. Other well-known architects are Eve Laron and Christine Vadasz in Australia; Itsuko Hasegawa in Japan; Odilfia Suarez in Argentina; Sol Madridejos and Marta Maiz in Spain; Minette DeSilva, Eulie Chowdhury, and Elizabeth Ghuman in India; Edith Girard, Marina Devillers, and Lena Perot in France; Gillian Hopwood in Nigeria; Diana Lee-Smith in Kenya; Gae Aulenti in Italy; Karla Kowalski in Austria; Natalya Zakharina in Russia; Ada Karmi-Melamede in Israel; and Elizabeth Hatz in Sweden. In the coming decades, the numbers of nationally and internationally known architects who are women will no doubt increase considerably, as will the impressive collection of books written to date by women in architectural education and practice on a wide range of subjects and the numbers of biographies and monographs documenting their lives and work.

Woman-Made Space

Women peripheral to professional architectural practice have had a major impact on the design and use of built environments. Since the early 1900s women have written books of domestic advice that have influenced their countries' national values, attitudes, and home design; and have developed models of cooperative housekeeping in which kitchenless houses and apartment hotels with communal dining, laundry, and day care would free women to work outside the home by paying other women to provide domestic services. At the turn of the century, women established more than 100 settlement houses in the immigrant ghettos and slums of cities in England and the United States to reform inadequate housing, neighborhood blight, and inhumane institutions. Globally, women have also played a leading role in neighborhood beautification programs, urban sanitation and public health, historic preservation, the parks and recreation movement, and, more recently, the environmental conservation movement.

At the community level, women have organized to solve the problems that directly affect them, their families, and their neighbors. In the United States, Bertha Gilke in St. Louis and Kimi Gray in Washington, D.C., formed self-management tenant organizations in some of the country's most shameful public housing developments, transforming these "projects" from places of neglect to homes that are safe and clean. Women worldwide have led rent strikes, formed housing committees, and sheltered one another.

Grassroots women's groups like the National Congress of Neighborhood Women in Brooklyn and the Women's Research and Development Center in Cincinnati have turned old, abandoned buildings into affordable housing with support services for low-income and elderly women. Canadian women have established numerous cooperative housing developments for women and formed an organization called METRAC—the Toronto Metro Action Committee on Public Violence Against Women and Children—that has raised awareness and affected public policy regarding the connections among transportation, safety, and women's participation in the workforce. The Pancha Carrasco Women's Cooperative in Costa Rica was formed by women, most of them housewives, who wanted to run small businesses from their homes so that they could look after their families and earn an income as well. The Nairobi-based organization Habitat International Coalition (HIC) Women and Shelter Network links people and organizations working on issues of women and shelter in Africa, Asia, Europe, Latin America, and North America.

In countries worldwide, women have created centers for day care, health care, and battered and homeless women and children. They have marched together to "take back the night," reclaiming public streets from pornographers and rapists; led sit-ins in public buildings and spaces to protest segregation; occupied vacant houses as urban squatters because their governments will not provide for them; and established peace camps at the sites of nuclear missile depots in defiance of the male war machine.

Housing, Development, and Social Justice for Women

Perhaps more than any other women's issue, the need for shelter has begun to unite women globally in a sisterhood of purpose that crosses the boundaries of race, class, and nationalism. Through international networking among women, there is an increasing realization that the needs of women in developing countries parallel those of low-income women in North America. From first world slums and public housing projects to third world squatter settlements, women live in appallingly overcrowded, hazardous, unsanitary dwellings that lack basic facilities—circumstances that worsen daily, exacerbated by global economic recessions, military spending, and debt crises that make affordable housing a low priority for many governments. Worldwide poverty among women means that many can afford only limited infrastructural services such as pit latrines, public water hydrants, open drains, and unpaved roads. Lack of adequate sanitation increases health risks. In Bangladesh and Middle Eastern countries, where the purdah system segregates the sexes, women who do not have private toilets are forced to defecate on rooftops and urinate only before sunrise or after sunset, which causes severe medical problems.

Women's generally low wages mean that fewer housing units are affordable and that household income is frequently insufficient to meet the eligibility criteria for subsidized housing. The high illiteracy rate among women worldwide limits their access to information on the availability of subsidized housing schemes, which is typically published in newspapers and public notices by housing authorities; the complexity of the application forms and

required documentation further prevents women from being successful applicants. In many countries women's legal standing denies them the right to own property, which means they cannot protect themselves and their children from domestic instability and violence or provide collateral to gain access to credit or capital.

An estimated one-third of the world's households are now headed by women. In parts of Africa and many urban areas, especially in Latin America, the figure is greater than 50 percent; in the squalid refugee camps in Central America and the deplorable public housing projects of North America, the figure exceeds 90 percent. Yet the universal favoritism bestowed on the male-headed family guarantees that the selection process for recipients of affordable rental and subsidized housing will screen out female-headed households. Moreover, households headed by women are more likely than any other households to be involuntarily displaced from their housing.

Homelessness among women is a common and widespread occurrence in many third world cities and is burgeoning across the United States as increasing displacement and domestic violence force women on to the streets and into welfare hotels and shelters, where they are once again frequently the victims of sexual assault by males. In fact, gender violence is among the leading causes of homelessness among women worldwide. The number of shelters everywhere, especially in rural areas, is scandalously few relative to the magnitude of the need.

Between the 1960s and the 1990s major wars around the world have created a vast population of some 30 million refugees, 75 percent of them women and children. Women refugees, made homeless and widowed by political upheaval, are systematically subjected to rape in the camps while they await resettlement, an act that is surely a form of political torture.

Violence against women also affects their use of public space and their participation in community and civic life. If the fear of sexual harassment on the streets causes women stress, the fear of rape keeps women off the streets at night, away from public parks and "dangerous" parts of town, and unconsciously afraid of half the human race. Women living in shanty towns and rural areas are also vulnerable to assault when they are forced to travel to desolate places to satisfy such basic needs as sanitation, water, and garbage removal.

As women from first world and third world countries share their varied housing experiences and strategies, they increase their ability to control their housing and communities, thereby claiming greater control over their own lives, their future, and the welfare of their children. The increasing realization among diverse women of their common, urgent need for safe shelter is contributing to a growing solidarity among white women and women of color, and migrant, native, rural, peasant, displaced, and refugee women.

Architecture, Feminism, and Social Change

The built environment exists fundamentally as the expression of an established social order. It is not easily changed until the society that produced it is changed. The establishment of dwellings, neighborhoods, public buildings, and cities that embody values which support human rights for women and expand women's life choices holds the potential to foster healthy, nurturing communities where all women, men, and children can live productive, fulfilling lives in relationships of equality and environmental wholeness. To achieve a future in which all people and all living things matter, we will have to recognize the interdependence among all of humanity, the natural world, and the built environment and learn to think and act out of that recognition.

See Also

BUILT ENVIRONMENT; DEVELOPMENT: OVERVIEW; DOMESTIC VIOLENCE; HOMELESSNESS; HOUSEHOLDS: OVERVIEW; HOUSING; REFUGEES; VIOLENCE: OVERVIEW

References and Further Reading

Adam, Peter. 1987. *Eileen Gray: Architect/designer.* New York: Abrams.

Berkeley, Ellen Perry, with Matilda McQuaid, eds. 1989. *Architecture: A place for women.* Washington, D.C.: Smithsonian Institution.

Boutelle, Sara. 1988. *Julia Morgan: Architect.* New York: Abbeville.

Colomina, Beatriz, ed. 1992. *Sexuality and space.* Princeton, N.J.: Princeton Architectural.

Dandekar, Hemalata, C., ed. 1929. *Shelter, women and development.* Ann Arbor, Mich: George Wahr.

Dutton, Thomas, ed. 1991. *Voices in architectural education: Cultural politics and pedagogy.* New York: Bergin and Garvey.

Franck, Karen A., and Sherry Ahrentzen, eds. 1989. *New households, new housing.* New York: Van Nostrand Reinhold.

Gray, Eileen. 1981. From eclecticism to doubt. *Heresies* (Issue II) 3(3): 72–72. Trans. Deborah F. Nevins. Originally published as De L'Eclestisme au doute, *L'Architecture Vivante* (1929): 17–21.

Hayden, Dolores. 1981. *The grand domestic revolution: A history of feminist designs for American homes, neighborhoods and cities.* Cambridge, Mass.: MIT Press.

———. 1984. *Redesigning the American dream: The future of housing, work, and family life.* New York: Norton.

Lorenz, Clare. 1990. *Women in architecture.* New York: Rizzoli.

Sprague, Joan Forrester. 1991. *More than housing: Lifeboats for women and children.* Boston: Butterworth Architecture.

Stevens, Mary Ottis. 1977. Struggle for place: Women in architecture. In Susana Torre, ed., *Women in American architecture: A historic and contemporary perspective.* New York: Whitney Library of Design.

Weisman, Leslie Kanes. 1992a. Designing differences: Women and architecture. In Cheris Kramarae and Dale Spender, eds., *The knowledge explosion: Generations of feminist scholarship.* New York: Teachers College Press.

———. 1992b. *Discrimination by design: A feminist critique of the man-made environment.* Urbana: University of Illinois Press.

Wekerle, Gerda R. 1988. *Women's housing projects in eight Canadian cities.* Ottawa: CMHC.

Leslie Kanes Weisman

ARMAMENT AND MILITARIZATION

Definition of Militarization

The term *militarization* refers to a process by which a group of human beings organize their lives and their work in preparation for fighting other human beings in wars. The first half of the twentieth century was characterized by world wars that involved almost all people on earth in fighting or in supplying those who were fighting. The second half of the twentieth century was characterized by regional wars in which the battlegrounds were localized. The warring parties were both local people and people from other nations. The people supplying the combatants included all the local people and most of the people who lived in the other participating nations.

Militarization is occurring in most nations in the world, although it takes different forms depending on the culture and political organization of each nation. In a representative democracy, militarization is often not perceived by the general public. Soldiers in uniform are not usually seen on the streets; military officers who participate in high-level decision-making groups with civilian leaders often are out of uniform and not identified by their rank in press releases. In a military dictatorship, soldiers in uniform with visible weapons may patrol the streets. The national leaders usually appear in uniform and are referred to by their military rank. Variations in these two political extremes occur depending on whether the nation is in a war or a nonwar period, whether there is a draft or a volunteer military force, and whether there is a high rate of preparedness or a more steady state of maintaining the forces.

Militarization is a process comparable to industrialization, which becomes part of every aspect of the civil order, adapting itself to existing institutions and practices. Military values are expressed throughout the culture, with an emphasis on authority and obedience, on aggression and violence, and on the acceptance of hardship and sacrifice. The purpose of militarization is preparation or readiness for war, which results in decision-making power and public tax money for the military, often greater than that for nonmilitary purposes.

Definition of Armament

Armament is necessary for the process of militarization, whether in the stage of continual readiness for war or in war itself. The political and economic systems of a nation are involved in the production of arms or weapons; the scientific and technological systems are involved in the design and development of arms; the military system selects the people and trains them in the use of arms. The most militarized nations in the world maintain their global power by the export of armament, especially weapons, equipment, and training, to the military of other nations. Four countries (United States, United Kingdom, France, and Russia) account for over 80 percent of arms exports, supplying military forces and regional and civil wars with armament and technical military personnel.

The term *armament* refers to a nation's total military strength—its soldiers, sailors, and air force personnel; its weapons and equipment; its vehicles, airplanes, missiles, battleships, and submarines—together with all the industries, manufactured products accumulated, and raw materials needed for war. Briefly, armament can be categorized as (1) people, (2) weapons, (3) factories, and (4) raw materials: the concrete, specific objects necessary for the process of militarization to occur. People are involved in different ways on the basis of their age, gender, race, and class, as they enter military service, or as producers of weapons of war, or as taxpayers, or as investors in the corporations producing armament.

Nuclear weapons are a special category of armament because of the effort by certain nuclear-armed nations (such as China, France, Russia, United Kingdom, and United States) to limit the export of nuclear weapons materials and technologies to other nations. As more nations acquire nuclear weapons and the capability of producing their own, the nuclear arms race is accelerated.

Feminist Theories and Perspectives

The women's suffrage movement before and during World War I produced theories and descriptions of militarization that are still relevant today. An essay on militarization and feminism by Ogden and Florence (1987) analyzed male despotism and patriarchy as the basic cause of militarism. They described how all aspects of social life were being directed by war and preparation for war, resulting in the continued subjection and oppression of women, and in the "perversion" of industry, religion, and education by militarism.

Current feminist theories on militarization also focus on male dominance in all societal institutions, especially the military and civilian government, corporations, and scientific and technical institutions. These theories are based on several disciplines, including economics, political science, social psychology, peace studies, and women's studies. The basic feminist thesis is that male dominance is inextricably linked to militarization. At the most fundamental level, men maintain their dominance by the threat or use of force: the threat to harm, injure, or kill, as well as actual harming, injuring, and killing. Feminist analysis describes militarization as the process that maintains male dominance or the patriarchy, in which preparation or readiness for war enables men to allocate most national resources to militarization and in which the actual conduct of war enables men to display the need for readiness and the need for all available resources. A war may defeat the enemy and at the same time reinforce the need for military supremacy in its own nation.

The Role of Women in Militarization and Armament

Women are central to the ongoing process of militarization and the production of armament. Women throughout the world take active and passive roles in militarization, depending on the nation in which they live, their class membership (upper, middle, or lower class), their race or ethnic identity, and their age. Their most active roles are as military personnel, enlisted or drafted into one of the military services, and as civilian personnel employed by the military services. Nations vary widely in the active participation of women, from those that prohibit military service for women to those that encourage young women to join the military.

Many women participate in militarization as workers in the war (or defense) industries producing equipment, weapons, and services. Prostitution and other forms of sex work accompany the military wherever armed forces are, including peacekeeping missions. It sometimes seems that the military could not function without prostitution, both forced and voluntary, and a steady stream of women and girls are produced for this function and related functions through the destruction of these women's civil societies and traditional occupations. Some of the least visible participants in militarization are female children, who participate in the male military cultural values and symbols propagated by media, schools, and manufacturers of children's toys and clothing; and elderly women whose retirement funds are invested in corporations that produce goods and services for the military and whose votes or support are sought in elections or public demonstrations.

In the military services, women are generally limited to noncombat occupations such as health care, administration, personnel, and supply services. They may be excluded from certain units such as infantry, armor, special forces, and submarine warfare. In scientific and technical fields, women may be limited by their lack of preparatory education in science and mathematics, or may be unable to find employment after such preparation. In the industrial world, many corporations are multipurpose, manufacturing for both military and civilian markets. Many military processes require security clearances in order to work in these factories, and women may not qualify. Women are the largest part of the labor force in all countries, as home workers whose work is unpaid and as paid workers who may work inside or outside the home. In some countries, women, who are half of the labor force, are limited to certain occupations, such as nurses, teachers, clerical workers, waitresses, and domestic workers. These occupations in both the military sector and the civil sector are an essential part of the maintenance of the militarization process.

Women's participation also is characterized by hardship and sacrifice that directly affect their work as homemakers. The use of most social goods for militarization and armament means that basic needs for food, water, shelter, heating, clothing, health care, and schooling are unmet or partially met at subsistence levels. The lives of women everywhere are affected by the meager proportion of national goods remaining from the militarization process.

See Also

DISARMAMENT; MILITARY; NUCLEAR WEAPONS; PACIFISM AND PEACE ACTIVISM; WAR

References and Further Reading

D'Amico, Francine, and Laurie Weinstein, eds. 1999. *Gender camouflage: Women and the U.S. military.* New York: New York University Press.

Enloe, Cynthia. 2000. *Maneuvers: The international politics of militarizing women's lives.* Berkeley: University of California Press.

Grossman, Lieutenant Colonel Dave. 1995. *On killing: The psychological cost of learning to kill in war and society.* Boston: Little, Brown.

Lumpe, Lora, and Jeff Donarski. 1998. *The arms trade revealed: A guide for investigators and activists.* Washington, D.C.: Federation of American Scientists Fund.

Mies, Maria. 1999. *Patriarchy and accumulation on a world scale: Women in the international division of labour.* London: Zed.

Ogden, C. K., and Mary Sargant Florence. 1987. Militarism versus feminism: An enquiry and policy demonstrating that militarism involves the subjection of women. In Margaret Kamester and Jo Vellacott, eds., *Militarism versus feminism: Writings on women and war: Catherine Marshall, C. K. Ogden, and Mary Sargant Florence,* 53–140. London: Virago.

Regan, Patrick M. 1994. *Organizing societies for war: The process and consequences of societal militarization.* Westport, Conn.: Praeger.

Russell, Diana E. H., ed. 1989. *Exposing nuclear phallacies.* New York: Pergamon.

U.S. Department of Defense, Office of the Executive Secretary. 2000. *Annual report to the president and the Congress.*

JoAn A. Saltzen

ARMED FORCES

See MILITARY.

ART

See ART PRACTICE: FEMINIST and FINE ARTS, *specific topics.*

ARTIFICIAL INSEMINATION

See REPRODUCTIVE TECHNOLOGIES.

ART PRACTICE: Feminist

Feminist art practice is a generic term, created by the women's art movement in the 1970s, to describe the relationship between the work of contemporary women artists, the larger feminist movement, and feminist theory. Feminist practices in art have not been dependent on specific media (for example, painting, photo-text or scriptovisual work, performance, film, video, and so on). They have been manifest through all the media available to artists, as well as many nontraditional media (such as the incorporation of domestic objects or clothing into artworks). The term itself should be thought of in the plural, as feminist practices in art do not represent the use of a specific style, medium, approach, or uniform methodology by women artists.

This is a contested term, constantly under redefinition, and the short history of its use also reflects broader tendencies in feminist theory, specifically the debates over essentialism and antiessentialism, which dominated the 1980s. When considered against a background of critical and historical terms, feminist art practices are part of the equally contested field represented by a shift from modernism and late modernism to postmodernism. Feminist art practices cannot be described as an "ism" in the modernist sense of an identifiable group of artists with a manifesto, producing work that can be characterized through formal or stylistic features. Historically, the "norm" for women artists within modernism was to be positioned as the "other," and, therefore, subject to the feminine stereotype—analyzed by Griselda Pollock and Rozsika Parker—where the category "art" is defined and appropriated by men and art produced by women falls under the separate and "lesser" category of "women's work" (Parker and Pollock, 1987: 84–87). Feminist art practices begin with a critique of this value system. It is useful to consider a feminist art practice as the result of a specific kind of intervention in meaning and method, drawing on analysis of the politics of representation and challenging conventional understandings in both art and feminism of "woman." Mary Kelly (1998) argued that the feminist critique of modernism also drew on many conceptual approaches to art in the 1970s, and that it offered a new means for women artists to contest the materiality, sociality, and sexuality of art and its values. Kelly used the term "the feminist problematic" to describe this field for challenging received ideas of femininity in feminist art practice.

In the mid-1980s, Craig Owens defined an apparent crossing-over between a feminist critique of patriarchy and the postmodern critique of representation in a group of women in New York whose work used postmodern strategies with imagery appropriated from the media and juxtaposed images and text to open up questions of intelligibility, subjectivity, and identification processes (Owens, 1985: 59). Feminist art practice could be characterized as a form of avant-gardism within the women's art movement, as it does

not encompass all women artists' practice or all kinds of collective collaboration between women artists on art projects or exhibitions. Feminist activism on social and political questions was fundamental to defining art practices as feminist in the 1970s. In the 1990s, the work of many women artists has been concerned with different questions of identity politics and transgression, from "bad girls" to lesbian identity politics or cyberfeminism. There also has been a renewed debate about the relationship of contemporary women's artwork to the legacy of feminist art practice in the 1970s.

Feminist practices in art have emerged as a truly international phenomenon, with a critique of both sexism and double standards in the art world, as well as through the collective action taken by women artists to increase their visibility and contest the current and dominant forms of representation of women. Demands for integration and recognition followed the first critiques of sexism in the art world, and there is a 30-year history of outstanding women artists' exhibitions in many countries worldwide.

Feminist art practice is not, however, concerned with a celebration of all women's creativity in the visual arts or culture. Although feminist artists have been eager to educate and develop projects with groups of women, distinction remains between sustaining a career as a professional visual artist because of specialized training and contributing creatively to a project on the basis of one's experience or specified knowledge. The separation between the women's art movement—as part of the broader women's movement—and the establishment of a more specialized and professional understanding of art practices as feminist among women artists working in the contemporary art market is important. The distinction rests on answers to the question: To what extent does a work of art enable political, aesthetic, or cultural change? The conclusions are determined by different feminist camps: Marxist, socialist culturalist, liberal, conservative, or anarchist.

Political and Ideological Aspects of Feminist Art Practice

Some women in the campaigns of the 1970s rejected the notion that visual art could contribute to political or ideological change except as a form of propaganda. Other women argued that all women's creativity was to be fostered and encouraged. The idea that some women possessed special skills as artists, while others did not, was anathema to the spirit of the women's movement as an inclusive movement. These two ideas from different camps led many women artists to withdraw from the women's movement, since either art was thought of as a luxury subordinate to political necessity or their specific professional training or knowledge was not respected as possessing any value. In the late 1970s, this division was institutionally reinforced by the developing curricula of women's studies, where art was rarely taught, while feminist artists continued to work—albeit often marginalized—in art schools and departments. In the late 1980s, with the increasing recognition of specialization within the academy, the situation shifted and even feminist philosophers looked to the work of visual artists for insights on questions of representation, ideology, and transformative potential among women.

Women artists did start working together as a direct result of the women's movement in the 1970s. Women artists' collaboration in public debates from the 1970s has led to numerous analyses of whether there is a separate women's culture, a female or feminine aesthetic, and how this is different from a feminist aesthetic. Women artists working professionally in well-established conventions or forms of art practice, who could be seen as producing an identifiably feminine response to emerging tendencies, were often distinguished from feminist artists who had a specific cultural agenda to reform the conception of art itself, redefine who the audience for contemporary art might be, and challenge familiar or stereotypical representations of women. In the 1970s and early 1980s, the notion that feminist art was by women, for women, and about women became an abbreviation for this idea. The biological sex of the maker did not guarantee that her work or approach would be understood as feminist, nor was this credo a justification for personal expression of all women's subjective viewpoints. How to define a woman artist's work as feminist rested on how the work could be read and integrated into a new collective context for understanding social and political questions in antiessentialist terms. How the personal could become political and how family relationships and social and political questions could be used as a source or reference point in a work (and be related to or differentiated from other women's experiences) became part of an important discussion of the context for the social and critical reception of the work of art.

Griselda Pollock (1998) argues that this is a question of reading, not making. For feminist artists, however, this is a question about the relevance of their work to cultural change and how questions of identity and social, cultural, and political problems could be addressed and challenged.

Conclusion

Feminist art practice has introduced new subject matter into art, which came directly from the impetus of the women's movement's analysis of many social and political questions. Feminists introduced into art many new subjects: the representation, ideology, and iconology of rape, incest, violence against women, domestic labor, homeworking, and homelessness; a reevaluation of the labor of women; a critique of traditional femininity, especially in revived and critical uses of traditional women's crafts; the representation of motherhood, of relationships between mothers and daughters and between women as lesbians; women's images of men; questions of racism, xenophobia, and representing the colonized and colonizer; women's sexuality from vaginal imagery to menstruation to pregnancy to images of sexual pleasure; the representation of the identity of the woman artist in relationship to her peers or to the history of other women artists; and subjects that played with traditional mythology and fairy tales.

Feminist practices in art also initiated collaborative and sometimes collective methods of working, which sought to challenge the notion of art as a product of the individual genius, toiling alone in the studio, through the development of group workshops, and through group art projects or exhibitions developed with consciousness-raising techniques or with other specific techniques and approaches, like phototherapy. Feminist practices in art have not been confined to the gallery or museum; social actions, media-staged events, agitprop, street theater, site-specific work, and community-based projects were all developed to expand the audience for art and specifically to engage the participation of groups of women in social and political issues concerning them.

See Also

AESTHETICS: FEMINIST; CREATIVITY; CULTURAL CRITICISM; CULTURE: WOMEN AS PRODUCERS; ESSENTIALISM; FINE ARTS: CRITICISM AND ART HISTORY; FINE ARTS: POLITICS OF REPRESENTATION; POSTMODERNISM: LITERARY THEORY

References and Further Reading

Arbour, Marie Rose, ed. 1982. *Art et féminisme*. Canada: Quebec, Musée d'Art Contemporain, Montréal and Ministère des Affaires Culturelles.

Broude, N., and M. Garrard, eds. 1994. *The power of feminist art: Emergence, impact and triumph of American feminist art movement.* New York: Abrams.

Burke, Janine. 1990. *Field of vision, Decade of change: Women's art in the 1970s.* Victoria, Australia: Viking.

La Centrale (Galerie Powerhouse). 1990, *Instabili: La question du sujet, The question of subject.* Montréal: La Centrale.

Deepwell, Katy, ed. 1995. *New feminist art criticism: Critical Strategies*. Manchester: Manchester University.

Dysart, Dinah, and Hanna Fink. 1996. *Asian women artists*. Roseville East, New South Wales, Australia: Craftsman House.

Ecker, Gisela. 1985. *Feminist aesthetics*. London: Women's Press.

Frueh, Joanna, Cassandra Langer, and Arlene Raven, eds. 1991. *Feminist art criticism; An anthology*. New York: HarperCollins.

Frueh, J., C. Langer, and A. Raven, eds. 1996. *Feminist criticism: Art, identity, action*. New York: HarperCollins.

Isaak, Jo-Anna. 1996. *Feminism and contemporary art: The revolutionary power of women's laughter*. London: Routledge.

Jones, Amelia. 1996. *Sexual politics: Judy Chicago's* The Dinner Party *in feminist art history*. Berkeley: University of California Press.

Kelly, Mary. 1998. Reviewing modernist criticism. In M. Kelly, *Imaging Desire*. Boston: MIT Press.

King-Hammond, Leslie. 1995. *Gumbo ya ya; Anthology of contemporary African-American women artists*. New York: Midmarch.

Kirby, Sandy. 1992. *Sightlines: Women, Art and Feminist Perspectives in Australia*. Roseville East, New South Wales, Australia, Craftsman House.

La Duke, Betty. 1985. *Compañeras: Women, art and social change in Latin America*. San Francisco: City Lights.

Lippard, Lucy. 1976. *From the center: Feminist essays on women's art*. New York: Dutton.

Loeb, Judy. 1979. *Feminist collage: Educating women in the visual arts*. New York: Teachers College.

Moore, Catriona, ed. 1994. *Dissonance: Feminism and the arts, 1970–1990*. St. Leonards, New South Wales, Australia: Allen and Unwin.

Owens, Craig. 1985. The discourse of others, in H. Foster, *Postmodern Culture*. London: Pluto.

Parker, Rozsika, and G. Pollock. 1987. *Framing feminism: Art and the women's movement, 1970–1985*. London: Routledge.

Pollock, Griselda, ed. 1996. *Generations and geographies*. London: Routledge.

Raven, Arlene. 1988. *Crossing over: Feminism and the art of social concern*. Ann Arbor: University of Michigan Press.

Robinson, Hilary, ed. 1987. *Visibly female*. London: Camden.

Rosen, R., and C. Brauer. 1989. *Making their mark: Women artists move into the mainstream, 1970–1985*. New York: Abbeville.

Roth, Moira. 1983. *The amazing decade: Women and performance art in America, 1970–1980*. Los Angeles, Astro Artz.

Siegel, Judy. 1992. *Mutiny and the mainstream: Talk that changed art, 1975–1990*. New York: Midmarch.

Sinha, Gayatri, ed. 1997. *Expressions and evocations: contemporary women artists of India*. New Delhi, Marg.

Witzling, Mara S., ed. 1994/1995. *Voicing today's visions*. London: Women's Press.

Web site: <n.pandoraonline>

Zegher, Catherine de, ed. 1996. *Inside the visible: An elliptical traverse of 20th century art, in, of and from the feminine*. Boston: ICA catalogue, MIT Press/ Kanaal Art Foundation.

Katy Deepwell

ASSERTIVENESS TRAINING

Assertiveness, according to Jean Baer, is making your own choices, standing up for yourself appropriately, and having an active orientation to life. Assertiveness training is the area of behavior therapy that concerns the skills of relating to people and the world around one (1976: 18, 20).

For a time in the 1970s and 1980s, particularly in the United States, many authors and trainers publicized assertiveness training programs as processes designed to enable women to change some of the limiting habitual patterns of their interaction. Directed primarily toward middle-class women, the training programs were popular among the many who read the books and practiced assertive techniques in workshops. Assertiveness training programs can help empower women to make appropriate choices for their families and their own welfare. While interest in the programs has decreased in recent years, such programs can still be useful in encouraging women to be courageous and to accept only dignified and respectful treatment. However, the programs also have critics.

In societies with double standards, assertiveness training can offer women alternative perspectives on negotiation techniques and communication styles (Winston, 1999: 50). Suzette Haden Elgin, a linguist, has developed a program to help people learn "the gentle art of verbal self-defense" (1997: 13). She criticizes the media's widespread acceptance of theories that women and men merely speak "different languages," and that communication problems between men and women can, basically, be solved if each learns the "other's" language. (These differing communication styles are described in popular terms in John Gray's best-selling series, which includes *Men Are from Mars and Women Are from Venus*.) Elgin points out that while the problems of physical violence are receiving increased attention, the problems of verbal violence have received relatively little.

Many programs suggest that women can be empowered to address their problems by changing their traditional behavior and thus changing the behavior of others. As a branch of behavior therapy, assertiveness training can educate women to be more expressive and candid. Baer's focus is primarily on life in the home, social relationships, and some workplace relationships. Pamela Butler uses the term "assertion," which she defines as "the freedom to state your feelings and opinions without anxiety or embarrassment, while at the same time allowing other people to have their own feelings and opinions" (1992: 3). Her focus is now on women's need to be assertive in expressing who they are as unique individuals rather on a basic style or behavior that needs to be altered.

Others have also been doubtful about the focus on changing individuals' behavior. While acknowledging that assertiveness training programs can provide guidance and support, these critics point out that the training can be largely cosmetic, helping some individuals at the expense of others. Assertive behavior involves an honest expression of one's feelings from one's own perspective. It does not attend to the other person's understanding of the truth. This method assumes that, if done properly, the interaction should not hurt the receiver (Janice, 1994: 71). However, often the suggested solutions can injure others, including other women. Also, the training programs usually pay little attention to the economics and social context of interactions. That is, the training may emphasize treating symptoms without acknowledging or working on the underlying problems of a society or considering the need for social change (Kramarae and Treichler, 1985: 59).

In a critique of the earlier assertiveness training programs, Nancy Henley (1979) wrote, "To focus on women's own minds and interaction styles as the source of their oppression is the most vicious sort of blaming the victim, right up there with curfews for women to save them from attack." Other critics have suggested that the programs reflect a notion—which seems characteristic of thinking in the United States—that major problems can be solved by individuals working through short training courses.

Some assertiveness training programs have been criticized as being based on traditional North American ideas of male leadership and behavior (Julia Wood, 1999). Today, as we are learning to live in a global environment, we need to be sensitive to a multicultural citizenry. We need to pay attention not only to the different expectations for and evaluations of women and women's behavior in the same culture, but also to the many cultural differences in how people worldwide express their honest feelings and exercise their personal rights without denying the rights of others.

See Also

COMMUNICATIONS: OVERVIEW; EMPOWERMENT; LEADERSHIP; MANAGEMENT; ORGANIZATIONAL THEORY

References and Further Reading

Baer, Jean. 1976. *How to be an assertive (not aggressive) woman: A classic guide to becoming a self-assured person.* New York: Signet.

Butler, Pamela E. 1992. *Self-assertion for women.* San Francisco: HarperCollins.

Elgin, Suzette Haden. 1997. *How to disagree without being disagreeable: Getting your point across with the gentle art of verbal self-defense.* New York: Wiley.

Henley, Nancy. 1979. Assertiveness training: Making the political personal. Paper given at the meeting of the Society for the Study of Social Problems (August).

Janice, Elizabeth. 1994. How to put your foot down without stepping on others. *Black Enterprise* 25(4): 71

Kramarae, Cheris, and Paula Treichler, with Ann Russo. 1985. *A feminist dictionary.* London: Pandora.

McMurrer, Daniel P., and Mark E. Van Buren. 1999. The Japanese training scene. *Training and Development* 53(8): 43.

Paik, Yongsun, and Rosalie L. Tung. 1999. Negotiating with east Asians. *Management International Review* 39 (2): 103.

Winston, Stephanie. 1999. *Getting out from under: Redefining your priorities in an overwhelming world.* Reading, Mass.: Perseus.

Wood, Julia T. 1999. *Gendered lives: Communication, gender, and culture.* 3rd ed. Belmont, Calif: Wadsworth.

Mary Thomas-Gallet

ASTRONAUTS

See SPACE.

ATHLETICS

See SPORT.

AUDIENCE ANALYSIS

See COMMUNICATIONS: AUDIENCE ANALYSIS.

AUTOBIOGRAPHICAL CRITICISM

The term *autobiographical criticism* describes a hybrid mode of scholarly writing now gaining increasing prominence, especially among American feminist literary scholars. Variously termed experimental critical writing, personal criticism, cross-genre writing, the new subjectivity, and narrative criticism, it is a politically and emotionally engaged, often belletristic mode that "freely mixes personal elements with research expertise" (Heller, 1992).

Although autobiographical criticism represents a radical shift in academic writing, its variants owe something to the essay tradition, with its writerly freedom; to the second-wave feminist tenet that the personal is the political; to a female psychology that allegedly favors "connected" over "separate" knowing (Belenky et al., 1986; Gilligan, 1982); and to a feminist epistemology that sees social location (the nexus of one's racial, religious, gender, class, geographic, sexual, familial, and institutional histories) as necessarily implicated (and thus needing to be articulated) in one's research (Harding, 1991; Rich, 1986).

Autobiographical *literary* criticism, the most common and widely published form of autobiographical criticism, owes something, in addition, to the increasing presence of poets in the academy, to the proliferation of creative writing programs, to the historically hybrid nature of poets' prose, and to the fact that English departments house poets and novelists along with composition teachers, textual critics, and literary and cultural theorists.

Autobiographical criticism thus shares, for example, composition theorists' emphasis on writing as process, not product; reader-response theorists' attention to the reactions of readers; and some French theorists' penchant for "crossing over genre lines, cross-pollinating autobiography, fiction and theory, and challenging traditional dividing lines between subject and object, self and others" (Flieger, 1994). Autobiographical criticism may also be indebted to such first-person cultural traditions as the Latin American *testimonio* and the African-American narrative of liberation and literacy. Perhaps China and Japan, two cultures with a strong tradition of "I" writing, will be the next great producers of and influences upon autobiographical criticism.

A short list of autobiographical-critical scholars might include Appiah (philosophy and Africana studies), Behar (anthropology); Field (Asian studies); Lipton (art history); Ruddick (philosophy); Williams (law); and Anzaldua, Atkins, Brownstein, Freedman, Gallop, hooks, Miller, and Tompkins (literature, theory, pedagogy) in the United States. In the United Kingdom, the list would include Steedman (sociology and psychoanalysis) and Jouve, Roe, and Wandor (literature). Gould (literary criticism and theory) works in Canada. (See also Freedman et al., 1993.)

Autobiographical literary critics challenge "objective" notions of literary interpretation and evaluation; they claim to know themselves through literature and to know literature from the perspective of their lives. Many concur with the sentiment Jane Tompkins expresses in a much-reprinted essay, "Me and My Shadow":

> The criticism I would like to write would always take off from personal experience, would always be in some way a chronicle of my hours and days, would speak in a voice which can talk about everything, would reach out to readers like me and touch me where I want to be touched. (1987)

Autobiographical criticism—in whatever discipline—has its detractors. As more of these experiments are being published, some critics have branded the "personal" as outdated, essentialist, antitheoretical, and solipsistic. Defenders respond that although women's studies have long connected lived experience and theory, one's work and one's life, most academic feminists continued to echo establishment forms in their work even if they challenged expectations about subject matter and research methodology. As to the charge of its being antitheoretical, Jane Gallop suggests that one can think or theorize through the body, while others see personal criticism as an extension of what is meant by theory. Others support autobiographical criticism for its accessibility and inclusivity—its potential for engaging readers beyond the halls of academe, an important goal of women's studies. As the anthropologist Ruth Behar (1993) has asserted, rather than being self-absorbed, the best autobiographical scholarship reaches out to its readers, beginning with personal discovery but finally producing "a redrawn map of social terrain."

See Also

AUTOBIOGRAPHY; LITERARY THEORY AND CRITICISM

References and Further Reading

Behar, Ruth. 1993. *Translated woman: Crossing the border with Esperanza's story.* Boston: Beacon.

Belenky, Mary field, et al. 1986. *Women's ways of knowing: The development of self, voice, and mind.* New York: Basic Books.

Flieger, Jerry Aline. 1994. Growing up theoretical: Across the divide. In Gayle Greene and Coppelia Kahn, eds., *Changing subjects: The making of feminist literary criticism.*

Freedman, Diane, et al., eds. 1993. *The intimate critique: Autobiographical literary criticism.* Durham, N.C.: Duke University Press.

Gallop, Jane. 1988. *Thinking through the body.* New York: Columbia University Press.

Gilligan, Carol. 1982. *In a different voice: Psychological theory and women's development,* Cambridge, Mass.: Harvard University Press.

Harding, Sandra. 1991. Who Knows? Identities and feminist epistemology. In Joan E. Hartman and Ellen Messer-Davidow, eds., *(En)gendering knowledge: Feminists in academe*. Knoxville: University of Tennessee Press.

Heller, Scott. 1992. Experience and expertise meet in new brand of scholarship. *Chronicle of Higher Education* (May): A7.

Rich, Adrienne. 1986. *Blood, bread, and poetry: Selected prose 1979–1985*. New York: Norton.

Tompkins, Jane. 1987. Me and my shadow. In *New Literary History*. 19: 169–178; reprinted in Diane Freedman et al., eds., *The intimate critique: Autobiographical literary criticism*, Durham, N.C.: Duke University Press, 1993.

Diane Freedman

AUTOBIOGRAPHY

Autobiography is a literary term that refers to a writer's account of his or her own life. Used to define a literary genre, *autobiography* means the retrospective narrative of the author's life. Feminist critics, however, have sometimes used the term more flexibly to include memoirs and journals, perceiving the ways that genre and gender are inextricably intertwined. Genre, used as a set of rules to define literary texts, can preserve a hierarchy of texts that are like each other. The assumption that autobiographical subjects can present a unified and coherent narrative about themselves, which is also representative of their era or even of humanity in general, prevents much of women's autobiographical writing from being included within generic classifications. The study of women's autobiography has therefore required questioning the accepted definitions and theories of autobiography, along with the discovery of women's texts and the identification of their historical and literary importance. Autobiographical writing by women spans different eras, cultures, and literary modes and forms a rich and diverse field; on the other hand, feminist critics have also traced through autobiographical texts the difficulty for women of telling their own story when culturally and historically they have been designated as object or "other" in forms of telling that assume a masculine subject. Approaches to autobiography have seen it both as a mode of witnessing or testimony to women's lives and women's experience and as evidence of the strategies of concealment, displacement, or splitting that women must use in relation to their own lives and writing.

The study of women's autobiography has been incorporated into many different disciplines and has provided the impetus for the questioning of disciplinary as well as generic boundaries. For feminist historians women's autobiographies provide not just source material about lives previously overlooked but a way of thinking about subjectivity and its form and place within historical accounts. Social scientists have thought about the effect of their own life histories on their research methods as well as the problem of using other women's life stories as research data. Within feminist teaching the reading and writing of autobiography have been used politically as a strategy of empowerment, as a way for women to use their own experience and to recognize themselves as subjects. Autobiography has played an important part, too, in feminist thinking about the diversity of women's lives and the differences between women: its engagement with specificity, with a particular point of view, and with the materiality of women's lives has posed a challenge to theoretical generalizations.

Within feminist debates, autobiography occupies an important place between theory and practice and has been a site of questioning of the relevance of postmodernist theory to a feminist political agenda; at the same time, it provides a focus for the development of complex arguments about subjectivity and about the danger of collapsing the "textual" or the "literary" into too simple or direct a notion of "experience." Julia Swindells argues that in their autobiographies, nineteenth-century working women turned to the "literary," to inherited models of melodrama or romance, as a response to the difficulty of writing about what is gender-specific. An understanding of subjectivity depends on reading the "textual" or the intertextual and being aware of "slippages" (1985).

Shari Benstock, using Virginia Woolf as her primary example, has explored the division within the autobiographical subject between writer and written, *je* and *moi*, conscious and unconscious. The autobiographer aspires to a knowledge of herself which she can never have, and which writing itself constantly defers. This problem of autobiography is intensified for women who are doubly alienated, situated as "other" within the symbolic system. Woolf exemplifies this in questioning both the status of the self and the written in the very act of writing (1988).

Bella Brodski and Celeste Schenk, on the other hand, have argued that an acknowledgment of the textual and of the constructed nature of the subject should not be allowed to cancel out the "bios," the lived element in autobiography (1988). To allow this is to lose the possibility of addressing the social subject and issues of class, race, and sexual orientation. It is also to deny the validation of women's agency and visibility that autobiography can bring; it is to deny the importance of autobiography to a feminist agenda and politics.

See also

AUTOBIOGRAPHICAL THEORY AND CRITICISM

References and Further Reading

Benstock, Shari, ed. 1988. *The private self: Theory and practice of women's autobiographical writing.* London: Routledge.

Brodski, Bella, and Celeste Schenck, eds. 1988. *Life/lines: Theorizing women's autobiography.* Ithaca, N.Y., and London: Cornell University Press.

Smith, Sidonie, and Julia Watson, eds. 1992. *De/colonizing the subject: The politics of gender in women's autobiography.* Minneapolis: Minnesota University Press.

Stanley, Liz. 1992. *The auto/biographical I: The theory and practice of feminist auto/biography.* England: Manchester University Press.

Swindells, Julia. 1985. *Victorian writing and working women.* Cambridge: Polity.

Linda Anderson

AUTOMATION

The term *automation* commonly refers to the partial replacement of human labor by machines. What makes this different from mechanization is that automation usually requires a combination of mechanical devices and systems for programming, monitoring, and control; this includes the capacity for a degree of self-adjustment in response to feedback.

Domestic central heating systems provide one simple illustration of this combination. The boiler and pump come on in response to an electric timer and to a thermostat set at a certain level; once the temperature in the house reaches this level, the heating switches off again. Examples in which automation is in use on a large scale include steel rolling mills, chemical processing plants, and major banks. In these contexts, automated systems are used to physically handle materials (a molten steel ingot, a batch of checks), and to monitor the processing of these within preset constraints (rolling the steel to a given thickness, sorting and recording written details within given formats).

There have been conflicting views about the scope and significance of automation; this article explores some of these with particular reference to gender relations, following a short overview of important features of the development of automated systems.

Automation: Historical Perspective

The principles that underlie automation can be identified in developments that began long before large-scale automated systems. For example, in the Jacquard loom, developed in France in the early 1800s, patterned fabrics were produced by using metal plates, punched with holes, to "program" repeating combinations of colored threads. There are recognizable similarities, here, with the later use of punched cards in the programming of early computers. As with many other aspects of the history of technology, much attention has been paid to the achievements of "great men" such as Jacquard. It has become difficult to distinguish the more diffuse processes through which large numbers of men and women have contributed to designing, implementing, and redesigning technologies. Similarly, the familiar landmarks in the history of automation tend to be located in what the novelist Doris Lessing has called the "north-west fringes" of the globe: northern Europe and North America. These landmarks include the following:

- 1920–1930s: partial automation of switching in telephone exchanges
- 1940s: introduction of automation in some areas of car assembly plants
- 1950s: development and use of the first automated machine tools
- 1960s: development of the first industrial robots
- 1970s: spread of word processing and other forms of office automation
- 1980s: development of "flexible manufacturing systems" (FMS), aiming to integrate computer-based systems that were previously separate, at shop floor, office, and management levels

Automation: Issues for Women and for Gender Relations

As with technology more generally, automation has been seen as bringing about both salvation and disaster. In 1964, for example, Robert Blauner's study predicted that automated systems would release workers from the drudgery of routine tasks; a decade later, Harry Braverman saw automation as part of a process in which technologies are used to "deskill" and degrade human labor, within a wider pattern of managerial control. Both views tended to see technology as a "cause" of change in its own right, rather than as an integral part of social and cultural relations. Both also saw women in the passive role of beneficiary or victim—rather than as active participants in technological change. But in practice, changes in the workplace, in mass communications, and in the home have proved double-edged and far more complex than either Blauner or Braverman could anticipate. Word processing, for example, has neither "freed" women clerical workers from routine typing nor destroyed women's employment in offices. Office computers can be used to speed up the large-scale production of standard letters and documents—intensifying the pressure of work for the clerical staff in a bank, for instance. Computers can also enable community or labor organizations to communicate rapidly across international boundaries, in order to share information and to develop political campaigns.

A number of studies by women have examined processes of automation from a gender perspective. Cynthia Cockburn (1983, 1985) has examined the ways in which technological systems—including automation—tend to be associated with masculinity in western societies; at the same time, she shows how processes of technological change and development can also create tension within established divisions of labor. Automation in printing or in garment manufacture, for instance, has brought an emphasis on keyboard skills rather than on crude physical strength. Cockburn describes the intense personal conflicts experienced by men contemplating the prospect of relying on skills previously associated with femininity—a blurring of previously clear-cut gender roles in the workplace.

Another dimension that has been of concern to feminists is the role of automation in countries that are currently becoming more intensively industrialized. Swasti Mitter (1986), for example, discusses the ways in which low-paid women factory workers and homeworkers, in countries such as India, are employed on casual terms by large multinational corporations. Both clerical operations and software production can be located "offshore" in this way, with potential long-term damage to local cultures, economies, and labor markets. The work involved in producing and checking silicon chips is a related concern: many women in the Pacific rim areas are employed in these activities, in which permanent damage to eyesight and other health risks can be involved.

Judy Wajcman's overview of feminist studies of science and technology (1991) illustrates the ways in which past studies of automation have tended to focus implicitly or explicitly on men's work (as with machine tools in engineering).

She also casts a skeptical eye over the vision of the "smart" or "self-servicing" automated house that has emerged in some social science literature: more high-tech systems in the home will be as open to differing interpretations and possibilities as those in the office or the factory.

Some of the most thought-provoking feminist assessments of automation (and technology more generally) have been developed in fiction. In her novel *The Female Man*, first published in 1975, Joanna Russ created a "smart house" that not only cleaned itself but also provided a very responsive artificial lover: an imaginative leap somewhat beyond the confines of interactive links between computer, cooker, vacuum cleaner, and washing machine. Two novels by Marge Piercy, published in 1979 and 1992, explore the contrasting political choices embodied in automated systems: intensified surveillance and entrenched inequality or cooperative networks, in which both men and women can literally wire themselves up to the Internet, and in which automated systems are a shared sphere of activity rather than an external threat or promise.

See Also

COMPUTING: OVERVIEW; DETERMINISM: ECONOMIC; INFORMATION TECHNOLOGY; NETWORKS: ELECTRONIC; TECHNOLOGY; TECHNOLOGY: WOMEN AND DEVELOPMENT

References and Further Reading

Blauner, Robert. 1964. *Alienation and freedom.* Chicago: University of Chicago Press.

Braverman, Harry. 1974. *Labor and monopoly capital.* New York: Monthly Review.

Cockburn, Cynthia. 1983. *Brothers: Male dominance and technological change.* London: Pluto.

———. 1985. *The machinery of dominance: Women, men and technical know-how.* London: Pluto.

Mitter, Swasti. 1986. *Common fate, common bond: Women in the global economy.* London: Pluto.

Piercy, Marge. 1992. *Body of glass.* London: Michael Joseph. (Published in the United States in 1991 under the title *He, she, it.*)

———. 1979. *Woman on the edge of time.* London: Women's Press.

Russ, Joanna. 1975. *The female man.* New York: Bantam.

Wajcman, Judy. 1991. *Feminism confronts technology.* London: Polity.

Jenny Owen

B

BABY-SITTING

See CHILD CARE.

BATTERY

Broadly, the term *battery,* or *battering,* refers to some form of physical or sexual violence perpetrated by one or more individuals against one or several others. In most of the world, battering has the additional connotation of gender-related violence. Questionnaires on the prevalence of assaults, police records, court appearances, sentencing data, and prison censuses all confirm that most victims of battering are women and children, and that the majority of assailants are men. The term *battering* is often restricted to assaults that occur in private between individuals who know one another, rather than to violence in public or perpetrated by strangers. Most cases of battering involve the physical or sexual abuse of women by their husbands, partners, or other family members. (This does not deny the existence of battering by women—abuse of women, children, and sometimes men by women. Battering in lesbian relationships and other forms of women-on-women battering do occur, but male-perpetrated assault is many times more frequent.)

Inclusion of Psychological Abuse

In some parts of the world, typically in developed western nations, psychological abuse may also be considered battery; however, this is a more recent association. Emotional abuse is destructive. While no form of abuse should be tolerated, and ideally, all members of society should work to minimize their harmful effects on others, problems remain in extending the definition of *battering* to include psycho-

logical abuse. First, there is concern that if the term is utilized too broadly, its import will be lessened when it is applied to physical or sexual violence. Second, any variation in the definitions of battery would make it difficult to compare its prevalence from one location to another and would raise problems for determining social or other policies aimed at improving the situation.

Prevalence of Battering: Geographical and Temporal Parameters

As mentioned above, it is difficult to find comparable data concerning the prevalence of battery of women around the world. Additional challenges for determining the prevalence of assault include the fact that domestic violence is typically hidden. People are often loath to acknowledge its occurrence, and therefore instances are not reported. In addition, various social agencies, such as the police, courts, and women's shelters, each deal with only a portion of the victims of battering, making it difficult to assemble a comprehensive overview of the prevalence of violence in families from these agencies' records.

Despite these documentation problems, the extant evidence demonstrates that battering does occur in most societies. In the contemporary well-documented world, an examination of just about any newspaper reveals evidence of battering. In the case of cultures which are comparatively less well documented in print media, similar evidence is found in the Human Relations Area Files (HRAF) cultural data archives, which are "a cross-indexed, cross-referenced collection of mostly primary ethnographic reports describing the ways of life of people in some 330 different cultural and ethnic groups from all regions of the world" (Levinson, 1989: 23). Levinson's study of these data demonstrates that "[w]ife beating is the most common form of family violence around the world. It occurs at least occasionally in 84.5 percent of the societies" in his sample. This is a disturbing finding for women, given that "[t]he sample is composed of 90 small-scale and peasant societies selected from the HRAF Probability Sample Files [which] is a stratified probability sample of 120 societies presumably representative of the 60 major geographical/cultural regions of the world" (1989: 31, 22). In other words, Levinson's research provides compelling evidence that battering is ubiquitous worldwide.

Documentation of the presence of battering is one thing; measuring its prevalence is another. The first methodologically rigorous attempt to do so was the American National Family Violence Survey of 1975. "This study [published by Straus, Gelles, and Steinmetz, 1980] measure[d] intrafamily violence in a large, nationally representative sample. This survey found that individuals faced the greatest risk of assault and physical injury in their own homes by members of their own families" (Jasinski and Williams, 1998: ix). This finding corroborated the experiences of women working in frontline community initiatives such as battered women's shelters or refuges and rape crisis organizations. Many of these organizations began to mobilize in the early 1970s in the United States, the United Kingdom, New Zealand, and other nations. At approximately the same time, the feminist movement began gaining momentum. All of these developments shared connections, and "[t]he discovery of violence against women as a major issue in Europe and North America coincided with the early stages of *feminist* theory development. In other parts of the world the convergence of *development*, *human rights*, and *feminist* praxis produced the framework for discovering the nature, forms, extent and pernicious effects of violence against women" (Schuler, 1992: 2; emphases in original).

Women's Studies and Research on Battering

The development of women's studies programs combined with the grassroots mobilization of feminists and the publication, in 1979, of both Lenore Walker's *The Battered Woman*, and Dobash and Dobash's *Violence Against Wives* stimulated further research into violence against women. From these initial publications, a flood of books and articles rapidly developed: "the 1990 ISIS International Bibliographic Survey of documentation on violence against women in the 1980s identified some 650 entries from around the world" (Schuler, 1992: 1). This prolific output resulted in significant advances in understanding battering and its causes.

Explanations for Battering

The many theories advanced to explain battering can be divided into four groups based on their premises: individual models, sociological models, sociostructural models, and ecological models. Individual models comprise approaches based on unique behavioral attributes, usually attributes of the perpetrators, such as low self-esteem, substance abuse, mental illness, or inability to ascribe blame.

Sociological models move beyond an analysis of individual characteristics to examine social dynamics within the group, usually the family. In this approach, root causes are attributed to goal-directed aggression, intergenerational transmission of violence, or other stresses. For example, resource theory suggests that each partner brings material and nonmaterial resources to the relationship. If one partner lacks resources, that partner may use violence as a means to gain power in domestic interactions. Neither the sociological nor the individual models advance understanding of why women typically are the victims of violence and men are usually its perpetrators.

In contrast to the somewhat static processes envisaged in sociological models, sociostructural models are based on the dynamic powerful opposition between males and females within family units. Feminist or postmodernist researchers often theorize in this framework. For example, social scientists using patriarchal theory view domestic violence as the result of women's subordination to men.

The ecological models incorporate various aspects of the other groups, with the addition of environmental factors. An example might be research to investigate domestic violence in the specific cultural context of Indian Fiji. These final two groups of theories have been of greatest interest to women's studies. Indeed, it has been suggested that "one of the great achievements of feminism was to define wife beating as a social problem, not merely a phenomenon of particular violent individuals or relationships" (Klein et al., 1997: 1). Following this line of reasoning, many activists propose that the problem of battering is intimately linked with the issue of women's subordination to men, and as long as gender equality proves elusive, so too will peaceful egalitarian relationships between the sexes. This linkage has strong implications for public policy initiatives.

Legal Sanctions and Public Policy

According to this reasoning, social policy to decrease domestic violence should be directed toward the social, political, and economic advancement of women in order to achieve gender equity. By this means, ultimately, male aggression toward women would be diminished.

However, most public policy and legal sanctions dealing with family violence penalize the individual perpetrators with fines or prison sentences, or in some cases mandatory attendance at reeducation programs, or penalties with regard to child custody or access. There has been relatively little governmental recognition—in terms of concrete policy—of the gender inequities that foster domestic violence.

Economic Costs of Battering

In attempts to impel governments both to acknowledge the costs of domestic violence and to enact effective policies to lessen the prevalence of battering, various researchers have quantified the economic costs of intrafamily abuse. The idea is to demonstrate that funds put into preventative programs are ultimately cost-effective in terms of decreasing the amount spent on individuals' and families' recovery. A study by Gelles in 1987 (reported in Browne and Herbert, 1997: 294), for example, suggested that family violence in the United States resulted in individual economic costs of "175,500 lost days from paid work; [and] with regard to the economy of society as a whole, $44 million were spent in direct medical costs in order to provide the necessary services to victims of family violence."

The long-term solution to violence against women entails a commitment to gender equality, described in Article 5(a) of the United Nations Convention on the Elimination of All Forms of Discrimination Against Women (1979). The goal must be to modify the social and cultural patterns of conduct of men and women, with a view to eliminating prejudices and all practices which are based on the idea of the inferiority or the superiority of either of the sexes or on stereotyped roles for men and women. Battery is a social problem which requires large-scale social policy such as ratification by individual nations of the Convention on the Elimination of All Forms of Discrimination Against Women. However, it must also be recognized that long-standing gender imbalances will not be corrected instantly. While societies are working for more equitable gender relations, short-term approaches such as strong legal sanctions against the perpetrators of battery are necessary for the safety of its victims.

See Also

ABUSE; ANGER; DOMESTIC VIOLENCE; FAMILY: POWER RELATIONS AND POWER STRUCTURE; FEMICIDE; MISOGYNY; PORNOGRAPHY AND VIOLENCE; RAPE; SEXUAL VIOLENCE; VIOLENCE, *specific entries*

References and Further Reading

Browne, Kevin, and Martin Herbert. 1997. *Preventing family violence.* Chichester, U.K.: Wiley.

Commonwealth Secretariat. 1992. *Confronting violence: A manual for commonwealth action (Revised).* London: Women and Development Programme, Human Resource Development Group, Commonwealth Secretariat.

Counts, Dorothy Ayers, ed. 1990. Special issue: Domestic violence in Oceania. *Pacific Studies* 13(3).

Dobash, R. Emerson, and Russell Dobash. 1979. *Violence against wives: A case against the patriarchy.* New York: Free Press.

Douglas, Kay. 1994. *Invisible wounds: A self-help guide for New Zealand women in destructive relationships.* Auckland: Penguin.

Jasinski, Jana L., and Linda M. Williams, eds. 1998. *Partner violence: A comprehensive review of 20 years of research.* Thousand Oaks, Calif.: Sage.

Jones, Ann. 1994. *Next time she'll be dead: Battering and how to stop it.* Boston: Beacon.

Klein, Ethel, Jacquelyn Campbell, Esta Soler, and Marissa Ghez. 1997. *Ending domestic violence: Changing public perceptions/halting the epidemic.* Thousand Oaks, Calif.: Sage.

Levinson, David. 1989. *Family violence in cross-cultural perspective.* Newbury Park, Calif.: Sage.

Schuler, Margaret, ed. 1992. *Freedom from violence: Women's strategies from around the world.* New York: UNIFEM.

Shepard, Melanie F., and Ellen L. Pence, eds. 1999. *Coordinating community responses to domestic violence: Lessons from Duluth and beyond.* Thousand Oaks, Calif.: Sage.

Walker, Lenore E. 1979. *The battered woman.* New York: Harper and Row.

Susan J. Wurtzburg

BEAUTY CONTESTS AND PAGEANTS

Beauty pageants are popular cultural events that take many forms, have many goals, and generate a host of often disparate expectations. Though the actual structure of pageants varies depending on the context, most beauty pageants have a familiar, recognizable format: women contestants enter a competitive event where they are judged on beauty, personality, talent, and the elusive "poise." A panel of judges evaluates each contestant, and the woman who garners the most points in the various categories of the pageant—often including swimsuit, evening gown, talent, and interview competitions—wins and is crowned "queen" (Banet-Weiser, 1999).

The United States sponsors many different pageants each year including the Miss America pageant, the Miss U.S.A. pageant, and the two most famous "global beauty pageants," the Miss World and the Miss Universe pageants. However, there are scores of smaller local and international pageants that focus less on the glamour and conventional constructions of femininity displayed on stages of larger pageants than with cementing and legitimating local and cultural identity (Cohen et al., 1996). Beauty pageants have different meanings depending on cultural and geographic differences, and they are often important, significant cultural events, where "local values and imported foreign [western] ones collide on stage" (Wilk, 1996). Smaller, less corporate international pageants are often sites where contradictions, conflicts, and claims of diversity are simultaneously constructed and maintained.

Feminist protests against beauty pageants began in 1968 at the Miss America pageant in Atlantic City, New Jersey. This protest is often noted as heralding the second wave of liberal feminism in the United States. At that time, feminists protested the pageant by throwing bras, girdles, and other "instruments of torture" into a "Freedom Trash Can" as a gesture of their refusal to be constrained by patriarchal society (Chapkis, 1986). Many feminists persuasively argued that pageants such as the Miss America pageant objectify and alienate women. Alice Echols (1997) added that this important argument calls attention to the way in which beauty practices and rituals constitute a particular kind of politics. The beauty pageant has often been understood in a feminist context as symbolic of the various regulatory practices and discriminatory acts of a sexist society. Objectifying and evaluating a woman's physical appearance—which constitutes the central focus of beauty pageants—has been interpreted as a microcosm of the way that patriarchal societies regulate and monitor women's bodies more generally.

Because of vocal feminist protests against the beauty pageant, the event itself has been fundamentally transformed. Beauty pageants continue to be a popular cultural form where women are evaluated on the basis of their physical appearance, but the pageant itself often appropriates liberal feminist rhetoric in terms of equal opportunity, access, and tolerance. Beauty pageants in the 1990s in the United States and elsewhere have been forced to confront and respond to demands that they accurately reflect racial and ethnic diversity, and that they adjust their format and goals to reflect the contemporary goals of women. However, because beauty pageants remain dedicated to the objectification of women's bodies, the goals of these events seem to remain contradictory and conflicted.

See Also

BODY; IMAGES OF WOMEN: OVERVIEW

References and Further Reading

Banet-Weiser, Sarah. 1999. *The most beautiful girl in the world: Beauty pageants and national identity.* Berkeley: University of California Press.

Chapkis, Wendy. 1986. *Beauty secrets: Women and the politics of appearance.* Boston: South End.

Cohen, Colleen Ballerino, Richard Wilk, and Berverly Stoeltje, eds. 1996. *Beauty queens on the global stage: Gender, contests, and power.* New York: Routledge.

Echols, Alice. 1997. Nothing distant about it: Women's liberation and sixties radicalism. In Cathy J. Cohen, Kathleen B. Jones, and Joan C. Tronto, eds., *Women transforming politics: An alternative reader.* New York: New York University Press.

Wilk, Richard. 1996. Introduction: Beauty queens on the global stage. In Colleen Ballerino Cohen, Richard Wilk, and Berverly Stoeltje, eds., *Beauty queens on the global stage: Gender, contests, and power.* New York: Routledge.

Sarah Banet-Weiser

BIAS

See DISCRIMINATION; HETEROPHOBIA AND HOMOPHOBIA; MISOGYNY; RACISM AND XENOPHOBIA; and SEXISM.

BIGAMY

Bigamy refers to the narrowly defined crime of having two wives or two husbands at the same time. While criminalizing marriage between individuals who already have a living spouse, bigamy does not address a wider range of behavioral practices that fall outside the boundaries of exclusive monogamous marriage: long-term consensual unions, adultery while residing with a spouse, premarital sex, and casual liaisons (Boyer, 1995). Although the term *bigamy* extends to marital behaviors of both men and women, in practice bigamy is largely understood as a crime committed by men who have two or more wives at once. The concept of bigamy as a crime appears to have its roots in Christian Europe, dating back at least to the Middle Ages.

Western colonial expansion and missionizing brought the European Christian belief in and practice of monogamy into conflict with the polygamous family relationships of many different peoples in the Americas, Africa, Australia, and Asia. Bigamy was a passionate issue for European colonialists and missionaries and often represented a lightning rod for the expression of tensions between indigenous and colonial ways of life (Hunt, 1991). Frequently, Europeans expressed the belief that plural marriages degraded women in the societies that openly practiced polygyny.

In the United States, controversy over bigamy peaked in the mid-nineteenth century and focused on the Mormons, whose church formally advocated polygamy until 1890. Opponents of Mormon polygamy claimed that plural marriages degraded Mormon women, that polygamy was lustful and immoral, and that the practice of plural marriages eroded the marital relationship. Antibigamy legislation, however, was used not to advance the position of Mormon women but to threaten Mormon civil rights and seize property of the church. During the antipolygamy campaigns of the late 1800s, many feminists, who equated polygamy with the oppression of women, were surprised to find Morman women publicly demonstrating in favor of the right to plural marriage as a matter of religious freedom.

In postcolonial times western and nonwestern feminists alike, who believe that polygamy erodes women's status and power, advocate its elimination. The liberation of women, especially in Muslim countries, is associated with the abolition of the practice of polygamy. For example, in 1957, after gaining independence from France, Tunisia attempted to establish formal equality between the sexes by guaranteeing women certain rights, among them the elimination of polygamy. The attempt to achieve liberation for women through the abolition of polygamy is not restricted to Muslim countries: in 1950 Communist China enacted a National Marriage Law that sought to enhance women's status by prohibiting a number of practices, among them polygamy.

See Also

ADULTERY; MARRIAGE: OVERVIEW; MORMONS; POLYGYNY AND POLYANDRY; WIFE

Reference and Further Readings

Boyer, Richard. 1995. *Lives of the bigamists: Marriage, family and community in colonial Mexico.* Albuquerque: University of New Mexico Press.

Clawson, Rudger. 1993. *Prisoner for polygamy: The memoirs and letters of Rudger Clawson at the Utah Territorial Penitentiary*

1884–87. Ed. Stan Larson. Urbana: University of Illinois Press.

Frost, Ginger. 1997. Bigamy and cohabitation in Victorian England. *Journal of Family History* 22(3: July): 286–306.

Hunt, Nancy. 1991. Noise over camouflaged polygamy: Colonial morality taxation and a woman-naming crisis in Belgian Africa. *Journal of African History* 32(3): 471–494.

Katherine T. McCaffrey

BIOETHICS: FEMINIST

Bioethics and second-wave feminism were both offspring of the civil rights movement in the United States in the 1960s, although they pursued different paths toward maturity. Persisting throughout many turns and twists in feminist thinking has been an unswerving commitment to identifying, analyzing, and subverting structures of power and authority that oppress women. However, few mainstream bioethicists have attended systematically to power imbalances in physician-patient and researcher-subject relationships or to the background conditions of such relationships. Bioethics has remained largely insensitive to hierarchical rankings that parcel people into more or less arbitrary groups—sex, race, ethnicity, age, and susceptibility to illness and disability. Feminist bioethics aims to rectify these imbalances.

The Emergence of Feminist Bioethics

Women have a long history of interest in health care issues extending back to midwifery and nursing before the medical profession took control of these practices. In the 1960s, women rose in protest over the increasing medicalization of their bodily functions, and interest in the fledgling women's health movement swelled. The first edition of *Our Bodies, Ourselves* appeared in 1969. By the mid-1970s, feminist scholars were decrying the erosion of access to abortion, supposedly secured by *Roe* v. *Wade*, and lamenting childbirth practices that sacrificed the humanity of the women to the convenience of her obstetrician and the presumably independent rights of her fetus. In the 1980s, feminists' interest in new reproductive technologies mounted, and the National Institutes of Health belatedly acknowledged the long-standing exclusion of women from clinical trials, the consequent dearth of research on diseases prevalent among women, and the differential effects of drugs on the female body. By then, work by feminist bioethicists was being widely circulated in feminist publications, and some was surfacing in bioethics journals. In 1981 Helen Bequaert Holmes and others published an anthology that was arguably the first book to link bioethics with systematic gender analysis.

It took almost another decade, however, before scholarship in feminist bioethics reached a critical mass. The feminist philosophy journal *Hypatia* devoted two special issues to feminist ethics and medicine in 1989, and in 1992 a collection based on these articles appeared as *Feminist Perspectives in Medical Ethics*. In the same year, the first book-length treatment of feminist bioethical theory appeared—Susan Sherwin's *No Longer Patient: Feminist Ethics and Health Care*. In the next year, works by Susan Bordo and Mary Mahowald appeared critiquing dominant medical and cultural attitudes toward women's bodies, and Anne Donchin and Helen Bequaert Holmes founded the International Network on Feminist Approaches to Bioethics (FAB). Recognizing the need for a cross-cultural perspective on bioethical issues that is responsive to nondominant social groups, FAB aimed to foster development of a more inclusive theory of bioethics.

As articulated in the work of feminist bioethicists and incorporated in FAB's aims, three goals have been central to development of feminist bioethics:

1. To extend bioethical theory to encompass women in all social locations as well as other social groups susceptible to harm through group identification and to assimilate the significance of race, ethnicity, and gender in bioethical theory and health care practice.

2. To reexamine the principles and legitimizing functions of bioethics insofar as they have been constructed from the standpoint of an elite group blinded to its own partiality. Dominant bioethical theory has overlooked such key components of moral life as context, partiality, and relational bonds and is often unresponsive to institutionalized injustices. Assimilation into theory and practice of these neglected moral dimensions can serve as corrective to the common tendency to regard patients only in their generality—as repeatable instances of generic care—ignoring particularities essential to understanding the situations of sick and vulnerable individuals.

3. To create new strategies and methodologies that can interject the standpoints of nondominant people into policy-making processes, catalyze change within both developing and developed countries, and empower marginalized people to address their problems in terms of their own cultural beliefs and interests.

Recent Developments and Future Directions

In the 1990s, feminist bioethics began to catch the attention of think tanks, journal editors, and textbook publishers, and it is now a credible topic for graduate students' dissertations. However, although more women are turning to bioethics scholarship, their influence on the field is still limited. The format of most bioethics texts has changed remarkably little. As though women's expertise were confined to childbearing issues, women's contributions to the more established bioethics anthologies have been relegated primarily to the sections on abortion, maternal-fetal relations, and reproductive technologies. Despite diversification in bioethical theory, the prestige of theoretical approaches that rely on abstract universal norms and regard concrete individuals as instances of generic "man" still remains high. Feminist critiques of mainstream bioethical theory tend to be classified along with communitarianism and casuistry as "alternative" approaches or subsumed under an "ethic of care." And, although bioethicists are better represented on public-policy panels and in medical school faculties, they include few women and virtually no feminists.

In other respects, too, feminist influence on the direction of bioethics scholarship and teaching remains peripheral. As globalization extends first world technologies into developing economies, American bioethicists are now exporting the very same affliction feminist bioethicists identified in the United States: a focus on abstract individuals and universal principles that slight concrete people and their lives. Moreover, as formerly socialist countries shift toward market economies, along with a tendency to appropriate morally dubious western technological practices comes a proclivity to view women's bodies as (often faulty) reproductive machines. Nonwestern leaders, by coupling western technology with social power, can intensify control over women by the medical establishment and utilize women's bodies to reproduce their own distinctive cultural norms. In both developed and developing countries, the effects of biomedical practices on women still tend to be viewed as only incidental side effects that raise "women's questions" which can readily be deferred.

Feminist bioethics, then, still has a considerable distance to travel before it can overcome the mistaken assumption that feminists are addressing only "women's concerns"—a special ethics for women. Like the broader feminist movement, which also aims to rectify systemic injustices, feminist bioethicists look forward to a future when both theory and practice have been transformed, when the voices of the socially marginalized are fully recognized, and the needs of all peoples are incorporated into a system of health care justice that is responsive to the differing conditions of human lives across all the earth.

See Also

ABORTION; DISABILITY: HEALTH AND SEXUALITY; ETHICS: FEMINIST; ETHICS: MEDICAL; ETHICS: SCIENTIFIC; EXPERIMENTS ON WOMEN; FETUS; HEALTH: OVERVIEW; MEDICAL CONTROL OF WOMEN; MEDICINE: INTERNAL, *I and II*; REPRODUCTIVE RIGHTS; REPRODUCTIVE TECHNOLOGIES; SCIENTIFIC SEXISM AND RACISM

References and Further Reading

Bordo, Susan. 1993. *Unbearable weight: Feminism, Western culture, and the body.* Berkeley: University of California Press.

Callahan, Joan C., ed. 1995. *Reproduction, ethics, and the law: Feminist perspectives.* Bloomington: Indiana University Press.

Donchin, Anne, and Laura M. Purdy, eds. 1999. *Embodying bioethics: Recent feminist advancers.* Lanham, Md.: Rowman and Littlefield.

Holmes, Helen Bequaert, and Laura M. Purdy, eds. 1992. *Feminist perspectives in medical ethics.* Bloomington: Indiana University Press.

———, B. Hoskins, and M. Gross, eds. 1981. *The custom-made child? Women-centered perspectives.* Totowa, N.J.: Humana.

Mahowald, Mary. 1993. *Women and children in health care.* New York: Oxford University Press.

Mahowald, Mary. 2000. *Genes, women, equality.* New York: Oxford University Press.

Purdy, Laura. 1996. *Reproducing persons: Issues in feminist bioethics.* Ithaca, N.Y.: Cornell University Press.

Sherwin, Susan. 1992. *No longer patient: Feminist ethics and health care.* Philadelphia: Temple University Press.

Tong, Rosemarie. 1997. *Feminist approaches to bioethics.* Boulder, Col.: Westview.

Wolf, Susan, ed. 1996. *Feminism and bioethics: Beyond reproduction.* New York: Oxford University Press.

Anne Donchin

BIOGRAPHY

The word *biography* was first defined in the *Oxford English Dictionary* in 1683. Since then, its central meaning has remained the same: the narrated life-course of a person. In the eighteenth and nineteenth centuries, lives of women were used to evoke humility and modesty in their female readers, as in Mrs. Mary Pilkington's *Biography for Girls* (1799) and biographies of women such as Florence Nightingale (Vicinus, in Shortland and Yeo, 1996). Nineteenth-century positivist approaches, which made literary, artistic, and political figures popular subjects, affirmed the place of biography as a means of recording heroic achievements in the public sphere.

In the twentieth century, several debates about the writing of biography led to a departure from the simple collection and narration of "facts." Tension developed between history and fiction; for example, Virginia Woolf described her biography of Roger Fry as "all too detailed and tied down," in contrast to her *Orlando*, a study of Vita Sackville-West, which she considered a "writer's holiday" (Edel, 1984: 208, 190).

The increasing links between biography, sociology, history, and psychology have provoked much discussion. The interdisciplinary journal *Biography*, published at the Center for Biographical Research at the University of Hawaii, has provided a medium for such cross-fertilization. Biographers' incorporation of Freudian ideas in exploring powerful women's inner lives, as in Leo Abse's study of Margaret Thatcher (1989), have provoked questions about how best to apply such models in interpreting a life.

Feminist biographers have destabilized the voice of the authoritative biographer by challenging us to reconsider versions of lives that glorify individual greatness and mask the social context that has produced the subject (Stanley, 1992). By introducing the voice of the author, some explore their own relationship to the subject as part of the text (Modjeska, 1990). The notion of a coherent "self" with a life-course recoverable by another has also prompted post-modern critiques of biography as a form (Rhiel and Suchoff, 1996).

The consumption of biographies by the book-buying public has created a profitable genre within the publishing industry. In 1994, a poll on reading habits in Britain found that biography was the most popular genre of nonfiction (Shortland and Yeo, 1996). Deirdre Bair and Claire Tomalin both have made their mark in this industry, Bair with her biographies of Simone de Beauvoir (1990) and Anaïs Nin (1995) and Tomalin with studies of Mary Wollstonecraft (1974), Katherine Mansfield (1987), and Jane Austen (1997). The public's desire to glimpse secrets of the famous has led to an industry of works that, like Andrew Morton's biography of Princess Diana, can change the way powerful figures are perceived and alter their place in the public sphere.

In her study of the various biographies of the poet Sylvia Plath, Janet Malcolm claimed that a biographer is like "the professional burglar, breaking into the house, rifling through certain drawers…and triumphantly bearing [the] loot away" (1994: 9). In the way biographers appear to transgress on the privacy of the subject, ethical issues arise about whose interests are served in the process of biography.

On the other hand, the recording of life-stories can convey a history that often is hidden from the public's gaze. Women of color, indigenous women, lesbians, working-class women, and women with disabilities may not see their lives reflected in mainstream culture, and biographies can help them claim their place in history. Biography can convey a synthesis of public and private because it describes the shaping of a life-project through self-discovery. This genre remains a growing and exciting field in women's studies through its depiction of the experience of resistance and acceptance.

See Also

AUTOBIOGRAPHICAL CRITICISM: AUTOBIOGRAPHY; CULTURAL CRITICISM; DIARIES AND JOURNALS; FICTION; HEROINE; HISTORY; JOURNALISM; LITERARY THEORY AND CRITICISM; LITERATURE: OVERVIEW; POSTMODERNISM: LITERARY THEORY

References and Further Reading

Abse, Leo. 1989. *Margaret, daughter of Beatrice: A politician's psycho-biography of Margaret Thatcher.* London: Cape.

Bair, Deirdre. 1990. *Simone de Beauvoir: A life.* New York: Summit.

———. 1995. *Anaïs Nin: A life.* New York: Putnam.

Edel, Leon. 1984. *Writing lives: Principia biographica.* New York: Norton.

Iles, Teresa, ed. 1992. *All sides of the subject: Women and biography.* New York: Teachers College Press, Columbia University.

Kadar, Melanie, ed. 1992. *Essays on life writing: From genre to critical practice.* Toronto: University of Toronto Press.

Malcolm, Janet. 1994. *The silent woman: Sylvia Plath and Ted Hughes.* London: Picado.

Modjeska, Drusilla. 1990. *Poppy.* Melbourne: Penguin.

———. *Stravinsky's lunch.* 1999. Sydney: Picador.

Pilkington, Mary. 1799. *Biography for girls, or, Moral and instructive examples for young ladies.* London: Vernor and Hood.

Rhiel, Mary, and David Suchoff, eds. 1996. *The seductions of biography.* New York: Routledge.

Shortland, Michael, and Richard Yeo. 1996. Introduction. In Shortland and Yeo, eds., *Telling lives in science: Essays on scientific biography.* Cambridge: Cambridge University Press, 1–44.

Stanley, Liz. 1992. *The auto/biographical: The theory and practice of feminist auto/biography.* Manchester: Manchester University Press.

Tomalin, Claire. 1997. *Jane Austen: A life.* London: Viking.

———. 1987. *Katherine Mansfield: A secret life.* London: Viking.

———. 1974. *The life and death of Mary Wollstonecraft.* New York: Harcourt Brace Jovanovich.

Belinda Robson

BIOLOGICAL DETERMINISM

Biological determinism is the belief that human behaviors may be attributed to a person's underlying essential genetic makeup. Popularly discussed in debates about nature versus nurture or heredity versus environment, deterministic thinking has its roots in evolutionary theory and dates back to the middle to late nineteenth century. Deterministic theories rose to prominence after Charles Darwin's theory of evolution by natural selection was popularized, and they became widespread in the United States and Europe in the mid-nineteenth and early twentieth centuries. Applications of biological determinism to social and cultural problems have usually coincided with periods of social upheaval (Bem, 1993; Bleier, 1984). Biological determinism has been used to discredit social movements such as antislavery, women's rights, and women's suffrage. Theories rising from biological determinism include eugenics, social Darwinism, and sociobiology.

Francis Galton applied—actually, misapplied—evolutionary thinking to heredity when he invented eugenics. Although Galton appreciated the interaction of heredity and environment, he still thought that selective mating would result in a superior populace—one that did not include racial mixing (Pearson, 1996). The Nazis applied such biological ideas to social and cultural institutions in the mid-twentieth century (Birke and Hubbard, 1995). Biological differences assumed enormous significance and resulted in gender segregation in schools as well as a continuum of racial superiority, which placed some races below animals. This was the worst manifestation of biology as destiny.

Throughout history, women have been subjugated in various cultures because of their assumed inherent nature (Bem, 1993). Seen as passive, nurturing, and dependent, women have been denied higher education, the right to vote, and other means for social and cultural advancement. Education was thought to be damaging to women's reproductive system. Even many nineteenth-century suffragists used deterministic beliefs about innate racial differences to promote their cause.

The sexual division of labor has long been assumed to be natural and universal, although, for example, Indian women contribute widely to agriculture and dairy farming. Recent studies reveal that in rural India agriculture is the major occupation of working women (Shiva, 1995)—a fact that often does not appear in statistics because of sexist definitions of "work."

In the late nineteenth century, Herbert Spencer used evolution to justify a conservative political and social agenda known as social Darwinism. Spencer used biology to justify restrictive Victorian constraints on women's roles. Although social Darwinism is no longer popular in its original version, a new form became popular in the twentieth century—sociobiology (Bleier, 1984). In the mid-1970s, E. O. Wilson published his first book on sociobiology, which casts the world in biological universals largely free from the influence of environment, learning, or culture.

This persistent manifestation of biological determinism reinforces cultural and racial stereotypes under the guise of genetic predisposition. These stereotypes continue to cast women as passive, manipulative, and dependent (Bleier, 1984). In the wake of the modern feminist movement, feminist critiques of science have included both critics and adherents of biologically deterministic thinking (Bem, 1993). Though no one perspective of biological determinism appears to be totally correct, women and society continue to benefit from the ongoing critique.

See Also

DIVISION OF LABOR; ESSENTIALISM; EUGENICS; NATURE-NURTURE DEBATE; SCIENCE: FEMINIST CRITIQUES

References and Further Reading

Bem, Sandra Lipsitz. 1993. *The lenses of gender: Transforming the debate in sexual inequality.* New Haven, Conn.: Yale University Press.

Birke, Lynda, and Ruth Hubbard, eds. 1995. *Reinventing biology: Respect for life and the creation of knowledge.* Bloomington: Indiana University Press.

Bleier, Ruth. 1984. *Science and gender: A critique of biology and its theories on women.* New York: Pergamon.

Pearson, Roger. 1996. *Heredity and humanity: Race, eugenics and modern science.* Washington, D.C.: Scott-Townsend.

Shiva, Vandana. 1995. Democratizing biology: Reinventing biology from a feminist, ecological, and third world perspective. In Lynda Birke and Ruth Hubbard, eds., *Reinventing biology: Respect for life and the creation of knowledge,* 50–71. Bloomington: Indiana University Press.

Barbara I. Bond

BIOLOGY

The impact of women's studies on the biological sciences can be best understood by exploring two distinct but related fields—"women in science" and "gender in science." The distinction between sex and gender, absent in scientific discourse, is a significant contribution of feminists and is central to feminist critiques of science. *Sex* generally refers to the biological categories male and female, whereas *gender* refers to the cultural categories masculine and feminine, shaped and defined by society.

Research on "women in science" includes the work of historians, philosophers, and sociologists who study the presence of women scientists and their political, social, and intellectual influence, past and present. Although a perusal of textbooks, Nobel laureates, and scientific "greats" would suggest a lack of women in biology, feminists have documented a long and rich history of women's participation in the field. This participation occurred despite strong social and political factors and speaks to the compelling interest, devotion, and commitment of women in the scientific enterprise.

In considering the factors that contribute to the continued underrepresentation of women in the biological sciences, two main arguments have been put forth. The first, largely from within the sciences, notes that with the increased visibility of women—thanks to women's movements—things have improved, especially in biology, a field that historically has had more women in its ranks, as contrasted with the physical sciences. Legal cases brought by women charging sex discrimination, sexual harassment, and unfair tenure and hiring practices have exposed unjust policies and opened the doors for the entry of more women. This camp argues that the problem lies not within science but in historical problems of women's "access" to scientific careers. Scholarships, fellowships, and aggressive affirmative action policies will provide access for women, and, once in science, women will be welcomed and included in the scientific enterprise. Many such arguments cite the increased participation of women in biology—in the United States, for instance, the proportion of women among employed biologists rose from 18.3 percent in 1978 to 41 percent in 1995.

The second argument is that science is a social enterprise and reflects a history of male domination in a "masculinist culture." Feminists supporting this view point out that although the overall numbers of women in biology have increased, women continue to be disproportionately represented in the lower ranks. These feminists argue that the problem lies in the "culture" of science and, therefore, programs to recruit women should work actively to retain women by transforming the culture of science rather than transforming women to fit into the culture.

Scholars have largely focused on white, western women scientists, but recent cross-cultural work suggests equivalent though culture-specific barriers for women scientists in other countries. Colonial and postcolonial policies have institutionalized western science across the globe in medicine, agriculture, and other fields in the guise of development replacing indigenous practices.

The greatest impact of scholarship in women's studies has been made by extensive work attacking the concept of science as gender-neutral and value-free. Influential figures include Ruth Bleier, Anne Fausto-Sterling, Donna Haraway, Sandra Harding, Ruth Hubbard, Evelyn Fox Keller, and Sue Rosser. Their work shifts the focus from biological sex and "human nature" to gender. Feminist scholars have argued that science constructs gender and vice versa, and that social policies use "scientific knowledge" to reinforce contemporary social stereotypes of masculine and feminine, thereby justifying the continued subjugation of women. They have found considerable evidence that science is socially constructed, citing various episodes in history when gender stereotypes of a culture were encoded into scientific theories. Thus, they argue, science constructing gender and gender constructing science have together proved a potent tool in maintaining the status quo—that is, social privilege is scientifically encoded into biological privilege.

Critiques of biological determinism are particularly significant because of its implications for women's lives and women's health. The view of women's biology as inherently inferior has a severe impact on the social and intellectual role of women in contemporary society. In addition to challenging the extension of data from men to women and the exclusion of women subjects from medical research, feminists have challenged the medical view of women as deviant from "normal" male biology—the "disease model" of women's biology, for example, premenstrual syndrome, menopause, and childbirth. Studies on sex differences span many disciplines where, it is held, complex traits have been reduced to being biologically determined by individual genes (like the fields of genetics, cell biology, and developmental biology); individual hormones (endocrinology); or structures in the brain or other organs (neuroscience and anatomy). Feminist critics have attacked these studies on grounds of poor experimental design, inadequate data, incorrect assumptions, poor controls, overstated conclusions, or extrapolation from studies of animals to humans (as in primatology and animal behavior). The mass media publicize these research studies because they validate the "status quo," but there are few data to support assertions that any group is biologically inferior.

Using close, careful historical documentation feminist scholars have argued that science has served the interest of white, western, heterosexual, upper-class men. Although scientific theories changed, the subordination of various groups remained, from eighteenth-century beliefs that educating women deprived the reproductive organs of blood (because the brain would need more) to current debates on mathematics and spatial ability. These theories seem Eurocentric and class-based and also illogical: if educating women reduces their fertility physiologically, why did racist and imperialist policies not involve mass education of all women of color?

If the history of science suggests that science mirrors society, how can we use this insight in the current practices and methodology of science? Feminist critics of science have developed a framework to explore questions of objectivity and subjectivity and new grounds for alternative epistemologies. An unfortunate historical fact is that many of the feminist critiques have developed outside the sciences, removed from the lives of women scientists, creating distrust between women scientists and feminist critics of science. It is increasingly evident that, over the next decade, women's studies needs to bridge this chasm with analyses beginning with "the question of where and how the force of beliefs, interests, and cultural norms enter into the process by which effective knowledge is generated" (Keller, 1987: 90).

See Also

ANATOMY; BIOLOGICAL DETERMINISM; EDUCATION: SCIENCE; ESSENTIALISM; HORMONES; NATURE-NURTURE DEBATE; PHYSIOLOGY; PRIMATOLOGY; PSYCHOLOGY: OVERVIEW; PSYCHOLOGY: NEUROSCIENCE AND BRAIN RESEARCH; REPRODUCTION: OVERVIEW; REPRODUCTIVE TECHNOLOGIES; SCIENCE: FEMINIST PHILOSOPHY; SCIENCE: OVERVIEW; SCIENCE: FEMINISM AND SCIENCE STUDIES;

SCIENCE: FEMINIST CRITIQUES; SCIENCE: TRADITIONAL AND INDIGENOUS KNOWLEDGE; SCIENTIFIC SEXISM AND RACISM

References and Further Reading

Bleier, Ruth. 1984. *Science and gender: A critique of biology and its theories on women.* Elmsford, N.Y.: Pergamon.

Fausto-Sterling, Anne. 1985. *Myths of gender* New York: Basic Books.

Haraway, Donna. 1997. *Modest_witness@second_millennium. femaleman.©_meets_oncomouse™.* New York: Routledge.

———. 1990. *Primate visions.* New York: Routledge.

Harding, Sandra. 1993. *The racial economy of science: Toward a democratic future.* Bloomington: Indiana University Press.

Hubbard, Ruth. 1995. *Refiguring life: Metaphors of twentieth-century biology.* New York: Columbia University Press.

———, and Marion Lowe, eds. 1983. *Women's nature: Rationalizations of inequality.* Elmsford, N.Y.: Pergamon.

Keller, Evelyn Fox. 1985. *Reflection on gender and science.* New Haven, Conn.: Yale University Press.

———. 1987. Women scientists and feminist critics of science. *Daedalus* 116(4): 77–91.

National Science Foundation. 1998. *Women, minorities, and persons with disabilities in science and engineering: 1998.*

Rosser, Sue. 1992. *Biology and feminism.* New York: Twayne.

Spanier, Bonnie B. 1995. *Im/partial science: Gender ideology in molecular biology.* Bloomington: Indiana University Press.

Banu Subramaniam

BIRTH

See CHILDBIRTH and PREGNANCY AND BIRTH.

BIRTH CONTROL

See CONTRACEPTIVES.

BISEXUALITY

The term *bisexual* has a checkered history and has undergone several shifts in meaning since its first recorded appearance in 1804. It originally meant "of two sexes," and it has often been associated with hermaphroditism or androgyny. However, most bisexual activists and theorists today use the term *bisexuality* to refer to sexual attraction to, desire for, or activity with more than one sex, and distinguish it from sexual attraction, desire, or activity directed exclusively toward one particular sex, which some bisexual theorists refer to as *monosexuality* (George, 1993; Rose et al., 1996).

According to some commentators, the convergence of second-wave feminism and the "sexual revolution" of the late 1960s and early 1970s created a climate in which bisexuality was regarded by many feminists as a sexual option, part of the sexual autonomy and freedom for women that were important feminist goals. This climate was short-lived, however, and the increasingly bitter "sex wars" of the late 1970s and 1980s saw the rise of feminist hostility toward bisexual women, who were often accused of undermining the women's movement by taking energy from women while putting their own energies into men, or of retreating behind "heterosexual privilege" when a political situation became too serious, or of simply lacking the courage to come out as lesbian (George, 1993; Rust, 1995). Feminists' negative attitude toward bisexual women was compounded by more general stereotypes of bisexuals as promiscuous, irresponsible, and—an effect of the "moral panic" regarding HIV/AIDS in the 1980s—carriers and spreaders of disease, either from gay communities to the "general" (that is, heterosexual) population, or, in some versions of the "moral panic," from men to lesbian communities (Rose et al., 1996). Bisexual theorists and activists coined the term *biphobia* to describe this kind of stereotyping and prejudice, which comes both from mainstream heterosexual society and from lesbian and gay communities (George, 1993).

Partly in response to biphobia of various kinds, bisexuality enjoyed something of a renaissance in the 1990s, although it did not immediately become clear to what extent one could speak of a coherent bisexual movement (Hutchins and Kaahumanu, 1991; Rose et al., 1996). Despite (or perhaps because of) the previously negative attitudes often encountered by bisexual women within feminism, some distinctively bisexual feminist analyses of gender, sexuality, and oppression began to emerge in the 1990s. These included a celebration of the sexual autonomy and freedom of choice represented by a sexuality not subordinated to gender roles or expectations, and an analysis of the specific forms of oppression of bisexual women as distinct from those faced by nonbisexual women and some men (George, 1993; Rust, 1995). Some bisexual feminists, more radically and ambitiously, claim that bisexuality subverts dominant constructions of gender and sexuality as binary or dichotomous (that is, divided into exactly two parts), and therefore has the potential to deconstruct the binary oppositions (conceptual pairings such as masculine-feminine, strong-weak, rational-emotional) that underpin sexism and heterosexism (Hemmings, 1993; Weise, 1992). Indeed, some argue that binary opposition and dualistic thinking underpin the whole tradition of western thought and that the mechanism of oppression itself is based on the hierarchical relations set up by this dualistic tradition; some bisexual feminists suggest that bisexuality may therefore have the potential not just to deconstruct current notions of gender and sexuality but even to deconstruct western dualism and hence the possibility of oppression itself (Rose et al., 1996; Weise, 1992). Although this perspective has many attractions and may gain popularity, it presents political and theoretical difficulties. Some formulations from within queer politics and theory suggest that gender and sexuality may not always be as straightforwardly binary or dichotomous as this perspective assumes, particularly in the light of transgendered sexualities (Nataf, 1996); in any case, it remains unclear, to say the least, how bisexuality is to make the leap from asserting itself as a feminist identity or practice to dismantling the entire edifice of western metaphysics.

Other recent work has investigated the ways in which bisexuality may covertly inform apparently nonbisexual lives, histories, and sexualities. One of the most common popular assumptions about bisexuality is that "everyone is bisexual really," meaning that all human beings are potentially bisexual; this view of bisexuality as potential is also current in psychology and psychoanalysis, from Freud onward (Garber, 1996; George, 1993). Many bisexual feminists now reject this as a myth, pointing out that not everyone is actually bisexual here and now and that human beings are probably neither more nor less potentially bisexual than they are potentially lesbian, gay, heterosexual, or anything else. Some have argued that bisexuality often functions as a subtext of other forms of sexual identity: as the excluded other that embodies the collective fears and desires of particular sexual groups (Rust, 1995), or as a sexual narrative which may emerge when sexuality is considered as a process in continuous flux rather than as a fixed state or identity (Garber, 1996). Such work suggests ways in which bisexuality may have importance for feminism, both as a concept and for the political goals and contributions of bisexual women.

See Also

AIDS AND HIV; EPISTEMOLOGY; HETEROPHOBIA AND HOMOPHOBIA; HETEROSEXISM; HETEROSEXUALITY; LESBIANISM; OTHER; QUEER THEORY; SEXUAL ORIENTATION; SEXUALITY: OVERVIEW; TRANSGENDER

References and Further Reading

Academic Intervention. 1997. *The bisexual imaginary: Representation, identity and desire.* London: Casell.

Bisexual Anthology Collective. 1995. *Plural desires: Writing bisexual women's realities.* Toronto: Sister Vision, Black Women and Women of Colour Press.

Garber, Marjorie. 1996. *Vice versa: Bisexuality and the eroticism of everyday life.* London: Hamish Hamilton.

George, Sue. 1993. *Women and bisexuality.* London: Scarlet.

Hemmings, Clare. 1993. Resituating the bisexual body: From identity to difference. In Joseph Bristow and Angelia R. Wilson, eds., *Activating theory: Lesbian, gay, bisexual politics,* 118–138. London: Lawrence and Wishart.

Hutchins, Loraine, and Lani Kaahumanu, eds. 1991. *Bi any other name: Bisexual people speak out.* Boston: Alyson.

Nataf, Zachary I. 1996. *Lesbians talk: Transgender.* London: Scarlet.

Rose, Sharon, Cris Stevens, et al., eds. 1996. *Bisexual horizons: Politics, histories, lives.* London: Lawrence and Wishart.

Rust, Paula C. 1995. *Bisexuality and the challenge to lesbian politics: Sex, loyalty, and revolution.* New York and London: New York University Press.

Storr, Merl. 1999. *Bisexuality: A critical reader.* London and New York: Routledge and Kegan Paul.

Weise, Elizabeth Reba, ed. 1992. *Closer to home: Bisexuality and feminism.* Seattle: Seal Press.

Web Sites

http://www.bi.org
http://www.bisexual.org

Merl Storr

BLACK FEMINISM

See FEMINISM: AFRICAN-AMERICAN and FEMINISM: BLACK BRITISH.

BLACKNESS AND WHITENESS

In sixteenth-century Europe, words for *black* had negative connotations of ill-fortune, impurity, and evil. Words for *white* had connotations of innocence, purity, and blessedness. When Europeans applied these terms to people, despite obvious physical inaccuracies, the words contributed to the perception that Africans and south Asians were the moral and physical opposite of Europeans: so different that they could be treated more like animals than humans.

In the late eighteenth century, western scientists linked color with cultural stereotypes to create the concept of race. In the first "scientific" racial taxonomy, the Swedish naturalist Carl von Linne divided people into four types:

Americanus or red—Tenacious, contented, free, ruled by custom

Europeanus or white—Light, lively, inventive, ruled by rites

Asiaticus or yellow—Stern, haughty, stingy, ruled by opinion

Africanus or black—Cunning, slow, negligent, ruled by caprice. (Corcos, 1997, p. 17)

Even after early twentieth-century scientists objected to the idea of biological races, color-specific concepts of race remained a central, if mutable, feature of western ideology and discourse.

Definitions of *white* and *nonwhite* have changed over time and across national boundaries. Eighteenth- and nineteenth-century slave owners in the United States categorized people with "one drop" of African blood as legally black, but people with mixed Native American and European ancestry could be legally white. American and northern European governments have at times considered Arab, Latino, Irish, Italian, and Jewish people white, and at other times nonwhite (Allen, 1994; Morsy, 1994; Sacks, 1994). Whereas colonial powers constructed race in binary terms, Latin American countries such as Brazil developed over one hundred words for racial identity and skin color (Rodriguez, 1994). Ruth Frankenburg observes that "'white' is as much as anything else an economic and political category maintained over time by a changing set of exclusionary practices both legislative and customary" (1993: 11–12).

Despite the racist ideology inherent in western concepts of race, oppressed minorities and colonized nations often constructed positive interpretations of racial identity. As Audre Lorde writes, "It is axiomatic that if we do not define ourselves for ourselves, we will be defined by others—for their use and to our detriment" (1984: 45). In the 1960s, the African-American "black power" movement consciously transformed the derogatory label *black* into a positive term, signifying strength, beauty, and unity. Native American activists similarly adopted the term "red power." These movements allied themselves with anticolonial struggles around the world and challenged western representations of the "other" with native articulations of ethnic pride and self-determination.

Patricia Hill Collins argues that Africans have identified with the social construction of blackness and race not only as a response to white racism but also because the concepts encompass "individual and group valuation of an independent, long-standing Afrocentric consciousness" (1991: 27). In contrast, contemporary white Europeans and Americans seldom describe whiteness as salient to their sense of self, and they often deny the cultural specificity of their worldviews (Garza and Herringer, 1987). Postcolonial scholars have described the absence of expressed white identity as a consequence of imperialism: western constructions of bounded, namable, subordinate "others" dialectically created whiteness as an empty, unmarked, normative category (Trinh, 1986/1987). In the last two decades of the twentieth century, feminist scholars and political activists devoted increasing attention to the investigation and articulation of relationships between gender identity and racial or ethnic identity, including whiteness (see, for instance, Davis, 1981; Frankenberg, 1993; Lorde, 1984; Moghadam, 1994; Moraga and Anzaldua, 1981; Trinh, 1986/1987).

See Also

ANTIRACIST AND CIVIL RIGHTS MOVEMENTS; APARTHEID, SEGREGATION, AND GHETTOIZATION; EDUCATION: ANTIRACIST; ETHNIC STUDIES; EUROCENTRISM: OTHER; RACE; RACISM AND XENOPHOBIA

References and Further Reading

Allen, Theodore. 1994. *The invention of the white race.* London: Verso.

Collins, Patricia Hill. 1991. *Black feminist thought: Knowledge, consciousness, and the politics of empowerment.* New York: Routledge.

Corcos, Alain. 1997. *The myth of human races.* East Lansing: Michigan State University Press.

Davis, Angela Y. 1981. *Women, race and class.* New York: Vintage.

Frankenberg, Ruth. 1993. *White women, race matters: The social construction of whiteness.* Minneapolis: University of Minnesota Press.

Garza, R. T., and L. G. Herringer. 1987. Social identity: A multidimensional approach. *Journal of Social Psychology* 127: 299–308.

Lorde, Audre. 1984. *Sister outsider: Essays and speeches.* Trumansburg, N.Y.: Crossing.

Moghadam, Valentine M., ed. 1994. *Identity politics and women: Cultural reassertions and feminisms in international perspective.* Boulder, Col.: Westview.

Moraga, Cherie, and Gloria Anzaldua, eds. 1981. *This bridge called my back: Writings by radical women of color.* Watertown, Mass.: Persephone.

Morsy, Soheir A. 1994. Beyond the honorary "white" classification of Egyptians: Societal identity in historical context. In

Steven Gregory and Roger Sanjek, eds., *Race,* 175–198. New Brunswick, N.J.: Rutgers University Press.

Rodriguez, Clara E. 1994. Challenging racial hegemony: Puerto Ricans in the United States. In Steven Gregory and Roger Sanjek, eds., *Race,* 131–145. New Brunswick, N.J.: Rutgers University Press.

Sacks, Karen Brodkin. 1994. How did Jews become white folks? In Steven Gregory and Roger Sanjek, eds., *Race,* 78–102. New Brunswick, N.J.: Rutgers University Press.

Trinh, T. Minh-ha. 1986/1987. Difference: A special third world women's issue. *Discourse* 8: 11–37.

Lori Blewett

BLENDED FAMILIES

See STEPFAMILIES.

BLUESTOCKINGS

The term *bluestocking* has been used since the beginning of the nineteenth century as a derogatory label for any woman whose ostentatious display of learning makes her behavior arrogant and immodest, hence "unfeminine." Although the primary objection is to the woman's appearance rather than to the improvement of her mind, the kind and degree of improvement are also at issue: the bluestocking typically dabbles in male pursuits such as mathematics, science, or philosophy. The term rapidly came to be used in a negative sense; but it originally had a positive connotation, referring first to intellectual men and then more specifically to a group of celebrated women in late-eighteenth-century London. Although the term has been applied to women actively engaged in promoting salons and intellectual culture in various countries, it properly refers only to the British group. The subsequent generalization and pejorative use of the term coincided with reaction against the French Revolution, as such reaction affected assumptions about gender, the social role of women, and changes in the political temper at the turn of the nineteenth century.

The Bluestocking Circle was the group of London hostesses whose imitation of the Parisian fashion for salons created for them a degree of fame. But, unlike the Parisian *salonières,* these women were less interested in re-creating a court atmosphere at home than in creating an outlet for female intellectualism during the London season. Dominated by Elizabeth Montagu (1720–1800), who became known as "queen of the Blues," this circle of intelligent and educated women created in their London mansions a social space for men and women to gather and engage in intellectual and literary debate. The original group included the hostesses and their close friends: Elizabeth Montagu, Elizabeth Vesey, Elizabeth Carter, Catherine Talbot, Mary Delany, Hester Chapone, and Frances Boscawen. Soon a younger and more literary generation of women joined: Hester Thrale, Fanny Burney, and Hannah More (whose poem "Bas Bleu; or Conversation," immortalized the group).

Montagu, Carter, and Vesey were the formative group whose friendship and correspondence began the exchanges in the 1760s that resulted in holding the London salons. Although their own use of the term *bluestocking* was originally in reference to male intellectualism—indeed, Vesey apparently coined the term for their philosophically minded friend Benjamin Stillingfleet, because he wore worsted blue stockings instead of white silk hose—they gradually began to use the term to refer to the kind of literate "conversation" they cultivated, finally calling it "blue stocking philosophy" to each other. Such conversations often included their favorite pastime, the promotion of women's education and intellectual endeavors. Elizabeth Carter's own classical scholarship, including her translation of the Stoic philosopher Epictetus (1758), provided Montagu in particular with a model of what female intellectualism could achieve. The Blues proved themselves women of letters with the publication of Carter's *Epictetus* (the first edition of which was printed by Samuel Richardson) and *Poems* (1762), in addition to her contributions to *Gentleman's Magazine;* Montagu's work of literary criticism *Essay on the Writings and Genius of Shakespeare* (1772) and her three *Dialogues of the Dead;* Catherine Talbot's *Reflections on the Seven Days of the Week* (1770) and *Essays on Various Subjects* (1772); and Hester Chapone's *Letters on the Improvement of the Mind* (1773) and *Miscellanies* (1775). They also supported women writers such as Charlotte Turner Smith, Mary Collyer, Sarah Fielding, Hannah More, Fanny Burney, Ann Yearsley, and Montagu's sister Sarah Scott. They were friends with men such as Samuel Johnson, David Garrick, Samuel Richardson, George Berkeley, George Lyttelton, Laurence Sterne, Horace Walpole, and Joshua Reynolds.

The salons were made possible by Edward Montagu's will, in which at his death in 1775 he left his estate to his wife. Elizabeth traveled to Paris, heard Voltaire speak at the Académie Française, and was herself received as an author. She was able to build a large house in Portman Square in London and entertain with "conversaziones" where aristocrats, intelligentsia, and artists mingled, as well as Parisian-style salons. While Montagu favored assemblies where debate was emphasized, Vesey developed a more informal style for which she became famous. The small rooms and spaces in Vesey's house encouraged her guests to gather in various groups for multiple conversations.

In addition to the creation of the London salons, the Bluestocking Circle also contributed much to making women's education acceptable, and to disarming the conventional and disabling association between women artists and sexual laxity. But with Montagu's death in 1800 the Bluestocking Circle was broken.

Even before this, younger women of intellectual inclination found little encouragement of the kind Burney and More had experienced when they were first introduced to the circle. By the late 1790s "bluestocking" had become a term of disapprobation and eventually misogyny. It began to mark a woman who was ungainly in society rather than a suave and sophisticated society hostess; the blue was by this time a woman unaware of how her learning detracted from her person by making her mentally and politically suspect. The blue was a bit mad, and possibly more than a bit jacobin à la Mary Wollstonecraft. By the time Jane Austen wrote *Pride and Prejudice,* the ungainly and unattractive sister Mary was cast as a bluestocking to oppose her essential antisocialism to Elizabeth's sociable but narrowly educated native wit.

The best-known visual tribute to the Bluestockings' importance remains Richard Samuel's painting *Nine Living Muses of Great Britain,* exhibited at the Royal Academy in 1779. The painting, now at the National Portrait Gallery, shows Elizabeth Montagu surrounded by other luminaries such as Charlotte Lennox and Catherine Macaulay, with Hannah More standing behind her. Montagu is shown sitting in critical judgment; this prominent placement in the composition is testimony to her centrality in the promotion of culture in London, and of women's intellectual and literary achievements.

References and Further Reading

Carter, Elizabeth. 1817. *Letters from Mrs. Elizabeth Carter to Mrs. Montagu between the years 1755 and 1800.* Ed. Montagu Pennington. 3 vols. London: R.C. and J. Rivington.

Huchon, René. 1907. *Mrs. Montagu and her friends, 1720–1800: A sketch.* London: John Murray.

Montagu, Elizabeth. 1906. *Elizabeth Montagu, the queen of the blue-stockings: Her correspondence from 1720 to 1761.* Ed. Emily J. Climenson. 2 vols. London: John Murray.

Myers, Sylvia Harcstark. 1990. *The Bluestocking Circle: Women, friendship, and the life of the mind in eighteenth-century England.* Oxford: Clarendon.

Tinker, Chancey Brewster. 1915. *The salon and English letters: Chapters on the interrelations of literature and society in the age of Johnson.* New York: Macmillan.

Elizabeth Fay

BODY

The female body as a general concept and actual individual women's bodies represent, of course, a very complex subject that can be approached in many ways and as part of many disciplines—anatomically, physiologically, historically, socially, aesthetically; in terms of health, of art, of literature, of economics; and on and on. This essay will discuss certain aspects of the body as a current sociocultural phenomenon.

The emergence of the feminist movement and the development of feminist theory have called into question the idea that biology is destiny. Social thought has been reoriented toward the study of the body as a social construct. Feminism, lesbian and gay politics, and the work of theorists such as Michel Foucault have led to an increased sensitivity to subtle forms of power that control and mold the body.

The ideas that any society develops regarding the human body can be thought of as receptors, organizers, and ordering codes that can project themselves into the social and physical spheres surrounding the body. In western societies, for instance, genital and reproductive distinctions between biological men and women have been considered a sufficient explanation for different identities, needs, and desires. Recent evidence suggests that our bodies are, in a sense, constructed of a complex web of beliefs, habits, ideologies, and social practices, although the relationships between these have yet to be investigated. We know, for example, that the dichotomy between mind and body is not as clear-cut in African cultures and traditional cultures as it tends to be in many other places. We also know that in some Asian cultures, sex is considered an integral part of healthy living and a way to achieve divinity.

The way we think shapes the way we live. There are many different and often contradictory discourses defining our bodies. Individual bodies are shaped and shape themselves in relation to preexisting sets of meaning, which regulate and control perceptions and behavior according to consciously and unconsciously accepted rules.

In western societies, the body, sexuality, and gender are intertwined and are heavily influenced by the fact that children, on the basis of their physiological characteristics, are assigned a gender at birth. This constitutes a set of cultural mandates that will order their sexuality and behavior. Gender, the social condition of being a woman or a man, and sexuality, the cultural way of living out our bodily experiences and desires, will be inextricably linked from that point on. Gender can be thought of as the corporeal locus of cultural meanings, both received and reconstructed, and sexuality as a way of fashioning one's identity in the experience of a body that is constituted from and around certain rules for socially accepted behavior.

In contemporary Judeo-Christian societies, the male body and male sexuality remain the norms by which we judge women's bodies. Despite all the debate that has taken place in recent decades, female sexuality continues to be a problem. Women's bodies are understood and acted upon by science, which involves a male-based model of social and natural reality. With regard to the female body, modern medicine concentrates on menstruation, reproduction, and menopause and may use metaphors based on these aspects of femaleness—while female sexuality is seen as an enigma. Since the late nineteenth century, the conventional image of female sexuality has been that it is basically passive, brought to life only through some sort of reproductive instinct.

Michel Foucault's idea of control of the body can give insights into how normative discourse about the human body has moved from religion to science. The modern female body has been constructed and given a name by biomedicine, which uses terms such as "natural" and "unnatural" or "healthy" and "sick" bodies and speaks of "differences" in sexuality.

Many women continue to have a sense of fragmentation and lack of autonomy because masculine gender norms imply a model of autonomy that denies the body. The modern idea of rationality implies a dichotomy between mind and body, in which the mind is the master that "controls" the body. This need to control one's own body reveals itself as estrangement from one's very existence. Simone de Beauvoir identified our cultural tradition as one in which men have been associated with the transcendent features of human existence and women with physical, "natural" existence. Thus women are defined by a masculine perspective that places them in the bodily sphere—the sphere that must be controlled. This mind-body split is a condition that forces a woman to "live in" her body in a special sense: the body is her essential, enslaving identity. Because society's perception of the human body is an androcentric view that separates flesh from spirit, women are led to deny their own bodies. The androcentric perspective of the human body has led many men and women to despise their body and its functions, to see the body as an enemy. For women it also has meant an estrangement from eroticism and sexuality, both of which are experienced as dangerous.

By the end of the twentieth century, health had become a prominent concern, even a vogue, in much of the western world, and various trends related to health popularized the concept of "body awareness." In part, this development was a result of increased preoccupation with old age and chronic illnesses. Body awareness, then, has transformed the body into an object that can be shaped and "preserved" by specific practices, such as aerobic activity and carefully controlled nutrition. Control of women's sexuality and eroticism is also very much a component of the new concern for the body; thus the concept of health continues, at least in part, to be an image of a lean body that appeals to men's sexuality precisely because it is lean.

The androcentric concept of the mind-body split is deeply imbedded in these new vogues because it makes the body an entity that must be "shaped," "monitored," or brought under control. During the 1970s, the feminist movement provoked discussion of the political implications of culturally constructed sexuality. It also drew attention to the idea that control of women's bodies is at the center of social organization and social domination, and that women's appropriation of their own bodies can be a point of departure for modeling new social relations. Even though the recent preoccupation with the body has, overall, had a positive impact on health, women still need to appropriate their own bodies. Males' naming of females' functions and desires has driven women away from their bodies; there is still a need for women to name their own bodily experience and their own sexuality. Women must develop knowledge based on systematic experimentation with body functions, sexuality, and eroticism.

In this process, the concept of "body consciousness" is important. Such consciousness can be achieved in various ways; for example, one exercise simply involves lying in a darkened room, breathing deeply, being still, feeling one's emotions and desires, being in contact with bodily processes, and listening to the body's needs—which may be as basic as needing to stay home and rest from the rush of being an "active woman." Body consciousness also has wider implications: it can be a process through which women seek and find identity, control, and power.

See Also

ANDROCENTRISM; BIOLOGICAL DETERMINISM; EROTICA; ESSENTIALISM; FEMINISM: OVERVIEW; GENDER STUDIES; IMAGES OF WOMEN: OVERVIEW; NAMING; SEXISM; SEXUALITY: OVERVIEW

References and Further Reading

Boston Women's Health Book Collective (BWHBC). 1998. *Our bodies, ourselves for the new century.* New York: Simon and Schuster.

———. *Nuestros cuerpos, nuestras vidas.* 2000. New York: Siete Cuentros/Seven Stories.

                              Irma Saucedo Gonzalez

BODY IMAGE

See ADVERTISING; BODY; EATING DISORDERS; and IMAGES OF WOMEN: OVERVIEW.

BOOK PUBLISHING

See PUBLISHING.

BOOKSHOPS

"Look, there's a women's bookshop!" There is incredulity in the voice. From inside the shop, the staff and regular customers silently respond in any number of ways: "Yes, and you'd better get used to it." Or "Where've you been—this is the twenty-first century." Or "It's a niche market like any other." Or "Well, then, sir [and occasionally madam], you've just had a learning experience."

Origins and Raison d'Être

The first wave of feminism concentrated on political action to win women the vote. The launch of the second wave of feminism is often credited to the publication of *The Second Sex* by Simone de Beauvoir (1949), *The Feminine Mystique* by Betty Friedan (1963), and *The Female Eunuch* by Germaine Greer (1970). *The Seven Demands of the Women's Liberation Movement* (Ruskin College, 1970) and further communication of ideas and consciousness-raising helped sustain this second wave. The slogan "The personal is political" was at the heart of the revolution.

The gatekeeping of knowledge was again, as access to education before it, a prime site of political struggle. Women's voices were demanding to be heard, and women realized that if this were to happen, they had to take control of their own communications. Authors and readers were there, but the means of linking them were often in indifferent or hostile hands. Women's publishing companies—including Daughters Inc. and Feminist Press in New York, Virago Press and Onlywomen Press in London, Naiad Press in Tallahassee, and Argument Verlag in Germany—led the way in changing this,

and women's bookstores followed. Because many first world feminists are fortunate enough not to have to spend many of their waking hours securing life's basic needs, such as food and clean water, women's bookstores developed first, and are still located primarily in, English-speaking first world countries.

The objectives of most women's bookshops are much like those expressed in the mission statement of Silver Moon Women's Bookshop in London: "To make available to the widest audience the works of women writers, feminist books and periodicals, many of which are not generally available due to the unsympathetic nature of the large distributors and the traditional policies of most bookshops." Working from this principle, women's bookshops the world over have listened to and created a demand for women's voices and politics. Women's voices are now heard and even sought at the highest levels. Maya Angelou, unpublished in the United Kingdom until Virago Press championed her, now has world renown. When Toni Morrison visited Silver Moon Women's Bookshop after publication of *Beloved*, other major bookstores were not much interested in the future Nobel laureate. Katherine V. Forrest's works are stocked in every lesbian section. Jeanette Winterson, now studied in schools and universities, was first presented by the feminist publisher Pandora Press and built a word-of-mouth following among lesbian and feminist booksellers. Voices of women in India have been gathered and recorded by the publishing house Kali. Without all this groundwork, the large publishers would not have recognized or pursued the talent of women such as Arundhati Roy or Michele Roberts. By taking on the infrastructure of distribution and controlling it, women's bookstores together with the publishers have connected the writers to their readers. They have created a circle that has produced a magnificent flowering of women's literature and knowledge of women's lives and concerns.

Women's bookstores do much more than sell books. To quote again from the mission statement of Silver Moon Women's Bookshop, the aim is "to provide a safe and comfortable forum where women may hold community and cultural events…[and] to provide a secure and welcoming meeting place." Everywhere, but particularly in the third world, women's bookstores are fundamentally a community resource. Women's bookstores make a huge effort to supply information such as legal advice, health and political information, and community news through notice boards and newsletters; to provide support for school projects and dissertations; to offer literacy classes; and so on. As destination stores they may also be tourist information centers. In many cases they are the first safe haven and contact for help

117

for a woman in distress from violence or sexual abuse. Women's bookstores are counselors for women coming out, for parents and daughters of lesbians, and for people in the caring and legal professions who are updating their attitudes and knowledge. Very much more than just a place to buy books!

As you can see, women's bookstores are not your garden-variety capitalist enterprise. For the women who start and run them, they are a mission, but one that must balance economic viability with a political commitment to feminism. The passion, dedication, and personal sacrifice of women's bookstore owners and workers all over the world are immense.

The grassroots and political origins of women's bookstores have also meant that probably all are undercapitalized, and many have also challenged traditional business organizational structures. Certainly in the 1970s working collectively and sharing skills were de rigeur among British feminists. Working in this different way was part of challenging patriarchal and hierarchical methodology. Mostly this theoretical position did not survive the pressures of the marketplace.

Different Contexts

Cultural specificity has given feminist bookstores quite different patterns of development. In the United States, Canada, and Australasia, the absence of any profound socialist or communist politics has meant that feminist bookstores broke new community ground. These areas have many bookstores in both large and small cities, which were founded exclusively as women's bookstores. In France, Spain, and England, which have longer centralized histories and stronger socialist traditions, women's bookstores have developed in a different pattern. Having spent years in the labor movement, many feminists in these European countries did not readily adapt to the entrepreneurial and capitalist spirit of American feminism. Furthermore, the established networks of radical booksellers sold feminist titles in their shops. Thus the openings for exclusively feminist shops were fewer. Those that exist are located in the capital cities. Italy and Germany have had yet another model of the development of women's bookstores. Both countries have strong socialist histories, but their citizens maintain local loyalties to their city, state, and *Länder* that go deeper than their fairly recent (mid-nineteenth-century) nationhood. Their pattern of bookstores looks American but derives from different roots. India's feminist bookstores Streelekha and those in Japan—Shokado in Osaka and Grayon House in Tokyo—are a tribute to the personal dynamism and courage of their founders.

At one point, *Feminist Bookstore News* counted 500 feminist bookstores in the United States, Canada, England, continental Europe, Australia, New Zealand, India, Japan, and Kenya.

The Future

Women's bookstores have been a huge success, but at the time of this writing many faced an uncertain future. Thirty-five percent of North America's feminist bookstores had closed, and Sisterwrite in London and Des Femmes in Paris were no more. Politically and culturally, women's bookstores have changed the world of reading and ideas. In the first world this success has brought two negative consequences. First, the assumption that feminists have achieved everything they wanted has depoliticized many young people. The battles won after so hard a fight—and those yet to be taken on—are accepted, forgotten, and subsumed in lifestyle, not political action. Second, the vibrant market for women's books is now an attractive target for ordinary commercial players. Book chains with deep pockets are cherry-picking the most profitable bits of the feminist market. The chains still ignore difficult politics and most lesbian works, but nevertheless they endanger the overall profitability of many feminist bookstores. And the chains provide little in the way of community resources or services.

In North America and Europe, there is considerable competition for market share in the book trade. This is not specifically an antifeminist backlash: all smaller and independent bookshops are imperiled. In North America, 40 percent of independents had gone out of business in the five or six years before this writing. Globalization and new technology, and the dominance of the English language in both, are creating volatile and challenging circumstances.

See Also

ENTREPRENEURSHIP; MANAGEMENT; PUBLISHING, *all entries;* WOMEN'S CENTERS

References and Further Reading

Federation of Radical Booksellers. 1985. *Starting a bookshop.*

Freeman, Jo. *The tyranny of structurelessness.* Self-published.

Garnham, Nicholas. 1989. *Concepts of culture, public policy and the cultural industries.* Discussion Paper. London: Greater London Council.

Redclift, Nanneke, and M. Thea Sinclair, eds. 1991. *Working women: International perspectives on labour and gender ideology.* London: Routledge.

Ruskin College. 1970. *The seven demands of the women's liberation movement.* England: Oxford University.

Russ, Joanna. 1983. *How to suppress women's writing.* Austin: University of Texas Press.

Spender, Dale. 1980. *man made language.* London:

Jane Cholmeley

BORDERS

Borders are usually defined as territorial lines that demarcate one sovereign nation-state from another, or, within the nation-state, one legal jurisdiction from another. Given men's virtual monopoly of government decision-making historically, one could say that borders are lines men have drawn. Rather than view borderlines as fixed and immutable, scholars increasingly treat borders as politically constructed, in order to explore when, why, and how they are drawn, and the consequences of peculiar borderlines. In *Imagined Communities* (1983), Anderson transformed thinking about nations, seeing them as "imaginations" that were made coherent by schools, languages, and compulsion.

Increasingly, borders are used in metaphorical ways to differentiate cultural and linguistic identities. Sometimes these identities are imposed on people (under apartheid, South Africa corralled its "Bantu-speakers" into "Bantustans"), but at other times people claim an identity for themselves (such as Chicanos and Chicanas or Latinos and Latinas in the United States, versus Hispanics or North Americans). Identities are likewise imposed on or claimed by diverse women, either within nation-states or across territorial and cultural borderlines.

Until relatively recently, few scholars theorized about or pursued research on women's containment within or agency across borders. Research on women, gender, and feminism blossomed only a quarter century ago, and when it did, writers often operated within disciplines that necessarily relied on territorial borders as units of analysis. Just as political science focuses on nation-states, their territorial borders, and relations between, among, and within them, the subfields of comparative politics and international relations (IR) also confined their analysis to nation-states, and IR paid little attention to women. (On the discipline, see Staudt and Weaver, 1997.)

In comparative women's studies, writers often take the nation-state as the unit of analysis. Many fine collections exist, including the 43-country study *Women and Politics Worldwide* (Nelson and Chowdhury, 1994). These works are important for contextualizing global movements and ideologies; *The Challenge of Local Feminisms* (Basu, 1995) is an example. Some collections have focused on women's participation in transitions to democracy, for instance, in Latin America and Eastern Europe (Jaquette and Wolchik, 1998).

Thanks to feminist theorizing in international relations, gender has become visible in constructions of nationalism. For example, in wordplay involving domestic imagery and the stark language of apartheid, Christine Sylvester situates women's homelessness and the homelands men have made (1994). Women assume agency in the nuanced constructions of *Feminist Nationalisms* (West, 1997).

Where does this leave women's transnational political agency across borders? At one level, those who analyze global movements and international organizations provide the broadest panorama (see, among many, Baden and Goetz, 1997). But the scope of such analysis does not extend to everyday transnationalism, such as migration and regional "free trade" schemes as some issue-oriented (Pettman, 1996) and regional political economy analyses (Staudt, 1998) have done. Conceptually, analysts need to attend more to cross-border networking and organizing with regard to specific issues and areas.

The European Union (EU) and North American Free Trade Agreement (NAFTA) provide manageable regional units of organizing within transnational political units ranging from narrow (NAFTA) to broad (EU) in policy and legal leverage. These regional communities show how new borders are drawn for finance, commerce, and occasionally migration, and old borders lose some of their traditional meaning. Still, national capital-to-capital organizing offers challenges regarding cultural, linguistic, and national identities that continue to affect women. Electronic communication, especially bilingual communication, eases cross-border exchanges, but the machinery is selectively available—that is, available mainly to the privileged. Ultimately, it is the person-to-person, cross-border organizing among women regarding health, immigration, human rights, and social justice that demonstrates the challenges and opportunities of contesting the national political machinery that men have made. Borders are policed, even militarized, with some ferocity, and immigration policies continue to draw real and metaphoric lines between "natives" and "foreigners."

Analysts cannot assume that women's solidarity will transcend borders. Rather, women are implicated in nationalism (McClintock, 1996), along with actions that seemingly protect jobs, encourage cheap consumer goods in the global economy, and mute or affirm national and cultural differences. Meanwhile, globalization in the new millennium will probably continue to be associated with simultaneous bordering, debordering, and rebordering (Spener and Staudt, 1998).

See Also

GLOBALIZATION; INTERNATIONAL RELATIONS; MIGRATION; NATION AND NATIONALISM; POLITICS AND THE STATE: OVERVIEW

References and Further Reading

Anderson, Benedict. 1983. *Imagined communities.* London: Verso.

Baden, Sally, and Anne Marie Goetz. 1997. Who needs [sex] when you can have [gender]? Conflicting discourses on gender at Beijing. In Kathleen Staudt, ed., *Women, international development and politics: The bureaucratic mire.* Philadelphia: Temple University Press.

Basu, Amrita, ed. 1995. *The challenge of local feminisms.* Boulder, Col.: Westview.

Jaquette, Jane, and Sharon Wolchik, eds. 1998. *Women and democracy: Latin American and Central and Eastern Europe.* Baltimore, Md.: Johns Hopkins University Press.

McClintock, Cynthia. 1996. "No longer a future heaven": Nationalism, gender, and race. In Geoff Eley and Ronald Suny, eds., *Becoming national: A reader.* New York: Oxford University Press.

Nelson, Barbara, and Najma Chowdhury, eds. 1994. *Women and politics worldwide.* New Haven: Yale University Press.

Pettman, Jendy. 1996. *Worlding women: A feminist international politics.* London: Routledge.

Spener, David, and Kathleen Staudt, eds. 1998. *The U.S.-Mexico border: Transcending divisions, contesting identities.* Boulder, Col.: Lynne Rienner.

Staudt, Kathleen. 1998. *Free trade? Informal economies at the U.S.-Mexico border.* Philadelphia: Temple University Press.

————, and William Weaver. 1997. *Political science and feminisms: Integration or transformation?* New York: Twayne Macmillan.

Sylvester, Christine. 1994. *Feminist theory and international relations in a postmodern era.* New York: Cambridge University Press.

West, Lois. 1997. *Feminist nationalisms.* London: Routledge.

Kathleen Staudt

BREAST

In many modern cultures, women's breasts are a target of lust, mockery, and objectification. Although women's sexuality may be arguably as important as physiology, we seem to have lost sight of the breast's main purpose: secreting and transporting milk for infants. A clinical perspective can provide insight into the importance of the breast as well as into breast health and the proper care of breasts.

Anatomy

Breast tissue extends from the collarbone to the inferior portion called the bra line, and from the breastbone to the middle of the armpit. In depth, breast tissue extends from the skin to the muscles of the chest. There is very little muscle tissue in the breast—only a small amount around the nipples.

Breasts come in all shapes and sizes. They may be symmetrical, but it is considered normal for the breasts to be different sizes. Usually, there is one nipple in the middle of each breast. It may protrude or lie flat or even be inverted; all these forms are generally considered normal. A change in the appearance or shape of the nipple, however, would warrant a visit to a health care practitioner for an examination. Some women have more than one nipple on each breast, or a nipple that is unusually placed. These extramammary nipples are not a sign of disease but rather a variation on the norm. Nipples contain spongy tissue that fills with blood. They respond to touch, cold weather, and a baby's suckling, and usually become taut or erect under those circumstances. The pigmented area around the base of the nipple is called the areola. The tiny pores or lumps on the areola are openings for the oil glands that lubricate the nipple and the areola itself during breast feeding.

Each breast is divided into 15 to 20 sections or lobes that are separated by Cooper's ligaments—bands of strong, flexible tissue that give the breast its support. Fat cells lie between and around the lobes and provide cushioning and shape to the breast. The fat cells, fibrous tissue, and other parts of the breast that do not produce, transport, or store milk are called the stroma. The milk-related parts of the breast are called the parenchyma.

Function

Within each lobe lie lobules that look like tiny bunches of grapes. Tiny gland cells lining the acinus (sac) at the end of each "grape" extract the ingredients needed to make milk from nearby blood vessels. For a few days after the birth of a baby, the gland cells extract water, sugar, fat, protein, and salts to make colostrum, the fluid that is nutritionally best for a newborn. As the infant grows, the formulation changes because the mother's hormones communicate to the gland cells that these cells are to make a different mixtures of ingredients. The milk is squeezed into the acinus and then into a small duct. These small ducts join to become larger ducts and transport the milk to a reservoir under the areola, where it stays until nursing time.

The breasts are rich in blood vessels that bring not only the ingredients for milk production but also hormones from the brain and ovaries as well as energy for the breast to do its work. The lymph system removes wastes from the breast and even recycles some of them. Lymph vessels connect the breasts and also drain each breast. Lymph nodes along the lymph channels filter and trap cells that cannot pass through.

Each month from adolescence through menopause, a woman's breasts physiologically prepare for a possible pregnancy. During the menstrual cycle, estrogen flows to the breasts from the ovaries and the adrenal glands. This estrogen reaches its peak during the middle two weeks of the cycle, counting from day one of the menstrual period. Estrogen tells the breast cells to prepare for milk production and transport.

When the ovary releases its egg, usually at midcycle, it begins to release progesterone. The blood supply to the breast then increases to prepare for the potential pregnancy. This increased blood supply plus some additional fluid may cause a sense of fullness, tenderness, discomfort, and sometimes even pain. This is a very typical premenstrual symptom for many women.

If no pregnancy occurs, the breasts begin to change again right after the menstrual period. The extra fluid returns to the body's general circulation through the lymph system. If pregnancy does occur, preparations for milk production begin to accelerate. The gland cells multiply, the lobules enlarge, the ducts lengthen, and the blood and lymph vessels become larger. By the end of a full-term pregnancy, the hormonal influence causes the glandular tissue to crowd out almost all the fat tissue. After pregnancy and lactation, the breasts and lymph system undergo a considerable adjustment of cells and structures for the breasts to revert to their prepregnancy state.

Life Changes

Women's breasts change not only during each menstrual cycle, pregnancy, and lactation, but also with age, body weight, and menopause. As women grow older, and especially after menopause, the proportions of parenchyma and stroma in the breasts keep changing. At some point, there is no working or lactating tissue left and the breasts become more fat and less glandular tissue. This fatty tissue makes it much easier to read mammograms. If a woman uses hormone replacement therapy after menopause, however, the breasts will still be influenced by hormones, although to a lesser degree than during the reproductive years.

Breast Conditions

Unusual breast conditions that are not cancerous are called benign problems. They include normal physiological changes such as minor tenderness, swelling, and lumpiness; mastalgia, or breast pain; infections and inflammations; discharge and other problems of the nipples; excessive lumpiness or nodules; and dominant lumps. For a woman, a dominant lump tends to be the most frightening discovery. Fortunately, most of the time the lump will be either a cyst or a harder benign lump called a fibroadenoma.

Some dominant lumps may in fact be cancerous. They tend to be harder but also can be minimal lumps that feel like a thickening. A cancerous lump can have other changes associated with it, such as swelling, dimpling, changes in skin color, visible blood vessels, enlarged pores, and changes in the nipple; nipple discharge; and microcalcifications or other observations visible on mammograms.

Caring for the Breasts

Three important methods are used to detect breast changes: self-examination of the breasts, mammography, and regular examinations by a health professional. No one method of detection is perfect, but the three work together. Each method has advantages and weaknesses. As science and medicine progress, new methods of breast cancer detection will evolve and improvements will be made.

One of the more meaningful risk factors for breast cancer is having a first-degree relative with breast cancer. Five to 10 percent of breast cancer cases occur in true "breast cancer families," in which mutated copies of the tumor suppressor genes BRCA1 or BRCA2 are passed from generation to generation. Since we receive genetic information from both parents, however, not every female in an affected family will inherit these genes. If a woman inherits the BRCA1 gene, her genes must still undergo other mutations that occur over a period of many years before cancer could occur, but these mutations may never happen. A woman born with a copy of a mutated gene does face an estimated 56 percent chance of developing breast cancer by age 70. BRCA1 is probably present in about 80 percent of families with a major history of both premenopausal breast cancer and ovarian cancer. Mutated BRCA2 may appear in up to 50 percent of all breast cancer families. A woman with mutated BRCA2 faces a chance of developing breast or ovarian cancer similar to the chance faced by a woman with mutated BRCA1.

Assertive prevention strategies become of vital importance for women with these inherited genes. Such strategies include adopting dietary habits that have been scientifically associated with lower rates of breast cancer (low fat, low animal fat, high fish fat, soy, fruits, vegetables, fiber, flaxseed, fewer calories); making changes in lifestyle that reduce risk (less alcohol, more exercise, less stress); reducing body weight; reducing exposure to estrogens (as from hormone replacement therapy, certain pesticides, some plastics, and chlorinated organic compounds); and reducing exposure to radiation. There are also pharmaceutical options for prevention (antiestrogen), as well as surgical options. Although more research is needed, there may also be some nutrients and herbs in supplement form that can reduce the risk of breast cancer, such as green tea, fish oils, flaxseed, vitamins C and D, and melatonin.

Empowering women to take charge of their health involves providing education and resources and improving self-esteem and overall quality of life. Depression, low self-worth, social degradation, poverty, poor-quality relationships, and violence are among the most damaging influences on women and women's health. For some women, breasts may be an integral part of these problems; some women may become depressed, for instance, because they do not believe they are sexy enough, or because they have received mistreatment related to sexuality and breasts. Low self-esteem is closely related to ways in which women are physically degraded because of their bodies, including their breasts. Relationships may be poor because they are oversexualized. Some women have been the victims of child or adult sexual abuse. As women gain more powerful positions in society, as men treat women more as equals, and as women grow and evolve with regard to self-care and power, the well-being of all women, including their emotional and physical health, is more likely to be achieved.

See Also

ANATOMY; BREAST FEEDING; CANCER; COSMETIC SURGERY; HORMONES

References and Further Reading

Arnot, Robert. 1998. *The breast cancer prevention diet: The powerful foods, supplements, and drugs that can save your life.* Boston: Little, Brown.

Austin, Steve, and Cathy Hitchcock. 1994. *Breast cancer: What you should know (but may not be told) about prevention, diagnosis, and treatment.* Rocklin, Calif.: Prima.

Guyton, Arthur C. 1997. *Human physiology and mechanisms of disease.* Philadelphia: Saunders.

Hudson, Tori. 1999. *Women's encyclopedia of natural medicine.* Lincolnwood, Ill.: Keats.

Keunke, Robin. 1988. *Total breast health.* New York: Kensington.

Love, Susan. 1995. *Susan Love's breast book.* Reading, Mass.: Addison-Wesley.

Novak, Edmund R., Howard Wilbur Jones III, Anne Colston Wentz, and Lonnie S. Burnett. 1988. *Novak's textbook of gynecology.* Baltimore, Md.: Williams and Wilkins.

Tori Hudson

BREAST CANCER

See CANCER and ENDOCRINE DISRUPTION.

BREAST FEEDING

Believed by many to be objects of sexual attractiveness, breasts in fact are intended by nature and actually used in most societies to provide milk to babies and small children. As western scientists reassess their opinion of what have sometimes been regarded as merely decorative appendages, they consider the following data:

- Colostrum, the first milk after the baby's birth, helps protect the baby from infection and disease. Colostrum is a laxative and helps clear the meconium out of the newborn's bowels. Breast-fed babies have fewer problem with allergies, constipation, ear infections, respiratory infections, diarrhea, and skin disorders than formula-fed babies (Boston Women's Health Book Collective, 1988; La Leche League, 1991).

- Human breast milk contains fats, carbohydrates, and proteins in the proportions and forms ideally suited for optimal absorption and metabolism by the baby (Kitzinger, 1989). The long-chain fatty acids (fats) in human milk are not duplicated in cow's milk, and fat intake (type and quantity) in infancy is critical to brain development. Minerals and salts from human milk are absorbed in a way that is healthiest for the human infant; for example, although human milk is low in iron, it is absorbed much better than is iron in cow's milk.

- Breast feeding reduces the health risks associated with being born in poverty, at least for the time that the breast feeding continues. Unless a woman is severely malnourished, her breast milk is as nutritious as that of an affluent, well-nourished woman. (However, the cost to a malnourished woman's health of repeated or closely spaced childbearing and nursing is considerable.)

The World Health Organization (WHO) and UNICEF, among other major agencies, have made increasing the incidence of breast feeding—as well as increasing its duration—critical goals. All over the world, formula makers provide samples of their product to expectant families or families with newborns. Using the samples instead of nursing can cause the mother's production of milk to stop; also, poor families may have to overdilute the formula or use contaminated water in the formula, which they then must continue to buy. Even when families can afford formula, it may be difficult for them to prepare and store it under sanitary conditions, with serious or even fatal results to children's health (Boston Women's Health Book Collective, 1998; La Leche League, 1991).

Even women who are secure in their decision to breast-feed can be intimidated by the reactions of others. Although it is clear that a nursing mother is simply feeding her baby, not engaging in a public display, there are those who can see prurience even in the act of nourishing an infant. Women whose milk letdown is inhibited by anxiety or nervousness may find it easier when breast-feeding to wear clothing loose enough to drape around the breast and the baby's head to cover the nipple during feeding; to go to another room to let the baby latch on, then rejoin the group once nursing has begun; and to nurse in areas in which it is possible to turn away from other people (Huggins, 1990). Women whose letdown is not inhibited may choose to nurse in public and simply ignore inappropriate attention.

Although breast-feeding women face pressure from advertisers and disapproving strangers, many women who prefer not to breast-feed or who are unable to do so feel another kind of pressure. A few women do not have sufficient glandular tissue; many others run into problems with nursing that are not resolved quickly. Long periods during which milk production is not adequately stimulated by the baby's sucking can lead to premature, involuntary weaning. (However, a high-quality breast pump, used frequently to mimic the baby's feeding patterns, may be used to maintain milk supply until the nursing problem is resolved.) A pacifier can reduce a baby's need to suck at the breast and can have a detrimental effect on milk production. Working inside or outside the home may make it difficult for a woman to breast-feed, and choosing formula may make her life much easier. Women who would like to breast-feed but cannot, or families for whom breast feeding is not the option chosen, should be assured that whether a child receives human milk or formula, love, security, and trust are the most important things consumed by the child during feeding and during life.

See Also

BODY; BREAST; CANCER; CHILDBIRTH; MATERNAL HEALTH AND MORBIDITY; MOTHER; MOTHERHOOD; NATURE-NURTURE DEBATE; SEX AND CULTURE

References and Further Reading

Blum, L. M. 1999. *At the breast: Ideologies of breastfeeding and motherhood in the contemporary United States.* Boston: Beacon.

Boston Women's Health Book Collective. 1998. *Our bodies, ourselves for the new century.* New York: Simon and Schuster.

La Leche League. 1991. *The womanly art of breastfeeding.* New York: Penguin.

Huggins, K. 1990. *The nursing mother's companion.* Boston: Harvard Common.

Kitzinger, S. 1989. *Breastfeeding your baby.* New York: Knopf.

Reukauf, M. D., and M. A. Traus. 1988. *Commonsense breastfeeding: A practical guide to the pleasures, problems, and solutions.* New York: Atheneum.

Brinlee Kramer

BRIDEPRICE

See DOWRY AND BRIDEPRICE.

BUDDHISM

Buddhism has been of particular interest to feminists in recent years for many reasons. It is a major religion, with 2,500-year-old traditions, which has spread beyond its homeland into very different cultures; throughout its history, Buddhist texts have included conflicting statements about the status of women; and within the male dominance of Buddhism, many women have lived as nuns or have become well-educated laypeople. Recently many western women have become dedicated Buddhists; they expect to study and practice along with men; to participate fully, and to take responsibility for propagating Buddhism.

Basic Tenets of Buddhism

Buddhism came into existence in the sixth century B.C.E. when a prince was born into a small tribal clan at the foot of the Himalaya mountains, in what is now Nepal. He was known as Prince Siddhartha. Soon after his birth, his horoscope was read, and it predicted that he would become either the "king of kings" or the "world renouncer." King Suddhodhana, his father, obviously preferred the first prediction and in order to make it come true provided the young prince with all worldly comforts. Yet when the prince was exposed to the realities of life—sickness, old age, and death—he became deeply concerned. His question was: How are we to rid ourselves of this human suffering? That question was the beginning of Buddhism. When his own son was born, the prince decided to go forth to seek the answer to his question, to save not only himself and his newborn child but also the human race.

After six years of both physical and mental journeys, the prince found his own spiritual path and became enlightened. He became known as the Buddha—the Enlightened One.

His first sermon, given to five ascetics, was in fact an exposition of what he had discovered in answer to his question about human suffering. He made two significant points before the actual sermon: first, he was self-enlightened, that is, the knowledge was not handed down to him by an outside factor; second, teaching is the middle path between the two extremes of idealism and materialism.

The sermon focused on the Four Noble Truths: Dukkha, Samudaya, Nirodha, and Marga. Dukkha—the First Noble Truth—is the realization that everyone born into life is subject to human suffering, in the form of sickness, old age, and death. Buddhism can help to free one from the suffering that is caused by clinging to the self as real or eternal. But suffering does not occur of its own accord. Since it is the result of something else, it must have a cause. This is the Second Noble Truth.

The Third Noble Truth confirms that even though there is suffering, it can be overcome. This is the cessation of suffering. The Buddha and his enlightened disciples were living proof of this truth.

The fourth Noble Truth asserts that there is a path to end this suffering. The Buddha prescribed, like a good physician, an Eightfold Path to be followed by those who realize suffering and desire to be free from it.

This, very briefly, is the message of Buddhism.

Oppressive and Liberating Factors for Women

In order to appreciate the liberating factors some women have experienced in Buddhism, one needs to understand the social context from which Buddhism arose. It started in India, amid a cultural background heavily laden with a patriarchal worldview. Some of the earlier social norms of Indian society can be found in Manu Dharma Shastra, the author-

itative Hindu ethical code written after the beginnings of Buddhism. In this text women are treated as commodities belonging to male members of the family. Women, considered impure, are not allowed to study the Veda, which is the most sacred Hindu text. Offerings by women alone are not accepted by the gods. In this vicious circle, women have no right to seek spiritual salvation. The only hope for salvation for women is through Bhakti (devotion), submission, and service to their husbands.

Buddhism, however, denies the absolute authority of the Vedic texts and does not recognize the caste distinctions so important to Hindu society. The Buddha was the first religious leader in the history of major world religions to proclaim the equal spiritual potential of both men and women.

It is important to distinguish between supramundane and mundane teachings in Buddhist literature. Supramundane teachings deal directly with the question of how to become enlightened. One becomes enlightened not as male or female. Enlightenment is beyond gender differences.

However, the teachings on the mundane level deal with life in society. It is at this level that social values play a prominent role. Early Buddhist society was Indian society. Oppressive elements prevalent in Indian society can be seen throughout Buddhist literature. Reading through that literature, one needs to be constantly reminded of the contextual history and must be able to sift Buddhism from the Indian social values handed down unconsciously. There are many liberating elements that are the real contribution of Buddhism to women in Indian society. Under Buddhism, women are free to strive for their own salvation without depending on their husbands or sons. Women, single or divorced, enjoy full rights to work out their own salvation. Spiritual life is allowed for women, and many of them have taken this opportunity.

Role of Women in Society

Women played very active roles in the Buddha's time and shared with men an equal responsibility to bring about the growth of Buddhism. The Buddha assigned this responsibility to four groups of Buddhists: monks, nuns, laymen, and laywomen. Laypeople are expected to provide the monks and nuns with four requirements: food, dwelling place, robes, and medicine. The monks and nuns, in return, should readily give spiritual guidance to the lay community. In the Buddha's time some laywomen were very advanced in the study and practice of Buddhism. Hence, they were in a position to offer advice to the ordained sangha (community of monks and nuns). The nuns were often well advanced in their practice and proved themselves equally qualified in propagating Buddhism.

At present, in some countries women are mostly seen as playing the role of supporters to the sangha; in some countries there are only monks, no nuns.

Contemporary Attempts at Emancipating Buddhist Women

In the past three decades women have become more active in Buddhism. The flow of Buddhists out of Tibet since 1959 is partly responsible for this phenomenon. More western women have been exposed to Buddhism, and many have chosen to follow the Tibetan lineage. Zen Buddhism as it is now commonly practiced in the West offers an opportunity for women to practice without emphasizing issues related to ordination.

In 1987 Sakyadhita, an international Buddhist women's association, came into existence after Buddhist women met for the first time at Bodh Gaya, India, where the Buddha attained enlightenment. This association promotes Buddhist education for women in general and supports full ordination of women in other countries. Sakyadhita is registered in the United States. The association organized five conferences, in India (1987), Thailand (1991), Sri Lanka (1995), Ladakh (1995), Cambodia (1997), and Nepal (2000), to bring about awareness of the status of women in Buddhism in each country where it is practiced. This heightened awareness should improve the role and status of Buddhist women.

Revival of Buddhist Nuns

In Buddhism, unlike Christianity, the order of fully ordained nuns (bhikkhuni, bhikshumi) was instituted by the founder of the faith, the Buddha; hence, the movement to revive the heritage of fully ordained nuns should be easier. In reality, however, Catholic and Buddhist sisters, particularly in Theravada countries, are not very different, particularly regarding the struggle to ordain women. Buddhism is traditionally divided roughly into two major schools: Theravada, the southern school, in Sri Lanka, Thailand, Myanmar, Laos, and Cambodia; and Mahayana, sometimes called the northern school, in China, Korea, Japan, Taiwan, and Vietnam. (Theravada tends to follow the letter of the teachings whereas Mahayana is more progressive and more assertive in social involvement) For the sake of convenience, Tibet is also included in the Mahayana category. The lineage of fully ordained nuns went from India to Sri Lanka in the third century B.C.E. during King Asoka's period and later spread to China, Korea, and elsewhere.

After the lineage in Sri Lanka died out, people in southeast Asia who practice Theravada were never ordained. Instead of the fully ordained nuns, there are local nuns in each country who hold much lower positions than monks.

In the last three decades of the twentieth century there were attempts to revive the nuns' lineage from abroad. Taiwan has been a stronghold for the revival of nuns. In 1988 Hsi-Lai Temple in Los Angeles, California, ordained 200 women from various traditions. In 1998 the same organization provided an international ordination in Bodh Gaya, India, for 135 nuns from various countries. In March 2000 there was another international ordination in Kaohsring, Taiwan. Full ordination can be obtained from Hsi-Lai Temple in Los Angeles or in Taiwan, where each year more women than men receive ordination.

Ordination is not a status to be claimed for purposes of equality only. Rather, it is a path in which one walks with full responsibility to develop one's spirituality and in that process help others along the path as well.

Feminist scholars have been interested not only in the differing treatment of women and men in Buddhist traditions, but also in the similarity of the Buddhist figure known as the Perfection of Wisdom to the Goddess of Wisdom, Sophia, in other traditions; and in the comparison of Buddhist explanations of suffering with principles of women-dominant religions where illness is not considered inevitable and where healing procedures are practiced as effective solutions to human suffering.

See Also

CASTE; FAMILY: RELIGIOUS AND LEGAL SYSTEMS—BUDDHIST TRADITIONS; HINDUISM; HOUSEHOLDS AND FAMILIES: SOUTH ASIA; HOUSEHOLDS AND FAMILIES: SOUTHEAST ASIA; NUNS; SACRED TEXTS; ZEN

References and Further Reading

Allione, Tsultrim. 1996. *Women of wisdom.* Boston: Arkana.

Boucher, Sandy. 1988. *Turning the wheel: American women creating the new Buddhism.* San Francisco: Harper and Row.

Chakravarty, U. 1981. The rise of Buddhism as experienced by women. *Mansui* 8: 6–10.

Chodroen, Thupten, ed. 1999. *Blossoms of the dharma.* Berkeley, Calif.: North Atlantic.

Findlay, Ellison, and Yvonne Haddad, eds. 1985. *Women, religions, and social change.* Albany: State University of New York Press.

Gross, Rita. 1993. *Buddhism after patriarchy: A feminist history, analysis, and reconstruction of Buddhism.* Albany: State University of New York Press.

Horner, I. B. 1930. *Women under primitive Buddhism: Laywomen and almswomen.* London: Routledge.

Kabilsingh, C. 1981. *A comparative study of bhikkhuni patimokkha.* India: Chowghambha Orientalia.

———. 1991. *Thai women and Buddhism.* Berkeley, Calif.: Parallax.

———, trans. 1998. *The bhikkhuni patimokkha of the six schools.* India: India Books Centre.

Macy, Joanna. 1985. *Dharma and development: Religion as resource in the Sarvodaya self-help movement.* West Hartford, Conn.: Kumarian.

Tsomo, Karma Lekshe. 1996. *Sisters in solitude: Two traditions of Buddhist monastic ethics for women.* Albany: State University of New York Press.

Chatsumarn Kabilsingh

BUILT ENVIRONMENT

"Feminist approaches to the built environment" covers a wide range of topics within gender studies. Fields covered include any that are related to human-made (built and unbuilt) environments, on any scale (geographical, architectural, and so on), for example, geography, urban planning, urban design, architecture, landscape architecture, history of architecture, and environmental psychology. The introduction of gender into the study and interpretation of the environment has not changed the epistemologies of these disciplines but rather has raised new theoretical questions, shifted angles, and revealed new perspectives and hypotheses.

Scholars have suggested the following hypotheses, aimed at "degendering" the environment: "Women's social experience is notably absent from the human-made environment and mechanisms by which this absence is perpetuated" (Boys et al., 1984: 1–2). "Women in design can use Social Science information in new and different ways." (Howell, 1983). "The man-made environment, through its production process, expresses or reinforces the social construction of genders, or, vice-versa, the social construction of genders is reproduced or reinforced through the human-made environment as a lived experience" (Tentokali, 1989). "Gender stratification is reinforced by spatial segregation. Gendered spaces that create distance between women and sources of masculine knowledge have the strongest association with gender stratification" (Spain, 1992: 27).

The theoretical corpus of gender studies of the environment can be divided into two general directions. The first theoretical direction, which deals with the construction of gender, explains the differences and similarities between human males and females within the environment. Gender is explored and interpreted in relation to its reciprocal links with the environment. Emphasis is placed on the ways of changing either the urban environment or gender relations. This direction includes two antithetical approaches (Borden, 1995): (1) An approach as a functional critique, which focuses mainly on the ways of changing the urban environment as a means for changing gender relations—or, more correctly, for changing social relations in general—to achieve a more equitable society. (Dolores Hayden's pioneer work belongs here.) (2) An approach as a more experimental and personal standpoint; instead of trying to change the fabric of the city according to a set of rules or provisions, it articulates ways of changing gender relations, exploring more libertarian ideas about what living in cities is (or should be) like. (The work of Elizabeth Wilson belongs here.)

The second theoretical direction consists of conceptual approaches, whose intent is not only to understand the architectural discourse but also to speculate on the meanings and representations of gender. These approaches incorporate the logocentrism of Derrida into the architectural discourse. As a consequence, they consider the notions of gender and space as texts and focus not only on what is present but also on what is not present in the text. "The logic in the system of architecture represses sex in two different ways: sex is understood in positive and negative terms, and woman [are] assigned the negative term (phallocentrism)" (Agrest, 1988). Under the constraints of Derrida's deconstruction, while philosophy, literary criticism, and psychoanalysis deal with the architectonics of the text, architecture adopts philosophical, literary, and psychoanalytical methods or concepts. The work of Mark Wigley and Beatrice Colomina belongs here.

See Also

AESTHETICS: FEMINIST; ARCHITECTURE; ENGINEERING; HOUSING; INTERIOR DESIGN AND DECORATION

References and Further Reading

Agrest, Diana, Patricia Conway, and Leslie Kanes Weisman, eds. 1996. *The sex of architecture.* New York: Abrams.

Borden, Iain. 1995. Gender and the city. In Iain Borden and David Dunster, eds., *Architecture and the sites of history,* 317–330. London: Butterworth Architecture.

Boys, Jos, Frances Bradshaw, Jane Darke, Benedicte Foo, Sue Francis, Barbara McFarlane, and Marion Roberts. 1984. *Making space: Women and the man-made environment.* London: Pluto.

Braidotti, Rosi. 1994. *Nomadic subjects, embodiment and sexual difference in contemporary feminist theory.* New York: Columbia University Press.

Colomina, Beatriz. 1992. Domesticity at war. *Assemblage* 16.

———, ed. 1994. *Privacy and publicity.* Cambridge, Mass.: MIT Press.

———, ed. 1992. *Sexuality and space.* Princeton, N.J.: Princeton Papers on Architecture.

Hayden, Dolores. 1981a. *The grand domestic revolution: A history of feminist designs for American homes, neighborhoods, and cities.* Cambridge, Mass.: MIT Press.

———. 1981b. *Seven American utopias: The architecture of communitarian socialism.* Cambridge, Mass.: MIT Press.

Howell, Sandra. 1983. Women, housing and habitability. Paper presented at the Symposium on Gender-Related Issues. Women in Housing. Seattle: University of Washington, 18–20 May.

Howell, Sandra, and Vana Tentokali. 1989. Domestic privacy: Gender, culture and development issues. In Low Shetha and Erving Chambers, eds. *Housing, culture and design: A comparative perspective.* Philadelphia: University of Pennsylvania Press.

Sellers, Susan, ed. 1988. *Writing differences: Readings from the seminar of Hélène Cixous.* Oxford: Open University Press.

Spain, Daphne. 1992. *Gendered spaces.* Chapel Hill: University of North Carolina Press.

Tentokali, Vana. 1989. *The spatial organization of the house as the expression of the family structure: The Organi case.* Thessaloniki: University Studio Press.

Webster's New World Dictionary. 1991. New York: Webster's New World.

Weddon, Chris. 1987. *Feminist practice and poststructuralist theory.* Oxford: Blackwell.

Wigley, Mark. 1992. Untitled: The housing of gender. In Beatriz Colomina, ed. *Sexuality and space,* 327–389. Princeton, N.J.: Princeton Papers on Architecture.

———. 1994. The domestication of the house: Deconstruction after architecture. In Brunette Peter and David Wills, eds. *Deconstruction and the visual arts: Art, media, architecture.* Cambridge: Cambridge University Press.

Wilson, Elizabeth. 1991. *The Sphinx and the city: Urban life, the control of disorder and women.* London: Virago.

Vana Tentokali

BULIMIA NERVOSA

Bulimia nervosa is an eating disorder characterized by recurring episodes of binge eating alternating with episodes of fasting or purging behaviors intended to prevent weight gain and undo the effects of the original binges. The health advocacy organization Anorexia Nervosa and Related Eating Disorders, Inc. (ANRED), classifies bulimia nervosa as a diet-binge-purge disorder and links it to anorexia nervosa (the relentless pursuit of thinness), anorexia athletica (compulsive exercising), and binge eating disorder (compulsive eating). The American Psychiatric Association classifies bulimia nervosa as a severe disturbance in eating behavior closely related to anorexia nervosa, but different from binge eating disorder, which does not include subsequent purging or fasting (American Psychiatric Assocation, 1994). Researchers are studying the physiology, psychology, and treatment of bulimia nervosa, but medical insurance companies in the United States do not pay for its treatment.

Bulimia nervosa occurs most frequently among white females in western cultures and affects young women about ten times more often than it affects young men. Onset occurs most often during the teenage years and early twenties (Academy for Eating Disorders, American Academy of Child and Adolescent Psychiatry, American Anorexia Bulimia Association). Statistics about prevalence are unreliable, however. Many girls with bulimia are able to maintain a normal or nearly normal body size, in contrast to girls with anorexia (whose bodies often show evidence of starvation and wasting) and girls with binge eating disorder (whose bodies show evidence of obesity). Many girls with bulimia conceal their eating disorder from their parents and doctors (although not necessarily from their peers), and doctors are not required to report cases of bulimia nervosa to public health authorities.

Bulimia Nervosa and the Body

Many girls and women are preoccupied with issues related to diet, exercise, thinness, and body image (Bordo, 1993; Thompson et al., 1999). A girl with bulimia nervosa experiences these preoccupations to the point of pathology, with signs and symptoms that include appetite disturbances, enforced fasts, enforced exercise sessions, insatiable hunger, and a sense of being unable to control her own behavior. During a bulimic binge, she stuffs her body with food. During a bulimic purge, she uses laxatives, diuretics, and self-induced vomiting to get rid of the food she has gorged, or she fasts or exercises relentlessly to get rid of the extra body weight that she fears. She may use stimulants, psychoactive drugs, and alcohol to cope with the anxiety, depression, and mood disorders that frequently accompany bulimia. She may experience side effects that include dehydration, electrolyte imbalances, neuroendocrine disturbances, menstrual irregularities, irritation of the esophagus, and erosion of dental enamel. Many researchers report a link between bulimic behaviors and episodes of shoplifting, obsessive-compulsive patterns that are not related to food, and self-mutilation (cutting). Whether the physical and emotional disturbances that accompany bulimia are a cause or an effect of repeated cycles of bingeing and purging is still unclear, but a powerfully reinforcing feedback loop does seem to be at work in either case.

Psychiatrists diagnose bulimia nervosa if cycles of bingeing and purging cycles recur, on average, at least twice a week for three months (American Psychiatric Association, 1994); many girls with bulimia report that their episodes occur as frequently as several times a day. Treatment may include antidepressant medication, family therapy, and cognitive-behavioral psychotherapy aimed at reducing impulsive behaviors, reducing relapses, and improving body image and self-esteem (Fairburn and Wilson, 1993; Tobin, 2000).

Bulimia Nervosa and Patriarchal Culture

Binging and purging are often accompanied by shame, secrecy, and self-loathing. These behaviors also appear to be linked to such important cultural issues as addictions, adolescent sexuality, food and nurturance, diet, pressure to be thin, body size, body image, power, and control (Bordo, 1993; Thompson et al., 1999). Princess Diana of Great Britain joked in public about having her head down the loo (the WC or toilet); and the actress Jane Fonda, who promoted and sold exercise videos, reported more than twenty years of bulimic behavior that sometimes involved binging and purging as frequently as twenty times a day.

Hilde Bruch linked the development of anorexia nervosa and bulimia nervosa to disturbances in the mother-child dyad (Bruch, 1985), and Marian Woodman expanded that theory to encompass repression of feminine power at the archetypal level (Woodman, 1980). According to this interpretation, when female power is stigmatized, thwarted, and legislated against in patriarchal cultures, the bingeing and purging characteristic of adolescent girls with bulimia nervosa can be interpreted as a ritual that represents alternating cycles of rebellion against and compliance with patriarchal requirements. During the binge portion of a bulimic episode, the girl's covert behavior resembles theft, as she consumes oversize amounts of forbidden foods. During the purse episode that follows the binge, the girl vomits up evidence of her crime or her sin and flushes it away, so that she seems outwardly to be in compliance with social rules once

again. Acting out the binge-purge cycle returns the girl to a calmer homeostatis (stability); but as the pressures of being a young girl in a patriarchal culture build up again, another destabilizing binge-purge episode is likely to follow. On this theory, it is not surprising that most researchers who study bulimia nervosa and other eating disorders report very high relapse rates. As long as patriarchal cultures continue to thwart and repress female power, there seems little likelihood of a reduction in the prevalence of bulimia nervosa among young women.

See Also

ANOREXIA NERVOSA; BODY; DRUG AND ALCOHOL ABUSE; EATING DISORDERS; FOOD AND CULTURE; PSYCHOLOGY: COGNITIVE *and* PSYCHOPATHOLOGY AND PSYCHOTHERAPY; SEXUALITY: ADOLESCENT SEXUALITY

References and Further Readings

Academy for Eating Disorders. *Bulimia nervosa.* <http://www .acadeatdis.org>.

American Academy of Child and Adolescent Psychiatry. 1998. *Teenagers with eating disorders.* <http://www.aacap.org /publications/factsfam/eating.htm>.

American Anorexia Bulimia Association, Inc. *Risk factors in the development of eating disorders.* <http://www.aabainc.org /riskfactors/index.html>.

American Psychiatric Association. 1994. *Diagnostic and statistical manual of mental disorders,* 4th ed. *(DSM-IV).* Washington, D.C.: American Psychiatric Association.

Anorexia Nervosa and Related Eating Disorders, Inc. (ANRED). *Statistics: How many people have eating and exercise disorders?* <http://www.anred.com/stats.html>.

Bordo, Susan. 1993. *Unbearable weight: Feminism, western culture, and the body.* Berkeley: University of California Press.

Bruch, Hilde. 1985. *Eating disorders: Obesity, anorexia nervosa, and the person within.* New York: Basic Books.

Fairburn, Christopher G., and G. Terence Wilson, eds. 1993. *Binge eating: Nature, assessment, and treatment.* New York: Guilford.

Thompson, J. Kevin, Leslie J. Heinberg, Madeline N. Altabe, and Stacey Tantleff-Dunn. 1999. *Exacting beauty: Theory, assessment, and treatment of body image disturbance.* Washington, D.C.: American Psychological Association.

Tobin, David I. 2000. *Coping strategies therapy for bulimia nervosa.* Washington, D.C.: American Psychological Association.

Woodman, Maria. 1980. *The owl was a baker's daughter: Obesity, anorexia nervosa, and the repressed feminine.* Toronto: Inner City.

Faye Zucker

BUREAUCRACY

"Women in bureaucracy" covers a number of topics or themes:

1. Women in bureaucratic types of organization, where the issue concerns whether "bureaucracy" as a type of social organization is inherently patriarchal, or whether this has been a historical circumstance of the development of this organizational form that can be altered.

2. Women in management positions in complex, bureaucratic organizations, both public and private, where it is assumed that organizational change of various kinds is needed for women to be adequately included in these positions.

3. Women in *public* bureaucratic types of organization, and the gender division of labor within the modern administrative state (see Siim, 1987; Yeatman, 1990: chapter 5).

4. A closely related topic, *femocracy*. *Femocrat* is the name that has been given to second-wave feminists in Australia and New Zealand who take up policy-related positions in government, which either directly promote the interests of women or promote generic policies such as equal opportunity that provide critical support for the promotion of women's interests.

The bureaucratic organizational form has underpinned the development of both the modern state and the modern capitalist firm (see Weber, 1968). The bureaucratic organizational form is fundamentally characterized by an ethos of "impersonality" as evidenced especially in the separation of the bureaucratic office from the private-domestic life and obligations of officials. This has been a peculiarly modern-western phenomenon, which has influenced—but not supplanted—the kinship-oriented organizational order of many nonwestern states. The issue is whether bureaucracy is inherently patriarchal, and, if it is, whether this also allows for a play of internal contradictions.

There have been three types of response to this question. The first type is liberal reformist (for example, Kanter, 1977; for discussion, see Savage and Witz, 1992: 13–18): the argument that bureaucratic organizations become less patriarchal the more they include women, that there is nothing inherent in the bureaucratic form itself that precludes gender equality. The second type is radical feminist (see Ferguson, 1984), arguing that the kind of rationality that structures the bureaucratic form is inherently masculine and patriarchal, requiring its practitioners to think and

work in ways which bracket out their embodied and domestic existence, an option that is simply not available to women as a group. Also, the bureaucratic type of organization is structured in terms of highly specialized jobs ordered in a hierarchical relationship to each other; in this hierarchy, masculine-patriarchal styles of operating are privileged, at the expense of the more cooperatively oriented and holistic approaches favored by women as a group. The third type is poststructuralist (for example, Pringle, 1989): this is the view that the bureaucratic type of organization is not as simple as it seems, that its dominant style of operating in terms of patriarchal rationality already contains, because it depends on, its opposite—what are typecast as feminine qualities of nurturance, sexualized or embodied presence, and informal patterns of cooperation. Just what *is* the bureaucratic order in any one particular organization is a dynamic and contested site of struggle between quite different interpretations of how this order should work.

Each perspective has insights as well as limitations. The liberal reformist view implies that the formal universalism of the bureaucratic organization may work to facilitate, even to invite, strategies that are oriented toward developing equal participation for not just women, but all social actors. The fundamental orientation of the bureaucratic form toward merit-based principles of selection and promotion encourages participation regardless of sex, race, ethnicity, and so on, even as it raises debates over what "merit" means and how it should be interpreted. The radical feminist view, by contrast, argues that the bureaucratic organizational form depends for its very existence on an internal gender division of labor: the typical bureaucratic style of disembodied, specialist, calculative rationality depends on a large number of poorly paid subordinates who do the bureaucrat's housekeeping both *inside* the organization (for example, secretaries, office cleaners) and *outside* (wives).

Thus, when some women are selected, on "merit," to become bureaucrats, they are contradictorily positioned as actors who are asked to assume a patriarchal-masculine style of organizational being but are also located within this category of society's housekeepers. The weakness of this view is that it cannot explain why some bureaucracies have proved to be more open to women's participation than others: for example, Australian femocracy indicates the relative openness of the Australian state to feminist participation and agendas between 1972 and 1987 (see Dowse, 1988; Sawer, 1990; Watson, 1990; Yeatman, 1990). If the radical feminist view tends to naturalize the masculine-patriarchal character of bureaucracy, the virtue of the poststructuralist perspective is its insistence on more open-ended dynamics of contested agendas and contradictions within any actual bureaucratic organization. This literature, however, is not cross-referenced with the traditional sociological critique of the Weberian model of bureaucracy for its neglect of the *informal*, nonbureaucratic relationships and styles of working on which the bureaucratic formal order depends.

None of these views locate their perspectives in relation to mainstream organizational theory and management policy literatures (see, for example, Mintzberg, 1979; Perrow, 1986). Nor do they respond adequately to the implications of the late-twentieth-century restructuring of the public sector in the liberal democracies for the bureaucratic form. Managerialism, devolution, and privatization have all fundamentally changed the organizational dynamics and structures of the public sector. Organizations tend now to be less hierarchical ("flatter"), less rule-bound, and more outcomes-oriented; less defensive in relation to outsiders; and more proactive in relation to what they perceive as a constantly changing context for their policy and management. This requires their personnel to become more flexible, intelligently proactive, strategic, multiskilled, and democratic. These developments do not fit the classical Weberian picture of bureaucracy. Because it favors more collegial, democratic, and intuitive styles of working, as well as requiring tough-minded and analytical policy skills, this new type of "postbureaucratic" organization has both "feminine" and "masculine" features. There is an emerging debate about how the postbureaucratic type of public sector organization (see Barzelay, 1992) relates to the older bureaucratic form: Does the former supplant or does it sediment over the latter? (For this debate, see Yeatman, 1994.) Certainly there is no suggestion by the exponents of the postbureaucratic type—such as Peters's and Waterman's antisytems models of management—that the ethical virtues of the bureaucratic type are jettisoned in today's business environment. These virtues are impersonality and due process. The democratic values of natural justice, equality, and accountability are fundamentally dependent on these virtues.

There is an inadequately elaborated and scattered literature on the participation of women in the development of the administrative state over the course of the twentieth century. There is a small literature on the participation of women in the staffing of the administrative state's services to the national citizenry in their early inception—the post office, for example (see Deacon, 1989; Zimmeck, 1992). This literature has not been cross-referenced with the sector-specific literatures on the participation of women in the staffing of a universal school system or in the various state administrative policy bureaus that underpinned the early development of welfare states (for example, the Children's Bureau created in 1912 under the leadership of Julia Lathrop in the United States). The Australasian literature on "femocracy" is concerned with the reform-oriented Australian and New Zealand social democratic administrations of the 1970s and 1980s. This literature is neither situated historically in relation to past patterns of women's participation in the administrative state, nor, as yet, reevaluated in terms of the implications of public sector restructuring for this participation. At the same time, there is a great deal of talk of a "glass ceiling" for women in private and public sector management, and this perspective is valid for most large organizations, especially global corporations. Information technology enables these organizations to centralize their strategic management, and to rebureaucratize the controls this central mind exercises over the many operations and functions it devolves or contracts out. Some individual women may cross the glass ceiling and become central organizational executives, but there will be a greater distance between them and women workers who staff service operations such as call centers. A good deal of new empirical research needs to be done on women in the context of these new organizational and bureaucratic forms.

See Also

FEMOCRAT; GOVERNMENT; HIERARCHY AND BUREAUCRACY; ORGANIZATIONAL THEORY

References and Further Reading

Barzelay, Michael. 1992. *Breaking through bureaucracy: A new vision for managing in government.* Berkeley and Los Angeles: University of California Press.

Deacon, Desley. 1989. *Managing gender: The state, the new middle class, and women workers, 1830–1930.* Melbourne: Oxford University Press.

Dowse, Sara. 1988. The women's movement fandango with the state: The movement's role in public policy since 1972. In Cora V. Baldock and Beltina Cass, eds., *Women, social welfare and the state* (2nd ed.), 205–227. Sydney: Allen and Unwin.

Ferguson, Kathy. 1984. *The feminist case against bureaucracy.* Philadelphia: Temple University Press.

Franzway, Suzanne, Dianne Court, and R. W. Connell. 1989. *Staking a claim: Feminism, bureaucracy and the state.* Sydney: Allen and Unwin.

Kanter, Rosabeth Moss. 1977. *Men and women of the corporation.* New York: Basic Books.

Mintzberg, Henry. 1979. *The structuring of organization: A synthesis of the research.* Englewood Cliffs, N.J.: Prentice Hall.

Perrow, Charles. 1986. *Complex organization: A critical essay,* 3rd ed. New York: Random House.

Peters, Thomas J., and Robert H. Waterman. 1984. *In search of excellence.* New York: Warner.

Pringle, Rosemary. 1989. *Secretaries talk: Sexuality, power and work.* London and New York: Verso.

Savage, Michael, and Anne Witz. 1992. The gender of organizations. In Savage and Witz, eds., *Gender and bureaucracy.* Oxford: Blackwell.

Sawer, Marian. 1990. *Sisters in suits: Women and public policy in Australia.* Sydney: Allen and Unwin.

Siim, Birta. 1987. The Scandinavian welfare states: Towards sexual equality or a new kind of male domination? *Acta Sociologica* 30: 255–270.

Watson, Sophie, ed. 1990. *Playing the state: Australian feminist interventions.* Sydney: Allen and Unwin.

Weber, Max. 1968. Bureaucracy. In *Economy and society,* Vol. 3: 956–1006. New York: Bedminster.

Yeatman, Anna. 1990. *Bureaucrats, technocrats, femocrats: Essays on the contemporary Australian state.* Sydney: Allen and Unwin.

———. 1994. The reform of public management: An overview. *Australian Journal of Public Administration* 53(3): 287–296.

Zimmeck, Meta. 1992. Marry in haste, repent at leisure: Women, bureaucracy and the post office, 1870–1920. In Michael Savage and Anne Witz, eds., *Gender and bureaucracy.* 65–94. Oxford: Blackwell.

Anna Yeatman

BUSINESS AND BUISNESSWOMEN

See ECONOMY: HISTORY OF WOMEN'S PARTICIPATION; ENTREPRENEURSHIP; FINANCE; LEADERSHIP; MANAGEMENT; and MULTINATIONAL CORPORATIONS.

BUTCH/FEMME

Butch and femme are two unique articulations of lesbian gender and desire. As a couplet, butch/femme (or butch-femme) is erotic dynamics cultivated through gender difference, between a masculine woman and feminine woman. It is a way of knowing and embodying desire through behaviors, mannerisms, deportment, style, and the negotiation and orchestration of sexual relations and practices. Butch/femme as gender and sexual identities produces its own particular social and erotic vocabularies, which facilitate desire and give expression and legitimation to lesbian genders and sexualities. Although gender difference is eroticized, it cannot be simply read as reproducing or mimicking heterosexuality and traditional gender roles. Butch/femme deploys and subverts traditional gender representations associated with heterosexuality by self-consciously appropriating and recontextualizing both masculinity and femininity and in the process radically transforming them both.

Although butch and femme share an important history as allies and companions, it is important to understand them as separate and distinct identities with different trajectories, unique childhood narratives, and distinct defining and developmental experiences. In order to have a richer understanding of what butch/femme means as erotic dynamics, it is crucial to understand who and what butch and femme are as separate identities.

Femme is a set of codes and behaviors that articulate desire in a seemingly traditionally feminine way. In actuality, however, femmes turn traditional femininity on its head. Although femmes may present a feminine appearance and mannerisms, they are not so easily dismissed. Femmes are women who vehemently reject the limitations imposed on them by a patriarchal society that seeks to control and manipulate women's bodies and sexualities. In directing their erotic impulses away from normative heterosexual relations, femmes take their desires into their own hands and, in the process, reshape femininity to satisfy their own wants and needs. Femmes reappropriate femininity and tease out its most dangerous and subversive elements. How femme femininity is articulated also has much to do with other variants such as race, class, religion, and region. Femme diversity is also manifested in the sexual arena. As many femmes may be attracted exclusively to butches, some are attracted to other femmes, and still others are also attracted to men and consider themselves bisexual. Femme variation, in addition to femme strength and bravery, has enriched lesbian communities throughout the twentieth century.

Butch is also set of behavior and codes that articulates and facilitates desire. Butches are born physically female but are more comfortable presenting and embodying a masculine gender and sexual identity. Many butches experience differing degrees of gender dysphoria, which means that they feel a certain amount of discomfort with the gender they were assigned at birth, based on their anatomical sex. To rectify their discomfort, butches appropriate and remake aspects of male masculinity to satisfy their own needs and desires. Many butches appropriate masculine clothing, haircuts, hobbies, and jobs in order to facilitate their masculine identification. As butches take masculinity out of its traditional context, they transform it into something new and unique. Masculinity layered over a female body disrupts conventional notions of gender as a natural outgrowth of anatomical sex. Butches threaten normative masculinity by usurping male privileges, particularly the right to conduct sexual relations with other women. Rather than see butchness as merely male mimicry, it is perhaps more accurate to understand it as resembling some aspects of male masculinity but as still being its own unique and separate gender expression. Butch masculinity, like femme femininity, is nuanced by other variables such as race, class, religion, and region. There is a diverse range of butch sexualities; for example, some butches may be exclusively attracted to femmes, some are attracted to other butches, and some may occasionally be attracted to gay men. These rich and diverse butch identities participated in the construction of lesbian communities throughout the twentieth century.

The historical development of butch/femme communities occured during the course of the twentieth century. During the 1910s and 1920s, groups of expatriates, artists, and upper-class women in New York, Paris, and London began living in romantic and sexual unions that resembled butch/femme relationships—perhaps the most-famous (or infamous) example was British author Radclyffe Hall and her lover Una Troubridge. The term butch/femme would have been categorically inconsequential, however, and incomprehensible to these women. As such, the terms and identities of butch and femme did not exist in these early milieus. Butch/femme emerged as an intelligible identity and signifier during the 1930s and 1940s, mostly in urban centers in the United States. Aided by historical forces such as the fundamental technological changes engendered by the second wave of the Industrial Revolution in the 1890s; the social, political, and artistic upheavals caused by the Great War; and the long process of steady urbanization that had begun a century before, new social and sexual landscapes were being formed. During World War II, which took many American men overseas, many women enjoyed access to better-paying jobs and less familial policing. It was during this period that butch/femme communities really flourished and carved a permanent—albeit often precarious—place for themselves on the urban landscape. In the 1930s and 1940s communities of primarily working-class women began organizing themselves around butch/femme erotics. For most of these communities the primary site for socializing was the bars, which afforded a sense of community and refuge from the hostile world outside. White working-class women and working-class women of color

often socialized together, although there were bars that catered more specifically to each crowd. However, because bar space was limited, especially in the early days, women of color and white women were often thrown together by circumstance. The heyday or "golden age" of butch/femme culture was the 1950s and early 1960s. During this period, butch/femme communities grew in size and number and flourished despite constant harassment, raids, and vicious assaults by the police and thugs. Butch/femme eroticism was the primary way in which working-class lesbians organized their sexual and romantic relationships and friendships. Tacit rules and etiquette provided instruction on courtship, romance, and sex, as well as friendship. Butches were expected to be the aggressors in sex and romance as well as in social situations. Butches also were expected to be attracted only to femmes and never to another butch; and, finally, butches were supposed to be sexually untouchable, or "stone." Femmes were expected to be more sexually receptive, gentle, and accommodating. Femmes were supposed to direct their sexual desires onto butches and never to other femmes; and, finally, they were not supposed to want to touch their butch lovers genitally. Although these were the rules and one could be ostracized for any publicized infraction, not everyone followed them all the time or interpreted them stringently. Many women found the rules perfectly compatible with their personalities and desires. Some women, however, did find them stultifying and felt trapped by them. The latter voices would hear their grievances elaborated and championed in the next decade.

As the 1960s progressed, liberation struggles and movements for social change took the center of the political and social stage. The black civil rights struggles, student movements, and antiwar movements bombarded popular consciousness with demands for social justice and change. It was in this climate that the women's liberation movement and lesbian feminism were born. During the course of the 1970s, lesbian feminism radically refigured what it meant to be a lesbian, which was predicated less on erotic preference and more on political allegiance. Any woman could be a lesbian as long as she placed the political and social causes and concerns of women above everything else. Butch/femme was rejected by lesbian feminists as derivative of heterosexuality and, therefore, inherently oppressive to women. Butch/femme relationships were reviled and devalued by the burgeoning lesbian feminist movement, and many butch and femme women were ostracized from these communities. Made to feel ashamed of their relationships, communities, and identities, butches and femmes were ridiculed and silenced by lesbian feminism. Many butches and femmes fought back and refused to be pushed out of lesbian communities; however, many others felt forced out and isolated.

With the start of the "sex wars" in the early 1980s—after a decade of forced silence and exile—butch/femme reemerged as a viable and desirable way to organize sexual relationships and gender and sexual identities. Academics, activists, and community members began to actively challenge lesbian feminist assumptions that butch/femme sexuality merely mirrored heterosexuality. Instead, they argued that butch/femme as a couple or as individual identities were unique and radical subjectivities that persisted, and sustained lesbians, throughout the twentieth century. Butch/femme pride was not only respected; it was actively encouraged. New scholarship and writing glorified butch/femme and lauded it as being instrumental to the construction of modern public lesbian identities. With the advent of queer theory in the late 1980s and 1990s, butch/femme identities were celebrated as sites of gender subversion. This revaluation and visible rearticulation of butch/femme have led to its renaissance in many lesbian communities around the United States and western Europe. Although butch/femme has remained a viable and common identification in working-class lesbian communities, it also has become more acceptable among younger middle-class lesbians.

Outside the United States and western Europe, there exist thriving sexual economies that resemble butch/femme but are distinct and unique to their particular cultures. Like the American butch/femme communities of the 1930s, 1940s, and 1950s, many of these communal formations are divided along class lines and have created their own unique language and codes to signify desire. In Greece, very masculine homosexual women are called *dalikes*. They are predominantly working-class and conduct romantic relationships with other very feminine working-class women called *carnivelesque women*. In the Philippines, masculine homosexual women are often referred to as tomboys or T-birds. More feminine women seem to be identified in relation to tomboys; they are the "wives" or "girlfriends" of tomboys. In the Philippines, masculine/feminine gender dynamics in female homosexual relationships are evident among the working and upper classes. These sexual unions and gender expressions resemble American and western European butch/femme couples but must be understood within the context of their location. Across cultures divergent attitudes toward gender, sexuality, and religion profoundly shape the worlds in which we live.

See Also

FEMINISM: LESBIAN; FEMINISM: RADICAL; GENDER; LESBIAN SEXUALITY; LESBIAN STUDIES; LESBIANISM; QUEER THEORY; SEXUAL DIFFERENCE; SEXUAL ORIENTATION; SEXUALITY: OVERVIEW

References and Further Reading

Halberstrom, Judith. 1998. *Female masculinity.* Durham, N.C., and London: Duke University Press.
Harris, Laura, and Elizabeth Crocker. 1997. *Femme: Feminists, lesbians and bad girls.* New York and London: Routledge.
Lapovsky, Elizabeth, and Madeline Davis. 1993. *Boots of leather, slippers of gold: The history of a lesbian community.* New York and London: Routledge.
Munt, Sally. 1998. *Butch/femme: Inside lesbian gender.* London: Cassell.
Nestle, Joan. 1992. *The persistent desire: A femme/butch reader.* Boston: Alyson.
———. 1987. *A restricted country.* Ithaca, N.Y.: Firebrand.

Sherry Breyette

C

CANCER

Physical, social, and economic factors influence a woman's experience of cancer. The kinds, causes, and treatments of cancer, the means of its prevention, and the incidence of mortality and morbidity are determined not only by the physical differences between men and women but also by the particular conditions in which they live. These conditions vary considerably by region and reflect disparities in political, economic, and medical resources available to women around the world in the fight against the disease.

General Definition

Cancer refers to several diseases with one common trait—the rapid, unrestrained growth and spread of cells that do not react to the body's normal mechanisms for limiting cell replication. Healthy, benign cells have specialized functions, and the body stimulates and regulates their rate of replication in order to restrict their growth to contact with other cells. Cancerous, or "malignant," cells lack what is called contact inhibition and so invade the surrounding tissue of other cells. This lack of inhibition causes solid tumors or lumps called carcinomas, which begin in the lining of organs and account for nearly 90 percent of all cancers. Other cancers affect the blood (leukemias), the lymph system (lymphomas), and bone and connective tissues (sarcomas). Cancerous cells can invade surrounding cells and enter the circulatory or the lymphatic system—the two systems that supply nutrients to the body's organs and carry away waste. When cancerous cells enter the circulatory or lymphatic system, they can spread to any tissue or organ in the body in a process called metastasis. The spreading of cancerous cells kills normal cells by depriving them of nutrients, thereby hindering or completely inhibiting the normal functioning of organs and glands and causing a host of debilitating symptoms and often death.

A Global Disease

Cancer affects people in all parts of the world. No reliable statistics exist on the number of cancer cases or the number of deaths from cancer worldwide, since many countries have no cancer registries. But available figures reveal that cancer is a major health problem everywhere. Dramatic increases in life expectancy and profound changes in lifestyles have caused the total number of new cancer cases to soar. The World Health Organization (WHO) estimates that by 2020 there will be 20 million new cancer patients each year, more than 70 percent of whom will live in developing countries. Although mortality rates in developing countries are still higher for communicable diseases that have been eradicated in developed nations, more than two out of three of the world's cancer patients will come from a developing country.

As global development increases, two factors will make cancer the leading cause of death worldwide: higher life expectancy and environmental contamination. Cancer is partially a disease of aging, and as life expectancy rises around the world, the number of cancer cases rises as well. In addition, as cancer-causing pollutants, particularly endocrine-disrupting chemicals, are released into the environment, the incidence of cancers that affect the reproductive organs of both women and men will increase.

Specific behaviors, such as eating certain kinds of food, drinking alcohol, and smoking cigarettes, also increase the risk of certain cancers. Cultural or economic encouragement of such behaviors influences the incidence and kind of cancer cases within a region. Such links help explain regional variations; for example, breast cancer has been relatively uncommon in Japan, but its incidence is now rising as the Japanese adopt western-style foods rich in saturated fats, a shift encouraged by commercial food manufacturing. Tobacco chewing in India explains why cancer of the oral cavity is more common there than in other countries. Factors associated with cancer include the following:

• Low fiber intake	Colon cancer
• High intake of salt-cured, smoked, and nitrate-cured foods	Esophagus and stomach cancer
• Tobacco chewing	Mouth and throat cancer
• Heavy drinking	Liver cancer
• Heavy smoking allied to heavy drinking	Mouth, throat, laryngeal, and esophagal cancer
• Overexposure to the sun	Skin cancer
• Cigarette smoking	Lung cancer (and as many as one-third of all cancer cases)

Other generally acknowledged risk factors are excessive exposure to X rays and, in a small number of cases, genetic inheritance (for example, there is evidence that genetic factors account for 5 to 10 percent of breast cancer). Hypertension, or stress, can be a factor as well and may have political, economic, or cultural causes specific to a region or lifestyle. Although personal choices and cultural context influence both the cause and the prevention of cancer, environmental and social factors also play a role in determining a community's ability to prevent or treat the disease. Historically, powerful corporations manufacturing chemicals and pesticides or dumping toxic wastes have downplayed the evidence linking these activities to cancer. As more affluent communities in the developed world organized against such dangers, companies began exporting toxic waste, pesticides, and chemicals, harming communities less economically able, or insufficiently politically organized, to defend themselves against such practices.

In an effort to account for specific trends related to cancer, some researchers distinguish between cancer in developed and underdeveloped nations and between cancers predominant in affluent countries and those common in poorer, generally less developed countries.

Women's Experience of Cancer

Cancers afflicting women conform in large measure to this pattern. Breast cancer is the leading cancer among women

in developed nations (often called "the North"), with the United Kingdom, the United States, and the Netherlands having the highest rates. By contrast, cervical cancer—the most preventable cause of death in women of reproductive age—is the leading cancer among women in developing regions (called "the South" or the third world), particularly east and central Africa, some areas in Asia, the Caribbean, and tropical South America. The factors contributing to such cancers are distinct and reflect the varying priorities of women from these different regions and from developed as opposed to developing countries. For breast cancer, contributing factors include late childbirth and few or no children; for cervical cancer, factors include early childbirth and multiple pregnancies. In addition, women from poor communities in the developed world may be susceptible to cancers typical of both developed and underdeveloped areas, and their mortality rates may be higher than those of more privileged women. For example, the incidence of cervical cancer is 2.5 times higher among African-American women than among white women, and while the incidence of breast cancer among African-Americans of all age groups is rising, the incidence of breast cancer among white women under age 50 is falling. Overall, 34 percent of indigenous women around the world and 38 percent of African-American women survive for five years after a diagnosis of cancer, compared with 50 percent of white women.

Although ethnic differences and class distinctions profoundly influence the risk of cancer and the chances of survival among women, gender itself unites women's experience of cancer and can serve as an important criterion for examining and combating the global increase in the disease.

Gender inequality and sexism are significant factors in the prevention and treatment of cancer. Cancers that affect women occur mainly in the reproductive-genital system. Worldwide cancer cases among women rank in the following order: breast, cervix, uterus, ovaries, vagina, placenta, and fallopian tubes. Such cancers affect the health and survival of women more severely than cancers of the male reproductive organs affect men. Among Latin American and Caribbean women, deaths from cancers of the reproductive organs are double or even triple those for men, and the female-to-male ratio for healthy years of life lost is 7 to 1. In the United States, the incidence of breast cancer is 1 in 2,000 for women age 20, 1 in 40 at age 50, and 1 in 8 at age 85.

Cancer afflicts women differently from men. A major risk factor is the prolonged presence of estrogen in the body, including estrogen that is produced naturally. The link between estrogen and cancer involves issues of reproductive health that are exclusive to women, including late childbirth and few or no children, early menstruation, late menopause, and no breast feeding. In addition to the natural link between estrogen and cancer, several factors compound this risk in one or more reproductive organs:

- Pesticides, drugs, fuels, and plastics that mimic the action of estrogen or alter the hormone's activity
- Alcohol, which increases estrogen production
- Long-term use of estrogen-heavy oral contraceptives
- Fat and obesity (because estrogen is produced not only in the bloodstream but also in fat cells)
- DES (diethylstilbestrol), a synthetic estrogen prescribed to prevent miscarriages, which gives the user's daughter an increased risk of cervical or vaginal cancer and the user herself a higher risk of cancers of the breast, uterus, cervix, and ovaries. DES, a drug made under about two hundred brand names, is banned in the developed world but is still prescribed in some developing countries.

Environmental pollutants and toxins, processed foods, alcohol, and undertested medicines increase the general risk of cancer for all, but they increase a woman's risk in ways that require distinct preventive measures.

In attempting to prevent cancer, a woman may need to make choices about cancer risks that are unique to her health needs. For example, a woman for whom estrogen is prescribed, perhaps to protect her from osteoporosis, must weigh her relative risk of osteoporosis, reproductive cancer, and other illness or disability in light of her own, and her family's, medical history. These choices affect the specific way a woman will experience cancer or the threat of it in her lifetime.

Society's views of women play a role in determining a woman's risk. The tendency of the pharmaceutical industry and the medical establishment to view reproduction as a mechanism and the female body as a machine that can be tinkered with has increased women's risk of certain cancers. Examples include the long dismissal of the dangers associated with the earliest oral contraceptives, the experiments in hormonal manipulation to regulate the ovulation of premenopausal women, and the attempt to induce false pregnancies in teenagers to counter the "incessant ovulation" blamed for breast cancer. These experiments illustrate that medical practices are susceptible to cultural misconceptions of women that increase women's risk of cancer.

Another example is male dominance in the private sphere. Because men often control the decision-making process in sexual relations, many young women have sex at an early age, and cervical cancer is associated with early sexual activity in women. In addition, men often make the decision whether or not to wear a condom, which could protect women against the cancer-related health risks associated with sexually transmitted diseases (STDs). Because societies often expect or even encourage male promiscuity, many women are at risk for STDs as well as for the HIV virus, which impairs or destroys their ability to resist disease. Crucial to cancer prevention is a woman's ability to control high-risk behaviors in her own life.

Women's Cancer Prevention

Women in many countries have organized to fight the preventable causes of cancer and are acquiring a greater claim to the economic and political resources for cancer prevention and treatment around the world.

A woman's most effective strategy against cancer is early detection. With early detection, some female cancers can be cured or put into remission, the temporary but sometimes long-term disappearance of symptoms. The Pap smear is a low-cost diagnostic tool for cervical cancer, which is almost 100 percent curable if detected early. Chances of surviving breast cancer also are greatly increased by early detection because deaths from breast cancer result not from the localized tumor in the breast but from metastasis, the spread of cancer beyond its primary site to the blood and lymph systems. Annual mammograms and examination of the breasts by a medical professional, together with monthly breast self-examination, are the most effective tools in early detection. Mammograms are sometimes considered not "cost-effective" for women under the age of 30 because "only 20 percent" of breast cancers occur in that age group; but it can be argued that this assumption disregards women who develop breast cancer at a young age, and particularly African-American women, a large proportion of whom develop breast cancer before age 40. Routine health examinations are an inexpensive yet often effective intervention—but they are not available to all women around the world.

Women also can initiate effective and personally empowering actions to enhance cancer prevention, detection, and survival. These include adopting lifestyle habits that detoxify the body, correct the metabolism, and strengthen the immune system, such as regular exercise and a diet high in fiber, low in saturated fats, and rich in vitamins A, C, and E as well as minerals and enzymes. It is important to maximize the body's capacity for self-healing by reducing hypertension and by incorporating emotional and mental health in preventing and caring for disease.

Women have made medical research increasingly sensitive to women's health issues. Because conventional chemotherapy has been less effective in treating several female reproductive organ cancers than in treating some other types of cancer, alternative therapies have been developed, with some success. Researchers have discovered a gene that may suppress tumor growth in breast and ovarian cancer and have developed a drug that controls cell division in metastatic ovarian and breast cancers which are unresponsive to chemotherapy. Research has also found that timing treatments to the body's natural daily rhythms reduces the toxicity of chemotherapy. Research continues on alternatives to radical procedures, such as mastectomies, that can cause severe physical and emotional damage to women's reproductive and sexual health.

In designing a global strategy of cancer prevention, consideration for the specific needs of regions and countries is crucial. Understanding the diverse patterns of cancer in the world helps tailor national prevention programs to the epidemiological and economic situation of a specific country. There is still a widespread misconception that noncommunicable diseases such as cancer do not afflict the developing world, that they are burdens of affluent societies only. As a result, many developing countries face an increased incidence of noncommunicable diseases along with their persistently high rates of communicable diseases.

Inexpensive but effective interventions, such as encouraging healthy eating and pressuring food manufacturers to decrease fat and increase fiber content in their products, can help prevent both cancers and cardiovascular diseases. As cancer-causing industries confront organized opposition in the developed world, they must not be allowed simply to migrate to developing countries. For example, WHO estimates that there are 200 million female smokers in the world, and tobacco industries are increasingly targeting developing regions as developed countries organize against cigarette smoking. In developed countries, 25 percent of women smoke, compared with 7 percent in developing countries. If prevailing trends continue, however, and the tobacco industry continues to target the developing world, it is estimated that by 2020 more than 1 million women will die each year from tobacco-related illnesses—twice the number in 2000. In India, for example, rates of tobacco-related cancers are already higher among women than the rate of breast cancer.

Access to resources is critical. One-third of all cancer cases are curable by applying current knowledge and technologies. Yet in many parts of the world, the population has no access to the basic cancer-fighting medical practices available in more affluent regions. The need for these effective resources will grow because the number of curable cases is expected to rise to one-half of cancer cases by 2025.

On a global scale, more must be done to bridge the gap between well-organized and well-financed women's advocacy groups in developed countries and the women of the poorest countries who have the fewest material resources for preventing and surviving cancer.

See Also

ENDOCRINE DISRUPTION; GLOBAL HEALTH MOVEMENT; HEALTH CHALLENGES; HEALTH EDUCATION; HORMONE REPLACEMENT THERAPY; LIFE EXPECTANCY; MENOPAUSE

References and Further Reading

Lorde, Audre. 1980. *The cancer journals.* San Francisco: Spinsters/Aunt Lutte.

———. 1988. *A burst of light.* Ithaca, N.Y.: Firebrand.

Proctor, Robert N. 1988. The politics of breast cancer. *Dissent* (Spring).

Rennie, Susan. 1993. The politics of breast cancer. *Ms.,* May–June.

Restrepo, Helen. 1993. Cancer epidemiology and control in women in Latin America and the Caribbean. In *Gender, women, and health in the Americas.* PAHO Scientific Publication no. 54.

Sontag, Susan. 1988. *Illness as metaphor.* New York: Farrar, Straus, and Giroux.

WHO Working Group on National Cancer Control Projects. 1991. *WHO report 1993.* Bauf, Canada, 25 September–1 October.

Willis, Claudia. 1991. A puzzling plague. *Time,* 14 January.

Andaiye

CAPITALISM

Capitalism usually refers to a form of economic or social organization characterized by the pervasive commodification of property, labor, and knowledge. It has been a focus for feminists in many different ways. In the 1970s, when Marxist vocabulary was a kind of lingua franca among left-leaning intellectuals, socialist feminists tried to construct a theoretical understanding of patriarchy by using the concepts associated with the Marxist analysis of capitalism as a theoretical template. Alongside this fairly abstract analysis, those concerned with shifts in gender relations, including women's place in economic organization, have necessarily had to understand changes in the relationship between local economies and the world market. These and other aspects of feminist analyses of capitalism and its relation to gender are usefully reviewed in Barrett (1988) and Andermahr et al. (1997), among others. However, for a number of reasons analyses that focus on capitalism fell out of favor in the 1990s.

Marxist Analysis of Capitalism

In classical Marxism, capitalism has a twofold character. Although it is defined by a unique type of exploitation—the construction of human labor as a commodity for which the worker is paid, but at less than the value of that labor—it also has a progressive role in the evolution of human historical development. Because production under capitalism is organized around the continuing accumulation of capital, as against other social or spiritual goals, it tends to revolutionize the forces of production through scientific and technological development. As it expands, it subordinates other, earlier modes of production, either appropriating their surplus or replacing them with capitalist forms of production. According to orthodox Marxists, however, the means of production created by capitalism will eventually outgrow their foundation in the exploitative capitalist relations that gave birth to them. Thus although capitalism alienates human labor and blocks the free development of human potential, class conflict engendered by the oppression of the proletariat would lead the working classes to join forces to overthrow bourgeois rule and create a socialist society in which the fruits of capitalist development could be enjoyed by all.

Ambivalence about capitalism in Marxism was also present in the ways it envisioned the relationship between capitalism and what second-wave feminism came to call gender relations. On the one hand, in the *Communist Manifesto* Marx drew a parallel between the power relation between wives and husbands as social categories and the oppression of the proletariat by the bourgeoisie, seeing the monopolization of property ownership as crucial in both cases. But Marxists have also tended to see capitalism as sweeping away all preexisting hierarchies and divisions, including women's oppression, and in nineteenth-century Europe the new economic independence of women employed in the factories spawned by the industrial revolution seemed evidence that this was occurring. Since then many theorists, feminist and other, have tried to posit a relationship between capitalism and sexuality. Marcuse (1964), for instance, initially assumed that capitalism required the repression of sexual pleasure but later argued that sexuality was deployed by capital in the interest of expanded consumption. In contrast, others have argued

that because modern urban capitalist development has made it possible for individuals to lead lives outside marriage, it is linked to the development of modern homosexual lifestyles and communities. In the 1990s, analysis of the commodification of sexuality also made reference to the expansion of capitalist investment into new spheres (Hawkes, 1996), but here (as was increasingly the case elsewhere) capitalism has tended to be defined in terms of commodification and market exchange rather than in terms of the social relations of labor.

Feminist Analysis of Capitalism

To begin with, second-wave feminist theory in the West turned to highly abstract analyses of capitalism as a mode of production with its own laws of development. The most influential text, initially, was Engels's late nineteenth-century work *The Origin of the Family, Private Property, and the State* (1972), which argued that modes of production incorporated systems of *re*production as well as systems of production, thereby creating a space for feminists to bring the analysis of sexual partnerships between men and women within Marxist theory. Feminist theorists extended the concept of reproduction to include not only biological, generational reproduction but also women's domestic labor, which reproduced the labor force on a day-to-day basis. They also drew heavily on the French Marxist philosopher Louis Althusser's analysis (Althusser and Balibar, 1970) of capitalism's dependence on its political and ideological levels, not merely its economic laws, in reproducing itself as a mode of production. Thus even though women may not have been as involved as men in capitalist relations in the workplace, their position in society was nonetheless determined by capitalism. The state, which was seen to reflect the interests of capital, played a particularly important role in cementing women's dependence on, and subordination to, men. However, the question whether the patriarchal basis of women's oppression was an aspect of capitalism or a separate but interacting system (dual systems theory) was much debated. Though it would be hard to say that the exact nature of the relationship between different aspects of gender relations and capitalism was ever resolved, these debates, which now seem rather arcane, put the situation of women at the center of theories of social formation rather than at their margins.

Since the collapse of the socialist regimes in eastern Europe and the marginalization of Marxist social theory more generally, capitalism as a focus for analysis has faded into the background. Even feminist researchers concerned with workplace issues have argued that the concepts Marxists developed to understand women's entry into industrial production under capitalism, such as the concept of the reserve army of labor, are not well suited to understanding women's concentration in reproductive labor or the service sector (Benhabib and Cornell, 1987). Studies of large-scale change have deployed concepts like globalization or post-Fordism (Fordism being a technological system that increases efficiency by breaking down and interlocking production operations, as on an assembly line, to mass-produce goods) or postindustrialism rather than focusing on capitalism as such. As examples one could compare writing from the 1970s and early 1980s on what was called "gender in development," in which the expansion of the capitalist world system was seen as a crucial determinant of transformations in gender relations (for example, Young, McCullagh, and Wolkowitz, 1985, first published in 1981; *Signs*, 1981), with later work (for example, Marchand and Parpart, 1995).

The marginalization of capitalism as an analytic focus has been particularly pronounced in western feminist thought, where the "cultural turn" privileging of the local, the personal, and the textual as against the structural and economic, play and choice as against constraint and oppression, has been particularly pronounced (Barrett, 1999). Foucauldian definitions of power, which refuse to see it based in any one sphere (such as the economy), have also turned attention away from relations of production. This analytic refocusing obviously has complicated roots and is linked to economic and social changes, not just shifting intellectual currents. But although calls for a feminist revival of materialist analysis as against cultural studies—for example, Ebert (1996)—may be justified, real changes in economic life and women's roles in it make a simple return to the analysis of gender and capitalism where it left off very unlikely. For instance, the proliferation of cultural and intellectual activities and their centrality to economic life make it difficult to contrast the cultural and the economic in any simple way. Indeed, the centrality of commodification to the expansion of feminist culture—through the purchase and sale of commodities such as books, journals, theater and cinema, and the development of electronic communication—suggests that feminist theory will have to take note of how feminism is itself linked to, if not dependent on, developments in late capitalism.

See Also

COMMUNISM; ECONOMY: OVERVIEW; ECONOMY: HISTORY OF WOMEN'S PARTICIPATION; MARXISM; SOCIALISM

References and Further Reading

Althusser, Louis, and Etienne Balibar. 1970. *Reading capital.* London: New Left.

Andermahr, S., T. Lovell, and C. Wolkowitz. 1997. *A glossary of feminist theory.* London: Arnold.

Barrett, Michèle. 1988. *Women's oppression today: The Marxist-feminist encounter,* 2nd ed. London: Verso.

———. 1999. Words and things. In M. Barrett, *Imagination in theory: Essays on writing and culture.* Cambridge: Polity.

Benhabib, Seyla, and Drucilla Cornell, eds. 1987. *Feminism as critique.* Oxford: Polity.

Ebert, Teresa. 1996. *Ludic feminism and after: Postmodernity, desire, and labor in late capitalism.* Ann Arbor: University of Michigan Press.

Engels, Friedrich. 1972. *The origin of the family, private property, and the state.* London: Lawrence and Wishart (originally published 1884).

Hawkes, Gail. 1996. *A sociology of sex and sexuality.* Buckingham: Open University Press.

Marchand, Marianne, and Jane L. Parpart, eds. 1995. *Feminism/postmodernism/development.* London: Routledge.

Marcuse, Herbert. 1964. *One dimensional man.* London: Routledge and Kegan Paul.

Signs, 1981. 7(2). Special issue on development and the sexual division of labor.

Young, K., R. McCullagh, and C. Wolkowitz, eds. 1985. *Of marriage and the market: Women's subordination in international perspective,* 2nd ed. London: Routledge and Kegan Paul.

Carol Wolkowitz

CAREGIVERS

Women's role as domestic caregivers—maintaining a household and the people in it—may be a source of both strength and oppression for them. Although women do most of the world's household work, domestic caregiving has varied over periods and cultures. Food preparation, cleaning, child care, and even nursing infants may be allocated among groups of women, children, and men. The distinction between domestic and nondomestic activities may be blurred or clear.

In industrialized countries the middle-class norm strongly associates domestic caregiving with mothering (Ruddick, 1989). Yet the extent to which women mother, and how mothering and other domestic tasks are arranged, will depend on social and economic conditions. When women move into paid work, domestic caregiving may be restructured; for example, cooking may be replaced by the purchase of prepared foods, older children may be assigned to child care. Kin and neighbors may participate in the division of caring labor. Same-sex households can divide caregiving without reference to gender roles. More affluent families often hire poor women to do some, if not most, domestic caregiving (Colen, 1989). As more women have entered paid work and feminist ideas have spread, men have been pressured and encouraged to share domestic caregiving.

Organization of Caring Activities

How societies organize caring activities greatly influences women's domestic work (Fisher and Tronto, 1990). Where a free-market economy prevails, women with money may buy caring services, whereas poorer women perform their own caring work or do without it. Where caring is organized into private or state bureaucracies or offered through community-based agencies, domestic caregivers must connect members of their households to caring services; for example, they must take a child to a child care center, help a disabled relative go to a clinic, or get home care for an aged parent. Because women are concentrated in the underpaid "caring professions," women domestic caregivers often find themselves pitted against women who work as paid caregivers (a mother against an overworked elementary-school teacher, a daughter against a nurse who is on strike). Without an increase in women's economic power, support for women as both paid and unpaid caregivers, and, perhaps, the full integration of men into domestic and nondomestic caring, such tensions are likely to continue.

See Also

CHILD CARE; DOMESTIC LABOR; ELDERLY CARE, *all topics;* HOUSEHOLD WORKERS; HOUSEHOLDS AND FAMILIES: OVERVIEW; HOUSEWORK; LONG-TERM CARE SERVICES

References and Further Reading

Colen, Shellee. 1989. "Just a little respect": West Indian domestic workers in New York City. In Elsa M. Chaney and Mary Garcia Castro, eds., *Muchachas no more: Household workers in Latin America and the Caribbean,* 171–194. Philadelphia: Temple University Press.

DeVault, Marjorie L. 1991. *Feeding the family: The social organization of caring as gendered work.* Chicago: University of Chicago Press.

Fisher, Berenice, and Joan Tronto. 1990. Toward a feminist theory of caring. In Emily K. Abel and Margaret K. Nelson, eds., *Circles of care: Work and identity in women's lives,* 35–62. Albany: State University of New York Press.

Ruddick, Sara. 1989. *Maternal thinking: Toward a politics of peace.* Boston: Beacon.

Berenice Fisher

CARTOONS AND COMICS

Women have worked in cartooning almost since its inception. Many women published cartoons in the early twentieth century, but several pioneers stand out.

Pioneers

In 1909, Rose O'Neill created her adorable, androgynous Kewpies. First featured in the *Ladies' Home Journal*, the "Kewpies" became a national craze and remained a staple of women's magazines and newspaper funny pages for decades. Nell Brinkley's glamorous Brinkley Girl became a pre–jazz age cultural ideal. Grace Drayton used the characters in her "Dimples" cartoon strip as models for her Campbell Kids, who appear on soup cans to this day. In England, Mary Caldwell Toutel's "Rupert Bear" series began running in 1874 and was still popular in the early twenty-first century. The strip "Bib and Bob," created by May Gibbs, Australia's first female cartoonist, ran from 1924 to 1967.

The first "continuity strip" to be penned by a woman was Edwina Dumm's classic boy-and-his-dog strip, "Cap Stubbs and Tippie," which began in 1918. Dumm also worked as an editorial cartoonist, for the *Columbus Monitor*, before women got the vote. Mary Orr's "Apple Mary," which later evolved into "Mary Worth," first appeared in 1932. Inspired by Brinkley, Dale Messick created "Brenda Starr, Reporter" in 1940, and this adventure strip with its implausibly glamorous heroine was still in syndication in 2000. Tarpe Mill's "Miss Fury," was the first major costumed action heroine and the only one created by a woman. Clad in a panther skin, Miss Fury fought crime from 1941 through 1949. Marge Henderson Buell's venerable "Little Lulu" first came into being in the 1930s.

Mainstream Publications

For most of the twentieth century, women cartoonists were absent from the pages of comic books and as creators of single-panel "gag cartoons," with the notable exception of Helen Hokinson, whose gently ironic portrayals of society matrons (cowritten with a man) ran in the *New Yorker* in the 1940s and 1950s. Despite the work of the pioneers, women cartoonists have also been underrepresented in the daily funny pages. Newspaper editors, many of whom are men, apparently assume that whereas material by men is of interest to all, a woman-centered strip is a special-interest niche, and they tend to carry only one woman-penned strip; the rest are by and often primarily about men.

This situation is changing, but slowly.

In wide-circulation magazines and in the daily newspapers, women cartoonists remain the exception rather than the rule. The Pulitzer Prize–winning editorial cartoonist Signe Wilkinson is a rarity. The *New Yorker*, the primary venue for single-panel gag cartoons, publishes only a few women, notably Roz Chast, Australia's Victoria Roberts, and, occasionally, Carol Lay.

"Brenda Starr" was for years the only woman-penned strip in the funny pages. It was finally joined in the 1970s by "Cathy," Cathy Guisewite's comic strip about a self-depreciating single working girl, and later by Lynn Johnston's reality-based domestic strip, "For Better or for Worse." In the 1990s, women-oriented strips such as Jan Eliot's "Stone Soup" and Barbara Brandon's "Where I'm Coming From" were picked up by the big syndicates. Brandon's was the first cartoon by an African-American woman to be nationally syndicated.

For the most part, however, comics and cartoons by women remained ghettoized in nonmainstream venues such as small-press comics, zines, alternative weekly newspapers, and the Internet.

Alternative Publications

In the 1960s, with the advent of underground comics, women were inspired to tell stories that, in the words of the cartoonist Trina Robbins (1999), "were more valid to my generation than…Sgt. Fury and His Howling Commandos." Although the underground movement liberated cartoonists with respect to subject matter, publication remained very much a "boys' club" in which male underground editors published comics primarily by men. *National Lampoon* in the 1970s was a rare exception, including Shary Flenniken's "Trots and Bonnie" as well as work by M. K. Brown and Mary Wilshire. Women cartoonists began founding their own underground publications, such as Robbins's "It Ain't Me, Babe," the first all-woman "alternative" comic book. The collectively published "Wimmen's Comix" first appeared in 1972. Joyce Farmer and Lynn Chevely's "Tits 'n' Clits," a comic book series about female sexuality, came out at this time, as did Roberta Gregory's "Dynamite Damsels," the first lesbian comic book. In 1976, Diane Noomin and Aline Komisky-Crumb pioneered "Twisted Sisters," a comic book showcasing work that was, in Noomin's words, "personal, self-depreciating, ironic, crude and in-your-face." Two influential "Twisted Sisters" anthologies followed. Also at this time, in France, Claire Bretecher began to pen her

groundbreaking multipage comics, mixing acerbic feminist humor with insightful social commentary.

Excluded from mainstream venues, women cartoonists such as Nicole Hollander ("Sylvia") and Lynda Barry ("Ernie Pook's Comeek") were able to reach an audience by self-syndicating their work to alternative weekly newspapers. They became so well known that they were staples of bookstore checkout counters. Others who went this route were Nina Paley ("Nina's Adventures"), Marian Henley ("Maxine"), and Carol Lay ("Story Minute"), as well as Alison Bechdel, whose "Dykes to Watch Out For" appeared in countless feminist and lesbian papers. All are strongly feminist, uncompromised voices.

Others, like Diane DiMassa ("Hothead Paisn, Homicidal Lesbian Terrorist"), self-published their work in zine form.

In the late 1990s, several editors and small presses began to specialize in publishing women cartoonists, among them England's Cath Tate and "Fanny Knockabout Comics," Italy's Luciana Tufani, and North America's Roz Warren and Deb Werksman (Hysteria Publications).

Also in the 1990s, the Internet emerged as a venue where women artists could easily and inexpensively publish their work, sidestepping the gatekeepers—the many male editors—to reach and build an audience. However, women artists continued to be underrepresented in the far more lucrative mainstream venues. Without the influence and financial rewards of mainstream syndication and publication, talented women cartoonists will continue to face major obstacles.

See Also

MAGAZINES; PUBLISHING; ZINES

References and Further Reading

Robbins, Trina. 1999. *From girls to grrrlz: A history of women's comics from teens to zines.* San Francisco: Chronicle.

Warren, Roz. 1995. *Dyke strippers: Lesbian cartoonists from A to Z.* Pittsburgh, Pa.: Cleis.

Roz Warren

CASTE

Caste is a hierarchical, hegemonic ranking of social groups found predominantly on the Indian subcontinent. A word of Portuguese and Spanish origin, *casta* in the early sixteenth century had several meanings, one of which was "purity of blood." By the eighteenth century, it designated two levels of groups on the subcontinent: the *jatis,* roughly 3,000 or more, loosely grouped into four *varnas,* systematically elaborated in the Brahmanic scriptures of the Vedic period.

Organization of the Caste System

In the upper-caste Brahman construction, which is elaborated in the Hindu Dharmasastras as part of a tradition of universal law, caste has its origin in the *varna* system, which was constituted by four orders: Brahman (priests), Kshtriya (warriors), Vaisya (traders), and Sudra (artisans, workers, peasants, and the like). Of these, the first three were the *dvija* (twice-born "clean") castes, the men of which are entitled to initiation into Hinduism. A fifth order, the panchama, or untouchables, made up of the slaves who performed menial chores (cleaning villages, washing clothes, and in general being engaged directly in production and connected closely to organic life), was included later.

Within this framework, women and slaves figure as subjects. Women are considered by nature fickle and unchaste, so their sexuality, bodies, and minds must be reined in by the dharma; the Manusmriti epitomizes this view. Evidence from the eighteenth century points to the vulnerability of all women, irrespective of *jati,* to enslavement for infringement of moral codes.

The panchamas, the untouchable castes, have for centuries been ghettoized in *vadas* (colonies), enslaved to the other four *varnas* in perpetual bondage. For women of these castes, the additional implication is sexual slavery. The word *asprsya* (literally "untouchable") was first used in the Visnusmrti, which calls for death for any member of these castes who deliberately touches a member of a higher caste. However, this proscription on physical contact did not extend to sexual relations between upper-caste men and untouchable women, because sexual labor was regarded as part of the physical labor provided by slave women and appropriated by the upper-caste owner or master.

With few exceptions, the caste system is patrilineal and patrilocal. There is evidence that seems to indicate the brief coexistence of patrilineality, patrilocality, and egalitarian gender relations in the early Rig Vedic period. Historical evidence also points to extremely fluid social groups with shifting occupational status and widely varying dietary practices among the four *varnas*: Sudra kings and Brahman military commanders, beef-eating Vedic Brahmans, and so on. Formal education, however, remained the preserve of the Brahman. Endogamy (specifically, the absolute proscription on upper-caste women engaging in marital or other physical relationships with lower-caste men), ritual purity, commensality, and slavery defined the caste system.

Critiques of Caste

The critique of caste has its origin in the work of Jotirao Phule and Savitribai Phule in Maharashtra in the nineteenth century, E. V. Ramaswami Naicker "Periyar" and Tamil Nadu in the early twentieth century, and B. R. Ambedkar in the later twentieth century.

Phule and his associates founded the Satyashodhak Samaj (Truth-Seeking Society) in 1873. The overarching theme of Phule's addresses at meetings of the Samaj was the character and unity of the working classes, the unequal division of labor between women of different castes, and the vital contribution of peasant women to production. Tarabai Shinde's Stree Purusha Tulana (1882), also part of the Satyashodhak tradition, confronts Brahmanic patriarchy as well as patriarchy within non-Brahman castes.

In mapping a non-Brahman worldview through the Self-Respect Movement, launched in 1925, Periyar stood the caste system on its head. The new social order could emerge only through a radical transformation of structures of feeling and material conditions. This immediately freed women and Adi Dravidas (Dalits) from caste-bound traditions, created a moral ground in which women exercised choice and consent in matters of both marriage and sexuality, and eliminated the priesthood and the chanting of Vedic hymns in marriage solemnities.

Ambedkar, an intrepid advocate of formal rights for the untouchables, belonged to the untouchable Mahar caste. He coined the word *Dalit* (literally "downtrodden") to designate untouchables as a political entity. During the struggle for independence in the early part of the twentieth century, Ambedkar's concerns centered on finding ways in which independence could bring freedom to the oppressed. As an architect of the Indian Constitution, he instituted constitutional safeguards for the depressed classes against exclusion (social boycott) and active discrimination by majority upper-caste Hindus in independent India. Significant among these provisions was the right to substantive equality through reservations in education and employment.

Articulations of caste by the Dalit Panther movement in Maharashtra and elsewhere in India since 1972 illustrate the intermeshing of gender with caste, although the connections are not made explicit. Dalit writing defines social location in terms of centrality in production processes. Dalit literature also articulates the playing out of nationality and citizenship on the bodies of women of lower castes, by juxtaposing, for instance, the fine of 50 rupees for molesting a Dalit woman against the fine of 300 rupees for disrespect to the national flag. This echoes the concerns of Pandita Ramabai, who, in the late nineteenth century, drew a parallel between English rule in India and the rule of high-caste men over low-caste men and women down the ages.

The National Dalit Women's Federation, formed in 1995, brings together the various perspectives in Dalit assertion and resistance, encapsulating a two-hundred-year history. The federation questions both upper-caste, Brahmanic hegemony in intercaste relations (particularly the antagonistic, often violent relations between upper castes and Dalit women, in a climate of increasing right-wing nationalism) and Dalit patriarchies from within. This approach by the federation brings into sharp focus current debates on the place of Dalit women in quotidian politics: Should Dalit women have a quota within the quota earmarked for reserved categories, or a quota within the quota reserved for women? That they might have a right to both is rarely acknowledged.

See Also

CLASS; HINDUISM

References and Further Reading

Ambedkar, B. R. 1990. *Writings and speeches.* Vol. 9. Bombay: Government of Maharashtra. Reprint.

Bapat, Ram. 1995. Pandita Ramabai: Faith and reason in the shadow of the East and West. In Vasudha Dalmia and Heinrich von Stietencron, eds., *Representing Hinduism: The construction of religious traditions and national identity,* 224–252. New Delhi: Sage.

Chatterjee, Indrani. 1999. *Gender, slavery, and law in colonial India.* New Delhi: Oxford University Press.

Dharampal-Frick, Gita. 1995. Shifting categories in the discourse on caste: Some historical observations. In Vasudha Dalmia and Heinrich von Stietencron, eds., *Representing Hinduism: The construction of religious traditions and national identity,* 82–100. New Delhi: Sage.

Geetha, V., and S. V. Rajadurai. 1998. *Towards a non-Brahmin millennium: From Iyothee Thass to Periyar.* Calcutta: Samya.

Guru, Gopal. 1995. Dalit women talk differently. *Economic and Political Weekly* 30(41, 42).

Hanlon, Rosalind. 1985. *Caste, conflict, and ideology: Mahatma Jotirao Phule and low caste protest in nineteenth century western India.* Hyderabad: Cambridge University Press and Orient Longman.

Ilaiah, Kancha. 1996. *Why I am not a Hindu.* Calcutta: Samya.

Jaiswal, Suvira. 1998. *Caste: Origin, function, and dimensions of change.* New Delhi: Manohar.

Kannabiran, Vasanth, and Kalpana Kannabiran. 1991. Caste and gender: Understanding dynamics of power and violence. *Economic and Political Weekly* 26(37).

Mendelsohn, Oliver, and Marika Vicziany. 1998. *The Untouchables: Subordination, poverty, and the state in modern India.* New Delhi: Cambridge University Press.

Omvedt, Gail. 1993. *Reinventing revolution: New social movements and the socialist tradition in India.* New York: Sharpe.

Phule, Mahatma Jotirao. 1991. *Selections: Collected works of Mahatma Jotirao Phule.* Vol. 2. Bombay: Government of Maharashtra. Reprint.

Kalpana Kannabiran

CATHOLICISM

See CHRISTIANITY and FAMILY: RELIGIOUS AND LEGAL SYSTEMS—CATHOLIC AND ORTHODOX.

CELIBACY: Religious

The term *celibacy* comes from the Latin *caelebs* ("unmarried") and denotes the state of remaining unmarried and abstaining from all sexual activity, whether through personal choice or force of circumstances. In the Roman Catholic and Orthodox Christian churches, "consecrated celibacy" designates the special state of persons who make a vow not to marry when they join a religious order. Male institutional celibates are present in many societies, but female celibacy is somewhat less common. This article addresses female celibacy in formal contexts.

Celibacy as a state of life is alien to the Old Testament tradition and Judaism. With their strong belief in the divine mandate to marry and have children, the Jews regarded willful celibacy as reprehensible. Thus, in the Bible, Jephthah's daughter bewails her virginity, and Hannah, mother of Samuel, grieves over her barrenness. It was rare for a Hebrew to embrace lifelong celibacy as an expression of exclusive devotion to God.

Celibacy in Christianity

Jesus departed from this tradition by modeling a life unfettered by family ties. According to Matthew 19:12, Jesus positively counseled that celibacy be chosen freely "for the sake of the Kingdom of Heaven." Since Jesus's time, the challenge to be celibate has inspired Christians to follow his example of total bodily surrender to the demands of faith. Nevertheless, it is clear that Jesus and his disciples (several of whom were married men) did not enjoin this state on all Christians.

Virginity as a state of religious power was already recognized in Rome, where the purity of the vestal virgins was a symbolic guarantor of the virtue and stability of the state. During the first four centuries after Christ, so many young women took vows of virginity that church authorities began to view the trend with alarm and addressed it at the Synod of Elvira (c. 306 C.E.). Some early Christian sects required that all their adherents be celibate, but, depending necessarily on a constant stream of converts, they were unable to persist. At first, Christian celibate communities included both men and women, but anxiety over possible scandal led to the sexes being separated.

In the Middle Ages, a monastic life for women came to fill social as well as religious needs. Convents offered a respectable, useful life to women who remained unmarried by choice, because their families could not provide adequate dowries, or because of a surplus of females in a population; many middle-aged widows also became nuns. Free from the demands of childbearing and child care, they devoted themselves not only to prayer but also to healing, teaching, and serving the indigent.

Protestants in the Reformation turned away abruptly from clerical celibacy, but the long equation of female virtue with celibacy retained some influence, and women celibate by choice were often accepted as church functionaries and teachers of children. All members of the Shaker sect, founded by Ann Lee in the eighteenth century and later widespread in the United States, were celibate.

Celibacy in Hinduism and in Taoism

On the Indian subcontinent, Hindu women did not begin entering the monastic life until the late nineteenth century. Buddhists, by contrast, have a long tradition of nuns who renounce attachment to worldly life and devote themselves to seeking enlightenment through restraint of the senses and meditation. Such women were not required to be virgins before joining their community but had to remain celibate thereafter. In some divisions of Buddhism, nuns (called *bhikshunis*) can preach and perform ritual functions as monks do. In the Jain religion, the Svetambara sect has a preponderance of celibate ("renunciant") nuns over male monastics; the other sect, the Digambara, discourages female renunciants but still includes a few.

Taoism, the indigenous religion of China, developed a monastic pattern during the Tang dynasty (618–907 C.E.), and there were female orders. Celibacy was recommended in at least some of these, but apparently not in all. In the modern period before the establishment of the People's Republic of China, a large number of women joined the Quanzhen order, which emphasized celibacy and meditation; it is not clear to what extent it has managed to survive under the current regime.

Celibacy in Other Religious Traditions

Beyond these major religious traditions, there is little evidence of female celibacy by choice on a large scale. Both Islam and Zoroastrianism reject the notion. In many cultures, however, women are expected to remain celibate before marriage and sometimes in widowhood. Ritual purifications throughout the world usually require that people abstain from sex in order to devote themselves to higher aims and to avoid contaminating holy times, places, and acts.

In the modern western world, consecrated celibacy is widely devalued in comparison with marriage. It is, however, gaining unprecedented meaning as a countercultural option against the backdrop of the market economy. Women may choose celibacy as a reaction against being commodified, reified, and bartered because of their sex. Their surrender of the body to their faith signals a decision in favor of human dignity, womanly freedom, and femininity liberated from the dictates of a patriarchal culture. As Mary John Mananzan has written, the meaning of celibacy today lies "in the freedom of the heart that is needed to be truly available to the many" (1993: 144).

See Also

CELIBACY: SECULAR; NUNS; RELIGION: OVERVIEW; SEXUALITY: OVERVIEW; SEXUALITY, *specific topics;* VIRGINITY

References and Further Reading

Abbot, Elizabeth. 2000. *A history of celibacy.* New York: Scribner.

Mananzan, Mary John. 1993. Redefining religious commitment today. In *Women religious now: Impact of the Second Vatican Council on women religious in the Philippines,* 138–149. Manila: Institute of Women's Studies.

Rees, Daniel, et al. 1978. Celibacy. In *Consider your call,* 154–188. London: Society for Propagation of Christian Knowledge.

Schneiders, Sandra. 1986. *New wineskins.* New York: Paulist.

The way. 1993. Supplement to no. 77, special issue on celibacy.

Sr. Irene Dabalus

CELIBACY: Secular

In Victorian times women were regarded as deviant if they enjoyed a genitally active sex life. Today women invite pejorative labels if they do not enjoy such a life. Some say that our orgasm-fixated society considers no sexual activity freakish except *no* sexual activity.

Historical Background

The original and primary meaning of celibacy was "the state of living unmarried," derived in the seventeenth century from Latin *caelibatus,* from *caelebs*. A secondary meaning is "abstention from sexual intercourse, especially by resolve or as an obligation."

The ancient view of celibacy in the West and elsewhere was positive singlehood conferring wisdom, health, and spiritual power. This idea of celibacy as a more elevated ideal than genital activity significantly contrasts with the centrality in many twentieth-century societies of heterosexuality and reproduction.

Chastity as an element of celibacy has been shrouded in myth in most religions. Christians are taught that Christ and Mary were virgins and that virginity was a holier state than sexual engagement. Catholics are taught to revere sexual abstinence. The European monastic movement offered its own example of celibacy as the highest purity. In medieval England the proportion of celibate men was as high as 5 percent of the male population and the proportion of celibate convent women only slightly lower.

In the nineteenth-century United States, three post–Civil War utopian societies—the Shakers, the Koreshans, and the Sanctificationists—substituted celibacy for sex, as a symbol which empowered their promotion of theoretical sexual equality and female social power (an early form of feminism). In these three religious groups, the support of women's economic and personal independence accompanied their acceptance of celibacy.

In nineteenth-century Britain, female celibates were denigrated as "prudes," a term that became a weapon for attacking suffragists and feminists who challenged men's abusive sexual behavior or who spurned heterosexual relationships.

Western European societies have long preached lifelong celibacy or delayed marriage, and non-European groups have also observed lengthy restrictions on sexual intercourse. A highly abstemious society is the Dani of Irian Jaya, Indonesia, who require a four- to six-year postpartum period of sexual abstinence, which is invariably observed and seems to lead to no signs of stress or misery in celibate abstainers.

Buddhist monastic life of poverty, chastity, and self-abnegation in places like Burma is remarkable for its firm renunciation of the society of women and "lustful" desires and for the degree to which it is part of ordinary people's daily lives.

In China in the 1960s and 1970s, a campaign to limit population growth was largely a campaign in favor of celibacy. Chinese adolescents were not expected to engage in any sexual activity. It was considered degenerate for girls not to control their sexual impulses; signs in factories stated, "Sex is a mental disease." By contrast, the current ethos is that celibacy is a mental disease.

Celibacy in Modern Societies

In the West at the turn of the twenty-first century, women are encouraged to engage in sexual—preferably heterosexual—activity, which, together with diets, beauty products, low wages, pornography, and violence, is part of a culture that limits women's progress and power. The multimillion-dollar pornography industry, which exists alongside a cosmetic surgery industry aimed at persuading women that it is healthy to be starved, snipped, and stitched in pursuit of a prolonged sexual shelf life, upholds an ideology that suggests that anyone who lacks interest in sexual activity must be in need of a cure. Given this oppressive climate, it is not surprising that women are deciding to abandon the sexual treadmill and find other, more fulfilling ways to express themselves. Many of today's celibates, then, are neither virgins-in-waiting nor the reluctantly single; they are women, married and single, heterosexual and lesbian, who have often found in celibacy the freedom and autonomy to redefine and celebrate their sexuality.

Research by the present author for her book *Women, Passion, and Celibacy* (Cline, 1993) found that a "genital myth" which prescribes genitally active behavior is accepted by women across social classes, cultures, ages, and sexual orientations. Celibate women today are labeled frigid or asexual despite an honorable male tradition that historically saw celibacy as a prestigious ideal.

Whereas the patriarchal definition of female celibacy is genital abstention, women are now redefining celibate identity and behavior as a mode of sexuality. Celibacy may be a choice to be without a sexual partner for positive reasons of political, personal, or spiritual growth. Women see it as a sexual independence that enables them to retain intimate connections yet define themselves autonomously. Though without the power struggles of a genitally active relationship, it remains a form of sexual practice. It focuses on women's personal development, and it is *not* about relating to other people.

"Ascetic celibates," who eschew any form of genital expression, see themselves as different from "sensual celibates," who enjoy masturbation, touching, and some physical intimacy. Some religious women today seeking spiritual growth, together with nuns, accept celibacy as a vocational requirement. Evidently, however, more women choose passion without possession, a key determinant of contemporary celibacy, for positive reasons of autonomy, a need for solitude, a search for passion, platonic companionship, time for their careers, improvement in communication with their partners, or antipathy toward possessiveness within partnerships. Some women become celibate as a consequence of widowhood, illness, disability, fear of AIDS or violence, dislike of penetration, sexual anxiety caused by childhood sexual abuse, or dislike of the unequal power dimension they perceive in genital relationships.

"Partnered" lesbian women experience less pressure about turning to celibacy than do partnered heterosexual women. All celibates in couples find it more difficult than single celibates to express their celibacy publicly, for fear of stigmatizing their partners. Still, many women find that celibacy enables them to view men as friends instead of lovers or enemies.

New definitions of contemporary female celibacy—which include defining it as a form of sexuality—change the philosophical meaning of the word. In the area of sexuality, women are not only breaking new ground philosophically but also making a cultural shift in the perception of celibacy, linguistically and practically.

See Also

CHASTITY: RELIGIOUS; MARRIAGE: OVERVIEW; SEXUALITY: OVERVIEW; SINGLE PEOPLE; VIRGINITY

References and Further Reading

Cline, Sally. 1993. *Women, passion, and celibacy.* London: André Deutsch.

Greer, Germaine. 1984. *Sex and destiny: The politics of human fertility.* London: Secker and Warburg.

Kitch, Sally L. 1989. *Chaste liberation: Celibacy and female cultural status.* Chicago and Urbana: University of Illinois Press.

McNamara, Jo Ann. 1985. *A new song: Celibate women in the first three Christian centuries.* New York: Harrington Park.

Rothblum, Esther D., and Kathleen A. Brehony, eds. 1993. *Boston marriages: Romantic but asexual relationships among contemporary lesbians.* Amherst: University of Massachusetts Press.

Sally Cline

CENSORSHIP

Censorship is an exercise of the critical faculty that is sanctioned by institutional authority. Authorities use censorship to control the power to name: the power to define what is true and what is right. Efforts by authorities to censor fallacious or dangerous ideas are integral and often palpable parts of their efforts to proclaim and propagate factual or felicitous views. Sense is made by censoring nonsense.

All societies, from ancient Sumer and Egypt to the corporate states that make up the emerging global cultures of the microchip, practice some form of censorship. Censorship not only assumes different forms—for example, official, subterranean, and self-censorship—but also frequently operates under other names, for example, patriotism, reason, competition, good taste, or national security.

Censorship is the knot that binds power and knowledge. Social order is created, and bodies of knowledge are assembled and organized by marking boundaries between conformity and deviance, reason and chaos. In some societies these boundaries are codified into law and enforced by formal administrative agencies, censorship boards, police, judicial officers, or their representatives. Every social group supplements or supplants formal controls with social pressures, conventions, rituals, and institutional practices that discourage dissent. Censorship is therefore a pervasive, intractable, and sociologically significant constituent of all human communities.

The Received History of Censorship

The word *censorship* and the practices conventionally associated with it are, however, usually more narrowly conceived within the discourses of contemporary scholars, jurists, and human rights advocates. Censorship is commonly thought of as a historical development that accompanied the rise of the modern state and the invention of the printing press (Lahav, 1989). Conversely, the great victories against censorship and for freedom of expression are regarded as outcomes both of the scientific revolutions that occurred in Europe in the sixteenth and seventeenth centuries and of the western Enlightenment that followed in the eighteenth century (Bury, 1913).

The emergence of liberal democracies is associated with these developments. The American and French Revolutions were, in part, precipitated by restrictions on press freedom. The First Amendment to the U.S. Constitution (1791) is regarded as a benchmark in the history of free expression. For the first time, a government formally barred itself from making any laws restricting freedom of speech, press, or religion. Subsequent legal controversies about censorship in the United States have therefore been largely restricted to: (1) issues of state or local censorships of books, the arts, and pornography; (2) questions related to the abuses of free speech and freedom of the press—for example, slander and libel; and (3) controversies about the forms and limits of press censorship during wartime and other national emergencies, as well as controversies that permit some prior censorship of the writings of government employees and former government employees. In western democracies, such as the United Kingdom, where church and state retain formal ties, publications or practices that are deemed blasphemous may also be proscribed by government regulation.

Etymology supports this historically circumscribed, Eurocentric understanding of the term. *Censorship* derives from the root *cense,* from the Latin *censure:* to estimate, rate, assess, be of the opinion, judge, reckon. Historically, the title "censor" was first used to designate two magistrates in ancient Rome who were responsible for the census, the official registry of citizens, as well as the supervision of public morals. Censorship was common in both Greece and Rome, but it was not systematically administered until technology extended access to the written word beyond nobles, aristocrats, and clerics. The invention of movable type by Johannes Gutenberg in Mainz, Germany (c. 1450), was followed almost immediately by a papal decree that established and enforced book censorship throughout all of Europe until the Protestant Reformation. The Reformation did not abolish censorship. Protestant reformers such as John Calvin set up far more rigorous censorial regimes than any envisioned by the papacy.

In reaction to what they regarded as the licentious corruptions of the Roman Catholic clergy, Protestants, especially the Puritan sects, instituted far more comprehensive regimens for disciplining the body than had prevailed under Catholicism. In the United States, fundamentalist Protestant groups continue to play leadership roles in organized efforts to prohibit or restrict sex education in public schools, to limit scientific inquiry in areas where science and Scripture conflict, to ban controversial books from public schools and libraries, and to influence textbook selections for public schools.

Women's Studies, History, and Censorship

From the perspective of women's studies, the received history of censorship is western, and patriarchal in origin. It recounts a familiar western myth of a progressive, almost oedipal, struggle of the forces of truth, justice, freedom, and enlightenment over tradition, superstition, ignorance, and punitive authority. All the featured players in this story are European men, and virtually all the action revolves around their struggles with one another.

Within this historical narrative, the Reformation marks an epochal triumph for freedom of conscience and reason. The fact that this freedom was achieved within cultures that regarded women, slaves, and servants as property, not as rational human beings, passes without comment. Liberal histories record the democratic revolutions of the eighteenth century as narratives of progress. They remain silent about the fact that the franchises for freedom of expression and freedom of the press secured by these revolutions were limited franchises extended only to citizens: free, white males who owned land, or, in the case of freedom of the press, those who owned printing presses, publishing house, or newspapers. These histories chronicle the daring deeds of great men. In short, they suggest that all the significant victories for freedom of expression took place in "a world without women" (Noble, 1992).

From Cato the Elder (234–149 B.C., Roman) to Anthony Comstock (1844–1915, American), the censors vilified in liberal histories of censorship were, to a man, defenders of the morals and manners of patriarchal gender orders. Their adversaries, the champions of free expression, posed no fundamental threats to that order. Indeed, with the exception of John Stuart Mill (1806–1873, British), they expressed little or no awareness of it. On the contrary, almost to a man, they struggled for the ascendancy of their respective political or social causes within the existing gender order. The great egalitarian revolutions of eighteenth-century liberalism were, for example, conceived within natural rights philosophies that understood the rights of *man* to be the rights of *men.*

In this view, the monotheistic, monocular, and monological assumptions of western thought naturalized the subordination of women. These constituent assumptions denied women both subjectivity and agency in historical processes. They provided the auspices for discursive forms that legitimated ignoring or, in the case of some historical writing, erasing women's participation in struggles for freedom of expression and freedom of the press. Consequently, repression and persecution of heresies like Gnosticism and witchcraft, which disproportionately targeted women, were not classified as censorship by historians. Yet church and state repression directed against these ideas and their advocates claimed more lives than many wars (Kors and Peters, 1972). Conversely, women's participation in the family-run clandestine presses that sprang up in many parts of Europe from the Inquisition until the French Revolution is not examined in histories of free expression. Yet women's work was essential to these enterprises, and widows often continued to operate illicit presses long after the death of their husbands.

Standard histories, it is argued, do not just fail to chronicle the experiences of European women. They also ignore the struggles of European men who belonged to subordinate or nonhegemonic categories of masculinity: homosexual men, landless men, servants, most laborers, and most members of non-Anglo-Saxon immigrant groups. In short, they exclude most of the European population. More significantly, they write all non-Europeans out of history. Liberal history frames its narratives in a periodizing schema—the Dark Ages, the Age of Reason, and so forth—that treats the achievements of prominent European men as universal. Within this schema, the Enlightenment marked the end of the great struggles against censorship. Yet most of the world's population was either disenfranchised or untouched by the "light" of the western Enlightenment.

When the chronology of liberal history is used to tell the stories of women, working-class, colonial, or postcolonial subjects, it reduces their struggles to attempts to amend or complete the received history of censorship. The liberal model ignores the differential social positioning of these people in time, place, and hierarchies of power and knowledge. It captures their resistances within its fictions of universal enlightenment.

The women's history movement abandons these narrative conventions. It treats gender as a primary category of historical analysis. Gender is conceived as a difference that makes a difference in how social order is created and how power relations are arranged, sustained, and contested. Received history is therefore not regarded simply as an incomplete record of the past. Rather, it is seen, for example by Joan Wallach Scott, as an active "participant in the production of knowledge that legitimized the exclusion or subordination of women" (1988: 26). The goal of women's history is not just to write women's achievements into the record. It is, Scott, a leader of this movement, points out, to write "histories that focus on women's experiences *and* analyze the ways in which politics construct gender and gender constructs politics" (1988: 27).

Women's history is only beginning to lay the groundwork for rewriting histories of censorship. It is, nevertheless, possible to identify some of the epistemological moves women's history must make to transcend the myopia of the received history of censorship. Sociological—rather than etymological or juridical—definitions of censorship are required to bring women's experience into focus. Alternative schemata for periodizing history need to be replaced with reflexive, contextual forms that recognize the uniqueness and multiplicity of diverse cultural experiences, discursive practices, and gender orders. Dichotomous concepts, like patriarchy, which provide a useful lens for understanding European experiences, may distort rather than enhance comprehension of the gender politics of nonwestern cul-

tures. Dualistic models do not, for example, advance analysis when applied to some Native American cultures where women are the primary producers of objects of aesthetic value, participate fully in political affairs, and yet play no part in important religious ceremonies.

Viewed from the perspective of women's history, liberal triumphs over church and state censorship require much fuller explanations. Using linear, positivistic theories of progress to theorize these developments greatly underestimates their complexity. These theories ignore the fact that victory within one of the multiple and mobile sets of social relations that make up the field of power is often accompanied by defeat within another (Foucault, 1980). The daring deeds of great men frequently require great sacrifices by their foot soldiers, servants, slaves, mothers, wives, sisters, and children. The free expression of such men often depends on the silence of their subordinates. A step forward in the historical process by some individuals or groups may signal steps backward by others. Women's history requires analysis of all the moves that take place within the field of power.

To cite a paradigmatic example: from the perspectives of standard historiography and women's history, Thomas Jefferson's arguments against censorship assume very different levels of significance. Liberal historians view history as a progressive development that culminates in the Enlightenment, free inquiry, and the rule of reason. Therefore, they regard the internal contradictions in Jefferson's discussions of censorship as inexplicable conundrums and relegate them to the museum of historical curiosities. In contrast, women's history theorizes power as a complex and conflictual process that constitutes the entire social body. As a result, it approaches Jefferson's contradictions as historical discoveries and rich resources for analysis. To bring women's experience of Jeffersonian liberalism into focus requires analysis of the fact that Jefferson vehemently condemned any form of state or local censorship in the American Republic, simultaneously advocating strict censorship of women's reading.

The goal of women's history is not to diminish Jefferson's achievements but to provide a fuller and more accurate account of their complexity. When historians examine the ways that "politics construct gender and gender constructs politics" in liberal democracies, the censorship of women's reading becomes a contradiction that requires explanation because men's reading is no longer subject to censorship. From this perspective, the American Enlightenment can be understood as both a reaffirmation of female subordination and a partial victory for women's struggles for emancipation. Even though it reproduced the gender order of the Old World, Jeffersonian liberalism also laid some of the philosophical and legal foundations for western feminist critiques of patriarchy.

Constituent and Regulative Censorship

Sociological definitions of censorship recognize the arbitrary, expansive, and fluid character of power relations and of the social structures and hierarchies they support. Two overlapping types of censorship can be distinguished: constituent and regulative (Jansen, 1988; Miller, 1962). Constituent censorship provides the epistemological foundations for the creation of social order and the legitimation of authority. It operates at the level of tacit or taken-for-granted assumptions. Constituent censorship is not ordinarily open to question or contestation except in periods of social tumult or transformation. Yet constituent censorship provides the precedent and anchor for regulative censorships. The gender order—what Gayle Rubin (1975: 157) describes as "the sex/gender system"—has served as a form of constituent censorship in virtually all known literate societies. Gender must therefore be understood as a fundamental constituent of all power relations, including the relationships of men with men.

Regulative censorship, by contrast, is generally both "visible and legible" (Sennett, 1980), even though it is often administered in inconsistent, arbitrary, or duplicitous ways. It involves formal, frequently bureaucratic, administration of written laws or rules. Regulative censorship is a legally constituted form of censorship practiced by church or state; it marks the limits of social permission and enforces sanctions against those who cross the boundaries of propriety, canon, or law. Liberal histories of censorship are histories of regulative censorships in the West.

Regulative censorship frequently contributes to the maintenance of the dominant sex or gender system in many cultures. It may, for example, be used variously to ban or restrict access to sexually explicit materials, including images and texts deemed pornographic or obscene; to censor materials that deal with homosexuality or lesbianism; and to restrict access to birth control information. In contemporary liberal democracies, regulation of sexuality has been a flash point for debates about censorship. Debates about regulating pornography framed within the terms of liberal discourse have deeply divided contemporary feminists in Europe and North America.

The distinction between constituent and regulative censorship is useful because it underscores both the intractability and the cultural variability of this suppression. It moves beyond and beneath western liberalism's circumscribed understanding of the concept. It opens up an approach that can begin to examine the diverse and distinctive ways that nonwestern cultures constitute their discourses and censorship. This approach allows censorship in Argentina, Azerbaijan, Indonesia, or Iran, for example, to be understood and critiqued on its own terms rather than within the terms of an alien screen of meaning that automatically codes difference as regressive, primitive, exotic, or unenlightened.

By emphasizing both the necessity and the difficulty of analyzing constituent forms of censorship, this terminological distinction also provides new ways of conceptualizing, contesting, and mediating current debates about censorship in the West. Groundbreaking works like Susan Griffin's *Pornography and Silence* (1981) and Carolyn Merchant's *The Death of Nature* (1980), which document historical repression and erasure of the female principle in the mythopoetics of western thought, acquire new significance. Viewed as probes of constituent censorship in western power and knowledge rather than as specialized studies of pornography or ecology, they begin the work of writing women's experience into the history of western censorship.

The challenge of rewriting the history of censorship through the lens of women's experience is a formidable one. A first step is to free the term *censorship* from the hegemony of western legal and semantic traditions. The next step is to develop a radical methodological reflectiveness that incorporates the lessons of both feminist and postcolonial examinations of the constituents of western thought. Then it may be possible to begin to build international forums where the multiple, disparate, and possibly irreconcilable voices of women's historical and contemporary experiences of censorship can be articulated.

For many women throughout the world, organized struggles for freedom of expression and against censorship are just beginning to gain momentum. These women are claiming a voice and making history in places like Dakar, Dublin, Lagos, Ljubljana, Los Angeles, Manchester, Manila, Phnom Penh, Santiago, and Tashkent. As historical subjects and agents, they are reconstructing gender, politics, and definitions of free expression.

See Also

DEMOCRACY; EROTICA; EUROCENTRISM; HUMAN RIGHTS; LITERATURE: OVERVIEW; PATRIARCHY: FEMINIST THEORY; PORNOGRAPHY IN ART AND LITERATURE; PUBLISHING; REPRESENTATION

References and Further Reading

Bury, J. B. 1913. *A history of freedom of thought.* London: Oxford University Press.

Butler, Judith, and Joan Wallach Scott, eds. 1992. *Feminists theorize the political*. New York: Routledge.

Chester, Gail, and Julienne Dickey, eds. 1988. *Feminism and censorship: The current debate*. Bridport, U.K.: Prism.

Coetzee, J. M. 1996. *Giving offense: Essays on censorship*. Chicago: University of Chicago Press.

Curry, Ann, and Robert Usherwood. 1996. *The limits of tolerance: Censorship and intellectual freedom in public libraries*. Lanham, Md.: Scarecrow.

Doherty, Thomas. 1999. *Pre-code Hollywood: Sex, immorality, and insurrection in American cinema, 1930–1934*. New York: Columbia University Press.

Foucault, Michel. 1980. *The history of sexuality*. Vol. 1: *An introduction*. New York: Vintage.

Griffin, Susan. 1981. *Pornography and silence: Culture's revenge against nature*. New York: Harper and Row.

Jansen, Sue Curry. 1988. *Censorship: The knot that binds power and knowledge*. New York: Oxford University Press.

Kors, Alan C., and Edward Peters. 1972. Introduction to *Witchcraft in Europe, 1100–1700: A documentary history*. Philadelphia: University of Pennsylvania Press.

Lahav, Pnina. 1989. Government censorship. In Erik Barnouw, ed., *International encyclopedia of communications*. Vol. 1, 246–249. New York: Oxford University Press.

Merchant, Carolyn. 1980. *The death of nature: Women, ecology, and the scientific revolution*. San Francisco: Harper and Row.

Miller, Jonathan. 1962. *Censorship and the limits of permission*. London: Oxford University Press.

Noble, David. 1992. *A world without women: The Christian clerical culture of western science*. New York: Knopf.

Rubin, Gayle. 1975. The traffic in women: Notes on the "political economy" of sex. In Rayna Rapp Reiter, ed., *Toward an anthropology of women*, 157–210. New York: Monthly Review.

Scott, Joan Wallach. 1988. *Gender and the politics of history*. New York: Columbia University Press.

Sennett, Richard. 1980. *Authority*. New York: Knopf.

Spender, Dale. 1982. *Women of ideas and what men have done to them: From Aphra Behn to Adrienne Rich*. London: Routledge and Kegan Paul.

Sue Curry Jansen

CENSUS

Throughout recorded history, elites and governments have conducted censuses as a means of keeping track of the material resources that they have owned or controlled (or have wished to own and control) within their borders. Most early censuses were conducted to enumerate the wealth and resources of the state for the purpose of assessing taxes and tributes due. Modern national censuses still provide economic information, but most states today conduct censuses primarily for broader social science purposes: the census, in most countries, is the main (often sole) document that aims to provide a comprehensive social survey of the nation. The most basic social census is designed to elicit information on the sex, age, marital status, family size, educational attainment, and economic status of each person enumerated; most national censuses go much further and include questions on health, welfare, housing conditions, consumption patterns, religious preference, and racial identity.

Conducting a regular census is considered a hallmark—and an obligation—of modern statehood; the United Nations issues guidelines on developing and conducting censuses. A decennial census (taken every 10 years) has become the international standard, but the ability of states to conduct regular censuses varies widely. A complex and costly infrastructure is required to conduct and interpret a national census, and in many poorer countries censuses are taken infrequently. On a global scale, then, the level of information available about the social and economic lives of women and men is wildly uneven; as a general rule, one can presume that the least information—or the least reliable information—is available for the poorest and more marginalized peoples and nations.

Uses of the Census

In many countries, the census is key to national government decision making—it is the primary document that provides the "factual" basis for a wide range of social, economic, and political policies. Most censuses are intended to be comprehensive social surveys, and most demographers, policy makers, and analysts who interpret census information have long assumed that this is what censuses provide. Recent critiques from social scientists, however, including feminists, particularly in western countries where census taking is a high-profile and high-expense government activity, have called into question presumptions about the comprehensiveness of modern censuses. It is increasingly clear that censuses provide, at best, a partial assessment of the "state of the state." It also is clear that the degree to which certain groups are rendered visible or invisible in a census will have important consequences in social and economic policy.

In some cases, certain peoples and groups may actively avoid being counted in national censuses; censuses are, after all, an arm of state surveillance, no matter how benign a function they may play in the national mechanisms of governance. Racial or ethnic minority groups, or peoples with particular political and religious affiliations, may feel they have good reason to resist being caught in the census net. However, intentional invisibility such as this probably accounts for only a small part of the underrepresentation that characterizes all censuses. *Undercounting,* which plagues most censuses, is more typically (though not always) unintentional and reflects the logistical difficulties of taking a census: certain groups, such as the homeless or people living in isolated parts of a country, are difficult to enumerate fully.

Censuses are also flawed by blind spots, which are the product of design predilections and presumptions built into the census itself. A census is a social construct, itself a social document; the questions that are asked or not asked on a census reflect presumptions about who and what are considered by the state to be "important" enough to count. Thus, the census as a social mirror seldom reflects all lives equally.

Racial and ethnic census classifications are especially problematic. Most censuses require people to identify themselves by one of a small number of preselected racial categories—the U.S. census, for example, allows for only five racial groupings. In most countries, this practice is coming under increasing criticism. Census racial classifications typically reflect stereotyped, simplistic, hierarchical, or imperialist classifications; once in place, such classifications narrow the nature of national debate and understanding about race relations; census categories give the impression that *race* is a fixed (and official) identity, and such categories can seldom accommodate multiracial identities.

Women's Invisibility in the Census

Throughout history, and in all countries, censuses, by both commission and omission, have rendered most of women's lives invisible most of the time. The invisibility of women in official statistics perpetuates the myth that what women do is less important, less noteworthy, and less significant than what men do. It is only relatively recently that women have been counted in censuses—literally. Although women are no longer counted merely as men's chattel, it is very much still the case that the basic categories and classifications used in most national censuses largely ignore women or misrepresent their social and economic roles.

For example, most censuses include questions about the participation of the population in economic activities. It is still the case, however, that most censuses define *economic activity* as "work" and define "work" in ways that mask women's economic contributions to family and state. Productive labor is typically defined solely as participation in the "waged" market economy. This renders invisible household labor, unpaid labor in family economic projects, unwaged agricultural labor, and volunteer activities, all of which have significant value to a national economy and all of which are feminized spheres of activity. In virtually every economy and family structure around the world, the greatest share of nonmonetary economic activity is done by women—and this sector of activity remains unaccounted for in most censuses (Waring, 1988).

The definition of *family* and of women's role as part of households is just as problematic in censuses as is the definition of economic activity—and, indeed, the two are linked (Folbre, 1991; Folbre and Abel, 1989). Most censuses take the "household," not the individual, as their basic unit of measure. The presumption built into most censuses that households have a single and identifiable "head" is usually paired with a default presumption that this "head of household" is male. Under these presumptions, married women who live with their husbands disappear, and women living in households without male heads become abnormalities. Allegiance to the notion that every family must have a head is strong, and in most national censuses this is still the norm, although women's protests have resulted in changes to these census categories in countries including Canada, the United States, Sweden, and New Zealand. Virtually all censuses continue to ignore non-kin residential arrangements, such as people living in communal groups or in same-sex partnerships. Mismeasurement of the extent of female residential independence contributes to an exaggerated perception of male family headship, which is then privileged by public policy. Men, women, and children within a household seldom have equal status, roles, aspirations, or access to money or amenities; aggregating data by household makes these differences *among* members of a household invisible and gives a false impression of homogeneity and intrafamily equality.

Despite their failings, censuses do provide baseline measurements on the state and status of a country's population, and census reports are a unique source of information useful to women and to feminists. For example, census reports have provided the empirical data for feminist analyses about the increasing feminization of poverty throughout western Europe and for analyses of the changing composition of households in Canada and the United States. Similarly, census data have provided the starkest evidence of the persistence of preference for sons and of female infanticide in India, Pakistan, and

China: sex ratios (the number of females per 1,000 males) are recognized as a good indicator of the status of women within society, and data on sex ratios are almost always available from even the most rudimentary census. In India, the census of 1991 reported a sex ratio of 929 females per 1,000 males, a drop since 1981, when the ratio was 934:1,000 (Barrett and O'Hare, 1992).

Feminists have developed sophisticated critiques of the politics of statistics, and in most countries women are struggling to insist that their national censuses reflect their lives more fully and accurately. Some of the greatest headway in this battle appears to have been made in New Zealand and in Canada, where the censuses have been significantly modified in response to women's critiques—although, as Marilyn Waring (1988) and others point out, there is still considerable room for improvement.

See Also

DEMOGRAPHY; ECONOMY: INFORMAL; FAMILY STRUCTURE; GEOGRAPHY; HOUSEHOLDS AND FAMILIES: OVERVIEW

References and Further Reading

Barrett, Hazel, and Greg O'Hare. 1992. India counts its people. *Geography* 77(2): 170–174.

Folbre, Nancy. 1991. The unproductive housewife: Her evolution in nineteenth-century economic thought. *Signs* 16(3): 463–484.

———, and Marjorie Abel. 1989. Women's work and women's households: Gender bias in the U.S. census. *Social Research* 56(3: Autumn): 545–569.

Waring, Marilyn. 1988. *If women counted: A new feminist economics.* New York: HarperCollins.

Joni Seager

CHADOR

See VEILING.

CHARITY

Generally, charity or philanthropy is associated with Christian doctrines of love and goodwill toward fellow beings. In late eighteenth- and nineteenth-century western industrial nations, the concept received a more specific meaning, that of benevolence toward the poor, in close association with the establishment of charitable organizations as the domain of upper-class women. The separation of home and work

that occurred at that time as a consequence of industrial capitalism was accompanied by an ideology of domesticity, which prescribed that, while men went out to paid work, women's place was in the household: charitable work, as an extension of domesticity, was the only activity suited to them. Many charitable organizations were run by women only (although men might be called on to chair meetings and donate money), and their activities were generally oriented toward working-class women and children. Upper-class women used these charitable pursuits "to wield power in societies intent upon rendering them powerless" (McCarthy, 1990: 1). In some countries—the United Kingdom, for example—these organizations were the forerunners of professional social work. In other instances—for example, in Mexico and Russia—well-to-do women directed their charity mainly to the church, raising funds for convents and other religious endeavors (McCarthy, 1990).

Interpretations of Charitable Activities

The charitable activities of nineteenth-century upper-class women have often been interpreted as instances of upper-class control over the working class. For example, Octavia Hill (1838–1912), a wealthy Englishwoman who provided cheap housing for the poor, exercised vigilant control over their morality and cleanliness. On the other hand, Jane Addams (1860–1935), a philanthropist and feminist who lived and worked among the poor in the United States, rejected the notion of charity as implying inequality and made every effort to assist poor people without patronizing or controlling them (Stebner, 1997).

During the twentieth century, professional social work came to the fore, and governments took on the responsibility for supporting the poor and disadvantaged through systems of social security. This, however, did not mean the demise of charitable organizations. Women continue to make a major, albeit often unacknowledged, contribution as leaders and workers in such organizations.

See Also

ALTRUISM; PHILANTHROPY; VOLUNTEERISM

References and Further Reading

McCarthy, Kathleen D. 1990. *Lady Bountiful revisited: Women, philanthropy, and power.* New Brunswick, N.J.: Rutgers University Press.

Stebner, E. J. 1997. *The women of Hull House: A study in spirituality, vocation, and friendship.* Albany: State University of New York Press.

Cora V. Baldock

CHASTITY

The word *chastity* has two related historical meanings. First, it refers to an abstention from almost all sexual activity: a chaste woman does not have sex. Second, it is used to describe a person whose only sexual interactions are with a spouse for the purpose of procreation: the chaste, faithful wife performs her uncomfortable generative duty. Unlike virginity, chastity does not depend on sexual purity and "innocence." Nonetheless, the terms are related in that they refer to qualities desired more from women than from men, placing primary value on women's sexual restraint and avoidance.

Chastity As a Female Virtue

Historically and across cultures, chastity has been a particularly female virtue. The cult of widow chastity, a phenomenon of early Chinese civilization, encouraged women not to remarry after a husband's death. Damage to "female honor and chastity" was the focus of a mid-nineteenth-century Russian rape code, an emphasis that highlighted the victim's status and downplayed the rapist's violence (Engelstein, 1992: 76). The eighteenth-century Scottish philosopher David Hume described chastity as such a necessary requirement of virtuous women that "bachelors, however debauch'd, cannot chuse but be shock'd with any instance of lewdness or impudence in women" (1990: 572).

The initial focus on women's chasteness as paramount and more necessary than men's sexual restraint comes from religious forces. Women were inextricably connected with the excesses and dangers of sexuality through a direct identification with the body. Polly Blue ties the foundations of sexual chastity to a "fear and loathing of the female body's functions; in identification of evil with the flesh, and flesh with women" (1987:59). This is apparent not only in the Judeo-Christian tradition, in which women's sinfulness and bodiliness began with Eve's collapse to temptation, but also in other religious thought.

Chastity and Property

In addition to religious influences, a societal emphasis on personal property and inheritance brought about chastity for women alone. Although Hume was characterizing the social mores of upper-class eighteenth-century Britain, his description of the rationale for the chaste woman is an effective one. According to the philosopher, a man will only support a child he is related to biologically; in order to be sure of his child's paternity, he must have no doubts of his wife's fidelity. Hence, writes Hume, society must ensure that women are faithful by overemphasizing the virtue of chastity. Further, women are the objects through which men procreate and pass on property; because of this dubious power, women's freedom of sexual expression is strictly limited through chastity.

See Also

CELIBACY: RELIGIOUS; CELIBACY: SECULAR; VIRGINITY

References and Further Reading

Blue, Polly. 1987. A time to refrain from embracing. In Linda Hurcombe, ed., *Sex and God*. New York: Routledge.

Engelstein, Laura. 1992. *The keys to happiness: Sex and the search for modernity in fin-de-siècle Russia*. Ithaca, N.Y.: Cornell University Press.

Hume, David. 1990. *A treatise on human nature*. Oxford: Oxford University Press.

Jennifer Casey

CHILD
See GIRL CHILD.

CHILD ABUSE
See ABUSE and CHILD LABOR.

CHILDBIRTH

A woman's capacity to conceive, gestate, and give birth to a human being is often described as a miracle, especially by those who have ever seen a baby slip from the enclosure of a woman's womb into the outside world. Pregnancy, labor, and birth, however, always take place in a societal context; the concept of birth as miraculous and the actual event of childbearing are mediated by the beliefs and practices of each culture (Jordan, 1978/1993). How women learn about childbearing and motherhood; whether and how they view themselves as spiritual, emotional, and practical agents of cultural continuity; and how their needs are met by customs and institutions related to maternity care are essential components of an understanding of childbearing. The understanding of childbirth reflected in this article, though by no means the only possible view, is a perspective shared by many today.

Needs of Mothers

Every pregnant woman deserves nurturance, encouragement, love, and support from family and friends: a safe work and home environment; good child care; adequate transportation; food, rest, and exercise; and a long enough leave from her work, with assurance that she can return to her job. She needs a skilled, wise, trustworthy practitioner to provide continuity of care throughout the time of childbearing, which is usually considered to be a year.

During labor, a woman needs a reassuring environment, as close to home and to her particular culture as possible, so that she can shape her labor as it unfolds. She needs attendants to help her relax and open up, to guide her and patiently observe the natural process of labor, and to be confident in her own intuitive and physical ability to give birth well. Labor progresses best when a woman can move around, change positions, and eat and drink as she desires to keep up her energy—and when she is surrounded by the people and objects that make her happiest and give her ease. She needs accessible medical resources nearby in case of an emergency.

After the birth, she needs time to be with her baby, as well as a helping hand during the following days and weeks to help her care for herself, the baby, and her family. She continues to need good food, rest, and exercise. A first-time parent needs information, encouragement, and the influence of experienced parents to help her be a good mother. She may want access to family-planning services so that she can plan any future pregnancies. Motherhood requires women to use their capacity for creativity, resilience, intuition, endurance, humor, and love, and to give so much of themselves that they deserve in turn to be well cared for.

How, then, do maternity care systems meet women's needs? Some questions to consider include these: Are women, mothers, and motherhood revered or discounted? Are women's birthing powers admired or feared? Do a society's practitioners and institutions support, control, or obliterate these powers?

Woman-Oriented Maternity Care

There are two main ideologies of childbearing and maternity: woman-oriented and obstetrical. The first, woman-oriented maternity care, or the midwifery model of care, in its ideal form, places mothers at the heart of the childbearing experience. Society, structured to value mothers' strengths and their perception of their own needs, pays careful attention to the social, economic, spiritual, and emotional circumstances of their lives. Childbearing and motherhood are viewed as creative, healthy, joyous life transitions, eluding

most efforts to measure and tame them and deserving of great respect. Women are treated with dignity and are trusted to know or to be able to learn what they need to know to be healthy, to give birth well, and to have healthy children. In this world, compassionate, experienced midwives "journey with" women during pregnancy, labor, and birth. Integral members of their communities, these midwives learn through apprenticeships, in midwifery schools, and occasionally in hospitals. Babies are born at home, in community birthing centers, or in hospitals when necessary. Every child is a wanted child. The community provides the resources to nurture and provide for every child. Family physicians and obstetricians hold women, motherhood, and midwifery in high regard. These practitioners, trained as medical and surgical specialists, provide backup when needed, in consultation with the attendant midwives, in homes, birth centers, or nearby hospitals, having carefully assessed the benefits and risks of any medical interventions they use. If this ideology were to become public policy, it would be consonant with women's needs; would come close to ensuring healthy, happy mothers and babies; and would cost society less money to implement and maintain than obstetrical care (Luce and Pincus, 1998; Rothman, 1982).

Obstetrics

Obstetrics, a surgical specialty, treats every woman's pregnancy as a potential illness, and birth as a medical event, to be "managed" and "controlled" in hospitals with drugs and technology. Within the hospital system, physicians (and nurse-midwives) may work in teams, so that a pregnant woman will not know whom she will see for her next appointment or who will assist her at the birth of her baby. Obstetrical care can be invaluable when it concentrates on medical surveillance and surgical rescue in times of crisis, but it is simply not appropriate for most women. Obstetricians are not trained to pay attention to a woman within the context of her life throughout the childbearing year; they are trained to examine her periodically very briefly during pregnancy, and then to enter the delivery room at the last moment to "deliver" the baby. They view labor as unbearably painful and much too long, and birth as excessively messy, risky, and dangerous. They rely on extensive testing, monitoring, probing, intrusion, and interference during pregnancy and labor, using drugs, devices, and procedures that have become the norm simply because they exist, their risks often undisclosed, their benefits—safety, necessity, effectiveness—unproven in any truly scientific way (Enkin et al., 1995; Goer, 1995).

Assuming that women's bodies don't work well by themselves, obstetrical practitioners impose a concatenation of interventions on labors that would ordinarily progress at a natural, harmonious rate in less coercive circumstances. Hospitals, modeled on factories, have rules, schedules, and routines of their own that interfere with the unique flow of each woman's labor; for example, each phase of labor must be accomplished within a predetermined amount of time. In industrialized societies, a "normal, standard hospital delivery" will involve the use of a hospital bed, a fetal monitor, an intravenous hookup, induction of labor, an epidural injection, and an episiotomy. All too often, over the last thirty years of the twentieth century—especially in the United States—labors ended in cesarean section, increasing both the expense and the risk of the birth, since a cesarean involves anesthesia, cutting into the woman's body, and possible postoperative infection.

The idea of the superiority of obstetrics prevails in almost all "developed" countries, where the obstetrical approach has become the norm. From the eighteenth century (and earlier) up to the turn of the twenty-first century, obstetricians have suppressed or eliminated midwifery practice, the result being that knowledge of some midwifery techniques and native medicine is lost (Murphy-Lawless, 1998; Wertz and Wertz, 1979/1989). Midwives and their advocates are harassed when they threaten obstetrical hegemony and medical practices. Most women do not know that alternatives exist, or they assume that midwifery care is inferior. They have their babies in hospitals, believing medicalized care to be the best and safest way. Ironically, because one intervention does lead to another (lying in bed slows labor; induction speeds it up, making it painful; drugs ease the pain; and so on), obstetrical technology ends up becoming "necessary."

Young women absorb the pervasive medical message permeating modern culture. Never having seen a woman actually giving birth, naturally or otherwise, they may fear the pain of labor and lack confidence in their bodies' capacity to give birth to a child. They learn from films and television shows that childbirth consists of hospitalized women lying on their backs in great distress, covered with sheets, under bright lights, surrounded by masked and gowned practitioners attending to a crisis, if not an emergency. In this age of technological proliferation, they tend to believe that medical technology will guarantee a healthy baby. If their intuition, their needs, and their desire for calmer, less intrusive treatment lead them to question routine experimental or invasive procedures, they are asked, "Don't you care about your baby?" and are made to feel selfish or guilty. They then go on to become mothers who carry on the message of medicalized birth to their daughters.

Childbirth Activism

In response to the efforts of childbirth activists and midwives, many hospitals in the United States have become more woman- and family-oriented, with birthing rooms and nurse-midwives as practitioners (Edwards and Waldorf, 1984). Birthing centers have sprung up to meet women's needs for a more homelike atmosphere. Doulas (birthing attendants) are accepted in many medical settings. A very few hospitals serve as backup for direct-entry midwives who attend women in their homes. These midwives themselves are seeking licensing laws that will enable them to receive reimbursement. Although these improvements offer some women more choices, they do not change the basic structure of maternity care.

Thus it is crucial for women, their families, and their advocates to support midwives and midwifery practiced in harmony with obstetrics when needed. It is essential that women bring to light stories about truly natural, individual births and describe pregnancy, labor, and birth as the flowing, organic, spiritual, sensual, and empowering experiences they can be. Positive, joyous birth stories serve to preserve women's awareness of their own capable, strong minds and bodies and of the benefits of midwifery (Gaskin, 1978; Mason, 1990). They counteract the technological bias of the present generation and add to the wealth of wisdom that enhances women's experiences wherever they give birth.

See Also

MEDICAL CONTROL OF WOMEN; MIDWIVES; OBSTETRICS; REPRODUCTION: OVERVIEW; REPRODUCTIVE HEALTH; REPRODUCTIVE PHYSIOLOGY

References and Further Reading

Edwards, M., and M. Waldorf. 1984. *Reclaiming birth: History and heroines of American childbirth reform.* Trumansburg, N.Y.: Crossing.

Enkin, M., M. J. N. C. Keirse, M. Renfrew, and J. Neilson. 1995. *A guide to effective care in pregnancy and childbirth.* New York: Oxford University Press.

Gaskin, I. M. 1978. *Spiritual midwifery.* Rev. ed. Summertown, Tenn.: Book Publishing.

Goer, H. 1995. *Obstetric myths versus research realities: A guide to the medical literature.* Westport, Conn.: Bergin and Garvey.

Jordan, B. 1978/1993. *Birth in four cultures.* Reprint, Prospect Heights, Ill.: Waveland.

Luce, J., and J. Pincus. 1998. Childbirth. In Boston Women's Health Book Collective, *Our bodies, ourselves for the new century.* New York: Simon and Schuster.

Mason, J. 1990. The meaning of birth stories. *Birth Gazette* 3: 14–19.

Murphy-Lawless, J. 1998. *Reading birth and death: A history of obstetric thinking.* Bloomington: Indiana University Press.

Rothman, B. K. 1982. *In labor: Women and power in the birthplace.* New York: Norton.

Wertz, R., and D. Wertz. 1979/1989. *Lying-in: A history of childbirth in America.* Reprint, New Haven, Conn.: Yale University Press.

Internet Resources

<http://www.ourbodiesourselves.org>; <http://www.feminist.com>

Jane Pincus

CHILD CARE

The Triple Roles of Women

For most of human history, women's multiple roles in life have been perceived as inseparable. Today, the significance of women's triple roles is recognized: women as worker, the productive economic role; as housewife and homemaker, the consumer role; and as mother, the bearer and rearer of children, the reproductive and caregiver role.

In preindustrial times and in many agrarian, pastoral, and other societies in the developing world, child care was part of the traditional female role, combined with production and consumption. In almost all times and places, however, care of the very young, as in primate societies, has been seen as *female* responsibility, to be handled by women of all age groups (grandmothers, aunts, sisters, and other female relatives) and not *solely* by the biological mother.

Rationale for Child Care

With the coming of the industrial revolution, profound social changes deeply affected the pattern of women's lives in the industrial world. Production moved into large factories, where groups of workers congregated, not only separating the workplace from the home but also creating working conditions that made it impossible to keep young children near their parents while they worked. More affluent women, who were not obliged to seek work under these conditions, found their responsibilities in the home gradually reduced to the tasks of home management; thus was born the "housewife" of modern times.

Along with the "housewifization" of women, the nuclearization of the family (increasingly becoming the "one-parent" family of postindustrial societies), declining fertility, and universal primary education (which left no more older siblings at home to mind the younger ones while they helped with the chores) were friendships that led to the emergence of child care as an identifiable task. Meanwhile, Marxist thinkers, in their analysis of industrial society, were describing women's roles as productive and reproductive, thereby collapsing the two important functions of homemaking and childbearing or -rearing into one, a conclusion that can justifiably be attributed to a male perspective.

At the same time, a revolution in thinking relating to human nature and human development, starting with Rousseau in the eighteenth century, led to a wider understanding that the child was a unique being in his or her own right, not just a miniature adult. The concept of childhood as a unique and precious period of life requiring special attention finally arrived, leading to an understanding of child care as a specialized activity.

The work of later psychologists and the growth of the discipline of child development in the twentieth century emphasized still more the importance of early childhood as a stage in human development, making it meaningful once again to speak of women's triple roles instead of the "double burden." The increasing unease felt by working mothers about the conflict between their maternal and economic roles came to a climax in the mid-twentieth century with the work of John Bowlby, who, by bringing powerful evidence of the severely detrimental and long-term effects on children of separation from their mothers at an early age, lent credence to the theory that working mothers of young children could damage these children's development.

The intellectual heritage of Freud and Marx thus provides the ideological base for some contemporary concepts of childhood, child care, and the mother alone as the primary or sole caregiver. Although these ideologies are influential worldwide, they are not equally accepted or equally applicable everywhere, because the objective conditions in which women and children find themselves differ widely across the globe. In most developing societies, the majority of women continue to work largely in the informal sector or in agriculture; the involvement of extended families in child care is the norm; school-age children participate in labor as well as in household chores, including care of younger siblings; and childhood itself is viewed in different ways in various cultures. Nevertheless, the importance of child care services, both as an instrument for child development and as a support for women as workers, has gradually come to be recognized in almost all countries and has become a plank of the women's movement in some. At the same time, the gradual recognition of group child care as a skilled activity has led to the growth of training and education and the emergence of a new profession.

Historical Review of Formal Child Care

The dawn of the twentieth century saw the beginnings of formal institutional child care in many countries of western Europe, a development that arose from both the growth of the labor movement and the influence of Fabian and socialist thought. Early labor legislation led to institutions such as *l'école maternelle* in France. The two world wars had a tremendous impact on women's work status and roles. A significant event of World War I was the Soviet revolution in Russia, with its emphasis on the liberation of women from the traditional roles of capitalist society and its declaration of commitment to state support for women workers in fulfilling their maternal roles. These policies were to be faithfully adopted by all the countries that embraced Soviet-style socialism in the years to come. In the western world, the entry of large numbers of married women with children into the workforce brought about profound social changes, which were, however, slow to be understood.

The second half of the twentieth century was characterized by the rise of alternative "models" of child care: on the one hand, the growth of institutionalized child care systems in the western world, both private and state-funded, responding to the needs of working women and children, with diversity both in quantity and in content; and on the other, the Soviet model of state-supported child care systems. The rest of the world, including many developing countries, attempted to copy one or the other, while the older informal kinds of "coping strategies," rather than systems, continued to predominate because of the slow, incomplete, and varied pace of "development."

Present Status

Child care services should include arrangements for the child from birth (or even before) up to the age at which the child begins to attend school full-time (and child care may continue part-time even after that age), but the nature of the provision required may vary with the age of the child. During the first few months of life, when breastfeeding is of greatest significance, mother and child need close proximity for both nutritional and psychic reasons; for the age group from 2 to 6 years, there are more possibilities for substitute caregiving within or outside the home. Child care services thus include two major elements:

- Maternity leave, now broadening into parental leave, including job protection, along with arrangements such as flexible work schedules, part-time work, home-based work, and so on, which enable the mother (or, in Europe,

the father) to stay away from work as much as possible in order to care for the child.

- Crèches (also known as nurseries or day care centers), which provide group substitute care for young children near the parents' workplace or their residence. This category increasingly includes family day care (also referred to as child minding or home-based care), which attempts to provide care in a homelike setting.

Data available from the International Labor Organization (1989) regarding provision for maternity benefits and child care for women workers in 135 countries reveal distinct patterns related to two groups of factors:

- Economic—level of development
- Political—degree of socialist or market orientation.

In the case of the formerly colonized countries, another powerful factor is the influence of the former imperial power.

In the *developed world*, child care ranges from high in Scandinavia, through continental western Europe, to low in Great Britain, Canada, Australia, and the United States, with the United States at the bottom of the heap, next to Japan. At its best, child care encompasses extensive maternity benefits, including maternity leave, and now increasingly parental leave (as much as 18 months to two years in some countries), as well as high-quality child care, in either group or family settings, with a high caregiver-child ratio. In Scandinavia, this may be attributed to the long history of welfare-oriented socialist governments and strong labor and women's movements in the context of high per capita income, dwindling family size, declining birthrates, universal nuclearization of the family, and increasing incidence of single-parent families. Several of these factors are equally applicable to western European countries, many of which have similar or somewhat lower and varying levels of provision. The table summarizes the extent of coverage of publicly funded child care services in some major European Union countries. However, there is a large and growing private and voluntary sector, which further disadvantages the most vulnerable.

At the other end of the spectrum, the poor record of the Anglo-Saxon countries may be related to the greater degree of market orientation and the policies of right-of-center governments. Significantly, in the United States, the most free market economy, there has been hardly any attention to maternity policy until recently; maternity leave (in some places quaintly termed *pregnancy disability*) is left primarily to private arrangements, and only very limited job protection is available.

Publicly funded early childhood services as percentage of all children in the age group, selected countries (1990)

	Date to which data refer	For children under 3 (%)	For children from 3 to compulsory school age (%)	Age when compulsory schooling begins (years)	Length of school day, including midday break (hours)	Care for primary-school children outside school hours (%)
Belgium	1988	20	95+	6	7	?
Denmark	1989	48	85+	7	3–5 1/2(a,b)	29
France	1988	20	95+	6	8	?
Greece	1988	4	85–70	5 1/2	4–5(b)	(–)
Ireland	1988	2	55	6	4 1/2–7 1/2(b)	(–)
Italy	1986	5	85+	6	4	?
Luxembourg	1989	2	55–60	5	4–8(a)	1
Netherlands	1989	2	50–55	5	6–7	1
Portugal	1988	6	35	6	6 1/2	8
Spain	1988	?	65–70	6	8	(–)
United Kingdom	1988	2	35–40	5	6 1/2	(–)

Key: ? = no information; (–) = less than 0.5; a = school hours vary from day to day; b = school hours increase as children get older

Notes: The table shows publicly funded services as a percentage of the child population; the percentage of children attending may be higher because some places offering services are used on a part-time basis. Play groups in the Netherlands have not been included, although 10 percent of children under 3 and 25 percent of children ages 3–4 attend, and most play groups receive public funds. Average hours of attendance—5 to 6 hours per week—are so much shorter than for other services that it would be difficult and potentially misleading to include them on the same basis as other services; however, play groups should not be forgotten in considering publicly funded care in the Netherlands.

Source: European Commission. 1990. *Childcare in the European Communities (1985–1990).* Brussels. In Peter Moss. 1992. *Perspectives from Europe.*

The *socialist world* shows a similar range of child care from the former U.S.S.R. and the more developed countries of eastern Europe to the poorer Asian and Latin American socialist countries. Common to all, however, is a strong political commitment to the care of children and support for working women.

In the former U.S.S.R. and the countries of eastern Europe, the services available have included extensive maternity benefits (with leave of up to two years in some cases), accessible crèches, and nurseries of medium to high quality, as well as financial incentives for protection of the family. These comments relate to the pre-1989 period. In light of the sweeping changes and political developments after 1989, reliable estimates of the present situation are difficult to locate, but there are indications that facilities have been substantially eroded.

In Vietnam, the poorest country in this group, crèches are extensively provided, though of low quality. Also found are imaginative schemes such as the involvement of elderly women in home-based day care services. About 35 percent of the 3–6 age group and 25 percent of the age group 0–3 are said to be covered by these arrangements. In China, the extensive network of crèches and day care centers is reported to be declining, and although maternity leave for 6 to 12 months is available, women are returning to work earlier in order to earn the full wage. The achievements in the smaller socialist countries of Latin America and Africa are also under threat.

Developing countries vary according to both the extent of market versus socialist orientation and the impact of the former imperial power. All Commonwealth countries, for example, have more or less the same pattern. India, a typical example, differs from China and Vietnam, at one end, and from Brazil, the Philippines, or Senegal at the other. Most follow the standard practice of three months' maternity leave (including both prenatal and postnatal periods).

Crèches are negligible in number, confined to urban areas, and more akin to preprimary schools, or altogether nonexistent. Among the developing countries, India has the largest and most comprehensive network of child care services, covering 12 percent of the child population below age 5 and more than 25 percent of the members of this age group below the poverty line. But, as in most third world countries, the services focus on survival, health, and nutrition, on the one hand, and preschool education as preparation for universal elementary education, on the other, with little commitment to day care as a support service for working women.

Although the majority of their women work in the unorganized sector, most of these countries have borrowed their legislation from the industrialized countries. The resulting policies are applicable to only a small minority of women, and few countries have made serious efforts to develop systems more suited to their economies. Crèches are legally mandated in many countries for the industrial sector, but because conditions are not conducive to their development, the laws often remain unheeded.

Professionalism in Child Care

With the emergence of the concept of child care as a specialized activity, recognition is emerging of the caregiver as a full-time skilled professional and of the need for training for this role. But caregiving is still a highly feminine profession, relatively low-paid, low-status, and with low visibility. The shift toward professionalism may signal a return to both an earlier acceptance of social, rather than merely individual, responsibility for the care and upbringing of children and an appreciation of quality as vital to the development of children at a crucial stage in their lives.

The impact of feminism and the women's movement worldwide, both on the development of child care services and on changing attitudes toward child care itself, has come from both directions because of the wide spectrum of opinion among feminists on this issue. Whereas there have been vociferous demands from some sectors, others have tended to downplay women's maternal role in order to compete "like men," and still other groups have voiced a need for communal child rearing in order to give women real choices. The impact has been mostly on the heightened visibility of the issue.

See Also

CAREGIVERS; CHILD DEVELOPMENT; EDUCATION: PRESCHOOL; HOUSEHOLDS AND FAMILIES: OVERVIEW; MATERNITY LEAVE; MOTHER; PARENTHOOD

References and Further Reading

Ariès, Philippe. 1962. *Centuries of childhood.* New York: Knopf.

Boserup, Esther. 1989. *Women's role in economic development.* London: Earthscan (originally published 1970).

Bowlby, John. 1953. *Childcare and the growth of love.* Harmondsworth, U.K.: Pelican.

Clarke-Stewart, Allison. 1982. *Day care* (The developing child series). London: Fontana.

Folbre, Nancy. 1994. *Who pays for the kids? Gender and the structures of constraint.* New York: Routledge.

Hewlett, Sylvia Ann. 1986. *A lesser life.* New York: Warner.

International Labor Organization (ILO). 1989. *Report on maternity and childcare provision.* Geneva: ILO (mimeo).

Lewenhak, Sheela. 1989. *Women and work.* London: Fontana.

Myers, Robert. 1992. *The twelve who survive.* London and Paris: Routledge/UNESCO/CGECCD.

Pugh, Gillian, ed. 1992. *Contemporary issues in the early years: Working collaboratively for children.* London: Paul Chapman/National Children's Bureau.

Sidel, Ruth. 1972. *Childcare in China.* New York: Hill and Wang.

Spiro, Melford. 1965. *Children of the kibbutz.* New York: Schocken.

Swaminathan, Mina. 1985. *Who cares? A study of childcare facilities for low-income working women in India.* New Delhi: Centre for Women's Development Studies.

———, ed. 1998. *The first five years: A critical perspective on early childhood care and education in India.* New Delhi: Sage.

Mina Swaminathan

CHILD DEVELOPMENT

In what ways do gender, ethnicity, and culture affect children? How do children understand everyday emotions? What can infants see? Why are relationships with family and friends important to children? The field of child development can answer these questions and many more, providing information about children's physical, cognitive, social, and emotional development (Berk, 1996). Child development is a field of study that has two primary responsibilities. The first is to formulate theories that make specific predictions about how and why children grow and change. The second is to use scientific research to obtain knowledge about development by testing the predictions that these theories make. This knowledge can then be used to guide parents, teachers, psychologists, and others who interact with children.

For any individual, child development begins at conception and continues through birth, infancy, childhood, and adolescence. After adolescence, individuals enter adulthood, which signals the end of child development and the beginning of adult development. Many aspects of child development are universal and occur in the same way for all children because of certain genes that are present in all humans. For example, all children carry genes that enable them to crawl before they are able to walk (Berk, 1996). This explains why all children, regardless of their sex or their ethnic or cultural background, develop in similar ways and have many commonalities. Each child, however, ultimately develops into a unique individual. This occurs for two reasons. First, all individuals have unique genes, as well as genes that are common to all humans. Second, all individuals experience different types and combinations of experiences. Thus biological influences (such as unique genes) and environmental influences (such as family and culture) interact to ensure that each child develops into a unique person.

Theories of Child Development

Theories about how children develop help researchers to organize and explain what is known and what is still unknown about development and to select topics to be explored in future research. Because children are complex individuals who develop in many different ways, no one theory can adequately explain all aspects of their development (Berk, 1996). Instead, many theories are needed. Some theories, such as Lawrence Kohlberg's theory of moral reasoning, offer explanations about how children make moral decisions. Other theories, such as Erik Erikson's theory of psychosocial development and Sigmund Freud's theory of psychosexual development, make predictions about how children's interactions with parents and other important people help them to develop healthy identities. Still other theories, such as Jean Piaget's theory of cognitive development and L.S. Vygotskii's sociocultural theory, make predictions about how children think about the world and develop new skills.

All these theorists—Kohlberg (a U.S. scientist), Erikson (a theorist born in Denmark but raised in Germany), Freud (an Austrian doctor), Piaget (a Swiss scholar), and Vygotskii (a psychologist from the former Soviet Union)—come from different cultural backgrounds, reflecting the fact that child development is an international field. Indeed, theorists and researchers from around the world have made important contributions to explaining how children develop (Adler, 1989). This has provided the field with a well-

rounded view of child development that is sensitive to cultural differences.

Not only have international scholars played an important role in the field of child development, but women also have contributed theories to the field. For instance, women such as Myrtle McGraw (a U.S. scholar), Eleanor Gibson (a U.S. researcher), Mary Ainsworth (working in Canada, Britain, Uganda, and the United States), and Nancy Bayley (a U.S. scientist) have contributed meaningful theories about topics such as physical growth (McGraw and Bayley), perception of visual, tactile, and auditory stimuli (Gibson), relationships between parents and infants (Ainsworth), and infant intelligence (Bayley).

The importance of gender in child development is apparent in another way. Several developmental theories have been designed specifically to explain children's gender-role development. These theories have focused on how children come to understand what it means to be a girl or a boy and why there are gender differences in children's personal qualities, behaviors, and social relationships (Ruble and Martin, 1998). The two major influences on children's gender-role development, according to these theories, are their social interactions and their cognitive abilities (that is, the way they think about the world). One way that children learn about gender is through their interactions with others, particularly parents, siblings, peers, and teachers. By watching and imitating those around them, children begin to learn at a very early age about the activities and behaviors that are associated with being a girl or a boy. In addition, as children begin to engage in different activities and behaviors, they also learn from the messages they receive from others about their actions. Parents, for example, may praise them when they behave in ways that girls or boys are supposed to act (according to cultural or societal beliefs). Or, parents may discourage or punish them when they engage in what are considered cross-gender activities (for example, if girls play with trucks). Thus children's social experiences are important because their gender-role development is influenced by what they observe others doing and by the feedback they receive from others when they behave in ways that are either consistent or inconsistent with their biological sex.

Child development theorists suggest that to understand children's gender-role development, it is not enough to consider their social interactions. Another important influence on gender-role development is how children think about or interpret the observations they make and the messages they receive from others. In order to begin to understand the world in a meaningful way, children simplify information by putting it into categories. In the many cultures where gender is an important part of everyday life, children organize information into gender categories (that is, feminine or masculine). These categories, which also are referred to as *gender schemes* (Ruble and Martin, 1998), are particularly important once children are able to label themselves as either a girl or a boy. When this happens, children use the gender categories they have developed to guide how they act and what they pay attention to in their environment (for example, at home, when playing with their peers). Thus children develop an understanding of gender through the way they think about and interpret the experiences they have with others and the observations they make on a daily basis.

A Feminist Perspective on Child Development

Feminist scholars have made substantial contributions to the study of child development (Jacklin and McBride-Chang, 1991). First, they have emphasized that girls' and women's issues are important and that the field of child development must pay attention to these issues (Osmond and Thorne, 1993). In this respect, feminists have criticized studies of child development because they have often neglected to consider girls' experiences and how girls' development may differ from boys'. Instead, the studies have focused primarily on boys' experiences (Jacklin and McBride-Chang, 1991). In fact, some of the most influential developmental theories, including Freud's psychoanalytic theory, Kohlberg's theory of moral reasoning, and Erikson's theory of psychosocial development, were based on information collected primarily from males or were formulated from a male standpoint, with little consideration for the special challenges that girls face (Jacklin and McBride-Chang, 1991; Muuss, 1996).

Kohlberg's theory of moral reasoning has received the most criticism from feminist scholars, particularly from Carol Gilligan (a U.S. scholar) and her colleagues (Gilligan, 1982; Gilligan and Attanucci, 1994). Gilligan and her colleagues (whose research involved white women in the United States) are concerned that Kohlberg's "male-based" model has been inappropriately applied to females and has led to the incorrect conclusion that girls are less skilled than boys in making moral decisions. This feminist debate has raised awareness that caution must be exercised when theories developed for males are applied to females. Furthermore, the ongoing discussion of gender differences sparked by feminists has fueled important research on moral reasoning. For example, researchers now know that moral decisions are based not only on what is fair or just, as Kohlberg suggested, but also on how others will be affected by the decision; that is, a "caring" orientation (Gilligan, 1982; Gilligan and Attanucci, 1994).

A second important contribution that feminist scholars have made to the field is in challenging the assumption that gender is determined by biological factors, such as genes or hormones (Osmond and Thorne, 1993). Feminists downplay biological explanations for differences between girls and boys because biological differences are often perceived to be inherent and unchangeable (Leaper, 2000). Suggesting that boys' greater interest in math and science careers is the result of boys' having more natural spatial and math abilities than girls, for example, implies that sex differences in career choice are inevitable.

Instead, feminists have argued that the meaning attached to gender is determined in each culture and society by the behaviors and roles assigned to girls and boys (or women and men). Thus feminists have suggested that gender differences in career pathways can be explained by differences in social expectations (for example, girls receive less encouragement in math and science than boys from parents and teachers) and in the opportunities that girls and boys have to develop math and science skills (for example, boys take more advanced math and science courses). The result is that, rather than accepting sex differences in career choices as unavoidable, girls are encouraged in "traditionally" masculine areas such as math, science, and engineering.

Conclusion

The field of child development provides valuable information about how girls and boys grow and develop and about how these changes are related to children's gender and cultural background. Feminists have been particularly influential in drawing attention to the role that gender plays in children's development, and scholars from a variety of cultural backgrounds have demonstrated the importance of cultural influences on children's development. In the years to come, this information will be beneficial in helping children around the world develop into healthy individuals.

See Also

ADOLESCENCE; CHILDBIRTH; CHILD CARE; EDUCATION, *selected topics;* GENDER CONSTRUCTIONS IN THE FAMILY; GENDERED PLAY; GENETICS AND GENETIC TECHNOLOGIES; GIRL CHILD; LIFE CYCLE; PARENTHOOD; PREGNANCY AND BIRTH; PSYCHOLOGY: OVERVIEW; PSYCHOLOGY: COGNITIVE; YOUTH CULTURE

References and Further Reading

Adler, Leonore Loeb, ed. 1989. *Cross-cultural research in human development.* New York: Praeger.

Berk, Laura E. 1996. *Infants, children, and adolescents.* Boston: Allyn and Bacon.

———, ed. 1999. *Landscapes of development: An anthology of readings.* Belmont, Calif.: Wadsworth.

Gilligan, Carol. 1982. *In a different voice: Psychological theory and women's development.* Cambridge, Mass.: Harvard University Press.

———, and Attanucci, Jane. 1994. Caring voices and women's moral frames: Gilligan's view. In *Moral development: A compendium.* Vol. 6, 123–137. New York: Garland.

Jacklin, Carol, and Catherine McBride-Chang. 1991. The effects of feminist scholarship on developmental psychology. *Psychology of Women Quarterly* 15: 549–556.

Leaper, Cam. 2000. The social construction and socialization of gender during development. In Patricia H. Miller and Ellin K. Scholnick, eds., *Toward a feminist developmental psychology,* 1–22. New York: Routledge.

Muuss, Rolf. 1996. *Theories of adolescence.* New York: McGraw-Hill.

Osmond, Marie W., and Barrie Thorne. 1993. Feminist theories: The social construction of gender in families and society. In Pauline G. Boss et al., eds., *Sourcebook of family theories and methods,* 591–623. New York: Plenum.

Ruble, Diane N., and Carol L. Martin. 1998. Gender development. In William Damon and Nancy Eisenberg, eds., *Handbook of child psychology,* 5th ed. Vol. 3, 933–1016. New York: Wiley.

Thomas, R. Murray. 2000. *Comparing theories of child development,* 5th ed. Stamford, Conn.: Wadsworth Thomson Learning.

Kimberly Updegraff
Laura Hanish

CHILD LABOR

Child labor is often regarded as exploitative because children are more subordinated than adults in work relations, but some types of work are also seen as giving children pride and status. In poor households, including some headed by women, children's labor and earnings contribute to survival.

Definitions

Questions arise in defining child labor. Definitions of childhood vary across societies and time and according to class and gender (Goddard and White, 1982). The concept of labor is also problematic. For instance, when does play with younger siblings become child care?

As members of the family unit of production in agrarian societies, children contribute unpaid labor to income-earning activities in the fields, in family enterprises, collecting and hunting, and so on. Children also do much unpaid domestic work, freeing adults from the burden of this time-consuming labor. In comparison with boys, girls carry out a disproportionate share. In a study by Benjamin White, rural Javanese girls aged 7 to 9 did 2.8 hours of domestic work per day compared with 1 hour by boys of the same age (Rodgers and Standing, 1981: 3). Children's involvement in work activities is thus part of the reproduction of gender roles. In some countries children may be bonded to wealthier households as low-paid apprentices or unpaid servants or else pledged by their parents as part of debt repayment. This is a factor in child prostitution.

Historical Changes

With industrialization, production is transferred from the family unit to industrial corporations. Children are valued as a source of cheap factory labor. In eighteenth- and nineteenth-century Europe, children were often hired as part of the family work group. Wages were paid directly to parents. Concern about children's conditions led to the passing of child labor laws in Europe from the early nineteenth century. Collusion among parents, employers, and often children themselves, and the lack of children's empowerment, mean that protective regulations and education requirements are frequently circumvented in both western and nonwestern countries. Outside the formal economy, children also engage in independent survival activities such as street vending, shoe shining, scavenging, begging, theft, and prostitution.

See Also

DIVISION OF LABOR; DOMESTIC LABOR; ECONOMY: HISTORY OF WOMEN'S PARTICIPATION; ECONOMY: INFORMAL; GIRL CHILD; PROSTITUTION

References and Further Reading

Goddard, Victoria, and Benjamin White. 1982. Child workers and capitalist development: An introductory note and bibliography. *Development and Change* 13: 465–477.

Reynolds, Pamela. 1991. *Dance, civet cat: Child labour in the Zambezi Valley.* London: Zed.

Rodgers, Gerry, and Guy Standing, eds. 1981. *Child work, poverty, and underdevelopment.* Geneva: International Labour Office.

Gaynor Dawson

CHILDREN'S LITERATURE

Children's literature is most simply defined as literature written for and read by children. The simplicity of this definition is deceptive, however, and for many years critics have debated whether there can be such a thing as "children's literature." Foremost among the issues in this debate is the relationship between the child and the text. For instance, since almost without exception children's books are written, published, marketed, and purchased by adults, in what sense do they belong to children? Are the characters in children's literature created to appeal to young readers, or are they products of adults' needs and fears? In an influential study, Jacqueline Rose (1984) proposes that children's literature is an impossibility and that the books in the children's canon are preoccupied with rescuing childhood for adults.

Children's literature is a relatively recent and geographically limited phenomenon. Before it is possible to have literature for children, it is necessary to have a concept of childhood as a distinct phase, with its own cognitive and emotional needs and interests. Literature is not essential for basic survival; in developing countries, reading is a skill that is primarily valued for its practical applications. Thus for cultural and economic reasons, literature for children—especially that concerned with cultivating the imagination—is at the bottom of the literary hierarchy. The low status of children's literature is compounded by the fact that in many countries books and stories for children are associated with women writers and storytellers, themselves placed low in the literary establishment.

The conditions necessary for the creation of a literature for children had been established in Great Britain by the seventeenth century, and Great Britain is generally accepted as the country with the longest and most developed tradition of writing for children. The Puritan movement is credited with developing children's literature in Great Britain because the Puritans recognized that children could learn (in this case about their sinful natures and the need to control them) from books.

The didactic nature of writing for children continues to be an important impetus and shaping force, though the nature of the message and the mode of its delivery have altered radically over the centuries. Initially children's literature was taught primarily through alternating stories of the exemplary with stories of the horribly punished and damned or by providing an indigestible diet of facts. Through the influence of educators, philosophers (notably Locke [1632–1704], Rousseau [1712–1778]), and the Romantic movement, the prevailing idea of childhood and children's needs was changed. Publishing for children began to combine its underlying drive to teach with an urge to entertain. The result is confusion about the criteria for assessing the merit of writing for children: Should it be judged by pedagogic, literary, or artistic standards?

By the end of the nineteenth century, most western countries had developed some form of a children's publishing industry. However, much of what was produced were imported and translated versions of texts that originated in Great Britain and, to a lesser extent, the United States, France, and Germany. Elsewhere this situation was compounded by the fact that printed material for children in the form of books, magazines, and tracts was frequently introduced by white missionaries and teachers and consisted of English-based stories translated into vernacular languages. Therefore, images of women generated by western, industrial-capitalist, patriarchal cultures dominated world publishing for children, a process that continued into the twenty-first century through the practice of buying and selling "world" copyrights (almost invariably including the North American market) and the need to attract copublishers in other countries. However, many governments have now recognized both that a literate population is essential in the modern world and that what young people read can profoundly affect how they understand the world. Explicit and implicit, consciously and unconsciously inscribed ideologies pervade literature for children. Newly affluent and emerging countries frequently use children's books to help create a sense of national identity through shared stories, vocabularies, and illustrations based on the traditional arts of a country or people. Examples of this can be seen in Australia (especially in relation to the indigenous, Aborigine population), India, Iran, and Israel and in the socialist realism of the former Soviet Union.

One woman who was particularly alert to the positive political potential of children's literature was the German-born Jella Lepman, who founded the International Board on Books for Young People (IBBY) at the end of World War II. Lepman believed that through exchanging and sharing books, young people would learn about and learn to value each other's cultures, thus reducing the possibility of future wars. IBBY is particularly concerned with encouraging children's literature in developing countries, where it fosters local publishing ventures, mobile libraries, and literacy plans.

Financial exigency means that in many countries an indigenous children's literature is prevented from developing. The paradoxical consequence is that it is often in host countries to large groups of immigrants or refugees that traditional tales first get printed. Through the complex networks of coeditions, such book may be produced in the United States, Great Britain, Germany, or France and subsequently exported to the countries from which they originate.

Women Writers

For most of the seventeenth, eighteenth, and nineteenth centuries, it was not regarded as appropriate for women to write scholarly or worldly books. However, women were immediately accepted as writers for children. Indeed, referring to Great Britain, Peter Hunt (1994) observed that "women have dominated children's books from the beginning." There are a number of explanations for this. For instance, women were regarded as children's "natural" caregivers; women were thought to have intellects not much more developed than children's and therefore to be able to communicate at their level; and writing for children was a low-status occupation and therefore relegated to women. Considerable evidence proves that many women *did* write for children primarily because it was an acceptable form of paid employment and a natural extension of other kinds of work in which they were already employed (for example, running Sunday schools and teaching children at home). However, some women writers of children's literature had other motivations. Crudely, these women can be divided into two kinds: those who used this approved forum to show that they were men's intellectual equals and to seek acceptance within the dominant discourses of their time; and those who discovered that in writing for children they found a voice and a vehicle (as well as an impressionable audience) to critique the society in which they lived.

Julia Briggs (1989) compares both kinds of writers and suggests that not until the end of the nineteenth century and the publication of innovative children's books by the British writer Edith Nesbit (1858–1924) did women begin to exploit the subversive and liberating potential of writing for children. Women writers began to see similarities between the situations of women and children: both groups were disparaged and repressed by the prevailing social order. No longer were all the women who wrote for young people interested in promoting and reproducing the values espoused by the male academic and social establishment— not least because their efforts were largely ignored. As women and as writers for children, they were doubly marginalized. This status encouraged some women writers to use children's literature to criticize and challenge the male establishment. Specifically, adopting the child's point of view and on occasion imitating the child's way of speaking helped women writers to break free from male-dominated literary modes and values.

In the 1990s, a number of women writers used children's literature explicitly to criticize social practice and to consider the treatment of women, including minority women, throughout history.

Women and Girl Characters

Folktales and fairy tales are the oldest branch of literature for children. They are particularly interesting to women not only because they contain many images of girls and women but also because they have traditionally been told and perpetuated by women. Feminist and Marxist critics have traced the history of the best-known tales and recovered others that have been omitted from the popular canon. In the process, several facts of interest to women have been uncovered. For instance, Jack Zipes (1983) argues that many of the negative female stereotypes characteristic of well-known fairy tales (wicked stepmothers, passive princesses) are distortions of more positive and powerful female archetypes. In oral versions generated before patriarchy became a dominant organizing principle in many societies, he argues, female characters were both good and powerful. The perversion of these earlier models was accelerated during the nineteenth century, when men such as the Grimm brothers (1785–1863; 1786–1859) and Andrew Lang (1844–1912) began collecting tales for patriotic and scholarly purposes. In line with the predominantly patriarchal and Christian values of their time, these retellings of old tales tended to diminish female characters from goddesses to wicked witches to mean stepmothers. Moreover, they often added a Christian dimension that linked curiosity and the rise of evil to women. In such stories, the only good females are pretty, passive, obedient, and domesticated, though feminists have been careful to show that "wicked" women are often made bad by a male-dominated society that values women only for their beauty and marriageability.

Feminist and Marxist critics have also focused attention on the importance of reading in the construction of identity and the dissemination of ideology. Because it is entirely bound up in language and images, reading can play a central role in determining the range of characters a young person identifies with and inhabits. By the 1970s gender-based stereotypes in all kinds of children's literature (including school reading texts) needed to be replaced with more realistic portrayals. As a consequence, girl characters are now frequently shown as active, clever, and innovative. Many feminists have returned to the books that impressed them as children and have sought to understand both the nature of the original appeal and the kinds of messages such stories transmit.

One work that has attracted considerable attention is Louisa May Alcott's *Little Women* (1868). Many women remember being attracted to that book's central character, Jo March, precisely because she seemed to embody rejection of the feminine ideal. However, some adult readers say that, at least superficially, Alcott's text forces Jo into the role of a "little woman," and that the reader colludes in this process because it is necessary for a conventional happy ending. Arguably, however, a closer scrutiny of the sexual politics of this novel shows that Alcott explored the destructive nature of the feminine ideal: Beth March, the character who is the quintessence of this ideal, is incapacitated by her self-sacrificing femininity, which ultimately leads to her death. Moreover, *Little Women*, which is set against the backdrop of the American Civil War, can be read as a book that celebrates matriarchy. The world of women and home functions well through collective effort; the manly sphere of politics, battle, and individual achievement has collapsed into destruction and disease.

Another influential female character in children's literature who has attracted the attention of feminist critics is Pippi Longstocking, created by the Swedish writer Astrid Lindgren (b. 1907). Pippi is the strongest girl in the world—she regularly carries her horse in her arms. Because her mother is dead and her father the king of a cannibal island, she lives on her own, precisely as she pleases. Pippi subverts the twin ideals of "child" and "girl" and celebrates qualities such as freedom and spontaneity over the habitual and correct. Through her writing for children, Lindgren has become a figure of national and international importance (her work has been translated into fifty-seven languages); with Pippi Longstocking she provides an original role model for girl readers around the world.

Children's literature has offered opportunities for women writers and has seen the creation of many original, powerful female characters. However, because so many women continue to be denied education and a public voice, and because they are frequently caught in the double traps of poverty and reproduction, women from many countries lag behind men even in this traditionally female sphere of publishing.

See Also

FAIRY TALES; LITERATURE: OVERVIEW

References and Further Reading

Briggs, Julia. 1989. Women writers and writing for children: From Sarah Fielding to E. Nesbit. In Gillian Avery and Julia Briggs, eds., *Children and their books: A celebration of the work of Iona and Peter Opie*. Oxford: Clarendon.

Carpenter, Humphrey, and Mari Prichard. 1984. *The Oxford companion to children's literature*. London: Oxford University Press.

Hunt, Peter. 1994. *An introduction to children's literature*. Oxford: Oxford University Press.

Landsberg, Michele. 1988. *The world of children's books: A guide to choosing the best*. London: Simon and Schuster.

Paul, Lissa. 1987. Enigma variations: What feminist theory knows about children's literature. *Signal* 54: 186–201.

Reynolds, Kimberley. 1994. *Children's literature, 1890–1990*. Plymouth: Northcote House/British Council.

———. 1990. *Girls only? Gender and popular children's fiction in Britain, 1880–1910*. Hemel Hempstead: Harvester Wheatsheaf.

Rose, Jacqueline. 1984. *The case of Peter Pan, or, The impossibility of children's fiction*. London: Macmillan.

Zipes, Jack. 1983. *Fairy tales and the art of subversion*. London: Heinemann.

Kimberley Reynolds

CHILLY CLIMATE

See EDUCATION: CHILLY CLIMATE IN THE CLASSROOM.

CHOREOGRAPHY

See DANCE: CHOREOGRAPHY.

CHRISTIANITY

As one of the three major western monotheistic traditions, Christianity affirms the existence of only one supreme being, a god who is intimately interested and involved in human affairs. However, Christianity differs sharply from Judaism and Islam when it comes to defining the nature of this deity. Whereas the other two traditions are resolute in their iconoclasm—that is, their insistence that God can be neither pictured nor adequately described in human terms—Christianity not only takes literally the idea that humans were created "in God's image" (Genesis 1:26) but also maintains that God took on human form in the historical person of Jesus of Nazareth (c. 6 or 5 B.C.–A.D. c. 30–33). The apparent conundrum of persons of both sexes being created "in the image" of one divine being, and the fact that in its human incarnation that being was a man, have made the position of women in the Christian traditions especially problematic.

Christian Origins

Christianity begins in the affirmation that Jesus was the Son of God. In declaring him to be the Messiah (Greek *Christos* = "Anointed One," whence the term *Christian*), his original followers asserted that his life, death, and reported resurrection constituted the fulfillment of Jewish messianic expectation. Little can be gleaned from extra-biblical sources about the career of Jesus of Nazareth, other than the facts that he did indeed live and die in first-century Judea; that he was an itinerant preacher who amassed a considerable following at a time of growing unrest among Jews chafing under Roman rule; and that, apparently concerned about the political implications of his popularity, the Roman governor Pontius Pilate had him executed. The rest of our information about Jesus comes primarily from the New Testament Gospel narratives, which were written less with concern for historical accuracy than to demonstrate that Jesus was indeed the Messiah.

Two facts about his public ministry do emerge clearly, however: Jesus preached a revolutionary message of radical love, equality, and justice; and, no doubt owing to this message, he counted among his closest friends and disciples a number of women. The prominence of these women among his core followers is affirmed at several key points in his story: he performed his first public miracle at the request of his mother; he praised Mary of Bethany's abandonment of housework in favor of religious study; it was Mary's sister Martha who declared Jesus to be "the Christ, the Son of God" (John 11:27); when all but one of his male apostles deserted him on the day of his crucifixion, the women stood by the foot of the cross; and when he rose from the dead, his first appearance was to a woman, Mary of Magdala, who appears to have been one of his closest associates. In addition, many of his most radical religious pronouncements were of especial concern to women: his rejection of divorce, in the context of a Jewish system that gave no rights to the wife; his intervention to prevent the stoning death of a woman convicted of adultery; his forgiving of the repentant prostitute (traditionally, if mistakenly, identified with Mary Magdalene); and his consistent championing of the interests of the socially subordinated (women, children, and slaves). Nowhere in the Gospels does Jesus employ a patriarchal vocabulary regarding the value of and distinctions among persons.

It is not clear that Jesus himself intended to found a "new" religion; he was a Jewish religious reformer. In this regard, he is very similar to Gotama Buddha, who six centuries earlier had sought to reform the Hinduism of his day. In both cases, while on one level the reform message is unintelligible without the context (Jewish or Hindu) that gave rise to it, on another level it became clear quite early that the teachings of Jesus and Buddha had implications well beyond their original environments. Hence, both Christianity and Buddhism developed into missionary religions, claiming universal appeal and global relevance that ultimately transcend cultural or ethnic boundaries.

Saul of Tarsus (c. 10–65/67 C.E.), who after his dramatic conversion to Christianity on the Damascus road went by his Roman name Paul, was the most influential among the first generation of Christian missionaries—so influential, indeed, that it may readily be argued that he, rather than Jesus, was the true "founder" of Christianity. The Jesus sect was rapidly spawning "house churches" throughout the Mediterranean world by the middle of the first century of the common era, and Paul's letters to these fledgling communities were the earliest written documents of the New Testament. In their blending of Jewish cosmology with Hellenistic philosophy, they set the model for the development of doctrine and theology that would preoccupy Christian thinkers for the next several centuries. It is clear from his letters that Paul, like Jesus, had a number of close and highly regarded female associates. Yet it is in Paul's own writings, along with others attributed to him, that one repeatedly finds statements that provide the scriptural foundations not only for the subordination of women in the Christian churches but also for the development of an oppressive theology of sexuality.

What accounts for this apparent contradiction? How could the same writer who proclaimed that "in Christ... there is neither male nor female" (Galatians 3:26–28) simultaneously instruct women to "keep silence in the churches. For they are not permitted to speak, but should be subordinate, as even the Law says" (1 Corinthians 14:34)? In part the answer lies in the fact that it was not the same writer: whereas the passage from Galatians most certainly represents Paul's own view, the oft-quoted passage from 1 Corinthians is generally regarded as a later interpolation into Paul's text. Additionally, all of Paul's statements about such social institutions as marriage and slavery (in the letter to Philemon he enjoins slaves to obey their masters) must be read in their apocalyptic context. Taking to heart Jesus's statements about the Kingdom of God being at hand, Paul apparently expected the world to end relatively soon, and he regarded spiritual renewal to be far more important than social reform. He may not have been, as some have argued, a protofeminist. But neither was he, as others have claimed, a misogynist. The same cannot be said for many of the theologians who would come after him.

The Early Church Fathers and the Development of a Theology of Sexuality

In the first few centuries of the common era, two parallel processes were at work, both of which would have a major impact on the shaping of Christian ideas about women in general and female sexuality in particular. The first was the process of canonization, that is, the creation of the Christian Bible. The second involved the development of several key theological concepts relating to the nature of God and Christ, original sin and the institution of marriage.

Christian theology actually begins in the creation of the canon. In the century following the life of Jesus of Nazareth, numerous texts appeared, attributed to various disciples and representing different—sometimes widely divergent—views regarding his teachings. As it gradually became clear that the world was not about to end, the Christian movement needed to become organized both socially in the form of the church and spiritually through the affirmation of a set of beliefs and practices held in common. The process of canonization (*canon,* from both Latin and Greek roots referring to a rule or measuring rod) involved coming to consensus on those texts that "measured up" to several criteria determined by the early church fathers. These criteria for canonicity also implied a standard of orthodoxy (from the Greek, meaning "right belief" or "straight thinking"). The texts that became the New Testament were the ones that shared a common, essentially Pauline point of view regarding the rudiments of Christian belief and practice, as well as four Gospel narratives, all of them written after and influenced by Paul's letters, that present a relatively coherent picture of the life and teachings of Jesus.

From the vantage point of women's history, what got left out of the New Testament is as important as what was included. This is especially true of the body of literature that has come to be known as the Gnostic Gospels. The Gnostics (Greek *gnosis* = "knowledge") were regarded as heretics by the early church fathers, and among their most heinous doctrinal errors, from the orthodox point of view, was their tendency to ascribe feminine qualities to God. The Apochryphon of John, for example, describes God as a trinity of Father, Son, and Mother; several other texts similarly assumed the Holy Spirit to be female. In addition, Mary Magdalene figures prominently in Gnostic writings; the Gospel of Mary establishes her as a major disciple and teacher. Women held positions of prominence equal to those of men in many Gnostic communities. It was clear to the early fathers of the church that if women were to be kept silent in the churches, the Gnostic materials must be kept out of the canon.

Those texts that did "measure up" supported a male-dominated hierarchy: in the canonical narratives the twelve apostles, Christ's major disciples, are all men, and what would come to be called the "apostolic succession" assumed that spiritual authority passed from one male to another. This is not altogether surprising, given the patriarchal con-

text in which the canon developed, and the male-dominated world for which it was intended. The best way for Christian missionaries to "sell" their message to their pagan contemporaries was to make it conform, by and large, to social assumptions with which they were already comfortable. The New Testament contains, at most, tantalizing hints regarding women's leadership in the earliest Christian communities, but the patriarchal overlay is so thick that we ultimately cannot penetrate it. Thus, for the last two thousand years, the orthodox Gospel (from the Greek, meaning "good news") has been far better news for men than for women. As recently as the 1990s, Pope John Paul II appealed to the idea of apostolic succession to reiterate that women cannot be priests because Christ "chose" all men for his apostles. In 2000, when the Southern Baptist Convention similarly reaffirmed that women could not be ministers, it could appeal to a long tradition of Scripture-based theological interpretation.

Just as there was no room for women in positions of religious leadership, as far as the early fathers of the church were concerned, there was no room for the feminine in the Christian godhead. Christian theology (Greek *theos* + *logos* = "god-talk") took several centuries to sort out the basic questions regarding the natures of God, man, and woman. God was understood to be triune in nature, and by the beginning of the third century the Latin father Tertullian (d. 230?) had developed the vocabulary to describe the Trinity as one God in three "Persons" (Latin *personae* = "masks" or "faces"): Father (the Creator), Son (incarnate in the figure of Jesus Christ), and a somewhat ephemeral but decidedly male Holy Spirit (generally symbolized by a dove). Trinitarian theology flatly rejected the female Holy Spirit of the Gnostics. It is hard to imagine Tertullian doing otherwise: one of the most incisive thinkers and eloquent writers among the early fathers, he was also among the most misogynistic. Reflecting on Eve—and by extension, on all women—he wrote: "The curse God pronounced on your sex weighs still on the world. Guilty, you must bear its hardships. You are the devil's gateway." The major framers of Christian theology agreed with him regarding women's fundamental corruption.

Jerome (c. 347–420), declaring, "Death came through Eve: life has come through Mary," exalted celibacy as the most appropriate lifestyle for Christian believers in general and for women in particular. Eve, who used her feminine wiles to trick Adam into eating the forbidden fruit, had been Satan's agent in humanity's fall and expulsion from the Garden of Eden. By contrast, the Virgin Mary was God's agent in the cosmic drama of redemption; she provided the human half of her divine Son's dual nature.

But in order for her to do this, she must have remained pure, without taint of sin (that is, sexuality). Here, Jerome and subsequent theologians misread the Old Testament prophecy that the Messiah would be born of a virgin (Hebrew *alma* = "maiden") in the light of their own mistrust of female sexuality. Not only was the female excluded from the godhead; she was also the "occasion of sin" for man and more intimately related to the forces of evil and death. Jerome's logic laid the groundwork both for the tradition of female asceticism (what the historian Rudolph Bell has termed "holy anorexia") in which sainthood is possible for women only to the extent that they renounce their own sexuality and for the witch craze during the Renaissance and Reformation periods of European history. This logic of female culpability and corruptibility was reinforced in the theology of the greatest of the Latin fathers, Augustine of Hippo (354–430). A libertine and heretic in his youth, Augustine well appreciated the power that temptation to sin could exert on both body and spirit. (He reports in his *Confessions* that prior to his conversion to Christianity, he would pray, "Lord, give me chastity, but not yet.") Yet his reading of Genesis led him to reject his contemporary Jerome's insistence on celibacy: God had, after all, instituted marriage in the Garden, before the fall. For Augustine, the Christian theology of marriage is, nevertheless, inextricably related to the "original sin" of Adam and Eve—a sin that passes, through procreation, to every successive human generation. Even within marriage, each act of sex is tainted with sin, just as even in the cradle, each infant is already a sinful being. Because God ordained the marriage bond for the purpose of procreation, however, sex is something of a necessary evil. Woman's purpose, in this scheme of things, is to seek salvation through reproducing children as well as through submission to male rule (Genesis 3:16). The Augustinian theology of marriage and sexuality set the pattern for orthodox Christian theology for the next fifteen hundred years.

Mystics, Heretics, Witches, and Protestants

Of course, for as long as Christian theologians have strived to guarantee orthodoxy, there have been heterodox thinkers. As the church in Rome solidified its authority throughout Europe, it developed means for containing or controlling individualistic thinkers lest they become free spirits in too literal a sense. Monasticism grew directly, and with church approval, out of the spiritual zeal that had led Christians in earlier centuries to either martyrdom or the hermitage. Originally, monasteries housed men and women together. However, in much the same fashion that

it has been claimed that the presence of women or of gay men would disrupt the male culture of the U.S. military, churchmen argued that the mere presence of women presented too great a sexual distraction to the monks. Female-only convents were therefore instituted as parallel institutions, and the role of nun (with Mary Magdalene, now identified with the repentant whore of Luke 7:37–39, as prototype) evolved as a church-sanctioned way for women to deny the body and devote themselves to the life of the spirit—most often under the direction of male spiritual advisers.

The medieval period saw not only the flowering of the monastic movement but also the rise of the cult of the Virgin Mary. The church was adamant in its insistence that the Mother of God was in no way herself divine; however, popular piety clearly ruled otherwise, and the Blessed Virgin attained a goddess-like stature. Indeed, many of her titles and the symbols associated with her were appropriated from earlier goddess traditions. As if to keep *her* under church control, Catholic theology stressed Mary's function as a role model for women, most of whom would be assigned the role of wife and mother. Given the Virgin's superhuman sinlessness, they would of course be destined to fall short of the ideal.

It was against the backdrop of the cult of the Virgin that Dame Julian of Norwich (1342–c. 1416) wrote of "Christ the Mother." There were many medieval women, like Julian, for whom neither the convent nor marriage provided spiritual satisfaction. Like their male counterparts, female mystics like Angela of Foligno (1248–1309), Catherine of Siena (1347–1380), and Margery Kempe (1373–c. 1439) sought direct, unmediated experience of the divine. Some women mystics were nuns, others were not; but all were, or became, celibate. Their visions were typically characterized by highly charged sexual imagery of their mystical marriage to Christ, while at the same time they engaged in often extreme forms of ascetic self-abasement, reinforcing the idea that the female body is the site of human sinfulness.

Mystics, of course, always risked being accused of heresy or witchcraft, and many divergent spirits went to their death. By the sixteenth century, for complex political and social reasons, the Roman church was no longer able to control religious divergence through either containment (as in the case of monastics and certain mystics) or expulsion and execution (as in the case of witches and heretics). With the Protestant Reformation, European Christianity became far more variegated in both belief and practice. Women experienced both gains and losses as a result.

Martin Luther, for example, abolished monasteries and convents and enjoined all good Christians to marry.

(The former monk was forced to be true to his word when the former nun Katharina von Bora insisted she would have none other than Luther himself; theirs turned out to be a long and loving union.) On the one hand, Lutheran theology took a far more positive view of the social role of wife and mother than did Catholic theology. On the other, it deprived women of any church-sanctioned religious role (the Lutheran churches would not begin ordaining women as ministers until well into the twentieth century, and some Lutheran denominations still bar women from the ministry). Similarly, John Calvin wrote that women should indeed be allowed to speak in church—but not to preach. The seventeenth-century Calvinist John Milton wrote movingly in his divorce tracts that marriage was first and foremost a spiritual and intellectual union between persons; yet in his masterwork *Paradise Lost* he depicted Eve as spiritually and intellectually inferior to Adam and as his sexual seducer into sin.

Women were more likely to attain something like genuine equality only in the more radical Protestant groups. Among the Quakers, for example, women and men were equally liable to be moved by the Holy Spirit to speak in Friends' meetings. Mother Ann Lee, the eighteenth-century founder of the Shakers, was regarded by her followers as the female Messiah. Fleeing from England to North America, the Shakers practiced a communal lifestyle in which the sexes were equal; they were, however, prohibited from intercourse on other than the spiritual plane.

Subsequent nineteenth- and early twentieth-century communitarian movements in the United States sought other ways to balance the sexes, either literally or symbolically. The Oneida Community practiced a variation on open marriage in which women were freed from many of the more onerous responsibilities of childbirth and child rearing. Two indigenous U.S. churches, the Mormons and the Seventh-Day Adventists, prayed to "Father/Mother God"; and in their early years both had female as well as male leaders, although in both women were eventually excluded from positions of leadership. Some women started their own churches: Ellen White (1827–1915) co-founded Adventism; Mary Baker Eddy (1821–1910) founded Christian Science; and Aimee Semple McPherson (1890–1944) founded the Foursquare Gospel Church. Interestingly, the female-founded U.S. churches tended to place considerable emphasis on physical health and spiritual healing—as if to counterbalance centuries of female denial of the body.

Twentieth-Century Developments

Three interrelated developments had a direct impact on women in, and in relationship to, Christianity in the twentieth century: globalization, the ecumenical movement, and the international women's movement.

Globalization. Christianity had been a "worldwide" religion nearly since its inception; but from the seventeenth century forward, its world became much larger. Catholic and Protestant missionaries brought their "good news" to Asia, Africa, and North and South America; in these generally imperialistic settings, conversion to Christianity usually meant adoption of European cultural values as well. However, by the twentieth century, it had become clear that the effort to "Europeanize" or "Americanize" native cultures ultimately did more harm than good to the natives in question. Moreover, in those cultures where Christianity had taken root, over time the symbolism had taken on more of a local color.

In patriarchal contexts—as in much of Catholic Latin America—male dominance was still the religious norm. However, revivalist movements like the Zionist churches in South Africa and Pentecostalism in South America drew on indigenous culture and opened up possibilities for women to experience the Holy Spirit and to testify and perform healing rituals on an equal footing with men. Arguably, the less God could be imaged as a white male, the greater the possibility over time for women, drawing on the authority of their own spiritual experience, to assert their spiritual equality with men.

The ecumenical movement. The Second Vatican Council (1962–1965), which brought Roman Catholicism into dialogue with Protestantism, was in a sense the culmination of a century of interreligious conversation among Christians, and between Christianity and other religions. What began as a conversation among religious professionals would have a revolutionary impact on believers: Roman Catholic ritual became much more immediate, with the Mass being performed in the vernacular rather than Latin and laypersons given a far greater role in the service. Much Catholic doctrine was similarly demystified. In a spirit of unity and mutual understanding, Protestants and Catholics discovered far more common ground, when it came to belief and practice, than earlier generations had suspected. Especially in the United States, where Catholicism was influenced by denominationalism, this led to increasing autonomy from Rome—at least on the parish level—and greater visibility and freedom for women within the religious community. The church continued to prohibit abortion and artificial contraception, to deny divorced Catholics the right to remarry in the church, and to refuse to ordain women as priests. Many Catholic women simply ignored the church's strictures on their sexual behavior. Others, influenced by the women's movement, called for a change in policy; by century's end, groups like Catholics for Free Choice and the Women's Ordination Conference had organized to demand reproductive rights, on the one hand, female priests, on the other.

The international women's movement. Throughout the so-called mainline Protestant churches, women have made terrific strides as a result of feminism. By the close of the twentieth century, women were becoming ministers in all but the most conservative denominations and accounted for roughly half the students in major divinity schools in the United States. The Episcopal and Anglican churches began to ordain women as priests, and the Episcopal church to consecrate female bishops. Issues of direct relevance to women—ranging from economic justice to reproductive freedom to world peace—were at or near the top of every church's agenda. Simultaneously, international women's conferences highlighted the role played by Christianity, as well as other religions, in the continuing oppression of women around the world and called for more aggressive action on the part of religious communities.

However, the late twentieth century also saw a resurgence of religious fundamentalism worldwide, which arguably represents a direct backlash against such gains as women have made. Christian conservatives, both Catholic and Protestant, bemoan the loss of "family values" and attribute that loss primarily to women's increased independence from male spiritual and economic control. They want to return Christianity to its roots: the patriarchal church and family, with men in charge and women willingly submitting to male rule. Christian feminists, ironically, are also calling for a return to Christianity's original spirit: that message of radical love, justice, and equality for which Jesus lived and died and around which the earliest Christian communities organized themselves. The shape that Christianity takes in the twenty-first century will depend, in large part, on which interpretation of "that good old-time religion" prevails.

See Also

CHRISTIANITY: FEMINIST CHRISTOLOGY; CHRISTIANITY: STATUS OF WOMEN IN THE CHURCH; HOLY SPIRIT; MARTYRS; MORMONS; MYSTICISM; QUAKERS; SHAKERS; THEOLOGIES: FEMINIST; WOMEN-CHURCH

References and Further Reading

Armstrong, Karen. 1987. *The gospel according to women: Christianity's creation of the sex war in the West.* New York: Anchor.

Bell, Rudolph. 1987. *Holy anorexia.* Chicago: University of Chicago Press.

Bynum, Caroline Walker. 1982. *Jesus as mother: Studies in the spirituality of the High Middle Ages.* Berkeley: University of California Press.

Clark, Elizabeth, and Herbert Richardson, eds. 1996. *Women and religion: The original sourcebook of women in Christian thought.* San Francisco: HarperCollins.

Heyward, Carter. 1999. *Saving Jesus from those who are right.* Philadelphia: Fortress.

Pagels, Elaine. 1988. *Adam, Eve, and the serpent.* New York: Vintage.

Ranke-Heinemann, Uta. 1991. *Eunuchs for the kingdom of heaven.* New York: Penguin.

Ruether, Rosemary Radford. 1983. *Sexism and God-talk: Toward a feminist theology.* Boston: Beacon.

Schüssler Fiorenza, Elisabeth. 1993. *Discipleship of equals: A critical feminist ekklesialogy of liberation.* New York: Crossroad.

———. 1987. *In memory of her: A feminist theological reconstruction of Christian origins.* New York: Crossroad.

Urban, Linwood. 1995. *A short history of Christian thought.* New York and Oxford: Oxford University Press.

Mary Zeiss Stange

CHRISTIANITY: Feminist Christology

Feminist Christology is part of an attempt by feminist theologians from all over the world to analyze and overcome the perceived patriarchal structures of Christianity and to reformulate the Christian faith from their own perspective and experience as women living in different contexts. During this process, feminist Christology increasingly revealed the crucial question whether feminism—women's struggle against all kinds of patriarchal oppression—and Christian belief are compatible. For feminist Christology, the Christian doctrine that the Jewish preacher Jesus of Nazareth is *the* Messiah (Christ), *the* universal savior for all people and the whole world, *the* unique, once-for-all, and full incarnation of God is not only the "heart" or center of Christianity but also one of the Christian doctrines most used to oppress women.

The Maleness of Christ

The first problem for women arises with regard to the maleness of Christ. The historical particularity of Jesus as male has been interpreted by the church throughout the ages to support and justify male dominance and the acceptance of it and female subordination and inferiority in church and society. On the basis of Hellenistic androcentric anthropology, the Christian church soon lifted the idea that the incarnation of God in a male was an *ontological* necessity: only the male represents full human nature and is by himself the complete image of God. Therefore, God had to choose the male sex to become human. Turning the historical particularity of Jesus's maleness into an ontological and Christological principle, the church not only emphasized the conceptualization of God as male but also denied that women were fully human, the image of the divine, and thus representative of the Christ. Christ became the male revealer of a male god whose full representative can only be male (Ruether, 1983). In the Catholic, Orthodox, and some Protestant churches, the maleness of Christ serves to exclude women from ordination even in the twenty-first century.

Some western feminists decided to leave Christianity because of the irreversibly sexist character of its central symbol (Daly, 1973). Other feminist theologians have tried to solve or reduce the problem of the maleness of Christ by rejecting the understanding of Jesus as the exclusive incarnation of God or by criticizing the deification of Jesus's maleness as a distortion of the Christian doctrine of incarnation and salvation. Women from the third world, who experience not only sexism but also poverty, neocolonialism, racism, and political oppression, emphasize that the maleness of Jesus is not a constitutive factor for his being Immanuel—"God with us"—or for the process of salvation. For them, Jesus is the representative of a new (redeemed) humanity that includes women and men equally, the incarnation not of a male but of a compassionate God who is with them in their daily struggle. For African-American women, as well, the male existence of Jesus is not the crucial point; they question whether Jesus is a white racist justifying slavery and white supremacy or whether he is on the side of black women, who suffer the triple oppression of racism, sexism, and classism (Grant, 1989). Some Asian feminist theologians understand the maleness of the historical Jesus as functional in a positive way: as a man having just and mutual relationships with women, Jesus challenged the patriarchal power system and the male definition of humanity (Fabella, 1993).

A Patriarchal and Imperial Christology

Feminist theologians criticize also the Christological doctrine, normatively defined at the church Councils of Nicaea (A.D. 325) and Chalcedon (A.D. 451), as the result of a patriarchalization of Christology during the first centuries of church history. The New Testament contains not one unique and standard Christology but a plurality of diverse contextual interpretations of who Jesus was for the people believing in him. But early on, the interpretation of Jesus as Logos of God, a term connoted with maleness, began to prevail over the very old Sophia-Christology (probably the oldest Christological tradition), which understands Jesus as the child/prophet or incarnation of the (female) Sophia, the divine wisdom. This patriarchalization culminated in the fourth century A.D. with the establishment of Christianity as the official state religion of the Roman Empire. The Christological dogmas of Nicaea and Chalcedon defining the one binding understanding of Jesus Christ as the Son of God not only made an end to the Christological controversies of various Christian groups but also served to guarantee the unity of the religious basis of the empire. Thus Christology, constructed in the context of political power, legitimated the patriarchal sociopolitical order of the Roman Empire and supported the establishment of a male hierarchical church. Christ became the head of the church (as man is the head of woman) and—like the Roman emperor—Pantocrator, that is, lord of the whole universe (Ruether, 1983).

Through the ages this patriarchal and imperial Christology not only oppressed alternative Christologies (for instance, Christologies more egalitarian in spirit) but also established the claim of Christ as being the unique way to salvation. Anti-Judaism, crusades, imperialistic conversions, and conquests of non-Christian peoples and cultures have been the cruel historical outcomes of this Christological model.

Feminist theologians from the third world therefore criticize not only the patriarchal but also the imperialistic character of western Christology, which has justified the colonization and exploitation of non-Christian continents and nations in the name of Jesus Christ, the lord of the whole universe. This colonial Christ also destroyed the indigenous religious and cultural traditions and worsened the situation of women in most cases. As African and Asian feminist theologians discovered in the history of their cultures, very often a patriarchal and Eurocentric Christianity added new forms of discrimination to the patriarchal structures of the indigenous cultures while repressing the traditional power of women, especially their spiritual power and agency (Chung, 1990; Kanyoro and Oduyoye, 1992). Most Asian and African feminist theologians reject this imperial "lordship" Christology for the patriarchal and colonialist oppression women have suffered in the name of the Lord. In the multireligious context of Asia, with its rich tradition of centuries-old salvation models, some feminist theologians also have questioned the Christian claim of the "uniqueness" of Jesus as the savior for all and the only full disclosure of God (Fabella, 1993).

Redemption through the Suffering and Sacrifice of Christ

Another problem for women in relation to traditional Christology is the Christological doctrine of redemption through the suffering, sacrifice, and death of Christ. As the U.S. feminist Mary Daly (1973) pointed out, the image of the suffering savior sacrificing himself for the sake of humanity has been used as a model, especially for women, to reinforce female "virtues" such as self-sacrifice and passive suffering and to render women subservient to various modes of domination. Some U.S. feminist theologians have further explored the relationship between the image of the suffering and self-sacrificing Christ and the legitimation of the victimization of women. For them, Christ, the son who suffers in obedience to his father's will, legitimizes, as an example to be imitated by those suffering patriarchal oppression, violence against women and children, especially domestic violence and sexual abuse (Brown and Bohn, 1989). For others, the Christological discourse of God sacrificing his innocent son for our sins reflects patriarchal views of divine power that sanction child abuse as divine behavior (Brock, 1988). Some womanist theologians criticize the Christian notion of Christ as surrogate figure standing in place of sinful humankind. This notion gives surrogacy an aura of the sacred and reinforces for African-American women the surrogacy roles as "mammies" they have been forced to perform since slavery (Williams, 1993).

In Latin America, Africa, and especially Asia, the image of the suffering Christ is claimed by many Christian women who suffer profoundly to give meaning to their own suffering. But feminist theologians from these continents warn their sisters not to accept every suffering as redemptive. Suffering inflected by oppressive and patriarchal structures and passively accepted by women does not lead to the new life Jesus lived and died for. Some Asian feminist theologians underscore the fact that the image of the suffering Christ or suffering servant has helped to promote the existing overemphasis on Asian women's self-denial and must be treated with caution (Fabella, 1993).

Feminist Reenvisioning of Christology

Aware of the various oppressive functions of traditional Christologies in the life of women, Christian women all over the world began to reenvision Christology in the context of their experience of oppression and their yearning for liberation and healing. For the first time in history women are giving individually and collectively their *own* answers to the Christological question: Who do you say that I am (Mark 8:29)? The answers are pluralistic and contextual, based on their *experiences* as women—experiences deeply influenced not only by gender but also by race, culture, and class. In Africa, where women endure extreme poverty and are subjected to oppressive cultural customs, Christian women discover the Jesus of the Gospels, who opposed religious and cultural practices oppressive for women in his time. Jesus is seen as liberator and healer, as companion and personal friend of women, and, like the African woman as the nurturer of life, as one who encourages the self-affirmation of African women (Fabella and Oduyoye, 1988).

For Christian women in Asia, Jesus is the one who transcends the evil order of patriarchy. In a continent of less than 3 percent Christians, where the majority of the poor and oppressed are women, most feminist theologians try to develop an understanding of Christ that is both liberating for women and respectful of religious pluralism (Fabella, 1993). Some Asian women also use religious imagery from their own cultural background to express who Jesus is for them in the context of modern Asia. They are transforming western Christology into a real Asian Christology based on their political, cultural, and spiritual experiences as Asian women (Chung, 1990). In Latin America, where women need liberation from both gender and politicoeconomic oppression, feminist theologians emphasize Christ's liberating mission by stressing aspects ignored by male liberation theologians: women's active participation in the Jesus movement, their equal status as disciples, Jesus's humanizing attitude toward women, and his criticism of patriarchal social and religious institutions (Aquino, 1993).

For black women in the United States, Jesus is the divine co-sufferer who is with them in times of trouble. In the past black women identified with Jesus because they believed that Jesus identified with them. The resurrection of Christ signified for them that their tridimensional oppression was not without end and inspired hope in the struggle for liberation. Therefore, Christ, in their experiences and community, is reimaged in womanist Christology as a black woman (Grant, 1989).

Most white feminist theologians in the United States and western Europe try to articulate a Christology that no longer supports sexism, anti-Judaism, racism, and western imperialism. Some understand Jesus as a messianic prophet, starting a process of liberation and redemption that must be carried on by his followers (Ruether, 1983). Some rediscover the Sophia-Christology of the New Testament, which interprets Jesus as the prophet or incarnation of the (female) Sophia, the divine wisdom (Schüssler Fiorenza, 1987). Others see Jesus as brother, showing us what it means to incarnate God—the power-in-relation—in our world and inviting us to do the same by living just and mutual relationships (Grey, 1989; Heyward, 1982). While this relational Christology does not confine Christ to the historical Jesus and leaves room for future revelations of the "Christic" power in our sisters and brothers, there are attempts to consider even the historical Jesus not as an isolated hero but as part of a healing community. Christ is seen as located in the (messianic) community of which Jesus was one historical part, and it is the community that generates the lifegiving and healing power and thus becomes the locus for redemption (Brock, 1988).

Despite the diversity of feminist Christologies in different sociopolitical and cultural contexts, they all share the belief that the Jesus traditions of the Bible contain liberating elements which Christian women today can reclaim as they struggle for dignity, self-affirmation, survival, and liberation in a patriarchal world.

See Also

PATRIARCHY: FEMINIST THEORY; THEOLOGIES: FEMINIST; WOMANIST THEOLOGY

References and Further Reading

Aquino, María Pilar. 1993. *Our cry for life: Feminist theology from Latin America.* Maryknoll, N.Y.: Orbis.

Brock, Rita Nakashima. 1988. *Journeys by heart: A Christology of erotic power.* New York: Crossroad.

Brown, Joanne Carlson, and Carol R. Bohn, eds. 1989. *Christianity, patriarchy, and abuse: A feminist critique.* New York: Pilgrim.

Chung, Hyun Kyung. 1990. *Struggle to be the sun again: Introducing Asian women's theology.* Maryknoll, N.Y.: Orbis.

Daly, Mary. 1973. *Beyond God the Father: Toward a philosophy of women's liberation.* Boston: Beacon.

Fabella, Virginia. 1993. *Beyond bonding: A third world woman's theological journey.* Manila: EATWOT and Institute of Women's Studies.

———, and Mercy Amba Oduyoye, eds. 1988. *With passion and compassion: Third world women doing theology.* Maryknoll, N.Y.: Orbis.

———, Lee Park, and Sun Ai, eds. 1989. *We dare to dream: Doing theology as Asian women.* Hong Kong: AWCCT and EATWOT.

Grant, Jacquelyn. 1989. *White women's Christ and black women's Jesus: Feminist Christology and womanist response.* Atlanta, Ga.: Scholars Press.

Grey, Mary. 1989. *Redeeming the dream: Feminism, redemption, and Christian tradition.* London: SPCK.

Heyward, Carter. 1982. *The redemption of God: A theology of mutual relation.* Lanham, Md.: University Press of America.

Kanyoro, Musimbi R. A., and Mercy Amba Oduyoye, eds. 1992. *The will to arise: Women, tradition, and the church in Africa.* Maryknoll, N.Y.: Orbis.

Ruether, Rosemary Radford. 1983. *Sexism and God-talk.* Boston: Beacon.

Schüssler Fiorenzina, Elisabeth. 1987. *In memory of her: A feminist theological reconstruction of Christian origins.* New York: Crossroad.

Williams, Delores S. 1993. *Sisters in the wilderness: The challenge of womanist God-talk.* Maryknoll, N.Y.: Orbis.

Doris Strahm

CHRISTIANITY:
Status of Women in the Church

Throughout history women have been active in the life and witness of the Christian church—supporting it by their faith and faithfulness, being its moral and spiritual energy at all times and all continents. Yet women have been denied a place as ordained clergy, in theological discourse, and in the preaching and teaching ministries of the church, as well as in its liturgical life and its administrative and decisionmaking processes. The church is often said to have remained a bastion of patriarchal power, in spite of the articulate voices of women and their active involvement in attempting to create an inclusive and just community of women and men. As Pauline Webb (1991) suggests, "There is a long history throughout the church of the lay ministry of women, of women in religious orders, diaconates and missionary service, and of the strength of women's movements within congregational life." But these women have been trivialized and silenced.

This article provides a glimpse of the status and role of women in the Christian church. It can only make broad generalizations because of the varied traditions, theologies, cultures, ecclesiologies, and administrative structures that have patterned the life and witness of the various denominations within the church. It is not always possible to speak in the same breath, for example, of the way the Eastern Orthodox churches in the Middle East or the Baptist churches in the southern United States or the African Independent churches in Nigeria would view the participation of women in their lives. Therefore, this article will concentrate on the way in which the World Council of Churches as a global ecumenical instrument of the Protestant and Orthodox churches has discussed some of the issues involved.

The Ecumenical Decade of the Churches in Solidarity with Women (1988–1998)

The Ecumenical Decade of the Churches in Solidarity with Women was launched by the World Council of Churches in 1988 as a response to the growing strength of the voices of women in the churches who seek more visible demonstrations of solidarity. It was also launched in order to challenge the churches to take forward the gains of the United Nations Decade for Women (1975–1985). The Ecumenical Decade called on the churches to stand with women in their struggles to achieve justice and human dignity. At the midpoint of the decade, four issues were identified for concerted action by the churches. The participation of women in the life of the church continued to be of central concern. The churches were urged to embrace the theological and spiritual gifts that women offer and to affirm the shared leadership of women in the life of the church. But the Decade was not intended to be merely inward looking. It invited the churches to deal with issues like the global economic crisis and its impact on women; the increasing violence against women in all its manifestations; and the many ways in which racism and xenophobia have torn apart women's lives. The churches were given a ten-year time frame within which to plan how they will act on the issues identified in order to ensure a significant change in the quality of life of women and men in church and society. The churches have not acted to ensure radical changes in their structures, as many women had expected and hoped. What has happened instead, in many contexts, is that women are in solidarity with the church more than the church is in solidarity with women.

Tradition: For or Against Women?

For the churches to be truly "in solidarity" with women, they must reconstruct some of their basic theological and ecclesiological foundations. Biblical literalists insist that the subordination of women and the leadership of men are divinely ordained, and they compound this by emphasizing that women can achieve happiness only if they live according to biblical dictates on "womanhood." Such a theological view has been at the heart of the Christian ideology of the sacredness of the Christian family, which in all regions of the world has often denied women their right to a life of dignity or, more seriously, has denied them their right to move from a

violent environment to a safe one. This theology, which determines narrowly what is expected of women, has penetrated many mainline churches, which formulate their ministries according to this tradition.

It is by falling back on tradition that the church has often silenced any attempts to transform itself into a true community of women and men. This tendency was challenged by the congregational-based Study on the Community of Women and Men that the World Council of Churches launched in 1975. At a global gathering in Sheffield, England, in 1981, which marked the culmination of this study process, an Orthodox woman, Elisabeth Behr-Sigel, maintained that it is only within the dynamics of the authentic tradition that one can find radical newness of the church, which is the basis of real community. Affirming the vision of the Orthodox tradition of living the Trinitarian life as the foundation of genuine community in the church, Behr-Sigel (1983) spoke of tradition as "the very life of the church and its continuity," as "an ever-renewed inspiration," and as the "dynamic of faith, hope and love." But she went on to say:

> Faithfulness to tradition does not mean sacralization of the past, of the history of the church. Tradition is not a kind of immutable monster, a prison in which we are confined forever. It is a stream of life driven and impregnated by the energies of the Holy Spirit, a stream which unavoidably carried historical and therefore transitory elements and even ashes and cinders, but under the rigid surface the clear waters of spring run. It is our task with the help of God's mercy, to break through the ice, especially the ice in our slumbering frozen hearts. In us and from us, the tradition will become a spring of living water again.

Tradition is often invoked when the issue of the ordination of women is considered. In South Korea, for example, ordination was discussed for sixty-two synod sessions of the Presbyterian church in Korea before it was finally decided on. The arguments against ordination are organizational and sometimes biblical, but in the analysis of women in Korean society, it is the Confucianist value system that causes the problem. The church hides behind the traditional values of the society and does not give space for the gospel to challenge injustices that the culture perpetuates. But more often it is the traditions of the church that oppose change. Patriarchal power and privilege of those with ecclesial authority lie at the heart of the unjust structures of the church. The institutional impunity that some have enjoyed over the centuries has numbed the church into inactivity, giving quasidivine sanctions to traditions that sustain this power. Added to this situation is the very androcentric theology that has governed the life of the church—diminishing women and legitimizing the unjust ways that women experience the truth.

In spite of the resistance to women in ordained ministry, denomination after denomination in the Protestant church family has had to respond to movements for the ordination of women, which have grown in every region of the world. A significant day in church history, 12 March 1994 was the first time in the 460-year history of that church that thirty-two women deacons of the Church of England were ordained as ministers. This action by the Church of England came late: Takahashi Hisano was ordained by the Presbyterian church (now a part of the United church of Tokyo, Kyodan) in 1933. There are now thousands of women ministers in all parts of the world belonging to the Anglican communion, as well as to many other Protestant denominations. It is also true that several churches have consecrated women as bishops. But there are also churches that still refuse women the right to read the Scriptures or pray aloud in the church. There are still many churches where the participation of women is token, where women are expected to be "good" and "obedient" in order to be accepted into the inner circles of power. Women who do not behave according to the rules set by men or who have the courage to articulate a new way of being in the church are rejected, denounced, and even branded as heretical.

Affirming Other Forms of Ministry

It is not only the question of ordination that preoccupies the minds of women in the church. There is another view among women that would challenge clericalism itself. What is needed today is perhaps not so much the clericalism that the institutionalized church tends to offer but rather the demands of priesthood set forth by St. Paul: a new and transformed lifestyle of sacrificial living, so that others may live. Women have established that ministry is more than a privileged role for a cleric. By their life of selfless service, women have demonstrated a more vibrant and enriching form of ministry. The suffering and sacrifice that women have been called on to bear by a society that has systematically devalued them make them preeminently equipped to offer the church a new vision of service and a new lifestyle of priesthood that the church and the world need today.

Women have served the church in multifarious ways through the centuries. These contributions, as indicated ear-

lier, have often been trivialized and discounted—seen as mere extensions of the housewifely role. The diaconal ministries of women, the teaching ministries of women in reaching out to the young, and the caring and nurturing ministries as women engage in many forms of healing and serving the community—these are all essential to the survival and witness of the church, and yet they are not generally considered central to the life of the church. They are often seen as the peripheral services, in which it is expected that women will play the major role. And yet women have through the centuries given of themselves so selflessly to the church and the community. How can these gifts that women have brought to the church be given the status that they deserve?

In many churches around the world, the traditions of the church—the forms of ministry they have followed and the structures they have established—are evoked to deny women participation. The church fathers had spoken and would accept no argument. Ecclesiastical patriarchy of this kind is part of church history. Tertullian captured the misogyny of the fathers when he wrote: "Women you ought to dress in mourning and rags, representing yourself as patients bathed in tears, redeeming thus the fault of having ruined the human race. You are the door to hell: you finally are the cause why Jesus Christ had to die" (quoted in Mananzan, 1992).

Such attitudes have followed women throughout history. Women who spoke out, who challenged misogyny, were branded and persecuted. It is estimated that more than one million women were burned at the stake in Europe between the thirteenth and eighteenth centuries because they were classified as witches. Churches no longer burn women to death as witches, but violence continues, sometimes in very subtle forms: in language and symbols that exclude the experiences of women, in denying women their participation and creativity. Unfortunately, violence in its most overt expressions, such as sexual abuse by the clergy in pastoral contexts, also exists and threatens to destroy the very fabric of the church.

This history of repression, misogyny, and violence has led many to ask why women stay in the church. It is true, of course, that many women have left the church, but it is also true that many women have stayed. One source of inspiration to many women is the newly emerging message of liberation that feminist theology highlights.

The Feminist Theology Movement—A Sign of Hope

It is ironic that it is the same Bible and biblical tradition that have been used, in some contexts, against women that are at the heart of the worldwide feminist theology movement.

Women seek ways to find sustenance and hope in their struggles for justice and survival and invoke the authority of the Bible to support them in their liberation. They draw particular strength from the Jesus movement, which is based on the radical newness of Jesus's life and teachings. In Jesus all old and odious distinctions were broken down, all barriers were torn down, and everyone found freedom and wholeness. In Jesus's community there were no fixed structures, nor did institutionalized leadership prevail. Such a holistic vision of an ecclesia of equals has inspired women to reimage faith, God, and Christ in a way that gives them meaning and hope. As women on every continent of the world reread the Bible with new eyes, they articulate a new paradigm that shifts from the traditional ways in which the Bible has been read and interpreted. While developing a "hermeneutics of suspicion" of traditional ways of understanding the Bible and the canonization process, which had selectively excluded several texts, women have formulated alternative, theologically liberating visions.

Many women have left the church because of its patriarchal, institutionalized power structures. The church, because of its conservatism and lack of vision, is causing deep hurt to women who stay within its structures. More and more women in many countries are leaving the church, which they believe has systematically dehumanized them. Some women have demonstrated a new liturgical and spiritual life experience in a new form of church—which women see as "a religious attempt, part of a global feminist effort to transform patriarchal structures of government, business, education as well as religions" (Hunt).

The church has much to do to ensure that the true community of equality and justice that Jesus came to establish is achieved. If the church is to give to the people of God the courage to live life meaningfully and fully, giving expression to what God means to them in their struggles and hopes, then the theological vision that women articulate takes on significance and relevance for the world today. This new voice of women needs to be nurtured, encouraged, and sustained. Women's cry within the church is a cry for a new ordering of church life, where all will find acceptance and dignity.

See Also

CHRISTIANITY; CHRISTIANITY: FEMINIST CHRISTOLOGY; MISOGYNY; THEOLOGIES: FEMINIST; WITCHES: WESTERN WORLD; WOMEN-CHURCH

References and Further Reading

Behr-Sigel, Elisabeth. 1983. The energizing force of tradition. In Constance F. Parvey, ed., *The community of women and men in the church,* 62. Geneva: World Council of Churches.

Gnanadason, Aruna. *Women's programme.* Geneva: World Council of Churches.

Hunt, Mary. Forthcoming. *Patriarchy and post-patriarchal possibilities.* Geneva: World Council of Churches.

Mananzan, Mary John. 1992. *Woman and religion.* Manila: Institute of Women's Studies, St. Scholastica's College.

Webb, Pauline. 1991. Women in church and society. In Nicholas Lossky, José Miguez Bonino, John S. Pobee, et al., eds., *Dictionary of the ecumenical movement,* 1069. Geneva: World Council of Churches.

Aruna Gnanadason

CHURCH

See CHRISTIANITY: STATUS OF WOMEN IN THE CHURCH.

CHURCH OF JESUS CHRIST OF LATTER-DAY SAINTS

See MORMONS.

CINEMA

See FILM.

CITIZENSHIP

The western idea of citizenship first appeared in the ancient Greek city-states, where it was defined by the Aristotelian notion of ruling as well as being ruled. In the Roman Empire, however, citizenship became associated with legal status and with specific rights and duties (Shafir, 1998). These two notions of citizenship came together in the construction of citizenship in the nation-state, where it first appeared during the French Revolution. The word *citoyen,* the French equivalent of *citizen,* implied a broad relationship between the individual and society. As with earlier forms, modern French revolutionary citizenship was constructed in a way that excluded women by virtue of their gender. Class and race were also exclusionary dimensions of early citizenship. Carol Pateman (1988) links the "social contract" of the republican "fraternity" in revolutionary France with a sexual contract giving men the right to rule and represent women and children in the public domain. Despite the exclusionary history of modern citizenship, the universalist terminology on which it was based would later be used by a variety of social movements of excluded citizens, including women, to demand their rights.

Models of Citizenship

The debate about women and citizenship has generally had two sides. The first is an evolutionary/progressive model of increasing female inclusion. This argument proposes that women are latecomers to citizenship as a result of historical disenfranchisement and exclusion from the public sphere; with growing equality between the sexes, however, their political exclusion will continue to attenuate gradually. This trope of evolving equality is the dominant folk model for female citizenship. The "postrevolutionary" cuts in women's citizenship rights in countries such as Iran and especially Afghanistan show that history does not always work in this inevitable progressive direction.

The other argument holds that the exclusion of women from full citizenship and women's association with the "private" domain have been part of the more general political project of the Enlightenment, which is at the root of modern citizenship. Fraternity, at the heart of enlightenment and citizenship, is not just about social solidarity or even "male bonding" among citizens. The concept refers to the transformation of society from a patriarchy, in which the father (or the king as a father figure) ruled over both men and women, to a fraternity, in which men have the right to rule over women in the private sphere but agree to equality in the public sphere. Women, therefore, were not excluded from the public sphere incidentally but as part of a bargain between the new regime and its member citizens (Pateman, 1988; Vogel, 1991; Walby, 1994).

Women's exclusion was part and parcel of men's entitlement to democratic participation, which conferred citizenship status not on individuals but on men as representatives of a family (that is, a group of noncitizens). The social philosophy at the center of modern state citizenship was therefore not truly universalist, as it claimed; it was constructed in terms of "rights of man" or, more specifically, "rights of white man" (Pateman, 1989).

There are many historical examples of the incomplete integration of women into the modern institution of citizenship. Britain was one of the outstanding early exemplars of modern citizenship. During Victorian times, however, women lost their citizenship when they married. This was particularly problematic for women who married foreigners and therefore lost juridical rights to their homeland. Women continued to lose their citizenship when they married foreign nationals until 1948. As late as 1981, the children of British women did not have the automatic right to citi-

zenship, although the children of British men did. At the end of the twentieth century, British citizenship rules still privileged, the male line, allowing citizenship to be conferred on children by their paternal grandfather but not by any other grandparents.

The basis for granting people in general and women in particular a formal citizenship varies among states. The "blood and soil" charters of most European countries define citizenship by blood relations. Such charters construct women as a national flag that must be protected—they are the carriers and reproducers of the nations but not necessarily by extension of the nation itself. Ethnic Germans who have lived in central Asia for generations can claim and have claimed German citizenship through an imagined or real blood connection to the soil of Germany.

Nazi Germany, perhaps the society most concerned with blood and soil, valued women predominantly as childbearers and claimed that they belonged in the domestic sphere. This belief was summed up in the slogan prescribing the role of women: "Kinder, Küche, Kirche" ("children, kitchen, church"). Many other national discourses have constructed women as symbols of the collectivity—its biological and cultural reproducers—and have therefore told women that it is their moral duty as citizens to have as many children as possible.

Nations, sometimes called settler states, that define their identity through their immigrant populations tend to place more emphasis on where one was born or where one's parents were born (though not on previous generations) when granting citizenship. It is difficult to imagine someone of Australian or Canadian descent claiming an ethnic identity based on bloodlines. Whereas the great-grandchildren of an Italian immigrant to the United States might call themselves Italian or Italian-American, there is really no analogous term for someone of Australian or Canadian parentage. Where blood is of less importance to the construction of a nation, the reproductive role of women is less significant to the perpetuation and identity of that nation.

Socialist countries tended to define citizenship in yet another way. Because their charters were connected to the idea of the proletariat, citizenship was constructed in terms of who lived and worked in a place. In the early years of the Soviet Union, there were no restrictions on citizenship; immigrants could immediately vote and be elected to the government. Although religious and other traditions that defined women's roles more in terms of gender persisted in many places, national charters generally valued women first and foremost as workers. This is reflected in the policies of Cuba and most of the former eastern bloc, where the recognition that persistent inequalities in child rearing and domestic duties lead women to do more work over their lifetimes was, and still is, compensated for by earlier retirement ages for women.

Marriage and Citizenship

Marriage is a universal means of gaining citizenship in a country where one was not born, regardless of how the nation is defined. However, strict citizenship regulations can make women particularly vulnerable to difficult or abusive situations. Existing gender inequalities can be compounded by the absence of full legal rights for a spouse whose citizenship is pending. This becomes particularly problematic when the immigrant is from a poorer, weaker country, so that her citizenship is of less value in the global context.

Women from poor backgrounds in countries where economic opportunities may be scarce can become entirely dependent on their husbands and are left with few options for confronting a bad marriage. With nowhere to return to and no rights in their adopted country, some women will endure abusive relationships when faced with the threat of deportation. In the mid-1990s, an Ecuadorian woman named Lorena Bobbitt, married to a U.S. citizen and living in the United States, appeared in newspapers and on television around the world after she cut off her husband's penis. She claimed that her actions were the result of her feelings of utter powerlessness in the face of an abusive marriage coupled with the threat of deportation if she left him.

"Mail-order brides," as they are euphemistically termed, are sometimes "marketed" for their submissive nature on the basis of cultural stereotypes as well as the vulnerability of their situation. Women from southeast Asia have been the most visible group. Since the collapse of the Soviet Union, Russian women have increasingly married foreigners as a means of escaping the country's economic problems. Although men also partake in marriages to gain citizenship, the transactions are more often a financial matter than an emotional or sexual one.

In the liberal tradition, individuals are presumed to have equal status and equal rights and duties with regard to status as citizens; inequalities deriving from gender, ethnicity, class, and other contexts are irrelevant. This individualist, "universalist" approach, in which differences among citizens are seen as irrelevant, can become exclusionary and discriminatory. Membership in a state, and resultant rights and responsibilities, are mediated by membership in other collectivities and polities, sub-, cross-, and supra-state. An individual's positioning in that respect, as well as in terms of class, gender, sexuality, age, ability, and so on, must be acknowledged in any citizenship project that would be inclusionary and democratic. Moreover, the distributive function of the welfare state, which constitutes much of what is known as "social citizenship," has been dependent on division of labor along gender lines within the family as well as in the public domain.

Domains of Citizenship

Feminist critiques of the influential comparative analysis of welfare states by Gosta Esping-Andersen (1990), like those of Ann Orloff (1993) and Julia O'Connor (1993), have pointed out the need to add the family domain to that of the state and the market when examining the ways in which countries organize the provision of welfare. This is an important correction. The family domain must also be added when discussing different locations for political organizations and power. This is especially important if we expand the comparative span of citizenship beyond the very limited western range of case studies to which most citizenship theorizations have referred.

It is misleading to see in the rise of the modern nation-state a completely different form of social organization from the premodern nation-state. In many states—especially postcolonial ones—for example, extended family and kinship relationships continue to be used as focal points of loyalty and organization, even when constructed as ideological political parties. Political, social, and probably even civil rights might depend on the familial positioning of the particular citizen. In these states, traditional social and especially familial relations continue to operate, and often women have either no formal citizenship rights or only very minimal rights. Paradoxically, where familial relations are important in the politics of a country, women who are widows or daughters of political leaders have the highest chance of becoming political leaders, as on the Indian subcontinent, for example.

It is important, therefore, to include the three domains—the familial, the civil, and that of state agencies that vary among states and societies—in the determination of the social, political, and civil rights of citizens. None of these spheres is ever homogeneous, because different parts of the state can act in ways that contradict the actions of other parts, with different effects on ethnic, class, and other groupings in the society as a result.

The role of gender in citizenship rights is evident in all these areas as well as in considering the kinds of rights that were not considered by T. H. Marshall (1950, 1981), the most influential theorist of citizenship. One such right is the right to enter a state and, having entered, to be allowed to reside there. Women and men tend to be treated differently when bringing dependent relatives or children into their state of residence (Bhabha and Shutter, 1994).

The question of cultural rights and their implications for the citizenship of women of specific ethnic communities is even more complex, because notions of cultures are often stereotyped, reified, and homogenized in multicultural policies. Such a perspective does not take into account internal differences and contestations of power within minority communities and can be detrimental to women who find themselves with the "burden of representation" of that abstract and static notion of culture (Mercer, 1990).

Women and Citizenship Duties

An often-debated issue in feminist and other circles is the connection between citizenship rights and duties in general and those of women in particular. Various definitions emphasize that citizenship is a two-way process, involving obligations as well as rights. This, of course, raises not only the thorny issue of whether specific rights should be conditioned by carrying out specific duties but also the more general question of the boundaries of citizenship in relation to people who are not able to carry out such duties (Meekosha and Dowse, 1997). For instance, defending one's own community and country is generally seen as the ultimate duty of citizenship—to die (as well as to kill) for the sake of the homeland or the nation (Yuval-Davis, 1991a, b). This duty has given rise to Kathleen Jones's claim (1990) that the body is a dimension in the definition of citizenship. Traditionally, she claims, citizenship has been linked with the ability to take part in armed struggle for national defense; this ability in turn has been equated with maleness, whereas weakness and the need for male protection have been equated with femaleness.

Some feminist organizations (NOW in the United States, ANMLAE in Nicaragua, and others) have fought for the equal inclusion of women in the military; they argue that once women share with men the ultimate citizens' duty—to die for one's country—they will also be able to gain equal citizenship rights. The experience of women who have served in the military, both in national liberation armies and, especially, in western military machines does not support this argument. Women in the military, as in the civil labor market, changed but did not abolish sexual divisions of labor and power. Moreover—and most significantly—the entrance en masse of women into western militaries (although they continue to constitute small minorities) usually occurs once the national draft has been abolished and military service is no longer a citizenship duty but, rather, a professional career choice (Enloe, 1983; Yuval-Davis, 1997a, b). The participation of women in the military, then, must become a question of equal opportunity as well as of general citizenship duty (of both men and women), to evaluate critically the roles of the military in local, national, and global communities.

The notion of global citizenship has become more popular with increasing globalization, and nongovernmental organizations and networks of women often operate across borders, sharing a belief that the rights of women should not be left only to the dictates of the state. In effect, many of these groups supporting women's rights counterpoise themselves to states, and women often benefit from the work and funding of these supra-state and interstate organizations, as patriarchal social and economic structures located within the state deny them effective autonomous access to money and power. The increasing ease of communicating and traveling around the globe means that people are often less bound by their nation of citizenship. This leaves them free to build cross-border identities and thus to identify with women on the other side of the world not as members of a foreign nation but simply as women with problems and challenges in common. At the same time, it is important to remember that the differential positioning of women who are citizens of different states is not symmetrical and is mediated by the relative power of their citizenship states in the international pecking order, as well as by membership in particular ethnic, racial, and other groupings within their states (Yuval-Davis and Werbner, 1999). Contemporary citizenships are best described as multilayered citizenships, in which we are all, simultaneously but in a relational way, citizens of our local, ethnic, national, trans-, and supra-national polities (Yuval-Davis, 1999).

See Also

References and Further Reading

Bhabha, Jacqueline, and Susan Shutter. 1994. *Women's movement: Women under immigration, nationality, and refugee law.* Stoke-on-Trent: Trentham.

Enloe, Cynthia. 1983. *Does khaki become you?* London: Pluto.

Esping-Andersen, Gosta. 1990. *The three worlds of welfare capitalism.* Cambridge: Polity.

Jones, Kathleen B. 1990. Citizenship in a woman-friendly polity. *Signs* 15(4).

Marshall, T. H. 1950. Citizenship and social class. Cambridge: Cambridge University Press.

———. 1981. *The right to welfare and other essays.* London: Heinemann Educational.

Meekosha, Helen, and Leanne Dowse. 1997. Enabling citizenship: Gender, disability, and citizenship in Australia. *Feminist Review* 57:49–72.

Mercer, Kubena. 1990. Welcome to the jungle: Identity and diversity in postmodern politics. In J. Rutherford, ed., *Identity, community, culture, difference.* London: Lawrence and Wishart.

O'Connor, Julia. 1993. Gender, class, and citizenship in the comparative analysis of welfare state regimes. *British Journal of Sociology* 44(3): 501–518.

Orloff, Ann. 1993. Gender and the social rights of citizenship: The comparative analysis of gender relations and welfare states. *American Sociological Review* 58(June): 303–328.

Pateman, Carol. 1989. *The disorder of women.* Cambridge: Polity.

———. 1988. *The sexual contract.* Cambridge: Polity.

Shafir, Gershon, ed. 1998. *The citizenship debates, a reader.* Minneapolis: University of Minnesota Press.

Vogel, Ursula. 1991. Is citizenship gender specific? In U. Vogel and M. Moran, eds., *The frontiers of citizenship.* Basingstock: Macmillan.

Walby, Sylvia. 1994. Is citizenship gendered? *Sociology* 28(2): 379–395.

Yuval-Davis, Nira. 1991a. The citizenship debate: Women, ethnic processes and the state. *Feminist Review* 39: 58–68.

———. 1991b. The gendered Gulf War: Women's citizenship and modern warfare. In Haim Bresheeth and Nira Yuval-Davis, *The Gulf War and the new world order.* London: Zed.

———. 1997a. *Gender and nation.* London: Sage.

———. 1997b. Women, citizenship, and difference. *Feminist Review* 57(Autumn).

———. 1999. The "multilayered citizen": Citizenship in the age of globalization. *International Feminist Journal of Politics* 1(1): 119–137.

———, Nira, and Pnina Werbner. 1999. *Women, citizenship, and difference.* London: Zed.

Nira Yuval-Davis
Jo Sanson

CIVIL RIGHTS MOVEMENT

See antiracist and civil rights movements.

CLASS

If the capitalist mode of production comprises the set of social, political, and economic structures through which human beings in the modern world system relate to nature and to each other, then class constitutes the fundamental social relationship through which the central processes of capitalism—*production,* or the material sustenance of the current generation; and *reproduction,* or the biological and social propagation of future generations—are organized.

Class Systems and Marxism

Any discussion of class must begin with Karl Marx's observation that all humans, as living, breathing, biological entities, must extract the means of their continued survival from nature: food, clothing, shelter, and warmth must be obtained from the organic and inorganic materials that make up the material world. In maintaining this continuous metabolic relationship with nature, labor—productive, energy-expending, physical interaction—constitutes the fundamental mediating mechanism between humans and their environment. Unlike other organisms, which must also interact with their surroundings to survive, humans possess the unique capacity to negotiate their relationship with nature through the conscious, deliberate, coordinated organization of labor. This capacity allows for a variety of subsistence arrangements. At various periods in human history, communities have developed distinct modes of production based on particular divisions of labor to sustain themselves. A society based on a class system, in which a massive working class bears the bulk of the responsibility for satisfying social needs, is one of many configurations through which human groups have historically organized their relationship to nature, and consequently to each other. Like other modes of production, class-based societies, such as capitalism, engender specific relationships between men and women, particularly as these relationships are rooted in the ownership of property and the sexual division of labor.

Much of the writing on class and gender has derived from the search for the social and historical roots of women's oppression. Such research has served to counter biological determinism, or the argument that male dominance follows "naturally" from the physiological differences between men and women, as well as to explain how different relations between the sexes obtain under different modes of production. Beginning with the publication of Friedrich Engels's *Origin of the Family, Private Property, and the State* in 1884, Marxists have argued that human history may be broadly conceived as a series of evolving stages based on emergent innovations in the social division of labor. As these divisions have changed, the status of women, women's access to the means of production, and their relationships to men have taken on new characteristics. Drawing on the work of the anthropologist Lewis

Henry Morgan, Engels posited three distinct phases of human history—hunter-gatherer, horticultural, and class society—based on particular divisions of labor, marital arrangements, and patterns of property ownership. As human communities moved through these periods, Engels argued, women gradually lost the status as reciprocal equals in the productive process that they enjoyed in the earliest stage of primitive communism. Land once held in common gave way to a system of private property, divisions of labor once based on sex alone were elaborated by the emergence of classes, and marriage systems once based on easily dissolved, loose associations of groups became restrictive and based on monogamous pairings.

According to this scenario, hunter-gatherer societies were based on purely sexual divisions of labor, loose forms of group marriage, and communal ownership of land. As these communistic bands gave way to horticultural societies, such relations became more restrictive; more complex divisions of labor arose, marriage came to be based on loose pairings of couples, and rudimentary forms of private property emerged with settled agriculture and the domestication of animals. The development of class society witnessed the emergence of private property, classes of exploiters and exploited, and the bourgeois state as an instrument of the ruling class. In the process, women not only lost access to land previously held in common but took on the characteristics of private property themselves, particularly within the institution of marriage. As class became the organizing principle of society, marriage came to be based exclusively on strict monogamy, the nuclear family became the basic economic unit of society, and women were relegated to the private or domestic realm of reproduction and lost access to the means of production, thereby becoming dependent on the wage labor of individual men. The extent to which real human societies "fit" into these categories—as well as the extent to which women have ever enjoyed true egalitarian status—has long been debated by anthropologists. What most recognize, however, is that different modes of production organize the subjugation of women in quite specific ways. In capitalist societies, the status of women is closely linked to the division of labor according to class.

Class Systems and Capitalism

Capitalist production is often described as dividing society into two economic categories: labor, the working class that produces social value out of nature and that must sell this capacity in exchange for a wage in order to survive; and capital, the nonworking class that owns the means of production (tools, land, raw materials, and capital) and that buys labor from the working class in order to produce com-

modities for sale. In terms of the metabolic process mentioned above, labor constitutes the class of society that transforms nature into the things human beings require for survival, while capital compels the working class to sell its labor by removing from it the other necessary elements of production, including nature as land and resources and the technologies required to transform nature efficiently. Through a series of historical developments rooted in feudalism and its dissolution, capital comes to monopolize the means of production, leaving labor with no way to satisfy its own needs, compelled to sell the only thing it does own: labor power, or the capacity to work. By crippling labor's capacity to produce for itself, capital compels labor to work for it. Devoid of land, tools, and capital, workers assemble in factories, where they sell their labor power for an hourly wage in the making of commodities. The exchange is not an even one, for labor generates more value in the production process than capital pays for it. This difference is the source of surplus value, which capital extracts from labor and invests in further production. Competition between individual capitals for increasingly larger portions of the social surplus results in a productive system whose primary motor force is the accumulation of profit rather than the satisfaction of human needs. The long historical transition to class-based capitalism thus represents a fundamental shift in the relationship between production and reproduction, from a state in which production occurs for the purpose of reproduction to one in which the reverse is true. Although this unequal relationship forms the basis of capital's exploitation of labor, it also provides a means for labor's emancipation, as capital's dependence on the working class to create its profits can be used as a weapon for seizing productive power through the collective capacity of laborers to refuse work.

In full-blown capitalism, participation in the wage-labor relation is not necessarily restricted to men. Some Marxists have conceptualized the entry of women into the sphere of capitalist production as a potential source of cheap labor, a reserve army used by capital to maintain leverage over men's wages. Yet drawing women into the wage labor force has potentially liberating consequences, because in theory it lends women access to their own means of subsistence and frees them from dependency on a breadwinning male: no longer slaves of the wage slave, they become wage slaves in their own right. Participation in capitalist production, however, does not necessarily free women from their reproductive roles. As feminist critics of Marxism have noted, the foregoing portrait of the capitalist organization of labor omits a crucial facet of working life in capitalist societies: unpaid labor. In order for capitalist relations to continue over generations, not only must workers be continually compelled to exchange their labor for a wage; they must be conceived, born, nurtured, and socialized. Though reproduction is subordinated to production under capitalism, it must still take place in order for capitalism to survive. For much of capitalism's history, reproduction has remained outside the sphere of wage labor, as well as outside the primary responsibility of women—even when they also are engaged in wage labor in addition to their reproductive roles. Reproduction entails a host of laborious activities, from the bearing, birth, and raising of children to household domestic chores to the organization and maintenance of kinship ties. Whereas responsibility for reproductive work falls primarily on women even in advanced capitalist nations, reproduction is not immune to the commoditizing effects of capitalist development. Child care, housework, even procreation itself have become profit-generating industries, driven by inputs of labor, capital, and technology. Thus women of the upper classes are more easily able to free themselves from certain reproductive labors by contracting them out to working-class women. Working-class women may find themselves responsible for their own unpaid reproductive labor at home, while simultaneously exchanging their reproductive labor with other women for a wage; their reproductive labor becomes the source of their productive labor as their mothering roles are commoditized.

Women As a Global Underclass

The widespread structural inequalities faced by women have led some to posit women as a global underclass in themselves. Yet the ways in which individuals construct their identities around class and gender under capitalism are complex, for the two relationships intersect. The working class comprises both male and female wage laborers, and constructions of gender strongly influence occupational segregation as well as unequal compensation for men's and women's work. At the same time, class differentiates the broad category of "women," producing vastly different experiences of life under capitalism among women of the working, middle, and capitalist classes. And both relationships are complicated by differential experiences of race, ethnicity, nationality, religion, age, and culture. Thus working women of color in the West, for example, encounter working-class life in different ways from working white women, even while they may encounter race in different ways from middle- or upper-class women of color. The geographical division of labor in the modern world system produces disparities among women not only within societies but between them. Women in advanced capitalist nations

may experience both class and gender in vastly different ways from women in "developing" nations, the poorest of whom confront decreased average life-expectancy rates and higher average infant-mortality rates, face restricted access to health care and reproductive technologies, and suffer the effects of exposure to more extreme forms of environmental degradation.

The complexity of such divisions has led many scholars to question the extent to which gender constitutes a fundamental category uniting all women. How is the project of women's liberation to be carried out in the face of such a wide variety of interests, experiences, and identities? Do women as a community of interest have enough in common with one another to override the class divisions that differentiate them? Does the working class as a community of interest have enough in common to override the divisions of gender that differentiates it? How should the emancipatory struggles of the working class relate to the liberatory struggles of women? How would a society free of both gendered and class-based oppression organize production and reproduction? How can the feminist project be incorporated into the socialist struggle to eliminate class, and how can the socialist project be incorporated into the feminist struggle to eliminate patriarchy?

Despite the difficulties feminists and socialists have encountered in allying their struggles, there remains little doubt that one cannot succeed absolutely unless accompanied by the absolute success of the other. The working class cannot obtain total freedom if half its members continue to live under patriarchal oppression; nor can women obtain universal liberation if the majority continue to labor under the yoke of class. The investigation of the relationship between class and gender entails not only analyzing the shifting past and sorting out the complex present but also imagining a just and equitable future, for women of all classes and workers of all genders.

See Also

CAPITALISM; CLASS AND FEMINISM; DIVISION OF LABOR; FEMINISM: MARXIST; MARXISM; POLITICS AND THE STATE: OVERVIEW; SOCIALISM

References and Further Reading

Barrett, Michèle. 1998. *Women's oppression today: The Marxist/ feminist encounter.* Rev. ed. London and New York: Verso.

Collins, Jane L., and Martha Gimenez, eds. 1990. *Work without wages: Comparative studies of domestic labor and self-employment.* Albany: State University of New York Press.

Coontz, Stephanie, and Peta Henderson, eds. 1986. *Women's work, men's property: The origins of gender and class.* London: Verso.

Engels, Friedrich. 1993. *The origin of the family, private property, and the state.* Ed. Eleanor Burke Leacock. New York: International.

Fox, Bonnie, ed. 1980. *Hidden in the household: Women's domestic labour under capitalism.* Toronto: Women's Press.

Ginsburg, Faye D., and Rayna Rapp, eds. 1995. *Conceiving the new world order: The global politics of reproduction.* Berkeley: University of California Press.

Hansen, Karen V., and Ilene J. Philipson, eds. 1990. *Women, class, and the feminist imagination: A socialist-feminist reader.* Philadelphia: Temple University Press.

Leacock, Eleanor Burke. 1981. *Myths of male dominance: Collected articles on women cross-culturally.* New York: Monthly Review.

Mullings, Leith. 1997. *On our own terms: Race, class, and gender in the lives of African American women.* New York and London: Routledge.

Nash, June, and María Patricia Fernández-Kelly, eds. 1983. *Women, men, and the international division of labor.* Albany: State University of New York Press.

Saffioti, Heleieth. 1978. *Women in class society.* Trans. Michael Vale. New York: Monthly Review.

Tilly, Louise A., and Joan W. Scott. 1987. *Women, work, and family.* New York and London: Routledge.

Eliza Darling

CLASS AND FEMINISM

Class is one of the central political concepts of Marxist theory and is connected centrally to Karl Marx's economic analysis of capitalist society. In the Marxist analysis, the way commodities are produced in capitalist society (the "capitalist mode of production") brings into existence three major classes of people, corresponding to the economic categories of capital and labor: wage laborers, capitalists, and landowners. For the purposes of this article, we will refer to just two classes: wage laborers (the working class, or proletariat) and capitalists (the ruling class, or bourgeoisie). We may do so because, technically, the landowning class is a rural formation of the urban, industrialized capitalist class and thus may be absorbed into this latter category.

Capitalist society, then, comprises two major classes of people (who are also further stratified into layers), whose class position depends on their relationship to the means of production (raw materials, machines, tools, and so on) within capitalist society. The ruling capitalist class is that very small group of human beings who own and control the means of production and thus also have control and ownership of the end products of commodity production, and consequently of most of the world's wealth. The human beings who constitute the ruling class control and own capital, which is the form of money that is found in capitalist society (by virtue of the nature of its circulation within the circuit of capitalist commodity production).

The working class is that majority of human beings who work the means of production but do not control or own the products of their labor and thus own little of the world's wealth. The human beings who constitute the working class draw a wage in return for selling their labor to the capitalist class, but this is not a voluntary arrangement: workers are compelled by capitalist society to sell the products of their labor in exchange for wages.

The Relationship of Class to Feminism

Human beings of different classes have *opposing* interests that are a consequence of the unequal distribution of wealth and resources created by differences in their relationship to the means of production. This opposition of material interests is accompanied by a severe power imbalance. Members of the same class have *common* interests, bringing about certain affinities and cultural similarities due to a common way of experiencing life. By virtue of belonging to the same class, people develop similar characteristics, as certain other characteristics are excluded by the nature of the lives they are likely to lead. This is determined by what they do: their daily labor. The way a worker experiences life will, in many ways, be the same as the way another worker experiences life. For instance, workers will be less physically healthy than capitalists because of the hard nature of their labor, will be generally less well educated, and will vote in similar patterns and engage in similar forms of cultural recreation.

It cannot be overemphasized how central the issue of class has traditionally been to feminism, and it may be argued that attitude toward class is the point from which the various formations of feminism have taken their departure. Feminists disagree about the importance of the role that class plays in the oppression of women. The political task for feminists has been to determine where to draw the line between the oppression women experience as a result of class disempowerment and the oppression they experience as a result of patriarchy. Roughly speaking, Marxist feminists deny that there is a system of oppression called patriarchy; they argue that women's oppression is caused by the stratification of society into classes and that the oppression of women commences with the advent of the privatization of the ownership of the means of production, the accumulation of capital by the capitalist class at the expense of the working class, and the resultant lack of democratic control of the means of life. Oppression specific to women exists only insofar as women's practices become different from men's under the capitalist mode of production. What is primary to this view is that women are women only insofar as they are human beings and, because there is no immutable or essential "human nature," there is no essential "women's nature." Rather, human nature is formed by the predominant type of labor in which human beings engage in any historical epoch. Women are no exception to this, and thus "women's nature" is manifold, reflecting the fact that women from different classes have engaged in varying types of labor over the course of history. Hence, women from the same class have more in common with one another as "workers" than they do as "women."

Oppression: Class versus Patriarchy

In direct opposition to the Marxist view, liberal feminists deny that class has played any oppressive function in the social subjugation of women. In the liberal feminist analysis, patriarchy is the only structure that causes the oppression of women. Between these two poles there exists a range of opinions. For example, some feminists maintain that class in the Marxist sense exists and provides the correct analysis of capitalist society but that it has not played the principal role in the oppression of women. Others reject the primacy of the category of "class" in favor of a feminist analysis of oppression that posits a difference between women's and men's way of experiencing the world. Feminists who subscribe to the latter belief are likely to be interested in what they consider the specificity of female experience.

How do Marxist feminists argue for the oppression of women in terms of class? The fact that the (lower and middle) working classes have possessed only their physical and mental abilities to labor to sell in the marketplace has meant that workers have been forced into commodity production in order to live. Because much of a worker's day is taken up with selling her or his labor power in productive activity, relatively little time is left for reproductive activities, which include all of those things that, together, maintain the worker's ability to take part in productive activity in return for wages in the marketplace: the cleaning of the home, the washing of clothes, the preparation of food, entertainment,

sleeping, and the procreation of children. The family unit, in this view, is simply a socially constructed way of forming a cohesive economic unit within the constraints of capitalism, but its construction is a result of the part orchestrated for women to play in capitalist society rather than a "natural" family arrangement. The term *family*, for Marxist feminists, refers to nothing more than a system of association and kinship dependent on the social and economic function that it serves. The Marxist feminist sees nothing "natural" about a heterosexual coupling in which children are produced to be raised by their biological parents on the basis of the blood tie.

This analysis poses a problem for Marxist feminists, who face the question of why it is women *in particular* who stay in the home while men take part in commodity production in the public sphere. If capitalism is gender-blind, this argument would suggest, then why have men not stayed at home? Why has the distribution of women and men over reproductive and productive activities not been equal? If women have almost exclusively performed reproductive activities rather than been involved in productive activities because their proximity to their children constitutes an economically convenient arrangement, then why do women stay at home longer than this formative period of child development in which they must be at home, for example, to breast-feed their babies?

The Marxist feminist argues that though it is true that women have stayed in the home, this is more likely to be a function of their class position. Working-class women simply do not stay at home after having their children, and most do, in fact, labor in the marketplace just as men do. If working-class women do stay at home until their children are of school age, then this is only because child care is unaffordable to them. Only bourgeois women face this type of exclusion from productive activity in that they are productively redundant in the eyes of the marketplace because they do not contribute to commodity production. Bourgeois women, according to Marxist feminists, become objects that belong to capitalist men because, unlike working-class women, they are supported by and dependent on capitalist men in living indirectly off the profits of the working class generated by their husbands. This economic enslavement of bourgeois women to bourgeois men gives bourgeois men a position of dominance over bourgeois women that working-class men have never had over working-class women, and this in turn leads to a particular sexist formulation of what Marx calls "false consciousness" in the distorted view of women's nature that it creates. Noteworthy here is the fact that Marxist feminist political activism, through "wages for housework" campaigns, has sought to address the problem of the "invisibility" of women's domestic labor and to expose the implicit dependency of capitalism on the reproductive labor that women perform.

Another problem for the class interpretation is to discover why, even when women have been involved in types of labor comparable to the labor of men, women's earnings have always been less than men's. The Marxist feminist must account for the empirical fact that even when women are in the marketplace, their work somehow comes to be socially undervalued and thus underpaid in comparison with male equivalents. There does not seem to be any reason determined by class that traditional women's work, such as nursing and teaching, should be paid less than traditional men's work, when such labor is just as socially indispensable as men's work. With respect to skilled labor, the class analysis may successfully extend as far as a demonstration that the very things that allow men to undertake skilled labor, such as postsecondary education and vocational training, have not been open to women until recently. The Marxist feminist is certainly correct in saying that this has occurred because education has usually been a privilege of the ruling classes and that the underrepresentation of women in positions of skilled labor is diminishing. But the question why men's ability to labor, and not women's, has taken them outside the home when the majority of commodity production does not require skills or qualities that are particular to men (such as a greater abundance or density of muscle) seems intractable. Hard physical labor constitutes only a small portion of the activity demanded by capitalist commodity production, and improvements in the type and quantity of machinery in the latter period of the industrial revolution and the technological revolution have reduced this proportion to even lower levels. Nevertheless, the actual distribution of men and women across the various types of laboring activities remains unequal.

It might seem that the Marxist feminist position would be simple enough to disprove by appealing to the fact that women's oppression predated industrial capitalist society as we know it, or that disadvantage of class is at least partially neutralized for the women's struggle because of the integration of global feminist discourse. But a refutation is not quite so easily achieved as this, because capitalist society has deep historical roots from which we may chart a continuous development from the ancient slave societies. Both historically and politically, it is perilous to assert that the forms of oppression that characterize capitalism's predecessor modes of production (such as feudalism) can be clearly distinguished from the forms of oppression that women experience today.

See Also

CAPITALISM; CLASS; ECONOMIC STATUS: COMPARATIVE ANALYSIS; FEMINISM: MARXIST; FEMINISM: RADICAL; FEMINISM: SOCIALIST; MARXISM; PATRIARCHY; SOCIALISM; WORK: FEMINIST THEORIES

References and Further Reading

Dixon, Marlene. 1978. *Women in class struggle.* San Francisco: Synthesis.

Engels, Friedrich. 1954. *The origin of the family, private property, and the state.* Moscow: Foreign Languages.

Ferrier, Carole. 1991. Publicising feminism. In Carole Ferrier and Bronwen Levy, eds., *Hecate* 17(1): 116–123.

Hansen, Karen V., and Ilene J. Philipson, eds. 1990. *Women, class, and the feminist imagination: A socialist-feminist reader.* Philadelphia: Temple University Press.

Jaggar, Alison M. 1983. *Feminist politics and human nature.* Lanham, Md.: Rowman and Littlefield.

Lerner, Gerda. 1986. *The creation of patriarchy.* Oxford: Oxford University Press.

Marx, Karl, and Friedrich Engels. 1948. *Manifesto of the Communist party.* New York: International Publishers.

Phillips, Anne. 1987. *Divided loyalties: Dilemmas of sex and class.* London: Virago.

Sargent, Lydia, ed. 1981. *Women and revolution: A discussion of the unhappy marriage of Marxism and feminism.* Boston: South End.

Walby, Sylvia. 1992. Post-post-modernism? Theorizing social complexity. In Michèle Barrett and Anne Phillips, eds., *Destabilizing theory: Contemporary feminist debates,* 31–52. Cambridge: Polity.

Melissa White

CLONING

Cloning is a reproductive technology that exploits natural cell division processes to produce identical copies of genetic material. The cloned offspring may be part of an organism or a complete organism—a plant or an animal. A clone may have more than one genetic parent, and these parents may be from different species, resulting in a "transgenic" offspring.

Technological progress can precede progress in social thought and institutions, and this is nowhere more compellingly true than in considering the implications of cloning. The ethical issues involved in cloning are complex and vary with the application.

Cloning of Animals

On 24 February 1997, a lamb named Dolly was born that had been cloned by a Scottish research team headed by Ian Wilmot. Dolly ushered in a new era of genetic engineering. To produce this clone, the researchers had removed the nuclei of unfertilized sheep eggs and replaced them with a nucleus containing DNA from the udder of a 6-year-old ewe (the genetic parent). These reconstructed eggs were artificially stimulated to begin embryonic growth and then were implanted in surrogate ewes, one of which gave birth to Dolly.

Since 1997 numerous animals of both sexes have been cloned, including rodents, primates, and other mammals. Cloning can be viewed as a way to improve the breeding of livestock and research animals. However, cloned animals may incur risks related to health and to survival itself: these animals are often frail, dying shortly after birth (Renard, 1999). Also, although cloning techniques are likely to improve with research and practice, the experience with the animals involved so far is of great concern to advocates of animals' rights. Cloning requires exploiting the reproductive capacities of female animals, and killing many of them. Dolly, for example, resulted from one of 29 implanted eggs: "In total, 62% of fetuses were lost, a significantly greater proportion than the estimate of 6% after natural mating.…At about day 110 of pregnancy, four fetuses were dead, all from embryo-derived cells, and postmortem analysis was possible after killing the ewes" (Wilmot and Campbell, 1997).

Scientific and Medical Applications

Transgenic cloning of animals promises significant advances in medicine and pharmaceutical science. A sheep has been cloned to carry a human gene for a blood-clotting factor used in treating hemophilia. Pigs have been cloned as suitable host animals for "xenotransplantation" of organs to humans: that is, human genes are transferred into pigs, and the organs of these transgenic pigs may be less likely to be rejected by a human recipient. Transgenic cloning may be done with human fetal cells as well as with reproductive cells (sperm and eggs). Through such methods, vital bodily parts or processes can be replaced with biomedical materials. Using nonfetal materials, people who have damaged or diseased organ tissue could provide their own somatic cells (that is, cells other than sperm and eggs) to grow stem cells—undifferentiated cells—which would in turn form whatever type of tissue was required for therapeutic purposes.

These technologies have, not surprisingly, given rise to ethical concerns. Those who believe that the human fetus possesses spiritual or ethical significance are opposed to fetal cloning. Others believe that advanced medical treatments based on cloning may disproportionately benefit the few and, further, that these methods may be too readily adaptable from medicine to unsuitable applications.

Human Cloning

The cloning of animals raises the possibility—and the issue—of cloning as a means of human reproduction. Feminists and others have pointed out that techniques originally used in animal husbandry, for example in vitro fertilization, are eventually practiced on humans, especially on women (Corea, 1985).

One application of cloning techniques involves genetically altering in vitro a sexually produced (noncloned) embryo, so that certain genes are suppressed or introduced in the new individual. Using this method to eliminate genetic diseases could of course be beneficial. However, some commentators see the process of predetermining a person's genetic makeup as a form of eugenics that could lead to socially engineered "designer babies."

The reproduction of a completely cloned person would involve procedures quite similar to those already in use with animals. The nucleus of a somatic cell of an existing (or previously existing) human being would be transferred to an ovum from which the nucleus had been removed. This reconstructed egg would be artificially stimulated to begin life, then transplanted into the uterus of a woman—a surrogate mother or genetic mother who would carry the cloned fetus in a pregnancy and give birth.

To ease public fears about human cloning, governmental and private bans were imposed in various nations in the late 1990s. In 1997 the president of the United States, Bill Clinton, barred federal funding for research involving cloning a person. In the same year, the minister of public health in Great Britain issued the following statement: "Under United Kingdom law, cloning of individual humans cannot take place whatever the origin of the material and whatever technique is used." The Federation of American Scientific Societies for Experimental Biology, a group representing more than 52,000 biologists, adopted a five-year voluntary moratorium on research involving cloning a person (FASSEB, 1997). At the turn of the twenty-first century, though, many nations had no laws prohibiting the practice, and scientists in some prestigious organizations were recommending opening the door to human reproductive cloning. Initially, reproductive cloning might be used to assist infertile women. Self-cloning is an additional possibility.

Cloning of human beings would challenge some concepts that have traditionally been associated with human life and human reproduction. Thus the ethical ramifications of human cloning must be addressed from religious, philosophical, and bioethical viewpoints. Moreover, with cloning—as with other reproductive technologies—feminist ethics must be in the forefront of the social dialogue, since ethical discourse should be grounded in the experience of those most likely to be affected.

The identity of a cloned person would constitute a somewhat novel situation affecting both the child and the family. A parent and a clone are analogous to identical twins, who, though sharing the same genes, develop obvious individuality through their different life experiences. Unlike a parent and clone, however, twins are contemporaries, and neither one is a deliberate copy of the other. An envisioned alternative to replacing the cell nucleus is called "embryo splitting"; with this method clones would be born, like identical twins, into the same environment.

As noted above, cloning would be likely to involve surrogate motherhood. This form of parentage, in which women bear children who are not their own genetic offspring, emerged in relation to artificial insemination and in vitro fertilization. Surrogacy, too, raises issues, because studies of surrogate mothers suggest that their long-term adjustment is problematic. With "surrogate cloning," the extraction of human ova, the insertion of the cloned embryo, the process of gestation and childbirth, and the subsequent emotional reactions may constitute a cost that is simply too high. Issues of class cannot be ignored; women from developing nations, as well as poor women and minority women in developed nations, are at greatest risk of exploitation by reproductive methods involving surrogate motherhood.

Human cloning would affect the family identity of all those involved—the genetic parent, the childbearing mother, the nurturing parent or parents, and the offspring. We may already have some clues to the complex identities implied by cloning: for instance, cloned offspring are likely to have some of the experiences of children resulting from artificial insemination (AI); and the experience of adoptive parents and children, surrogate mothers, and identical twins and other multiple births may also be relevant in some ways. These considerations too will need to become a part of the reality and ethics of cloning.

See Also

BIOETHICS; MEDICAL CONTROL OF WOMEN; REPRODUCTION: OVERVIEW; REPRODUCTIVE HEALTH; REPRODUCTIVE PHYSIOLOGY; REPRODUCTIVE TECHNOLOGIES; SURROGACY

References and Further Reading

Corea, Gena. 1985. *The mother machine: Reproductive technologies from artificial insemination to artificial wombs.* New York: Harper and Row.

FASSEB (Federation of American Scientific Societies for Experimental Biology). 1997. Statement (September).

Human Genome Advisory Commission. 1998. Cloning issues in reproduction, science, and medicine. Paper (December).

Kolata, G. 1997. *Clone: The road to Dolly and the path ahead.* New York: Morrow.

Pretorius, Diederika. 1996. *Surrogate motherhood: A worldwide view of the issues.* American Series in Behavioral Science and Law. Springfield, Ill.: Thomas.

Renard, Jean-Paul. 1999. *British Medical Journal* 318(8: May): 1230.

Sorosky, Arthur D., Annette Baran, and Reuben Pannor. 1989. *The adoption triangle: The effects of the sealed record on adoptees, birth parents, and adoptive parents.* Garden City, N.Y.: Doubleday.

Stacey, M. 1996. The new genetics: A feminist perspective. In T. Marteau and M. Richards, eds., *The troubled helix: Social and psychological implications of the new human genetics.* Cambridge: Cambridge University Press.

Transgenic sheep expressing human factor IX. 1997. *Science* 278: 2130–2133.

Viable offspring derived from fetal and adult mammalian cells. 1997. *Nature* 385: 881.

Wilmot, Ian, and Keith H. S. Campbell. 1997. Statement of the Roslin Institute, Edinburgh.

Celeste Newbrough

CLOTHING

See DRESS and FASHION.

COEDUCATION

See EDUCATION: SINGLE-SEX AND COEDUCATION.

COHABITATION

The term *cohabitation* refers to a heterosexual couple living together in a more or less permanent relationship without being legally married (Trost, 1979). Among the peasantry of northern and central Europe in the Middle Ages, marriages would often take place after proof of fertility was produced through cohabitation. When socially condoned, cohabitation is variously called living together, common-law marriage, quasi marriage, trial marriage, and consensus marriage. Cohabitation has met with disapproval at various historical times and in different regions of the world. Terms such as "living in sin" or "shacking up" reflect this disapproval.

In the twentieth century, the number of common-law unions increased in most western countries as marriage rates declined. However, cohabiting unions have been found more prone to dissolution than legal marriages. This relative ease of dissolution may be part of the attraction of cohabitation as compared with traditional marriage. McRae (1993) suggests that the more acceptable cohabitation becomes, the more likely the unions are to last. She also reports that, paradoxically, cohabiting couples who marry are more likely to have unstable marriages and are more likely to divorce. A 17-nation study (Stack and Eshelman, 1998) found support for the thesis that marriage is associated with higher levels of personal well-being than cohabitation.

Heterosexual cohabiting couples in western countries hold less traditional views of gender relations than married couples but are not likely to differ with regard to the division of household labor by gender (McRae, 1993). The fact that cohabitation holds the potential for an increasing equality in male-female relationships could have an appeal for women who hold feminist ideals.

In the twentieth century, unmarried cohabitation was first observed and studied in Scandinavia and in the northern and central European countries, as well as in Canada and the United States. Reflecting increased social acceptance since the 1960s, common-law marriages have gradually become legally recognized in western countries. Three general patterns of cohabitation have been found in Europe: (1) countries where cohabitation is a relatively established phenomenon (Sweden and Denmark); (2) countries where cohabitation is emerging as a significant pattern (the Netherlands, France, Finland, Norway, Austria, Switzerland, and Britain); and (3) countries with very little cohabitation (Italy, Spain, Portugal, Greece, and Ireland) (McRae, 1993). Canada and the United States follow the second pattern. In the first pattern, cohabitation may be seen as an alternative to marriage, whereas in the second grouping, cohabitation is more likely to be seen as a part of courtship, leading to marriage.

Nonwestern and less industrialized countries, especially those with strong religious sanctions, fall into the third category, likening cohabitation to adultery. A double standard prevails: women are more severely ostracized or punished for cohabitation than men and may be considered concu-bines or prostitutes. In some industrializing countries, married cohabitation is becoming less common. With increased migration, working men are more likely to leave their wives and children behind, increasing the number of single-parent, female-headed households.

See Also

ADULTERY; COURTSHIP; DIVISION OF LABOR; HOUSEHOLDS AND FAMILIES: OVERVIEW; MARRIAGE: OVERVIEW; MARRIAGE: REGIONAL TRADITIONS AND PRACTICES

References and Further Reading

Eekelaar, John M. 1980. *Marriage and cohabitation in contemporary societies: Areas of legal, social, and ethical change: An international and interdisciplinary study.* Toronto: Butterworths.

McRae, Susan. 1993. *Cohabiting mother: Changing marriage and motherhood?* London: Policy Studies Institute.

Stack, Steven, and J. Ross Eshelman. 1998. Marital status and happiness: A 17-nation study. *Journal of Marriage and the Family* 60(2): 527–537.

Trost, Jan. 1979. *Unmarried cohabitation.* Vasterås: International Library.

Vappu Tyyska

COLLEGES

See EDUCATION: HIGHER EDUCATION and EDUCATORS: HIGHER EDUCATION.

COLONIALISM AND POSTCOLONIALISM

The Colonial Experience

Colonialism is the domination of poorer, weaker countries by wealthier, more technically advanced nations. The term is generally used when a formal system of political dependency is constructed by one country over people of a different ethnicity and also designates the political frameworks through which control is established and maintained. Colonialism has been practiced since ancient times by cultures all over the world, but the modern colonial period began with European overseas expansion into Asia, India, the Middle East, Africa, and South and North America in the seventeeth century and continued into the twentieth century.

During the colonial period economists and politicians emphasized social mores as well as the political economy of the colonies. In his *History of India,* J. S. Mill (1806–1873) wrote,

"The condition of women is one of the most remarkable circumstances in the manner of nations. Among rude people the women are generally degraded, among civilised people they are exalted." This concept was often used to justify colonization (Liddle and Rai, 1998) and also reflects early developmentalism: civilization was regarded as both social and economic.

Relations between men and women in the colonized countries were considered symptomatic of degeneration. Colonized men, for example, were said to be brutal to women—not only when these men were described as martial, aggressive, and boorish (examples are Aryan groups such as the Afghans and Sikhs) but even when they were "feminized" by stressing their small stature and their presumed frailty; thus colonized women were rescued from them by an external, modernist authority. In colonial discourse, then, men's relationship to women mediated east-west relations.

For the colonial powers, civility implied modernity: modern social relations were spoken of in the same breath as capitalist individuation. Colonialism was seen as a "sharing of progress," either by modifying indigenous mores (as the orientalists demanded for India) or through completely new arrangements (as in the Americas)—through colonization itself (Cowen and Shenton, 1996: 42–59). One aspect of this process was recasting the social relations of colonized men and women, among other means by direct and indirect humiliation.

In the first stages of colonial conquest, humiliation was direct. In Latin America, "for the vast majority of indigenous women, the Conquest [by the Spanish and Portuguese] meant the loss of material, political and ritual privileges; exploitation of their labour, and sexual abuse by the invading soldiers and priests who crucified them in bed under the pretext of saving their souls" (Stolcke, 1994: 8). Often, women who were sexually abused by the conquerors were then rejected by their own male relatives in the name of honor and purity. Often, too, rejected women became part of the political economy of colonial war by "servicing" soldiers. Socially, prostitution at first placed women in a gray area—vulnerable, forgotten, abused, the responsibility of no one. However, as a colonial power settled in, prostitutes were generally regulated; an example is the implementation of the Contagious Diseases Acts in British colonial states in the late nineteenth century.

Humiliation was also indirect, as when customary relations between men and women were refashioned. This affected economic arrangements such as property rights and the organization of labor, and also social arrangements such as marriage and education; and it reflected power relations between colonial and colonized men: "All too often in male nationalisms *gender* difference between women and men

serves to symbolically define the limits of *national* difference and power between *men*" (McClintock, 1993: 62).

In British India, the Permanent Settlement Act of 1793 is an example of the far-reaching effects of property relations (Metcalf, 1995). Under this act, *zamindars*, the traditional tax collectors, who had earlier been dependent on feudal *nawabs*, were given property rights. The resulting commercialization of Indian agriculture changed social relations, and the sequestering of common land meant that women had little access to an important means of economic survival. Also, under this act cash replaced kind in the payment of taxes; and cash crops changed patterns of agricultural production, including the division of family labor (Mackenzie, 1995). Women's labor became concentrated in providing food for the family and so was invisible within the new financial arrangements, while men's contribution to the family income became more visible. Thus property rights and land management changed relations between peasants and landholders, and also the position of women. These new social realities were then given a legal framework. Particularly under the British, the idea of the "rule of law" was central to the "improvement" of the colonies.

One issue that continues today is access to natural resources. Modern capitalism involved the state more in exploiting resources; and terracing, logging, irrigating, conservation, and infrastructure projects were often used the forced labor of colonized men and women. While resistance was widespread, it was also gendered, as in the Chipko movement in India and the renegotiation of the traditional Matengo pit system of cultivation in Tanganyika (Mackenzie, 1995). The Chipko movement originated in the 1970s as a protest by village women against logging abuses in Uttar Pradesh in the Himalayas; it led to bans on clear felling in several regions and influenced natural resource policy. *Chipko* comes from a word meaning "embrace": the women practiced *satagraha*—nonviolent resistance—interposing their bodies between the trees and the contractors' axes. The Matengo system involves labor-intensive crop rotation done in large part by women, who have defended this environmentally sound agriculture against the threat of high-yield methods that ravage the land.

The Nationalist Response

The colonial discourse on gender relations was challenged, but some of it was also absorbed into postcolonial nationalist thinking (Metcalf, 1995: xi). Often, a nation in the making was described idealistically, even as sacred. The terms "fatherland" and (more generally) "motherland" symbolized familial relations; thus the home, the family, and the concept of womanhood became critical in the discourse of nationalism (Papanek, 1994: 46–47): "Certain ideals of womanhood are propagated as indispensable to the attainment of an ideal society. These ideals apply to women's personal behaviour, dress, sexual activity, choice of partner, and the reproductive options.... Women [are] the 'carriers of tradition' or 'the center of the family' especially during periods of rapid social change." Women's "actions and appearance should alter less quickly than that of men, or should not be seen to change at all"; and women should "conform to prescriptive norms of a *collective* identity that is seen as advancing the goals of the group." Societal ideals, then, become attached to notions of appropriate behavior of women, and restoring social order means imposing stringent controls over women rather than addressing more structural issues.

In India, for instance, the ideal home and the ideal woman were upper-class or high-caste concepts of familial space and relations (Liddle and Joshi, 1988). However, they became the basis of a "national" understanding of social relations and were legally codified, perhaps because nationalism was viewed not simply as an ideology but as similar to kinship and religion (Moghadem, 1994: 4).

The "home-nation" stood for security, familiarity, and tradition and remained the domain of indigenous male elites. Indeed, colonizers allowed patriarchal autonomy within the home in the hope of undermining anticolonial resistance. In northern Rhodesia-Zambia and Nyasaland-Malawi, according to Martin Chanock, male elders allied themselves with colonial rulers to reestablish control over women through a contrived "customary law" (Parpart and Staudt, 1989: 7). In India, when the British tried to refashion familial relations through legislation on the age of consent (*sati*), modern nationalists supported them but nationalists such as Tilak were bitterly opposed. The home, then, was an integral part of nationalist discourse and was seen as threatened from without (by the colonizers) and from within—by traditionalists who were endangering the future or by modernists who were polluting the authentic culture (Kandiyoti, 1991).

Authentic culture was embodied by the woman within the home: "Only the women of the nation are the beautiful ones" (Pettman, 1996: 51). National identity was linked to boundaries, purity, and chastity and was in jeopardy if women's role in the home was compromised. The woman created future generations and ensured cultural continuity through her own appropriate social conduct and the religious and cultural education of her children. Male elites might disagree about changes in women's outer garb, but they agreed that her inner core, like the idea of the nation, was immutable; thus modernity might include the woman while still leaving her untouched within the home—a reflection of a broader distinction between technology and tradi-

tional culture. In China, for instance, this distinction allowed a compromise between the communists and the peasant elites on the "woman question" (Stacey, 1983).

An important factor in the delineation of women was the growth of print capitalism. Vernacular journals carried women's own voices, becoming a vehicle for the first feminist challenges to both colonial and nationalistic ideas about women's position in society (Talwar, 1993). However, feminist agendas did not gain equality with those of male nationalists, perhaps partly because feminists also needed to keep "the woman" as a recognizable, stable entity: at this stage, the struggle did not center on diversity. Women were mobilized in the nationalist cause—and such mobilization became the basis of women's first demands in their own interest.

Nationalist Movements and Women's "Self-Determination"

For women, nationalism created new spaces but also posed challenges. The greatest challenge involved unity: anticolonialism demanded discipline and sacrifice. "Particular interests" were seen as a threat to the national agenda, and the rights of particular groups might have to be compromised. Recognizable social relations—such as the figure of the woman within the home—cemented political unity.

Most women's groups accepted the urgency of the nationalist struggle, but they were also aware that it marginalized their interests. Nongendered citizenship appealed to women in the language of equality even though they were aware of differences between women's and men's lives, publicly and privately. Women's groups rebelled against being cast as victims of their own society and asserted their cultural identity; but when they were recast as new women of a new nation-state, they were aware of the gap between political rhetoric and social reality. Despite their voluntary code of silence, women's groups were uncomfortable with male nationalists' articulation of women's "place." The demand for unity and solidarity was, then, often a dilemma for women: "Women had been assigned a place in society which could not be challenged without questioning both the past and the future" (Helie-Lucas, 1991: 58).

Anticolonialism led to an "era of patriotic feminism." In Turkey, "no less than a dozen women's associations [were] founded between 1908 and 1916, ranging from primarily philanthropic organisations to those more explicitly committed to struggle for women's rights" (Kandiyoti, 1991: 28–29); and this same phenomenon existed in other countries engaged in nationalist transformations. Often, however, women's organizations were established by and with the support of men, or—given the primacy of unity—existing women's groups were incorporated into dominant nationalist parties. In Turkey in the 1920s, under Mustafa Kemal, the "new woman" symbolized a break with the past, but Kemal's paternalistic (though benevolent) regime hindered women's political initiatives. Kemal refused to authorize the Women's People's Party in 1923; he advised women's groups to establish a Turkish Women's Federation—an association rather than a party—but even this was disbanded in 1935, only a few days after it had hosted the Twelfth Congress of the International Federation of Women.

The issue of unity was sharpened by disagreement within women's groups on modernism versus culture and on different types of feminism. Most women who became leaders during nationalist movements were bourgeois—educated, well connected, from politicalized families, symbolic of modernity, but also circumscribed within upper-class boundaries. Motherhood, for instance, held an important but contested place. Malathi de Alwis observed of motherhood in Sri Lanka that it "can be defined as not only incorporating the act of reproduction . . . but also the nursing, feeding and looking after of babies, adolescents, the sick, the old and even grown women and men, including one's husband" (Maunaguru, 1995: 160). In other words, motherhood was contained within recognizable family forms, validated by the nationalist elite, and part of the iconography of patriotism. Similarly, matters of class, ethnic diversity, and religion became blurred and would later emerge as divisive issues for women's movements. In India, for instance, women who subscribed to the secularization of social and public life were often accused of cultural ignorance, insensitivity, class bias, and a slavish acceptance of western ideas. Thus when women's groups supported one articulation of nationalism, that could be presented as denying other identities.

Another problem for local and national feminism was feminist intervention from the outside, especially from western "maternal imperialists" (Ramusack, quoted in Liddle and Rai, 1998). Nationalist feminists who accepted western liberalism became a target for traditionalists—solidarity with western feminists, therefore, came at a high price.

Codifying Patriotism as Development

Struggles within nationalist movements over women's role reflect an acceptance of modernity and are important for understanding alternative visions of postcolonial development. In most nationalist movements, a bourgeois liberal elite became dominant, as did its idea of women's place in the new nation-state: "The women of the peasantry were . . . proletarianised, those of the bourgeoisie were trained to accept new social roles in conformity with the emerging bourgeois ideology of the period" (Jayawardene, 1987: 9). Postcolonial constitutional reforms remained largely politi-

cal: legal equality for women; rescinding of obviously discriminatory practices; the right to the vote, to education, and usually to own property; and laws forbidding violence against women.

Postcolonial nationalists—liberal, socialist, or Marxist—saw themselves as regenerating their countries through independence, progressivism, modernism, and industrialization. These concepts had direct consequences for gender relations. Industrialization, for example, implied a focus on male employment; commercial; mechanized agriculture in rural societies implied a marginalization of women's work; and new infrastructure (such as damming rivers for hydroelectric projects—Nehru called these dams the "temples of modern India") implied displacing populations, a situation in which women are particularly vulnerable. Modernization was often equated with the preferred political system, restricting the space in which women could challenge their marginalization. Except in Marxist nationalist states, private property was taken as given; in terms of agrarian gender relations, this meant that under "cultural regimes," women could rarely inherit land.

Thus postcolonial nationalism was deeply gendered, but this was seldom acknowledged. National development was the primary issue; "the woman" continued to have a shadowy existence on the periphery of nationalist consciousness—mobilized in its cause but confined within the home, which was also the nation.

At the point when a nationalist movement became the dominant political force in an independent nation-state, most women's groups remained convinced of its agenda and were reluctant to seek special dispensations. In India, for example, the All India Women's Committee, the Women's Indian Association, and the Central Committee of the National Council of Women demanded political equality for women but rejected "any form of preferential treatment" (Sharma and Rai, 2000: 154).

However, differing visions of the future of the nation-state determined women's position within different political systems. In liberal contexts, although women were individualized as citizens, they might also be regarded as markers of a group identity. This was true of Indian women: after partition at the time of independence—in the interest of political stability—Muslim women were denied many rights that Hindu and Christian women were granted. For Muslims, such matters as polygamy, divorce, and inheritance were decided according to Islamic family law rather than Indian constitutional law. In Algeria, a more authoritarian context, the revolutionary state tried to maintain both a "socialist" and an "Islamist" identity but was unable to placate the fundamentalists while also providing economic goods. The political situation deteriorated, with tragic consequences for the country and for Algerian women (Bouatta and Cherifati-Merabtine, 1994). In Marxist states, citizenship and nationalism were subsumed under ideology: gender was subordinated to economic development and political power. Thus at one point in China, "having children was a social duty, failure to observe which 'should be severely criticized by the party'" (Evans, 1997: 31, 44); and concerns about women's appropriate behavior within the family were implicitly accepted in policy making (Stacey, 1983: 188). In all three political contexts, at the moment of victory for a decolonized nation-state, women seemed to be shut out of the institutional design.

In sum, while social reform was a priority, postcolonial states also emphasized an "essential distinction between the social roles of men and women in terms of material and spiritual virtues" (Chatterjee, 1989: 243). Though unacknowledged, this distinction became part of law and state policy in various ways. As Carol Smart has argued, "we can begin to analyse law as a process of producing fixed gender identities rather than simply as the application of law to previously gendered subjects" (1991: 9). Although most postcolonial states used the language of equality, citizenship remained different for men and women; and women remained very much targets, not agents. Women's struggle to translate the language of equality into political agency has continued in postcolonial states with varying degrees of success.

See Also

INDIGENOUS WOMEN'S RIGHTS; NATION AND NATIONALISM; POSTCOLONIALISM: THEORY AND CRITICISM

References and Further Reading

Bouatta , Cherifa, and Doria Cherifati-Merabtine. 1994. The social represenation of women in Algeria's Islamist movement. In V. Moghadem, ed., *Identity politics and women: Cultural reassertions and feminisms in international perspective*. Boulder, Col.: Westview.

Chatterjee, P. 1989. The nationalist resolution of the women's question. In K. Sangari and S. Vaid, eds., *Recasting women*. New Delhi, Kali for Women.

Cowen, M. P., and R. W. Shenton. 1996. *Doctrines of development*. London: Routledge.

Evans, H. 1997. *Gender and sexuality in China*. Cambridge: Polity.

Helie-Lucas, M. 1991. Women in the Algerian liberation struggle. In T. Wallace and C. March, eds., *Changing perceptions: Writings on gender and development*. Oxford: Oxfam.

Jayawardene, K. 1987. *Feminism and nationalism in the third world*. London: Zed.

Kandiyoti, D. 1991. Bargaining with patriarchy. *Gender and Society* 2(3).

Liddle, J., and R. Joshi. 1988. *Daughters of independence*. London: Zed.

———, and S. Rai, 1998. Orientalism and feminism: The challenge of the "Indian woman." *Women's Journal of History* 25(4).

Mackenzie, F. 1995. Selective silence: A feminist encounter with environmental discourse in colonial Africa. In J. Crush, ed., *Power of development*. London: Routledge.

Maunaguru, S. 1995. Gendering Tamil nationalism: The Construction of "woman" in projects of protest and control. In P. Jeganathan and Q. Ismail, eds., *Unmaking the nation: The politics of identity and history in modern Sri Lanka*. Colombo: Social Scientists' Association.

McClintock, A. 1993. Family feuds: Gender, nationalism, and the family. *Feminist Review* (44: Summer).

Metcalf, T. R. 1995. *Ideologies of the Raj*. Cambridge: Cambridge University Press.

Moghadem, V., ed. 1994. *Identity politics and women: Cultural reassertions and feminisms in international perspective*. Boulder, Col.: Westview.

Oberoi, P. 1996. *Social reform, sexuality, and the state*. New Delhi, Sage.

Papanek, Hannah. 1994. Ideal woman and ideal society: Control and autonomy in the construction of identity." In V. Moghadem, ed., *Identity politics and women: Cultural reassertions and feminisms in international perspective*. Boulder, Col.: Westview.

Parpart , J., and K. Staudt. 1989. *Women and the state in Africa*. Boulder, Col: Lynne Rienner.

Pettman, J. J. 1996. *Worlding women: A feminist international politics*. London: Routledge.

Sharma, K., and S. Rai. 2000. Democratising the Indian parliament: The "reservation for women" debate. In S. Rai, ed., *International perspectives on gender and democratisation*. Basingstoke, England: Macmillan.

Smart, Carol. 1991. The woman of legal discourse. *Social Legal Studies* 1(1).

Stacey, J. 1983. *Patriarchy and socialist revolution in China*. Berkeley: University of California Press.

Stolcke, V. 1994. Invaded women: Sex, race, and class in the formation of colonial society. *European Journal of Development Research* 6(2). Special Issue: *Ethnicity, gender, and the subversion of nationalism*.

Talwar, V. B. 1989. Feminist consciousness in women's journals in Hindi: 1910–1920. In K. Sangari and S. Vaid, eds., *Recasting women*. New Delhi: Kali for Women.

Shirin M. Rai

COMEDY

See HUMOR.

COMMODITY CULTURE

A commodity culture is a culture in which people define themselves and make sense of their world primarily through their relationship to manufactured products. The idea that a person is defined by the acquisition of commodities is summed up in the contemporary maxims "I shop, therefore I am," and "You are what you shop." In addition to having a practical use as a material object, a commodity stands for a set of culturally specific meanings and desires. In buying a fashionable article of clothing, for example, a woman buys certain culturally constructed images of sexual attractiveness, modernity, and style. The notion of commodity culture helps explain how gender and sexual identities are formed and transformed in western industrialized societies.

The idea that the commodity acquires a social value through the process of exchange has its origins in the Marxist analysis of capitalism. The concept of commodity culture generally has negative connotations in Marxist and feminist thought. Leftist critics have argued that the rapid growth of commodity culture in the twentieth century co-opted class conflict and contributed to the so-called Americanization of immigrant populations. Feminists have argued that mass marketing techniques have produced stereotypical and demeaning images of women. The mass media, pornography, and prostitution turn women into products—more specifically, into sexualized bodies or body parts—to be used and exchanged by and for the pleasure of men. Women and, some argue, lately even feminism become commodities in a culture that commodifies everything.

The subject of women *as* commodities has attracted more feminist attention than have the implications of women *having* commodities that are imbued with gendered meanings. As the gendered division of retail space in department stores used to indicate, retailers and marketing experts have viewed most goods as unambiguously "male" or "female" in character. Many commodities are still marketed to either women or men. Commodities can thus function conservatively as powerful symbols of ideal femininity, masculinity, and heterosexuality. By reinforcing apparently fundamental differences between the sexes, commodities help maintain the cultural boundaries that mark the feminine as different from, and often inferior to, the masculine.

Each commodity culture lends consumer goods its own specific repertoire of social and sexual meanings. Rather than assuming a monolithic, Anglocentric concept of a commodity culture, then, some researchers have begun to study the diversity and regional specificity of consumer practices and their implications for relations between the sexes. In Japan. for example, clothes (purchased, as they are in most English-speaking cultures, primarily by women) are emblems of status and correctness: hence the uniformlike skirts and white blouses considered appropriate for "office ladies." Packaging is important in a society that stresses aesthetics and "taste." Thus the wrapping attached to each commodity in Japan carries a cultural significance that would be unknown to most western consumers.

John Clammer (Shields, 1992) argues that Japan's urban consumer culture is manifestly postmodern. In contrast to those who hold that consumer culture exploits and oppresses women, students of postmodern culture suggest that a woman's choice of commodities allows her to play with, experiment with, and literally refashion herself. If commodities in a modernist commodity culture rigidly prescribed fixed sexual meanings, in postmodernity the commodity becomes an empty category waiting to be filled, or added to. Shopping is increasingly associated with leisure and entertainment, rather than work. Buying different commodities permits women (and men) to "try on" and change social identities. Fashion, described by Gail Faurschou (1987) as the postmodern commodity par excellence, "becomes a data base of aesthetic categories." Many feminists believe that postmodern commodity cultures offer new opportunities for renegotiating sexual identities previously thought to be essential and unchangeable.

See Also

CAPITALISM; FASHION; MARXISM; POSTMODERNISM: FEMINIST CRITIQUES

References and Further Reading

Farschou, Gail. 1987. Fashion and the cultural logic of postmodernity. In Arthur Kroker and Marilouise Kroker, eds., *Body invaders: Panic sex in America.* New York: St. Martin's.

Irigaray, Luce. 1985. *This sex which is not one.* Trans. Catherine Porter with Carolyn Burke. Ithaca, N.Y.: Cornell University Press.

McCracken, Grant. 1988. *Culture and consumption: New approaches to the symbolic character of consumer goods and activities.* Bloomington: Indiana University Press.

Shields, Rob, ed. 1992. *Lifestyle shopping: The subject of consumption.* London and New York: Routledge.

Strasser, Susan. 1989. *Satisfaction guaranteed: The making of the American mass market.* New York: Pantheon.

Gail Reekie

COMMUNICATIONS: Overview

The term *communications* generally brings to mind attention to the symbolic messages of the human species; the processes involved in creating, sending, and receiving these messages; and the myriad historical, political, economic, cultural, psychological, and sociological contexts in which these processes are embedded.

The rise of communication studies and the rise of women's studies were historically contemporaneous, with calls for both in the 1930s and again in the 1970s. Both have shifted perspective from more essentialist to more interpretive approaches. Where communication studies and women's studies intersect, this change is illustrated by the difference in conceptualizing gender as cause versus effect. When gender is thought of as cause, questions focus, for instance, on how men and women differ in their communication styles, or how they are portrayed differently in the media. When gender is thought of as effect, questions become more interpretively focused on which forces create and maintain gender differences: in essence, how human beings, human artifacts, and human structures become gendered. In the earlier stages, gender is assumed to be a biological distinction; in the latter stages, it is understood as created in communication.

Over time, women's studies has evolved to challenge communications studies to extend its understanding of communication to incorporate women's experience and to see communication as political. At the same time, communication studies has challenged women's studies to go beyond a polarized concept of the political, from feminism to feminisms, from one view to multiple views. Inherent within this movement has been a journey from a liberal concept of gendered communication (how women are treated unfairly) to a radical concept (how women differ inherently) to a socialist concept (how power structures hold inequities in place) to a discourse concept (how gender is created, maintained, and changed in discourse).

This evolution has also led to a call for methodological innovation. One result is a move from reductionist, non-holistic ways of analyzing gendered messages to richer approaches that focus on revealing the subtle ways in which power is embedded in discourse. A second result is a call for interpretive studies of audiences, which open up studies of communication to voices other than those of privileged researchers.

Because communication studies is an emergent focus that cuts across disciplines, one finds emphasis on gendered communication in a bewildering number of locales that indicate differing degrees and qualities of attention. As one example, women's studies has had a longer influence on media studies than on interpersonal communication studies, so, whereas media studies advanced beyond sex-role differences in the early 1980s, interpersonal communication began to do so only in the 1990s. Likewise, branches of communication studies arising from social scientific traditions have been slower to attend to gendered discourse than branches arising from humanities traditions.

In general, there are three major thrusts or focuses in studies of gendered communication. One focus is on the nature of the structures within which messages are created, including the study of the political, economic, and other forces that affect the creators of messages. The second focus is on the nature of texts and involves analyses of representations of gendered discourse in, for example, popular culture or defined communities. The third focus is on audiences and their reception of gendered messages, or the way they make sense of those messages.

In the mid-1990s, these once-distinct divisions blurred as feminist studies of communication begin to address two issues. One was how to conceptualize the relationship between structures (which contain and reinforce gendered practices) and human actors (who maintain these structures and also resist and transform them). The second issue was how to study gendered communication so that neither an entirely structuralist view nor an entirely individualistic view would be privileged. The former perspective is identified more frequently with socialist and critical perspectives; the latter more frequently with liberal and postmodern perspectives. By the end of the 1990s, what began to emerge strongly was a call for a synergy or, at least, a communion between these usually polarized perspectives.

See Also

COMMUNICATIONS, *all entries;* MEDIA: OVERVIEW

References and Further Reading

Carter, Kathryn, and Carole Spitzack, eds. 1989. *Doing research on women's communication.* Norwood, N.J.: Ablex.

Dervin, Brenda. 1987. The potential contribution of feminist scholarship to the field of communication. *Journal of Communication* 37(4): 107–120.

Lont, Cynthia, ed. 1995. *Women and media: Content/career s/criticism.* New York: Wadsworth.

Pearson, J., L. Turner, and W. Todd-Mancillas. 1991. *Gender and communication,* 2nd ed. Dubuque, Iowa: Brown.

Steeves, Leslie H. 1987. Feminist theories and media studies. *Critical Studies in Mass Communication* 4(2): 95–135.

Shields, Vickie R., and Brenda Dervin. 1993. Sense-making in feminist social science research: A call to enlarge the methodological options of feminist studies. *Women's Studies International Forum* 16(1):65–81.

Valdivia, Angharad N., ed. 1995. *Feminism, multiculturalism, and the media: Global diversities.* Thousand Oaks, Calif.: Sage.

Van, Zoonen, L. 1994. *Feminist media studies.* London: Sage.

Brenda Dervin

COMMUNICATIONS: Audience Analysis

Why study the audiences for mass media and popular culture? From a feminist perspective, there are many potential reasons. Products of mass media and popular culture permeate our cultural experience in complex societies and, increasingly, in all areas of the globe. Because, in a sense, we are all members of the audience all the time, in the postmodern world audience study has been transformed into a more general analysis of how we receive culture in everyday life, in addition to the more specific study of actual audiences constituted to receive particular products of popular culture.

This situation raises interesting questions for feminists concerned with cultural and media studies. If we come of age in a cultural climate awash with the products of popular culture, then popular culture is an extremely important influence on the development of our gender identities and orientations. Yet, if it is true that popular culture is as ubiquitous in the postmodern world as most scholars believe, it is difficult to study its influence using traditional scientific methods, which require the ability to manipulate variables and to control for their respective influences. In fact, many feminist scholars now argue that these traditional approaches to audience analysis, predicated on the assumption that the influence of popular culture can be controlled, have underestimated the actual influence of popular culture on women and others.

As a result of their dissatisfaction with traditional approaches, feminists have investigated nontraditional methods of studying the influence of popular culture and media on the women in their audience. Approaches they have pursued include combining different types of traditional methodologies (for example, mixing qualitative and quantitative methods) as well as developing more in-depth, interpretive approaches to studying media as part of the general cultural environment.

Feminist study of the audience for popular culture has grown over the last several decades. It now constitutes a sizable body of work with its own history, subfields, criticism, and problems. In addition, whereas traditionally the focus of audience study has been on the particular media of film and television, recent studies have broadened this narrow concentration to include consideration of popular music and audiences' reception of and participation in other popular forms such as romance novels. Finally, recent theoretical perspectives in the field have emphasized the diversity and fragmentation of the female audience for popular culture and have produced studies of the receptive experiences and activities of racially, ethnically, socioeconomically, and sexually diverse groups within this general category.

Film and Television Study

Although most film scholars have come out of humanities traditions in universities and have studied film as art, television scholarship has been rooted primarily in the social sciences and has been governed by quite different traditions.

Film study: As has been true of much literary criticism of the past several decades, and in keeping with its base in the humanities disciplines, film audience theory has utilized psychoanalytic theory to describe modes of reception. Scholars studying film reception have generally "theorized" about "the spectator" rather than applying social scientific methods to the empirical study of actual film viewers. The tradition can be traced to the early work of scholars like Christian Metz (1982), who argued that psychoanalytic theory was necessary to understand the "dreamlike" state to which the film audience regressed in the darkened movie theater. Problems inherent in this body of work stem from a lack of historical and cultural context in most psychoanalytic writing, generally. The psychoanalytic literature often falsely universalizes a white, middle-class, heterosexual nuclear family, ignoring the experience of members of racial, ethnic, and sexual minority groups. In contrast to the abstract theorizing popular in film literature, the television audience has been primarily studied by social scientists who use survey methods, interviews, or other research methods to gather data about actual audience members, their thoughts, and their habits.

Gender and the film spectator: The dominant narratives of the classic Hollywood film often deemphasize women's subjectivity or activity, emphasizing instead the woman as a passive object, decorated with the finery of consumer society. Many theorists have discussed the prevalence of men as the central agents in most mainstream popular films, with women serving as the decorative objects of their actions or desires (Kaplan, 1983; Mulvey, 1975; Silverman, 1983). These scholars note that women are "looked at" in films—as the object of the male gaze—more than they actively look at others. Feminist film scholars have hypothesized that these conventions encourage women to view themselves as passive objects rather than active agents taking charge of their own lives.

Feminist scholars have developed some rather complicated theories in their attempt to explain the pleasure that many women (often including themselves) derive from watching dominant Hollywood cinema. Most prominent among these is Laura Mulvey's famous essay, "Visual Pleasure in Narrative Cinema" (1975). Using psychoanalytic theory to develop her ideas about how spectators derive pleasure from films generally, Mulvey theorizes that women watching Hollywood films actually identify with the male spectator to whom most films are addressed. Taking the part of men, then, in their viewing, women get the same pleasure that men do when they watch other women in the film who are framed as beautiful objects to be looked at.

Other feminist scholars have challenged Mulvey's theories. Arbuthnot and Seneca (1982), for example, use the example of a popular Hollywood musical of the 1950s, *Gentlemen Prefer Blondes,* to counter Mulvey's argument. In this film, Jane Russell and Marilyn Monroe, the stars, were often shown actively looking at men or "returning the gaze" of the men looking at them. Many feminist theorists have argued that film noir, which features extremely sexual images of women, also can be read as showcasing women's strength, rather than their objectlike status (Kaplan, 1998).

Current feminist work on film often questions the supposed lack of women in many aspects of film production (Kaplan, 1983). These authors discuss innovative films made by feminist producers, writers, and directors, which often challenge the dominant conventions of Hollywood narrative films and posit a different type of female audience member. Some films, such as Laura Mulvey and Peter Wollen's *Riddles of the Sphinx* (1976), or Michelle Citron's *Daughter-Rite* (1978), challenge the conventions of narrative itself, moving nonlinearly so that no story is told in the traditional sense. Others, such as Chantal Akerman's *Jeanne Dielman* (1975), challenge the dominant notion of time in the Hollywood film by creating a filmic time that mirrors actual time. This film follows several slow-moving

hours in the domestic life of a woman, following her through the movements of her day. Rather than, in Hollywood style, glamorizing the domestic arena and women's role within it, Ranier highlights the work involved in domestic life, showing it as very repetitive, tedious, and dull. This sort of reality is rarely presented in the dominant cinema we view most often. Audience theorists hypothesize that such films disrupt, in a critical manner, conventional female subjectivity for the women who watch them; they therefore are considered to have critical potential for feminists.

Current films made by women—and current critical feminist film theorists such as Bobo (1995)—often challenge the lack of racial, class, ethnic, and sexual diversity that characterizes both classical Hollywood cinema and much other contemporary cinema. These films, and the new film theories as well, often focus on the experiences of nonwhite women, working-class women, or women living in nonwestern cultures, or they have central characters who are lesbian or bisexual. In these ways, both feminist filmmakers and feminist theorists are changing many of the conventions of traditional film and creating new patterns and models. Feminists theorize that the ultimate impact of these images on audiences will be to challenge the hegemony of white, upper-class individuals in our society.

Gender and the television audience: Because television study is rooted in the social sciences, a plethora of social scientific methodologies have been applied to the study of the television audience, and in particular, to gender differences in that audience; these include traditional social scientific methodologies such as survey research, as well as "softer," more qualitative techniques such as in-depth interviewing or ethnographic investigations. The study of the television audience is no exception. There have been several interesting qualitative studies of the television audience in recent years using in-depth interviewing or ethnographic techniques. One such study, *Family Television* by David Morley (1986), employed a vast team of researchers who used ethnographic and interviewing techniques to investigate the way television is received in the context of the family. Studying a group of primarily working-class families in London, researchers found strong gender dynamics in families watching together during prime-time viewing hours. Men, it was discovered, often hold the remote control for the television and determine the fare of the family's collective viewing. Specifically "women's genres" of television such as melodramas, soap operas, or romantic shows or movies, are more likely to be viewed by women alone at times when men and other family members who devalue such shows are not present.

Other investigators (Ang, 1985; Hobson, 1982) have examined how women view particularly female genres such as soap operas, and what meanings they make of them. Hobson's study involved participant observation and depth-interviewing with British working-class women fans of a very popular nighttime soap opera called *Crossroads*. She discussed the intricate ways in which women weave their reception of soap operas around their domestic labor and their relationships with family and friends in their homes. *Crossroads,* Hobson found, played an important role in the lives of lonely—and emotionally isolated—female viewers. Women were able to develop relationships with the soap opera characters, which were vibrant and real for them. Ang (1985) discusses the importance of soap opera characters and relationships, in terms of the emotional lives of women fans of the show *Dallas*. Ang hypothesizes that *Dallas,* stereotypical as its female characters are in some ways, offers women valuable forms of pleasure and escape, which may encourage their feminist imaginations in important ways rather than merely contributing to their oppression in patriarchal society. Such works opened up the possibility that soap opera, so often disparaged as "low-level" entertainment and assumed by even feminist scholars to be degrading to women, is in fact worthy of serious attention by feminist scholars because of its widespread consumption and the obvious pleasure it affords its many women viewers.

Some scholars have focused on women's reactions to prime-time television entertainment (Press, 1991, 1992; Press and Cole, 1999). In particular, their work has explored differences in reactions among women of different social classes and generations. *Women Watching Television: Gender, Class, and Generation in the American Television Experience* is based on the present author's open-ended in-depth interviews with a sample of working-class and middle-class women of different social classes and age groups (Press, 1991). Essentially, I asked women to "tell me about television" and the meaning it had in their lives. Using their responses as data, I theorized about the fundamentally different ways in which television influences working-class and middle-class women, and women of different generations, in our society. Working-class women are more likely to notice aspects of television related to social class while middle-class women are more likely to notice gender-related content. Working-class women tend to construct from television a vision of middle-class life as "normal." This causes them to see their own lives, very different from that reality, as evolving toward it, and to discount the aspects of their own lives which indicate that

they live very differently from this "norm." For middle-class women, the class-related aspects of television are less important. Instead, they are more likely to discuss the relationships between men and women, and within the family, which they view on television, and to use television as a way to explore alternative relationships or possible solutions to relationship problems that they themselves may be experiencing.

Women's Genres and Female Readers

Many feminist audience scholars have focused exclusively on what are traditionally thought of as "female genres," a category applied to the analysis of many different media including books, television, and films. So-called female genres—romance novels, television soap operas, cinematic melodramas—are thought to appeal specifically to women, and, as in each of these examples, are consumed by many more women than men (although of course there are some male consumers in each case).

Perhaps the most famous reception study which focuses on a female genre is Janice Radway's *Reading the Romance* (1984). In her study, Radway used several methods including questionnaires, individual and group interviews, and ethnographic participant-observation to study a small group of white, middle-class midwestern women in the United States who were avid readers of romance novels. In 1984, Radway's book was revolutionary in its methodology and its claims, when considered in the context of the feminist literature about romances current at the time. With the new approach of audience analysis—for example, actually using as data women readers' own explanations of their fondness for romance novels—Radway theorized that romances in several ways were symbols and tools of resistance to patriarchy, rather than a means by which women were enslaved by a patriarchal system. Women liked, and sought, the most independent heroines romances had to offer, for example, and were more likely to dislike romantic heroines who were too docile or spiritless. They disliked scenes in which heroines showed no spunk or resistance against senseless brutality or violence. They enjoyed the happy endings of romances, which helped them interpret their lives and prospects positively, even in the face of adversity. In addition, and perhaps most important, these readers, who were most often married and consumed with the very demanding tasks of being wives, homemakers, and mothers, used the *act* of reading as a means of carving out time for themselves in the midst of the numerous and competing demands of their families. Reading romances was often the only time these women had for themselves. The very act of becoming a regular romance reader was a sort of rebellion against their families, and the minimum care they themselves received within the family. As caretakers to all, these women suffered from the lack of a caretaker of their own; time for reading was, in a sense, a substitute. If no one was assigned to take care of these women, they could make sure they took the time to care for themselves by asserting the importance of their reading habit. In these ways, Radway challenged prevailing feminist criticism of the romance genre, and developed a new theory that gave more credit to its female audience. Women, rather than being negatively influenced by romances, instead used them creatively to resist the oppressive features of patriarchal culture.

Popular Music

One of the most interesting new areas of study in the field of the female audience for popular culture is the audience for popular music. With regard to popular music, and the music videos that have become its accompaniment, feminist scholars have engaged in some of the most interesting debates in the field, involving issues both of general reception of music and of fan groups and their specific modes of reception.

One of the most controversial phenomena in this area has been the study of the image of pop star Madonna. Fiske (1987) and Schwichtenberg (1992) use both textual research and some audience research to argue that Madonna is a liberatory image for women, challenging many stereotypes (such as those of the demure, "pure," virginal woman) with her blatant displays of female sexuality and desire in her live performances, her films, and her music videos. Quoting young teenage fans, Fiske argues that for them, Madonna symbolizes individuality, independence, and freedom and is an image that explicitly challenges many of the more traditional teachings still predominating in our gender culture (1987: 125–126). Whereas more traditional feminist analysis might say that Madonna's early image is sexist, in that it flaunts what is in some ways the very traditional garb of female sexuality—heavy makeup, lacy undergarments, a vampy look overall—Fisk's theory highlights the irony in Madonna's presentation of these features. She is using them, he intimates, to critique, or at least to expose, traditional assumptions about female sexual behavior. She is "playing" with these assumptions and, through her play, opens the possibility of criticizing them and ultimately subverting them. In Fiske's analysis, Madonna's image is extremely feminist. The many contributors to Schwichtenberg's edited volume *The Madonna Connection* (1992) make a series of sophisticated arguments about what Madonna signifies for girls, feminism, and feminist politics in particular. Schwichtenberg herself offers an interesting analysis of Madonna's play on the concept of "femininity" in the different incarnations her image has taken, referring to Baudrillard's notion of simulation to explain, in postmodern terms, what Madonna's image signifies (1992: 132–133).

In general, feminist discussion of popular music has been critical of the field for excluding women from many of its dimensions. Other than as singers, few women musicians really "make it" in the world of music. As is the case in many other professions feminist scholars study, the reasons for this are complex and very difficult to isolate; clearly, it is a problem that requires further study. The impact of this fact is unfortunate, though scholars disagree as to what the particular impact is in the case of popular music. Lewis's interesting studies of female musicians and fans (1990, 1992) chronicle the careers of some of the few top female rock stars, their music, their video products, and their fans, from a feminist perspective.

Other feminists discuss their ambivalence about female fans of rock and roll stars. Wise (1990) offers an interesting argument based on her own experience growing up as a fan of Elvis Presley. It has been assumed, Wise argues, that rock stars such as Elvis are sex symbols for female fans, either strong, macho figures or cuddly teddy-bear types. This interpretation of the popularity of male rock stars serves male interests, Wise argues. It assumes that female fans are merely "responding" to manipulation and control by the strong figure of the star. Instead, she argues that the star figure himself is the object of the fans, and that the way to find out the true meaning of rock stars for female fans would be to ask the fans themselves, something that has rarely been done, and has never been done in the case of Elvis Presley. Wise argues that in her own case, she knows that Elvis functioned more as a friend than a sex symbol during a lonely, stormy adolescence in which she felt essentially friendless and alienated. (Later, she found out that her emerging lesbian sexuality, still concealed at the time, was one cause of this loneliness.) She hypothesizes that for other fans he may have functioned similarly.

Current work in the field is beginning to investigate the meaning of "fandom" from the female point of view. Petrusso (1992), for example, interviewed and observed a group of female fans of what is normally considered an exclusively male genre, heavy metal music. Whereas it is normally assumed that women participating in heavy metal culture are there only to be sexual groupies of the male stars, Petrusso found that many women were interested in the music, which they found meaningful in itself. These women considered the "groupie" stereotype of women fans extremely demeaning, and not at all representative of their own relationship to popular music culture.

Other feminist scholars challenge specific genres of popular music for blatant and, they fear, harmful sexism (Peterson-Lewis, 1991). But Rose (1994) argues that, although there is some misogyny in rap music lyrics, there also are discernibly feminist songs. Emphasizing the music of female rappers, she shows how many female rap artists take the opportunity to address issues of interest to women in the African-American community—sometimes explicitly addressing male rappers about their potentially misogynist and exploitive lyrics. Rose's argument raises interesting questions for audience analysis.

Conclusion

Much work has been done in analyzing the female audience for different types of popular culture. Many studies employ qualitative, interpretive methodologies that are sensitive to the difficulties involved in assessing actual "effects" of media and culture on individual and group beliefs, values, and actions. In addition, variations in the experiences of different groups within the female audience, especially those differentiated by race, class, and sexual orientation, have been discussed. Newer studies often seek to combine qualitative and quantitative data, thus presenting as complete a picture as current social science analysis will allow. Some, particularly those influenced by postmodernist analyses that question the unity and value of the notion of the subject, consider the future of audience analyses. For these scholars, the very term "audience" is laden with indefensible assumptions about characteristics that popular culture itself maps onto its alleged recipients. Until those espousing such perspectives re-create a social science capable of studying the true audience more effectively than can be done with the methods currently in use, however, audience analysis will continue to be a vital part of feminist cultural and media studies.

See Also

COMMUNICATIONS: OVERVIEW; CULTURE: WOMEN AS CONSUMERS OF CULTURE; MUSIC: ROCK AND POP; POPULAR CULTURE; SOAP OPERAS; TELEVISION

References and Further Reading

Ang, Ien. 1985. *Watching* Dallas: *Soap operas and the melodramatic imagination.* London: Methuen.

Arbuthnot, Lucie, and Gail Seneca. 1982. Pre-text and text in *Gentlemen Prefer Blondes. Film Reader* 5:13–23.

Bobo, Jacqueline. 1995. *Black women as cultural readers.* New York: Columbia University Press.

Fiske, John. 1987. *Television culture.* New York: Methuen.

Hobson, Dorothy. 1982. Crossroads: *The drama of a soap opera.* London: Methuen.

Kaplan, E. Ann. 1983. *Women and film: Both sides of the camera.* New York: Methuen.

———, ed. 1998. *Women in film noir.* London: British Film Institute.

Lewis, Lisa A. 1990. *Gender politics and MTV: Voicing the difference.* Philadelphia: Temple University Press.

———. 1992. *The adorning audience: Fan culture and popular media.* London: Routledge.

Metz, Christian. 1982. *The imaginary signifier: Psychoanalysis and the cinema.* Bloomington: Indiana University Press.

Morley, David. 1986. *Family television.* London: Comedia.

Mulvey, Laura. 1975. Visual pleasure and narrative cinema. *Screen* 16(3: Autumn): 6–18.

Peterson-Lewis, Sonja. 1991. A feminist analysis of the defenses of obscene rap lyrics. *Black sacred music: A journal of theomusicology* 5 (1: Spring): 68–79.

Petrusso, Annette. 1992. *Women fans of heavy metal.* Ann Arbor: Unpublished honors' thesis, Residential College, University of Michigan.

Press, Andrea L., and Elizabeth R. Cole. 1994. Women like us: Working-class women respond to television representations of abortion. In Jon Cruz, Sut Jhally, and Cathy Schwichtenberg, eds., *Reading, Viewing, Listening: Audiences and Cultural Reception.* Boulder, Col.: Westview Press.

———, and Terry Strathman. 1993. Work, family, and social class in television images of women: Prime-time television and the construction of postfeminism. *Women and Language* 16(2): 7–15.

Radway, Janice. 1984. *Reading the romance: Women, patriarchy, and popular literature.* Chapel Hill: University of North Carolina Press.

Rose, Tricia. 1994. *Black noise: Rap music and black culture in contemporary America.* Hanover and London: Wesleyan University Press.

Schwichtenberg, Cathy, ed. 1992. *The Madonna connection: Representational politics, subcultural identities, and cultural theory.* Boulder, Col.: Westview.

Silverman, Kaja. 1983. *The subject of semiotics.* New York: Oxford University Press.

Wise, Sue. 1990. Sexing Elvis. In Simon Frith and Andrew Goodwin, eds., *On record,* 390–409. New York: Pantheon.

Andrea Press

COMMUNICATIONS:
Content and Discourse Analysis

Content and discourse analysis are two distinct analytical methods used in the study of communication. Both can be applied to various types of communication, including interpersonal exchange, mass media such as television drama and newspaper editorials, and political discourse. Both analytical methods may be used to examine linguistic elements or more generalized themes and issues. Both have been used extensively to document bias related to race, class, gender, nationality, sexual identity, and so forth. Beyond these similarities, the two methodologies should be considered distinct and will be treated as such here. The primary use of these methods has been in the analysis of mass communications.

Content Analysis

Content analysis uses a quantitative approach to identify, categorize, and describe themes, issues, or subjects in order to record bias or differences in representation, reveal or examine trends in a particular medium, or make a comparison between different media. The aim of content analysis is to assess the degree of importance or attention given to the elements under examination. Feminist scholars and others interested in relations of power have made use of content analysis that calculates the prevalence and types of imagery in representations of women and minorities. The edited volume *Hearth and Home: Images of Women in the Mass Media* (Tuchman et al., 1978), which documents the dearth of representations of women in mass media in the United States, is an excellent and well-known early example.

Although content analysis has frequently been used by scholars interested in relations of power and has been useful in documenting both lack of representation and various negative portrayals of minorities and women in the mass media, it has also come under criticism by feminists and others for its lack of a theoretical and explanatory framework. Although high-quality content-analytical work can overcome such objections, the tendency has often been comparative counting of representations of racial groups, for example, without an accompanying discussion of significance, interpretation, or purpose. For example, simply determining that few women characters portrayed are in positions of power in prime-time television programming does not explain: (1) why it is important to count their representation; (2) why the inclusion of such characters might be rare; (3) what course, if any,

should be followed to correct this gap in representation; (4) whether any such correction would be accompanied by change beyond the world of televised representation; or (5) what is the significance or meaning of this observed fact. In addition, content analyses tend to assume an objective reality against which representations can and should be measured. Content-analytical work that does not address these questions is of limited usefulness for obvious reasons: although it may record a fact about representation, it is not sufficiently connected to a rationale or goal for change and cannot explain its findings. Content analysis is defended on the grounds that it reveals something about the values and attitudes of mass media producers and audiences.

Discourse Analysis

Discourse analysis is a qualitative method that aims at revealing the ways in which communication legitimizes or maintains ideology. This work offers a means for understanding how language, particularly patterns and habits of usage, reflects and reproduces biased patterns of thought, decision making, and distribution of power. Discourse analysis examines the language used within a given text or interaction: it assumes that relations of power are embedded in language and attempts to deconstruct the ways in which this occurs. Individual analyses of discourse might take a variety of approaches to identifying patterns of articulation and absence, including the observation of dominant metaphors and analogies, the recognition of cultural myths and stereotypes, the examination of available frames of meaning, or simply an analysis of central terms or clusters of key terms within a text. Such work is designed to reveal values, perspectives, and interests which are not explicitly stated in the text but which convey subtle ideological messages such as who or what is dangerous or threatening. Discourse analysis is used by feminists to reveal the subtle ways in which communication transmits familiar ideas about gender, such as the idea that women are emotional and men are rational.

Discourse analysis is based on the assumption that a sense of reality is constructed through the use of language and is often interested in revealing how racism, sexism, class differences, and other inequalities are subtly furthered. Thus, discourse analysis can be used to reveal gender or racial bias within a language or within a particular usage pattern or text, such as the observation that women and girls are often in a grammatically "passive" position while males are grammatically "active," or the finding that mainstream news makes use of traditional ideas about rape to structure its coverage of sexual assault. In its emphasis on the deconstruction of ideolog-

201

ical power within texts, this work can sometimes make use of highly abstract scholarly jargon that is difficult even for readers with graduate-level education. As such, it has been accused of being detached from or unrelated to practical issues of social change. Discourse analysts claim that only limited social change can take place without accompanying change at the level of language and language use, and thus assert that their work is a sort of praxis aimed at the transformation of elements of social life such as what a group accepts as reality, truth, normality, and knowledge.

For current essays employing discourse analysis, consult the journal *Discourse and Society,* edited by Teun A. van Dijk and published by Sage.

See Also

COMMUNICATIONS: AUDIENCE ANALYSIS; COMMUNICATIONS: SPEECH; LINGUISTICS; MEDIA: OVERVIEW

References and Further Reading

Bell, Allan, and Peter Garrett, eds. 1998. *Approaches to media discourse.* Oxford: Blackwell.

Berelson, Bernard. 1952. *Content analysis in communications research.* New York: Free Press.

Foucault, Michel. 1972. *The archaeology of knowledge and the discourse on language.* New York: Pantheon.

Greenberg, Bradley S. 1980. *Life on television: Content analysis of US TV drama.* Norwood, N.J.: Ablex.

Holsti, O. R. 1969. *Content analysis for the social sciences and humanities.* Reading, Mass.: Addison-Wesley.

Lentz, Leo, and Henk Pander Maat, eds. 1997. *Discourse analysis and evaluation: Functional approaches.* Amsterdam: Rodopi.

Thomas, Sari. 1994. Artifactual study in the analysis of culture: A defense of content analysis in a postmodern age. *Communication Research* 21 (6 December): 683–697.

Tuchman, Gaye, Arlene Kaplan Daniels, and James Benet, eds. 1978. *Hearth and home: Images of women in the mass media.* New York: Oxford University Press.

van Dijk, Teun. 1985. *Handbook of discourse analysis.* Vols. 1–4. New York: Academic.

———. 1988. *News as discourse.* Hillsdale, N.J.: Erlbaum.

Lisa Cuklanz

COMMUNICATIONS: Speech

The study of speech communications includes the analysis of verbal and nonverbal interaction at interpersonal, small-group, and organizational levels. This article distinguishes speech communications from public communications, such as speeches presented to large groups in openly accessible settings, and mass communications, such as broadcast or print media messages reaching huge audiences. *Interpersonal communication* refers to dyadic (two-person) interaction; *small-group communication* designates interactions among a cluster of usually 10 or fewer individuals; and *organizational communication* signifies interpersonal and small-group interactions within formally structured environments focused on task-oriented goals.

Speech communications research has historically been dominated by studies of white, English-speaking, heterosexual, middle-class, able-bodied individuals living in the United States (where communication programs are well established). As a result, the experiences of people of color, non-English-speaking, homosexual or bisexual, low-income, and disabled persons in the United States and around the world have generally been excluded from mainstream research. The studies reviewed in this article should be evaluated in light of these limitations.

Interpersonal and Small-Group Communication: Gender, Competence, Power, and Context

Since the mid-1970s, feminist research in speech communications has often focused on the controversial relationship of sex and gender to interpersonal communication. Scholars studying female-male verbal communication have contended that women generally communicate in a more expressive and empathic manner than men, developing topics at length and utilizing questions and verbal minimal responses (such as "uh-huh") to maintain conversation (see Henley and Kramarae, 1994: 388–389). Research on nonverbal communication has suggested that women use vocal and facial displays to communicate emotion more often than men and employ body movements and gestures to signify positive affect. Further, women utilize touch and seek greater physical contact than men, assuming less personal space and tolerating greater spatial intrusion (see Burgoon, 1994: 247). Numerous studies have documented observed differences in female and male speech communication, but debate arises among feminist scholars about whether this diversity results from biology or gender enculturation or is an effect of women's oppression in patriarchal societies (Henley and Kramarae, 1994).

Related to studies of gendered conversational dynamics and power are analyses of impression formation and communicative competence. Analyzing responses from 94 participants in the United States, Scott (1980) found that stereotypically feminine communication traits, such as "gentle" or "smooth" speech, were consistently rated as more socially desirable than stereotypically masculine traits, such as "forceful" or "direct" speech. Moreover, respondents in Scott's study described the sex-generic "adult competent communicator" in terms of traditionally feminized behaviors. Yet, despite these positive evaluations, Scott cautioned that socially desirable or competent communication may not imply effective communication for women lacking relational power in a given context.

Similar to interpersonal communication research, feminist marital and family communication studies have primarily emphasized sex or gender differences and power differentials that affect communicative patterns. Empirical research on marital and family communication in the United States has most often focused on the dyadic or interpersonal level, concentrating on middle-class heterosexual courtship, spousal, and parent-child interactions. Feminist researchers studying dominance and control in marital interactions have argued that women utilize questions and minimal responses to facilitate communication, while men use silence to control length, pace, and topic. Additionally, research has suggested that power in decision making is frequently under dispute for Caucasian and African-American couples, with final authority often resting on a husband's occupational prestige, income, and education (see Kramarae, 1981).

Research further indicates that gender and power relations that characterize spousal communication are replicated in parent-child interaction. In a study of preschool children, Esther Blank Greif (1980) found that fathers were more likely than mothers to interrupt and speak simultaneously with children. However, both parents were more likely to interrupt or interfere with daughters' speech than sons' speech. Greif's research suggested that women learn stereotypically feminine, passive communication roles in childhood, as girls' speech is often hindered.

Although feminist speech communication research has often considered gender the dominant influence on women's communicative behavior, multicultural studies of women's speech communities have demonstrated that gender is one of many social and cultural factors that affect communication. Feminist scholars investigating women's speech communities have examined the way female social roles and activities and gender relations in specific sociocultural contexts shape communication patterns. Penelope Brown's study (1994) of women speakers in a community of peasant Mayan Indians in Tenejapa, Mexico, illustrated the importance of context for understanding the dynamic meanings of gendered speech. Comparing women's use of the Tzeltal language in "amicable, cooperative, 'ordinary'" interactions and "angry" courtroom confrontations, Brown found that the function of politeness, which is characteristic of Tenejapan women's speech across contexts, varies widely. While women's use of polite forms signifies affect, empathy, and cooperation in "ordinary" conversation, women's display of polite speech behaviors in court communicates opposite meanings, including discontent, hostility, and disagreement. Brown's study stressed that no universal conclusions should be drawn concerning the positive or negative affect conveyed by communication, because speech behaviors may denote vastly different meanings in different contexts.

Organizational and Task-Oriented Communication: Gender, Leadership, Health, and Group Behavior

Feminist research in organizational communication has frequently examined the influence of gender on managerial behavior. Recurring topics of inquiry in superior-subordinate communication research are managerial efforts to obtain compliance and conflict management. Although research has documented many similarities in the tactics utilized by female and male managers to shape employees' behavior, a number of differences have also been uncovered. In a meta-analysis of research on gender and managerial influence, Kathleen J. Krone et al. (1994) found that female and male managers display similar preferences for rational persuasion and altruism in employee relations but tend to differ in the use of rewards and coercive strategies. Because observed differences in managerial influence tactics do not always correspond to gender-role stereotypes, Krone et al. concluded that managerial behavior results from a combination of gender and organizational socialization. These researchers also concluded that managers' use of influence strategies emerges from a complex interrelationship between gender, situational confidence, structural position, and self-perception of power in the organization.

In contrast to managerial influence research, which cites gender as one of many factors shaping communication, meta-analyses of sex differences in conflict management see gender as a key element in decision making. Aggregating results from several studies, Barbara Mae Gayle et al. (1994) concluded that males are 27 percent more likely than females to employ competitive or aggressive conflict resolution tactics, while, conversely, females are 27 percent more likely than males to use compromising, relationally driven strategies. Noting stability in managers' use of conflict management strategies across contexts, the researchers concluded that compromising and competitive tactics are "intrinsically tied to gender roles rather than processes that emerge over the length of the conflict interaction" (19). How and why female and male managers sometimes deviate from gender-related patterns of conflict management remains at issue.

A key context for the study of superior-subordinate communication has been health care. Scholars examining interpersonal health communication have focused primarily on practitioner-client relationships, analyzing such issues as power relations in medical interactions, effective communication by providers, clients' satisfaction, and compliance with care. Many feminist studies of physician-client communication have focused on obstetric/gynecologic (OB/GYN) interactions. After two and a half years of observations of gynecologist-client interactions in private offices and community clinics, Alexandra Dundas Todd (1989) concluded that gynecologists consistently initiate, direct, and close conversation with clients, dominating questioning, selecting topics, and monopolizing the distribution of talk. Because 80 percent of gynecologist-client interactions in the United States involve female-male communication, physicians in the OB/GYN context may assert communicative power as medical experts and as men (Todd, 1989). Further impeding communication between gynecologists and clients are a range of sociocultural influences, including race, ethnicity, language barriers, sexual identity, stereotypes, and beliefs about the body and illness. For example, the gynecological disorders of women of color have often been misdiagnosed and falsely attributed to sexual promiscuity on the basis of prejudicial stereotypes. Effective gynecologist-client communication hinges on both parties' competent negotiation of contextual variables.

Along with superior-subordinate contexts, feminist researchers studying organizational communication have also investigated women's communicative roles in work groups. Analyzing mixed-sex groups, researchers have found that men generally tend to be assigned overall leadership roles, while women are relegated to socioemotional leadership roles on the basis of gender-related expectations about communication. However, as task complexity and group longevity increase, studies suggest that men are proportionately less likely to assume general leadership positions. The gender composition of groups also plays a key role in shaping communication patterns, as men speak more often with longer utterances and women speak more tentatively (using disclaimers and hedges) in mixed-sex groups. Furthermore, both males and females have been found to enact stereotypically gendered communication behaviors more frequently in same-sex groups (see Berger, 1994, for a full review). In sum, work group research reinforces gender as an important but inconsistent influence on communication, because group or task characteristics may lead individuals to transcend traditional gender roles.

Future Directions in Feminist Studies of Speech Communications

"Gender difference" theories of speech communications, which have been the basis of many feminist analyses, have come under scrutiny in recent years for evaluating female speech against a masculine norm. The concept of gender difference has been further criticized for its inability to account for the complexity of women's speech. Encouraging greater attention to the social and cultural context of speech communications, many feminist researchers are calling for the consideration of multiple and sometimes competing influences (such as gender, race, class, and sexual identity) on communicative behaviors. The construction of gender as a stable, unproblematic category is also increasingly questioned in feminist research. Regarding gender as a fluid construct, many feminist researchers are investigating the ways in which the communication patterns of both sexes are shaped by power structures that foster particular forms of gendered (feminized or masculinized) communication in specific cultural contexts and historical moments (Henley and Kramarae, 1994). Contemporary feminist studies of speech communications analyze gender as part of an interrelated matrix of factors that constitute the social field of communication.

See Also

COMMUNICATIONS: OVERVIEW; COMMUNICATIONS: AUDIENCE ANALYSIS; COMMUNICATIONS: CONTENT AND DISCOURSE ANALYSIS; CONVERSATION

References and Further Reading

Berger, Charles R. 1994. Power, dominance, and social interaction. In Mark L. Knapp and Gerald R. Miller, eds., *Handbook of interpersonal communication*, 2nd ed., 450–507. Thousand Oaks, Calif.: Sage.

Brown, Penelope. 1994. Gender, politeness, and confrontation in Tenejapa. In Camille Roman, Suzanne Juhasz, and Cristanne Miller, eds., *The women and language debate*, 322–339. New Brunswick, N.J.: Rutgers University Press.

Burgoon, Judee K. 1994. Nonverbal signals. In Mark L. Knapp and Gerald R. Miller, eds. *Handbook of interpersonal communication*, 2nd ed., 229–285. Thousand Oaks, Calif.: Sage.

Gayle, Barbara Mae, Raymond W. Preiss, and Mike Allen. 1994. Gender differences and the use of conflict strategies. In Lynn H. Turner and Helen M. Sterk, eds., *Differences that make a difference*, 13–26. Westport, Conn.: Bergin and Garvey.

Greif, Esther Blank. 1980. Sex differences in parent-child conversation. *Women's Studies International Quarterly* 3(2/3): 253–258.

Henley, Nancy M., and Cheris Kramarae. 1994. Gender, power, and miscommunication. In Camille Roman, Suzanne Juhasz, and Cristanne Miller, eds. *The women and language debate*, 383–406. New Brunswick, N.J.: Rutgers University Press.

Kramarae, Cheris. 1981. *Women and men speaking.* Rowley, Mass.: Newbury House.

Krone, Kathleen J., Mike Allen, and John Ludlum. 1994. A meta-analysis of gender research in managerial influence. In Lynn H. Turner and Helen M. Sterk, eds. *Differences that make a difference*, 73–84. Westport, Conn.: Bergin and Garvey.

Scott, Kathryn P. 1980. Perceptions of communication competence: What's good for the goose is not good for the gander. In Cheris Kramarae, ed., *The voices and words of women and men*, 199–208. Oxford: Pergamon.

Todd, Alexandra Dundas. 1989. *Intimate adversaries.* Philadelphia: University of Pennsylvania Press.

Lisa Sanmiguel

COMMUNISM

Marxist socialists analyzed gender relations from a materialist perspective best articulated by Engels in his book *Family, Private Property and the State.* Engels argued that the subordination of women is an aspect of class oppression. The transference of private property from father to son meant ensuring a monogamous relationship between man and woman, which further needed the continued material dependence of women on men within marriage. The argument, therefore, was that with the abolition of private property under socialism the subordination of women would be at an end. With economic independence derived from inclusion into "waged" work (that is, work earning wages), women would be equal to men in the productive and, therefore, social spheres. Marriage in such a context would lose its constraining characteristics and become a union of independent partners.

Property Relations and Gender Relations

Property relations lay at the heart of this analysis and took the social form of marriage. There were two foci for women's struggles. Class struggle was the way forward for women wanting economic independence. If capitalist property relations were changed, women would benefit. This was because capitalism treated women as what Marx called a "reserve army" of cheap labor, subsidizing its economic outlays by providing facilities—cleaning, ironing, looking after children, and so on—which if paid for as part of the (male) worker's wages would cost the capitalist system enormously. If capitalism were replaced by a fairer economic system, such expropriation of women's labor would be replaced by their inclusion in a waged economy. Women also had to struggle against the social form of property relations—marriage was the everyday site of a woman's oppression and needed to be replaced by a relationship not enforced by the state—one that would be based not on economic and legal dependence but on mutual respect. This analysis was adopted by most communist parties and leaders as the basis on which to formulate the "woman question," and it inspired the strategies and policies to empower women pursued by subsequent state institutions. Participation in waged work would be a feature of a new socialist society; therefore, women's liberation from the yoke of marriage and social subordination was dependent on their participation in the socialist revolution. Mobilization of women followed as these revolutionary movements gained ground. For example, in Russia on International Women's Day in 1917 women textile workers went on strike, and this action helped delegitimize the provisional government. In China, women participated in great numbers in the May Fourth Movement in 1919 and supported the armed struggle of the Communist Party against both the Guomindang government and the Japanese.

Problems with a Materialist Analysis of Gender Relations

There were several problems with this materialist understanding of gender relations. The first set of problems arose from the importance of property and class relations in this analysis. There was no recognition of the fact that many aspects of women's subordination cannot be explained simply by reference to property, let alone to the bourgeois family form. Because of the emphasis on class relations, there also was a universalizing of the family without any sensitivity to the various family arrangements in different cultures, historical periods, and social groups. Such an analysis allowed the assumption that women's social status was exclusively bound up with property relations, and, therefore, the alteration of these relations would automatically result in a fundamental change in their position. It was because of these assumptions that Stalin could declare the "woman question" resolved in 1930.

A second set of problems with this analysis of gender relations stemmed from the emphasis on class relations and class structures in social transformation. When discussing the Jewish socialists' demand for a separate forum within the Socialist International to discuss particular issues pertaining to the Jewish community (for example, anti-Semitism),

Marx argued that any such separate identity for a group would be divisive and thus detrimental to the working-class struggle against the bourgeoisie. By the same argument women, too, could not seek a separate space within the working-class socialist movement. On the one hand, this resulted in suppressing debate about gender relations; on the other hand, it also had the effect of creating hierarchies of oppression. For example, in China, Mao Zedong declared that the class struggle was the "primary contradiction" that needed to be resolved before all others. The postponement of other struggles—including women's issues —was to become a permanent feature of state socialist regimes.

This materialist construction of the woman question, when linked to a hierarchy of oppressions set out by male party elites, posed difficult issues for the women's movements and for groups struggling to organize in their own interests. If a socialist revolution was the primary goal of the party organization, then strategic decisions had been made that might or might not support the struggles of women. Judith Stacey (1983) has argued, for example, that the Chinese Communist Party (CCP) made compromises with a socially conservative peasant patriarchy for its support of the revolution at the expense of women's rights. Whether this compromise was a conscious device for gaining support of peasant male heads of households, or whether the logic of "primary contradiction" led the CCP to this position, is arguable. What is pertinent here is that the materialist understanding of history and gender relations allowed the communist state to focus on one form of oppression (class-based) rather than another (gender). Marxist theory, while making gender relations integral to its critique of property regimes, especially under capitalism, does not let women's specific experiences contribute to revolutionary transformations other than through participation in party-organized class struggles.

The forms that the revolutionary states took also pose issues for gender relations. The Leninist party organization was a rigid, hierarchical structure with clear vertical lines of authority ensuring discipline within its ranks. Representation of special interests was difficult within the rubric of Marxist politics. The debates that raged within the Bolshevik party before the setting up of a separate women's organization (*Zhenotdel*) indicate the passion with which specific interests of women were denied, and also the determination with which women within the Bolshevik party fought for them to be recognized. Once the battle for a separate organization was won, however, a second struggle—pertaining to its agenda—was launched. The party was more successful in this battle.

Benefits of a Materialist Analysis of Gender Relations

The materialist understanding of gender relations did, however, lead to some real improvements in the economic and legal position of women. In 1922, for example, the Soviet Land Code was passed, which distributed land to "all citizens" and gave women the right to land ownership for the first time, even though some patterns of social relations within the family and the community remained unchallenged. The woman left her natal village to go to her husband's. Once accepted as part of a household, however, she owned land not because of the presence of her husband or son, but because of her own membership in the *dvor* (household). What made matters more complex was the Family Code, which allowed women to leave households with their property rights protected. Whereas the Land Code guaranteed the rights of households, the Family Code protected the rights of women—tension was inevitable in this context. Variations at the levels of implementation meant that women frequently did not get what was due to them, though the legal position was in their favor.

We find similar issues and tensions in the Chinese communists' attempt at reforming the old system through the Land and Marriage Laws of the 1950s. Considerations of political stability were often in conflict with the reformist impulses of the communist parties; however, the reformist impulses in themselves did not always challenge customary practices or discourses. This was most evident in the ways in which the traditional patriarchal monogamous family continued to be recognized as the norm and was privileged politically as ensuring social stability. In China, for example, the Marriage Law of 1950 presented the "new democratic family" as constituted by a monogamous heterosexual couple—monogamy as "natural" and the basis of a new socialist "morality." During the campaigns to publicize the law, the emphasis was not on women's claiming of rights but on harmonizing interests within the household, with concessions made by women to patriarchal rituals and practices in the wider interests of social cohesion so much needed by a state engaged in a process of economic reconstruction. The images of women that were constructed at different periods bore the imprint of this particularized understanding of gender relations within the boundaries of the nation-state—at different points in time, women were "comrades," "heroine mothers," or revolutionary workers.

An area of public policy where the immediate concerns of the state were paramount was demographic control. Pro- and antinatal policies were implemented in communist states, and they reflect the concerns of these political systems and the range of choices denied to women. Access to, and choice of, contraception has formed an important part of the demographic story in these countries. Whereas the Soviet Union and eastern European countries largely pursued pronatalist policies, the Chinese state implemented an antinatalist policy. In the first group of countries, women were denied access to contraception; as a result, multiple abortions became the last resort for millions of women. The implications for the health and welfare of women are obvious. In China, by contrast, the antinatalist perspective resulted in the implementation of the "one child policy." Women, especially urban women, experienced extraordinary state control over their reproductive capacities and choices. The state has used several measures of control—wide provision of contraception, surveillance of women to ensure the use of contraception, and significant disincentives for women and their families in case of the birth of a second child. The national agenda has been privileged over the rights of choice of women in these countries. The inclusion of women in public life under communist parties took place in specific and particular ways. Whereas the mobilization of women into waged work was extremely successful, the redistribution of nonwaged housework, which depends on a reordering of gender relations, remained largely undisturbed. A "double burden"—a dual responsibility—was placed on women: to be good workers as well as good mothers, wives, and daughters. Women's participation in political life remained limited.

Women resisted both the economic mobilization and the demographic policies implemented by the state. This resistance, however, did not have organized expression, because of the lack of political space within the communist political systems for the articulation and mobilization of special interests. In the formal political sphere, dominated by the communist parties, women also did not fare well. For example, "of the 30 people who have sat on the Standing Committee of the Political Bureau of the Central Committee of the Chinese Communist Party between 1969 and 1990s, not one was a woman. Among the 15 people who served as Chair and Vice-chairmen of the Central Committee, not one was a woman, and among almost 725 people who served as members of the Central Committee in that period only 35 were women" (Christiansen and Rai, 1996: 115–116). Although in most communist states proportional representation determined by the communist party ensured a presence of women in legislative bodies, the absence of women was pronounced in decision-making bodies. The organizations set up to represent women's interests—such as the Chinese Women's Federation—operated under the "leadership of the communist party" and were part of the state and party system. As such, they were able to represent the views of their members only so long as they did not conflict with communist party policies. Given the suspicion of special interest representation, the dominance of the communist party, and the only partial reorganization of gender relations in these countries, women have lacked choice in their lives.

Gender relations in communist states were, thus, considered subsidiary to the agendas set by a party or state that is complicit in the perpetuation of patriarchal value systems and material relations. The narrow confines of a materialist analysis of gender relations proved inadequate for challenging patriarchy within the communist framework. The one-party political state also restricted the avenues open to women to mobilize independently in their own various interests. Although the materialist analysis of gender relations provided a powerful critique of property-based relations between men and women under capitalism, it has been unable to deliver on the promise of equality and justice for women within the confines of state communism.

See Also

CLASS AND FEMINISM; FEMINISM: MARXIST; HOUSEHOLDS AND FAMILIES: COMMONWEALTH OF INDEPENDENT STATES; HOUSEHOLDS AND FAMILIES: EAST ASIA; HOUSEHOLDS AND FAMILIES: EASTERN EUROPE; MARXISM; POLITICS AND THE STATE: COMMONWEALTH OF INDEPENDENT STATES; POLITICS AND THE STATE: EAST ASIA; POLITICS AND THE STATE: EASTERN EUROPE; SOCIALISM

References and Further Reading

Buckley, Mary. 1989. *Women and ideology in the Soviet Union* Hemel Hempstead: Harvester-Wheatsheaf.

Christiansen, Flemming, and Shirin M. Rai. 1996. *Chinese politics and society: An introduction.* Hemel Hempstead: Harvester-Wheatsheaf.

Einhorn, Barbara. 1992. *Cinderella goes to the market.* London: Verso.

Engels, Fredrick. 1968. The origins of family, private property and the state. In Karl Marx and Fredrick Engels, *Selected works.* London: Lawrence and Wishart.

Evans, Harriet. 1997. *Gender and sexuality in China.* Cambridge: Polity.

Kruks, Sonia, Rayna Rapp, and Marilyn B. Young, eds. 1989. *Promissory notes: Women in transition to socialism.* New York: Monthly Review.

Rai, Shirin, Hilary Pilkington, and Annie Phizacklea, eds. 1992. *Women in the face of change: Eastern Europe, Soviet Union and China.* London: Routledge.

Stacey, Judith. 1983. *Patriarchy and socialist revolution in China.* Berkeley: University of California Press.

Wolfe, Margery. 1985. *Revolution postponed: Women in contemporary China.* London: Methuen.

Shirin M. Rai

COMMUNITY

"Community," of course, has many meanings. For activists in the women's movement, community is defined as a process. It can be described as a creative process through which they explore, challenge, and validate female identity in a male-dominated society. It can also be described as a process of creating a cohesive, supportive group from a collection of people who, although diverse, share a commitment to work through issues of gender peacefully and nonagressively.

The Creation of Community

A fundamental aspect of this community is that it is not limited to a static place, time, or group but is something to be created. Because much of society is designed by men, whose perspective is that of power, women throughout history have created groups—salons, clubs, societies, consciousness-raising circles, and now on-line networks, where issues and needs could be explored from a female perspective. Such groups may also have a religious character. Rev. Kittredge Cherry of the Universe Fellowship of Metropolitan Community Churches, for instance, has said, "Building women's community is one of my passions, and creating community among women is also part of my profession as a minister."

Another fundamental aspect of community is that it is something to which each of us belongs, physically, mentally, or both. Our personal identity reflects the communities to which we belong and is in turn reflected in them. In this regard community is sometimes compared explicitly to a family: "I have this need to feel a part of a community. It is not that I want to be a member of this or that group but to be part of a larger 'family.' This is important to me" (*Utne Reader,* 1992).

Although one conventional understanding of community is related primarily to a particular site, community can be defined as a shared sense of purpose, values, or identity. In this sense, then, we can speak of the civil rights community, the environmental community, or the Jewish community. As the word itself implies, community is often described in terms of ideas held in common. For eample, Tania Adbulahad wrote in 1992, in the magazine *Women of*

Power, "I think community is…people with whom I've developed not only a history, but a connectedness, a kinship, around some common areas." And Mary Cross, an activist in Washington, D.C., wrote in the same issue, "A community is…based on a set of values that people share or want to build together."

The Women's Community

The women's community is characterized not only by the obvious bond of being female, and of having a shared commitment to actively change a male-dominated world, but even more importantly by a commitment to engage in the process of connecting with other sectors and other populations. Shared values are clearly important, but if a community is to be more than a homogeneous enclave, it must also stress inclusivity and open-mindedness—and act accordingly.

Bernice Johnson (1981) described this situation as follows:

> Now every once in a while there is a need for people to try to clean out corners and bar the doors and check everybody who comes in the door and check what they carry in and say, "Humph; inside this place the only thing we are going to deal with is X or Y or Z. And so only the X's or Y's or Z's get to come in." That place can then become a nurturing place or a very destructive place.

This concept of community as both sharing and inclusiveness has resulted in an ongoing effort to make and maintain connections, and it has also involved meeting the challenge of recognizing and overcoming barriers to community. In other words, community, for women, combines activism, inclusion, and self-examination to identify barriers to inclusion. To activists in the women's movement, community has always meant more than simply a place to feel "at home." It is a way to build connections and develop shared values, and, at its best, a process of overcoming obstacles to unity. The following illustrations from the United States have many counterparts in other societies.

Developments in the United States

In the United States, a significant connection has been made between academics and grassroots activists. During the second wave of the women's mvement, the recognition that women had been largely omitted from history and from educational leadership led to nationwide calls for women's studies programs. In 1969, Cornell University in New York state offered the first course in women's studies, New York University (in New York City) offered the first course in women's law, and San Diego State College in California offered the first women's studies program, consisting of 10 courses. By 1974, more than 1,000 colleges and universites in the United States had courses in women's studies, and 80 had full programs. This development resulted both from ideology—a heightened consciousness of women's issues—and from direct action: a campaign by the National Organization for Women (NOW) to promote women's studies. Thus the new academic courses and programs were directly connected to pragmatic activism.

These developments in the United States also incorporated the commitment to overcome barriers to community. Women's studies programs and women's centers were established that required learners to participate in off-campus advocacy; to ground their research in the need for understanding women's daily lives (for instance, how to define and measure violence against women, leadership by women, and women's educational advancement); and to promote new centers to address research findings and fill in researchers' omissions. Examples include the Center for Women Policy Studies, which began by focusing on domestic violence and then expanded its coverage to address a range of issues critical to women's equity; the National Women's Law Center, which has examined and advocated for equity in legal status; the Project on the Status of Women and Girls in Education, which has confronted the issue of sexual assault, and women's safety in general, on campuses; and Women's Alliance for Theology, Ethics, and Ritual (WATER), which has sought to update Christian teachings to reflect, and change, women's lives and needs.

Today, most colleges and universities in the United States have not only women's studies programs but also centers for women and women's research centers. Such centers take an interest in topics concerning women in society and also maintain links with the world outside academia. The Wellesley College Center for Research on Women (in Massachesetts) has guest researchers who are in residence for up to a year, studying and writing. The Union Institute—a nontraditional university in Washington, D.C., that specializes in individualized learning—has a Center for Women whose mission is to form coalitions between academics and local residents that will work on overcoming societal impediments to women's achievement.

Activism, of course, tends to imply at least some degree of conflict. Mary Cross spoke of this too in *Women in Power*. "I think we have to have conflict; otherwise, we're making assumptions about those values and beliefs that maybe we don't all share. And without that conflict, we are missing an opportunity to build that community a little bit stronger than it was before."

And community itself can have many broader implications. In 1994, participants in a conference called "Sustaining Definable Communities" suggested some ramifications of community: "If we are committed to sustainability, then we are committed to overcoming inequity, racism, and ethnic conflict." "Quality of life means more than clean air and solving traffic problems—it means addressing concentration of wealth." "A sustainable community requires commitment to engage in a dynamic natural process that enables a coalescence of diversity toward a common purpose."

Whether conventional or unconventional, a collaborative process of change is essential to our understanding of the women's community.

See Also

FEMINISM: SECOND-WAVE NORTH AMERICAN; WOMEN'S CENTERS; WOMEN'S MOVEMENT, *specific topics;* WOMEN'S STUDIES: OVERVIEW; WOMEN'S STUDIES: UNITED STATES

References and Further Reading

Johnson, Bernice. 1981. Coalition politics: Turning the century. Speech at the West Coast Women's Music Festival.
Utne Reader. 1992 (July–August): 86.
Women of Power. 1992. No. 22: 7.

Sharon Parker

COMMUNITY POLITICS

The meaning of the term *community politics* varies considerably depending on the cultural and political context. It became popular in the United States in the 1960s and 1970s to refer to the grassroots, locally based activism associated with popular democratic protests, such as the civil rights, black power, women's, and environmental movements. In these contexts, community politics was counterposed to "traditional," "mainstream," or "electoral" politics, and carried with it assumptions about the connections between new forms of political participation and popular empowerment. In many other contexts, however, particularly in India (and south Asia, more generally), in the United Kingdom, and increasingly in the countries of the Commonwealth of Independent States, eastern Europe, the Middle East, and north Africa, it has come to be associated with what is also termed *communalism,* a politics characterized by the mobilization of people on the bases of religious identification, often of a fundamentalist sort. With respect to both uses of the term, key issues are how *community* is defined and who participates in creating—and maintaining—that definition.

History of the Concept of Community

Raymond Plant (1978) noted that community has long been a contested concept in political theory and practice. Although the term generally has positive connotations, evoking images of home, belonging, and connection and providing a powerful impetus for mobilization, the other side of inclusion and belonging is exclusion. The concept of community has also been used to exclude those defined as other, and to dominate those defined as members of a given community on the basis of purported "community values." Many of these issues have proved to be topics of intense debate among contemporary Anglo-American political philosophers, presented under the general rubric of "liberalism versus communitarianism."

For some, *community* refers to a geographic area and is effectively synonymous with *neighborhood* in the sense of a physical environment. Others emphasize the significance of interpersonal relationships and argue that community is essentially a social construct, the viability of which depends on ongoing interactions among its members. Still others focus on what Beth Roy refers to as "metaphoric" communities, based on presumed cultural or other commonalities among individuals—for example, the "black community," the "women's community," the "Jewish community." Although there may sometimes be a congruence between such culturally or geographically defined communities and class-based divisions, "community politics" often tends to treat issues of class as somewhat less fundamental than those of ethnicity, culture, or identity.

Linking the construction of community to a sort of "identity politics," however, highlights the problematic nature of both communities and community politics. The language of "the community" implies that there is a single, homogeneous, unified (if not monolithic) group that shares certain critical characteristics or a particular set of political perspectives. But a sense of community must be created; it does not arise naturally simply from living in a particular place or from being born into a particular group. And although a sense of community can be empowering—if it mobilizes new participants into the political arena and enables them to find their voice—it also can serve to reinforce, or protect from scrutiny, existing relations of domination and subordination (particularly of men over women, for example, or of traditionalists over modernizers) within particular communities and within larger political entities, on the basis of what may be represented as community values, tradition, or community autonomy.

Although these problematic uses of community have been brought to the fore quite dramatically in those areas where communalism is the dominant form of community

politics, they have also begun to be addressed in Anglo-American contexts. Critics and activists in both arenas (see, for example, Young, 1991; and Howard, 1993) note that definitions of *community* cannot be separated from the structuring of ideology, power, and inequality in any particular society, and that no community, however defined, will ever be totally homogeneous: its membership will be differentiated by sex, age, life stage, class, and other factors. How those differences are welcomed, denied, or otherwise negotiated must become a critical question of "community politics." Why are some identities (out of the whole complex of possibilities) chosen as "central" in any particular context? Who chooses? How are those choices enforced? Who defines what constitutes membership in a community or what constitutes appropriate behavior for members? How are the boundaries of membership created and maintained?

Women's Roles

Feminist historians and anthropologists have noted the importance of women to the creation and maintenance of community values and boundaries (Kaplan, 1982; Rosaldo and Lamphere, 1974; Ruddick, 1989). One could argue, in fact, that in the United States, such political participation as most women engaged in during the nineteenth and early twentieth centuries was primarily what might be termed "community politics" (see Baker, 1984), expressing "quality-of-life" concerns. Some feminist theorists in the United States have argued (Kaplan, 1980; Ruddick, 1989) that community-based mobilization around these quality-of-life or survival issues represents the predominant form of women's political participation cross-culturally. They suggest that (in most societies) women's responsibility for nurturing children and family results in a particular propensity to engage in such struggles and explains the disproportionate presence of women in these forms of activism in many cultural contexts.

Closely connected with these perspectives on community politics and participation is a view of the relationship between participation and "empowerment." Classical theorists of democratic participation such as John Stuart Mill and Alexis de Tocqueville argued that participation in public affairs has important educative effects on those who participate: it engages them in "public business," increases their sense of belonging to the larger political entity, and increases their commitment to broader democratic process. Similarly, some contemporary feminist and participatory democratic critics have argued that the participation of working-class women and women of ethnic and racial minorities in community-based politics has provided opportunities for both individual and community empowerment of those who were previously marginalized and ignored, and generated radical critiques of the workings of power in the formal political institutions and processes of the larger society (Cockburn, 1977; Evans and Boyte, 1986).

Nevertheless, both in the context of "communalist" politics and within U.S.-style community politics, women can be ignored or relegated to secondary status by those who claim to represent "authentic" community values. What is clear, then, is that neither "communities" nor "community politics"—as concepts or practices—are necessarily either liberating or oppressive to women or to other so-called "marginalized" groups. Definitions of marginality, themselves, are the products of complex, and dynamic, interactions between and among "communities" and the institutions of the state.

In short, questions of identity, community, and power are at the center of many contemporary political struggles. As participants in those conflicts, women in a variety of cultural contexts will continue both to affect and to be affected by the ways those questions are posed and answered.

See Also

COMMUNITY; DEMOCRACY; IDENTITY POLITICS; LIBERALISM

References and Further Reading

Ackelsberg, Martha A. 1995. Identity politics, political identities: Thoughts toward a multicultural politics. In *Frontiers: A Journal of Women's Studies* (Fall).

Baker, Paula. 1984. The domestication of politics: Women and American political society, 1780–1920. *American Historial Review*, 89: 620–647.

Cockburn, Cynthia. 1977. *The local state.* London: Pluto.

Evans, Sara, and Harry Boyte. 1986. *Free spaces: The sources of democratic change in America.* New York: Harper and Row.

Freitag, Sandria B. 1989. *Collective action and community: Public arenas and the emergence of communalism in North India.* Berkeley: University of California Press

Howard, Rhoda E. 1993. Cultural absolutism and the nostalgia for community. *Human Rights Quarterly* 15: 315–338.

Kaplan, Temma. 1982. Female consciousness and collective action: The case of Barcelona, 1910–1918. *Signs: Journal of Women in Culture and Society* 7(3): 545–566.

Plant, Raymond R. 1978. Community: Concept, conception, and ideology. *Politics and Society* 8(1): 79–107.

Rosaldo, Michelle Zimbalist, and Louise Lamphere. 1974. *Woman, culture and society.* Stanford, Calif.: Stanford University Press.

Roy, Beth. 1994. *Some trouble with cows: Making sense of social conflict.* Berkeley: University of California Press.

Ruddick, Sara. 1989. *Maternal thinking: Toward a politics of peace.* Boston: Beacon.

Young, Iris Marion. 1991. *Justice and the politics of difference.* Princeton, N.J.: Princeton University Press.

Martha A. Ackelsberg

COMPOSERS

See MUSIC: COMPOSERS.

COMPULSORY HETEROSEXUALITY

See FEMINISM: LESBIAN.

COMPUTER SCIENCE

Computer science is one of the three subfields in informatics—information technology and information systems science being the other two. They share the same basic knowledge, but the directions of specialization differ. Computer science is more theoretically oriented, including programming and databases at the professional level and artificial intelligence and algorithms at the research level. In working life, computer scientists are people who design, run, and maintain information systems.

The introduction of new technology was expected to help break down the gender division in the labor market and narrow the wage gap between women and men. However, there is no evidence that technological change has so far had any impact in promoting equality in these essential aspects. A negative attitude toward technology has also been present—for example, among the West German women's movement in the 1970s until the mid-1980s. Computer technology was considered male-dominated, while the women's movement focused on the social implications of technology.

The Role of Women in Computer Science

The early history of computer programming includes a number of women pioneers. The best known is Lady Ada Lovelace, considered the first programmer (1843, United Kingdom). Her role as a programmer is overemphasized, but the programming language ADA bears her name, and she became a female "role model" in the field. Grace Hopper (United States) supervised a group at the Eckert-Mauchly Computer Corporation which created the first compiler (1952). This group also developed the longest-lived programming language, COBOL. Another female computer pioneer, Jean Sammet (United States) taught the first computer courses in American universities.

Women have gained admittance into low-skilled data entry jobs and professional software programming. Female computer scientists are also found at the management level and as technical personnel, programmers, analysts, computer operators, teachers, and researchers. Higher up in the hierarchy there are, however, very few women, and overall women are underrepresented in computer science.

A commonplace view is that women are not interested in technology or in computers. There are attitudinal and cultural obstacles, from differences in the upbringing of boys and girls to workplace culture. Men and women also often emphasize different aspects of computers—technology versus implications. Courses in management information systems (MIS) have emerged at many business schools as an alternative for students desiring to enter the computing profession. Women are better represented in MIS than in computer science. The explanation for this choice may provide an answer to the declining number of female computer scientists.

Barriers to Women in the Profession

Attitudinal and cultural barriers to computer science certainly differ between countries. In Scandinavia, for example, the opportunities are relatively fair.

In Germany female computer scientists have problems with obtaining equal qualification status and with social differences. They try to counter such shortcomings with special qualifications and, in many cases, advance their career at the expense of their family situation: only 5 percent of female computer scientists have children, compared with 62 percent of men.

In Spain women's presence in the labor market is low compared with other OECD (Organization for Economic Cooperation and Development) countries, and they are less qualified than men. They are notably absent from technical studies and therefore from computer science.

In Africa women's work is often invisible, because they generally work in the informal sector. A Nigerian report tells of lower salaries and lower status for female computer scientists, although their capabilities and work tasks are the same as those of their male colleagues. It is also reported to be almost impossible to combine a profession with home and children.

In the United States the computer culture is not friendly to women. Two studies of female engineers and engineering undergraduates found that 70 percent of women felt they had to work harder than their male counterparts to get comparable pay; 58 percent felt that harassment of some sort was prevalent in the workplace; 50 percent felt that they viewed ethical issues differently from men; 39 percent felt they would be penalized if they took maternity leave; and 78 percent felt they received comparable pay when they started but were not promoted as rapidly as their male colleagues.

Barriers to Women in Computer Science Education

Another barrier to entry is the educational system. Segregation starts early; boys have more access to computers than girls, and much software is designed to attract boys. Science is not made interesting in schools, and girls are not encouraged to pursue sciences.

For undergraduates, four problems to entry and completion of computer science studies are reported. First, girls have difficulties with self-esteem. Second, there is a lack of mentoring and role models. Third, gender discrimination is perceived. Fourth, there are difficulties in balancing career and family responsibilities. Instead of fighting these problems women often opt out of computer science.

At universities, "pipeline shrinkage" is noticeable (as women move along the academic pipeline, their percentage continues to shrink). Although somewhat more than 50 percent of university students are female in the United States (as in most western countries), relatively few take a bachelor's degree in computer science, and even fewer take a master's or doctor's degree. Less than 10 percent of computer science faculty members at universities are female.

Two severe barriers are identified. First, the "tenure clock versus the biological clock" often results in dropouts to industry or an independent career—for example, as a consultant. Second, female doctoral students usually prefer a female mentor, but the number of female faculty members is low. The resulting supervision problem is twofold: national backgrounds can influence how male mentors treat female students, and research interests may differ. In artificial intelligence, for example, designing tutoring systems attracts women more than men. There are also women interested in basic theoretical research and software engineering, which are by no means gender-biased and should not present a supervision problem.

Increasing the Number of Female Computer Scientists

The shortage of qualified people in computer science and female underrepresentation in the field have led to national initiatives. Britain, for example, has a "Women in IT" (information technology) campaign, educational schemes such as "Girls into Science and Technology," and a host of women's training workshops. In West Germany a working group within the Society for Computer Science was established in 1986 and became a specialized group called Women's Work and Computer Science. In the United States the Association for Women in Computing (AWC) was established. The introduction of the Equal Status Law (United States) is reported to have increased the percentage of female engineering students. There are also several groups—for example, the Women's Action Alliance and Educational Equity Concepts—that organize courses for teachers. Networks such as Systers (mostly U.S.-based) and WITI (an international network of women in technology) provide a medium for mentoring among female computer science professionals in business and academia. There are also conferences, seminars, and workshops for researchers in computer science—for example, the conference on women, work, and computerization supported by the International Federation for Information Processing.

See Also

COMPUTING: OVERVIEW; CYBERSPACE AND VIRTUAL REALITY; EDUCATION: TECHNOLOGY; INFORMATION REVOLUTION; INFORMATION TECHNOLOGY; NETWORKS, ELECTRONIC

References and Further Reading

Adam, Alison, and Jenny Owen, eds. 1994. *Proceedings of the fifth international conference on women, work and computerization: Breaking old boundaries, building new forms.* Manchester: UMIST.

Bromley, H., and M. Apple, eds. 1988. *Education/technology/power.* Albany: State University of New York Press.

Communications of the ACM. 1990. Vol. 33, no. 11 (November: Special issue on "Women and computing").

———. 1995. Vol. 38, no. 1 (January: Special issue on "Women in computing"): 26–82.

Eriksson, Inger V., Barbara A. Kitchenham, and Kea G. Tijdens, eds. 1991. *Women, work and computerization: Understanding and overcoming bias in work and education.* Amsterdam: North-Holland.

Grundy, A. E., et al., eds. 1997. *Women, work, and computerization: spinning a web from past to future. Proceedings of the sixth international IFIP conference.* Bonn, Germany, 24–27, May. Berlin: Springer.

Kick, Russel C., Jr., and F. Stuart Wells. 1993. Women in computer science. *SIGCSE Bulletin* 25(1): 203–207.

Stein, Dorothy. 1987. Sex and the COBOL cabal. *New Scientist,* 17 Sept.: 79–80.

Inger V. Eriksson

COMPUTING: Overview

Information technology is radically transforming society in ways that have made significant parts of our lives unrecognizable in the twenty-first century. Central to shifts in education, work, entertainment, and private life is the increasing dominance of the computer. This article briefly traces the history of women in computing and notes some of the major issues that have concerned feminists working in the area for the past 25 years. The rapid growth of computing since World War II has prompted predictions of a major social transformation (Olerup et al., 1985). Feminists in the field ask if a new technology alone can create social change. Further, can that change benefit women? Many feminist writers fear that current inequalities between men and women will be perpetuated and widened by developments in computing.

Gender and Computing

Although technology itself might be construed as neutral, many observers have described the contexts and culture of computing, in common with many other technologies, as deeply gendered (Cockburn, 1980; Cockburn and Ormrod, 1993; Game and Pringle, 1983; Greenbaum, 1994; Perry and Greber, 1990).

The increasing recognition of the stratified nature of computer work, of computer education, and of the language and meanings surrounding computing has led during the last twenty-five years of the twentieth century to a virtual avalanche of women's publications, special editions of journals, and meetings—for example, the now well established "Women, Work, and Computerization" conferences. A major strength of this activity is the diversity of disciplinary backgrounds from which it springs and the richness of the debates it initiates.

Historical Background

Machines for mechanical computation have been known for almost three hundred years. The historical record lists notables such as the Frenchman Blaise Pascal and the German Gottfried von Leibniz. Women are not entirely absent. In the earliest period, Ada Lovelace, daughter of the English poet Lord Byron, played a significant role in developing a computer program for the "analytic engine" designed by Charles Babbage in the nineteenth century. The contribution of Ada Lovelace was recognized by the U.S. Department of Defense when it named a powerful computer language "Ada."

The computer did not develop on a significant scale until after World War II. Wartime needs in North America and Great Britain led to the development of machines with calculating power vastly superior to that provided by women using hand calculators (Perry and Greber, 1990). The links between the military and the development of the computer continue to shape its acceptability and patterns of work in computing.

Women have been associated with computer software since the earliest days, although their contribution is yet to be fully documented. Grace Hopper, an American, had a significant impact on the computer language COBOL; Adele Goldstine is thought to have been involved in designing software for the United States' large computer ENIAC during World War II (Perry and Greber, 1990). Yet the occupation rapidly became sex-typed. Men operated the large early computers while women fed them data (Game and Pringle, 1983). With the increasing demarcation of hardware (machines) and software (programs), men became associated with the development of machines and women with data entry. The emerging area of programming, though initially attractive to women, has become associated with men, at least at the higher levels. In the developed world in the early 1990s, women held roughly one-third of positions overall in systems analysis, programming, consulting, and informatics (Mackinnon et al., 1993).

The gendered nature of higher education worldwide exacerbates the sex typing of computer work. In universities and technical colleges, women students constitute a tiny minority in electronic engineering, the training ground for the architects of supercomputing and artificial intelligence. The number of women in computer science in the developd world is decreasing, a phenomenon that has been attributed, paradoxically, to the introduction of microcomputers in schools and to the violence and competitiveness of computer games, which do not, in general, appeal to girls.

The Global Village and the Electronic Cottage

The computer, allied with communication technologies such as satellites, propels vast amounts of information around the world, making national boundaries more permeable and bridging vast distances. This shrinking is encapsulated in Marshall McLuhan's famous expression "the global village." Ownership and control of the large media and electronic companies that encircle the globe is vested in men, usually from a handful of wealthy developed countries, whose decisions influence national and international economic policy. In order to maximize profits, large corporations shift work sites to developing countries where labor costs are cheaper, often employing women workers in conditions that would be unacceptable in their own, more regulated economies.

The ensuing international division of labor destabilizes work patterns in developed countries, where full-time jobs are shrinking and "contingent" work (temporary, short-term, contract, casual) is increasing (Greenbaum, 1994). Thus, the destinies of women in both developing and developed countries are linked in ways over which they have little control. The increasing casualization of work in the developed world has been characterized as a "feminizing" of work, with more men from white-collar and blue-collar occupations having to adapt to contingent patterns of work previously associated with women (Haraway, 1991).

At the same time, the computer presents possibilities for a break in the pattern of work that has prevailed in the developed world since the industrial revolution. The separation of home and work, which occurred when mechanized work was transferred to large factories, underpinned the separation of public life (usually associated with men) from private life (usually the domain of women). This separation in turn justified the sexual division of labor—a resilient division that undervalues women's work in the home and declares paid labor in the factory or office the domain of men. This sharply defined boundary between home and work may well be blurred as the computer allows for the possibility of performing paid work from one's home. With the assistance of telephones, facsimile machines, and photocopiers, employees in many businesses can now conduct their work without leaving their dwelling.

This new form of work, variously called telework, telecommuting, or remote work, has significant benefits for the environment (less time is taken up in travel, traffic jams are avoided, the atmosphere is less polluted by fossil fuels) and for regional redevelopment. The "electronic cottage" allows, in theory, a blending of the nurturant and the income-generating work of the household. Yet feminists monitoring this new working style observe that women who lack significant professional skills are disadvantaged, often experiencing isolation, exploitation, and the horrors of the sweated laborer of the nineteenth century or the developing country (Huws, 1984; Wajcman and Probert, 1988).

The issue of telework raises again the central question relevant to the entire computing field. Does computing enhance women's public and private lives, or does it reinforce the sexual division of labor? Can new technology create social change? Curiously, as telecommuting has become increasingly attractive for professionals, the concern expressed by feminists for lower-paid workers has virtually disappeared from the literature. Few women are currently writing about the phenomenon. Telework has not developed on the major scale predicted in the 1980s partly because of managers' concerns about loss of control and employees' fears of isolation and exploitation. However, it is likely to become increasingly important as work continues to become more flexible and more jobs are lost from the core workforce (Greenbaum, 1994). Feminists' concerns that the electronic cottage may consign women to the home and child care at a time when women have made many advances in education and paid work ensure that the issue will continue to arouse lively debate.

Patterns of Debate

Feminist analysis of women in computing has paralleled major theoretical developments in feminism and in the social sciences and humanities since the 1970s. Writers have generally avoided arguing that technology determines social change, attempting instead to map the location of women in the computer industry and to highlight women's exclusion from computer education, software design, and computer work due to underlying patterns of male dominance. Drawing on the feminist notion of the sexual division of labor, writers demonstrated the way in which computing education and work became sex-typed (Game and Pringle, 1983). In order to explain the relegation of women to the menial level of computing work, writers drew on the Marxist "deskilling" hypothesis developed by Braverman, which suggested that the erosion of the skills of low-paid workers was a necessary step in capitalists' increasing appetite for control over the workplace (Wajcman, 1991). Braverman's labor process theory and the sexual division of labor together provided a framework for explanations of women's exclusion.

By the 1980s arguments that stressed the social construction of masculinity and femininity were increasingly used to explain the differential access of boys and girls to computer education and of men and women to particular forms of computer work. Writers such as Cynthia Cockburn (1985; Cockburn and Ormrod, 1993) demonstrated that the sexual division of labor was involved in the conception and design of technologies. Writers also implicated the military's continuing connection with developments in computing. It has been argued that the military represents our culture's definition of masculinity in its clearest form (Perry and Greber, 1990). The association of computing with masculinity is reinforced by computer games, often the first point of contact with computers for young people. The socially constructed nature of masculinity and femininity remains of central importance as an explanation for the continuing division of labor in computing and for the decreasing numbers of girls and young women in computing classes in school and in undergraduate courses.

Language, Meaning, and Feminist Epistemology

More recently writers have drawn from postmodernist and poststructuralist debates in order to deconstruct the languages, meanings, and representations surrounding the culture of computing. There they find themes of domination, control, competition, and escape, themes that are not generally associated with women's patterns of socialization. They question the style of thinking dominant in computer programming, claiming that the formal, abstract, linear thinking central to computer programming is less hospitable to women (Turkle and Papert, 1990).

The most influential feminist poststructuralist writer is undoubtedly Donna Haraway, whose frequently cited work is a clarion call for women to "refuse an anti-science metaphysics, a demonology of technology," to "embrace the skillful task of reconstructing the boundaries of daily life" (1991: 181). Haraway exhorts women to take responsibility for the "social relations of science and technology," to see the subversive potential of computing and information technology, to form alliances with other marginalized groups, and to appropriate computing and information technology to their own ends (see also Plant, 1997; Herring, 1996). It remains to be seen if current patterns of gender bias in computing can be disrupted and the promise of information technology realized for all.

See Also

COMPUTER SCIENCE; COMPUTING: PARTICIPATORY AND FEMINIST DESIGN; CYBERSPACE AND VIRTUAL REALITY; CYBORG ANTHROPOLOGY; EDUCATION: TECHNOLOGY; INFORMATION TECHNOLOGY; NETWORKS, ELECTRONIC; PART-TIME AND CASUAL WORK; TELEWORKING; WORK: OCCUPATIONAL SEGREGATION; WORK: PATTERNS

References and Further Reading

Cockburn, Cynthia. 1985. *Machinery of dominance: Women, men, and technical know-how.* London: Pluto.

———, and S. Ormrod. 1993. *Gender and technology in the making.* London: Sage.

Erisson, I. V., B. A. Kitchenham, and K. G. Tijdens, eds. 1991. *Women, work and computerization: Understanding and overcoming bias in work and education.* Amsterdam: Elsevier.

Game, Ann, and Rosemary Pringle, 1983. *Gender at work.* Sydney: Allen and Unwin.

Greenbaum, Joan. 1994. Windows on the workplace: The temporization of work. In Alison Adam and Jenny Owen, eds. *Breaking old boundaries: Building new forms.* Proceedings of the Fifth International Conference on Women, Work and Computerization, Manchester.

Haraway, Donna. 1991. *Simians, cyborgs and women (The reinvention of nature).* London: Routledge.

Herring, Susan, ed. 1996. *Computer-mediated communication: Linguistic, social and cross-cultural perspectives.* Amsterdam: Benjamins.

Huws, Ursula. 1986. New technology homeworkers. *Employment Gazette* (January): 13–1.

Mackinnon, Alison, Martha Blomqvist, and Maria Vehviläinen. 1993. Gendering computer work: An international comparison. in *AI and Society* 7(4): 280–294.

Olerup, A., L. Schneider, and E. Monod, eds. 1985. *Women, work and computerization: Opportunities and disadvantages.* Amsterdam: Elsevier.

Perry, R., and L. Greber. 1990. Women and computers: An introduction. *Signs: Journal of Women in Culture and Society* 16(1): 74–101.

Plant, Sadie. 1997. *Zeroes and ones: Digital women and the new technoculture.* London: Fourth Estate.

Turkle, Sherry, and Seymour Papert. 1990. Epistemological pluralism: Style and voices within the computer culture. *Signs: Journal of Women in Culture and Society* 16(1): 128–157.

Wajcman, Judy. 1991. *Feminism confronts technology.* London: Polity.

Wajcman, Judy, and Belinda Probert. 1988. New technology outwork. In E. Willis, ed. *Technology and the labour process: Australian case studies.* Sydney: Allen and Unwin.

Alison Mackinnon

COMPUTING:
Participatory and Feminist Design

Participatory design and feminist design are not finished products but processes. Participatory design means that future users of a computer-based system take part in developing it. Feminist design is used here to talk about computer design processes in which women's interests and perspectives are taken into account.

Participatory Design

How users are involved in designing a computer-based system varies: they can act as representatives of a larger user community, can be directly involved in the design, can be consultants, can be actual collaborators, and can have more or less influence—that is, greater or lesser power to make design decisions.

Common reasons for using a participatory process to design computer systems are:

1. To improve the "fit" between the system and the work it will perform.
2. To help users develop realistic expectations about the system and reduce their resistance to change.
3. To increase workplace democracy.

The first two reasons are practical. The third, which is based on experiments on "working life democracy" in Scandinavia in the early 1960s, is partly political but also practical: participation was seen as means of increasing productivity and efficiency.

A large-scale program for improving working life and enhancing industrial democracy was conducted by the Norwegian Federation of Trade Unions (which wanted to empower workers), in cooperation with the Norwegian Employers' Federation (which wanted to rationalize and improve organizational development). Scandinavian unions initiated a series of associated research projects in the 1970s and 1980s to develop alternative views and knowledge about computers in the workplace, and to strengthen workers (labor) relative to employers (capital). In Norway, the most important result of the democracy program was legislation specifying that workers and their representatives would be kept informed about systems used for planning and performing work, and about proposed changes in such systems. The law emphasized sufficient education for using the systems, and participation in the design process, the main idea being that the workers themselves should control work and be responsible for performing it. Similar laws were passed in Denmark and Sweden.

In the 1980s and and 1990s, Scandinavian approaches to system design were critical in attitude and were user-oriented rather than management-oriented. Techniques were developed for users' participation in analysis, design, and implementation of computer-based systems; and because of the practical benefits of involving users in design, other European, North American, and Australian researchers have also worked on creating techniques for participatory design. The Scandinavian participatory design projects involved large, tailored in-house computer systems, with users from strong, cooperative trade unions. Techniques for system description and system presentation (such as prototyping) with users have also been developed, expanding the objective from helping system designers to enhancing communication and discussion between designers and users; the term *cooperative design* describes this approach more accurately.

Feminist Design

To discuss feminist design, one has to consider system design from a feminist perspective. This feminist perspective can be applied to criticize methods and work styles in system design, as well as the values underlying system design as a discipline and a profession. A starting point is to look at the consequences of using computers at work and in society.

Analyses of technology by feminist theorists, such as Cockburn's discussion of technology in the printing industry (1983), tend to conclude that neither technology development nor technology itself is neutral. In systems design, most traditional methods and work styles seem to operate within a reductionist, rationalistic, scientific paradigm. This implies that work processes can be described precisely and then automated—a belief that excludes informal, social, and tacit knowledge. The same ways of formalizing work processes have been used in traditional industry (as on assembly lines) and in office work (such as typing pools), so they have affected not only predominantly male industrial workers but also predominantly female office workers. Even when the methods seem to be more sophisticated—for example, when they incorporate techniques for describing tacit and informal aspects of work—the familiar metaphor of the assembly line is still considered valid for describing modern workflows.

Participatory design in general and feminist design in particular represent an alternative to this rationalistic approach. Involving future users in computer design may mean emphasizing aspects of work other than those most easily described and formalized; focusing on reproduction of information or on the security of information may run counter to a highly rationalistic, formal, and efficient information flow. Female-dominated work tends to be oriented toward reproduction and care of information as well as toward people and artifacts; thus a feminist design process needs to include nonformalizable aspects of work—something that can be done only by engaging and involving workers in the design process. A feminist perspective allows alternative views on computer systems and on the work organization these systems are meant to support. Thus introducing multiple voices—other disciplines and other methods—can challenge and change system design.

A feminist perspective can also be used to examine the basis and and values of system design. Often, women tend to be interested in technology because it helps them do their work—not because it is "advanced" or because it confers status. Women are generally interested in technology that is useful, easy to learn, and easy to use. For example, researchers have found that women generally do not learn all the features of the latest version of a word processing program unless they recognize a need for these features. (Not only women react this way, of course; thus an initially simpler computer system, which could be made more complex as the user becomes more skillful and requires more sophistication, is often suggested. Interestingly, however, such a system is just as difficult to build as an initially complex system.)

At least one lesson of participatory and feminist computer design would seem to be, then, that a computer system useful in work represents a new basis for evaluating the success of the system—and that this may be more appropriate than many traditional design methods and projects.

See Also

COMPUTER SCIENCE; COMPUTING: OVERVIEW; CYBERSPACE AND VIRTUAL REALITY; EDUCATION: TECHNOLOGY; TECHNOLOGY

References and Further Reading

Adam, A., et al., eds. 1994. *Women, work, and computerization: Breaking old boundaries, building new forms.* Proceedings of Fifth International Conference, Manchester. Amsterdam and New York: Elsevier.

Bjerknes, G., P. Ehn, and M. Kyng, eds. 1987. *Computers and democracy: A Scandinavian challenge.* Aldershot: Avebury.

Cockburn, C. 1983. *Brothers, male dominance, and technological change.* London: Pluto.

Ehn, P. 1989. *Work-oriented design of computer artifacts.* Hillsdale, N.J.: Erlbaum.

Emery, M., ed. 1993. *Participative design for participative democracy.* Centre for Continuing Education, Australian National University.

Eriksson, I. V., et al., eds. 1991. *Women, work and computerization: Understanding and overcoming bias in work and education.* Proceedings of Conference, Helsinki. Amsterdam and New York: North-Holland Elsevier.

Green, E., et al., eds. 1991. *Gendered by design?* London: Taylor and Francis.

Greenbaum, J., and M. Kyng, eds. 1991. *Design at work: Cooperative design of computer systems.* Hillsdale, N.J.: Erlbaum.

Gustavsen, B. 1992. *Dialogue and development.* Assen/Maastricht: Arbetslivscentrum and Van Gorcum.

Mumford, E. 1983. *Designing human systems.* Manchester, U.K.: Manchester Business School.

Tijdens, K., et al., eds. 1989. *Women, work, and computerization: Forming new alliances.* Proceedings of Conference, Amsterdam. Amsterdam and New York: North-Holland Elsevier.

Tone Bratteteig

CONFLICT RESOLUTION:
Mediation and Negotiation

Conflict—a pervasive part of life—can be defined as disagreement or dispute over issues, attitudes, opinions, or behavior. It can take many forms, from words to violence, and people engaged in a conflict can range from two individuals to virtually the entire world. Women (like men) have caused and participated in conflicts and have also been instrumental in solving them.

Conflict and Power

Power is a significant element in conflicts. In this regard, psychology contributes to escalation or deescalation of a conflict because, consciously or unconsciously, the contending parties form a perception of their relative strength. This perception of power is based on one or more of its facets: power can be, for example, intellectual, hierarchical, material, military, cultural, traditional, customary, legal, or related to nationality, class, or gender. When power on both sides of a conflict is more or less equal, it is often described as *symmetrical;* when power is unequal, it is said to be *asymmetrical.*

Those who regard relationships in terms of wielding power may not value human dignity, and that in itself is a source of conflict. Individual, group, and national interests will eventually cause conflict if relationships are exclusively competitive and are not mutually rewarding.

Not all conflict is destructive; some conflicts remain harmless and inconsequential, and some can even be beneficial. Conflict between individuals, for instance, can reduce tension and lead them to a better understanding of each other. In general, conflicts can enhance understanding when those involved, whether individuals or groups, demonstrate caring and want to resolve the conflict. By contrast, conflicts tend to escalate when the relationship is based on power rather than on caring.

Conflict Resolution

Conflict resolution, mediation, and negotiation are concerned with human nature, needs, and aspirations.

Conflict resolution is the process by which individuals and groups mediate and negotiate to deescalate and settle a dispute. This process is often described as an art: it requires time, interest, skill, specific techniques for addressing the conflicting parties, knowledge of the situation, and an understanding of the factors—ideological, structural, or cultural—that led to the conflict. Conflict resolution is most likely to succeed in contexts of symmetrical power relationships.

A *mediator* is an individual who intervenes in a conflict, usually by request. The mediator's aim may be to settle the conflict; however, a mediator has no power to impose a settlement but can only offer advice or recommendations. To ensure the success of the intervention, the mediator should have the trust, respect, and confidence of the contending parties; have influence over both sides; and be able to communicate effectively with both. Mediators are often used in traditional societies, in large corporations, and in regional, national, and international political conflicts, among other settings.

A *negotiator,* in the simplest sense of the term, is an individual who bargains. Such a person can negotiate a commercial or political agreement or, at times, legislation. Negotiation in all three settings—commerce, politics, and law—often involves applying psychology. A skilled negotiator should be able to reach an agreement acceptable to both parties; in some cases, a negotiator can impose an agreement.

Conflict resolution, as an art and a technique, has flourished in recent years in much of the western world, particularly in Anglo-Saxon countries. Its practitioners often base their approach on several assumptions: that there is goodness in every human being; that peace is better than war; and that in every conflict the parties will sooner or later reach a point where they need to negotiate and need a mediator to enhance the negotiation process.

It should be noted that these assumptions are not universally held, nor is conflict resolution universally practiced: for example, throughout history there have been those who believe that war is inevitable or even desirable and those (usually the powerful) who believe that power always rules; and advocates of nonviolence, such as conscientious objectors, often lack the strength to intervene in conflicts. Also, the process of conflict resolution has drawn criticism: in 1995, a report by the Refugees Studies Program argued that this approach "does not take the element of power and control into consideration."

Conflict resolution can be assessed by considering those who receive training in the process; by measuring the deescalation of strife when these techniques are introduced; by noting whether the parties to a conflict are indeed engaged in finding mutually beneficial soloutions; by asking whether the approach does increase conscientiousness; and by determining to what degree the parties have internalized the concept—that is, adopted it as a value of their own. The assessment is likely to vary, depending on the context.

In the Middle East, for instance, conflicts have generally ended with one party losing and the other succeeding, or in a stalemate. Negotiations involving mediation have often been based on such an asymmetrical power relationship that one party views them as invalid—as with agreements negotiated between Israel and the Palestinians. In this region, hegemony tends to be an obstacle to conflict resolution: each contending party tries to dominate. Another obstacle, in some Middle Eastern conflicts, is that one party ignores the existence of the other: conflict has escalated in this way in Algeria, Turkey, Iran, and the Sudan. It is probably fair to say that in many conflicts in the Middle East, neither party has taken sufficient account of the rights or dignity of the other, or of the benefits that could be derived from mutual recognition.

In some contexts, conflicts have been resolved by an imposed peace—that is, a peace imposed on both of the contending parties by a superior power. This is a dangerous situation, because it leaves both parties dissatisfied; when regional, national, or international circumstances allow, either party may escalate the conflict again.

Not surprisingly, conflict resolution is easier when—as in Lebanon—people can draw on earlier experiences with the process and when the necessary resources are already in place to serve as a basis for their future coexistence. In other situations, innovative, imaginative methods of resolution are required, such as appealing to historical coexistence, a shared cultural heritage, or common goals for the future. In the Middle East, for instance, mediation and negotiation are an integral part of Arab-Islamic culture; consensus is fundamental to communal life; and there is abundant literature on mediation and negotiation between warring peoples—made possible by shared values, beliefs, social makeup, and territory. However, any such innovative concepts should be based on a symmetrical power relationship if their effect is to be long-lasting.

Women and Conflict Resolution

Women's role in conflict resolution also varies with the context. Women have always mediated and negotiated in family, neighborhood, and school conflicts. In some societies their influence has theoretically been limited to these spheres, or to just the family—but even there, women have not been completely isolated from the contemporary culture of conflict resolution.

To return to our example of the Middle East, women have begun to work as trainers in conflict resolution and nonviolence (see Ougarit Younan in Osseiran, 1994). A Lebanese trainer, Randa Slim, became a resource person in conflict resolution not only in the Middle East but elsewhere as well (*Report on Training of Trainers,* 1994). By the year 2000, there were still only a few women trainers in the Middle East (and not many more men); but some commentators were urging that more women be trained in all types of conflicts in this region, on the theory that women trainers would bring an element of concern for life, compassion, and cooperation. It was also argued that women's

professionalism in this work would have a positive effect on values regarding women's rights and women's role in Middle Eastern society, perhaps especially as decision makers; and that more training would enhance women's role in society as citizens and active partners. Women's activity in regional nongovernmental organizations (NGOs), their ability to assess power relationships within their own organizations, their demands for a greater voice in public policy, and their increasing networking, not only locally but also with international NGOs, were all expected to have an impact.

Significant developments include the women in Lebanon who demonstrated to call for an end to the Lebanese conflict and the country's war machine; and the Israeli and Palestinian women who started working together to build peace. Still, such trends have been seen mainly, if not exclusively, among elite women, whereas true conflict resolution may need to start from the bottom up. Women who toil daily to earn a living for themselves and their families often have violence inflicted on them, and their voices must be part of the contemporary wave of conflict resolution. When women's rights and abilities are acknowledged, in the Middle East and worldwide, they have much to contribute to the nonviolent resolution of conflicts.

See Also

PEACE EDUCATION; PEACEKEEPING; PEACE MOVEMENTS, *specific regions*

References and Further Reading

Baruch Bush, A. Robert, and P. Joseph Folger. 1994. *The promise of mediation.* San Francisco: Jossey-Bass.

Cornelius, Helena, and Shoshana Faire. 1989. *Everyone can win.* Sydney, Australia: Simon and Schuster.

ESCWA. 1994. *Arab regional preparatory meeting for the Fourth World Conference on Women, 6–10 November.* Amman, Jordan: Publication No. ESCWA A/SD/1994/WG-3-WOM/4.

International Alert. 1993. *Conflict resolution Training in the north Caucasus and Georgia: Nalchick seminar.* London: International Alert, November.

———. 1994. *Internal conflicts in Africa.* London: International Alert, January.

———, Gernika Gogoratuz Peace Research Centre (1993). *Intercultural conflict research training.* London: International Alert, April.

Migauda, Edith. 1994. Harnessing internal local resources for conflict resolution and self-sustaining peace in the face of ethnic violence. Paper presented at IPRA Conference, Valetta, Malta, November.

Morton, Deutsch. 1991. Subjective features of conflict resolution: Psychological, social, and cultural influences. In International Social Sciences Council (ISSC), ed., *New directions in conflict theory*. London: Sage.

Moussala, Ahmad. 1993. An Islamic theoretical model for political conflict resolution: Takhim (arbitration). Paper presented at AUB Conference on Conflict Resolution, Larnaca, Cyprus, July.

Nasr, N. Waddah. 1993. Nonviolence as a means for resolving conflict and its relevance to the Arab world. Paper presented at AUB Conference on Conflict Resolution, Larnaca, Cypurs, July.

Osseiran, Sanàa. 1994. *Handbook of teaching and resource material in conflict resolution: Education for human rights, peace, and democracy*. Paris: IPRA/UNESCO.

———. 1990. *Peace building and development in Lebanon*. Paris: IPRA/UNESCO, April.

———. 1993. *Training in conflict resolution in Lebanon*. Paris: IPRA/UNESCO, April.

———. 1995. *Training in conflict resolution: Jal-el-Deeb*. Paris: IPRA/International Alert, March.

Paye, Olivier, and Eric Remacle. 1994. Conflicts in Abkhazia and Nagorno-Karabakh. Paper presented at IPRA Conference, Valletta, Malta, November.

Report on Training of Trainers. 1994. Paris: IPRA/UNESCO, February.

Ryan, Stephan. 1990. The United Nations and the resolution of ethnic conflicts. Paper presented at IPRA Conference, Groningen, Netherlands.

Sanàa Osseiran

CONFUCIANISM

Confucianism is a system of thought dominant in China and parts of east Asia for more than 2,000 years. The name Confucius is a Latin rendering of Master Kong (c. 551–479 B.C.E.), the Chinese name of a wise man from the state of Lu (modern Shantung), who proclaimed his love for the learning of antiquity. "I transmit but do not create," he said; "I love antiquity and am faithful to it." Kong had a strong sense of his own mission, associated with teaching. He appears to have been a modest, religious man, who sought to understand and follow heaven's will. But he lived in an age of turmoil, during which the ancient religious beliefs were questioned, and he contributed to the rationalist atmosphere of philosophical reflection. His teachings are best found in the Analects—the record of his conversations with his disciples. But Confucianism regards as its special texts the Classics—books of widely divergent genres. In his time there were six, including the Book of Changes or Yijing, well known today in the West as a divination manual; the Book of Historical Documents or Shujing; the Book of Songs or Poetry or Shijing; the Classic of Rites or Lijing; the Spring-Autumn Annals, a chronicle of Kong's native state of Lu; and a sixth, the Book of Music, which is no longer extant.

Relationships within Confucianism

Within Confucianism, the well-known Five Relationships include ruler–minister, father–son, husband–wife, elder and younger brother, and friend and friend. Three of these are family relationships, and the other two are usually conceived in terms of the family models. For example, the ruler–minister relationship resembles father–son, and friendship resembles brotherliness. For this reason, Confucian society regards itself as a large family: "Within the four seas all men are brothers" (Analects 12: 5). The responsibilities ensuing from these relationships are supposed to be mutual and reciprocal, but the relationships emphasize the vertical sense of hierarchy. And the duty of filial piety, the need of procuring progeny for the sake of ensuring the continuance of the ancestral cult, has been for centuries an ethical justification for polygamy. Kong supported the patriarchal character of society in general. He said: "Women and people of low birth are very hard to deal with. If you are familiar with them, they get out of hand. If you keep your distance, they resent it" (Analects 17: 25).

Social Behavior and Religious Rituals

Confucianism is not just about social behavior. It gives a definite importance to rituals, including religious rituals. The central doctrine is of the virtue of *ren*, which is associated with loyalty (*zhong*), loyalty to one's own heart and conscience; and reciprocity (*shu*), respect of and consideration for others (Analects 4: 25). *Ren* is translated variously as goodness, benevolence, humanity, and human-heartedness. It was formerly a particular virtue, the kindness that distinguished the gentleman in his behavior toward his inferiors. Kong transformed it into a universal virtue, that which makes the perfect human being, the sage.

Confucius's later follower in the fifth century B.C.E., the philosopher Mencius, emphasized that human nature is originally good and thus perfectible. He therefore taught that every person could become a sage (Mencius 6B: 2)—a teaching that has served to strengthen a basic belief in human equality. Mencius also emphasized that the taboo between the sexes should not prevent a man from helping to rescue a drowning woman, such as his sister-in-law (Mencius 4A:

17), thus putting human life and dignity before ritual law. And Confucian political philosophy promotes a benevolent government from above, which is different from western democracy. Yet Confucianism also taught that the ruler could govern only with a mandate from heaven, which he stood to lose if he became unworthy. Indeed, Mencius explicitly taught that people had a right to rebel against an unjust ruler (Mencius 1B: 8, 7B: 14).

Confucianism became the established orthodoxy for the Chinese state in the second century B.C.E. and remained dominant for most of premodern times, spreading to Korea, Japan, and Vietnam. Its later movement is sometimes known as Neo-Confucianism, a western coinage. Neo-Confucian thinkers concentrated their attention on the Four Books: the Analects of Confucius; the Book of Mencius, also a collection of conversations; and the Great Learning and the Doctrine of the Mean, two short treatises derived from the Book of Rites. The movement oriented itself increasingly toward metaphysical and spiritual questions and assimilated much from Buddhist and Daoist philosophies. Zhu Xi (or Chu Hsi) (1130–1200) is the best known and the most prolific Neo-Confucian scholar. His commentaries (on the Four Books) were eventually integrated into the curriculum of the civil service examinations (1313), making his philosophy the new state orthodoxy for six centuries.

In the late nineteenth century, when China was shaken politically and psychologically by western intrusion, Confucianism was regarded by many as intellectual shackles, preventing modernization and stifling human freedom and individual initiative in the name of passive, conformist virtues. With the Communists' takeover of the mainland (1949), vigorous debates took place over the merits and demerits of the Confucian tradition. Succeeding decades witnessed the rise of Japan as an economic giant and the rapid economic and political growth of the Pacific rim countries, where Confucianism was never formally rejected. Now it is credited with offering a work ethic and family solidarity for Chinese, Japanese, Koreans, and Vietnamese and promoting their economic development. This claim is being increasingly recognized in western society.

Confucianism has often been criticized for subjugating women to men. Actually, the process began before Confucius, with the development of a patriarchal kinship system (zongfa or tsung-fa) associated with the ancestral cult. The ritual texts speak about "three obediences," subjecting women to their fathers, to their husbands, and then to their sons during widowhood.

Speaking generally, women's position deteriorated in Chinese history, a process that was intensified by Zhu Xi's

school, which taught that wives were to husbands as ministers were to rulers, thereby discouraging the remarriage of widows, which had been much more commonplace earlier. And while it was never part of the school's teaching, Confucianism did not discourage the custom of foot binding for young girls, which became widespread in China after the fourteenth century and was abrogated only in the twentieth century.

See Also

HOUSEHOLDS AND FAMILIES: EAST ASIA; POLITICS AND THE STATE: EAST ASIA; RELIGION: OVERVIEW

References and Further Reading

Andors, Phyllis. 1983. *The unfinished liberation of Chinese women, 1949–1980*. Bloomington: Indiana University Press.

Ching, Julia. 1997. *Mysticism and sagehood in China*. Cambridge: Cambridge University Press.

Johnson, Kay. 1985. *Women, the family, and peasant revolution in China*. Chicago: University of Chicago Press.

Karim, Wazir Jahan, ed. 1995. *"Male" and "female" in developing southeast Asia*. Washington, D.C.: Berg.

Kit-Wah, Eva Man. 1993. Chinese women in the family: A Confucian perspective. *Tripod* 77: 19–28.

Sharma, Arvind, ed. 1994. *Today's women in world religions*. Albany: State University of New York Press.

Julia Ching

CONSCIOUSNESS-RAISING

Consciousness-raising is a central activity of the women's liberation movement, enabling women as a group to share problems, experiences, and feelings. It allows women to recognize that what they perceive as personal problems—"problems that have no name"—are shared with others. It also enables women to realize that what they think of as resulting from their own personal inadequacy, or their own inability, may be a result of living in a patriarchal society—that the personal is often political.

Consciousness-raising can be seen as enabling women to overcome false consciousness—to throw off the man-made model of women, come to a realization of their own potential, and move from self-deluded dependence to autonomy and self-reliance. This view is reflected in the "consciousness-raising novels" of the 1970s—for example, Marilyn French's *The Women's Room* (1977). Liz Stanley and Sue Wise (1983) point out that consciousness-raising is not just a series of stages—going from a prefeminist consciousness to one of true understanding, a feminist consciousness—but an ongoing process. It is a process that brings about personal and collaborative change as opposed to structural change. The need for ongoing discussion—in small groups or informally—is, they suggest, central to being a feminist.

See Also

FEMININE MYSTIQUE; FEMINISM: OVERVIEW; SLOGANS: "THE PERSONAL IS THE POLITICAL"; WOMEN'S MOVEMENT, *specific topics*

References and Further Reading

Robinson, Victoria. 1993. Introducing women's studies. In D. Richardson and V. Robinson, eds., *Introducing women's studies*. London: Macmillan.

Stanley, Liz, and Sue Wise. 1983. *Breaking out*. London: Routledge and Kegan Paul (2nd ed. 1993).

Pamela Abbott

CONSERVATISM

The Evolution of Western Conservatism

Lamenting the challenges and utopian ideals offered by Enlightenment rationalist philosophers of the late eighteenth century, Edmund Burke produced the seminal work on conservatism in 1790. His *Reflections on the Revolution in France* criticized the assumption that drastically altering the political system in order to promote abstract ideals such as liberty, equality, and fraternity would result in positive societal change. Burke emphasized instead slow change through existing institutions that have at their center history, religion, and tradition. It is not the case that conservatism resists all change; rather, as Burke proposed, conservatism should reflect the willingness to "change in order to conserve."

Although Burke is generally credited with establishing the central tenets of conservatism, it is difficult to equate the history of conservatism and conservative principles with Burkean philosophy or even with the history of England or France. Unlike Marxism, socialism, or communism, all of which are tied in more explicit ways to specific historical figures or events, conservatism has evolved differently in response to changes in governmental structures, such as the transition from monarchy to representative government, technological changes such as industrialization, and the ideological challenge of feminism. Despite the variations within

conservatism, there are several elements that are central to all conservative ideologies. These include commitment to the defense of tradition, support for authority, a defense of the right to own private property, an assumption that humans are imperfect and fallible (and a distrust in the ability of government to solve the problems of society related to human imperfection), a willingness to limit individual freedom in order to preserve traditional values or maintain social order, an organic view of society, and, to varying degrees, support for free market economic principles.

Conservatives are committed to defending tradition, which is assumed to reflect the wisdom of those who have gone before and who have made decisions with the benefit of long experience. For this reason, conservatives tend to resist change unless change is necessary in order for society to evolve in a nonrevolutionary manner. Part and parcel of conservative ideology is that it is important for people to have the right to own property privately, although the conservative view should not be assumed to be congruent with the classical liberal principle of property ownership, which entitles owners to use their property however they see fit. For conservatives, property ownership not only provides an individual with a vested interest in society, especially in maintaining order; it also entails certain obligations and, in the case of inheritance of property, reflects the conservative commitment to preserving tradition.

A further defining element of conservatism is the assumption that humans are imperfect, flawed creatures who need the guidance provided by strong family structures and government-enforced law and order to exist together peaceably. Whereas conservatives generally support a strong state in order to promote the law and order deemed necessary by the imperfect nature of the human condition, it is important to note that conservatives do not support the notion that government should or can intervene to try to improve people (Oakeshott, 1962). The exception to this principle is that conservatives do support government intervention in the case of preserving traditional values, or at least in preserving what they deem the best moral standards that the past represents (Kirk, 1954). Government involvement in economic matters has been an inconsistent element of conservatism, ranging from support for the laissez-faire economic principles of Adam Smith in the 1800s to the more interventionist policies of John Maynard Keynes in the early twentieth century, and back to more laissez-faire principles in the late twentieth century. The economic policies of Margaret Thatcher and John Major in the United Kingdom and of Ronald Reagan and George Bush in the United States illustrate this shift from Keynesianism to less government intervention in economic policies, and, perhaps more important, illustrate one contemporary branch of conservatism: neoconservatism (the new right). Neoconservatives subscribe to a distinctively libertarian economic philosophy that is coupled with a clearly conservative social philosophy, at least to the extent that social order must be maintained even while economic freedom is expanded (Nozick, 1974).

Conservatism and Women's Politics

It is against this backdrop that the conservative view of society as organic becomes most important in considering the role of conservatism in women's politics. Their organic view of society means that conservatives consider family structures to be "natural" and the basis of the larger structure of society. Contrary to liberalism, conservatism holds that membership in both the family and society cannot be seen as based on either tacit or voluntary consent, and, in this sense, cannot be viewed as approximating a social contract. Rather, the family, because it is the basic unit on which all other social institutions are formed, in the conservative view, must be preserved and defended at all costs. For conservatives, this is so even if patriarchy and inequality are fostered by traditional familial relationships. As women are necessarily disadvantaged by the patriarchy and inequality that may be argued to be inherent in traditional familial structures, conservatism has posed a particular paradox for women. To defend conservatism is tantamount to accepting or even supporting traditional, patriarchal familial structures. By contrast, to oppose conservatism is to undermine the most abiding element of women's status in the social order, that of wife, mother, and moral guardian. That the price of equality has meant at various times in history abandoning those roles, or at least redefining them, has placed conservatism squarely in the center of women's politics. Whether the distinction is between women as social conservatives or economic conservatives (Klatch, 1987) or between women as either conservative or feminist, the ideological battleground of women's politics has often contained an element of conservatism.

Perhaps more than in any other country, this can be seen in the politics of women's movements in the United States. The distinctive historical context provided by a country that was built on assumptions about property rights and individual freedom, that had a strong religious foundation, and that experienced very early in its history the Industrial Revolution, created an environment in which ideological battles centering on conservatism were bound to proliferate. Whether we consider the temperance movement of the late nineteenth century, the struggle for suffrage in the late nineteenth and early twentieth centuries,

or the second-wave feminist movement of the 1960s, women's involvement with these elements of conservatism—either as opponents or as defenders—has been complex and fluid.

Temperance and Suffrage in the United States

The temperance movement is an intriguing historical example of the complex intersection of gender and ideology. Frances Willard, founder of the Women's Christian Temperance Union (WCTU), was able to mobilize many traditional, conservative women to join the temperance movement, because the call for prohibition was worded in the language of protecting the family. For example, prohibitionists argued that men wasted money on alcohol instead of providing for their families, and that alcohol contributed to domestic violence and promoted prostitution. This approach made possible the mobilization of thousands of conservative women, yet Willard herself was far from conservative (Fowler, Hertzke, and Olson, 1999). Dean of a women's college, and professor of aesthetics, Willard used the WCTU to promote the creation of kindergartens, reforms in child labor laws, and, perhaps most important, women's suffrage. The WCTU was able to convince the conservative women it had mobilized that prohibition would come only if women got the vote. In this manner, the WCTU mobilized conservative women to participate in a struggle for women's rights that in some regards seemed to contradict conservative ideology.

Suffrage was not, however, an issue that was clearly defined ideologically. Influential leaders of the early women's movement, such as Susan B. Anthony and Elizabeth Cady Stanton, were far more liberal than the majority of women who supported suffrage. Many women who supported suffrage did so not because they embraced feminist or liberal ideals but because they believed that in doing so they were acting in the best interest of their families. Embracing their "natural" roles as wives and mothers, these women supported suffrage as a means of securing the ability to influence legislation regarding child labor, working conditions for women, and better government. In this manner, their conservatism did not contradict their support of suffrage; rather, it was a logical extension of their commitment to their traditional roles, despite the fact that it placed them alongside their feminist and liberal sisters (McGlen and O'Connor, 1998).

Conservatism and Second-Wave Feminism in the United States

An important recent addition to the discussion of women and conservatism in United States politics centers on the second-wave feminism of the 1960s that provided the impetus for the proposed Equal Rights Amendment (ERA) to the U.S. Constitution in 1972. This is especially important in understanding the evolution of the most recent manifestation of conservatism: neoconservatism. Partly in response to the permissiveness of the 1960s—which was evidenced by student radicalism, civil disobedience, sexual freedom, a growing illegal drug culture, and the willingness to challenge and question authority—and partly in response to the reemergence of feminism as an influential political ideology, neoconservatism flourished in the 1980s. Although it was certainly not their intention, feminist activists in the United States helped to fan the flames of neoconservatism.

Neoconservatives called for a return to "family values" (what Thatcher called "Victorian values" in the United Kingdom) and social order against the backdrop of a deregulated economy and a commitment to strong national defense. This new face of conservatism was a direct response to a perceived upheaval in social institutions such as traditional familial relationships and traditional gender roles. The battle over the ERA in the United States is one example that clearly illustrates the way in which conservatism structured the battle for women's rights for both feminists and neoconservatives.

Proposed as an amendment to the U.S. Constitution in 1972, the ERA was the first tangible piece of legislation that spelled out the equality that feminist women in the United States were seeking. The ERA was perceived by neoconservatives as a threat to—even a destruction of—everything that they believed was important about women and women's traditional roles. The ERA, by bringing equal legal status to men and women, was seen by neoconservative women as threatening not only their specific roles as wives and mothers but the "family values" that they believed were central to maintaining the very structure of society. In this manner, the ERA was a specific issue that reflected the general trend toward a more permissive society in which the roles of men and women would no longer clearly be differentiated. Traditional values, it seemed, would no longer have any safe haven, as their very existence required a clear sense of difference in gender roles; and the ERA, its opponents argued, would eliminate any legal difference between the sexes. This strategy, employed by anti-ERA activists such as Phyllis Schlafly, was to a certain extent successful, as many women came to believe that the ERA would actually undermine the status of women and, hence, they mobilized against it. Although the ratification of the ERA seemed assured, because in 1972 it had overwhelming support (especially in the U.S. Senate), the battle for ratification in the

state legislatures was doomed to fail. Thirty-eight states would have to ratify the amendment for it to become a law, and despite an initial flurry of support, by 1982, even though extensions were granted by the U.S. Supreme Court, only 35 states had voted to ratify. The failure of the ERA to be ratified is due in large part to the activism of neoconservative women who mobilized against feminist women around the issue of women's legal equality. In this manner, even for an issue that seems so clearly linked to feminism, the importance of conservatism and its influence on women's politics cannot be overlooked.

As the battle over the ERA illustrates, there are profound differences between feminists and conservatives in terms of ideologies and values. Conservative women in the antifeminist movement argue that sex differences are innate and biologically determined. Thus, women are unique and different from men and any attempt to equalize men and women has the potential to threaten the institution of the family and women's roles as wives and mothers. For conservatives, to do this is tantamount to destroying the very cement of society, because the family for them is the basic social unit on which all other societal institutions are built.

Women and Contemporary Nonwestern Conservatism

Although our previous discussion of women's politics emphasized the clash of conservatism with a liberal feminist movement, it should be noted that this clash between the two core ideologies—that is, liberalism and conservatism—in the United States does not always represent the conflict about gender politics in other parts of the world. For instance, gender politics in postcommunist eastern European countries has to be at least partially understood as a response to the experience of communism.

The western idea that patriarchy and capitalism are at the heart of women's oppression does not adequately describe eastern European and post-Soviet gender politics. Many eastern European and former Soviet countries are characterized by an "intensification of gender segregations in the economy and society as a whole" (Molyneux, 1994: 293). Studies on the role of women in these countries (for example, Heitlinger, 1996) show that vehement antifeminism is not only based on a conservative ideology that values motherhood and family but also represents a backlash against communism and state socialism—ideologies that favored, at last officially, the "emancipation" of women. In fact, there is evidence suggesting that Russian, Lithuanian, and Ukrainian women are more skeptical about democratization and capitalism than their male counterparts, possibly because the new capitalistic market systems are not perceived as dealing as effectively with women's concerns as the old communist systems (Hesli and Miller, 1993).

Gender relations in many developing countries are characterized by a resurgence of nationalism and religious fundamentalism. For instance, an analysis of the politics of gender in Islamic nations shows that western feminist discourse contributes only little to an understanding of women's roles. Whereas conservative women from advanced industrialized western nations assert that legal equality between men and women has already been achieved, women in many Middle Eastern countries, parts of Africa, and the Asia-Pacific regions live in societies that are deeply segregated along gender lines. Those women are subject to a deep-rooted social and cultural conservatism, which is often justified by religious doctrine. Although fundamentalist movements are far from monolithic, they tend to converge in their opposition to women's equality. This opposition is not so much the result of religious beliefs as prescribed by the Qur'an, the Sunnah, or the Hadith—the three sources of Islamic religion—but rather stems from a particularly modern interpretation of these writings that justifies women's subordination and sexually repressive practices.

Although much of the literature on women in developing nations emphasizes women's roles as victims, it ignores the significant presence of women's movements in most of these nations and the significant activism of women. Obviously, women who live in societies in which religion continues to regulate all aspects of daily life and is a source of personal identity apply different benchmarks to measure the success of women. Western standards of progress, such as economic equality and access to legalized abortions, are of less significance to women struggling for elementary rights, such as access to education or the right to protect their bodies from violence. Given the many social, cultural, and economic constraints, women's activism has developed in dialogue with prevailing cultural contexts. Women in Islamic nations draw on the universal concept of human rights; however, they, along with many of their African sisters, reject western notions of extreme individualism. Instead of rejecting religion, they seek to reinterpret religious doctrine to end centuries of discrimination against women.

Despite these profound differences in women's activism, there are many unifying features. Similar to the United States women's temperance and early suffrage movements, many of the women's movements all over the world emerged from more traditional women's concerns over the family. For instance, the initial organizing of women in many Latin American countries was not political in the conventional sense, but reinforced traditional women's roles as mothers, wives, and sisters. An example that stands out is the Mothers of the Plaza de Mayo, an Argentinian group of women who protested the disappearance of their family members under military dictatorship. Instead of basing their protests on their rights as citizens, these women used their traditional gender identity as mothers, wives, and grandmothers to politicize their demands. Their activities, which were seemingly apolitical, made it possible for women to occupy political spaces that were previously vacant (Jacquette and Wolchik, 1998; Marshall, 2000).

Toward the Future of Conservatism

It is undeniable that one of the major elements of conservatism, limited government involvement as long as social order is not threatened, has become increasingly important for the twenty-first century. The demise of communist and socialist governments has given way to a privatized and deregulated economic system in many parts of the world. At the same time, economic freedom and the consequent free market values that it engenders may create particular problems for conservatism in the future. Heywood (1998) argues the values and behaviors created by late twentieth-century conservatism (particularly by neoconservatism) have produced an environment that promotes self-seeking competitiveness (the heart of free market economics) at the expense of social order and stability, something that would seem anathema to conservatism. Because conservatism requires government-mandated social order and the preservation of tradition, it is possible that the individualistic and egoistic behaviors and values created by the economic principles of the most recent wave of conservatism may prove to be its own worst enemy. In the absence of communism and socialism as serious economic or ideological challenges to contemporary conservatism, this apparent internal paradox may be the new threat to twenty-first-century conservatism.

See Also

FUNDAMENTALISM; FUNDAMENTALISM AND PUBLIC POLICY; LIBERALISM; POLITICS AND THE STATE: OVERVIEW

References and Further Reading

Fowler, Robert Booth, Allen D. Hertzke, and Laura R. Olson. 1999. *Religion and politics in America.* Boulder, Col.: Westview.

Heitlinger, Alena. 1996. Framing feminism in the postcommunist Czech Republic. *Communist and Post-Communist Studies* 29(1): 77–93.

Hesli, Vicki L., and Arthur Miller. 1993. The gender base of institutional support in Lithuania, Ukraine and Russia. *Europe-Asia Studies* 45(3): 505–533.

Heywood, Andrew. 1998. *Political ideologies.* New York: Worth.

Jaquette, Jane, and Sharon L. Wolchik. 1998. *Women and democracy: Latin American and Central and Eastern Europe.* Baltimore, Md.: Johns Hopkins University Press.

Kirk, Russell. 1954. *A program for conservatives.* Chicago: Henry Regnery.

Klatch, Rebekah. 1987. *Women of the New Right.* Philadelphia: Temple University Press.

Marshall, Barbara L. 2000. *Configuring gender: Explorations in theory and politics.* Peterborough, Ont.: Broadview.

Molyneux, Maxine. 1994. Women's rights and the international context: Some reflections on the postcommunist states. *Millennium* 23(2): 287–313.

McGlen, Nancy E., and Karen O'Connor. 1998. *Women, politics, and American society.* Upper Saddle River, N.J.: Prentice Hall.

Nozick, Robert. 1974. *Anarchy, state and utopia.* Oxford: Blackwell.

Oakeshott, Michael. 1962. *Rationalism in politics and other essays.* New York: Basic Books.

Lorraine Bernotsky
Frauke Schnell

CONSTITUTIONS

The constitution of a nation-state specifies political goals and institutions, and defines relationships between people and the state. The practice of codifying basic principles dates from the eighteenth century. The United States (1787) and France (1789 and 1791) set a pattern, granting limited powers to government and individual rights to certain men. In the twentieth century, in the wake of wars, colonialism, and communism, writing a constitution became a part of the founding process of every new state. Today, all but three nations (Israel, New Zealand, and the United Kingdom) have a codified constitution (collected in Blaustein and Flanz, 1971+). Constitutions carry exceptional authority. They stand above and regulate legislation and governmental actions, legitimate and delegitimize certain goals and groups, and often symbolize national identity and social ideals.

The doctrine that constitutions derive authority from the consent of free and rational individuals is problematic for women. Pateman (1989: 79–81) believes there has never been equal respect for the consent of women and men. Women's consent has been proxied, assumed, or falsified. Some theorists argue that individualism misrepresents the moral vision and experience of women, who live in a web of relationships with men, women, and children (Gilligan, 1982). Bills of rights for individuals are alleged to divide and isolate women, disguising the structural nature of oppression. The prevalent liberal model, originating in western thought, has been contested as colonization through constitutionalism.

Regardless, the authority of constitutions lends significance to their treatment of women. Constitutional texts may speak directly of women. But their silences also contribute to the construction of gender norms and roles. The language of many constitutions makes women invisible, granting universal rights in the generic masculine ("words importing the masculine gender shall be taken to include females," Pakistan, Art. 263). Ostensibly neutral words may conceal gender bias, as when "citizenship" is transmitted through the male line or bears responsibilities like military service sometimes barred to women. Some recent texts speak directly of women and men (Hungary, 1989; Nicaragua, 1987; South Africa, 1996). Yet all contain provisions that affect women and men differently, through language and through institutions such as federalism that divide power in ways that have an impact on women. And constitutions almost without exception are heterosexual documents, rarely even acknowledging discrimination on grounds of sexual orientation (South Africa, Art. 9).

Contradictions in Constitutions

The writing of constitutions is a political process, and textual compromises and contradictions abound. Constitutions typically make simple, skeletal declarations that cannot match the complexity of the roles of women in families, economies, and states. One problem is to reconcile individual freedom and equality with still-respected but inegalitarian traditional cultures and customary law. The constitution of South Africa prioritizes "nonsexism" (Sections 30, 31, 39, 212); it also protects language, cultural and religious freedom, and traditional authorities (Section 1), leaving open the question whether both are possible. When paternal transmission of citizenship was challenged in Botswana, it was said that "if gender discrimination were outlawed in customary law, very little of customary law would be left at all" (Bazilli, 1991: 259). Customary property rights, inheritance laws, and hierarchies conflict with individual rights from Africa to southeast Asia and the Aboriginal nations of Australia.

Contradictions between rights and religions also leave women's status contested. In Islamic nations, constitutions may recognize both religious law and women's rights. Algeria affirms political and labor equality and an Islamic Family Code of obedience to husbands. Egypt guarantees equality and coordination between "the duties of the woman toward the family and her work in the society, considering her equal with man in the fields of political, social, cultural and economic life without violation of the rules of Islamic jurisprudence" (Arts. 8, 10). In the Catholic tradition, Ireland's guarantee of equality "shall not be held to mean that the State shall not ... have due regard to differences of capacity, physical and moral, and of social function" (Art. 40), categories of difference most often used to subordinate women's roles.

The family, sexuality, and reproductive rights are critical issues for constitutionalism, exemplifying the allocation of power over women's lives. Gender difference, historically centered on these concerns, conflicts with secular as well as traditional and religious beliefs, with the aspirations to equality raised by liberal constitutionalism, and with women's full participation in economic and political life. In a characteristic evasion, women are often constructed simultaneously as free and equal individuals and in the circumscribed roles of wife, mother, and dependent: "Men and women are equal before the law. The law shall protect the organization and development of the family" (Mexico, Art. 4). Alternatively, the Irish constitution states the equal right to life of unborn and mother, and elevates the family as bearer of rights "antecedent and superior to all positive laws" (Art. 40, 41). Mexico's Article 4 grants "every person" the right to decide in a "free, responsible, and informed manner on the number and spacing of ... children," but this gender-neutral statement brings its own problems, giving men equal rights in decisions about women's bodies. Where, as in the United States, a constitution is silent on family and reproductive issues, women still seek constitutional recognition, but their claims may be insecurely resolved by inference from rights to equality or privacy.

Interpretation of Constitutions

What a constitution fails to specify or prioritize, legislators and courts will interpret: "In view of the different legal and institutional starting position with regard to the employment of mothers and fathers, it shall be the task of the all-German legislator to shape the legal situation in such a way as to allow a reconciliation of family and occupational life" (German Treaty of Unification, 1990, Art. 31). The paper powers of constitutions become political forces through human agency. Most constitutions embody dominant assumptions and biases from the time of their writing. Stiff requirements for amending these texts, along with the practice of interpretation and enforcement through courts, commonly led by men, make them resistant to change. Two centuries of American constitutionalism (with two female Supreme Court justices out of 108) show only slow and uncertain progress. Often there is no attempt to make a constitution work, and declarations of equality remain pious hopes. The Japanese equal rights clauses (1946, Arts. 14, 24) were little used for decades, although lately, Japanese women have used the constitution to advance legal equality through litigation and legislation. Thus constitutional equality on its own does not guarantee substantive change in women's lives. Gains for women in protection and social rights to education, welfare, or housing contained in new eastern European constitutions have been negated by the disproportionate economic loss, increased violence, and restricted reproductive rights suffered during the postcommunist transition (Scheppele, 1995: 66).

Many features of national constitutions recur in international conventions (Peters and Wolper, 1995). The influential European Convention on the Protection of Human Rights (1950) grants civil right such as "respect for his private and family life, his home," without "discrimination on any ground such as sex." United Nations conventions on the political and marital rights of women (1952, 1957, 1962) and the Elimination of All Forms of Discrimination Against Women (1979, with 151 signatory states by 1996) proscribe discrimination, seek to reconcile family and individual rights through aligning the responsibilities of women and men, and in most cases comprehensively endorse women's need for social as well as civil rights. Educational and symbolic at first, these instruments and national constitutions are now monitored by an international women's rights movement (see Sisterhood Is Global Institute, 2000). But their role remains educational and symbolic, without adequate means for enforcement. International Labor Organization conventions and the single gender-specific clause of the European Economic Community Treaty of Rome (1957, Art. 119), requiring equal pay for equal work, have also made some gains for women in the workforce but still fail to reconcile work with reproductive and family roles.

Why, then, have women found some hopeful prospects in constitutional politics? First, inclusion gives symbolic standing and recognition. And, second, even a right that is contradicted, overruled, or ignored in practice creates a resource for women. Women have contested constitutional constructions of gender, used existing texts to their benefit, and demanded change. Women in the United States failed to win an Equal Rights Amendment. Canadian women demanded a guarantee of equality in the Charter of Rights and Freedoms (Canada, 1982, s. 28) and have used this to win a measure of social change. Women in Brazil (Verucci, 1991), postcommunist East Germany (Scheppele, 1995), South Africa, and elsewhere have seized the initiative in the formative phases of constitutions (Bazilli, 1991). As women recognize the pervasive presence of constitutions in twenty-first-century politics, they are increasingly appropriating these authoritative texts for their own needs.

See Also

CITIZENSHIP; GOVERNMENT; HUMAN RIGHTS

References and Further Reading

Bazilli, Susan, ed. 1991. *Putting women on the agenda.* Johannesburg: Ravan.

Blaustein, Albert F., and Gilbert H. Flanz, eds. 1971+. *Constitutions of the countries of the world.* Dobbs Ferry, N.Y.: Oceana.

Connelly, Alpha. 1999. Women and the constitution of Ireland. In Yvonne Galligan, Ellis Ward, and Rick Wilford, eds., *Contesting politics: Women in Ireland, north and south,* 18–37. Boulder, Col.: Westview.

Dobrowolsky, Alexandra. 2000. *The politics of pragmatism: Women, representation, and constitutionalism in Canada.* Don Mills, Ont.: Oxford University Press.

Gilligan, Carol. 1982. In *a different voice: Psychological theory and women's development.* Cambridge, Mass.: Harvard University Press, chapter 5.

Pateman, Carole. 1989. *The disorder of women.* Stanford, Calif.: Stanford University Press.

Peters, Anne. 1999. *Women, quotas and constitutions.* The Hague: Kluwer Law.

Peters, Julie, and Andrea Wolper. 1995. *Women's rights, human rights: International feminist perspectives.* London and New York: Routledge.

Scheppele, Kim Lane. 1995. Women's rights in eastern Europe. *East European Constitutional Review* 4: 66–69.

Tétreault, Mary Ann, and Haya al-Mughni. 2000. From subjects to citizens: Women and the nation in Kuwait. In Sita Ranchod Nilsson and Mary Ann Tétreault, eds., *Women, states, and nationalism.* London and New York: Routledge.

Verucci, Florisa. 1991. Women and the new Brazilian constitution. *Feminist Studies* 17: 551–68.

Internet Sources

International Constitutional Law. 2000. <http://www.uni-wuerzburg.de/law/>

Sisterhood Is Global Institute. 2000. <http://www.sigi.org/>

Vivien Hart

CONTRACEPTION

Numerous options for contraception are available for women, many of them highly effective. Each method is reviewed here. Female methods are described first, and then male methods are discussed, each category in order from most effective to least effective.

The *failure rate* for a contraceptive method is defined as follows. If 100 women use the method for a year, the number who are pregnant by the end of the year is the failure rate. Failure rates are further classed as *perfect-user* and *typical-user* failure rates. The typical-user failure rate refers to actual use of the method and includes mistakes made by users, such as forgetting to take a pill or neglecting to use a diaphragm. The perfect-user failure rate is just that—the failure rate for a person using the method perfectly.

Sterilization

Two surgical procedures are available for female sterilization: minilaparotomy and laparoscopy ("having the tubes tied," or tubal ligation). Both are performed under either local or general anesthesia and involve blocking the fallopian tubes so that sperm and egg cannot meet. In both cases, the physician makes a small incision in the abdomen, identifies each fallopian tube, severs it, and then blocks each end with a small clip or by tying or electrocoagulation.

Following the surgery, the ovaries continue to function normally and, therefore, the production of sex hormones continues. The failure rate is 0.5 percent (occasionally, the ends of the tubes will rejoin).

Female sterilization should be considered a permanent method of contraception, although researchers are developing increasingly effective methods for reversing the procedure if a woman changes her mind and wishes to have a child.

Sterilization is a common method of birth control; in the United States, for example, it is the most common method for married couples. In 1990, 30 percent of married white women and 48 percent of married black women in the United States were sterilized, as were 20 percent of married white men and 2 percent of married black men (Mosher, 1990).

Implants and Injectables

Norplant consists of six rod-shaped capsules, each about the size of a matchbook match, that are implanted under the skin in the upper arm. Depo-Provera (DMPA) is administered by injection. Both methods deliver progestin (a synthetic progesterone) at a steady rate.

Norplant and Depo-Provera work by inhibiting ovulation; in addition, they thicken the cervical mucus, making it difficult for sperm to penetrate it; and they reduce the lining of the uterus (endometrium) so that it will not provide an adequate environment for implantation should a fertilized egg arrive.

Norplant has a failure rate of only 0.05 percent. It lasts for five years and then must be replaced. Depo-Provera has a typical-user failure rate of less than 1 percent. Women using Depo-Provera must obtain a new shot every three months, because it is effective only for that length of time.

Few side effects have been documented for either method. Many women using these methods experience menstrual irregularities, such as amenorrhea (absence of menstruation), because of the interference with natural hormone levels.

The Pill

Three basic types of pills are available: the combination pill, which provides a steady high dose of both estrogen and progestin; the triphasic pill, which provides a steady level of estrogen but varying levels of progestin corresponding roughly to the natural cycle; and the progestin-only pill, which contains progestin but no estrogen. Most of the discussion that follows focuses on the combination pill, because it is the one most widely used.

The Pill works by preventing ovulation; it provides backup effects as well, thickening the cervical mucus so that it is difficult for sperm to penetrate, and changing the lining of the uterus so that, if a fertilized egg does arrive, it will have little chance of successfully implanting and growing.

The Pill has a perfect-user failure rate of 0.1 percent and a typical-user failure rate of 5 percent. Failures occur primarily because the woman forgets to take a pill. If she forgets one pill, she should take it as soon as she remembers it and then take the next one at the regular time. If she forgets two pills, the chance of pregnancy increases and she should use a backup method for the rest of the cycle.

The IUD

The intrauterine device (IUD) is a small piece of plastic that is inserted into the uterus by a medical professional. Different types of IUD may also contain progestin or copper, both of which are intended to improve effectiveness. The IUD can remain effective for long periods of time, up to five or ten years.

The mechanism for the effectiveness of the IUD has been somewhat murky. It is thought to prevent fertilization by creating an environment in the uterus that immobilizes sperm. The addition of copper reduces the chance of implantation. Added progestin thickens cervical mucus and reduces the chance of ovulation.

The IUD with copper has a failure rate of 0.8 percent in the first year and a lower failure rate after that. Most failures result from expulsion of the IUD, which is more likely in women who have not had children.

A rare but serious potential side effect of the IUD is pelvic inflammatory disease (PID), which is an infection of the uterus or fallopian tubes. The IUD may increase menstrual cramps and produce increased menstrual flow.

The Diaphragm and Cervical Cap

The diaphragm is a circular, dome-shaped device made of thin rubber, with a rubber-covered rim of flexible metal. A woman inserts it so that it covers her cervix. The cervical cap is quite similar except that the shape is somewhat different; it fits more snugly over the uterus. Each comes in different sizes and must be properly fitted by a medical professional.

Both the diaphragm and the cervical cap work by covering the entrance to the uterus, thus preventing sperm from reaching the egg. For proper use, both must be lined, before insertion, with a spermicidal cream, which kills any sperm that may get past the barrier of the device. They must be left in place for at least six hours after intercourse.

The typical-user failure rate for the diaphragm is around 20 percent. Most failures are due to improper use: a woman may not use the diaphragm, may not keep it in long enough, or may fail to use a spermicide with it. The cervical cap has a typical-user failure rate of around 18 percent, with most failures occurring for the same reasons as diaphragm failures.

The Female Condom

The female condom is made of polyurethane and resembles a clear balloon. It contains two rings, one at the top and one at the bottom. The smaller ring, with polyurethane reaching across it, is inserted by the woman into the vagina like a diaphragm, so that it covers the cervix. The other ring remains external and covers much of the vulva. Polyurethane then lines the vagina. The female condom is available over the counter; each condom should be used only once.

The female condom became available only in 1994, so data on its effectiveness are less certain than those for older methods. Early results indicate a typical-user failure rate of 21 percent.

No side effects appear to be associated with the female condom. A major advantage is that it provides some protection against sexually transmitted diseases (STDs).

Foams and Other Spermicides

Contraceptive foams, cream, jellies, and inserts are all spermicides, that is, sperm killers. They are inserted into the vagina before intercourse and are effective for only one act of intercourse.

Spermicides work in two ways. First, they contain chemicals that kill sperm. Second, the inert base, ideally, covers the entrance to the cervix so that sperm cannot swim into the uterus.

Spermicides are not very effective, with typical-user failure rates of 26 percent. In addition, some women are allergic to them. One advantage is that they are an over-the-counter method, not requiring a visit to a doctor or clinic. In addition, they may provide some protection from bacterial STDs such as chlamydia and gonorrhea; there is no evidence, however, that they provide protection against HIV.

Rhythm

Rhythm, or "fertility awareness," methods are a form of "natural" family planning and, as such, are the only methods approved by the Roman Catholic church. The essence of these methods is determining when the woman ovulates and abstaining from intercourse for several days before and after that date. Several variations exist, then, depending on the method used to determine the date of ovulation.

The calendar method is based on the assumption—well supported by the evidence—that women ovulate 14 days before the onset of menstruation. To implement the calendar method, a woman keeps track of her menstrual cycles for at least six months and preferably for a year. She then knows the length of her longest and shortest cycles and, from that information, can deduce the earliest and latest times in the cycle when she ovulates. She abstains from intercourse from four days before the earliest day of ovulation until three days after the latest date. Clearly, this method works best for women who have a very regular cycle. With an irregular cycle, it is difficult to pinpoint the day of ovulation, and two weeks of abstinence may be required.

The basal body temperature method makes use of the fact that a woman's first morning temperature drops on the day of ovulation and then rises the next day and stays somewhat higher for the rest of the cycle. This method can be combined with the calendar method for more accurate identification of ovulation.

The cervical mucus, or ovulation, method relies on well-documented changes in the consistency of the mucus produced by the cervix over the course of the cycle. A woman can be trained to "read" her cervical mucus and use it to determine the day of ovulation.

Home ovulation tests were developed only in the 1990s, so it is too early to know their effectiveness.

The typical-user failure rate is around 25 percent for all rhythm methods. Thus this method is not adequate for absolute prevention of pregnancy, but it may be adequate if the goal is to space children. In addition, the rhythm method may be combined with another method, such as the diaphragm, to increase its effectiveness.

Male Methods

Male methods of contraception have an enormous impact on women and therefore are reviewed here as well. At the beginning of the twenty-first century, only two male methods are available—sterilization and the condom—but other methods are under development. These potential methods include a male hormonal oral contraceptive (a male Pill) and hormonal implants (analogous to Norplant), both of which would reduce or stop sperm production.

The male sterilization procedure is known as vasectomy, because it involves severing and tying off the vas deferens, the tube that carries sperm from the testes to mix with the ejaculate. The procedure can be done in a physician's office and requires only about 20 minutes to perform. After the surgery, sperm are still manufactured, but they are prevented from moving through the duct structure, so that the ejaculate contains no sperm. The one exception is that a few stray sperm may linger postsurgically, so the man needs to have several ejaculations and a sperm count for verification. Then the method is 100 percent effective. It is a permanent method of contraception.

The male condom is a thin sheath that fits over the penis and, thus, prevents ejaculate from entering a woman's vagina. Condoms may be made of latex ("rubber"), polyurethane, or the intestinal skin of lambs. Latex condoms are by far the most frequently used. A major benefit is that they provide protection from several STDs. As a method of contraception, the condom has a 14 percent failure rate for typical users but a much lower failure rate, 3 percent, for perfect users.

Conclusion

A wide variety of contraceptive options are available to women today. Selection of the best method depends on the individual. If, for example, a woman has intercourse frequently (several times a week), she needs one of the highly effective methods such as Depo-Provera or the Pill. If she has intercourse infrequently (for example, once a month), a diaphragm may provide adequate protection. If she feels embarrassed about using a diaphragm or condom and may therefore not use it consistently, she will be better off with a method such as the Pill, which is unconnected with intercourse. If she needs protection from STDs, the condom—perhaps combined with a second method—is a good choice. If, however, she is in a monogamous relationship with an uninfected partner and she is uninfected as well, then the Pill or Depo-Provera is a good choice. Thus, the method, the individual, and her situation must all be considered in arriving at a "best" choice.

See Also

CONTRACEPTIVES: DEVELOPMENT; HEALTH: OVERVIEW; NORPLANT; THE PILL; REPRODUCTION: OVERVIEW; REPRODUCTIVE PHYSIOLOGY; REPRODUCTIVE RIGHTS; REPRODUCTIVE TECHNOLOGIES; RU 486

References and Further Reading

Hatcher, Robert A., et al. 1998. *Contraceptive technology*, 17th ed. New York: Ardent Media.

Hyde, J. S., and J. D. DeLamater. 2000. *Understanding human sexuality*, 7th ed. New York: McGraw-Hill.

Kaunitz, A. M. 1997. Reappearance of the intrauterine device: A "user-friendly" contraceptive. *International Journal of Fertility* 42: 120–127.

Marquette, C. M., L. M. Koonin, L. Antaish, P. M. Gargiullo, and J. C. Smith. 1995. Vasectomy in the United States, 1991. *American Journal of Public Health* 8: 644—649.

Mosher, W. D. 1990. Contraceptive practice in the United States, 1982—1988. *Family Planning Perspectives* 22: 198–205.

Janet Shibley Hyde

CONTRACEPTIVES: Development

Modern contraceptive development has a distinct history compared with that of other industrially manufactured drugs or devices: the decision concerning which birth control method to develop (or not to develop) has been determined primarily by the intersecting interests of population control institutions and the scientific community, rather than by the profit motives of the pharmaceutical industry—or by concern for women.

History before 1970

Throughout the ages and in many cultures, women have wanted means to gain greater control over their own fertility. Their wishes, however, have had only a marginal influence on the direction of modern contraceptive research. Until the 1960s, mainstream scientists and the pharmaceutical industry were reluctant to engage in contraceptive research because they did not want to confront social taboos concerning women's sexual freedom and reproductive self-determination.

Thus, although the pharmaceutical industry and mainstream scientists had the knowledge needed to develop a contraceptive pill as early as the 1920s, it was left to Gregory Pincus, a reproductive scientist who conducted contract research at a private foundation, to do much of the research into the oral contraceptive that became known as "the Pill." Pincus formulated the Pill in the 1950s, at the behest of Margaret Sanger of the Planned Parenthood Federation, who wanted women to have access to a contraceptive that would be easy to use. Sanger, like many of her contemporaries in the United States and elsewhere, was worried about "race suicide"; she feared that poor people, particularly black people, would "outbreed" white middle-class Americans. Though initially women-centered, Sanger's family-planning perspective had shifted toward a eugenic view, captured in her declaration: "More children from the fit, less from the unfit—that is the chief issue of birth control" (Gordon, 1990: 277). Sanger considered poor people to be less adept at using the contraceptive methods that were then available, such as the diaphragm, vaginal douches, condoms, the rhythm method, and withdrawal.

Unexpectedly, however, white, middle-class women enthusiastically took up the Pill when it became available in the early 1960s. Many mainstream accounts of contraceptive research hailed the Pill as a milestone of women's emancipation—but this was an unintended outcome of the technology and not in fact the intention behind its development. Feminist research has shown that the rise of the population control ideology in the late 1950s and early 1960s was the decisive factor in turning contraceptive development from an effort that scientists had shied away from into a socially acceptable, even desirable, endeavor (Clarke, 1998; Hartmann, 1995).

The negotiations that ultimately determined the nature of modern contraceptives took place primarily between 1925 and 1945 in western countries such as the United States and Germany. The main actors were advocates of birth control (including feminists who wanted reproductive self-determination, medical professionals who wanted to reduce maternal mortality, and eugenicists and neo-Malthusians who wanted population control) and reproductive scientists. Parallel to a shift from birth control as an issue of individual self-determination to an issue of population was a shift from "simple" user-controlled means of contraception to contraception that was under professional control (Clarke, 1998).

From the start of research into modern contraceptives, corporate and private foundations in the United States, such as the Rockefeller and Ford Foundations, were instrumental in creating institutions and networks of scientists to engage in contraceptive development. In the 1960s, lobbying by proponents of population control resulted in a substantial flow of public funds for contraceptive research and distribution. During the 1960s, however, the major part of the research funds came from pharmaceutical companies, attracted by the potentially enormous market for products to be used by women worldwide throughout their fertile years.

Developments after 1970

During the 1970s, this situation changed. Most large American companies started to pull out of research into and development of new contraceptives, partly in reaction to protests over inadequate testing of contraceptives. In addition, liability suits over the misleading safety claims of the first generation of (high-dose) pills and intrauterine devices (IUDs, in particular the Dalkon shield), had resulted in tighter standards for research prior to registration of a product; consequently, the cost of research and development increased. Women's associations and third world solidarity groups also opposed the introduction of unsafe products, especially the injectable hormonal contraceptive Depo-Provera. As a result, large pharmaceutical companies decided that other biomedical products would be more profitable and less controversial than birth control methods (Mastroianni, 1990: 61).

By the early 1990s, there was a clear dual research agenda for birth control methods: larger pharmaceutical companies tended to leave the financial risks of research on new contraceptives to governments, national and international organizations, and small entrepreneurial firms, while concentrating their own efforts on improving existing hormonal contraceptives for customers who could afford to pay for them (Gelijns and Pannenborg, 1993).

Nonprofit investment was focusing on new contraceptives that would be highly effective in preventing pregnancy, would have long-term action, and would pose a low risk of "user failure." These contraceptives were intended primarily for subsidized population programs in the third world. Preoccupation with "user failure" made little distinction between (1) incorrect use of contraceptives such as the Pill because of insufficient prior information about correct use and (2) cases where women deliberately stopped taking the

Pill because of its adverse effects (or because of a lack of care and compassion on the part of the services when users felt uncomfortable with hormonal contraception). "User failure" was also an easy (if inaccurate) label for pregnancies that occurred as a result of substandard quality or an irregular supply of contraceptives.

Large pharmaceutical companies have been willing to help perfect and market new contraceptives only if they were satisfied about the profit potential—and only after the initial research institutions had fostered public acceptance of these methods.

What was the result of the combination of scientists working in a narrow, biomedical framework that sees a woman's body as a reproductive machine—often with little consideration of the real-life situation of women—and a population framework that is preoccupied with bringing birthrates down? The outcome has been that the safety of contraceptives was given a lower priority than their efficacy. The focus on long-action methods with low rates of user failure resulted in the development of high-technology contraceptive methods with a significant potential for abuse. After the Pill, which a woman could discontinue at any time, came intrauterine devices (IUDs), injectable hormones, and implants, which act for months or years at a time, so that women have to wait until the contraceptive effect wears off or depend on a medically trained person for removal. (Two exceptions will be vaginal rings and skin patches, both hormonal methods that at the time of this writing were said to be close to market introduction; women can remove them at any time without professional help).

Research on barrier methods (such as diaphragms and male and female condoms), improvement of natural methods of family planning, and research into traditional methods and practices of fertility control and male contraceptives received only a fraction of worldwide contraceptive funding.

Contraceptive Research after Cairo

The women's movement has lobbied consistently for a reversal of this trend. In 1994, just before the International Conference on Population and Development in Cairo, some highly placed individuals within the contraceptive research establishment started calling for a reorientation of contraceptive research—away from "demographically driven goals" and toward addressing the "still unmet needs of women." But, because this reorientation was portrayed as "one of the best strategies for saving the planet" (Fatallah, 1994: 229), many participants in the women's and people's rights movements felt that, to some degree, it might actually represent a shift from "hard" to "soft" population control, a shift from coercion toward more subtle manipulation. A true reorientation of contraceptive development, they argued, cannot be achieved simply by adding a few more contraceptives to the gamut developed within a framework that is not people-centered. The women's movement also argued that in making decisions about the direction of contraceptive research, the research community must take the AIDS epidemic into account.

At the beginning of the twenty-first century, there are finally some substantial shifts in contraceptive development. More funds are now being allocated to research on barrier methods and microbicides. However, the challenge remains to reevaluate all birth control methods still being developed, such as the chemical sterilant Quinacrine and antifertility "vaccines"—a new class of contraceptives which act by turning the immune system against reproductive hormones or egg or sperm cells, and which a number of articles in scientific and popular media have described as offering unprecedented effectiveness for demographic control (Richter, 1996: 81–89). There is a great difference between a framework for development and distribution of contraceptives that aims to bring birthrates down and a framework designed to support women's reproductive self-determination and give men more methods to share the burdens of birth control. It is the difference between birth control as a duty and birth control as a right.

See Also

CONTRACEPTION; EUGENICS; FAMILY PLANNING; GLOBAL HEALTH MOVEMENT; NORPLANT; THE PILL; POPULATION CONTROL; PRO-CHOICE MOVEMENT; REPRODUCTIVE RIGHTS; REPRODUCTIVE TECHNOLOGIES; STERILIZATION

References and Further Reading

Clarke, Adele E. (1998). *Disciplining reproduction: Modernity, American life sciences, and the problem of sex.* Berkeley: University of California Press.

Corréa, Sonia. 1994. *Population and reproductive rights: Feminist perspectives from the South.* London: Zed, in association with Development Alternatives with Women for a New Era (DAWN).

Fathallah, Mahmoud F. (1994). "Fertility control technology: A women-centered approach to research." In Gita Sen et al., eds., *Population policies reconsidered: Health, empowerment, and rights.* Boston, Mass.: Harvard University Press.

Freedman, A. M. (1998). Two Americans export chemical sterilization to the third world. *Wall Street Journal* 1: A10, A11.

Gelijns, Anne Christine, and C. O. Pannenborg (1993). "The development of contraceptive technology: Case studies of incentives and disincentives to innovation." *International Journal of Technology Assessment and Health Care* 9(2): 210–232.

Gordon, Linda. 1990. *Women's body, women's right: Birth control in America,* rev. ed. New York: Penguin.

Hartmann, Betsy. 1995. *Reproductive rights and wrongs: The global politics of population control and contraceptive choice,* 2nd ed., 173–286. Boston: South End.

LaCheen, Cary. 1986. Population control and the pharmaceutical industry. In Kathleen McDonnell, ed., *Adverse effects: women and the pharmaceutical industry.* Penang: International Organization of Consumers Unions, Regional Office for Asia and the Pacific.

Mastroianni, Luigi, et al., eds. 1990. *Developing new contraceptives: Obstacles and opportunities.* Washington, D.C.: National Academy Press.

Ollila, E. (1999). *Norplant in the context of population and drug policies.* Helsinki: STAKES, National Research and Development Center for Welfare and Health.

Richter, J. (1996). *Vaccination against pregnancy: Miracle or menace?* London and New Jersey: Zed; Melbourne, Australia: Spinifex.

Wajcman, Judy (1994). Delivered into men's hands? The social construction of reproductive technology. In Gita Sen and Rachel C. Snow, eds., *Power and decision: The social control of reproduction.* Cambridge, Mass.: Harvard University Press, 153–175.

Judith Richter

CONVERSATION

The concept of gendered conversational dynamics refers to generalizable differences in the communication of women and men, as groups. In recent years scholars have identified a number of distinctions between women's and men's communication. This article summarizes differences reported by researchers, examines alternative explanations of the differences, and highlights implications of gendered conversational dynamics.

Sex Differences in Communication

Gender-related differences in interpersonal communication were most studied in the United States in the late twentieth century. Researchers have documented relatively consistent and generalizable distinctions between the conversational behaviors of the sexes (Aries, 1987; Henley, 1977; Noller, 1986; Tannen, 1990; Wood, 2000). The table on page 234 summarizes a number of specific differences reported in the verbal and nonverbal communication of western women and men.

Rather than catalog particular differences in verbal and nonverbal behaviors, this article surveys broader gender differences in the goals, content, and styles generally characteristic of women's and men's interpersonal communication.

Goals of Communication

Women and men appear to pursue dissimilar primary goals in interpersonal communication. As a rule, women use communication to build relationships with others; they do this by sharing feelings and ideas, expressing empathy, including and responding to others, and giving verbal support. As a rule, men are more likely to use communication to establish and assert individual status, give information, achieve results, and gain and keep the conversational stage. The terms *expressive* and *instrumental*, respectively, capture the communicative goals of women and men. The linguist Deborah Tannen (1990) refers to these differences as "rapport" (feminine) and "report" (masculine) talk. These are general differences only, and it must be remembered that both sexes pursue expressive and instrumental objectives, although each sex may emphasize one goal more than the other. Also, not all women use communication primarily for expressive reasons, and not all men talk primarily for instrumental purposes.

Content of Communication

Scholars have also reported generalizable, although not universal, differences in the content of women's and men's communication. Whereas women's talk tends to focus on personal topics such as intimate issues, feelings, and relationships, men's talk typically concentrates more on what have been labeled impersonal topics such as sports, politics, work, and activities being done while talking. Also, women's talk often includes attention to mundane daily issues and is typically sprinkled with many details and asides. Neither abundant detail nor attention to everyday matters seems as typical of men's talk (Wood, 1993, 1998, 2000). These dissimilarities in content suggest that women often connect with others through verbal sharing of feelings and experiences, while men build connections through common interests, contexts, and activities. Paralleling the expressive-instrumental goals of communication, gender-differentiated content of communication reflects a feminine preference for "closeness in dialogue" (Aries, 1987) and a masculine inclination toward "closeness in the doing" (Cancian, 1987; Swain, 1989).

A sampling of gender differences in communication

Verbal differences

1. Women take shorter speaking turns.
2. Women respond more personally and expressively.
3. Women maintain conversations by inviting others to speak, asking questions, and so forth.
4. Men interrupt more.
5. Men more often reroute conversations to topics that interest them, or they highlight such topics.
6. Men give "minimum response cues," which show minimum interest in another's talk.
7. Women's talk is more detailed.
8. Women communicate interactively, whereas men communicate using sequential monologues.

Nonverbal differences

1. Men assume more space and enter others' space.
2. Women engage in more eye contact when interacting with others.
3. Caucasian women smile more.
4. Women tilt the head to show attentiveness.
5. Women use more facial expressions, both in response to others and to create their messages.
6. Women use touch to indicate liking; men use touch to demonstrate or gain power.

Styles of Communication

In general, women and men also adopt distinct styles of interpersonal communication. The contrast most often noted is between women's conversational emphasis on process and men's emphasis on outcome. In practice, this is evidenced by women's greater attention to the dynamics of communication, or how the process of interaction unfolds: How is the conversation going? Is everyone having a chance to speak? Are we being responsive to what everyone says? Are we feeling close, angry, and so forth, in this interaction? As a group, men adopt a more instrumental style that focuses on results of talk. In other words, men regard communication as a means to other ends, whereas women perceive communication as an end in itself.

Consistent with other differences in style, women tend to communicate interactively, whereas men are more likely to communicate using sequential monologues. Thus, talk between women friends typically involves rapidly executed back-and-forth exchanges in which the conversational floor is shared as each speaker talks for only short periods before the other speaks. More characteristic of men's conversational style are extended monologues in which speakers talk in sequence and each speaker holds the conversational floor for a longer period of unshared time. The interactive-monologic distinction renders feminine communication more informal and evolving and masculine communication more formal and preset (Wood, 1998, 2000).

Another gender-related difference in style concerns how the content of talk is narrated. Men generally follow a linear style of presentation in which events are highlighted in a climactic sequence. Thus, a story has a clearly defined plot through which it progresses from the start through key events to a clear apex. Women tend to follow a weblike, or multiple-track, style of presentation in which events, people, relationships, and feelings are described within contexts, sometimes multiple contexts that are richly portrayed. A pronounced plot and a climactic sequence are not necessarily found in women's narrative style, since people, relationships, and feelings are more emphasized than an event-focused plot (Hall and Langellier, 1988; Wood, 2000). Thus, women's narration moves fluidly from topic to topic, and a given conversation may include several lines of talk that are woven together in the process of communicating.

Explanations for Sex Differences

Several explanations have been advanced for gendered conversational dynamics. At present, no one theory or explanation has eclipsed others, and there is substantial controversy over the reasons for and meaning of identified differences. The explanations developed fall into two broad and oppositional categories: essentialist and constructionist accounts.

Essentialist explanations: Essentialist explanations share the fundamental premise that some essential, innate quality in women and men accounts for their distinct communication behaviors. The most obvious form of essentialist explanation is rooted in biology and genetics. For example, men's more aggressive communication style is explained by the greater presence of the hormone testosterone; women's nurturing, inclusive communication style is explained by the greater presence of the hormone estrogen. Another version of biological explanation traces communication differences to differential hemispheric specialization in the brains of the two sexes. Men have greater development of the left lobe, which enables the linear, analytic thought more characteristic of men's communication; in women the left hemisphere and corpus

callosum connecting the two lobes are more developed, and these govern integrative and synthetic thinking, which is reflected in the weblike structure of women's communication. Some scholars, particularly French feminists, claim that women's bodies and biology tie them to natural rhythms and interdependence that are not promoted by male biology. Yet a third type of essentialist explanation accounts for communication differences as matters of divine law. Thus, goes the reasoning, God or another deity designed women to be nurturing and deferential and men to be instrumental and dominating. The conversational differences, like other differences between the sexes, are part of a divine design.

Constructionist explanations: The second broad genre of explanation for communication disparities is constructionist theories, which currently enjoy a greater following than essentialist theories. Common to the many specific constructionist explanations is the basic assumption that gender is socially constructed, not innate. Constructionists believe that aside from a few quite obvious differences (for example, reproductive organs and abilities, secondary sex characteristics) that result from biological sex, differences between women and men are constructed and sustained through social practices that reflect the prevailing ideologies in various societies.

Cultural theorists argue that the institutions, also called structures, and practices that make up cultures reflect and reproduce distinctly gendered identities. Institutions such as religion, the military, and schools are hierarchically organized, with men consistently occupying positions of greater power than those assigned to women. Practices such as granting maternity leave, but not paternity leave, embody and perpetuate the cultural expectation that women should be the primary caregivers (Wood, 1994). In concert, the structures and practices of a culture reflect and continuously re-create gendered identities and associated communication differences.

A recent and important addition to the cultural group of accounts is standpoint theory, which notes that the position a social group occupies in a culture shapes what and how members of a group know (Harding, 1991). Standpoint theorists trace how intersections among gender, race, class, and other bases of social groupings influence group members' experiences and, thus, the identities they form and the patterns of communication they develop. Sara Ruddick (1989) argues that women's traditional placement in domestic relationships cultivates "maternal thinking," which emphasizes noticing and responding to others and their needs.

Standpoint thinking provides a theoretical foundation for research on gendered communication cultures. Some scholars (Johnson, 1989) believe that males and females are socialized into different communication cultures that inculcate distinct understandings of how to communicate. Daniel Maltz and Ruth Borker's classic study of children's play (1982) suggests that the games girls and boys play teach the sexes different rules about communication. War and football, which are typical boys' games, emphasize competition and instrumental goals, whereas house and jump rope, games more usual for girls, place a priority on cooperation and relationship goals.

More than other theories, standpoint reasoning sheds light on documented differences between women of different races. For example, Caucasian women tend to smile more than African-Americans, and African-American women are more verbally assertive and dramatic than Caucasians. The greater protection or patronization imposed on white women in western culture may explain why, as a group, they have had less need than black women to develop assertiveness.

Complementary to cultural accounts are social learning theory (Bandura and Walters, 1963; Mischel, 1966), which claims that individuals learn to behave in masculine or feminine ways through observing and imitating others and by reinforcement from others; and cognitive development theories (Gilligan, 1982; Kohlberg, 1958; Piaget, 1932), which assert that individuals develop a constant sense of their gender by age 3, and that they actively work to become competent in meeting social expectations for their gender. These kindred theories propose that girls learn to communicate in cooperative, responsive, caring ways by modeling themselves after women, and boys learn to communicate in competitive, assertive, instrumental ways by modeling themselves after men.

A final constructionist view is psychoanalytic, or psychodynamic, theory. While other constructionist accounts focus on conscious and observable ways that gender is formed, psychoanalytic theory deals with unconscious processes of identification and internalization through which gender is constructed. In his original psychoanalytic theorizing, Sigmund Freud contended that "anatomy is destiny." By this he meant that a child's genitals determine with which sex she or he will identify, and that a penis is a source of envy for girls and a source of fear for boys (that is, boys fear castration).

A large number of scholars and clinicians who reject Freud's biological determinism and his reverence for the penis endorse alternative psychoanalytic theories (Chodorow, 1978; Wood, 1994, 2001). The basic principle

of newer psychoanalytic accounts is that core personality is shaped by relationships in the early years of life. As the usual first primary caregiver, mothers form distinct relationships with sons and daughters. Between daughters and mothers there is a basic identification, so that girls typically develop gender identity *within a relationship* and internalize the mother as part of themselves. Since boys do not share the sex of mothers, they must establish their gender identity *apart from a relationship*. Because males carve out their identity relatively independently of others, and females establish their identity in relation to others, the two sexes develop fundamentally different orientations to relationships and interpersonal communication. Women's documented tendency to use communication to build connections, create and express empathy, and engage in personal disclosures can be explained by their earliest relationships, which featured intimacy, openness, and identification with one another. The lack of identification between sons and mothers and the sons' need to define gender identity independently of the bond with the mother could explain men's use of communication to assert individual status, their emotional reserve, and their preference for doing over talking as a way to create and express closeness.

No one theory has emerged as clearly superior, although constructionist theories have gained wider adherence than essentialist theories.

Consequences of Sex Differences

Regardless of how differences in women's and men's communication are explained, they have pragmatic consequences for personal identity and interpersonal relationships. Women's tendency to sense others' feelings, provide emotional support, and monitor interpersonal dynamics imposes on them primary responsibility for maintaining conversations and relationships. More than men, women take care of others, express empathy, resolve tension, and otherwise keep relationships amiable (Cancian, 1987; Tavris, 1992). Because women's attentiveness to others and to relationships ties them more closely to others, these tendencies may reflect and perpetuate their low power relative to men (Kramarae, 1981). Women's communication style also encourages their emotional expression and growth, which may be inhibited by the communication patterns men tend to favor.

Gendered conversational dynamics may also complicate interaction between women and men. Because the two sexes, in general, use communication in different ways and to accomplish distinct goals, they often misunderstand one another (Tannen, 1990). A woman may discuss a problem with a man to build a connection with him and in the hope of receiving empathy and emotional support. However, the instrumental communication style typical of men may lead them to show they care by doing something—diverting the conversation to less painful topics or offering advice instead of emotional connection. Anne Wilson Schaef (1981), among others, claims that women are often disappointed and frustrated in relationships with men because women reveal themselves and reach out for connection while men maintain emotional reserve and independence. Conversely, men may be unsatisfied when women respond to their problems by providing empathy and emotional support instead of instrumental assistance.

Women and men may also fail to understand and appreciate one another's narrative patterns. Women may be frustrated by the lack of details and contextualizing in men's narrative method, and men may be equally frustrated by the presence of rich detailing and contextualizing in women's narratives. As a rule, men assume that conversation in general and stories in particular move relatively systematically toward a clear point, defined as a plot and climax. Yet women generally regard the primary point of conversation not as a recounting of events but as making personal connections, a goal that may lead narrators beyond plot-focused accounts. These and other misunderstandings between the sexes reflect gendered communication dynamics.

Conclusion

The gendered conversational dynamics identified by researchers are generalizations that do not apply to all women and men everywhere and do not represent absolute dichotomies between the sexes. Research is continuing, and is increasingly focused on on-line discussions, which take place all over the world. (Herring, 1999, is an example of such research.)

See Also

COMMUNICATIONS: SPEECH; DIVISION OF LABOR; ESSENTIALISM; FAMILY: POWER RELATIONS AND POWER STRUCTURES; GENDER CONSTRUCTIONS IN THE FAMILY; LANGUAGE; SILENCE

References and Further Reading

Aries, Elizabeth. 1987. Gender and communication. In Phillip Shaver and Clyde Hendrick, eds., *Sex and gender*, 149–176. Newbury Park, Calif.: Sage.

Bandura, A., and R. H. Walters. 1963. *Social learning and personality development.* New York: Holt, Rinehart and Winston.

Cancian, Francesco. 1987. *Love in America.* Cambridge: Cambridge University Press.

Chodorow, Nancy. 1978. *The reproduction of mothering: Psychoanalysis and the sociology of gender.* Berkeley: University of California Press.

Gilligan, Carol. 1982. *In a different voice: Psychological theory and women's development.* Cambridge, Mass.: Harvard University Press.

Hall, Deana, and Kristin Langellier. 1988. Storytelling strategies in mother-daughter communication. In Barbara Bate and Anita Taylor, eds., *Women communicating: Studies of women's talk.* Norwood, N.J.: Ablex.

Harding, Sandra. 1991. *Whose science? Whose knowledge: Thinking from women's lives.* Ithaca, N.Y.: Cornell University Press.

Henley, Nancy. 1977. *Body politics: Power, sex and nonverbal communicating.* Englewood Cliffs, N.J.: Prentice Hall.

Herring, Susan. 1999. The rhetorical dynamics of gender harassment online. *Information Society* 5(3):157–167.

Johnson, Fern L. 1989. Women's culture and communication: An analytical perspective. In Cynthia Lont and S. A. Friedley, eds., *Beyond boundaries: Sex and gender diversity in communication,* 301–316. Fairfax, Va.: George Mason University Press.

Kohlberg, Lawrence. 1958. The development of modes of thinking and moral choice in the years 10 to 16. Ph.D. dissertation, University of Chicago.

Kramarae, Cheris. 1981. *Women and men speaking: Frameworks for analysis.* Rowley, Mass.: Newbury House.

Maltz, Daniel, and Ruth Borker. 1982. A cultural approach to male-female miscommunication. In John Gumpertz, ed., *Language and social identity,* 196–216. Cambridge: Cambridge University Press.

Mischel, Walter. 1966. A social learning view of sex differences in behavior. In Eleanor Maccoby, ed., *The development of sex differences,* 93–106. Stanford, Calif.: Stanford University Press.

Noller, Patricia. 1986. Sex differences in nonverbal communication: Advantage lost or supremacy regained? *Australian Journal of Psychology* 38; 23–32.

Piaget, Jean. 1932. *The moral judgment of the child.* New York: Free Press.

Puka, Bill. 1990. The liberation of caring: A different voice for Gilligan's different voice. *Hypatia* 5: 59–82.

Ruddick, Sara. 1989. *Maternal thinking: Towards a politics of peace.* Boston: Beacon.

Schaef, Anne Wilson. 1981. *Women's reality.* St. Paul, Minn.: Winston.

Swain, Scott. 1989. Covert intimacy: Closeness in men's friendships. In Barbara Risman and Pepper Schwartz, eds. *Gender and intimate relationships,* 71–86. Belmont, Calif.: Wadsworth.

Tannen, Deborah. 1990. *You just don't understand: Women and men in conversation.* New York: Morrow.

Tavris, Carol. 1992. *The mismeasure of woman.* New York: Simon and Schuster.

Wood, Julia T. 1993. Enlarging conceptual boundaries: Research in interpersonal communication. In Sheryl P. Bowen and Nancy J. Wyatt, eds., *Transforming visions: Feminist critiques of speech communication,* 19–49. Cresskill, N.J.: Hampton.

———. 1994. *Who cares: Women, care, and culture.* Carbondale: Southern Illinois University Press.

———. 1998. *But I thought you meant…: Misunderstandings in human communication.* Mountainview, Calif.: Mayfield.

———. 2000. He says, she says. In Dawn O. Braithwaite and Julia T. Wood, eds., *Case studies in interpersonal communication,* 93–100. Belmont, Calif.: Wadsworth.

———. 2001. *Gendered lives: Communication, gender, and culture,* 4th ed. Belmont, Calif.: Wadsworth.

Julia T. Wood

COOKING

The ethnologist Claude Lévi-Strauss wrote, "The role of fire in transforming food from raw to cooked…marked… the emergence of humanity" (1993: 36–37). Women, less mobile than men while pregnant and raising young children, became specialists in the preparation of food at the hunter-gatherers' hearth. They also specialized in gathering plant and small animal foods and eventually in cultivating crops. When human societies stopped roaming and built permanent shelters, the hearth—which eventually became a separate room, the kitchen—was the domain of mother and wife.

This is still true, around the world, but male cooks have come to dominate in certain elite, industrial, and ritual settings. The ancient Egyptians and Roman emperors employed men as cooks, and this practice was continued by medieval European kings, who hired cooks from the armies, where they had learned to feed large groups. By the eleventh century, royal cooks, bakers, caterers, and butchers had formed guilds that excluded women and admitted members through patrilineal descent or payment of fees. In medieval China and Japan, such elite cooks were males from the lower classes. Only in Africa did women normally cook at ruling courts, but they were usually the king's wives.

In many cultures, there are specific situations in which men assume the task of cooking normally done by women. Some religions prohibit women from handling and eating certain foods; among the Northern Athabaskan Indians, for example, women avoid bear meat, which is prepared and eaten by men. Men participating in rituals may cook special meats to prevent women's ritual impurity from contaminating it. Military and hunting groups usually have designated male cooks. In modern western society, men typically preside at outdoor barbecues that imitate the meat-centered meals of hunting parties.

The male-dominated kitchen based on a military model remained intact in Europe throughout the nineteenth century. In 1898, the French chef and culinary writer Auguste Escoffier instituted a hierarchical system called the "brigade" for food preparation, which was soon imitated widely by professional cooks. American restaurant and elite cooks of the time were usually from Europe and imported the brigade system to North America. The brigade system, still utilized in many large kitchens, is one in which the hierarchical structure is similar to that of the military. A typical brigade would include chef, sous chef, and numerous chefs de cuisine (line chefs) as well as a pastry chef and a saucier.

Women's entrance into professional cooking in the West came primarily through cookbooks and the establishment of cooking schools in the late nineteenth century. Fannie Farmer, whose *Boston Cooking School Cookbook* appeared in 1896 and eventually sold more than four million copies, has been credited with developing consistency in measurement and uniformity of instructions in recipes. The twentieth century's most popular cookbook, *The Joy of Cooking,* was written originally by Irma Rombauer. These and other female cookbook writers enhanced women's reputation as cooks and encouraged them to improve their skills, but women nevertheless were excluded from professional kitchens until the latter half of the century.

After Farmer opened her Boston Cooking School, a number of cooking schools were founded by women. The most notable is the Culinary Institute of America in New York, which opened in 1946 under the direction of Frances Roth and Katherine Angell. It was established to retrain male World War II veterans funded by the GI Bill, however, and did not graduate a woman until 1970. In the United States and England, cooks who were female were generally regarded as domestic servants (the U.S. Department of Labor designated all cooks as domestics until 1976) rather than professional workers.

In the 1960s a wave of innovative female chefs and authors, led by Julia Child and her now classic *Mastering* the Art of French Cooking, swept over the culinary scene. Child's television cooking show debuted in 1963 and inspired women to take up "serious" cooking, first at home and eventually as caterers and restaurant chefs. By 1992, *Food Arts* magazine had presented "Women Chefs: Role Models for the 1990s" and the James Beard Society had held "A Salute to Women Chefs in America," with Alice Waters named "best chef" and her influential restaurant, Chez Panisse, named the United States' "best restaurant." Today, women graduate in large numbers from culinary academies and work alongside men as peers in most of North America's and Great Britain's fine restaurants, though they continue to be a smaller presence in professional kitchens elsewhere in the world. Although 43 percent of all chefs and cooks in the United States are women, less than 15 percent are executive chefs.

Many facets of home cooking have recently been studied by sociologists, anthropologists, historians, and gender theorists. Some commentators see the kitchen as a place where women exert more social and economic control than they may be permitted elsewhere; others (for example, McIntosh and Zey, 1982) point out that even though women enact the role of cook, men may still order it. Social scientists study women's role as "gatekeepers" controlling family nutrition and eating habits, a perception that leads government programs to target women in attempts to fight hunger and poor nutrition. Economists look at how reducing the demands of domestic cooking can free women to make other contributions to a society's production.

Acquiring food by gathering, cultivating, or shopping can consume much of women's time in nonindustrialized societies. In countries where homes lack refrigerators, fresh foods must be purchased almost daily—an activity that may require women who live in rural areas to walk long distances to market. Moreover, these women may have to provide fuel for cooking by gathering wood or dried animal dung. More hours may be spent in garden plots. Until recently, the processing of many staple foods was done laboriously in the home; ethnographers estimate that it took two to eight hours a day to prepare the maize (corn) consumed by a traditional Mesoamerican family. In most of these tasks, women are assisted by their daughters, who may be less likely to obtain education because their labor is needed at home. The demands of cooking thus become a social and development issue, and aid agencies are now paying attention to projects that will lighten women's cooking-related work.

Through most of history and still today in most of the world, women have learned to cook in the home from their mothers and other female relatives. Institutional education for girls, however, has long included cooking instruction. European convents taught young girls to cook in preparation for domestic life, and missionary schools used culinary instruction as a way to acculturate indigenous populations to European consumption habits. In the eighteenth and nineteenth centuries, schools for upper-class girls in Britain and Europe trained students to plan menus, administer kitchens, and instruct their cooks about elite food preferences. In the United States, high schools instituted "home economics" classes, in which students—until recently, only females—were taught the principles of nutrition and food preparations; before 1960, most girls in public schools were required to take at least one "home ec" class. These institutional systems reinforced the view that women belong in the domestic sphere as well as mainstream cultural views of "proper" eating habits (many of which have now been rejected by nutritionists), but they also served as an entry point for young women to pursue higher education and careers in the food industry.

See Also

AGRICULTURE; DIVISION OF LABOR; DOMESTIC LABOR; EDUCATION: DOMESTIC SCIENCE AND HOME ECONOMICS; FOOD, HUNGER, AND FAMINE; HOUSEHOLD WORKERS; HOUSEWORK; NUTRITION, *I and II;* WORK: OCCUPATIONAL SEGREGATION

References and Further Reading

Cooper, A. 1998. *A women's place is in the kitchen: The evolution of women chefs.* New York: Wiley.

Counihan, Carole M., and Steven L. Kaplan, eds. 1998. *Food and gender: Identity and power.* Amsterdam: Harwood Academic.

Fitzgerald, Thomas K., ed. 1977. *Nutrition and anthropology in action.* Assen, Netherlands: Van Gorcum.

Goody, Jack. 1982. *Cooking, cuisine and class.* Cambridge: Cambridge University Press.

Lévi-Strauss, Claude. 1993. *The raw and the cooked: An introduction to a science of mythology.* Trans. John Weightman and Doreen Weightman. New York: Harper and Row (originally published 1969).

McIntosh, Alex, and Mary Zey. 1998. Women as gatekeepers. In Carole M. Counihan and Steven L. Kaplan, eds., *Food and gender: Identity and power,* 125–144. Amsterdam: Harwood Academic.

Wheaton, Barbara. 1983. *Savoring the past: The French kitchen and table from 1300 to 1789.* Philadelphia: University of Pennsylvania Press.

Ann Cooper

COSMETIC SURGERY

Cosmetic plastic surgery, sometimes called aesthetic surgery, alters the appearance of a person who has normal body functioning. It differs from reconstructive plastic surgery, which corrects an injury or disfigurement. In some cases, the distinction between reconstructive and cosmetic surgery is not sharp, but the focus here will be on the cosmetic aspects, from a mainly feminist, critical standpoint. Other, more positive views can be found, of course, in many media; but it is important to be aware of the issues—theoretical and practical—surrounding such surgery. Most cosmetic surgery is done on women.

Motivations

Cosmetic surgery is a medical "solution" for a purely social problem—self-perceived ugliness, low self-esteem, insecurity in relationships, or, in some cases, lack of access to jobs. Cosmetic surgeons are, in a sense, selling dreams: the dream of attaining a culturally defined image of beauty, often based on the young, thin, northern European ideal; the dream of success in love and life. These fantasies are related to—and reinforce—the belief that physical beauty is more important for women than for men.

Until the late twentieth century, only rich people could afford cosmetic surgery, and for this reason it was associated with high social status. Today it has become more widespread, as the number of cosmetic surgeons has increased, necessitating an increase in the number of surgeries performed to support these surgeons. This has increased the pressure for surgical procedures to become part of a woman's "normal" pursuit of "improving" her looks, like hairstyling or makeup. Cosmetic surgery can also be viewed as "job insurance" that can help women enter, succeed in, and remain in certain careers; and in fact women who meet the cultural ideal of beauty often are rewarded with higher status and access to more money.

Cosmetic Surgery and Women's Role

Cosmetic surgery reinforces the role of women as objects for men's use rather than as people who can be accomplished in their own right. It upholds and strengthens polar, stereotypical images of male and female by reshaping the body to make it more "feminine" or "masculine." The social endorsement of reshaping women to fit a certain image leads directly to the concept of woman as commodity. To the extent that women see themselves as "improvable" objects, the female body comes to be seen as isolated, changeable, mechanical parts, subject to evaluation based on appearance. Messages from partners, employers, and the media, as well as real discrimination against certain groups of people, can all have an impact on a woman's aesthetic sense of her own body that may coerce her—subtly or explicitly—to think that she needs surgery.

Cosmetic surgeons claim that they should not act as arbiters of what is acceptable by denying surgical body changes to those who wish to conform to a cultural ideal. They also assert that by providing bodily changes, they increase a person's life choices. In response, however, it can certainly be argued that by advocating cutting and reshaping the body as a reasonable first option in addressing a woman's dissatisfaction with her physical appearance, cosmetic surgeons actually reinforce the cultural status quo. In particular, they make age, weight, and ethnic and racial differences less visible. If the range of acceptable looks becomes narrower, the choices available to women—in friendships, love, and work—become more limited. In this way, then, surgery itself shapes standards as doctors replace a natural range of looks with an artificial sameness.

Risks and Outcomes

The expected improvement in attractiveness and self-esteem from cosmetic surger is supposed to occur painlessly and effortlessly. In fact, one reason many women are willing to undergo cosmetic surgery is that it is made to seem easy. Both the media and the surgeons themselves present the surgery in ways that minimize the risks, so that clients often do not realize what chances they are taking with their health.

The risks, however, are significant, including a loss of physical functioning from nerve or muscle damage, as well as rare cases of paralysis or death. The device used for liposuction, for example, rips up the underpinnings of the skin and then vacuums them away. Yet descriptions in the popular literature of most of the cosmetic surgeries minimize the association with surgery and present the risks as if they were on a par with those involved in coloring hair or applying makeup. Terms used in the United States for some of the procedures reflect how the risks are downplayed: a face-lift is described as a "freshening"; an abdominal rearrangement of muscles and skin, a major operation, is given the infantilizing name "tummy tuck." When the results of a procedure are unacceptable, the subsequent corrective surgeries are called "revisions" or "touch-ups." Women usually do not hear much about complications until after they have decided to go ahead with the surgery.

The Practice of Cosmetic Surgery

Cosmetic surgeons may relabel normal bodies as "pathological," as in a statement by the American Society of Plastic and Reconstructive Surgeons in 1982 describing small breasts as "deformities [that] are really a disease which in most patients result[s] in feelings of inadequacy, lack of self-confidence, distortion of body image and a total lack of well-being due to a lack of self-perceived femininity"—a definition that ignores the question of whether, or how well, a woman's breasts function sexually or for nursing, not to mention the changing fashions in "ideal" breast size. Nearly twenty years later, the message, though perhaps more subtle, was basically unchanged: the American Society of Plastic Surgeons used the slogan "Life is what you make it" in a national media campaign "to educate patients on the value of plastic surgery," with advertisements in magazines like *Cosmopolitan* and *Allure* (American Society of Plastic Surgeons, 2000).

Cosmetic surgery is an unusual branch of medicine and surgery in that its chief benefit is psychological, yet cosmetic surgeons have rarely done serious studies on whether or how a particular procedure changes the client's psychological state. They argue in support of the effectiveness of their work by citing their own clinical impressions and testimonials from clients, often in the form of poorly designed self-evaluation questionnaires. Follow-up of clients usually lasts only for a few months, though the effects of the surgery may last a lifetime. In addition, the surgeons pay little attention to how undesirable results affect their clients.

Cosmetic surgeons are not always well regulated. In the United States, for instance, any person with a medical degree can legally perform cosmetic surgery. Because most of these surgeries are prepaid and are performed outside of a hospital, there is usually no quality oversight by peers, hospital boards, or insurance companies.

Cosmetic Surgery and Feminism

From a feminist perspective, it is important for women to find ways of increasing self-esteem that do not depend on altering their appearance through cosmetic surgery. Women can reconceptualize how they view and describe their bodies, so that "droopy eyelids," for example, are transformed into "wisdom curves," "unsightly wrinkles" are seen as "experience lines," and breasts that "sag" after nursing become, instead, "relaxed and flowing." Workshops and support groups can help women learn to be more assertive, to change negative patterns of thinking, to accept the diversity of women's appearance, and to love their own bodies as they are.

See Also

ADVERTISING; BODY; COSMETICS; ETHICS: FEMINIST; FASHION; IMAGES OF WOMEN: OVERVIEW; SURGERY

References and Further Reading

American Society of Plastic Surgeons. 2000. Plastic Surgery Information Service. <http://www.plasticsurgery.org/>

Anderson, Lenora Wright. 1989. Synthetic beauty: American women and cosmetic surgery. Unpublished PhD thesis available through University Microfilms International, 300 North Zeeb Road, Ann Arbor, Mich. 48106-1346, United States, order number 9012773.

Cash, Thomas F., and Thomas Pruzinsky. 1990. *Body images: Development, deviance, and change.* New York and London: Guilford.

Dull, Diana, and Candace West. 1991. Accounting for cosmetic surgery: The accomplishment of gender. *Social Problems* 38(6): 54–70.

Zones, Jane Sprague. 1992. The political and social context of silicon breast implant use in the United States. *Journal of Long-Term Effects of Medical Implants* 1(3): 225–241.

Esther Rome

COSMETICS

Cosmetics are salves, face paints, and chemicals used to change a person's natural appearance, usually to improve it according to current standards of beauty. Their use is practically universal, throughout the world and throughout time. For most women with free choice in the matter (that is, women who are not constrained by religious, societal, family, or economic considerations), the use or nonuse of makeup is a statement. How or whether we wear makeup tells others something about the kind of people we are: practical, too busy, down-to-earth, shy, conservative, traditional, narcissistic, free-spirited, wild. The use or avoidance of cosmetics—the choice to blend in with the majority of women in a peer group or purposely not to look like its members—is particularly telling in women outside that group. For example, "lipstick lesbians" may be making a statement about who they are by differentiating themselves from lesbians who don't want or feel the need to spend their time and energy on cosmetics—or maybe they just like the way they look in makeup.

Historical and Cultural Background

The use of makeup as a means of self-expression may almost be a primal instinct; Neanderthals are believed to have used body paints (though perhaps more for religious or tribal reasons than for the sake of mere appearance). Among the ancient Egyptians and Romans, both men and women, particularly aristocrats, certainly took a great deal of care over their appearance; however, among the ancient Greeks, heavy makeup was associated more with prostitutes than with women of the upper classes. Throughout western history, much could be gleaned from a woman's or girl's appearance: whether she was married or unmarried, chaste or unchaste, rich or poor (and a woman's marital and reproductive status is revealed, overtly or implicitly, in her jewelry, makeup, or clothing in societies all over the world). And although the poetic ideal of womanhood (aspired to by those who had the time and money to spare for the pursuit) has generally been unpainted, natural loveliness, the reality of infrequent bathing, poor health, poor nutrition, and tooth decay even among the upper classes meant that women who wished to appear attractive had no choice but to resort to artifice. Men may have been naive about the reality of what it took for women to be such visions of loveliness—in 1770, the English parliament passed a law to protect men who had been tricked into marriage by women using "scents, paints, cosmetic washes, artificial teeth, false hair, … high-heeled shoes and bolstered hips" to snare them. The women were to be punished as if for witchcraft and the marriages rendered null and void. (There is no evidence, however, that the law was ever enforced.)

This attitude probably accounts for the acute distinction that was once made in advertisements between improving the skin and masking it. Starch and rice powders protected the skin and were usually socially acceptable; tinted makeup and lead-based powders, which whitened the skin, were considered "paint" and were not. This is not to say that lead-based powders were not used: they were, and their dangers are obvious to us now. Women have died for beauty. Although cosmetics, at least in the United States, are fairly safe today because the Food and Drug Administration (FDA) has established manufacturing guidelines, tests of a makeup's safety do not have to be reviewed by the FDA before the product is sold. It is also interesting to note that the law does not require a cosmetic's performance to live up to the manufacturer's claims. Moreover, animal rights groups have pointed out that animals have paid the price for humans' beauty by suffering through painful or even fatal safety testing of cosmetics.

Race and Cosmetics

If even white-skinned women were trying to make themselves paler, what were brown-skinned women living in societies dominated by Caucasians trying to do? Many were also trying to make themselves paler. Because the influence of European colonialism reached around the world by the second half of the nineteenth century, so did the European ideal of beauty. During and after the years of slavery in the United States, black women were often considered presumptuous if they tried to look more like white women; but in cartoons exaggerated characteristics of African-Americans (such as hair, nose, or lips) were used to promote the idea that whites were evolutionarily superior. Small wonder, then, that products which promised to straighten hair and lighten skin were used by African-Americans, even as early as the 1850s. However, the African-American women whose names are most closely linked to such beauty products—Annie Turnbo Malone and Madam C. J. Walker (Sarah Breedlove)—never sold skin bleaches and promoted their hair products as hair growers and "glossines" rather than straighteners. Even at that time there was awareness, and criticism, of the fact that many beauty products for African-Americans had as their goal a European appearance, but the aim of these two entrepreneurs was to increase their customers' dignity and sense of womanhood. Walker's stance is beautifully summarized in a speech she gave to the National Negro Business League in 1912: "I am not ashamed of my past; I am not ashamed of my humble beginning. Don't think because you have to go down in the wash-tub that you are any less a lady!" In addition to deliberately not trying to mold their customers into copies of white women, both she and Malone promoted, and were financially supportive of, the social well-being of blacks. Only after Walker's death did her company produce a skin bleach.

With regard to race, the most obvious criticism of the idea of cosmetics is that they are generally used to make the wearer more closely resemble an ideal—in many cases a European ideal. There are now cosmetics specifically designed for women of color, but the widespread availability of these is relatively recent. It is worth pointing out in this context that on occasion white women have tried to give themselves an "exotic" look: the "Sheba type" or the "Cleopatra type" or a dark-haired Spanish beauty. However, unlike those "exotic" types, African-American women were almost never held up as an ideal in advertising aimed at white women.

Current Trends

The use of cosmetics by women can have implications for racial identity, social status, ageism, and other social issues. (It also can be no more than a response to advertising or a desire to fit in with one's peer group.) For most men, it is a nonissue. Today, only at the extremes of society do men have to deal with the question of whether to wear obvious cosmetics: in the cultures reached by advertising or other media, it is almost unthinkable for all but the most out-of-the-closet gay men, cross-dressers, or transvestites, and when they wear makeup in public they are most definitely making a statement about who they are. This is not to say that men do not go under the surgeon's knife or spend long hours at the gym to improve their appearance, but vanity rarely extends to wearing obvious makeup.

Whether or not we intend or even want to convey anything by our appearance, others respond to it. Thus, it is understandable that many women, including feminists, are deliberate about the image they present to the world; a woman politician, for example, shouldn't be too pretty or she won't be taken seriously, but she'd better not be too plain, either. It need hardly be pointed out that politics is full of men at one end of the attractiveness spectrum, even though men who are considered to be at the other are not hurt by being thought handsome. Makeup itself is not the issue; Wolf (1991) writes "The problem with cosmetics exists only when women feel invisible or inadequate without them.... When a woman is forced to adorn herself to buy a hearing, when she needs her grooming to protect her identity,...when she must attract a lover so that she can take care of her children, that is exactly what makes 'beauty' hurt.... Many mammals groom, and every culture uses adornment. The real problem is our lack of choice" (1991: 272–273).

See Also

ADVERTISING; BEAUTY CONTESTS AND PAGEANTS; COSMETIC SURGERY; GAZE; IMAGES OF WOMEN: OVERVIEW; MEDIA: MAINSTREAM

References and Further Reading

Etcoff, Nancy. 1999. *Survival of the prettiest: The science of beauty.* New York: Doubleday.

Foulke, Judith E. 1994. Decoding the Cosmetic Label. *FDA Consumer Magazine.* Department of Health and Human Services. Rockville, Md.: U.S. Government Printing Office.

Gunn, Fenja. 1973. *The artificial face: A history of cosmetics.* New York: Hippocrene.

Peiss, Kathy. 1998. *Hope in a jar: The making of America's beauty culture.* New York: Metropolitan.

Scranton, Philip, ed. 2000. *Beauty and business: Commerce, gender, and culture in the United States.* New York: Routledge.

Wolf, Naomi. 1991. *The beauty myth: How images of beauty are used against women.* New York: Morrow.

Brinlee Kramer

COSTUME

See DRESS.

COURTSHIP

Heterosexual courtship can be defined as "the institutional way that men and women become acquainted before marriage" (McCormick and Jesser, 1991). *Courtship* should be distinguished from a related term, *dating.* Whereas courtship refers to the selection of a potential mate, dating involves a more casual interaction between women and men, without a chaperone and without specific commitment (Cate and Lloyd, 1992).

Traditional Courtship

In societies where boys and girls are kept apart as much as possible during puberty and the early adult years, courtship is a way of introducing young men and women to their prospective mates. Traditional courting behavior consists of formal visits between young women and men, with parental consent, either in the presence of a chaperone (a parent or some other adult) or with parental consent and approval and with strict limitations on the quantity and nature of time spent together. Sexual self-control in courtship is valued, and there are severe restrictions as to whom one can court and what takes place during courtship. Supervision and protection of daughters form the basis of traditional courtship. A double standard prevails, however, whereby women are expected to be virgins but men are allowed sexual indiscretions. As noted by Humphries (1988), for example, formally courting couples in Edwardian England could engage in sex, whether it was forced by the man or mutually agreed upon; but if a pregnancy followed and a marriage could not be arranged, the shame was primarily carried by the woman.

In the traditional pattern of courtship, parents are extensively involved. Such courtship usually ends in marriage, with parents exercising power over the selection of a suitable mate. Parental power over courtship is often used as a means of forging or perpetuating economic or political alliances between families. The courtship that follows between the future bride and groom contributes to community stability. Once such a courtship is initiated, cancellation or interruption is not customary.

Traditional courtship is still somewhat prevalent in southern Europe, especially in those countries where Catholicism is the dominant religion. It is also normative in large parts of Asia and the Middle East. In India and in Muslim societies, for example, courtship may be fairly short in duration, involving a few formal visits between the families of the future marital partners, during which the future bride and groom have a chance to see each other face to face. In some areas where traditional courtship is practiced, such as in southern Africa, it is increasingly possible for the young men and women themselves to indicate whom they would prefer as a potential mate, but the final decision still rest mostly with their parents (Mullan, 1984).

Dating as a Pattern of Courtship

As pointed out by McCormick and Jesser (1991), intergenerational power is an integral part of courtship. With industrialization and urbanization, kin and the immediate family lose some of their control over young people, and unmarried people themselves gain the power to determine their courtship patterns. Dating then becomes important. With the relaxation of controls on sexual behavior in the latter part of the twentieth century, sexuality and intimacy became more accepted parts of young people's lives. Today, it is assumed in many societies that dating partners will become lovers.

Dating is practiced in western countries and is presumed to have begun in North America after World War I. Dating also developed around the same time in northern and western Europe as well as in Australia and New Zealand. Intergenerational conflicts may arise over dating, particularly in ethnically diverse societies where mainstream values are adopted by young people while their parents hold onto norms of courtship (Dhruvarajan, 1996).

Unlike courtship, dating assumes that young people select their own marital partners and that marriage should be based on romantic love. Dating becomes a way of finding potential partners without committing oneself from the beginning. In addition to being a form of selection, dating can also be a form of recreation or of socialization. Dating is casual; boyfriends and girlfriends can have fun together in a relationship that involves flirtation or a sequence of verbal and nonverbal behaviors that create intimacy (McCormick and Jesser, 1991).

Dating is also called going out with or seeing someone. Albas, Albas, and Rennie (1994) describe dating, going out, and seeing someone as a three-step process in which *dating* refers to the initial, less serious phase of finding out about someone, and *going out* and *seeing someone* indicate a more serious intent that can be a step toward marriage.

McCormick and Jesser's research (1991) suggests that traditional gender roles still prevail in dating relationships in that men are more likely to take the initiative, including asking a woman for a date or initiating first sexual intercourse. However, there are also observable challenges to old norms.

Sexually experienced women are more likely to be independent and to take the initiative in dating and sex. The double standard seems to have been diminished, allowing women to use strategies previously reserved for men.

Men's traditional power in relationships is often expressed in physical violence and sexual aggression. Even when physical violence is reciprocal, men's greater strength means that women are more likely to be victims of violence. Sexual aggression is defined as sexual interaction gained through the force, arguments, pressure, threats of force, or the use of alcohol, drugs, or one's position of authority. When this takes place in a dating relationship, it is called date rape. It is estimated that in the United States 15 to 28 percent of women may have experienced date rape. (Care and Lloyd, 1992).

See Also

HETEROSEXUALITY; MARRIAGE: OVERVIEW; ROMANCE; VIRGINITY

References and Further Reading

Albas, Cheryl, Daniel Albas, and Douglas Rennie. 1994. Dating, seeing, and going out with: An ethnography of contemporary courtship. *International Journal of Contemporary Family and Marriage* 1(1): 61–81.

Care, Rodney M., and Sally A. Lloyd. 1992. *Courtship.* Newbury Park, Calif.: Sage.

Dhruvarajan, Vanaja. 1996. Hindu Indo-Canadian families. In Marion Lynn, ed., *Voices: Essays on Canadian families,* 301–328. Toronto: Nelson Canada.

Humphries, Steve. 1988. *A secret world of sex: Forbidden fruit: The British experience 1900–1950.* London: Sidgwick and Jackson.

Kurian, George. 1979. *Cross-cultural perspectives on mate selection and marriage.* Westport, Conn.: Greenwood.

McCormick, Naomi B., and Clinton J. Jesser. 1991. The courtship game: Power in the sexual encounter. In Jean E. Veever, ed., *Continuity and change in marriage and family,* 134–151. Toronto: Holt, Rinehart and Winston.

Mullan, Bob. 1984. *The mating trade.* London: Routledge and Kegan Paul.

Vappu Tyyska

CRAFTS

Craft is a term that denotes the products of human skills that are manual and involve varying degrees of experiential knowledge and apprenticeship or training, directed by different categories of intention. The products are referred to in a general way as *artifacts,* and the categories of intention on the part of the maker, together with distinctions in the mode of consumption, provide for connotative definitions of the term.

Crafts are functional objects which may receive aesthetic appreciation but which blossom fully in use. The act of consumption involves understanding and knowledge of the symbolic and material conditions of the object. Some crafts, however, have been placed into categories of art, as for example during the European Renaissance, when the economic and ideological demands of early capitalism transformed some artisanal work into "art." Here the intention of the work was to refer beyond society's general use and valuation, to account for the subjective or aesthetic demands of the dominant leaders. The internationalization of culture in the latter part of the twentieth century placed similar strains on definitions. In this case the export of craftwork into alien cultures, often through consumption by tourists, does not necessarily allow proper understanding and knowledge of the artifact, which in such circumstances will function only as art. Such movements in the valuation and consumption of categories of crafts over time have created shifting hierarchies among the various mediums. Higher-status crafts are those which have been professionalized; these tend to require long training together with professional practice for local or official recognition of expertise. An example of such a craft is pottery, which has long hovered on a border between art and craft. Today, some pottery, such as that by the Pueblo Indians of New Mexico or the "artist-potters" of Europe, is an artifact which demands aesthetic response before functional use.

Sexual Division of Crafts

There are no inherent differences between the crafts of women and those of men. At different times in most societies crafts will have been practiced predominantly by one gender or the other, depending on the sexual division of labor. Among the Suni peoples of New Mexico, for instance, women are by tradition responsible for all matters connected with the home. They are the builders and make all clay products; they make the adobe blocks for their buildings and also practice associated skills, such as bricklaying and plastering. In addition, these women produce functional and decorative pottery of great beauty.

In some societies a general craft category may be practiced by both genders. Among the Australian Aboriginals of Arnhem Land, although it is the women who are responsible for fiber crafts, men are the weavers. This has arisen because men perform ceremonial rituals, and thus

are responsible for the associated ritual items, including woven artifacts. This led them to undertake the weaving of objects for daily use as well. Nevertheless, it is the general case that textile crafts are predominantly practiced by women.

Mechanization and Leisure Crafts

Concurrent with the professionalization of some crafts in the late nineteenth and the twentieth centuries has occurred the mechanization of many. Together, those phenomena have changed the economic and cultural position of traditional crafts. Artifacts made from fibers, glass, clay, metals, wood, and so on are produced more quickly, cheaply, and in greater quantities than has ever been possible by hand. They are standardized and often more reliable than those made by hand. Mechanization removed the necessity for the creation of handmade objects and, particularly for women, fostered an increased practice of such skills as a leisure activity.

Crafts have been embraced as leisure activities not only because they are pleasurably creative but also because they have a utility value, fulfilling the moral injunction on women to be industrious. The case has been made by Rozsika Parker (1984), for example, that for several hundred years since the seventeenth century, women of the leisured classes in Great Britain have been socialized into the ideal of the feminine through embroidery. Through this craft women learned submissiveness, patience, perseverance, and the habit of selfless service to others. A similar syndrome was apparent in Great Britain in the 1920s and 1930s when married women were increasingly confined to unpaid work in the home. The prevalent requirements of upward mobility demanded that works of craft be produced in quantity for the maintenance of family and home. Women as homemakers were measured by their industry in the production of such artifacts as clothing and home furnishings of various kinds.

Personal and Political

In the work of feminist cultural theorists during the last twenty years of the twentieth century, women's crafts were considered traditionally representative of female popular culture. Carrying personal and political meanings, craftwork is often perceived by women as providing a vehicle for feminine values as well as for creative expression. One example was the work of grandmothers, mothers, and wives of the "disappeared" in Chile. In a clandestine act of subversion, women used a traditional South American craft—patchwork and embroidered pictures—to communicate the violations of human rights in their country. Their example inspired the Sisters of Soweto in South Africa to work together in similar fashion on a variety of crafts in protest against apartheid. And in the 1980s the women of Greenham Common in Britain initiated a renaissance of banner-making in a collective enterprise of peace and protest against nuclear weaponry. In these ways, groups of women have been enabled by public, sisterly recognition to use crafts as carriers of political messages beyond local boundaries.

See Also

ART PRACTICE: FEMINIST; FINE ARTS: OVERVIEW

References and Further Reading

Elinor, Gillian, et al. 1987. *Women and craft.* Virago.
Fan Craft. 1988. 2(6).
Koplos, Janet. 1992. *Considering crafts criticism.* Haystack Mountain School of Crafts.
Parker, Rozsika. 1984. *The subversive stitch : Embroidery and the making of the feminine.* London: Women's Press.
———, and Griselda Pollock. 1981. Crafty women and the hierarchy of the arts. *Old mistresses: Women, art, and ideology.* London: Routledge and Kegan Paul.
Women's Art Magazine. 1991. (Special issue 43 on women's crafts).

Gillian Elinor

CREATION STORIES

Most human cultures have produced myths that recount how the world and its creatures originated; these are called creation, origin, or primal stories. The technical term for the creation of the universe is *cosmogony*. In recent decades women scholars have investigated these stories in search of information about earlier matricentral social systems, the role of women in intellectual cultures, and the development of present patterns of gender relations. Such studies are necessarily speculative, and it is crucial that they utilize reliable primary evidence and analyze it in the light of a broadly contextualized knowledge and understanding of the cultures that generated it. The discussion that follows centers on the presence or absence of female creators in only a few of the world's mythologies; for more information, the reader should consult the works cited.

When one draws on reported myths, one must bear in mind that written sources give only one of several or many versions that were present in oral tradition over the centuries. Moreover, the writers are likely to have selected and reinterpreted elements to serve religiopolitical agendas or to reflect their private philosophical views. This is true even of

reports of oral tradition: folklorists and ethnographers may have been influenced by ideological currents of their time, and informants—native intellectuals—sometimes produced idiosyncratic versions of stories.

Modern science has challenged the myths and empirical observation on which these earlier creations stories were based. It is now evident that the cosmos is far older (10 to 15 billion years) and far larger than ancient people realized. New poets are perhaps needed to take new scientific knowledge and write it in language that can inspire religious awe and ethical responsibility for the interdependency that links humans with one another and the rest of the cosmos.

Eastern Mediterranean

Christianity inherited creation stories from three traditions: the monotheistic creation of the Hebrews, recounted in Genesis 1–2; the Sumero-Babylonian myth complex; and the Greek philosophical cosmology expressed by Plato in the *Timaeus* (Jowett, 1937). Early Christians read the biblical story through the lens of Greek thought.

The classic text of the Babylonian creation story is the *Enuma Elish* of the second millennium B.C.E. In it, the divine is plural, multigenerational, and both male and female. The cosmogony is the account of the generation of the gods from the monstrous mother goddess Tiamat and her consort, where strife reigns among the divine parents, children, and grandchildren and defines the struggle between chaos and cosmic order. In the climax of the story, a battle ensues between Tiamat and her grandchild, Marduk, the champion of the younger gods. He repels Tiamat's attack, slays her, and treads her body underfoot. Marduk splits the body in half to make heaven and earth. He then mixes the blood of Tiamat's slain consort with clay and from it makes humans to be "slaves of the gods."

This story suggests a more ancient matricentric society that is overthrown to create the new world of patricentric states out of military battle and death. The matricentric world was gestated, but the new world is made out of the dead matter of the old by a warrior-architect. The gods are masters of their human slaves, the immortal counterpart of the earthly, military aristocracy ruling a slaveholding economy.

The Hebrew priestly account in *Genesis* banishes plurality of gender and generation in the divine: God is one, male, disembodied word, above the swirling chaos and in serene control of it. Only a hint of Tiamat remains in the formless void and dark waters. For the Hebrews, the master-slave relation was also a metaphor for that of God to creatures; however, Adam is not a slave but a vicegerent who represents his lord by caring for the creation. God both works and rests, and he commands this pattern for all humans, animals, and land. Although the primal human is defined as both male and female, in Hebrew law the collective human community is represented by the patriarchal male, ruling women, children, and slaves. Yet because this was not spelled out explicitly, Genesis 1:26–27 has been read in modern times as an egalitarian text in which women as well as men are created in God's image and share the governance of creation.

The highly intellectualized version of classical Greek cosmogony reported in the *Timaeus* (Jowett, 1937) defines the primal nature of reality as a split between mind and matter. The demiurge (*demiourgos*), or creator, looks to the eternal ideas for a model by which to shape matter into a spherical and hierarchical cosmos. He mixes the power of life or soul and infuses it into the cosmic body to put it in motion. The residue of this cosmic soul is divided up to make human souls and is sown in the stars, where these souls gain a preincarnate vision of truth. Then they are incarnated and placed on earth, which is seen as the lowest level of the cosmic hierarchy.

Christianity adopted several key ideas from Plato. One was that earthly life was not the true state of the soul, but rather a fallen state from which the soul must extract itself to return to its true home in the heavens. This idea, however, contradicted the Hebrew belief in the resurrection of the body and a blessed, transformed earth. Christian eschatology (thought about the afterlife) tried to bridge the two ideas with the concept of a "spiritual body" that would someday rise in a new creation redeemed from mortality.

Western Christian thinkers rejected Greek and Hebrew ideas of preexistent matter from which the creator shapes the world in favor of a belief that God created the world from nothing. This led to an ongoing debate about whether created matter, mortal and finite, is a substance alien to that of god, or whether creation proceeds out of the substance of God and is therefore to be identified with God's body, or sacramental self-manifestation.

Christianity also rejected the Platonic idea of the preexistent soul, and so eliminated its explanation for gender and class hierarchy. Each soul was created separately at the time of conception for one existence on earth, to be continued in an immortal future. Female subjugation was explained by reference to ideas in Genesis that woman was created after Adam and was primarily responsible for disobedience to God and expulsion from paradise.

The Qur'an, the holy book of Islam, does not contain a unitary creation myth like that found in Genesis, but statements in separate *suras* (chapters) offer ideas similar to those of the Hebrew Old Testament, which were familiar to the Prophet Muhammad. God—single, male, without antecedents—created heaven, earth, and humanity with the command "Be!" He made all this in six days and ordered the elements in hierarchical fashion. Unlike Genesis, the Qur'an does not mention the separate creation of male and female humans.

Attempts have been made, notably by the poet and scholar Robert Graves (1955), to reconstruct from fragmentary sources an ancient, female-centered cosmogony believed to have existed in Asia Minor and Greece before the Homeric age. In Graves's version, the goddess Eurynome arises alone from primordial chaos, conceives after intercourse with a serpent, and lays an egg from which all creation hatches. She then banishes the serpent to the underworld and creates the secondary deities and the first (male) human.

Pre-Christian Europe

In the eighth century B.C.E., the Greek poet Hesiod drew on tradition to compose the *Theogony* (origin of the gods), in which creation begins with four spontaneously arisen deities, one of whom—Gaea or Ge (Earth)—is female. From her marriage with Ouranos (Heaven) descends the complex lineage of the Greek gods. Mortal humans, we learn from Hesiod's *Works and Days,* were created by the gods (specifically, male gods) in several cycles, which have become known as the golden, silver, bronze, and iron ages. The present "fifth race" was made by the patriarchal deity Zeus.

An alternative Greek cosmology seems to have been espoused by the Orphic cults, which drew from sources to the east and are known only from fragments. Their primal deity, Phanes, was bisexual, born from an egg. Phanes created a daughter, Nyx (Night), and with her begat Gaea, Ouranos, and the earth-lord Cronus.

When Rome rose to dominate the Italic and Etruscan peoples, indigenous religious beliefs were syncretized with the traditions of the Greeks, who dominated Mediterranean intellectual life. By the time from which written documentation has come down to us, this process of assimilation was pervasive. We know many names of pre-Roman deities and some of their associations, but not their stories.

Early Celtic cosmogony, reconstructed from evidence in archaeological finds and Roman writings, seems to have resembled that reported by Hesiod. Earth was the female member of the primal couple, mother of the succeeding gods. Early Scandinavians, too, imagined a genealogy in which the first female seems to have been the sun; the first mortals were a man, made by the sky gods from an ash tree, and a woman, from an elm.

These related mythologies are Indo-European, but alongside them existed the western Finno-Ugric peoples. The *Kalevala,* an eighteenth-century C.E. compilation of folk tradition, depicts the creator as a female, the Mother of Waters. Like Graves's reconstructed creator-goddess, she lays eggs from which the rest of creation hatches.

Ancient Egypt

The religion of ancient Egypt was not monolithic; instead, it was syncretized from various local mythologies, which remained to some extent discrete through Egypt's long history. The two primary theologies, called Memphite and Heliopolitan from their leading cities, had different cosmogonies. Both posited a male primal creator: Ptah in Memphis, Atum in Heliopolis. Atum, thought by some scholars to be androgynous, achieved creation through masturbation, while Ptah worked through language. Both created divine offspring, male and female, who assumed specific divine responsibilities related to the primal elements. The ordering of the universe took place through both cooperation and conflict among the gods, in which goddesses were often as active as their male counterparts.

Sub-Saharan Africa

African origin myths often posit a primal couple. Their acts and those of their divine children, which often mirror familiar human activities such as war and the use of technology, form the world known to humans. These myths tend to depict humans not as the result of a specified act of creation; instead, they come to the earth from the heavens or emerge from below earth's surface or from water, already differentiated by gender.

Recorded African creation myths display great variety. The Bushongo (Congo) recount how a single male god produces the universe by vomiting its first elements; his three sons, in the role of demiurges (secondary creators), refine and order its contents. In a Ngombe story, humans first reach earth when a woman annoys the creator-god and is lowered from heaven with her son and daughter. The Dogon (Mali) told how differentiated creation arose from the copulation of a male god with the earth, which the god had rendered unequivocally female through a primal act of genital excision. Some myths trace human ancestry to primal male–female twin pairs, and some to androgynous persons. In general, the active creators are male, though the Fon (Benin) tell of an androgynous primal deity; women tend to appear as receptive earth-mothers and as agents of conflict.

India

The eastern Indo-Europeans created Hinduism from their polytheistic tradition. Its earliest documents, the Vedic hymns, refer to the creation of the universe from chaos by Prajapati, a male primal god. His descendants create the present world from the dismembered parts of Parusha, a primeval man. The role of the creator in scriptures created some centuries later is assigned to the asexual Brahman, an egg-born entity which wills all subsequent creation into existence. Brahman creates the masculine Brahma, a demiurge responsible for the differentiation and ordering of the universe. The other great religions of India—Jainism and Buddhism—reject the Hindu cosmogony and envision an eternal, uncreated universe.

Eastern Asia

Known ancient Chinese creation myths involve the combination of the principles *yin* (masculine, sky) and *yang* (feminine, earth), arisen out of chaos, to produce the elements and a primal human male. In some versions, this man acts as a demiurge; in others, he is sacrificed and creation stems from his parts. This conception was borrowed and combined with native Shinto beliefs in Japan, where more anthropomorphic deities, both male and female, appear as active myth personalities.

Other Asian traditions have been recorded much more recently and reflect borrowings from Buddhism, Orthodox Christianity, Islam, and Iranian sects. Male creators and male primeval humans predominate.

The Americas

The creation myths of Native Americans are as varied as their societies and language families, but some overarching themes are apparent. The physical world exists before the "action" of peopling and ordering it begins, often after a great flood. The creator is envisioned as male and often has a semidivine male helper whom he provides with a woman, the mother of all succeeding humans. (In Hopi myth, the male demiurge has his own demiurgic helper, Spider Woman, who in turn makes humans; some South American cultures recognize a primal couple.) Incest often figures significantly in creation stories—perhaps reflecting attitudes of small migrating groups who were unable to practice exogamy—and female participants in incest may become important deities, such as the sun. Earth, when personified, tends to be female. Anthropomorphized animals, mostly presented as male, are prominent actors in differentiating the world and establishing customs. The only pre-Columbian American societies that left written records were the Maya and Aztec peoples of Mesoamerica. The Quiché Maya book, the *Popol Vuh,* records a cosmogony with male primal creators who have both male and female helpers; they make male and female humans at the same time but of different substances. The elaborate and violent Aztec cosmogony actually begins with a female deity who gives birth to further gods; a salient episode in the ordering of the world is the overthrow of an evil goddess by a hero-god, Tezcatlipoca.

Australia and Oceania

The widespread Australian Aboriginal creation myth called the Djanggawul cycle recounts the ordering of a preexistent world by a man and his two sisters; the sisters gave birth to a great many beings. The women were more active until their objects of power were stolen by their brother and other men, who then further limit the women's power by excising their originally large genitals. In another Aboriginal myth, a male creator gives birth to animals and male humans from his navel and armpits. In contrast, the Kakadu people of northern Australia told of creation by a fecund female who left her consort and traveled alone.

Female creators are reported from the Malay Peninsula (a divine couple) and West Ceram in eastern Indonesia (three goddesses). Pacific Island cultures posit male or asexual creators, though Maori myth offers a primal couple, Heaven (male) and Earth (female), whose rebellious offspring choose to remain closer to their mother. Tahitians believed that the first human created was male and wicked, but he was given a semidivine wife whose goodness rescued worldly order, though she could not keep her husband from condemning people to mortality. The *Kamulipo,* a creation poem from Hawaii, records the simultaneous, spontaneous generation of male and female progenitors.

See Also

CHRISTIANITY: FEMINIST CHRISTOLOGY; CHRISTIANITY: STATUS OF WOMEN IN THE CHURCH; GAIA HYPOTHESIS; GODDESS; HINDUISM; MYTH; RELIGION: OVERVIEW; WOMANIST THEOLOGY

References and Further Reading

Berry, Thomas, and Brian Swimme. 1992. *The universe story.* San Francisco: Harper.

Bird, Phyllis. 1992. Male and female he created them. In Karri Borresen, ed., *Image of God and gender models,* 11–34. Oslo: Solum.

Jowett, Benjamin, ed. and trans. 1937. Timaeus. In *The dialogues of Plato,* 3–70. New York: Random House.

Lovelock, James. 1979. *Gaia: A new look at life on earth.* Oxford: Oxford University Press.

Mendelsohn, Isaac. 1955. *Religions of the ancient near east: Sumero-Akkadian religious texts and Ugaritic epics.* New York: Liberal Arts.

Ruether, Rosemary. 1992. *Gaia and God: An ecofeminist theology of earth healing.* San Francisco: Harper.

Sproul, Barbara C. 1991. *Primal myths: Creation myths around the world.* San Francisco: Harper.

Rosemary Ruether

CREATIVITY

Creativity has many meanings, but one common thread in the various definitions, descriptions, and analyses is uniqueness: what is created is in some way new. Thus, according to Clarissa Pinkola Estés (1994: 316):

> Creativity is the ability to respond to all that goes on around us, to choose from the hundreds of possibilities of thought, feeling, action, and reaction and to put these together in a unique response, expression, or message that carries moment, passion, and meaning.

A consideration of women's creativity can reasonably draw attention to feminist issues, such as the status and role of the body in women's consciousness, and the extent to which women can borrow existing patriarchal concepts without colluding in and perpetuating their own and other women's colonization. Should women try to fit in? Or is creativity a key to women' survival and health, and to feminist interventions?

Contexts of Women's Creativity

Women's history as producers of knowledge and agents of social transformation—sustaining and maintaining relationships and domestic, social, and ecological systems—testifies to their ability to integrate creativity within day-to-day living. Their creativity may also have symbolic and mythic signficance, as in the concepts of the "goddess" and the "wild women," archetypes recurring in stories and myths across diverse cultures and eras:

> Earth-centred, not heaven-centred, of this world not otherwordly, body-affirming not body-denying, holistic not dualistic, . . . the Goddess was the life force. (Gadon, 1989: xii)

The Wild Woman carries the bundles for healing: she carries everything a woman needs to be and know. She carries the medicine for all things. She carries stories and dreams and words and songs and signs and symbols. She is both vehicle and destination. (Pinkola Estés, 1994: 12)

There is widespread evidence that women's creativity has been seen as a process of healing and becoming—"identifying our pain and imaginatively constructing maps for healing" (hooks, 1993: ii)—and of connecting the self, others, and the environment. In India, for example, Prakriti is understood as "a living and creative process...from which all life arises,...nonviolence as power,...an embodiment and manifestation of the feminine principle" (Shiva, 1989: xviii, 1, 40). Both integration and expansion characterize creativity as a process of self-maintenance and healing:

My fullest concentration of energy is available to me only when I integrate all the parts of who I am, openly, allow power from particular sources of my living to flow back and forth freely through all the different selves, without the restriction of externally imposed definition. (Lorde, 1984: 120–121)

Creativity and Patriarchy

Feminist analysis often sees a conflict between patriarchy and women's creativity. Thus the Enlightenment, the scientific revolution, and colonialism devalued women's creative heritage as primitiveness, prehistory, or magic that had been superseded by civilization, modernity, and rationality:

Activity, productivity, and creativity which were associated with the feminine principle are expropriated as qualities of nature and women, and transformed into the exclusive qualities of man....From being the creators and sustainers of life, nature and women are reduced to being "resources." (Shiva, 1989: 6)

In this regard the western concept of "genius" as "the famale male" (Battersby, 1989: 107) is also significant, making the idea of women as creative seem paradoxical. When "femaleness" is taboo, women face a crisis—if creativity cannot be embodied in women, then creative women are forced into self-denial and disguises, trying to be men.

Creativity and Politics

From this perspective, feminism as a form of creativity involves working with the materials of women's internalized oppression, such as their deep-seated self-doubt. If regarding genius as the "female male," or making creativity a male domain, can be said to be a patriarchal reversal, creative feminism must in turn reverse that reversal: it must deprivatize creativity by developing contexts in which women can collaborate, form networks, and engage in co-creativity. This is a politics of becoming, in which women imagine and create not just social forms and cultural artifacts but themselves and each other.

Such a process is not academic; it cannot be simply another method, an approved professional activity, or certain kinds of products. Instead, it moves toward something that is described as feminist poetics-politics, which realizes women's potential for loving and living: their confidence in, and their attentive listening to, both the inner self and other women. This entails recognizing nonverbal and bodily phenomena as central to feminist consciousness, creativity, and politics—a recognition, however, that goes against academic norms and conventions which put language and displays of authority and power in a privileged position.

Obstacles to Feminist Identity and Community

The western patriarchal concept of genius incorporates "professionalism" and specialization, such as art and science. The roots of women's creativity are often said to lie elsewhere, in diversity, mutliple identities, and integrated engagement with life-sustaining processes. If male "genius" is a function of privilege, women's creativity can be seen as a function of necessity. If western rationality and professionalism require a denial of bodily processes and identification, one result may be that women are embarrassed by the history of the "goddess" and the "wild woman" and their meaning as symbols of "the core self, the instinctual self" (Pinkola Estés, 1994: 472).

Women's creativity, in this kind of feminist analysis, is necessarily a struggle for liberation, an intensification and an enactment of women's femaleness and wildness, not a fixed identity but a process. That concept is rendered contentious, if not taboo, by some western postmodern theory, which opposes any identification of women with nature or nature with women and rejects "woman" as a subjective position from which to speak.

Consequently, creativity and intellectuality may persist as opposites within women's studies. Women can "adopt" intellectuality (identified with masculinity and language) without feeling overly compromised; but the western patri-archal concept of creativity—sexualized and colonial—becomes a site of struggle, both among women and between women and men. Feminist creativity, in particu-lar interdisciplinary methods and transdisciplinary goals, may be stereotyped as "entertainment": turbulent, exotic, and associated with women who are lower down in the social and academic hierarchy. By identifying some women with the intellect, rationality, the mind, and culture while "the others" are identified with creativity, emotionality, the body, and nature, women's studies may perpetuate patriar-chal hierarchies and women's fear of themselves, of one another, and of community. Alienating women from their female biographies, then, curtails their potential for femi-nist creativity and perpetuates their subjugation to patriar-chal values.

See Also

AESTHETICS: FEMINIST; ARCHETYPE; ART PRACTICE: FEMINIST; COMMUNITY; FINE ARTS: OVERVIEW; GODDESS; LITERATURE: OVERVIEW; PATRIARCHY: FEMINIST THEORY; PERFORMANCE ART; POETRY: OVERVIEW

References and Further Reading

Battersby, Christine. 1989. *Gender and genius: Toward a feminist aesthetics.* London: Women's Press (reprinted 1994).

Gablik, Suzi. 1991. *The reenactment of art.* London: Thames and Hudson.

Gadon, Elinor W. 1989. *The once and future goddess: A symbol for our time.* Wellingborough: Aquarian.

hooks, bell. 1991. *Yearning: Race, gender, and cultural politics.* London: Turnaround.

———. 1993. *Sisters of the yam: Black women and self-recovery.* London: Turnaround.

Lorde, Audre. 1984. *Sister outsider.* Trumansberg, N.Y.: Cross-ing.

Pinkola Estés, Clarissa. 1994. *Women who run with the wolves: Contacting the power of the wild woman.* London: Rider.

Raven, Arlen. 1988. *Crossing over: Feminism and the art of social concern.* Ann Arbor and London: University of Michigan Research Press.

Shiva, Vandana. 1989. Unbounded women? Feminism, creativ-ity, and embodiment. In Ghaiss Jasser, Margit van der Steen, and Mieke Verloo, eds., *Feminism in Europe: Cul-tural and political practices.* Utrecht, Netherlands: Women's International Studies Europe (WISE).

Val Walsh

CREED

In Christianity, a creed (from the Latin *credo,* "I believe") is a significant part of religious identity, marking the bound-ary between true and false belief. Brief, creedlike formulas may be found in the New Testament—for example, Martha's "confession" in John 11:27: "I believe that thou art the Christ, the Son of God, which should come into the world." More characteristically, both in the New Testament and in second- and third-century writings of the Christian era, a three-part pattern emerged, as a result of question-and-answer preparation of candidates for baptism, and in order to distinguish true from false teaching. The pattern reflects "trinitarian" belief—that is, God as "three in one."

The titles of Christian creeds may be misleading—for example, the Apostles' Creed developed, not from the orig-inal apostles, but from a creed used in the church in Rome in the middle of the fourth century. The Nicene Creed was agreed on at the Council of Constantinople in 381, extend-ing the formula of the Council of Nicea in 325. From the earliest days, confessions of belief of varying lengths have proliferated.

The major issue that arises for feminists of both sexes with respect to the Christian creeds is the language used for the divine. An important theological rule is that God tran-scends both sex (biological differentiation) and gender (cul-tural meaning associated with sex). God is ultimately mysterious and beyond "saying." The creeds used in Christ-ian worship and other statements of belief manifestly do not "say" God in humanly inclusive ways, though much spiritu-ality and prayer has used gender-inclusive language for God and has more adequately reflected the cultural diversity and richness of gender differences. This is no merely "verbal" mat-ter; it is arguable that the value or devaluation of women and the "feminine," as well as of men and the "masculine," are at stake, not only as co-procreators of human life but also as expressed in and through all realms of experience.

The dynamics of tradition require attention to mark-ers of truth and identity and to responsibility for those mark-ers in widely differing contexts. It does not therefore follow that no sense may be made of the language of divine father-hood if God in the Christian sense is believed to be both given and apprehended in gender-inclusive ways. Nor can there be any ultimate justification for refusing to explore the way in which divine motherhood may express the tran-scendence of God.

Also, Christian understanding of divine humility, God's commitment to humanity expressed in "taking flesh" in the sexual and gendered life of Jesus of Nazareth through the body of his mother, may represent the promise of gender reconciliation when that promise is associated with Spirit, given and giving. The trinitarian language of the creeds may well be capable of yielding creative compassion and the seeking of justice in human relationships, though there is to date no interchurch creed that has assimilated what is after all very recent feminist criticism. It will probably be most productive both to explore what the tradition may yet have to offer, given the extraordinary variety of contexts in which Christianity is to be found, and to accept the necessity of theologically imaginative experimentation with new statements of belief.

See Also

CHRISTIANITY; CHRISTIANITY: FEMINIST CHRISTOLOGY; DEITY; FAITH; PRAYER

References and Further Reading

La Cugna, Catherine Mowry, ed. 1993. *Freeing theology: the essentials of theology in feminist perspective.* New York: Harper-Collins.

Leith, John, ed. 1973. *Creeds of the churches: A reader in Christian doctrine from the Bible to the present.* Oxford: Blackwell.

Young, Frances. 1991. *The making of the creeds.* London: SCM; Philadelphia: Trinity.

Ann Loades

CRIME AND PUNISHMENT

Arguably, the social control of women involves the interlocking spheres of economic exclusion, domestic violence, and punishment within criminal justice systems. Daily struggles with poverty, violence against women, and imprisonment are interrelated forms of punishment, and they can all be seen as dimensions of social control integrally related to women's reproductive capacities and societal roles. Historically, the most poignant and entrenched forms of social control for women have been within the institutions of the family and the economy: gendered violence, poverty, and marginalization. In the contemporary world, social control exercised through criminal justice systems is becoming central to this matrix of domination.

Major feminist concerns include the criminalization of women's behaviors, the demonization of women offenders, and the gendered and excessive forms of punishment to which women are subjected. In many countries, punishment encompasses increasingly punitive responses to nonviolent offenders, a harsh "punishment tax" inflicted on women and their children, and the psychological, physical, and sexual abuse of incarcerated women. Equally important but often ignored are the links between structural inequality, punitive social policies, and the victimization, crime, and punishment of women.

A monumental obstacle to the feminist analysis of crime and punishment is the lack of systematic data and research on which to base that analysis, policy recommendations, or collective actions. There is a paucity of comprehensive data regarding worldwide crime and justice, and those data that do exist commonly ignore issues of gender. For example, in the United Nations Global Report on Crime and Justice of 1999, women are invisible. International and national data that are available must be scrutinized carefully, for they reflect not just women's criminality but, rather, the combination and confluence of women's behavior, responses by the criminal justice system, and the power structures in which both occur.

"Unnatural" Criminals

On the basis of existing information, it is clear that crime and violence (corporate, political, and street crime) are overwhelmingly the province of men and boys. But, although women participate in illegal behavior far less than men, those who do are commonly portrayed as exceptionally deviant, supercriminals, or inhumane monsters. Images of women offenders as singularly and uniformly violent, "unwomanly," "unfit mothers," and "unnatural criminals" have been pervasive historically and are still powerful in the contemporary world.

The majority of women become enmeshed in criminal justice systems because of drug-related offenses and offenses against property or public order. Worldwide, women are far more likely to be victims of violence than to perpetrate it. Relatively few women are arrested for violent crimes, and those few arrests often reflect desperate acts by violated women, including assaulting or killing abusive male partners. In the many countries where drug use is criminalized, drug-related offenses account for much of the increase in the arrest, conviction, and incarceration of women. Accordingly, women's involvement in criminal justice systems is a direct result of increasingly punitive responses to drug use and related crimes to support drug habits, such as prostitution and, especially, theft. In this age of increased surveillance and punishment, the greatest increases have been in the number of incarcerated women and the length of their incarceration. The massive rise in women's arrest and imprisonment in numerous countries reflects changes in social policy far more than increases in women's criminality.

International monitoring agencies, such as Human Rights Watch, suggest that many women are often arrested, detained, or incarcerated because of either discriminatory laws or the discriminatory application of laws. Although it is not the focus of this article, it also must be acknowledged that women worldwide are held as political prisoners and, even when women are arrested for "ordinary street crimes," the criminal justice process is deeply imbued with power struggles. The very definition of what constitutes crime, the decision-making processes related to criminal prosecution, and the rise of a global prison industrial complex are issues of urgent concern to feminists, as is the fact that throughout the world indigenous women and women from racial and ethnic minorities are overrepresented among those who are charged with and punished for crimes. This punishment goes particularly to the heart of their existence as women and, for the vast majority, as mothers.

Gendered Punishment

Specific forms of punishment vary throughout the world, but widely used sanctions include fines, probation, imprisonment, parole, and, in some countries, capital punishment. Many feminist issues are involved in this, including the punitive and gendered nature of much public policy, especially the long-term confinement of women for drug-related offenses; the long-term confinement of women for killing abusive partners; the multiple ways in which experiences within criminal justice systems are determined by gender, race, and class; the exclusion of women offenders and their children from cultural emphases on family integrity and the preeminence of "family values"; and exploration of the potential for change within jails and prisons through feminist activism and the advancement of women's rights within the global community. Especially crucial are the isolation, the lack of services, and the harsh, often abusive, conditions of women's punishment, as well as the multitude of ways in which they are affected by offenders' complex status as stigmatized women.

The punitive measures applied against women offenders take specific forms that subject these women to intensified punishment that is especially virulent for women. While the policies and practices of a few nations incorporate women-centered approaches, in most instances there is an added punishment—a "gender tax"—inflicted on women offenders. The abridgment of their reproductive and human rights and their exclusion from mainstream society are exacerbated, an effect that includes the long-term consequences of the disruption and destruction of countless families.

Women's imprisonment presents a microcosm of the myriad controversies surrounding both contemporary systems of punishment and women's place in society. Incarceration intensifies and perpetuates the degradation of women, and involves multiple systematic ways in which they are stripped of their identity as women, mothers, and contributing members of society. Policy changes surrounding punishment and prisons are evidence of contradictory and conflicting responses to women's needs and life situations. Some feminists advocate equity or parity in response to stereotypic treatment and markedly inferior services that perpetuate the subservient status of women. Yet superficial or nominal equity for women leads to unacknowledged additional punishment, because "equality" inevitably means inferiority when the context and standards are inherently male-oriented.

For example, equity in sentencing means relatively harsher punishment for countless women because of the acutely painful nature of their separation from their children. Likewise, the isolation experienced by most prisoners is heightened for women. Especially when prisons are designed as massive, centralized institutions, many women are incarcerated at significant distances from their homes. Control and discipline are frequently harsher for women than in men's facilities, as well as disproportionate to the less serious nature of most women's offenses. For example, research in the United States suggests that, even though they are less violent than their male counterparts, women receive a greater number of disciplinary citations for less serious infractions, are subjected to harsher standards of parole, and have fewer opportunities to be housed in minimum-security facilities.

Equally important, because women's numbers are small compared with men and because of the masculinist orientation of prisons, there is a grave lack of services tailored to the specific needs of women, including education and vocational and career training. This is often legitimated in the name of organizational expediency and the security needs of prisons, but it also has become an explicit strategy in the political demonization of prisoners as "undeserving of privilege." Increases in public funding are used primarily for the construction of more jails and prisons; far less is allocated to hiring and training staffs, and prison budgets are characterized by deep cuts in funding for academic or vocational education. The resulting lack of educational services is especially consequential for the future of poor and imprisoned women and their children. In turn, the inability of these women to provide for their children may be used to justify efforts to expedite the termination of their parental rights.

Another critical area of concern is health care. Women clearly have specific needs for health care, but the care provided varies greatly depending on the social and economic policies of specific societies. Where imprisonment is synonymous with deprivation and degradation, the gendered penalties of prison are clearly evident in the unavailability and poor quality of health services. The seriously inadequate care for poor women in many societies is epitomized by the neglect of imprisoned women's reproductive needs, including general gynecological services, prenatal and postpartum care, safe and unharassed childbirth, and medical counsel during menopause. The availability and quality of gynecological care vary greatly, including access to regular exams, Pap smears, and mammograms, as well as women-specific drug treatment and comprehensive services for women living with physical disabilities or HIV and AIDS, and those who are terminally ill.

Few societies address the specific needs of pregnant prisoners, such as appropriate diets, prenatal care, or lighter work assignments. Nor do most prisons have the resources to deal with miscarriages, premature births, or even routine deliveries. In most cases, prisoners' experiences during pregnancy and childbirth are far removed from public view and scrutiny, but available reports depict degraded and inhumane conditions. Because few prisons have facilities for giving birth, woman are transferred to local hospitals, and after giving birth most are immediately separated from their child and returned to prison. Prison guards are stationed near hospital rooms, prisoners' newborns are taken immediately or within two days, and most frequently women give birth without support from friends and family. Indeed, a vivid symbol of the prioritization of punishment over mothers and children is the vision of women shackled during childbirth.

Punishing Mothers and Children

There are unacknowledged surplus penalties for women prisoners, and the experiences of all incarcerated mothers give reason for feminists to be concerned. Obviously, incarceration severely damages women's relationships with their children, often irreparably. Primary issues include who cares for the children of incarcerated women; the lack of support services for incarcerated women's children, including transportation to jails and prisons for visitation; and the general lack of cooperation between foster parents and incarcerated mothers.

Despair is especially pronounced for imprisoned mothers who do not have a supportive family and must leave their children with unreliable persons, and for women whose children are placed in foster care or adopted. In the best circumstances, imprisoned women feel powerless to provide the nurturance and support their children need; in worse situations, they may not even know where their children are or whether the children are being subjected to neglect or abuse. Imprisoned women feel anguish concerning their children, but they also often live in fear that they will not be able to regain custody when released from prison. Reuniting is more likely when children are cared for by the incarcerated woman's parents, sisters, or other relatives, but the loss of children becomes imminent when no relatives are acceptable to authorities, so that the children become wards of the state and are placed in foster homes, often separated from brothers and sisters. In some situations, the imprisonment of women results in homelessness and abject poverty for their children.

Tremendous disruption, and sometimes permanent dissolution, of their relationships with their children is a well-documented aspect of women's imprisonment, a hidden and unacknowledged aggrandizement of women's punishments. But perhaps the ultimate, most overwhelming penalty for imprisoned women is the enormous guilt that accompanies their frequent or perpetual sense of inability to control their children's lives. Feminist analysts have suggested that a state of permanent guilt is integral to women's experiences within patriarchal society, but heightened guilt and self-condemnation are prevalent among imprisoned women. These feelings are intensified further by the contradiction of being responsible mothers while subjected to the infantalization of prison life, where women are routinely treated like children devoid of decision-making ability.

Abuses against Women in Custody

Throughout the world, women in custody lack physical security and dignity, and they are highly vulnerable to emotional, physical, and sexual abuse. Although few systematic data are available, investigations and reports such as those conducted by Amnesty International document official mistreatment ranging from humiliation and harassment to rape and torture. The specific country or cultural context greatly influences these conditions and possible remedies.

The increased surveillance of contemporary prisons is accompanied by gender-specific dangers for women. The constant surveillance and denial of privileges—particularly in maximum control units—heighten women's vulnerability to sexual harassment and abuse. These are the extreme of everyday experiences of many imprisoned women where prison architecture and policies purposefully deny privacy and subject them to surveillance during even their most personal moments, for example, when showering and using the toilet. Strip searches are commonly conducted in the name of security or in search of contraband but also as preparation for visitation.

Imprisoned women are subjected to harassment, abuse, and rape by guards, and this emotional and sexual abuse perpetuates the domination of many women who have been abused prior to incarceration. Societal indifference to crimes against women, in the home and on the street, is mirrored in the disregard for the violation of imprisoned women. This is most evident in the minimalization of guards' accountability or punishment for abusing women prisoners. Despite guards' tremendous power over the day-to-day well-being of prisoners, women's sexual involvement with guards, in exchange for privileges or goods from their keepers, is commonly viewed as "consensual" rather than exploitive and abusive.

Brutal rape and terror are often met with indifference. Violation of imprisoned women—as of women in society—is often not treated as a true crime; this attitude is similar to the pervasive response to domestic violence. When abuses occur, there may be no grievance process; if there is a process, women often are uninformed regarding it; offenses are commonly handled as internal administrative (rather than criminal) matters, with minor sanctions; there is a high possibility of retaliation from abusive officers; and women's grievances are rarely investigated by external, independent review boards. Degradation and mistreatment, even rape and torture, become part of women's punishment.

Conclusion

Economic exclusion, domestic violence, and punishment within criminal justice systems are significant aspects of the social control of women throughout the world. Each provides brazenly overt as well as insidious avenues to patriarchal subjugation and domination of women. The punitive role of criminal justice systems has become especially preeminent in many countries and requires close feminist scrutiny. The criminalization of women's behaviors, the demonization of women offenders, and highly gender-determined forms of punishment merit our careful attention and highest commitment. In order to challenge women's fate within these structures of power and ideology, feminists must confront and counter both the lack of sys-

tematic women-centered information and research and the extensive exclusion of women offenders from feminist communities.

See Also

CRIME AND PUNISHMENT: CASE STUDY—WOMEN IN PRISONS IN THE UNITED STATES; CRIMINOLOGY; DOMESTIC VIOLENCE; DRUG AND ALCOHOL ABUSE; PROSTITUTION

References and Further Reading

Cook, Sandy, and Susanne Davis, eds. 1999. *Harsh punishment: International experiences of women's imprisonment*. Boston: Northeastern University Press.

Howe, Adrian. 1994. *Punish and critique: Toward a feminist analysis of penality*. London and New York: Routledge.

Stern, Vivien. 1998. *A sin against the future: Imprisonment in the world*, chapter 7. Boston: Northeastern University Press.

Peg Bortner
Jolan Hsieh

CRIME AND PUNISHMENT: Case Study— Women in Prisons in the United States

The United States currently has the highest rate of incarceration in the world, exceeding the rates of the former Soviet Union and South Africa (Irwin and Austin, 2001). In the United States crime control became increasingly punitive in the latter half of the twentieth century. At the end of the century, federal, state, and local authorities came to rely more heavily on incarceration as a means of punishing people who violate the criminal code. *Incarceration*, as used here, refers to the use of institutionalized supervision in either a jail, for short-term confinement, or prisons for sentences of more than one year.

While women offenders represent a numerical minority in the overall prison population, they also represent the fastest-growing portion of incarcerated people. Popular explanations for the increased number of women in prison often cite increases in women's criminality or growing violence among female offenders. Such accounts fail to reflect accurately the political, social, and economic variables that contribute to the environment in which women commit crimes and are punished with prison or jail terms. Regardless of the means by which women enter prison, once they are incarcerated there is little intervention to increase the likelihood that they will return to society as law-abiding citizens and remain law-abiding. Given the high incarceration rates and the growing population of women prisoners, this article will focus entirely on incarceration and women imprisoned in the United States.

Increased Numbers of Women in Prison

The Bureau of Justice Statistics (BJS, 1991, 1999) reported a 200 percent increase in the women's prison population during the 1980s. The men's prison population increased 112 percent during the same period. Through the mid-1990s, the women's population continued to increase by an annual average of 11.2 percent while men's numbers grew 7.9 percent. Signs show that the growth of the prison population is slowing, but the number of women prisoners is still increasing at nearly 6 percent annually while the population of men averages less than 5 percent annual growth.

The numbers may indicate that more women are entering prison, but the statistics do not impart *why* more women are being incarcerated. The majority of women offenders are incarcerated for nonviolent property offenses (36 percent) or drug crimes (39.1 percent). The largest portion of property crimes committed by women offenders consists of larceny theft and fraud (Ditton and Wilson, 1999). Although these same categories of offenses also apply to men, differences in the damages caused by women are distinct. Women are reportedly more likely than men to engage in shoplifting (larceny theft), welfare fraud, and writing bad checks—crimes that produce low profit for the offenders and relatively small economic damage to the victims (Chesney-Lind, 1997; Feinmen, 1994). Many of the women arrested for drug crimes are cited for possession only. Women who are sentenced for drug distribution or trafficking are generally small-time dealers who engage in multiple transactions and are caught because of their visibility on the streets. When women do commit violent crimes, the offenses are often the result of an ongoing violent relationship in which women have been abused by partners or other family members, and their abusers become the targets of violence. Patterns of women's criminality are reported to have remained stable since the early 1980s. If this is true, it invalidates the claim that women are more involved in crime and violent acts now than in the past (Belknap, 1996).

Some women offenders may not be exercising free choice but, rather, may have been pushed into criminality. Those who are sentenced to prison or jail are disproportionately women of color, poor, and undereducated, with few legitimate employment skills. Approximately 67 percent of the women held in local jails and state and federal

prisons are women of color (BJS, 1999). The distribution of prisoners along racial and ethnic lines is comparable in men's institutions, where black and Hispanic prisoners are the numerical majority. The disproportionate overrepresentation of people of color, including women of color, in prison is important to address but exceeds the scope of this article. Often these same women are financially and emotionally responsible for the care of dependent children. Many are survivors of physical, emotional, and sexual abuse that took place either during their childhood or when they were adults. The overall portrait of incarcerated women is a dismal one that has led some researchers to suggest that criminal behavior may be the only avenue open for women with marginal employment skills, few resources, and the responsibility to provide for their children (Chesney-Lind, 1997).

Once women have been brought into the criminal justice system, there are few options to help them address their needs in addition to serving their punishment. The growing movement in the United States toward harsher penalties includes changes in sentencing structures. For example, mandatory minimum sentences require a set number of years to be served in prison before a prisoner becomes eligible for parole. "Habitual offender" statutes enhance penalties for repeat offenders. Finally, truth-in-sentencing policies require that prisoners convicted of violent crimes and certain types of drug offenses serve approximately 85 percent of an incarcerative sentence before consideration for parole. All of these changes in sentencing structures channel more women offenders toward institutionalized punishment where few opportunities exist to receive counseling or job training that would enable them to live crime-free (Owen, 1998).

In addition to the deprivations of prison life, women prisoners are also at risk of further victimization. The Human Rights Watch report *All Too Familiar: Sexual Abuse of Women in U.S. State Prisons* (1996), provided an in-depth study of the sexual victimization that women prisoners experience at the hands of correctional officers and staffs. Despite policies that prohibit sexual contact between staff members and prisoners, day-to-day prison operations provide many opportunities for guards to be present while women prisoners are disrobed and to touch the prisoners through pat-downs and body searches. Women prisoners have few legal channels through which to pursue their assailants, and so the cycle of sexual victimization continues. The physical and emotional damage done to these women by abusive staffers only compounds their troubled personal histories and further diminishes their potential for rehabilitation and reintegration into society.

Separation from Children

BJS (1994) reported that about 66 percent of women in prison have at least one child under the age of 18. Prior to being incarcerated, 72 percent of these mothers were living with their children. In many cases the fathers of the children are not present; only about 25 percent of mothers in prison report that their children are living with their fathers. In comparison, only about 50 percent of incarcerated men are fathers, and the majority of fathers (90 percent) reported that their children were living with their mothers.

In most U.S. women's prisons, mothers are not permitted to keep infants with them who are born during the incarceration or to bring children with them to the institution. Two notable exceptions to this general policy are the Bedford Hills Correctional Facility in New York and the Nebraska Center for Women in York, Nebraska. Each of these facilities operates nursery programs that enable women prisoners who have given birth in prison to keep their infants with them for one to two years. These options are generally reserved for women who are serving short sentences and will be released from prison at the same time that their children would be required to leave the nursery program. Researchers who have studied the mother–child connection note the importance of maintaining contact between mothers and their offspring. These relationships are viewed as crucial to the health and well-being of both mother and child. Research regarding the impact of a parent's incarceration on the child has found that children of imprisoned parents often have emotional and behavioral problems linked to loss of contact with their parent, including anger, depression, poor school performance, and nightmares (Johnston, 1995). Often caregivers for the children are unwilling to address truthfully where the mother is or what is happening to her while she is away. Rather than comforting the child, the lack of communication about where the mother is and when she will be back can produce confusion, anger, and anxiety.

These behavioral and emotional problems of children can escalate to the point where the children could come under social control, as a result of such matters as truancy, running away from home, or criminal behavior. While research does not identify a direct causal relationship between a parent's incarceration and the misconduct of a child, some researchers have reported that as many as one-third of juvenile offenders have one or more parents who are or have been in prison (Muse, 1994). Factors contributing to criminality and incarceration are numerous and complex, and this brief overview is not intended to suggest that there are crime-prone families. Rather, research on the links between separation of parents from children and the subsequent behavior of the children must continue.

Children are not the only ones negatively affected by separation. Mothers in prison report feeling guilt, anxiety, fear, and sadness stemming from the loss of contact with their children (Synder-Joy and Carlo, 1998). More research is needed on how the feelings of the mother, combined with the stress of incarceration, may contribute to emotional and behavioral problems during institutionalization and after release from prison.

Life in Women's Prisons

The pain of separation from children is not the only consequence of incarceration. Life in women's prisons is characterized by many losses, mainly the loss of freedom and autonomy. Incarcerated women are removed from society and placed in institutions that often do not provide meaningful ways for women to occupy their time or prepare for return to outside society. Barbara Owen's book *In the Mix* (1998) provides an in-depth study of life in California's women's correctional facilities. Owen reports that the punitive focus of prisons does little to address the needs of women offenders. As noted earlier, women enter prison with low employment skills, few resources, and histories of physical, emotional, and substance abuse. The programmatic offerings in prisons do not include the in-depth counseling necessary to help women cope with their own experiences of abuse or patterns of addiction. Instead, many of the women who enter prison directly or indirectly as a result of their own social and emotional needs will leave prison having gained very little to help them change for the better (Belknap, 1996).

Vocational training and education programs are also lacking in women's prisons. Women prisoners are trained primarily for work as cosmetologists, seamstresses, secretaries, and filing clerks, and other low-paying, low-status occupations (Belknap, 1996). If women do manage to secure employment in these fields after their release, the pay they receive will probably not move them out of poverty and will probably not provide sufficient income to care for their families. Without legitimate employment skills, the women may well feed again the financial and social pressure to engage in criminal activity to care for themselves and their children. Thus, a cycle of poverty, powerlessness, and incarceration can be maintained.

Summary

The future for women brought into the U.S. criminal justice system is uncertain. The emphasis on strict state social control through incarceration does little, if anything, to intervene in or change the conditions that contributed to the women's contact with the state to begin with. The social problems of domestic violence, substance abuse, and poverty are not addressed on a structural level. Rather, individualization of criminality results in punishment for women—primarily institutionalization—which does little to change their situation or their behavior. Added to the needs of women are the needs of young children separated from their mothers.

For women brought into the criminal justice system, intervention rather than incarceration is needed to provide viable options to empower women in society and reduce the need for formal social control. Community-based programs designed to help women address histories and patterns of abuse, provide legitimate job skills to earn a living wage, and enable women to remain connected or to reconnect with their children are central issues for the new century.

See Also

ABUSE; CHILD ABUSE; CRIME AND PUNISHMENT; CRIMINOLOGY; DOMESTIC VIOLENCE; HOUSEHOLDS: FEMALE-HEADED AND FEMALE-SUPPORTED; POVERTY; TORTURE

References and Further Reading

Austin, James, and John Irwin. 2001. *It's about time: America's imprisonment binge.* 3rd ed. Belmont, Calif.: Wadsworth/Thompson Learning.

Belknap, Joanne. 1996. *The invisible woman.* Belmont, Calif.: Wadsworth.

Bureau of Justice Statistics (BJS). 1999. *Prisoner and jail inmates at midyear 1998.* Washington, D.C.: U.S. Department of Justice.

———. 1991. *Women in prison.* Washington, D.C.: U.S. Department of Justice.

———. 1994. *Women in prison.* Washington, D.C.: U.S. Department of Justice.

Chesney-Lind, Meda. 1997. *The female offender.* Thousand Oaks, Calif.: Sage.

Ditton, Pamela, and Doris James Wilson. 1999. *Truth in sentencing in state prisons.* Bureau of Justice Statistics Special Report, U.S. Department of Justice, Office of Justice Programs, CJ 170032.

Feinman, Clarice. 1994. *Women in the criminal justice system.* West Point, N.Y.: Preager.

Human Rights Watch. 1996. *All too familiar: Sexual abuse of women in U.S. state prisons.* New York: Human Rights Watch.

Johnston, Denise. 1995. Effects of parental incarceration. In Kristin Gabel and Denise Johnston, eds., *Children of incarcerated parents,* 59–88. New York: Lexington.

Muse, Daphne. 1994. Parenting from prison. *Mothering* (Fall): 99–105.

Owen, Barbara. 1998. *"In the mix": Struggle and survival in a women's prison.* Albany: State University of New York Press.

Snyder-Joy, Zoann, and Teresa Carlo. 1998. Parenting through prison walls: Incarcerated mothers and children's visitation programs. In Susan Miller, ed., *Crime control and women,* 130–150. Thousand Oaks, Calif.: Sage.

Zoann Snyder

CRIME FICTION

See DETECTIVE FICTION and LESBIAN WRITING: CRIME FICTION.

CRIMINOLOGY

The academic study of criminology is often confused with (or overlaps) criminal justice studies, which offer practical preparation for careers in criminal justice. In western nations, women generally constitute less than 20 percent of criminal justice workers (apart from office workers and women's prison staffs), just as women make up about 20 percent of the international American Society of Criminology (close to 2,500 total). Women are also a distinct minority among people criminalized (that small proportion of lawbreakers processed, labeled, and punished as "criminal").

Globally, women are convicted of between 5 and 20 percent of all criminal offenses; because their crimes are generally minor and nonviolent, women compose only between 2 and 10 percent of adult prison populations.

Feminist Revision of Criminology

Since the 1970s, feminist scholars in criminology have given attention to women as *subjects* (rather than objects) of research, and power relations with regard to sex and gender, social class, race, ethnicity, and so on. Criminology invites critical, sociolegal investigation of social control mechanisms, such as political economy, medicine and psychiatry, family and welfare law, social service and judicial agencies, the military, the media, and education. These and other channels of coercion or force, all considered "gendered," constitute the discursive links that make up the state. All affect and are affected by criminal justice agencies.

Research on women in criminal justice professions has focused primarily on their effectiveness in a "masculinist" environment; generally women perform at a high standard—including tasks requiring physical stamina, strength, and quick reflex. Policewomen are often more effective than men in working with victims (usually female) of rape, battering, or other physical and sexual abuse.

Cesare Lombroso, the late-nineteenth-century Italian "father of criminology," recycled the theory that the "born criminal" woman was more evil and dangerous than the worst of men because of her biological inadequacy. In 1973 Dorie Klein published her pathbreaking critical analysis of early theories on the "female offender," starting with Lombroso. Interest in this area rapidly increased. Other early researchers, from three continents, included Meda Chesney-Lind, Estelle Freedman, Nicole Rafter, Freda Adler, Nancy Stoller, Zelma Henriques, and Darryl Steffensmeier in the United States; Marie Andrée Bertrand, André LaChance, J. M. Beattie, and Constance Backhouse in Canada; Christine Alder, Naffine Ngaire, Suzanne Hatty, and Anne Summers in Australia; and Frances Heidensohn, Carol Smart, Mary McIntosh, Allison Morris, Pat Carlen, Elizabeth Stanko, Susan Edwards, R. Emerson Dobash, and Russell P. Dobash, in the United Kingdom. These were among the first women and men to advance scholarship on women, crime, and punishment. Many other feminist researchers and activists continue to "deconstruct" criminology, exposing what they identify as misogynist myths, and they examine gender, race, and class in the social construction of crime, criminals, criminal justice agencies, and institutions, as well as the androcentricity of criminology itself. There is also an enormous literature on criminal violence *against* women and children.

The Sex Factor

Age, color, and sex (young, minority, male) are the significant factors in predicting who will be convicted of street crime (which is much more likely to be prosecuted than white-collar crime). Mary Eaton and Kathleen Daly, among others, have found that the sentencing stage following conviction, for both males and females, is positively influenced by a defendant's demonstrated commitment to meeting parental responsibilities.

Embodying modern western cultural attitudes toward women (which are changing in many societies), prostitution epitomizes the duality between good girl (madonna) and bad girl (whore). The prosecution of prostitutes in the nineteenth century revived the sexualization of female crime and the criminalization of female sex. Scientists, following Freud, look for the causes of prostitution in women's bodies and psyches. Feminists point to the objectification and commodifi-cation of female bodies, as promoted by pornography and prostitution, to the pervasive violence against sex workers, and to the rising incidence of child and female sex slavery in Asia, for example. Other women, in Europe, the Commonwealth, and the United States, organize to defend adult prostitution as a "chosen job" in societies characterized by limited choices and by class and gender stratification.

Sameness and Difference

A key feminist analysis in both criminal and civic disputes involves the question of whether to plead *gender neutrality* or *gender specificity.* When do women plead equality on the grounds of *sameness* with men (specifically property owners, in whose interests most laws were written), and when do women plead for special treatment on the grounds of *differences*? Disadvantaged victims cannot be perceived as equal, but achieving equity requires recognition of subordination. For example, historically, rape was a property crime, the violation of one man's daughter or wife by another man; the victim's suffering was of no consequence. The issue of "sameness or difference" relates to the issue of biological essentialism. For example, blaming crime on premenstrual syndrome or on postpartum depression perpetuates the notion that women's bodies harbor dangerous, uncontrollable impulses.

Prison

As noted, between 2 and 10 percent of all adult prisoners are women, a lower per capita rate than in the late nineteenth century, when Elizabeth Fry began her reform work in the United Kingdom. Early twenty-first-century issues include separating children from their mothers; inadequate health care education and job training; the internationalization of women's imprisonment, primarily as a result of the jailing of drug couriers ("mules") in the countries where they are arrested; accelerated construction of women's prisons in the 1980s and 1990s (attributed to the United States' "war on drugs"); and disproportionate representation of the lowest economic stratum. Universally, women's prisons are mainly occupied by unemployed single mothers, with a disproportionate number from colonized or persecuted minority groups.

Boys are seldom locked up for status offences. The vanguard research of Meda Chesney-Lind, beginning in the early 1970s, shows how girls innocent of any crime have been sent to reformatories to "protect" them from sexual immorality. "Female offenders" of all ages, whether jailed for minor offenses or sent to prison for a long term, follow this "victimization–criminalization continuum." For example, research in North America suggests that most adult street prostitutes ran away from abusive homes in their youth. Abolitionists or decarcerationists (who would limit prisons to violent people) argue that it is economically wasteful and destructive to invest in institutions of punishment for such women. What is needed is services and job training to assist women recovering from abuse, and overall reduced violence.

The Crimes

Some mass media in the mid-1970s trumpeted the myth that emancipated women become "like men," with the prediction that "women's lib" would produce more violent crime by women. This has not occurred. In most western nations, women are convicted of between 10 and 20 percent of crimes against the person, a historical constant. In homicides by women, the victim is often a man who has abused the woman; some defendants are receiving acquittals or eventual clemency on grounds of "battered woman syndrome," a term coined by Lenore Walker.

Historically, women have been executed or imprisoned for a wide array of offenses: witchcraft, scolding their husbands, infanticide, adultery, working as midwives, assisting with abortion, distributing information about birth control, using bad language in the street, demonstrating for the vote, and otherwise challenging "women's place." In Canada in the 1990s, women were convicted of up to a third of minor property crimes, including shoplifting and welfare fraud (with increases attributed to a steady rise in the "feminization of poverty"). They were charged with less than 15 percent of drug crimes, and less than 8 percent of robberies and breaking and entering, both considered "masculine" crimes. Overall, on both sides of the law and in every country, criminal justice is substantively and significantly a world of men.

See Also

CRIME AND PUNISHMENT

References and Further Reading

Adelberg, Ellen, and Claudia Currie, eds. 1993. *In conflict with the law: Women and the Canadian justice system.* Vancouver: Press Gang.

Allen, Judith. 1990. *Sex and secrets: Crimes involving Australian women since 1880.* Melbourne: Oxford University Press.

Belknap, Joanne. 1996. *The invisible woman: Gender, crime and justice.* Belmont, Calif.: Wadsworth.

Boyd, Susan. 1999. *Mothers and illicit drug use: Transcending the myths.* Toronto: University of Toronto Press.

Boritch, Helen. 1996. *Fallen women: Female crime and criminal justice in Canada.* Scarborough, Ont.: Nelson.

Brock, Deborah R. 1998. *Making work, making trouble: Prostitution as a social problem.* Toronto: University of Toronto Press.

Carlen, Pat. 1998. *Women's imprisonment at the millennium.* London: Macmillan.

Chesney-Lind, Meda. 1997. *The female offender: Girls, women and crime.* Thousand Oaks, Calif.: Sage.

Comack, Elizabeth. 1996. *Women in trouble.* Halifax: Fernwood.

Cook, Sandy, and Susanne Davies, eds. 1999. *Harsh punishment: International experiences of women's imprisonment.* Boston: Northeastern University Press.

Daly, Kathleen. 1994. *Gender, crime and punishment.* New Haven, Conn.: Yale University Press.

DeKeseredy, Walter S. 2000. *Women, crime and the Canadian criminal justice system.* Cincinnati, Ohio: Anderson.

Dobash, R. Emerson, Russell P. Dobash, and Leslie Noaks. 1995. *Gender and crime.* Cardiff: University of Wales Press.

Eaton, Mary. 1993. *Women after prison.* Buckingham: Open University Press.

Faith, Karlene. 1994. *Unruly women: The politics of confinement and resistance.* Vancouver: Press Gang.

Feinman, Clarice. 1994. *Women in the criminal justice system.* Westport, Conn.: Praeger.

Fishman, Laura. 1990. *Women at the wall.* Albany: State University of New York Press.

Fletcher, Beverley, Lynda Shaver, and Dreama Moon. 1996. *Women prisoners: A forgotten population.* Westport, Conn.: Praeger.

Gelsthorpe, Loraine, and Allison Morris, eds. 1990. *Feminist perspectives in criminology.* Buckingham: Open University Press.

Hampton, Blanche. 1993. *Prisons and women.* Sydney: University of New South Wales Press.

Hannah-Moffat, Kelly, and Margaret Shaw, eds. 2000. *An ideal prison? Critical essays on women's imprisonment in Canada.* Halifax: Fernwood.

Heidensohn, Frances. 1996. *Women and crime,* 2nd ed. Basingstoke, U.K.: Macmillan.

Howe, Adrian. 1994. *Punish and critique: Towards a feminist analysis of penality.* London and New York: Routledge.

Maden, Tony. 1996. *Women, prisons, and psychiatry.* Oxford: Butterworth-Heinemann.

Maher, Lisa. 1997. *Sexed work: Gender, race, and resistance in a Brooklyn drug market.* London: Clarendon.

Mann, Coramae. 1993. *Unequal justice: A question of color.* Bloomington: Indiana University Press.

Messerschmidt, James W. 1993. *Capitalism, patriarchy and crime: Toward a socialist feminist criminology.* Totowa, N.J.: Rowman and Littlefield.

Miller, S. L., ed. 1998. *Women: Feminist implications of criminal justice policy.* Thousand Oaks, Calif.: Sage.

Moyer, Imogene L. 1992. *The changing roles of women in the criminal justice system: Offenders, victims and professionals,* 2nd ed. Prospect Heights, N.Y.: Waveland.

Muraskin, Roslyn, and Ted Alleman, eds. 1993. *It's a crime: Women and justice.* Englewood Cliffs, N.J.: Regents–Prentice Hall.

Owen, Barbara. 1998. *In the mix: Struggle and survival in a women's prison.* Albany: State University of New York Press.

Naffine, Ngaire, ed. 1994. *Gender, crime and feminism.* Aldershot, U.K.: Dartmouth.

Pollock-Byrne, Joycelyn M. 1999. *Criminal women.* Cincinnati, Ohio: Anderson.

Price, Barbara Raffel, and Natalie J. Sokoloff, eds. 1995. *The criminal justice system and women,* 2nd ed. New York: McGraw-Hill.

Rafter, Nicole, and Frances Heidensohn. eds. 1995. *International feminist perspectives in criminology: Engendering a discipline.* Buckingham, U.K.: Open University Press.

Rock, Paul. 1996. *Reconstructing a women's prison: The Holloway Redevelopment Project 1968–1988.* Oxford: Clarendon.

Simon, Rita J., and Jean Landis. 1991. *The crimes women commit, the punishments they receive.* Lexington, Mass.: Lexington.

Stanko, Elizabeth. 1995. *Everyday violence: How women and men experience physical and sexual danger.* London: Pandora.

Watterson, Kathryn. 1996. *Women in prison: Inside the concrete womb.* Boston: Northeastern University Press.

Wiebe, Rudy, and Yvonne Johnson. 1998. *Stolen life: The journey of a Cree woman.* Toronto: Knopf.

Zedner, Lucia. 1991. *Women, crime and custody in Victorian England.* Oxford: Clarendon.

See also the scholarly journal *Women and Criminal Justice* (Haworth Press). Editor Donna Hale.

Karlene Faith

CRITICAL AND CULTURAL THEORY

From the beginning, feminists have taken an intense but critical interest in culture. It is within the cultural domain that gendered subjects are socialized. Culture also yields a public domain of shared (and competing) meanings and values, wherein norms and symbols of sexual difference are reproduced. Alongside more materialist strands of feminism concerned with women's socioeconomic conditions, cultural theory investigates the ways in which ideas of femininity (and masculinity) are inscribed within the language and images of everyday life, at the point where society and the self mesh. More narrowly, culture is also composed of the artistic and literary creations that particular societies prize and that help to tell their members who they are. Women's contributions to and exclusion from this realm, as well as the way they have been represented and represent themselves there, have all been abiding concerns of feminist cultural theory.

Approaches to Feminist Cultural Theory

A range of approaches emerged in the course of these feminist explorations: critical analysis of the male, or masculine, bias of mainstream culture and its related denigration of all that is coded "feminine" or associated with women; a bringing to visibility of women's previously marginalized cultural creations; a celebration of either a different feminine culture, newly retrieved, or a woman-centered one, yet to be invented. Both equality and difference are important in these approaches, which generally operate within an opposition between women and men, feminine and masculine. They may broadly be classified as modernist, as opposed to recent postmodern strategies aiming to subvert such oppositional thinking, whose very structure is now deemed phallocentric.

Postmodernists also emphasize the cultural diversity, rather than the universality, of women, as well as the precariousness and heterogeneity of feminine identity. Although culturally innovative, such tactics seem paradoxical in light of feminist concerns about a generalized patriarchal culture and a woman-centered alternative developed collectively by women whose shared oppression yields a common identity and a basis for political solidarity. Yet in considering difference, feminists find themselves obliged to consider more explicitly their own cultural interventions regarding location and context: questions arise as to who is speaking or listening to, or about, whom and from what position, and about where authorship and authority are interwoven. From all these perspectives, cultural theory is concerned with the exercise of power in and through culture and is therefore thoroughly political.

Feminists have always drawn attention to the ways in which patriarchal culture constructs norms of femininity into which women are then socialized and within which they are disciplined. For early liberal and Marxist feminists, femininity was imposed on women through poor education and trivial, domestic pursuits; it meant a generally impoverished personality from which equal rights would emancipate women for full participation in human (male) culture. However, there were others who considered feminine traits superior and anticipated their culturally transformative effects, once women were free to express themselves publicly. A similar dialectic, between those who seek gender equality within an androgynous ideal and a nonsexist culture on the one hand, and on the other hand those who value women's difference and its cultural radicalism, has persisted through the twentieth century, where it is interwoven with debates concerning whether gender is contingent or essential. On the whole feminists have seen gender unfolding within culture, rather than being ascribed by nature. This is why they have been so concerned with cultural theory.

Simone de Beauvoir and "The Second Sex"

It is difficult to overemphasize the contribution of Simone de Beauvoir's study of women as the second sex (1972). Women, she declared, are made, not born, but their common fate is to be constituted as man's "other." Examining myths, biographies, scientific theories, and life cycles, de Beauvoir concluded that women had been excluded from history and culture, where their status as goddesses, wives, and mothers relegated them to otherworldly or passive roles and to uncreative and repetitive tasks, as opposed to men's active engagement in cultural projects and practices of freedom. Both a pervasive cultural symbolism and a sexual division of labor excluded women from acting as subjects. To a large extent, de Beauvoir's solution was cultural—socialize women like men and grant them the same opportunities for active subjectivity—but she doubted that liberated women would create a different culture specific to themselves. Despite subsequent feminist criticism of de Beauvoir's conclusions—for example, her negative evaluation of motherhood, her acceptance of male norms of the humanly valuable, and her neglect of women's particular cultural traditions—her approach to analyzing the way mainstream culture denigrates the images of women it constructs has remained central to feminist critical theory. Kate Millett's *Sexual Politics* (1977) is a good example of early radical feminist cultural analysis, tracing misogynist currents through fashionable social scientific and literary works into everyday culture. Subsequent studies in this critical genre have excavated more profoundly the foundations of western culture and subjectivity, to argue that fantasy, desire, and language are thoroughly encoded with sexual difference, misogyny, and phallocentrism.

Restoring the Neglected Feminine

The other side of the coin is a feminism that aims to make visible the neglected feminine, or woman-centered culture

that patriarchy has marginalized. Both representations of women's experiences and representations by women themselves have been silenced within mainstream culture. Feminists have retrieved many cultural creations by women, which had simply been denied a public or ascribed male authorship, thereby establishing their predecessors' virtuosity. However, because women have generally been denied space for what is considered high culture, scholars have also emphasized women's own skills and crafts, such as embroidery or quilting, which mainstream (male) culture had dismissed. Others have pursued new genres in writing, or new artistic symbolism associated with a feminine imaginary or the female body, suggesting an alternative feminine (or feminist) aesthetic.

A Woman-Centered Culture

Although this approach sometimes seems to court essentialism, feminists have on the whole insisted that feminine expressions are associated with skills and orientations learned within culture. Besides a feminine aesthetic, they explore the notion of a different epistemology and vision—a gendered way of knowing and seeing the world—and ethics. To avoid charges of essentialism, feminists sometimes argue that these radical alternatives are only conventionally labeled "feminine" and could in principle be adopted by women or men, or that they are feminist rather than feminine. Emphasis on a woman-centered culture to be constructed, rather than on a feminine culture to be retrieved, is important here, although this still leaves open the question of what it is that women, or feminists, share. Recent cultural analysis reveals acute awareness of the dangers of overgeneralizing. In line with trends toward postmodernism, feminists are eager to point out the rich variety of women's creativity and the cultural diversity of feminine identities and feminist aspirations. Nevertheless, there is often tension between such emphases and the project of an alternative, woman-centered culture. Central to the latter is a refusal to evaluate women's culture according to male norms, and to a large extent it is only this logic that lesbian or African-American women (for example) deploy when they establish their own criteria and voices, accusing feminism of universalizing certain culturally privileged norms of its own. Thus African-centered feminist analyses describe a specific maternal culture and mode of being in the world, and such examples of woman-centered cultures, with their own images of femininity, ideals, and oppression, abound. This emphasis on differences as well as difference, on the empowerment of previously marginalized voices, and on the location of audiences and authorities within broader structures of power leads feminist cultural studies, almost inevitably, in a postmodern direction.

Postmodernism and Poststructuralism

A considerable amount of cultural theory in the last decade of the twentieth century fell under the broad heading of *postmodernism,* although this term is both contested and a general category subsuming various dimensions. The idea of postmodernity suggests a significant historical shift in the ways that, for example, production and consumption take place within a context of rapid technological innovation, where processes of economic and cultural globalization are accompanied by fragmentation of previously relatively stable structures such as the nation-state, family, gender, and class. These sorts of change are more readily amenable to social scientific study, although postmodernism itself stresses cultural approaches and this orientation is followed by most of its feminist adherents. Poststructuralism, which is closely, if not unproblematically, associated with postmodernism, reinforces this cultural focus. Although such an approach was already common among radical feminists, ideas of women's liberation as an escape from and destruction of patriarchal power are now displaced by notions of an ongoing struggle in a mobile context where (patriarchal) power is constantly reproduced yet also contested. Politically, the aim is not merely to expose the gender bias of mainstream culture or to make visible women's suppressed activities there, but to engage directly in cultural practices that subvert the foundations of western, and especially modern, modes of representation themselves.

For poststructuralists, reality is in principle unknowable because language, rather than communicating something "out there," constructs meaning. It is in the way such meaning unfolds that feminists detect profound processes of privilege and exclusion that operate according to sexual difference. The structures of syntax; the quest for stable definitions and a language that conceptually mirrors, or masters, reality; the binary but hierarchical oppositions (such as masculine-feminine) that structure meaning; the deployment of the feminine as a metaphor for all that is unruly, nonrational, and a threat to orderly significance; the repression of desire and of preoedipal bodily rhythms and their pleasures in discourse—all these aspects of (western) symbolism render it phallocentric. The feminine, excluded and literally unrepresentable within it, thus emerges as a subversive force that shatters language and destabilizes the quest for mastery (e.g., through avant-garde poetry, motherhood, or *écriture féminine*), while transgressing the oppositions that had defined woman only as man's other, mirror, or lack

(phallic-nonphallic). Difference without opposition is pursued instead. In this context a distinction must be made between thinkers like Julia Kristeva, for whom women and the feminine are only contingently related and interventions are primarily negative, and those like Luce Irigaray, for whom there is a specific relationship mediated by the morphology of the female body and a utopian vision of feminine countersymbolism. For all of them, however, the feminine emerges not as a specific or authentic identity, but as a heterogeneous, complex, and open process that defies the rigid either-or sexual opposition imposed by patriarchy and phallocentrism.

While this excursion into the foundations of language and the unconscious may appear abstruse, there are other levels on which postmodernism has inspired intervention within popular culture to great effect. The way discourses name, define, and construct groups profoundly affects their identity and efficacy, especially among those such as women who have been designated "other" and silenced accordingly. Postmodern concerns with culture simultaneously yield political strategies that empower these others and celebrate difference. The way images of women are represented, as well as the structure of the male gaze, also suggest a politics of representation and of vision. Postmodernists insist not merely that these representations are degrading or misrepresentative of something more valid, but that they actually construct and reproduce both gendered subjects and a culture thoroughly inscribed with sexual difference. Because this form of power operates below the level of reflection, through bodies and symbols, it is often more amenable to aesthetic, rather than rational and analytical, strategies. Thus postmodern feminist aesthetic practices—for example, in films or paintings that disrupt the opposition between the active male gaze and the passive female object, or in art that resists representations of the female body designed to satisfy male fantasies, or in contests over terminology—are perceived as politically efficacious. To deconstruct, or transgress, binary oppositions is to render phallocentric culture unworkable. The central question that divides feminists is what, if anything, will replace it. What is certain is that for feminism, cultural theory and political practice are indissoluble.

See Also

References and Further Reading

Alcoff, Linda. 1988. Cultural feminism versus poststructuralism: The identity crisis in feminist theory. *Signs* 13(3): 405–437.

Beauvoir, Simone de. 1972. *The second sex.* Harmondsworth, U.K.: Penguin (originally published 1949).

Bonner, Frances, Lizbeth Goodman, Richard Allen, Linda Janes, and Catherine King, eds. 1992. *Imagining women: Cultural representations and gender.* Cambridge: Polity.

Butler, Judith. 1990. *Gender trouble.* London: Routledge.

Collins, Patricia Hill. 1990. *Black feminist thought.* London: Unwin Hyman.

Dean, Jodi, ed. 1997. *Feminism and the new democracy: Resiting the political.* London: Sage.

hooks, bell. 1991. *Yearning: Race gender, and cultural politics.* London: Turnaround.

Hutcheon, Linda. 1989. *The politics of postmodernism.* London: Routledge.

Millett, Kate. 1977. *Sexual politics.* London: Virago.

Moi, Toril, ed. 1986. *The Kristeva reader.* Oxford: Blackwell.

Rose, Jackqueline. 1986. *Sexuality in the field of vision.* London: Verso.

Squires, Judith. 1999. *Gender in political theory.* Cambridge: Polity.

Weedon, Chris. 1987. *Feminist practice and poststructuralist theory.*

Diana Coole

CROSS-DRESSING

See BUTCH/FEMME and TRANSGENDER.

CULTS

See SECTS AND CULTS.

CULTURAL CRITICISM

Cultural criticism is an extremely broad term that is generally used to refer to the analysis of both "elite" and popular culture using the theoretical tools of literary and critical theory. This method of study gained special popularity in a number of mainly western academic establishments in the 1950s and early 1960s, when judgments regarding the aesthetic "value" of the literary text were increasingly called into question. Many writers and critics began to cast into doubt the primacy of the written text over other, equally interesting forms of process and experience to which it also might be relevant to apply critical tools, such as discourse analysis, semiotics, deconstruction, and psychoanalytic theory. Cultural criticism paved the way for a number of nonliterary areas of discourse to become "respectable" fields of academic debate, leading to the growth in popularity—in the 1970s and early 1980s—of sympathetic, analytical studies of television, soap opera, shopping, comic strips, housework, and horror films. Although the terms of cultural criticism initially remained tied to the literary analysis of discourse, these terms soon broadened to take into account all kinds of diverse areas of nonliterary texts and aesthetic experiences, which could then be analyzed according to their own individual sign-systems, ideas, ceremonies, techniques, codes, conventions, and stylistic discourse.

Cultural Criticism and Cultural Studies

The popularity of cultural criticism was partly responsible for the development of cultural studies as a field of academic interest in universities, especially in the United States and western Europe. It continues to be one of the most popular courses among students. For women academics in this field, the important work of Janice Radway (1984) on popular romance fiction and of Judith Williamson (1978) on advertising suggests that this might be an area in which critics and thinkers could define a space to theorize about the special meanings of women's lives apart from the patriarchal discourse of the academic literary establishment. Cultural criticism allowed for the analysis of women's texts and women's experiences of cultural processes to become "acceptable" areas of theoretical debate and conceptual study. This situation provided a background to the important work of women academics such as Ien Ang (1985) on *Dallas,* Angela McRobbie (1990) on girls' subcultures, Dorothy Hobson (1982) on *Crossroads,* and Tania Modleski (1982) on romance fiction. In Britain, Australia, and the United States, women writers and critics such as Helen Taylor, Deirdre Pribram, Valerie Walkerdine, Meaghan Morris, and Elspeth Probyn have continued to produce important and influential work. Theoretical perspectives in these studies include the writing of women's histories and the establishment of "traditions," reevaluating texts, notions of class and audiences, ideologies of mass culture, the female imagination, the popular audience, mass marketing, and criticisms of the cultural "divide." Whereas structuralism and semiology were fashionable, influential, and central to debates in cultural criticism within European academia in the late 1970s, by the mid-1980s the focus had turned to how women can make their own meanings of pleasure out of popular texts inscribed within a patriarchal discourse.

In western Europe and the United States, however, cultural criticism remains a male-oriented field of academic study, closely engaged with structuralist hermeneutics and the shifting paradigms of capitalism, heavily influenced by Marxism and the "seduction" of the text's rhetorical and semiotic devices. Feminist cultural critics—particularly those working within nonwestern traditions such as Kobena Mercer, Fatmagül Berktay, and Bhikhu Parekh—have essentially been marginalized by the lasting influence of male-based, Marxist-oriented criticism on the one hand and early French semiotics on the other. What began as a radical means of theoretical progression from a narrow patriarchal academic canon is increasingly being reabsorbed as an orthodox component of the very tradition it was developed to attack.

See Also

COMMUNICATIONS: AUDIENCE ANALYSIS; CRITICAL AND CULTURAL THEORY; CULTURAL STUDIES; FEMINISM: CULTURAL; LITERARY THEORY AND CRITICISM; POPULAR CULTURE

References and Further Reading

Ang, Ien. 1985. *Watching "Dallas": Soap opera and the melodramatic imagination.* London: Methuen.

Hobson, Dorothy. 1982. *Crossroads: The drama of a soap opera.* London: Methuen.

McRobbie, Angela. 1990. *Feminism and youth culture: From "Jackie" to "Just Seventeen."* London: Macmillan.

Modleski, Tania. 1982. *Loving with a vengeance: Mass-produced fantasies for women.* Hamden, Conn.: Archon.

Radway, Janice. 1984. *Reading the romance: Women, patriarchy and popular literature.* Chapel Hill: University of North Carolina Press.

Williamson, Judith. 1978. *Decoding advertisements: Ideology and meaning in advertising.* London: Marion Boyars.

Mikita Brottman

CULTURAL FEMINISM

See FEMINISM: CULTURAL.

CULTURAL STUDIES

By the mid-1990s, the term *cultural studies* had been used to describe a wide range of scholarship, intellectual practices, and political projects. Although this open-endedness is one of the abiding strengths of cultural studies, it obscures the fact that the term has a specific, albeit contested, history

of its own. It is both a *project* that resides in the academy—borrowing methods and analytical frameworks from the traditional disciplines—and a *way* of doing academic work that is steadfastly critical of disciplinary demarcations. This critical focus has not inhibited the more "traditional" academic disciplines from staking a claim to the name of cultural studies, however; scholars from sociology, anthropology, literary studies, history, media studies, and comparative literature each have at different times, with different degrees of investment, recast their disciplinary projects as cultural studies. Without a doubt these academic disciplines could also offer histories of the development or appropriation of the term *cultural studies*. What follows, instead, is a situated account of the institutional evolution of the identity of cultural studies as a specifically *inter*disciplinary and *critical* enterprise. This brief review also describes the rich engagement between cultural studies and feminist studies since the late 1970s—an engagement that has been structured, from the very beginning, around two important projects: (1) the development of *multi*disciplinary, critical frameworks of analysis and (2) an investigation of the politics of academic work. The best way to begin the work of defining cultural studies is to approach it historically, which is to say that there is no *essential* definition of cultural studies. This article considers definition to mean a project of historical mapping, and in this sense could be understood to address the broad coordinates of a such a map. The four sections roughly sketch out the shape of the historical evolution of the engagement between feminist studies and cultural studies from the late 1970s to the 1990s in the service of describing the development of what has come to be known as "feminist cultural studies."

The Early Work

The term *cultural studies* is inherited from early work by scholars associated with the Centre for Contemporary Cultural Studies (CCCS) in Birmingham, England. Annual reports from the CCCS, beginning in the mid-1960s, use the term "cultural studies"—set off in quotation marks—to identify a specific cross-disciplinary project: the critical analysis of the ideological work of English Studies. As the study of English literature became institutionalized in the United Kingdom, scholars began to investigate the ideological impact of such educational efforts to bring "high" culture to working-class students. Cast as the "literature-society" debates, this critical project combined the methods and analytical frameworks of sociology and literary criticism; from the outset the point was to investigate the social effects of certain educational practices—"teaching" the canon of great books to bring "culture" to the working class and to instill a particular nationalistic identity. Although literature was the first "mode" of "culture" analyzed in this way, scholars soon expanded their studies to investigate other aspects of everyday life such as television, music, popular literature, and sports—cultural forms that were also seen as operating ideologically to create a certain effect in the reader, listener, or audience member. In these studies, cultural studies borrowed sociological methods such as participant observation and ethnography as means of investigating the social phenomenon of identity construction and group (subculture) formation. These critical projects, as well as those in social history more generally, grew out of a long-standing engagement with an earlier tradition of British Marxism that was in need of reconstruction and reinvention.

The trajectory that describes the further development of cultural studies is neither smooth nor unidirectional. Although cultural studies continues to show traces of an early Marxist influence, in that these projects seek to understand the interrelations among cultural processes, social relations, and institutional formations, and to constitute "culture" as a terrain of struggle and power relations, Marxism is only one of the bodies of cultural theory that inform cultural studies. Indeed, in the service of developing a formulation of how the abstract (culture) was related to the particular (concrete social practices), cultural studies engaged, in turn, most of the key intellectual movements of the past two decades: structuralism, poststructuralism, psychoanalysis, social history, feminism, postcolonialism, queer theory, and postmodernism. This is to say that the development of cultural studies proceeded most significantly through a series of engagements with other forms of cultural theory and less through its encounters with institutionalized academic disciplines. In this sense, one can trace how cultural studies articulates its projects or "problematics" through various cultural theories, while it borrows from the academic disciplines for its methods of description and analysis—that is, close reading, encoding and decoding, historiography, ethnography, and semiotics.

At the broadest level, cultural studies is centrally concerned with the complex ways in which subjectivity and consciousness are shaped and inhabited; this leads to a preoccupation with language, signification, and discourse (Johnson, 1987). But it is important to note here that this does not translate into a narrow focus on textual artifacts—which is what distinguishes cultural studies from literary studies more generally. On the contrary, one of the key contributions of cultural studies has been to insist on the notion of the *circulation* of meaning that occurs through the production and reading of various textual forms. The

aim is to try to understand how such meanings are implicated in the construction of subjectivity in everyday life. How, specifically, does "meaning," which circulates in popular texts and forms of discourse, determine or influence the construction "subjectivity"? This also requires attention to the ways in which "meanings" inform other cultural productions and are transformed in the process, thus asserting that the construction of meaning is a dynamic cultural process which involves agents of production and agents of reception who, although often displaced in space and time, are engaged in a mutual project: constructing reality. Texts, accordingly, are treated as productive cultural forms not only by the agents who are their authors (or, for that matter, by the cultural "moment" from which they emerge) but also by the agents who are situated as readers, audiences, and viewers.

Feminism and Cultural Studies

Feminist engagement with cultural studies takes shape first in Britain as part of the evolution of British socialist feminism. One of its beginning points is the work associated with the feminist historians who were part of the "history workshop" movement begun in the 1960s (Davidoff and Hall, 1987; Turner, 1990). The influence of historicist cultural materialism is marked by the commitment, in feminist cultural theory, to resist the temptation of grand theorizing in favor of developing a model of study that produces historically specific cultural analyses. Another beginning can be traced to the influence of British socialist feminists who, although they rely on Marxist theory, marked their critical difference from it because of its economic determinism and its inadequate treatment of the role of women under capitalism. Although the encounters among members of these sometimes overlapping intellectual communities and their engagement with the central figures of cultural studies (Marx, Althusser, and Williams, among others) have their own interesting history, what was shared and passed on was a commitment to investigate the material conditions of women's lives under capitalism (Barrett, 1988; Barrett and McIntosh, 1982; Brunt and Rowan, 1982; Coward, 1983; Kuhn and Wolpe, 1978).

One of the first books to explicitly address the intersections between feminist studies and cultural studies is the edited collection *Women Take Issue: Aspects of Women's Subordination* (Women's Studies Group, 1978), which includes essays and an introduction written by members of the Women's Studies Group at the CCCS. In the introduction, the editorial group "takes issue" with the "invisibility" of women not only in relation to the articles in the early volumes of *Working Papers in Cultural Studies* but also in "much of the intellectual work done within the Centre." Consequently, *Women Take Issue* illuminates two important aspects of the cultural formation that would later be called feminist cultural studies. On the one hand, the working group explicitly attempted to construct a descriptive statement about the process of "doing" feminist intellectual work, both in relation to the CCCS and within the broader context of the British women's liberation movement (see Lovell, 1990). As a result, from early on, feminists interested in cultural studies demonstrated a reflexive mode of analysis that took seriously the responsibility to elucidate its own conditions of possibility in an academic institution, as well as its political accountability to a broader social movement. A second equally important contribution of this early engagement was to address the structured absence of feminist work and "woman" from the theoretical frameworks and problematics that animated scholars at the CCCS at the time. This is to stress that the early feminist engagement with cultural studies was already defined as a critical intervention in a field that was itself an emergent formation. In addition to establishing a feminist presence in the work of the CCCS, the book represents a characteristic move or stance that will become more pronounced in the later development of feminist cultural studies, by including a range of diverse feminist perspectives that explicitly take "culture" to be a focal point of the production of feminist criticism.

Two issues, however, are conspicuously missing from this collection: (1) a sustained analysis of race and racism within those same feminist projects, and (2) an account of the construction and bias of nationalist or imperialist feminist identities. These absences are telling in that they mark a characteristic blind spot of feminism more broadly during the late 1970s. Even with these notable absences, the *Women Take Issue* collection is an important event in the development of feminist cultural studies for several reasons. In the first place, these essays employ a more inclusive model of culture and subcultures that emphasizes the importance of everyday life and domestic space in the reproduction of relations of power. The contribution was more than a shift of emphasis to what superficially might be recognized as the private sphere of collective life. Drawing on the wisdom of the women's movement more broadly, and feminist historians more specifically, this shift reflected a slightly different understanding of the feminist slogan "The personal is political." Taken together, the essays describe the many ways in which the "private" sphere is determined and constrained by structures of power. Second, these essays contribute to the development of an understanding of the *articulation* of sex, gender, and class

in the organization of social relations and the disposition of power at a *specific* historical moment. To summarize, the impact of these essays is to focus on both women's subordination and class subordination and how the interconnections between them determine: (1) "women's structural position within the production and reproduction of material life," (2) "how this is understood and represented politically, and ideologically," and (3) "how women live their lives within and through these terms" (Women's Studies Group, 1978: 23). Like cultural studies more broadly, this feminist work takes up the issue of the social construction of subjectivity and the role this plays in practices of everyday life. These three levels of analysis are characteristic of the projects that emerge during the 1980s as feminist cultural studies turns to psychoanalysis and poststructuralism to elucidate the relations between gendered and class subjectivities and everyday life.

Ethnography and Autobiography: The Practice of Writing Cultural Criticism

The relationship between culture and the subject was a preoccupation of much feminist cultural studies during the 1980s, either implicitly in the work of feminist literary and film critics or more explicitly as part of the work that theorizes the practices of autobiography and ethnography. These practices all concern the process of "doing research on women" and consider at great length the politics of representing those who are usually denied self-representation. For example, Angela McRobbie takes issue with the masculine focus of the CCCS tradition of ethnographic study of British youth, arguing not only that girls' subcultures have a specificity of their own, but also that methods of subculture research need to be scrutinized for relations of power and exploitation. One of the major contributions from this line of feminist cultural studies is attention to the politics and practices of writing cultural criticism.

Angela McRobbie argues that the ethnographic accounts produced in the process of doing subcultural research necessarily provoke tension between the "anarchy of talk and the order and formality of written work" (1983: 50). In reflecting on her own research on women's and girls' subcultures, McRobbie points out that the research situation includes social relations and practices that, left unexamined, threaten to undermine crucial feminist political commitments. It is clear that feminist ethnographers rely on women's talk and their willingness to share personal stories. The ethnographer, for her part, interviews, listens in, asks questions—all in the attempt to generate more talk. From there she orders the talk, summarizes it, selects from it, rephrases it, surrounds it with theory, and finally, but never simply, represents it; in constructing a representation of women's talk, the ethnographer offers an interpretation that is unavoidably partial and political because of the talk that was left out, ignored, and transformed through the process of transcription and transcoding itself. In this sense, the best ethnographies can produce only partial truths that are always politically inflected. Far from closing off ethnography for feminist cultural studies, these insights reinforce the understanding that all knowledge, both the kind that is fiercely personal and the kind that is contoured according to more public sensibilities, is discursively constructed and culturally determined.

Another very different project of feminist cultural studies contributes to a broader theoretical understanding of how everyday life is constructed mutually from the stuff of biography as well as of history. In relying on psychoanalysis and poststructuralism to provide models by which to understand the cultural determination of subjectivity and biography, Frigga Haug and the Frauenformen Collective (1987) invented a new method of feminist ethnography. In the process, they drew attention to the writing practices involved in the construction of cultural criticism. *Memory work,* the term they use for their ethnographic practice, focuses on the act of writing as an investigative strategy. Each member of the collective contributed a written account of a memory or "body story" that represented a moment of learning a sexualized interpretation of the female body. Through a laborious process of remembering, writing, reading, and rewriting, the collective began to identify ways in which women as individuals construct themselves into already existing or determined social structures, cultural narratives, and power relations. Simultaneously, they were uncovering the production of individual consciousness out of the stuff of culture and everyday life. Through collaborative writing and self-interrogation, the collective worked to uncover the status of truth and authenticity that operates in women's subjectivity by focusing on how cultural narratives get "taken up" in the construction of the "self."

Both of these projects, by McRobbie and by the Frauenformen Collective, investigate the role of writing practices in the production of feminist cultural criticism. In so doing, they illuminate a model for feminist cultural politics that is not just vaguely determined by the general political aims of the women's movement, but, more important, is concerned to show specifically how subjectivity is produced (that is, through writing, through close reading); how subjective changes can be empowering (that is, through the construction of a speaking position); and, finally, how one can revise dominant narratives of gender, race, and class identity (see

Wallace, 1990). This emphasis on the theoretical elaboration of the practices of reading culture and writing cultural criticism continued to distinguish much of feminist cultural studies in the 1990s.

Feminist Cultural Politics

One of the key issues to emerge from the engagement between feminism and cultural studies has been the investigation of the politics of culture. Early attempts to theorize about the politics of representation enabled a discussion among feminists who themselves were wrestling with issues of identity construction and the politics of "difference." Taking the lead in structuring these discussions were both activists and scholars of black identity, postcolonialism, and queer theory. As these discussions expanded, so too did the notion that cultural studies needed to be situated in a global context. This has led, more recently, to efforts to engage work by scholars and activists in various national contexts: Africa, Asia, Australia, Canada, Japan, and South America.

In their editorial "Challenging Imperial Feminism," Valerie Amos and Pratibha Parmar remind their readers that "it is the autonomous activities of Black women which have forced the white women's movement away from a celebration of universality and sameness, to be concerned with the implications of differences among women's experiences and understanding the political factors at work in those differences" (1984: 7; see also Introduction to Barrett, 1988). The critique initiated and most fully developed by black feminist critics and postcolonial scholars establishes two broad objectives for feminist cultural studies. One is to challenge the often implicit assumption that there is general consensus among feminists regarding the appropriate political aims of critical feminist work. A second challenge requires the development of more complex criticism of the oppression inherent in the gendered and class relations within a racist society. The issue, according to Hazel Carby, will be one not of simply making visible the invisible "black woman," but, rather, of redefining the "central categories and assumptions of mainstream feminist thought" to take account of the interconnection of class, gender and race and of the "existence of racism . . . as a structuring feature of our relations with white women" (1982: 213–14; see also Carby, 1987). The importance of this work for the development of feminist cultural studies rests with its attention to the articulation of a politics of location that means, in Chandra Mohanty's words, attention to "the historical, geographical, cultural, psychic and imaginative boundaries which provide the ground for political definition and self-definition for U.S. feminists" (1987: 31).

A second thread of work in feminist cultural studies is the cultural politics of science and technology. An earlier feminist criticism that condemned science and technology as masculinist cults of rationality has given way to a serious engagement with a cluster of related questions that concern not only the development of new sciences and the deployment of new technologies (genetic engineering, for example) but also the philosophical frameworks that structure the social organization of the production of truth and knowledge. This refers to a range of feminist work that addresses such issues as the methodological frameworks of the social sciences, epistemological questions about scientific discourse, and the close reading of scientific "findings" that support culturally determined and ideological theories of sexual difference (Bleier, 1984; Harding, 1986; Harding and Hintikka, 1983; Jacobus et al., 1990; Keller, 1985; Rothschild, 1983; Zimmerman, 1983). Many of these projects consider the relation of women to the discourses of science and technology, in terms of their participation in its production as well as their subjugation to its "truth." While the technophobia of earlier feminist criticism has been displaced, much of this feminist work remains critical of the aims of contemporary science and technology. One of the consequences of this feminist cultural criticism is an expanding argument for the transformation of scientific and technological practices.

One of the most influential critical feminist cultural analyses to emerge in the 1980s is outlined in Donna Haraway's essay "A Manifesto for Cyborgs: Science, Technology, and Socialist Feminism in the 1980s" (1985), in which she develops a broad-ranging analysis of the contemporary scene of multinational science and technology in the interest of developing a framework for a socialist, materialist feminism that would be equipped to critically engage that scene (see also Haraway, 1990). Haraway argues that social responsibility will not be well served by an "anti-science metaphysics [or] a demonology of technology" or by an equally problematic belief in technological progress or the benign deployment of scientific knowledge. Rather, Haraway maintains that science and technology, as discourses, as social relations, are cultural productions that cannot be ceded to a hegemonic ruling bloc. It is simply not tenable, therefore, for feminists to write off those productions because they institutionalize masculinist values—rationality, conquest, domination. Haraway also suggests that the notions of woman that inform many feminist "standpoint" arguments are similarly constructed cultural representations. Although these representations enable feminists to critique the politics of

science and technology in the name of an "essentialist" identity of "woman," they are not, she argues, innocent reflections of some transhistorical reality of gender identity. Rather, in Haraway's cyborg cosmology, identity (feminist, woman's, or something else) is always partial, recombinant, implicated, and in process. Drawing inspiration from all of this work, feminist cultural studies involves the production of cultural criticism that explicitly accounts for the construction of fragmented, fluid identities. In the process, it also identifies specific cultural sites for feminist intervention, infiltration, and reconstruction.

See Also

CRITICAL AND CULTURAL THEORY; CULTURAL CRITICISM; FEMINISM: SOCIALIST; HUMANITIES AND SOCIAL SCIENCES: FEMINIST CRITIQUE; LITERARY THEORY AND CRITICISM; POPULAR CULTURE

References and Further Reading

Amos, Valerie, and Pratibha Parmar. 1984. Challenging imperial feminism. *Feminist Review* (Autumn): 3–19.

Balsamo, Anne. 1991. Feminism and Cultural Studies. *Journal of the Midwest Modern Language Association* 24(1: Spring): 50–73.

Barrett, Michele. 1988. *Women's oppression today: The Marxist/ feminist encounter,* 2nd ed. London: Verso (1st ed. 1980).

———, and Mary McIntosh. 1982. *The anti-social family.* London: Verso.

Bleier, Ruth. 1984. *Science and gender: A critique of biology and its theories on women.* New York: Pergamon.

Brunt, Rosalind, and Caroline Rowan, eds. 1982. *Feminism, culture and politics.* London: Lawrence and Wishart.

Carby, Hazel V. 1987. *Reconstructing womanhood: The emergence of the Afro-American woman novelist.* New York: Oxford University Press.

———. 1982. White woman listen! Black feminism and the boundaries of sisterhood. In Centre for Contemporary Cultural Studies, *The empire strikes back: Race and racism in '70s Britain,* 212–235. London: Hutchinson.

Coward, Rosalind. 1983. *Patriarchal precedents: Sexuality and social relations.* London: Routledge.

Davidoff, Lenore, and Catherine Hall. 1987. *Family fortunes: Men and women in the English middle class 1780–1850.* London: Hutchinson.

Grossberg, Lawrence, Cary Nelson, and Paula Treichler, eds. 1992. *Cultural Studies.* New York: Routledge.

Hall, Stuart, Dorothy Hobson, Andrew Lowe, and Paul Willis. 1980. *Culture, media, language: Working papers in Cultural Studies 1972–1979.* London: Unwin Hyman.

Haraway, Donna. 1985. A manifesto for cyborgs: Science, technology, and socialist feminism in the 1980s. *Socialist Review* 80 (2): 65–108.

———. 1990. *Primate visions: Gender, race, and nature in the world of modern science.* New York: Routledge.

Harding, Sandra. 1986. *The science question in feminism.* Ithaca, N.Y.: Cornell University Press.

———, and Merrill Hintikka, eds., 1983. *Discovering reality: Feminist perspectives on epistemology, metaphysics, methodology and philosophy of science.* Dordrecht: Reidel.

Haug, Frigga, and the Frauenformen Collective, eds. 1987. *Female sexualization: A collective work of memory.* London: Verso.

Jacobus, Mary, Evelyn Fox Keller, and Sally Shuttleworth, eds. 1990. *Body politics: Women and the discourses of science.* New York: Routledge.

Johnson, Richard. 1987. What is cultural studies anyway? *Social Text* 6(1): 33–80.

Jordon, Glenn, and Chris Weedon. 1995. *Cultural politics: Class, gender, race and the postmodern world.* Oxford: Blackwell.

Keller, Evelyn Fox. 1985. *Reflection on gender and science.* New Haven, Conn.: Yale University Press.

Kuhn, Annette, and AnnMarie Wolpe, eds. 1978. *Feminism and materialism.* London: Routledge.

Lovell, Terry, ed. 1990. *British feminist thought: A reader.* Oxford: Blackwell.

McRobbie, Angela. 1983. The politics of feminist research: Between talk, text, and action. *Feminist Review* 12: 46–57.

Mohanty, Chandra Talpade. 1987. Feminist encounters: Locating the politics of experience. *Copyright* 1 (Fall): 30–44.

Rothschild, Joan, ed. 1983. *Machina ex dea: Feminist perspectives on technology.* New York: Pergamon.

Turner, Graeme. 1990. *British cultural studies: An introduction.* Boston: Unwin Hyman.

Wallace, Michele. 1990. Negative images: Towards a black feminist cultural criticism. In Michele Wallace, ed., *Invisibility blues: From pop to theory.* London: Verso.

Women's Studies Group. 1978. *Women take issue: Aspects of women's subordination.* London: Hutchinson.

Zimmerman, Jan, ed. 1983. *The technological woman: Interfacing with tomorrow.* New York: Praeger.

Anne Balsamo

CULTURAL THEORY

See CRITICAL AND CULTURAL THEORY.

CULTURE: Overview

Culture, as Raymond Williams noted, "is one of the two or three most complicated words in the English language" (1976: 87). It is a term at the center of several scholarly debates among advocates from distinct academic disciplines that seek to establish the right to determine its meaning. Since the late 1980s, the word also has been used to describe the political ferment generated by changes in college curricula in the United States. Dubbed the "culture wars" by the mass media, this political ferment has been provoked (in part) by the success of teachers and students of women's studies in calling for a reexamination of traditional programs of study and pedagogical practices. In participating in these debates, whether as members of academic disciplines or as contributors to reports of these debates in the mass media, feminist scholars have asserted that any discussion of culture also must take into account issues of gender and race. Sometimes this means arguing for the centrality of gender and race within disciplinary definitions of culture; at other times, it means attending to the role played by gender and race in establishing the parameters and the consequences of the debates. The term describes a dynamic concept both maddeningly imprecise because of its cross-disciplinary usage and powerfully descriptive for naming a critically important dimension of collective social life.

Culture in the Disciplines

Williams details the historical development of the term *culture* along two lines: (1) as a noun of process that means, in an agricultural sense, to cultivate something, and (2) as a synonym for the word *civilization* (1976: 89). Over time, the two senses of the term began to refer to each other in that the notion of being cultured was also what was implied by the notion of being civilized. This semiotic blending of the notions of being cultured and being civilized invokes connotations of breeding and social class, so that the word now carries with it a more modern sense of something that has high social value. This use in turn implies another sense, one in which "culture" is the product of those who are "cultured." Thus, we inherit (according to Williams) three senses of the word *culture*: (1) as a process of the cultivation of human characteristics, (2) as a name for the collective life of human beings, and (3) as the term for highly valued human products and expressive practices.

Theses three senses are emphasized to different degrees within different academic domains. In the humanities, the meaning of culture connotes highly valued human products and expressive practices: music, literature, and visual and performing arts. In the social sciences, the term is used most often to refer to the collective life of human beings within particular, bounded social arrangements. Common across the disciplines is the specification of taxonomies of types of cultures or types of cultural practices. Although different disciplines begin with different understandings of the term *culture*, they are united in their attempts to create categories of practices or products as a way of making sense of cultural differences. These disciplinary taxonomies can be seen as an attempt to impose order on inherently dynamic and unwieldy human phenomenon.

Cultural studies scholars have developed a theory of culture that seeks to merge the insights of the humanities and the social sciences to forge a concept incorporating both the material and symbolic-expressive senses of the term. Although they, too, attempt to categorize cultural differences, they have focused more intently on the temporal dimension of cultural transformations. In addition to attending to the way in which cultural phenomena change over time, they also have focused on what they consider debased or devalued cultural categories of the traditional disciplines. For example, where literary studies was preoccupied with works of "high culture," cultural studies examined the significance of popular forms of mass culture. There were several reasons for this interest, not the least of which was the fact that cultural studies was built on a foundation of Marxist social theory and feminist theory—theoretical traditions that call for the critical examination of systems of demarcation that establish differential value for practices and forms of expression.

Disciplinary Taxonomies and Frameworks of Analysis

In the field of literary studies, literature is considered a form of cultural expression that often has been categorized according to a taxonomy opposing high and low culture. Although the aesthetic quality of a work of literature evaluated as "high culture" is assessed according to different value categories, one of these is based on an evaluation of how well the literary text illuminates universal human characteristics. Literary works that belong to the category of "low culture" include popular forms of fiction such as romance and detective novels, as well as science fiction. For a significant period in the history of literary studies, literature written by women (with a few notable exceptions) was dismissed summarily as low culture. The reasons for this dismissal differed. For example, Kate Chopin was identi-

fied as a "regional writer" who wrote novels of local color. Zora Neale Hurston was dismissed as a "black writer" whose use of dialect and stories about black characters had little, if anything, to say about the "universal human condition." Joanna Russ was accused of writing from personal experience with a sense of feminist outrage that disqualified her work as serious literature.

More recently, feminist literary scholars have provoked a wide-ranging disciplinary reconsideration of the division between high and low culture. Joined by black studies and cultural studies scholars, feminist literary critics have examined the social and racial class biases built into the notion of culture when it is used as the basis for creating a taxonomy of literary value. In this way, a critical examination of the use of the term *culture* grounds debates about the formation of canons. This examination argues that the works that belong to the category of "high" culture often reflect the values of an elite, white, privileged class of people who have had, historically, the social power to determine what gets institutionalized and idealized as "universal" values in literature and in other expressive cultural practices. This critique sets the stage for a wide range of feminist studies of women's writing and has stimulated the study of the way in which cultural values are implicitly expressed in other discipline-specific textual genres, such as ethnography and science writing.

Culture, in an anthropological sense, names the collective social life of a group of people who share geographic location, national traditions, or a particular ethnic identity. Cultural taxonomies are based on either national and geographic boundaries or types of culture. For example, some anthropologists distinguish between traditional or folk culture on the one hand, and urban or industrialized culture on the other. Central to the traditional anthropological project is a focus on comparative studies of the secular process of human development. *Culture* is the term used not only to name the production of material artifacts and arts but also for the structures and practices of collective life, including social arrangements such as kinship networks, expressive practices such as mythmaking, and social habits and conventions. This use of *culture* is more encompassing than its use among literary scholars, because it refers to the entire ensemble of human practices, both expressive and material. This is not to say that the anthropological use of the term eclipses its literary sense; on the contrary, anthropologists (following the work of Paul Ricoeur and Clifford Geertz) often employ interpretive theories (borrowed to a great extent from literary studies) to make sense of the structured patterns they uncover. In this case, cultural practices are themselves considered a text to be read and interpreted according to an analytical framework. The "interpretive term" in anthropology has spawned a vigorous theoretical debate about the relationship between practices or actions and textual representations (see Clifford and Marcus, 1986). But it is also the case, following the work of several feminist anthropologists, that the ethnographer's textual accounts and representations of other people's cultural practices also are subjected to interpretive scrutiny. This work focuses attention on the practices of constructing and interpreting meaning on the part of the anthropologists themselves. In this way, feminist anthropologists call for a self-reflexive analysis not only of how they construct interpretations of the cultural practices of others but also of their own cultural practices.

More recently, cultural anthropologists have turned their attention to site-specific cultures that are not delimited by national or geographic boundaries. For example, some feminist anthropologists have begun to study the social patterns and meaning-making practices of people who work in particular industries, such as the culture of scientists and technologists in the laboratory (see Traweek, 1988). These ethnographic investigations rely on a notion of culture as something that is produced by people who interact in a common space of daily life but who may not share anything that looks like "traditional" cultural characteristics, such as national identity, geographic location, or material practices. These cultural markers of group identity become even more elusive to track for those anthropologists who are moving away from the study of *actual* social sites to the study of *virtual* environments. The question they ask in these situations is: What counts as a shared culture when all that is shared is textual exchanges in cyberspace? Although it is common for advocates of cyberspace to claim that communication networks are race- and gender-blind spaces of human interaction, feminist ethnographers of on-line communication investigate the way that gender continues to influence social interactions, even when these interactions are limited to the disembodied textual exchanges mediated through electronic communication technologies. One of the consequences of such studies is that the notion of culture is broadened not only to name the interactions among people who share geographic spaces or ethnic traditions but also to identify the sense of community and the framework of cultural meanings that emerge among people who may never interact within embodied space.

A similar notion of culture is also invoked to describe the cultural sensibility of groups of people who are categorized by demographic characteristics. Sociologists study culture by analyzing patterns of social interaction among people who belong to particular groups but who may never interact in a shared embodied space. Taxonomies used to divide people into cultural groups are sometimes based on socioeconomic indicators such as income level—that is, working class versus middle class—or on generational distinctions such as those that distinguish the "baby boomers" from their "generation X" offspring. An earlier classification that set up an opposition between "mainstream" culture and "deviant" subcultures has been replaced with a less normative one, which differentiates dominant cultural groups from oppositional subcultures.

The "turn to culture" in sociology has been driven by the work of three groups of sociologists: (1) those who study the structural organization of the culture industries, (2) those who work in the tradition of symbolic interactionism to investigate the ways in which people negotiate cultural contexts, and (3) those who have taken up the issue of the "body" within a sociological framework. Whereas the scholars and researchers who study the culture industries employ traditional methods of structural analysis to describe the institutional organization of the mass media, symbolic interactionists borrow methodological approaches from anthropology and literary studies to investigate the social accomplishment of cultural meaning (Becker and McCall, 1990). Employing techniques of participant observation and interpretive analysis, these sociologists analyze the process of constructing meaning at the level of everyday life.

The issue of human embodiment has recently emerged from the shadows of sociological thinking as a topic of study and debate. This interest in the body is due in part to a growing sociological interest in a broader culture—specifically postmodern culture, where the body plays an important role as a key symbolic resource and an expressive medium (see Featherstone et al., 1991). Feminist sociologists have taken up the issue of the body in various ways. For example, Virginia Olesen (1992) studies the embodied self and the cultural construction of health and illness. A tradition of feminist studies of "deviant" bodies that include Janice Raymond's study of transsexuality (1979) and Jennifer Terry and Jacqueline Urla's investigation of queer bodies (1995) ironically reclaims the term *deviant* to describe bodies that transgress social and cultural norms. The important contribution offered by these feminist "body studies" is that culture must be understood as an embodied phenomenon even when it emerges in disembodied spaces (see Balsamo, 1995). Thus, these feminists assert that although discursive interpretive frameworks of analysis are a useful way to investigate the construction of cultural meaning and practices, a robust understanding of culture also must take account of its material, embodied, and institutional foundation, which includes but is not limited to taking account of the gendered, racial, and sexual identities of participants in the culture.

Culture As a Signifying System

Early in *The Sociology of Culture* (1981), Raymond Williams summarizes the history of the concept of culture, putting in place an understanding of the term that reflects the convergence of its discipline-specific meanings. Culture includes both:

> (a) an emphasis on the "informing spirit" of a whole way of life, which is manifest over the whole range of social activities but is most evident in "specifically cultural" activities—a language, styles of art, kinds of intellectual work; and (b) an emphasis on "a whole social order" within which a specifiable culture, in styles of art and kinds of intellectual work, is seen as the direct or indirect product of an order primarily constituted by other social activities. (12)

This passage delineates both an "idealist" sense of culture and a "materialist" position on culture. Offering a synthesis of the term, Williams suggests that culture is the "signifying system through which necessarily…a social order is communicated, reproduced, experienced and explored" (13). This meaning combines the anthropological and sociological senses of the term and "the more specialized if also more common sense of culture as 'artistic and intellectual activities'" (13). Thus, Williams puts in place a notion of culture as the term for a range of signifying practices that include "not only the traditional arts and forms of intellectual production but also all the 'signifying practices'—from language through the arts and philosophy to journalism, fashion and advertising" (13).

In this sense, cultural studies borrows widely from different disciplines to forge an understanding of the term *culture* that captures the ways in which its various senses are interrelated. Not only do cultural studies scholars seek to investigate material cultural practices and actual cultural forms (that is, literature, film, advertising), but they also study the institutions and formations within which such forms are produced. The aim is to produce analyses of the relations between moments of cultural signification and the structural relations that give rise to those moments.

Instead of working with taxonomies of cultural types, cultural studies has focused more specifically on the dynamic nature of cultural transformation. Williams himself stressed the importance of a historical sensibility. Writing about the process of cultural reproduction, he uses the terms *dominant, residual,* and *emergent* to name different domains of cultural practice (1981). *Dominant* forms of cultural production are usually seen as "natural and necessary" (204), set in place by a well-organized, institutionalized system of power and knowledge. *Residual* cultural practices include "work made in earlier and often different societies and times, yet still available and significant" (204). *Emergent* cultural forms include new work and practices of various sorts. To elucidate the complex interactions among dominant, residual, and emergent cultural forms at a particular historical moment requires making connections between practices and formations, between forms of symbolic expression and institutional arrangements, and between specific manifestations of culture and broad forms of ideological reproduction. In more practical terms, this means working to elaborate the connections between forms of expression (such as specific works of literature) and the institutional arrangements that structure the reception and evaluation of such forms. It means specifying the relations between cultural myths that circulate in the mass media and the way in which these myths inform the individual practices of identity construction. It means situating practices of representation within broader cultural patterns of signification.

This brief overview of the term *culture* implicitly argues against seeing culture as an "object of study" isolated from a historical, social, or material context. As is evident in the broad body of work in feminist cultural studies, culture is a complex dynamic quality of human existence. This understanding illuminates some of the reasons for the recent tension surrounding debates about culture that have been identified in the media as the "culture wars." What began as a discussion about the criteria of inclusion on the list of "great books" in the U.S. literary canon has expanded into a debate about cultural literacy and the type of knowledge that should be taught in U.S. educational systems. Whereas dictionaries of cultural literacy implicitly define culture as a decontextualized collection of facts and historical trivia, cultural studies scholars understand that it is a multifaceted system for the construction of meaning.

See Also

ANTHROPOLOGY; CLASS; CRITICAL AND CULTURAL THEORY; CULTURAL CRITICISM; CULTURAL STUDIES; CULTURE: WOMEN AS CONSUMERS OF CULTURE; CULTURE: WOMEN AS PRODUCERS OF CULTURE; CYBORG ANTHROPOLOGY; LITERARY THEORY AND CRITICISM; POPULAR CULTURE; SOCIOLOGY

References and Further Reading

Balsamo, Anne. 1995. *Technologies of the gendered body: Reading cyborg women*. Durham, N.C.: Duke University Press.

Becker, Howard, and Michal McCall, eds. 1990. *Symbolic interaction and cultural studies*. Chicago: University of Chicago Press.

Clifford, James, and George E. Marcus, eds. 1986. *Writing culture: The poetics and politics of ethnography*. Berkeley: University of California Press.

Featherstone, Mike, Mike Hepworth, and Bryan S. Turner, eds. 1991. *The body: Social process and cultural theory*. Newbury Park, Calif.: Sage.

Hall, Stuart, Dorothy Hobson, Andrew Lowe, and Paul Willis. 1980. *Culture, media, language: Working papers in cultural studies 1972–1979*. London: Unwin Hyman.

Olesen, Virginia. 1992. Extra-ordinary events and mundane ailments: The contextual dialectics of the embodied self. In Carolyn Ellis and Michael G. Flaerty, eds., *Investigating subjectivity: Research on lived experience*, 205–220. Newbury Park, Calif.: Sage.

Raymond, Janice. 1979. *The transsexual empire*. Boston: Beacon.

Shiach, Moraq. 1999. *Feminism and cultural studies*. Oxford: Oxford University Press.

Terry, Jennifer. 1999. *An American obsession: Science, medicine and the place of homosexuality in modern society*. Chicago: University of Chicago Press.

———, and Jacqueline Urla, eds. 1995. *Deviant bodies: Perspectives on difference in science and popular culture*. Bloomington: Indiana University Press.

Traweek, Sharon. 1988. *Beamtimes and lifetimes: The world of high energy physics*. Cambridge, Mass.: Harvard University Press.

Triechler, Paula. 1999. *How to have theory in an epidemic: Cultural chronicles of AIDS*. Durham, N.C.: Duke University Press.

Williams, Raymond. 1976. *Keywords: A vocabulary of culture and society*. New York: Oxford University Press (rev. ed. 1983).

———. 1981. *The sociology of culture*. New York: Schocken.

Anne Balsamo

CULTURE:
Women as Consumers of Culture

A broad continuum of women's consumption practices includes formally organized reading groups and informal fanship networks. While it may seem that women's consumption of popular culture, particularly the media, would reinforce their integration into patriarchal culture, a look at the research about women's reading and viewing practices shows that women use popular culture in a variety of ways. Women actively consume popular culture, and they can just as actively construct meanings for themselves out of it. Women find pleasure in such socially condoned activities as book-reading groups, in such less socially acceptable fanship practices as reading romance novels or watching soap operas, and in such masculine-defined activities as punk rock slam dancing or watching professional wrestling. A number of women's consumption practices are highlighted here with an emphasis on the tension between their relationship to patriarchal ideologies of femininity and feminist notions of strength and independent thinking.

Femininity and Social Norms

Elizabeth Long (1987) has studied organized reading groups, looking at how they choose books and interpret their reading. She found that women's, men's, and mixed-sex reading groups all "use their readership to mark a boundary between themselves and their neighbors, and the elite among such reading groups distinguish themselves from people who 'only read trash'" (306). Even the exclusively women's book groups she investigated defer to established authorities and traditional academic hierarchies when choosing books. For example, their choices range from the classics, at the top of the hierarchy, to other "serious" works but never include formula novels. Cultural authorities like academics were consulted for the selection of books, but once they read the books the women in Long's groups analyzed them in decidedly nonscholarly ways. The discussants gave a wide variety of interpretations, often linked to personal experiences. They often viewed characters as though they were real and were generally "playful" in their discussions of a particular text.

Oprah Winfrey's book club has succeeded in breaking down the reliance on academic hierarchies in choosing books. Winfrey selects books according to her own value system. Her choices have given her, and by extension other women, a heightened awareness of the credibility of their choice of what to read, and also their interpretations of these choices. Debra Grodin (1991), in a study of readers of self-help books, a largely feminine genre, found that her readers sought commonality and connectedness from their reading experience in order to assure themselves that what they were thinking and feeling fell within the boundaries of the "normal." The readers' concerns seemed to indicate the uncertainties women feel in adjusting to hegemonic power relationships. The readers in her study were largely middle-class and college-educated.

Music videos have been found to encourage female fans to push against cultural definitions of femininity. Lisa Lewis (1990) points out that female fans of rock stars such as Cindy Lauper and Madonna sometimes create visible signs of female significance and formulate new responses to gender inequality. In the 1980s Lewis found that "female address videos" were made by women rock artists to appeal to young women who identified them as representations of their own cultural experience. This meant that girls refocused their attention and adoration from male to female rock stars. Angela McRobbie (1984) theorizes similarly about dance, noting that it allows girls to experience power through the use of their bodies. This power is in their control and is female-centered even though dance is often seen as existing for masculine voyeuristic pleasure.

Readership, Class, and Ethnicity

Andrea Press (1991) has drawn distinctions between how working-class and middle-class women in the United States relate to television texts. Working-class women, she found, valued realism in their television viewing more than middle-class women. They also judged television's depiction of middle-class life unrealistic. Since the working-class women were more likely to accept television's version of middle-class life as normal in our society, Press felt that they were, to some degree, alienated from their own material experience and that this alienation accentuated their social oppression. Her middle-class subjects were more likely to identify with characters on a personal level, and to fall prey to television's portrayals of physical or behavioral ideals of womanhood. From this research, it appears that class differences may influence how women construct meanings in relation to their personal lives. Other research about women's television viewing in the context of families supports this conclusion while emphasizing gender differences in viewing styles within class and ethnic differences.

David Morley (1993), looking at a group of working-class British families, concluded that men and women watched television in fundamentally different ways. The women described television viewing as a social activity that involved ongoing conversations and sometimes the performance of some other domestic activity like ironing. The men had a clear preference for viewing in silence, attentively, and without interruption. Not only did the men and boys watch more television than the women and girls, but the men usually checked the newspapers or other guides to plan their viewing, operated the video recorders, sat in possession of the remote control when they watched, and in general watched what they preferred to watch when they wanted to watch it. Morley describes women viewers as uninterested. The inattentiveness of these women may be due to the fact that, for some women, home is a place not of leisure but of work. Hence, it is difficult for women to concentrate on and uncomplicatedly enjoy television viewing. In the case of a group of Korean families living in the United States, Lee and Cho (1990) found that "women rarely do what they want to do for themselves [in the home], and this is most evident in television watching" (32). However, both in these Korean families and in the British families observed by Morley (1986) and Gray (1987), the women found a way to enjoy television and films on videotape despite their husbands' disapproval. Some formed what the Korean women called video clubs in order not only to watch what they wanted to watch but to watch it in an atmosphere where they could talk and do as they pleased.

Sexually and racially subordinated groups frequently make use of what culture has to offer through "cultural poaching" (Jenkins, 1992)—using a cultural artifact in ways that were not intended. Cultural poaching may occur when artifacts produced in dominant cultures fail to speak to certain groups, so these groups simply use the available cultural resources for their own ends. For example, Cathy Griggers (1993) suggests the possibility of an "aberrant" reading that essentially makes fun of a text, including partial identifications and nonlinear rewriting of the narrative. This process, she maintains, is particularly apparent in, though not necessarily confined to, gay camp readings. Lesbian feminist audiences often apply interpretive strategies that reject or alter the representational practices of Hollywood cinema (Ellsworth, 1990).

Female soap opera fans also use their viewing to establish group networks in which they talk, not only about soap operas, but also about relationships, families, social possibilities, and the way they can conceptualize life in general. Even though watching soap operas can be a solitary experience, most often the experience is discussed with others who form a community of viewers of particular soap operas. Discursive networks constructed around soap operas can work as a spoken text. The constant, active, and playful discussions about soap operas that take place in women's oral networks are an integral part of the cultural experience of the text (Brown, 1994).

Another segment of the population that engages in active interpretation of cultural texts is the women in the science fiction fan community. Although the science fiction fanship community is predominantly male, the fanzine community is more than 90 percent female—editing and writing stories, poems, songs, and vignettes, and producing artwork, photographs, and videotapes about the characters who populate *Star Trek, Blake's 7, Star Trek: The Next Generation, Doctor Who,* and other television and film source products. Between 1977 and 1988 10,000 community members from both English-speaking and non-English-speaking countries produced more than 34,000 items (Bacon-Smith, 1992). Besides its literary output, the fanzine community also supports close-knit friendship circles that produce and distribute the fanzines and gather the work produced by other circles. Although there are large conventions of all types of *Star Trek* and science fiction fans, the core groups within the fanship community are the circles, usually of not more than 15 women who range in age from late teenagers to women in their seventies. Their work is issued on-line or is still sometimes produced on 8 1/2-by-11-inch paper, photocopied, and distributed to their circles free or exchanged for the work of other circles (Bacon-Smith, 1992; Jenkins, 1992; Penley, 1991). This alternative literary network not only indicates a vast community of women taking part in a non-vertical network in which there is no head, focus, or center, but is also one in which its participants are consciously outside the consumer economy.

Race and the Oppositional Reading

bell hooks (1993) argues for an oppositional gaze, or the right to look, on the part of black female spectators. Slaves were punished for looking, and the gaze has subsequently become a site of resistance mainly concerned with race and racism. Because racial domination of blacks by whites has overdetermined representation, black looks were rarely concerned with gender. This is why a film like *The Color Purple* (1982) which, on the surface, told a black women's story, but structurally created a negative depiction of black women harking back to earlier stereotypes, was read positively by many black women. According to Jacqueline Bobo (1993), many black women responded sympathetically because this film connected them to a strong tradition of black women writers. Their gaze defied evaluations by professional film critics and instead was a matter of resonance in their own lives.

Thus, although a vast range of women consume popular culture, their responses to it are not all uniform or predictable. The pressure to conform to social expectations regarding beauty and behavior cannot be ignored. However, women and girls often use popular culture either to assert themselves

or to struggle against their ideological positioning as passive or against their "looked-at-ness," or even to construct alternative systems of distribution that fly in the face of capitalism. Women's consumption of popular culture is replete with the contradictions that make up the lives of women and other oppressed groups. For these groups, pleasure is not simple but complex. The pleasure women find in consumption of popular culture may come not only from absorbing the dominant ideology but also from conscious resistance to that ideology.

See Also

COMMUNICATIONS: AUDIENCE ANALYSIS; LEISURE; POPULAR CULTURE; ROMANTIC FICTION; SCIENCE FICTION; SOAP OPERAS; TELEVISION

References and Further Reading

Bacon-Smith, C. 1992. *Enterprising women: Television fandom and the creation of popular myth*. Philadelphia: University of Pennsylvania Press.

Bobo, J. 1993. Reading through the text: The black women as audience. In M. Diawara, ed., *Black American cinema*, 272–287. New York: Routledge.

Brown, M. E. 1994. *Soap opera and women's talk: The pleasure of resistance*. Thousand Oaks, Calif.: Sage.

Ellsworth, E. 1990. Illicit pleasures: Feminist spectators and *Personal Best*. In P. Erens, ed., *Issues in feminist film criticism*, 183–196. Bloomington: Indiana University Press.

Gray, A. 1987. Behind closed doors: Video recorders in the home. In H. Baehr and G. Dyer, eds., *Boxed in: Women and television*, 38–54. London: Pandora.

Griggers, C. 1993. *Thelma and Louise* and the cultural generation of the new butch-femme. In A. Collins, J. Collins, and H. Radner, eds., *Film theory goes to the movies*. London: Routledge.

Grodin, D. 1991. The interpreting audience: The therapeutics of self-help book reading. *Critical Studies in Mass Communication* 7: 117–128.

hooks, b. 1993. The oppositional gaze: Black female spectators. In Manthia Diawara, ed., *Black American cinema*, 288–302. New York: Routledge.

Jenkins, H. 1992. *Textual poachers: Television fans and participatory culture*. London: Routledge.

Lee, M., and C. H. Cho. 1990. Women watching together: An ethnographic study of Korean soap opera fans in the US. *Cultural Studies* 4: 30–44.

McRobbie, A. 1984. Dance and social fantasy. In A. McRobbie and M. Nava, eds., *Gender and generations*, 130–162. London: Macmillan.

Lewis, L.A. 1990. *Gender politics and MTV: Voicing the difference.* Philadelphia: Temple University Press.

Long, E. 1987. Reading groups and the postmodern crisis of cultural authority. *Cultural Studies* 1: 306–327.

Morley, D. 1986. *Family television: Cultural power and domestic leisure.* London: Comedia.

———. 1993. *Television, audiences and cultural studies.* London: Routledge.

Penley, C. 1991. Brownian motion: Women, tactics, and technologies. In C. Penley and A. Ross, eds., *Technoculture*. Minneapolis: University of Minnesota Press.

Press, A. L. 1991. *Women watching television: Gender, class and generation in the American television experience.* Philadelphia: University of Pennsylvania Press.

Mary Ellen Brown

CULTURE:
Women as Producers of Culture

The possibility of access to media technology and expertise has often shifted the position of women from consumers to producers. When women become producers of culture rather than consumers, a variety of possibilities emerge. Women musicians, artists, writers, media producers, and Internet activists who make decisions to create as well as consume culture are in a position to shape new possibilities for themselves and for other women. When they work in groups, they become part of a collective experience that not only involves the celebration of women's lives, histories, processes, and emotions, but also fosters criticism of and reflection about the status quo.

In developing countries, many forms of collective activism have been used by women: print, small-format media, drama, and, particularly since the 1960s, radio. Radio is available in rural environments and adapts well to oral forms of transmission. Oral transmission can take the form of speaking through loudspeakers, recording cassettes, or establishing clandestine radio stations (Rodriguez, 1994). Women in developing countries have also gained access to video production via art and community centers. From the Far East to South America, all across North America and Europe, individual women, as well as collectives of women, have produced visual diaries, social documentaries, and commentaries on their own life situations. When aired on local cable stations, the faces of community activists, elders, neighbors, and family are inserted into a space previously reserved for consumer-driven images of extreme wealth,

beauty, and romance. Clemencia Rodriguez describes the impact of such productions on the women themselves as a process of identity deconstruction, personal and group empowerment, demystification of mainstream media, reversal of power roles, and increasing collective strengths (1994).

In developed countries, women's cultural production can take place alongside and within the mainstream culture of music, art museums, publishing, and film or television presentations. Even though there are constraints and difficulties because economic power resides with the dominant groups, women have been able to explore topics relevant to masked, suppressed, or nondominant constructions of culture.

Women and Science Fiction

Language is the basis of culture. Arguably, the producers of language dictate its implications, its issues, and its use in the recording of history. On this view, language, especially in western civilization, is gendered and male. For women to write in a way that can be understood by their readers is an important part of why women seek access to the production of culture. Women science fiction writers, for example, present speculative narratives, opening up for fictional women the possibilities of alternative environments where they live independently of men. Many women sci-fi writers also create new languages for their women characters. These languages have evolved, and readers have added words, ideas, and new meanings to old concepts through fanzines: low-budget on-line or photocopied publications that are produced by fans and distributed to other fans. The roles of producer and consumer overlap here. One popular mode of resistance among consumers is to refuse to consume cultural artifacts in the socially prescribed manner, as when some women watch soap operas without buying into the ideology they embody (Brown, 1994). In science fiction, a whole new discourse about romantic relationships between some of *Star Trek*'s male characters has been created through fanzines (Penley, 1991).

Pamela Sargent (1995) notes that women have maintained a stronghold within the various divisions of science fiction, from traditional narratives to cyberpunk. Some work by Ursula K. Le Guin and Margaret Atwood falls into the category of utopian science fiction. The British writer Gwyneth Jones writes about postholocaust matriarchy in her book *Divine Endurance* (1984). Also in this category is Suzette Haden Elgin, whose books *Native Tongue* (1984) and *Native Tongue II: The Judas Rose* (1987) illustrate how some female science fiction women writers have created a distinct language for their female characters, a language that exists outside of that used by the male occupants of the specific planet or arena about which they write. With regard to feminism and women sci-fi writers, Sargent (1995) quotes the critic Joan Gordon, "[recent female science fiction writers] don't neglect feminist thought: they assume, apply, subsume it in their texts" (1995: 19).

Women Musicians and Performers

From rock to performance art, from country to gospel, women have used their positions as performers, songwriters, and producers to tell about the multifaceted aspects of women's lives. Whether it be protest rock or rap, women musicians have used the words of their own anger, personal experiences, and political causes—as well as the words of women novelists—in their music as a means of infiltrating the music industry, which has been traditionally seen as exclusionary and male. As in the case of authors and readers of women's science fiction, women's music fanzines and gatherings continue and elaborate the discussions opened on the stage.

The most successful fanzine, Riot Grrrl, can be loosely described as a punk rock feminist movement and is easily accessible on the World Wide Web. Through these fanzines women musicians network and encourage other women to create bands. Lucy O'Brien (1996) writes in her book *She Bop,* "It was as much about speaking out, decoding verbal expression and manipulating visual images as it was about playing in bands" and quotes the Riot Grrrl Chia Pet as stating, "Music is an integral part of youth culture that makes it possible for girls to infiltrate male-dominated society" (1996: 160). The most commercially successful women's music festival was Lilith Fair, a summer tour celebrating women in music by presenting all female soloists and women-fronted bands. The festival was originated by the singer Sarah McLachlan in 1996 and produced summer tours until 1999.

O'Brien found that African-American female rappers frequently include in their songs narratives by well-known African-American women writers including Toni Morrison, Alice Walker, Ntozake Shange, and Toni Cade Bambara. These African-American writers, O'Brien states, "showed a reinvention of language through jive talk, folklore, and literary metaphor. Female rappers continue in this tradition, articulating their generation's experience through the bold originality of their own language" (1996: 312). O'Brien notes that rap lyrics, like the characters in Toni Morrison's book *Beloved* (1987), utilize "re-memory," a reclamation of the "dis-remembered" in the history of African-Americans, resurrecting them as positive, strong role models for the com-

munity at large. Female rappers often give themselves names like Queen Latifah and Nefertiti as a means of "naming" which, according to O'Brien, "countered anonymity, the legacy of women silenced through slavery" (p. 313). She also found that female rappers "evolve their own cast of characters, from fly girl to earth mother to mackstress to blacksista" (p. 300). These women are producing culture through the deconstruction and rewriting of history, articulating what their mothers and grandmothers may have been unable to speak.

Just as science fiction writers deal with complex issues of racism, sexuality, and violence within their fictional landscapes, female musicians often use lyrics that articulate similar concerns. The country music singer Mary Chapin Carpenter, for example, often inserts the desires and fantasies of her enormous female audience into traditional country narratives. One song in particular, "He Thinks He'll Keep Her," is about the liberation of a woman from the assumptions of her husband, suggested by the sexism inherent in the words of the title. The Dixie Chicks attack violence against women in their song "Good-Bye Earl," released on CD in 1999. Similarly, performance artists like Laurie Anderson, Karen Finley, and Diamanda Galas use their music and narratives as cultural and political activism, deconstructing notions of what music is and which music should be heard.

Women Novelists

In addition to Morrison, Walker, Shange, and Bambara, women novelists including Kathy Aker, Amy Tan, Louise Erdrich, Jamaica Kincaid, and Sandra Cisneros have used generational and societal influences to express individual and collective identities. Their narratives dethrone man as the central figure in women's lives and give recognition to grandmothers, mothers, aunts, sisters, and daughters as powerful figures in changing their desires or in creating the identities they aspire to. These writers produce female characters who resist uniformity and represent the panoply of personalities of real women. They are given dialogues that celebrate what is often referred to as "non-sense": intuition, spirituality, discernment, and women's knowledge based on experiences outside masculine authorship.

Visual Artists

The production of art that dispels the mainstream notion of woman as passive and as desired objects replaces this notion with works by women artists which bridge the binaries woman-nature and man-culture. In western society, women have traditionally been products for male consumption rather than producers of culture. Their bodies have been idealized, and their intellectual identity has been systematically appropriated. The fragmentation of women's bodies for male pleasure and the constant dissemination of such ideals has had a devastating effect on women, which has led to depression, anorexia, bulimia, self-loathing, and suicide. The perfect body is not swollen with pregnancy or vulnerable to disease, and it never ages. It is a body or text coded in terms of pleasure and possession. Women artists have produced works countering these phallocentric concepts.

Two such artists, Jo Spence and Hannah Wilke, decode while resignifying the female body. By photographing their own cancer-stricken nude bodies, they reveal the hidden. They claim possession of their own bodies, casting aside preconceived concepts of beauty. Spence wrote that her work represents "not merely a history of victimization and injury, nor a shift into a utopian world of 'positive images,' but [rather] the continuous struggle to speak, to redefine, to name, [to come] into being" (1995: 163). Wilke's photographs of her illness are especially startling when contrasted with those taken of herself in the early 1970s. These early images utilize her youthful and beautiful nude body pictured in such a way as to parody the traditional use of women's bodies in art. Collectively, Wilke's photographs document the evolution of the female body through youth, aging, disease, and, ultimately, death. Jean Dykstra (1995) writes that "autobiographical photographs of bodies marked by disease signify a forceful challenge to codes of representation and cultural ideologies about the female body" (1995: 12). Similarly, the work of the Mexican artist Frida Kahlo represents the fragmentation of the female body not by the male gaze but by injury and illness. Whitney Chadwick writes, "Kahlo used painting as a means of exploring the reality of her own body and her consciousness of that reality" (1990: 295).

Women artists such as Mary Kelly, Jenny Holzer, Carrie Mae Weems, and Lorna Simpson couple the written word with the visual image as a means of positioning a feminine text within their art. This feminine text articulates what has traditionally been censored within the modern art world. Kelly and Holzer challenge patriarchal notions of female subjectivity, from motherhood to consumerism. Holzer's "truisms," such as the work of art entitled "Protect Me from What I Want," speak of the rejection of a product-driven society. Weems and Simpson combine counter-hegemonic or socially unacceptable images dealing with black identity and fragments of language, stating concepts which could be developed only after the period of history when rich nations colonized poor ones. bell hooks writes, "Lorna Simpson's images of black female bodies are provoca-

tive and progressive precisely because she calls attention to aspects of black female identity that tend to be erased or overlooked in a racist, sexist culture. Her work counters the stereotype" (1995: 97).

Women Filmmakers

The feminist film critic Annette Kuhn defines a feminine text within women's film as one that depends on an interplay between the text and the reader. Kuhn states, "This challenging relationship is one in which, in the act of reading, meanings are grasped as shifting and constantly in process, and the subject-reader is placed in an active relationship to those meanings" (1982: 12).

There is not just one fixed meaning conveyed by a film. Particularly in a feminine text or film—which is constructed in such a way that its very narrative conventions go against accepted notions of how a film should be constructed—the film can open the way to unconventional meanings. For example, the classical Hollywood narrative begins with stability, the stability is disrupted, the story of the film is about reestablishing the world of the story, and in the end that world is stabilized. However, this classical narrative is disrupted when the ending is ambiguous or the chronological sequence is out of order. The narrative of this type of film does not attempt to speak to a certain type of viewer; rather, it addresses any number of types of viewers.

Women filmmakers like Julie Dash, Chantal Akerman, and Trinh T. Minh-ha use the floating signifiers or open meanings of feminine texts. Their films are in contrast to those of classical Hollywood cinema that position women characters (with a few exceptions) as saints, victims, or whores. Dash's film *Daughters of the Dust* (1992) breaks narrative, linguistic, and cultural conventions. In this film, Dash confronts the audience with a history outside of university textbooks, a history of black slaves and descendants of slaves on the coast of South Carolina who remember and try to understand their historical past—even that part which does not fit the images explained in written history. This is a reclaiming of the "dis-remembered" similar to that of black women authors discussed earlier. The film challenges the audience not to dismiss what they have borne witness to through viewing it.

Several films by the Dutch filmmaker Chantal Akerman draw on the mundane. Out of this mundaneness, however, emerges a poetry of the ordinary, the daily, and the routine that excludes no one and therefore decenters the protagonist or star figure. Akerman's work also deconstructs concepts and ideals of gender that are often encoded into language, society, and film.

The Vietnamese-American filmmaker Trinh T. Minhha intends to break down the language of conventional anthropological films. Her "subjective documentary" style has the effect of repositioning or eliminating the voyeuristic gaze of the viewer and the filmmaker. Producing cinematic collages of female imagery accompanied by the female voice, whether speaking or singing, Minh-ha counters traditional ethnographic depictions of third world women as "other."

Within or outside the mainstream, women construct and produce culture. They disseminate their language and iconography across an international network both consumed and maintained by the audience. Sherry Ortner writes that a woman is "a full-fledged human being endowed with human consciousness just as man is; she is half the race, without whose cooperation the whole enterprise would collapse.... Having consciousness, she thinks and speaks; she generates, communicates, and manipulates symbols, categories, and values" (1974: 76). By challenging the status quo, women as producers of culture can carve out a space to communicate as women.

See Also

ART PRACTICE, FEMINIST; CREATIVITY; CULTURE: OVERVIEW; CULTURE: WOMEN AS CONSUMERS OF CULTURE; FILM; LANGUAGE; MEDIA: OVERVIEW; MUSIC: ROCK AND POP; PERFORMANCE ART

References and Suggested Reading

Brown, Mary Ellen. 1994. *Soap opera and women's talk: The pleasure of resistance.* Thousand Oaks, Calif.: Sage.

Chadwick, Whitney. 1990. *Women, art and society.* London: Thames and Hudson.

Dykstra, Jean. 1995. Putting herself in the picture: Autobiographical images of illness and the body. *Afterimage 16* (September–October).

hooks, bell. 1995. *Art on my mind.* New York: New Press.

Kuhn, Annette. 1982. *Women's pictures.* London: Verso.

Minh-ha, Trinh T. 1991. *When the moon waxes red: Representation, gender and cultural politics.* New York: Routledge.

O'Brien, Lucy. 1996. *She bop.* New York: Penguin.

Ortner, Sherry B. 1974. Is female to male as nature is to culture? In Michelle Zimbalist Rosaldo and Louise Lamphere, eds., *Woman, culture and society.* Palo Alto, Calif.: Stanford University Press.

Penley, C. 1991. Brownian motion: Women, tactics, and technologies. In C. Penley and A. Ross, eds., *Technoculture.* Minneapolis: University of Minnesota Press.

Rodriguez, Clemencia. 1994. A process of identity deconstruction: Latin American women producing video stories. In Pilar Riano, ed., *Women in grassroots communication: Furthering social change.* Thousand Oaks, Calif.: Sage.

Sargent, Pamela, ed. 1995. *Women of wonder: The contemporary years.* San Diego, Calif.: Harcourt Brace.

Spence, Jo. 1995. *Cultural snippings.* London: Routledge.

Mary Ellen Brown
Susan Dyer

CURRICULUM

See EDUCATION: CURRICULUM IN SCHOOLS.

CURRICULUM TRANSFORMATION MOVEMENT

In women's studies, the term *curriculum transformation* refers to efforts in the United States to develop a curriculum that includes the experiences, perspectives, and scholarship of women in all their diversity. By the end of the 1970s, after some 300 women's studies programs had been established, feminist academics began to turn their attention to integrating the new scholarship on women into the curriculum as a whole. During the 1970s and 1980s, scholars working in women's studies and, as it was then called, black studies began to document the absence of women of all ethnic groups and men of color, as well as lesbian women, gay men, and working-class people, from the curriculum and scholarship. Early efforts were often referred to as "curriculum integration projects" and had as their goal the integration of missing women into the traditional curriculum, which was understood to be narrowly white, biased in favor of males, Eurocentric, and heterosexist. In spite of their good intentions, many early curriculum efforts were faulted for failing to reflect the scholarship and the experiences of women of color, who were often marginalized in women's studies much as women in general had been marginalized within black studies and traditional scholarship.

As women's studies and feminist scholarship continued to develop, it became clear that adding previously excluded voices to the curriculum raised serious questions about the ways in which the disciplines themselves had been constructed. "Curriculum transformation," in contrast to "curriculum integration," challenges the basic assumptions, models, paradigms, and language used throughout the disciplines and works toward a transformed understanding of what constitutes knowledge and reality. Because knowledge is understood to be socially constructed, close attention is paid to the position and values of the knower, and the necessity of having a diverse community of knowledge-seekers is recognized. As Patricia Hill Collins and others have observed, women in the academy in general, and women of color in particular, because of their status as "outsiders within," are uniquely suited to reflect on the ways in which the traditional disciplines have been constructed.

Curriculum transformation projects at different institutions and in different regions of the country have been shaped by the special needs and specific resources of those who participate. Some institutions have created large faculty development projects that seek to transform the entire institution and rely on visits from national scholars who lecture and consult on a regular basis. They offer the resident faculty release time to revise course offerings and encourage both junior and senior scholars to participate. Other projects, with less funding or less faculty or administrative support, have created smaller initiatives that focus on selected disciplines or courses and rely primarily on the expertise of their own faculty members, who meet on a regular basis to rethink the curriculum and scholarship. While some projects have targeted introductory courses for revision, others have focused on general education or core requirements; still others have sought to revise electives or create new courses, some of which are interdisciplinary in nature. Some projects do all three.

In addition to providing a range of faculty development experiences and opportunities during the regular academic year, many curriculum transformation projects have created, or arranged for the faculty to participate in, summer institutes where participants have an opportunity for intensive study. In addition to focusing on curriculum and scholarship, curriculum transformation projects examine issues of pedagogy and classroom process, seeking to transform these relations in the course of rethinking content. Projects collect, create, and disseminate bibliography, syllabi, films, and other teaching resources, and many have published the results of their efforts in book or pamphlet form. Materials generated by these projects are being collected by the National Center for Curriculum Transformation Resources on Women at Towson State University, Towson, Maryland.

Among the early and best-known curriculum projects were those at Montana State University, directed by Betty Schmitz; Southwest Institute for Research on Women (SIROW), directed by Myra Dinnerstein; the Wheaton College Project on Balancing the Curriculum, directed by Bonnie Spanier; the Mellon Seminars at the Wellesley Center, organized by Peggy McIntosh; and the Black Studies/Women's Studies Project, directed by Johnnella Butler, then at Smith College, and Margo Culley, University of Massachusetts, Amherst. Other important projects include the Project to Incorporate Black Women's Studies into the Liberal Arts Curriculum at Spelman College, directed by Beverly Guy-Sheftall; projects at Memphis State University and at Towson State University in Maryland; and the Project on the Status and Education of Women at the Association of American Colleges and Universities. In 1986, the New Jersey Project: Integrating the Scholarship on Gender became the first such statewide project in higher education.

Second-generation projects have been designed to emphasize the incorporation of the scholarship and perspective of women of color into the curriculum, to encourage curriculum projects at two-year institutions, and to integrate international perspectives into women's studies. Funding for these initiatives has come from internal funding by individual institutions, government agencies such as the Fund for the Improvement of Post-Secondary Education (FIPSE), the National Endowment for the Humanities (NEH), and the Women's Educational Equity Act (WEEA), and from private foundations such as the Ford Foundation, the Mellon Foundation, and the Carnegie Endowment.

During the early 1980s, some members of women's studies faculties expressed the fear that curriculum transformation or "mainstreaming" projects would divert funding and energy from women's studies departments and programs that were already underfunded and understaffed. By 1983, plenary speakers at the National Women's Studies Association's annual conference agreed that the dual strategies were complementary, not antagonistic, reflecting the view that long-term change would require both involving a broad spectrum of faculty members in transformation efforts and simultaneously strengthening women's studies and ethnic studies departments. In practice it has turned out that the more successful curriculum projects have been those carried out under the direction of a strong "core" women's studies faculty. During the 1990s, many feminist academics became involved in campuswide curriculum transformation initiatives to create broadly interdisciplinary "diversity" requirements or specific courses combining the study of race and ethnicity, class, gender, and sexuality.

See Also

EDUCATION: CURRICULUM IN SCHOOLS; ETHNIC STUDIES; LESBIAN STUDIES; WOMEN'S STUDIES, *specific entries*

References and Further Reading

Fiol-Matt, Liza, and Mariam Chamberlain, eds. 1994. *Women of color and the multicultural curriculum: Transforming the college classroom.* New York: Feminist Press.

Friedman, Ellen, Wendy Kolmar, Charley Flint, and Paula Rothenberg, eds. 1996. *Creating an inclusive college curriculum.* New York: Athene.

Hull, Gloria, Patricia Bell-Scott, and Barbara Smith, eds. 1982. *All the women are white, all the blacks are men, but some of us are brave: Black women's studies.* Old Westbury, N.Y.: Feminist Press.

Rothenberg, Paula. 2000. *Race, class, and gender in the United States: An integrated study,* 5th ed. New York: St. Martin's.

Schuster, Marilyn, and Susan Van Dyne, eds. 1985. *Women's place in the academy: Transforming the liberal arts curriculum.* Totowa, N.J.: Rowman.

Spanier, Bonnie, Alexander Bloom, and Darlene Boroviak, eds. 1984. *Toward a balanced curriculum.* Cambridge, Mass.: Schenkman. (Includes Peggy McIntosh's classic essay "Interactive Phases of Curriculum Re-vision.")

Women's Studies Quarterly 1990. Special issue: "Curricular and institutional change" 18 (1–2: Spring–Summer).

Paula Rothenberg

CURSE

A curse is a form of divine punishment for violating religious or moral law. When an individual, rather than a deity, curses another person, it is a form of calling down a spiritually powerful external retribution in the name of the sacred law that the cursed one has transgressed. The strength and power of a curse depend on the cursed person's internalization of the moral or religious law she or he has violated. To be cursed is to feel a profound sense of guilt, shame, and damnation, which provokes submissive and even suicidal behavior.

The curse has long been used by patriarchal social and religious systems to dominate and control women. In this way, it has served as a form of religious violence. As patriarchal religious systems overthrew older matrifocal societies, they effected an ethical inversion, whereby women, formerly associated with the principle of life, became cursed as the origin of evil and death.

In patriarchal religions, women's cursed status can serve to justify their divinely sanctioned inferiority and sexual submission to men. One example of this process can be seen in the mythical figure of Lilith. Originally a revered Sumero-Babylonian deity, she was incorporated into Hebraic tradition as Adam's first wife. When Adam tried to force her to lie beneath him during sex, she cursed him, flew away, and coupled with demons. The curse of Lilith came to be used to explain men's nocturnal emissions; "wet dreams" were caused by this she-demon copulating with men in their sleep. Through the Middle Ages, Jewish, Catholic, and Muslim traditions continued to use Lilith-like figures (lilim, night hags, succubae) to represent a curse imposed on those who would reverse the divinely sanctioned male-superior sexual position.

Women's status as cursed and women's ability to invoke calamity or suffeirng by cursing evildoers have been primarily associated in many cultures with female powers: menstruation, childbirth, and "mother right."

The Curse of Menstruation

The religious association of menstrual blood with the curse of evil or pollution reflects an inversion of an earlier cultural association of power with the sacred, "wise," or magic blood of women. Thus, in the Talmud it is said that if a menstruating women walked between two men, one of the men would die. Persian religion shared a belief with many of its Middle Eastern counterparts that to lie with a menstruating woman would cause a man to be cursed in various ways: he would beget a demon, he would fall sick and die, and so on. Ancient myths in general held that a menstruating woman was capable of invoking a variety of evils. For the Greeks, the glance of a menstruating woman could paralyze a man like the glance of a Gorgon. Pliny said a menstruating woman's touch could blast the fruits of the field, sour wine, cloud mirrors, rust iron, and blunt the edges of knives.

This view of menstruating women as cursed can also be found in Judaism. Rabbinical tradition says that Eve began to menstruate only after she had copulated with the serpent in Eden. Orthodox Jews refuse to shake hands with a woman because she might be menstruating. Jews also seem to have adopted a warning from Hesiod never to wash in the same water as a woman because it might be tainted by menstrual blood.

Christianity, too, inherited the ancient patriarchs' view of menstruating women as cursed. St. Jerome wrote: "Nothing is so unclean as a woman in her periods; what she touches she causes to become unclean." From the seventh to the eleventh centuries, many church laws forbade menstruating women to take communion or even to enter a church. The extension of menstrual pollution to the condition of being a woman in general is reflected in the *Ancrene Wisse,* a Middle English guide for female ascetics: "Are you not come of foul slime, are you not a vat of filth?" (White,

1993: 129). The Catholic church has used the notion that a menstruating "priestess" would pollute the altar as an argument against the ordination of women.

Medical authorities of the sixteenth century still believed that demons were produced from menstrual blood. Nineteenth-century doctors gave a more modern scientific gloss to the curse of menstrual blood, maintaining that men contracted gonorrhea and other diseases from copulating with menstruating women.

This is the tradition from which the contemporary woman's slang reference to her period as "the curse" is derived.

The Curse of Childbirth

Orthodox Judeo-Christian tradition holds Eve responsible for God's cursing the human race with death, a curse that can be removed only by the spiritual death and rebirth of the Savior. As Mary Daly (1973: 69) has put it, Eve's curse is fundamental in masculinist Christian theology: "Take the snake, the fruit-tree, and the woman from the tableau, and we have no fall, no frowning Judge, no Inferno, no everlasting punishment—hence, no need of a Savior." Eve's sin also brought a sex-specific curse on all women: "I will greatly multiply your pain in childbearing; in pain you shall bring forth children, yet your desire shall be for your husband and he shall rule over you" (Genesis 3:16).

While Eve is perhaps the example most often cited, the idea that women's bodies before, during, and after childbirth are unclean and capable of bringing divine retribution on others is not simply a western cultural bias. As Adrienne Rich (1986: 163) notes, "The idea of birth as defilement is widespread. Indian village midwives are usually of the 'untouchable' caste, and in some parts of India the mother is supposedly 'untouchable' during birth and for ten days after." Chinese and Japanese religious tenets have also held pregnant women to be "defiled": in Japan, "if menstruating or pregnant, a woman could not walk through the *torii*, or arches, of shrines" (quoted in Rich, 1986: 137).

Mother's Curse

Many cultural traditions reflect a great fear of being cursed in vengeance by the matrifocal traditions overthrown by patriarchy. In ancient Asian belief, a mother's curse meant certain death. Post-Vedic holy law held that "the houses on which female relations, not being duly honored, pronounce a curse, perish completely, as if destroyed by magic" (Bullough, 1973: 232–33).

The orthodox Christian justification of Eve's curse is turned back on God the Father in some Gnostic texts which tell various versions of the Adam and Eve story. In one ver-

sion, God is a villain who cursed Adam and Eve and expelled them from paradise out of jealousy. In other versions, Eve reprimands Jehovah, curses him, or casts him into the abyss because he arrogantly pretended to be the sole creator (Pagels, 1979: 57–59).

Another important example of a mythic tradition in which a female principle curses those who violate or ignore the more ancient matrifocal blood ties is to be found in the Greek Erinyes (Furies), defenders of ancient "mother right." The blood of a slain mother caused the murderer to be tainted with the mother's curse, called miasma, a spiritual pollution that would lead the Furies to pursue the murderer's clan for generations. Aeschylus's trilogy *The Oresteia* dramatizes the Furies pursuing Orestes for killing his mother, insisting on their right to punish him for violating the more ancient maternal-bloodline clan system.

See Also

MENSTRUATION; MISOGYNY; MYTH; SIN; TABOO

References and Further Reading

Briffault, Robert. 1927. *The mothers.* New York: Macmillan.

Bullough, Vern. 1973. *The subordinate sex.* Chicago: University of Illinois Press.

Daly, Mary. 1973. *Beyond God the Father.* Boston: Beacon.

Pagels, Elaine. 1979. *The Gnostic gospels.* New York: Random House.

Rich, Adrienne. 1986. *Of woman born: Motherhood as experience and institution.* New York: Norton.

Sharma, Arvind, and Katherine Young. 1999. *Feminism and world religions.* Albany: State University of New York Press.

Spretnak, Charlene. 1982. *The politics of women's spirituality.* New York: Doubleday.

White, Hugh, trans. 1993. *Ancrene Wisse: Guide for anchoresses.* New York: Penguin.

Young, Serinity, ed. 1999. *Encyclopedia of women and world religion.* New York: Macmillan.

Ivone Gebara
Cathy Peppers

CYBERSPACE AND VIRTUAL REALITY

As we enter the twenty-first century, information technology is becoming pervasive. Digital information and communication networks are linking up, producing a global web of connections. This web is unevenly distributed but increasingly dense, and it is coming to define a new—and sometimes exclusionary—sense of the global. *Cyberspace* is the name given to a new kind of space located "within" these networks.

Cyberspace is more than cables and computers. It emerges as humans use computer networks and as they represent these activities, this new space, and this new connection with technology—to themselves and to each other. Cyberspace is thus partly an imagined space and also a shared one. As Margaret Wertheim (1999: 304) puts it: "the 'production of space'—any kind of space—is *necessarily* a communal activity." The science fiction writer William Gibson (1986: 67), who coined the term *cyberspace* in the novel *Neuromancer,* expressed this by describing cyberspace as a "consensual hallucination."

Today millions of people contribute to this hallucination. Cyperspace is becoming a significant new sphere of human action. It may also be a place where something as basic as "what it is to be human" is being substantially rethought. Life on the screen might involve the production of new kinds of subjectivities and identities, adapted to suit a virtual world.

For all these reasons, it is important that women are involved in the development of cyberspace. Lamis Alshejni (1999), a Yemeni woman, articulates this when she states that Arab women need to contribute to the developing "Net" culture, in order that they can be "subjects not objects of a shared cyberculture." Similarly, Dale Spender (1996: 168) fears "the marginalization of women at that place where increasingly 'we make sense of the world.'"

"Being there," contributing to cyberculture, might be more problematic for women than men in that technology and the use of technology are gendered; in most societies technology is "coded masculine." A central issue cyberspace raises for women, therefore, is whether what Judy Wacjman (1991: 159) has characterized as the "close connection" between men and machines still holds in this new sphere. The promise of cyberspace for many women, particularly for those who have a feminist constructivist view of technology, lies in its potential to disturb that connection. Wacjman has argued that "the correspondence between men and machines is…neither essential nor immutable, and therefore the potential exists for its transformation." There are implications here not only for how societies "think" technology but also for how they understand gender and sexual difference.

Cyber-Enthusiasm

Many women participated in the wave of popular enthusiasm for getting on-line that launched the Internet into everyday life in many countries. Mapping this activity is important. It provides evidence of a new—and more positive—engagement between women and technology.

Some women have produced women-only services. An early example was *Women's Wire,* launched in 1994, which proclaimed itself "an information clearing house" and "conversational on-line gathering place." Other women are active in all kinds of open forums on the Internet. These are public spaces in which sexual difference might be irrelevant, given the anonymity of the Net, which produces a degree of gender confusion. With bodies "hidden" behind texts (or avatars), women are free to conceal their gender (and age, race, and class). For these reasons the Net has been celebrated as a new public space which is gender-blind and which may foster new and more equal forms of participation for women in civil society.

Gender switching as part of a wider identity is a common phenomenon on some parts of the Net, particularly in multiuser domains (MUDs) and chat rooms. Women have been involved in these fantasy spaces, which might be understood as laboratories for the production of new kinds of selves, possibly even multiple selves (Stone, 1995). Researchers such as Sherry Turkle (1996) have studied how users create partial, multitasking, and fluid identities on-line, cycling through identities depending on which "window" they are operating within. Turkle has argued that these postmodern forms of subjectivity might come closer to feminist concepts of the self than they do to masculinist concepts of autarky of the subject.

Finally, some very visible female celebrators of cyberspace are geekgirls. These are (young) women who identify strongly with information technology. Geekgirls regard access to the Net, and technological competence, not as a gender transgression but as an essential component of modern womanhood, linking grrrl power with geekgirl power, as one activist, Rosie X, put it in "Grrrls Need Modems" (Wakeford, 1997: 61). Other activists who have contributed to a feisty female presence on the Net include the Australian artist collective VNS Matrix, which used the metaphor of viral contagion to argue that the Net may be productively "infected" with feminine values.

The Pleasures of Connection

The geekgirls' central assertion is that the pleasures of an intimate relationship with technology can be feminine as much as masculine. A growing body of theoretical and fictional writing by women explores this possibility.

Cyberspace has been widely celebrated in male science fiction, and in much writing about the Net, as an escape from the "meat," an escape out of nature. In contrast, many technophile women writers have understood the potential of cyberspace to be located not in transcendence but rather in connection. The allure of the virtual, for women, can be understood not in terms of what William Gibson called the "bodiless exaltation of cyberspace" (Wertheim, 1999: 23), but rather in terms of fusions and leakages between bodies and machines.

An important theoretical reference point is Donna Haraway's influential *Cyborg Manifesto* (1991), which can also be understood as a response to ecofeminists' technophobia. Some ecofeminists hold that technology, understood as masculine in essence, is inimical to feminine values, and that women should therefore resist technological "progress." *A Cyborg Manifesto* accepts that information technologies are bridging divisions between nature and culture, human and nonhuman. Against these ecofeminists, however, Haraway argues that the blending of those categories, which underpin—and naturalize—sexual difference, can have productive possibilities for women and other subordinated groups.

This potential is explored through the cyborg, an imaginary creature, simultaneously flesh and machine, and therefore beyond those dualisms that determine gender and sexual difference. The cyborg raises the possibility of a new kind of information society, one not defined in terms of the culmination of masculine strategies of domination over nature. This is also expressed in terms of a contest for language, the embodied cyborg standing against the pure logic of cybernetic code. Haraway defines cyborg politics as "the struggle for language and the struggle against perfect communication, against the one code that translates all meaning perfectly, the central dogma of phallogocentrism" (1991: 176).

Haraway's cyborg politics have been influential. Later writers, however, have developed different—often more essentialist—versions of technophilia, in their writings about the Internet.

A leading exponent of this new writing in the United Kingdom is the cyberfeminist Sadie Plant (1996: 170). Plant understands the Internet as an emergent system twisting beyond the control of its makers. For her, cyberfeminism is the revolt of this emergent system—a system that includes women and computers—against the worldview and material reality of a patriarchy that seeks to subdue them. Plant's cyberfeminism is about the identity of women with emergent machines. For Plant, technology is thus revealed as feminine.

The rhetoric of cyberfeminism is at once defiant—promising infiltration and corruption—and triumphalist, in that the necessary conditions for the overthrow of patriarchy are understood to have already arrived. Women are already "in the process, turned on with the machines" (Plant, 1996: 182). The cyborg future, speculative for Haraway, has here arrived. Commentators such as Judith Squires (1996: 209) have noted that this leaves open the possibility that not only gender, but also the need for feminism of any kind, might have expired in the matrix.

Situating Cyberspace in Social Relations

Many commentators, while applauding the energy of the geekgirls and the rhetorical power of cyberfeminism, argue that these are elements of a more complex weave, with other more problematic threads. As Rosie Braidotti (1996: 20) has put it, "There is a strong indication… that the shifting of conventional boundaries between the sexes and the proliferation of all kinds of differences through the new technologies will not be nearly as liberating as the cyberartists and internet addicts would want us to believe."

Most basically not all women have a similar stake in the system. While in the United States increasing numbers of Net users are women, in other parts of the world connection rates in general are likely to remain low. Globally, most women are excluded from the Net.

Many women find cyberspace a hostile environment. Among the problems documented are "flaming" and other exclusionary tactics deployed by males in public spaces, harassment, male-dominated content—including pornography, which is increasingly prevalent—and the poverty of interactions in disembodied, nonaccountable chat rooms. Women-only areas, seen in this light, might be understood as defensive.

Finally, while gender switching is widespread on-line, gendered identities on the Net are often very traditional. Without real bodies in evidence, normative notions of the feminine might actually be said to operate in a heightened way in cyberspace, as gender is reduced to a stylized set of stereotypical injunctions (Bassett, 1997). As Margaret Morse (1997: 27) has put it, "interactions and subjectivities on-line are caught up in the same dualisms which structure the outside world; values [including those of sex and gender] encoded in the symbolic system prevail in the minds of users."

Women's experiences of cyberspace are uneven. Some argue that it tends to flatten out gender difference. Others have found sexual difference reinforced and gendered hierarchies reintroduced in this new space. Does this undermine claims made for cyberspace as a place that might facilitate new kinds of relationships between women and the technologies? Perhaps it complicates this picture rather than destroys it. Many feminists are cautious about accounts which focus on such absolute categories as "women" and "technology," arguing that they tend to ignore differences between women. Dale Spender (1996), for one, has called for assessments of cyberspace that start by understanding both information technology and women as embedded in existing social relations. From this situated perspective, a more complex and less total account of the possible significance of cyberspace for different women emerges. This new picture might underscore the continued necessity for feminist interventions—activist, theoretical, political, artistic—in this new sphere.

See Also

COMMUNICATIONS: OVERVIEW; COMPUTER SCIENCE; COMPUTING: OVERVIEW; CYBORG ANTHROPOLOGY; INFORMATION REVOLUTION; INFORMATION TECHNOLOGY; INTERNET POLITICS AND STATES; MEDIA: OVERVIEW; FEMINIST PHILOSOPHIES; FEMINISM: POSTMODERN; SEXUAL DIFFERENCE; TECHNOLOGY: OVERVIEW

Reference and Further Reading

Alshejni, Lamis. 1999. Unveiling the Arab woman's voice through the Net. In Wendy Harcourt, ed., *Woman*. London: Zed.

Bassett, Caroline. 1997. Virtually gendered. In Sarah Thornton and Ken Gelder, eds., *The subcultures reader*, 537–551. London: Routledge.

Braidotti, Rosie. 1996. Cyberfeminism with a difference. *New Formations* 29 (Summer): 9–25.

Gibson, William. 1986. *Neuromancer*. Harmondsworth: Penguin.

Haraway, Donna J. 1991. A cyborg manifesto: Science, technology, and socialist-feminism in the late twentieth century. In *Simians, cyborgs and women: The reinvention of nature*, 149–181. London: Routledge.

Morse, Margaret. 1997. Virtual identity. In Jennifer Terry and Melanie Calvert, eds., *Processed lives: Gender and technology in everyday life*, 23–36. London: Routledge.

Plant, Sadie 1996. On the matrix, cyberfeminist simulations. In Rob Shields, ed., *Cultures of Internet: Virtual spaces, real histories, living bodies*, 170–183. London: Sage.

Spender, Dale. 1996. *Nattering on the net*. Toronto: Garamond.

Squires, Judith. 1996. Fabulous feminist futures. In Jon Dovey, ed., *Fractal dreams, new media in social context*, 194–216. London: Lawrence and Wishart.

Stone, Allucquere Rosanne. 1995. *The war of desire and technology at the close of the mechanical age*. London: MIT.

Turkle, Sherry. 1996. *Life on the screen*. London: Weidenfeld and Nicolson.

Wakeford, Nina. 1997. Networking women and grrrls with information/communication technology. In Jennifer Terry and Melanie Calvert, eds., *Processed lives: Gender and technology in everyday life*, 51–66. London: Routledge.

Wajcman, Judy. 1991. *Feminism confronts technology*. Cambridge: Polity.

Wertheim, Margaret. 1999. *The pearly gates of cyberspace*. London: Virago.

Caroline Bassett

CYBORG ANTHROPOLOGY

A *cyborg* (shorthand for "cybernetic organism") is a symbiotic fusion of human and machine. Humans have always developed technologies to help themselves survive and thrive, but in recent decades the rapid escalation and intensification of the interface between humans and technology have exceeded anything heretofore known. From satellite communications to genetic engineering, high technology has penetrated and permeated the human and natural realms. Indeed, so profoundly are humans altering their biological and physical landscapes that some have openly suggested that the proper object of anthropological study should be cyborgs rather than humans, for, as Donna Haraway (1991) says, we are all cyborgs now.

Cyborg Anthropology As a Subspecialty of Anthropology

Anthropology, the study of humans, has traditionally concentrated on discovering the process of evolution through which the human came to be (physical anthropology) or on understanding the beliefs, languages, and behaviors of past or present human groups (archaeology, linguistics, cultural anthropology). Cyborg anthropology is a recent subspecialty launched at the Annual Meetings of the American Anthropological Association (AAA) in 1993. Within the AAA, cyborg anthropology is associated with the Committee for the Anthropology of Science, Technology, and Computing (CASTAC). From the start cyborg anthropologists have located themselves within the larger transdisciplinary field of science and technology studies (STS); they have attended the annual meetings of the Society for the Social Studies of Science (SSSS) and have applied cyborgian perspectives to a wide research spectrum ranging from the culture of physicists in Japan (Traweek, 1988) to organ donation in Germany (Hogle, 1999) to extended work on the new reproductive technologies.

Both the transdisciplinary nature of cyborg studies and their strongly feminist orientation were established by Donna Haraway with her famous article "Cyborg Manifesto: Science, Technology, and Socialist-Feminism in the Late Twentieth Century" (1986), which is included in her book of essays *Simians, Cyborgs, and Women* (1991). Following Haraway's lead, despite the breadth of its inquiry—which encompasses all aspects of the human-technology interface—cyborg anthropology has retained a focus on feminist issues and women's concerns, intervening directly in the long-standing problem of women's relationship to technology. Technology often provides choices that were not available before and extends the abilities of humans—empowering, for example, many women with disabilities to live better lives. But technologies are embedded in their socioeconomic and cultural contexts and can equally well be used to constrain, survey, and disempower. A feminist cyborg anthropology is always attentive to which women benefit from a specific technology and which women do not.

The Implications of New Diagnostic Technologies

New diagnostic technologies, from genetic tests to brain imaging, and new therapeutics, from antidepressants like Prozac to organ transplants, create new ways of living and deciding that are at once exciting and troubling. For instance, testing for the breast cancer gene BRCA-1, which identifies an increased risk of cancer in some women, often restructures a woman's relationship to the health care system, to her family, and to herself. Taking the test can lead to losing insurance coverage and to accelerated treatment choices like prophylactic mastectomy; in other words, identification of genetic risk can result in a women's being treated as if she already had breast cancer. This test thus creates a new cyborgian category—the presymptomatically ill—and a new set of risks posed by the "prophylactic" treatments prescribed for its members.

Cyborg Anthropology and Women's Studies

The most developed cyborg anthropological work in women's studies concerns reproduction, addressing everything from technologies of conception and prenatal diagnosis and treatment (Rapp, 2000) to the technologization of birth to the commodification of disability and pregnancy loss (Layne, 2000). For example, Rayna Rapp's long-term fieldwork among genetic counselors and her attention to racial, class, and religious differences in how women make choices given uncertain information about amniocentesis constitute outstanding examples of simultaneous attention to technology, its mediators, and its implications for women. In the contemporary developed world, there is almost no such thing as "normal" birth: giving birth without prenatal testing, hospitals, electronic fetal monitoring,

drugs, and forceps is generally considered unsafe, despite the demonstrated safety of midwife-attended out-of-hospital births. The mothers and children whose lives are structured and whose bodies and development are altered by birth technologies can be fruitfully analyzed as cyborgs who demonstrate the full range of ambiguity and possibility this concept encompasses. Various chapters in *Cyborg Babies* (Davis-Floyd and Dumit, 1998) probe these ambiguities, asking whether the sense of control provided to women and practitioners by the routine application of such technologies compensates for the very real physical damage they often do.

Other exemplary ethnographies in the wider arena of cyborg studies include Emily Martin's work on immunological science, Deborah Heath's work on the science and activism regarding Marfan's syndrome, Diana Forsythe's studies of artificial intelligence and expert systems, Joseph Dumit's studies of brain imaging practices, and Karen-Sue Taussig's work on genetics clinics in the Netherlands. As the location of these studies makes clear, however, much work needs to be done to expand cyborg anthropology to address non-middle-class and nonwestern issues such as the multiple effects of pollution, pesticides, and bioengineering in agricultural production and racial and gendered exclusions from access to cyborg technologies. The strength of cyborg anthropology is its ability to combine attention to scientific practices and working technologies with critical analyses of technophilia (cultural fascination with high technologies), social control, and hegemonic and popular appropriations of technology. Its weakness is that the same fascinating lure of science and technology keeps its practitioners focused on the "cyberdazzle" of the newest technologies, "big science," and western market power.

See Also

ANTHROPOLOGY; CYBERSPACE AND VIRTUAL REALITY; ETHICS: SCIENTIFIC; GENETICS AND GENETIC TECHNOLOGIES; REPRODUCTIVE TECHNOLOGIES

References and Further Reading

Davis-Floyd, Robbie, and Joseph Dumit. 1998. *Cyborg babies: From techno-sex to techno-tots.* New York: Routledge.

Downey, Gary Lee, and Joseph Dumit, eds. 1997. *Cyborgs and citadels: Anthropological interventions in emerging sciences, technologies and medicines.* Seattle: SAR/University of Washington Press. (Includes essays by Joseph Dumit, Deborah Heath, and Rayna Rapp.)

Forsythe, Diana. 2001. *Toward an anthropology of informatics: Ethnographic analyses of knowledge engineering and artificial intelligence.* Stanford, Calif.: Stanford University Press.

Gray, Christ Hables, ed., with Heidi J. Figueroa-Sarriera and Steven Mentor. 1995. *The cyborg handbook.* New York: Routledge.

Haraway, Donna. 1991. *Simians, cyborgs, and women: The reinvention of nature.* London: Free Association.

Hogle, Linda F. 1999. *Recovering the nation's body: Cultural memory, medicine, and the politics of redemption.* New Brunswick, N.J.: Rutgers University Press.

Layne, Linda, ed. 2000. *Transformative motherhood: On giving and getting in a consumer culture.* New York: New York University Press.

Martin, Emily. *Flexible bodies: Tracking immunity in America from the days of polio to the age of AIDS.* Boston: Beacon.

Rapp, Rayna, 2000. *Testing women, testing the fetus: The social impact of amniocentesis in America.* New York: Routledge.

Taussig, Karen-Sue. Forthcoming. *Just be ordinary: Normalizing the future through genetic research and practice.* Berkeley: University of California Press.

Traweek, Sharon. 1988. *Beamtimes and lifetimes: The world of high energy physicists.* Cambridge, Mass.: Harvard University Press.

Robbie Davis-Floyd

D

DANCE: Overview

The activity that is recognized as dancing in the West takes a number of different forms and can be found in a variety of different social contexts, covering the spectrum from high art to popular culture. In dance—as a performance art, as light entertainment, or as a leisure activity—the body is the primary instrument and means of expression. The word *dance,* however, must be used with caution. Anthropologists have found that the term *dance* is "essentially ethnocentric or culture specific" (Blacking, 1983: 89), being based on common concepts of dance in western cultures (Buckland, 1999). A number of societies have no generic word for *dance* as it is understood in the West but subsume similar kinds of movement activities under other categories, such as play, music, or worship. This point is exemplified by the work of pan-African dance ensembles such as Adzido, where drumming and dancing are inextricably linked. Some anthropologists (Kaeppler, 1991: 12) consider that in order to take a wider view of "structured movement systems" the term *human movement* should be used rather than *dance.* As this article is focused primarily on providing an overview of women's roles in western performance or art dance, however, the term *dance* is deemed appropriate.

History of Recording Dance

It is difficult to review dance as an art form because, unlike other arts such as painting, literature, or sculpture, a dance tradition does not leave behind it a large body of artifacts to be examined and reassessed by contemporary or future generations. As a performance art, dance has a transient quality: as it is seen, so it has gone. This makes the study of dance more elusive than that of literature or art. Although drama and music are also performance arts, they are more accessi-

ble to study than dance because a text or a score can be consulted and the work reconstructed or reinterpreted. No commonly accepted system of notation for recording or preserving dance exists, although there have been a number of notable attempts to generate a system of movement notation over the centuries (Guest, 1984). However, two systems developed in the twentieth century have been used to record western theater dance: the Benesh system of choreology, and Labanotation. The Benesh system was developed in the 1960s to record ballet and is used by the British Royal Ballet, among other classical companies. Labanotation was developed from a system devised by the dancer and theorist Rodolf Laban (1879–1958), who was also a major influence on central European modern dance. Modern dance choreographers such as Mary Wigman (1886–1973) in Europe and Doris Humphrey (1895–1958) in the United States had some of their dances recorded in Labanotation. The system has been used to notate and reconstruct many forms of dance: ballet, folk, modern dance, and nonwestern dance forms. The Dance Notation Bureau in New York was founded by Ann Hutchinson, among others, in 1940, with the express aim of advancing the art of dance through the use of a notation system.

Although dance history and dance aesthetics lag behind the analysis of other art forms, they too have developed within the context of the western humanist tradition of thought, and their discussions have been overwhelmingly directed toward the analysis of western theater art dance, which, until the 1930s, meant ballet. Ballet, as it is known today, is the codified system of movement formulated on the classical style or *danse d'école* which was developed by French, Italian, and English professional dancing masters and dancers over a long period beginning in the latter part of the seventeenth century. The form had its roots in the

French and Italian courts of the sixteenth century. As other dance genres have developed in the twentieth century, such as modern dance and, later, postmodern dance, the discussions have been widened to take account of shifts and breaks within and across the various dance genres.

It is also important to note that performance or art dance is not restricted to the West. Many societies in south Asia, east Asia, and southeast Asia have strong performance dance traditions that reach back farther in history than classical ballet. To provide a wider perspective, this article will also draw attention to the role of women in Indian classical dance and to the concerns of certain contemporary women dancers and choreographers from that tradition.

Contribution of Women

The history of western theater dance, from ballet to modern dance to postmodern dance, reveals that women have made considerable contributions to the development of dance, as performers, as choreographers, and as prime advocates in the institutional development and establishment of certain dance genres. For example, dancers and choreographers such as Isadora Duncan (1878–1927) and Ruth St. Denis (1879–1968) were a source of inspiration as well as a point of departure for dancers of the next generation, such as Martha Graham (1894–1991) and Doris Humphrey (1895–1958), who in turn were key figures in the formation and establishment of American modern dance from the late 1920s to the 1950s. It should be noted, however, that there were a number of other contributors to the movement who have been left out of the story of modern dance (see Graff, 1997). Once modern dance was established, it lost its avant-gardist edge, and it too became subject to dismantling just as ballet and the interpretive dance of St. Denis and Duncan had been before.

Although dance writers have noted the primacy of women in the formation and the early development of modern dance as dancers and choreographers, this has not generally been the case with regard to ballet. Until recently, histories of mainstream ballet focused primarily on women's contribution as performers, to the neglect of the other aspects indicated here. There are exceptions to this general overview. For example, Dame Marie Rambert (1888–1982) and Dame Ninette de Valois (b. 1898) were innovative figures in the development of British ballet. Both women had worked with Serge Diaghilev (1872–1929) whose Ballets Russes revolutionized and revitalized ballet in the early twentieth century. In 1931, with the assistance of Lillian Baylis (1874–1937), de Valois founded the Vic-Wells Ballet, which later became the Sadler Wells Ballet, and in 1956 she became the director of the Royal Ballet. Also in 1931, Ram-

bert, with her playwright husband, established the Ballet Club at the Mercury Theatre in London; the company was later renamed Ballet Rambert. Where de Valois had a talent for organization, Rambert's gifts lay in discovering and nurturing talents in dancers and choreographers. Most of the latter were men, with a few exceptions such as Andrée Howard (1910–1968). Thus the creative and organizational mantle of British ballet was passed to male choreographers and directors, with women retaining their traditional role as dancers.

Postmodern Dance

Postmodern dance began to emerge in the early 1960s in the United States as a reaction to what dancers such as Yvonne Rainer (b. 1934) and Trisha Brown (b. 1936), who were members of the Judson Dance Theater in New York (a collective dance venture that included artists, composers, and writers), perceived to be the failure of modern dance to fulfill its radical potential (Banes, 1987). Whereas modern dance was primarily a women's movement in its formative stage, postmodern dance was forged by both women and men. Rainer, however, was by far the most polemical of this group of choreographers and dancers, and her work, like that of a number of others, was influenced by the feminist concerns that began to come to the fore in the 1960s. Rainer used the term "post-modern" (as opposed to *postmodern*) to indicate that she was part of a generation that came after modern dance. There is some dispute among dance critics and historians as to whether the work of the Judson Dance Theater corresponds to what is now generally agreed to be postmodernism in the other arts (Jordan, 1992: 4–5). Although aesthetic postmodernism defies a fixed definition, it may be characterized by pastiche, irony, a mixing and matching of styles and genres, and a collapsing of the distinction between high art and popular culture (see Thomas, 1995: 14–20). Postmodern dance (the hyphen has now been dropped generally), like its predecessor, modern dance, constitutes a large body of diverse work from the 1960s to the 1980s, some of which appears to fit in more with the canons of modernism than postmodernism.

Unlike the United States, Great Britain did not have a strong tradition of contemporary or modern dance to react against in the 1960s. In the mid-1960s, "the Graham technique of contemporary dance became the first established alternative to ballet in Britain" (Jordan, 1992: 1) as a result of the creation of the London School of Contemporary Dance (1966) and the London Contemporary Dance Theatre (1967) and the shift of direction of Ballet Rambert to a contemporary dance company. What is commonly thought of as postmodern dance in the United States and Canada resonates with experimental work or *new dance* in the United Kingdom, which emerged in the late 1970s and 1980s. In its early stages the majority of new dance choreographers and performers were women (see Adair, 1992: 182–198). One of the forces of this alternative dance movement in the United Kingdom was the X6 Collective (1976–1980), founded by Jacky Lansley, Maedée Duprès, Emilyn Claid, Mary Prestige, and Fergus Early. Concerned with working in new ways, the Collective was influenced by the politics of feminism and western Marxism. The X6 Collective founded *New Dance* magazine to explore alternative attitudes toward dance and social issues. Like postmodern dancers, New Dance choreographers such as X6 abandoned traditional ideas of technique, dance clothes, and the star image of the choreographer and performer in favor of different collective ways of working.

Feminist and Cultural Influences

The influence of feminist theory and cultural studies on dance research since the mid-1980s has contributed to a critical reappraisal of the place of women in the tradition of classical ballet, and a reevaluation of the influence of feminism on the founders of modern dance and on postmodern or new dance (see Adair, 1992; Banes, 1998; and Manning, 1993). Central to these developments in dance research has been a consideration of the ways in which women have been represented in dance through their bodies (Cooper Albright, 1997; Daly, 1995). Several leading ballet dancers—Gelsey Kirkland—(b. 1952) for example, call attention to the ways in which women's bodies in ballet were disciplined and subjugated to the demands of the system and choreographers' concerns (Kirkland, 1987). Other choreographers, such as Pina Bausch (b. 1940), challenge and explore the conventions and contradictions of male-female sexuality in dance and in culture.

Black dancers and choreographers in general, and especially black women, have had to struggle to achieve a place in the western dance canon, particularly in ballet (see Burt, 1998; Emery, 1988). Some black dance companies seek to combine the possibilities of contemporary dance and African dance traditions. For example, the contemporary choreographer Jowole Willa Jo Zollar, through her all-female company Urban Bush Women, seeks to challenge the conventions of the western aesthetic of the female dancing body by combining her African heritage with her American experience (Cooper Albright, 1997, 150–217).

As with classical ballet in the West, the choreography, the teaching, and the production of classical Indian dance have traditionally been controlled by men. The influence of feminist perspectives is very recent among Indian classical dancers. Manjusri Chaki-Sircar, a contemporary Indian dancer, sees the history of classical Indian dance as a repressive system which has exploited women (Hanna, 1993: 119, 132). She draws on and integrates a number of styles of Indian classical dance, martial arts, and yoga poses, incorporating the traditional footwork of classical dance but rejecting the symmetry and the centering of the body. In the brochure of her Dancers' Guild of Calcutta, Chaki-Sircar states: "The contemporary dancer here wishes to develop an ethos that questions the traditional one of Brahmanic patriarchy creed so deeply enmeshed in Shastric classicism" (Hanna, 1993: 119).

Another contemporary choreographer, Shobhana Jeyasingh, has gained acclaim for her work in the United Kingdom. She challenges the traditional divide in dance between Ease and West. Jeyasingh collaborates with contemporary western composers such as Michael Nyman and combines Bharatha Natyam technique with the techniques of contemporary dance, intentionally blurring the boundaries between the forms (Roy, 1997: 68–86).

See Also

DANCE: CHOREOGRAPHY; DANCE: CLASSICAL; DANCE: MODERN; DRUMMING; POSTMODERNISM: LITERARY THEORY

References and Further Reading

Adair, Christy. 1992. *Women and dance: Sylphs and sirens.* London: Macmillan.

Banes, S. 1988. *Dancing women: Female bodies on stage.* London: Routledge.

———. 1987. *Terpsichore in sneakers: Post-modern dance.* Boston: Houghton Mifflin.

Blacking, John. 1983. Movement and meaning: Dance in social anthropological perspective. *Dance Research* 1 (Spring: 1): 89–99.

Buckland, T. J., ed. 1999. *Dance in the field.* Basingstoke: Macmillan.

Burt, R. 1998. *Alien bodies: Representations of modernity, "race" and nation in early modern dance.* London: Routledge.

Cooper Albright, A. 1997. *Choreography difference: The body and identity in contemporary dance.* Hanover, N.H.: University Press of New England.

Daly, A. 1995. *Done into dance: Isadora Duncan in America.* Bloomington: Indiana University Press.

Emery, Lynne Fauley. 1988. *Black dance from 1619 to today,* 2nd ed. London: Dance Books.

Graff, E. 1997. *Stepping left: Dance and politics in New York City, 1928–1942.* Durham, N.C.: Duke University Press.

Guest, Ann Hutchinson. 1984. *Dance notation: The process of recording movement on paper.* London: Dance Books.

Hanna, Judith Lynne. 1993. Classical Indian dance and women's status. In H. Thomas, ed., *Dance, gender and cultures.* Basingstoke: Macmillan.

Jordan, Stephanie. 1992. *Striding out.* London: Dance Books.

Kaeppler, Adrienne. 1991. American approaches to the study of dance. *Yearbook of Traditional Music* 23: 11–21.

Kirkland, Gelsey, with Greg Lawrence. 1987. *Dancing on my grave.* New York: Jove.

Manning, S.A. 1993. *Ecstacy and the demon: Feminism and nationalism in the dances of Mary Wigman.* Berkeley: University of California Press.

Roy, S. 1997. Dirt, noise, traffic: Contemporary Indian dance in the western city: Modernity, ethnicity and hybridity. In H. Thomas, ed., *Dance in the city,* 68–87. Basingstoke: Macmillan.

Thomas, Helen. 1995. *Dance, modernity and culture: Explorations in the sociology of dance.* London: Routledge.

Helen Thomas

DANCE: Choreography

In western dance, women's contributions to choreography have varied according to the form. Modern dance, from the beginning a genre concerned largely with the expression of experience and emotion, was pioneered largely by female artists. Ballet, a form stressing line and bursts of explosive energy, has historically been choreographed and directed by males. This dichotomy may account for the aesthetic and philosophical division between the two; or perhaps the reverse is true and the differences explain why women have been ascendant in some areas, men in others.

Ballet

Traditionally, women have gained influence in ballet as performers, with a notable few rising to prominence in choreography or as company directors. Several have guided the development of choreography as company directors with power to select and produce the work of others. Among these have been Lucia Chase (1907–1986), codirector of the American Ballet Theater from 1945 to 1980; Marie Rambert (1888–1982), who directed the Ballet Rambert in London from 1931 until her death; and the Cuban ballerina Alicia Alonso (b. 1921), who, in the 1940s, began a long career as choreographer and ballet director when she founded the company now called the Ballet Nacional de Cuba.

Those considered significant choreographers as well as directors include Ninette de Valois (b. 1898), the architect of London's Royal Ballet. She headed the company from 1931 to 1963 and established the standard for ballet in Britain. The Swedish choreographer Birgit Cullberg (1908–1999) directed the Cullberg Ballet from 1967 to 1981 and pioneered the fusion of classical dance with modern that today pervades the form.

Other important artists include Bronislava Nijinksa (1891–1972), who experimented with a modernist aesthetic in the 1920s, creating *Les Noces* and *Les Biches* (called the first feminist ballet) for Diaghilev's Ballets Russes; and Agnes de Mille (1905–1993), whose work blended classical dancing with American rhythms. Her choreography for the Broadway musical *Oklahoma!* in 1943 used dancing to further the plot, a development that changed the nature of musical theater.

Modern Dance

Isadora Duncan (1878–1927) and Ruth St. Denis (1880–1968), two U.S. dancers working separately during the first decade of the twentieth century, laid the foundation for modern dance. Duncan was seeking natural ways of moving, challenging tradition not only in dance but also in sexual mores, clothing, and women's roles. St. Denis's influence was seen in the development, with her husband Ted Shawn, of Denishawn, a school and company that, from 1915 to 1930, provided a training ground for the next generation of modern dancers. Whereas Duncan's impact stemmed from her life and philophical writings, St. Denis is credited with developing a nonclassical touring company and an approach to dance education that developed the mind as well as the body.

Doris Humphrey (1895–1958) and Martha Graham (1894–1991), the revolutionary choreographers of the next generation, were students of St. Denis and Shawn; both rebelled against the eclecticism of the Denishawn repertoire. Each experimented with developing an American form of dance and sought ways of moving that expressed life in contemporary times. Graham worked with the contraction and release of breathing that carried her into powerful, emotion-packed movement. Humphrey experimented with gravity to devise a theory and style based on fall and recovery. Though rivals, these two created movement that reveals weight and effort and built modern dance into a credo of individualism and social relevance, a point of view that prevails today.

Other notable choreographers of the time included Mary Wigman (1886–1973), a German artist of somber intensity whose work often portrayed the primitive drives that exist in civilized people; and her protégée, Hanya Holm (1898–1992), who, being sent to the United States in 1931, developed the Wigman style for American bodies and temperaments. During the 1940s, Katherine Dunham (b. 1912) and Pearl Primus (1919–1994) became important influences. They were black, university-trained anthropologists, as well as choreographers, and each worked with African, Caribbean, and African-American themes and set the stage for today's black dance.

Since the 1960s, choreographic authority in the field has shifted to male artists, although some women do stand out. Yvonne Rainer (b. 1934) and Trisha Brown (b. 1936) were leaders in the Judson group, which pioneered the pedestrian, task-oriented choreography of the 1960s. Pina Bausch (b. 1940) of Germany and Meredith Monk (b. 1943) and Kei Takei (b. 1946) in the United States are important for their imagistic movement-theater works. Twyla Tharp (b. 1941) has successfully blended high and popular art through an inventive fusion of styles. Today her work is produced by both ballet and modern dance companies.

See Also

DANCE: OVERVIEW; DANCE: CLASSICAL; DANCE: MODERN

References and Further Reading

Adair, Christy. 1992. *Women and dance.* New York: New York University Press.
Anderson, Jack. 1992. *Ballet and modern dance: A concise history.* Princeton, N.J.: Princeton Book.

Jan van Dyke

DANCE: Classical

In its general sense, the term *classical* may be used to describe a variety of dance activities in a wide range of historical, geographic, and cultural contexts. For example, the dance of ancient Greece and its aesthetic legacy in the work of Isadora Duncan are considered classical. Even modern dance works that emphasize structure, clarity of spatial design, and dance itself over expressive content may be described as classical in their values. The term is also applied to certain forms of dance from south Asia, but its most popular usage is in relation to ballet. Although ballet is a broad genre that embraces styles such as romantic and modern, which in a strict sense can be distinguished from classical, the term *classical* tends to be applied to popular concepts of all styles of ballet.

Women as Dancers and as Creators of Dance

Dance is one of the few art forms where women, as executants, have far outnumbered men. Although dance was initially a male art form, soon after its professionalization ballerinas took center stage, with the first appearing in 1681. Key figures in the public perception of its history include Marie Sall and Marie Camargo in the eighteenth century; romantic-era dancers such as Marie Taglioni and Fanny Elssler, whose names became household words; the cult figures of Russia's golden age of ballet in the late nineteenth century; the mythologized Anna Pavlova; Britain's Margot Fonteyn and the contemporary athletes of Europe, North America, and the Far East. Spreading across Europe from its origins in France and Italy, the art form today is practiced and, through modern media, disseminated to a worldwide audience. Codified syllabi and their concomitant performance values, traditions, and differentiation between the training of the male and female dancer now form the international basis of the dancer's experience. Since the 1960s male dancers have tended to achieve high, even glamorous, status; but wherever ballet is performed, it is still synonymous with women.

However, women's contribution as creators or directors has been less well recorded in historiography. Before the twentieth century the ballerina often choreographed her own solos, but in public documentation this work was subsumed under the name of the ballet master. In the twentieth century Bronislava Nijinska, best known for her work with the Ballets Russes, was a rare exception as a named choreographer. There were others—among them Andre Howard for the Ballet Rambert—but some of their names are now lost. More prominent were women such as Ninette de Valois (Royal Ballet), Marie Rambert (Ballet Rambert), and Lucia Chase (American Ballet Theater), who directed large companies; some also choreographed or encouraged the creative endeavors of others. However, it is rare, either historically or in contemporary theater, for women to hold key positions of authority or power. Generally, women have become known through the role of performing muse of a male creator.

Feminist Perspectives on Ballet

This image has provided a fruitful source of investigation for feminist scholarship, but the reputation of classical ballet as elite or specialized practice and the ephemeral nature of dance in general have hindered the extensive scrutiny accorded to other forms of art or popular culture. As the body is the prime site for the construction of gender, dance offers a rewarding field for analysis, but the relationship between ballet and feminism has been an uneasy one. The narratives of nineteenth-century classics such as *Giselle* (Perrot/Coralli, 1841) and *Swan Lake* (Petipa/Ivanov, 1895) are seen to support the dichotomous categories of women's perceived essential nature as chaste or impure, good or evil. A similar duality is seen in the ballerina and the members of the corps de ballet, which rarely has a place in historiography. By the nature of the codified vocabulary itself—which is based on, among other key elements, turnout and full exposure of the body to the audience—the dancer has been seen as femininity objectified, the embodiment of patriarchal ideology (Daly, 1987/1988; Adair, 1992). For example, it is argued that the pas de deux, for the ballerina and her lead male partner, embodies the traditional attributes of femininity and masculinity. She appears to be supported, manipulated, by him; he displays her to the spectator. Concealing her strength, she gives the appearance of fragility and moves within her own kinesphere, the private space around her body. In contrast, he demonstrates his strength and power with soaring virtuosic leaps across the public space of the stage.

Feminist writing has drawn on critical and cultural theories from film studies, semiotics, or psychoanalysis, thus adding new perspectives to the symbolic construction of women in ballet. While these methodological tools have enhanced both dance and feminist scholarship, the human agency of the dancer and her human identity have tended to be lost. This difficulty is discussed by Aalten (1995), who, using her own experience as a case study, explores the problematic nature of the ballerina in relation to the gender ideologies of ballet. It is a challenge for women's studies to explore the personal and creative contribution of women in classical ballet without losing sight of their function in a patriarchal society.

See Also

DANCE: OVERVIEW; DANCE: CHOREOGRAPHY; DANCE: MODERN; DANCE: SOUTH ASIA

References and Further Reading

Aalten, Anna. 1995. Femininity as performance/performing femininity: Constructing the body of the ballerina. *Border tensions: Dance and discourse,* 118. Guildford: University of Surrey.

Adair, Christy. 1992. *Women and dance: Sylphs and sirens.* London: Macmillan.

Banes, Sally. 1998. *Dancing women: Female bodies on stage.* London: Routledge.

Carter, Alexandra. 1999. Dying swan or sitting duck? A critical reflection on feminist gazes at ballet. *Performance Research* 4(3): 9198.

Daly, Ann. 1987/1988. Classical ballet: A discourse of difference. *Women and Performance* (2) 5767.

Foster, Susan Leigh, ed. 1995. The ballerina's phallic pointe. *Corporealities.* London: Routledge.

Alexandra Carter

DANCE: Modern

Although modern dance does not constitute a single system or style of dancing, it can be defined in general as western performance art dance that is not founded on the principles of the European tradition of ballet, romantic or interpretive dance, or various forms of "popular" dance entertainment (Thomas, 1995). Women were dominant in the foundation of modern dance in the first decade of the twentieth century and in its development. Like modernism in the other arts, modern dance has taken on a variety of "-isms": expressionism, cubism, absolutism, and so on (Martin, 1965). Its history, similarly, has been characterized by rapid cyclical changes: "revolution to institution; institution to revolution" (Banes, 1980: 5). As modern dance became established in the 1950s, a number of men became well-known choreographers. However, it was a woman, Martha Graham, whose name became almost synonymous with the term *modern dance.*

Historical Background

The history of modern dance is best understood as a "point of view" (Martin, 1965: 20) that was pioneered and developed in the late 1920s and 1930s through the highly individual work of iconclasts: Martha Graham (1894–1991); Doris Humphrey (1895–1958) and her partner, Charles Weidman (1901–1975); and Helen Tamiris (1905–1966) in the United States. Although modern dance is generally associated with the United States, a similar form—central European modern dance—evolved independently in Germany ten years earlier through the work of Mary Wigman (1886–1973), Harold Kreutzberg (1902–1968), and Kurt Jooss (1905–1978).

Wigman was a central figure in central European modern dance for fifty years. She established branches of her school in Germany in the 1920s, and the Wigman New York School was set up in New York in 1931 with her former student Hanya Holm (1898–1992) as the principal. The influence of central European modern dance was curtailed by the rise of the Nazi movement and World War II. Wigman did not publicly detach herself from the Nazi regime in Germany in the 1930s. In light of the growing opposition in the United States to fascism in Europe, Holm came to see Wigman's form of expressionist dance, which was bound up with the idea of humanity and its fate, as inappropriate for U.S. dancers. In 1936, she set up her own school and company and evolved her own style. Holm became one of the "big four" of U.S. modern dance when she, along with Graham, Humphrey, and Weidman, was invited to participate in the Bennington College School of the Dance in the 1930s (Lloyd, [1949] 1974).

Graham, Tamiris, and other modern dancers worked to create new dance forms that reflected the twentieth-century urban scene in the United States. Following Loie Fuller (1862–1928), Isadora Duncan (1878–1927), and Ruth St. Denis (1879–1968), they set out to establish modern dance as an art form in its own right. They abandoned the received ideas and images of western theatrical dance of the day and, like those earlier revolutionaries, choreographed and performed their own images. This contrasted with the traditional convention whereby the ballet master and choreographer created the dance for the female dancer.

Dance as "Significant Movement"

Fuller, Duncan, and St. Denis had been instrumental in helping to promote new attitudes toward women's bodies and in freeing the body of the modern dancer from the constraints of pointe shoes and the traditional attire of the female ballet dancer. Duncan and St. Denis relied on music and drew their inspiration from the past cultures of Greece and Asia, respectively. Graham, Humphrey, and Tamiris discarded the romantic or interpretive tradition of dance that had come through Duncan and St. Denis. They turned inward to their own bodies to discover the first principles of dance, which they found in "significant movement," that is, movement expressing an idea or an emotion. They insisted that movement take precedence over all other elements of theatrical performance.

Modern dance began by rejecting aesthetic formalism. The various techniques that emerged in its name were created out of the requirements of the individual choreographers. This is in contrast to ballet, in which the choreographer works with an impersonal, abstract, prescribed technical system that has evolved for four hundred years (Banes, 1980).

Some modern dancers, such as Tamiris and the left-wing dancers who performed under the auspices of the Workers' Dance League (formed in 1932), stressed that politics and art are inseparable and that dance should make a social comment. The New Dance Group (formed in 1932 by members of the Wigman New York School) wanted dance to be a vehicle for the masses, not just for themselves as artists. While the left-wing dancers performed for mass audiences in trade union halls, Humphrey and Graham, whose eyes were firmly set on establishing modern dance as a serious art form, generally performed for small, dedicated audiences. The Workers' Dance League provided the first challenge to the emerging modern dance establishment (Lloyd, 1974). Other performers, such as Katherine Dunham (b. 1912) and Pearl Primus (1919–1994), attempted to create a space for black performers by fusing black dance and modern dance.

A number of the early figures in the second generation of modern dance, such as José Limon (1908–1972), Anna Sokolow (b. 1915), Sophie Maslow (b. 1910?), Jane Dudley (b. 1912), Erick Hawkins (1917–1994), and Merce Cunningham (b. 1919), developed their own choreography while performing in the companies of the big four, contributing further to the diversity of modern dance.

By the 1950s, however, the aesthetics of modern dance had become established in concert halls and colleges and universities in the United States. With the exception of Graham, most of the acknowledged choreographers of the next generation were men, and that has continued to the present. Graham's technique has become almost as established as that of ballet.

This orthodoxy was challenged by a few modern dancers, such as Cunningham and Ann Halprin (b. 1920); and such challenges influenced the subsequent emergence of what came to be called postmodern dance in the 1960s. Postmodern dance has been characterized by difference and heterogeneity. A significant number of postmodern innovators have been women, such as Yvonne Rainer (b. 1934), Simone Forti (b. 1935), Trisha Brown (b. 1936), Deborah Hay (b. 1941), Lucinda Childs (b. 1940), and Twyla Tharp (b. 1941).

See Also

DANCE: OVERVIEW; DANCE: CHOREOGRAPHY; DANCE: CLASSICAL; DANCE: SOUTH ASIA

References and Further Reading

Banes, Sally. 1980. *Terpsichore in sneakers: Post-modern dance.* Boston: Houghton Mifflin.

Lloyd, Margaret. 1974. *Borzoi book of modern dance.* New York: Dance Horizons. (Originally published 1949.)

Martin, John. 1965. *The modern dance.* New York: Dance Horizons. (Originally published 1933.)

Thomas, Helen. 1995. *Dance, modernity and culture: Explorations in the sociology of dance.* London: Routledge.

Helen Thomas

DANCE: South Asia

India has seven main classical styles: bharatha natyam, kuchipudi, mohini attam, and kathakali from the south and the kathak, manipuri, and odissi styles from the north. Apart from these classical forms, there are hundreds of folk styles and tribal dance forms. Each state in India has its own folk dances—for example, tamasha in Maharashtra, bhangra in Punjab, and ottamthullal in Kerala.

The Classical Styles

Classical dance styles in India are based on the theoretical treatise *Natya Sastra* (second century B.C.E to third century C.E)—in Sanskrit, "the theory of theater." Some styles use later commentaries and discussions on *Natya Sastra,* such as the *Abhinaya Darpana.* All the classical styles are mythological in their narrative content and use the rich tapestry of the stories of gods and demons from Hindu mythology.

The major performers in most styles, with the exception of kathakali, are female. However, the artists who have revived most of the styles and are the "gurus" of many of these performers are males, usually descended from the original performing and teaching lineage associated with a particular style. For example, Vempati Chinna Satyam, who is credited with the revival of kuchipudi, belongs to the family of Brahmans originally chosen many generations ago by Siddhendra Yogi to perform kuchipudi. Although his female students, such as Sobha Naidu, have been the instruments of his genius, it is interesting to note that his son, Vempati Ravi Shankar, is the "chosen" one to carry on his lineage.

Almost all styles of Indian dance have significant gender issues involved in their transition from temple dances into self-conscious "art" modes. The exceptions are kathak and mohini attam, which were court dance styles.

Of all the styles of dance, bharatha natyam is the most popular. It was originally practiced by devadasis, or temple dancers, in the region now predominantly covered by the state of Tamil Nadu. During the British rule in India, the devadasi system was outlawed, as it was narrowly seen as a system of prostitution. It was Rukmini Devi Arundale, a highly respectable Brahman woman, who spearheaded a revival of bharatha natyam. She worked with Anna Pavlova and brought back to the Indian style some of the ensemble techniques and slickness of western ballet styles. She established "Kalakshetra" in Madras, which is one of the major centers of bharatha natyam in India. This revival was very conscious of respectability. The dance form was now in the hands of middle-class, urban Brahman girls, and its devadasi origins were discussed and acknowledged only in a historical context.

Kuchipudi was originally practiced by male Brahmans in the village of Kuchipudi in Andhra Pradesh. Kuchipudi derived from dance drama and, hence, gives equal importance to pure dance (*nritta*) and to emotional and narrative

exposition (*abhinaya*). It differed from kathakali in that the female roles were predominant—for example, the role of Satyabhama. The male dancers dressed as women; this exaggerated the sensuousness of the form. Men had more freedom to be explicit in their erotic sentiments than females performing the same narratives in other styles. Some of the ribald humor in the style derived from the use of transvestite characters, such as Madhava-Madhavi in the famous traditional dance drama "Bhamakalapam." In its evolution from an all-male style to one that has both a male and a female dance vocabulary, kuchipudi has an interesting history. In the 1960s, Vempati Chinna Satyam left the village and brought this form to Madras, the center for dance in south India. He opened up the style to women, and some of his early students, such as Yamini Krishnamurthy, were highly skilled performers who popularized kuchipudi. When women first began performing the style, there was much criticism of its untempered, "vulgar" sexuality. Since then, Satyam's choreography has deliberately moved away from the modes still practiced in the village of Kuchipudi to create a style that is urban and middle-class in its sophisticated restraint. Satyam has also turned the tables by casting female dancers in male roles—for example, the role of Krishna or even that of the fiery male god Siva. He has developed a strong male vocabulary, which was missing in the form's original emphasis on female roles. Vempati Chinna Satyam's center in Madras, the Kuchipudi Art Academy, remains the main training institute for this style.

Kathakali is a very theatrical dance style with a highly evolved, complex movement vocabulary. It was an exclusively male style, but the state of Kerala now has an all-female kathakali dance company. The training is long, rigorous, and physically demanding; it includes many massage techniques, and some argue that these are not safe for a woman's body. Women are still a rarity in kathakali.

Lesser known dance forms include chau, a vigorous all-male form from the northeast of India, which has been taken up by a significant number of female exponents.

The "New Dance" Movement

In the growing movement for "new dance" in India, some dancers and choreographers use their formidable knowledge of the traditional forms to create a more modern dance vocabulary. Foremost in this endeavor in India is Chandralekha. One of the first dancers to take this path, Chandralekha has, for thirty years, created work, such as "Praana" and "Angika," that has challenged some of the traditional parameters of classical styles. She fought a hard and often lonely battle for a contemporary voice in Indian dance, a movement away from the repetitive mythological narratives and toward something more integral and essential to a modern Indian. Her efforts gained more recognition overseas than in India.

Conclusion

Although Indian dance has a large number of male performers, it is dominated by female practitioners. Nevertheless, in terms of their influence on the choreographic evolution of the various styles, the male "gurus" of Indian dance are still more powerful than the women. The various "schools" of any traditional dance style are still controlled by men, usually from families that have been practicing the art forms for several generations. Exceptions—such as Padma Subramaniam, who has used her research of theoretical texts to transform Bharatha Natyam and establish her own school of dance, which she calls Bhaaratha Natyam or the dance of India ("Bhaarath")—are becoming more common.

Indian forms have influenced dance forms elsewhere in south Asia. Bharatha Natyam is prevalent in Sri Lanka, particularly among the Tamils. Kandyan dancing takes various forms, including some male forms. In Bangladesh, variations of the styles taught in Shantiniketan in West Bengal and other forms, such as Kathak and Bharatha Natyam, are practiced.

See Also

DANCE: OVERVIEW; DANCE: CHOREOGRAPHY; DANCE: MODERN; HINDUISM; MUSIC: SOUTH ASIA

References and Further Reading
Bharucha, Rustom. 1995. *Chandralekha—Woman dance resistance.* New Delhi: Indus/HarperCollins.
Devi, Ragni. 1953. *Dances of India.* Calcutta: Gupta.
Ghosh, Manomohan, trans. 1975. *Nandikesvara's Abinaya darpana: A manual of gesture and posture used in ancient Indian dance and drama.* 3rd. ed. Calcutta: Manisha Granthalaya.
Kismore, B.R. 1998. *Dances of India.* Surrey, Canada: Asian.
Natyasatra. 1996. Trans. Adya Rangacharga. Columbus, Ohio: Coronet. (This work, attributed to the legendary Bharatha Muni, is also available in other translations and in the original Sanskrit.)
Note: Marg Publications, Mumbai: (Bombay), has issued a series of books on Indian dance.

Padma Menon

DARWINISM

See BIOLOGICAL DETERMINISM; and EVOLUTION.

DATING

See COURTSHIP.

DAUGHTER

The kin term *daughter* refers to female offspring of biological genitors, although the relationship of daughter to parent often connotes social obligations—filial respect and responsibility for the emotional and financial needs of parents. Although not all women become sisters, wives, mothers, or grandmothers, all women are, or once were, daughters. The rights and obligations common to the role are various, starting in earliest childhood, when parents typically begin investing in children, both economically and in terms of training for adulthood. Daughters in many societies are household helpers, providing female household members with invaluable assistance in economic tasks and, often, in extradomestic responsibilities as well. A common assignment for daughters is the care of younger siblings, which serves to socialize young women for future motherhood. Another common form of parental investment in daughters is dowry, which is actually a woman's inheritance, received at the time of marriage.

Rites of Passage for Daughters

The period of adolescence is often accompanied by initiation rites or rites of passage for daughters, which are prerequisites for the passage into adulthood. In industrialized societies the educational system, the military, and marriage ceremonies normally serve this function, but many nonindustrialized societies stage coming-of-age rituals specifically for this purpose. Among the Apache, the *nai'es,* the ritual of "getting her ready" for adulthood, fertility, and motherhood (also known as the sunrise dance) is a demanding coming-of-age rite for girls that incorporates the entire community and celebrates the curing powers of this "changing woman" (Basso, 1970). The elima, or puberty ceremony, for girls among the Mbuti of Zaire is, similarly, an announcement of a girl's readiness for motherhood and lasts from one to two months (Turnbull, 1960). Victor Turner (1967) speaks of adolescence as a liminal phase—that is, an ambiguous stage between the clearly demarcated periods of childhood and adulthood. Coming-of-age rituals usher the individual from one phase to the next and often mark the beginnings of sexual activity.

Preference for Male Offspring

In the West, adolescence for both genders is generally much more protracted than in most other societies, in part because the interval of schooling is correspondingly prolonged. In some societies daughters are perceived as more costly than sons. In societies with patrilocal residence rules, a daughter goes to live with her in-laws upon marriage, and parents often justify the harsher treatment of daughters relative to sons with the rationale that they are raising their daughters for someone else—that is, for a future husband's family. Patrilineal societies, those in which descent is organized through the father's line, take this even further, because the daughter's children will belong to her husband's patrilineage and not to her natal kin group. This fact serves as a disincentive to treat female children as equal to male children, who will remain with the family of origin. Traditional Chinese, Indian, and Islamic societies organized kinship, descent, and postmarital residence rules in this manner. A further justification for the preference for sons over daughters in traditional China and India was that daughters, unlike sons, could not perform funerary rites for parents.

Female infanticide, the killing of female children, and selective neglect, the withholding of food or other necessities of life, are extreme examples of the outcome of the tendency to favor sons over daughters. In India, the high cost of dowries also increases pressure on parents to terminate pregnancies selectively with the aid of amniocentesis testing; in adulthood, a new bride may be an object of abuse by her husband's family, sometimes to the point of death, because of an insufficient dowry.

See Also

ADOLESCENCE; DOWRY AND BRIDEPRICE; FAMILY: RELIGIOUS AND LEGAL SYSTEMS, *specific regions;* FEMICIDE; GENDER CONSTRUCTIONS IN THE FAMILY; GIRL CHILD; INFANTICIDE; INITIATION RITES; SISTER

References and Further Reading

Basso, Keith. 1970. *The Cibecue Apache.* New York: Holt, Rinehart and Winston.

Turnbull, Colin. 1960. The elima: A premarital festival among the BaMbuti Pygmies. *Zaire* 14: 175–192.

Turner, Victor. 1967. *The forest of symbols.* Ithaca, N.Y.: Cornell University Press.

Maria Ramona Hart

DAWN MOVEMENT

DAWN—Development Alternatives with Women for a New Era—is an expanding network of women, researchers, and activists from the economic "South" (Latin America, the Caribbean, Africa, Asia, and the Pacific Islands). The network promotes alternative approaches to development as well as stimulating the building of coalitions and platforms for articulating the perspectives of poor women from these regions. An analysis (Jain, 1983) of the impact of development on poor women found that whatever the region and whatever the thrust of a project, it seemed to worsen poor women's position and simultaneously deepen the crisis in that locality. This paper was circulated to individual women who had been participating in international forums for development as feminists, who were receptive to the findings and enthusiastically translated this analysis into a framework for dissemination. Thus was born the first meeting of women that converted itself into the DAWN network. Following this initial meeting in Bangalore, India, in August 1984, on the eve of the Third United Nations Conference on Women, the network prepared a platform document that was used as the basis of a series of panels and workshops at the NGO (nongovernmental organization) Forum in Nairobi in 1985. The network was formally launched the following year in Rio de Janeiro, where a secretariat was established.

As a feminist organization, DAWN has consciously avoided building up a formal structure or establishing a permanent secretariat or location. Thus it was located in India at its inception in August 1984, but the secretariat—the focal point—shifted to Latin America (Rio de Janeiro, Brazil) after the UN World Conference on Women, held in Nairobi in 1985. In 1990 the focal point shifted again, this time to the Caribbean (Barbados). Since 1998, DAWN has been based in Fiji.

DAWN's specific contribution to the achievement of a model of development that is people-centered, holistic, and sustainable, and that empowers women, has been to serve as a catalyst for debates on key developmental issues. To provide a voice for women of the developing world, DAWN works in a consultative role to create platform documents and carry them to national, subnational, regional, and international forums. Currently the network has approximately four hundred members. It generates its activities through regional focal points, usually individuals located in already established institutions who are interested in DAWN's activities and willing to take responsibility for them.

In seeking paradigms for development, DAWN's aim is to develop a framework based on an analysis of the issues from the perspective of women in the "South." DAWN's analysis attempts to reflect the diversity of regional experiences and to relate the experience of women at the microlevel of the household and community to an understanding of macroeconomic policies and global trends.

The women who participate in DAWN believe that locating analysis and affirmative action in particular political contexts is crucial to their success. Thus, DAWN participates in world coalitions of women, whether on issues of the environment, health, employment, leadership, or any other matters related to justice and peace.

Through a process of consultation, DAWN developed a platform document (Sen and Grown, 1987) that was offered for discussion in several panels at Nairobi. In this document, a shift was made in frameworks of development analysis, particularly in relation to poor women. The key innovative element of this shift was that it located the "woman issue" in the context of macrocrises, differentiated according to region—for example, food in Africa, debt in Latin America, cultural cross fire in the Arabic region, and poverty and unemployment in Asia.

DAWN has developed other platform documents, which sometimes evolve into books (for example, Correa, 1994), in response to global discourse on specific subjects such as the environment, population, social policy, and global economic management. DAWN also reflects the perspectives of, and advocates on behalf of, poor women of the "South" through participation in numerous forums across the globe, including UN structures and the preparatory committees for world conferences, as well as the national and regional committees for such events.

In its quest to substantiate feminism, DAWN has hesitated to define feminism or to build any single model, as the movement is continually evolving, acting as a receptacle for ideas from its constituency and recycling these ideas. One idea that has persisted, however, is sustaining a method and process that will allow space for evolution, for accommodating difference, for converging and dispersing, for engaging in dialogue and collective decision making. Platforms are built on issues that cut across differences and on viewpoints or quests that seem to echo widespread anxiety or an inspiration. This approach—echoing a widespread common concern and building that concern into papers and books for joint advocacy—has continued to be an underlying pattern and one ethic of DAWN's work.

A second ethic that runs through DAWN's quest for understanding is that poor women, no less than men, are capable, creative, and thoughtful, and that development needs to spring from these women; or, in more objective terms, that poverty does not mean ignorance or incapacity.

A third ethic is the rejection of dichotomies, such as those between research and action, between intellect and practice (Jain, 1993), between ethics and development, and

between economic and social categories that impinge on the human being.

The current work of DAWN includes responding with alternative economic frameworks to the general disillusionment with global management, to widespread distress among poor nations and poor people, and to widespread doubts about the efficacy of the international financial institutions.

See Also

DEVELOPMENT: OVERVIEW; DEVELOPMENT, *specific regions;* ECONOMY: OVERVIEW; POVERTY

References and Further Reading

Correa, Sonia, in collaboration with Rebecca Reichmann. 1994. *Population and reproductive rights: Feminist perspectives from the south.* London: Zed.

Jain, Devaki. 1992. Can we have a women's agenda for global development. Keynote address at Five Years after Nairobi Conference, 1990. *Development: Journal of the Society for International Development.* Rome: SID.

———. 1983. Development as if women mattered; or, Can women build a new paradigm? Lecture given at OECD/ DAC meeting, Paris.

———. 1993. The leadership gap: A challenge to feminists. Address to the Sixth National Conference of the Indian Association for Women's Studies, New Delhi.

Sen, Gita, and Caren Grown. 1987. *Development, crises and alternative visions: Third world women's perspectives.* New York: Monthly Review.

Wiltshire, Rosina. 1992. *Environment and development: Grass roots women's perspectives.* Barbados: DAWN.

Devaki Jain

DAY CARE

See CHILD CARE.

DEATH

Feminists have written a great deal about death. For example, they have studied infant and child mortality and maternal death, death in refugee camps, wars, "bride burning" in India and elsewhere, starvation, violence of everyday life, stalking and death threats, rates of breast and cervical cancer, septic abortions around the world, and the spread of HIV.

Women, in general, are less likely than men to romanticize death in war. Many women and children die as a corollary of wars, and the deaths of boys and men in war often have catastrophic effects on women and children.

Women are the chief caregivers for the sick and dying; they cook and help feed, clean, and monitor those in their care, often in addition to their other work. In western countries, the responsibility for taking care of ill and dying relatives often falls on single women, who are thought to have the time for it.

Mourning

In many religions and societies women wash and watch over a body until burial and are active in mourning rituals. Often death rituals differ for women and men. For example, in the Belize Black Caribs religion (a composite of African, Amerindian, and Roman Catholic elements) traditionally women have done the mourning while men and children do not formally mourn. In Black Caribs communities (where women are the religious leaders), as well as in many other groups, death rituals involve much food preparation by female kin and neighbors.

Implications of Death

Death, the "great leveler," is of crucial importance to religions that preach a dualistic values: self-denial in the here and now will be made good and crowned by high favors and achievements in the hereafter. The biological fact of annihilation of the living organism is recognized by the legal concept that death cancels a contract. In both instances the understanding of death is that it is an event which closes a person's life.

Precisely when death has happened is a matter of considerable debate and speculation for physicists and ethicists. Death was once defined as taking place when the heart stopped beating, but now it is often defined as the end of activity in the brain stem. With ever more sophisticated precision instruments, "brain death" in turn no doubt will be overtaken by another measurement.

For many people with financial means, the ebbing away of life has been sanitized and largely put into the hands of medical experts, so that dying takes place away from relatives or friends. (Religious and medical practices are often closely linked. For example, in the United States, many medical centers have histories of religious affiliation.)

But death is not just a measurable event. Death, for many, is connected with renewal. The rupture death brings is often accompanied by a theme of resurrection, analogous to the cycle of nature, leading to a renewal of life. Creation

stories from around the world echo this organic understanding of a necessary link between life and death, of the necessity of death to make place for life.

Immortality is a concept that is important in dualistic patriarchal religions, which base justice systems on obedience to structures in the here and now. Feminist writings have argued that such concepts are manifestations of self-perpetuation beyond death, an egotistic mind-set in contradistinction to a value system of rationality and life-affirming views.

In the cosmology of many cultures there has been a realm of death, an underworld where the dead live—figured variously, for example, as Xibalba for the ancient Maya, Amenti for the ancient Egyptians, or the netherworld presided over by Ereshkigal in ancient Sumer. In pre- and nonpatriarchal religions, this underworld is often understood as the cosmic womb of an Earth mother or goddess. In cosmologies where living and dying are seen as complementary aspects of the same cycle, human birth, death, and rebirth are parallel to birth, death, and rebirth cycles in nature.

This vision of the realm where the dead live as a place of regeneration is different from the Judeo-Christian vision of heaven and hell, in which hell is a place for punishing those whose lives made them unworthy of heaven. In the history of the Jews, especially in the experience of the exile and of God's promises to an obedient people, views of regeneration shifted to a different concept, the awakening from death. And when Greek philosophical thought of the immortal spirit soul flowed into Christianity, the immortality of the soul was purchased by baptism. Death as the gateway to the underworld became death as the gateway to either eternal life or eternal damnation.

This traditional Christian view of welcoming death as the harbinger of a redress of injustices suffered on Earth is contrasted in feminist theology with a revaluing of one's mortal life. If there is celebration of life in the here and now, there is no need to console the living with a vision of a glorious afterlife. But life is often a cheap commodity; women, men, and children are murdered by warfare, callous neglect, and man-made disasters. This, according to feminists, was a reason for patriarchal religions to envision a "reward in heaven" and to encourage another attitude—enduring injustice, not complaining, and "offering the other cheek," in the sure knowledge that after death one will have a place in paradise and a reunion of the just.

In a feminist theological interpretation, death no longer ushers in eternal condemnation or happiness. Once the crutches of dualism—punishment and reward—are removed, one need no longer see death in the guise of the great leveler. The cyclicality of life and death gives way to a wavelike movement of life, with ups and downs. The task of making life in all its facets endurable, enjoyable, and enriching becomes more important. In women-led religions, such as the Shakers, notions of a life hereafter are often present, but ideas of a hell (with eternal suffering) are generally absent, as are other dualistic notions such as cosmic wars between good and evil. In Christian Science, founded by Mary Baker Eddy, there is no judgment after death—no heaven or hell. In the religion called Witchcraft, Old Religion, or simply the Craft—a religion whose origins go back before Christianity, Judaism, Islam, Buddhism, and Hinduism—death is merely the end of the physical form that allows the spirit to prepare for a new life.

The metaphor "dying to the world," which, from early Christianity onward, has been associated with sexual renunciation, has had disastrous effects on women in particular. Their bodies came to be seen as in need of control, including public control by clergy. This has, arguably, warped the understanding of the body and of sexuality.

The concept of death as the great leveler, as an equalizing mechanism, or as retributive justice can be seen as a construct that keeps people dependent and obedient, despite the crippling effects of unjust structures. Many feminists place more emphasis on relationality (equitable relations), which can overcome the social death of uncaring and unsharing egotism.

See Also

LIFE CYCLE; MEDICINE: INTERNAL I; MEDICINE: INTERNAL II; MYTH; SUTTEE (SATI); THEOLOGIES: FEMINIST

References and Further Reading

Brown, Peter. 1990. *The body and society: Men, women and sexual renunciation in early Christianity.* London and Boston: Faber and Faber.

Clinton, Sally. 1997. *Lifting the taboo: Women, death, and dying.* New York: New York University Press.

Ruether, Rosemary Radford. 1983. *Sexism and God-talk: Towards feminist theology.* London: SCM.

Sölle, Dorothee, and F. Steffensky. 1983. *Nicht nur Ja und Amen. Von Christen in Widerstand.* Reinbek: Rowohlt Rotfuchs TB 324.

Starhawk. 1979. *The spiral dance: A rebirth of the ancient religion of the great goddess.* San Francisco: Harper and Row. (2nd ed. 1989).

Dorothea McEwan

DEITY

Deity refers to divine beings or powers believed to underlie and sustain all reality. In human religions deity has been thought of in many ways, as impersonal and as personal, as single or as plural, as male or female or both. Christians, as well as Jews and Muslims, assume that a personal male monotheistic God is the normative view of deity; all other views that are more impersonal, are plural, and include the female are wrong—either idolatrous worship of false "gods" or "primitive" views that have been surpassed by the fullest and highest view.

This article will discuss the development of the male monotheistic concept of deity in relation to earlier plural and dual-gender views, as well as the challenges to the exclusively male view of deity from contemporary feminist theologians. It will also argue that underneath the official Jewish and Christian views of God as a single male lurk remnants of ideas of deity as complex and as including female and male.

Ancient Deities

Ancient Near Eastern and Greek religious myths and cults, as well as some found in most tribal and early urban societies, assumed that the divine was plural and could be of both genders. Sometimes the divine is seen as existing on several levels, with the ultimate level being more impersonal, gender-neutral, or androgynous. Some paleoanthropologists have suggested that the earliest human concept of the divine was female, such as a great mother or a womb that encompassed all things, from which heaven and earth and gods and earth creatures came forth. The oldest religious images, widespread in ancient cultures from Europe to Asia, show female figures, either pregnant or slim, with uplifted arms.

Since we have no texts from this period, we can only guess how such figures were understood theologically. By the time we have religious texts from the third millennium B.C.E. from Egyptian or Sumerian and Babylonian civilizations, deity is assumed to be plural, multigenerational, and consisting of both males and females in each generation. However, in several of these stories, such as the Babylonian creation story, the *Enuma Elish*, there is a suggestion that deity evolved from a dominant female in the most ancient stage to a dominant male with subordinate females in the later stages. Thus, these stories may themselves suggest a religious development from a matricentric to a patriarchal view of deity.

Monotheism

The Jews particularly gave to world culture an insistence that God is one and transcendent and that humans should "have no other gods before Me." All other deities are rejected as idols. Both Christianity and Islam accepted this concept of deity as single, male, and transcendent, as well as the exclusivist rejection of gods from other religious traditions. Through military colonization and evangelization these two progeny of Hebrew monotheism have often sought to spread this view throughout the world and to suppress the worship of other deities. Yet other views have not died but persist as the religions of more than half of humanity.

Although Hebrew monotheism imagined God as a patriarchal male, standing outside and above creation and ruling over it with sovereign authority, the more sophisticated thinkers of the tradition do not see God as literally male. For them, God is not human and has neither a body nor gender but is an all-encompassing spirit. Theologians have stressed that all artistic and verbal "pictures" of God are mere metaphors drawn from human experiences with other realities and so are not to be taken literally. To take such pictures literally is itself idolatry.

Although the images used for God in Hebrew scripture favor male-identified, powerful roles, such as lord and king, there is an implicit recognition that such names are not to be taken literally and that it is sometimes appropriate to imagine God as like a female. Some texts (for example, Isaiah 42:13–17) compare God with both a warrior and a woman giving birth. The "wisdom literature" of the later Hebrew Bible develops the female-identified figure of Sophia, who is the immanent expression of the transcendent God in the work of creation, revelation, and redemption. "Wisdom" imagery also appears in the New Testament as a way of speaking about the divine reality manifest in Jesus Christ (I Corinthians 1:23–24).

Jewish mysticism continues the female metaphor for divine immanence in the figure of the Shekinah, or divine presence, that accompanies Israel in its historic journey and brings reconciliation with the transcendent God. The image of Sophia for both the Holy Spirit and the divine person of Christ continues in early and medieval Christianity. Second-century Syriac Christianity favored an image of the female Wisdom as the divine power present in baptism, fertilizing the womb wherein Christians are reborn. Medieval women mystics, such as Julian of Norwich, stressed the motherhood of Christ.

Protestantism

In the seventeenth and eighteenth centuries Protestant mystics, such as Jakob Böhme and Emanuel Swedenborg, recovered earlier concepts of divine androgyny. Utopian groups, such as the Anglo-American Shakers, built on these traditions to insist that God is both Mother and Father and that redemption must be manifest in both a male and a female messiah. The Shakers thought of their founder, Mother Ann Lee, as a female messiah who was the manifestation of the Mother or Wisdom aspect of God.

In the second half of the twentieth century to the first years of the twenty-first, as increasing numbers of women obtained a theological education and became ministers or theological teachers, the maleness of God became a central issue. Feminist theology argues that the exclusive male concept of God exalts the male as the representative image of God and suggests that females are inferior, representing the body and the created world but unable to be an image of God.

Some women (and men) desire female images of God to provide the loving and nurturing aspects of God that they feel have been denied in concepts of God modeled after patriarchal males. Other theologians stress that God is beyond gender and consider it idolatrous to think of God as literally male, female, or even human. We may need to expand our images of God to include all aspects of transforming goodness in a way that can help both males and females to become whole persons. The patriarchal concept of God is sometimes said to be blasphemous because it associates God with unjust domination and violence. These arguments over gender imagery for deity represent a profound conflict in the understanding of God and of human gender relations.

See Also

CREATION STORIES; GODDESS; MYTH; SACRED TEXTS; SHAKERS; THEOLOGIES: FEMINIST

References and Further Reading

Bynum, Caroline. 1982. *Jesus as mother.* Berkeley: University of California Press.

James, E. O. 1959. *The cult of the mother goddess.* New York: Barnes and Noble.

———. 1963. *The worship of the sky god.* London: Athlone.

Johnson, Elizabeth. 1993. *She who is: The mystery of God in feminist theological discourse.* New York: Crossroads.

Ochshorn, Judith. 1980. *Female experience and the nature of the divine.* Bloomington: Indiana University Press.

Patai, Raphael, 1967. *The Hebrew goddess.* Philadelphia, Pa.: KTAV.

Ruether, Rosemary. 1993. *Sexism and God-talk: Toward a feminist theology.* Boston: Beacon.

Rosemary Ruether

DEMOCRACY

"For feminists, democracy has never existed; women have never been and still are not admitted as full and equal members and citizens in any country known as a 'democracy'" (Pateman, 1989: 210).

Democracy is most simply defined by its Greek root words *demos* ("people") and *kratos* ("rule"), meaning rule by the people. What exactly constitutes "rule by the people" has caused much debate and even bloodshed for centuries. From the ancient period when democracy was associated with mob rule by the poor, to the modern period of bourgeois revolutions establishing representative government in the United States and western Europe, to contemporary nationalist and socialist revolutions striving to achieve self-government, autonomy, and economic development, democracy has undergone numerous theoretical conceptualizations and practical experiments. Many international struggles have occurred throughout the course of history in the name of "freedom," "equality," "fraternity," and "social justice," most people claiming that all of these concepts have something to do with democracy.

The role of women in democracies around the world and the impact of feminism on both the theory and the practice of democracy have become important aspects of study. Throughout history, democracies have consistently denied women, as well as people of color, the right to participation as full citizens. In the ancient Greek city-state, women—along with slaves and resident foreigners—were not considered citizens and thus did not have the rights of democratic citizenship. In the United States, where the founding fathers worked hard to preserve "the spirit of form" of popular government without codifying "pure democracy"—which they associated with majority tyranny—only property-owning white men had the right to vote until property qualifications were dropped in the 1830s, racial qualifications in 1870, and, finally, gender qualifications in 1920. In South Africa, where blacks constituted a majority of the population living under the minority white system of apartheid, men and women waited in line for days to vote in the country's first democratic elections in 1994.

Women have been active participants in struggles for democracy around the world, from the suffrage movements in the nineteenth century to the anticolonial wars in Africa and the antiauthoritarian struggles in Latin America in the twentieth century to the fall of the Soviet Union in Russia and eastern Europe in the 1980s. Although women have fought to guarantee the basic political and civil rights of liberal capitalist democracy in the public sphere of the state, they have also fought for economic, social, and cultural rights in society, the market, and the family, and have done so through an ever-increasing role in autonomous organizations in civil society. Feminist theory and international women's movements have expanded not only the sphere to which democracy should apply but also the fundamental understanding of what democracy should constitute in everyday life.

Definitions of Democracy

Definitions of democracy usually break down into three categories: (1) direct versus indirect; (2) procedural versus substantive; and (3) political versus socioeconomic. Direct democracy, in the spirit of the ancient Greek city-state or *polis,* is based on the direct participation of all members of the political community. As such, direct democracy is usually associated with a model of discourse and deliberation in which the whole is seen as greater than the sum of its parts. This notion is best understood through the modern political thought of Jean-Jacques Rousseau (1712–1778), in which the will of all, the sum of individual private interests, is seen as distinct from the general will, or the public interest, discerned through participation, communication, and consensual decision making. The contemporary theory of Jürgen Habermas is also based on a communicative ethic, which stresses discourse and deliberation. Direct democracies are often assumed to be limited to small communities. Proponents of direct democracy are usually supporters of a more substantive definition of democracy, which connects political participation with economic equality and social justice.

Indirect democracy—also known as representative democracy—has become the accepted definition of democracy in the contemporary period of large nation-states. It relies on a procedural understanding of democracy as the creation of political institutions, which protect people's basic civil rights and political freedoms—most important, the right to vote. Representative government gives citizens the opportunity to elect representatives who will make substantive decisions based on either their perceptions of the demands of their constituencies; the demands of the strongest voting members of their constituencies; the demands of the most powerful interest groups supporting their campaigns; or their assessment of what is in the "public interest." On the basis of the work of Joseph Schumpeter (1942), representative democracy is expected to include the following minimal characteristics: (1) a government based on the rule of law; (2) a written constitution; (3) free, fair, competitive, multiparty, periodic elections; (4) universal suffrage; and (5) basic political and civil rights. These are the minimal standards that have become accepted today around the world as the necessary components of liberal capitalist democracy.

Many scholars and activists, however, feel that while these minimal standards may be necessary for establishing democratic government, they are not sufficient for establishing democracy as a political system in its fullest sense. Proponents of a more substantive definition of democracy are concerned not just with setting up a democratic process but with ensuring democratic outcomes, particularly in terms of social and economic justice. Many theorists and practitioners around the world have argued that a meaningful definition of democracy as the exercise of political rights cannot exist without a connected notion of economic rights. The social democracies of Western Europe have been more concerned than the United States with establishing an economic safety net through various welfare state models based on granting economic rights to workers specifically or citizens universally. The revolutions in the nations of the developing world have sought to establish "People's Republics," which have included various models of state-run socialisms, anticolonial and antiimperialist nationalisms, and mixed economies.

One example of a revolutionary regime in the developing world that attempted to link political and economic aspects of democracy is Sandinista Nicaragua. According to Katherine Hoyt (1997), the Sandinista revolution in Nicaragua attempted to combine three essential aspects of democracy: (1) political, or representative, democracy—which establishes a republican form of government based on periodic elections and universal suffrage; (2) participatory or mass democracy—which incorporates citizen participation through mass organizations in civil society; and (3) economic democracy—which attempts to establish a more equitable distribution of wealth and more democratic control of the people over the resources and economic decision making of the nation. In Nicaragua at the turn of the twenty-first century, after the electoral defeat of the Sandinistas in 1990 and again in 1996, many people argue that while there is greater political democracy given the decreasing role of the state and the party and the increasing role of autonomous organizations in civil society, there is less economic democracy because of the decreasing commitment of the state to an equitable distribution of wealth and the increasing privatization of the market. Democracy seen only as representative government would not produce such a nuanced understanding of the political and economic forces that shape people's everyday lives.

Democracy and Feminism

Most of the dominant literature on democracy (for example, Schumpeter, 1942; and Stephens, and Stephens, 1992) has been willing to ignore gender qualifications for voting, defining universal suffrage as (male) suffrage or democracy as "one man, one vote," and thus, it is argued, revealing the gendered nature of the very concept of "democracy." The first struggle for feminism, then, has been simply to include women in the minimal standards of liberal democratic citizenship by guaranteeing that universal suffrage is truly universal.

The first country to grant women the right to vote was New Zealand, in 1893. Only 33 out of 174 countries in the United Nations Human Development Report, or 19 percent, had granted women the right to vote by 1930; 40 percent, or 70 out of 174 countries, granted women's suffrage by 1950. By 1970, women had the right to vote in 88 percent, or 153 out of 174 countries, around the world. Women did not get the right to vote in France until 1944, or in Canada until 1950. Women secured the right to vote in Portugal in 1976; in Switzerland, in 1971; in Namibia, in 1989; in the United Arab Emirates, in 1997. At the time of this writing, women still did not have the right to vote in Brunei Darussalam, Kuwait, Qatar, Saudi Arabia, or Oman.

Global feminism has brought a great deal to the discussion of democracy. Not only have feminists focused on the more substantive dimensions of democracy as social justice, but they have demanded the full participation of women, people of color, the poor, and other marginalized groups in the struggles to achieve democratization around the world and to decide what that vision of democracy should look like. In addition, by challenging the dichotomy between the public and the private and insisting that "the personal is political," feminists have begun to demand the democratization not just of the state and the market but of civil society and the family as well. When democracy is viewed through a feminist lens, it becomes not just a political system or a form of government but a way of life that transforms the actual functioning of power in all spheres of everyday life.

Some feminist theorists have challenged the accepted definition of democracy as representative government and suggest new conceptualizations from a feminist perspective. Jane Mansbridge (1980) has argued that the concept of democracy as electoral representation, majority rule, and "one citizen one vote" by secret ballot presupposes that the interests of citizens are in constant conflict, and, therefore, she calls this concept of democracy *adversary democracy*. Mansbridge has offered another concept of democracy, based on the experiences of a town-meeting government and a participatory workplace, which she calls unitary democracy. Unitary democracy involves face-to-face participation and consensual decision making among equals, presupposes common interests among citizens, and is closer in practice—many would argue—to European forms of consociational democracy or revolutionary one-party states in the developing world.

Other feminist theorists have challenged the division between public and private, which reserves democracy for the public sphere, keeping intact various inequalities that exist in the private sphere. Carole Pateman (1989) argues that the separation of the public and the private in liberal Enlightenment values precludes democracy for women, because the mere extension of liberal values to women in the public sphere does not address unequal power relations between women and men in the private sphere of the family. Making a similar argument based on class rather than gender inequality, Ellen Meiksins Wood (1995) holds that the separation between public politics and private economics in liberal capitalist democracy allows capitalism to privatize political power. For Meiksins Wood, unequal capitalist private power manifested through private ownership prevents the possibility of equal democratic public power.

Many feminist theorists have argued that the sexual division of labor around the world and women's unequal roles within the patriarchal family have prevented the development of democracy for women. According to Carole Pateman, who has examined the marriage contract, the slave contract, and the wage labor contract and maintains that a sexual contract of women's subordination underlies all social contract theories, "A patriarchal family with the despotic husband at its head is no basis for democratic citizenship; but nor, on its own, is an egalitarian family (1989 : 217). For Pateman, "Democratic ideals and politics have to be put into practice in the kitchen, the nursery and the bedroom.... A democratic theory and practice that is not at the same time feminist merely serves to maintain a fundamental form of domination and so makes a mockery of the ideals and values that democracy is held to embody" (1989: 222–223). Participation in a variety of institutions and spheres, then, is necessary for women and men to become fully functioning participants in a democratic polity.

The result for women globally, however, has become the double burden of labor. As women's participation in the public sphere of politics and paid, "productive" labor in the market has increased, men's participation in the unpaid labor of the private sphere of household and family has not increased proportionately. Women are still expected to perform the unpaid "reproductive" labor of food preparation, child rearing, cleaning, and subsistence agriculture in most cultures and societies. Jane Jaquette has argued that for women, democratic political participation actually produces "a triple burden of housework, income generation, and community organizing, and they may also pay the price of male resentment and even domestic abuse" (1994: 226).

What all of these arguments have in common is their assertion that women need to be included equally in the constructions of the individual, the person, and the citizen, and that if these categories are constructed from the perspective of women's daily lives, democratic citizenship will look very different. Many feminist scholars have argued that identity differences such as sex, gender, race, sexuality, ethnicity, and culture must be acknowledged within any kind of democratic theorizing. Much of the canon of democratic theory and political theory in general has apparently assumed genderless, raceless, and classless human subjects. For most of the modern period, the nature of man has been analyzed from the perspective of European property-owning men, as if these men were representative of a universal human experience. Even in contemporary theory, ignoring the identity of human subjects or hiding identity behind a "veil of ignorance" has been proposed as a desirable way to construct norms of fairness, equality, and justice (Rawls, 1971).

Instead of considering practical political norms and democratic values from behind a "veil of ignorance" as John Rawls does, many feminists have argued that we must examine democracy from the perspective of human subjects who do indeed have gender, race, and class. As Iris Marion Young argues (1995), the group precedes the individual. We are all born into identity categories and larger systems of oppression, which shape the way that we will be treated and the decisions that we will make as individuals. Much work has been done within critical theory, postmodern theory, and feminist theory regarding the concept of radical democracy. Radical democracy, first articulated by Laclau and Mouffe (1985), recognizes that all individuals occupy multiple subjective positions simultaneously, and identifies as its goal the eradication of all relationships of domination and subordination within society, which prevent the development of actual democracy.

The most interesting work being done at the turn of the twenty-first century in the area of international women's studies is on issues of intersectionality. Third world feminism and writings by women of color from the perspective of women located at the intersections of multiple oppressions, including gender, race, class, sexuality, nationality, and postcoloniality—to name a few—have had a tremendous impact on the theory and practice of democracy.

See Also

CITIZENSHIP; DEMOCRATIZATION; POLITICAL PARTICIPATION; POLITICAL REPRESENTATION; POLITICS AND THE STATE: OVERVIEW; SUFFRAGE; WORK: FEMINIST THEORIES

References and Further Reading

Alexander, M. Jacqui, and Chandra Mohanty, eds. 1997. *Feminist genealogies, colonial legacies, democratic futures.* New York: Routledge.

Cohen, Cathy, Kathleen B. Jones, and Joan Tronto, eds. 1997. *Women transforming politics: An alternative reader.* New York: New York University.

Dean, Jodi, 1997. *Feminism and the new democracy: Resiting the political.* London: Sage.

Hoyt, Katherine. 1997. *The many faces of Sandinista democracy.* Ohio: Ohio University Center for International Studies.

Jaquette, Jane, ed. 1994. *The women's movement in Latin America: Participation and democracy.* Boulder, Col.: Westview.

Jones, Kathleen. 1993. *Compassionate authority: Democracy and the representation of women.* New York: Routledge.

Laclau, Ernesto, and Chantal Mouffe. 1985. *Hegemony and socialist strategy: Towards a radical democratic politics.* New York: Verso.

Mansbridge, Jane. 1980. *Beyond adversary democracy.* Chicago: University of Chicago Press.

Meiksins Wood, Ellen. 1995. *Democracy against capitalism: Renewing historical materialism.* New York: Cambridge University Press.

Pateman, Carol. 1989. *The disorder of women: Democracy, feminism and political theory.* Stanford, Calif.: Stanford University Press.

———. 1970. *Participation and democratic theory.* Cambridge: Cambridge University Press.

Phillips, Anne. 1991. *Engendering democracy.* University Park: Pennsylvania State University Press.

Rawls, John. 1971. *The theory of justice.* Cambridge: Cambridge University Press.

Schumpeter, Joseph A. 1942. *Capitalism, socialism and democracy.* New York: Harper and Row.

Trend, David. 1996. *Radical democracy: Identity, citizenship and the state.* New York: Routledge.

Young, Iris Marion. 1995. *Justice, gender and the politics of difference.* New Haven, Conn.: Yale University Press.

Jennifer Disney

DEMOCRATIZATION

Since the 1970s, the world has witnessed the so-called third wave of democratization. Beginning in the Iberian peninsula in the mid-1970s, and continuing in much of Latin America in the 1980s and in eastern Europe and parts of Asia and Africa in the late 1980s and 1990s, there was a widespread movement toward competitive electoral politics. Democratization is therefore seen by many political scientists as one of the most significant trends of the late twentieth century. A vast literature on democratization has been produced since the mid-1980s. But this large political science literature has so far made very little mention of gender or more specifically women, despite the evidence of the significant role women and women's movements have played, for example, in the return to democratic politics in Latin America. The process of democratization has been subdivided into three phases: the initial breakdown of authoritarian rule, the transition to competitive electoral politics, and the consolidation of competitive electoral politics. The majority of the literature on gender and all phases of transitions has focused on Latin America. Up until the mid-1990s it has concentrated on the extent of women's mobilization under authoritarianism, examining the different types of women's movements that directly and indirectly challenged the military, demanding greater participation and rights as citizens. The role played by women's movements in the subsequent phases of the transition to and the process of the consolidation of democratic rule has only just begun to be considered in the same depth.

To develop a framework for the analysis of both the role played by women in the process of transition and the impact of democratization and democratic consolidation on gender relations, five key questions emerge. These questions can be used to explain the very different processes of transition and outcomes—for example, in Latin America and eastern Europe, where women's movements played an important role in the former and a minimal role in the latter.

To Organize or Not to Organize

The first question is, therefore, why women choose to organize or not to organize in different contexts. The contrasting cases of eastern Europe and Latin America demonstrate that, whereas some "political space" existed for women's organizing under authoritarian regimes, very little existed under state socialism as civil society was comprehensively suppressed. The attempts by military regimes in the "southern cone" to abolish male-dominated politics, shutting down or restricting the activities of congresses, political parties, and trades unions, shifted the locus of whatever political activity (widely defined) could take place away from these institutions of the conventional political arena to the community, where women often found it easier to participate. The identification of women as apolitical, and therefore of women's activities as not being political, initially gave women some room to maneuver (room that was unavailable to men) before their activities where seen as subversive. The repression of the conventional political arena, therefore, created a "political space" that allowed women's activities to achieve a relatively high profile outside of it, while the impact of the debt crisis and the resulting "structural adjustment packages" pushed women into adopting collective survival strategies.

The Nature of Women's Movements

The second question considers the nature of these movements where they exist. Despite the attempts of the military to depoliticize society in the southern cone of Latin America, the late 1970s and 1980s saw the emergence of strong and heterogeneous women's movements operating outside the conventional arena, in part a combination of authoritarianism and economic recession. Three main types of oppositional women's movements can be discerned, although the sometime shifting boundaries between them makes clear delineations difficult. Two of these, human rights groups and urban popular movements, had women as the majority of their members and pressed primarily social and economic demands. Women entered the public sphere on the basis of the politicization of their social roles, that is, as mothers and household providers; this led to some politicization of the private sphere. The period of military rule also saw the reemergence of feminist movements comprising women organizing together to press gender-based demands.

The human rights groups grew out of the experiences of relatives trying to ascertain the whereabouts of family members who had disappeared as a result of the activities of military regimes or associated paramilitary groups. The Madres of the Plaza de Mayo, formed in Argentina in April 1977, are the best-known group. Similar groups, such as AFDD in Chile, Comrades in El Salvador, and GAM and CONAVIGUA in Guatemala, were formed in other parts of Latin America. Human rights groups such as the Madres are renowned for the innovative forms as well as the content of their protests. The Madres used the military's very traditional notions of a women's proper role, that they should be at home with their children, as the pivot of their protests. They argued that the disappearances prevented them from fulfilling this role and forced them to search for their children. The Madres were well known for their

demonstrations on Thursday afternoons in the Plaza de Mayo, the main government square in Buenos Aires. They would march in a circle wearing white kerchiefs embroidered with the names of their missing children or grandchildren; later, they carried pictures of these missing relatives, demanding that they be returned alive.

Popular organizations also emerged in primarily poor urban working-class districts; they focused on the "politics of everyday life," particularly consumption issues, and were organized on a neighborhood basis. The majority of the members of these organizations were women, often operating under the auspices of the church and NGOs in the face of repression and recession. Many popular organizations implemented collective survival strategies either by providing necessities such as soup kitchens or through income-generating projects, such as producing marketable goods and services. The Chilean soup kitchens were seen by many of the women involved as an important visible protest, because their existence demonstrated the extent of hunger and unemployment, whereas the military judged any collective activity in poor districts to be subversive.

After a period of "feminist silence" that followed the suffrage movements active earlier in the century, feminist groups began to form in the 1970s and 1980s, engaging in a variety of activities focused on women's inequality and subordination. Women's centers were set up, and feminist publications were produced. Umbrella organizations were also established to coordinate the activities of the various groups into national movements. Feminist movements argued that authoritarian power relations were not simply confined to the public sphere but were present in the household and family as well. The slogan of the Chilean movement was "democracy in the country and the home." Popular feminism, which saw itself as distinct from this predominantly middle-class feminism, also emerged in this period from the experience of poor women organizing and campaigning self-consciously as women in the community organizations described above.

The Role of Popular Movements in Political Change

The third question looks at the interaction between women's political activities and the process of transition. What prompts change in coercive regimes, and what is the role of popular movements, particularly women's movements in promoting that change in very different contexts? It is clear that during the initial phase of the breakdown of authoritarian rule, the political initiative often lay outside the largely inoperative conventional political arena. Women's movements such as the Madres played a key role in bringing about an "end of fear" and creating the initial opening. Military governments were often prompted by mass mobilizations to begin negotiations with civilian elites about the return to competitive electoral politics.

The Impact of Democratization

The fourth question shifts the focus to the outcomes of transition and asks about the impact of democratization and democratic consolidation on gender relations. Before analyzing outcomes, it is necessary to establish what impact the form taken by the previous regime and the nature of the transition to competitive electoral politics has on structuring not only the politics of the subsequent regime but also gender relations and women's activities. The premise is, first, that institutional democratization does not necessarily entail a democratization of power relations in society at large, particularly between men and women; and, second, that there is no necessary connection between playing an important role in any stage of the process of democratization and having any particular role during the period of consolidation. Many commentators have argued that women's movements, which played a key role in the breakdown of authoritarian rule, have found it hard to convert their activities into political representation once conventional political activity has resumed. Next, one must therefore examine what happens to the various women's movements that were active before democratization: Can they sustain their activities? Some women's movements, primarily some middle-class feminist groups, have opted for a strategy of critical negotiation with the state and political parties and have had some limited success in achieving their aims. Other groups, however, primarily popular movements, autonomous feminists, and human rights organizations, have tended to stay outside the conventional political arena and have been less effective; often, their activities have declined.

Political Structure and Women's Participation

The role of women in the new institutional politics also must be explored. Thus a fifth question is whether different types of political structures have differing effects on women's participation. There is some evidence from Chile that, although resistant to change, an institutionalized party system can make it easier for women activists both inside and outside political parties to exert pressure for institutionalized changes than a weak party system. In contrast, more arbitrary populist political systems or high levels of presidentialism make institutionalized change harder to achieve. Finally, "women's issues," particularly the extent to which they enter policy agendas, must also be considered. In Chile, feminists active in the political parties of the center-left before the return to

competitive electoral politics managed to get a plan for a women's ministry incorporated into the election manifesto of the center-left coalition that won the first election. Servicio Nacional de la Majur (SERNAM) was established in 1990 to oversee government policies on women and has had some limited impact on policy making. Although women have frequently played a key role in initiating transitions, however, they have not often translated this into influence over conventional political activity during the consolidation of competitive electoral politics.

See Also

DEMOCRACY; LIBERATION MOVEMENTS; POLITICS AND THE STATE: CENTRAL AND SOUTH AMERICA; POLITICS AND THE STATE: EASTERN EUROPE

References and Further Reading

Alvarez, Sonia. 1990. *Engendering democracy in Brazil: Women's movements in transition politics.* Princeton, N.J.: Princeton University Press.

Friedman, Elisabeth. 2000. *Unfinished transitions: Women and the gendered development of democracy in Venezuela 1936–1996.* Philadelphia, Pa.: Penn State University Press.

Jaquette, Jane, ed. 1994. *The women's movement in Latin America: Participation and democracy.* Boulder, Col.: Westview.

Jaquette, Jane, and Sharon Wolchik, Sharon, eds. 1998. *Women and democracy: Latin America and eastern Europe.* Baltimore, Md.: Johns Hopkins University Press.

Waylen, Georgina. 2000. Gender and democratic politics: A comparative analysis of consolidation in Argentina and Chile. *Journal of Latin American Studies* 32: 3.

————. 1994. Women and democratization: Conceptualizing gender relations in transition politics. *World Politics* 46(3): 327–353.

Georgina Waylen

DEMOGRAPHY

Few feminists take any serious interest in the academic field of demography. This is curious because one of demography's central concerns—the long-run decline in fertility since the nineteenth century—has shaped women's lives today in immeasurable ways. The major decline in numbers of children born, the increasing proportion of the world's women with access to birth control, and the separation of sexuality from reproduction have, in differing degrees, assisted women to gain emancipation from their narrow roles within the household. Questions of population growth (or lack of it) are vital for women, who have often been pawns in government-backed schemes to increase births at times of national need, such as war or a high demand for labor. At the beginning of the twenty-first century these issues claim more attention as populations of developed nations stabilize or drop, owing to declining birthrates (Teitelbaum and Winter, 1998). In all probability those nations will look to immigration to restore their numbers. Where immigration is less desired politically, they might revert to pronatalism. The example of countries where access to contraception and abortion has been curtailed (Obermeyer, 1994) leaves us in no doubt that such a reversal is possible, if politically less probable, in the West. The importance of these questions alone should alert us to the ongoing significance of demographic research.

A small band of feminist researchers have taken up these issues, usually from disciplines such as social and women's history (Gittens, 1982; Mackinnon, 1997), economics (Folbre, 1983), anthropology (Greenhalgh, 1995; Riley, 1997), population and development studies (Sen and Snow, 1994), and even demography itself (Federici et al., 1993; Mason, 1997; Watkins, 1993). A major stumbling block, as many of these writers point out, is demography's reliance on numbers—on positivist, large-scale aggregate studies from which it seems unlikely that any sense of individual lives positioned within rich social contexts can be gained (Scheper-Hughes, 1997). For many feminists, qualitative and interpretative methods have won the day, and a deep-seated suspicion surrounds studies with endless tables and sophisticated statistical techniques. Further, such studies have often been linked to conservative agendas, unresponsive to women's needs (Scheper-Hughes, 1997). As Nancy Riley points out, demography is in the early stages of creating intellectual space for gender studies (1997: 115). As a pragmatic social science where little interpretative or deconstructive work is done, demography is less hospitable to new frameworks and epistemological challenges.

Nevertheless, challenges have begun. Within the field of demography Susan Watkins (1993) threw down the gauntlet in an aptly titled piece, "If All We Knew About Women Was What We Read in [the journal] *Demography*, What Would We Know?" An important collection, *Women's Position and Demographic Change* (Federici et al., 1993), attempted to bring together two major transformations of the twentieth century—demographic transition and change in women's position. While much helpful work was included, the editorial introduction reveals an inability to accept the finding of a link between the two phenomena, largely, it seems, because it cannot be quantified.

More radical approaches have come from anthropological demography. Susan Greenhalgh's collection *Situating Fertility* (1995) argues strongly for "a reconceptualization of … fertility of reproduction…and new thinking on four aspects of reproductive dynamics: culture, history, gender and power" (5; see also Sen and Snow, 1994). Those four aspects are part of any argument that places women at center stage. Nancy Folbre pointed out in 1983 that shifts in bargaining power between men and women were crucial in reproductive decision making. Historians have demonstrated in countless studies the contextual factors that have influenced this bargaining power, from participation in the labor market (for example, Gittens, 1982) to the impact of education (Mackinnon, 1997; Gillis et al., 1992). Demography has moved toward acknowledging the primacy of cultural factors, recognizing the importance of gender equity for maintaining fertility (McDonald, 1997), and putting more emphasis on context. These trends and the increasing numbers of female graduate students asking perceptive new questions and using mixed methodologies, offer considerable hope for a fruitful engagement between demography and feminism.

See Also

GEOGRAPHY; POLITICAL ECONOMY; POPULATION: OVERVIEW; POPULATION CONTROL; REPRODUCTIVE RIGHTS; SOCIAL SCIENCES: FEMINIST METHODS

References and Further Reading

Federici, Nora, Karen Oppenheim Mason, and Solvi Sogner, eds. 1993. *Women's position and demographic change.* Oxford: Clarendon.

Folbre, Nancy. 1983. Of patriarchy born: The political economy of fertility decisions. *Feminist Studies* 9.

Gillis, John, Louse Tilly, and David Levine, eds. 1992. *The European experience of declining fertility: A quiet revolution 1850–1970.* Cambridge: Blackwell.

Gittens, Diana. 1982. *Fair sex: Family size and structure 1900–1939.* London: Hutchinson.

Greenhalgh, Susan, ed. 1995. *Situating fertility: Anthropology and demographic inquiry.* Cambridge: Cambridge University Press.

Mackinnon, Alison. 1997. *Love and freedom: Professional women and the reshaping of personal life.* Cambridge: Cambridge University Press.

———. 1995. Were women present at the demographic transition? Questions from a feminist historian to historical demographers. *Gender and History* 7(2).

Mason, Karen Oppenheim. 1997. Gender and demographic change: What do we know? In Gavin Jones, Robert Douglas, John Caldwell, and Rennie D'Souza, eds., *The continuing demographic transition*. Oxford: Clarendon.

McDonald, Peter. 1997. Gender equity, social institutions and the future of fertility. *Working Papers in Demography* 69. Canberra: Australian National University.

Obermeyer, Carla Makhlouf. 1994. Religious doctrine, state ideology, and reproductive options in Islam. In Gita Sen and Rachel Snow, eds., *Power and decision: The social control of reproduction*. Boston: Harvard Series on Population and International Health.

Riley, Nancy E. 1997. Similarities and differences: Anthropological and demographic perspectives on gender. In David Kertzer and Tom Fricke, eds. *Anthropological demography: Towards a new synthesis*. Chicago: University of Chicago Press.

Scheper-Hughes, Nancy. 1997. Demography without numbers. In David Kertzer and Tom Fricke, eds., *Anthropological demography: Towards a new synthesis*. Chicago: University of Chicago Press.

Sen, Gita, and Rachel Snow. 1994. *Power and decision: The social control of reproduction*. Boston: Harvard Series on Population and International Health.

Teitelbaum, M., and J. Winter. 1998. *A question of numbers: High migration, low fertility and the politics of national identity*. New York: Hill and Wang.

Watkins, Susan Cotts. 1993. If all we knew about women was what we read in *Demography*, what would we know? *Demography* 30(4).

Alison Mackinnon

DEMONIZATION

The demonic female is a recurring archetype in western cultures. Women who possess or are possessed by evil spirits play leading roles in patriarchal drama, myth, metaphor, religion, military campaigns, and judicial systems. A demonic tale often tells the story of a good male who is harmed by an evil female who uses unfair power to upset the status quo. The demonic story may lead to the male using heroic violence against the female to defeat her evil spirit and restore the earlier balance of power, which favors the male principle (patriarchy). In most versions of the story, demonization of women is a prerequisite to violence against women, as primal fear of evil replaces individual acts of reason, conscience, and judgment. In some versions of the story, the hero receives a good female as an additional reward for eliminating the evil female. Examples of demonic females in the western cultural tradition include Adam's first wife Lilith,

who left her husband to couple with demons; Adam's second wife Eve and the serpent in Genesis; Scylla, Charybdis, and the Sirens in Homer's *Odyssey;* the gorgon Medusa; the wicked stepmother who threatens Cinderella, Sleeping Beauty, Snow White, or Rapunzel; the Baba Yaga; the bad girl of detective fiction and film noir; the militant feminist of modern western satire and caricature; the real women murdered in crimes of passion and honor killings; and the European women executed during the witch-hunts of the thirteenth to seventeenth centuries.

Witchcraft Executions and the *Malleus Maleficarum*

During the witchcraft trials, male judges and priests used the full power of church and government to save their souls and their communities from women accused of intimate partnerships with demons and devils.

Authorized by Pope Innocent VIII in a papal bull dated 5 December 1484, the rules governing the witchcraft inquisition and holocaust were codified by the fifteenth-century theologians Heinrich Kramer and James Sprenger into a judicial volume called *Malleus Maleficarum* ("hammer of witches"). Included among its many topics were how infidelity, ambition, and lust are female vices; why ambitious women are more deeply infected by filthy lusts than women without ambition; how midwives steal babies and are more wicked than other women; how women's feeble minds and bodies leave them more vulnerable than men to the spell of witchcraft; how women copulate with devils; how abortions harm men; how women have special methods to injure men and steal their sexual organs; how the devil prevents women from being hurt during "ordeal by red-hot iron"; and upward of 350,000 additional words of (male) religious and judicial wisdom based on the principle that "when a woman thinks alone, she thinks evil" (*Malleus Maleficarum,* 1971: Part I, Question 6). *Malleus Maleficarum* also describes how men may become involved with demons and witchcraft, but scholars estimate that upward of 80 percent of witchcraft executions targeted women (Ehrenreich and English, 1973; Noddings, 1989).

Feminist Scholarship about the Demonization of Women

Many academic disciplines offer evidence that demonization of women by men is a consistent pattern throughout recorded history, with philosophy, psychology, anthropology, sociobiology, theology, and jurisprudence all offering theory and explanation.

The criminologist Anne Campbell (1993) traces how the pattern identifies aggression as an acceptable rule-governed male norm but a female anomaly that threatens the social order. The theologian Wendy Doniger (1999) offers evidence that the pattern pervades Indo-European cultures and religions and can be linked to a "double standard" in biological sciences and sexual politic. The philosopher and educator Nel Noddings (1989) links the pattern to a "morality of evil" and to efforts to control women's sexuality. The journalists Barbara Ehrenreich and Deirdre English (1973) show how demonization of women healers and midwives in medieval Europe contributed to the sexism that pervades modern medical practice. Perhaps the most useful insights come from psychology, which links the archetypal demonic female to the Freudian concept of displacement of men's instinctual wishes and to the Jungian concepts of the shadow, the repressed anima, and the content of the collective unconscious (Harding, 1971), particularly evident in the fairy tales told to children during their developmental years (Jacoby, Kast, and Riedel, 1992; von Franz, 1993). Primate studies (for example, de Waal, 1996; Wrangham and Peterson, 1996) confirm the stability of male violence against females as an ongoing pattern of male-dominated cultures (although alpha male chimpanzees and gorillas presumably spend less time anthropomorphizing evil spirits than human males do), but also offer intriguing new evidence that female-dominated ape cultures (bonobos) can thrive by using sexuality rather than violence to resolve conflicts.

Women are not the only representatives of demonic content in the collective unconscious of western patriarchy. Bats, cats, goats, sharks, snakes, and gorillas often represent evil spirits in story and myth, and demonic males (Satan, Lucifer, Mephistopheles, Dracula, Dorian Gray, Dr. Jekyll's Mr. Hyde, Darth Vader) also form a common cultural motif. Demonization of minority men by majority men contributes to racism, homophobia, and wars of ethnic cleansing and genocide.

Nor, of course, are women always demonized; sanctification of women is also a recurring pattern. This version of mythic material focuses more on the madonna side of the madonna-whore dyad. The female may be a wise and kind mother (Mary of the New Testament, Sophia of Greek tradition, the nurse Florence Nightingale, the good mother of Victorian-era Britain), or she may be the mating female whom the male pursues. The sanctified woman also is a patriarchal archetype, resulting in a failure of equity in male-female power structures. Once the good female accepts her placement on the metaphoric pedestal, she can no longer reach for male rights, privileges, and responsibilities.

Women demonize men, too. This article, for example, uses "patriarchy" as the evil spirit that shifts power away from

its right and proper position (male-female equity). Because this is a feminist article, however, violence is not part of its story line. Recognizing that demonic content belongs in myth and metaphor but not in government and society could go a long way toward reducing violence by men against women and girls, still perhaps the most pervasive violation of human rights in the world today.

See Also

ARCHETYPE; FAIRY TALES; IMAGES OF WOMEN: OVERVIEW; MYTH; WICCA; WITCHES: ASIA; WITCHES: WESTERN WORLD

References and Further Reading

Campbell, Anne. 1993. *Men, women, and aggression.* New York: Basic Books.

de Waal, Frans. 1996. *Good natural: The origins of right and wrong in humans and other animals.* Cambridge, Mass: Harvard University Press.

Doniger, Wendy. 1999. *Splitting the difference: Gender and myth in ancient Greece and India.* Chicago: University of Chicago Press.

Ehrenreich, Barbara, and Deirdre English. 1973. *Witches, midwives, and nurses: A history of women healers.* New York: Feminist Press.

Harding, M. Esther. 1971. *Woman's mysteries ancient and modern: A psychological interpretation of the feminine principle as portrayed in myth, story, and dreams.* New York: Harper and Row.

Jacoby, Mario, Verena Kast, and Ingrid Riedel. 1992. *Witches, ogres, and the Devil's daughter: Encounter with evil in fairy tales.* Boston: Shambhala.

Malleus Maleficarum of Heinrich Kramer and James Sprenger. 1971. Ed. and trans. Montague Summers. New York: Dover.

Noddings, Nel. 1989. *Women and evil.* Berkeley: University of California Press.

von Franz, Marie-Louise. 1993. *The feminine in fairy tales.* Rev. ed. Boston: Shambhala.

Wrangham, Richard, and Dale Peterson. 1996. *Demonic males: Apes and the origins of human violence.* Boston: Houghton Mifflin.

Faye Zucker

DEPRESSION

Depression is a pervasive and sustained emotional state characterized by feelings of sadness, despondency, discouragement, pessimism, and despair. Other terms that are often used to characterize this state are: melancholia, blues, sorrow, neurosis, doldrums, or dumps. Depression is often accompanied by a decrease in activity level, motivation, or emotional responsiveness. Physical problems such as heart palpitations, stomach pains, or headaches also may be symptoms of depression. The overt manifestations of depression can be highly variable, as are the methods of managing depression. Different cultures throughout the world have widely disparate characterizations for depression. For example, in many cultures, depression frequently manifests itself only as somatizations, for example, physical symptoms with no apparent physical cause. There also are cultures that have no concept of or language for depression, such as the Kaluli of New Guinea and the Hopi of North America.

There are many situations in which depression may be a normal state, including bereavement, life changes, or unexpected reversals of fortune. When feelings of depression persist for long periods of time and interfere with life functions and personal vitality, however, it becomes a condition that should be attended to by others.

Forms of Depression

Individual experiences of depression can range from mild to severe. The specific indications of depression include feelings of sadness; noticeably diminished interest or pleasure in most, if not all activities; significant changes in body weight; marked changes in sleeping patterns; diminished ability to think, concentrate, attend, or make decisions; feelings of worthlessness; and inappropriate guilt. For a diagnosis of depression these symptoms should be present for at least two weeks and should represent a marked change in the previous level of functioning. This characterizes a major, unipolar depression. Another form of depression, dysthymia, involves a chronically depressed mood but usually involves less severe symptoms. A study by the World Organization (WHO) found that worldwide, anxiety is one of the most prevalent forms of depression.

Bipolar disorder, often called manic-depression, is also a form of depression. This condition involves cycles of highs (mania) and lows (depression). These mood swings can be gradual or sudden and dramatic. Features of the manic cycle include inflated self-esteem, increased talkativeness, reduced impulse control, racing thoughts, distractibility, and agitation.

Seasonal affective disorder (SAD) is a periodic form of depression that seems to be connected to reduced daylight during the winter months. Women may also suffer from postpartum depression. It is estimated that 7 out of 10 new mothers experience depression. This depression may be due to the precipitous hormone changes that a woman experiences after giving birth.

With every form of depression there is a heightened risk of suicide. However, all forms of depression are known to be treatable and over 80 percent of people who receive treatment report an improvement. Unfortunately, only about 3 out of every 10 people suffering the effects of depression seek out professional assistance.

The classifications for depression are made in the *Diagnostic and Statistical Manual of Mental Disorders—Fourth Edition* (DSM-IV) and by the *International Classification of Diseases and Related Health Problems—Tenth Revision* (ICD-10). It is important to consider, however, that these definitions are dominated by Eurocentric considerations. Therefore, in some cultures, depression is viewed as illness, a conceptualization that follows from the medical model. In many other cultures, the classic western symptoms of depression are viewed more from a cultural, spiritual, or religious perspective. From a historical perspective, the characterization of depression has always been a competition between scientific and religious perspectives. When various world cultures are examined, this dichotomous approach can be clearly seen.

Cultural Differences

Cultures use different constructs to convey a sense of loss, grief, or personal distress. The Tuareg, a nomadic people of the central and western Sahara, describe individuals who are listless, withdrawn, and avoidant. They believe loss, adversity, or a disruption in one's social routine causes these symptoms. They consider the cure for this condition to be music, jokes, and noise (Leff, 1994). Eastern cultures are more likely to see depression in terms of somatic symptoms. Bodily expressions of depression often include problems such as heart, stomach, or head pains. The Chinese refer to these symptoms as *shenjing shuairuo,* and when this is diagnosed it also would meet the diagnostic criteria for depression or anxiety in western medicine. In west Africa, symptoms such as these are called "brain fag." Somatic complaints, usually of pain in the head and neck, as well as blurred vision and sensations of burning accompany brain fag.

In Mexico, depressive symptoms are often treated by a *curandera,* or folk healer. *Curanderas* often facilitate relief for the sufferer by enacting culturally expected roles that validate the individual's sense of what has caused the depression. The *curandera* thereby eliminates any culturally caused stress before seeking other methods of intervention (Javier and Herron, 1998). People with depressive symptoms were compared in Indonesia and Germany. In Indonesia the research subjects described their symptoms as somatic and in Germany the symptoms were described as "guilt and suicidal ideas" (Pfeiffer, 1968). In cultures that follow Indian practices based on the Vedas or Upanishads, *chakras* are considered at the center of life force energy. Although *chakras* themselves are not physical entities, it is believed that they have a strong impact on the body and an integral relationship to physical functioning. It is thought that depression arises from a deficiency in the third *chakra*, where the energy of the body is literally depressed. This represents a very close tie between the function of the mind and the body and acknowledges that emotions can and do affect physical states.

In the West, depression is more often seen as an illness. As such, it is often treated with antidepressant medication—for example, Prozac, Celaxa, or Zoloft—and psychotherapy. Many individuals also "self-medicate" through the use of natural substances such as St. John's wort or with alcohol or other drugs. By combining medication and psychotherapy, mental health professionals can address both the physiological and the psychological causes of depression. One way psychologists have treated depression is to consider how people react to life experiences. People generally tend to react in one of two ways: either they interpret the experiences as the result of external forces or they blame themselves. Self-blame is often a faulty attribution that can induce depression. This explains depression as "learned helplessness" (Abramson et al., 1978). If the sociocultural climate represses individuals, they easily learn to blame themselves for their circumstances.

Aaron Beck, a leader in cognitive therapy, attributes depression to distorted views of self, unexpressed beliefs, and logical errors (Beck, 1976). Beck suggests that if a therapist works with patients to uncover cognitive distortions and articulate underlying beliefs and assumptions, the patients can restructure their minds and relieve their depression. This view also must be considered within the sociopolitical environment that a patient occupies.

Given the varied experiences of depression across cultures, it is important to consider the cultural constraints that produce these differences.

Women and Depression

The most significant risk factor for depression is being a woman. In every country of the world where research has been conducted, women are two to three times more at risk of depression than men are. Worldwide, women's risk of depression throughout the life span is 7.4 percent, whereas the risk for men is only 2.8 percent. The risk varies from cul-

ture to culture, however. For example, in a study done in 10 countries, rates of depression ranged from a low of 1.5 percent in Taiwan to a high of 19 percent in Lebanon (Weissman, 1996). Numerous studies in developing countries have found depression rates of close to 30 percent for women versus 12.6 percent for men (World Health Organization, 2000). A study across nine European countries has also found that in depression among the elderly, rates for women predominate over those for men (Copeland et al., 1999).

There are many theories about why women are more prone to depression. A negative, stereotypic view of depression dates back to the early Greeks, who theorized that women have "weaker constitutions." Modern science as well as feminist thinking and research has refuted this. There are, however, some interesting physiological or physiobiological theories. Researchers have studied the effects of neurotransmitters, sex hormones, stress hormones such as cortisol, and thyroid hormones on gender and depression. These studies suggest that a woman's chemical makeup predisposes her to depression. Researchers at McGill University studied the synthesis rate of serotonin in men and women. They found that men synthesize serotonin at a rate that is 52 percent higher than women. Other studies have shown that serotonin reuptake inhibitors (SSRIs)—for example, antidepressant medications that keep serotonin available in the nervous system for longer periods of time—relieve depression. Unfortunately, it is not known how serotonin itself contributes to depression or how interactions with other neurotransmitters may affect depression. Science seems quite far from understanding the complex physiological causes of depression.

The biological underpinnings of depression also seem to be supported by studies of adolescents. At around age 11, which is often the onset of menses for girls, there is a sharp drop in girls' psychological resilience. Puberty seems to be the onset of the marked differences between female and male rates of depression (Seligman, 1991). But the social changes that occur for many girls around this age also may contribute to the changing rate of depression.

Sociocultural influences are another explanation for high rates of female depression. In most cultures women are considered to be second-class and inferior to men. This discriminatory position has a devastating impact on the psychological well-being of women. Depression rates are higher among lower socioeconomic classes, and women generally have a lower socioeconomic status than men. Women continue to experience significant stress within society as a result of discrimination, abuse, and their multiple roles as caregivers and breadwinners. Many studies have cited the socialization of women as an explanation for the high rate of depression.

Women are much more likely than men to experience physical and sexual abuse. Cultural tolerance of this violence has a major impact on the stress women suffer and the depression that follows.

These biological and sociocultural factors are paired with psychological states. Women are more likely to respond to stress by developing low self-esteem, self-hate, inwardly focused anger and aggression, and ego helplessness. These states are all known to contribute to depression. But it is difficult to determine whether these factors are inherent in women's psychological composition or a result of cultural forces. The biological, psychological, and sociocultural factors that cause depression are so intertwined that it may be erroneous to disregard any one.

Depression is a complicated emotional state, and research is just beginning to grasp the complexity of the factors that may be involved. Research, however, has dispelled the notion that depression is the individual's fault. Depression is not the result of a character flaw; contemporary approaches to depression consider it a serious condition that negatively affects a woman's life.

See Also

DEPRESSION: CASE STUDY—CHINESE MEDICINE; MENTAL HEALTH I, MENTAL HEALTH II

References and Further Reading

Abramson, L. Y., M. E. P. Seligman, and J. D. Teasdale. 1978. Learned helplessness in humans: Critique and reformulation. *Journal of Abnormal Psychology* 87: 49–74.

Beck, A. T. 1976. *Cognitive therapy and emotional distress.* New York: International Universities Press.

Copeland, J. R., et.al. 1999. Depression in Europe: Geographical distribution among older people. *British Journal of Psychiatry* 174: 312–321.

Javier, R. A., and W. G. Herron, eds. 1998. *Personality development and psychotherapy in our diverse society: A sourcebook.* Northvale, N.J.: Jason Aronson.

Kleinman, A., and B. Good, eds. 1985. *Culture and depression.* Berkeley: University of California Press.

Leff, J. 1994. Cultural influences on psychiatry. *Current Opinion in Psychiatry* 197–201.

Pfeiffer, W. 1968. The symptomatology of depression viewed transculturally. *Transcultural Psychiatric Research Review* 5: 121–123.

Seligman, M. E. P. 1991. *Learned optimism.* New York: Random House.

Weisman, M. M. 1996. Cross-national epidemiology of major depression and bipolar disorder. *Journal of the American Medical Association* 276: 293–299.

World Health Organization. 2000. Women and mental health. Fact Sheet No. 248.

Joan E. Huebl

DEPRESSION: Case Study— Chinese Medicine

Depression is perhaps twice as prevalent in women as in men (Nolen-Hoeksema, 1987). The conventional approach to its treatment is psychotherapeutic or pharmacological. Principles of Chinese medicine provide alternative and complementary treatment modalities—for example, acupuncture—integrating psychological and physiological factors.

In Chinese medicine, the depressed person is considered a body-mind continuum; thus somatic and psychological symptoms are equally important. By focusing on detecting energetic imbalances rather than on diagnosing and treating disease, Chinese medicine relates physiological (somatic) and psychological events—which tend to be considered as separate phenomena in the western medical model—thereby helping to close the gap between soma and psyche. Furthermore, Chinese medicine provides a framework for understanding distinct syndromes and treating each pattern with an individually tailored therapy (Schnyer and Allen, 2001).

Qi, Yin, and Yang

Chinese medical theory is based on the concept of *qi* (pronounced "chee"), or "vital energy," which represents the capacity of life to maintain and transform itself (Kaptchuk, 1987). Life is manifested as an interaction between two complementary forces, yin and yang, which represent the totality of the dynamic equilibrium (Beinfield and Korngold, 1991). Health is defined as a balance between yin and yang, which is sustained by the proper circulation of *qi* along energetic pathways, or meridians. The meridians form a network that connects the surface of the body with the internal organs; the organs are defined by their functions and interrelations rather than by structure or anatomical location. Organs represent a complete set of functions that reflect energetic relationships among physiological and psychological events and are referred to as "organ networks." Meridians and organ networks both work in pairs, with one yin and one yang function interconnected; each organ network is considered to have a yin (storing, nourishing, cooling) component and a yang (activating, protective, warming) component (Seem, 1987). Yin confers rest, tranquillity, and quiescence as well as a capacity to unfold gracefully while being content and quiet. When yin is deficient, we lack receptivity and contemplation and become agitated, unsettled, or nervously uneasy. Yang, by contrast, causes transformation and change, providing us with the capacity to engage life, to react, and to respond. When yang is deficient, we find ourselves paralyzed with fear, confused, indecisive, hopeless, and unable to express what we want (Kaptchuk, 1987).

Implications for Depression

A relative deficiency (hypoactivity) or excess (hyperactivity) of either yin or yang precipitates personal patterns of reaction. If, when a person is confronted with an emotional stressor, the metabolic response is increased in preparation for "fight or flight," activating a response in the sympathetic nervous system, yang becomes excessive and yin deficient (Seem , 1987). In this case, depression is characterized by anxiety, agitation, and insomnia. If a person's tendency is to withdraw from external activity, allowing the organism to "rest and digest," yin becomes relatively excessive and yang is deficient. Depression of this type is characterized by lethargy, decreased motivation, loss of appetite, and an excessive desire to sleep.

The relationship between yin and yang is further divided into stages that describe the process of change. These stages correspond to a set of meridians, a set of organ networks that, in turn, each have physiological and psychological functions as well as specific associated emotions. Emotions are expressions of *qi,* and any emotion that finds no release through verbal expression or physical activity becomes stagnant energy—or noxious energy—that does not circulate properly (Hammer, 1990). Stagnation of *qi* combines with the tendency toward excessive or deficient yin or yang, adding complexity to this picture. The experience of a disorder and the nature of the symptoms, as well as the protocol and outcome of the treatment, will vary greatly depending on which organ networks are weak, which ones are most affected by stagnation, and how much the individual's organizing force has been disrupted.

The organ network responsible for the smooth flow of *qi* is also responsible for regulating the storage and distribution of blood (that is, menstruation), as well as for digestion, evenness of emotion, and consistent behavior. The pathway of the meridian that corresponds to this organ tra-

verses the pelvis, abdomen, breasts, throat, gingiva, and vertex of the head. In addition, the cyclic flow of *qi* describes the rise and flow of hormones in the body. Significantly, the physical and emotional changes that characterize premenstrual syndrome (PMS) and other symptoms at specific phases of the menstrual cycle correspond to symptoms that arise from the stagnation of *qi* along the pathway of the meridian (for example, dysmenorrhea, abdominal bloating, breast distension, and headache), or they are associated with one of the functions of this organ network (for example, menopathy, increased or decreased appetite, and emotional lability). It is also interesting that a number of women experience some PMS symptoms consistent with depression, or an aggravation of existing depressive symptoms, during the week preceding the onset of menses (Schnyer, 1995). Furthermore, some symptoms of depression correspond to PMS: for example, emotional lability, persistent anger or irritability, depressed mood, lack of interest or enthusiasm, lack of energy, and changes in appetite and sleep.

See Also

DEPRESSION; ENERGY; HOLISTIC HEALTH; MENSTRUATION; MENTAL HEALTH; PREMENSTRUAL SYNDROME (PMS); TRADITIONAL HEALING: EAST AND SOUTHEAST ASIA; ZEN

References and Further Reading

Allen, J. J. B., and R. N. Schnyer. 1998. Depression and acupuncture. In E.A. Blechman and K. Brownell, eds., *Behavioral medicine for women: A comprehensive handbook.* New York: Guildford.

Allen, J. J. B., R. N. Schnyer, and S. K. Hitt. 1998. The efficacy of acupuncture in the treatment of major depression in women. *Journal of Psychological Science* 9:397–401.

Beinfield, H., and Korngold, E. 1991. *Between heaven and earth: A guide to Chinese medicine.*New York: Ballantine.

Flaws, Bob. 1991. *PMS: Its cause, diagnosis, and treatment according to traditional Chinese medicine.* Boulder, Col.: Blue Poppy.

Hammer, L. 1990. *Dragon rises, red bird flies: Psychology and Chinese medicine.* New York: Station Hill.

Kaptchuk, T. J. 1987. Chinese herbal medicine course; personal communication.

———. 1987. *Jade pharmacy clinical manual.* (Available from Crane Enterprises.)

———. 1983. *The web that has no weaver: Understanding Chinese medicine.* New York. Congdon and Weed.

Larre, C., and E. Rochat de la Vallée. 1991. *The heart in lingshu.* Cambridge: Monkey.

Noelen-Hoeksema, S. 1987. Sex differences in unipolar depression: Evidence and theory. *Psychological Bulletin* 101:259–282.

Schnyer, R. N., and Allen, J. J. B. 2001. Depression and mental illness. In C. M. Cassidy and M. Micozzi, eds., *Contemporary practice of acupuncture and oriental medicine*. Philadelphia, Pa.: Saunders.

Schnyer, R. N., J. J. B. Allen, S. Hitt, and R. Manber. (Forthcoming.) *Acupuncture in the treatment of depression: A manual for research and practice*. (Manuscript.)

Schnyer, R. N., and Bob Flaws. 1988. *Curing depression naturally with Chinese medicine*. Boulder, Col.: Blue Poppy.

Seem, M. 1987. *Bodymind energetics: Toward a dynamic model of health*. Rochester, Vt.: Thorsons.

Wiseman, N., and F. Ye. 1998. *A practical dictionary of Chinese medicine*. 2nd ed. Brookline, Mass.: Paradigm.

Rosa N. Schnyer

DETECTIVE FICTION

Detective fiction has been significantly influenced since the early 1980s by the entry of feminist authors into the field and by feminist critics' historical and literary analysis. That analysis is the focus of this article.

The genre began with Edgar Allen Poe's invention of the first fictional detective in *Murders in the Rue Morgue* (1841), then Conan Doyle's creation of his archetypal detective hero, Sherlock Holmes. Although detective fiction is sometimes said to be inherently masculine, women have been writing it almost from the start. *Dead Letter* (1866), by North American Seeley Register, is now considered the first detective fiction by a woman; the golden age of classic detective fiction is usually dated from the publication of Agatha Christie's first novel in 1920 to Dorothy L. Sayers's last in 1937. Christie, England's biggest-selling author, perfected the form of mystery narrative in which the reader joins the detective in solving the crime. A shift occurred in the 1920s in North America, with the increasing dominance of hard-boiled private-eye fiction; Raymond Chandler's Philip Marlow was a typical hero.

Contemporary feminist critics see a recent overt feminization of detective fiction and contend that actually it was taking place covertly since women began using the genre. Earlier infiltrations were strategically subversive. They are evident in the creation of independent women investigators like Sayers's Harriet Vane as models of female agency; in rendering of crime and its solution as domestic and private, notably in the psychological thrillers of writers like Patricia Highsmith and Ruth Rendell; in the way female "networks" might replace of the male protagonist, whose mythic social status is acquired through his uncanny knowledge or physical superiority; and in the use of female stereotypes to challenge the codes used in the representation of male investigators. Christie's Miss Marple, the elderly gentlewoman whose brilliantly incisive detecting skills are masked by her apparently haphazard arrival at a solution of the crime, is one example.

Contemporary Writers

Perhaps ironically, the highly coded nature of detective fiction has made it very attractive to contemporary women writers. Freed from the constraints of realism, they are able to hypothesize alternative realities that implicitly or explicitly criticize their own culture, while at the same time reconsidering the form and potential of the genre. A popular mode, however, must conform to the conventions of the genre; thus such writers run the risk that their radical politics will be absorbed by the conventions they seek to challenge. Nevertheless, feminine and feminist strategies of reading and writing are forms of cultural resistance, and detective fiction offers plenty of scope for serious or parodic reworkings of its strict formulas as well as for disruptive humor. An example is Sarah Paretsky's female private eye, V.I. Warshawski, whose name gives her an androgynous identity; she is socially aware but often physically and emotionally vulnerable, and she relies on women friends for professional and personal advice. She represents an alternative to the male fantasy of the private eye, a lone individual who lives hard, confronts overwhelming odds, and always triumphs. Another example is Barbara Neely's black detective, Blanche—a housekeeper who succeeds as a sleuth partly because her white employers undervalue her talent and commitment to justice.

For feminist critics and writers, patriarchal control over women is embedded in detective fiction, which characteristically represents women either as threatening seductresses, sexualized victims, or generalized targets of male violence. Feminist crime fiction is dedicated to undermining these modes of representation. Contemporary women writers are also often less concerned with the traditionally palliative function of crime fiction, the discovery and solution of crimes, than with the socially disruptive effects of crime: the suffering it inflicts on communities and individuals, and the compromised or corrupt nature of systems of justice.

See Also

FICTION; LESBIAN WRITING: CRIME FICTION

References and Further Reading

Carr, Helen, ed. 1989. *From my guy to scifi: Genre and women's writing in the postmodern world*. London: Pandora.

Irons, Glenwood, ed. 1995. *Feminism in women's detective fiction*. Toronto: University of Toronto Press.

Merivale, Patricia. 1996. An unsuitable genre for a woman. *Contemporary Literature* 37 (4) 1: 693–700.

Messent, Paul, ed. 19979. *Criminal proceedings: the contemporary American crime novel*. Chicago: Pluto .

Munt, Sally R. 1994. *Murder by the book? Feminism and the crime novel*. London: Routledge and Kegan Paul.

Reddy, Maureen T. 1988. *Sisters in crime: Feminism and the crime novel*. New York: Continuum.

Slung, Michele. 1975. *Crime on her mind*. New York: Random House/Pantheon.

Delys Margaret Bira

DETERMINISM: Economic

Economic determinism is a concept derived from Marxist social theory (for example, Marx, 1904) that explains the human condition in terms of the material circumstances and the economic structures (for example, feudalism or capitalism) that human beings invent to ensure their livelihood. Such economic structures, according to economic determinists, are the cause of all other facets of life, including family structure, religion, ideology, and culture. The concept when applied to the position of women would explain women's subordination in terms of economics and social class. This implies, for example, that the position of women would improve if and when socialism replaces capitalism. It also suggests that women's involvement in paid work is central to their politicization and liberation. Although some feminists have attempted to work within the context of this theory, most have resisted such economic explanations, concentrating more on the impact of noneconomic factors on the condition of women. Some (for example, O'Brien, 1983) have argued that an exclusive focus on productive relations ignores the importance of reproductive processes (life is not only about finding food and shelter but also about reproducing offspring); others (for example, Lerner, 1986) have argued that patriarchal relations precede and override changes in economic organization. Feminists (for example, Beasley, 1994) have also argued that a preoccupation with economic

relations precludes recognition of caring, loving relationships associated with the private sphere and the world of women.

See also:

DEVELOPMENT: CENTRAL AND EASTERN EUROPE; ECONOMICS: FEMINIST CRITIQUES; ECONOMY: HISTORY OF WOMEN'S PARTICIPATION; FEMINISM: MARXIST; FEMINISM: RADICAL; SOCIALISM; WORK: FEMINIST THEORIES

References and Further Readings

Beasley, Chris. 1994. *Sexual economyths: Conceiving a feminist economics*. Sydney: Allen and Unwin.

Lerner, Gerda. 1986. *The creation of patriarchy*. New York: Oxford University Press.

Marx, Karl. 1904. *A contribution to the critique of political economy*. Chicago: Kerr.

O'Brien, Mary. 1983. *The politics of reproduction*. London: Routledge.

Cora V. Baldock

DEVELOPING COUNTRIES
See THIRD WORLD.

DEVELOPMENT: Overview

Mainstream development theories conceptualized "development" through a male lens. This ignored women's link with economic, social, and environmental issues in the development process in countries of the "South" (also called developing or third world countries). The women's movement in the 1970s and the recognition given to the ideas of feminism, women, and development during the United Nations (UN) Decade for Women 1976–1985, have resulted in the inclusion of women in development programs to various degrees. Policy approaches to women and development have evolved from a focus on welfare to issues such as equity, antipoverty, income generation, and empowerment. Each of these approaches is based on a particular understanding of women's role in development. There is a substantial literature both examining the effects of these strategies on women and challenging the assumptions on which they are based.

Theoretical Concepts

Although the term *women in development* (WID) was first used by the Women's Committee of the Society for

International Development in Washington, D.C., it was Esther Boserup, from Denmark, who provided the conceptual foundation for the field with her book *Women's Role in Economic Development* in 1970. This was one of a series of three books on economic development in relation to agriculture, women, and population that were stimulated by her research in India. In examining the global sexual division of labor in agrarian economies, Boserup was the first to point out the differential impact of modernization and technology on the work of men and women. Boserup argued that women's contribution was substantial in family production in subsistence economies. The problem of women's unequal participation arose with the shift to specialized production of goods and services when women's work was replaced by economic activities outside the home—activities, to which their access was limited. Modernization benefited men much more than women. In agriculture women's traditional economic roles were displaced by technology, which became the realm of men. Industrialization increased job opportunities for women in urban areas, but women were seen as surplus labor in the lowest-paying jobs. Modern land reforms changed the practice of common cultivation in which both men and women worked. Through the introduction of private property, land titles were transferred to men, making only men eligible for loans and agricultural extension services. Women thus became unpaid family workers. Economic development changes women's work, their fertility, and their role in the family and society. Although Boserup has been criticized for not capturing all the complexities of women's lives, she was the first to use gender analysis on generally available data.

During the colonial period from the last quarter of the nineteenth century up to the mid-twentieth century, women's position deteriorated further. Colonial administrations favored the education of boys, and women were excluded from the economic sphere of work. With independence, the major change for women was the spread in opportunities for education and paid work.

The concept of development arose after decolonization, from western notions of linear economic development that were based on ideas of rationality, individuality, and patriarchy. The idea of integrating women into development (women in development) was closely aligned to the modernization and human capital theories of the 1950s–1970s. Boserup's analysis of women's work in agriculture legitimized a focus on women in the development process and argued that development assistance should reach women as well as men. The call for better integration of women into development focused on minimizing the disadvantages of women

in the productive sector, as well as adjusting the imbalance of education and technological training between men and women. It was assumed that expansion of education and health services would ultimately reach women, but they were not considered separately in this linear vision of development.

Soon it was clear that (1) educational enrollments of females were lower at all levels, but especially at the second and third levels; (2) women were in the lowest-paying jobs because of lower education and the supplementary nature of their work; and (3) the new technologies were being introduced to men.

The focus of women in development (WID) was how to equalize educational and employment opportunities for women within existing development programs. This did not involve taking historical and cultural factors and class differences into account. It meant that development projects tended to "add on" women's issues in a welfare approach focusing on income generation and training in crafts, or in child care and health science. The assumption was that income generation would solve women's problems without consideration of who controls that income. The focus was exclusively on the productive aspects of women's lives, with no recognition of their reproductive roles. While *production* refers to making goods and services that have economic value, *reproduction* not only means producing children but also involves the daily tasks of the household, such as cooking, cleaning, and care of children and the elderly, which have no economic value when performed within the family.

By the mid 1970s, neo-Marxist feminists and dependency theorists turned their focus away from strategies for the integration of women (women *in* development, WID) to look at the relationship between women *and* development (WAD), especially in terms of class. The unequal position of women was linked to a framework of global and class inequalities, but the emphasis on class grouped oppressed women with oppressed men, disregarding women's subordination by patriarchy, and other differences such as race and ethnicity. Women's work in the family and the economy was recognized as essential to society, but only work that had economic value was recognized. Thus WAD, like WID, focused on the productive, not the reproductive, sector, so that interventions were aimed at income generation and equity policies (for greater participation in the economic sector) without consideration of the double burden of work for women. Development projects were to aim at developing skills, and women's work was recognized as being in the public domain. Western biases and a lack of understanding of women's work in developing societies reinforced a false but sharp division between the public and private spheres, so that household work and care of children and the elderly were given no economic value.

The *gender and development* approach (GAD) of the 1980s was influenced by social feminism and postmodern postcolonial theories. It combined aspects of culture, power, hegemony (dominance maintained by power and ideology), and patriarchy (dominance of men over women) in defining women's position in the political process that is development. It was a holistic approach that took into account the totality of women's lives (inside and outside the home) and rejected the dichotomy between public and private that has been used to devalue women's work at home. Feminist theory sees women's oppression as intersecting with class, race, and culture, and as being embedded in history. While class distinctions are important, patriarchy is seen as cutting across class lines. The family (power relations and work distribution inside the home) was outside the framework of WID and WAD, but GAD saw oppression of women in the family as significantly related to development. There was a fundamental recognition of the social construction of gender relations in productive and reproductive roles, and this was seen as the basis of women's oppression.

Feminist scholars have started questioning the predominantly male understanding of development and offering women's perspectives on development through a different "voice." This is central to the identity of women as "subjects" rather than as "objects" of development, as agents of change rather than as recipients of welfare. The focus is on the process through which different forms of knowledge are prioritized and valued as development even when they lead to oppression and violence; on what development means in terms of justice and values, and as an aspect of a culture in the process of human evolution; and on the relationship between power and consciousness and human dignity (Freire, 1970). According to this analysis, it is the power of women that we must focus on if women are to move from the margin to the center (hooks, 1989). Empowerment for women is a sense of control over their lives.

Feminism and Development

Initially, western feminists did not include imperialism, colonialism, or racism in their analysis of women's situations. Nor were they sensitive to differences in the economic realities of women's lives in developing countries, to the organization of family and kinship groups, or even to the values regarding these institutions. The slogan for the UN Decade (Mexico City, 1975) symbolized the differences in priorities for women in different parts of the world: "Equality, Development, and Peace." The first of these concepts represented the priorities of women in the West; the second represented women in the socialist bloc; the last represented women in the third world. By the end of the decade (Nairobi Conference, 1985), it was realized that equality, peace, and development were inextricably interrelated because there can be neither peace nor equality without economic justice. More important, a global perspective was needed to address the universal subordination of, and violence against, women. The growth of indigenous women's movements throughout the developing world, along with the merging of women's perspectives on development, gave rise to global feminism.

While different feminist perspectives still exist, there is a general consensus now about rethinking the very concept of development. The assumption of WID and WAD was that development and growth were in themselves the ideal within which women were to be integrated. The call for "another development" (Dakar seminar on "Another Development with Women," 1985) to replace dependent development emphasized interdependence among people at all levels and rejection of existing structures of domination at the international, national, and household levels. Empowerment and the need for women to define themselves was further reiterated by Development Alternatives with Women for a New Era (DAWN; see Sen and Grown, 1987), which focused on the need for ethical and nurturing aspects of women's lives to be incorporated in the concept of development. A new vision of development means depicting it in feminist terms because of the close relationship between women's subordination and socioeconomic and political aspects of society.

An important aspect of a new vision of development is the environment. Ecofeminists from industrialized and third world countries have developed theoretical insights linking women's intimate relationship with nature to their daily lives. Western-style progress based on unrestrained exploitation of the earth's finite resources not only has endangered our planet's existence but has been especially detrimental to the majority of women who live in rural areas and are involved in getting food, fuel, water, and medicine, as well as in activities such as farming and raising animals. Environmental degradation causes droughts and imbalances in the ecosystem, which particularly affect the health of women for whom nature is a vital source of sustenance. Women in some areas (such as desert and dry regions) spend considerable energy and time gathering food and fuel and collecting water. Several indigenous women's environmental movements have shown that women are a source of power and creativity in the concept of sustainable development—the type of development that sustains and protects the environment and biological diversity. Agenda 21 of the UN Conference on Environment and Development (Rio de Janerio, 1992), which brought together the values and ideas of 1,500 women from the "North" and the "South," recognized women's integral role in environmental management and outlined ways to achieve a sustainable world with the help of women.

Women's Issues

What constitutes women's issues in development? This is not a list of concerns; rather, it is a political perspective on women's lives that links the themes of their roles, image, and the desirable society. Women tend to have a differing worldview, a more humane economics. For example, some studies have found that women in small enterprises in south Asia often use profit to improve family nutrition and educate their children rather than simply reinvest it (Tinker, 1987). Women's responsibilities vary by class and involve a complex balance of wage and nonwage activities. While there are class and regional variations, the majority of women in poor countries work up to 12 to 14 hours a day in the home as well as being farmers, food processors, providers of water and fuel, craft makers, weavers, and potters. And none of this is considered work. One reason is that a key factor in measuring development has been statistics—aggregate data that ignore differences based on gender, class, geographical region, and age. Disaggregated statistics create "illusions" of growth and development. For example, development and modernization create conflict and commodification, which devalue women, resulting in, for example, female infanticide, trafficking in women, and an increase in dowries in India (although this is forbidden by the constitution).

Indicators

If development is measured only by economic indicators such as income of women, then the important goal of well-being is missed. However, economic indicators are a means to an end. The importance of income and an increasing GNP should not be underestimated, not only because of the obvious link to prevention of diseases and death, but also because a sound economy enables the provision of better social services.

The shift from purely economic factors in the concept of development to human factor led, in the 1970s and 1980s, to the "basic needs" approach in development indicators. This included data on education, health, nutrition, housing, safe water, and sanitation. By 1990, the UN Development Program introduced the Human Development Index in an attempt to capture both social and economic indicators such as life expectancy, education, and income. However, qualitative factors are not easily measured. For example, capacity development is a participatory process, and self-confidence, empowerment, and consciousness raising are significant aspects of development for women.

Patriarchy

While emphasis on the daily needs of women is very important in development projects, there is a danger of overlooking structural and strategic issues and neglecting women's interests. Endorsement of equal rights is not sufficient for prevention of discrimination, because oppressive practices are passively tolerated. The total life experiences of women—their work in bearing and rearing children and caring for the sick and elderly, and their household chores, on the one hand, and their paid labor in the public sphere, on the other—cannot and should not be separated. Even though they are often overworked, women are less valued economically than men; their daughters are put to work in the house and are less valued than their sons. Quite often their work in microenterprises (such as food processing in rural areas and street vending in cities) is perceived as an extension of their domestic activity. Moreover, if women's ventures are successful, men tend to take them over.

The structural causes of women's subordination (class and patriarchy) are complicated by religion, ethnicity, and caste (in India). Patriarchy is maintained through modernization because households are characterized by patriarchal bargains (that is, conflicts and cooperation) that are structured along gender lines. These shape women's consciousness of inequality, conditioning them for control of their labor (Sen, 1990). Female mortality rates and skewed sex ratios are linked to (1) availability of services in health care and education and (2) intrahousehold power and allotments of food and care.

Structures of subordination reinforce one another through the family, the media, and the education system. With modernization there has been a disappearance of certain traditional norms that protected women from some forms of sexual aggression. Religious revivalism and fundamentalist movements restore the power of patriarchy in new forms. On the whole there is an increase in media reports on new forms of violence against women within as well as outside the home. Reducing violence is as related to development as is the notion of equality. The hope is that since inequality and violent behavior are socially constructed and learned, they can be unlearned.

Education

Changes in women's position (especially in higher education) took place over the last decades of the twentieth century in most developing countries. But inequality in education and employment is still pervasive. While there are fewer visible constraints, social norms, role conflict, and discrimination in the home and employment (often subtle) prevent equality of opportunity. Education of girls at all levels of the system continues to be a problem because availability of educational opportunities does not ensure their utilization. Class is an important determinant of educational and professional opportunities for females. With a large percentage of the population in extreme poverty, the value of work which must be given up to educate girls (a course that is seen as risky), and cultural disparities, enforce a legacy of limited opportunities for girls in the education system. The real beneficiaries of legislation regarding education and equality have been urban middle-class women, who constitute a small minority. Purdah and the related concept of female chastity and honor remain factors in early withdrawal from school and in the fear of coeducational institutions, particularly in rural areas.

Technology

The sociopolitical context of technological change results in differential access to training in technology, and, therefore, a decline in women's status. Technology and education perpetuate social relations of gender, but access to them is a necessary if not a sufficient condition for improvement in women's status. Has technology improved women's lives and given them more leisure? What are the sociocultural, economic, and political barriers to training in technology for women? While the development of appropriate technology built indigenously has indeed helped women in some countries of the "South," too much reliance on such technology may ghettoize women in the midst of wider technological changes.

Health

All south Asian countries are "female-deficit" countries as indicated by mortality and ratios of females to males. The female deficit in India alone, as calculated by Sen (1993), means that 37 million women are missing if 1.02 is used as the average ratio. Sen found that women in south Asian countries have to be more seriously ill than men to be taken to a hospital and that calorie intake is far less for females than for men. The male household head is the most favored, and young female children receive the least in nutrition. The factors that influence patterns of intrahousehold food distribution and calorie intake are linked to women's economic power.

Work

There is general agreement that paidwork is a necessary but not a sufficient condition of high status for women. However, the form of earning and who controls the earning are important because in some cultures men appropriate women's wages. Ironically, increasing women's opportunity to work often results in overwork, with no accompanying improvement in status.

In most cases, women's ability to do skilled work outside the home enhances their social standing and the care they receive within the family. When women have more money to spend, they usually have a greater say in decisions regarding family welfare, which affects intrahousehold distribution and the nutritional status of children. However, with economic development, there has been a shift from time-intensive traditional foods to time-saving foods, which are often less nutritious.

Economic Liberalization and Its Impact on Women

There is a ongoing debate on the probable positive and negative impact on women of newly introduced economic liberalization programs in many third world countries. The issues are (1) the complex area of women's work, both productive and reproductive work (such as children's sustenance and upbringing); (2) women's health, education, and training; (3) their employment opportunities; (4) their time and leisure; and (5) the amount of stress and bargaining power created in family cooperation and conflict. *Economic liberalization* refers to economic and industrial restructuring along the lines of capitalism, in which private ownership, profit, and a market framework regulate activity. In both private and state-run enterprises there has been a change in the nature of employment that has led to more flexible hiring of casuals and temporaries. These policies result in a decline in wage employment of both male and female members, leading to a decline in total household income.

There is much literature examining economic liberalization policies in developing countries from a gender perspective, mostly at the societal (macro) level. There are increased job opportunities due to feminization of the workforce, but it is generally agreed that during the liberalization period women bear the cost of transition. This is because market processes undervalue anything not directly calculable in terms of money. Overall, the effects of policies on women's roles lead to increased demands on women's already overstretched time and have adverse effects on women's nutrition and health. Evidence from Latin America, sub-Saharan Africa, and southeast Asia indicates that during structural changes there is usually a sharp reduction of budget-fiscal deficit, requiring a reduction of subsidies for activities not valued by the market, and leading to cutbacks in public-sector jobs.

First, restructuring in public services transfers work from the paid to the unpaid economy. Cutbacks in health shift the burden of care to the community and household, and thus to females. Second, opening domestic markets to competition leads to sharp increases in consumerism that, combined with patriarchal structures, restrict females' freedom. Third, privatization reduces women's social as well as collective rights as citizens in terms of economic assets. Fourth, inflation and devaluation of national currency (usually a component of economic restructuring) result in rising prices. Higher food prices affect nutritional levels of women, who, traditionally, keep the worst for themselves. This results in time pressures on women because they spend more time looking for cheaper prices and preparing food. Finally, greater economic integration of the global economy is changing the structure and conditions of employment (more part-time, nonunionized labor).

Economic liberalization policies and liberating market forces consider only the productive economy (paid labor), not unpaid labor. They are, therefore, structurally biased against women, since it is women who undertake most unpaid work. Relationships that are not intrinsically gendered, such as monetary and commercial relations, become unequal between males and females (Whitehead, 1979) because of the sexual division of labor. The subordination of women constrains their choices, and overwork can bring them to the breaking point (Elson, 1991).

Conclusion

Changes in women's position result from development efforts that perpetuate their subordination by responding to their practical (work) and material (money) needs, rather than their strategic interest (empowerment). Wage work, literacy, and education tend to improve the overall status of women. Literacy and education raise women's consciousness, and working outside the home exposes women to the world and empowers them to challenge the traditional socioeconomic order. A distinction must be made between the condition of women and their position. *Condition* refers to their material state (poverty, lack of access to education, technology, and credit, burden of work); *position* refers to their social and economic location in society relative to men. The politics of loca-

tion (their powerlessness) influences women's strategic interests. What is needed is to increase women's earning capacity (practical need) while simultaneously empowering them (strategic need).

See Also

DAWN; ECOFEMINISM; ECONOMY, *specific entries;* FAMILY: POWER RELATIONS AND POWER STRUCTURES; MODERNIZATION; TECHNOLOGY: WOMEN AND DEVELOPMENT

References and Further Reading

Another development with women. 1982. *Development Dialogue* 1:2.

Boserup, Ether. 1970. *Women's role in economic development.* New York: St. Martin's.

Elson, D, ed. 1991. *Male bias in the development process.* Manchester: Manchester University Press.

Freire, P. 1970. *Pedagogy of the oppressed.* New York: Continuum.

hooks, bell. 1989. *Feminist theory from margin to center.* Boston: South End.

Krishnaraj, M., R. M. Sudarshan, and A. Shariff, eds. 1998. *Gender, population and development.* Delhi and New York: Oxford University Press.

Sachs, C. E. ed. 1997. *Women working in the environment.* Washington, D.C., and London: Taylor and Francis.

Sen., A. K. 1993. Economics of life and death. *Scientific American* 268 (5: May): 40–47.

———. 1990. Gender and cooperative conflicts. In I. Tinker, ed., *Persistent Inequalities.* Oxford: Oxford University Press.

Sen, G., and C. Grown, 1987. *Development, crisis, and alternative visions.* New York: Monthly Review.

Tinker, I. 1987. The human economy of micro-entrepreneurs. Paper presented at the International Seminar on Women in Micro- and Small-Scale Enterprise Development, 26 October, Ottawa, Canada.

Whitehead, A. 1979. Some preliminary notes on the subordination of women. *IDS Bulletin* 10 (3).

Ratna Ghosh

DEVELOPMENT:
Australia and New Zealand

Similarities between Australia and New Zealand were few before European settlement in the eighteenth century. Since that time, however, a common Anglo-Celtic ancestry of the white populations, together with location and other geographical similarities, has dominated the socioeconomic development of both countries. In particular, the period since the early 1970s has been one of parallel socioeconomic and political change, which has generated a common set of socioeconomic problems for the women of both countries. Indigenous and ethnic subgroups in each country face additional problems arising from racial and religious intolerance in the face of an increasing desire for the maintenance or reestablishment of their cultural identity.

The economic issues arising from these changes are associated with the need for women of all ethnic and class backgrounds to be treated equitably in the workplace and under the taxation and welfare systems. Equity in the workplace involves equal access for all women to the full range of available work within the official market sector of the economy; equal access to promotion for those who are working; access to appropriate education and training in order to place women in a position where they can reasonably expect to have access to the full range of jobs and promotions opportunities; equal pay for work of equal value; and extension of the full range of nonwage employment conditions and provisions, including superannuation, security of tenure, holiday, sickness, and parental leave, to women in all sectors of the workforce.

Equity under the taxation and welfare systems involves a restructuring of these systems to eliminate distortions that lead to socioeconomic deprivation, in particular for those women with responsibility for the care of children. This restructuring involves the elimination of poverty traps; provision of sufficient, good-quality, subsidized child care; and provision of sufficient financial support for low-income mothers, including those without partners.

Welfare Systems

Unlike the social insurance schemes common in Europe and the United States, which rely on the contributions of individuals from their market earnings, the welfare systems in Australia and New Zealand are categorical and funded out of general taxation revenue. As such, they are relatively more equitable, with a common set of regulations and income support applying to all in the targeted group irrespective of previous market earnings and taxation contributions. This is advantageous for women, especially those who spend relatively small amounts of time in work. The disadvantages are (1) the relatively low levels of income support available and (2) use of the household in assessing eligibility for support, rather than the individual, as is done in both countries for taxation purposes. Feminists have argued that either the existing system should be changed to evaluate eligibility on an individual basis or that a new integrated taxation and wel-

fare system should be put in place to provide a minimum level of income support to all adults, irrespective of their circumstances, and abated progressively as additional income is earned (Hyman, 1994).

Except for the issues facing indigenous and ethnic subgroups, the socioeconomic changes affecting women in Australia and New Zealand are similar to those affecting women throughout the developed world. The most important of these are the rise in the number of sole-parent families, the aging of the population, and the increasing participation of married women in the labor force.

Women represent more than 80 percent of all sole parents and an increasing proportion of the aged population. Poverty and the attendant problem of socioeconomic isolation are the major issues these women must face. The increasing feminization of poverty in Australia and New Zealand is due largely to the dominance of women in these two expanding population subgroups. More than 70 percent of Australian and New Zealand female sole parents are receiving government-funded income support. These women also have high rates of joblessness and low rates of home ownership, which contribute to their increasing predominance at the bottom of the income distribution for all families.

Female sole parents, together with all Australian and New Zealand women, face a labor market distorted by industrial relations structures that operate against women, particularly women with responsibility for children. Of more urgent concern for sole parents, however, is the inequitable treatment they receive under the taxation and welfare systems. The level of income support they receive is typically insufficient to provide them with an acceptable standard of living. More important, the interaction of the taxation and welfare systems generates high effective marginal tax rates that in some circumstances result in workers' losing more than 100 percent of any increased income they gain from other sources, usually market work. (High effective marginal tax rates occur because of an overlap between pension losses and taxation payments. For example, in Australia pension recipients lose their pension at a rate of 50 cents for every dollar earned above $300 per week. Before all of the pension income is lost, the pension recipient also reaches a point where income from all sources is taxed. With a tax rate of, say, 20 cents on the dollar, the effective marginal tax rate becomes 70 percent. At the point where all pension income is lost because of increased income from other sources, the pension recipient also loses the Pensioner Fringe Benefits Card, which entitles the bearer of reductions on things such as public transportation, entertainment, telephone and electricity charges, and pharmaceuticals. The loss of these entitlements also represents an effective loss of income that, in some circumstances, is high enough to raise the effective marginal tax rate to more than 100 percent. Poverty traps are generated by similar conditions in New Zealand.) These high effective marginal tax rates generate poverty traps for women in that they make it impossible to improve one's economic circumstances through paid employment. Poverty traps, together with an insufficient level of income support from official welfare programs, are a potent force keeping women in poverty. Poverty traps have also been largely responsible for the recent increase in imprisonment of women with children. Being unable to alleviate their poverty through official means, these women often work in the unofficial market (which is often termed the *underground economy*) without reporting their earnings to the government department administering the income support program. Increasing expenditure by these departments on the surveillance of welfare recipients has led to many women's being discovered in this practice and subsequently imprisoned.

The distorting effect of poverty traps in reducing participation in the workforce is reinforced for women with children because of the financial and other costs associated with the provision of childcare. The cost of child care is also a major factor inhibiting sole parents from engaging in education and training programs and taking part in other activities that would alleviate the socioeconomic isolation suffered by many of these women.

In general, a lack of commitment by government in both countries to the provision of adequate income support for low-income families and the provision of adequate child care facilities disadvantages all women. In this regard, Australian women are somewhat better off than their New Zealand counterparts, because a universal allowance for caregivers was instituted in Australia in 1994 to provide income support to low-income women who remain at home to care for their children. A scheme similar to this was abolished in New Zealand in 1990.

The growing aged population in both countries has heightened awareness of both the needs of an aged population and the costliness of meeting these needs. Income support is provided in both countries from general revenue, although the structure of the New Zealand system is preferable in that it provides an independent income for all aged individuals regardless of their family circumstances. In Australia, although wives receive their pension allowance independently from their partners, this allowance is paid at a lower married-couple rate to couples who live together in de jure or de facto relationships. However, the major concern for aged women is the progressive

withdrawal of government support for residential care. This is worsening the socioeconomic deprivation of the aged, in particular aged women, whose powerlessness also is often made worse by increasing physical or intellectual feebleness. The severe neglect within which many aged women pass the final days of their lives is a pressing social issue that is intensified by the increasing aging of the population.

Women's Position in Paid Work

The growing workforce participation of all women, and in particular married women, has emerged from, as well as contributed to, women's changing perceptions of themselves and the changing status of women within the community and the family. In 1947, 24.9 percent of Australian women were in the official labor market. By June 1994 this figure had more than doubled, to 52.3 percent. These figures for Australia include all women who worked for at least one hour each week or were looking for either full-time or part-time work. The closest comparable figures for New Zealand are for 1945, when 28.5 percent of all New Zealand women worked at least 20 hours each week or were looking for either full-time or part-time work. In 1994, 54.4 percent of all New Zealand women worked at least one hour each week or were looking for either full-time or part-time work.

The increase in married women's participation in the official labor market has been even more spectacular. In 1947, 6.5 percent of Australian married women either worked or wanted to work. The closest figure for New Zealand is for 1945 when, 7.7 percent of married women either worked or wanted to work. By 1994 these figures had increased to 53.4 percent for Australia and 58.8 percent for New Zealand. Over these same periods, married women's share of the total female labor force increased from 15.3 percent to 59.4 percent in Australia and from 23.2 percent to 63 percent in New Zealand (Lambert and Petridis, 1994; Statistics New Zealand, 1993).

For all working women, workplace equity is a major issue. There has been significant progress in this regard in both countries in terms of equal pay and policies toward equal employment opportunity. Equal pay for equal work, equal pay for work of equal value, and antidiscrimination legislation were established progressively in Australia over a decade and a half from the late 1960s to the mid-1980s. In New Zealand equal pay for equal work was established in the public sector in 1960 and in the remainder of the economy progressively between 1973 and 1977, with antidiscrimination legislation enacted in 1977 and its scope extended in 1993. Less progress has been made in New

Zealand on equal pay for work of equal value and compulsory equal employment opportunity plans; legislation covering both was passed by Labour government in 1990 but was repealed by the incoming National government in the same year.

Women's increasing share of total employment is also indicative of an improvement in the economic circumstances of many women. However, earnings differentiated by gender, persistent high levels of occupational segregation, and relatively lower levels of workplace training suggest a continuing lack of workplace equity in both countries. Women in both countries are concentrated in part-time employment and in small workplaces where earnings and other conditions of work such as superannuation, vacations, sickness and parental leave, and job security are limited to the minimum code, which may itself not be strongly enforced. Although some married women are moving into well-paid full-time work, an increasing majority remain in the traditional female sectors, where employment outcomes are poorest. In Australia this is particularly true for young women in full-time employment. In 1983, the gender earnings differential for ordinary-time hourly earnings (that is, without overtime) stood at 76.3 percent for Australia and 79 percent for New Zealand. By 1993, this had improved only slightly, to 79.8 percent in Australia and 81 percent in New Zealand (Hyman, 1994; Lambert and Petridis, 1994).

Economic Changes

Politically generated economic changes, some of them arising surprisingly from populist labor governments in both countries, are continuing to have a major impact on the economic circumstances of Australia and New Zealand women. From the early 1980s both economies have been engaged in a process of restructuring through progressive deregulation in the financial sector, the overseas sector, and the labor market. This deregulation has been accompanied by privatization of government enterprises and instrumentalities and a reduction in staffing levels in the remaining sectors of government. Falling employment in the public sector and deregulation of the labor market have been particularly important for women, for whom the public sector has been an important source of high-quality employment. In Australia in particular, reduced employment opportunities in the public sector are forcing more women into less stable, less well remunerated private sector employment.

Labor market deregulation is progressing through reductions in centralized wage determination and a movement toward bargaining between employers and employees within individual enterprises. Women who have gained entry to the male-dominated sectors of the economy may benefit from such a change. However, the vast majority of women are likely to suffer losses, both in pay and in working conditions, because of their lower levels of unionization in the private sector, their concentration in small workplaces and service industries, and the casual or part-time nature of much of this employment. This is exacerbated by high levels of unemployment, arising from recession and a drive for increased productivity, which have given employers more power in negotiations.

Moreover, the industrial relations structures of both countries have evolved under the domination of men and therefore contain little consideration of the particular workforce issues relevant to women. For example, few industrial awards contain provision for parental leave or any other consideration for workers with the care and responsibility of children. The move to a system of enterprise bargaining significantly weakens women workers' ability to change the industrial relations structures to reflect their need for work-based child care, parental leave, or further education and training. Without family-friendly workplaces and more equal sharing within households, women are inclined to suffer a double burden and have fewer opportunities in paid work.

The politically fashionable ideology of the free market, from which the deregulation policies have evolved, is also affecting the ability of women, in particular older women, to gain the education levels necessary to compete on an equal basis with men for the full range of better jobs. The Australian federal government has reduced its per capita real spending on all forms of tertiary education and, at the same time, has directed the tertiary sector of the educational system to give preference to recent graduates over older applicants for places in their institutions. This will have an impact on the participation of older women in higher education. In both countries, measures such as increased fees and a loan system where repayment favors the higher-paid are likely to deter many women from entering tertiary education. These measures were introduced on the basis of arguments that emphasized the private gains, in terms of higher earnings, resulting from higher education. Other arguments, emphasizing the public benefit associated with higher education, were given little weight. In both countries these changes are likely to reduce women's current relatively high levels of education, placing women at a further disadvantage, relative to men, in the labor market. They will also further decrease participation in higher education by Aboriginal and Torres Strait Islander women, Maori women, and other disadvantaged groups.

Impacts on Indigenous Women

While the issues discussed above operate to disadvantage all women, it is unfortunately true in Australia and New Zealand, as it is elsewhere, that the most disadvantaged are those from indigenous or non-English-speaking backgrounds. These women must carry the additional burden of racial intolerance as they strive to maintain or recapture their cultural identity, while seeking to establish themselves as equal members within the wider socioeconomic community. Both the New Zealand Maori and the Australian Aboriginal and Torres Strait Islanders fare badly on all socioeconomic measures, including earnings, education, and rates of imprisonment, morbidity, and mortality. Issues of self-determination, land rights, and other means of redressing these and other long-standing grievances are crucial to the indigenous peoples of both countries.

The European patriarchal structures that have been imposed on indigenous peoples in both countries are particularly inappropriate in the case of the Australian Aborigines and Torres Strait Islanders. In particular, they have forced indigenous Australian women to bear the major burden of responsibility for support of their families and, thus, the major burden of the overall socioeconomic disadvantage suffered by these people.

Maori, the *tangata whenua* (indigenous people) of Aotearoa-New Zealand, form a larger proportion of the population than do Australian Aboriginal and Torres Strait Islanders: about 14 percent against 3 percent. This is largely a consequence of the relatively poorer treatment of indigenous peoples that occurred in Australia after European settlement. There, numbers of indigenous peoples were severely depleted, partly because of their isolation on reserves and the removal of many of their children. Such experiences were not shared to the same extent by the New Zealand Maori. The relatively better treatment of the Maori by the colonizing Europeans is partly responsible for the earlier progress on the Maori claims for recognition and compensation than has been the case in Australia. The Treaty of Waitangi, signed with the British crown in 1840, and the Waitangi Tribunal have also been important in this regard. The Waitangi Tribunal has been crucial to the settling of Maori claims over the past 10 years, whereas in Australia claims progressed very slowly and without official recognition before the Mabo decision in 1994, which granted land rights to Aborigines and Torres Strait Islanders.

In New Zealand, biculturalism, through recognition of the Maori people as the indigenous ethnic minority, has been given priority over multiculturalism. This is evidenced in the recognition of Maori alongside English as an official language; in the very successful development by Maori women of Kohango Reo, that is, Maori immersion kindergarten education; and in the arguments by many Maori groups for devolution of funding and provision of services such as education and health to tribal and extended family groups (the *iwi* and *whanau*). In addition, Maori women have taken a claim to the Waitangi Tribunal to secure access to decision-making bodies of all types. More recently, the position and needs of other ethnic groups, particularly Pacific Islanders, some of whom have automatic immigrant rights, have been receiving attention.

In Australia, multiculturalism has been of greater importance; it is recognized that the diverse immigrant communities have both shared and varied concerns that require social and political expression. The Mabo decision in 1994 was a major policy shift in the path to full recognition of and reconciliation with the indigenous peoples of Australia.

Conclusion

Although there have been important legislative changes aimed at reducing economic discrimination against women, in particular in the workplace, many Australian and New Zealand women still face considerable socioeconomic hardship. Moreover, current political and economic changes are having the effect of increasing this hardship through reducing the incentives and opportunities for women to engage in further education and by bringing about changes in the labor market that further reduce the ability of women to eliminate the industrial relations biases that operate against them.

These changes, together with the increasing feminization of poverty, indicate a growing disparity not only between men and women but also among women themselves, with relatively few women gaining significantly, while the majority are becoming increasingly economically disadvantaged through increasingly poor and insecure employment and high rates of welfare dependence. Economic theory, systems, and policies inevitably reflect philosophies and values. Recent trends toward deregulation and a reliance on the operation of markets place an emphasis on individual choice without due consideration of the systematic differences in constraints, power, and resources possessed by different groups. This can only emphasize existing biases against women, ethnic minorities, and those of lower socioeconomic status. The goal of economic independence for all, including women, on which voluntary and community systems of interdependence can be built, is still a long way off in Australia and New Zealand.

See Also

References and Further Reading

Briar, Celia, Robyn Mumford, and Mary Nash, eds. 1992. *Superwomen, where are you? Social policy and women's experience.* Palmerston North, N.Z.: Dunmore.

Else, Anne. 1996. *False economy: New Zealanders face the conflict between paid and unpaid work.* Birkenhead, N.Z.: Tandem.

Hyman, Prue. 1994. *Women and economics: A New Zealand feminist perspective.* Wellington, N.Z.: Bridget Williams.

Kelsey, Jane. 1999. *Reclaiming the future: New Zealand and the global economy.* Wellington, N.Z.: Bridget Williams.

Lambert, Sue F,. and Ray Petridis. 1994. *Occupational segregation and female employment over the trade cycle.* Canberra, Australia: Women's Policy Section, Department of Employment, Education and Training.

O'Donnell, Christine, and Philippa Hall. 1988. *Getting equal: Labour market regulation and women's work.* Sydney: Allen and Unwin.

Sharp, Rhonda, and Ray Broomhill. 1988. *Shortchanged: Women and economic policies.* Sydney: Allen and Unwin.

Statistics New Zealand. 1993. *All about women in New Zealand.* Wellington, N.Z.: Statistics of New Zealand.

Statistics New Zealand and Ministry of Women's Affairs. 1999. *New Zealand now—Women, 1998 edition.* Wellington, N.Z.: Statistics New Zealand.

Sue Lambert
Prue Hyman

DEVELOPMENT:
Central and Eastern Europe

The situation of women in central and eastern Europe reflects the impact of the transition from communist rule in both the political and the economic realm. Women's roles and opportunities also continue to be conditioned by the legacy of communist rule as well as by values, attitudes, and practices that predate the communist era.

The end of communist rule in central and eastern Europe has brought many new opportunities for both women and men in the region. At the same time, the transition to the market and the effort to reintroduce democratic political life have had negative effects on many women. As in the case of men, the impact on women of the reintroduction of the market and of efforts to create democratic political institutions has depended on other factors. Women who are younger, are better educated, and live in urban areas have been better positioned to take advantage of the new opportunities that the end of communist rule has created. Older, less well educated women have suffered more hardships. Elderly women and single mothers have been particularly vulnerable to the economic disruptions the move to the market has created.

Women and the Shift to the Market

With the end of communist rule, political leaders in central and eastern Europe began the complicated process of re-creating a market economy. In certain countries, such as Poland and Hungary, leaders were able to build on the earlier efforts of communist party leaders to introduce elements of the market. In others, such as Czechoslovakia, Bulgaria, Albania, and Romania, economic life was almost entirely in the hands of the state prior to the end of communist rule, and the introduction of the market required greater effort.

Women can now form private businesses or work in private-sector enterprises. They can also practice their occupations without the ideological interference that was a common feature of the communist era. Survey research conducted in several of these countries indicates that women are less supportive than men of the move to the market (see Jaquette and Wolchik, 1998). However, women are entering the private sphere as both entrepreneurs and workers.

The shift to the market has also brought benefits to women as consumers. In contrast to the situation during the communist era, when shortages of basic goods needed to run a household were frequent in most countries, a wide variety of goods and an increasing assortment of services are now readily available for those who are able to pay for them.

Women have encountered problems in both of these areas, however. The period immediately after the end of communism saw many women as well as men react to the pattern of changes in gender roles that had occurred under communist rule. Under communism, the proportion of women in the labor force increased dramatically in all of the countries in the region. Women's educational levels also increased markedly. But while women's employment outside the home became an accepted fact during the communist period, many inequalities remained in the workplace. More women entered technical fields than previously, but there was still a good deal of occupational segregation by gender. This situation in part reflected the different educational specializations of men and women, as girls and boys chose and were channeled into different areas of education. Women's wages were generally 60 to 70 percent less than those of men, and women were far less likely than men to hold leading economic positions, even in areas of the economy in which they predominated, such as education and medicine.

After the end of censorship, many voices in these countries called for women to return to the home. Many women activists also felt that women's levels of employment were too high and called for women to have a choice concerning paid employment. Survey research suggests that many women in the region are ambivalent about their jobs. Most women indicated, as men did when asked similar questions, that they worked primarily for economic reasons. However, many, particularly those who were younger and better educated, also said that they would continue to work even if it were not necessary. Similar attitudes have been documented by survey research conducted after the end of communism in the region (see Wolchik and Rueschemeyer entries in Rueschemeyer, 1994).

In practice, financial considerations prevent most women from withdrawing from the labor force voluntarily. As in the communist period, two incomes are necessary for most families to survive. Economic uncertainty and other elements of the move to the market, such as the closing of unprofitable enterprises, have increased the importance to families of having two incomes. Women's labor force participation has declined in most countries of the region, but this decline has occurred largely as the result of worsening unemployment rather than choice on the part of women.

Women are more likely to be unemployed in all of these countries with the exception of Hungary. This situation has been particularly difficult in the former East Germany, where overall unemployment rates are particularly high. Women who become unemployed also have a more difficult time than their male counterparts in finding new positions and are more likely to become "discouraged workers," those who no longer actively seek new jobs.

Women also face new demands at the workplace and, in many cases, increasingly open discrimination. In the first area, women have come under pressure to work more efficiently, work longer hours, and improve their skills. These demands affect men as well, but many of the new kinds of expertise and the nature of the work required of employees disadvantage women, given the lack of change in gender roles in the home. Women are no longer able to use working time to take care of family business, as many were able to do during the communist era.

The end of communism has also seen increasingly open forms of discrimination in the workplace. These range from

lower wages for women to degrading requests for sexual services. It is common for job advertisements to specify the gender of the prospective employee, and older women in particular are vulnerable to being replaced by younger women who are presumed to be more attractive. Women's wages continue to be lower than those of men with similar education in similar occupations. Foreign corporations appear to contribute to these practices. Many hire young men for management training positions while hiring young women with comparable educational background and qualifications primarily as clerical workers.

Women face increased competition from men in areas of the economy that were largely women's preserves because they offered lower-than-average wages, such as services, banking, tourism, and financial management. As these fields become more financially attractive, more men are entering them. The situation of older women is particularly difficult. Although pensions have increased to account for increased prices of food and most other goods and services, many older women live in poverty.

The decline in the standard of living of the population that accompanied the introduction of the market also has had a disproportionately negative impact on women. Because it is still women who care for the home and family, the need to stretch the family budget to cover the increased expense of goods and services necessary for running a family has fallen largely on women's shoulders. Improvements in economic performance in many of these countries suggest that living standards should soon improve, but many families will continue to find it difficult to meet their needs for some time to come.

Changes in the organization of services have also complicated women's lives. The need to make a profit has led some factories to close their child care facilities; lack of funds has prompted many municipal governments to do the same. The decline in public spending on other services and the shift to a needs-based system of providing social benefits has also had an impact on family budgets.

Social and Psychological Issues Raised by the Transition

In addition to dealing with economic change, women have had to cope with the uncertainty and other social and psychological costs of the transition. Men have also been affected by these factors. However, in these as well as other societies, women continue to be primarily responsible for the emotional well-being of the family and so must help other family members cope with the disruptions caused by the large-scale changes that have occurred.

The opening of borders and the end of tight political control have exacerbated many existing social problems and created new ones. Drug abuse and violence against women have increased. Pornography and prostitution have also increased, as have other forms of sexual exploitation of women.

In the former Yugoslavia, the end of communist rule has had devastating consequences for most women outside of Slovenia. As a result of the civil war, many women became refugees or died. Others were forced to endure dislocation, hunger, rape, and other forms of violence. These were particularly severe in Kosovo, where much of the Albanian population was forced to leave the country in the first half of 1999 as the result of Serbian ethnic cleansing policies. Most refugees returned to Kosovo after an intensive NATO bombing campaign forced Serbian leaders to agree to the presence of international peacekeeping forces. However, daily life still bears the marks of dislocation and ethnic violence. Although the impact on women has not been as great as in the former Yugoslavia, women in a number of other countries in the region have also been subjected to nationalist rhetoric and mobilization.

Women and Politics in Postcommunist Central and Eastern Europe

The elimination of censorship and end of the Communist Party's monopoly on power were followed by a rapid pluralization of political life in central and eastern Europe. Women as well as men have been able to take advantage of these new opportunities to be active in political life—to articulate their preferences, organize with others who share similar views, and pressure political leaders to take action on issues of concern to them. They also have new opportunities to run for political office themselves.

However, as in the economic realm, the re-creation of democratic political life has led to difficulties for women. During the communist era, women in rural areas became aware of being part of a larger political community. Most women, as well as men, voted in the single-candidate elections that were typical during the communist period, because voting was required in all countries except the former Yugoslavia. As many women as men participated in the symbolic demonstrations of support organized by the regime on important anniversaries and holidays. Women were well represented in the symbolic or governmental elites, but they formed a smaller proportion of Communist Party members than men and were far less frequently found in the top party leadership.

After the end of communist rule, women's marginalization in politics continued. Although women participated in large numbers in the mass demonstrations that brought about the collapse of communism in East Germany, Czechoslovakia, and Romania, women's representation in the national legislatures dropped significantly in all countries. This decline in the number of women legislators does not signify as large a decrease in women's exercise of political power as it might seem, because the women who served in the governmental and party elites under communism differed in important ways from their male counterparts and exercised little real influence. Though fewer in numbers, women leaders now have educational backgrounds and career patterns that more closely resemble those of their male colleagues. The small number of women leaders is important, however, because it is one of the factors limiting women's ability to use the political process to raise issues of particular concern to them.

Since the end of communist rule, women have been able to organize independently. Numerous women's groups have formed in all of the formerly communist countries. Most do not consider themselves to be feminist, and many deny that they are political at all. Instead, many of the new groups focus on women's roles as mothers and wives, which they see as having been neglected during the communist period. Nonetheless, these groups provide women with a forum to articulate their views and meet with others who share similar interests. Many organize lectures and discussions for women that relate to political issues or aspects of the move to the market. Others have organized demonstrations to call attention to public problems such as the lack of safety of the food supply in Czechoslovakia and problems with water shortages in Bulgaria.

Feminist groups also exist. These are small and generally consist of educated women professionals in large cities. However, although they have had little impact on the making of public policy, these groups play an important role in their societies. In Poland, for example, women's groups organized to fight the restrictive abortion law. In Slovakia, women intellectuals who publish a feminist journal have succeeded in getting gender issues into public discourse among intellectuals for the first time.

In the near future, it is unlikely that there will be significant changes in women's situation in these countries. Political leaders will not be likely to take action to remedy existing gender inequalities without pressure from women, and most women do not appear to be willing to engage in such action at present. Women are more likely to participate in nonpartisan activities, and many are involved in nongovernmental organizations. Few, however, are involved in positions of leadership in political parties or hold political office. However, continued experience with the workings of a market economy, coupled with increased contact with the rest of the world, can be expected to increase support for women's movements. Such experiences may also lead to the development of a feminist agenda, particularly among young women.

See also:

EDUCATION: EASTERN EUROPE; ENVIRONMENT: CENTRAL AND EASTERN EUROPE; FEMINISM: EASTERN EUROPE; POLITICS AND THE STATE: EASTERN EUROPE.

References and Further Reading

Einhorn, Barbara. 1993. *Cinderella goes to market: Citizenship, gender and women's movements in East Central Europe.* London: Verso.

Funk, Nanette, and Magda Mueller, eds. 1993. *Gender politics and postcommunism.* New York: Routledge.

Jancar, Barbara Wolfe. 1978. *Women under communism.* Baltimore, Md.: John Hopkins University Press.

Jaquette, Jane, and Sharon Wolchik, eds. 1998. *Women and democracy: Latin America and central and eastern Europe.* Baltimore, Md.: Johns Hopkins University Press.

Moghadam, Valentine M., ed. 1993. *Democratic reform and the position of women in transitional economies.* Oxford: Clarendon.

Renne, Tanya. 1997. *Ana's land.* Boulder, Col.: Westview.

Rueschemeyer, Marilyn, ed. 1994. *Women in the politics of post-communist Eastern Europe.* Armonk, N.Y.: Sharpe.

Wolchik, Sharon L., and Alfred G. Meyer, eds. 1985. *Women, state, and party in eastern Europe.* Durham, N.C.: Duke University Press.

Sharon L. Wolchik

DEVELOPMENT: Central and South America and the Caribbean

Occupied by Spain and (in the case of Brazil only) Portugal for about 300 years and formally independent for over 170 years, Latin America still bears the imprint of a strongly male-dominated culture and endorses racial distinctions and prejudices, which are reflected in its social classes. Most of the Caribbean was under British control until the mid-twentieth century. This fact and the long-lasting effects of slavery on the family have produced weaker male-centered norms in the Caribbean.

Latin America and the Caribbean make up a diverse region in terms of population and economic development. It ranges from highly industrialized areas such as São Paulo to survival agrarian economies such as that of Haiti. Its social

indicators on infant mortality and illiteracy vary widely; illiteracy, for example, is almost negligible in Argentina but reaches 47 percent in Haiti (UNDP, 1993). As a whole, the region has a diversified economic production, with the participation of all three sectors (agriculture, industry, and service), yet it has the most uneven income distribution in the world.

The region is increasingly urban; as of the year 2000, about 77 percent of the population lived in cities. Although the region embarked with much optimism on an import-substitution development model (which emphasized national industrialization) in the early 1960s, today it has declined in the global economy, having been surpassed by the growing production of several Asian countries. The failure of the strategy of industrialization for the purpose of creating a self-sustaining market in many countries, the endorsement of a free trade economic system, and the enduring burden of foreign debt have led to the restructuring of the economies of most Latin American and Caribbean countries. This restructuring has often been characterized by reduced government participation in, and greater privatization of, the productive sectors. These changes have had negative effects on the Latin American working class and, in particular, on women in low-income groups.

Economic hardships continue to be serious in this region. By 1994, fewer than 33 percent of the countries of Latin America and the Caribbean had regained the income per capita they had in 1980 (Inter-American Dialogue, 1994). In Venezuela, which used to be one of the wealthiest Latin American countries, the proportion of households in extreme poverty (that is, having an income less than would purchase the "basket" of staple goods needed for survival) went from 11 percent in 1982 to 20 percent in 1987 (Benería, 1992). In Peru in 1994, 50 percent of the population were classified as poor (of these, 20 percent were categorized as extremely poor). Some countries have had economic success, such as Chile, Brazil, and Mexico (before the devaluation of the peso in 1995). However, economists have observed that this economic growth has benefited at most 50 percent of the population, or 70 percent in places with "economic" miracles, such as Chile (Benería, 1992).

Indigenous and black women suffer the most in terms of access to remunerated work, education, and other public benefits. Women of these minority groups usually occupy the lowest jobs: they constitute a large number of those in domestic work, an area where workers' benefits—despite some legislation to protect them—are practically nonexistent.

Latin America is a predominantly Catholic region. Yet, in defiance of church precepts, societal norms about birth control have been changing, with the result that the fertility rate had decreased in 1990 by about 50 percent compared with that in 1960 (UNDP, 1993). This is facilitating women's access to the labor force and to further schooling.

Unmitigated political violence in Central America, first in Nicaragua and later in El Salvador and Guatemala, has caused substantial population shifts. Large migratory movements to the United States have substantially increased the Latino population of that country. Migration from the Caribbean has been steady, with mostly men moving to Canada and the United States. Latin America has also seen considerable internal migration, as rural populations, impelled by poverty and fear of armed violence in the countryside, have gone to the cities. Migration has resulted in a high degree of family fragmentation, producing a steady rise in the number of female-headed households.

General Economic Conditions

In the past few decades there has been considerable economic slowdown in Latin America. One-third of the countries have shown negative growth since about 1970, and another third at most a 1.6 percent growth per year (Psacharopoulos and Tzannatos, 1992). During the import-substitution phase, women participated in industry, especially in textiles and food production. In recent decades there has been less demand for industrial labor, so women have moved into commerce, services, and self-employment. Women's unemployment is two to three times higher than that of men in the same age groups. Women's salaries are lower than those of men in all the countries in the region (see the table). More than half of all women receive salaries below the minimum wages established by their countries (Kirsch, 1975). The informal sector of the economy (jobs characterized by very low pay and outside the framework of workers' rights and protections) is prominent today, and the family has become a site of collective action for economic survival.

The number of female-headed households is growing, in part because of younger, unpartnered mothers and in part because of the increased number of widows or displaced women and children. Although there are conceptual problems in the definition and measurement of "head of household," there is agreement that the category of female-headed households is expanding and that women are becoming less dependent on male income.

With the globalization of the economy and the concomitant emergence of low-paying industrial jobs for women, more women entered the labor force during economic contraction in Chile and Uruguay in the 1970s and in Brazil and Costa Rica in the early 1980s, but since there

were more workers than jobs, the formal unemployment of women increased sharply. In rural Mexico, the decreased purchasing power of wages has obliged women to withdraw children from school and make them work in agriculture (Chinery-Hesse et al., 1989).

According to household survey data gathered in 14 Latin American countries and Jamaica, the average rate of participation in the labor force for women in the late 1980s was 31 percent, and women's pay was 71 percent of that of men. The early increase in the employment of women is considered the result of expansionary government policies, since the governmental sector is a larger employer of women than the private sectors (Psacharopoulos and Tzannatos, 1992). Despite the increased role of women as workers and heads of families, institutional resources such as technical assistance and bank credit still favor men. This is especially true in the agricultural sector.

While the number of women in the labor force increased substantially in the past decades, they have taken

Female Participation Rate and Female Pay Relative to Male Pay (F/M)

Country (age group)	Year	Female participation rate (percent)	Year	Relative F/M pay (percent)
Argentina (20–60)	1980	33.1	1985	64.5
Bolivia (20–64)	1976	32.1	1989	62.3
Brazil (20–60)	1980	33.0	1980	61.2
Chile (20–60)	1982	28.9	1987	65.4
Colombia (25–60)	1985	39.4	1988	84.6
Costa Rica (20–60)	1984	26.4	1989	80.8
Eucador (20–60)	1982	22.6	1987	63.7
Guatemala (20–60)	1981	14.7	1989	76.8
Honduras (20–60)	1974	18.0	1989	81.3
Jamaica (20–60)	1982	48.2	1989	57.7
Mexico (20–60)	1980	32.7	1984	85.6
Panama (20–60)	1980	35.7	1989	79.6
Peru (20–60)	1981	29.0	1990	65.7
Uruguay (20–60)	1985	46.0	1989	57.4
Venezuela (20–60)	1981	35.0	1989	70.6
Average		**31.1**		**70.5**

Notes: Participation of prime-age women (aged 20 to 60 years). Weekly earnings in Venezuela, Mexico, Colombia, Jamaica, Honduras, Chile, and Bolivia, and monthly earnings in all other countries. Participation: Constructed from ILO (1990), table 1. Relative pay: based on information provided in the companion volume.

Source: Psacharopoulos and Tzannatos, 1992: 5. The trends indicated by these figures have continued.

a higher proportion of subordinate positions compared with men, whether in the industrial sector or the informal sector of the economy. And women are becoming members of the labor force without being released from their domestic responsibilities and their reproductive functions. The reduction of social services by the state has further affected women, as they have had to provide social services no longer supplied by public agencies. Men, on the other hand, tend to be more accepted into the formal sector of the labor market than women.

Agriculture

Latin America is usually described as a "male farming system" (where men do most of the agricultural work). However, microstudies show a trend toward "feminization of farming," as men emigrate, become seasonal migrants, or engage in off-farm labor. It is estimated that women generate on average one-third of the household cash derived from small-scale marketing and the feeding and selling of small animals (Ashby and Gomez, 1985). Research comparing men and women has focused on field operations (land preparation, planting, cultivation, harvesting) but has neglected types of crop. There is some gender selectivity in these activities; for instance, women participate much more in the production of tobacco than maize crops.

Macrostatistical data reporting women's low participation in agriculture have been found to be misleading because of conceptual problems of measurement, such as women's self-description as "housewife," census definitions of what constitutes economic activity by unpaid female workers, and time reference periods of census interviews that do not capture the seasonal nature of women's work. Reviewing census data for several Latin American and Caribbean countries, Recchini de Lattes and Wainerman (1982) estimate that census data, in contrast to more precise household surveys, underestimate women's agricultural work by between 14 and 33 percent and that of men by 2 to 6 percent. Moreover, statistics continue to confuse domestic tasks with unremunerated family labor, particularly agricultural production and processing.

Manufacturing and Industry

The participation of women in the industrial sector is low compared with their involvement in services and in the informal sector. But their participation in manufacturing is increasing in the free export zones (FEZs). In Mexico, where many women work in export-processing plants, there is a clear intersection between gender and age in hiring patterns. Unmarried women who have completed primary schooling, or more, work in *maquiladora* (assembly) plants, while older

and less-educated women work in economically decaying textile industries. In Brazil women have a sizable representation in industry, most of it in São Paulo, where young women are employed in nontraditional sectors such as metalwork, steel, plastics, and electrical appliances, and in more traditional sectors such as garments, shoe manufacturing, and, though decreasingly, textiles. In the entire region there is a tendency to recruit young, single, and more educated women for nonmanual occupations and industrial employment, while older or uneducated women prevail in domestic work and informal activities.

Services

Women's involvement in the service sector of the economy is manifested primarily in the informal sector, domestic work, and governmental services. By endorsing starkly different gender roles, the patriarchal family contributes to the subordination and exploitation of women in the labor force. As a result (except as noted above), most economically active women work in the service sector, where the largest category is domestic work. According to data for 1992 from the United Nations (UN) Economic Commission for Latin America and the Caribbean, about 30 percent of the women in the labor force are in domestic service, and this figure constitutes more than 90 percent of low-income women working in the tertiary sector. In Brazil, domestic work involves one of every three female workers. It has been observed that the importance of remunerated domestic work increases in inverse relation to family income. The need for economic survival among low-income women has led to the development of extensive kinship networks and neighborhood organizations that give one another assistance. The growth of popular kitchens and neighborhood dining halls in Peru, Colombia, Chile, and Argentina is an example of the increased economic role of women. Not surprisingly, women in Buenos Aires have been found to face working days of 13 to 14 hours (Feijóo and Jelín, 1987). Similarly heavy schedules have been observed among poor women in São Paulo. Their days become longer as they seek stores with the cheapest food prices, work in community self-help groups, and conduct at-home services for others that during better times would have been bought in the marketplace.

Most of the women who work as maids rely on unwritten contracts; this allows arbitrary control by patrons—usually women from middle and upper social classes. Domestic workers earn low salaries, since they seldom have the leverage to negotiate. Their labor earns neither workers' benefits nor related legal protection. The prevalence of women in domestic work and the inequities associated with such work are one of the strongest obstacles to class-integrated feminism in Latin America.

Studies of the informal sector in six Central American countries have found that women engage in mostly subsistence activities with little possibility of economic improvement. The women thus engaged face a heavy double work day. Most of their participation in the informal sector enables them merely to make ends meet rather than to accumulate capital for future investment. In the case of men, self-defined objectives and limited responsibilities for domestic duties enable them in some cases to involve themselves in "dynamic informality" (meaning profit-making participation and concomitant management in the informal economy). In the case of women, domestic and family obligations limit economic progress (Pérez Sáinz and Larín, 1994: 447).

Current structural adjustment programs in Latin America and the Caribbean, which have reduced public social services, have led to increased participation by women in the informal sector of the economy. These jobs are marginal and poorly remunerated. In the absence of government efforts to provide these women with training and some capital, it will be very difficult for them to move beyond the subsistence level.

Another important aspect of women's participation in the service sector involves those working for public agencies and state-owned enterprises. It has been found that women are better paid in all types of jobs in the public sector, earning about twice what they would receive in the private sector. With structural adjustment programs now in effect, most of which include a decrease in government expenditures as well as the privatization of industries, state bureaucracies have been drastically downsized. Consequently, many women have lost relatively well-paying jobs.

With regard to labor statistics, it has been noted that women's strong participation in informal-sector services still underestimates their involvement in productive work (Fort et al., 1994).

Wage Differentials

A negative view of the economic realities in Latin America and the Caribbean sees a growing deterioration in the standard of living, with many men and women suffering from this. A more sanguine view sees an emergence of economic dualism, with some areas becoming highly industrialized and others remaining backward and exploited.

Amid this uneven economic panorama, strong gender differentials in wages have been detected. The lowest gender differentials have been observed in Mexico and Colombia and the highest differentials in Uruguay and Jamaica.

Women earn less because they enter a limited number of occupations and generally work overtime less than men, but there are also other reasons. In Venezuela, where women earn 71 percent of men's wages, the rather slight differential has been explained in terms of several factors, such as a larger number of Venezuelan women with tertiary education compared with men (10 versus 6 percent). The country also has acute shortages of managerial personnel, skilled workers, and technicians; equal pay legislation was enacted in the 1970s, which may have encouraged more egalitarian salaries.

Psacharopoulos and Tzannatos found that on average only 20 percent of the wage differential in the region could be explained by differences in the amount of learning and training men and women have acquired. They found that an additional 20 percent could be attributed to women's selecting (or being in) lower-paying jobs than men. The unexplained 60 percent was attributed to discrimination (1992: 23). Discrimination operates in several ways: women must have more education and experience to qualify for the same jobs; women receive lower wages for the same work; or—the most common pattern—women enter a gender-segregated labor force, where jobs defined as feminine pay less.

The full impact of the liberalized economies of Latin America is yet to be documented, but some economists (such as, Benería, 1992) hold that opening markets has resulted in moving wages toward the lowest common denominator. With women working for survival, it is difficult to imagine that they will have the time to work for their social and economic improvement. A contrary view holds that the severe economic crisis and the presence of authoritarian governments in Latin America in the 1970s created an unintended social space for women that enabled them to leave the house and emerge as new social subjects. According to this view, women have gained valuable economic and political experience and have become able to address and interact with the state on issues regarding material survival and ethics (human rights).

Labor Unions

Although women workers in the formal sector constitute a smaller group than men, they are supposed to receive significant economic and legal benefits; their membership in labor unions is assumed to ensure the defense of their rights as workers. There are few studies of what labor unions do for women. Cortina's study of teachers' unions in Mexico (1992) found that women teachers did not participate in decision making, and thus union policies did not take their needs into account.

On the other hand, it has been noted that protective legislation for women in many Latin American countries prohibits women from certain deleterious activities and allows long periods of absence for reasons related to maternity. There is an increasing consensus among social scientists that these requirements may perpetuate sex stereotypes and result in discrimination against women during employers' recruitment and promotion of workers (Feijóo and Jelín, 1987; Psacharopoulos and Tzannatos, 1992).

Work and the Domestic Sphere

Benería and Roldáno (1987) have observed that while several studies of female industrial workers exist for some countries, the examination of the relationship between gender and class factors within family, factory, and trade union settings has been weak thus far.

Women continue to face the old problems of occupational segregation, inadequate income, and differential wage distribution compared with men. Particularly as a result of structural adjustment programs, low-income women continue to experience double and triple burdens every day (Benería, 1992; Chinery-Hess et al., 1989). These problems may be difficult to resolve because women are absent from spaces where public policies are decided. (Their power is expressed mainly through demonstrations and occasional lobbying.) Some changes, however, are taking place. More women are staying in the labor force despite having children, unlike the situation in the 1970s. As a result of the crisis, but also reflecting their desire, more women are now entering the labor force.

Benería (1992) remarks that the household now faces many tensions—between men and women, and between brothers and sisters. She sees the main strategies for income generation taking place through the interdependence of family members. In her view, this is creating a forced unity within the family as well as perpetuating patriarchal rule. There is evidence that the economic crisis is affecting family composition. Glimpses from Ecuador—a median country in per capita income for the region—reveal that the number of nuclear and extended families has remained constant, but the composition of extended families has changed, with more married sons and daughters and their income-earning partners remaining at home (Moser, 1993). This arrangement has been increasingly observed in several other Latin American countries as well.

Bauer (1994) and others predict that privatization is likely to increase concentrations in the distribution of income: it may cause large layoffs as new owners try to improve the efficiency of their firms. This may lead to price increases in electricity and transportation and other goods and services. This situation will generate greater survival needs among low-income sectors, which are likely to result in greater demands made on female labor in the home and elsewhere in order to compensate for increased family expenditures.

Women's integration into the global market will generate more income for women and will probably facilitate their adoption of individualistic norms. With increased financial autonomy and assertiveness, women may counter the oppressive practices of parents and husbands. Some evidence for such a trend was presented by Fernández-Kelly (1983), who noted that Mexican women working in *maquiladora* plants were gaining new social spaces such as women's bars. Mummert, conducting research in Mexico several years later, also found that young women working in export agricultural firms felt less obliged to obey their fathers' proscriptions (1992).

Conclusions

Women are now participating to a greater extent in the economy, and this has the positive result of giving them access to an independent income, however limited. Unfortunately, the concurrent implementation of structural adjustment programs has debilitated the state, which has cut social services and thus augmented women's domestic labor. Under these conditions, women in Latin America and the Caribbean may see their capacity to question patriarchal rules reduced.

See Also

EDUCATION: CENTRAL AND SOUTH AMERICA AND THE CARIBBEAN; ENVIRONMENT: CARIBBEAN; ENVIRONMENT: CENTRAL AND SOUTH AMERICA; FEMINISM: CARIBBEAN; FEMINISM: CENTRAL AND SOUTH AMERICA; POLITICS AND THE STATE: CARIBBEAN; POLITICS AND THE STATE: CENTRAL AND SOUTH AMERICA.

References and Further Reading

Ashby, Jacqueline, and Stella Gomez, eds. 1985. *Women, agriculture and rural development in Latin America.* Cali, Colombia: Centro Internacional de Agricultura Tropical.

Bauer, Werner. 1994. Privatization in Latin America. *World Economy* 17 (4): 509–28.

Benería, Lourdes. 1992 (February). Contextualizing women's struggles for livelihood: The household, the market, and beyond. Paper presented at the conference on Learning from Latin America: Women's Struggles for Livelihood. Los Angeles: University of California at Los Angeles.

Benería, Lourdes, and Martha Roldáno. 1987. *The crossroads of class and gender: Industrial homework, subcontracting, and household dynamics in Mexico City.* Chicago: Chicago University Press.

Chinery-Hesse, Mary, et al. 1989. *Engendering adjustment for the 1990s.* London: Commonwealth Secretariat.

Cortina, Regina. 1992. Gender and power in the teachers' union of Mexico. In Nelly P. Stromquist, ed., *Women and education in Latin America.* Boulder, Col.: Lynne Rienner.

Feijóo, María del Carmen, and Elizabeth Jelín. 1987. Women from low income sectors: Economic recession and democratization of politics in Argentina. In UNICEF, eds., *The invisible adjustment: Poor women and the economic crisis,* 27-54. Santiago: UNICEF.

Fernández-Kelly, Patricia. 1983. *For we are sold: I and my people.* Albany: State University of New York Press.

Fort, Lucia, Mona Danner, and Gay Young. 1994. Gender inequality around the world: Comparing fifteen nations in five world regions. In Gay Young and Bette Dickerson, eds., *Color, class, and country: Experiences of gender,* 131–153. London: Zed.

Inter-American Dialogue. 1994. *The Americas in 1994: A time for leadership.* Washington, D.C.: Inter-American Dialogue.

Kirsch, Henry. 1975. La participación de la mujer en los mercados laborales latinoamericanos. In CEPAL, ed., *Mujeres in América Latina.* Mexico: Fondo de Cultura Económica.

Moser, Caroline. 1993. Adjustment from below. In Sarah Radcliffe and Sallie Westwood, eds., *Viva: Women and popular protest in Latin America,* 173–196. London: Routledge.

Mummert, Gail. 1992 (February). Rural Mexican women's struggle for family livelihood. Paper presented at the conference on Learning from Latin America: Women's Struggles for Livelihood. Los Angeles: University of California at Los Angeles.

Pérez Sáinz, J. and Menjívar Larín. 1994. Central American men and women in the informal sector. *Journal of Latin American Studies* 26: 431–147.

Psacharopoulos, George, and Zafiris Tzannatos. 1992. *Women's employment and pay in Latin America: Overview and methodology.* Washington, D.C.: World Bank.

Recchini de Lattes, Zulma, and Catalina Wainerman. 1982. *Female workers undercounted: The case of Latin American and Caribbean censuses.* New York: Population Council.

United Nations Development Program. 1993. *Human development report 1993.* New York: United Nations Development Program.

Nelly P. Stromquist

DEVELOPMENT: China

Since coming to power in 1949, the Chinese Communist Party (CCP) has instituted various measures aimed, on the one hand, at maximizing the use of women's labor for economic development, and, on the other, at ensuring that the benefits of economic development are shared equally by women and men. After a brief section providing a historical perspective to the modern period, this article outlines the ways in which the CCP's aims have been pursued and the extent to which they have been achieved. While the situation of women in general is covered, the focus is on rural women, because they constitute between 70 and 80 percent of the female population.

Historical Perspective

Before 1949, women's involvement in the economy was circumscribed by Confucian ideology, which deemed women inferior and subservient to men. Fundamental to this system was a concern for the maintenance of the patrilineal family. Marriages were arranged by the older generation and were usually patrilocal and exogamous, which meant that on marriage, a woman most commonly joined her husband's household in a different village. This system meant that women were treated as temporary residents in their natal family and as outsiders to the family and village after marriage. Daughters were considered less valuable than sons, and fewer resources were devoted to raising them because doing so was seen as "watering another man's garden." After marriage, women were expected to serve and submit to the authority of their parents-in-law. Women's power was decreased further because they could not own or inherit property or get a divorce.

Confucianism taught that women should not take part in public affairs and that their work should be confined to the home. This ideal was, to some extent, enforced in reality through the practice of foot binding, in which a young girl's feet were wrapped tightly to prevent them from growing beyond three-inch stumps. This meant that for the rest of the girl's life, walking would be slow and painful.

Confucian ideals could not always be maintained, however. The degree to which women were confined to the home, for example, differed according to class and according to the economic necessities of the time and place (Davin, 1976: 117–122), but it was only the women of the gentry who led truly secluded lives. In peasant families, women devoted most of their time to domestic work, but this included activities such as fetching firewood and water and going to market, which involved travel and contact with outsiders. Women often did their domestic tasks together, forming valuable friendships and support networks in the process.

Women also undertook spinning and weaving at home, and poorer women often worked as peddlers, prostitutes, and servants, although this work was not considered respectable (Pruitt, 1945). In agriculture, women's participation rates varied between regions, but on average they performed only about 13 percent of field labor (Davin, 1976: 116–118).

The early stages of industrialization in China, as in Europe, drew heavily on young women from the countryside. Consequently, by the 1920s, although they constituted only a small proportion of the population, the absolute number of young women working in factories, especially textile factories, in coastal Chinese cities such as Shanghai and Tianjin was quite large. For most, factory work was a miserable experience, characterized by exploitation and appalling living and working conditions. However, these women did gain some independence from their families and were exposed to new ideas; many participated in the labor movement (Croll, 1978: 102–6).

Among the wealthier classes the 1910s and 1920s saw an improvement in women's education and political participation. In the 1930s the Nationalist Party passed laws giving women and men equal rights in marriage and divorce, ownership of property, and employment (Croll, 1978: 155–56). However, little effort was devoted to implementing the laws, even in the cities, and few people heard about them in the countryside. It was not until after communism that legislation such as this was successfully translated into substantial improvements in women's lives on a broad scale.

The Period 1949–1976

After coming to power, the CCP initiated a program for development that drew heavily on that of the Soviet Union. This program included a commitment to gender equality and efforts to achieve both economic growth and a reduction in class inequality, through the redistribution of land from the minority gentry class to the peasants, followed by collectivization and the nationalization of industry.

The key principle underpinning CCP approaches to gender issues was Friedrich Engels's argument (1977: 74) that women will be liberated only once they are involved in paid production and their domestic duties are reduced to a minimum.

However, over the years, the degree to which this principle was acted out in practice varied according to the perceived needs of the economy. In fact, after 1949 there was a

rough pattern in which CCP policies related to women's work swung from an emphasis on women's participation in paid labor, in one period, to a deemphasis on their paid labor and a greater stress on their domestic labor in the next. Thus, the years 1949–1952, and 1957–1965 were periods in which women's participation in paid production was deemphasized. This pattern corresponded roughly to changes in the economy and, more particularly, to changes in overall economic and political strategies.

The greatest efforts to fulfill Engels's requirements for women's liberation were made during the "great leap forward" (GLF) period of 1957–1960. GLF was a development strategy that aimed to overcome problems due to lack of technology, expertise, and capital through mass mobilization of China's one plentiful resource: human labor.

In rural areas, collectivization was undertaken at a rapid pace. An important result for women was a loosening of the authority of the (usually male) head of the family over other family members. Under the collective system, the production team leader, rather than individual male heads of families, made the important decisions concerning the use of women's labor. In many places this played an important role in improving the situation of women, since party policy put pressure on production team leaders to treat women and men equally.

In addition, large numbers of women were drawn into paid production, and the income they earned helped to improve their status in the family. As a result of GLF, from this time on, even though the proportion of women employed would not increase at a constant rate, it was generally accepted, indeed expected, that women would work in paid production.

A further aspect of GLF was that for the first, and to date the last, time in the history of the CCP, large-scale efforts were made to socialize domestic work. Each commune ran several nurseries and kindergartens, and families were urged to eat in communal dining halls. Other services that developed on a wide scale during this period included sewing workshops, grain mills, and health services.

However, the GLF period also revealed limitations and problems associated with Engels's approach to women's liberation. One problem was that the program for the socialization of domestic labor ran into difficulties because it was considered too costly. After GLF a large proportion of communal services in rural areas were closed, although they fared somewhat better in urban areas.

Other limitations stemmed from the failure to challenge the continued practice of patrilocal marriage in rural areas. This practice led to the mistreatment of young daughters and a reluctance to teach them skills that would be lost to another family, and—resulting from this and from the fact that, on marriage, they were moved into an alien environment—an inability on the part of many young women to participate in production outside the home and in the political affairs of the village.

Another phenomenon that remained largely unchallenged during GLF was the gender division of labor in paid work. Women were concentrated in the least prestigious areas of the economy, and despite a policy of "equal pay for equal work," it was common, especially in rural communes and small collective industries, for women to receive less pay than men, even for performing the same tasks (Croll, 1978: 285–286).

The obstacles to women's liberation made apparent during GLF received some attention during subsequent years and especially in the years just following the Cultural Revolution, that is, from 1969 to 1976. During these years campaigns were run in rural areas to persuade men to share housework with their wives, matrilocal marriages were promoted, and women's participation in political affairs was encouraged. In most areas, however, the campaigns were short-lived and not very effective.

Contemporary China

After the death of Mao Zedong in 1976, the CCP instituted a set of radical reforms aimed at increasing economic growth through modernization and the development of a market economy. The reforms engendered rapid economic development and improvements in living conditions, but also increases in inequalities, including those between women and men and between rural and urban women.

In rural areas communes were dismantled in the late 1970s and early 1980s and a form of household farming once more became the norm. In addition, a number of measures were taken to encourage diversification and commercialization of the rural economy, and in 1979 a one-child family policy was introduced in both rural and urban areas in order to curb population growth.

These reforms had some serious negative consequences for women. For example, the introduction of household farming resulted in declines in collective funds available for education. This led to increases in school fees, so that numerous poor families could no longer afford to send all their children to school. Many families kept their sons in school but withdrew their daughters. This resulted in an erosion of earlier gains in rural female education, with an alarming rise in illiteracy among young girls.

In contrast to urban areas, where one- or two-child families were already the norm, there has been enormous resis-

tance in the countryside to the policy of one child per family. This is in part because more labor means more income in a peasant family, and in part because, with no old-age pension system, parents depend on children for support in their later years. Particularly, they depend on sons, because under the patrilocal marriage system, which continues to prevail in the countryside, daughters leave their natal family when they marry. Where the one-child policy has been successful, women have benefited from a reduced workload and less strain on their health. However, women have also borne the brunt of the conflicts over reproduction that have become common between peasant families and state officials. Some have been forced by local officials to have late abortions, while others have been beaten and abused by their families for giving birth to daughters. There have also been reports of female infanticide in some provinces. Concern over these issues led the government to modify the one-child policy in the late 1980s, so that rural couples who gave birth to a girl would be allowed to have another child. This has led to a decline in the violence against women associated with the one-child policy, but at the same time the new concessions reinforce the perception that females are inferior to males (Davin, 1990).

In terms of production and employment, reforms introduced in rural areas spurred a growth in agricultural productivity, a diversification of the rural economy, and very rapid industrialization. These changes affected women and men rather differently. Thus, one of the most striking trends to have emerged in recent years is the "feminization" of agriculture, a corollary of industrialization noted in many other countries besides China. With the development of nonagricultural employment opportunities, farming has come to be seen as the least desirable form of employment. Rural men, and, to a lesser extent, young rural women, have been the first to leave the farm, while married women have taken over responsibility for agriculture (Judd, 1994; Jacka, 1997: 120–142).

Cottage industries and household-based animal husbandry have become a major avenue for rural women's employment. Their work in this sector has been promoted by the government as a way of reducing the demand for industrial employment and maximizing the use of a flexible, cheap workforce. At the same time, women themselves have sought such work, in some cases because they have no alternative but in others because, although it usually generates only a low income, this type of work is more easily combined with domestic duties and offers women more autonomy and scope for self-development than employment in large-scale industry (Jacka, 1997: 143–161; Judd, 1994: 153–163).

While industry employs fewer rural women than men, during the 1980s and 1990s increasingly large numbers of young, unmarried rural women were drawn into industrial employment. The majority work in local township enterprises. There they constitute about 33 percent of the workforce, on average, but as much as 95 percent in some textile factories (Duan Daohuai et al., 1988).

With the development of a market economy, previously very strict restrictions on rural-urban migration have been considerably relaxed, although it is still extremely difficult for a peasant to obtain permanent residence in an urban area. It is estimated that there are currently some 100 million peasants living temporarily in cities or towns. Of these, approximately 30 percent are women, although the proportion varies from one region to the next. A large proportion work as domestic servants in urban households, while others are employed as temporary laborers in unskilled jobs in textile industries and in private street stalls and restaurants and as prostitutes. These are all jobs that urban women shun as low-paid, low-status, unpleasant work.

Young rural women also form the majority of the workforce in the manufacturing industries of the Special Economic Zones, which were first established at the end of the 1970s to attract foreign investment and technology with tax incentives and cheap labor. The situation of women in this sector of the Chinese economy is similar to that of the female workers in the export-processing zones of southeast Asia, and, sadly, is also reminiscent of the exploitation of women in industrial employment in the early part of the twentieth century. Women are drawn to such work because of the scarcity of income-generating work on the farm and because of the lure of high wages and a modern lifestyle. Yet reports abound of women, many of them below age 16, working very long hours in dangerous, unhealthy conditions for below-subsistence wages (Lee, 1998: 109–136).

Urban women today, as previously, are considerably better off than their rural counterparts, but recent reforms have also brought them problems. In particular, these reforms have contributed to increases in discrimination against women in employment.

In state-run industries, managers have been given more autonomy as a result of urban reforms and have been put under more pressure to maximize profitability. Consequently, many have tried to "streamline" production by reducing their workforce. Women have been the first to lose their jobs, in part because the requirement for paid maternity leave makes women workers more expensive in employers' eyes. There have also been frequent reports of direct discrimination against women in the recruitment of new workers. As a result, women constitute about 70 per-cent of the urban unemployed. In addition, within the urban workforce, the average female worker receives only 42 to 55 percent of the wages earned by the average male worker. These figures are comparable to those reported in other east Asian economies and are due in large measure to the concentration of women in the poorest paying occupations and sectors of the economy (Rawski and Zhang, 1999).

These trends in employment are reinforced through gender typing in education and the media. During the 1970s it was claimed that "what men can do, women can do too," and women were portrayed in the media as industrial workers and peasants, almost indistinguishable in appearance from men. Today, however, physiological differences between women and men are stressed, as is the desirability of a traditional division of labor between the sexes, and the most common images of women in the media are mothers, housewives, and sex objects (Honig and Hershatter, 1988; Hooper, 1999).

Conclusion

In the 1960s and early 1970s, Communist China was hailed enthusiastically by feminists across the world as a model of how concerns for gender equality could be successfully incorporated into development strategies. Today, the achievements of the Communist Party and of women in China are still impressive. Women are no longer considered men's chattels, almost all women work in paid employment, and outstanding improvements have been made in female education.

Yet, since the 1970s, outside observers have spoken, more often than not, of the "unfinished" liberation of women in China, and Chinese women themselves believe that China is still a long way from achieving gender equality, especially in the countryside. As in other parts of the world, Chinese women continue to suffer a heavy "double burden" of domestic and nondomestic work; they are concentrated in the lower-paid, less prestigious sectors of the economy; and they frequently face discrimination.

See Also

EDUCATION: EAST ASIA; ENVIRONMENT: EAST ASIA (CHINA); FEMINISM: CHINA; HOUSEHOLDS AND FAMILIES: EAST ASIA; POLITICS AND THE STATE: EAST ASIA

References and Further Reading

Croll, Elisabeth. 1978. *Feminism and socialism in China.* London: Routledge and Kegan Paul.

Davin, Delia. 1976. *Woman-work: Women and the party in revolutionary China.* Oxford: Clarendon.

Davin, Delia. 1990. Never mind if it's a girl, you can have another try. In Jorgen Delman, Clemens Stubbe Ostergaard, and Flemming Christiansen, eds., *Remaking peasant China: Problems of rural development and institutions at the start of the 1990s*, 81–91. Denmark: Aarhus University Press.

Duan Daohuai, Jin Zhenji, Zhang Zhunying, and Shi Suoda. 1988. Building a new countryside: Chinese women in rural enterprises. In Noeleen Heyzer, *Daughters in industry: Work skills and consciousness of women workers in Asia*. Kuala Lumpur: Asian and Pacific Development Centre.

Engels, Friedrich. 1977 [1884]. *The origin of the family, private property and the state*. Moscow: Progress.

Honig, Gail, and Emily Hershatter. 1988. *Personal voices: Chinese women in the 1980s*. Stanford, Calif.: Stanford University Press.

Hooper, Beverley. 1999. Researching women's lives in contemporary China. In Antonia Finnane and Anne McLaren, eds. *Dress, sex and text in Chinese culture*, 243–262. Australia: Monash Asia Institute, Monash University.

Jacka, Tamara. 1997. *Women's work in rural China: Change and continuity in an era of reform*. Cambridge, New York, and Melbourne: Cambridge University Press.

Judd, Ellen. 1994. *Gender and power in rural North China*. Stanford, Calif.: Stanford University Press.

Lee, Ching Kwan. 1998. *Gender and the South China miracle: Two worlds of factory women*. Berkeley, Los Angeles, and London: University of California Press.

Pruitt, Ida. 1945 *A daughter of Han: Autobiography of a Chinese working woman*. Stanford, Calif.: Stanford University Press.

Tamara Jacka

DEVELOPMENT: Chinese Case Study— Rural Women

China is a large agricultural country with a rural population that has reached 900 million, accounting for 75 percent of the total population. Since the early 1980s, because of rural economic reform, steady development in China's agriculture—especially food production—has provided a solid foundation for national economic growth. It is astounding but true that, in China, cultivation of 7 percent of the world's farmland feeds 22 percent of the world's population.

The rural women of China are an immense human resource and have played a key role in agricultural development in China since the establishment of the Household Responsibility System in 1978. With the establishment of rural industrial structure and the changes in the rural indus-

trial system as well as the rapid emergence of township enterprises, many male laborers have turned to nonagricultural work or have moved to urban areas for employment. Women have, therefore, become a key factor in agriculture. In some areas, the number of female laborers has exceeded 70 percent. According to 1998 statistics provided by the All China Women's Federation (ACWF), rural female laborers had reached 21 million, accounting for 65.6 percent of the total rural labor force, and their contributions were responsible for 50 to 60 percent of the total value of agricultural production. As a more localized example, 4.5 million women in Shandong farmed 60 percent of the total farmland in the province, and 2.8 million women in Hebei Province have been responsible for the production of 65 percent of the cotton fields in the province. Approximately 12 million women in China voluntarily take part in tree-planting and watershed projects every year.

Women are also actively involved in multibusiness activities. It has been determined that among 187 township markets in Songhuajiang District, Heilongjiang Province, 80 percent of the business has been conducted by women. Fifty-two thousand women in Nanzhao County, Henan Province, market agricultural and sideline products, and at least 200 of those women were believed to hold an average of one million yuan in assets. Fifty million women workers in Guangdong Province provide 43 percent of the total labor force in township enterprises.

These figures lead us to the conclusion that rural reform and development in China have created new opportunities for women's full participation. Although women's active participation has accelerated and facilitated the smooth reform of the development process, and has opened new doors to employment, Li (1999) examined women's critical issues and found that those opportunities have brought about serious challenges to women who have to confront growing social and psychological stress.

Economic development in China has created imbalances for a variety of natural, physical, social, economic, and historical reasons. Major problems encountered by rural women can be examined from the following vantage points:

1. *Heavy physical labor*: Rural women engaged in farming are subject to heavy physical demands because of the extreme need for agricultural productivity, the use of heavy and out-of-date farm tools, and the conventional farming system. Women often suffer from contagious and gynecological diseases caused in part by their exhausting physical labor.

2. *Lower education level*: The ACWF reported in 1998 that among 21 million rural female laborers, those who have

a primary or middle school education are most prevalent. There are still 20 million illiterate females aged 15 to 40 in rural China. Women's cultural position has sometimes prevented them from acquiring information and using agricultural science and technology or responding to the challenge of a market economic system.

3. *Poor access to technological information*: Women's access to technological information is affected by male-dominated cultural traditions, a poor extension service system, weakness in communication and information networks, poverty, and a lack of credit.

Women have less access than men to technical training, community activities, and connections to the outside world owing to their inferior social, cultural, and economic status relative to men. Women face the pressure of triple roles: reproduction, production, and community management. Traditionally, women have been confined at home and expected to perform the full reproductive role including childbearing, child care, looking after a husband and the old, preparing food and clothing, cleaning the house, and so on. In the late twentieth century, the Chinese government advocated only one child per couple.

Understandably, there is a strong desire to raise a healthy and clever child, and this is of primary importance to each family. Women are required to shoulder child rearing duties, in addition to farming and other income-producing activities. The stress and challenge of these multiple roles often prevent women from finding time to attend training or to obtain current technical information.

The ACWF (Urban and Rural Department, 1998) reported that there are still about 10 thousand townships in rural China without an agricultural extension system. Even with the existence of an extension system in some areas, Liu (1997) argues that women's specific needs tend to be ignored.

Gao (1999) assessed women's organizations in China. The ACWF is recognized as the biggest women's organization. It has networks at provincial, county, township, and village levels. Women's federations represent and protect women's rights, promote gender equality, and facilitate women's participation at all levels by organizing nationwide campaigns and training activities, implementing poverty alleviation projects, and so on. Their commitment and contributions are highly valued; however, the method of conventional top-down and supply-driven management has been considered to be a negative influence in the attempt to stimulate more effective work.

Liu (1997) points out that women lack self-help groups at the grassroots level as well as local aid organizations to provide technical service. Therefore, informal face-to-face interactions are considered by women to be their most preferred, reliable, economic, and effective way to gather information and exchange ideas. Credit is necessary for women to do efficient farming or to embark on diversified activities. This is especially true for the women who continue to strive just for survival. It continues to be difficult for women to obtain the credit they need.

Zhang (1999) determined that 20 million people and 20 million head of large livestock lacked adequate drinking water in 592 poor counties in China. The poor population is mostly located in scattered harsh mountainous areas, desert or plateau areas, and remote minority-nationality regions. It is estimated that 35.6 percent of the poor inhabit central China and 56.7 percent inhabit western China. Poor women, comprising over half of the population, are the most underprivileged, impoverished, and vulnerable group.

Zhang (1999) attributed difficulty in generating family income to three major factors: the falling price for agricultural produce because of abundant market supply; a declining need of township enterprises for surplus labor; and decreased wages and job opportunity caused by an increasing number of laid-off urban workers.

Participation by rural women in work and development opportunities is encouraged and supported by both the family and the society. Government policy makers, women workers, researchers, and practitioners from public, private, or voluntary sectors—including national and international NGOs—it is hoped, will gain a better awareness of gender issues, developing good strategies, designing appropriate policy approaches, and initiating effective intervention programs to best respond to women's needs.

See Also

AGRICULTURE; DEVELOPMENT: CHINA; DIVISION OF LABOR; EDUCATION: EAST ASIA; ENVIRONMENT: EAST ASIA (CHINA); MEDIA: CHINESE CASE STUDY

References and Further Reading

Gao Xiao-xian. 1999. Assessment and rethinking of rural women and rural development. *Chinese Women's Movement* 3.

Li Xiao-yun. 1999. Current status and prospects for women and rural development. *Chinese Women's Movement* 3.

Liu Feng-qin. 1997. Information transfer and rural women's development—with reference to women in rural China. Unpublished MA dissertation paper.

Urban and Rural Department, ACWF. 1998. A report on China's rural women and agricultural development. Unpublished.

Zhang lei. 1999. A report on tasks and current status of China's poverty alleviation.

Feng-qin Liu

DEVELOPMENT:
Commonwealth of Independent States

The joint demise of communism and the Soviet Union have had an important effect on the status of women in the Commonwealth of Independent States (CIS). In the Soviet Union, communist commitment to gender equality translated into significant privileges and advancements for women. At the same time, communism hardly resolved the question of equality between men and women. Contrary to communist ideals and Soviet accounts, women experienced systematic discrimination in the workforce and by the Communist Party. Female workers suffered from lower wages and less professional mobility, and relationships between men and women were characterized by the latter's subordination and obedience rather than equality and partnership (Malysheva, 1992). The continued transformation of this region and the establishment of independent states with distinctive gender policies presents women in the CIS with tremendous challenges and uncertainty.

The Position of Women in the Soviet Union

The trends affecting women in the CIS have been conditioned by communist ideology and patterns of economic development and political authority that developed during the Soviet era. According to socialist theory, if women could work outside the home while child care facilities, communal kitchens, and other means of socializing housework were available, their oppression would be eliminated, and communism would bring about equality between the sexes. Studies conducted in the 1950s confirmed that despite differences in cultural traditions and levels of economic development across the 15 republics and among the over 100 ethnic groups, communism both improved women's status and influenced their role in similar ways throughout the Soviet Union.

The position of Soviet women was affected by three main factors: increased access to education, the government's desire to move women into the paid labor force, and the establishment of generous social welfare programs and child care facilities (Lapidus, 1978). Free, universal primary education was introduced in the Soviet Union in the 1930s. Within 40 years, Soviet women were slightly better educated than men, constituting over half of the students in higher education and more than 60 percent of all skilled workers with higher or secondary specialized education.

According to the Soviet modernization strategy, educated and technically trained women were necessary to expand the Soviet labor force. As a result, for most of the post–World War II period women represented approximately half of the Soviet labor force. Women's involvement in the labor force, however, varied across the republics. In the 1980s, Latvian and Estonian women constituted approximately 55 percent of the workforce in their republics, while women in central Asia, where traditional cultures were most resistant to Soviet mobilization efforts, constituted less than 40 percent of workers.

Women's high education levels, their substantial presence in the workforce, and Soviet law, which guaranteed equal pay regardless of sex, did not mean there were no differences between Soviet men and women in the economic and political spheres. Despite the image of Soviet women as tractor drivers and scientists, most female workers were found in the education, medical, and trade sectors of the economy. "Horizontal divisions" such as these meant that these "feminized" sectors of the economy received less pay and little prestige compared with the industrial and military sectors, dominated coincidentally by male workers.

Horizontal divisions of the workforce only partially explain the reason for women's lower salaries, as women remained highly concentrated in low-paying, "nonproductive" spheres of the economy. Further insight into women's status can be gained by examining the "vertical divisions" of the Soviet labor force, which left female workers at lower and mid-level positions. Consequently, even *within* sectors of the economy, there were substantial differences between women's and men's salaries and their ability to reach positions of authority. In the late 1980s, Soviet women represented well over half of all engineers, economists, and medical workers, yet they represented less than 10 percent of the country's top administrators (Fong, 1993). In the Transcaucasian republics and in central Asia, the number of female directors or women in positions of authority was negligible (Pilkington, 1992).

While communist theory strongly supported the mobilization of women into the labor force, many communists believed that women's participation in paid labor was separate from women's involvement in politics. Lenin himself recognized that most male communists regarded agitation and propaganda work among woman with suspicion, either because they considered specific women's sections unnecessary or because they felt that women's work had nothing to do with party goals (Heitlinger, 1979). Compared with many industrialized countries, the Soviet Union boasted a large percentage of women in political office. Yet, according to Joel Moses's research (1977), women in the Soviet Union were most often recruited for positions involving either indoctrination or issues related to health or education, but they were virtually denied access to important political posts. All studies conducted conclude that despite the significant presence of women in the workforce and public life, they were virtually absent from high-level decision-making bodies.

The Position of Women in the CIS

The economic, political, and social destabilization following the collapse of the Soviet Union has been tremendously difficult for all citizens living within its former boundaries. Economic restructuring and growing social conservatism, however, have proved particularly damaging to the status of women in Soviet society. Although gender equality was never fully realized in the Soviet Union, the division of this country into independent states, none of which have articulated an interest in women's equality and all of which are moving rapidly toward the uncertainties of market economies, is, indeed, ominous. At present, economic and political changes have left women in the Commonwealth facing high unemployment, fewer political opportunities, and tremendous pressure to embrace traditional feminine roles.

Women in the former Soviet Union are most threatened by economic restructuring, as these states seek to become more economically efficient and productive. The future of CIS economies relies on strong, expanding private sectors, and women (far more than men) are both less able and more reluctant to participate in this high-risk sphere. Data thus far indicate that while Commonwealth states do not prevent women from starting their own businesses, women are more fearful of getting involved with what were not so long ago considered "black market" activities. In addition, women lack business connections or have little access to start-up capital to move independently into the private sector (McMahon, 1994).

In theory, ongoing structural changes in the economy could prove beneficial to women, as the emphasis on heavy industry is replaced by the development of a service sector. Females in these "nonproductive" sectors of the economy would, thus, have much to gain from the increased need for and prestige of white-collar positions. In reality, however, women are being forced out of positions in previously feminized sectors, such as banking, economics, and finance, which are attractive and lucrative in capitalist systems.

Detailed statistics on women's unemployment in all of the commonwealth states are not available, but studies con-

ducted in the last years of the Soviet Union and in post-Soviet Russia and Ukraine confirm that female workers will predominate among the unemployed in the CIS. In the last phase of communist rule, the marginalization of women in the workforce and their return to the home became the unofficial answer to the need to scale back the labor force and combat social ills. From 1985 to 1987, for example, more than 80 percent of all labor cutbacks were made at the expense of female workers. In 1989–1990 this trend intensified, and women constituted over 60 percent of those who had lost their jobs.

In most cases, the Soviet state and post-Soviet governments have discouraged women from working by extending maternity leave for new mothers or by replacing full-time work with part-time positions with flexible hours. Initially, many women were attracted to the notion of extra time for their families and the opportunity to shop for affordable products. However, the liberalization of prices, the move toward the market, and the rising number of female-headed households have together made the contribution provided by women's labor an economic necessity for most families in the CIS.

Economic reasons to terminate female workers are exacerbated by post-Soviet societies' desire to throw off the vestiges of communist thinking in all spheres. Indeed, as Commonwealth states establish their own economic and social welfare policies, many of their citizens, men and women alike, have begun to question the Soviet commitment to gender equality. To varying degrees, the appropriate position of women in society and their role in the workforce have come under intense scrutiny. In some states, such as Russia, the backlash against the Soviet experiment with egalitarianism has resulted in calls both for women to return to the home and to their "natural" role as wife and mother, and for the "resexualization" of society.

Women, thus, not only suffer from higher unemployment but also are less likely to find employment in the emerging market economies. According to all reports, the "typical" unemployed CIS citizen is a middle-aged, professional woman with higher or at least secondary education. These women have a difficult time finding suitable employment, especially in an environment where foreign and domestic firms advertise job openings according to gender and age. Newspapers are filled with job advertisements seeking "young and pretty girls" to become secretaries and personal assistants, and on occasion sexual relations with the boss are implied. Without the threat of reprisal from the Communist Party, and with the virtual elimination of affirmative action policies in post-Soviet states, women have little protection against such discrimination.

During the Soviet period, women's obligations in the paid sector were made more bearable by a generous system of paid maternity leave, extended leave for mothers with young children, and other compensations. However, the collapse of the Soviet government transferred the responsibility of financing such benefits to individual states' control. In an effort to increase economic efficiency, many of the Commonwealth states have, in turn, placed the responsibility of welfare entitlements and child care facilities on local enterprises. As these companies face the pressures of a competitive marketplace, the attractiveness of employing women is further diminished.

Democratization of the political sphere promises equal opportunity for all citizens. Yet in the former Soviet Union this promise has translated into a further marginalization of women in the official political sphere. Since the late 1980s and the elimination of political quotas, which appropriated a certain number of political positions for female candidates, there has been a steady drop in the number of women in political office. Given these societies' reactions against Soviet demands for women's involvement in politics and the lack of genuine changes in perceptions of gender roles, many voters see female politicians as the least desirable candidates for political office. Consequently, every postcommunist government in the region has witnessed a decline in the number of women elected to political office. Moreover, few of the CIS governments have nominated women to become cabinet members or high-level advisers.

The dearth of women in political office and as party leaders does not mean that they have not taken advantage of the new political environment. Mary Buckley (1992) and others point to the important role that women's organizations played in many of the movements for national liberation during the last stage of the Gorbachev era. In Lithuania, for example, the Popular Front Movement created "women's sections" because many female activists believed that independence from Soviet control was a necessary step toward the liberation of Lithuanian women.

Today, the intersection of nationalism and women's rights is most prevalent in Commonwealth states with high percentages of ethnic Russians, such as Kazakhstan and Estonia. Russian women are finding that many of the rights they took for granted as Soviet citizens, such as a woman's right to self-determination through the control of her body, are threatened by growing religious fundamentalism and social conservatism. Russian women living in central Asia, for example, started women's organizations and support groups, lobbied their respective central Asian governments, and appealed to then-President Yeltsin to support the rights of Russian women.

Reasons for Optimism

Despite the difficulties facing women in the CIS, recent changes have not been wholly negative. Although unemployment, the elimination of political quotas, and the conservative backlash present women with significant challenges, women have not been mere observers of change. The emergence of civil societies has already translated into a proliferation of independent women's organizations, such as economic networks, research institutes, and consciousness-raising groups. Economic and political changes are, thus, seen by some women as an opportunity to confront ongoing threats to women's status and to make genuine advances in gender equality. For those who feel that communism forced radical, alien concepts on their societies, thereby yielding more burdens than benefits, the transformation of these societies is viewed with concern but also relief. Their activities emphasize women's roles as wives and mothers and seek to promote women's traditional values in society.

Women in the CIS are faced with both obstacles and opportunities. At present, the enormousness of these obstacles tends to overshadow any potential benefits. However, the numerous women's organizations and a growing consciousness among women of the problems affecting their gender are positive signs that, despite different orientations, women are beginning to assert an independent voice. With women slowly but steadily realizing that they alone have the power to define the future role they will play in post-Soviet life, communism's demise and the emergence of independent, democratically oriented states should perhaps be seen as a potential blessing in disguise.

See Also

DEVELOPMENT: OVERVIEW; EDUCATION: COMMONWEALTH OF INDEPENDENT STATES; POLITICS AND THE STATE: COMMONWEALTH OF INDEPENDENT STATES

References and Further Reading

Buckley, Mary. 1992. *Perestroika and Soviet women.* Cambridge: Cambridge University Press.

Berry, Ellen E. 1995. *Postcommunism and the body politic.* New York: New York University Press.

Einhorn, Barbara. 1993. *Cinderella goes to market.* London: Verso.

Fong, Monica. 1993. *The role of women in rebuilding the Russian economy.* Washington, D.C.: World Bank.

Funk, Nanette, and Magda Mueller, eds. 1993. *Gender politics and postcommunism.* New York: Routledge.

Heitlinger, Alena. 1979. *Women and state socialism: Sex inequality in the Soviet Union and Czechoslovakia.* London: Macmillan.

Lapidus, Gail Warshofsky. 1978. *Women in Soviet society.* Berkeley: University of California Press.

Malysheva, Marina. 1992. The politics of gender in Russia. *Women in Literature and Society*, Occasional Bradford Vocational Papers, no 7: 74–85.

McMahon, Patrice. 1994. The effect of economic and political reforms on Soviet/Russian women. In Nahid Aslanbeijui, Steven Pressman, and Gale Summerfield, eds., *Women in the age of economic transformation*. London: Routledge.

Moses, Joel, C. 1977. Women in political roles. In Dorothy Atkinson, ed., *Women in Russia*. Stanford, Calif.: Stanford University Press.

Pilkington, Hilary. 1992. Russia and the former Soviet republics. In Chris Corrin, ed., *Superwomen and the double burden: Women's experience of change in central and eastern Europe and the former Soviet Union*. London: Scarlet Press.

Renee, Tanya, ed. 1997. *Ana's land*. Boulder, Col.: Westview.

Rueschemeyer, Marilyn, ed. 1994. *Women in the politics of postcommunist Eastern Europe*. Armonk, N.Y.: M. E. Sharpe.

Patrice McMahon

DEVELOPMENT: Japan

Women have always played a vital part in the Japanese economy, contributing to social and economic development through paid and unpaid labor. Until the 1950s women were engaged in farming and family businesses, largely controlling their own work. Drastic changes in women's work came with changes in the Japanese economy in the 1960s and 1970s as women took paid employment outside the home. Women's employment changed again by 2000 from an emphasis on manufacturing to the service sector. Today, about 80 percent of employed Japanese women are in white-collar jobs and about 20 percent in blue-collar jobs. As more educated women enter the labor force, they are taking more diverse work, ranging from traditionally male-only jobs to new jobs in emerging fields (Ministry of Labor, 1999). Employment has become the norm for women as more women balance paid and unpaid labor.

Women nonetheless still have secondary status in the labor market. Their salaries equal only 60 percent of those of male workers. Promotion is limited. Only a few women occupy managerial positions. About 37 percent are engaged in part-time work (less than 35 hours per week). Women constitute about 67 percent of the part-time labor force. Their secondary status in the economy can be attributed to this gender inequality in the workplace.

Patriarchal Ideology

Patriarchy in Japan originates in the prewar traditional family system in which the male head exercised power over women. The traditional family system, while inheriting Confucian ethics of the feudal era and the imperial power of the Meiji era, empowered the father to control his daughter's life. Although there was not a sharp gender division of labor in the household and family business, the daughter was confined mainly to domestic work and was expected to be married and become a wife and mother (Fukutake, 1989). Patriarchy put women in secondary roles in the economy. The nuclear family replaced the traditional family system in contemporary Japan. But patriarchal ideology has remained, in the form of a clear-cut gender division of labor between men and women in the capitalist nuclear family. The gender division of labor in the home sustains and reinforces gender inequality in the economy. The gender division of labor is the primary cause of women's secondary status in the labor market; but other institutions like the enterprise system and the state have played a role, too.

Gender Inequality in the Enterprise System

Institutional changes brought women into the mainstream of the labor force during the 1980s and 1990s. Fifty-one percent of the total female population aged 15 and older were in the labor market in 1992. More women (40 percent of female high school graduates) than men (36 percent of male high school graduates) went on to colleges and universities and entered the labor market with more education. In 1992, 80.4 percent of women college graduates and 79.7 percent of their male counterparts were employed. A labor shortage and corporate restructuring toward a more flexible economy increased the demand for female labor. Equal employment legislation and other government measures helped women balance family and work.

These institutional changes have led to growing segmentation within the female labor market. The wage gap between regular and part-time women workers has widened, and wage inequality between men and women has also increased. The segmented female labor market has not however changed the general pattern of Japanese women's participation in the labor force, indicating that gender itself continues to play an important role in women's disadvantaged position in the economy.

Women have moved into the enterprise system, filling labor shortages and occupying strategic functions. Corporations have created new forms of employment and personnel policies to accommodate the influx of women. Some corporations have gone beyond the clerical and managerial dual-track system and are now offering women multicareer paths. Others have totally abolished gender disparities. But as long as corporations retain the enterprise system, women will have to work like men. In this sense, the elimination of gender disparities does not offer much to women. An old problem remains. When a woman decides to have a child, she must drop out of the labor market. Abundant child care centers (more than 20,000 in Japan) and the child care leave system are not sufficient to support the longer working hours that the enterprise system requires of women. The inadequate support system for working women makes it difficult for them to have simultaneous involvement in the family and workplace.

The enterprise system is characterized by long working hours, employment for life, seniority-based wages and promotion, and on-the-job training (Dore, 1987). These characteristics conflict with a woman's life cycle. The enterprise system requires women to keep working without interruption of employment and is therefore probably the strongest institutional support for patriarchal ideology. Under the enterprise system, working women must be company women devoted to the firm and in need of a "househusband" if they are to combine child rearing and work. In the absence of a househusband, women have no choice but to quit work to care for their children. Thus, the enterprise system creates a rigid gender division of labor between workplace and home.

The enterprise system is harsh on women because it has been created by and for men and supported by women's unpaid labor in the home. The male-only club of the enterprise environment also discourages women's career aspirations. When they face their life cycle choice, women pursue their desire to have a family, deliberately choosing their autonomy over the enterprise system. Women prefer their life plan over total devotion to the enterprise.

Japanese women's participation in the labor force thus takes the shape of an M-shaped curve, which may be attributable to the patriarchal enterprise system. Women's first peak (75.6 percent) in their participation rate is in their early twenties (20–24). Women continue to work until their early thirties, when they have a child. The early thirties(30–34) is the bottom (52.7 percent) of the M-shaped curve. When the children enter school, women go back into the labor market, creating the second peak (72 percent) of the curve in their forties (45-49) (Ministry of Labor Women's Bureau, 1999). In some advanced societies, women's labor force participation describes either a much milder M curve or a continuous pattern, indicating that women keep working during their reproductive years.

When Japanese women return to the labor market in their early forties, they tend to take part-time jobs, simply because the enterprise system makes it impossible to balance family and full-time regular work. During the economic expansion of the 1960s and 1970s, female part-time workers did mostly unskilled and semiskilled production work. Employers used women to adjust their business to cyclical ups and downs in the economy, defining them as peripheral employees (Fujita, 1988).

The entry of women college graduates into the part-time labor market in the 1980s and 1990s changed women's employment structure. Women are no longer functioning primarily as economic cushions but are staffing expanding businesses and filling restructured corporate positions. The most striking change is the emergence of female part-time professionals, particularly in the information industry. Employers are using women part-time professionals not as cheap labor but as strategically crucial, flexibly specialized employees. This new type of demand for female part-time professionals makes women's paid work more compatible with their preference for personal autonomy while meeting employers' requirements for a flexible labor pool. Many women are refusing full-time work, seeing it as limiting the realization of their potential (Fujita, 1991).

The Rigid Gender Division of Labor in the Home

The enterprise system compounds a gender division of labor in the home. Having a "company man" turns a woman into a "worker bee" primarily responsible for the family. Men primarily value the enterprise community, where they work in a web of human relations. The welfare of the family is less important than their devotion to the enterprise. Women thus take primary responsibility for the family and take part in the community where the family lives. They, too, live in a web of social relations, but in much wider and looser terms. They are mothers, wives, daughters, sisters, caretakers for their parents, friends, volunteers in recycling campaigns, members of health food co-ops, members of peace and environmental movements, members of parent-teacher associations, and activists in local politics. In Japan, where smooth relations with others are stressed, the internal and external pressures to fill these roles are quite high. When women quit work to have a child, they tend to give priority to child care, but still aspire to a career. Placing paid work in a secondary position, many women play multiple roles.

The linkage of the nuclear family to the enterprise system thus leads to a rigid gender division of labor in Japan. Men are confined to the workplace while women extend their activities communitywide. Women communicate with and support one another through horizontal networks that are the obverse of the vertical enterprise system.

The State as Orchestrator of Patriarchal Ideology

The state has launched several policies to keep women in the labor market. A leave system was enacted in 1992 to ease the burden of child care for men and women. The state also enacted leave so that employees could attend to elderly parents.

Although these laws address both sexes, men working in the enterprise system are less likely to use them. The laws are really aimed at women. Women are expected to take employment while simultaneously caring for children and elderly parents. Arguably, the state, far from liberating women or giving them equal opportunity to compete with men, keeps women in secondary roles in the labor market. If the state is serious about gender equality, the Japanese enterprise system must be changed to accommodate women's interests. As yet, there is no sign that the state is intent on changing the enterprise system; on the contrary, the state supports it with every available means.

The Japanese state is "developmental," engineering the country's economic development. It also engages in reaching consensus about the future direction of Japanese society (Hill and Fujita, 1995). Yet it is remarkably gender-blind in its economic policies, none of which addresses women explicitly. Women exist in the state's blueprint, along with the aged, as a secondary labor force available in times of labor shortage. Otherwise, women do not appear except as part of the state's emphasis on a healthy and sound family to reproduce male labor power and the next generation's labor force. The state shares responsibility for gender inequality in the labor market because of its failure to intervene in the labor market on behalf of women's interests. Gender-blind policy has reinforced male dominance in the enterprise system, the workplace, and the home (Fujita, 1987).

Facing an aging society, the state uses women to keep its welfare program to a minimum. In the Japanese welfare system, the family is the primary caregiver for elderly parents. But it is women who actually take responsibility for aged parents, often quitting work to take care of them. By using women in this way, the state achieves a low-cost welfare policy. The state's failure to provide alternatives such as nursing care facilities for the elderly reveals the presumption that women, as primary homemakers in the family and secondary workers in the labor market, can assume the burden of caring for the elderly as well.

Conclusion

Employers need women's labor power. Labor shortages and restructuring in the economy require women's paid labor. The family needs women's unpaid labor. Men in the home, accustomed to the gender division of labor and the enterprise system, cannot conceive of taking family responsibility, whether child rearing or nursing elderly parents. The state meets employers' and men's needs. It makes women's paid labor available to employers through social policies like the equal employment opportunity law and the childcare leave system and by mobilizing women to take employment through campaigns touting the ideal woman as both homemaker and worker. The state also assures men of unpaid housekeeping at home and eases their anxiety about having women as job competitors by keeping women in second-class status in the economy. In addition, the state uses women as primary caregivers to the elderly to keep welfare expenditures to a minimum.

Women are aware of all this, yet they choose to go along with their state, employment, and family roles—partly to get the most out of their current limited situation and partly because they believe they are engaged in a process of social change no matter how trivial their community activities are. Women's way may be the future model for the Japanese enterprise system and for Japanese society as a whole (Iwao, 1993). At least one survey conducted by the prime minister's office supports this future model: it found that more men now consider home and family important in their lives and that they would like to shift their lifestyle from a business orientation to a family orientation (Nuita, 1994).

See Also

EDUCATION: EAST ASIA; ENVIRONMENT: EAST ASIA (JAPAN); HOUSEHOLDS: POLITICAL ECONOMY; PATRIARCHY; POLITICS AND THE STATE: EAST ASIA: WORK: OCCUPATIONAL SEGREGATION

References and Further Reading

Dore, Ronald. 1987. *Taking Japan seriously.* Stanford, Calif.: Stanford University Press.

Fujita, Kuniko. 1987. Gender, state and industrial policy in Japan. *Women's Studies International Forum* 10 (6): 589–597.

———. 1991. Women workers and flexible specialization: The case of Tokyo. *Economy and Society* 20 (3: August): 260–282.

———. 1988. Women workers, state policy, and the international division of labor: the case of silicon island in Japan. *Bulletin of Concerned Asian Scholars* 20 (3): 42–53.

Fukutake, Tadashi. 1989. *The Japanese social structure.* 2nd ed. Tokyo: Tokyo University Press.

Hill, Richard C., and Kuniko Fujita. 1995. Product cycles and international division of labor: Contrasts between the U.S.A. and Japan. In David Smith and Jozsef Borocz, eds., *A new work order? Global transformation in the late 20th century.* New York: Greenwood.

Iwao, Sumiko. 1993. *The Japanese woman: Traditional image and changing reality.* Cambridge, Mass.: Harvard University Press.

Ministry of Labor Women's Bureau. 1999. *Hataraku fujin no jitsujo* (Working women in Japan). Tokyo: Ministry of Finance Printing Bureau.

Nuita, Yoko. 1994. Survey. *Japanese Women* 72:3.

Kuniko Fujita

DEVELOPMENT:
Middle East and the Arab Region

The Middle East and the Arab region includes Turkey, Iran, Israel, Jordan, Iraq, Palestine, Syria, Lebanon, Kuwait, Oman, Qatar, Saudi Arabia, the United Arab Emirates, Yemen, Mauritania, Somalia, Sudan, Djibouti, Morocco, Tunisia, Algeria, Libya, Egypt, and Ethiopia. There are substantial differences in the levels of economic development among the countries in the region, making comparison of women's status between countries difficult. For example, a comparison of the position of woman in Saudi Arabia and Sudan would be strongly influenced by the vastly different levels of economic development of these two countries. This would make it difficult to ascertain the effect of other parameters. It is also necessary to acknowledge that the Middle East and the Arab region include several different religions and that religious differences have influenced women's status and participation in economic development.

Development policies in most countries of the region have displaced women from their traditional roles in subsistence activities and yet limited their opportunities to engage in nontraditional economic activities. Various case studies have been chosen to examine the role of women in economic development and their status in different countries.

Women's Participation in the Labor Force

It is well known that the total labor force as a proportion of the population in the Middle East and in the Arab region is low (except in Israel and Turkey). The participation rate has variously been estimated as ranging between 20 percent and 30 percent of the total population in the late 1980s (Hijab, 1988). Reasons for the relatively small labor force include the youthfulness of the population and the fact that women constitute a very small proportion of the labor force. A World Bank report in the 1990s estimated labor force participation by women from a high of 34 percent in Turkey and Israel to only 8 percent in Saudi Arabia (World Bank, 1994). In Israel, only 15 percent of Arab women were in the labor force compared with 45 percent of Jewish women (Semyonov and Lewin-Epstein, 1994). But the small proportion of women in the labor force does not mean that few Middle Eastern women work, or even that few earn money. Official statistics rarely reflect the real number of economically active men and women. They tend to define work as labor for wages. This means that most working women in rural areas and urban slums are not categorized as working.

For example, national statistics in Egypt in 1970 reported that only 3.6 percent of the agricultural labor force were women, but a study in 1970 of women in rural households throughout the country revealed that half the wives plowed and leveled the land in Lower Egypt, and between 55 percent and 70 percent participated in agricultural production activities (Hijab, 1988).

A report on Moroccan peasants (cited in Hijab, 1988: 73) found that the population was divided into five categories: (1) actively employed, (2) unemployed, (3) students, (4) housewives, and (5) other inactive people. As noted by Mernissi (cited in Hijab, 1988: 73), 92 percent of the women classified as housewives and other inactive people would hardly have recognized themselves from this description. Anyone who took a walk through a Moroccan village would see women engaged in indispensable tasks.

Despite the widespread recognition of the unreliability of official statistics on the rate of female participation in the labor force and the limited value of these statistics as indicators of the economic status of women, they are still used as major indicators of the economic status of women in the Middle East and the Arab region. The traditional view among commentators and policymakers has been that women would find themselves in a better position if their labor force participation rates were similar to those of men. Youssef (1976), for example, argues that participation in the economic system is a prerequisite to women's eventually recognizing their own economic power.

The determinants of women's official labor force participation in the Middle East are discussed in a considerable

Table 1: Status of women in selected countries of the Middle East and the Arab region: General indicators (percent)

Country	Women in labor force (% of total 1990–1992)	Crude adult literacy rate (% of age 15+) 1992	Birthrate per 1,000 pop.) 1992
Egypt	29	35	32
Jordan	10	72	39
Saudi Arabia	7	50	36
Turkey	31	72	29
Iran	10	45	41

Note: Data for Israel are not included in United Nations Development Program (UNDP 1994).

Source: United Nations Development Program (1994: 138, 162, 174).

number of studies. For example, Abu Nasr, Khoury, Azzam, and Moskoff use data from different countries in the Middle East (Egypt, Saudi Arabia, Jordan, Israel, Turkey, and Iran are included) to estimate the determinants of female labor force participation. The variables they used are crude birthrate, age at marriage, and the female illiteracy rate (Abu Nasr et al., 1985; Moskoff, 1982). Crude birthrates per thousand of population in most countries of the region are well above 30, which is quite high. The World Bank report estimated crude birthrates from a high of 38 in Jordan to only 21 in Israel (1994). Traditionally, a woman gains power and status when she has children, particularly sons, and establishes control of her own household. Associated with high birthrates is the early age at which women marry. More than half of all women between the ages of 18 and 22 are married in Middle Eastern countries. Very few reach the age of 30 without being married.

Education is another determinant of women's official labor force participation. There is a negative correlation between women's participation rate and the illiteracy rate. The literacy rate for females varies among the countries of the region. For example, the highest adult literacy rate (72 percent) is found in Turkey and Jordan and the lowest (35 percent) in Egypt (see the table).

Most of the literature focuses on the impact of social factors restricting women's participation in the formal labor force. Hijab (1988) discusses the factors keeping women's participation rate low in most of the Middle Eastern countries. She argues that there are three conditions to be met before women can be integrated into the wage labor force: need,

opportunity, and ability. If any one of these conditions is not met, then women's participation rates will continue to be low. These conditions must be met at the state and local levels. At the state level, *need* refers to a country's staffing requirements, *opportunity* refers to official efforts to create the proper environment for employment (through planning and legislation), and *ability* refers to the government's efforts to train people in required skills. At the local level, *need* refers to a family's or an individual's requirements for income, *opportunity* refers to social obstacles to women's participation in paid work, and *ability* refers to an individual's skills.

There is a tendency to blame the low participation of Middle Eastern women in the formal labor force mainly on sociocultural factors, but these factors are not always the main determinants of low participation rates. The situation differs with changing economic needs and opportunities. Hijab gives the example of labor migration in the Arab region as one of the factors creating a need and an opportunity at state and local levels for the involvement of Arab women in the wage labor force. In some cases, women have been encouraged to join the workforce as replacements for male migrants. In other cases, a rise in the cost of living, partly the result of migration, has created a need for women to work in the paid labor force. In Jordan, Egypt, Syria, and Yemen, officials attributed the increase in women's participation in the paid workforce during the 1970s to the gap left by the number of men who had migrated to the oil-rich states of the region for better-paying jobs.

In Egypt, Khafagy's study in 1977 (cited in Hijab, 1988: 79) of a village south of Cairo where male villagers worked abroad found some evidence of a change in women's roles. Emigrant workers' wives, who had stayed at home, managed the remittances sent back by their husbands. In addition they dealt with individuals and institutions outside the household, such as merchants or the village agricultural cooperative, and sometimes they hired workers and negotiated the workers' wages. Although the wives' workload had increased, most of the women did not mind this and viewed labor migration in a positive light. The husbands were seen to have become more dependent on their wives' advice and turned more frequently to them during decision making. It was concluded that women were doing more than filling the gap until their husbands' return, and that this was likely to have some lasting effects.

In Turkey—in contrast to Egypt—Kandiyoti (1977) points out that when wage labor jobs took Turkish men away from depressed areas and offered them a fixed regular wage, their absence placed the responsibility of agricultural production on women, who were left with a double burden. Women were left without husbands for long periods of time and had to act as heads of households. But this situation did not enrich women or allow them more room to negotiate their own needs or rights with the men of their families. This was not only because women had to work twice as hard, but also because they did not usually control the cash flow from their fathers, sons, or husbands, as was the case in preindustrial rural Turkish society.

Looking at a different aspect of the changing role of women, El Solh's study in 1985 (cited in Hijab, 1988: 79) examined the lives of Egyptian settlers in Iraq to assess changes in the role of women. Women settlers coming from rural Egypt were involved in marketing activities, which meant mixing with male strangers. The women explained the changes by saying they were in a foreign country where no one knew them, or that their situation differed, since their husband could not rely on anyone else. As El Solh noted, when ideals and reality clashed, economic self-interest came first, although the fiction of adhering to customs and tradition was upheld.

In Israel, as mentioned earlier, the participation of Jewish women in the paid labor force has steadily increased and is much higher than for women in other countries in the Middle East (except Turkey). In Israel, women's participation is determined by a number of factors. It is positively correlated with level of education and is negatively correlated with number of children; these are relationships that are found in other countries. Not surprisingly, the presence of preschool children exerts the greatest influence against women's working, while older children exert the least influence (Moskoff, 1982).

It is interesting that Israeli women born in either Africa or Asia have a lower participation rate than women born in North America or Europe. This reflects several things. First, the culture they were brought up in has an impact. Also, African- and Asian-origin women are likely to have married younger. However, the most important factor may be that their level of education is likely to be lower than that of other groups of Jewish women.

Asian or African origin is not the only factor militating against Israeli women's labor force participation. A severe constraint on women's labor market activity is the dual labor market. Moskoff (1982) argues that female participation is dependent on expansion of the tertiary sector of the economy, since women's admission to traditional male occupations is quite limited. He concludes that there is a lack of institutional support for working women. Most schools close at noon, which necessitates that mothers be home in the afternoon to care for their children. This suggests that part-time work is the only alternative for married women with children.

As regards the patterns of women's paid employment, Middle Eastern and Arab women are concentrated in professional occupations. The high incidence of women workers in professional and technical occupations in most countries may be the outcome of occupational segregation prevalent in the region, where women cluster in specific jobs such as teaching and nursing (Moghadam, 1993). It may also be a function of the relationship between class, income, and work participation, in that women from elite families are most likely to be those who are in paid employment, especially in the Gulf countries. In terms of occupational distribution, all countries have few women in administrative and managerial occupations. There also appears to be a marked disinclination for women to enter sales work or even clerical work, except in Israel (Moghadam, 1993). Mujahid (cited in Moghadam, 1993: 51) explains women's avoidance of such jobs in terms of cultural norms, because these are occupations with the highest likelihood of indiscriminate contact with outsiders.

The kinds of occupations open to women varied among the countries of the region. For example, in Israel, 28.9 percent of the workforce in the professional, technical category were women, while in agriculture, forestry, fishing, and hunting only 1.6 percent were women. In Turkey, the female participation rate ranged from a high of 69 percent in agriculture and hunting to only 0.1 percent in administration and managerial workers (Moghadam, 1993: 51).

Women, Work, and Ideology

In the Middle East and in the Arab region the majority of people are Muslims (except in Israel). Religion-based ideology and culture have influenced women's economic position and role in development. However, Islam is only one of the many contributory factors that shape the lives of women in the Middle East, and therefore it cannot be seen as the primary causal element that has led to the low level of female participation in the paid labor force. It is essential to recognize the different historical and cultural contexts in which the laws of Islam have been interpreted, as alterations and adjustments to these laws have arisen from socioeconomic and political needs.

There is a widespread belief that the ideology of Islam is hostile to women's participation in the paid labor force. Some empirical studies (for example, Moskoff, 1982) have used simple statistical comparisons to argue that female labor force participation rates are lower in Muslim countries and, therefore, a strong case has been made that a number of elements within Islamic culture combine to produce a low female participation rate. However, it is not clear whether this relationship is a result of supply factors (Muslim women being unwilling to participate) or demand factors (Muslim employers being unwilling to hire women) or some other set of factors common to Muslim countries but unrelated to religious values.

There is a considerable body of literature that has used interviews with Muslim women to assess their attitudes to work. For example, a study by Sanad and Tessler (1988) considered the attitudes of a random sample of Kuwaiti women. This study was typical of a large number of studies that did not find general opposition to the idea of women working. Sanad and Tessler also developed indicators of religiosity and concluded that Islam did not appear to be an important independent contributor to the economic conservatism of older Kuwaiti women. In other words, whatever was causing the negative attitudes toward working wives in Kuwait, it did not appear to be Islam.

Although there is considerable literature dealing with the effect of Islam on women's attitudes to employment, there are very few studies that examine the attitudes of employers in Islamic countries. Al-Meer (1988) administered a questionnaire to a small sample of western, Asian, and Saudi men in a variety of companies in order to assess their attitudes toward women as managers. Although he found that western men had more positive attitudes toward women as managers, he found no significant difference between Asians and Saudis. While this is only one study with a small sample, these results are remarkable, since Saudis are among the most conservative Muslims. Al-Meer comments that negative attitudes seem to be a function of the level of development of the country.

A study on women, work, and ideology was conducted by the World Bank in four countries (Jordan, Egypt, Morocco, and Turkey) in 1990. It examined the attitudes of women and employers in these countries. The main findings of this study (cited in Afshar, 1993) can be summarized as follows:

1. The study was consistent with the existing literature, which generally found little independent direct effect of an Islamic ideology producing hostile attitudes to women's paid employment.
2. The major constraint that women perceived on their employment outside the home was the lack of satisfactory arrangements for the care of their children. They did not feel constrained by the attitudes of their menfolk.
3. Employment opportunities for women in firms surveyed seemed to be relatively favorable. Women were relatively overrepresented in the higher grades, and a considerable number of managers perceived benefit from employing women.
4. On the other hand, there were also a number of firms that were reluctant to consider hiring women in various capacities. The firms that perceived disadvantages to hiring women mentioned factors such as unsatisfactory levels of education and training. Again, religious objections appeared relatively unimportant.

With regard to attitudes of employers to the employment of women in Islamic countries, it is worth mentioning an extensive statistical study carried out by Anker and Hein in 1986 (cited in Afshar, 1993: 113). This research focused mainly on the reasons for labor discrimination in developing countries. Anker and Hein found the following:

1. The main complaint made by employers against women was high absentee rates, and the authors found this complaint to be justified by the evidence available.
2. The possibility of pregnancy was also mentioned frequently as a reason for not hiring women.
3. Employers provided a long list of jobs for which women were considered less suitable than men. Only teaching was mentioned as a job for which women would be more suitable than men.
4. Women were considered less suitable than men because they were considered to have less muscular strength and to lack supervisory skills, and because some jobs were considered to be male jobs.

Most of the information cited above concerns Muslim Arab countries. In the case of Iran, no study had been undertaken as of this writing that examined the role of religion in women's economic status although, according to many scholars, a principal objective of the leaders of the present Iranian regime had been to restore women to what they considered women's primary role in society: domestic responsibility (Moghadam, 1988). A woman's religious duty requires her to concentrate on fulfilling her "real" tasks as wife and mother.

Turkey replaced the Islamic personal status laws with a civil law code regulating personal and family relations and equalizing the duties and responsibilities of the sexes. In the 1920s, Turkey introduced secular legal codes based on western models. Such legal codes provided an important basis for changing the status of women, and of women's work, in Turkey.

In Israel an ideology concerning "the primacy of men's role as chief provider and women's role as family-tender has been strongly reinforced by the powerful religious establishment and is embodied in the social policy of both the welfare service and the National Insurance" (Bernstein, 1983: 284).

The effect of ideology had not (at the time of this writing) been included in assessing women's participation in the paid labor force in most of the Middle East and the Arab region, yet its effect could be dramatic. For example, in Saudi Arabia women are forbidden to work outside the home in the company of men, but in Egypt many women must work to support families, though social customs might hinder them.

Women and Development in the Middle East and the Arab Region

Before about 1970, it was thought that the development process affected men and women in the same way. Productivity was equated with the wage economy, and so most traditional women's work was ignored. When it became apparent that economic development did not automatically eradicate poverty through trickle-down effects, the problems of distribution and equality of benefit to the various segments of the population took on major importance in development theory.

The role of women in development in the Middle East has rarely been acknowledged and has often been misunderstood. One reason for this has been western ethnocentrism (Fernea, 1986).

The "general good" assumption about development is one found in the West. It is an ethnocentric view of the world in which it is believed that only when third world countries implement development patterns and industrial patterns common in the West will they triumph over poverty. As for women, the assumption is that only when Middle Eastern women cast off their cultural backwardness, their traditional homebound roles as wives and mothers within the family unit, and participate in the public world of production will their difficulties cease. Such a view ignores the realities of what women are doing today and have done in the past in Middle Eastern society. These realities include the fact that women always participated in many different ways in the preindustrial labor market; women were already laboring in local industries, both privately and publicly owned; and women continue to provide domestic labor as they have always done, not only in the home, but in what is called the informal sector of the old economy, without which labor in the modern economy could not proceed.

Mernissi (cited in Moghadam 1993: 63) argued that modernization reduces, marginalizes, and devalues women's work. Her research suggests a link between the deterioration of women's position and their preexisting dependence on men. Her interviews with Moroccan women working in various craft industries (such as weaving, textiles, and rugs) indicate how dependent women are on men as intermediaries, a situation that worsens their precarious economic position. She concludes that the increasing capitalist penetration of such industries has had the consequence of further degrading women.

The complex and contradictory nature of the relationship between development and women's status has been explored by a number of Turkish and Iranian researchers. Kandiyoti's research conducted in the 1970s (cited in Moghadam, 1993: 64) comparing the status of Turkish women in nomadic tribes, peasant villages, rural towns, and cities found that the influence of the patrilineal extended household—where the father dominates younger men and all women, and there is a hierarchy by age among the women—was pervasive in all sectors, but less so in the towns and cities because of smaller (unextended) family groups and the diminished importance of elders. Compared with peasant and nomadic women, urban women played a reduced role in the productive process, even though they were more likely to head their own households. But peasant and nomadic women did not receive recognition for their own labor.

Esther Boserup (1970) was one of the first scholars to suggest that ethnocentric western-style development plans, particularly in agriculture, ignored the realities of women's participation, and that this myopic view had a negative impact not only on women but on the overall developing economy. One of her examples involved Africa—and is applicable to north African Arab countries—where western-style agricultural development plans were drawn up in which men were allotted land and given tools and seeds. The plan totally ignored the previously existing situation in the African countries, in which women, not men, were the actual cultivators. Men in these countries had not farmed before, and thus, not surprisingly, the agricultural plan failed. The lesson of Boserup's work seems clear: ethnocentricity hinders, not helps, development plans.

Ethnocentricity also clouds the definitions of labor and production on which development plans are based. Labor and production, according to western criteria, are defined as work performed outside the home for fixed wages. This definition probably accounts for more confused western pictures of men's and women's labor in Middle Eastern societies than any other single idea. Defining labor as wage labor outside the home ignores the paid and unpaid labor of women and men in agriculture in every Middle Eastern country. Women, men, and children also engage in domestic production. In addition to housework and child rearing, many other economic activities take place in the domestic sphere, such as raising animals; managing and serving in small shops; performing medical, social, and religious roles such as midwife, matchmaker, and mullah (religious adviser); and producing small craft items such as clothing, rugs, and pottery. These domestic production activities, sometimes called informal-sector production, do not feature in official statistical analyses of labor force participation. Hence, official analyses and reports on which national and international development plans are based discuss only one layer of the society that is being analyzed. Such analyses are based on western assumptions that the Middle East is merely replicating the experience of the West following the industrial revolution, and hence these informal-sector activities will soon disappear. This assumption is basically false, for the area is changing in very different ways from the West and over a much more extended time. What is actually happening to women in different parts of the Middle East and in different classes of these societies is ignored, particularly if it contradicts western assumptions.

Since the early 1980s, a new approach has appeared, criticizing the western-oriented development approach. Huda Zurayk (1979) and Sonia Ali (1979) discuss the shortcomings of the methods used in the measurement of women's economic participation. Carla Makhlouf Obermeyer (1979) sees a necessity for new definitions of women's work from within Middle Eastern society itself. Nawal El Saadawi (1981) asserts that almost half the labor force in Egypt is female, though this fact is not recorded in publications of international agencies. Rural versus urban experience is also important but, again, seldom included in the official statistics. Further, development plans in the Middle East have neglected the phenomenon of households headed by women. Thus plans assume that women are being supported rather than supporting others and do not include women in work benefit schemes, loan arrangements, and other supporting mechanisms.

Most of the development plans in the Middle East and in the Arab region focus on urban development and industry. Urban industrial development has had adverse effects on women's lives and economic status in both urban and rural areas, because factories do not offer equal pay, decent conditions, or reasonable working hours to women. Rather, this kind of development gives women a double burden (work at home and labor in the workplace).

In Iran during the 1980s, development plans concentrated on the role of women in society in terms of their domestic responsibility and their real tasks as wife and mother. The same approach has been applied in Saudi Arabia.

Government Policies and Women's Status

Since the 1960s, state expansion, economic development, oil wealth, and increased integration within the world system have combined to create educational and employment opportunities favorable to women.

During the 1970s the large countries, such as Egypt, Iraq, Turkey, and Iran, were importing machinery to run local industries producing consumer goods. This strategy was associated with an economic system characterized by central planning and a large public sector, and it opened some employment opportunities for women, mainly in the expanded civil service but also in state-run factories or industrial plants in the private sector receiving state support and foreign investment (Moghadam, 1993). The rise of oil prices in the early 1970s led to a proliferation of development projects in the Organization of Petroleum Exporting Countries (OPEC).

A large percentage of male workers migrated from capital-poor to oil-rich countries, and considerable intraregional investment and development assistance took place in the region as a whole. This was followed by increased male employment and an increase in the portion of the labor force involved in industry and services. These changes also affected women, who were increasingly brought into the paid labor force. For relatively well-educated women, services (teaching, health, and welfare) offered the greatest possibilities, while in the more developed Middle Eastern and Arab countries (such as Turkey and Egypt) women's participation increased in commercial and industrial enterprises and public administration.

During this period of rapid growth, some governments provided generous benefits to working women. Kuwait in 1976 and Jordan in 1978 instituted comprehensive social security systems for workers, including women. Iran adopted the International Labor Organization (ILO) Convention No. 3, which applies to all women employed in industrial and commercial undertakings and provides for 12 weeks' maternity leave, to be taken in two parts, one before and one after childbirth, the latter being compulsory. Legislation in nearly all Middle Eastern countries protected a female employee from dismissal during pregnancy or maternity leave, and in some cases (Jordan, Syria, and Iraq) provided for the establishment of workplace nurseries and breast-feeding breaks (Moghadam, 1993).

In the 1980s all Middle Eastern and Arab countries faced economic and political difficulties, which affected women's economic status and employment opportunities. The economic crisis in the Middle East and Arab region occurred in the context of a worldwide crisis resulting in part from a drop in real prices of primary commodities, including oil. Austerity measures were introduced in Egypt, Jordan, Algeria, Morocco, and Syria, the availability of development aid decreased, and major development projects were reevaluated or suspended. The Iraqi invasion of Kuwait in August 1990 raised the price of oil again, but the damage had already been done. Arab countries in North Africa experienced low or negative economic growth rates. Turkey was placed on the World Bank's list of severely indebted middle-income countries. The livelihood of lower-middle-class, and working-class women was adversely affected, especially in Iran, Egypt, Morocco, and Algeria. In Israel, the official state policy toward female employment saw women as a reserve of labor only after men were employed (Bernstein, 1983). Women were seen as secondary providers; men are the heads of family. Policymakers perpetuated the existing division of labor within the family in order to maintain social stability and social order. Israel received aid from the United States; but elsewhere, tough economic reforms, along with poverty and unemployment, had a negative impact on the economic status of women. Political pressures throughout the region have also discouraged women's integration into the development process.

Summary

In most Middle Eastern and Arab countries women remain an underutilized human resource because of an ideology stressing women's family roles, and because of ambivalence on the part of governments toward the full participation of women in development. Women's official labor force participation in the Middle East and in the Arab region is still very low (except in Turkey and Israel). Islam is only one of the many contributory factors shaping the lives of women in the Middle East, and it cannot be seen as the primary causal element that has led to the low level of female participation in the paid labor force. Political forces and economic needs and opportunities have strongly affected the level of female participation in this sector. The role of women in economic development has rarely been acknowledged and has often been misunderstood. Defining labor as wage labor outside the home ignores the paid and unpaid labor of women in agriculture in every Middle Eastern and Arab society. In conclusion, the following factors have most influenced the economic status of women in the Middle East and in the Arab region: level of development, economic crises (oil price fluctuations, inflation), men's and employers' attitudes toward women working, women's educational levels, and women's class position. It is necessary to stress the importance of appropriate economic development, legal reform, and educational opportunities for women. These will have a significant impact on the role of women and their participation in development in the Middle East and the Arab region in the future.

See Also:

EDUCATION: MIDDLE EAST AND NORTH AFRICA; ENVIRONMENT: MIDDLE EAST; FEMINISM: MIDDLE EAST; ISLAM; POLITICS AND THE STATE: MIDDLE EAST AND NORTH AFRICA; WORK: OCCUPATIONAL SEGREGATION

References and Further Reading

Abu-Nasr, J. Ulinda, Nabil F. Khoury, and H. T. Azzam. 1985. *Women, employment, and development in the Arab world.* Berlin: Mouton.

Afshar, Haleh. 1993. *Women in the Middle East: Perception, realities, and struggles for liberation.* London: Macmillan.

A-Meer, Abdulrahim. 1988. Attitudes towards women as managers: A comparison of Asians, Saudis, and westerners. *Arab Journal of the Social Sciences* 3 (1): 139–149.

Ali, Sonia. 1979. Women in labor force data in Egypt. In *The measurement of women's economic participation: Report of a study group,* 51–55. Beirut, Lebanon: Population Council, West Asia and North Africa Region (October 12–13).

Bernstein, Deborah. 1983. Economic growth and female labor: The case of Israel. *Sociological Review* 31: 263–287.

Boserup, Esther. 1970. *Women's role in economic development.* London: Allen and Unwin.

Fernea, Elizabeth. 1986. Women and family in development plans in the Arab East. *Journal of Asian and African Studies* 21 (1–2): 81–87.

Hijab, Nadia. 1988. *Womenpower: The Arab debate on women at work.* Cambridge: Cambridge University Press.

Kandiyoti, Deniz. 1977. Sex roles and social change: A comparative study of Turkey's women. *Signs* 3: 57–73.

Moghadam, Valentine. 1993. *Modernizing women: Gender and social change in the Middle East.* London: Lynne Rienner.

———. 1988. Women, work and ideology in the Islamic republic. *International Journal of Middle East Studies* 20: 221–243.

Moskoff, William. 1982. Women and work in Israel and the Islamic Middle East. *Quarterly Review of Economics and Business* 22 (4): 89–104.

Obermeyer, Carla Makhlouf. 1979. Some notes on women's economic participation in North Yemen. In *The measurement of women's economic participation: Report of a study group,* 39–42. Beirut, Lebanon: Population Council, West Asia and North Africa Region (Octorber 12–13).

Saadawi, Nawal, El. 1981. *The hidden face of Eve.* London: Zed.

Sanad, Jamal A., and Mark. A. Tessler. 1988. The economic orientation of Kuwaiti women: Their nature, determinants and consequences. *International Journal of Middle East Studies* 20: 443–68.

Semyonov, Moshe, and Noah Lewin-Epstein. 1994. Ethnic labor markets, gender and socioeconomic inequality: A study of Arabs in the Israeli labor force. *Sociological Quarterly* 35 (1): 51–68.

United Nations Development Program (UNDP). 1994. *Human development report.* Oxford: Oxford University Press.

World Bank. 1994. *World development report: Infrastructure for development.* Oxford: Oxford University Press.

Youssef, Nadia. 1976. Education and female modernism in the Muslim world. *Journal of International Affairs* 30(2): 191–210.

Zuryk, Huda. 1979. Measuring women's economic participation. In *The measurement of women's economic participation: Report of study group,* 5–38. Beruit, Lebanon: Population Council, West Asia and North Africa Region (October 12–13).

Dalma Al-Khudairi

DEVELOPMENT: North America

This article discusses the position of women in the economies of Canada and the United States. It briefly describes populations, ethnic composition, and histories of migration. It then discusses the nature of labor markets, the labor force participation of women, the wage differences between women and men, the extent of unemployment and poverty, and the increasing "feminization of poverty" in these two countries.

Canada's Population, Size, and Brief Ethnic History

Canada is the second largest country in the world in area, with a comparatively small population (28 million). With the coming of Europeans, the original 1 million (approximately) native people rapidly declined to 125,000 by 1967 owing to disease, starvation, and warfare. By 1994, they had increased to 586,000, or 2 percent of the population.

The first European settlers in Canada were predominantly of French and British origins. Quebec, where those of mainly French origin settled, differs from the rest of Canada in culture, language, and civil law. In terms of religion, most Quebecers of French origin officially claim to be Roman Catholic (97 percent), whereas the British are mainly Protestant. In 1994, those of French ancestry in Canada made up about 31 percent and the British about 45 percent of the nation's population.

African Canadians first arrived with the Loyalists from New England or the West Indies as slaves. Others arrived through the "underground railway" (a network to aid runaway slaves fleeing the United States). By 1996, Canadian blacks came from many diverse places and constituted about 2 percent of the population.

Although migration to Canada was mainly from Europe, more recently there has been increasing migration from Asia, Africa, Latin America, and the Caribbean, creating what is called a "visible" minority. Canada has a policy of multiculturalism, which supports cultural diversity. It is, however, still a hierarchy of ethnic groups, or, as the sociologist John Porter (1965) referred to it, a "vertical mosaic." Moreover, women have been and continue to be disadvantaged relative to men within this vertical mosaic.

The United States's Population, Size, and Brief Ethnic History

The United States is the fourth largest country in area, with the third largest population in the world (249 million). It has been a recipient country for both voluntary migrants and involuntary refugees since its inception; even the native peoples migrated from Asia. Besides the Native Americans, blacks, and Hispanics, the largest migrant groups arrived from Germany, Ireland, England, Italy, France, Poland, and the Netherlands. Before the 1960s the United States was thought of as a "melting pot" where migrants assimilated into the American way of life. The civil rights movement and the rise of ethnic consciousness in the 1960s and 1970s changed this idea. Now, ethnic groups are proud of their heritage and some have passed their original languages on to succeeding generations. This may be more the case with the visible migrants who have more recently come in large numbers from Asia and South America. European migrants have more successfully competed with mainstream Americans, whereas migrants of color have met discrimination and have not been as successful in competing with whites. Rural blacks, especially black females, remain among the most economically disadvantaged groups in the United States. Some regard this situation as a continuing legacy of the southern slave and plantation economy (Lichter, 1989).

Whites make up about 80 percent of the country's population. Blacks form the largest minority group (about 12 percent); others are smaller minorities, such as Hispanics (1 percent), Asians (3 percent) and Native Americans (1 percent). As well as ethnic and gender stratification within the economy, there are also regional differences and differences between urban and rural areas.

Nature of the Labor Markets

Both these countries are highly developed industrially, and most people have a high standard of material living. However, there is obvious inequality in the distribution of wealth among the various ethnic populations, and groups of color suffer markedly more poverty overall.

A historical overview of the Canadian and U.S. economies shows that at the end of the nineteenth century and the beginning of the twentieth, the factory system was replacing the family as the main productive unit. Factory work involved long hours, low wages, and often brutal working conditions. Jobs for women were limited in number, and there was strong sentiment against married women working outside the home, motivated by fear of cheap female labor undercutting men's wages.

During World War I, women did men's jobs; but they received lower wages. At the end of the war, women were strongly encouraged to leave the workforce. The expansionary period of the 1920s was cut short by the depression, and unemployment skyrocketed. With World War II, the economy recovered. Production expanded enormously and so did employment. When men went to war, single and then married women were again called to do men's jobs, again for lower wages. This time, however, many stayed and found employment in the expanding number of "female" jobs in the service sector of the economy (Connelly, 1978; Milkman, 1987; Reskin and Padavic, 1994).

The 1950s were a period of rapid economic expansion. The shift from agriculture to manufacturing increased the amount of consumer goods. This, in turn, created a need for services, such as marketing and advertising, and many of the new jobs created were in the "female" occupations of teaching, nursing, sales, and clerical work.

Generally, women earn less than men because of their location in the labor market. The labor market has been described as dichotomized between primary jobs and secondary jobs. Men are overrepresented in the primary jobs in core corporations, where they are in permanent positions with higher salaries, benefits, and opportunities for promotion, whereas women are overrepresented in the secondary jobs in the peripheral and smaller firms, where jobs are low-paid, unstable, with few benefits and little chance for mobility (Armstrong and Armstrong, 1994; Connelly and MacDonald, 1990; England and Browne, 1992).

This type of occupational sex segregation has declined somewhat since women have begun to move into male professions, managerial occupations, and even some manufacturing and high-technology jobs, but even in these occupations women tend to meet a "glass ceiling" where it is difficult to gain promotion and reach positions at the top (Reskin and Padavic, 1994). In the United States in 1990, less than 0.5 percent of the highest-paid directors were women (Fierman, 1990). In the field of law in 1990, one in three associates in large firms was a woman, but only one in eleven was a partner (Epstein, 1993).

Labor markets are differentiated not only by occupation but also by economic sector and geographical area. For example, women tend to fare better in the public sector than in the private sector, in the larger cities, and in the more prosperous states and provinces. Affirmative action strategies within federal, state, and provincial agencies have made some difference to career mobility for women and minorities.

Services accounted for most new jobs created in the 1980s (70 percent of paid workers in both countries were in the service sector), but many were part-time jobs. With economic restructuring, many full-time jobs are being converted to part-time or to piecework done at home with corresponding loss of income, benefits, and security (Connelly and MacDonald, 1996). Traditionally women have been overrepresented in nonstandard forms of work, such as part-time, part-year, short-term, or temporary (in Canada 31 percent women as opposed to 16 percent men). As full-time jobs disappear, men's percentage in nonstandard forms of work increases.

Labor Force Participation

In Canada in 1901 women made up 13 percent of the labor force, and by 1951 they had increased this share to 22 percent. Another two decades (by 1971) saw this figure climb to 34 percent, and by 1981 women were 41 percent of the labor force. In 1986, women of Aboriginal origin had a lower participation rate (40 percent) than non-Aboriginal women (56 percent). By 1994, the majority (60 percent) of Canadian women were working or looking for work outside the home.

The same dramatic increase after World War II was witnessed in the United States. In 1890, 19 percent of women were in the labor force. By 1950, there was an increase to 30 percent; by 1970 the figure had increased to 41 percent; and by 1992, to 58 percent. At the beginning of the twentieth century, there was a large difference in labor force participation between white (16 percent) and black (40 percent) women. By the end of the twentieth century, white women had narrowed the gap in their labor force participation so that by 1987, 56 percent of white women and 58 percent of black women were working (England and Browne, 1992).

Wage Differences between Women and Men

Despite increases in women's labor force participation over the past century, there remains a gap between the wages of women and men. This is mainly because the higher the percentage of females in an occupation, the lower its wages. It has been estimated that between 35 and 40 percent of the sex differences in wages in the United States is a result of occupational sex segregation. Over time, the gap in annual earnings has narrowed, but there has been little movement over the past few decades. The ratio of women's annual earnings to men's was 46 percent in 1890, 55 percent in 1930, 64 percent in 1955, 64 percent in 1983 and 74 percent in 1997. African-American women earned only 86 percent and Hispanic women just 74 percent as much as white women. African-American women earned 63 percent as much as white men, and Hispanic women earned 54 percent as much. In actual incomes, though, white men earn the most, followed by black and Hispanic men, then white, black, and Hispanic women (England and Browne, 1992).

In Canada, wages fell for the decade 1980 to 1990 and workers were not able to bargain for higher wages in the current economic climate. Men's wages decreased more than women's wages, and for this reason the gap between female and male average wages narrowed to 70 percent in 1991 (Armstrong, 1996). Women who are members of visable minorities earn the least. As in the United States, white men have the highest income, followed by nonwhite men, then white women, and, only marginally lower, nonwhite women (Li, 1992).

Unemployment, Poverty, and the Homeless

In 1994, 1.7 million people in Canada were unemployed, and there had been a sharp increase in long-term unemployment. Unemployment was significantly higher for Native Canadians. As jobs become more difficult to obtain, firms find it easier to reduce wages and extract other concessions from workers. As a result, the conditions of work are eroding, and the standard of living is dropping. Maintaining a reasonable standard of living is a particular problem for the nearly one million Canadian families headed by single parents, of which 82 percent are headed by women. According to Statistics Canada (1992), 62 percent of single mothers live on incomes well below the poverty line.

A number of groups in the United States live below the poverty line. Besides blacks and Hispanics, who form a large proportion of poor Americans, more recent migrants from Asia often live in poverty. A study of Indochinese refugees (Jones and Strand, 1986) found that most households (Vietnamese, Lao, Hmong, and Cambodian) were earning an income below poverty level, with Cambodians the poorest and Vietnamese somewhat better off. Not all Asian-Americans live below the poverty line, however. Asian Indians (second to Japanese-Americans), as a minority, earn high salaries, though not commensurate with their education, and males earn on average twice as much as females (Barringer and Kassebaum, 1989).

Just as there is heterogeneity among and within migrant groups, so there is among the black population. There is a growing black middle class, but chronic problems persist among the black "underclass," and there are major differences between blacks living in rural and urban areas. In rural areas, two out of every five blacks are without jobs, cannot find a full-time job, or cannot earn enough to raise themselves significantly above poverty thresholds. In the 1980s, more than 50 percent of young blacks in cities were jobless, working at part-time jobs involuntarily (wanting full-time jobs), or earning poverty-level wages (Lichter, 1989).

Whether black or white, most families on welfare live in poverty. The percentage of female-headed households is increasing, and more women have been categorized as poor adults, leading to the term *feminization of poverty*. In the United States, half of all female-headed families with children under 18 are below the federal poverty line. Female-headed families are far more likely to be poor if they are black (56 percent) or Hispanic (55 percent) than if they are white (28 percent) (McLanahan, et al., 1989; Northrop, 1990).

Another group increasingly at risk of living in poverty is aged women. Close to three out of four older people who are poor are women. Women who are widowed and other women living alone are among the poorest. Ann Hartman argues that "aging is a feminist issue. The poorest segment of American society is elderly Black women; 82 percent were poor or near poor at the time of the 1980 census " (1990: 388). One reason that women face a greater risk of poverty is the wage gap between men and women, which carries over into retirement, when benefits depend on income during their working lives.

Government cutbacks to welfare programs eventually translate into increases in poverty rates. In both countries, governments are shedding many welfare responsibilities, more often than not, resulting in increased workloads for women. Working or not, generally women still do the bulk of household management and domestic work.

Homelessness in late twentieth-century North America was a sign that "safety net" programs for the prevention of extreme destitution have diminished. It was estimated in 1987 that there were 194,000 homeless adults in large U.S. cities. Although most homeless people are single men (about 73 percent), there was a rise in the presence of homeless families toward the end of the 1980s, and a large majority of these families were female-headed, single-parent households (Burt and Cohen, 1989).

Strategies for Equality

In both countries, since the 1960s, women have been organizing to demand greater equality. The women's movement raised consciousness and emphasized women's right to independence and control of their own lives. Women joined unions and other organizations in greater numbers. They debated issues such as wages for housework, affirmative action, equal pay, parental leave, adequate day care, reproductive rights, and protection against sexual harassment and violence. In recent years women have begun to struggle against cutbacks in government services.

In the United States there was a spate of legislation that started with the Equal Pay Act of 1963, continued with Title VII of the Civil Rights Act of 1964 and Title IX of the Higher Education Act of 1972, and ended in the same year with the passage by Congress of an equal rights amendment. Similar bills have been enacted in Canada. Each of these bills attempted to remove some barriers to equality. Yet together they have had little discernible impact for women as a whole. Even the addition of affirmative action and comparable worth has not brought anticipated gains. As Alice Kessler-Harris has suggested, "gender equality will be achieved only when the values of the home are brought to the work place where they can transform work itself. It opens the possibility that an ethnic of compassion or tolerance, a sense of group responsibility to the world at large (instead of to self), might in fact penetrate the work place." (1985: 157).

See Also

DEVELOPMENT: OVERVIEW; DIVISION OF LABOR; ECONOMY: HISTORY OF WOMEN'S PARTICIPATION; ECONOMY: WELFARE AND THE ECONOMY; WORK, *specific topics.*

References and Further Reading

Armstrong, Pat. 1996. The feminization of the labor force: Harmonizing down in a global economy. In Isabella Bakker, ed., *Rethinking restructuring: Gender and change in Canada.* Toronto: University of Toronto Press.

———, and Hugh Armstrong. 1994. *The double ghetto: Canadian women and their segregated work* 3rd ed.. Toronto: McClellan and Stewart.

Barringer, Herbert, and Gene Kassebaum. 1989. Asian Indians as a minority in the U.S.: The effect of education, occupations and gender on income. *Sociological Perspectives* 32 (4): 501–520.

Burt, Martha, and Barbara Cohen. 1989. Differences among homeless single women, women with children, and single men. *Social Problems* 36 (5: December.): 508–520.

Clio Collective. 1987. *Quebec women.* Toronto: Women's Press.

Connelly, Patricia. 1978. *Last hired, first fired: Women and the Canadian work force.* Toronto: Women's Press.

Connelly, Patricia, and Martha MacDonald. 1996. The labor market, the state, and the reorganization of work: Policy impacts. In Isabella Bakker, ed., *Rethinking restructuring: Gender and change in Canada.* Toronto: University of Toronto Press.

———. 1990. *Women and the labor force: Focus on Canada.* Ottawa: Statistics Canada.

England, Paula, and Irene Browne. 1992. Trends in women's economic status. In *Sociological Perspectives* 35 (1): 17–51.

Epstein, Cynthia F. 1993. *Women in law.* Urbana: University of Illinois Press.

Fierman, Jaclyn. 1990. Why women still don't hit the top. *Fortune* (30 July): 40, 42, 46, 50, 54, 58, 62.

Hartman, Ann. 1990. Aging as a feminist issue. *Social Work* 35 (5: September): 387–388.

Jones, Woodrow, Jr., and Paul Strand. 1986. Adaptation and adjustment problems among Indochinese refugees. *Social Science Review* 71 (1: October): 42–46.

Kessler-Harris, Alice. 1985. The debate over equality for women in the workplace: Recognizing differences. In Laurie Larwood, Ann Strombert, and Barbara Gutek, eds. *Women and work: Annual review* 1: 141–161. Beverly Hills, Calif.: Sage.

Li, Peter. 1992. Race and gender as bases of class fractions and their effects on earnings. *Canadian Review of Sociology and Anthropology* 29 (4): 488–510.

Lichter, Daniel. 1989. Race, employment hardship, and inequality in the American nonmetropolitan South. *American Sociological Review* 54 (June): 436–446.

McLanahan, Sara S., Annemette Sorensen, and Dorothy Watson. 1989. Sex differences in poverty, 1950-1980. *Signs: Journal of Women in Culture and Society* 15 (1): 102–122.

Milkman, Ruth. 1987. *Gender at work.* Urbana: University of Illinois Press.

Northrop, Emily M. 1990. The feminization of poverty: The demographic factor and the composition of economic growth. *Journal of Economic Issues* 24 (1: March): 145–160.

Porter, John. 1965. *The vertical mosaic: An analysis of social class and power in Canada.* Toronto: University of Toronto Press.

Reskin, Barbara, and Irene Padavic. 1994. *Women and men at work.* Thousand Oaks, Calif.: Pine Forge.

Statistics Canada. 1992. *Families: Number, type and structure.* Ottawa: Government Press.

Janice Currie

DEVELOPMENT: Postmodern Perspectives

See POSTMODERNISM AND DEVELOPMENT.

DEVELOPMENT: South Asia

This article discusses the position of women in five countries of the south Asian region. It looks at their social and cultural status, marital status, education, and labor force participation; and the impact of capitalism and patriarchal institutions; and issues that seem to affect their position owing to the recent development processes.

South Asia has a disproportionate number of the developing world's poor. While 30 percent of the developing world's population is concentrated in the region, it has 47 percent of its poor. Nearly 51 percent of the population in south Asia is considered to be below the poverty line, compared with 33 percent of the total population of the developing world (*Human Development Report 1994*).

Women appear to share the major burden of this state of development; more than 70 percent of adult females were illiterate in three out of five countries in the region (Table 1). In countries like Banglaesh, India, and Pakistan, high maternal mortality rates indicate that women lack access to basic medical facilities; the rates also reflect malnutrition, anemia, and complications related to reproductive health. The position of women in these countries poses many contradictions. Powerful Hindu goddesses and female political leaders coexist side by side with cultures of hierarchic male authority. In south Asia it is misleading to refer to women as a class in terms of their economic position or as a group with shared interests and common problems. Although women in general may be more oppressed than men, the nature and extent of their oppression will vary according to their class, caste, ethnicity, and religion. Development issues concerning women in south Asia are also linked to the impact of imperialism and capitalism and the influence of traditional patriarchal structures. The varying impact of all these forces on the status and lives of the women in these countries leads to considerable difference in their conditions.

Sri Lanka

In terms of gender relations and the general status of women, Sri Lanka occupies a special place among other countries in south Asia. Sri Lankan women gained the right to vote as early as 1931, three years after women in Great Britain (Sastri, 1993). Women in postindependence Sri Lanka have achieved very high literacy rates, and they outnumber men in some sectors of tertiary education. In 1960 Sri Lanka made history by becoming the first country to have a woman lead its democratically elected government. Demographic improvements are also apparent, such as a rise in the age of marriage, a sharp decline in fertility rates, and higher life expectancy. Most of these trends are unusual by third world standards, and Sri Lankan women cannot claim to face serious disadvantages compared with women in other south Asian countries. Yet the majority of women in Sri Lanka, like their sisters elsewhere in the region, are confronted with many issues that contribute to the deterioration of their overall quality of life.

The protracted ethnic conflict in the north and the east has resulted in substantial social dislocation and trauma, affecting on the lives of many women and their families. The increasing financial cost of the war has led to a deterioration in the quality of health and education services and in the quality of life of people in the country.

Bangladesh

Bangladeshi women are usually seen as dependent and vulnerable. Although women contribute immensely to domestic labor and economic production, this is not acknowledged (*Women in Development,* 1986). On the other hand, they are subject to social ostracism if they fail to produce sons or if they have sick children. It is the responsibility of the women to produce a son or sons to acquire status. If a woman's marriage ends when she is young or old with no son to support her, she may either return to her family of birth or live in poverty. The most noted social custom in Bangladesh is seclusion, or purdah.

India

India inherits a caste-linked patriarchy. The system of kinship has been patrilineal and patrilocal throughout the subcontinent except among the Nayars and related castes in Kerala. With regard to seclusion, controls on women vary, since lower castes allow women greater independence, which is necessary to their work and survival. Traditions that allow child marriage, patriliny, and dowry deaths still remain, while androgyny and female power (*shakti*) exist only at the ideological level. The cultural reality for most Indian women is *pativarta* (one who worships her husband). Postcolonial economic development has increased the gap between the organized and the unorganized sectors as well as the gap between men and women. Capitalism in the form of commercial tree felling, large-scale construction projects, mining development, and factories (especially in the forest and mountainous areas) has invaded the traditional sources of livelihood for most tribal women. These developments have at the same time united poor women in protecting the environment, finding employment, and fighting violence.

Nepal

Nepal is one of the least developed countries in the world; the majority of the population is dependent on low-productive agriculture. The legal status of women appears to be mixed. While the constitution of 1990 guarantees fundamental rights to all citizens without discrimination on the basis of caste, ethnicity, sex, or religion, there is no supportive leglislation. On the other hand, family laws that govern marriage, divorce, property rights, and inheritance reinforce patriarchy and restrict women's power over economic resources (Women in Nepal; 1999). Early marriage, high fertility rates, and lower life expectancy rates are more the rule than the exception. Women also bear the risk of early widowhood, owing to the practice of early marriage and to poor health facilities in the country. The female literacy rate is low, and few women have been able to obtain higher education. Women's participation in political and administrative fields is marginal, with few employed at the decision-making levels in the government sector. Acknowledgement of women's contribution to the national economy is limited, because the majority are omitted from labor force statistics. The predominance of the idea of patrilineage and male superiority, the high value placed on chastity, and the notion that women should not live independently all contribute to the low status of women in Nepal.

Pakistan

The low status of women in Pakistan is one of the main impediments to the achievement of developmental goals. The extended family is a basic functional unit in Pakistani society, and for most people it is the only source of security. Family structure is based on descent through the male line and acceptance of male authority. Early marriage and the ability to produce children after marriage, especially sons,

Table 1. South Asia: Basic indicators

	Sri Lanka	India	Bangladesh	Pakistan	Nepal
GNP per capita dollars	810	430	175	480	210
Average annual growth rate	nd	4.2	3.4	2.5	−0.1
Adult illiteracy rate, male/female					
% of people 15 and above	6/12	33/61	50/73	45/75	44/79
Maternal mortality rate per 100,000 live births	30	440	850	340	220
Population, millions 1998	19	980	126	132	2.3
Fertility rate 1997	2.2	2.8	3.2	5.0	4.4

Source: World Development Report 1999/2000: 230; 232; 242.

determine a woman's position within the family. Religious values are used to provide guidance on relationships between the sexes, marriage, divorce, inheritance, and family matters. At the same time they are used to restrict women from openly participating in educational, economic, political, and other activities.

Social and Cultural Status of Women

In the developing nations of south Asia, women's access to power and positions of influence is determined to a large extent by traditional norms and religious values. The majority of women in south Asia belong to the religious traditions of Hinduism, Islam, and Buddhism, with a minority of Christian groups. Stemming from these religious beliefs are values about appropriate behavior for men and women. The social and cultural status of women in south Asia therefore varies according to the nature and intensity of religious influences, together with the social class position of women and the remoteness of a region from modernized urban sectors.

On the Indian subcontinent women enjoyed many privileges and religious rights in common with men during the Vedic era, but a gradual erosion of their status resulted after the laws of Manu were written down. According to these laws, a female must be subjected to her father in childhood, to her husband during youth, and, when her lord is dead, to her sons; a woman must never be independent

(Manu: V: 147, cited in Altekar 1950: 329). What was expected of a woman was unquestioning obedience to her husband and unlimited service to him, however unfair his demands and however low he may have been. In the classical texts such a woman was called a *pativarta,* or one who worships her lord: the ideal woman in Hinduism. In marriage a Hindu woman has to be chaste and bear sons for the performance of funeral rites for her husband. During the early periods, excessive practices—such as suttee *(sati),* or the burning of a widow on the funeral pyre of the husband—were carried out. Even in modern times widows are expected to follow strict codes of conduct such as wearing plain clothes, disposing of jewels and ornaments, and behaving in ways that reflect Hindu renunciation. These beliefs are internalized by women and passed on to younger generations. From early childhood females are taught to play subservient roles, to be docile, submissive, and passive. They are socialized to expect that they will spend their lives as mothers and housewives and will have responsibility for child care and housework. In the Hindu tradition, women derive their status from fertility in the exalted status of mother goddesses, while infertility is considered a curse (Kasarda, Billy, and West 1986). However, women have no control over their own fertility. Childbirth and lactation force women to withdraw from active economic work and make them dependent on their men. Religious notions have reinforced patriarchal values, which have shaped the lives and behavior of the majority of women in south Asia.

In Sri Lanka the majority of women are followers of Buddhism, and to a great extent their lives are influenced by Buddhist values. Although Buddhism as a liberal reaction against orthodox Brahmanism elevated the status of women, in practice it tends to favor men. For instance, the Buddha allowed women into the order under the "eight high ordinances," yet the first one asked nuns, even those ordained a hundred years ago, to show respect to a monk just ordained. There is still no possibility for women to become ordained as Buddhist nuns, and in Sri Lanka there have been heated discussions on this issue. The idea of mother as a self-sacrificing and benevolent figure is very much present in Buddhist thought. Yasodara, the devoted wife of Prince Siddharta, Amara in Ummaga Jataka, and Kinneri in Sandakinduru Jataka are religious images that have made a great impact on Buddhist women, like the influence of Sita on Hindu women.

Islam and Christianity both have ruling male gods (Allah and God the Father), male prophets (Muhammad, Jesus, John the Baptist), and male priests. Women are denied a place in the priesthood and are often excluded from mosques. The majority of women in Pakistan and Bangladesh are subjected to Islamic rules and are also influenced by local customs, traditions, and tribal laws. In the less populated provinces of Baluchistan and Northwest Frontier Province in Pakistan, a woman's life is governed by a rigid code of tribal beliefs and patterns of behavior, and any deviations from these codes may have grave consequences (Shaheed, 1989). Thousands of Pakistani women and girls are stabbed, burned, or maimed every year by husbands or other male relatives, who think the women have brought them dishonor. The most common reasons for such assaults are for being unfaithful, seeking a divorce, eloping with a lover, or refusing to marry a man chosen by the family. If the victim dies, the crime is interpreted as a "honor killing," an action that is seldom punished by law.

Although women's status is closely linked to their class in Islamic countries, women are generally considered subordinate to men both in their families and in society. In Pakistan, even the position of the former prime minister (Benazir Bhutto) was threatened by religiopolitical parties which argued that a woman cannot be a head of state in Islam. The trend toward politicizing religion and toward Islamization has adversely affected the position of women in countries like Pakistan and Bangladesh. In these countries women are also conditioned by such notions as gender segregation and honor, and by the prescriptions of purdah (that is, female seclusion).

Purdah, female seclusion, creates a sexually segregated world that identifies men with the public or social sphere and women with the private domestic sphere. Its outward symbol is the *purkah,* a concealing garment that women don when they leave the household and enter the "male space." Along with other elements of the system at both ideological and structural levels, purdah sets and maintains the limits to women's access to power and autonomy. In Bangladesh purdah is practiced by middle- and upper-class women, while poor women do not conform to these controls, because they are pushed out to seek contractual forms of wage labor (*Women in Development,* 1986). Customs related to purdah have prevented women's mobility, access to information and education, skills, and work opportunities. Purdah often leads women to withdraw from institutions at puberty and discourages them from attending schools at any distance from their homes. Rural areas in Baluchistan and Northwest Frontier Province, which have the most extensive purdah restrictions, also record the lowest literacy levels. In the long term these practices create barriers to women's participation in all spheres of activity, including the

Table 2. Indicators of marital status

	Sri Lanka	India	Bangladesh	Pakistan	Nepal
Mean age at marriage	24.4	16.7	18.7	19.8	17.9
% women currently married 15–19 years	9.7	65.4	43.5	29.1	50.1
% women currently married 25 plus*	59	77	74	73	81
Women currently divorced	0.5	2.8	0.8	0.5	0.4

Source: The World's Women 1995: Trends and Statistics, page 36.

*The World's Women (1979–1990) Trends and Statistics; 1991 pages 28–29.

political and legal spheres that could help to promote their rights and status.

Marriage: Customs and Practices that Affect Women's Status

The status of women in any society can be gauged by the forms of negotiation involved in marriage. In south Asian countries it is considered the duty of the family to get females married, whether they be daughters or sisters. This focus on marriage tends to distract parents from concentrating on important areas such as the education and training of girls for the labor market. Originally the dowry meant that the marriage of a daughter was often accompanied by small gifts, including cash, clothing and jewelry that the bride kept as her personal property. In India, although the dowry was banned by the Dowry Prohibition Act of 1961, it is easily evaded because gifts made at the time of the wedding are not included in the legal definition of dowry. Today it has become a form of extortion, with young brides being harassed, beaten, tortured, and in extreme cases murdered if the husband's family considers the dowry inadequate.

In Sri Lanka during early times, marriage between cross-cousins was considered the ideal, and marriages between families of the same caste in the same or neighboring villages were common. In these marriages the dowry was more of a gift to the daughter in the form of jewelry or property. Later, arranged marriages through a matchmaker (*kapuwa*) became the accepted norm, especially among the middle classes. Although caste, family, religion, horoscopes,

and place of birth (whether up-country or low country) were important considerations in a marriage, dowry tended to assume greater importance. At present, with the impact of commercialism, marriage and dowry have assumed new dimensions, and capitalistic attributes such as class background, occupation, education, wealth, and in extreme cases foreign exchange (for dowry payment) play an important role.

Social, cultural, and religious traditions affect women's reproductive role. With the exception of Sri Lanka, women in the region are married, on average, by age 19 (Table 2). Men tend to marry later, and in countries like Bangladesh men are on average seven years older than women who marry for the first time (*World's Women 1970–1990*, 1991). This gap would increase women's dependence on their husbands even if women contribute to the family income. It further indicates that because of their responsibilities for child care few women complete secondary school or work outside the home. In most countries of the region a woman fulfills her most important responsibility and acquires status when she produces a son. To fulfill this obligation females are married off at puberty and then are locked into high-fertility patterns. Failure to produce a son may sometimes lead to desertion or divorce.

Education and Training

Despite broad progress in education, there is a huge discrepancy in literacy between men and women, especially rural women, in south Asian countries (Table 3). Secondary and tertiary education have also been limited compared with countries in Latin America, the Carribean, and other parts in Asia (*World's Women 1995*: 92). As in the countries of sub-Saharan Africa, generations of educational neglect have left high illiteracy rates among older women, with more than 70 percent of women aged 25 and over being illiterate (*World's Women 1995*: 88). In this gloomy scenario Sri Lanka's performance is unique in achieving high literacy rates. The impressive educational achievement in Sri Lanka is attributed to the interventions in education in the early years of this century and to the availability of free education immediately after independence. In the rest of the region it will take many years to reduce the gender gap in literacy due to the historical deficit in women's education. This literacy gap is paralleled by an educational gap at every level of the educational system. In secondary enrollments girls lag behind, and one reason could be early childbearing in countries like Bangladesh and Pakistan. Except for Sri Lanka, the countries in the region enroll fewer than 40 women per 100 men in higher education.

Table 3. Indicators of education

	Sri Lanka	India	Bangladesh	Pakistan	Nepal
Adult literacy rate 1995 Male/ Female (a)	93/87	65/37	50/24	49/26	40/14
Females per 100 males enrolled at first level (c)	93.0	65.0	50.0	66.0	41.0
Female enrolment in secondary education (b) 1997	79.3	48.0	21.0	15.6	39.7
Female tertiary students-per 100,00 women (a)	388	445	238	188	231

Source: (a) Human Development Report 1998

(b) United Nations Development Fund for Women-Targets and Indicators 2000

(c) *The World's Women 1995: Trends and Statistics, 1995.*

Women and Work

The ability to participate in economic activities and gain control over one's income is an important indicator of women's status in general. The extent of women's participation in the labor market and the nature of the activities performed would reveal women's status as well as the variations of status across socioeconomic classes (see Table 4).

Developmental processes have differential impact on women in south Asia. For example, domestic work, which is often considered the second shift of women's work, is class-differentiated. The availability of cheap female and child labor as low-wage domestic servants provides time for middle-class women to enter the professions and participate in political decision making. The availability of cheap domestic service may also explain the lack of a female middle-class voice demanding that males share domestic labor. Apart from class, patriarchy and caste are also interactive elements in determining women's work. In India, for example, women's work is stratified and determined by norms of appropriate work related to one's class or caste position (Bhadran, 1991). Casual, low-paid, and laboring jobs will not attract women of upper-class and upper-caste families.

Women from the landowning classes in the rural sector often have control over the labor of poor peasant women and others who work in their households. In the urban areas women professionals have different working lives from factory workers, construction workers, casual laborers, and vendors.

In countries in south Asia, women who are at the bottom of the socioeconomic hierarchy are the landless poor who work as casual workers in rural and urban informal sectors. Two-fifths of all working women in India are low-paid casual laborers, and of this group, the majority are tribal and outcaste women. This phenomenon could be attributed to patterns of economic development such as logging of forests, which have forced tribal people out of their forest-based subsistence (Bhadran, 1991).

In Bangladesh, although women are restricted by purdah, poor women work outside the home as low-paid domestics in rich households, construction workers, and daily laborers in unskilled rural nonfarm work (Feldman, 1993). In urban areas a small percentage of women hold professional jobs, in fields such as teaching, medicine, and social welfare. In recent years, with the creation and expansion of garment factories, there has been an increase of women in the manufacturing sector. Segregation of women in lower categories of work leads to problems of unemployment, underemployment, insecurity, and irregularity of jobs, as well as lower remuneration. This is also true in Pakistan, where increasing numbers of women are employed in factories and production units such as electronic industries and garment industries. In the unorganized or nonformal sector the activities of women are not recognized and go unreported. For example, women working in quarries, although forming 50 percent of the labor force, are not recognized as laborers, and their wages are paid to the male head of the family.

In Sri Lanka, the majority of women are engaged in rural agriculture, the so-called informal sector, where women laborers, especially those engaged in paddy cultivation, are paid less than men for performing the same tasks. Women employed in the formal sector are governed by labor legislation, and in 1985 women public-sector employees gained the right to three months' maternity leave for the first two live births, as well as social security benefits available to male public-sector employees. According to the socioeconomic surveys carried out by the Central Bank in Sri Lanka, there has been an increase of 1.4 percent in the urban sector, which could be attributed to the increase of the service and manufacturing industries, particularly those in the free trade zones

Table 4. Indicators of economic activity

	Sri Lanka	India	Bangladesh	Pakistan	Nepal
Female % of labor force 1998 (a)	36	32	28	42	40
Women's share of earned income (b)	36	25	21	23	n.d.
Female administrators and managers 1992–1996 (b)	16.2	2.3	3.9	4.9	n.d.
Female professional and technical workers 1992–1996 (b)	19.4	20.5	19.5	34.7	n.d.
Women in government at ministerial level % 1995 (b)	12	4.2	3.7	4.5	0

Source: (a) World Development Report; 2000.

(b) Human Development Report 1998 or 2000.

South Asian women in general are subject to considerable pressure to conform to the domestic roles of wife and mother, as well as to religious ideologies, which emphasize female inferiority. Arranged marriages, the dowry system, purdah, and new patterns of economic development all contribute to reinforce women's social and economic dependence. Although these discriminatory conditions have been identified, few steps have been taken to address them.

Gaps in policy, development, and income deprive many south Asian women of the long overdue recognition for their work in the home, labor force, and services to the community.

See Also

BUDDHISM; COLONIALISM AND POSTCOLONIALISM; DOMESTIC LABOR; FEMINISM: SOUTH ASIA; HINDUISM; POLITICS AND THE STATE: SOUTH ASIA, *I and II;* SHAKTI

References and Further Reading

Altekar, A. S. 1950. *The position of women in Hindu civilization from pre-historic times to the present day.* Delhi: Motilal Baranarsidas.

Bhadran, Kalpana. 1991. Women and feminism in a stratified society: Recent developments in India. In Sally J. M. Sutherland, ed. *Bridging worlds: Studies on women in South Asia.* Berkeley: University of California Press.

Feldman, Shelley. 1993. Contradictions of gender inequality: Urban class formation in contemporary bangladesh. In Alice Clark ed., *Gender and political economy: Explorations of South Asian systems,* 215–43. Oxford: Oxford University Press.

Human development report 1994. (1994. United Nations Human Development Report 1998. UNDP; New York Oxford University Press Development Program.) New York: Oxford University Press.

Karsada, John. D, John. D.G. Billy, and Kirsten West. 1986. *Status enhancement and fertility.* Academic Press Inc. New York.

Sastri, Amita. 1993. Women in development and politics: The changing situation in Sri Landa. In Alice Clark, ed., *Gender and political economy: Explorations of South Asian systems,* 246–41. Oxford: Oxford University Press.

Shaheed, Farida. 1989. *An analytical description of women in Pakistan (NORAD).* Islamabad: Royal Norwegian Embassy.

The state of world population. 1994. New York: UNFPA.

Women in development: Country briefing paper. 1986. Asian Development Bank.

Women in Nepal: Country briefing paper. 1999. Asian Development Bank.

World development report: Infrastructure for development. 1994. World Bank. New York: Oxford University Press.

World development report: Entering the 21st Centry. 1999/2000. World Bank. New York: Oxford University Press.

The world's women 1970–1990: Trends and statistics. 1991. New York: United Nations.

The world's women 1995: Trends and statistics. 1995. New York: United Nations.

Thalatha Seneviratne

DEVELOPMENT:
Sub-Saharan and Southern Africa

Women today play a prominent role in the economic development of Africa. Since prehistoric times, as reflected in instructional myths of origin, women have generated and sustained life. They have contributed substantially to the economic welfare of African societies as the main producers of staple foods; they have processed the food crops and provided the daily sustenance of extended families. Women's status has similarities throughout the continent, though there are also variations based on historical experience and modes of livelihood in different ecological zones. Differences in precolonial histories and cultures, the history of the slave trade, the impact of religion, colonial occupation, rule by different foreign powers, varying national struggles for independence, the political and economic systems the countries adopted, and increasing pressure from the world economic systems are all factors that have influenced women's contributions to and potential for development in different parts of southern and sub-Saharan Africa. Sub-Saharan Africa consists of all the countries within and south of the Sahara: Angola, Zambia, and Tanzania are the northern border countries of southern Africa. North Africa includes Algeria, Egypt, Libya, Morocco, and Tunisia, which thus fall outside the geographical area of this article.

Patterns Inherited from Precolonial African Society

In the woodlands and mountains of precolonial African society there was a division of work between men and women. This division allotted men the task of hunting game for food and skins for clothing, felling and hauling trees for constructing houses, making weapons and tools, and carving utensils. In order to stalk prey and acquire materials, men had to veer outside the domestic area. Women tended the hearth and food stores; they gave birth and nurtured offspring. Male young people were initiated into wilderness survival, while females were initiated into regenerative domestic tasks. The border between the human habitat and wilderness demarcated the division of work between men and women, as it later did between public life and the domestic sphere. This is the historical basis for the division of labor even in changing societies.

Men claimed the right to mobility for clan, tribal, or interstate politics and trade, much as they have done until today. Occasionally women have become chiefs. In Tanzania the hereditary Mwami of the Nyiha, Mangi Mayanka of the Chagga, elected because of her personal qualities, led her subjects to war against neighboring chiefs (Swantz, 1985). The Rain Queen of the Lovedu maintained authority by remaining invisible to her subjects.

Women were healers, shamans, diviners, and, in general, central actors in ritual celebrations. For the most part, however, large state celebrations for kings, rulers, and tribal elders constituted the men's domain. Women were precluded from defending themselves or even from participating in public proceedings.

The myths of origin of domestic plants among the Zaramo of Tanzania explain that women discovered edible plants and initiated their cultivation (Swantz, 1985: 25–27). Where cultivation was the basis for subsistence, settlements had a degree of permanency. In the woodlands, shifting slash-and-burn cultivation required men to cut forests for fields while women took care of family sustenance. Women managed all domestic work, as they have continued to do in rural areas until today, even if the nature of the work has changed.

Together with men or alone, women cleared felled trees and prepared fields for sowing; they hoed, weeded, and harvested; they processed the crops, cooked the meals, and carried water and firewood. Women bore and nurtured children and cared for the general well-being of their families. Where plows were in use, men's share of the work was larger. Similarly, where the skill of weaving was developed, men were the weavers, as in west Africa and Ethiopia and in a few other parts of Africa.

Scattered groups—the !Kung San ("Bushmen") of Botswana and Namibia, the Hadzapi and Tindiga of Tanzania, and the Efe or Mbuti ("Pygmies") in the borderlands of Congo and Uganda—chose to remain hunters and gatherers until the changes that have recently been forced on them. Women gathered wild grasses, roots, leaves, fruits, and nuts, occasionally benefiting from a swarm of locusts or flying ants, while men tracked their prey deep in uninhabited terrain. Even here territorial distances conditioned the division of work. These groups have been pushed out to survive in marginal lands; they have collided with modernizing national policies in Tanzania; and they have suffered from wars in their territories, especially in southern Africa, where South African troops exploited their skills of orientation and survival in deserts and forests.

Herding in arid lands created a cattle-based culture with seasonal migration to better grazing grounds. Among persistent pastoralists, the basic life pattern has remained unchanged since precolonial times. Women have tended small stock near the home kraals, milked cows, and worked with beads and leather. Moving the kraal has been seasonal or has followed weather conditions in years of drought. Indigenous methods of spacing children were imposed for the sake of mobility. A child had to walk before another was born; a mother could not carry two children. Even today, women remain with a child until he or she walks and "can take a gourd of milk" to the father. Polygamous marriages permit time for the mother to recover after childbirth.

Many traditionally nomadic herders have until recent times seldom engaged in cultivation. However, the vast arid lands in Sahel, where precipitation is concentrated in one relatively short season a year, have lent themselves to extensive plow cultivation. Suitable weather conditions created areas for combined cattle herding and cultivation in countries like the Hausaland of northern Nigeria, Burkina Faso, Niger, and Mali, or in northern Tanzania, to mention a few. Neither extensive plow cultivation nor herding has been principally women's work. Since tractors have replaced the plow here, both the work and control of the produce for cash crops have slid into the hands of men. In general, extensive agriculture and the use of the plow, and later the tractor, have kept much agricultural work in the hands of men. When herders began cultivating, they not only hired labor but also preferred tractors to oxen for fear that their livestock would suffer if they were turned into beasts of burden. Nonetheless, women's participation in weeding, harvesting, and processing is greater than commonly recognized. The change from extensive to more intensive cultivation of groundnuts, as an export crop to Europe from Senegal and Burkina Faso, increased women's workload, but, here as elsewhere, women were usually obliged to give the cash to their husbands.

Cattle herding has been male-dominated, even if cattle are transferred from one family or lineage to another through women. For example, in the Parakuyo of Tanzania, head of cattle are counted as a man's property even if he holds the stock in the name of his wives. The man controls the herd, but he cannot dispose of such cattle without the permission of the particular wife. The herd symbolizes social relationships in the kraal. Women's dependence on men's authority has gradually decreased, however, as women discover their de facto economic power.

Prehistoric penetration of pastoralists into the areas of sedentary cultivators in the regions of central African lakes created differentiations between cattle owners and sedentary cultivators, the latter becoming servants, even slaves, to the wealthier cattle owners. Male-dominated feudal class societies were born among the peoples around the lakes. In the 1980s and 1990s the world witnessed a sequence of bloody internal wars in this region.

The slave trade, which was carried out from the western coast of Africa to the Americas, and from the eastern coast to Asia and Arabia as well as to the French-ruled islands of the Seychelles and Mauritius in the Indian Ocean till the latter part of the nineteenth century, reached the heart of inland Africa and had a devastating impact on social relations. Along the slave route women were traded as pawns or concubines, valuable for the labor and sexual services they could render for internal and intertribal power struggles as well as for external transactions. Marcia Wright's studies on redeemed women slaves after the abolition of slavery is

an important piece of women's history on which most other history books are mute (1975, 1993). Many slave girls were bought by missions or they themselves escaped to freedom. Since they had no kinship ties to surrounding communities, they were the first women to receive an education and to become helpers in mission stations or teachers of children and other women.

Christianity and Islam, as historical religions based on written traditions, have old roots in the northern parts of Africa. The Orthodox church gave shape to the culture of Ethiopia; Islam spread from the northeast over the Saharan states and through large parts of west Africa.

Since the early centuries of the second millennium (according to the western calendar), traders and craftsmen from Persia (Shiraz), the Arabian peninsula, India, and even China and Indonesia came with their boats to the east coast of Africa. They traded, invaded, intermarried, and settled on the islands of Lamu, Zanzibar, Pemba, and Kilwa, and on the shores of the mainland. Their penetration to inland regions began later with long-distance trade. Africa was a land not only of slaves but also of ivory, animal trophies, and, above all, gold. On the islands and along the coastline flourishing settlements were created. The chronicles and ruins of extensive stone structures of palaces and mosques tell of the wealth of the black women who, as early as the Middle Ages, bathed in palace pools and dressed in silk gowns and golden ornaments. Engravings on centuries-old gravestones indicate that the towering tombstones were erected in honor of notable women as well as men. Moreover, old Swahili poetry records women poets whose manuscripts have been preserved in family chests as heirlooms. Islam also changed African traditional architecture; women's seclusion became more pronounced than earlier because houses that had been on open ground became fenced in (Weule, 1909). Islamic social practice on the eastern coast has influenced women's economic activities differently in west Africa. It has kept women away from the markets and other public places. In western Africa, in Ghana, Nigeria, and Senegal, women control the market trade with their tightly organized yet flexible informal systems.

Colonial Africa

Only the fortresses of Mombasa and Kilwa remain as physical reminders of the 200-year-long Portuguese occupation—from the end of the fifteenth century—of the Tanzanian and Kenyan coast. But in Angola and Mozambique and to a certain extent in Guinea-Bissau and Cape Verde, Portuguese rule left behind traumatic development and severe national birth pains.

The era of accelerated long-distance trade had caused movement of peoples and goods, including the sale of women, as already indicated. It whetted the appetite of the powerful nations of Europe: Britain, France, Belgium, and Germany. In Berlin in 1885 representatives of European governments sat around a table and sliced the map of Africa into sections for colonization. Subsequently, these countries sent emissaries to usurp the designated lands. This marked the beginning of the colonial era in Africa.

The introduction of Christianity to sub-Saharan Africa in the middle of the nineteenth century through foreign missionaries, and to a greater extent through indigenous evangelists and Christians, coincided to a large degree with the colonial period. Where the mission agencies were active, Christianity influenced women's position. Women in subservient social situations could experience new forms of personal freedom (Larsson, 1991); hospitals and clinics provided health services especially for parturient women and infants, and elementary schools were established for girls as well as boys. Christian churches also introduced monogamous marriage rules, which changed the social fabric. Women's workload increased in single-wife marriages, as did the number of children borne by one mother. Women received elementary education in mission and church schools, but institutions of higher learning were opened later for young women than for men. The pattern of education varied in different colonial systems. In francophone Africa a selected number of highly competent students, eventually including a number of women were integrated into the French educational system. Some students from Africa were welcomed at the Sorbonne and other academic institutions in France, but the majority of the people received little or no education. Most women remained illiterate under French rule, as they had been under Portuguese rule.

The primary concern of all colonialists was to secure the workforce required for lower posts within the colonial administrative system. First the Germans, then the British aimed at building a broad-based system of primary and middle schools but few secondary schools. A few top students were sent to the academic institutions of Britain. In the 1920s the number of girls in government schools was negligible, though the church schools provided rudimentary education to children of both sexes. With the help of voluntary agencies, above all Christian churches and missions, the number of schools grew substantially. They were eager to educate the wives of men who had become Christians.

Employment opportunities later opened for educated women in government, the church, and other institutions. After World War II women began to be trained as teachers,

nurses, and clerks and started looking for employment as domestic servants and industrial workers. The accompanying changes affected local cultural and social systems profoundly. Women did not always gain a better position within the household in monogamous marriages as male rule persisted, and the institutional churches also created new male hierarchies.

The increased need for labor in public works, for agricultural workers on plantations, and for mining industry led to extensive labor migration. The colonial governments recruited laborers through imposition of head and hut taxes. To pay the taxes, men were forced to migrate to towns and plantations for wage employment, or men were introduced to cotton, coffee, or tea production for cash crops. Labor migration reinforced the gender-based division of work, which to a great extent has remained until today, even if the lifestyles of the people have changed. Men's long absences and extramarital relations in towns had grave consequences for family life and the health of women and children who were left behind to care for their own well-being. On the other hand, when women had to assume greater responsibility for the management of households and cash crops, the construction of houses, and the education of children, their management skills and economic independence increased, even when men controlled the cash earned from crops.

The male-dominated urban centers attracted women whom the social system could not accommodate: widows or divorced women with no land for cultivation and women in search of more personal freedom (Larsson, 1991). When wages improved, whole families could accompany the man. Town life also dramatically changed the pattern of women's daily lives.

After Independence

African countries gained their independence over a period of 35 years. Ghana was the first in 1957; the French colonies were granted independence by de Gaulle in 1960; and Tanzania became independent in 1961, a few years before other east African countries. Independence has meant a strong emphasis on development in all the African countries, with mixed results. Women have played an increasingly central role in sustainable development.

Women's central role in sustaining life has always been of fundamental importance in Africa, and it is even more important today, though during the first decades of development the international community hardly recognized their contribution. African political leaders, intent on modernizing and developing, treated women as traditionalists who had to be admonished to come out from their kitchens.

Internal and external development agents similarly treated women at first as passive beneficiaries of development; they were invisible as long as the thrust of development was on technological modernization. Little acknowledgment was given to the role women played as producers and providers of family sustenance.

In the 1970s two approaches to women's issues became common. The one-sided emphasis in development rhetoric on economic growth and technological modernization was balanced by "basic needs" policies. When women's heavy workloads were acknowledged, public discourse turned women into victims requiring salvation from excessive labor, ignorance, ill health, and illiteracy. In general, the gender imbalance was beginning to be recognized, as was the fact that women were often deprived of basic rights. Another approach, which women themselves began to promote through national and international women's movements, and which was first stated in 1970 in an international forum in the Second International Development Decade United Nations document, was to "integrate women into development" (Joekes, 1987). The international community began to realize that women are not only targets of action or beneficiaries and victims of welfare; they are also actors in their own right. Women have increasingly become conscious of the great significance that their productive, reproductive, and nurturing work has always had, not only for their own families and communities, but for the economic development of their countries in general.

International Women's Year was declared by the United Nations General Assembly in 1975. The Women's Decade, which the first World Conference on Women initiated in Mexico City in that year, had a great influence on women's positions all over the world (Pietilä and Vickers, 1994). The fact that women had their own International Year and a subsequent Women's Decade became a general topic of discussion at all levels of society. National preparations for the four international women's conferences that followed Mexico—the second in Copenhagen in 1980, the third in Nairobi in 1985—became international events that permanently established women on the development agenda both nationally and internationally. The conference in Nairobi adopted a document entitled "Forward-Looking Strategies for the Advancement of Women," which the United Nations General Assembly later legitimized, thus obliging all member governments to implement it. This document has played an important role in establishing women's issues in subsequent development policies in Africa as elsewhere.

The 1980s were referred to as the "lost decade" for Africa because most countries on the continent suffered steep economic decline, having invested in large construction and industrial projects that depended on external funding. The expansion was too fast, and too little thought was given to operating expenses or maintenance costs. Aid money was gradually decreased or totally withdrawn, and many large projects could no longer be sustained.

As in developing countries elsewhere, African countries south of the Sahara became heavily indebted. The interest payments alone consumed a large portion, up to 30–40 percent, of their export earnings. Policymakers did not recognize that the production of export crops in order to gain foreign currency depended on the work of women cultivators. If they were unable to produce enough, the countries were unable to pay the interest or to reimburse the debt that the industrial sector had incurred. The problem was exacerbated when young people went to school or moved to town in search of a better life, leaving most of the agricultural work to older and fewer women in the rural areas. Droughts in the late 1960s and early 1970s, especially in the Sahel countries, in the 1980s in east Africa, and in the early 1990s in the southern parts of Africa, impaired the productive capacity of African countries even more.

Under considerable pressure, the countries began one by one to concede to implement a "structural adjustment program" (SAP), which the International Monetary Fund (IMF) jointly with the World Bank demanded as a precondition for further loan money. The SAP measures hit women in charge of families the hardest. Radical cuts in health and educational expenditures affected women and children most acutely, because they were the prime users of social services. With rapid inflation, wages lost buying power as food prices rocketed. This resulted in a rapid growth of the informal economy, nontaxable gray work, black markets, and smuggling of goods across borders. Since women were the providers of daily food and other basic needs for the family, they also became involved in manifold ways of producing, processing, or exchanging goods for sale and trading them and in providing a variety of services. Liberalization of trade also legalized transactions that earlier were out of legal bounds. This development has also helped women find legal, albeit informal, forms of microentrepreneurship and has lifted them, especially in urban centers, from inactive consumers' roles to become major economic actors. Women have gained new economic opportunities especially within the informal market but also in the formal market system during the recession and the economic crisis of the late 1980s.

In precolonial society women had no separate economic role apart from the generation of life and the maintenance of family livelihood in general. Today we are conceptually returning to that same situation: women at the grassroots have retained the complex pattern of everyday living out of necessity. Women continue to combine their domestic and economic roles. Economic life cannot be partitioned into a separate domain.

Although it is widely recognized today that women, after the economic crisis of the 1980s, emerged from their hidden domestic role as the main economic actors in large parts of Africa, official statistics do not acknowledge their work as economically significant. Statistics are able to include women's work only in situations where products are exchanged at the marketplace and given added value. Gross domestic product (GDP) includes only produce that is assigned monetary value in national statistics. Until today women have been accorded credit only in rhetorical discourse about development. Yet women's work within the informal economic sphere has grown to such proportions that in countries like Tanzania it now covers more than one-half of the national economy. Of the household incomes in Dar es Salaam at about the time of this writing, between 80 and 90 percent was earned by women through their "projects" (Tripp, 1997).

Future Perspectives

Women's situation in today's Africa is radically different from what it was 50 years ago. The dismantling of colonial societies, the often painful process of building independent states, and the onslaught of the world economic system have changed the structures of societies and influenced the status of women profoundly. Each country has built its politics on its own history, some achieving independence since the early 1960s through a relatively peaceful struggle. Other countries, like Mozambique, Angola, and Zimbabwe, and later Namibia and South Africa, have gone through prolonged wars and bitter political processes.

There have been some homogenizing forces at work through multi- and bilateral development agencies. Multi- and bilateral organizations specializing in issues of health, work, family planning, and women's rights have also gained influence through international conferences, which have passed recommendations for the improvement of women's plight. National governments have signed conventions and have agreed on strategies that have given women opportunities for their own action. Women have been organized in national movements often controlled by parties and governments, but more recently by self-initiated women's organizations. Through these organizations and movements women are beginning to influence decision making on different levels. Through them they also

form linkages that enable individuals to fulfill their economic and social obligations.

The continental economic crisis has placed huge demands on women. It has loaded them with heavy work, but the increased economic responsibility has also afforded them more personal freedom and social authority. Women play a central role in the economies of the African countries through their income-earning activities and entrepreneurship. Their activities are often informal and small in scale, and this provides women the flexibility required to manage their manifold daily tasks. Another notable aspect of women's economy is the readiness and ability to combine service with income generation. By necessity, women operate by standards other than the profit motive that mainstream economics prescribes. Their businesses do not always aim at growth; rather, they represent an opportunity for family members and neighbors whom they feel responsible for to earn a living (Tripp, 1997). They multiply horizontally, making room for many small enterprises, instead of growing in size. The economy thus remains manageable by women as well as men and serves as a model for economies of the poor in general.

Health problems have always affected women even more than men because of their reproductive tasks and their primary responsibility for children. Many parts of Africa have suffered droughts and wars, which have had dire consequences for the food situation. During the 1990s the HIV virus became an even greater killer of women than of men, and its spread still continues, with very few success stories in arresting it.

In dealing with women's issues there has been a shift from a discussion of "basic needs" to a focus on "human rights." This has accompanied a shift from women's developmental issues emphasizing income generation and welfare concerns to questions of how women could attain political power.

Women's political participation in Africa increased dramatically over the 1990s as new actors claimed political space. As a few African countries moved toward electoral democratization in the 1990s, most remained basically authoritarian or semiauthoritarian but incorporated some democratic innovations. Thus, the rules for authoritarian regimes changed in some fundamental ways, so that such regimes differed markedly from the autocracies of the earlier postindependence period.

The nature of women's political activities underwent transformation as a result of these political openings. Whereas earlier organizational efforts focused on income generation, in the 1990s women's organizations began to focus more intensively on formal political power. Women politicians and organizations began to lobby actively for constitutional and legislative reforms to improve the status of women. Nonpartisan women's organizations made concerted efforts to increase female representation in parliaments. For the first time, women began to aspire to the presidency in countries like Tanzania, Nigeria, and Kenya, and women started and led political parties. On the electoral front, women's associations and women politicians were beginning to question the political manipulations of ethnicity. In Tanzania, women's efforts to develop nonpartisan, nongovernmental associations sparked conflict and debate over the nature of politics and citizenship and the limits of the right to organize. Similar struggles over associational autonomy intensified throughout Africa (Tripp, 2000).

See Also

DEVELOPMENT: MIDDLE EAST AND THE ARAB REGION; EDUCATION: SOUTHERN AFRICA; EDUCATION: SUB-SAHARAN AFRICA; ENVIRONMENT: SUB-SAHARAN AND SOUTHERN AFRICA; POLITICS AND THE STATE: SOUTHERN AFRICA; POLITICS AND THE STATE: SUB-SAHARAN AFRICA

References and Further Readings

Boserup, Esther. 1970. *Woman's role in economic development.* New York: St. Martin's.

Bryceson, Deborah, ed. 1995. *Women wielding the hoe. Lessons from rural Africa for feminist theory and development practice.* Oxford/Washington: Berg.

Joekes, Susanne. 1987. *Women in the world economy: An INSTRAW study.* New York: Oxford University Press.

Larsson, Birgitta. 1991. *Conversion to greater freedom? Women, church and social change in Northwestern Tanzania under colonial rule.* Uppsala: Almqvist and Wicksell.

Pietilä, Hilkka, and Jeanne Vickers. 1994. *Making women matter: The role of the United Nations.* Updated and expanded ed. with a foreword by Gertrude Mongella, Secretary General of the Fourth Conference on Women. London: Zed.

Swantz, Marja Liisa. 1985. *Women in development: A creative role denied? The case of Tanzania.* London: C. Hurst; New York: St. Martin's.

Tripp, Aili Mari. 1997. *Changing the rules: The politics of liberalization and the urban informal economy in Tanzania.* Berkeley: University of California Press.

———. 2000. *Women and politics in Uganda.* Madison: University of Wisconsin Press; Oxford: James Currey and Kampala: Fountain.

Weule, Karl. 1909. *Native life in east Africa.* New York: Appleton.

Wright, Marcia. 1975. Women in peril: A commentary of the life stories of captives in nineteenth-century east-central Africa. *African Social Research* 20 (December.): 800–819.

———. 1993. *Strategies of slaves and women: Life stories from east/central Africa.* New York: Lillian Barber.

Marja Liisa Swantz

DEVELOPMENT: Western Europe

The Meaning of "Women and Development" in the European Context

The concept "women and development" is relatively new to western Europe. It has evolved from consideration of the developing world rather than of Europe itself. At the international summit in Rio de Janeiro (1992), an undertaking was announced that the industrial world would increase assistance for development to over 0.7 percent of national budgets. In fact, only a few countries (Denmark, Norway, Sweden, and the Netherlands) have done this. In all other western European countries (as well as in the United States), the contributions to bilateral and multilateral agreements have declined since 1992. Furthermore, the strict monetary and fiscal policies necessary for joining and remaining in the European Monetary Union (EMU), which was launched on 1 January 1999, have constrained national budgets so that future increases are unlikely. In addition, recommendations at the Fourth Women's Conference in Beijing in 1995 about improving gender equality in pay and working conditions began to be seriously considered by the European Union (EU) only in 2000.

In European eyes, there is a need to maintain levels of assistance to ex-communist and developing world countries even if only about 5 percent of the world's asylum seekers and refugees come to European countries. Of all industrialized nations, New World countries such as Canada, Australia, and the United States continue to take proportionally higher percentage per capita of refugees. Overall, the western European record of accepting refugees has been poor. Some agreements now exist to encourage asylum seekers and economic refugees to return to their home countries by providing short-term financial incentives. Sweden has the highest per capita intake of refugees of all western European countries (1 refugee per 62 inhabitants), followed by Denmark (1:173), Norway, (1:175), and France (1:263). By far the poorest per capita intake in western Europe occurs in Germany (1:782), Spain (1:993), and Great Britain (1:3,108) (*Aktuell '95*, 1994). In Scandinavian countries and in the Netherlands, the intake of refugees (particularly the intake of Vietnamese in Norway) has been managed by an integrative community approach that has generally avoided the worst ravages of displacement. In other countries, refugees often suffer the ill effects of a generally hostile reception, with concomitant lack of work, lack of money, limits to access the social infrastructure, and even racial attacks, adding to the pool of Europe's poor. The dramatic increase in the number of refugees seeking asylum caused by ethnic conflict in the former Yugoslavia has created domestic pressure to limit immigration and cut back on the acceptance of refugees.

Even though the issue of "development" is meant to refer to the developing world, the term is by no means irrelevant to European countries. There are several main factors to support the concept of women in development within Europe itself. One is that economic development amongst European nations has remained very uneven and there are wide variations in gross national product (GNP). The substantial differences between European countries, with concomitant variations in living standards, are elucidated by examining per capita GNP figures (Table 1):

Table 1. West European national incomes (GNP) per capita per year (1999)

Country	Per capita income (U.S. dollars)
Andorra	16,114
Austria	25,550
Belgium	23,792
Denmark	32,119
Finland	23,162
France	23,786
Germany	25,592
Greece	11,688
Iceland	26,869
Ireland	19,612
Italy	19,912
Liechtenstein	40,703
Luxembourg	46,634
Netherlands	21,370
Norway	34.864
Portugal	10,789
Spain	13,511
Sweden	25,735
Switzerland	35,978
United Kingdom	21,823

Source: UN, 1999.

Whereas the low earners in Europe are the Balkan countries, parts of southern Europe and all eastern bloc countries have standards of living not unlike those in South American and some African countries. Even within western Europe, however, there are wide variations in income. Western Europe is heavily populated, with some 380 million people, and much of the continued population growth is among the poorer nations. For instance, in 1998, the overall birthrate of the EU nations was 1.44, but Ireland's rate was 1.92, while Turkey's was 4.36. Such population pressures continue to exert themselves most selectively on those groups that are already in vulnerable positions.

Causes and Symptoms of Underdevelopment in Western Europe

Although absolute poverty is rare, relative poverty can be widespread and substantial. *Relative poverty* refers to the situation of households having less than half of the national average wage at their disposal. In western European countries, there are a number of causes of underdevelopment. Although these are extremely complex, it is at least possible to identify some key elements. The firmness of the class structures and the relatively limited income mobility in some countries (especially pronounced in some southern European countries) have contributed to perpetuating an underserviced, underprivileged, and underprovided group, the main sufferers being women. There are areas in western Europe that are without water and electricity and have few or no health services and few of any of the modern amenities to which the western world in general has grown accustomed. Beggars, homeless occupiers of public park benches (called *clochards* in Paris), are a familiar sight in western Europe. Entire subsections of the population live by sifting through garbage cans or by petty thievery. These are not just people ravaged by drug and alcohol abuse but also those ravaged by poverty, class-based, and work-based structural inequalities. In recent times, these groups have been joined by refugees and asylum seekers who spend their time in the limbo of rootlessness and unemployment. Youth unemployment is high in some areas of western Europe; at times gangs form and turn to violence, mainly against victims of another kind, such as the old, the gay, the foreign, or women.

Income distribution plays a role in living standards as well as in the social and service infrastructure. Lack of social infrastructure and limited opportunities for education have been particularly detrimental for women. These differences exist not only because of national differences in economic success but also because of social attitudes.

For example, depending on how much or how little power the church or the military (seen as pillars of a misogynist past) manage to exert on state affairs, women's rights can be supported or severely curtailed. The western European example suggests that the more secular and "civil" a country is, the more progressive its social practices are in terms of gender justice and freedom of expression for women.

Furthermore, a rising number of female-based households has severely affected living standards. In pockets of the population, illiteracy has remained a problem, even within Europe. In 1990, about every third women in the world was unable to read and write. Whereas nearly 80 percent of all illiterate women were to be found in 10 countries of the developing world, Europe (including the former Soviet Union) had nearly 20 million illiterate people, of whom 64 percent were women (data from UNESCO's World Education Report). In western Europe, the proportion of single-parent households headed by women in the lower-income bracket is three times the number in the general population, and in the United Kingdom and Ireland the number is five times higher.

Infant mortality, reflecting the general health of women and the level of health services available, is generally low in Europe. Indeed, Europe has the lowest infant mortality rates in the world (except Japan). The countries with the lowest infant death rates are Sweden (3.6 per 1,000) and Austria (5 per 1,000); the highest number is in Portugal (7 per 1,000). All other western European countries are below 10 deaths per 1,000 live births. In contrast, Turkey's rate is 42 deaths per 1,000 births and Romania's is 22 deaths per 1,000 births. Compared with developing countries, which may have over 200 deaths per 1,000 live births, these figures are deemed negligible.

The situation is different for measures of schooling and labor force participation. In general, school attendance of females even in poorer western European countries improved dramatically over the last two decades of the twentieth century, and the gaps between males and females are beginning to close. This is not yet true of university education, although here the differences are related not necessarily to the wealth or poverty of the country concerned but to social attitudes. Hence, wealthy Switzerland still has a low level of women attending universities, while Greece, a much poorer country, has relatively high levels of enrollment of women at universities.

The Human Development Report (1994) indexed countries according to some of these basic measures, including education, labor force participation, and life expectancy. Whereas western European countries were amongst the highest-ranking, they were also distributed widely, between 2 and 76 for Europe as a whole and between 2 and 46 for western Europe. According to this report, Canada had the highest rating (1) and other non-European countries were among the first 20 ranks, for example, Japan (3), Australia (7), the United States (8), New Zealand (18), and Israel (19). There was a weak relationship between education, labor force participation, and wages.

Now that most women receive some form of education, the continuation of low earnings for women is a new issue. For every 100 males who are employed full-time, there are only 52 women in full-time employment. Sweden has the largest percentage of women in the workforce, with 68.7 percent employed in 1999, followed by Denmark (67.4 percent) and the United Kingdom (62.3 percent). The nations with the lowest percentage of women in the workforce were Spain (32.2 percent), Italy (36.1 percent), and Greece (38.5 percent). Many women in western Europe cite family commitments as the main reason for not seeking employment. Some 97 percent of women who were not seeking employment in Germany and 95 percent of women in Spain cited family obligations as preventing them from taking non-home-based jobs (EU, 2000). Average monthly earnings for males outweighed wages for women in all of the EU nations. The largest differences were in the Netherlands and Belgium. This confirms that change must encompass far more than mere formal change in policies and legislation.

Table 2. West European unemployment rates (1999)

Country	Men	Women
Austria	4.4	5.0
Belgium	7.0	10.9
Denmark	3.3	5.0
Finland	9.4	10.8
France	8.5	12.4
Germany	8.3	9.7
Ireland	5.8	5.9
Italy	8.6	14.9
Luxembourg	1.7	3.9
Netherlands	2.0	3.6
Portugal	3.7	4.7
Spain	10.4	21.6
Sweden	7.1	6.0
United Kingdom	6.4	5.3

Source: EU, 2000.

Overall, countries with ailing economies that joined the European community now find themselves increasingly better off.

Developments in Southern Europe

The term *development* has a more hopeful sound in poorer western European countries than in some of the developing countries. In the 1950s and 1960s, all four southern European nations (Portugal, Spain, Italy, and Greece) were the poor cousins of the rest of western Europe. They also shared a dismal record of oppression and dictatorships, lasting longer than anywhere else in western Europe. The postdictatorial phases in these countries set in motion a hasty restructuring of the economy and a transformation of social life. Political turmoil followed such restructuring. Portugal had no less than nine governments in three postrevolutionary years; Italy had 31 governments in less than 25 postwar years. The Greek form of government vacillated between a military junta and a parliamentary democracy, and Spain suffered a fate similar to that of Portugal.

Until rather recently, the economies of most southern European countries were predominantly based on agriculture and steeped in the preindustrial manufacturing mode of highly exploitative rural home-based labor, which typically fell to women and, sometimes, children. Women thus had few if any rights, and they were often not much better off than slaves. Rarely, if ever, had they any reprieve from total paternal-patriarchal supervision, from childbearing and low-paid or unpaid work. Topics such as sexuality or any form of birth control were entirely taboo, and a large number of women, mostly in rural areas, received little or no medical attention. With the exception of Italy, death rates of mothers in childbirth and infant mortality rates were high well into the 1970s. Changing the social infrastructure has been at the forefront of social policies, but the rate of change required to improve the worst positions of women is enormous and often beyond the capacity of the country in question.

As a result of the violent political conflicts, however, the postdictatorial constitutions of these four countries are now among the most progressive in Europe, enshrining women's rights in work, marriage, and education. Moreover, two of the southern European countries have experienced important economic successes: Italy now belongs among the leading industrialized nations of the world, and Spain has moved to a comfortable middle-level position within western Europe.

Rurality

Rurality is one of the chief factors in low levels for development, poor infrastructure, and the survival of customs that more often than not work against women. In most of western Europe the rural sector has declined sharply, now often constituting no more than 1 to 3 percent of the labor market in a given country. By contrast, Portugal and Greece are still today overwhelmingly rural nations, a fact that is reflected in female employment in agriculture in Greece (35.4 percent) and in Portugal (27.3 percent)—the highest figures in all of western Europe (EU, 1999). Their development must overcome an extreme lack of mobility.

In Portugal, before the revolution in 1974, social immobility was extreme. The upper class, a semifeudal oligarchy, was a small, rich, and separate entity that controlled most of the country's economic fortunes. Eighty percent of the national economy was in the hands of eight families. The bulk of the population was proletarian—chiefly agricultural (over 80 percent of the population lived in rural communities). Every third women and every fifth man was illiterate. In rural and semirural communities, the figure might have been as high as 80 percent for women (Kaplan, 1992). Women were the property of their husbands in reality if not in name; the husband could determine every aspect of family life. By law, domestic work was compulsory for women after marriage. The penal code went so far as to implicitly permit a husband to kill his unfaithful wife, because the crime did not incur a prision sentence; the law merely stipulated that he had to leave his province for three months. Contraceptives were unknown and in any case unavailable. Abortion was a serious crime, punishable by at least eight years' imprisonment. General ignorance was worsened by the unavailability of newspapers, of books, and often of radio and television. Social security provision hardly existed. Schools, hospitals, and medical services functioned only in some of the largest cities. Basic services such as transportation, electricity, and water often were lacking in rural and semirural areas. The rural sector was depressed, and hardly any change—either technological or social—had occurred in Portugal over centuries. Portugal had the lowest per capita income in western Europe, together with the highest rates of illiteracy, infant mortality, and infectious diseases (Kaplan, 1992).

Figures show, however, that Portugal has begun to climb out of its social and economic ills. Moreover, the national constitution of 1976 was a milestone in Portuguese women's history. Women regained the vote and were declared equal in all aspects of life. In 1980, Portugal ratified the United Nations convention on the elimination of any discrimination against women. At the same time, the government began to create the social infrastructure that Portuguese society has almost totally lacked. In 1986,

Portugal joined the European Communities as its youngest and poorest member, and pledged to improve the position of women, along with a multitude of other obligations and rules.

Acquiring standards of education, health, and social services to which most other western European countries had been accustomed for some time has necessitated drastic steps. The great need for educating the population, even at the most basic level, can be beyond the scope of available resources. In many areas primary school classes, for instance, may accommodate up to 100 students. Teaching may be done in shifts and school buildings are often used until 11 P.M. for routine instruction of students. There have been drastic shortages of teachers at all levels of schooling—trade and postsecondary education—especially in southern European countries, as the constant brain drain to the richer nations continued. Nevertheless, illiteracy rates are falling steadily, although in 1988 it still stood at about 11 percent for men and 21 percent for women in Portugal and averaged 7 percent in Greece in 1992.

Changes in Greece have followed patterns similar in Portugal. Over the last two decades of the twentieth century, developments were perhaps even more remarkable, in terms of the rise in general living standards and in terms of women's issues. For example, in the controversial area of reproduction and sexuality, Greece is among the most progressive countries in Europe. Contraceptives were made available cheaply and readily. In June 1986, one of the most advanced laws in Europe was passed, allowing abortion on demand for the first 12 weeks of pregnancy and up to 19 to 24 weeks in case of rape or for any medical reason related to the mother or fetus. Abortion, moreover, is low-cost or covered by health insurance.

Greece, perhaps more clearly than any other western European nation, lives at least on three levels of tradition and modernity. Large segments of the urban population are western in outlook, progressive, and even radical. Another stratum lives in a state of tension between traditional values and some modern "imports." In a third group, most often found in rural areas, there is little evidence of a change of pace, lifestyle, customs, or views. One example is the *prika*—the dowry—which the government abolished along with its family law reforms in 1982. In several parts of Greece, the system of dowry has remained a social practice. In families that adhere to the dowry system, a girl is an expensive item. Brothers usually cannot afford to marry until the sister is married off, for they, along with the father, have to save for her dowry. Arranged marriages are still being practiced (although their numbers are declining steadily), and girls in many families are unable to move about by themselves. In some families a new bride is still judged by the mother-in-law in terms of whether she is likely to be willing to accept the mother's regime. In some mountain regions, the chief criterion for approval or disapproval of the new bride is how much weight she can carry on her back (Kaplan, 1992).

Spain and Italy have made impressive economic advances in the post–World War II period, although here, too, certain regions—usually rural—are very depressed. In Spain during the Franco regime in the 1960s, 2.9 percent of landowners owned 80 percent of all pasture lands in Spain, and 18 percent of the upper echelon of Spanish society collected well over 50 percent of the nation's total GNP. Illiteracy rates for women stood at 18.3 percent in 1950 (Seager and Olson, 1986) and have now dropped to below 5 percent. The legal provisions that affect women most in their family life and in reproduction, however, have remained very limited and of dubious efficacy. Rape is severely punished in Spain (by 12 to 20 years' imprisonment), but it is rare that a sentence can be pronounced on a rapist, because of one important clause: the victim has the "power" to pardon the rapist. In small communities—as well as in cities—the mechanisms of "persuading" the victim to let the rapist go free are extremely powerful and rather unsavory.

As in all countries, it is difficult to describe the status of women overall. In pockets of rural Spain, it was reported in the late 1970s that water was in short supply and needed to be carted from wells. This was done only by women, irrespective of whether they were old, pregnant, or sick. Electricity was often nonexistent. The entire burden of raising children and looking after a rural household without appliances fell exclusively on the women. In addition, women very often had to help with the harvest or cook in a family restaurant or sell goods in a family-owned store. Women in rural Spain worked for well below the national minimum wage, worked longer hours than elsewhere (12-hour days), and were given no holidays to which were legally entitled, while they continued to be under the strictest parental supervision. It is conceivable that these observations may well hold true for pockets throughout Europe, particularly in countries that have been identified at the bottom end of GNP.

Conditions for married women in rural areas have remained problematic in many other ways. For instance, when wives were beaten by their husbands, there was nowhere for them to turn for support, and the distance between women's centers remains a problem today. The conditions of childbearing in some customary rural areas can only be described as "barbaric." Even difficult births often take place without the assistance of painkillers or anesthetics. To prevent some problems at birth, in the 1970s it still was common for the vaginal opening to be cut automatically while the woman was fully conscious—a practice, it is to be hoped, that is no longer possible. Women were often so traumatized by the experience of giving birth that they never wanted to have another child. In 1984, however, only 26 percent of women used the Pill, and 10 percent of men used condoms. By the end of the 1990s, those figures had doubled, and the birthrate in Spain had fallen to 1.5 percent.

Women in rural areas usually remain unpaid labor in family concerns, with a working day of 14 to 16 hours. They are marginalized in jobs that carry no benefits. With the crumbling of old beliefs and practices, there also has been an increase of loneliness, of isolation in old age, and of the misery associated with the whole gamut of modern urban living.

Women in Poverty in Rich Nations

Pockets of poverty for women also exist in the well-to-do countries and even in the richest countries of Europe. Although the matter is too complex to unravel here, there are several chief factors (rurality aside) that continue to foster poverty. One is class. Class-based poverty is relatively fixed, and neither government nor population policies tend to be geared toward the permanent underclass. Another factor is the rising number of female-headed households. A newer factor is the clash between free or mixed market (capitalist) economies and state-run (socialist) economies. For example, when Germany was unified and the five former states of the German Democratic Republic (GDR, East Germany) were incorporated into the new nation, women saw their economic independence crumble. The GDR had maintained a high employment rate for women (about 90 percent), as indeed was the case in most other eastern bloc economies, upheld by an infrastructure that supported women's work. Following unification, infrastructure support was lost and unemployment rose sharply in the wake of rationalizations for purposes of profit. Unemployment, therefore, was one of the first experiences of unification for a substantial number of women. Not only unemployment but also cuts in the budget for creches and kindergartens hit female-headed households especially hard. Every third child in the former GDR was born out of wedlock; 2.2 million children were being raised by single mothers. By 1991, unemployment in former GDR territories had risen to 56.1 percent. At the same time, the female unemployment rate in the old Federal Republic (FRG, West Germany) fell to

14.8 percent (EU, 1991). Women as heads of households who live solely on unemployment benefits cannot do well, because in Germany, as in many other western European countries, unemployment benefits are dependent on the last income (that is, on previous active labor force participation), and staggered as a percentage of income. As incomes in the GDR were substantially below those in the FRG, benefits for women in the former GDR were usually below the poverty line. The feminization of poverty, although contentious in some circles, gains new meaning in the case of German unification.

Another factor in poverty is age, and most old people are women. German regulations, not unlike those in the United States and elsewhere, make pension entitlements and unemployment benefits dependent on the active participation in the labor force across the entire life span. Moreover, pension and unemployment entitlements are fixed incomes, while the free market economy uses property and housing for speculation. East Germans are no longer protected by stable rental costs. FRG law allows owners of real estate to increase the rent every three years by 30 percent of the final rent, widening the gulf between haves and have-nots. Women are in a precarious situation indeed, and women of the former GDR have shown a marked anxiety about the future.

Central and eastern European countries have some experiences akin to the southern Europe decades earlier. The transition to parliamentary democracies and capitalist market forces has not been entirely favorable to all women in Europe. It is also worth remembering that capitalist societies in the West have played their role in creating and maintaining an underclass, as just one of the symptoms of the structured inequality on which the economic model functions. Systemic poverty is present in even the richest countries of western Europe. Although homelessness is rare among women, the isolation and harshness of poverty retain all their force in certain regions and age groups, and particularly among women.

See Also

DEVELOPMENT: OVERVIEW; EDUCATION: WESTERN EUROPE; HEALTH CARE: WESTERN EUROPE; HOUSEHOLDS AND FAMILIES: WESTERN EUROPE; POLITICS AND THE STATE: WESTERN EUROPE

References and Further Reading

Aktuell '95. 1994. Dortmund: Harenberg Lexikon Verlag.
European Commission. 1993. *European economy: Social Europe, 1993, reports and studies, No. 3, Commission of the European*

Communities. Brussels: Directorate-General for Economic and Financial Affairs, Directorate-General for Employment, Industrial Relations and Social Affairs.

———. 2000. Eurozone Unemployment. *Eurostat*. Brussels, EU.

———. 1986. *Women and development, 1986*. Supplement No. 17 to *Women of Europe*. Brussels: Commission of the European Communities.

———. 1991. *Women in Europe, 1991*. No. 69. Brussels: Commission of the European Communities.

———. 1999. Women in the European Community. *Eurostat*. Brussels: Commission of the European Communities.

Kaplan, Gisela. 1992. *Contemporary Western European feminism*. New York: New York University Press.

Netherlands, Ministry of Education and Science. 1993. *Woman, man and family: The division of labour within the family in southern European countries*. Newsletter, no. 9. Zoetermeer: ENWS.

Seager, Joni, and Ann Olsen. 1986. *Women of the world: An international atlas*. London: Pan.

UN. 1994. *Human Development Report, 1994*. New York: United Nations Development Program.

———. 1999. *UN/ECE yearbook: Trends in Europe and North America*. New York: United Nations.

———. 1991. *The world's women 1970–1990: Trends and statistics*. New York: United Nations Statistical Office.

Gisela Kaplan

DIARIES AND JOURNALS

Diaries and journals are forms of personal writing—sometimes referred to as "personal chronicles"—generally associated with the regular recording of daily events and frequently with only the writer as audience. Autobiographies, memoirs, and reminiscences are related forms but are written in the first person ("I"), are usually a life story, are often "recollected" (or reconstructed from a diary or notes) after the events have occurred, and are more likely to be intended for publication. A diary or journal can be a record of events, and, like all personal forms of writing, it can assist with self-development, self-analysis, or sanity. A biography is also the story of a life, but it differs from diaries or journals in that it is told by someone other than the subject and is generally written in the third person ("she" or "he"), though there are some exceptions. (For example, the English writer Fay Weldon wrote a "biography" of Rebecca West in the first person, as if she were Rebecca West—an indication that some boundaries are now being broken in this genre.) Because all these forms of personal chronicle depend upon the ability to read and write, they are primarily a product of literate societies. However, here too there are exceptions.

Scribes and Slave Narratives

Some women have used scribes to record their life stories. One example is Margery Kempe (an Englishwoman born c. 1373), who called on two scribes to take down her account; the manuscript—recorded in the hand of yet a third scribe—was identified in 1934 and is held to be the first autobiography in English. More recent examples are accounts by American slaves who, prohibited from learning to read and write, turned to a scribe or a white sponsor to set down their narratives.

Gatekeeping: Editorial Intervention

The use of scribes or editors raises a number of questions about authorial versus editorial control. In her study of Harriet Brent Jacobs's *Incidents in the Life of a Slave Girl: Written by Herself*, Alice Deck (1987) points out that in editing this manuscript for publication, Lydia Maria Child introduced her own values, with the result that it is possible to identify not one but two voices in the published text. In fact, the issue of whose story it is arises frequently in relation to diaries, memoirs, reminiscences, autobiographies (and of course, biographies), particularly when these are being prepared for publication and are edited by the author or someone else.

One interesting example of the changes that can be made in the editorial process is provided by the journals of Katherine Mansfield (1888–1923), who was born in New Zealand. Mansfield did not keep a regular diary during her lifetime; her *Journals* were published posthumously and were the direct result of her husband's efforts. A question arising from John Middleton Murry's piecing together of the "scraps" (papers, notes, unmailed letters, and the like) is whether Katherine Mansfield can be the "author" of a product that did not exist in her lifetime.

Editorial intervention is are not uncommon when diaries and journals—and letters—that were written in private are made public after the writer's death by people who have a vested interest in portraying the author in the best possible light and who may also be concerned to protect certain individuals from embarrassing (or worse) revelations; on this basis damaging and incriminating material can be excluded or destroyed. So, for instance, passionate passages in the letters of the American poet Emily Dickinson (1830–1886) to Sue Gilbert were omitted by the editor Martha Dickinson Bianchi, who was Emily Dickinson's niece and Sue Gilbert's daughter. And on the ground that it was their children and not the writer whom he was protecting, Ted Hughes burned sections of the journals of his former wife, the U.S. author Sylvia Plath (1932–1963), including entries that she had made just two days before her suicide.

In the interest of presenting a writer more positively, some editors have gone so far as to add their own contribution to the original work. For example, not only did Ralph Waldo Emerson, William E. Channing, and James Freeman Clarke alter the prose of the U.S. transcendentalist Margaret Fuller (1810–1850) and excise some passages; they also inserted their own "better" commentary in her *Memoirs*—as if it were her own words—in order to make her more "respectable." When editors cut uninteresting parts to construct a "good story," they can misrepresent a writer, particularly a woman whose purpose was to suggest something of the boredom and tedium of a woman's day. The problem is not just that what might be uninteresting to an editor could be of great interest to a writer or reader, but that some women writers have definitely not wanted to present their lives as a good story.

Of course, all writing is to some extent filtered. Even when there is no external editor, a process of self-editing, according to the purpose of the writing and the intended audience, is taking place. Theoretically, some diaries could be written for the self alone and could therefore receive little or no editing for any other audience, but perhaps no one puts words on paper without acknowledging the possibility that they might someday be read by someone else.

Also, there is nothing to prevent a writer from returning to a diary or journal and revising it, or from changing it at a later date by using it as a basis for an autobiography, memoirs, or reminiscences or even as a source for a work of fiction. For example, the Australian-born writer Annabella Boswell (1826–1916) "recast" her very early diaries for her children's benefit, so that she sometimes retains her own childish forms but sometimes overwrites them with mature polish and judgment. Given that it is possible for a writer to have more than one voice—at different times, in different moods, at different stages in life—the definition of a single, "spontaneous" *self* as author is difficult to formulate and not always useful to apply.

The Double Standard

It is partly because women's personal chronicles have long been excluded from the literary canon and from serious study and analysis that so many misapprehensions about the form arise. In the past, a gender bias has operated in relation to diaries: the personal chronicles of men have been seen as objective (and have become enshrined as authoritative historical documents, as in the case of Samuel Pepys), whereas those of women have been treated as subjective, "confessional," idiosyncratic documents that can make no contribution to the general picture. Such a double standard is, of course, absurd; women diarists (like women letter writers) have frequently commented on the public world. An example is the *Memoirs* of Ann Fanshawe (1632–1680), who wrote about the Civil War in England from a much more involved and exciting perspective than that of Samuel Pepys. Women have had much to say about the private world as well and have made observations about the discrepancies between it and the public world.

Diarists and Their Themes

Early diarists: There were women who could read and write before the sixteenth century in Europe: among others, Hypatia (370–415), who was born in Alexandria at the time of the Roman Empire; the German abbess Hildegard of Bingen (1098–1179); and Christine de Pizan in France (c. 1364–1431). Still, it is interesting to note that within the English tradition diaries and journals are a relatively recent development. Among the first English diarists are Grace Sherrington Mildmay (1553–1620), who kept a diary from 1570 to 1617; and Lady Margaret Hoby (c. 1571–1633), whose diary entries run from August 1599 to July 1605 (they were published in 1930). For both Mildmay and Hoby, devotional records are fundamentally important, although references are also made to law, household items, recipes, and cures, or "physic."

Japanese examples: The personal chronicle flourished in Japan during the Heian period, from 794 to 1185. The diaries of noblewomen and ladies-in-waiting were often cast in poetic form; were frequently concerned with romantic affairs at court; and included quotations, personal commentary, and records of events. Although such a chronicle was written by one individual, it would generally be passed around for others to read, thereby crossing the boundary between private and public.

Among the Heian diaries are Murasaki Shikibu's *Her Diary and Poetic Memoirs* and an anonymous work called *The Gossamer Years: A Diary by a Noblewoman of Heian Japan,* which spans a period of twenty-one years. Lady Daibu (born in 1157) left a poetic diary-memoir; and Fujiwara no Nagako, lady-in-waiting to Emperor Horikawa (who died in 1107), also left a diary, which details court practices of the period. "Lady Sarashina" (b. 1058), whose real name is unknown, wrote a diary, and her reminiscences, *As I Crossed the Bridge of Dreams: Recollections of a Woman in Eleventh-Century Japan* (1971), document her life from ages 12 to 50. *The Pillow Book* of Sei Shonagon covers the period 990–1000. *The Confessions of Lady Nijo* (published in 1983) was written about 1308 and covers the period 1271–1306, during which time Lady Nijo became (at age 14) the concubine of a retired emperor and, in her later years, a Buddhist nun. Karen Brazell, who translated Lady Nijo's autobiography, holds it to be "one of the finest works in classical Japanese literature."

Travel diaries: In recounting her wanderings as a nun, Lady Nijo provides one of the earliest women's travel diaries, although she was not the first—even within the Japanese tradition—to keep a record of her journeys: Nun Aktsu, who died in 1283, documented in a poetic diary her trip from Kyoto to Kamakaru.

As overseas travel expanded, and as women accompanied men who served as soldiers and administrators in colonial empires, the opportunity to provide tales of adventure in the form of diaries (as well as letters and novels) was greatly extended. Some women of the nineteenth-century Victorian period chose travel as a way of life. Missionaries also wrote accounts of people and practices in places such as Africa, India, South America, and China. To this day, in fact, many of the published sources on India and China are by western travelers rather than indigenous authors; the writings of Toru Dutt (1856–1877) in India and the Chinese soldier Hsieh Pingying (born in 1903), author of *Letters of a Chinese Amazon* (1930), are notable exceptions.

Isolation, loneliness, and hiding: In direct contrast to travel writing, and more common, are the journals women have kept (and the letters they have sent) when they were isolated or immobilized. Sickness, for example, has often prompted a woman to take up her pen as a way of overcoming loneliness and pain, and of sharing her experiences in the face of fear, despair, and danger.

There are also moving accounts by girls and women who were forced into hiding; Anne Frank's diary, written in the Netherlands during the Nazi occupation, is one of the most remarkable. There are the chronicles of women who have been imprisoned, such as the Irish nationalist Constance Markievicz (1868–1927), who was found guilty of treason and wrote many letters to her sister Eva Gore Booth. There have been women who were prisoners of war and women who were imprisoned in concentration camps.

Travel itself could, in effect, represent isolation. For many of the wives and daughters who accompanied their men to Dutch, Spanish, French, and British colonies, there was no element of choice about their destination. And many women who migrated permanently to new countries—particularly those who left the old world for the new—were in a sense isolated and turned to diaries for comfort, companionship, and consolation. Quite fre-

quently, a diary or journal, which might also serve as a series of letters sent to those at home, was the only "confidante" available to these pioneers. For some women who went west in the United States, keeping a diary was a form of conversation and a means of self-actualization.

Age: Older women sometimes use a diary as an *aide-memoire,* and younger women as a means of creating their own world. Although few girls' diaries have been published, the attraction of diaries for young women is widely recognized. Many girls' diaries come with a lock and key, indicating the importance of secrecy. These writings are also a means of self-exploration, self-expression, rehearsing identity, and responding to reality.

Today, as more girls set up their own Web sites and "publish" their self-representations on the Internet, the secret diary might give way to the public personal chronicle (many such chronicles are being added each day). Another contemporary trend, increasingly common among women of all ages, is keeping and collating their E-mail as a record of daily life.

Self-improvement and religion: From the earliest records, women have used diaries for self-improvement; Quaker diaries are a notable example. Although some of today's diaries still serve this purpose, contemporary diaries in the western world seem to focus more on self-analysis, catharsis, or therapy than on spiritual perfectibility. As a conversation with the self, the diary does provide an opportunity for self-reflection; and, of course, in the act of writing—of organizing and arranging thoughts—new understandings can be reached and new connections forged. In letters, too, women can generate new meanings in the process of representing the everyday and familiar.

One of the most renowned diarists, Anaïs Nin (1903–1977), an American who was born in France, wrote that "life only became real when I wrote about it," yet she was also extremely influential in having women's diaries accepted as an art form. In explaining the particular appeal of journal-keeping for women, Nin suggested that it was the diary that allowed them to explore discrepancies between public (patriarchal) demands and the private (woman-centered) self; her own diary, she wrote, "helped me to make the separation between my real self and the role playing a woman is called upon to do." That the "real" experiences and values of women are encoded within their diaries and represent their history (which is often at variance with the public records of men) is another argument advanced for the significance and status of women's personal chronicles.

It is precisely because they confound the categories of public and private—and because they provide a form of validation for women's lives—that women's diaries, journals, autobiographies, memoirs, and reminiscences have such continuing importance in women's history.

See Also

AUTOBIOGRAPHICAL CRITICISM; AUTOBIOGRAPHY; BIOGRAPHY; TRAVEL WRITING

References and Further Reading

Addis, Patricia K. 1983. *Through a woman's I: An annotated bibliography of American women's autobiographical writings, 1946–1976.* Metuchen, N.J.: Scarecrow.

Benstock, Sheri, ed. 1988. *The private self: theory and practice of women's autobiographical writings.* Chapel Hill: University of North Carolina Press.

Blodgett, Harriet. 1988. *Centuries of female days: Englishwomen's private diaries.* New Brunswick, N.J.: Rutgers University Press.

Bloom, Lynn Z. 1987. Till death do us part: Men's and women's interpretations of wartime internment. *Women's Studies International Forum* 10(1): 75–84.

Brazell, Karen. Introduction. 1985. In *The confessions of Lady Nijo,* vii–xxvii. Trans. Karen Brazell. Middlesex: Zenith/Hamlyn.

Brodzki, Bella, and Celeste Schenck, eds. 1988. *Life/lines: Theorizing women's autobiography.* Ithaca, N.Y.: Cornell University Press.

Bunkers, Suzanne L. 1967. Faithful friend: Nineteenth-century midwestern American women's unpublished diaries. *Women's Studies International Forum* 10(1): 7–18.

Cline, Cheryl 1989. *Women's diaries, journals, and letters: An annotated bibliography,* Garland Reference Library of the Humanities, vol. 780. New York: Garland.

Culley, Margo, ed. 1985. *A day at a time: The diary literature of American women from 1764 to the present.* New York: Feminist Press, City University of New York.

Deck, Alice. 1987. Whose book is this? Authorial versus editorial control of Harriet Brent Jacobs's *Incidents in the life of a slave girl: Written by herself. Women's Studies International Forum* 10(1): 33–40.

Durova, Nadezhda. 1990. *The cavalry maiden: Journals of a female Russian officer in the Napoleonic wars.* Trans. Mary Fleming Zirin. London: Paladin/Grafton.

Franklin, Penelope, ed. 1986. *Private pages: Diaries of American women, 1830s–1970s.* New York: Ballantine.

Huff, Cynthia. 1985. *British women's diaries: A descriptive bibliography of selected nineteenth-century women's manuscript diaries.* New York: AMS.

Huff, Cynthia. 1987. Chronicles of confinement: Reactions to childbirth in British women's diaries. *Women's Studies International Forum* 19(1) 63–68.

Isles, Teresa, ed. 1991. *All sides of the subject: Women and biography.* New York: Athene, Pergamon.

Jelinek, Estelle C. ed. 1980. *Women's autobiography: Essays in criticism.* Bloomington and London: Indiana University Press.

Jelinek, Estelle C. 1986. *The tradition of women's autobiography: From antiquity to the present.* Boston, Twayne.

Jelinek, Estelle C. 1987. Disguise autobiographies: Women masquerading as men. *Women's Studies International Forum* 10(1) 53–62.

Personal Narratives Group, eds. 1989. *Interpreting women's lives: Feminist theory and personal narrative.* Bloomington and Indianapolis: Indiana University Press.

Robinson, Jane. 1991. *Wayward women: A guide to women travellers.* Oxford: Oxford University Press.

Russell, Mary. 1986. *The blessings of a good thick skirt: Women travellers and their world.* London: Collins.

Schiessel, Lillian. 1982. *Women's diaries of the westward journey.* New York: Schocken.

Smith, Sidonie. 1987. *A poetics of women's autobiography: Marginality and the fictions of self-representation.* Bloomington and Indiana: University of Indiana Press.

Spender, Dale, ed. 1987. Personal chronicles: Women's autobiographical writings. Special Issue. *Women's Studies International Forum* 10(1).

———. 1989. *The writing or the sex? Or Why you don't have to read women's writing to know it's no good.* New York: Athene/Teachers College Press.

Stanley, Liz. 1987. Biography as microscope or Kaleidoscope? The case of "power" in Hannah Cullwick's relationship with Arthur Munby. *Women's Studies International Forum* 10(1): 19–32.

Stanton, Donna C., ed. 1984. *The female autograph: Theory and practice of autobiography from the tenth to the twentieth century.* Illinois and London: University of Chicago Press.

Dale Spender

DIETING

See ANOREXIA NERVOSA and FOOD AND CULTURE.

DIFFERENCE I

Difference is an important issue in contemporary feminist debate. It refers to sexual difference and to discussions in linguistics, philosophy, psychoanalysis, politics, and science.

The term *difference* occurs in the work of the Swiss linguist Ferdinand de Saussure (1857–1913). In his *Course* in *General Linguistics* (1988), Saussure described language as a convenient system we utilize to structure and transmit our experience of the world. He argued that words do not contain meaning, but that meaning arises from the compositional differences between words. The French critic Jacques Derrida (b. 1930) developed Saussure's theory to suggest that meaning is also a process of deferral. Linguistic meaning not only results from the differences between words but also is a ceaseless and unstable interaction between both present and "absent" differences. Derrida coined the term *differance* to denote this. He argued that language continually evokes different meanings that exceed and disrupt any intended meaning.

The French philosopher and historian Michel Foucault (1926–1984) extended this notion that meaning is a result of difference to explore its formative role in the construction of identity. Foucault suggested that perceptions of sameness and difference organize the way we think, speak, and define ourselves in relation to others. In the nineteenth century, the German philosopher Georg Hegel (1770–1831) provided a metaphor for the way difference is ordered through opposition and hierarchy in his model of a master and slave. The model refers to the procedure whereby a master defines himself in relation to his slave, good is designated with reference to evil, white in contradistinction to black. The French feminist philosopher and writer Simone de Beauvoir (1908–1986), in her pioneering study *The Second Sex* (1949), developed the paradigm to argue that man has appropriated, negated, and made use of woman's difference in order to guarantee his position as master.

Psychoanalysis has contributed to the debate on difference. The French psychoanalyst Jacques Lacan (1901–1981), drawing on the pioneering work of the Austrian Sigmund Freud (1856–1939), argued that language structures identity and that our perceptions of difference, including sexual and gender differences, are culturally determined.

The issue of difference has been discussed by feminist commentators. The feminist critics Hélène Cixous (b. 1938), Julia Kristeva (b. 1941), and Luce Irigaray (b. 1930) insist that men have repressed or employed women's differences to establish patriarchal rule. In her study *Speculum of the Other Woman* (1974), the French philosopher and psychoanalyst Luce Irigaray argues that our conception of difference derives from a single, male view. She examines the premises of western metaphysics and concludes that our entire system of thinking has been determined with the result that women exist within it only as the inverted other of men. She argues that this bias is encoded in language, reducing women to silence. The Bulgarian-born linguist and psychoanalyst Julia Kristeva believes that the monotheism of western culture is sustained by differentiating between the sexes, since only by designating another sex can patriarchy institute the "one law" on which it depends. The French critic and writer Hélène Cixous also takes this view, and in her essay "Sorties" (1975) she argues that women must inscribe their differences in order to shatter the patriarchal state.

This insistence that the exploration of difference will provide an impetus for change has in turn been challenged. Anglo-American feminism, with its background in the grassroots women's movements that emerged in the aftermath of the U.S. civil rights campaigns in the 1960s and 1970s, has tended to promote sexual equality rather than sexual difference. It has been suggested that the focus on difference, and especially the view that linguistic revolution will instigate change, detracts from the struggle to end women's legal and economic oppression.

There have been various attacks based on biological reduction or essentialism. *Essentialism* refers to the belief that there are innate physiological differences between the sexes and that these give rise to different perspectives and patterns of behavior.

Other critiques maintain that sexual difference can be understood only in the context of the differences that operate between women, such as the differences of race, class, wealth, education, political persuasion, and sexual preference. The Indian critic Gayatri Chakravorty Spivak (b. 1941), for example, has criticized western feminism for its exclusion of black women, its insularity, and its assumptions concerning those women it perceives as inhabiting a "third world." Spivak points out that these differences, too, have been appropriated or ignored. With regard to sexual orientation, critics such as the Italian-born Teresa de Lauretis (b. 1938) have argued that lesbianism must be considered in terms of its difference. Her view—that lesbian sexuality constitutes an important source of identity—is in contrast to broader definitions, such as that expressed by the North American writer Adrienne Rich (b. 1929), who argues for a "lesbian continuum" of relationships between women. Other feminists have identified differences in wealth, class, and education as crucial factors in distinguishing between women's experiences and opportunities.

In science, difference is similarly an important issue. Recent research has suggested that the traditional allocation of X and Y chromosomes (whereby a woman has two X chromosomes and a man one X and one Y) is overstated and that sexual difference derives from a single gene (SRY). This gene produces a protein responsible for transforming the otherwise female-destined embryo into a male. Breakthroughs in genetic, surgical, and hormone engineering have further reduced the boundaries of difference. The realities of fetal implants, drug therapy, and the plastic construction of sexual organs seem set to challenge our ideas of sexual difference.

See Also

BIOLOGICAL DETERMINISM; DIFFERENCE II; ESSENTIALISM; LINGUISTICS; PATRIARCHY; FEMINIST THEORY; PSYCHOANALYSIS; SEXUAL DIFFERENCE

References and Further Reading

Beauvoir, Simone de. 1949. *Le deuxième sexe* (The second sex). Paris: Gallimard.

Cixous, Hélène. 1975. Sorties. In Hélène Cixous (with Catherine Clément), *La jeune née* (The newly born woman). Paris: Union Générale d'Editions.

Irigaray, Luce. 1974. *Speculum de l'autre femme* (Speculum of the other woman). Paris: Minuit.

Kristeva, Julia. 1974. *La Révolution du langage poétique* (Revolution in poetic language). Paris: Seuil.

Lauretis, Teresa de. 1987. *Technologies of gender: Essays on theory, film, and fiction.* Bloomington, Ind.: Indiana University Press.

Rich, Adrienne. 1986. Compulsory heterosexuality and lesbian existence. In *Bread, blood, and poetry: Selected prose 1979–1985.* New York: Norton.

Saussure, Ferdinand de. 1988. *Cours de linguistique générale* (Course in general linguistics). Reprint, Paris: Payot. (Originally published 1916.)

Sellers, Susan. 1991. *Language and sexual difference: Feminist writing in France.* Basingstoke, U.K.: Macmillan.

Spivak, Gayatri Chakravorty. 1987. *In other worlds: Essays in cultural politics.* London: Roatledge.

Susan Sellers

DIFFERENCE II

Difference is a philosophical concept that attempts to give the oppression of women an appropriate theoretical explanation by denying the existence of universal selfhood and positing a specific female selfhood. The substantive claim of "difference feminists," or "feminists of difference," is that the female body not only determines the type of gender socialization a female child is likely to undergo but is also a determinant of the structure of women's consciousness. According to this concept, women have a form of consciousness different from men's, precisely because their bodily experiences are different from men's.

Feminists divide, roughly, into those who affirm and those who deny the existence of difference in this sense. In general, feminists who deny difference argue that achieving equality is sufficient to overthrow oppression. Feminists who affirm difference hold that there are intrinsic and essential facts about being a woman which would continue to be a source of oppression even if equality was achieved in all the relevant socioeconomic categories. Difference feminists argue that the aim of reaching equality is severely limited as an object of feminism, since it is based on reaching equality with men; thus this goal implies and depends on an assumption that men's achievements and men's values are the universally correct or best standards of measurement. Some feminists of difference also hold that since men are the dominant group in society, men's experiences and values are encoded in reason and language in such a way that women do not have access to them, but that reason and language have come to be regarded as universal vehicles of expression rather than as gendered instruments for privileged male expression.

Difference feminists claim that women are different from men and, accordingly, women need to assert their own social values and priorities so that they stand independent of male standards of well-being and achievement. The liberation of women is not entirely reducible to equality with men in certain socioeconomic categories: women lack equal representation and power in the civil structures of society not just because they are "held back" by men and kept in positions of subservience (although this is true), but also because women, themselves, do not value institutional positions of power in the same way as men do. This, it is argued, is because women do not produce relations of power in the way men do or in the way these positions exist within a patriarchal order.

Thus difference feminists hold that patriarchy and phallocentrism—not just sexism—are accountable for the oppression of women. Consequently, in the metaphysics of feminism of difference, patriarchy is ontologically elevated as a source of oppression, because individual cases of sexism in society, when considered collectively, are unable to account completely for why women continue to be oppressed. "Patriarchy" and "phallocentrism" are terms expressing the contention that women have a different phenomenological experience of the world based on their bodily differences from men, and these terms highlight the belief of difference feminists that the reason men still find themselves holding most of the world's wealth and power has to do with what men want and value rather than with any natural inferiority of women. Given that the usual socioeconomic measures of equality reflect only the values and priorities of men and are not universal indicators of well-being or success, then, according to feminists of difference, women who achieve equality with men achieve only material equality and cannot be said to be liberated from oppression—because participation in patriarchal structures does not permit the expression of specifically female ways of relating to the world that arise from the singular female consciousness.

This has raised an obvious problem: if feminists of difference are right, the oppression of women is more thoroughgoing than it first appears and cannot be addressed solely by achieving equality with men. If femaleness cannot be affirmed under current patriarchal societal arrangements, and if human reason is not universal, then women must seek the necessary space outside the confines of patriarchal rule and phallocentric discourse in order to be able to express "women's thoughts" and to counterpoise "women's rationality" against the dominant masculine norms and models of discourse.

Another problem is essentialism: difference feminists have often been accused of relying on a notion of "essence" to support their claims about the specificity of female experience. This is an issue because, philosophically, essentialist accounts of femaleness are at risk of establishing a psychological or biological fixity that may undermine the goals of difference feminism and, more important, may support a view that differences between men and women are ideologically more fundamental than class or racial differences between women—a view which ignores the fact that difference is, to a large degree, constructed by politics.

Feminism of difference does cite examples—such as the menstrual cycle and childbearing—as evidence for its claim that the female body structures reason, thought, and language into specifically female configurations; however, it should be noted that this claim really lies beyond the scope of empirical verification. In the face of this, some feminists have seen the concept of difference not as a factual statement about women but rather as a theoretical strategy required to give the political agenda of feminism the conceptual tools it needs if women's intellectual empowerment is to be independent of men's.

Feminism of difference has very complex origins but owes its existence largely to the response of French feminists to Sigmund Freud's psychoanalytic theory. Freud constructs his psychoanalytic account of women's psychic condition by positing a lack based on their envy of the male penis. Feminism of difference attempts to overturn Freud's picture of women as merely the negation of a "real

sex" by giving women a positive content of their own. In other words, difference feminists seek to discredit the theory that women are a "nonsex" in order to provide an alternative metaphysical view of women—the view required to give the feminist project rational legitimacy. Historically, the textual point of departure for the debate between difference and equality begins with Simone de Beauvoir's book *The Second Sex*.

See Also

DIFFERENCE I; ESSENTIALISM; FEMINISM: CULTURAL; FEMINISM: RADICAL; FEMINISM: SECOND-WAVE EUROPEAN; GENDER; KNOWLEDGE; PATRIARCHY: FEMINIST THEORY; PHALLOCENTRISM; PSYCHOANALYSIS

References and Further Reading

de Beauvior, Simone. 1953. *The second sex*. Trans. H. M. Parshley. London: Picador.

Fuss, Diana, 1989. *Essentially speaking: Feminism, nature, difference*. New York and London: Routledge.

Gatens, Moira, 1983. A critique of the sex/gender distinction. In J. Allen and P. Patton, eds., *Beyond Marxism? Interventions after Marx*, 143–160. Australia: Intervention.

Grosz, Elizabeth, 1989. *Sexual subversions: Three French feminists*. North Sydney: Allen and Unwin.

Irigaray, Luce. 1985. *This sex which is not one*. Trans. Catherine Porter. Ithaca, N.Y.: Cornell University Press.

Lloyd, Genevieve. 1984. *The man of reason: "Male" and "female" in western philosophy*. London: Methuen.

Mitchell, Juliet, 1975. *Psychoanalysis and feminism*. New York: Vintage.

Schor, N., and E. Weed, eds. 1994. *The essential difference*. Bloomington and Indianapolis: Indiana University Press.

Young, Iris Marion. 1990. *Throwing like a girl and other essays in feminist and social theory*. Bloomington and Indianapolis: Indiana University Press.

Melissa White

DIFFERENTLY ABLED WOMEN

See DISABILITY AND FEMINISM.

DIGITAL DIVIDE

As computer technology becomes increasingly important to economic, political, and social success, part of humanity finds itself in a digital chasm. Many developing countries do not have access to the latest technology or Internet access, unlike their affluent counterparts in the western world. Information technology has the potential to dramatically transform the ways in which the global community can interact. Around the world, the Internet is becoming a tool for personal success and professional advancement. People use it to find jobs, contact friends and family, locate public information, and take courses on-line. Electronic commerce is increasingly helping small companies and entrepreneurs, including those in remote areas, flourish. People in developing nations can make contact with global markets, find products, or sell their products worldwide.

However, a "digital divide" hinders worldwide distribution of information and communication technology. This divide is the result of disparities in income levels, in educational levels, among demographic groups, and between genders. The concept of information has broadened to include access to information services, and a considerable portion of commerce, communication, and research takes place on the Internet. Access to computers and networks is today as important as access to traditional telephone services.

In the United States, technology has created economic change, which in turn has influenced social change. Income level is a strong determinant of an individual's or household's Internet access. Minorities and women lag behind overall in the U.S. with regard to telephone penetration and computer ownership. In rural areas, the difference is even more pronounced. Minorities and women have less access to the Internet at any location (home, work, school, or library).

Education levels also affect Internet access. The more education an individual has, the greater the likelihood that this individual has a phone, computer, or modem. Again, this difference is even more distinct in rural areas.

Family structure can also make a significant difference in who has access to information. Very few women around the world have professions based on information technology. Women are overall the least well paid and occupy the least prestigious jobs. Therefore, a disparity in technology access across gender lines still exists. Households composed of married couples with children are roughly twice as likely to own a computer and have on-line access as are single-parent households headed by a male. Single-parent female households are the least likely to own a computer and have on-line access.

However, the digital divide among Americans pales next to the gap separating developing countries from the industrialized West and Japan. The information superhighway does not easily stretch to villages in southeast Asia

or sub-Saharan Africa. Technical know-how, financial banking, electrical infrastructure, and telephone access are unequally spread across the world.

High costs make it difficult for many African countries to access the Internet. Furthermore, a lack of telephones and adequate electrical supply makes it impossible for most people to go on-line. As most computers are manufactured in the West, developing nations usually incur the cost of importing the computers and parts. In addition, lack of training and technological know-how hampers Africans from "catching up" with technology. Increasing the digital chasm, the content of the Internet is generally based on North American culture.

Gender roles further determine who has access to technology. A woman's place in African society is distinct from that of men, and, as a result, women are generally poorer than men. Households without a male head—which make up one third of households in developing nations—are the poorest of all. Women also rank among the least educated. In many African countries more than half of women are illiterate. Even educated women tend not to pursue technological courses because of their cultural roles and expectations. For both illiterate and literate women, information technology is often disconnected from their lives.

On the other hand, African women are engaging in formal and informal entrepreneurial activities, and as economies become more and more information-driven, women may find a place in the world of information technology.

See Also

COMMUNICATIONS: OVERVIEW; COMPUTING: OVERVIEW; COMPUTING: PARTICIPATORY AND FEMINIST DESIGN; INFORMATION REVOLUTION; INFORMATION TECHNOLOGY; NETWORKS, ELECTRONIC; PUBLISHING; TECHNOLOGY

References and Further Reading

At what price? Economic constraints to the effective use of telecommunication in education, science, culture and in the circulation of information. 1988. CII-98/WS/2. Paris: UNESCO.

d'orville, Hans. 1996. *Technology revolution study: Communications and knowledge-based technologies for sustainable human development.* Report to the Assistant Administrator and Director, Bureau for Policy and Programme Support (BPPS). New York: United Nations Development Programme (UNDP), 30 April.

Ntalaja-Nzongola, Georges. 1996. Africa in the twenty-first century: Confronting cultural, economic, and technological diversity. *TransAfrica Forum* 6(3, 4): 71–76.

National Telecommunication Information Administration—
    NTIA. 1999. *Bridging the digital divide.* http://ntia.gov>
UNESCO. 1997. *The challenges of the information highways.* 150
    Ex 15. Paris: UNESCO, 16 August.

Veronique Maingi-Dozier

DISABILITY AND FEMINISM

Feminism is complex and multifaceted, yet one idea underlies all its manifestations—that biology is not destiny. This assertion also underpins disabled people's activism throughout the world. Disability, like gender, is a social construct: people who experience physical, sensory, or intellectual impairment or difficulties related to mental health are disabled by the social context in which they live rather than by their bodily characteristics in themselves.

This social model of disability involves focusing not on what is "wrong" with people's bodies or minds but on what is wrong with the way society is organized—focusing on prejudice, inaccessible physical and communication environments, the failure to put resources into enabling technology, and other socially created barriers. *Sexism* and *racism* refer to oppression experienced by women and by minority ethnic people; *disability* refers to oppression experienced by people with physical, sensory, or intellectual impairments or with mental or emotional distress.

The assertion that biology is not destiny—that the quality of life is determined not by impairment as such but by its social context—has been as liberating for disabled people as feminism has been for women. Gwyneth Ferguson Matthews's *Voices from the Shadows* was groundbreaking in the way she brought her personal experience to bear on her research and analysis of the lives of 45 Canadian women disabled by society's reactions to their physical impairments. Susan Hannaford's *Living Outside Inside* was similarly impelled by her own experience but was also a more deliberate attempt to bring together feminism and disability rights. Both are examples of the importance to disabled women of the feminist principle of making the personal political, a task that has also been undertaken by the more personal writings of disabled women like Anne Finger (1990) and in anthologies such as *With the Power of Each Breath* (Browne, Connors, and Stern, 1985) and *Mustn't Grumble* (Keith, 1994).

Most published work easily available concerns the experiences of disabled women in the developed world, although an international anthology published by Diane Driedger and Susan Gray in 1992 does include writings by women from developing countries. Disabled People's International (which has more than fifty national assembly members from developing countries) and Disability Awareness in Action (an international public education campaign) have each sought to promote the concerns of disabled women worldwide.

Although a key text published by Michelle Fine and Adrienne Asch in 1988 (see also Begum, 1992) firmly claimed a place for disabled women's experiences on the academic agenda, most feminist theory and research and many feminist activists, have continued to ignore these experiences. The exclusion of disabled women from mainstream feminism means that the accounts of women's experiences per se are incomplete. Moreover, feminist theory is the poorer for the lack of understanding of the interactions between the two social constructs of gender and disability.

What little analysis there is of the lives of disabled women appears as a "special" area of study and is often couched in terms of asking whether and how women with physical or sensory impairments or learning difficulties encounter a "double disadvantage" because of their experience of sexism and of disability. Such an approach has been criticized as treating disabled women as passive victims of oppression. In contrast, work that is informed by personal experience of disability and that combines a feminist perspective and a disability rights perspective is rooted in resistance to oppression. This work is part of the struggle against the discrimination and prejudice that disabled women experience and, as such, focuses not just on exclusion but also on survival (Morris, 1991).

Reproductive Rights

Disabled women's right to reproduce and to parent is often threatened by assumptions that they are unable to care for others. Women with learning difficulties are perhaps particularly at risk. However, the most controversial aspect of reproductive rights for disabled women is the way that the debate over abortion tends to assume that a "handicapped fetus" inevitably means a poor quality of life for both child and mother. Genetic testing has, arguably, been motivated by oppressive ideas of normality and what it is to be human. There is an urgent need for a dialogue between the feminist and disabled people's movements on this issue.

Abuse and Violence

The naming of and response to domestic violence and sexual abuse experienced by nondisabled girls and women has been one of the most important achievements of western feminism. Feminist investigations of violence and disabled women would highlight abuse in homes and by perpetrators who are paid carers as well as those who are family members. Denial of autonomy is a daily feature of many disabled people's lives, and there has been some recognition, especially in the United States, of institutional abuse. Feminist research and analysis have a key role to play in putting these experiences under the same kind of spotlight that has been brought to nondisabled women's lives.

Independent Living

The international Independent Living Movement asserts that physical, sensory, or intellectual impairment does not *in itself* mean that people cannot exercise choice and control in their lives. However, campaigns for empowering forms of personal assistance tend to focus on the public aspects of people's lives—on employment and leisure. For women, giving personal assistance and support to others within the private world of the household is also important. Disabled women want personal assistance that enables them to look after children, run a home, and look after parents or others who need help themselves. While the public world of work is of course important for disabled women, independent living must also be concerned with the private world of the family and personal relationships.

Disabled women in many countries have campaigned at local, national, and international levels on all these issues. To give just one example, in Britain, Nasa Begum initiated a successful campaign by disabled and nondisabled women to establish a refuge for women with learning difficulties who have experienced abuse.

Feminism promotes the independence in women's lives that is achieved by equal rights to housing, employment, education, equal status under the law, and choice and control over sexuality and reproduction. Feminism is also about feeling good about being a woman, recognizing the worth and value of women. Choice and control, and the rights and access necessary to attain these, are also aims of disabled people's movements. Disabled women also want to assert the value of their lives, to feel good about themselves. An increasing number of disabled women are bringing together feminist and disability rights perspectives in a liberating analysis of the oppression and injustice they experience (Morris, 1996).

See Also

DISABILITY: ELITE BODY; DISABILITY: HEALTH AND SEXUALITY; DISABILITY: QUALITY OF LIFE

References and Further Reading

Begum, Nasa. 1992. Disabled women and the feminist agenda. *Feminist Review* 40: 70–84.

Browne, Susan E., Debra Connors, and Nanci Stern, eds. 1985. *With the power of each breath: A disabled women's anthology.* Pittsburgh, Pa.: Cleis.

Campbell, J., and M. Oliver. 1996. *Disability, difference, discrimination.* Lanham, Md.: Rowman and Littlefield.

Conversations—Feminist research on disability: Newsletter of the Women's Research Network. Ontario: Roeher Institute.

Dreidger, Diane, and Susan Gray, eds. 1992. *Imprinting our image: An international anthology by women with disabilities.* Charlottetown, Canada: Synergy.

Fine, Michelle, and Adrienne Asch, eds. 1988. *Women with disabilities: Essays in psychology, culture, and politics.* Philadelphia, Pa.: Temple University Press.

Finger, Anne. 1990. *Past due: A story of disability, pregnancy, and birth.* Seattle: Seal; London: Women's Press.

Hannaford, Susan. 1985. *Living outside inside: A disabled woman's experience—towards a social and political perspective.* Berkeley, Calif.: Canterbury.

Keith, Lois, ed. 1994. *Mustn't grumble: Writing by disabled women.* London: Women's Press. (Also published as *What happened to you? Writing by disabled women,* New York: New Press.)

Matthews, Gwyneth Ferguson. 1983. *Voices from the shadows: Women with disabilities speak out.* Ontario, Canada: Women's Educational Press.

Morris, Jenny. 1991. *Pride against prejudice: Transforming attitudes to disability.* London: Women's Press; Philadelphia, Pa.: New Society.

———, ed. 1996. *Encounters with strangers: Feminism and disability.* London: Women's Press.

Silvers, Anita, David Hasserman and Mary B. Mahowald, eds. 1997. *Disability politics: Understanding our past, changing our future.* London: Routledge.

Jenny Morris

DISABILITY: Elite Body

The western concept of the body fragments into a number of categorizations (abstractions) that are the province of different specialists and "experts" (professionals): the physical body (medical or aesthetic); the social body ("normal" or "deviant"); the occupational body (useful or disposable); the textual body (abstract and safe for academics). These are coded as opposites sometimes called binaries: perfect-imperfect, ideal-flawed, intact-damaged, good-bad, right-wrong. Binaries are pure and conflicting categories, unlike lived experience, where, for example, "we are not either ill or healthy, weak or strong" (Keith, 1994: 6). Some commentators argue that patriarchal consumer capitalism constructs a myth of an elite body—forever young, male, heterosexual, white, superdeveloped, mobile, inexhaustible, nondisabled, and pain-free. Evidence of "inadequacy" (for example, femaleness, fatigue, aging) is accompanied by loss of "human" status: "having control" and "being human" are clearly, sometimes fiercely, connected. Feminists have highlighted the significance of the body (woman as sex or nature) and desire (straight or gay) as variously motivating or disruptive of men's intellectual and cultural production and male-dominated institutions, and have tried to undermine the dominance of medical and academic models that separate to control. But disabled women have often been overlooked within these debates and campaigns. The claim that "gender and disability both inhabit all discourse" (Garland Thomson, 1994: 592) and intersect has been slow to win acceptance. Western thought continues to see the body as an obstacle to rationality or mind, denying that theories, for example, are always a result of specific acts of labor or production (Potts and Price, 1995: 102–103). Disembodiment, even as prerequisite for an attribute of thought, is both a feminist and a disability issue: "We must return ourselves to a state of embodiment in order to deconstruct the way power has been traditionally orchestrated in the classroom, denying subjectivity to some groups and according it to others" (hooks, 1994: 139).

See Also

BODY; DISABILITY AND FEMINISM; DISABILITY: HEALTH AND SEXUALITY; DISABILITY: QUALITY OF LIFE

References and Further Reading

Begum, Nasa. 1992. Disabled women and the feminist agenda. In Hilary Hinds, Ann Phoenix, and Jackie Stacey, eds. *Working out: New directions for women's studies* 61–73. London: Falmer.

Flax, Jane. 1992. Beyond equality: Gender, justice and difference. In Gisela Bock and Susan James, eds., *Beyond equality and difference: Citizenship, feminist politics, female subjectivity,* 193–210. London and New York: Routledge.

Garland Thomas, Rosemarie. 1994. Redrawing the boundaries of feminist disability studies. *Feminist Studies* 20(3: Fall): 583–95.

Hawthorne, Susan. 1996. From theories of indifference to a wild politics. In Diane Bell and Renate Klein, eds., *Radically speaking: Feminism reclaimed.* 483–501. London: Zed.

hooks, bell. 1994. *Teaching to transgress: Education as the practice of freedom.* London: Routledge.

Keith, Lois, ed. 1994. *Mustn't grumble: Writing by disabled women.* London: Women's Press.

Morris, Jenny. 1991. *Pride against prejudice: Transforming attitudes to disability.* London: Women's Press.

Potts, Tracy, and Janet Price. 1995. "Out of the blood and spirit of our lives": The place of the body in academic feminism. In Louise Morley and Val Walsh, eds. *Feminist academics: Creative agents for change,* 102–115. London: Taylor and Francis.

Val Walsh

DISABILITY: Health and Sexuality

The United Nations estimates that, worldwide, there are 500 million people with mental, physical, and sensory disabilities. Over 80 percent live in developing countries, and more than half are women. As more people grow older, and more survive accidents and illness, the number of disabled women will continue to increase. Disability crosses all boundaries; women with disabilities can be found in every nation, every race, and every class. A disproportionate number of disabled women, however, live in poverty.

Women with disabilities share the same health, reproductive, and sexual needs and concerns as other women. In addition, disabled women face additional problems and bring up particular issues related to health, reproduction, and sexuality. Around the world, women with disabilities are raising their expectations for self-determination and quality of life. Increasingly, disabled women are demanding the right to live independently, to be integrated into their communities, to set their own goals, and to make their own choices. In so doing, they challenge their societies to be more accessible, supportive, and inclusive.

The phrase "independent living" is often used to describe the guiding philosophy of the disability-rights movement: the conviction that anyone, regardless of the nature or extent of a disability, can function in the community as a free and equal participant. In this sense, "independence" does not mean complete self-sufficiency; rather, it denotes having maximum control over one's own life, using whatever resources are necessary and available.

Terminology—the language used to describe disability—has been a topic of much discussion both within and outside the disability community. Phrases such as "handicapped," "crippled," "wheelchair-bound," "feeble-minded," and "imbecile" have been rejected by many as being loaded, stereotyped, and negative. Some have put forward more "positive" descriptors, including "physically challenged" and "differently abled," as alternatives. Generally, disability-rights activists favor language that is straightforward and accurate—phrases such as "people with disabilities," "people with intellectual (or cognitive) disabilities," "wheelchair users," and so on. This article will refer to "women with disabilities," and "disabled women."

Disability and Health

Disability is a natural phenomenon that occurs in every society, in every generation. Disabilities may result from several causes: prenatal factors, birth injuries, disease, traumatic injuries, and physical or mental stress.

Disability is not an illness, although some disabilities are caused by illness. Rather, disability is a chronic or long-term condition that substantially limits an individual in performing one or more activities of daily living (ADLs). ADLs include walking, seeing, hearing, learning, caring for oneself, breathing, lifting, and so on.

Disability is not necessarily incompatible with good health. Many women with disabilities make it a high priority to maintain or improve their health. Disabled women seeking health care may have both typical and special needs. These needs can include the following:

- General health care and obstetrical and gynecological (ob/gyn) care. Disabled women have the same needs for general and preventive health care as other women. When disabled women present health problems, practitioners should not assume that these problems are related to the disability—or that the disability makes treatment impossible or unnecessary. Disabled women should receive the same careful diagnoses and appropriate remedies as other patients. Like all women, disabled women should have regular breast and pelvic examinations, practice safe sex, and have access to family planning and birth control services.
- Prevention of secondary disabilities. Some disabilities can lead to additional, preventable health problems. For example, a woman who spends much of her time in a wheelchair may be susceptible to problems such as poor circulation or pressure sores. Some secondary disabilities can be serious, even life-threatening. Women with disabilities should be taught techniques to prevent secondary health problems and should be assisted in taking these preventative measures.
- Services to support independent living. In order to live independently, to fulfill family or work responsibilities,

and to maintain their health, women with significant disabilities may need personal assistance, mobility assistance, housekeeping support, monitoring or supervision, skills training, or other services. Assistance should be available in different settings—home, school, work, community—and should support a range of activities, including personal care, menstrual care, sexual hygiene, employment, volunteer activities, study, socializing, parenting, political activities, religious activities, and so on. Studies have shown that women who are able to avoid institutionalization and who can choose and control their own environment tend to live longer and stay healthier.

- Assistive technology. Devices such as wheelchairs, braces, crutches, walkers, canes, and shower seats—sometimes called "durable medical equipment"—are designed to aid disabled people in performing necessary functions: moving around, personal care, and so on. In addition, items such as adapted tools and utensils, Braille writers, adapted telecommunications devices, and modified computers can significantly increase the health, independence, mobility, productivity, and quality of life of women with disabilities. Some assistive devices are "high-tech," using sophisticated electronic or mechanical components. These kinds of devices can perform a range of complex functions, but they may be expensive and difficult to acquire and maintain. Other devices are "low-tech," involving relatively simple, commonsense applications of ordinary materials. Whether high-tech or low-tech, assistive devices should be appropriate to the needs of the individual disabled woman, and she should be offered training in utilizing the devices effectively.
- Violence prevention and intervention. Women with disabilities are subject to a higher-than-average incidence of violence, abuse, and neglect. This can create or aggravate health problems, including serious physical injuries, emotional stress, emotional illness, sexually transmitted diseases, unwanted pregnancy, poor hygiene, skin breakdowns, malnutrition, dehydration, and death. Disabled women are especially likely to be victimized by people they know, including family members, spouses, and care providers. Women with disabilities need support in empowering themselves through assertiveness training, self-defense training, and independent living skills and resources. In addition, disabled women who experience violence, abuse, or neglect need to be able to obtain intervention and assistance from the criminal justice system, providers of victim services, battered women's shelters, rape crisis organizations, counseling programs, and other appropriate services.

Barriers to Health Care

Women with disabilities often encounter physical, attitudinal, and policy barriers in seeking to meet their health care needs. Physical barriers include lack of transportation; stairs and narrow doorways into clinics, doctors' offices, and so on; written information, such as intake forms and patient education materials, not available in alternative formats (that is, Braille, tape, or large print); high examining tables that prevent transfer by women using wheelchairs; mammogram machines that require patients to stand; and lack of personal assistance during clinic visits to women who need it. These barriers may be remedied through accessibility planning and modifications; availability of written materials in alternative formats; obtaining "adaptable" equipment, such as tables that can be raised and lowered; and provision of trained, appropriate assistance in mobility and other personal care needs.

Attitudinal barriers arise from negative societal beliefs about the worth of women with disabilities. These barriers may include disrespect or discomfort on the part of medical professionals; unwillingness to communicate with women whose speech or hearing is impaired; professionals' lack of knowledge about particular disabling conditions; and a focus on the disability to the exclusion of other health needs. Some practitioners wrongly believe that disability inevitably diminishes a disabled woman's value or quality of life. They may therefore fail to explore or offer all treatment options, assuming instead that death is preferable to living with a significant disability. Doctors, nurses, and other clinical and hospital staff people may benefit from training and education in these areas. In addition, women with disabilities should be fully informed about their rights as patients.

Policy barriers may be imposed by hospital or clinic regulations, by insurance companies, or by other third-party payers such as Medicare and Medicaid. Some insurance providers discriminate against individuals with disabilities by barring coverage for "preexisting conditions" or by cost-capping services that may be essential for managing a disability. Another major barrier is that some necessary services—such as in-home personal assistance services, prescription medications, durable medical equipment, holistic health services, assistive technology, preventive care, certain therapies, and abortion services—may not be covered by private or government-funded insurance plans. Government and private policies also may have an "institutional bias"— that is, they offer services primarily in nursing homes, rehabilitation hospitals, and other large long-term care facilities, but not in the disabled woman's own home, where she can be part of her family and community. Ending this institutional bias, and securing more support for independent living (IL) and community-based rehabilitation (CBR), is a major focus of disability-rights advocates in many countries.

Disability and Sexuality

Women with disabilities experience a full range of sexual feelings, desires, needs, and problems. Prominent issues of sexuality and disability include the following:

- Sex education and information. Because of factors such as social isolation, exclusion from mainstream schools, negative assumptions about their sexuality, and barriers to communication (that is, the unavailability of information by sign language, in Braille, on tape, or in other accessible formats), girls and women with disabilities may not receive adequate education and information about sexuality. Age-appropriate sex education should be available to all girls and women. When necessary, this information should be adapted for different communication needs, learning styles, and abilities. Information also should be available about the potential impact on sexuality of different types of disabilities.

- Sexual self-determination. Independence is a prerequisite for making choices regarding sexuality. Women with disabilities who have access to resources that let them live independently can define their own sexual identity and desires and may lead full, satisfying sexual lives. By contrast, disabled women who live in institutions, or with their parents or other family members, may be severely inhibited in exploring and expressing their sexuality. Limitations may be due to any of the following: lack of privacy; others' discomfort with disabled women's sexuality; homophobia; lack of access to information about sexuality; lack of access to sexual stimulation devices, birth control devices, or safe-sex materials; and policies that explicitly restrict sexual activity.

- Body image and self-esteem. Girls and women with disabilities, especially physical disabilities, often notice that they do not conform to dominant cultural and commercial images of feminine beauty. The mass media, as well as individual interactions, seem to emphasize a particular ideal of perfection, which disabled women may feel is unattainable. Women who are able to understand, analyze, and reject those images may develop a stronger sense of their own unique beauty. Disabled girls and women may benefit from counseling and other support services that help them to enhance and reinforce their self-concept as strong, attractive women. Role models— other disabled women who convey strength and self-confidence—also can encourage personal growth and self-respect in girls and women with disabilities.

- Relationships. Even for many healthy, confident women with disabilities, difficulties may arise in initiating and maintaining sexual and romantic relationships. Potential partners may have misconceptions about disabled women and their sexual potential, or they may doubt the ability of disabled women to reciprocate pleasure, companionship, and love. In addition, they may be unwilling to face the social stigma that they fear would accompany a relationship with a disabled woman. These feelings may prevent a relationship from beginning or may create conflict within a relationship. Many disabled women, however, do develop healthy, mutually supportive relationships with their partners. As with most couples, qualities such as trust, self-esteem, mutual respect, shared interests, willingness to give and take, and good communication help to promote successful relationships between disabled women and their partners. Some disabled women prefer partners who also have disabilities, finding in these relationships a sense of camaraderie, shared values, and common backgrounds. Other women with disabilities seek nondisabled partners, and still others assert that they have no preference in this regard.
- Sexual activity. The presence of a disability does not preclude sexual activity, although it may necessitate adaptation to accommodate limited movement, fatigue, sensitivity to pain, lack of sensation, or other disability-related factors. Mutually satisfying sex is more likely if the partners communicate honestly and clearly, discuss their desires and barriers, and attempt to solve problems creatively.
- Safe sex and birth control. Women with disabilities should be as careful as other women in avoiding unwanted pregnancy and in preventing the spread of sexually transmitted diseases. Women with all kinds of disabilities should be fully informed about risks and prevention techniques. In order to take effective precautions, some disabled women may need assistance or support. A woman with limited movement, for example, may require help in taking birth control pills or inserting a diaphragm. If her partner is unable or unwilling to provide this assistance, the woman may need help from an attendant.
- Sexual identity and sexual orientation. Women with disabilities who are lesbian or bisexual may face double or triple discrimination, based on disability, gender, and sexual orientation. These women sometimes find it difficult to obtain information and resources to support their sexual activities and relationships. Gaining access to lesbian communities is often difficult, because of the same kinds of physical and attitudinal barriers that exist

in society as a whole. In addition to offering contact with potential partners, however, such communities can be an important source of support and self-discovery. In order to make contact with these communities and form relationships, some women with disabilities may need assistance, including information and referral to events and organizations, accessible transportation, attendant services, and interpreting services.

Reproductive Issues: Mothers with Disabilities

Reproductive choice is essential to the self-determination of women with disabilities. Like other women, disabled women suffer when poverty, governmental restrictions, or religious pronouncements deny them access to birth control and abortion services. Unlike most other women, however, women with disabilities also face restrictions on their right to have children. Involuntary sterilization of women with physical or mental disabilities continues in many countries, including the United States. (Although most states in the United States have either amended or repealed their sterilization statutes, most of the remaining statutes are based on negative presumptions about disabled women's competence, or even their worth.) In addition, doctors, family members, and others routinely advise women with disabilities to avoid or terminate pregnancy, even when these women demonstrate the desire and the ability to bear and raise children.

These legal and cultural pressures arise from persistent biases regarding the childbearing and parenting abilities of women with disabilities. Such biases arise from myths and misconceptions, including the fear that a disabling condition may be passed on to a child; the assumption that disabled women cannot nurture, care for, or discipline children; the belief that mobility is essential for child rearing; and the notion that a mother's disability would be a hardship to her children.

All of these assumptions are inaccurate, misguided, or both. Most disabilities are not inherited. Even in situations where a woman's disability may be passed on to her children, she may choose to bear children anyway—and this may be a valid, responsible decision. The disabled woman may know better than anyone else the value and quality of a life with her particular disability.

Many disabled women are independently able to perform most or all of the tasks involved in raising children. Even women with more significant physical or mental disabilities, however, can be effective parents, with the help of support services. Such support may include the help of a spouse or partner, friends, or family; attendant services; in-home child care; accessible day care; assistive devices; and parenting classes.

Reproductive Rights: Children with Disabilities

Just as disabled women want the right to bear children without confronting antidisability bias, women who risk giving birth to a disabled child also must have the right to bear that child. With the growing use and sophistication of prenatal testing techniques, women face increasing pressure to terminate a pregnancy when a potential disability is detected. Pressure may come from doctors who warn that abortion is the only "responsible" decision; from friends and neighbors who may blame the mother for the child's disability; or, increasingly, from insurance companies that deny coverage for "preventable" conditions.

Pregnant women should be able to refuse tests that they do not want. Women carrying a fetus with a disability should be given accurate and complete information about that disability—not simply a medical prognosis but also information about community resources, legal rights, and opportunities for people with disabilities to attain independence and a good quality of life. They should have the chance to meet adults who have the disability and parents of children who have it. Women should be able to make their own decisions about bearing children with disabilities—decisions free of misinformation, coercion, or penalty.

Conclusion

The health rights, sexual rights, and reproductive rights of women with disabilities are part of two large, multifaceted movements: the disability-rights movement and the feminist movement. Both movements, at times, fail to recognize these rights as essential human rights issues. Both have yet to make disabled women's access to health care, disabled women's sexual self-determination, and disabled women's reproductive freedom high priorities on their agendas. Disabled women themselves, however, are charting new territory in human rights and taking control of their own destiny—through self-help and political advocacy, through grassroots organizing and international networking, and through changing attitudes and changing policies.

See Also

ANTIDISCRIMINATION; DISABILITY AND FEMINISM; DISABILITY: ELITE BODY; DISABILITY: QUALITY OF LIFE; EDUCATION: SPECIAL NEEDS; NURSING HOMES; WORK: EQUAL PAY AND CONDITIONS

References and Further Reading

Browne, Susan E., Debra Connors, and Nanci Stern, eds. 1985. *With the power of each breath: A disabled women's anthology.* Pittsburgh, Pa.: Cleis.

Fine, Michelle, and Adrienne Asch, eds. 1989. *Women with disabilities.* Philadelphia, Pa.: Temple University Press.

Rogers, Judi, and Molleen Matsumura. 1991. *Mother to be: A guide to pregnancy and birth for women with disabilities.* New York: Demos.

Shapiro, Joseph P. 1993. *No pity: People with disabilities forging a new civil rights movement.* New York: Times Books/Random House.

Shaw, Barrett, ed. 1994. *The ragged edge.* Louisville, Ky.: Advocado.

Laura Hershey

DISABILITY: Quality of Life

In many western European and North American countries, pregnant women routinely undergo prenatal tests such as amniocentesis. These tests are designed to show if a woman is at risk of giving birth to a disabled child. When there is such a risk, a woman is given the option of aborting the pregnancy. Disabled feminists have responded critically to prenatal testing. This has informed the position they adopt in debates on abortion and the genetic technology that underpins prenatal testing. In particular, disabled feminists have challenged the rationale behind prenatal testing. This rationale assumes that the quality of life of a disabled child would be so poor that it is right to question whether such a child should be born at all. A similar assumption about the poor quality of life of disabled people can be found in debates about euthanasia and nontreatment of disabled infants.

Disabled feminists argue that assumptions about quality of life are based on nondisabled people's misconceptions of disability. Disabled people are often marginalized or segregated from mainstream society; thus nondisabled people have little opportunity to know about disabled people's lives. Instead, disability is regarded as something out of the ordinary. It is feared because it reminds people of their own vulnerability. Moreover, in many cultures, the meaning given to disability is that it is a tragedy, with a disabled person destined for a life of dependency and pain.

The liberation movement of disabled people sees these ideas as oppressive, limiting, and denigrating of the experiences of disabled people. Disabled feminists are part of this movement and argue that "disability is socially constructed, . . . so economic and social forces which now restrict our [disabled people's] lives can and will change" (Finger, 1984). It follows from this that a disabled person's quality of life is shaped by social circumstances. Having an impairment may cause a person physical and emotional pain. But rarely does this completely determine the person's life. Moreover, if it does, the individual may not necessarily judge her life not worth living. Such a judgment is personal and subjective. It will vary from individual to individual (Finger, 1991; Morris, 1991).

For these reasons, disabled feminists see assumptions about quality of life as invalid and nothing but a reflection of society's prejudices toward disability. They also argue that these assumptions have a negative impact on the situation of all disabled people. Alison Davies writes that prenatal testing and subsequent abortion "denies us [disabled people] an identity as equal human beings worthy of respect, and calls into question the place in society of disabled individuals" (Davies, 1987).

Assumptions about quality of life perpetuate the idea that disability is only a medical problem. This encourages governments to think that they have no responsibility for solving the problems faced by disabled people. It is argued that if governments were wholeheartedly committed to preventing impairment, then they would tackle poverty rather than fund prenatal testing, particularly in developing countries. That would do more to reduce disability and stop suffering (Knudsen, 1995). An argument is also made that where the state funds prenatal testing, it may reduce services to disabled children and their parents. It is believed that the governments' reasoning would be: "We enabled a woman to 'choose' not to have a disabled child, but she decided to have the child, and therefore it is her responsibility to raise the child" (Morris, 1991).

The use of prenatal testing raises the fear of eugenics—that is, that governments will promote the use of prenatal testing in order to eliminate disabled people because they are considered "bad" for society. This point is made by drawing a parallel with Nazi Germany in the 1930s and 1940s. There, 70,000 disabled people were killed under a "euthanasia" program. The Nazis were motivated in part by thinking that it was a kindness to kill disabled people in order to prevent their suffering. This echoes the argument made by some nondisabled commentators today that it is in the interest of the disabled fetus not to be born. The Nazis were also motivated by economics, by a desire to reduce the cost to the state of providing facilities for disabled people. Again, this echoes the argument used in debates about policy that preventing the birth of disabled people saves the state the "lifetime costs" of supporting a disabled child (Morris, 1991).

One difference between Nazi Germany and most governments today is that the former held a fascist ideology. Among other things, this meant that individual rights were totally disregarded. However, the point that disabled feminists make is that judgments about quality of life have a strong emotive appeal in political debate. This may make societies less willing to spot or speak out against abuses of prenatal testing and its negative social effects.

Disabled feminists have expressed disappointment at the apparent readiness with which nondisabled feminists have used arguments about quality of life. They feel the reproductive rights movement has exploited fears of disability to argue for abortion on grounds of fetal impairment. Nonetheless, most disabled feminists support a woman's right to have an abortion, though with some important qualifications. A woman must be given accurate information about any impairment that her fetus has. In making a decision about abortion, a woman has to take into account the resources she has to raise the child. But there must also be an awareness of the discrimination disabled people face and how this may affect the woman's judgment and the advice she gets from people around her (Saxton, 1984).

See Also

DISABILITY AND FEMINISM; DISABILITY: HEALTH AND SEXUALITY; EUGENICS: REPRODUCTIVE RIGHTS

References and Further Reading

Davies, Alison. 1987. Women with disabilities: Abortion and liberation. *Disability, handicap, and society* 2 (3): 275–284.

Finger, Anne. 1984. Claiming all our bodies: Reproductive rights and disability. In Rita Arditti, Renee Duelli Klein, and Shelly Minden, *Test tube women: What future for motherhood?* London: Pandora.

———. 1991. *Past due: A story of disability, pregnancy and birth.* London: Women's Press.

Knudsen, Janne Sander. 1995. Danish women with disabilities—Opening of the workshop at NGO-Forum, March 1995. In Eve K. Damm et al., eds., *Perfect babies in a perfect world: Who has the right to life?* Report from workshop in NGO–Forum, Valby, Denmark, on Danish women with disabilities.

Morris, Jenny. 1991. *Pride against prejudice: Transforming attitudes to disability.* London: Women's Press.

Saxton, Marsha. 1984. Born and unborn: The implications of reproductive technology for people with disabilities. In Rita Arditti, Renee Duelli Klein, and Shelly Minden, *Test tube women: What future for motherhood?* London: Pandora.

Ruth Bailey

DISARMAMENT

Disarmament, in recent years, has been a response to pressure from democratic movements, and to a perceived need for the great industrial countries, mainly the former Soviet Union and the United States, to end the ruinous and dangerous arms race that developed during the cold war and was accelerated after the fall of the Soviet empire.

About two decades ago, the United Nations reported that women composed 63 percent of the peace movement throughout the world—recalling the early twentieth century, when feminism was associated with antimilitarism and U.S. suffragists created the Women's Peace Party (Boulding, 1976)—and the theme of the International Decade of Women (1975–1985), organized by the United Nations, was "Peace, Equality, Development." The great military powers' hostility to disarmament impeded the organization of international peace conferences by nongovernmental organizations. However, women are still a crucial component of peace movements, with support from the international community.

The feminist movements that emerged in the western world in the 1970s included many antimilitarist women, who joined with others and created new women's movements for peace. They applied their considerable creativity—which, they felt, had been made invisible in male culture—to originate actions expressing their resistance to war. They rejected militarization as a means to make peace and solve conflicts, taking instead an innovative theoretical approach.

Women As Innovative Actors in the Disarmament Process

Most sociopolitical actors, particularly nation-states, claim their commitment to peace even as they prepare, provoke, or wage a war. It was in the the name of "peace maintenance" that many cruise and Pershing missiles were deployed in western Europe; these were partially dismantled when disarmament agreements were signed between the Soviet Union and the United States. It was also to

"defend peace" that, in 1990, the great Western powers organized a coalition to wage war against Iraq and prolong it by a blockade that killed or injured several thousands of people each month for the following years. The blockade was still in force at the end of the twentieth century. In both cases, women were in the vanguard of resistance.

In 1981 British antimilitarist women organized the Greenham Common Camp next door to a military base where 96 American cruise missiles were to be deployed; women also organized peace camps around 20 other bases where more missiles were to be deployed, but Greenham Common was the most famous. There, women lived in tents for five years enduring hunger, cold, disease, and discomfort and risking harassment and imprisonment by the authorities. This experience pointed up the importance of organizing resistance to become efficient and the benefit of women-only groups to give women a space for freedom of speech and feminine solidarity. It also suggested that participating in political parties was not an appropriate way to raise British people's consciousness about the dangers of the arms race (Jones, 1983). Greenham common was widely admired and drew support from women throughout the world.

Also in England, women started Women Oppose the Nuclear Threat (WONT). This movement was based on the premise that feminism should not be limited to women's problems, such as rape, abortion, or health; the women of WONT held that there was a close relationship between nuclear arms and men's domination of women, and that in a pacifist society, this domination would be overcome more easily (Jones, 1983).

In the United States, under the leadership of Helen Caldicott (an Australian), Women for Action for Nuclear Disarmament (WAND) gathered thousands of women for public antinuclear demonstrations and also mobilized them for educative action. WAND isued booklets based on the idea that prevention is the only defense.

Women Pentagon Action (WPA) organized symbolic activities that included civil disobedience (women encircled and blocked the Pentagon's entrances) and distributing "awareness-raising" pamphlets to the Pentagon's employees. Like their counterparts of Greenham Common, some leaders of these actions were sentenced to jail for ten days or a month (Jones, 1983).

In Germany, there was intense resistance to missile deployment under the leadership of Eva Quistorp and Petra Kelly (Kelly, 1992). In France, which was not a member of the North Atlantic Treaty Organization (NATO) and thus was not a site for missle deployment, resistance took a different form (Danielsson and Danielsson, 1986). Solange Fernex, deputy to the European Parliament and president of Women for Peace, Marie-Laure Bovy (Stop-Essais), Madeleine Briselance (SOS-Tahiti), and Marie-Thérèse Danielsson mobilized women to end France's nuclear tests in French Polynesia, where these tests were having a disastrous impact. François Mitterand declared a moratorium after several dozen tests had been conducted, but his successor as president, Jacques Chirac, planned to resume them, causing antimilitarist women to increase their resistance. Similarly, indigenous women from islands destroyed or damaged by American and British nuclear tests (Bikini, Marshall Islands, Mariana Islands) toured England and the United States to inform people about the irreversible harm inflicted on women and children by nuclear testing in that part of the Pacific (Oxford Green Line, 1987).

Antiwar sentiment ins another aspect of disarmement. In 1991, for example, according to public opinion polls, a majority of women in Japan (75%), the United States (73%), England, (59%), and France (54) opposed the war against Iraq, though a majority of men approved it (Michel, 1995). More recently, the war in Yugoslavia mobilized western women and in particular feminists against military violence toward women. Consequently, they obtained from the United Nations the creation of an International Tribunal on Violence toward Women to prosecute war criminals and crimes against humanity.

There are many more instances of women's actions related to disarmament and mobilization for peace in Asia, Latin America, and Africa, where dozens of armed conflicts have taken place. Often, these efforts go unreported by the mass media and are identified only in alternative literature (International Peace Bureau, 1996). Before the Gulf War, in November 1990, Arab women organized a Boat of Arab Women for Peace (Al Sadoon, 1996). Gathering women from Morocco, Indonesia, the United States, Sweden, and elsewhere, they sailed from Algiers to Bassora to demonstrate their desire to end the conflict in a nonviolent manner. At the African Conference on Women in Dakar, Senegal, in 1994, African Women's Movements for Peace adopted a resolution demanding that African states stop buying arms and suggesting that women become peace ambassadors. In the second half of the 1990s, two women, one from Latin America and the other from Asia, won the Nobel Peace Prize. These women represent thousands of invisible women who fight every day for peace, justice, and disarmament—generally, women do not separate these three goals.

Women As Innovative Thinkers on Disarmament

The prevention of armed conflicts by decreasing military expenses and resisting arms production and deployment must be reinforced by efforts to expose the prejudices and stereotypes that lead people to leave their security in the hands of political and military powers, socioeconomic formations called the military-industrial complex.

Preventing militarization and war requires rejecting arms as the sole way of solving conflicts among social classes, regions, ethnicities, nations, states, or interstate conglomerates. Nonviolence, justice, and bargaining are the best means to solve conflicts and prevent wars. If women are more numerous than men in peace movements, it may be because more often than men, they reject the proverb "If you want peace, prepare for war" and replace it with "If you want peace, prepare for peace."

Women have also discounted other widely held beliefs. For instance, militarization is often perceived as a source of jobs and innovative technologies. But Marion Anderson and her associates (1986) reported that during Ronald Reagan's first term as U.S. presisdent (1981–1985), when military expenses reached a peak, more than 1.2 million jobs were lost, and 80 percent of them were women's jobs (Anderson et al., 1986).

Another idea—that low-level nuclear radiation is safe, was challenged by Alice Steward, a British doctor, whose report that these emissions were harmful led to the undertaking of studies by nongovernmental agencies and independent scientists.

Rosalie Bertell (1988) wrote an exhaustive report on victims of the military and civil use of nuclear power throughout the world since Hiroshima and Nagasaki. She argued that the nuclear industry, with its enormous concentration of financial and technological power, was interfering with the democratic process through its suppression or distortion of research findings, its politics of secrecy, its neglect of human health, and so on. For instance, American authorities did not register radiation levels of the geographic zones downwind while nuclear tests took place in the Nevada desert, for fear that the results would raise resistance to testing. Today, with cancer striking perhaps one woman out of eight in the United States, Women's Environment and Development Organization (WEDO) has asked the government to start an epidemiological study on the environmental effects of radiation.

Scilla McLean (1986) studied the "decision-making power" of the nuclear arms complex and concluded that the civil nuclear industry is incompatible with democracy. She argued that in the presumably democratic societies (England, France, the United States), much decision-making is done not by government but by the military-industrial complex—sociopolitical clans composed of high-ranking military men, politicians, bankers, businessmen from the defense industry, and directors of defense research laboratories. Most of them come from the same social strata, and the same academic background: *"grandes écoles"* (France) or elite universities (England, United States). These men decide, for example, on military expenses and on research and development for new, sophisticated nuclear weapons. McLean also concluded from her research that a similar military-industrial complex makes such decisions in China and the former Soviet Union as well.

Resistance to militarization requires accurate information concerning the level of military expenses in the world. In the United States, well before the United Nations Development Program (UNDP), Ruth Leger Sivard compared the level of military spending with spending on health and education in various conturies. She was opposed by the Pentagon, which feared that this information would create resistance to military budgets. Hence, she set up her own research foundation, World Priorities, and periodically releases reports about military expenses in the world (Leger Sivard, 1993).

Resistance to war requires convincing people that violence is not a genetic characteristic of the human species—particularly of males—and that passivity is not a genetic characteristic of females. In the United States and Europe, feminist researchers have argued that male violence and female passivity are not innate but result of socialization. From an early age, they believe, males are socialized for violence and females for passivity (Brocke-Utne, 1985; Reardon, 1985). Evelyne Accad (1999) argues that the different reactions of men and women to war are part of the gender structural relationships that characterize the patriarchal system. This system is a social creation, particularly strong in Middle Eastern societies, where male domination and female submissiveness are characteristic.

Preventing militarization and war also implies convincing women that joining the army does not symbolize women's emancipation or equality with men. Cynthia Enloe (1983) concluded that the military system is "the archetype of the patriarchal system" and that it accepts women only in subordinate roles, as instruments of the patriarchal system of which militarization is the main component.

The present author, Andrée Michel (1995), has argued that women are the main victims of violence generated by armament and contemporary wars and should not leave their security to the military industrial-complex or give men the means to achieve security by military violence. Michel believes that citizenship can be achieved only when men and women resist the military-industrial complex and work to achieve their own security. If women are the victims of war, they also are the main social actors who can prevent and resist it efficiently and innovatively.

Women play a very important role in the disarmament process. Antimilitarist women, for example, promote disarmament by challenging the notion that war is prevented by armament and that militarization has a positive effect on employment, the economy, and technology. Some women have been particularly innovative in opposing the deployment of new nuclear or conventional arms.

But women have rarely intervened when military budgets are discussed in parliaments or among high officials. It is important for more women to understand that preventing war and achieving security for all should begin with reducing military expenses and channeling these funds into health and education programs. The Women's International League for Peace and Freedom (WILPF, 1996) has created and disseminated a "women's budget" to counteract the U.S. federal budget by converting the enormous military expenses into investments in education, infrastructure, job training, and the renewal of the federal guarantee of income support for poor children.

Women's action for disarmament and peace does not entail submission to injustice, totalitarianism, or sexism; in fact, quite the opposite is true. Algerian women's resistance to violence is a well-known example. In spite of death threats and numerous assassinations, Algerian girls and women have continued to attend schools and universities, to practice their occupations, and to refuse to be veiled. Simultaneously, they organized mass demonstrations opposing the government's bargaining with Muslim fundamentalists who want to apply the Shari'a to women.

These Algerian women—and many others like them—prove to the world that women can risk their lives and that their love of peace and their rejection of violence are compatible with defending the universal values of freedom and respect for human dignity.

See Also

ARMAMENT AND MILITARIZATION; MILITARY; NUCLEAR
WEAPONS; PACIFISM AND PEACE ACTIVISM; PEACE
MOVEMENTS, *specific regions;* WAR

References and Further Reading

Accad, Evelyne. 1989. *Sexuality, war, and literature in the Middle East.* New York: New York University Press.

Al Sadoon, Nasra. 1996. *Le bateau des femmes arabes pour la paix.* Paris: l'Harmattan.

Anderson, Marion, Michael Frish, and Michael Oden. 1986. *The empty pork barrel: The employment cost of the military buildup, 1981–1985.* Lansing, Mich.: Employment Research Associates.

Bertell, Rosalie. 1988. *No immediate danger? Prognosis for a radioactive earth.* London: Women's Press.

Boulding, Elise. 1976. *The underside of history: A view of women through time.* Boulder, Col.: Westview.

Brock-Utne, Birgit. 1985. *Educating for peace: A feminist perspective.* New York: Pergamon.

Caldicott, Helen. 1980. *Nuclear madness.* New York: Bantam.

Danielsson, Bengt, and Marie-Thérèse Danielsson. (1986). *Poisoned reign: French nuclear colonialism in the Pacific.* Harmondsworth, England: Penguin.

Enloe, Cynthia. 1983. *Does khaki become you?* Boston: South End.

Fernex, Solange. 1983. *La vie pour la vie.* Paris: Utovie.

International Peace Bureau (IPB). 1996. *International Women's Day for Peace and Disarmament.* Geneva: IPB.

Jones, Lynne. 1983. On common ground: The women's peace camp at Greenham Common. In Lynne Jonnes, ed., *Keeping the peace, 79–97.* London: Women's Press.

Kelly, Petra. 1992. *Nonviolence speaks to power.* Honolulu: University of Hawaii Press.

Leger Sivard, Ruth. 1993. *World military and social expenditures 1987–1988.* 12th ed. Washington, D.C.: World Priorities.

McLean, Scilla. 1986. *How nuclear weapons decisions are made.* London: Macmillan and Oxford Research Group.

Michel, Andrée, 1985. Le complexe militaro-industriel et les violences à l'égard des femmes. *Nouvelles Questions Féministes,* 11–12: 9–73.

———. 1995. *Surarmement, pouvoirs, democratic.* Paris: Harmattan.

Michel, Andrée, and Floh. 1999. *Citogennes militairement incorrectes.* Paris: Harmattan.

Oxford Green Line. 1987. *Pacific women speak.* Oxford:

Reardon, Betty. 1985. *Sexism and the war system.* New York: Teachers College.

Turpin, Jennifer, and Lois Ann Lorentzen. 1996. *The gendered new order: Militarism, development, and the environment.* New York and London: Routledge.

West, Lois A., ed. 1997. *Feminist nationalism.* New York and London: Routledge.

Women's International League for Peace and Freedom. 1996. *Women's budget.* Special ed. Philadelphia, Pa: Women's International League for Peace and Freedom.

Andrée Michel

DISCIPLINE IN SCHOOLS

Discipline in schools is often defined as the maintenance of an orderly system that creates the conditions necessary for learning. The term *discipline* also describes students' behavior that is desired by and acceptable to teachers (and dominant power groups within society) and the practices and procedures applied by a school to achieve it.

Purpose of Discipline

While it can be argued that discipline is essential to the creation of an orderly learning environment, it is important to note that within schools there are many disciplinary practices that have little bearing on providing the necessary conditions for academic learning. Rather, these practices are designed to socialize and control students in particular desired ways. Desirable conduct is determined by the values, ideology, and moral and cultural imperatives of a society. Acceptable behavior thus differs according to what is considered "desirable" behavior for students—females and males of a particular age, class, sector, or ethnic or religious group.

Discipline—A Gender Issue

In its broadest sense, then, *discipline* often reflects values that different societies see as being important to the quality of their future. Within this context it is significant to note that in western countries research on discipline problems at schools has focused predominantly on boys. As Adler (1988: 61) points out, school is just as central to the everyday lives of girls, and yet this fact tends to be ignored in explanations of delinquency and troublesome behavior. The preoccupation with boys' more spectacular indiscipline is also of concern because little attention has been given to the less "visible" ways some girls resist schooling (Davies, 1984; Wolpe, 1988). Discipline is thus an important factor in examining the outcomes of schooling for girls.

Disciplinary Traditions

It is difficult to generalize about the differing models of discipline applied within schools throughout the world. Taking a very broad perspective, it could be argued that discipline models reflect the way a society sees education as meeting either collective or individual needs. For example, in China there has been a tradition that children should be socialized as early as possible to conform to cultural expectations. This meant that in China not only was attendance compulsory but so also was achievement (Cheng, 1990: 164). Disciplinary practices have been undertaken in a collectivist spirit with the intention of forming "good" behaviors. In countries such as China and India there are strong masculinist traditions in the teacher-pupil relationship, and yet this field of research, school discipline and gender, is still to be fully developed.

In countries such as Australia, Britain, and the United States, models of discipline have been strongly influenced by behavioral psychology. Educational psychologists drawing on behaviorism argue that students' behavior can be modified by the use of rewards and punishments. In this model of discipline misbehavior is seen as an individual "defect" that needs remedial attention. Some of the most popular models in this field include Glasser's *Control Theory* (1985) and *The Quality School* (1990); Canter and Canter's *Assertive Discipline* (1976); and Rogers's "Decisive Discipline" (1991). Critics express the concern that these models are not underpinned by an educational theory of discipline; they are concerned primarily with the control or management of students rather than the educational value of a disciplinary regime (Knight, 1988; Slee, 1995).

Gender and Discipline

Another concern is the failure to conceptualize students' behavior and school discipline in ways that address the significance of gender (Slee, 1995). Research has found that girls and boys are disciplined differently in schools; and some researchers conclude that these differences reinforce patriarchal power relationships (Delamont, 1980; Robinson, 1992; Spender, 1982; Wolpe, 1988;). Boys' behavior or misbehavior is perceived by teachers (and others) as a natural part of boys' growing up—they are "naturally" boisterous, competitive, and aggressive. The same behavior when exhibited by girls, however, is seen as problematic (Robinson, 1992).

Such researchers argue that girls who break school rules are doubly punished because they are also seen as breaking with the rules of "nature." Girls are expected to be passive, polite, and obedient. Girls who resist these constructions of femininity are likely to be labeled as "tarts," "sluts," or "slags" (Lees, 1986; Wolpe, 1988). Such unfounded judgements about morality endangers a girl's potential value in the heterosexual marriage market.

There are further concerns about the ways girls are punished for transgressing the norms of adolescence, femininity, sexuality, and schooling. Carrington (1993) describes how a number of girls fall into the hands of welfare and juvenile justice authorities not so much for criminal activity as for sexual conduct. Cook and Slee (1993) describe the same phenomenon in China. On their visits to Chinese *gongdu* schools (juvenile detention centers), they found that the majority of boys were sent to these institutions for crimes against property or crimes of violence, while girls had been sent for what their interpreter described as "sexual insults." Arguably, this gender-differentiated policing of girls' perceived "immorality" constructs and perpetuates patriarchal gender relations. Aboriginal, Afro-Caribbean, and African-American girls are evidently subjected to even more intense surveillance, are often more severely disciplined, and are seen as being more prone to "promiscuity" (Carrington, 1993). It is important to note the different ways in which race, gender, and class contextualize students' experiences of discipline in school.

Arguably too, dominant versions of masculinity and femininity operate in tandem to produce a hidden "curriculum" of the female body, one that is policed by both students and teachers (Fine and Macpherson, 1994). Particular constructions of masculinity and femininity dominate disciplinary practices, and yet the nature of gender-constructed power and control in behavior-management policies, programs, and practices in schools has yet to be considered systematically.

See Also

EDUCATION: ACHIEVEMENT; CHILD DEVELOPMENT; FEMININITY; SEXUALITY: ADOLESCENT SEXUALITY

References and Further Reading

Adler, C. 1988. Girls, schooling, and trouble. In R. Slee, ed., *Discipline and schools: A curriculum perspective.* Melbourne: Macmillan.

Canter, L., and M. Canter. 1976. *Assertive discipline: A take charge approach for today's education.* Calif.: Canter.

Carrington, K. 1993. *Offending girls: Sex, youth, and justice.* Sydney: Allen and Unwin.

Cheng, Kai Ming. 1990. The culture of schooling in east Asia. In N. Entwistle, ed., *Handbook of educational practices.* London: Routledge.

Cook, S., and R. Slee. 1993. Removing dust from flowers: A Chinese model for correctional education. In R. Semmens, ed., *Yearbook of correctional education.* Calif.: Center for Study of Correctional Education.

Davies, L. 1984. *Pupil power: Deviance and gender in school.* Lewes, U.K.: Falmer.

Delamont, S. 1980. *Sex roles and the school.* London: Methuen.

Fine, M., and P. Macpherson. 1994. Over dinner: Feminism and adolescent female bodies. In H. L. Radtke and H. J. Stam, eds., *Power/gender: Social relations in theory and practice.* London: Sage.

Glasser, W. 1985. *Control theory in the classroom.* New York: Harper and Row.

———. 1990. *The quality school: Managing students without coercion.* New York: Harper Perennial.

Knight, T. 1988. Student discipline as a curriculum concern. In R. Slee, ed., *Discipline and schools: A curriculum perspective.* Melbourne. Macmillan.

Lees, S. 1986. *Losing out: sexuality and adolescent girls.* London: Hutchinson.

Radtke, H. L., and H. J. Stam. 1994. *Power/gender: Social relations in theory and practice.* London: Sage.

Robinson, K. 1992. Classroom discipline: Power, resistance and gender. A look at teacher perspectives. *Gender and Education* 4 (3): 273–87.

Rogers, W. 1991. Decisive discipline. In M. N. Lovegrove and R. Lewis, eds. *Classroom discipline.* Melbourne: Longman and Cheshire.

Slee, R. 1995. *Changing theories and practices of discipline.* London: Falmer.

———. 1988. *Discipline in schools: A curriculum perspective.* Melbourne: Macmillan.

Spender, D. 1982. *Invisible women: The schooling scandal.* London: Writers and Readers.

Wolpe, A. M. 1988. *Within school walls: The role of discipline, sexuality, and the curriculum.* London: Routledge.

Delia Hart

DISCRIMINATION

Discrimination may be defined as the denial of equal enjoyment of rights. It can occur on the basis of sex, race, religion, political belief, caste, social class, disability, age, or sexual orientation, or a combination of these and other attributes. Discrimination need not be intentional—it covers actions or policies that have the *effect* of discriminating.

Three types of discrimination are usually distinguished: direct discrimination, indirect discrimination, and systemic discrimination. The examples given here will focus on sex discrimination.

In the case of *direct discrimination* a woman is disadvantaged or less favorably treated simply because she is a woman; because of characteristics associated with being a woman, such as the capacity to have children; or because of characteristics attributed to women, such as a propensity to value relationships over career achievement. Discrimination can also occur when women fail to conform to gender stereotypes. For example, a woman who displays the competitiveness or results-orientation expected of the senior staff within an organization may be judged as overly aggressive or lacking in interpersonal skills.

Another form of direct discrimination against women is sexual harassment. Legal acceptance of sexual harassment as a form of sex discrimination largely stems from the work of the U.S. feminist Catharine MacKinnon (1979). Sexual harassment is defined as unwelcome sexual conduct, particularly in employment or education, that creates a hostile work environment for the victim and is associated with structural inequalities of power between men and women. Women are also subjected to sexual harassment from coworkers, particularly when they are attempting to enter areas of work traditionally thought of as "masculine." In most jurisdictions employers have vicarious liability for this as well as other forms of sex discrimination, unless they can show that they took reasonable steps to prevent it.

Indirect discrimination occurs when policies or practices that appear to be gender-neutral have the effect of discriminating against women and cannot be justified on grounds such as business necessity. The requirement of full-time hours of work for a woman returning from maternity leave, for example, has been found to constitute indirect discrimination. The requirement of continuity of service in order to be eligible for promotion would be another example of a policy that has disparate impact, because women are more likely to have interrupted work histories. Indirect discrimination also occurs when equal treatment compounds the effects of earlier discrimination—as when the "last on, first off" rule is applied to women who have only recently been allowed into certain jobs.

The concept of indirect discrimination was endorsed by the United States Supreme Court in 1971 in the case of *Griggs* v. *Duke Power Co.* The acknowledgment that equal treatment (as in this case, the requirement of a high school education) may be discriminatory has been an important breakthrough in thinking about discrimination. It means that treating people as if they were the same as a norm from which they differ in significant ways is just as discriminatory as penalizing them directly for their difference (Hunter, 1992).

Some people have been concerned that the recognition of difference which underlies the concept of indirect discrimination may result in the perpetuation of inequality. One alternative that has been proposed is the "subordination principle" (MacKinnon, 1987). This judges both gender-neutral treatment and treatment based on accommodation of difference by the standard of whether such treatment serves to maintain or overcome women's subordination to men.

Systemic discrimination refers to the whole range of gender-based assumptions and expectations that form part of the socialization and education process. These give rise to the gender segregation of the labor market and are built into the structure and culture of organizations. For example, girls may be steered toward gender-appropriate subjects and occupations, with their careers being viewed as subsidiary to their roles as wives and mothers.

This systemic bias means that women are relegated to the "secondary labor market," including the part-time and casual jobs deemed compatible with their familial responsibilities. It also shows up in the devaluing of "female" skills, including interpersonal skills, and the low work value assigned to "female" jobs, such as those involving responsibility for children.

Organizations may be designed around an assumed split between public and private life. There is often an expectation that employees in promotional positions can engage in full-time and continuous work and that career structures do not need to accommodate family responsibilities. Women can rarely conform to these organizational expectations.

Inflexible work hours and career patterns also prevent men from taking on a more active parenting or caring role and from sharing the load of unpaid work more equally. This failure of organizations to accommodate the realities of parenting and other family responsibilities has achieved legal recognition not only through the prohibition of indirect discrimination on the grounds of sex but also through the more recent prohibition of discrimination on the grounds of family or carer responsibilities.

Organizations are often characterized by homosocial reproduction—that is, like recruiting like (Lipman-Blumen, 1976). Managers feel more comfortable with those who are like themselves, who "fit in." Social similarity simplifies communication and increases predictability of response. Characteristics of the dominant group become incorporated into the way "merit" is construed in the organization. This is one explanation of discrimination against those who are "different," who might do a job in a different though equally effective way. Social similarity also makes it easier for senior members of an organization to identify with more junior ones and to act as mentors for them.

Another form of systemic discrimination that has received increased international attention in recent years is the cultural tolerance of violence against women. Gender-based violence has been recognized by the United Nations as a form of discrimination that prevents women's equal participation in public and private life and contributes to their subordination.

The concepts of indirect and systemic discrimination are still unfamiliar to most people. Many believe that as long as requirements are the same for everyone and there is no explicit intention to discriminate, then everything that needs to be done in the name of equity has been done—regardless of differential access to the enjoyment of human rights.

See Also

ANTIDISCRIMINATION; EQUAL OPPORTUNITIES; EQUALITY; SEXUAL HARASSMENT; STEREOTYPES

References and Further Reading

Australian Law Reform Commission. 1993. *Equality before the law.* Discussion Paper 54. Sydney: Australian Law Reform Commission.

Hunter, Rosemary. 1992. *Indirect discrimination in the workplace.* Annandale, New South Wales, Australia: Federation.

Lipman-Blumen, Jean. 1976. Towards a homosocial theory of sex roles: An explanation of the sex segregation of social institutions. In Martha Blaxall and Barbara Reagan, eds., *Women and the workplace: The implications of occupational segregation.* Chicago: University of Chicago Press.

MacKinnon, Catharine. 1987. *Feminism unmodified.* Cambridge, Mass.: Harvard University Press.

———. 1979. *The sexual harassment of working women.* New Haven: Yale University Press.

Marian Sawer

DISCOURSE ANALYSIS

See COMMUNICATIONS: CONTENT AND DISCOURSE ANALYSIS.

DISEASE

The human body is remarkably adaptable to a variety of living conditions. When the stresses of the environment, aging, or everyday life overwhelm our ability to accommodate, however, dysfunction may result.

The medical definition of disease focuses on the interruption, cessation, or disorder of body functions, systems, or organs. In medicine, a disease entity must have two of the following: recognizable causes, recognizable symptoms, and consistent anatomical changes. While the term *disease* is considered objective, *illness* refers to the patient in context: it encompasses the physical, social, cultural, emotional, intellectual, and philosophical milieu in which the patient exists and is therefore a more subjective term.

There are diseases that exist primarily in certain cultures. *Anorexia nervosa,* for example, is mainly a disease of modern western culture; there is a specific psychosis in Malaysia called *amok* that involves running around waving knives and threatening people (this is the source of the term "running amok"). In cultures in which status rises with age, women have fewer symptoms that they attribute to menopause.

In most parts of the world, women have different patterns of disease and death from men. In developed societies, women have higher rates of chronic illness but also a longer life span than men do. In developing countries, malnutrition, infectious diseases, and pregnancy-related mortality (both from complications of childbirth and, if abortion is illegal or difficult to obtain, from complications of unskilled abortions) greatly decrease a woman's life expectancy.

Sexism plays a significant role in what is considered disease in women. A key sexist notion is that the female body is inherently weaker than the male body. The female body must be viewed as distinct from and inferior to male bodies in order to provide a rationale for different treatment.

Historically, women's strength has been challenged on the basis of physical accomplishments without regard for the ways in which females of higher social status have been discouraged or prohibited from participating in exercise, sports, or manual labor. Working-class or immigrant women, on the other hand, are viewed as capable of physical work but are viewed as bearers of disease (Ehrenreich and English, 1973). Typhoid Mary is probably the most famous disease-bearer in history; far fewer people have heard of Patient Zero, the handsome male flight attendant believed to have been responsible for infecting an inordinate number of men in the early days of AIDS. Female commercial sex workers, who have been hit hard by the AIDS epidemic, are viewed not as victims of a male-borne disease but as carriers of the disease to men. And women of all classes are blamed for conveying mental disorders to their children, whose problems are attributed not to absent fathers or an unsupportive society but only to bad mothering.

Within the medical system, many female disorders have been dismissed as psychogenic (emotionally caused): menstrual pain used to be attributed to problems in accepting one's feminine or maternal role; problems related to silicone breast implants have for many years been dismissed as emotional rather than physical. One outcome of this perspective is a paucity of research that examines physiological processes in common women's complaints.

Conversely, women have been targeted for unnecessary and unethical medical and surgical interventions in order to increase the market for health care services. In the United States, the number of surgeries varies in proportion to the number of surgeons, regardless of actual need, and many unnecessary cesarean deliveries, hysterectomies, and "prophylactic" mastectomies occur each year. As the number of physicians grows (and competition for medical funding and income increases) the territory of what is considered appropriate for medical intervention expands.

Menopause, reproduction, the menstrual cycle, aging, and appearance have each been targeted as medical disorders. The medicalization of naturally occurring phenomena generates great outlays of money for procedures and products to deal with concerns that are socially manufactured rather than medical. Western society has tended to medicalize normal processes from womb to tomb; women give birth in hospitals, hooked up to monitoring machines during labor, often on their backs, the most inefficient position. Menopause is viewed as a hormone deficiency disease rather than a normal part of a woman's life cycle.

Self-hatred is a lucrative commodity: in 1982, the American Society of Plastic and Reconstructive Surgeons stated that small breasts are a "deformity...a disease which in most patients results in ... a total lack of well-being due to a lack of self-perceived femininity" (Porterfield, 1982).

It has become acceptable in preventive medicine to decrease the incidence of one disease while increasing the risk of another. For instance, at the time of this writing the United States government was spending $68 million to study whether tamoxifen, a drug used to treat breast cancer, actually prevents breast cancer, even though it is known to increase the risk of endometrial cancer. Such trials promote "disease substitution" rather than prevention.

Women—as providers and consumers—have sought holistic or alternative care in greater numbers than men, in part because of their alienation from a male-dominated care system—and in part because holistic healing assumes that the mind and body are integrated, that we are capable of healing ourselves, and that any explanation of individual health conditions is grounded in the physical and social environment.

A true understanding of disease cannot be had without a contrasting understanding of health, a state of optimal physical, emotional, and spiritual functioning, which involves not only one's inner resources but the interrelationships among humans, and between humans and their environment.

See Also

ANOREXIA NERVOSA; BREAST; BULIMIA NERVOSA; CANCER; EATING DISORDERS; ETHICS: MEDICAL; HEALERS; HEALTH: OVERVIEW; HOLISTIC HEALTH, *I and II*; MEDICINE: INTERNAL, *I and II*; SURGERY; TOXICOLOGY

References and Further Reading

Ehrenreich, Barbara, and Deirdre English. 1973. *Complaints and disorders: The sexual politics of sickness.* New York: Feminist Press.

Porterfield, H. W. 1982. *Comments on the proposed classification of inflatable breast prostheses and silicone gel-filled breast prostheses.* American Society of Plastic and Reconstructive Surgeons.

Jane Zones
Adriane Fugh-Berman

DISPLACED PERSONS

See REFUGEES.

DISTANCE LEARNING

See EDUCATION: DISTANCE EDUCATION.

DIVISION OF LABOR

The term *division of labor* refers to the separation of work into component tasks to be executed by given social groupings divided by class, caste, age category, or gender. While all human societies practice a division of labor of some kind, industrial societies extend the more basic divisions based on class, gender, and age to include those divisions based on skill; educational achievement; profession (craft specialization); mental, manual, and machine labor; and even ethnic or caste origin.

The sexual or gender division of labor involves "women's work and "men's work,"which are often complementary, even though the specific types of work assigned to men and women vary enormously cross-culturally. Each society justifies the partition of tasks by gender on culturally defined so-called natural differences based on sex. The "naturalness" of the tasks assigned to men and women is reinforced by specific cultural explanations, which are then invoked to explain gender inequality. The age division of labor usually means that lighter tasks are assigned to the very old and the very young. Although all societies have ideas about those most able to fill particular labor requirements, very little is fixed by actual biological considerations. The only firm requirement of the sexual or gender division of labor seems to be that women give birth to and breastfeed infants. Yet in many societies, subsistence activities are fluid and cross both gender and age lines; it is chiefly in more industrialized societies that increasing specialization is prevalent. Such specialization is, according to Adam Smith (1723–1790), the basis of further subdivisions of the labor process.

Background: Division of Labor in Industrial Societies

Smith coined the term *division of labor* to refer to the fact that, with industrialization, people had become specialists rather than generalists. With the introduction of the factory system, people were now responsible for a specific task or series of tasks, rather than the entire production process, as in artisanal or preindustrial commodity production. The production of any item can be subdivided extensively. According to Smith, the specialists' concentration on a single task leads to ever greater innovation through experimentation because the time taken to complete each step is continually reduced. Karl Bucher, a contemporary of Smith's, noted that the division of labor now included both those who operated machines and those who made them.

The division of labor can be applied to nations as well as individuals, according to Smith. Immanuel Wallerstein (1974) theorizes that the global division of labor among nations originated in the late fifteenth and early sixteenth century. There are marked differences between what Wallerstein terms the *core*, western Europe, and the *periphery,* Latin America, the Caribbean, Asia, and Africa. The periphery produces low-profit, low-capital intensive goods for the export market, earning only small profits for those who provide the capital and bare subsistence wages for the nonfree or coerced labor force that actually manufactures them. The core, on the other hand, produces high-profit, highly capital-intensive goods and pays high wages to the free labor force that produces them. With European expansion into the periphery, a deliberate process of underdevelopment virtually ensured that cheap raw materials from the areas under European control (sugar, cotton, lumber, and tobacco, to name a few) would make their way to the European market and the European consumer.

In England, which underwent its first industrial spurt between 1750 and 1850 and was the first European nation to industrialize, the rise of the factory system was based both on the ready availability of these cheap imported raw materials from abroad, and on locally available cheap human labor. With the replacement of precapitalist modes of production by industrial manufacture, free labor had become cheaper than slave labor. Now that workers in the factories and towns were paid by the hour or by the piece (the quantity produced), the housing, food, and clothing of the worker did not have to be paid for by the capitalist, as was typical in precapitalist modes of production. The social reproduction of the workforce was no longer the capitalists' concern. Families now had to feed, clothe, school, and care for their children through the earnings of their members. Because of insufficient wages, the most common recourse was to put all able-bodied family members to work, and women and children began to enter the factory workforce in ever-increasing numbers, until this was stopped by the advent of protective legislation in the twentieth century. Ultimately harmful to women, so-called protective legislation in many countries began as an attempt to end the exploitative conditions inside the factories for women and children; however, such legislation permitted the continued exploitation of men.

Exploitative conditions often led to the alienation of the worker from the labor process, owing to the endless repetition of a limited number of steps. The harmfulness of repetitive motion to the worker's mental and physical health was noted by Smith, who was cognizant of its importance to capitalism but realized that it would lead to "stupidity and ignorance" on the part of the worker (1965). Émile Durkheim (1858–1917) theorized that specialization, or an excessive division of labor, would lead to a state of normlessness or anomie, and eventually to societal breakdown. Georg Lukacs (1885–1971) argued that the expansion of the division of labor unduly favored economic relations while reinforcing unequal relations between human beings. Marx stated that the worker, stunted by the division of labor in modern society, was a "crippled monstrosity...riveted to a single fractional task," and hence, ripe for revolution.

With the solidification of the factory system, production was removed from the domestic sphere, and a separation of work and residence was the result. European and American women, who before were able to combine wage work with activities essential to the smooth operation of the household, now had to work twice as hard in the labor market and inside the home. Because of the persistence of a gender division of labor, women still found themselves responsible for the reproductive activities of the household, that is, preparing and preserving food, cooking, sewing, mending, cleaning, and caring for children. By contrast, in many nonindustrial, agrarian societies, there is less of a dichotomy between work "in" the household and work "for" the household. In these societies, the home is most often the site of production, consumption, and reproduction, and a more equal division of labor sometimes exists.

Historical Changes in the Sexual Division of Labor

A large body of evidence links strategies for procuring food with differences in the sexual division of labor. With the changeover from a foraging-gathering-hunting or a horticultural subsistence base to intensive agriculture in many parts of the world, women's contribution to cultivation decreased. At the same time, and especially among better-off women, attention to domestic tasks increased. This is true for several reasons. First, with the changeover to agriculture as a means of subsistence, cereal foods became more important than ever before. The time required for cooking and processing is proportionately greater for cultivated cereal crops than for the root crops commonly found in horticultural systems. Unlike root crops (yams, potatoes, manioc, and cassava), cereal grains (wheat, barley, corn or maize) must be processed prior to consumption. A Mayan woman in the Americas might spend several hours each day grinding maize into flour and shaping flour into tortillas, using her hands constantly. The same kind of work is necessary in the preparation of bread, pasta, and other grain-based staples. By contrast, a Mabuti woman in central Africa preparing manioc is able to leave the manioc to boil for hours in a pot that needs to be supervised only every once in a while. Because she spends less time in food preparation, the Mabuti woman may engage in a wider range of activities and may need to remain at home less.

Since the fifteenth century, with the opening up of the Americas, Africa, and Asia to European colonization, many indigenous lifeways, customs, and beliefs were altered as new ideas influenced by European thought began to penetrate and intermix with the old. Foremost among these were cultural definitions of the tasks appropriate for men and women. Especially in areas where a mestizo, ladino, or mixed-blood group formed a dominant class, often strongly influenced by Spanish, Portuguese, British, or French customs, indigenous belief structures were profoundly shaken. Women, who at times held preeminence in given areas of expertise in preindustrial, premercantilist, and precapitalist systems—for example, in religion and medicine, or in agriculture, as in much of Africa—were often stripped of their duties as these tasks came to be seen as more appropriately male. Among the Baule of the Ivory Coast, cloth production long epitomized the cooperative nature of the sexual division of labor. Women grew cotton (as an intercrop between rows of yams, the staple) and spun it into thread, while men wove the thread into traditional designs. When a demand for cash, introduced with taxes imposed by the French colonial government (which had to be paid by men, considered the household heads by the French), the traditional sexual division of labor began to break down. Before this period the labor division was in many respects balanced. Ironically, with the introduction of foreign capital and means of control into Baule society, the raising of cotton, now a cash crop, was entrusted to men. Yet it is important to examine the changes due to foreign capital on a case-by-case basis. Afonja emphasizes that capitalist production was not entirely imposed on African society from the outside; rather, "entrepreneurial Yoruba men were active in developing cash crop production and in controlling trade, and, as local enterprises grew, women's marketing activities were reduced to a secondary place in Yoruba economy" (cited in Leacock, 1981: 489).

More recently, the sexual division of labor has undergone profound changes as a result of external influences in many parts of Africa, Latin America, and Asia, most notably in the form of monetary aid for rural development projects such as those underwritten by the International Monetary Fund and the World Bank. Often this means that women, traditionally horticulturalists and agriculturalists in much of Africa, are overlooked as loans and monetary support are entrusted to men. Another recent development in the sexual division of labor is the advent of manufacturing jobs in multinational corporations throughout the world, especially in designated "export processing zones" of the so-called third world. Such multinational firms are often underwritten or explicitly financed by foreign capital, especially U.S. capital, even when company management is indigenous. To save labor costs, these jobs are given with increasing frequency to women—jobs that are among the most tedious and painstaking, involv-

ing repetitive motion and, increasingly, injury to eyes, respiration, and hearing. The justification for hiring women comes from women's supposed affinity for such detail-oriented work as a result of their traditional work on tasks such as sewing and cooking. In other words, cultural designations of women as workers in the home are often reinforced by high-tech industry. This is known as the "nimble fingers" hypothesis. Women are increasingly channeled into work in electronics assembly, food processing, and clothing production because these jobs are thought to be appropriately "feminine." While men often work as tailors and designers, women are far more likely to work in areas of production that do not lead to advancement. This segregation of women leads to sex-specific abuses. Because women are often seen as a docile workforce, accepting harsh working conditions and low wages, such expectations are then enforced, often to the point of sexual and psychological abuse.

Export processing zones have proliferated throughout those parts of the world where wages can be kept artificially low, and that are still accessible to cheap transport and shipping routes. Such areas include the northern Mexican border state of Chihuahua, where they are known as *maquiladora* industry, the Philippines, Singapore, Taiwan, and the Caribbean. Increasingly, particularly in communications industries such as satellite-driven customer service operations, peripheral European states like Ireland are sought out for the development of new industry. Perhaps the newest such site of operations is India, which, along with Ireland and the Caribbean, has a highly educated English-speaking workforce in a society beset by high unemployment rates. The preference for hiring women in such areas has led to artificially high unemployment rates for men, and means that women, rather than men, often become the household breadwinners (Safa, 1995).

Because notions of patriarchy—the control of women by men—are present, the hiring of women rather than men has exacerbated already existing social problems such as alcoholism in men. This combination of factors has also often led to household dissolution, abandonment of wives, and migration by men in search of employment elsewhere. Traditional household practices and beliefs are thus further upset even though women are empowered in some sense. The rise of such industries is a double-edged sword; although workers are paid wages that are far below those in the developed world, pay scales are often proportionately greater than in surrounding areas. Hence, the export processing zones have become a magnet for women who want a better life, and these zones have caused further migration from and depopulation of rural areas.

Patterns in the Sexual Division of Labor

The sexual or gender division of labor has certain features that can be observed cross-culturally. In most societies men are usually responsible for hunting and trapping animals, both large and small; for procuring and cutting lumber; for mining; for constructing boats, musical instruments, and ornamental objects (of bone, horn, and shell); and for engaging in combat. In many societies, men fish, herd, and tend large animals; collect wild honey; clear land; prepare soil for planting; butcher animals; build houses; make nets and rope; and are political leaders. Tasks which are assigned to either one gender for specific cultural reasons, or to one or both indiscriminately, are collecting shellfish; caring for small animals; planting, tending, and harvesting crops; milking animals; preserving meat and fish; and preparing skins, leather, baskets, mats, clothing, or pottery. Cross-culturally, women usually gather wild plant foods, care for children, cook, prepare foods (this includes cutting, grinding, smoking, or preserving), launder cloth items, fetch water, collect fuel (usually firewood but also animal dung), and spin yarn. In addition, women almost always care for infants; this care includes breastfeeding.

One interesting fact about the sexual division of labor is that work seen as appropriate for women in some cultures is more appropriate for men in others, and vice versa. In addition to bearing and raising children and cooking, "women's work" for Efe pygmies of Zaire includes agricultural work, chopping and carrying firewood, and carrying meat. Carrying heavy loads is so strongly associated with women's work rather than men's that when men kill an animal, especially a large game animal, they will walk all the way back to camp in order to procure women to carry the load for them. Women shoulder burdens even when pregnant, although not as often. In addition, women cook, trade, and work as agricultural laborers for the Lese, their neighbors. When work is done by women, it tends to be considered "easy"; when the same work is done by men, it is likely to be considered "hard." An example reported by some observers is pulling and transplanting rice seedlings in India.

The cultural explanations that are given for the division of labor are normally made to seem natural and immutable to change. Guyer (1984) reports that among the Beti, a formerly migratory population in Cameroon that now concentrates on the production of rubber and palm for export and on cocoa for the local market, male work may be perceived as involving vertical movement

and dealing with wood, creating erectness or height, while female work involves bending and circular, dealing with soil or foliage. Among the Beti, Guyer reports, men's work includes tree cultivation, yam-staking and harvesting, as well as tomato cultivation with long-handled hoes. Women's work centers on tasks that can be completed with the short-handled hoe, cooking over the fire, building mud houses, and tending to the cultivation of the groundnut. After the harvest, women spread groundnuts out to dry in the sun; according to Guyer, the harvest has taken on increased importance because it gives women some control over their lives The groundnut has come to be seen as a "woman's crop"—an interesting historical change related to the penetration of capital into the countryside. This change also represents the process by which a task can come to be seen as natural to one gender or the other.

Theories of the Sexual Division of Labor

Many theories have been proposed to explain why every society divides its work into male and female tasks. While what is seen as appropriate for men and women differs in almost all societies, there is very little agreement on what these tasks actually are, and many theories have been devised to explain this variation.

In the 1930s, George Murdock conducted a cross-cultural comparison of 224 societies and documented extensive evidence to corroborate a cross-cultural sexual division of labor. Murdock argued that strength was an important component of men's activities, as was being away from the home base for extended periods. Men's tasks typically involved a high degree of cooperation. According to Murdock, women's activities required less strength and involved considerably less travel.

Another hypothesis has to do with "economy of effort." It suggests why men produce the majority of manufactured goods in so many societies. Goods manufactured by men range from simple objects, like eating utensils and pots to more complex ones, like musical instruments, even though these items are small and portable and could as easily have been produced by women. According to this theory, because men more often procure lumber (although rarely firewood), it costs less in terms of time, effort, and energy for them to transform wood from its raw to its finished state, as a useful object, than it would for a woman to finish the task.

Another theory, known as expendability theory, proposes an explanation for men's propensity to perform work that is commonly seen as perilous. According to this theory, such work is assigned to men because individual men are more "expendable" than individual women. It is women who gestate the unborn while caring for young children who need protection. Because of the biological requirements of sexual reproduction, fewer men than women are needed for the successful reproduction of the group. This is evidenced by the many societies which are organized polygynously, that is, in which men can have more than one wife.

What has come to be called the child care compatibility hypothesis, first put forth by Judith K. Brown in 1970, suggests that women's contribution to subsistence work depends on the compatibility of the subsistence activity with child care. Women are much more likely to be entrusted with child care than men are, and thus are less mobile than men. Small children can be carried only so far; thus women often concentrate on tasks such as cooking, food preparation or storage, and agricultural work, which allow them to remain close to home.

Another hypothesis explores the possibility that fertility may be a factor in the sexual division of labor. Patricia Draper has studied the !Kung San of southern Africa and the division of labor by gender among men and women among this group of (former) gatherer-hunters. Draper reports that environmental conditions in southern Africa are harsh, because of especially poor growing conditions and scarce water in the hottest months. The !Kung say that a woman carrying a child on her back as well as in her belly has a "permanent backache" and that allowing this situation would be foolish. Draper argues that lactating women with small children rarely become pregnant, owing to the suppression of fertility brought about by both breast feeding and amenorrhea, which is caused by extensive physical activities. On the savannah, !Kung women were constantly on the move in the search for food and water, and, as a result, experienced extremely low fertility. Hence, one explanation for women remaining closer to home and walking less may be the increased likelihood of conception. This is borne out by the much higher fertility levels of agricultural societies relative to migratory ones.

Cross-Cultural Variation in the Sexual Division of Labor

Some societies have practically no gender division of labor at all or have fluid gender divisions. According to a one study of the Agta of the Philippines, women regularly form hunting groups to track deer and wild pigs, and this activity is an important part of women's contribution to group subsistence. Turnbull's classic study of the Mbuti

pygmies of the Congo (1968) indicates that the Mbuti have almost no gender division of labor. The Mundurucu of Brazil (Murphy, 1974) have a marked gender division of labor, with men living in men's houses in the center of the village, and women living with their children in separate houses. In addition to separate living quarters, each gender has separate working activities and spends the majority of its time apart. There is also a high degree of "gender parallelism" among the Yoruba of Nigeria. Historically, women were chiefs and cult leaders and could participate in royal councils and operate as market officials or as heads of craft guilds. Among the Yoruba, both women and men participated in every aspect of life, and this social structure still affects rituals, economics, politics, and the family.

Class and Status Variables in the Sexual Division of Labor: The Andean Case

Deere and Leon de Leal (1985) distinguish between production and reproduction in regard to the sexual division of labor. They stress that while most women still do tend toward human reproduction (defined as the reproduction of labor power on a daily basis and the reproduction of labor power over time, as in child rearing), the sexual division of labor in productive activities (that is, work) may vary by class, status, position, region, and time. In other words, the division of labor by sex is not merely culturally determined but is tempered by the material conditions of production.

Examining three cases in Andean agriculture in highland Colombia and Peru, Deere and Leon de Leal found differential results of the mode of production. In the first case, a region of "noncapitalist" production, women predominated in tasks centering on the care of animals and in services relating to agricultural production, such as cooking for field hands who did the actual agricultural work. Here, only half the women became involved in agricultural processing activities themselves, and even fewer did any agricultural work. In the region of "advanced capitalist" penetration—the second case—women were much more likely to market agricultural produce and it was even rarer for them to participate in agricultural work. In the region of mixed capitalist and noncapitalist production—the third case—elements of both systems were present, with women involved in all kinds of productive work. Even when men and women ostensibly did the same things, there was a technical division of labor within tasks. In planting, for example, men dug holes in the ground and women put in the plants.

As is often the case, both men and women placed most importance on men's tasks rather than women's. In fact, both sexes considered women to be merely "helping out." This contrasts with another agrarian society: Friedl (1962) reported that in Vasilika, a Greek peasant community, neither men's nor women's work had any prestige. Both were regarded as "distasteful" but necessary, and either sex would do the work of the other with no shame attached.

The undervaluation of women's labor highlights an ambiguity often present in the theoretical relationship between the sexual division of labor and women's subordination. Is women's lower position a result or a cause of the division of labor by sex? Deere and Leon de Leal argue for an examination of the material conditions of production in answering such a question. In the Andes, among groups engaging in capitalist relations of production, women are paid much less than men because they are segregated by sex, in this case, in tobacco processing and textile production. Giving women the most labor-intensive yet "low-productivity" jobs seems to justify paying them less. Hence, capitalist relations of production put women and men in different economic positions. By contrast, poverty, especially rural poverty, seems to be something of an equalizer—when farming becomes less important as a family economic strategy, women seem to engage in it more. Thus poverty may be a factor in breaking down established sex roles.

Conclusion

Although the advent of new technology and ways of working has altered the kinds of work that men and women do, sometimes making it possible for women to engage in strenuous and dangerous work formerly reserved for men, a gender division of labor to persists. Advancing technology has not been a social leveler as is sometimes thought. Three decades of feminism and as many cohorts of feminist anthropologists, sociologists, theorists, and activists have attempted to explain why this is the case. The depiction of tasks as "natural" to one gender or another within cultural settings accounts for continued gender inequality in the workplace in many cases. However, continued differential pay scales for men and women in most societies are more difficult to explain, though they suggest the differential worth of men and women in many advanced capitalist societies. Such analyses leave many unanswered questions but are critical for the eradication of persistent inequality.

See Also

AGRICULTURE; BIOLOGICAL DETERMINISM; DOMESTIC LABOR; DOMESTIC TECHNOLOGY; ECONOMY: OVERVIEW; GLOBALIZATION; HOUSEWORK; PATRIARCHY: DEVELOPMENT; WORK: *specific topics*

References and Further Reading

Anker, Richard. 1998. *Gender and jobs: Sex segregation of occupations in the world.* Geneva: International Labour Organization (ILO).

Blau, Francine, Mariane A. Ferber, and Anne E. Winkler, eds. 1999. *The economics of women, men and work.* Upper Saddle River, N.J.: Prentice Hall.

Deere, Carmen, and Magdalena Leon de Leal. 1985. *Women in Andean agriculture.* 2nd ed. Washington, D.C.: Internationation Labor Office.

Dex, Shirley. 1985. *The sexual division of work: Conceptual revolutions in the social sciences.* New York: St. Martin's.

Friedl, Ernestine. 1962. *Vasilika: A village in modern Greece.* New York: Holt, Rinehart and Winston.

Guyer, Jane I. 1984. *Family and farm in southern Cameroon.* Boston, Mass.: Boston University, African Studies Center.

Kleinberg, S. Jay. 1998. *Retrieving women's history: Changing perceptions of the role of women in politics and society.* New York: Berg.

Leacock, Eleanor. 1981. *Myths of male dominance: Collected articles on women cross-culturally.* New York: Monthly Review.

Mies, Maria. 1998. *Patriarchy and accumulation on a world scale: Women in the new international division of labour.* London: Zed.

Murphy, Yolanda. 1974. *Women of the forest.* New York: Columbia University Press.

Peoples, James G., and Garrick Bailey. 1996. *Humanity: An introduction to cultural anthropology.* 4th ed., Minneapolis-St. Paul, Minn.: West.

Safa, Helen. 1995. *The myth of the male breadwinner: Women and industrialization in the Caribbean.* Boulder, Col.: Westview.

Smith, Adam. 1965. *An inquiry into the nature and causes of the wealth of nations.* New York: Modern Library. (Originally published 1778.)

Towery, Matt A. 1998. *Powerchicks: How women will dominate America.* Atlanta, Ga.: Longstreet.

Turnbull, Colin. 1968. *The forest people.* New York: Simon and Schuster.

Wallerstein, Immanuel. 1974. *The modern world system.* New York: Academic.

Maria Ramona Hart

DIVORCE

Divorce reflects societal changes in morality, economics, mobility, and gender roles. The same issues appear worldwide: attribution of blame for ending a marriage, acceptable grounds for divorce, distribution of assets and liabilities, spousal support, and responsibility for children.

Statistics

In the last decades of the twentieth century, the divorce rate rose substantially in most western countries, with the highest rates found in the United States and the Scandinavian countries, followed by Canada and the other western and eastern European countries. In Sweden and the United States (according to some methods of counting) one of two marriages ends in divorce. In the Baltic states divorce is common; Estonia equals its Scandinavian neighbors; and in some countries of the former Soviet Union more than one-third of marriages end in divorce. In the Caucasus and the central Asian states, divorce is less common.

In the countries of southern Europe divorce has increased moderately since 1980. In Malta divorce is illegal; in Ireland it was legalized in 1995. In Greece and Portugal divorce rates did not exceed 20 percent until the late 1990s.

In Albania, Bulgaria, Poland, Romania, and Yugoslavia, divorce rates are moderate and fairly stable—10 to 20 percent of marriages end in divorce—whereas in the former Czechoslovakia, the former German Democratic Republic, and Hungary, rates rose steadily from 1980 to 1990 before stabilizing at about 30 percent (United Nations, 1995).

Reasons for Divorce

In general, women do not divorce casually or for trivial reasons. Although women's economic status, family arrangements, educational attainment, cultural background, and personal preferences vary greatly, their reasons for divorcing can sometimes be traced to the hardships that contemporary marriages cause women through the different pleasures, burdens, and duties husbands and wives experience in their roles. Some women are frustrated by their husbands' attempts to control their time, their friends, or their work. Other women are angry that their husbands, who insist on their own point of view, do not listen to their wives or value their opinions. Even women who do not directly experience violence in their marriages report being intimidated by their husbands' anger. Violence (physical and emotional) is a factor, and so are hard living (alcohol and drug abuse, husbands' "running around" and absent-ing themselves from the home), disproportionate child care and family responsibilities, and financial inequality. Many women report being left for other women.

Consequences of Divorce

Divorced women often suffer diminished returns on their marital investment as a result of legal, social, and economic policies. Children, too, are financial and emotional victims of divorce (U.S. Census Bureau, 1999). Once male parents are separated from their wives, they often avoid taking economic responsibility for their children. Child custody agreements may become a battleground for former spouses; the Hague Convention on International Child Abduction of 1986 establishes legal rights and procedures for the return of children abducted across national boundaries.

What distinguishes a marriage that lasts from one that does not is not how good or bad the marriage is but how tolerable the partners find it. How a marriage ends affects a woman's assessment of her divorce. A woman who is left by her husband against her wishes may see herself as having lost a major opportunity because of divorce, whereas a woman whose ex-husband was abusive may feel that divorce has given her the opportunity to pursue a more fulfilling life.

Despite the obstacles (social, religious, practical, and financial), women continue to pursue divorce because changes in thinking must be accompanied by action to change reality. Wives today have options that were unavailable to their mothers and grandmothers. Now, a woman in a difficult marriage can say, "No, I do not need to live this way, and I will not do it anymore. This is not right."

See Also

ADULTERY; DOMESTIC VIOLENCE; MARRIAGE: OVERVIEW; MARRIAGE: REMARRIAGE

References and Further Reading

Boston Women's Health Book Collective. 1992. *The new our bodies, ourselves.* New York: Simon and Schuster.

Engel, Margorie. 1994. *Divorce help sourcebook: Resources and references for legal, financial, and personal issues.* Detroit: Gale Research/Visible Ink.

United Nations. 1995. *The world's women: 1995 trends and statistics.* Social Statistics and Indicators, Series K, No. 12. New York: United Nations.

United States Census Bureau, U.S. Department of Commerce. 1999. Child support for custodial mothers and fathers: 1995. In *Current Population Reports,* Series P-60, No. 196, March 1999.

Margorie Engel

DOMESTIC CONSUMPTION

See HOUSEHOLDS: DOMESTIC CONSUMPTION.

DOMESTIC LABOR

Domestic labor refers to unpaid work carried out by household members for themselves and one another. This can include both routine work (such as cooking, cleaning, and washing) and nonroutine work (such as gardening, do-it-yourself tasks, and car maintenance). However, the term *domestic labor* is frequently used to denote routine unpaid work carried out by women for their families. The activities commonly associated with domestic labor are found in all societies, with women being assigned to similar types of tasks in all contexts. In preindustrial societies, however, although a strict gender division of tasks may exist, productive and reproductive tasks are not separated in time or space. Consequently, women's domestic activities count as work. It is only in industrial societies where the place of employment is separated from the household that women's household activities have not been defined traditionally as work. Indeed, the concept of domestic labor was originally developed within women's studies and the feminist movement in the 1960s and 1970s in North America and Europe as part of a strategy to emphasize both the practical significance of women's work in the home to the functioning society and the economy and, more important, the theoretical significance of women's responsibility for this labor in explaining their oppression.

Methodological Problems Relating to Domestic Labor

The methodological problems relating to the study of domestic labor concern how to measure and evaluate the quantity of this work and how to discover the nature and extent of the gender division of domestic labor. A principal source of such information is the data produced by the large-scale time-budget studies carried out sporadically in a number of European and North American countries, for example, Britain, France, the United States, and Canada (Gershuny and Jones, 1986). A time budget study is a technique for data collection whereby the research participants complete diaries chronicling the number of minutes spent on a range of activities. From these diaries, it is possible to calculate time spent on domestic labor. Similar results have been found in all the countries concerned.

Two main results have come from time-budget studies. First, these studies have found that at least as much time is spent on domestic labor as is spent on employment. This testifies to the fact that the family has not lost its pro-ductive functions under capitalism. Second, the studies have found that women continue to spend much more time engaged in domestic labor than men do, even when they also spend long hours in employment. Even when a broad definition of domestic labor is used (encompassing traditionally masculine tasks), employed women still spend roughly twice as much time on domestic tasks as employed men. Time-budget studies have shown unequivocally that the gender division of domestic labor is far from equal. When it comes to understanding women's and men's differing relationship to domestic labor, however, measurements in time of this kind have a number of shortcomings, which obscure the true extent of the domestic labor burden for women. First, time-budget studies often do not take into account the possibility that an individual will carry out two tasks simultaneously. Undertaking multiple activities is a characteristic of women's domestic labor (for example, a woman may be recorded as at leisure even though she is minding the children while watching television). Second, time-budget studies can measure an individual's commitment in time only to a concrete activity. They cannot capture the time and effort involved in planning and managing one's own and others' activities. This work often falls on the shoulders of women. Third, women's domestic labor cannot be measured in time in the same way that employment can because a woman's relationship to her family is not the same as an employee's relationship to his or her company. Employees are financially compensated for specific tasks completed or for a specific amount of time spent "at work." In contrast, women must be permanently available to their families and must fit their activities around their families' needs. For a woman, even time not actually spent in the service of the family may still be constrained time. Fourth, women's caring and emotional work undertaken for the benefit of husbands and children cannot be calculated in time alone.

Given the vast amounts of time devoted to domestic labor, it is not surprising that the absence of any reference to this activity (and thus to the majority of women's work) in the models for national accounting has been questioned by some women researchers. In some third world countries there have been attempts to calculate the importance of "self-provisioning" work, which crosscuts women's domestic labor; but in the industrialized nations (as of this writing) only one study—conducted in France in the 1980s by Chadeau and Fouquet (1981)—has made a serious attempt to evaluate domestic labor in monetary terms. More recent literature has taken up the call for domestic labor to be valued in this way (James, 1994; Luxton, 1997). Chadeau and Fouquet tested three methods of calculation, which they applied to time-budget data collected for France for 1975. Two methods are based on a principle called "lack of necessity to spend," and calculate what households would have to pay a third party if they substituted paid goods and services for their own domestic labor. The first method applies the salary paid to a domestic servant to the time spent in all domestic tasks, regardless of their nature, while the second applies the salary rates of different types of worker depending on the specific activities undertaken. The third method uses "opportunity cost" model to calculate what household members could earn if they spent the time that they spend on domestic labor in paid employment instead.

Although more time was spent on domestic labor in 1975 in France than was spent on employment, when evaluated in monetary terms, domestic labor was worth only one-half of the gross national product (GNP) according to the first and third methods (which use women's wage rates as a basis of calculation) and two-thirds of GNP according to the second method (which uses wage rates current for men as well as women). One major problem occurs in all these methods of calculation: by using equivalent values borrowed from the formal labor market to assess the "worth" of domestic labor, such calculations reflect the lowly status of women in the labor market and the low value placed on their routine domestic activities in society at large.

Until the early 1970s in North American and Europe, not only was the economic importance of domestic labor ignored, but the relationship between women and domestic labor was deemed natural within mainstream sociology. The dominant view of the family was Talcott Parsons's, in which women's role as homemaker was seen as functional, and thus indispensable, to the stability of society (1955). From the 1970s onward, the validity of conceiving of the family in this way came under fire, particularly in feminist circles. From then on, it was argued that understanding why women maintain the relationship they do to domestic labor was a key to understanding women's oppression. In the late twentieth century, the major debates surrounding domestic labor have focused on explaining why women have come to be responsible for it and what role domestic labor plays in the functioning of society.

Domestic Labor—Productive or Unproductive?

With the arrival of the feminist movement in the late 1960s and early 1970s, Marxist-inspired feminist theories began to question the lack of concern within orthodox Marxism for women's oppression, and the inability of Marxism to explain women's relationship to domestic labor. The principal work on women in capitalism until that time was Engels's analysis of the family (1972, originally 1884). Engels contended that the family was an anachronism that was marginal to the survival of capitalism, because it was a part of the social superstructure and, therefore, had no material justification. Marxist feminists set out to explain that women's oppression within capitalism does indeed have a material and not merely an ideological basis. That material basis is domestic labor. Indeed, the study of domestic labor in the early 1970s was very much a part of feminists' struggle to find an identity apart from socialism and Marxist structuralist analysis, which had sidelined women's particular concerns and problems.

Marxist feminists argued that capital depends for its survival on the unpaid work performed within the family by women, because the role of women as reproducers of the workforce and as a "reserve army of labor" is essential and not marginal to the extraction of surplus value. Women's domestic labor is productive of certain goods and services that are necessary for the maintenance and reproduction of labor power—that is, the clothing and feeding of the current generation of workers for capital and the procreation and education of the next generation.

Within Marxist feminism, however, there was a debate that took up much time and energy during the 1970s, concerning whether women's domestic labor was unproductive or productive in a Marxist sense. Some argued that domestic labor is unproductive because, to be productive in the original Marxist sense, an activity must fulfill both of two criteria: first, it must be exchanged on the market against a wage; second, it must work directly with capital's means of production to produce commodities that have a calculable exchange value from which surplus value is directly extracted. Domestic labor fulfills neither of these criteria. Domestic labor produces only "use values" for consumption in the home, not exchange values or surplus value. Because housewives are not employed by capital, their contribution to profit, though necessary, is not direct. Women's production of use values is outside the exchange of labor for wages, although it is economically part of the creation of surplus value (see, for example, contributions to Barker and Allen, 1978).

Other Marxist feminists realized, however, that labeling domestic labor "unproductive" relegated it to a place of secondary importance behind wage labor and consequently once again made women's oppression a side issue of the class struggle. These women argued that domestic labor was indeed productive. The initiators of the "productive labor thesis" were Dalla Costa and James (1972), who contended that the main product of domestic labor,

407

the human being, is no different in nature from any other commodity. Women's domestic labor produces something that is sold to capitalists—namely, labor power—even if women have no legal ownership of it. Domestic labor is therefore productive.

Out of this "productive labor thesis" grew the "wages for housework" campaign. This school of thought rejected the idea of liberation through work (Dalla Costa and James, 1972), because it would mean that women should merely become wage slaves alongside men. Because the only difference between wage labor and domestic labor is said to be that domestic labor is unpaid, feminists instead should demand wages for housework, which would show women's oppression to be a function of capitalism. Wages for housework would place the burden of reproduction on the shoulders of the oppressors. The fight for wages for housework was therefore intended to be a part of the class struggle because, in paying such a wage, the state and capitalists would incur reproduction as a direct cost. However, the "wages for housework" campaign never drew widespread support, because on a practical level it coincided with right-wing proposals to entice women back into the home.

Women As Domestic Laborers— Servants of Capitalism or Patriarchy?

Other theoretical perspectives have questioned Marxism further by asking whether domestic labor serves capitalism or patriarchy or a combination of the two, and whether in fact domestic labor is part of the capitalist mode of production, the "patriarchal" mode of production, or both.

Not all socialist women argue that domestic labor is first and foremost functional to capital, nor do all agree that there is only one mode of production—the capitalist mode. In the middle to late 1970s, a school of thought developed that could be described as feminist-Marxist, which challenged Marxist-feminist analyses to explain why it is women and not men who undertake domestic work. Marxist-feminist analysis tells us only that domestic labor is essential to capitalism, not why *women* should carry out that domestic labor. The feminist Marxists' answer to this question is that women's oppression and domestic labor are situated at the point of interaction between patriarchy and capitalism.

For this type of feminism, the fact that domestic labor does not fit into the criteria set out to describe wage labor—and thus constitutes reproduction as opposed to production—indicates that women's domestic responsibilities need to be examined as part of the patriarchal sys-

tem. In this school of thought, the benefits derived from women's unpaid work in the home by men as well as by capitalism are a proper cause for concern. In this analysis women (and their domestic labor) belong to men first and capital second. Women's confinement to the domestic role puts them in their specifically disadvantaged position. Women's responsibility for domestic labor means that they are not free to sell their labor power on the market. Taken to its logical conclusion, capitalism would have freed women from the home in order to put men's and women's labor power into complete competition. This did not happen because capitalism had to accommodate the patriarchal social structure that predated it—for example, by paying "family wages" and by introducing regulations regarding child and female labor and laws preventing wives from seeking employment without their husbands' consent (Hartmann, 1981, and Kuhn and Wolpe, 1978).

Many of these propositions are not questioned by a further school of thought that can be described as social constructionist radical feminism. Its major exponent is the French theorist Christine Delphy (1984). Delphy's theoretical position derives from her political perspective, which seeks to cast women's struggle against patriarchy as independent of the proletarian struggle against capitalism. For her, domestic labor is not a mode of reproduction within the capitalist system, nor is patriarchy a historic concept that has influenced the structure of capitalism. Instead, patriarchy develops historically, having, like capitalism, a mode of production. Delphy calls this the domestic mode of production, in which women's unpaid labor for the family is exploited by men. The domestic mode of production is embodied in the social institution of marriage. It is through marriage that men appropriate women's domestic labor. The mechanism by which this appropriation takes place is very different from that which exists within the capitalist mode of production, in that the wife's time is appropriated as a whole by her husband. In return, the wife is "kept." She is not given a set sum per hour for her domestic labor, as an employee would be given for his or her wage labor.

Neoclassical Explanation of Women's Responsibility for Domestic Labor

All of the foregoing explanations of women's relationship to domestic labor can be termed *structuralist* in the sense that they perceive society in terms of conflicting social groups, the existence and relative power of which rest on and characterize a particular social structure. In contrast, neoclassicists reject the view that domestic labor is the material basis of women's oppression. Instead, they see women's responsibility for domestic labor in terms of "rational choices made under constraint" by couples who are attempting to maximize their "utility."

It was a member of the Chicago school in the United States—G. S. Becker—who first developed a neoclassical conceptualization of women's responsibility for domestic labor. Before Becker's new home economics theory, the microeconomic model of the offer of labor had been based on the idea that an individual chooses between more work and more leisure. Thus, women's seeking employment in increasing numbers could be explained by microeconomists only as a change of preference for work as opposed to leisure. This seemed to contradict the social values of the time. To explain this phenomenon, Becker introduced the factor of "household production" to his analyses. The combination of market goods and household time is "household production." Consequently, gender roles within the couple could be theorized as a division of labor and a choice between market production or domestic production.

Applying Becker's model, microeconomists analyze how couples choose rationally (or intentionally) to divide their combined time between professional work and domestic labor according to the economic circumstances in which they find themselves and their own abilities and preferences. Becker asserts that women specialize in domestic labor when their "opportunity costs" of working in the market are too great—that is, when the cost of paying for market alternatives to their domestic production is not adequately covered by what they could earn in a job. Husbands and wives specialize in professional and domestic labor respectively when the husband can earn more on the market than his wife and when the wife cannot cover the costs of running the home with her potential salary. It should be emphasized that in this model it is assumed that men and women have a common utility function. In other words, they have common interests to which end they specialize in different forms of activity and exchange their specialized skills. All the while, they attempt to maximize the satisfaction derived from their efforts by mobilizing their forces in market and domestic production in the most efficient way possible.

The Role of Biological Reproduction in Linking Women to Domestic Labor

The extent to which progress can occur in women's situation with regard to domestic labor depends on one's assessment of the significance of women's childbearing role in determining their responsibility for domestic labor and, ultimately, their social and economic status. Within a neoclassical framework, women's role in childbearing is a significant factor. Neoclassicists do not attempt to eliminate the physiological factor of having children in explaining women's position. They see women as having an absolute advantage over men in specializing in domestic labor because of their childbearing role.

The various types of feminist analysis have sought to explain women's relationship to the family as being purely socioeconomic rather than biological, but not all these theories actually manage to "erase" women's identity as a biological group in order to replace it with a socioeconomic identity. One of the basic difficulties with which Marxist feminists have struggled is that it is easy enough to explain the vital importance of the reproduction of the labor force to capitalism and the logic of carrying out this work within the family, but how does one explain why capital needs women and not men to perform this labor? The implicit answer is that reproduction is compatible with the biological role of childbearing. It is implied that biological differences led to the exclusion of women from production and their confinement in the role of reproducers of the workforce in the first place.

Feminist Marxists acknowledge that women constitute a group economically exploited by men as well as by capital, but their analyses of women's situation with regard to domestic labor still have some biological undertones. They base their theories on the possibility of differentiating between those tasks and social relations relevant to the production of goods and services and those that concern the reproduction of human beings. What, however, is reproduction as opposed to production if it is not those tasks and social relations that are the prolongation of childbearing?

Perhaps it is inevitable that, despite the considerable progress made in understanding the social relations of gender, "women" first and foremost is still perceived as a biological category, and the explanation of gender difference and a gender division of domestic labor cannot escape this cultural assumption. However, Delphy's radical feminism perhaps comes nearest to escaping it. Delphy argues that women's difference must be discussed in material, historical, and political context. Then, difference is exposed as synonymous with women's oppression. This is a theory of women's oppression based on the notion of "sex classes" with men as a class benefiting from the oppression of women as a class. Delphy refuses to describe the situation of women as being based on their exclusion from the market and production because this would imply that women are something other than a socially constructed category—that is, a product of a certain set of social relations. Just as the social class of the proletariat does not exist outside its relationship to the means of production, neither does the gender class of women exist outside its place in the patriarchal mode of production. Delphy rejects the dichotomy of production and reproduction, conceptualizing society instead as being composed of two separate modes of production.

Is the Division of Domestic Labor Changing?

A crucial question of the contemporary period is to what extent women's increased participation in the labor force, and the relative financial power that this participation has given them within the couple, has led to a more equal gender division of domestic labor. It is clear that men's involvement in domestic labor has not increased to match women's involvement in the labor market. However, some argue that the small changes recorded in men's domestic activities are evidence of a "lagged adaptation" of the gender division of domestic labor to women's role in employment (Gershuny, Godwin, and Jones, 1994). This argument suggests that adjustment to work roles takes place not through a short-term redistribution of responsibilities but through an extended process of household negotiation (and perhaps reconstitution) extending over many years and, indeed, across generations. Others argue that the continued unequal division of domestic labor is a sign that patriarchy is now located more than ever in the private sphere of the family. If patriarchy is viewed as a set of social relations in which men dominate women, then one way for patriarchy to adapt to women's newfound independence on the employment market is to ensure that patriarchal relations persist within the home (Delphy and Leonard, 1992).

See Also

CAREGIVERS; CHILD CARE; DIVISION OF LABOR; ECONOMICS: FEMINIST CRITIQUES; FAMILY STRUCTURES; HOUSEHOLDS: POLITICAL ECONOMY; HOUSEWORK; MARRIAGE: OVERVIEW; MARXISM; WORK: FEMINIST THEORIES

References and Further Reading

Barker, D., and Shiela Allen, eds. 1978. *Dependence and exploitation in work and marriage.* Harlow, U.K.: Longman.

Becker, Gary S. 1981. *A treatise on the family.* Cambridge, Mass.: Harvard University Press.

Bittman, M., G. Matheson, and G. Meagher. 1999. The changing boundary between home and market: Australian trends in outsourcing domestic labour. *Work Employment and Society* 13 (2): 249–273.

Chadeau, Ann, and Annie Fouquet. 1981. Peut-on mesurer le travail domestique? *Economie et Statistique* 136: 29–42.

Dalla Costa, Mariarosa, and Selma James. 1972. *The power of women and the subversion of the community.* Bristol, U.K.: Falling Wall.

Delphy, Christine. 1984. *Close to home.* London: Hutchinson.

Delphy, Christine, and Diane Leonard. 1992. *Familiar exploitation.* Cambridge: Polity.

Engels, Frederick. 1972. *The origin of the family, private property and the state.* London: Lawrence and Wishart. (Originally published 1884.)

Gershuny, Jonathan, and Sally Jones. 1986. *Time use in seven countries 1961–1984.* Shankill: European Foundation for the Improvement of Living and Working Conditions.

Gershuny, Jonathan, Michael Godwin, and Sally Jones. 1994. The domestic labour revolution: A process of lagged adaptation. In Michael Anderson, Frank Bechhofer, and Jonathan Gershuny, eds., *The social and political economy of the household,* 151–197. Oxford: Oxford University Press.

Hartmann, Heidi. 1981. *The unhappy marriage of Marxism and feminism.* London: Pluto.

James, Selma. 1994. Women's unwaged work: The heart of the informal sector. In M. Evans, ed., *The woman question* London: Sage.

Jarvis, H. 1999. The tangled webs we weave: Household strategies to coordinate home and work. *Work, Employment, and Society* 13(2): 225–247.

Kuhn, Annette, and Anne M. Wolpe. 1978. *Feminism and materialism: Women and modes of production.* London: Routledge and Kegan Paul.

Luxton, M. 1997. The UN, women, and household labor: Measuring and valuing unpaid work. *Women's Studies International Forum* 20(3): 431–439.

Oakely, Ann. 1974. *The sociology of housework.* Oxford: Martin Robinson.

Parsons, Talcott. 1955. *Family socialization and interaction process.* Glencoe, Ill.: Free Press.

Riley, P. J., and G. Kiger. 1999. Moral discourse on domestic labor: Gender, power, and identity in families. *Social Science Journal* 36(3): 541–548.

Windebank, Jan. 1994. Explaining women's relationship to domestic labour: Structuralism, individualism, and empiricism. *Women's Studies International Forum* 17(5): 499–509.

Jan Windebank

DOMESTIC SCIENCE

See EDUCATION: DOMESTIC SCIENCE AND HOME ECONOMICS.

DOMESTIC TECHNOLOGY

Domestic technology is the application of scientific principles and engineering methods from industry to develop mechanized tools for household work. It includes larger appliances such as stoves, refrigerators, clothes washers and dryers; smaller appliances such as vacuum cleaners, coffeemakers, and food processors; and underlying technology such as sewer systems, electricity, and indoor plumbing (Wajcman, 1992). Domestic technology was first mass-produced and distributed in the United States and Britain between 1890 and 1920 (Strasser, 1982). Although there have been technological developments for homes in other countries, much of the technology adopted in the last two centuries seems to be a result of the more industrialized, capitalistic influence of countries in the "North," specifically the United States and Britain.

The development and widespread influence of domestic technology have a much more complex and culturally embedded history than may at first appear. As the feminist scholar Cheris Kramarae pointed out, technology includes more than its products; it is a tool that regulates social relations (1988: 2). Just as technology helped usher in major social change with the industrial revolution in the United States and Britain in the late 1800s to the 1900s, it also helped bring about major social change in the home, redefining presumed ideal gender roles for women and men. These changes had profound effects, particularly on women assigned to the home by these gender roles; however, domestic technology is not commonly included in historical accounts of technological development and the industrial revolution because of its inferior social status (Cockburn, 1997).

The Promise of Efficiency

When domestic technology is discussed, the emphasis is commonly on claims of efficiency and the liberation of women from mundane tasks. Surveys from the United States, Britain, Canada, Norway, Denmark, and the Netherlands from the 1960s to the 1980s found that, in some cases, technology made work more efficient (e.g., cooking and cleaning) but additional technology created new tasks (e.g., ironing), and studies of child rearing in these countries found that demands on women rose with the influx of technology (Wajcman, 1992). In general, domestic technology has not liberated women from housework. Technology or no technology, women world-wide, particularly poor women, have been the primary caretakers and homemakers, whether they have paid jobs outside the home or not.

As noted above, technology has made some jobs, such as laundering and cooking, less labor-intensive. One need only look to the lives of many women in countries of the "South," where technology and wealth are limited, to illustrate this point. In these countries, wood is one of the most important sources of renewable fuel energy, and women and children are primarily responsible for collecting it in most of the countries of that region. As wooded areas in Africa, parts of Asia, and Latin America become increasingly barren, owing to industry, collecting wood has become even more labor-intensive. In parts of Sudan, for example, the time needed to gather firewood was multiplied by four in the 1980s, consuming the majority of one's day (Agarwal, 1992: 267). While industry has contributed to this problem, collaborative technological development has helped ease many women's lives in villages of northwest India. The woman of the house works with the builder to design a stove that meets her home's unique needs. The result has been more efficient technology.

This type of partnership in developing domestic technology has not happened in any commercially successful way in most industrialized cities and countries. For example, in a study of clothing washing machine technology in Barcelona, Spain, Carme Alemany Gomez found that newer designs were guided more by production savings than by any concern to ease the work involved in using the machine, which required stooping, bending, and kneeling—efforts a top loading design does not entail. In an extensive study from 1988–1992 in eight European countries, women researchers found an almost complete absence of women among design engineers. There were no women involved in developing the food processor, washing machine, or central vacuum system (Cockburn and Fürst-Dilíc, 1994). Technology originally intended for industry has typically been adapted for the home by men, and is not as efficient as it might be if the women using the products had been involved in the design.

The Selling of Predominant Social Ideology

Women have been involved in developing alternative domestic technology, but most of these developments have not survived. For example, commercial steam laundries were successful in Britain and the United States during the later 1800s until the electric home washer was introduced in 1914. As the cost of home washers decreased and household experts in women's magazines cautioned women not to trust their delicate clothing to commercial laundries, the popularity of commercial laundries declined. The same problem occurred with attempts to run commercial laundries where neighbors or paid workers did the work. Eventually these laundries could not compete with commercial coin-operated laundries, and they were also criticized as being socialist (Cowan, 1983).

It was well into the twentieth century before domestic technology became affordable for working-class people. Today, U.S. kitchens contain from 12 to 20 motorized appliances, only one of which—the refrigerator—is used continuously (Wajcman, 1992). Advertisers helped create a demand for such goods by selling new tasks for women (such as family transportation), sentimentalizing housework (a "good" mother starches and presses all clothes), and raising the standards of housework. Domestic technology became a status symbol, a sign of affluence and of a well-kept home (Cowan, 1983). Families across social classes wanted to be the first in their neighborhood to own an electric washing machine, which promised convenience and independence for nuclear families.

Technology-Prescribed Gender and Sexuality

Household technology and the predominant social ideology accompanying it helped to solidify the idea that the proper place of women was in the home. Gender roles—prescribed expectations for women's and men's place in society—became more dichotomous, rigid, and unequal. Men belonged in the public sphere, where more valued, better-paid production occurred. The private sphere was men's leisure place and women, as heterosexual mates, were responsible for making this a haven. Women belonged in the private sphere, where productivity was presumed not to exist, since food, clothing, and furniture were predominantly made by industry. The home, and thus women, became more dependent on others owing to the image of being a consumer only.

In reality, the public versus the private sphere was a false dichotomy. Minority and poor women around the world have a long history of working in both spheres. Domestic workers' paid employment (public sphere) is someone else's private sphere (the home; see, for example, Martens and Mitter, 1994). The split between public and private life represented predominant stereotypes of appropriate behavior for women and men, as defined by white middle-class U.S. and British standards, to which many of

the less privileged came to aspire. Furthermore, what happened in the public sphere—technology and capitalism—greatly affected women's role in the home; the home was never a haven from external influence. Not only was domestic technology a tool designed in the "public" sphere; it also designated the user (Cockburn and Fürst-Dilíc, 1994) as well as the user's gender identity and sexual orientation. Moreover, the concept of public versus private sphere imposed other images of necessary, complementary relationships: woman-man, wife-husband, and homemaker-breadwinner. These helped legitimize the unequal status of women.

This emphasis on separate spheres and women's place was reinforced by advertisers and by household experts in popular advice literature. Susan Strasser, an American historian, argues in her classic book, *Never Done: A History of American Housework* (1982), that the advice literature reflects a predominant white middle-class social ideology about housework, "a set of doctrines about women's work" (xv). This trend in advice literature began in the 1800s and continued through the 1900s in what is called the "domestic science movement." Most notably, Christine Frederick, who wrote articles in women's magazines and popular books in the early 1900s, intertwined advice for women with the tenet that women's place was in the home and that women should approach housework like a science and a business. Women were told to apply the business principles of time management, technology, and work scheduling to create a loving home.

These ideas of the home and women's role in it remained more or less intact into the 1960s and early 1970s in the United States, where the isolated white middle-class suburban housewife was still a common phenomenon (Oakley, 1974). By the 1980s, women in the United States and Britain were entering paid employment in greater numbers than ever before, challenging the notion of public and private spheres; yet their responsibilities in the home did not seem to be changing at the same rate. Gender-stratified domestic technology was still occurring, as evidenced by the development of the microwave oven. This invention originated in the male-dominated British military; women had only minor roles in adapting the ovens for home use, though women were the targeted consumers as the ovens became popular in the 1980s (Cockburn and Ormrod, 1993).

In Australia in 1992 a national survey of 7,000 persons found that women did more of the unpaid labor in the home (133.3 million hours per week) than men (94.2 hours; Ironmonger, 1994). In the United States, by contrast, as women have increasingly entered employment outside the home, standards for cleanliness have been reduced and men in heterosexual relationships seem to be doing more housework. A telephone survey of 10,000 people in the United States found that men had increased their time cooking by 45 percent from 1965 to 1995 (1.6 hours per week) and cleaning by 240 percent (1.7 hours), and women had decreased their cooking time (50 percent, 4.6 hours) and cleaning time (7 percent, 6.7 hours). However, the comparative differences in workload in the home are still substantial (Dodge, 1999). Furthermore, Judy Wajcman (1992), a sociologist from Australia, has pointed out that as with children, the presence of men in the home increases the time women spend on housework. In contrast, men living with women, regardless of the ages and number of children, do less housework than men living alone.

Thus, at a time when domestic technology is most affordable, when more women are working in paid employment, and more women are presumably gaining purchasing power in the home, domestic technology has not significantly improved women's lives. Unequal gender relations continue to influence the development of technology, and technology reinforces unequal gender relations. History suggests that improvement would require a change in predominant white, capitalistic, patriarchal values.

See Also

AUTOMATION; CHILD CARE; EDUCATION: DOMESTIC SCIENCE AND HOME ECONOMICS; DOMESTIC LABOR; GENDER CONSTRUCTIONS IN THE FAMILY; FAMILY: POWER RELATIONS AND POWER STRUCTURES; HOUSEWORK; TECHNOLOGY; TECHNOLOGY: WOMEN AND DEVELOPMENT

References and Further Reading

Agarwal, Bina. 1992. Cold hearths and barren slopes: The woodfuel crisis in the third world. In Gill Kirkup and Laurie Smith Keller, eds., *Inventing women: Science. technology and gender,* 255–265. Cambridge: Polity.

Cockburn, Cynthia. 1997. Domestic technologies: Cinderella and the engineers. *Women's Studies International Forum 20* (3) 361–371.

——, and Susan Ormrod. 1993. *Gender and technology in the making.* London: Sage.

——, and Ruza Fürst-Dilíc, eds. 1994. *Bringing technology home: Gender and technology in a changing Europe.* Buckingham and Philadelphia, Pa.: Open University Press.

Cowan, Ruth Schwartz. 1983. *More work for mother: The ironies of household technology from the open hearth to the microwave.* New York: Basic Books.

Dodge, Susan. 1999. Men do their home work—sometimes. *Chicago Sun-Times,* NWS (27 July): 1.

Gomez, M. Carme Alemany. 1994. Bodies, machines, and male power. In Cynthia Cockburn and Ruza Fürst-Dilíc, eds., *Bringing technology home: Gender and technology in a changing Europe.* Buckingham and Philadelphia, Pa.: Open University Press.

Ironmonger, Duncan. 1994. The value of care and nurture provided by unpaid household work. *Family Matters 37,* 46–51.

Kramarae, Cheris. 1988. Gotta go, Myrtle, technology's at the door. In Cheris Kramarae, ed., *Technology and women's voices: Keeping in touch,* 1–14. New York: Routledge and Kegan Paul.

Leto, Victoria. 1988. "Washing, seems it's all we do": Washing technology and women's communication. In Cheris Kramarae, ed., *Technology and women's voices: Keeping in touch,* 161–179. New York: Routledge and Kegan Paul.

Martens, Margaret Hosmer, and Swatsi Mitter. 1994. *Women in trade unions: Organizing the unorganized.* Geneva: International Labor Office.

Oakley, Ann. 1974. *Woman's work: The housewife, past and present.* New York: Pantheon.

Strasser, Susan. 1982. *Never done: A history of American housework.* New York: Pantheon.

Wajcman, Judy. 1992. Domestic technology: Labour-saving or enslaving. In Gill Kirkup and Laurie Smith Keller, eds., *Inventing women: Science, technology, and gender,* 238–54. Cambridge: Polity.

——. 1991. *Feminism confronts technology.* Cambridge: Polity.

Victoria Leto DeFrancisco

DOMESTIC VIOLENCE

Domestic violence is a common term generally used to refer to physical violence perpetrated by one adult intimate partner against another.

Domestic violence describes the threat or use of physical force to coerce and control an adult intimate partner; it occurs in intimate relationships regardless of sexual orientation or marital status. "Two key aspects of violence are threat and control. That is, the effects of battering are seen not only in the actual physical assaults, but in how fear of being hurt is used to manipulate and control a [partner] via threats" (Adams, 1994: 12).

There are certainly other forms of abuse that occur within the immediate or extended family: the physical, sexual, and emotional abuse or neglect of children by parents or caretakers, or of the elderly by adult children or caretakers. It is not unusual to find these forms correlated with the abuse of the adult partner. However, these forms will not be discussed here.

Problems

Although the term *domestic violence* may describe the geography of the violence (that is, within the "domestic" sphere of the family), from the perspective of a feminist analysis its euphemistic tone presents at least two problems (Jones, 1994).

First, the term does not indicate agency: Who is doing what to whom? As with the term *battered woman,* the agent who chooses to use violence—in 95 percent of cases in the United States a man (Adams, 1994: 7)—is unidentified.

Also, the term obscures the gender of the victim and perpetrator so that the gendered nature of most domestic violence—the implementation of male dominance against a female partner—is not apparent.

A Feminist Analysis

A feminist analysis provides a behaviorally based typology of domestic violence (first developed by Anne Ganley, 1981). For assessment purposes, five forms of domestic violence have been identified.

1. Physical battering. This is the most visible and life-threatening form of domestic violence and usually establishes the basis for the coercive effect of psychological battering. Physical battering includes punching, kicking, grabbing, throwing a person against a wall or down the stairs, and the use of weapons such as guns, knives, bats, acid, automobiles, and so on, in such a way that serious physical injury or death may result.

2. Sexual battering. This is a subset of physical battering. Sexual battering involves forced sexual activity or physical violence directed at the genital area or breasts. It is often referred to as "marital rape," although the marital status of the individuals is not a determinative factor in the definition. Sexual battering often follows a physical attack on a partner and can therefore be confused with "love making" or "making up."

3. Psychological battering. Psychological battering is the pattern of psychological pressure used by an abuser to coerce and control the victim. Its efficacy is a function of the real threat of physical harm already introduced into the intimate relationship by the abuser. Psychological battering is analogous to brainwashing experienced by prisoners of war or hostages and can include forced isolation; impris-

onment in the home; denial of access to money, education, or health care; and so on.

4. Destruction of property. While the destruction of property is a common behavior for the abuser, it is not often identified as part of domestic violence. It is not a random destruction of property but rather the intentional destruction of the victim's possessions such as photos, books, family heirlooms, which were very important to her. The message of this behavior is clear: this time it is your property; next time it will be you. Thus the destruction of property contributes to psychological battering.

5. Harm to animals. Again, this is not random harm to animals (usually family pets) but harm directed at an animal who is important to the victim. The animal may be threatened, injured, or killed by the abuser. In a single act, then, the abuser may deprive his victim of a valued relationship while also communicating that her safety, too, is in jeopardy (Ganley, 1981: 8; Adams, 1995).

The value of these categories is the recognition of the interrelatedness of different kinds of behavior and the identification of phenomena that are not ordinarily perceived as domestic violence (such as destruction of property and harm to animals). Understanding battering behaviorally (that is, understanding that battering is behavior deliberately chosen by the abuser) transforms the traditional understanding of battering as a victim's problem (and thus a private problem) to a recognition that it is the abuser's problem—and thus a community problem. As a community problem, it requires aversive consequences for the abuser, established and enforced by the community, especially but not exclusively by the criminal justice system. Consequences are discussed below.

In its impact, domestic violence is analogous to political violence. As Judith Herman demonstrates in *Trauma and Recovery,* the consequences of domestic violence and political terror are very similar for the victim. One similarity is that the victim may subsequently suffer from posttraumatic stress disorder. The psychologist Alfred D. Biderman studied of brainwashed American soldiers and codified the results in a chart of coercion that was published by Amnesty International. In *Rape in Marriage,* Diana Russell argued that Biderman's chart could also be used to understand the effects of torture on wives, as well as those who are seen ordinarily as "hostages." This chart of coercion is now used in battered women's shelters to help them identify the controlling tactics of their partners.

Patriarchy and Domestic Violence

It appears that domestic violence is a common behavior for men in every contemporary patriarchal culture. Wherever there is a history of male domination in politics, economics, and religion, women report being abused by male partners. Feminists maintain that judicial, religious, and political leaders to respond very slowly articulations of women's experiences of domestic violence and that this is a predictable result of these institutions' patriarchal foundations. It is true that relatively few men actually exercise public power in class- and race-stratified patriarchal cultures, but men's self-interest in sustaining these structures is appealed to by the corresponding power permitted them in the domestic sphere, where their violence is often exercised with impunity.

That domestic violence is an enacting of male dominance is suggested by evidence from batterers themselves. Professionals in the United States who work with men who batter have observed that assaultive men believe stereotypes about male and female roles, and overidentify with the stereotypic male role. Because of this overidentification they feel that they have a right to control anyone with less power or status (such as women, children, and animals). As a result, "husband-dominance is also a predictor of child abuse" (Adams, 1994: 14). The inflexible adherence to traditional expectations for men in relation to women is one of the forces that make wives "appropriate victims" (Dobash and Dobash, 1979: 31–47).

Domestic Violence and Control

When a man hits a woman he has not lost control of himself; rather, he achieves and maintains control of his partner. *It is not so much what is done but what is accomplished.* Not only is he achieving and maintaining control but he is reminding the woman of her subordinate status in the world:

> Battering may be done intentionally to inflict suffering. For example, the man may physically punish a victim for thinking/behaving in a way that is contrary to the perpetrator's views. Or battering may be done simply to establish control in a conversation without intending harm. Regardless of the intent, the violence has the same impact on the victim and on the relationship. It establishes a system of coercive control. (Ganley, 1989:203)

Men who batter not only believe they have the right to use violence but receive a reward for behaving in this manner—obedience from their partners. Battering guarantees that the man "wins" disputes and that the status quo in the relationship is maintained.

In response to domestic violence, the victim changes something about herself in an effort to accommodate the perpetrator. Frequently, this involves restricting her choices, ending relationships with friends or family to whom he has objected (which is usually all of her friends and family, since they all pose a threat to his control), or even quitting her job. Often his behavior limits her access to a car or her ability even to leave the house. Meanwhile, she attempts to soothe and please the controlling man, complying with his demands, agreeing with his opinions, denouncing his enemies. She accepts blame for things that are not her fault and squelches her anger for fear of igniting his. She makes excuses for him—all to no avail. "When a woman tries to keep a partner calm by pleasing him, he gains exactly what he wants. He exercises his power over her and gets his way on a daily basis. It is ironic that she thinks she is 'managing' best when in fact she is most under his control" (Jones and Schecter, 1992: 35, 36).

Misconceptions about Causes of Domestic Violence

Stress? Stress does not cause men to batter. Many people who live stressful lives (battered women, for example) do not batter. Moreover, men who batter and attribute this to stress generally do not batter strangers, neighbors, or coworkers.

Alcohol and drugs? Some men who batter drink or use drugs; others do not. Of those who do drink or use drugs, some batter only when drunk or high; others batter only when sober. The majority of known alcoholics do not beat their wives, and the majority of wife abusers have not been diagnosed as alcoholics (Adams, 1994:14). Wife abusers, however, may become intoxicated in order to carry out violence. Abusive alcoholic or drug-dependent men have two problems: chemical dependency and woman-battering. Sobriety alone will not eliminate battering.

Violence in family of origin? Until recently the theory that boys who were abused or witnessed abuse grew up to abuse others seemed convincing. But the research on which this theory was based did not include control groups (more than 90 percent of families in the United States believe that corporal punishment of children is acceptable). "In fact, several studies indicate that an estimated 65 to 85 percent of adults who were abused as children *do not grow up to abuse their children*" (Jones and Schecter, 1992: 58). Brothers of batterers, who presumably witnessed the same abuse, do not necessarily grow up to become abusers.

Anger? Domestic violence is not a matter of anger but a matter of control. An abusive man chooses to lose his temper. He is already in control. His partner thinks, "If he would only express his emotions," but he already is expressing them, and quite effectively. What is needed for batterers is less self-expression of anger; giving vent to anger increases rather than lessens the person's angry state. "Therapists who encourage abusive people to 'vent their emotions' give them what they want: authoritative support for their explosive tirades." Such advice is "dangerous, even deadly when it is handed out to controlling and perhaps violent men" (Jones and Schecter, 1992: 65).

Victim's provocation? This question presumes that the woman has control over her partner's behavior. She does not. The abuser's violence is a consequence of his decision to control his intimate partner; it is not in any way caused by the woman. No matter what the woman's behavior, he still chooses to be violent. While a batterer may claim that his partner provoked him, no documentation exists to show that women are more verbally aggressive than men or that men hit only when women are verbally aggressive (Ganley, 1989). In fact, one study found that "physically abusive husbands were more verbally aggressive than their wives" (Ganley, 1989: 207). A man may be upset about his partner's verbal response to him, but such as verbal response is not battering: "These men have not been assaulted by their mates and they [the men] are not terrorized by them" (Ganley, 1981: 13).

A woman's behavior may irritate or anger her partner. She may be intoxicated or assertive, or may even be having an affair (which is rarely the case but is often assumed by the abuser); but none of these behaviors on her part justifies his beating her. The only justification for the use of physical force is self-defense in the face of imminent threat of physical danger. It is very difficult for a woman to pose a physical threat to a man unless she has a weapon.

Perpetrators may have multiple problems: they may be alcoholics, veterans suffering from post traumatic stress disorder, survivors of child abuse, or victims of racism, but these are not the reasons why they abuse someone else. The abusive man's behavior is the problem; explaining why he is abusive will not bring about any change in his behavior and usually contributes to his avoidance of responsibility for his behavior. No matter how compelling the explanations can be, identifying an explanation will not and cannot stop the abuse (Jones and Schecter, 1992: 49–73). This is because abusive behavior is something that can be controlled only by the abuser He exercises a great deal of self-control in other situations where he experiences stress. He has to learn to do the same in his intimate relationships.

Domestic Violence and Accountability: Aversive Consequences

The most effective way to stop domestic violence is to hold the abuser accountable. The most effective way to accomplish this is a coordinated, comprehensive community response that relies on a consistent response from all institutions of the community. In its review of developments in the law in response to domestic violence, the *Harvard Law Review* describes a coordinated community response to controlling assailants through "stringently enforced protection orders and vigorous prosecution, combined with community education" ("Developments in the Law," 1993: 1522). In counseling sessions which are a part of such a community response, this means that focusing on the man's decision to act in a violent manner is essential. Aversive consequences—especially arrest, accompanied by court-mandated counseling and sometimes loss of his job, separation from his family, or time in jail—demonstrate that domestic violence does not work. Its rewards are negated by the consequences. "Court-mandated treatment is necessary for many who batter. Due to their personality characteristics of denial, minimization, externalization, and impulsivity, many batters will either avoid or fail to complete voluntary treatment programs" (Ganley, 1981: 1). The dropout rate for voluntary treatment continues to be high (Jones and Schecter, 1992: 108), but court-mandated treatment imposes a degree of accountability that allows for monitoring the batterer's commitment to change, support for his efforts to change, and provides consequences if he does not change.

While legal interventions such as probable-cause arrest of batterers and unequivocal legal consequences are beginning to show some success in North American contexts, there are difficulties, particularly in minority communities. The issue of domestic violence may be seen by some as yet another excuse for the dominant culture to patrol the lives of minority people. In these situations, the police are not often seen as a resource and battered women may be fearful to call on them for help and also anxious about what the legal system may do to their male partner if he is arrested. This is also an issue for immigrants, who may be afraid to call on any resource for fear of encountering immigration officials.

In some communities, the police are not welcome under any circumstances. For example, in poor urban communities in the Philippines, women community leaders are developing alternative interventions that do not involve the police at all. In one community, the women gather around the home of the batterer and demand that he stop beating his wife. Because of the close proximity of living units, it is possible for the community to monitor his behavior and hold him accountable. Whether the intervention is highly organized and carried out by formal institutions such as the police and the judiciary, or whether it is informal and community-based, the strategy is the same: a coordinated, comprehensive community response. This response "deprivatizes" domestic violence, gives support to the victim, and calls the batterer to account. Privacy and silence, then, no longer serve to protect the batterer from consequences and to isolate the victim from support.

"War Brides," "Mail-Order Brides," Immigrant Women, and Minority Women

Immigrant women who are being battered face extraordinary difficulties in finding safety. Whether they come to a new country as wives of foreign military personnel who were stationed in their native country, as "mail-order brides," or as members of families immigrating together, they are particularly vulnerable and generally very isolated. War brides and mail-order brides are essentially dependent upon their husbands economically and socially. If a husband chooses, he can easily control and manipulate his partner by limiting her access to resources, to social contacts, to learning a new language, and so on, and he can literally hold her immigration papers in order to keep her with him. Documented and undocumented immigrant women are often fearful of immigration authorities and thus are unlikely to seek out community resources. Community resources are not often available that provide a context where an immigrant woman can speak her own language and feel comfortable in her own cultural setting.

Any battered woman who is a member of a minority community faces the difficulty of disclosing her victimization to anyone outside of her community. She is often caught in a double bind. As a member of a minority community that faces oppression from a dominant community, she has learned not to talk about community problems outside of the community for fear of fueling the prejudice of the dominant community. But she also is likely to avoid disclosing her abuse within her own community for fear of lack of support. Where does she turn? Whether she is African-American, Jewish, Aboriginal, Native Canadian, Muslim, or lesbian, she struggles with issues of loyalty to her community versus her need for resources and support to help her find safety.

Stalking and Other Forms of Separation Assault

The time of separation from an abuser and afterward is extremely dangerous for the battered woman. Violence often intensifies at the point of separation, as the batterer attempts to coerce his victim to return or retaliates against her for leaving him. Up to 50 percent of men who batter have sought out and continued to beat and otherwise terrorize their wives after they have left.

What is often referred to as "stalking," should instead, according to Martha R. Mahoney, be called "separation assault." This term identifies the struggle for control that occurs when a woman decides to separate or when she begins to prepare to separate. Mahoney maintains, *"Separation assault is the attack on woman's body and volition in which her partner seeks to prevent her from leaving, retaliate for the separation, or force her to return. It aims at overbearing her will as to where and with whom she will live, and coercing her in order to enforce connection in a relationship. It is an attempt to gain, retain, or regain power in a relationship, or to punish the woman for ending the relationship"* (Mahoney, 1991: 65–6).

Self-Defense

One of the most difficult issues for many battered women is the situation in which the woman finally chooses to defend herself and her children in the face of the brutality of her abuser. If she kills her abuser, she most likely come up against the judicial system, and she may face a long prison sentence. Battered women and their supporters are waging campaigns in many countries to bring about a recognition within judicial systems of the fact that battered women often act in self-defense. Many campaigns focus on changing laws that have historically defined self-defense in terms of men's experiences and neglected the particulars of women's self-defense. Some battered women who have killed abusers are mounting successful defenses and being acquitted. Others who have been convicted and are serving prison time are campaigning for clemency, with some success.

Terminology

The terminology that is chosen to name domestic violence and to name those who use it and those upon whom it is used is very significant. As indicated above, even naming the problem is difficult. But one particular linguistic distinction should be indicated here. Many who work on these issues distinguish between "victims" and "survivors" or between "battered women" and "formerly battered women." The purpose of these different terms is to indicate that at some point in time, an individual is in fact victimized—that is, made a victim—by the actions of an abuser. But this condition is not permanent; that is, it is possible for the individual to find safety and no longer to be in that particular situation of imminent danger. At this point (which is based on the victim's own assessment of her circumstances) she becomes a survivor or a formerly battered woman. Her experience of battering is an important part of her history, but it is not definitive in her future.

Religious Issues

Religious questions are common for battered women in many cultures. To the extent to which religious teachings promote a patriarchal agenda, they tend to reinforce the supposed patriarchal prerogatives of male intimate partners. Some religious doctrines tend to support the attitudes and actions of men who batter; such teachings include the permanence of marriage (without the option of divorce), the right of a husband and father to physically chastise his wife and children, the sanctity of suffering, and the expectation of forgiveness without justice. Unless religious leaders take the initiative to challenge these doctrines or the misinterpretations of doctrine on which they are based, religious institutions are invariably complicit in the abuse of women and children.

Cultural Imperialism and Domestic Violence

The prevalence of domestic violence in most cultures raises serious questions for activists. For example, the protocol for researching the transnational issue of domestic violence is a concern. Euro-American women researchers have been urged to restrict their research to their own countries, and thus allow their sisters in other countries to pursue their own research projects. Otherwise, research projects may be tainted by cultural imperialism. At the same time, it is crucial that activists be in contact across national borders in order to share information, ideas, strategies, and critical feedback. The commitment from Euro-American activists should be to avoid imposing a framework upon the experiences of women in another culture and to avoid appropriation of the work of activists in another culture. The common challenge is finding ways to communicate and share resources that may be useful to the shared goal of ending domestic violence in all cultures.

Domestic Violence and the Concept of the Private versus the Public

Conceptually, a reconsideration of the term *domestic violence* is necessary in light of feminist critiques of the division between "public" and "private" in patriarchal culture. This distinction has kept domestic violence from being seen as a public concern; according to feminists, it is inherently gender-based and thus conceptually flawed. Historically, in western culture, female gender-identified traits have been associated with the private ("domestic," "home") sphere, while male gender-identified traits have been associated with the public ("civic," "political") sphere. Those who are equated with the public sphere (most frequently white men) are seen as having higher value, status, and so on, than those who are equated with the domestic sphere (women of all colors). Both the geography of violence (domestic rather than political or civic) and the usual victim of violence (female rather than male) contribute to keeping domestic violence invisible. Until recently, violence in the "domestic" sphere was not closely scrutinized by the public sphere. The concept of privacy for the domestic sphere also contributed to making domestic violence a nonissue by keeping it nonpublic, and thus unable to be scrutinized. In the absence of scrutiny and any accompanying consequences for violent behavior, domestic violence is left unchallenged. The idea of the division between domestic and public protects the private domain from being the focus of certain ethical and philosophical concerns—such as justice—which are often presumed to pertain only to the public realm. An ongoing aspect of feminism has been its insistance that ethical, religious, and philosophical concerns are domestic as well as public, and that it is urgent to guarantee each woman's bodily integrity and safety.

See Also

ABUSE; BATTERY; PATRIARCHY: FEMINIST THEORY; SEXUAL VIOLENCE; VIOLENCE, *specific entries*

References and Further Reading

Adams, Carol J. 1994. *Woman-battering*. Minneapolis: Fortress.

———. 1995. Woman-battering and harm to animals. In Carol J. Adams and Josephine Donovan, eds. *Animals and women: Feminist theoretical explorations*. Durham, N.C.: Duke University Press.

———, and Marie M. Fortune. 1995. *Violence against women and children: A christian theological sourcebook*. New York: The Continuum Publishing Company.

Developments in the law—Legal responses to domestic violence. 1993. *Harvard Law Review* 106(7): 1498-1620.

Dobash, R. E., and R. P. Dobash. 1979. *Violence against wives: A case against the patriarchy*. New York: Free Press.

Fortune, Marie M. 1987. *Keeping the faith: Guidance for christian women facing abuse*. San Francisco: Harper and Row.

Ganley, Anne L. 1981. *Court-mandated counseling for men who batter*. Washington, D.C.: Center for Women Policy Studies.

———. 1989. Integrating feminist and social learning analyses of aggression. In P. Lynn Caesar et al., eds., *Treating men who batter*. New York: Springer.

Herman, Judith. 1992. *Trauma and recovery.* New York: Basic Books.

Jones, Ann. 1994. *Next time she'll be dead.* Boston: Beacon.

Jones, Ann, and Susan Schecter. 1992. *When loves goes wrong.* New York: HarperCollins.

Mahoney, Martha R. 1991. Legal images of battered women. *Michigan Law Review* 90(1).

Russell, Evelyn. 1985. *Chain chain chain: For black women dealing with physical and emotional abuse.* Seattle: Seal.

Marie M. Fortune
Carol J. Adams

DOMESTIC WORKERS

See DOMESTIC LABOR and HOUSEHOLD WORKERS.

DOWRY AND BRIDEPRICE

Dowry and *brideprice* (also known as *bridewealth*) refer to customs and practices involving material transactions between two families (nuclear or extended) at the time of drawing up a marriage contract or alliance between the partners and their respective families, covering both movable and immovable property.

One crucial difference between the two is the direction of the flow of goods or wealth, which includes the woman as part of the package. *Dowry* connotes movement of both women and wealth in the direction of the household formed with the partner in marriage or the existing household of which the male partner is a member. *Brideprice* involves movement of material goods or wealth and women in the opposite direction. In brideprice transactions it is rare for control over this wealth to be exercised either by the female, for whom the price has been paid, or by the partners jointly. Control over the brideprice is the perogative of the household from which the female partner came.

The other critical difference (theoretically speaking) between the two systems of transactions is operational at the time of divorce or dissolution of the marriage. In most instances, if the female is the one to dissolve the marriage, brideprice is expected to be returned by the parents, or by other members of the female's maternal home on whom responsibility can be affixed in the absence of the parents, or—if she should leave in order to marry someone else—by the new male partner. In the case of dowry, in theory it can be taken back by the female partner.

In both systems problems arise at the time of reclaiming because the manner in which the respective amounts have been spent, the nature of legal title to the wealth exchanged, and the degree of control over it are all variables.

There is, however, one striking similarity between the two systems. In neither system, at or after the dissolution of marriage, does the woman independently—without involvement of her maternal household, her conjugal household, or the household of the male partner—have the right to place a market value on herself, and offer herself, in the case of brideprice, or to decide on her own the amount payable in the form of dowry, if another alliance is being entered into. In marriage alliances the transactions and exchanges are finalized on the basis of criteria such as agreement about the amount of wealth that will be exchanged or transferred. These variables include factors and determinants such as class, caste, social status of the families, definition, and customary value—all of which vary in turn with the society, the woman's capacity to work, and her fertility. The woman's status as an individual has not found any space within either dowry or brideprice.

There is considerable variation between societies in how dowry and brideprice function, depending on region; predominant cultural features (for example, whether a society is agrarian or industrialized); religion; legal codes pertaining to property rights and inheritance; lineage patterns; household forms; and finally, customary practices and changes taking place in the economy or polity.

There is a wide range of interpretations of the two systems of transactions conceptually and practically, in relation to their role and function in society. Both dowry and brideprice are primarily considered at the time of marriage, divorce, or separation. However, because payments may be staggered in some societies, issues related to these payments may persist for years. The issues and concerns involving the transactions at the time of marriage, or as the marriage continues, or when it is discontinued, are not restricted to the partners. They also become the concerns of the households of the partners and the society or community; and they are affected by the economic and social status of the two families and the law of the country. The system of dowry and brideprice is therefore not a matter of individual choice or decision; it is a social matter. As a result, the kind of questions that have become pertinent inslude these: Why is there a system of dowry and brideprice? How did the system evolve? In what ways is it related to the structure of the economy and society? Why is it associated only with a marriage alliance and with deviations from a particular alliance? Should dowry and brideprice transactions be defined as one-time gifts or as continuous throughout the term of the alliance? Is a dowry or brideprice an exchange of goods and wealth for either partner, or a fee for the alliance? How is it valued—as a transfer of property rights separate from inheritance rights; as compensation for loss of inheritance (this question is particularly relevant in the case of dowry); as a purchase price for the labor of the female partner, decided on by the household concerned, according to the requirements of the economy of that household (as the term *brideprice* indicates); or as a demand made by the maternal household of either of the two partners of a future alliance, (in which case factors determining the nature and form of the demand become important)?

As both dowry and brideprice center on the female partner's endowment, price, or enabling capacity, in various combinations and weights, an important related question is: Who finally has control over the transacted amount? Is the wealth controlled by the female partner, the male partner, or their respective households, or is it held jointly by the partners? What purpose is met by the transacted amount? Who makes decisions, about the manner in which the transacted amount is to be used?

The kind of goods or wealth that are exchanged under both systems vary in form and amount. Beyond the form or the amount, it is important to unravel the ways in which the system or practice is affected by societal evolution, differentiation among classes, and other social segmenations, and in what ways the systems redistribute property and are therefore linked with the formation and economy of a state. Some examples of the nature of goods and wealth transferred may help to explain why the systems are linked with larger processes in a society.

The goods and wealth include cattle, land (ownership or usufruct rights); gold, silver, and other precious metals; clothes and utensils; furniture; houses; cash; vehicles; and so on. The form of these items changes with changes in agricultural practices, degree of industrialization, technology, and consumerism.

Dowry and brideprice are not specific to any particular country or region historically. They have taken different forms, have performed different functions, and have been linked with different stages of development of societies. Country-based studies become important for legislating, for raising specific demands, and for bringing about changes in the existing practices.

Thus there are many variations in all aspects of both systems, and there are also several interpretations of both systems.

See Also

CASTE; CLASS; FAMILY: RELIGIOUS AND LEGAL SYSTEMS, *specific entries*; MARRIAGE: REGIONAL TRADITIONS AND PRACTICES; POLYGYNY AND POLYANDRY

References and Further Reading

Bleie, T. 1990. *Dowry and bridewealth presentations in rural Bangladesh: Commodities, gifts, or hybrid forms?* Bergen: Christian Michelsen Institute.

Dumont, Louis. 1970. *Homo hierarchicus: The caste system and its implications.* London: Weidenfeld and Nicolson.

Goody, Jack, and S. J. Tambiah. 1973. *Bridewealth and dowry.* Cambridge: Cambridge University Press.

Gupta, Jayoti. 1990. Class relations, family structure, and bondage of women. In L. Dube, and R. Palriwala, eds., *Structures and strategies: Women, work, and family.* Delhi: Sage.

Meillassoux, C. 1981. *Maidens, meal, and money: Capitalism and the domestic community.* Cambridge: Cambridge University Press.

Sharma, U. 1984. Dowry in north India: Its consequences for women. In R. Hirschon, ed. *Women and property—women as property.* London: Croom Helm.

Jayoti Gupta

DRAMA

The history of women's participation in drama is also a history of banishment from the public stage. Nevertheless there have been few cultures in which women have not taken active roles, and none in which they are not present on stage as characters. It is possible that women performed in Greek drama earlier, though not later, than the sixth century B.C. However, Aeschylus, who wrote when all performers were male, exploits the dramatic properties of gender difference, giving opposite sexual identities to chorus and protagonist. One problem is how to retrieve women's history and promote women's future in this field, and how to interpret the characterizations of women by male dramatists in cultures where only men are actors.

Women in religious communities in the medieval period are known to have expressed both their learning and their devotion in drama. Abbess Hildegard von Bingen

(1098–1179) wrote words and music for a play representing her own visionary experience, *Ordo Virtutem*. The tenth-century nun Hrotswitha wrote Christianized imitations of the plays of Terence, and there is an extensive eyewitness account of a passion play performed in the fourteenth century by the nuns of Barking Abbey in Essex, directed by the abbess. In a secular context, some sixteenth- and early seventeenth-century Englishwomen wrote plays to be performed (or perhaps just read) by members of their own households (for example, Mary Sidney and Elizabeth Cary), and they probably also took parts in these.

Lucerne, Metz, and Saragossa provide evidence of medieval women acting in the civic drama performed by the trade guilds. The first professional actors, the *commedia dell'arte* troupes from Italy, included female performers who, since the genre is improvisatory, should also be regarded as creative artists. The same is true of Jane, the female fool of Princess Mary Tudor's court in the 1530s.

Theater is often a politically subversive activity, and many cultures have sought to control it under the guise of religion by characterizing it as morally subversive. Female behavior is usually the first to be scrutinized in such circumstances. The all-male kabuki theater of Japan was actually invented in 1603 by a woman, Okuni, who played robust parts in male attire (Yoko, 1994). Women (and subsequently boys) were soon banned from performing, necessitating the invention of the role of the *onnagate*. This adult male actor presents an idealized masquerade of womanly charm and feeling that is more feminine than real. Originally he was also required to live his personal life dressed as a woman, which must have set him outside of the society of both genders. During the Cultural Revolution in China, women characters in drama (now played by women) were likewise given a politically determined identity as desexualized fighters for the revolution (Chen, 1997).

The women's suffrage movement inspired a number of plays, such as those written by the actor Elizabeth Robins of the United States. Many other women in the first half of the twentieth century, however, wrote plays under male pseudonyms in order to get them performed and to attract impartial reviews. Ironically, the standard drawing room setting for plays of that period, compounded with the notion of women's domestic sphere, encouraged disparagement and neglect (at the time by male theater critics and more recently in academic histories). There were, nevertheless, nearly a thousand plays by women produced in the British commercial theater between 1918 and 1958, nearly 29 percent of which achieved runs of over 50 performances, which is roughly the same percentage as for plays by men (Gale, 1994). The term *kitchen sink drama* was coined to describe the reaction against drawing room drama of the "angry young men" playwrights of the 1950s but this kitchen-sink theater did not always concerned itself with the experience of the gender that is still more likely to inhabit kitchens.

The concept of *mimesis* is significant here. Originally denoting the representation of a platonic ideal, whether an immortal figure or a quality (such as womanliness), *mimesis* came to mean simply "imitation of life." When women's roles are circumscribed in real life, a realistic theatrical aesthetic serves to reinforce oppression, producing strongly normative gender stereotyping. For example, the incidence of rape in English plays increased exponentially after actresses began to perform on the public stage in 1660, as dramatists came to rely on the physical allure of real, but helpless, women's bodies (Howe, 1992). Late seventeenth-century adaptations of Shakespeare, which held the stage until the mid-nineteenth century, likewise weakened the female characters according to notions of propriety and perceived "feminine" traits. By contrast, a dislocation in gender between actor and character can set up a dialectic in the viewer's mind that calls social conventions into question. In the case of men playing women it can, as in the comedies of Aristophanes, enable the writing of much stronger language and behavior for female characters than the society for which the play was written would normally publicly countenance.

Such variation in the representation of women can now be found in theater in the third world. In postcolonial francophone African culture, for example, performance by women has, until recently, rarely progressed beyond displays of traditional dance for visiting dignitaries. Theater is, however, now being used in development programes as a palatable way to inculcate educational messages on matters such as health and nutrition. More radically, forum theater techniques empower real women, under cover of a character, to speak to their communities about their own lives in terms which would not be possible in direct conversation with village elders. At the other extreme, Werewere Liking, one of the very few female dramatists of Cameroon, has created a form of ritualistic theater that incorporates traditional African methods for training the body and the memory, in order to promote a new concept of feminine identity (Orlando, 1998).

In the 1970s Caryl Churchill and the Joint Stock Company pioneered a way of writing drama that is often described as "female" because it involves extensive, collaborative "workshopping" of ideas with actors and directors. It is now a recognized way of developing works by playwrights of both genders. Churchill also used cross-gender casting in *Cloud Nine* in order to question role stereotyping. Pam Gems, on the other hand, rejects being described as a feminist playwright because the term implies polemic, and polemic involves changing things in a direct, political way. Drama is subversive (Goodman, 1993).

The flowering of British women dramatists in the 1970s and 1980s has, according to Timberlake Wertenbaker, given way to a new male dominance in British theater (in which she feels the violent plays of Sara Kane can be included): "I don't think women have ever been a welcome voice. . . . Men judge the plays and, on the whole, run the theatres" (Billington, 1999).

See Also

LESBIAN DRAMA; PERFORMANCE TEXTS; THEATER: OVERVIEW; THEATER: WOMEN IN THEATER

References and Further Reading

Billington, Michael. 1999. In conversation with Timberlake Wertenbaker. Men judge the plays, put on the plays, and run the theatres. *Guardian,* (25 November).

Case, Sue-Ellen. 1988. *Feminism and theater.* New York: Methuen.

Chen, Xiao-mei. 1997. A stage of their own: The problematics of women's theater in post-Mao China. *Journal of Asian Studies* 56(1): 3–25.

Diamond, Elin. 1997. *Unmaking mimesis.* London and New York: Routledge.

Gale, Maggie. 1994. A need for reappraisal: Women playwrights on the London sage, 1918–1958. *Women: A Cultural Review* 5 (2: Autumn).

Goodman, Lizbeth. 1993. *Contemporary feminist theatres.* London: Routledge.

Howe, Elizabeth. 1992. *The first English actresses: Women and drama, 1660–1700.* Cambridge: Cambridge University Press.

Henderson, Jeffrey, trans. and ed. 1996. *Three plays by Aristophanes: Staging women.* London and New York: Routledge.

Laughlin, Karen, and Catherine Schuler, eds. 1995. *Theatre and feminist aesthetics.* Madison, N.J.: Fairleigh Dickinson University Press, Associated University Presses.

Meredith, Peter, and John E. Tailby, eds. 1983. *The staging of religious drama in Europe in the later middle ages: Texts and documents in English translation.* Kalamazoo: Western Michigan University, Medieval Institute Publications, Early Drama, Art, and Music Monograph Series, 4.

Mlama, Peninan Muhand. 1991. *Culture and development: The popular theater approach in Africa.* Uppsala: Nordiska Afrikainstitutet.

Morgan, Fidelis, ed. 1981. *The female wits: Women playwrights on the London stage 1660–1720.* London: Virago.

Orgel, Stephen. 1992. *Impersonations: The performance of gender in Shakespearian England.* Cambridge: Cambridge University Press.

Orlando, Valerie. 1998. Werewere Liking: The development of ritual Francophone theatre in Cameroon—Towards a new feminine theatre for Africa. In Kamal Salhi, ed., *African theatre for development: Art for self-determination.* Exeter: Intellect.

Perkins, Kathy A. ed., 1999. *Black South African women: An anthology of plays.* New York: Routledge.

Soufas, Teresa Scott, ed. 1997. *Women's acts: Plays by women dramatists of Spain's golden age.* Lexington: University Press of Kentucky.

Stowell, Sheila. 1992. *A stage of their own: Feminist playwrights of the suffrage era.* Manchester: Manchester University Press.

Yoko, Takakuwa. 1994. Masquerading womanliness: The Onnagata's theatrical performance of femininity in Kabuki. *Women: A cultural review* 5 (2: Autumn).

Ros King

DRAMA: Lesbian

See LESBIAN DRAMA.

DRESS

Dress is a system of nonverbal communication that enhances human beings' interaction as they move in space and time. As a coded sensory system, dressing the body occurs when human beings modify their bodies visually or through other sensory measures by manipulating color, texture, scent, sound, and taste or by supplementing their bodies with articles of clothing, accessories, and jewelry. Dress ordinarily precedes and facilitates or hinders verbal or other communication. Codes of dress set off cognitive and affective processes, which result in recognition or lack of recognition by the viewer. Any system of body modifications and supplements can mark several identities of an individual, such as age, gender, occupation, religion, community, and ethnicity. Dress encompasses more than either clothing or fashion, words that are often used as synonyms for dress.

Designating gender by dress is common throughout the world and has been associated with both prescriptive and proscriptive behaviors. Items of dress protect men's and women's bodies from the elements and from soil and grime. Women have, however, more often than men either chosen to or been forced to use garb for sexual protection, to conceal their bodies from the gaze of others and from male predators. This raises the issue of dress and its relationship to the definition of sexual allure for men and women within a cultural context.

Writers over the ages have been intrigued with the meaning of dress. In the nineteenth century, practical, philosophical, and academic views of dress were developed, with implications for the understanding of dress and gender. Amelia Bloomer advocated a trousered outfit for women as a reform measure against corsets and other constricting garments. Oscar Wilde and others pursued a philosophy of "aesthetic dress" that allowed freedom of movement and freedom from the dictates of fashion. Both men and women scholars have written about dress since the late nineteenth century from the prevailing viewpoints of their respective disciplines—anthropology, art history, economics, psychology, and sociology—particularly analyzing clothing and fashion.

Cross-disciplinary analyses of dressing the body developed in home economics and domestic science in the United States and Great Britain, beginning in the early twentieth century; this field was founded and dominated primarily by women. Early concerns in these disciplines focused on the care and selection as well as the construction of clothing, and on teaching these skills to those training to be teachers; later, the focus expanded to include textile design and research on textile properties and clothing practices. Women as well as men are prominent in high fashion in the twentieth and early twenty-first century; earlier, women occupied themselves in, and perhaps dominated, the practices of millinery, dressmaking, and tailoring.

Women have historically been significant in work throughout the world related to farming and production of many items of dress, particularly clothing, such as the planting and harvesting of cotton and flax, the tending of sheep, spinning, weaving, crocheting, knitting, and felting of cloth, as well as chewing and gnawing animal hides and decorating garments and cloth with needle and beadwork. With industrialization, women moved into weaving mills and garment factories or contributed labor through piecework in cottage industry production of apparel.

As interest in women's studies grew, some feminists viewed the study of dress and fashion negatively, citing Thorstein B. Veblen's theory of the leisure class, which focused on men displaying the dress of their wives and children as status symbols for the family and the enhancement of the man's reputation. In addition, the study of dress, textiles, and home science was often devalued by males, because practical work related to the home was seen as less important than either work outside the home or intellectual pursuits in academia. Some feminists claimed that differentiation by dress reinforced inequity in power relations between men and women and rejected the study of fashion and the idea of "being in fashion" as superficial concerns. They sought to display equity by wearing items or complete ensembles of men's clothing. Others claimed that women did not have to copy men and that dress defined as feminine, including the use of cosmetics, was appropriate and even a sign of power, as signified by the statement, "Beauty is power."

Toward the end of the twentieth century, research on dress expanded to include marketing specialists as well as academics. Concern with the body as the armature for dress has increased, sometimes to a point where the importance of body coverings is neglected. Scholars of dress recognize that varieties of styles exist not just within western fashion but worldwide. Simple descriptions of gender differences at a point in time ignore the ubiquity of change and the variability in, as well as the complexity of, the meaning of dress.

See Also

FASHION; FURS; TEXTILES

References and Further Reading

Baizerman, Sue, Joanne B. Eicher, and Catherine Cerny. 1993. Eurocentrism in the study of ethnic dress. In *Dress* 20: 19–32.

Barber, Elizabeth Wayland. 1994. *Women's work: The first 20,000 years.* New York: Norton

Benedict, Ruth. 1931. Dress. In *Encyclopaedia of the social sciences.* Vol. 5, 235–237. New York: Macmillan.

Eicher, Joanne B., and M. E. Roach-Higgins. 1992. Describing and classifying dress: Implications for the study of gender. In Ruth Barnes, and Joanne B. Eicher, eds., *Dress and gender: Marking and meaning,* 8–28. New York: St. Martin's.

Evans, Elizabeth, and Minna Thornton. 1989. *Women and fashion: A new look.* London: Quartet.

Polhemus, Ted. 1994. *Streetstyle: From sidewalk to catwalk.* London: Thames and Hudson.

Roach-Higgins, Mary Ellen, and Joanne B. Eicher. 1992. Dress and identity. *Clothing and Textile Research Journal* 10(4): 1–8.

Joanne Eicher

DRUG AND ALCOHOL ABUSE

Drug and alcohol use is reported in most countries throughout the world. Variations in use and abuse among populations worldwide are most frequently attributed to religious or political prohibitions, economic conditions, and the general availability of these substances.

Drugs and alcohol comprise a broad category of substances that cause changes in the central nervous system of humans by affecting particular neurotransmitters. They are often referred to as psychotropic or psychoactive substances. The changes caused in the functioning of the central nervous system produce a wide range of effects. These range from pleasure (induced by stimulants), for example, the exhilarating effects of alcohol, cocaine, or caffeine; to pain reduction (induced by sedatives), for example, the numbing or calming effects of heroin or Valium; to altered perception and euphoria, for example, the hallucinogenic effects of cannabis (marijuana) or PCP (phencyclidine). Individual users can have a wide range of reactions to these substances because of individual tolerance or the amount consumed. Reactions may range from a mild relaxing effect, which provides relief from the ordinary stresses of the day, to a substance-induced stupor, which leaves the individual in a state of unconsciousness.

Alcohol and drugs have long been a part of social and cultural history. Over time, they have had numerous ceremonial uses. Examples include the Roman Catholic mass (in which wine is used), Native American rituals (which use peyote), and some Hindu marriage ceremonies (which use opium). Drugs and alcohol have also been culturally significant by their absence, as in Muslim culture, which prohibits the use of alcohol. Their absence can also be politically significant, as during the Prohibition era in the United States, when alcohol use was illegal.

Drugs and alcohol have a long economic and commercial history as well. Alcohol has been an important source of commerce since the earliest known civilizations. Archaeological evidence shows that alcohol trading flourished around the Mediterranean and throughout China before 2500 b.c.e The poppy trade (poppies are used to make opium) has been recorded in prehistoric sites throughout central Asia. The worldwide economy continues to profit from both licit and illicit alcohol and drug commerce. For example, it is estimated that the annual income from Colombian drug trafficking fluctuates between U.S. $2 billion and $5 billion (United Nations International Drug Control Programme, 1997).

There are many categories of drugs, encompassing a broad array of psychoactive substances from legal, or licit, prescription drugs such as Valium or Prozac to illicit drugs such as heroin, cocaine, and marijuana. The category of illicit drugs also includes synthetic, or "designer," drugs. These synthetic drugs are substances such as amphetamine-type stimulants (ATS)—for example, methamphetamines or MDMA (methylenedioxy-methamphetamine), known as ecstasy, and LSD (lysergic acid diethylamide). Synthetic drugs are the fastest-growing segment of abused substances.

Inhalants are another category of drugs. Substances that are intentionally inhaled include glue, paint thinners, gasoline, and aerosol sprays. Usage is prevalent in both developed and developing countries and is an increasing problem among young people. In many countries, usage is high among street children and indigenous young people because inhalants are accessible and cheap and produce a rapid "high."

Alcohol is a colorless, inflammable liquid that causes intoxication. Substances such as beer, wine, and distilled spirits are considered alcoholic beverages. Worldwide, over 750,000 alcohol-related deaths are recorded annually. Typically, about one-half as many women as men abuse alcohol.

Nicotine and caffeine are two other psychotropic substances considered to be part of the overall problem of drug abuse worldwide. Nicotine is most often consumed through tobacco products such as cigarettes and smokeless tobacco, which is chewed or used as snuff. Nicotine is now known to be highly addictive, and its detrimental impact on health is well documented. Over one-third of the global population (1.1 billion people) use nicotine (World Health Organization, 1996). Twelve percent of women worldwide use nicotine. In the United States, deaths related to nicotine use are the leading cause of cancer fatalities among women aged 55 to 74.

Caffeine is found in many beverages such as coffee, tea, and carbonated soft drinks; foods such as chocolate and yogurt; and many over-the-counter medications. Caffeine is an addictive substance and, although it may not present the serious problems seen with other drugs and alcohol, its use is frequently associated with other substances and is thought to foster a climate of drug acceptability.

Substance Abuse

Drug and alcohol abuse is generally referred to under the broad heading of substance abuse (SA). Abuse of any of these substances occurs along a broad continuum of consumption and behaviors. The least problematic forms of substance abuse are those that allow users to continue functioning in their everyday lives. However, such users function with considerable impairments, most often seen in the following areas: (1) failure to fulfill major obligations, (2) substance use in physically hazardous situations, (3) legal problems, and (4) social or interpersonal problems (APA, 1994). The user has an increased tolerance for the substance, which means that increasing amounts are needed to achieve the desired effect or intoxication. Often, this is specifically what is referred to as substance abuse. For example, a woman who consumes 12 alcoholic drinks per week is considered to be "at risk" of substance abuse. One drink is the equivalent of 12 grams of pure alcohol. This is the amount found in 12 ounces (0.75 liter) of beer, 5 ounces (0.36 liter) of wine, or 1.5 ounces (42.5 grams) of distilled spirits.

The most severe form of substance abuse is called substance dependence or addiction. Usage at this level includes all the problems known to occur with abuse as defined above and, in addition, is causes physiological and psychological harm to the user (World Health Organization, 1992). Dependence or addiction is also characterized by withdrawal, which takes place when the substance is not used, because the user has developed a physiological need for the substance. Cultures around the world have very different degrees of tolerance for substance use. Given these cultural differences, worldwide norms have not yet been established for defining deviant or abnormal substance use.

Women and Substance Abuse

For many years, worldwide, research and survey techniques focused on substance use among men. More recent research methodologies, as well as a greater awareness of gender issues, have significantly changed the understanding of women and substance abuse. These changing methods have found an alarming scenario for women. Women are involved with drugs in many ways, from their own use to their presence as nonusers in drug-abusing families or relationships. Women are often subjected to a dual stigmatization when they are substance abusers. First, like all substance abusers, they are deviant in relation to the social norms; second, they are "doubly deviant" in not conforming to the traditional role of mother, woman, and nurturer (Fagan, 1999). Even though women's traditional gender roles are changing around the world, women continue to be judged more harshly than men for substance use. For many women, such stigmatization leads to denial of the abuse; and failure to recognize and seek treatment for substance abuse leads to more serious problems. For women of childbearing age, substance abuse presents serious health issues for their unborn children. A single drinking binge by a pregnant woman can be enough to permanently damage the brain of her fetus—this is known as fetal alcohol syndrome (FAS), and it is one of the leading known causes of mental retardation. Children born to substance-dependent women are known to suffer withdrawal symptoms following birth. They also experience health problems at birth that are intensified by poor caretaking, stress, and chaos, because of the mother's lifestyle as a drug abuser. Infants born to mothers who smoke nicotine are three times more likely to die from sudden infant death syndrome, SIDS (National Clearinghouse for Alcohol and Drug Information, 1999). The intense guilt and shame that often accompany abuse and denial cause women to become even more isolated from the social systems that could provide support. This phenomenon is referred to as role engulfment (Stephens, 1991).

The gradual emancipation and economic independence of women over the past three decades have also placed additional stresses on women, which may contribute to the increase in substance abuse. As gender stereotyping has lessened, traditional protective attitudes toward women have eroded. These new freedoms have removed many of the barriers to drug and alcohol access that formerly insulated many women.

Family problems and other relationship problems, along with psychological and physical problems, are often cited as factors contributing more heavily to substance abuse among women than men. Studies in the Czech and Slovak republics have shown that the social upheavals of war, refugee status, and economic uncertainty all have contributed to a rise in substance abuse among women (World Health Organization, 1993). Physical violence against women also increases their susceptibility to substance abuse. One out of every three women worldwide has been beaten, raped, or seriously mistreated. Such injuries often cause the victim to turn to drugs or alcohol as a way to cope with her situation. In the United States, as many as 75 percent of survivors of abusive trauma report alcohol abuse (National Center for PTSD). Similarly, female alcoholics are more likely to have experienced sexual abuse, physical violence, or father-daughter verbal aggression than females in the general population.

In addition to the tremendous social and personal losses substance abuse represents, there are even more serious health issues. For example, the mortality rate for women who are alcoholics is 5.2 times greater than the corresponding rate in the general public. Physiologically, women have a lower tolerance than men for these substances, which leads to earlier and more serious health issues, including damage to the liver, brain, and heart. Substance abuse also worsens any other health or mental conditions, such as congenital heart problems or depression.

Special Considerations for Women

Women typically begin using substances at a later age than men. However, given their lower tolerance to substance abuse, they can experience more serious health consequences in a shorter period of time. Women are more likely to have a high rate of coexisting psychological problems, such as depression and anxiety. When women are substance abusers, they are more likely to abuse multiple substances—most often prescription drugs. A North American study found that physicians prescribe psychoactive drugs 2.5 times more often to women over 60 than to men of the same age group (United Nations International Drug Control Programme, 1997). Another study found that physicians regularly misdiagnose alcohol abuse among women over age 59 as depression and then prescribe sedatives or antidepressants, which are often lethal in combination with alcohol (National Center on Addiction and Substance Abuse). Women may trade sex for drugs and thus be at risk of sexually transmitted diseases (STDs) such as HIV. For example, Thailand has a large commercial sex trade and a high incidence of drug abuse and HIV. Its government, however, does not report statistics by gender, and so it is difficult to determine the impact of drug abuse on the health of Thai women. Among substance abusers, women are more likely to attempt suicide, and they have higher mortality rates than men.

Although the symptoms and consequences of substance abuse are more severe for women, they seem to do at least as well as men when they receive treatment. This is true despite the fact that there are barriers making it difficult for women to enter treatment and pressures for them to drop out of treatment. Researchers have not adequately studied gender differences in health behaviors and cannot yet explain these apparent paradoxes. As gender roles change throughout the world, additional investment should be made for the study, prevention, and treatment of substance abuse among women.

See Also

CRIME AND PUNISHMENT; DEPRESSION; DISEASE; EATING DISORDERS; HEALTH: OVERVIEW; HIV AND AIDS; MATERNAL HEALTH AND MORBIDITY; PHARMACEUTICALS; SAFER SEX

References and Further Reading

Alcohol tied to unborns' brain damage. 2000. *Los Angeles Times* (11 February): A46.

Ames, G., C. Schmidt, L. Klee, and R. Saltz. 1996. Combining methods to identify new measures of women's drinking problems, Part I: The ethnographic stage. *Addiction* 91(6): 829–844.

American Psychiatric Association (APA). 1994. *Diagnostic and statistical manual of mental disorders.* 4th ed. Washington, D.C.: APA.

Dreher, D. M. 1995. Women and drugs: Case studies from Jamaica. *Drugs: Education, Prevention, and Policy* 2(2): 167–176.

Fagan, J. 1999. Women and drugs revisited: Female participation in the cocaine economy. *Journal of Drug Issues* 24(2):179–225.

McCrady, B. S., and E. E. Epstein, eds. 1999. *Addictions: A comprehensive guidebook.* New York: Oxford University Press.

Miller, B. A., W. R. Downs, and M. Testa. 1993. Interrelationships between victimization experiences and women's alcohol use. *Journal on the Study of Alcohol* Supplement 11: 109–117.

National Center on Addiction and Substance Abuse. *Under the rug: Substance abuse and the mature woman.* On-line: <http://casacolumbia.org/publications 1456/publications _show.html>

National Center for PTSD. *PTSD and problems with alcohol use: A fact sheet.* On-line: <http://www.ncptsd.org/FS _Alcohol.html>

National Clearinghouse for Alcohol and Drug Information. 1999. *Healthy women/healthy lifestyles: What you should know about alcohol and other drugs.* Rockville, Md.: National Clearninghouse.

National Institute on Alcohol Abuse and Alcoholism. 1999. Are women more vulnerable to alcohol's effects? *Alcohol Alert* 46. On-line: <http://www.niaaa.nih.gov>

Stephens, R. C. 1991. *The street addict role: A theory of heroin addiction.* Albany: State University of New York Press.

Study calls violence against women a global health issue. 2000. *Los Angeles Times* (22 January): A19.

United Nations International Drug Control Programme. 1997. *World drug report.* Oxford: Oxford University Press.

World Health Organization (WHO). 1992. *International classification of diseases and related health problems.* 10th rev. ed. Geneva: WHO.

———. 1996. *Trends in substance use and associated health problems.* On-line: <www.who.org>

———. 1993. *Women and substance abuse.* Public Service Announcement 93.12.

Joan E. Huebl

DRUGS: Medicinal

See PHARMACEUTICALS.

DRUMMING

The drum is one of the oldest and most widespread musical instruments. The first known drum was the frame drum, painted on a wall of a shrine room in the Neolithic city of Catal Huyuk (present-day Turkey) in 5600 B.C.E. There are occasional representations of hourglass-shaped drums, barrel drums, and kettledrums, but the frame drum is by far the most prominent in the ancient civilizations of Mesopotamia, Egypt, Greece, and Rome. For at least 3,500 years, 3000 B.C.E. to 500 C.E., it was the primary percussive instrument, and it was played almost exclusively by women, with their bare hands. During this period there are comparatively few representations of drums of any kind played with sticks.

The frame drum of the ancient Mediterranean cultures was usually hoop-shaped, with a diameter much wider than the depth of its shell; however, some frame drums were square or rectangular. The common round frame drum was shaped like a grain sieve and probably shared the same origin.

Most often, the frame drum had a skin on only one side, although sometimes it had skins stretched across both sides. Bells or jingling and rattling implements may have been attached to the inside rim. Drums often were painted red, the color of blood, or sometimes green, the color of living vegetation. Mystical designs and symbols were also painted on the skin or the wooden frame.

Although the Mediterranean frame drum was similar in appearance to the shaman's drum found throughout Asia and North America, there was a major difference in how they were played. The shaman's drum was struck with a bone, horn, or stick, whereas the Mediterranean frame drum was played with bare hands. This difference in stroke technique led to differences in construction. The inner edge of the rim of the Mediterranean frame drum was beveled, and its skin was usually thinner, to enhance the sounds produced by fingers and hands. While striking a frame drum with a stick gives a single, deep, resonant sound, finger techniques allow more variety: a deep, open tone, a slap, a high-pitched rim sound, a soft brushing sound. It is not clear which technique is older: the shaman's drum played with a stick or the frame drum played with bare hands. The uses and basic constructions of the drums were so similar that, without a doubt, they emerged from the same root techniques of altering consciousness for religious or healing purposes. In many cultures from Siberia to China and into Alaska, women have functioned and still do function as shamans, playing frame drums with sticks.

Between 3000 and 2000 B.C.E., many representations of frame drums begin to appear, the earliest of which were from Sumer and then Mesopotamia. At least 95 percent of the performers depicted in all the ancient cultures were women, and most of these women were priestesses of various goddesses and gods. The earliest named drummer in history was the spiritual, financial, and administrative head (the *en*) of the Ekisnugal, a temple in Ur, around 2300 B.C.E. Her name was Lipushiau, and she was described as the player of the balag-di drum, a small, round frame drum.

Many ancient goddesses are depicted playing a frame drum with their hands. Although it was used in secular contexts at banquets and festivals, the frame drum was primarily a sacred instrument used as a rhythmic support for the chanted and sung liturgies of the ancient religions. The drum is mentioned frequently in religious texts from Sumer, Babylonia, Egypt, Anatolia, Israel, Greece, and Rome. The references to the training of the temple musicians noted that it was thorough and took many years.

From the third millennium B.C.E., written records of the Sumerians describe the goddess Inanna as the creator of the frame drum, along with all other musical instruments. The scriptures tell of Inanna's priestesses, who sang and chanted to the rhythms of round and square frame drums. Along with the written texts, numerous figurines of women playing small frame drums have been found. These drumming rituals depicted in the texts and in visual representations were carried into the later worship of Ishtar, Asherah, Ashtoreth, Astarte, and Anat in Babylonia, Phoenicia, Palestine, and Assyria.

During the second millennium B.C.E., frame drums began to appear in Egypt. During the Middle Kingdom, the records show not only that the drummers were primarily women, but that most professional musicians of the courts and temples were also women. These priestess-musicians functioned as the composers and choreographers of the sacred music and dance used on religious occasions in the temples. In the Cairo Museum there is an actual rectangular frame drum from 1400 B.C.E. that was found in the tomb of a woman named Hatnofer, the mother of the architect who built Queen Hatshepsut's funeral complex. Also surviving from the Ptolemaic period is the skin head of a frame drum on whose surface is painted a woman playing a frame drum in front of the goddess Isis. The drummers were always depicted playing with their bare hands; in fact there is no evidence of stick drumming from ancient Egypt.

The Old Testament of the Bible refers to the frame drum as the *toph*, which has also been translated as the timbrel and the tabret. Exodus 15:20 reads: "And Miriam, the prophetess, sister of Aaron, took a timbrel in her hand, and the women went out after her with timbrels and with dances." The frame drum was used in ancient Israel to celebrate joyous occasions and great feasts, in ritualized welcomes and farewells of beloved people, and in the worship of Yahweh, the biblical God. This drum was also played by important groups of women musicians as part of state rituals welcoming home victorious warriors. The frame drum was prominent in rites of mourning, and female drumming figurines have been found in grave sites.

In Greece some of the most beautiful representations of the frame drum are found on the red-figured vase paintings from the fifth century B.C.E. It is theorized that the music and religion of Greece developed from Asian and Egyptian sources—both of which used the frame drum in ceremonial and secular contexts. The frame drum entered Greece from several different directions—from Cyprus, one of the main centers of the cult of Aphrodite, where the frame drum was prominent from at least 1000 B.C.E.; and also from Crete, where it was used in the rituals of Ariadne, Rhea, and Dionysos.

Preclassical Greece also saw the introduction of the cult of the goddess Cybele, from western Anatolia. The *tympanum,* the Greek name for the frame drum, was used pervasively by the maenads (women initiates) in the worship of Cybele and Dionysos and was also played by the priestesses of Artemis, Demeter, Persephone, and Aphrodite. Both single-headed and double-headed frame drums appear, once again played almost exclusively by women with their bare hands.

The Romans saw the last great flowering of these rites when the religion of Cybele was brought to Rome in April of 204 B.C.E. Cybele was described as "the All-Begetting Mother, who beat a drum to mark the rhythm of life." Her worship flourished until the Roman Empire officially adopted Christianity in the fourth century C.E.

In the first two centuries of our era, Rome was the cultural center for the mystery religions of Cybele, Dionysos, Isis, and Dea Syria—all of which used the frame drum in their ceremonies. With the ascendancy of Christianity, Cybele's great temple in Rome was destroyed, the Vatican was built on the site, and the new priesthood banned the priestesses, instruments, and music associated with her rites. With the rise of the new religions of Judaism, Christianity, and Islam, women were prohibited from functioning as priestesses or musicians in the new religious traditions, and this marked the beginning of their disappearance in history as professional drummers and musicians.

In these trans-Mediterranean cultures there is conclusive evidence of the tradition of women's performance ensembles rooted in drumming, which also included singing and dancing and playing flute and lyre . The music of this period was primarily rhythmically structured. As the main percussive element, the frame drum was the center of this music, and—significantly—it was played by women.

After the frame drum was banned by the Christian church, it survived as a folk instrument, still played today by women and men in the villages of Italy, Spain, and Portugal. In north Africa and the Middle East it is used in religious and classical traditions from which women are still excluded, although there is evidence that women play frame drums and other types of hand drums in secular situations within the community and usually within the confines of the home.

Stick drumming as a military enterprise entered Europe from Turkey during the Crusades in the twelfth and thirteenth century C.E. as a completely male occupation. It proved to be an extremely effective technique for organizing for warfare and spread rapidly throughout Europe. By the Renaissance the military drum had been transformed into an instrument used in the world of courtly and classical music, which appeared also to be a completely male profession.

In the twentieth century, black jazz players in the United States transformed the military marching drums into the drum set. The drum set and classical percussion were rarely played by women in this century. Not until the 1970s did women begin entering into the profession of drumming on a larger scale again. Although drumming as a profession is still male-dominated, more and more women are reaching new levels of visibility and success as performers and soloists.

See Also

References and Further Reading

Blades, James. 1984. *Percussion instruments and their history.* London: Faber and Faber.

Drinker, Sophie. 1995. *Women and music.* New York: Feminist Press, City University of New York.

Quasten, Jonannes. 1973. *Music and worship in pagan and Christian antiquity.* Washington, D.C.: National Association of Pastorial Musicians.

Redmond, Layne. 1997. *When the drummers were women.* New York: Three Rivers Press.

Layne Redmond

DYING

See DEATH.

E

EARTH

Ground of our being, matrix of all known life, Earth has been seen as a nurturing mother in many folk cultures around the world for thousands of years. The most familiar record of this ancient idea for Europeans and Americans is Greek mythology, which begins with Gaia, or Earth, emerging from formless, undifferentiated Chaos. This female deity is described as the "ever-sure foundation of all the deathless ones" and in the "Homeric Hymn to Earth" is called "Panmhteiran" and "HyUemeUlon" ("mother of all" and "most ancient of beings" (Evelyn-White, 1977: 86–87, 466). This Greek concept of Mother Earth descends from much older traditions all over the world, emerging out of prehistoric ways of understanding the absolute dependence of all creatures on the living landscape. Glimpses of these origins can be caught in the twenty-five-thousand-year-old art and symbols from the caves of northern Europe, in which images of plants and animals are associated with large female sculptures, often called Venuses, whose reproductive functions are suggested in their accentuated hips and breasts. In later (Neolithic and Bronze Age) cultures votive clay figurines of the female body, inscribed with signs for water and growing plants, were produced by the thousands to indicate the idea of the common ability of Earth and women's bodies to produce new life and nourishment. In *Goddesses and Gods of Old Europe* (1982) and *The Language of the Goddess* (1989), Marija Gimbutas has reproduced and discussed hundreds of the thousands of such figurines and images recovered by archaeologists in the twentieth century. Although Gimbutas's theories have always been controversial, they are closely argued and based on a vast body of archaeological fieldwork, much of which she conducted herself. Her work supports earlier scholarship on pre-Celtic cultures in northwestern Europe and on pre-Hellenic Greece, Egypt, Mesopotamia, and the Levant that describes a widespread cultural focus on Earth and its powers associated with the feminine. (See, for example, Marshack, Nilsson, Drews, Harrison, Mellaart, Kramer, Clark, Pagels, Patai, Piggot, Driver, and Gottlieb.) Most scholars of ancient Mediterranean, Mesopotamian, and Indo-European civilizations accept the general import of Gimbutas's assertion that cultures based on the worship of Earth goddesses were supplanted by patriarchal value systems that focused on sky gods and on ideas of spiritually transcending Earth. (See, for example, Lerner, 1986: 146–153; Mallory, 1989: 182–185 and 222–272; and Baring and Cashford, 1991: 447–546.)

Earth and Patriarchal Tendencies

As written languages developed in Mesopotamia, China, and India, concepts of Earth as mother and female body became part of the earliest literatures. However, patriarchal ideologies in China, Japan, and India erased or suppressed many early records of such thinking. What survive are fragments, as in Chinese references to the goddess Nü Kua (Birrell, 1993: 2–35), Dravidian folk deities and rituals representing pre-Indic traditions of chthonic belief (that is, belief deities associated with Earth's powers) on the Indian subcontinent; and linguistic traces of the archaic Indic supernatural ancestress Áditi (Puhvel, 1987: 47). Among the earliest literatures, remnants of early chthonic worship are clearest in Mesopotamian culture, particularly the literature of Sumer and Babylon. Four-thousand-year-old hymns to the Sumerian goddess Inanna describe her body as synonymous with the fertile earth (Wolkstein and Kramer, 1983). The traditional associations of the goddess and Earth continue through the two thousand years of transmission of the *Epic of Gilgamesh* in Mesopotamia, even though by the time of the Babylonians, the epic had come to express a masculine value system that moves the locus of authority away from Earth and into the dominating figure of the young king who makes his reputation by destroying a forest sacred to the goddess. Most tribal cultures around the world continued to think of Earth as nurturing mother even as the intellectual traditions of literate civilizations abstracted themselves further and further from earlier traditions of reverence and identification with Earth's power. The historian Gerda Lerner (1986) has suggested that the creation of patriarchal cultures grew out of the domestication of animals and plants during the Neolithic era, leading men to consider themselves masters of all reproductive sources—Earth, plants, domestic animals, and women. The classicist Page DuBois chronicles the intellectual evolution of masculinist movement in ancient Greek culture away from the respectful interrelation with the fertile landscape and the feminine in her book *Sowing the Body* (1988). A similar evolution occurred in the Judaic scriptures, which led to the erasure of most traditions of reverence for Earth from the texts that came to form the Hebrew and Christian canons. Thus in Genesis, Earth and Eve are both cursed by Yahweh for Eve's initial disobedience in the Garden of Eden; nature is "fallen" and separate from mankind, just as woman is. Traces of the older Middle Eastern traditions of reverence, from which early stories of the Torah descend, can be glimpsed in the Hebrew people's tendency to worship the Golden Calf when patriarchs, like Moses, are absent. The Golden Calf may be associated with worship of a Palestinian goddess, Asherah, related to Ishtar, the later form of Earth goddess Inanna; reversion to this older orientation was anathema to the patriarchs, who were strenuously defining a new order ruled by a transcendent, immaterial father god (Johnson, 1988: 304). Given the saturation of European culture by Indo-European and Hebraic intellectual and religious traditions, it is clear why the ancient honor for Earth as a female center of life was eroded. Many folk traditions retain the older attitudes, but they have been consistently devalued and overlaid by ideas of human, and especially masculine, domination of nature.

As modern science and technology have advanced from the Renaissance through the present, Earth has come to seem more and more a separate, inert object in the intellectual tradition of the global human community. Miners and engineers have dug deep tunnels and chasms, blown the tops off mountains, changed the course of rivers, and built ribbons of asphalt and concrete over the land. Soils have been chemically altered and poisoned. The seas have been raked and swept for food, devastating many marine communities. The air is full of sounds and currents of energy that have changed the environment for migrating birds, and it has grown noticeably warmer since the industrial revolution stimulated increasingly intense combustion of fossil fuels.

Though humankind, particularly masculine industrial culture, has dramatically changed the life of Earth with inventions and interventions, American nature writers and conservationists such as Henry David Thoreau, John Muir, and Aldo Leopold established a countertradition to this arrogant humanism. The environmental movements of the second half of the twentieth-century began to question the industrial exploitation of Earth. With her book *Silent Spring* (1962), Rachel Carson was the first to awaken attention to the devastation caused to Earth's life by industrial chemicals. Since Carson, environmental concern for the health of Earth has steadily increased in the United States and spread over the globe. Environmental organizations such as the Sierra Club and Greenpeace have supported an ever-increasing movement to restore reverence for Earth.

The Challenge of Ecofeminism

By the end of the twentieth century, a multifaceted ecological feminism—or ecofeminism—had directly challenged the prevailing concepts of humanity's separateness from and superiority to an inert Earth. The term *ecofeminism* seems to have been coined by the French feminist Françoise d'Eaubonne in a 1974 essay issuing a scathing indictment of masculine industrial culture and a call for its overthrow by women worldwide. American ecofeminist thinkers such as Annette Kolodny, Carolyn Merchant, Mary Daly, Susan Griffin, Charlene Spretnack, and Irene Diamond have defined the destructive misogyny that has accompanied the European conquest of the globe and the natural world from the Renaissance to the present, cataloging the ways that gendering Earth as female has been used to justify devastating exploitation of landscapes and communities of plants and animals. They have shown how ancient traditions of reverence for a vast, nurturing matrix of life have been turned upside down. Internationally many women activists and writers have initiated movements to restore health to devastated landscapes. One such movement is a tree-planting campaign in Kenya. Another is outlined in Vandana Shiva's book *Staying Alive* (1998), which describes the disaster caused to the landscape of India by the so-called Green Revolution of industrial agriculture. Shiva urges a return to sustainable farming that can restore life to the soil and bring back vital forests and watersheds. Ecofeminism is a multifaceted movement that includes intense controversies, such as the debate between "essentialists" and "constructionists," as well as many different orientations toward other environmental movements, for instance, "deep ecology." Some ecofeminists urge continued use of the female metaphor for the planet, but others argue that the cultural gender wars of the nineteenth and twentieth centuries indicate how dangerous such a strategy can be. Most agree, however, in seeing profound relationships between mistreatment of Earth and of women.

In fact, Earth is not a female animal but a huge living planet orbiting around a star that energizes its life. Human beings live within Earth's community, completely intertwined with all its life, as the philosopher Maurice Merleau-Ponty spent his life explaining. The British scientist J. E. Lovelock developed a new paradigm for thinking about Earth when he published *Gaia: A New Look at Life on Earth* in 1979. Basing his hypothesis on the remarkable stability of Earth's temperature and the chemical mixture of normally unstable gases that make up the atmosphere, Lovelock argued that Earth is an enormous living system that creates the proper conditions for its own life. Thus Earth's living community continually adapts its many processes to maintain the crucial temperature and atmosphere for its survival. Lovelock explains that such adaptation does not necessarily favor any particular species but it does maintain life itself in ever-evolving forms. Humans could be wiped out—or wipe themselves out—just as most forms of anaerobic bacteria did millions of years ago. Or a large meteor could so change the atmosphere for a time that most large creatures could, like the dinosaurs, be suddenly destroyed. Lovelock's close associate the American biologist Lynn Margulis has supported his work in many ways, among them her book *Symbiotic Planet: A New Look at Evolution* (1998), which argues that cooperation among species is much likelier than simplistic Darwinian competition to have led to evolutionary change. New thinking of this kind is beginning to have a profound influence in many scientific disciplines and also in the social sciences and philosophy. Earth is once again being seen as a living matrix within which humans have their being in relationship with the whole of its mysterious and vital community.

See Also

ECOFEMINISM; GAIA HYPOTHESIS; GEOGRAPHY; GREEN MOVEMENT; POLLUTION; POPULATION: OVERVIEW

References and Further Reading

Baring, Ann, and Jules Cashford. 1991. *The myth of the goddess.* New York: Viking.

Birrell, Anne. 1993. *Chinese mythology.* Baltimore: Johns Hopkins University Press.

Carson, Rachel. 1962. *Silent Spring.* Boston: Houghton Mifflin.

Clark, R. T. Rundle. 1978. *Myth and symbol in ancient Egypt.* London: Thames and Hudson.

Drews, Robert. 1988. *The coming of the Greeks: Indo-European conquests in the Aegean and the Near East.* Princeton, N.J.: Princeton University Press.

Driver, G. R. 1956. *Canaanite myths and legends.* Edinburgh: T. and T. Clark.

DuBois, Page. 1988. *Sowing the body: Psychoanalysis and ancient representations of women.* Chicago: University of Chicago Press.

Eaubonne, Françoise d'. 1994. The time for ecofeminism. Trans. Ruth Hottell. In Carolyn Merchant, ed., *Ecology.* Atlantic Highlands, N.J.: Humanities.

Eveyln-White, Hugh G. 1977. *Hesiod, the Homeric hymns, and Homerica.* Cambridge, Mass.: Harvard University Press.

Gimbutas, Marija. 1982. *Goddesses and gods of old Europe.* Berkeley: University of California Press (originally published as *The gods and goddesses of old Europe*, London: Thames and Hudson, 1974).

———. 1989. *The language of the goddess.* San Francisco: Harper and Row.

Gottlieb, Freema. 1989. *The lamp of God: Shekhinah as light.* London: Aaronson.

Harrison, Jane Ellen. 1922. *Prolegomena to the study of Greek religion.* Cambridge: Cambridge University Press.

Johnson, Buffie. 1988. *Lady of the beasts: Ancient images of the goddess and her sacred animals.* San Francisco: Harper.

Kramer, Samuel Noah. 1969. *The sacred marriage rite: Aspects of faith, myth, and ritual in ancient Sumer.* Bloomington: Indiana University Press.

Lerner, Gerda. 1986. *The creation of patriarchy.* New York: Oxford University Press.

Lovelock, J. E. 1979. *Gaia: A new look at life on earth.* Oxford: Oxford University Press.

Mallory, J. P. 1989. *In search of the Indo-Europeans.* London: Thames and Hudson.

Margulis, Lynn. 1998. *Symbiotic planet: A new look at evolution.* New York: Basic.

Marshack, Alexander. 1971. *The roots of civilization.* New York: McGraw-Hill.

Mellaart, James. 1967. *Catal Huyuk: A neolithic town in Anatolia.* New York: McGraw-Hill.

———. 1965. *Earliest civilizations of the Near East.* New York: McGraw-Hill.

Merleau-Ponty, Maurice. 1962. *Phenomenology of perception.* Trans. Colin Smith. London: Routledge and Kegan Paul.

———. 1968. *The visible and the invisible.* Trans. Alphonso Lingis. Evanston, Ill.: Northwestern University Press.

Nilsson, Martin P. 1927. *The Minoan-Mycenaean religion and its survival in Greek religion.* Lund: C. W. K. Gleerup.

———. 1988. *Adam, Eve, and the serpent.* London: Weidenfeld and Nicolson.

Pagels, Elaine. 1980. *The Gnostic gospels.* London: Weidenfeld and Nicolson.

Patai, Raphael. 1990. *The Hebrew goddess,* 3rd ed. Detroit: Wayne State University Press.

Piggot, Stuart. 1950. *Prehistoric India.* Harmondsworth: Penguin.

Puhvel, Jaan. 1987. *Comparative mythology.* Baltimore: Johns Hopkins University Press.

Shiva, Vandana. 1988. *Staying alive: Women, ecology, and survival in India.* New Delhi: Kali for Women.

Wolkstein, Diane, and Samuel Noah Kramer. 1983. *Inanna: Queen of heaven and earth.* New York: Harper and Row.

Louise Westling

EATING DISORDERS

The term *eating disorders* refers to severe disturbances in attitudes and behaviors related to eating, usually but not exclusively experienced by girls and women. "Eating disorders" is a broad clinical category, encompassing a number of diagnostic subtypes of disordered eating (American Psychiatric Association, 1994). The two principal subtypes are anorexia nervosa, which is characterized by an intense fear of fatness, an extreme reduction in food intake, and a refusal to maintain a minimally "normal" body weight; and bulimia nervosa, which is characterized by cycles of binge eating followed by purging behaviors such as vomiting and abuse of laxatives. Other subtypes of disordered eating, including obesity, bulimarexia, compulsive eating, binge-eating disorder (without regular purging), and dietary chaos syndrome, have also been suggested but remain contentious.

Many women diagnosed with an eating disorder also experience disturbances in body image—that is, in their perception of their own bodies. Body size and weight may be overestimated so that, for example, a woman may perceive herself to be fat even if she is actually emaciated. Eating disorders also are associated with profound psychological distress, particularly with low self-esteem and a poorly defined sense of self; with feelings of helplessness; and with lack of control and autonomy (Bruch, 1974). Hence, disordered eating—such as bingeing, purging, and self-starvation—may

be expressive of underlying inter- and intra-personal difficulties and may be experienced as a pseudo solution to these problems (Bruch, 1974). The intense control of eating and body weight in anorexia, for example, may be a means of achieving the sense of control that a woman feels she lacks in the rest of her life. By exercising this control, she may feel that she is thereby developing a more autonomous identity for herself. Like other women and girls, however, those diagnosed with eating disorders are a heterogeneous group. It is not always helpful to make universal or even broad generalizations about so-called typical "anorexic" or "bulimic" personalities or about psychological difficulties. It is important to understand, therefore, that in eating disorders the psychological meanings of symptoms are neither fixed nor universal: they may vary between girls and women as individuals and in different sociocultural contexts. Similarly, for any one individual, symptoms may sustain many complex and even contradictory meanings, which also may vary over time.

Diagnoses of eating disorders seem to have a quite specific historical, cultural, and demographic distribution (Swartz, 1985). Although eating disorders have existed as a clinical category in the form of anorexia nervosa since the end of the nineteenth century, it is only since the 1960s that diagnoses appear to have increased dramatically, at least in the West. Until recently, few studies examined eating disorders in nonwestern cultures, but research composing prevalence has found considerably higher rates among western girls and women. If prevalence is rising elsewhere, that may be due to a globalization of western culture.

The majority—approximately 90 to 95 percent—of those diagnosed with eating disorders are girls and young women, and traditionally, these disorders have been considered more common among the middle and upper social classes and among white rather than black or Asian women in Europe and North America (Hsu, 1989). Research in the 1990s, however, suggested that disordered eating had become increasingly common among all social classes and age groups (Cosford and Arnold, 1992; Hill and Robinson, 1991) and among girls and women of all ethnic backgrounds (Edwards-Hewitt and Gray, 1993).

There is a vast body of literature providing numerous explanations of the possible causes of eating disorders from a variety of different perspectives. Researchers have sought to explain eating disorders in terms of biological dysfunction, genetic predisposition, cognitive distortions, psychodynamic difficulties, dysfunctional family background (including but not confined to child abuse), and sociocultural and gender-political factors (see Malson, 1998, for a review). Although much of this literature is valuable, there is no conclusive evidence for any one etiology, and no single perspective can adequately explain the complex multi-dimensional aspects of eating disorders. It is, however, recognized more and more that women's disordered eating must be understood within its sociocultural and gender-specific contexts (Fallon et al., 1994; Malson, 1998). The cultural idealization of the youthful, thin female body has been well documented, as has the high prevalence of body dissatisfaction, preoccupation with weight and food, dieting, and bingeing and purging among western women and girls. Within this context, the distinction between disordered and so-called normal eating becomes less clear, and eating disorders are being viewed more often as part of a continuum that also encompasses women's "normal"—yet often distressing—experiences of eating and dieting. The alternative term *eating distress* emphasizes this view by countering the concept of eating disorders as individual pathologies that might somehow be understood separately from their sociocultural context.

In short, if we locate eating disorders within the contemporary cultural and gender-specific context in which so many girls and women are dissatisfied with their bodies, wish to be thinner, worry about their caloric intake, and habitually diet and engage in other weight-reducing behaviors such as purging and laxative abuse, then it becomes impossible to see "eating disorders" as a pathological deviation from so-called normal women's experience. Instead, we can reconceptualize "eating disorders" as a collection of distressed and damaging experiences and body-management practices that are a part of (rather than distinct from) the gender ideologies and normative practices that shape and regulate the lives of all women in contemporary western cultures (Bordo, 1993; Malson, 1998).

The thin body as a cultural ideal of feminine beauty and the accompanying pressure on girls and women to diet clearly form a very important aspect of the social context from which "eating disorders" emerge. However, as numerous feminist scholars have argued (for example, Chernin, 1983; Katzman and Sing, 1997; Lawrence, 1984; Malson, 1998; Orbach, 1993), a much wider array of social and gender-political issues are also relevant in understanding how "eating disorders" are culturally produced. Eating disorders can be understood not only as an intensified pursuit of a heterosexually attractive feminine body but also as a rejection of or ambivalence toward traditionally defined "femininity" (Orbach, 1993) and as an expression of women's relative powerlessness and lack of status in patriarchal cultural contexts (Chernin, 1983; Lawrence, 1984). Eating disorders can thus be understood to be expressive of cultural concerns and issues about femininity and about feminism. But they can also be interpreted as

expressing cultural concerns about, for example, individual competitiveness and personal display (Brumberg, 1988), the ethics of mass consumption, experiences of the body within contemporary consumer culture, and the dilemmas created by the cultural requirement that we inhabit the antithetical identities of self-controlled disciplined worker and self-indulgent consumer (Bordo, 1992, 1993; Brumberg, 1988; Malson, 1989; Turner, 1992).

"Eating disorders" can then be understood as manifestations of profound personal psychological distress expressed through eating behaviors that cause serious physical damage and sometimes even death. At the same time, "eating disorders" are expressive of a range of sociocultural and political concerns about the body, control, and consumption and about gender, power, and identity (Bordo, 1993; Brumberg, 1988; Fallon et al., 1994; Malson, 1998). Conceptualizing "eating disorders" in terms of individual psychopathology (see Malson, 1998) risks ignoring or diminishing the importance of these multiple and complex cultural-political contexts that shape girl's and women's experiences of themselves and their bodies.

See Also

ADOLESCENCE; ANOREXIA NERVOSA; BEAUTY CONTESTS AND PAGEANTS; BODY; BULIMIA NERVOSA; DEPRESSION; FASHION; IMAGES OF WOMEN: OVERVIEW; PATRIARCHY: FEMINIST THEORY; STRESS

References and Further Reading

American Psychiatric Association. 1994. *Diagnostic and statistical manual of mental disorders,* 4th ed. Washington, D.C.: American Psychiatric Association.

Bordo, Susan. 1992. Anorexia nervosa: Psychopathology as the crystallization of culture. In H. Crowley and S. Himmelweit, eds., *Knowing women: Feminism and knowledge.* Cambridge and Oxford: Polity Press in association with Open University Press.

———. 1993. *Unbearable weight: Feminism, western culture, and the body.* Berkeley: University of California Press.

Bruch, Hilde. 1974. *Eating disorders: Obesity and anorexia nervosa and the person within.* London: Routledge.

Brumberg, Joan. 1988. *Fasting girls: The emergence of anorexia nervosa as a modern disease.* Cambridge, Mass.: Harvard University Press.

Chernin, Kim. 1983. *Womansize: The tyranny of slenderness.* London: Women's.

Cosford, P. A., and E. Arnold. 1992. Eating disorders in later life: A review. *International Journal of Geriatric Psychiatry* 7(7): 491–498.

Edwards-Hewitt, Terilee, and James Gray. 1993. The prevalence of disordered eating attitudes and behaviours in Black-American and White-American college women: Ethnic, regional, class, and media differences. *Eating Disorders Review* 1(1): 41–54.

Fallon, Patricia, Melanie A. Katzman, and Susan C. Wooley, eds. 1994. *Feminist perspectives on eating disorders.* London: Guilford.

Hill, A. J., and A. Robinson. 1991. Dieting concerns have a functional effect on the behaviour of nine year old girls. *British Journal of Clinical Psychology* 30: 265–267.

Hsu, L. K. George. 1989. The gender gap in eating disorders: Why are the eating disorders more common among women? *Clinical Psychology Review* 9: 393–407.

Katzman, Melanie A., and Lee Sing. 1997. Beyond body image: The integration of feminist and transcultural theories in the understanding of self-starvation. *International Journal of Eating Disorders* 22(4): 385–394.

Lawrence, Marilyn. 1984. *The anorexic experience.* London: Women's.

Malson, Helen. 1998. *The thin woman: Feminism, post-structuralism, and the social psychology of anorexia nervosa.* London: Routledge.

Orbach, Suzie. 1993. *Hunger strike.* London: Penguin.

Swartz, L. 1985. Anorexia nervosa as a culture-bound syndrome. *Social Science and Medicine* 20(7):725–730

Turner, Bryan S. 1992. *Regulating bodies: Essays in medical sociology.* London: Routledge.

Helen Malson

ECOFEMINISM

The term *ecofeminism* refers both to the global intersection of women's movements and ecological movements in the late twentieth century and to the worldview that contends there is a connection between the degradation and devastation of the earth and the domination of women. This new consciousness of a relationship between a culture's treatment of women and its treatment of the nonhuman natural world, sometimes labeled the "third wave of feminism," is extremely diverse and contains positions and political commitments that sometimes conflict. As the term was increasingly used by activists, writers, and academics in the 1980s and 1990s, this heterogeneity of ecofeminism was often noted. Some critics saw this lack of a unified position or theory as evidence of ecofeminism's incoherence; those who were more sympathetic thought this lack of unity spoke to the move-

ment's quintessentially postmodern character. There are no clear boundaries between the thought and practice of ecofeminism and those of other movements originating in the late twentieth century that deal with issues of nonviolence, social justice, health, and the natural world. Moreover, ecofeminism, as an outgrowth of feminist, environmental, and postcolonial movements, is not immune to many of the political divisions and intellectual debates found in these movements. Precisely because ecofeminism's roots and alliances are so varied, one's understanding of the potential and problems of this global tapestry is heavily shaped by the affinities of the particular interpreter. Nonetheless, there are certain assumptions common to all ecofeminisms that warrant its designation as a distinct form of consciousness and political practice.

Giving Value to Women's Voices

Like feminism, ecofeminism strives to give value to women's voices and to challenge cultural and political practices that assume women's inferiority. However, ecofeminism also strives to revalue the nonhuman natural world, for this world is understood as an active subject with agency of its own. Because of this dual focus, ecofeminism does not assume that women's freedom is contingent on severing women's historical association with nature. The liberation of women is seen to be intimately associated with the liberation or revaluation of the natural world, whereas the foundation of patriarchy is understood as deriving from the denigration or "othering" of both women and nature. In ecofeminist visions—whether they be political platforms, science fiction stories, or theoretical treatises—struggles for women's rights and freedom are viewed as inseparable from struggles to repair the living systems of the earth that sustain life. Nature is not assumed to be inferior to human culture: indeed, ecofeminist theorists strive to challenge the very dualism of nature and culture that is typically assumed rather than questioned in much social and political thought.

Shared Tenets of Ecofeminism

In addition to this revaluation of nature and the natural world, another commonly shared tenet of ecofeminism—one that infuses the worldviews of political activists, academic scholars, and spiritually focused practitioners—is a belief in the interconnectedness of life. Indeed, this recognition of the relational manner of all existence, which for some participants is the impetus toward spiritual accounts of life on Earth, provides the link between ecofeminist political initiatives and the theoretical accounts of women's condition and the ecological crisis. Whether it be efforts to save forests, struggles around industrialized agriculture, movements against toxic contamination, or antimilitarism campaigns, these initiatives are typically conducted in modes that bring to the fore the question of how people's survival and well-being are intimately linked to the well-being of the earth. And for theorists of ecofeminism—whether advocates of Goddess spirituality, philosophers who focus on explicating the connections between the oppression of women and the oppression of nature, theologians who explore the symbols and myths that structure creation stories, historians who examine the impact of western science and capitalism on the survival strategies of third world women farmers, or ecocritics who explore the images of gender and nature in literature—the interconnections among the phenomena of the social and natural worlds are a uniform feature of the diverse accounts. The domination of women and the domination of nature are viewed as interconnected, both in cultural and religious myths and symbols and in social and economic structures. The devaluation of both women and nature is understood in terms of a particularly deleterious construction of masculine consciousness that denigrates and manipulates everything defined as "other," whether nature, women, colonized cultures, or marginalized races.

There is some disagreement over the coinage of the term *ecofeminism*. The French writer Françoise d'Eaubonne used the term in a text entitled *Le féminisme ou la mort* (1974; Feminism or death). D'Eaubonne argued that "male control of production and of women's sexuality had brought about the twin crises of environmental destruction through surplus production and overpopulation through surplus birth." Ecofeminism represented women's potential for bringing about an ecological revolution to ensure human survival on the planet. Such an ecological revolution would entail new gender relations between women and men and between humans and the earth. D'Eaubonne's coinage of the term was noted in Mary Daly's *Gyn/ecology*, which was published in the United States in 1978. Students of Daly in Boston were introduced to d'Eaubonne, but most users of the term, whether academic scholars, writers, or activists, were not aware of Daly's genealogical investigation, and thus coinage is not appropriately traced in any straightforward manner to d'Eaubonne. Much evidence suggests that the term began to be used spontaneously across a number of continents in the mid-1970s by women's movement activists focused on issues of peace and the ecological costs of science, technology, and development. The United

States–based Institute for Social Ecology began holding seminars on women and ecology during this period; and Ynestra King, a teacher at the institute and an activist in the antimilitarism movement who went on to organize the 1980 Conference on Women and Life on Earth: Ecofeminism for the 1980s, is often credited with developing the term in the U.S. context. The 1987 conference "Ecofeminist Perspectives: Nature, Culture, and Theory," held at the University of Southern California in Los Angeles, brought together academics and writers associated with the term, women activists working on environmental issues, and leading philosophers of deep ecology. The conference received international press coverage outside the feminist community and served to catalyze interest in ecofeminism among participants in and observers of the environmental movement. The 1990 volume *Reweaving the World: The Emergence of Ecofeminism* (Diamond and Orenstein), which grew out of the conference, generated interest in this new constellation in a range of intellectual and political communities around the globe. In 1988, the Indian physicist Vandana Shiva published *Staying Alive: Women, Ecology, and Survival in India*. Although Shiva had initially resisted the term *ecofeminism* because of its association with the West, in 1993 she published *Ecofeminism* with the German sociologist Maria Mies. Shiva's combining neo-Marxist theories with relentless activism around the globe on issues of development, global trade, and bioengineering moved the term *ecofeminism* into the realms of international policy making on women and global political and environmental discourse. Although the movement's philosophical and political merits were still heavily contested, Shiva's embrace of the word shifted the terms of the debate. Ecofeminism could no longer be seen as a product of western feminism.

Continuing Debate

Debates among identifiers with the movement and among outside observers center on the issues of essentialism, spirituality, animal rights, and science. Critics are often wary of the alleged essentialism of ecofeminism, while identifiers either strive to refute such charges or claim that ecofeminism employs essentialist rhetoric for strategic purposes. One significant form of ecofeminism draws heavily on second-wave feminism's rediscovery and embrace of goddess-revering cultures that are reputed to be more respectful of women and the natural world. This association is the most contentious issue dividing ecofeminists and is the primary reason ecofeminism is attacked or dismissed as nonsignificant by nonidentifiers. Within the movement, the centrality of Goddess spirituality is either embraced, critiqued, or minimized. Many ecofeminist activities in western nations focus on animal rights issues, and this work is central to the theoretical accounts of a small number of ecofeminist theorists. Political attacks from outside are often directed at this work. Within the movement, the centrality of animal rights is rarely debated; but when it is, it is extremely contentious. Many ecofeminist texts document the deleterious impacts of modern science, and outside observers often dismiss ecofeminism for its alleged vilification of science. There is relatively little debate about science within the movement, because the antiscience stance is often internal to the explication of the worldview or simply assumed. As the movement expanded in the last decade of the twentieth century, its use of scientific findings in political campaigns was often noted, and there were internal calls for more complex positions on science.

See Also

EARTH; ENVIRONMENT: OVERVIEW AND REGIONAL ENTRIES; GODDESS; GREEN MOVEMENT; GYN/ECOLOGY; NATURE; NATURE: PHILOSOPHY AND SPIRITUALITY

References and Further Reading

Daly, Mary. 1978. *Gyn/ecology*. New York: Beacon.

Diamond, Irene, and Gloria Orenstein, eds. 1990. *Reweaving the world: The emergence of ecofeminism*. San Francisco: Sierra Club.

Eaubonne, Françoise d'. 1974. *Le féminisme ou la mort*. Paris: P. Horay.

Gaard, Greta, ed. 1993. *Ecofeminism*. Philadelphia: Temple University Press.

Mellor, Mary. 1997. *Feminism and ecology*. New York: New York University Press.

Merchant, Carolyn. 1980. *The death of nature: Women ecology and the scientific revolution*. San Francisco: Harper and Row.

Mies, Maria, and Vandana Shiva. 1993. *Ecofeminism*. London: Zed.

Plumwood, Val. 1993. *Feminism and the mastery of nature*. New York: Routledge.

Ruether, Rosemary Radford. 1996. *Women healing earth: Third world women on ecology, feminism, and religion*. New York: Orbis.

Salleh, Ariel. 1997. *Ecofeminism as politics*. London: Zed.

Shiva, Vandana. 1988. *Staying alive: Women, ecology, and survival in India*. New Delhi: Kali for Women.

Sturgeon, Noel. 1992. *Ecofeminist natures*. New York: Routledge.

Irene Diamond

ECOLOGY

See ECOSYSTEM and ENVIRONMENT: OVERVIEW.

ECONOMIC DETERMINISM

See DETERMINISM: ECONOMIC.

ECONOMIC DEVELOPMENT

See DEVELOPMENT, SPECIFIC ENTRIES; and ECONOMY: OVERVIEW.

ECONOMIC STATUS:
Comparative Analysis

The economic status of women throughout the world is generally lower than that of men. Measurements of the economic value of work that determine status have been devised and applied by men for at least 7,000 years. They have also been implemented by women to create and maintain a supply of cheap labor to perform with the hardest, most repetitive jobs. Girls and women form the bulk of the world's cheap labor force. They supply most of the labor in the world, including unpaid labor. The work women do in their homes for their families forms the economic basis of every society. In today's world every kind of economic and social structure coexists, ranging from electronic, computerized finance capitalism to Stone Age tribalism.

Tribalism

In the 1990s—the United Nations Decade of the Indigenous Peoples—more than 150 million indigenous and tribal people were estimated to be living in Asia and millions more in Australia, Africa, Latin America, North America, and Europe. Tribal women are often included in official ceremonies designed to help the local economy, such as those devoted to rainmaking and to enhancing the fertility of the soil. Most plant deities are female; some South American Indians, now put to work in sugar factories, still sing songs to the Earth Mother Nungui. However, men sometimes claim a prior right to paid jobs; this claim may have originated in their special responsibility for long-distance hunting. The claim may also be related to men's responsiblity for defense, which evidently developed along with the development of defined territories.

Slavery

Slavery permeates the whole of human society. Tribal peoples recognized women's economic importance, but they also initiated slavery, which developed along with settled agriculture. The common human practice of forcing the disadvantaged to do the hardest and most unpleasant work persists in feudal, capitalist, and socialist states today, and the sale of human beings is still rife.

Slavery today exists in agriculture, domestic work, manufacturing of clothing and textiles, and prostitution, all trades involving large numbers of women. The United Nations Economic and Social Council in 1983 passed a resolution (no. 30) asking member states to ratify the Convention for the Suppression of the Traffic in Persons passed 34 years earlier in 1949. In 1991 UNESCO set up a working group to assist the implementation of this convention. In the twenty-first century ancient forms of slavery exist in the Sudan and Mauritania; people are traded in open markets in Karnataka, India; they are used as forced labor in Brazil and Haiti; and child slaves work openly on the streets of Gabon. Anti-Slavery International, the International Abolitionist Federation specializing in combating prostitution, the International Labor Organization, and other United Nations agencies and institutions have all failed to stop the trade in persons.

Serfdom

Serfdom developed late among tribal peoples, originating in settled farming. Today it is the mode of economic existence for millions of women as well as men. However, it is most visible as the basis of feudalism. Under feudalism serfs are tenants who pay for the right to a small farm not only in cash and produce but also by working for their landlords. The serf tenant has to provide not only his own labor but also that of his wife and children. This system is common today in Latin American and southeast Asian countries, and vestiges of it are only now dying out in industrialized countries. To a landlord, the advantage of serfdom over slavery is that a serf family feeds and maintains itself, whereas slaves must be maintained by the landlords. Often free peasants, owing to bad harvests, have to borrow in order to survive. High interest rates charged for loans to buy food and seed prevent families from paying off their debts: the system is known as debt slavery or bonded labor. To repay the debt, a male peasant, as in classic serfdom, pledges not only the product of his own labor but also that of his whole family.

In free peasant families, marriage requires a woman to provide agricultural labor, to collect fuel and water, and to bear children and perform household work. Unless she personally markets some of her own produce and establishes an incontrovertible cash value for that part of her work, her economic contribution, being unpaid, is valued less than that of a paid servant.

Serfs, bonded families, and females whose work in food production for their families is unacknowledged lower the status of free paid workers doing the same jobs. The taint of servility sticks not only to agriculture but also to other work done for landlords mainly by women: cleaning, laundering, making and mending clothes, and preparing food are still termed *menial*. The status of a worker in agriculture has risen to equal that of a worker in manufacturing only in the last 100 years as farming has been increasingly mechanized in industrialized countries.

Making Goods for the Market: Female Labor

The economic status of craft manufactures, in which people provide their own raw materials and in which women often participate, is high in preindustrial societies. Women also play a significant part in land-based commerce, especially when they can sell their own products locally, and, in West Africa, much farther afield. Less commonly, they engage in seaborne trade; for example, the Mamas Benz of Lomé in Togoland import foreign goods like cigarettes and whiskey.

The status of all workers deteriorated when merchants, usually male, began providing raw materials and paying outworkers to turn them into finished products. Landless people, unable to grow their own food and therefore unable to support themselves in this new ecomonic environment, became virtual employees of a raw material supplier; their numbers increased with the growth of towns. As in serfdom and bonded labor, whole families are employed in this way. Large numbers of women are involved because of their skill in making clothes, accessories, and soft furnishings. The low "piece rates" paid compel them to work at unhealthily intensive speeds for overlong hours so they become "sweated labor." Homework cuts employers' overhead, for the employee in her own home pays for the power, light, heat, water, and premises and the work may be hidden so employers do not pay any statutory social insurance.

The ease with which people with little bargaining strength could be induced to accept low wages resulted in their not being paid much when machines were introduced that required a power source not available in people's homes and manufacturing moved into factories. Girls from peasant families in southeast Asia, India, Mozambique, and other parts of Africa, and from Latin America and the West Indies, are employed in local factories and compete with female labor in old industrialized countries not only in textiles, clothing, and printing but also in manufacturing the most up-to-date electronics components. This competition is so strong that the European Union (EU) has tried to limit clothing and textile imports and the United States has tried to reduce competition in electronic goods.

The governments of newly industrializing countries (NICs) compete with one another for foreign investment. The earliest NICs—South Korea, Hong Kong, and Taiwan—lost their competitive edge to Singapore, Malaysia, Thailand, and the Philippines, which in turn have been overtaken by Indonesia, China, Bangladesh, Sri Lanka, and Vietnam. The prime attractions are readily available and cheap female labor in special economic processing zones and lax health and safety regulations and laws. Criticism by some western companies of bad conditions in the factories of their Asian subcontractors has been seen as protectionism against Asian competition. However, in industrialized countries, too, depressed areas compete with one another and with Asian countries to attract investment and jobs. This policy of locating businesses where the cheapest competent labor is available is now also being applied to office work. For example, a U.S. company outsources its data processing to Barbados rather then having it done in New York City. In industrializing, as in industrialized countries, women predominate in these often low-paid clerical and related jobs.

Some argue that the cheapness of female labor protects women's jobs and may create opportunities for work. For instance, in self-service supermarkets, much that used to be done by experienced, knowledgeable men grocers is now done by computerized ordering and by women operating sophisticated adding machines at checkouts.

However, not only low pay but also increasing job insecurity undermines economic status. White-collar jobs in offices and banks are no longer secure in industrialized countries like Britain that are more and more using short-term contractors.

Cheap female labor is still a feature of skilled occupations largely staffed by women. Semiskilled women engineers, employed because of their ability to deal with tiny components, emerged from the unskilled classification only at the end of the twentieth century. In the Russian Federation, the medical field, at all but the highest specialist level, and teaching are largely staffed by women, as they were in the Soviet Union earlier. Yet they have always been low paid and today, like other public servants, have to struggle for wages owed to them by the state because public finance is chaotic.

The twentieth century was marked by global financial crises, notably in the late 1920s and 1930s and in the 1980s and 1990s. In the intensified effort to survive, people competed for jobs, undercutting one another's wages: to gain work, women accepted less money than men, and youngsters of both sexes accepted less money than women.

Raising Women's Economic Status

Unions and informal organizations. The reaction to low pay and poor work conditions has been to organize. In industrialized countries women have been a part of trade unionism since it began in the late eighteenth century. From the beginning, however, women found it necessary to set up unions separate from those initiated by men. Within trade unions in some countries women workers are still cold-shouldered by men not only because many women are classed as unskilled whatever their expertise but also because men want the major share of any wage increases.

Throughout the twentieth century and beyond, women continued to set up their own unions. For example, in Hong Kong in 1988, women household workers formed the Asian Domestic Workers Union, whose 1,700 members came from many countries in the region.

There is also a powerful informal organization of women domestic workers in Delhi who pass the word around if one manages to persuade an employer to raise her pay; then the rest follow, pushing up their rates. That these workers live near one another in the same quarter of the city makes it easier for them to cooperate in improving their working conditions. Concentration in factories and offices became important for workers' organization only as transportation developed, enabling people who work together to live far apart.

The women in Delhi have one big advantage. Each works on a part-time daily basis for more than one employer. Each woman specializes in a particular household job, which she does for several households during a week. Each woman is therefore much less vulnerable than an employee working for a single employer, however high-grade the work. People in the latest form of homework, telework, have likewise found they obtain better pay if they work for several employers and not just one; this may also help to compensate for the fact that they neither live in the same area nor work in the same office.

Part-time workers. Part-time work is popular with women because it leaves them time and energy to do family and household jobs while allowing them to earn. The British government's claims that the number of unemployed was much lower in Great Britain than in other EU countries were based on the mass of women part-timers. These women were a form of cheap labor with none of the rights of full-time employees until the early 1980s, when unions began to support them in legal claims of sex discrimination. So much part-time work was done by women that the EU equated their lack of rights with sex discrimination. With trade union help, women have established a European Union directive, giving part-timers pro rata equality of treatment in a range of rights and benefits, including share options, pensions, and holidays. The directive was formally adopted into member states law in 1999 and became operational in 2000.

Banks and credit circles. Some men, like Dr. Muhammad Yunus of Bangladesh, champion poor, illiterate women. Yunus founded the Grameen Bank to enable the rural poor, particularly women, to start making small incomes for themselves. The bank provides credit for loans to small groups; the groups monitor loan repayments, so that the rate of default is very low. The bank's success has inspired similar institutions in 30 other countries. However, men in their roles as heads of families often misuse the bank's loans, diverting then to purposes not approved by the bank: women borrowers are then burdened with more debt.

Informal credit circles were popular in Asia before banks appeared. In Vietnam they are now extremely important, and women run these circles from their homes.

The informal sector. Among women's initiatives to raise their economic status, the most widespread is still the marketing on a small, local scale of surplus produce from gardens and cottage industries. This so-called informal sector escapes official notice and goes unmeasured and untaxed. In trade what matters is numeracy. Literacy becomes important only with the growth of bureaucracies and world trade. Then people have to be able to read regulations and deal with government departments.

International recognition for the self-employed. Ela Bhatt's Self-Employed Women's Association (SEWA), an offshoot of the Women's Wing of the Textile Labor Association of Ahmadabad, Gujarat State, India, assists the organization of petty traders, workers in service jobs and manual labor in agriculture, construction, transportation, cleaning, health, and catering and domestic help, and home-based workers in a variety of trades. It sponsors 40 cooperatives a pioneered women's savings banks that provide women with working capital. Exclusion from national accounts and economic indicators may enable women to escape taxation. Recognition, however, could bring a minimum wage, maternity benefits, worker's compensation, and other welfare measures. Ela Bhatt was one of the six eminent persons whom the president of India is permitted to nominate to uncontested seats

in the Raja Sabha, the upper house of the Indian parliment. She served from 1986 to 1990, and although she retired as SEWA General Secretary in 1996, she and SEWA continue to influence national and international policies. As a result of their campaigning, the International Confederation of Free Trade Unions in 1988 passed the first-ever international resolution on the Recognition and Protection of Home-Based Workers, which benefits women worldwide.

Discrimination or protection. To improve women's economic competitiveness with men, some women in the United States and Latin America propose extending their working hours by lifting bans on their working overnight and in dangerous manufacturing processes. Women struggling for access to paid jobs often believe that limitations on their work hours are intended to cut competition for jobs that men usually do. The limitations are allegedly protecting women's motherhood function. However, in various parts of the world women do what are conventionally regarded as "men's jobs," just as men do "women's jobs"— with the one universal exception of procreation. Proposals to end bans are, however, counterproductive when work is being destroyed by machines and unemployment is high or rising, as two French trade union organizations, Force Ouvrière and the Confédération Générale du Travail, have pointed out. To reduce unemployment and the resulting drain on social security funds, a cut in working hours for both sexes is necessary, banning night work in manufacturing and in offices.

Education, training, and more women in higher-grade jobs. One way to raise women's economic status is by giving girls the same educational opportunities as boys. Traditionally boys have been given better opportunities because of their gender rather than their innate capabilities. This tradition remains strongest in less industrialized countries, but some have recognized the problem and have begun taking steps to repair it. For instance, in Zimbabwe the Department of Women's Affairs stated in 1992 that a comprehensive education program should begin with parents, as a first step toward giving girls more access to education and careers.

Women in industrialized countries worked long and hard to establish educational equality for girls, and they largely succeeded in the last quarter of the twentieth century. Still, there is only a small minority of women in top-level jobs. Attempts to help women into professional jobs must often contend with perceptions of favoritism on the part of ethnic minorities and those engaged in lower-grade work, as the United States discovered when it implemented programs to help undo sexual bias in education and employment. The Equal Employment Opportunity Commission

439

and other federal government agencies from the 1970s had to combat the perception that affirmative action under legislation like the Civil Rights Acts mainly helped educated white women already in higher-grade posts. In the mid-1990s over a third of managers and administrators in industrialized countries were women. But this proportion was as high in some developing countries, notably in Latin America, where some women from rich families still have feudal advantages, such as cheap domestic labor, which enables them to work outside the home. Many women in higher-grade jobs today rely on their own earnings to buy services to ease their double workload, and they have benefited from the mechanization of housework.

It is no use, however, educating and training girls for unemployment. Many high-tech processes, which girls have learned in order to gain well-paid jobs, are being rapidly overtaken by new technological developments. Rates of unemployment in Germany, France, Italy, and Spain are boosted because proportionately more women than men are looking for paid jobs, not only in traditional women's work like textiles and clothing but also in modernized office work. A growing number of girls in western industrialized countries who attend college are opting for training in the one expanding field of employment—the environment, in subjects from veterinary science to geology. They may have less chance of financial success but better job security.

Unpaid Work

The economic status of motherhood and family care.
Childbearing has a recognized economic value in non- and newly industrializing countries, especially where social security is nonexistent or weak. Children, as well as being expected to care for the elderly and infirm, are valued for their labor because they can help with family work from an early age, can be sold, or can earn in paid jobs, although payments are pitifully low. Motherhood generally had no publicly acknowledged value in most industrialized countries until, beginning in the mid-twentieth century, a number of governments began to develop social security provisions for maternity leave to which employers as well as employees have to contribute. As a result some female and male managers and employers—for instance, in Latin American countries and Britain—were found by labor and women's organizations to be reluctant to add to overheads by employing women. In some countries, for example, the United States, with its Family and Medical Leave Act of 1993, maternity leave is unpaid, but employers have to continue to pay health insurance, and employees are entitled

to return to the same or an equivalent job; payment has to be claimed under disability benefit; some U.S. states, however, provide more generously. Moves in Scandinavian countries, Canada, and the European Union to give men some responsibility for families are intended to redress the imbalance so that employers have fewer grounds for preferring men. With the appearance of "rent-a-womb" agencies in the 1980s, childbearing has been given a price, which may help to reestablish the notion that motherhood has an economic value and that childbearing and child rearing are forms of work.

In the former socialist countries of eastern Europe, there was a huge increase in state provision of child care in order to enable women to go out to paid jobs. In the aftermath of the collapse of the socialist system, child care facilities have been closed down. On the other hand, the Cuban State Marriage Service of 1974 required marriage partners to share the work of running their homes. In China there was less socialization of household work following the establishment of the People's Republic in 1949; however, along with girls' equal access to education, many nurseries and kindergartens have been provided. Following initiatives during the revolutionary struggle of the 1930s and 1940s, in 1950 a law decreed that a wife's work in the family home was equivalent to that of a husband outside the home and gave her equal rights to the family property. From the 1980s the numbers of Chinese women in wage employment have risen with the demand for female labor, especially in tourism and in economic processing zones, and more men have been taking on household jobs. However, Confucian and feudal traditions of men having a higher economic status have persisted in the countryside. The All-China Women's Federation hopes that the current shortage of women—particularly in rural farming communities due to female infanticide and the migration of poor women to towns—will increase recognition of women's economic importance. Asian women leaders are well aware that rising populations impede women's efforts to raise their economic status. Children are future competitors for their parents' jobs.

By the late 1990s, under growing pressure from women citizens, more countries had officially taken steps to acknowledge the importance of unpaid work: Trinidad and Tobago in 1996 passed a law; Canada and Switzerland included relevant questions in censuses; New Zealand and Spain initiated "time-use" studies. However, the adoption of "time-use" as a means of measuring the economic worth of unpaid work devalues it. Only the lowest status, least skilled paid jobs are remunerated on time rates of pay; skill and energy are taken into account in most paid jobs.

Geographically small states experience pressure more than large ones. In Belgium, the Netherlands, and parts of Britain there are more people per square hectare than in most other countries, including China and India. Striking a balance between population growth, a country's area and natural resources, and the foreseeable demand for labor is a priority for raising women's economic status, especially where there is high unemployment.

Men's economic measurements. So long as women's economic status is determined by measurements developed by men—gross domestic product (GDP) and gross national product (GNP), which value work in terms of cash or equivalents like oil—the true value of women's economic contributions will remain invisible. For example, the governments of the various Indian states set what they considered a fair payment for work on small and marginal farms. On that basis the women on these farms in the late 1980s were adding about U.S. $62.5 million a day to India's GDP that was never counted.

Beginning in the United States in 1920, women, sometimes supported by men, have been insisting that household and family work has an economic value. In 1947 the International Labor Organization began to include in its statistical yearbooks numbers of female and male "Unpaid Family Workers" in family economic enterprises—that is, in farming, manufacturing, shops, and so on. All unpaid jobs in homes are also done for pay outside; this provides a basis for estimating values through market rates, negotiated agreements, insurance company premiums for replacement of wives and mothers, agency rates, and so on. However, work done for no pay results in low pay for many jobs done for the market. In the 1970s estimates of the cash value of unpaid household work amounted to about a third of GNP in the United States, and 40 percent or just over half, in Canada, depending on whether women's or men's earnings were used for the calculation. That difference in itself was an illustration of women's lesser earnings. In Japan, calculating on the basis of women's earnings would have added only 8.7 percent to the GNP. In Finland, in 1981, the calculated figure was only somewhat higher—an additon of 9.6 percent for house cleaning and child care alone.

The United Nations Children's Fund and the United Nations Development Program in the 1990s began to create alternative measurements to GDP and GNP. Health, education, a clean environment, and free participation all count in the United Nations Development Program's Human Development Index, in which countries with very low GNP per capita rank higher than some ascribed greater GNP values.

The members of the United Nations Commission on the Status of Women are mostly from educated female elites who feel their professional achievements may be belittled if the economic value of unpaid home and family work is acknowledged. The strategic objectives that emerged from the 1995 Women's World Conference supported women's need for paid help with children and family care, but apparently these functions were not counted as economic and part of the labor market. The present United Nations view is that putting a notional value on unpaid work and including it in GDP should be left to individual countries.

No country can afford to pay women for their unpaid work. Countries can, however, acknowledge its value loudly and publicly, and work can be redefined—no longer limited to what is paid for in cash—as effort—all effort—in order to live.

See Also

CAREGIVERS; CASTE; CHILD CARE; CLASS; DOMESTIC LABOR; ECONOMY: OVERVIEW; HOUSEWORK; MATERNITY LEAVE; MULTINATIONAL CORPORATIONS; POVERTY; SLAVERY; VOLUNTEERISM; WORK: FEMINIST THEORIES

References and Further Reading

Anderson, Bridget. 2000. *Doing the dirty work: The global politics of domestic labour.* London: Zed.

Anti-Slavery International. Newsletters. 1993–. London: Anti-Slavery International.

Bales, Kevin. 1999. *Disposable people: New slavery in the global economy.* Berkeley: University of California Press.

Barot, Ronit, Harriet Brady, and Steve Fenton, eds. 1999. *Ethnicity, gender, and social change.* London: Macmillan.

Bhatt, Ela. 1991. Organizing self-employed women toward self-reliance. *Women's Information Network for Asia and the Pacific Newsletter,* nos. 8–9 (Dec.): 15.

Goldschmidt-Clermont, Luisella. 1982. *Unpaid work in the household.* Women, Work, and Development Series 1. Geneva: International Labour Office.

International Labor and Working-Class History 56 (Fall 1999).

Lewenhak, Sheila. 1988. *The revaluation of women's work.* London: Croom Helm.

Lim, Lin Lean. 1996. *More and better jobs for women: An action guide.* Geneva: International Labour Office.

Melkas, Helena, and Richard Anker. 1998. *Gender equality and occupational segregation in Nordic labour markets.* Geneva: International Labour Office.

Survival International. 1994. *Survival Newsletter 33*. London: Survival International.

Waring, Marilyn. 1988. *If women counted*. London: Macmillan.

Sheila Lewenhak

ECONOMICS: Feminist Critiques

Economics is a male-dominated discipline, in terms of practitioners, subject matter, and approach. Feminists both outside and inside economics have sought to develop a feminist interpretation of the economy and have challenged the male bias of the formal discipline. The feminist critique of economics concerns its treatment of women and the limitations of its analysis resulting from its inadequate inclusion of gender.

Economics claims as its domain the whole of reproduction, distribution, and consumption in society: the use of resources, human and physical, to meet human needs. Such a broad definition should include women; however, economics is essentially about male experience or a male view of the world. This is not surprising, given that the majority of economists are male. Throughout the 1990s women made up about 13 percent of the economics faculty at Ph.D.-granting institutions in the United States (Committee on the Status of Women in the Economics Profession, 1999). In New Zealand in 1992 only two of thirty senior staff in economics departments were women (Hyman, 1994: 49).

Furthermore, research on the history of economic thought has shown that a more inclusive view of the economy was systematically undermined (Pujol, 1992). Economics has overwhelmingly concentrated on the public sphere, on the buying and selling of inputs and goods in the market. This focus on price (and wage) determination means that much of the economic activity of women is ignored, because it is unpaid. This partly reflects the actual undervaluing and nonrecognition of women in the real world, of concern to feminists everywhere. It also ignores the underlying relations between the paid and unpaid economies and between household production and market production.

Feminists expose the male bias in the theory and concepts of economics and in the inability of economics to deal adequately with feminist concerns such as gender inequality in the paid market, the gender division of labor, distributional issues within households, and the economic importance of unpaid work. In discussing these issues, explicit account must be taken of differences among the three major paradigms or approaches in economics. The

dominant mainstream approach, called neoclassical economics is characterized by its use of a behavioral model of constrained choice, where individual units (be they persons or firms) maximize their self-interest, and these choices generate the supply and demand of commodities and resources in markets, where prices are determined. The radical paradigm, on the other hand, with more or less explicit roots in the Marxist tradition, emphasizes factors beyond the control of the individual, focusing on the structural forces in the economy that limit and shape the choices people have. The relations of production (class) are central to the analysis. The institutional paradigm, while somewhat diverse and eclectic, draws attention to culture and the inseparability of the political, economic, and social spheres. The institutional context of decision making is of critical importance and leads to more complex, multidisciplinary explanations of economic behavior. Feminists working within each tradition have challenged and critiqued each approach.

Neoclassical Economics

Neoclassical economics has perhaps come under the most attack. The critique includes both the gender biases in the concepts and methods and the problems with traditional economic analysis of women. Neoclassical economics rests on an analysis of how scarcity and choice underlie the allocation of resources. As Becker wrote, "The combined assumptions of maximizing behavior, market equilibrium and stable preferences, used relentlessly and unflinchingly, form the heart of the economic approach" (quoted in Hyman, 1994: 23). Feminist economists join others in challenging how economics has become defined and limited by this approach. They argue that economics should be defined by subject matter, not by one approach. Nelson (1993: 32) suggests that economics should focus on "the provisioning of human life, that is on the commodities and processes necessary to human survival," which would include, but not be limited to, the study of choice.

Feminists have long criticized the concept of the rational economic man, which is the cornerstone of the model of choice in microeconomic theory. The primary unit of analysis is the individual decision maker who makes rational choices among alternatives in accordance with mathematical principles of constrained optimization. The consumer maximizes well-being, termed *utility*, and the producer maximizes profit, subject to constraints. Is this a reasonable approximation of human motivation and behavior? Does it apply more to the behavior of men than women? Individualism and self-reliance are key behavioral attributes built into the models and implicitly championed by the analysis.

Feminists object to how the analysis of the rational economic agent focuses on *choice,* rather than on constraints. People are all dependent at some stage of life, and individuals differ in how much real choice they have in their various economic transactions. The focus on choice tends to translate into laissez-faire attitudes, assuming that economic outcomes are freely and rationally chosen.

The neoclassical model, with its focus on the individual, does not capture the relational aspects of decision making. The model assumes that tastes or preferences are exogenous rather than analyzing the interdependence of tastes and endogenous preference changes (England, 1993; Woolley, 1993). The model also assumes that interpersonal utility comparisons are impossible, because utility is the satisfaction of subjective desires. This rests on a notion of a separative self rather than on an assumption of interconnectedness (England, 1993). It denies absolute measures of well-being and comparisons of group well-being. The model also assumes self-interested behavior, which often translates into selfish behavior. This conception again rests on an individualistic notion of human nature and in turn reinforces individualistic behavior. Only in neoclassical models of the household (the new home economics) is altruism introduced as a form of self-interested behavior, in order to allow for a joint utility function among household members. Feminist critiques of this household model are discussed later. "Overlapping generations" models in new growth theory analysis build on this work on altruism and joint utility functions.

The concept of rational man–economic action is also subject to the general feminist philosophy of science critique of positivism for its implicit gender bias (Nelson, 1992), as well as to the postmodern critique of the universalist claims of positive science. The feminist critique of science draws attention to the dualisms, such as mind/body, objective/subjective, rational/emotional, on which positive science is based. Claims of objectivity and value neutrality are challenged. Science is identified with masculine values and a male standpoint, while the claim is made that such science is value-free and neutral, uncovering universal principles and truths. The feminist critique of science emphasizes the implicit hierarchical duality in this form of analysis—objective versus subjective; hard versus soft science; masculinity versus femininity. Neoclassical economics provides clear examples of this (Nelson, 1995).

In the feminist critique, it is not that economics has simply not yet turned its attention to feminist concerns; rather, the whole construction of the theory and methodology of the discipline reflects the social devaluation of "femininity" and has erased from view feminine reality and nonmasculine worldviews, values, and ways of knowing. Choice, independence of action, competition, individualism—all core aspects of the economic model—are identified in many cultures with masculinity. A related aspect is the defining of male behavior as the norm, implicitly leaving female as the "other." Feminist theory argues that disciplines like economics have an implicitly male standpoint and that this must be balanced by analysis based on a female standpoint. This will require theoretical and methodological tools different from those that have been honed to the male standpoint.

The feminist critique also questions the obsessive mathematical focus of neoclassical economics. Feminist economists do not advocate abandoning mathematics; they advocate opening the discourse to other forms of analysis and argument and emphasize possibilities for other lenses to view economic reality, other rules of the game in the economics discipline. Julie Nelson(1993: 33–34) puts it this way: "I am not claiming or advocating that men do one kind of economics and women another. Nor do I believe that the problem can be solved by asking economists who want a richer approach to simply remove themselves to sociology (as has been suggested more than once)....Rather than keeping high-status economics as it is and pushing all dissidents out, I suggest that the term economics be reclaimed. Let us start by speaking of the mathematical theory of individual choice, as 'the mathematical theory of individual choice,' instead of as 'economic theory'; or the choice-theoretic approach as the 'choice-theoretic approach,' instead of as '*the* economic approach.'"

In addition to critiquing of the conceptual and methodological basis of neoclassical economics, feminists challenge specific applications of the analysis. Women are rendered invisible by the focus on market transactions. The distinction between *production* and *consumption* also makes invisible women's labor by consigning nonmarket production to the sphere of consumption. Much of what women contribute to the economy is explicitly outside the domain of traditional economics. In the simple models of labor supply, the activities of women in the home are labeled "leisure," and only paid work is counted as "work." This invisibility of women's work is most clearly apparent in the *national accounts,* where most nonmarket work is not valued. The standard comment in introductory economics is that gross national product (GNP) goes down if a man marries his housekeeper. The woman's actual work does not change, but it is no longer counted as part of the production of goods and services in the economy. Although this is often acknowledged as an unfortunate oversight, feminist scholars have revealed conscious gen-

443

dered decision making, which turned home production into leisure and eliminated it from "economic activity" (Benería, 1981; Folbre, 1991; Waring, 1988). The definitions of economic activity in the national accounts not only render women's work invisible but also count activities that damage the environment and thus overstate the "value" of our production. Because economic concepts and measures take a narrow and shortsighted view of the economy, they do not provide a full accounting of the value of resources used and output produced. Thus neoclassical economics fails at its own goal of analyzing efficient resource allocation. In the late twentieth century the efforts of women led to significant steps to take better account of unpaid work, through changes to the UN System of National Accounts and the development of satellite accounts by some countries (Benería, 1992).

Neoclassical economics has increasingly turned its attention to household decision making and household production in the *new home economics* (Becker, 1981). Although feminists applaud this focus, they have been highly critical of the analysis. The "new home economics" takes the basic neoclassical model discussed above, with its analysis of maximizing behavior and choice, and applies it to decision making on issues ranging from choice of marriage partner, to time allocation between home and market, to number of children. The subject matter is expanded, but the conceptualization of human behavior is not. This work does not at all satisfactorily address feminist questions about the gender division of labor and the relationship of unpaid domestic work to the paid market sphere. At most it describes the vicious circle women are in, whereby household responsibilities undermine their labor market work and help justify lower wages and lower wages then perpetuate the household sexual division of labor. It fails, however, to shed light on the raison d'être of these gender relationships. It is unable to address issues concerning the function of this unpaid domestic work in the broader economy, as opposed to its utility to the individual household unit. It cannot resolve questions about overall resource allocation, including market and nonmarket activities.

These models of household behavior have to be based on assumptions about how decisions are made. The initial models assumed a joint or family utility function, with no conflict or differences in preferences. Becker (1981) showed that you could reconcile separate individual utility functions with a single household utility function by assuming an altruistic head who made decisions in everyone's best interests. Thus, whereas the market models of rational choice are driven by selfishness, the home models are driven by altruism. Feminists point out the need to recognize elements of

both altruism and selfishness in both spheres. The minimum requirement for a feminist model of the household is one that allows for conflict of interests and patriarchal power relations within and outside the family. Bargaining models have been developed based on cooperative and noncooperative game theory (Hyman, 1994; Lundberg and Pollack, 1996; McElroy and Horney, 1981). Such models assume that individuals within households have different preferences and experiences. All these "collective models" also share the idea that control of market income may influence decision-making power within the household and affect outcomes such as expenditure patterns and labor supply. They challenge the standard economic assumption of the household as an income-pooling unit.

Each household model has to capture the asymmetries between men and women (Woolley, 1993). There are problems with all these models, however, because they all rely on the general neoclassical principle of constrained optimization, with its limited focus. While intrahousehold inequality is now a recognized issue within economics, the neoclassical approach does not provide adequate insight into this central feminist concern. The whole area of the economics of social reproduction remains marginalized and inadequately understood, with profound implications for policy issues in areas such as social security and child welfare (Elson, 1991; Folbre, 1986; Humphries and Rubery, 1984; MacDonald, 1998).

Another crucial topic for feminists that is inadequately addressed in the neoclassical approach is *gender inequality in the labor market*. Feminists are concerned about the gender division of labor and the inequality of outcomes in the labor market. Why do women earn less than men? Neoclassical economics has paid a lot of attention to the analysis of wage differentials. Given the emphasis on competition and individual choice, the neoclassical approach draws attention to productivity-related characteristics that might account for wage differences (such as the amount or type of education "chosen" by the individual) or job attributes that might result in a wage difference due to the forces of supply and demand (such as "heavy" work). To the extent that the gender wage gap can be explained by such factors, it is considered to reflect a well-functioning labor market. There is no interest in the systemic factors that might privilege men in this regard.

Neoclassical theories of discrimination suffer from a focus on the individual (who may have a "taste" for discrimination) and a lack of attention to institutional and social processes. The empirical methodology of neoclassical economics retains this focus on the individual. Research on gender wage differentials uses data on individual employees and their attributes. The analysis proceeds in the tradition of looking at industry, occupation, union/nonunion, or public/private sector wage differences. However, feminists working with such wage equations quickly find that most of the variance is unexplained, using the variables that neoclassical economic theory draws attention to. Neoclassical economics does not facilitate an understanding of the origins, nature, and function of sexism or patriarchy, as manifested in the gender division of labor in the home and in occupational segregation and the glass ceiling in the workplace. These are the "invisible" determinants of wage inequality in the neoclassical literature.

The feminist critique of applied neoclassical economics has tended to focus on its analysis of household and labor market inequalities, but increasing attention is being paid to problems with other topic areas. For example, macroeconomics is increasingly under attack for its implicit male bias and neglect of the sphere of economic reproduction (Bakker, 1994; Cagatay, Elson and Grown, 1995; Elson, 1991). Its focus on market production gives a distorted understanding of the economy. Feminists emphasize the interrelationships between the productive and reproductive sphere and the feedback effects created when the reproductive sphere is unduly stressed, as it was in developing countries undergoing structural adjustment in the late twentieth century (Elson, 1991). Third world feminists have been very active in critiquing the modernization approach to development, with its roots in neoclassical economics (Sen and Grown, 1987), and in developing alternative gender and development analyses.

Radical Economics

Radical economics, or political economy, has a long tradition in economics as an alternative to the neoclassical approach. The radical paradigm, with more or less explicit roots in the Marxist tradition, emphasizes factors beyond the control of the individual, focusing on the structural forces in the economy that limit and shape the choices people have. Issues of power are central to the analysis. This gives it an appeal to feminists attuned to systemic gender inequality, and feminist work in economics is better established within this tradition than within the neoclassical approach. However, radical economics has traditionally focused more on the relations of production and class than of reproduction and gender. The economy that has been studied is the same money economy as in neoclassical economics, and the methodologies of the two approaches are both in the tradition of scientific rationalism and are subject to the same general feminist philosophy of science critiques.

The Marxist tradition, however, has always paid some attention to the unpaid work of women. For example, the analysis of the transformation from the domestic mode of production to capitalism includes its impact on the family and the sexual division of labor. Another example is the relationship of the cost of social reproduction of labor power (including unpaid work) to the production of value. Thus gender relations are more visible in Marxist economics, though they have traditionally been of only peripheral interest in the development of the paradigm. Only the feminists working within this approach have seriously tried to expand the analysis of the relations of reproduction and production under patriarchy and capitalism (Gardiner, 1975; Hartmann, 1979; MacDonald, 1984).

The methodology of radical economics, which emphasizes historical analysis, class conflict, and relations of power, has both attractions and traps as a framework for feminist economics. It is appealing in its fundamental recognition of conflicting interests and systemic power differences among groups and in the questions raised about the family wage and the importance of the reproduction of labor power (Albelda, 1997; Hyman, 1994; MacDonald, 1984). It is disappointing, however, in its emphasis on class divisions, which consistently dwarf or marginalize concerns with other divisions, such as gender or race. Feminist economists did not readily find answers to their concerns about gender inequality in this paradigm. Women have been introduced in certain fields as a topic; however, the overall approach has not been altered by incorporating feminist concerns and analyses.

Feminist critiques of the radical approach focus on the two topic areas discussed in the neoclassical critique: the analysis of the household and the unpaid work of women, and the analysis of gender inequalities in the labor market. These critiques arise from the experience of feminist economists trying to ground their work within the radical approach (Folbre, 1982; Hartmann, 1979).

The radical analysis of the household focuses more on the role of domestic labor in relation to the external economy than on the choices of the individual woman and her family, as in neoclassical analysis. However, as Humphries and Rubery (1984) point out, Marxist economics as well as neoclassical economics treats the family either as totally autonomous (exogenous) or in a reductionist/functionalist way (subsumed to the interests of capital). Marxist economics is also silent on the issue of inequality within the home (Folbre, 1986).

Feminists have tried to bend, stretch, and reinterpret Marxist categories to accommodate gender concerns. For example, the work done by socialist feminists in the area of women's paid and unpaid work and its economic meaning has taken two tracks, drawing on traditional Marxist analytic categories (MacDonald, 1984). The reserve army of labor analysis has been modified to address questions of female labor force participation, and the relationship between reproduction and production in the creation of value has been analyzed at length in the domestic labor debate (Gardiner, 1975). These categories have proved inadequate, and feminist political economists are increasingly moving beyond the straitjacket of traditional concepts (Folbre, 1994).

The radical approach pays considerable attention to the systemic creation of inequalities within the labor market, and this has provided a home for feminists concerned about gender inequalities. They have argued for an analysis of the labor process as inherently gendered, exploring relationships between capitalism and patriarchy (in endless variations) (Hartmann, 1976). In the 1990s considerable attention began to be devoted to racial issues, recognizing the differences among women (Amott and Matthaei, 1991). Despite the considerable body of work on the labor market by feminists within the radical approach, they are still frustrated by the failure of the approach to incorporate gender into the core of its analytic framework. For most economists gender is not a factor unless one is studying household or labor market issues. The more fundamental gendered nature of the economy goes largely unrecognized.

Institutional Economics

The third approach in economics is the institutional tradition. This approach combines the American tradition of Thorstein Veblen with the European tradition of Karl Polanyi and Gunnar Myrdal (Jennings, 1993). The "new institutionalism" associated with Oliver Williamson is not part of this approach but is basically an application of neoclassical principles to the analysis of institutions. Institutionalism constitutes a critique of the neoclassical approach and is in agreement with many elements of the feminist critique. Its focus on culture, historical processes, and collective activity is more in keeping with feminist concerns. Institutionalism, like feminist philosophy, rejects dualistic constructions.

Thus the institutional approach, like the radical approach, views the economy in a holistic way that offers the potential to incorporate feminist analysis. The flavor of the analysis is more interdisciplinary, the view of human behavior more complex than the neoclassical approach. However, that is not to say that institutionalist work has made gender central to its analysis (Peterson and Brown, 1994). Gender blindness characterizes much of this work, as

it does in the related disciplines of anthropology, sociology, and history.

There is also a related institutional literature in labor economics that emphasizes the social context of labor markets and the importance of institutional structures. It exists in opposition to aspects of the neoclassical and radical approaches. Institutional labor economics is less abstract and mathematical than its neoclassical counterpart. There is a more interdisciplinary flavor in both theory and methods. While interested in issues of power, inequality, and conflict, institutionalists do not embrace Marxist categories or method. Institutional work on wage inequality has focused on internal labor markets—the complex job and wage structures of firms that create a world somewhat insulated from competitive market pressures. Institutionalists emphasize rigidities and systemic inequalities in the labor market that give rise to labor market segmentation (MacDonald, 1984). Structural factors, rather than individual choice, are emphasized in explanations of labor market inequality. Systemic inequalities related to race and gender are analyzed. While this approach addresses feminist concerns, its emphasis on "women and other minorities" does not elucidate the fundamental gendered nature of the economy and the particular subordination of women. The focus is paid work and the norm is the good, implicitly male job —with women and minorities cast in the position of "other." Feminists working in this tradition are struggling to have gender and household made more central to the analysis.

Conclusion

Economic theory has failed to provide answers to the most fundamental feminist concerns about the economy, including the pervasive economic subordination of women and the relationship of the unpaid work of women to the formal economy. The critique of neoclassical economics is especially strong, and feminists are also challenging radical and institutional economics. Many feminist issues are essentially economic, yet economics has not provided answers or even frameworks capable of formulating the questions. The critiques outlined in this article are being reiterated by feminists around the globe—in developing and industrialized countries. The hegemony of the neoclassical market model and its dominance in policy making affect women everywhere. Feminists both within and outside the discipline of economics are increasingly challenging this approach. Feminist economics is beginning to take shape, drawing on elements of each of the traditional approaches but fundamentally transforming them in the process. The International Association for Feminist Economics has been active since the early 1990s in promoting feminist inquiry into economic issues, including publishing the journal *Feminist Economics* and holding annual conferences. The literature in feminist economics has grown exponentially and shows every indication of continuing to flourish.

See Also

DIVISION OF LABOR; ECONOMIC STATUS: COMPARATIVE ANLYSIS; ECONOMY: INFORMAL; MARXISM; THIRD WORLD; WORK: FEMINIST THEORIES

References and Further Reading

Albelda, Randy. 1997. *Economics and feminism: Disturbances in the field.* New York: Twayne.

Amott, Teresa, and Julie Matthaei. 1991. *Race, gender, and work: A multicultural economic history of women in the United States.* Boston: South End.

Bakker, Isabella, ed. 1994. *The strategic silence: Gender and economic policy.* London: Zed.

Becker, Gary. 1981. *A treatise on the family.* Cambridge, Mass.: Harvard University Press.

Benería, Lourdes. 1981. Conceptualizing the labor force: The underestimation of women's economic activities. *Journal of Development Studies* 17(3): 11–28.

———. 1992. Accounting for women's work: The progress of two decades. *World Development* 20(11): 1547–1560.

Cagatay, N., D. Elson, and C. Grown, eds. 1995. *Gender, adjustment, and macroeconomics.* Special issue of *World Development* 23(11).

Committee on the Status of Women in the Economics Profession. 1999. *1999 annual report* (www.cswep.org).

Elson, Diane, ed. 1991. *Male bias in the development process.* Manchester: Manchester University Press.

England, Paula. 1993. The separative self: Androcentric bias in neoclassical assumption. In Marianne Ferber and Julie Nelson, eds., *Beyond economic man: Feminist theory and economics.* Chicago: University of Chicago Press.

Ferber, Marianne, and Julie Nelson, eds. 1993. *Beyond economic man: Feminist theory and economics.* Chicago: University of Chicago Press.

Folbre, Nancy. 1982. Exploitation comes home: A critique of the Marxian theory of family labour. *Cambridge Journal of Economics* 6(4): 317–329.

———. 1986. Hearts and spades: Paradigms of household economics. *World Development* 14(2): 245–255.

———. 1991. The unproductive housewife: Her evolution in nineteenth-century economic thought. *Signs* 16(3): 463–484.

———. 1994. *Who pays for the kids? Gender and the structures of constraint.* London: Routledge.

Gardiner, Jean. 1975. Women's domestic labor. *New Left Review,* no. 89.

Hartmann, Heidi. 1976. Capitalism, patriarchy, and segregation by sex. *Signs* 1(3).

———. 1979. The unhappy marriage of Marxism and feminism: Towards a more progressive union. *Capital and Class,* no. 8.

Humphries, Jane, ed. 1995. *Gender and economics.* Aldershot, U.K.: Edward Elgar.

Humphries, Jane, and Jill Rubery. 1984. The reconstitution of the supply side of the labour market. *Cambridge Journal of Economics* 8(4): 331–346.

Hyman, Prue. 1994. *Women and economics: A New Zealand feminist perspective.* Wellington, N. Z.: Bridget Williams.

Jennings, Ann. 1993. Public or private? Institutional economics and feminism. In Marianne Ferber and Julie Nelson, eds., *Beyond economic man: Feminist theory and economics.* Chicago: University of Chicago Press.

Kuiper, Edith, and Jolande Sap, eds. 1995. *Out of the margin: Feminist perspectives on economics.* New York and London: Routledge.

Lundberg, Shelly, and Robert Pollack. 1996. Bargaining and distribution within marriage. *Journal of Economic Perspectives* 10.

MacDonald, Martha. 1984. Economics and feminism: The dismal science? *Studies in Political Economy* 15: 151–178.

———. 1998. Gender and social security policy: Pitfalls and possibilities. *Feminist Economics* 4(1): 1–25.

McElroy, M. J., and M. B. Horney. 1981. Nash bargained household decision-making. *International Economic Review* 22: 333–349.

Nelson, Julie. 1992. Gender, metaphor, and the definition of economics. *Economics and Philosophy* 8(1): 103–125.

———. 1993. The study of choice or the study of provisioning? Gender and the definition of economics. In Marianne Ferber and Julie Nelson, eds., *Beyond economic man: Feminist theory and economics.* Chicago: University of Chicago Press.

———. 1995. Feminism and economics. *Journal of Economic Perspectives* 9(2): 131–148.

Peterson, Janice, and Doug Brown, eds. 1994. *The economic status of women under capitalism: Institutional economics and feminist theory.* Aldershot, U.K.: Edward Elgar.

Peterson, Janice, and Margaret Lewis, eds. 1999. *The Elgar companion to feminist economics.* Northhampton, Mass.: Edward Elgar.

Pujol, Michele. 1992. *Feminism and anti-feminism in early economic thought.* Aldershot, U.K.: Edward Elgar.

Sen, Gita, and Caren Grown, eds. 1987. *Development crises and alternative visions.* New York: Monthly Review.

Waring, Marilyn. 1988. *If women counted.* San Francisco: Harper-Collins.

Woolley, Frances. 1993. The feminist challenge to neoclassical economics. *Cambridge Journal of Economics* 17: 485–500.

Martha MacDonald

ECONOMY: Overview

Everywhere in the world women make a crucial contribution to the economy—that is, to the production of goods and services essential for human survival. But everywhere women's economic status is lower than that of men. Much of women's economic activity is "unwaged" (unpaid) or poorly paid. Very few women are financially independent or participate in economic decision making as business entrepreneurs, as directors of banks and other financial institutions, or as traders in financial markets. There are considerable cross-cultural and cross-class differences in the opportunities available to women and the type of economic activities in which they engage: women of color generally are less well off than white women; women in industrial countries have a wider and different range of economic activities available to them than women in agrarian societies. Religion, education, class, and ethnicity all play a part. But all women have in common the fact that their economic contribution, however extensive, tends to be ignored or underrated and that their economic status and power are less than that of men.

Discourses on Economy and Development

According to many thinkers, the lack of attention to women's economic contribution is a consequence of the predominance of (male) mainstream economic thinking, which renders unwaged work invisible, gives attention only to economic activities that take place in the formal labor market, and undervalues the waged work of women. Writers such as Marilyn Waring (1988), for example, have drawn attention to the distorted view of the economy produced by the collection of government statistics that ignore most of women's productive work. This distorted view is reflected in male-centered definitions of concepts such as work, unemployment, leisure, the informal economy, and development, rendering such definitions inappropriate for the analysis of women's work.

Current literature in economics includes a wide range of works that redress the bias of conventional scholarship on the economy, labor, and development. Such works are written by feminist anthropologists, historians, political scientists, and sociologists from across the globe. Scholarship along these lines may differ in emphasis, but in general it highlights the importance of women's contributions to waged and unwaged labor, the extent of job segregation caused by the sexual division of labor, and the serious economic disadvantages faced by women. It describes differences and similarities in the experiences of women between countries and cultures and emphasizes women's capacity to "fight back," their persistent efforts to carry on with their important daily tasks and to improve the quality of life for their children, their community, and themselves.

Feminist explanations of women's position in the economy and in work and development focus on the nature of patriarchy. Feminists reject theories of rational choice, developed by neoclassical economics, which assume that women *choose* not to take a major role in "market" economic activities. Feminists are also critical of "radical economics," or political economy perspectives, which argue that women's position can be explained solely by the economic processes of capitalism. Instead they argue for the development of feminist economic and social theories that acknowledge the importance of women's unwaged work, explain the connection between women's waged and unwaged work, and—while recognizing the relevance of class, ethnicity, and cultural differences among women—give central attention to patriarchal structures, created by men for men, as the reasons for women's economic disadvantage.

Economy

A fruitful starting point for analysis is the history of women's participation in the economy. A review of this history reveals profound differences in the position of women between gatherer-hunter, agrarian, feudal, industrial capitalist, industrial socialist, and colonized nonwestern societies. Studies indicate gradual deterioration in women's economic status as economic surplus increased: whereas women were central to the survival of their communities in gatherer-hunter societies, they became subordinate to men in subsistence agricultural societies—although they were still major participants in economic activities. For example, Gerda Lerner (1986), describing economic developments in Mesopotamia in the Neolithic period, argued that it was at the time of the development of agriculture that women became sexual and reproductive subordinates, "traded" between men of different tribes as part of warfare and economic exchange. Industrial capitalism brought a new dimension to women's subordination with its sharp distinction between home and work and with its new definitions of the categories of paid work suitable for men and women. It was in this context that the productive work carried out by women in the home became defined as nonwork—being work that did not take place in the public sphere and was not paid.

During the second half of the twentieth century a major economic restructuring took place that rendered the entire world a "global supermarket." In those regions most affected, globalization of agriculture has led to the demise of subsistence economies and therefore of the livelihood of women. Whereas they had once been subsistence producers together with men, women now became defined as "housewives" whose livelihood depended on men (Mies, 1986). Where globalization of industry (for example, in electronics or textiles) occurred, young women were the preferred workers because they could be forced to accept low wages and submit to employers' strict work regimes. As Maria Mies has noted, the processes are similar in developed and developing countries. They involve deregulation, flexibility of labor, "housewifization," and an increase in informal sector work and home-based (sweated) labor.

The poor economic status of women has meant a strong reliance by women on state welfare in those countries—generally only industrialized capitalist countries—where state welfare is provided to modify the negative effects of the market economy. However, in the late twentieth century government policies of privatization eroded such welfare provisions. This led to a reduction in paid-work opportunities for women (traditionally women are employed to provide these state welfare services) and an increased reliance on the unwaged work of women as informal carers and volunteers. In countries without developed welfare systems, women's welfare is normally dependent on family support and their own involvement in subsistence agriculture or paid employment. Where global restructuring has undermined women's opportunities to gain a livelihood through trading or wage labor, without the safety net of state welfare, abject poverty is common. Marginal, unregulated activities such as street vending, work as a domestic servant, and prostitution are the symptoms.

Work

For an analysis of the nature of women's work it is important to reiterate that waged *and* unwaged work need to be considered. Both waged work and unwaged work are extremely varied. Women's unwaged work commonly involves the many physical tasks of being a wife and mother such as food production, meal preparation and feeding of children, water carrying, fuel collection, cleaning, washing,

sewing; it also involves the complex and never-ending emotional labor associated with caring for children and partners. In addition it may include unwaged informal care of the elderly and chronically ill in family and community and volunteer work for charitable organizations. Being a wife may also encompass unwaged work for husbands: doctors' wives act as office receptionist, wives of tradesmen keep the books and answer the telephone, church ministers' wives carry out innumerable social and pastoral tasks, and businessmen's wives are expected to play hostess to important guests (Finch, 1983). In agricultural societies women's work as food producers and traders provides much of the subsistence for their families. Such "informal" work is still common in industrial settings: women take in boarders, baby-sit, clean houses, take in washing and ironing, or do "outwork" within their homes—all work activities that they are paid for but that are not defined as part of the formal labor market (Chen et al., 1999). When in the formal labor market, women are commonly found in low-paying casual and part-time jobs and in areas typically defined as "women's work" in retail, clerical, domestic, service, and so-called caring labor. They tend to work in smaller enterprises, may work in isolated sites (for example, providing domiciliary care to the elderly), and may not have the protection of industrial unions. Especially when they are employed in "caring labor," which is deemed women's natural province, their work is often defined as unskilled.

Women's entry in the professions is generally seen as a benchmark of their progress toward equality. However, the professions remain segregated, with women predominating in lower-status professions and in the lower echelons of high-status professions. The very few women who make it to the top are expected to fit in with the dominant male culture and frequently experience strong resistance from male colleagues. The same applies in the case of senior management and government bureaucracies (see, for example, Cockburn, 1991). The public service sector is an important employer of women in industrialized capitalist countries. This is why the process of privatization—that is, the cutting of government expenditure through transfer of services to the nongovernment profit or not-for-profit sector—has serious implications for women, robbing them of stable job opportunities and relegating the services back to them without pay.

For most women their hours of paid work and the location and type of paid work they undertake are affected by domestic contingencies. When women's paid and unpaid working hours are combined, they work much longer hours than men, and the necessity of juggling their paid and unpaid work often has a deleterious effect on their advancement in paid work. This problem has been recognized in legislation facilitating the combination of paid and family work through the provision of child care, maternity leave, and parental leave. The recognition that women face discrimination when seeking (advancement in) paid work has also led to equal opportunity and antidiscrimination legislation.

Development

The concept of development has frequently been associated with processes of modernization and westernization in so-called developing (sometimes called third world) countries. Since the 1970s feminists have criticized such processes as detrimental to women: they observed that development policies marginalized women's contributions to the economy and inevitably led to a reduction in women's economic opportunities. The feminist preoccupation was to rewrite the "development" agenda so as to emphasize the necessity for a global perspective that focuses on human rather than exclusively economic factors and on a humane economics for an environmentally sustainable, nondestructive economy (Mies, 1997–1998; Shiva, 1989).

The economic opportunities of women in industrialized capitalist countries are also an aspect of development. There are vast differences in the position of women between and within countries in terms of economic structures, educational levels and religious and other cultural factors. For instance, the enterprise system in Japan assumes a worker's lifelong total devotion to one firm (a notion that is difficult to reconcile with a woman's family life cycle); and sex segregation still prevails in some Middle Eastern countries, where women are forbidden to work outside the home in the company of men. It appears that everywhere—even in the most privileged settings of North America, western Europe, Australia, and New Zealand—women are subservient to men, carrying out waged and unwaged economic activities that underpin the wage economy and support men's paid work.

See Also

Specific topics: DEVELOPMENT; ECONOMY; WORK

References and Further Reading

Chen, Martha, Lesley O'Connell, and Jennifer Sebstad. 1999. Counting the invisible workforce: The case of homebased workers. *World Development* 27(3: March): 603–608.

Cockburn, Cynthia. 1991. *In the way of women: Men's resistance to sex equality in organizations.* London: Macmillan.

Finch, Janet. 1983. *Married to the job: Wives' incorporation in men's work.* London: Allen and Unwin.

Lerner, Gerda. 1986. *The creation of patriarchy.* New York: Oxford University Press.

Mies, Maria. 1986. *Patriarchy and accumulation on a world scale.* London: Zed.

———. 1997–1998. Women and work in a sustainable society. *Cross Currents,* no. 47 (Winter): 473–492.

Shiva, Vandana. 1989. *Staying alive: Women, ecology, and development.* London: Zed.

Waring, Marilyn. 1988. *Counting for nothing.* Wellington, N. Z.: Allen and Unwin.

Cora Vellekoop Baldock

ECONOMY: Families and Households

See HOUSEHOLDS: DOMESTIC CONSUMPTION; HOUSEHOLDS: POLITICAL ECONOMY; and HOUSEHOLDS: RESOURCES.

ECONOMY: Global Restructuring

The term *global restructuring* refers to the process of the globalization of the market economy. Although this process started with the beginning of colonialism in the sixteenth century and with the development of capitalism as a world system (Wallerstein, 1974), late twentieth-century discourse on globalization or global restructuring of the economy means that practically all regions and countries of the world are now integrated into the capitalist economy of commodity production and consumption. In this process goods produced in different and distant parts of the world, particularly in the developing or poor countries of the "South," are being sold and consumed in the affluent countries and the "North." This process has had far-reaching consequences for societies in both the South and the North, particularly for women and their work.

In the following overview three stages of global restructuring will be discussed: (1) the colonial period; (2) the period beginning with the early 1970s, which has also been called the new international division of labor; and (3) the period from the late 1980s through the 1990s. When people talk of global restructuring, they usually refer to this last stage, in which global institutions like the World Bank and the International Monetary Fund (IMF) and agreements like the General Agreement on Tariffs and Trade (GATT), which was institutionalized in the World Trade Organization (WTO) in 1995, and the (failed) Multilateral Agreement on Investments (MAI) have been organizing the whole world economy into one global supermarket. The following analysis of this process will focus on its impact on women, particularly on their work, both in the South and in the North.

Colonial Restructuring and Women's Work

As Wallerstein (1974) pointed out, the new economic system that started with colonialism in the sixteenth century was from the beginning a "world system," aiming at dividing the whole world up in to "metropoles," or "core countries," and "colonies," or "peripheries." In this dualistic and hierarchical division of the world the colonies—usually through direct violence and coercion—provided the cheap raw material and the cheap labor for industrialization and the accumulation of ever more capital and wealth in the core countries. In the colonies large masses of people were forcibly taken away from their subsistence base and transported to other parts of the world, where they had to work as slaves or indentured laborers for their colonial masters. In the phase of slavery these masters calculated that it was cheaper "to purchase than to breed" slaves. Therefore, slave women were not allowed to marry or have children and a family. They were treated merely as physical labor power (Reddock, 1994).

Colonial plunder and exploitation are the base on which the modern capitalist industrial society was built. Capitalism also restructured women's lives, work, and identities in the metropoles. Whereas formerly women had been subsistence producers, together with men, they were now defined as "housewives," whose livelihood depended on a male "breadwinner" for the nuclear family. This "housewifization" of women became the complement to the proletarianization of men. But whereas the proletarian sells his labor power for a wage or salary to an employer, the housewife does not get a wage for her work. Because housewives' nonwaged work takes place in the private sphere of the family, it is hidden, together with colonial exploitation and the exploitation of nature, from the eyes of economists and politicians. It does not appear in the UN System of National Accounting (UNSNA) (Waring, 1988) or in national statistics. The exclusion of nonwaged labor and of nature from the concepts, theories, and policies of the formal economy is one of the secrets of its paradigm of permanent growth or accumulation (Bennholdt-Thomsen and Mies, 1999; Mies, 1999).

The New International Division of Labor (NIDL)

The fundamentally colonial structure of the capitalist world economy was not abolished when most of the former colonies won their political independence after World War II. This was the period when old-style colonialism was replaced by the development discourse, which suggested that the former colonial countries could reach the living standard and the wealth of the former metropoles by "catching-up-development" and industrialization (Mies and Shiva, 1993).

By the beginning of the 1970s, particularly after the oil shock (1972), it became clear that this independent development of "underdeveloped" countries had not happened. At the same time the leading economies of the world, and the transnational corporations (TNCs), were confronted with high-wage demands from workers and a flood of petrodollars that they could not profitably invest in their countries. The solution was a restructuring of the international division of labor. In the old international division of labor, the colonies had been used as sources of raw material, which then was manufactured into commodities in the metropoles. Now the TNCs of the United States, Europe, and Japan relocated entire factories to so-called cheap labor countries, particularly southeast Asia and Mexico, later also Tunisia, Sri Lanka, Bangladesh, and other poor countries. The relocated firms had a very high percentage of female workers. The industries that were first relocated were electronics, textiles and garments, toys, and plastics. This transfer was made possible by new inventions in the field of electronics, by cheap transport costs, and by special concessions that the host countries gave to these companies. These concessions included relaxation of labor laws, exemption from import/export tariffs, tax holidays, lax environmental laws, and prohibition of strikes. The relocated production units were established in special areas—Free Production Zones (FPZs), World Market Factories (WMFs), Export Processing Zones (EPZs)—because at this stage the production was not for a home market but for consumers in the North. The TNCs chose these countries because of their low labor costs. In 1994 a production worker in Germany earned $25 per hour, a worker in the United States $16, in Mexico $2.40, in Poland $1.40, in India, China, and Indonesia $0.50 (Woodall, 1994).

Labor costs are so low in the third world not only because these countries are generally poor and have a large pool of unemployed but also because up to 90 percent of workers in the global factories are young, unmarried women. One of the main reasons for hiring young women is that they are assumed to have acquired a "housewife ideology" and to have mastered certain skills related to housework, such as sewing and knitting. They are also supposed to have "nimble fingers" and to be "docile." Moreover, when they get married and have children, many either leave the job or are fired. Also, in the housewife ideology the woman's wage is seen only as a supplement to the man's wage. Because most of these women come from impoverished households, they accept appalling working conditions, including working up to 12 hours per day, an inhuman work speed, sexual harassment, practically coerced labor discipline, and safety and health risks that would not be permitted in northern countries (Mies, 1999).

The global restructuring of the capitalist economy is not restricted to the industries in the EPZs; it has also penetrated agriculture and has created an enormous expansion of what has been called the informal sector in rural and urban areas. It is, above all, the exploitation and overexploitation of women's labor in this informal sector that explain how people in rich countries and classes can buy garments, handicrafts, flowers, fruit, or vegetables year-round from Asia, Africa, and Latin America at a very low price. Owing to the process of modern development in agriculture, particularly the "green revolution," many peasants lost their land or were pauperized. Many had to migrate to the cities, where their women then had to take up domestic service, work in a sweatshop, or work from their homes as homeworkers, organized along the lines of the putting-out system. The sex industry, including prostitution tourism, is also an outcome of this process. It is characteristic of this informal sector that women are defined not as workers but as housewives and therefore do not appear in labor statistics, are not protected by labor laws, and are atomized and consequently not organized. The main features of such work for the global market were analyzed in *The Lace Makers of Narsapur: Indian Housewives Produce for the World Market* (Mies, 1982). In the lace-making industry the women's wages could be much lower than even the minimum wages of a female agricultural laborer. Therefore it is not surprising that in the last decade of the twentieth century the putting-out system and working in the home have been rediscovered by international capital as the optimal form of labor organization—an informal sector that includes both women and men, both in the South and in the North (Werlhof, 1988).

Globalization without a "Human Face"

The third stage of global restructuring began with the recession around 1990. It is characterized by an unprecedented penetration of all regions of the globe and all areas of life by the logic and practice of capital accumulation, epitomized as global free trade. Moreover, owing to the breakdown of "actually existing socialism" in eastern Europe, there no longer seems to be any alternative to this global economic system.

In this stage most of the changes brought about in the second stage of the restructuring of the world economy have continued, but there have been quantitative and qualitative differences. The system of relocating manufacturing industries to low-wage countries has vastly expanded and includes today not only practically all poor countries of the world but also the economically bankrupt eastern European countries, Russia, and China. The closing down of labor-intensive, environmentally polluting plants and relocating them to cheap-labor countries has now also affected other industries in the rich countries like steel, coal mining, and ship and car production. It has led to a massive layoff of skilled workers, mainly male, in Europe and the United States. Moreover, when, due to workers' protests, wages rise in one of the cheap-labor countries, the companies move to a country that is even cheaper—for example, from South Korea to Bangladesh (Bennholdt-Thomsen and Mies, 1999; Elson, 1994).

The restructuring of the global economy in the direction of ever more export-led industrialization, also in the South and in the East, is driven by the big TNCs. In their hands more and more capital and power are concentrated. TNCs control not only most of the world's consumer-goods markets, like computers, cars, household equipment, textiles, and garments, but also almost all primary commodities, like food. Cargill, one of the biggest TNCs, controls 60 percent of the world's trade in cereals. The same concentration can be observed in the field of telecommunication. Almost half of the TNCs are located in the United States, the rest in Europe and Japan. Thus the third world is virtually excluded from this concentration of money and power (Lang and Hines, 1993).

This neocolonial structure of the global economy— Michel Chossudovsky (1994) talks of "market colonialism"—is politically and ideologically upheld by a few global institutions and agreements, such as the World Bank, the IMF, GATT, and the WTO.

The WTO believes that trade barriers, which countries have set up to protect certain areas of their economy and society, have to be removed; the countries have to open their markets to goods and corporations from all over the world. This neoliberal free-trade policy assumes that all trading partners are equal and that by using the principle of comparative advantages, all will benefit equally. But in practice the weaker partners, particularly third world countries, will be forced to accept regulations that threaten their national sovereignty. They have to make their agricultural sector dependent on the TNCs and abandon their policy of food self-sufficiency. They have to allow northern firms to set up their "dirty" industries in their territory. They have to open themselves up to northern banks and insurance companies and, above all, through the GATT clause on trade-related intellectual property rights (TRIPs), allow foreign companies and scientists as patent holders to privatize, monopolize, and commercialize their biological and cultural heritage and common property.

TRIPs are particularly dangerous for the third world against the backdrop of the development of biotechnology, of gene and reproductive engineering. This technology is considered unprecedented in its potential to change the world. Biotechnology TNCs are trying to gain monopoly control over all life-forms, plants, animals, even human genes, above all in the South. This will affect women in particular, who in many countries are responsible for the preservation of seeds (Akhter, 1998; Shiva, 1993).

But the genetic manipulation of plants, animals, and eventually human beings will also have detrimental consequences in the North. Most consumers in the North already depend on TNCs for their food, and they will lose the freedom to choose food that is not manipulated. Because biotechnology is increasingly seen as *the* growth industry, ethical considerations are more and more pushed aside. In these processes women and their capacity to generate new human life are of strategic importance. Reproductive technology is being expanded all over the globe. It opens the way for eugenic, racist, and sexist manipulations and treats women's bodies increasingly as reservoirs of biological raw material for scientific experiments and for bioindustry. Already scientists are asking women to produce "fetal material" for research or for the development of spare parts for organ transplants (Klein, 1989; Mies and Shiva, 1993; Raymond, 1993).

Another consequence of globalization is an increasing polarization of the rich and the poor in the South as well as in the North. One reason for this is the Structural Adjustment Programs (SAPs), which were imposed on indebted third world countries in order to bring their economies under the discipline of the neoliberal "free market." These SAPs have had disastrous consequences, particularly for poor women. The austerity program that the IMF prescribes under the SAPs usually consists in devaluing a country's currency, privatizing hitherto state-run enterprises and institutions; dismantling social programs for the poor, such as primary health care, free education, and subsidies for basic food items; liberalizing trade and promoting export-oriented production; and removing import barriers for foreign consumer goods. In practically all countries of the South and in the former Soviet-block countries, these SAPs have led to an immediate rise in the price of basic goods like bread, an increase in unemployment, and the collapse of basic health care. Primary health care centers were closed down and replaced by family planning centers in many third world countries. In desperation the poor in many countries revolted against the SAPs of the IMF, but their protests were usually brutally suppressed by police forces. In many parts of the world the economic crisis and the increase of poverty and social polarization, sparked off by the neoliberal austerity programs, have led to more violence against women, to social strife, and even ethnic, religious, and racial wars (Chossudovsky, 1994). In the second phase of globalization the poor could still hope that the state would eventually take care of them, but this illusion is no longer possible. The poor and particularly poor women are virtually left to fend for themselves. They are practically expendable, both as producers and as consumers. That is why poor women are the main target of population control.

On the other hand, the new global restructuring has improved the situation of the elites in the third world, so much so that their lifestyle is more or less similar to that of the middle classes in the North (Mies and Shiva, 1993; Sklair, 1994). Until 1997 the fastest growing economies were some of the newly industrializing countries in Asia, such as Thailand, Indonesia, China, and India. Their middle classes are keen to buy western-produced consumer goods, and, according to an analysis by Pam Woodall (1994:13), they helped "to pull the rich world out of the recession of the early 1990s." According to an estimate by the Organization for Economic Cooperation and Development in the early 1990s, the number of consumers in India, China, and Indonesia will total 700 million by 2010. But some argue that the gap between these elite consumers and the poor in their countries will widen further. This trend even continued after the financial meltdown in Indonesia and Thailand in 1997, which made millions of people jobless.

A similar situation can be observed in the North. The computer "revolution" and the relocation of industries to the third world have led to increased unemployment, wage loss, and poverty in the United States and Europe, and the strategies to "solve" this crisis are similar to those being applied in the South: privatization, deregulation, and "flexibilization" of labor; housewifization; and increasingly informal labor relations, with more homeworking. The creation of a cheap labor sector *within* a country, particularly one made up largely of women, the gradual dismantling of the welfare state, the elimination of subsidies, particularly for peasants, follow the same pattern as SAPs in the third world. Owing to all these measures, poverty has returned to the rich countries of the North. Also in the North the polarization between the poor and the rich is increasing. From 1980 to 1990 the income of the richest 5 percent of U.S. citizens rose by 23 percent. In the same period that of the poorest 10 percent sank by 15 percent (George, 1999). Global restructuring has not brought, as its spokespeople promised, more wealth, more equality, and development to *all;* on the contrary, the global capitalist economy can grow only as long as it maintains and re-creates inequality between and within countries as well as between men and women. This was clearly spelled out by Woodall in 1994: "The benefits of international trade come from allowing countries to exploit their comparative advantage, not from requiring them to be identical. And much of the Third World's comparative advantage lies, in one way or another, in the fact of its poverty, in particular, cheap labor and a greater tolerance of pollution" (42). Although the process of neoliberal restructuring of the world economy is still going on, the people most negatively affected by it are increasingly rebelling against further deregulation, privatization, and globalization. Peasants and indigenous people in the South were the first to reject neoliberal globalisation. But since 1998 they have been joined by large protest movements of various NGOs and initiatives in the North. These movements contributed to bringing the MAI to a halt in 1998. And their successful opposition to a further comprehensive round of global trade liberalization helped to turn the third Ministerial Meeting of the WTO in Seattle, at the end of 1999, into a fiasco. In all these movements women have played an important role.

See Also

ECONOMY: OVERVIEW; GLOBALIZATION; INTERNATIONAL RELATIONS; POLITICAL ECONOMY

References and Further Reading

Akhter, Farida. 1992. *Depopulating Bangladesh.* Dhaka: Narigrantha Prabartana.

———. 1998. *Naya Krishi Andolon* (A peasants' movement for food, security, and a happy life in Bangladesh). Dhaka: UBINIG.

Bennholdt-Thomsen, Veronika, and Maria Mies. 1999. *The subsistence perspective: Beyond the globalised economy.* London: Zed.

Chossudovsky, Michel. 1994. *The globalisation of poverty: Impact of the IMF and World Bank reforms,* London: Zed.

Elson, Diana. 1994. Uneven development and the textiles and clothing industry. In Leslie Sklair, ed., *Capitalism and development.* London: Routledge.

George, Susan. 1999. A short history of neoliberalism: Twenty years of elitist economics and chances for structural change. Paper presented at the Conference on Economic Sovereignty in a Globalising World, March, Bangkok.

Klein, Renate D. 1989. *Infertility: Women speak out about their experiences of reproductive medicine.* London: Pandora.

Lang, Tim, and Colin Hines. 1993. *The new protectionism: Protecting the future against free trade.* London: Earthscan.

Mies, Maria. 1982. *The lace makers of Narsapur: Indian housewives produce for the world market.* London: Zed.

———. 1999. *Patriarchy and accumulation on a world scale: Women in the international division of labor.* New ed. London: Zed.

———, and Vandana Shiva. 1993. *Ecofeminism.* London: Zed.

———, Veronika Bennholdt-Thomsen, and Claudia Werlhof. 1988. *Women: The last colony.* London: Zed.

Raymond, Janice. 1993. *Women as wombs: Reproductive technologies and the battle over women's freedom.* San Francisco: Harper.

Reddock, Rhoda. 1994. *Women, labour, and politics in Trinidad and Tobago: A history.* London: Zed.

Shiva, Vandana. 1993. Women's indigenous knowledge and biodiversity. In Maria Mies and Vandana Shiva, *Ecofeminism.* London: Zed.

Sklair, Leslie. 1994. Capitalism and development in global capitalism. In Leslie Sklair, ed., *Capitalism and development.* London: Routledge.

Wallerstein, Immanuel. 1974. *The modern world system: Capitalist agriculture and the origin of the European world economy in the sixteenth century.* New York: Academic.

Waring, Marilyn. 1988. *If women counted: A new feminist economics.* London: Macmillan.

Werlhof, Claudia von. 1988. The proletarian is dead: Long live the housewife! In Maria Mies, Veronika Bennholdt-Thomsen, and Claudia von Werlhof, eds., *Women: The last colony,* 168. London: Zed .

Woodall, Pam. 1994. The global economy. *Economist,* 1 Oct.

Maria Mies

ECONOMY:
History of Women's Participation

Conventionally, economists define economic activity in terms of paid work or labor performed in the production of surplus value. In consequence, women's work that is unpaid and carried out within the home is invariably invisible in official statistics. Food processing, the production of clothing, or the provision of health care through the market are formally recognized as productive work. But the same activities carried out unrecompensed within the home are not counted despite functioning in an identical way to serve basic needs. Feminist writings challenge such orthodox definitions of labor to include both paid and unpaid work: that which creates surplus value, as well as that which relates to subsistence needs, household maintenance, the social exchange of services, child care, and childbirth (Waring, 1988).

Scholarly interpretations of the history of women's participation in the economy have been dominated by the socialist-feminist tradition influenced by the nineteenth-century writings of Lewis Henry Morgan and Friedrich Engels. Fundamentally, this position asserts that the sexual division of labor and women's involvement in production are adversely affected by changing property relations and that segregated spheres focused on production in the "economy" and reproduction in the "family" emerge with the development of class divisions in society.

Critiques of the Engels thesis refute underlying assumptions of the natural basis of the sexual division of labor and the artificial distinctions between economy and family, public and private, production and consumption that follow from adopting constructions of the economy founded in modern capitalism. Also challenged is the lineal evolutionary model of social development that provides the framework for the Morgan-Engels thesis.

A great deal of historical and anthropological research has since been devoted to the comparative analysis of empirical evidence on women's work in different modes of production. Of critical importance has been the research of anthropologists and historians on gatherer-hunter and agrarian societies where production within the household or domestic sphere is the basis of economic provisioning. These studies, alongside research on unpaid work in industrial societies, show that the nature and allocation of productive and reproductive tasks in this more widely constructed understanding of the economy vary considerably across time and cultures (Moore, 1988).

Gatherer-Hunter Societies

Feminist research on foraging societies has deconstructed the myth of "man-the-hunter," which placed male hunting activities at the heart of human evolution in general and of the economy of what are conventionally termed *hunter-gatherer* systems in particular. The discovery that women were major providers of subsistence, contributing up to three-quarters of the food supply (Lee, 1979), challenged assumptions of the marginality of women's contribution in the productive sphere. These findings altered widely held essentialist views that tied women's work to the reproductive sphere, while men dominated economic production as the primary providers of subsistence. Ethnographic research also uncovered a much less exclusive sexual division of labor among some gatherer-hunter groups than had previously been thought. Women were found to be competent hunters, and men actively participated in child care in many gatherer-hunter societies.

Women in these societies used various methods to space and limit the number of children. The difficulties of carrying and feeding more than one young child in such a mobile lifestyle, and the fact that in small groups there was a limited pool of people to assist with child care, have been suggested as motivations for women's decisions regarding whether to bear a child or to keep it after birth. Motherhood has often been assumed to limit women's productive work, but there is evidence that women in these societies restricted their activities for only a short time after childbirth and that child care was adjusted according to the demands of other work (Dahlberg, 1981: 20–23).

Research on gatherer-hunter groups settling and adopting new economic bases in the contemporary period supports the general thesis that women's roles have become restricted with the shift to other modes of production. A decline in the relative valuation of women's economic contribution tends to be accompanied by a loss of autonomy and status as agriculture, trade, or wage labor supplant the traditional gathering subsistence base. For an interesting case study, see Howell's (1983) research on socioeconomic change among the Chewong.

Agrarian Societies

Ester Boserup's classic study, *Woman's Role in Economic Development* (1970), redressed previously prevailing stereotypes of the sexual division of labor in agrarian societies. Although it is true that women were restricted or excluded from working in the fields in regions such as Europe and parts of Asia, where male-controlled plow technology was (and still is) dominant, the situation is markedly different under other farming regimes. Shifting cultivation, the typical farming pattern among nonstate societies in Africa, South America, and Asia, has involved high rates of female participation, as does wet-rice cultivation in southeast Asia. In shifting cultivation, an extensive form of agriculture that does not involve plowing the soil or irrigation, the heavy labor of felling trees is normally a male activity. Women usually sow, weed, and harvest the crop. The disproportionate amount of farming labor carried out by women in African shifting-cultivation economies led Boserup to term these *female farming systems* (16–24).

The prominent role of women in the labor force of the wet-rice cultivating societies of southeast Asia is a notable exception to the evidence on intensive cultivation. In this case, the considerable labor demands of transplanting, weeding, and harvesting encouraged a system where male and female participation was roughly equal and in some cases undifferentiated. Boserup (1970: 35) argued that population densities determined the kind of farming regime needed to support the population and that technology and labor demands within each of these productive systems determined that in general women controlled agriculture in shifting cultivation; men dominated extensive plow-farming systems; and both sexes contributed the heavy labor demanded by intensive irrigated agriculture.

Cross-cultural studies by Jack Goody (1976, 1990) presented a complementary interpretation of the role of women in agrarian economies but focused on the transmission of property through marriage and inheritance rather than treating demography and technology as the pivotal variables, as did Boserup. An important contribution of Goody's approach was a recognition that in precapitalist agrarian societies such as China, which had a highly developed state and class structure, there was a marked difference between the economic roles and positions of elite and peasant women.

Although there remains considerable debate about causal relationships, the work of Boserup and Goody presented convincing evidence of the interconnections between patterns of kinship, demography, modes of production, and the role and status of women cross-culturally. However, both schlolars shared an emphasis on economic structures and material determinants that many feminist analysts regard as inadequate to explain the widespread devaluation of women's work, even in many societies where women's substantive contribution to the economy is visible and recognized. Feminists have looked to theories of patriarchy to explain how ideology and culture associated with the reproductive and domestic spheres are linked to social and economic structures with adverse material consequences for women.

Thus Gerda Lerner (1986), for example, argued that with the initial development of agriculture in the Neolithic period, women's sexuality and their reproductive capacity became commodified under arrangements controlled by men. Women became a "resource" as they were "exchanged" between tribal groups in order to create marriage alliances, thereby reducing the incidence of warfare between groups. The acquisition of women and their reproduction of children were important for male prestige, while women's labor contributed to the accumulation of surplus.

In early agrarian state societies, such as that of Mesopotamia, the patriarchal family became institutionalized. Male family heads represented their households in the public realm and were dependent on the king or state bureaucracy for the allocation of resources. The state enacted numerous laws to regulate female sexuality. These power relations were mirrored at the household level in the male family heads control over both resources, and their female kin's production and sexuality. Daughters of the poor were sold by their families as brides or into prostitution. Women, as slaves, were required to provide sexual services as part of their labor, and their children became the property of their masters (Lerner, 1986).

European Feudal Society

In medieval Europe, although women were generally excluded from political life, they played an active economic role. There was a wide variation in the assignment of tasks between men and women, but husband and wife were mutually dependent and both supported their children. Rural women in general worked in the house, barn, farmyard, and garden, and much less often in the fields. They ventured infrequently into village and public life, except for marketing. Research indicates that in feudal England key activities such as plowing brought men "into the political arena of feudal services and obligations, emphasizing their public role as representative of the household" (Bradley, 1989: 35).

In the city, women worked in the home or shop along with men. However, they performed different tasks from men and did not take finished articles to the marketplace. Whereas men tended to specialize, women were more likely to generalize and to take on less valued types of work. Their jobs were usually linked to their marital status and their location in the life cycle and were frequently considered a "sideline" activity. Often women obtained work through male relatives, such as husbands or fathers. When they were employed for wages, their pay was less than that of men. As in the twentieth century, women's work histories were fragmented and intermittent, unlike those of men, who remained at their chosen craft throughout their working life (Bradley, 1989: 35).

Women were members of artisan guilds, but this was often through their husbands or fathers, rather than as independent craftswomen. Some guilds were exclusively filled by women (for example, Paris and Cologne), but these were administered by men, with the result that women were excluded from positions through which they could achieve high social status. Women appear clustered in a number of occupations outside guild-organized crafts. The most common of these were spinning, brewing, retailing, and general provisioning (Charles, 1985: 7).

Debates range over the nature of the power relationships within marriage. Some authors, such as Louise Tilly and Joan Scott (1978), saw the partnership of husband and wife as complementary in that although men and women performed different roles, both were essential to the family economy and one was not subordinate to the other. Others, such as Lindsey Charles (1985), argued that women were relegated to more marginalized and secondary work roles and that this was because men held ultimate power within the family. This power difference is argued to be reflected in the lower value men assigned to women's work and their reluctance to take part in such work, a point also conceded by Boserup (Bradley, 1989: 37–38).

Part of the difficulty in coming to an agreement in the debate is that the evidence available indicates that there was great variability in the sexual division of labor between regions and even within communities. There were expectations regarding gender roles, but the sexual division of labor was flexible. This enabled some women to challenge the rules and achieve and maintain economic independence, particularly in early and middle medieval times.

The Beguine movement, which sprang up during the Middle Ages in the Low Countries, Germany, and France, offered women the opportunity for independent self-supporting livelihoods outside the confines of marriage and convent. Beguines competed with guilds in the cloth-making industry until guild restrictions on their use of tools forced them to rely on work in the non-competing areas of education and nursing. They undertook literary and scholarly work, some of which was regarded by church authorities as challenging orthodox theology.

Medieval women also contested prescribed domestic roles by entering one of the many convents that flourished during this period. Although working in the male-dominated confines of the Catholic church, nuns and abbesses were free to pursue their activities in a protected environment. They made substantial contributions to science, the arts, and the establishment of social services. However, by the late Middle Ages the influence of churchwomen had waned. Outside the church, women's opportunities external to the domestic setting were also rapidly narrowing. One manifestation of this was the diminishing guild membership of women and the suppression of the Beguines by guild restriction and church authorities (Shahar, 1983)

Industrial Capitalism

In the process of capitalist industrialization in Europe during the eighteenth and nineteenth centuries, new definitions of the division of labor emerged in the types of work allocated to women and men and through the separation of home and workplace. In the early period of European industrial capitalism, the range of opportunities for some women to earn a cash income within their home increased. For instance, in Britain the introduction of the "flying shuttle" circa 1760 made male weavers more efficient. This created a demand for more thread. In the 1770s the "spinning jenny" became widely used by women and children working within their homes. A few years later, with the introduction of Arkwright's water frame, the production of warp moved to the factory, where men were employed to work the new machines. For a short time, spinning within the home was maintained in combination with the male-operated factory production, but with further technological developments the entire spinning process was moved into the factory. "Women's work" of spinning became "men's work," not only because of the separation between home and workplace but because women were denied access to the new technology.

In the factories and workshops women were allocated the lowest paid, unskilled, and semiskilled types of work, which were often seen as extensions of their tasks in the home. Greater social value was given to men as workers and to the work they did. Training and use of new technology was therefore provided for men, who were seen as the more important workers.

However, while some women lost work opportunities, an increased demand for cotton cloth and the absence of men during the French revolutionary wars created openings for women in the previously male-dominated weaving industry. Eventually women constituted a high proportion of weavers, but as a group they were still subordinate to male weavers. Few had been apprenticed, and they lacked formal qualifications. Most were dependent on skilled male weavers to set up their looms. Women were paid at a lower rate than men, and because of their presumed lesser skills and the oversupply of labor, their wages rapidly dropped below that which was sufficient for their own reproduction

(Pinchbeck, 1969: 166–82). Working-class women participated extensively in such economic activities outside the home and in paid domestic work, but middle-class women had a different experience. They were increasingly confined to the home to carry out their duties as "housewives" as the ideal of separate public and domestic spheres became institutionalized.

In Britain in the latter part of the nineteenth century, women were increasingly excluded from competition with men for jobs. Opportunities for women in agriculture and domestic industry decreased, and light industry was largely replaced by heavy industry in which mostly male workers were employed. By the end of the nineteenth century only a limited range of waged employment was available for women, and many women lived in poverty. Domestic service continued to be an important source of women's work. Employment opportunities did not expand until the twentieth century, with the creation of the "white-collar" service sector and during wartime.

The contraction in women's wage labor opportunities in the late nineteenth century was linked to social definitions of women's domestic and child-rearing obligations. When production had been located within the home, women's work was only briefly interrupted by childbirth. Women could continue spinning or working at other activities while babies slept or crawled around their feet, and older children helped. Because working-class women's wages were necessary for the family unit's survival, it was necessary for them to work whenever possible. Children were left with elderly relatives or paid baby-sitters, and wet-nursing was widespread. Child mortality rates were high, and not many more than six out of ten children could be expected to live to 20 years of age. At the end of the nineteenth century, legislation was passed regulating wet-nursing and child care, limiting the hours of women's paid work, and prohibiting women from returning to the workforce soon after childbirth. By the early twentieth century, fertility rates among the working class declined as couples deliberately controlled family size. The participation of working-class women in the workforce became periodic or part-time, and the mark of a respectable working-class husband was the ability to keep his wife at home, where she could devote herself to the raising of the children and to household duties (Tilly and Scott, 1978: 228).

Capitalism and the Industrialization of the Nonwestern World

Colonization was stimulated in the nineteenth century as the industrial revolution created a demand for raw materials and new markets. The economic autonomy, status, and rights of colonized women were eroded as the indigenous economy was transformed in the interest of the colonial powers (Etienne and Leacock, 1980). Colonized men were the focus of intervention. They were absorbed into the administration, introduced to new technology, and favored in the production of cash crops and access to resources. Women, whose economically dependent position within a patriarchal nuclear family was assumed by colonial administrators, were excluded from these opportunities. Increasingly, they were identified only with subsistence production. Changes in land tenure from collective rights in land to private property also advantaged men (Boserup, 1970: 58–63; Rogers, 1980: 122–147). Indigenous women were often forced to provide domestic and other services for colonial administrators, landowners, magistrates, and their wives. The work of Christian missionaries in altering beliefs and attitudes was also detrimental to indigenous women's economic position, because their roles were redefined to eclipse traditional forms of female authority and they were made dependent on men.

The processes of capitalization in the nonwestern world and the imposition of western patriarchal values and technologies through "development" policies have been traced by a number of writers. Barbara Rogers (1980) and Maria Mies (1986) argued that capitalism and westernization have compounded patriarchal restrictions in nonwestern cultures, often resulting in a more narrowly constructed "domestic" sphere being reconstituted as women's place. Rogers described the process as one of "domestication," Mies as "housewifization." Both focused on the structural exclusion of women from full participation in the economy and on the role of gender ideologies in producing and reproducing this effect. Since the United Nations' sponsored International Women's Year in 1975, more attention has focused on women and the development process. Yet even programs under the aegis of "women in development" reinforce women's domestic role at the expense of their wider economic participation.

The Capitalization of Agriculture

The global capitalization of agriculture has replaced the predominantly self-subsistent systems of peasant production for the domestic unit with production for the market. Throughout the nonwestern world this process had its beginnings in the colonial period, but it accelerated rapidly in the last half of the twentieth century with the introduction of the green revolution. This "masculinist paradigm of food production," as Vandana Shiva (1989: 96) described capitalist-industrial agriculture, increased productivity per unit of land and labor by introducing substantial capital inputs (hybrid seeds, chemical fertilizers, pesticides, and machinery). Depending on credit and these nonrenewable inputs available only outside the domestic economy, the green revolution shifted the basis of food production from a labor-intensive, subsistence orientation to a mechanized, profit-driven system. The structural and technological changes that accompanied the intensification of rural agricultural production have disporportionately displaced women, whose households traditionally depended on their income from labor-intensive composting, weeding, harvesting, and threshing.

With the displacement of women from traditional occupations, growing landlessness, and the incapacity of the agricultural sector to absorb more labor, many women have migrated in search of work. The international migration of women as domestic workers has been a growing trend since the 1970s, but most movement is within countries and overwhelmingly from rural to urban areas. Industrializing urban areas attract women because of the greater diversity of formal and informal income-earning activities available. Migration of men from rural areas also has important consequences for women's participation in the economy. In many regions, women are increasingly taking over subsistence production, contributing to the "feminization" of agriculture (Moore, 1988: 75).

The Globalization of Industry

Taking advantage of low incomes and displaced labor from the countryside are globally integrated industries seeking a cheap, controllable workforce. In the 1950s and 1960s, rising production costs led corporations to search for new locations with abundant supplies of cheap labor outside the industrialized countries. Many were attracted to Export Processing Zones, which offered lucrative incentives to foreign investors. The effects of the new international division of labor have been double sided for women in developing countries. On the one hand, some aspects of the sexual division of labor prevailing under precapitalist systems are being eroded as women choose, or are forced by the decline of traditional economies, to seek new kinds of work in the expanding industrial sector. On the other hand, global factories are attracted to these new sites of production precisely because they can rely for their profits on the invisibility and devaluation of women's skills acquired in the domestic sphere. Patriarchal gender ideologies continue to ensure low wages and rapid turnover in the female workforce that is the backbone of rapidly changing industries such as electronics (Heyzer and Sen, 1994).

As "gender typing" locates women's work disproportionately at the bottom rung of the occupational hierarchy in the factories and offices of the modern world system, the effects of the construction of the feminine around the domestic and reproductive are even more explicit for the large number of women who must find work outside the "formal" sector of factory and office in the modern economy. These women find themselves on the margins of the urban environment in the often unregulated and sometimes illegal economy of the "informal" sector as street vendors, prostitutes, or domestic servants.

Women are also marginalized in home industry and the "putting-out" system, in which the interconnections between production and reproduction are strikingly apparent. As producers in their own homes, women are part of national and international economies and at the same time juggle their domestic and child care responsibilities. The system is characterized by long working hours and low pay at piece rates, yet the atomization of workers makes it difficult for women to organize against their exploitative conditions (Mies, 1982).

Despite the introduction of equal opportunity legislation in postindustrial societies, women everywhere earn lower incomes than do men. In the United States the median annual earning of full-time working women was 76 percent that of men in 1998 (U.S. Bureau of Labor Statistics, 1999). Even in the former socialist countries of eastern Europe, which claim a commitment to equality and the "emancipation of women," women's wages are on average lower than men's. Their employment is gender typed and restricted to lower-status positions within the occupation. For instance, in the former Soviet Union almost all principals of schools for children up to the age of 7 were women. However, in schools for children from the ages of 8 to 17 only 40 percent of principals were women (Lewenhak, 1992: 189).

Women's collective political and organizational efforts are an important dimension in the struggle to confront the structural and legal bases of economic inequalities. In western and nonwestern countries, women's organizations and self-help groups offer a means by which women can improve their access to resources, training, and political power, offsetting to some extent the forces producing and reproducing gender disparities (Pearson and Jackson, 1998). In Bolivia women have formed production, marketing, and consumer cooperatives to counter their restriction to domestic-centered economic activities. Women in other countries have successfully organized to gain title and rights to land and access to credit. Women's farmer cooperatives in Kenya have flourished, and some have become large-scale businesses (Lewenhak, 1992: 106–108).

In Bangladesh, ordinary women were responsible for the remarkable success of the Grameen Bank micro-credit scheme. In India, urban women in the informal sector organized to protect themselves through SEWA, the Self-Employed Workers Association (Kabeer, 1994).

Organization and self-help do have the potential to empower women and transform society, as Gita Sen and Caren Grown (1987) discuss. Nevertheless, both formal and informal organizations tend to represent particular interest groups rather than women as a whole. There remain many challenges and new problems surrounding women's participation in the economy.

Not least among the issues raised by feminist scholarship has been the "double burden" induced or accentuated by women's increasing participation in the paid workforce. Asymmetries are compounded when income-generating activities are added to women's responsibilities in the reproductive sphere. Women in Development (WID) policies were criticized for their one-dimensional focus on economic participation, while failing to recognize the broader context of gendered power relations that have to be addressed for women's empowerment (Kabeer, 1994). Caroline Moser (1993) points to a third dimension of the gendered division of labor revolving around the largely unrecognized collective consumption and community management tasks women perform. She argues that a "triple role framework" is required for a more complete analysis and appropriate interventions, particularly for women in the low-income part of the globablizing economy.

Finally, the relationship among gender, the economy, and the global ecological crisis is one of urgent concern. Shiva has written extensively on the destruction of women's knowledge about and control over food production throughout human history. Tied to that loss of knowledge and control is the fate of the poorest segments of the world's population and the environment itself (1989: 104–121). Shiva describes the privatization of property, knowledge, and value, which have paralleled the history of women's displacement from their central roles in the production and reproduction of life in the late twentieth century, as the last phase of capitalism's relentless drive toward enclosure of the commons. The objective of economic participation—production for human needs—has been subverted by capitalist processes divorced from substantive criteria for measuring real worth. Shiva argues that women need to recover the commons, where nature and women's energy and knowledge are again recognized and respected as living capital resources and where local needs for water, food, and fuel

again become the basis for managing the economy (93–95, 220–224).

See Also

CHILD CARE; CHILD LABOR; ECONOMY: INFORMAL; FERTILITY AND FERTILITY TREATMENT; HOUSEHOLDS AND FAMILIES: OVERVIEW; POLITICAL ECONOMY; PROSTITUTION; REPRODUCTION: OVERVIEW; WORK: OCCUPATIONAL EXPERIENCES; WORK: PATTERNS

References and Further Reading

Boserup, Esther. 1970. *Woman's role in economic development.* New York: St. Martin's.

Bradley, Harriet. 1989. *Men's work, women's work: A sociological history of the sexual division of labour in employment.* Cambridge: Polity.

Charles, Lindsey. 1985. Introduction to Lindsey Charles and Lorna Duffin, eds., *Women and work in pre-industrial England,* 1–23. London: Croom Helm.

Dahlberg, Frances, ed. 1981. *Woman the gatherer.* New Haven, Conn.: Yale University Press.

Etienne, Mona, and Eleanor Leacock, eds. 1980. *Women and colonization: Anthropological perspectives.* New York: Praeger.

Goody, Jack. 1976. *Production and reproduction.* Cambridge: Cambridge University Press.

———. 1990. *The Oriental, the ancient, and the primitive: Systems of the family in pre-industrial societies of Eurasia.* Cambridge: Cambridge University Press.

Heyzer, Noelina, and Gita Sen. 1994. *Gender, economic growth, and poverty: Market growth and state planning in Asia and the Pacific.* New Delhi: Kali for Women.

Howell, Signe. 1983. Chewong women in transition: The effects of monetization on a hunter-gatherer society in Malaysia. In *Women and development in southeast Asia.* Occasional Paper no. 1, Women and Development in Southeast Asia I. Canterbury, U.K.: University of Kent.

Kabeer, Naila. 1994. *Reversed realities: Gender hierarchies in development thought.* London: Verso.

Lee, Richard B. 1979. *The !Kung San: Men, women, and work in a foraging society.* Cambridge: Cambridge University Press.

Lerner, Gerda. 1986. *The creation of patriarchy.* New York: Oxford University Press.

Lewenhak, Sheila. 1992. *The revaluation of women's work,* 2nd ed. London: Earthscan.

Mies, Maria. 1982. *The lace makers of Narsapur.* London: Zed.

———. 1986. *Patriarchy and accumulation on a world scale.* London: Zed.

Moore, Henrietta. 1988. *Feminism and anthropology.* Oxford: Basil Blackwell.

Moser, Caroline. 1993. *Gender planning and development: Theory, practice, and training.* London: Routledge.

Pearson, Ruth, and C. Jackson. 1998. *Feminist visions of development: Gender analysis and policy.* London: Routledge.

Pinchbeck, Ivy. 1969. *Women workers and the industrial revolution, 1750–1850.* London: Frank Cass.

Rogers, Barbara. 1980. *The domestication of women: Discrimination in developing societies.* London: Tavistock.

Sen, Gita, and Caren Grown. 1987. *Development, crises, and alternative visions.* New York: Monthly Review.

Shahar, Shulamith. 1983. *The fourth estate: A history of women in the Middle Ages.* London: Methuen.

Shiva, Vandana. 1989. *Staying alive: Women, ecology, and development.* London: Zed.

Tilly, Louise A., and Joan W. Scott. 1978. *Women, work, and family.* New York: Holt, Rinehart, and Winston.

U.S. Bureau of Labor Statistics. 1999. *Highlights of women's earnings in 1998.* Report 928 (http://stats.bls.gov/cpswom98.htm).

Waring, Marilyn. 1988. *Counting for nothing: What men value and what women are worth.* Wellington, N. Z.: Allen and Unwin.

Carol Warren
Gaynor Dawson

ECONOMY: Informal

Informal economy is a term that defines "unregulated" and "unrecorded" small-scale activities that people undertake in order to generate income. These types of economic activity include production, provision of services, and trading of goods. In the developed countries the informal economy is often equated with the "black economy" because many informal activities like construction of a veranda for one's neighbor or baby-sitting are not registered and therefore not taxed. Some would thus call them illegal activities. (Various types of criminal activity are also considered part of the informal economy.) Developing countries have a much broader notion of the informal economy which includes the very diversified activities that are often the main income of households. In developing countries the problem of taxation is often of limited importance because the taxation system is much less regulated than in developed countries.

The notion of an informal economy came about in the 1970s to distinguish a certain kind of economic activity from the kind that goes on in the formal economy: the regulated, registered production by workers who are employed on contracts and the delivery of information about wages to the tax authorities. Women are often highly concentrated in the informal economy, and therefore feminists became interested in analyzing and understanding the dynamics of the informal economy.

Debates about the informal economy have included discussions about both the definition of *informal economy* in general and the role of gender. It is important to stress that it was a *debate,* because the term *informal economy* or *informal sector* covers a wide variety of definitions. Moreover, the approach of discussions about the informal economy in developing and developed countries has been very different.

Interest in the role of women in the informal economy was almost absent in the early debate. This was due partly to the level of abstraction of the analysis but also to the "invisible" nature of women's work. When feminists discuss informal economy, they often prefer the term *informal work,* because a great deal of women's work is informal, due to its reproductive nature, but is not considered illegal. Nursing children, taking care of the elderly, cooking, and so forth, cannot be considered illegal work. When women's studies became more engaged in this field, the concept had to be broadened.

The concept of informal economy was first identified in a 1971 study of Ghana by J. K. Hart, but a report by the International Labour Office (ILO) about Kenya is often mentioned as the point when the concept became well known. In the Kenya report (ILO, 1972), the focus shifted from employment to unemployment, and a category of workers called the working poor was identified. The working poor were employed in the informal sector and were considered to have a very low income compared with the workers in the formal economy.

The characteristics given in the ILO studies of the informal economy in developing countries usually include the following:

1. Ease of entry
2. Reliance on indigenous resources
3. Family ownership of enterprise
4. Small-scale operations
5. Labor-intensive and adapted technology
6. Skills acquired outside the formal school system
7. Unregulated and competitive markets
8. Lack of attention from or direct discouragement by governments

On the other hand, activities in the formal economy are characterized by the following:

1. Difficulty of entry
2. Frequent reliance on overseas resources
3. Corporate ownership
4. Large-scale operations
5. Capital-intensive and often imported technology
6. Formally acquired skills, often obtained abroad
7. Protected markets (tariffs, quotas, and trade licenses)
8. Governmental encouragement

The differences between the two types of economic organization would appear clear-cut, but many questions have been raised about the most salient differences. For example, was the central difference that the informal sector involved small-scale production and was adaptable to local conditions, unlike the formal sector? Was it the difference in income between wage labor and self-employment? Or was the issue the labor market—protected in the formal sector, unprotected in the informal sector?

Moreover, the concept of informal sector was severely criticized for grouping everything that was not formal together, even if there were big differences within the sector between productive activities, trade, domestic service, prostitution, beggary, or income-generating criminal activities. Public policy toward the various activities also differed greatly. Furthermore, the original concern of the ILO was the problem of employment in big cities, and researchers on the informal sector were criticized for not including small-scale nonfarming activities in rural areas.

A further point was basically theoretical: the formal-informal dichotomy pointed to a dual economy in which each sector was independent, driven by its own rules and dynamics, whereas it would be more meaningful to speak of the sectors as interrelated, with one being dominant. The strongest criticism came from Marxist scholars, who pointed out the dependency of the informal economy on the capitalist sector. This school analyzed the informal economy as "petty commodity production," which is a transitional mode of production used to describe a phase in the development of capitalism in Europe in the nineteenth century. That sort of production was never considered an independent or dominant mode, and Marx himself held that the capitalist mode would transform all other forms of commodity production to capitalist production. In reality this petty commodity production has increased rather than decreased. Therefore, Marxists developed the concept of petty commodity production as a mode at the margins of capitalist production but nevertheless integrated and subordinated. Some anticipated that only a small part of the

proletariat would have stable wage employment (Gerry, 1974, 1987).

At this point feminists became much more engaged in the discussion. The gender role had been a very subordinated issue, even if the debate hit on the hot issue of women's increasing participation in the labor market, in the household, and in household production. For male authors, the 1970s were still a period when gender roles were seldom taken into consideration, and the official development policy toward the informal sector focused on males. In the early 1980s the debate about the informal economy was revived and redirected by female researchers such as Noeleen Heyzer and Caroline Moser at the Institute of Development Studies in Sussex, England (for example, Moser, 1978; Moser and Young, 1981).

When the most dynamic economies in developing countries turned to export production, women often constituted a large share of the new labor force. The dominance of female labor accelerated the development of a segment with lower wages in the labor market. For a time this type of "world market factories" attracted the attention of researchers.

The attention now shifted, however, from the previous foci to look at *women's* work. It became clear that young women were employed in the formal labor market, but at the same time a process of informalization of labor was also taking place—that is, women worked increasingly in short-term wage work, subcontracting, or self-employment. Many of these activities took place in the household, and because of ideological assumptions about women as housewives usually dependent on their husbands, their work was not considered important: it was "invisible." Apart from the evident role of reproduction, women are considered responsible for the maintenance of daily life—cooking, sewing, creation of a home environment, taking care of the socialization of children, and so on. It was suggested that because of their multiple roles, women could combine these with work only in the informal sector (Heyzer, 1981). The informal activities were considered "survival strategies," especially for women in poor female-headed households. The dominant approach was, however, that the informal sector was an undesirable adjunct to the formal capitalist economy.

In the early 1980s the informal economy was becoming a focus also in mainstream sociological research of developed societies; but even if women's work was included in the research, it was mainly regarded as an addition to the male-centered account (Pahl, 1984).

Socialist feminists reacted angrily to the fact that women increasingly were employed in informal household activities in the developing world. They saw expanding capitalism as interfering in more and more areas of life and economy, which led to a deterioration of conditions for survival and of human life (Mies et al., 1988). In the mid-1980s, the world economy was characterized by crises of accumulation of national and international capital. Socialist feminists concluded that under these circumstances workers in the formal economy would disappear due to underproductivity and be replaced by low-paid female home labor (Mies et al., 1988: 10). The term *informal economy* was changed to other expressions like *housewifization, marginalized labor processes,* or *households,* which were "seen neither as isolated nor as small units of social organization related to national economies, but instead as basic units of an emerging world-system" (Roldan, 1987). Because of the new trends in the international division of labor, the process of informalization was considered a central characteristic: high-technology firms make use of subcontracting that increasingly involves the informalization of female labor.

Alejandro Portes (1983) suggested a definition of the informal sector that turned the picture on its head by saying that this sector was the area in which the majority of people were employed in developing countries. It included all activities that were not part of contractual and legally regulated employment. This definition embraces various modes of production and allows for a historical point of view: informal sector work did not occur only in the expanding city conglomerates of the third world in the 1960s, but could also be found in the countryside in earlier periods of history. On the other hand, the definition was still not gender oriented per se and, for example, did not include work that was not income generating. In some respects it was back to square one of the early discussion of formal versus informal, yet inverted.

Nevertheless, Portes's concept of informality opened an approach that distinguished informal versus formal work. By including all types of work carried out, except for direct leisure activities, his approach made women's work visible to the same degree as men's, including non-income-generating work; all types of work are important for the production and reproduction of individuals and households (Nørlund, 1990). The question about the relation between the world economy and the local economy is not determined strictly in the definition of informal work, and we need not presume that the relation to capital necessarily leads to increased exploitation. Rather, we should recognize that the relations of production are changing, and the important factor is how these changing relations relate to existing family and gender structures.

The focus on informal work instead of the informal economy or sector bridges the debate of developing and developed societies. Probably owing to the Eurocentrism of the perspectives adopted, the relations between local and global conditions are much more dominant in the debate of developing countries. The international impact on developed countries is not very important in the discussion, but of course the economic crises—at both the national and the global level—of the 1970s and 1980s led to an increase in the informal economy, strengthened by the new information technology.

A striking difference in the debate on the economy in developing and developed countries is that feminist researchers in developing countries were much less engaged in the specific differences between women's and men's work, which became a core issue in the debate in developed countries. In the 1970s in developed countries feminists found trends of de-skilling in women's informal labor in the household because of the competition with mass-produced consumer goods. In the 1980s a new trend of feminist analysis acknowledged the low evaluation of women's skills, a devaluing of women's work whether it was income generating or not, due to dominant male ideology (Baldock, 1990). The central point is that women's work and activities differ substantially from men's, and this is probably the best way of understanding both the low evaluation of and lower wages for work carried out by women. In most developing countries, giving birth to children and raising and educating them are some of the central tasks in life, and, following from this, marriage and reproduction are the central issues for women. Even if marriage and childbearing are less important in western ideology, and even if bringing up children and nursing and taking care of elderly people are tasks that to a higher degree are assumed by the welfare state, still, women's work and activities are more related to the household than men's. This difference is debated by feminists in developed countries as the dichotomy between the private and the public. In developing countries this has not been discussed so thoroughly. It is certain, however, that feminist research on informal work has enhanced our understanding of women's and men's lives in both developing and developed countries.

See Also

DOMESTIC LABOR; ECONOMICS: FEMINIST CRITIQUES; FEMINISM: SOCIALIST; UNEMPLOYMENT; VOLUNTEERISM

References and Further Reading

Baldock, Cora Vellekoop. 1990. *Volunteers in welfare.* Sydney: Allen and Unwin.

Gerry, Chris. 1974. *Petty producers and the urban economy: A case study of Dakar.* WEP Urbanization and Employment Research Program, Working Paper no. 8. Geneva: International Labour Office.

———. 1987. Developing economies and the informal sector in historical perspective. *Annals of the American Academy of Political and Social Sciences,* "The Informal Economy."

Hart, J. K. 1971. Informal income opportunities and urban employment in Ghana. Paper presented at a conference at the Institute of Development Studies, Sussex, U.K. September; later published in revised form in *Journal of Modern African Studies* 11(1973): 61–89.

Heyzer, Noeleen. 1981. *Women, subsistence, and the informal sector: Towards a framework of analysis.* Discussion paper. Sussex, U.K: Institute of Development Studies.

International Labour Office (ILO). 1972. *Employment, incomes, and inequality: A strategy for increasing productive employment in Kenya.* Geneva: International Labour Office.

Mies, Maria, Veronika Bennholdt-Thomsen, and Claudia von Werlhof. 1988. *Women: The last colony.* Zed.

Moser, Caroline. 1978. Informal sector or petty commodity production: Dualism or dependence in urban development? *World Development* 6(9/10: Sept./Oct.): 1041–1064. Special issue on "The Urban Informal Sector: Critical Perspectives."

———, and Kate Young. 1981. Women of the working poor. *Bulletin.* 12(3: July): 3–7. Special issue on "Women and the Informal Sector." Sussex, U.K.: Institute of Development Studies.

Nørlund, Irene. 1990. Informal work: Textile women in Vietnam and the Philippines. In Satya Datta, *Third world urbanization: Reappraisals and new perspectives.* Stockholm: Swedish Council for Research in the Humanities and Social Sciences.

Pahl, R. E. 1984. *Division of labor.* Oxford: Basil Blackwell.

Portes, Alejandro. 1983. The informal sector: Definitions, controversy, and relation to national development. *Review* 7(1): 151–174.

Roldan, Martha. 1987. Yet another meeting on the informal sector? Or the politics of designation and economic restructuring in a gendered world. In *The Informal Sector as an Integral Part of the National Economy,* 22–68. Proceedings of conference in Denmark, 28–30 September. Roskilde: Danish Association of Development Researchers.

Irene Nørlund

ECONOMY: Patterns of Work

See WORK: PATTERNS.

ECONOMY: Welfare and the Economy

Historically, *welfare* has been used as a specialized term to refer to the intervention of the state in capitalist industrialized countries to modify the negative effects of the market economy. If people have to rely solely on paid work for their support, many suffer hardship, and hence welfare states provide an alternative source of income for those unable to participate in paid employment. Welfare state programs have also historically encompassed the collective provision of basic services such as education and health, so that these are not available only to those who can afford to pay for them. As welfare states have matured, they have responded to a wider range of social needs and claims, including those of women. It remains the case, however, that welfare and the economy can only be understood in relation to each other both at the societal and at the individual level. This fundamental relationship was highlighted by policy trends in the 1980s and 1990s that led in most countries to privatization of collective assets and services, cuts to welfare state expenditure, and a reemphasis on the market economy.

Dual Welfare States and the Public-Private Dichotomy

Second-wave feminist writers have been well aware that women's and men's citizenship can only be understood in terms of their differing relations to the economy and the welfare system. This has led to the observation that it is not really accurate to speak of one welfare state; rather, there is a dual system. Effectively there are two welfare states, one for women and one for men, though from the latter decades of the twentieth century these have shown increasing signs of convergence. Nonetheless women's position is still affected by their association with traditional caring roles and an assumed economic dependence on a male breadwinner, despite the reality that rates of employment among married women are high and increasing in many countries and that many women are breadwinners.

Whereas women's welfare state is formed around an assumed location of women within the family or private sphere, men's welfare state is formed around men's location within the public sphere, as breadwinners and as workers within the market economy. This breadwinner role has historically been recognized within men's welfare states through a range of entitlements for a dependent spouse and in some countries, such as Australia and the United Kingdom, through the provision for men of a family wage. The association of women with the private sphere and men with the public is highly significant for gender equality because the public sphere is associated with far greater economic and social rewards and is the sphere in which political power is exercised (Bryson, 1992; Fraser, 1989; Hernes, 1987).

That different welfare states are experienced by men and women is highlighted by the legislation that was enacted in many countries from the 1970s explicitly to address the issues of gender inequality, particularly in relation to employment. The Scandinavian collective term *equality policies* neatly encapsulates the cluster of policies variously referred to in other countries as antidiscrimination, equal employment opportunity, and affirmative action. These policies involve women being responded to as workers, not only as wives and mothers. For example, child care is provided by some states to facilitate women's employment, and when their children are no longer dependent, women may be restricted from claiming entitlements as widows or mothers. Some provisions, for example the sole parent benefit and parental leave to care for young children, were extended to fathers (Sainsbury, 1996), though men are not eagerly taking up these options.

The degree of formal convergence of women's and men's welfare states varies considerably from country to country, with the Scandinavian countries generally the most advanced. These nations tend to be the only states that systematically promote women's independent rather than family status, though other countries, including Australia, are moving in this direction. Nonetheless, even in the Scandinavian nations the effects of former patriarchal structures are still evident. Women still undertake most of the public caring work of the society, particularly of the hands-on kind, as well as taking major responsibility for private caring work. This is linked with lower earnings, lower-status and highly sex-segregated jobs, and high levels of part-time employment. The rate of part-time male and female employment rose during the 1990s and in 1997, among the European Union countries, was 32 percent of all women's employment compared with 6 percent of men's (European Commission, 1999).

The Development of Dual Welfare States

Gendered patterns were built into the very fabric of modern western welfare states, whose origins are traced to various nineteenth-century European poor laws, with the British Poor Laws having been particularly influential. Poor laws generally provided an entitlement to a level of subsistence to those who, for example, through ill health and/or old age, were unable to support themselves through working within the emerging market economy. Assistance was based on an absolute definition of poverty—that is, it was kept to the minimum necessary to keep people alive rather than aiming to provide any level of comfort (Bryson, 1992; chaps. 2 and 3). Where nations are deemed welfare states today, their regimes are based on a relative definition of poverty. This relative approach is aimed not just at subsistence but at providing life chances that compare reasonably with those enjoyed by the nonpoor.

Much nongovernment charitable welfare activity directed to the poor of many countries remains of the subsistence kind, and the poorest countries, where needs are greatest, are unlikely to have institutionalized welfare systems. In countries that are without developed state welfare systems, an individual's welfare is normally dependent on paid employment and families. Hence, for all societies—not just those designated welfare states—to understand women's position, analysis must focus on the interplay of the three key social systems: the family, the market economy, and the state.

Contemporary welfare states also encompass the right of individuals to be fully participating members of their society, and it is on this that the claims of women to equality are based. These rights assume liberal notions of social justice, and although these cannot deliver the radical changes that many feminists would like to see, such as a world at peace and a society more concerned about caring than profit, they have provided an invaluable basis for claims to full citizenship.

Dual Constructions of Entitlement

The seeds of later dual welfare states are evident in the focus of the early poor laws on women as mothers. A major concern was to prevent women having children independent of a male breadwinner and then claiming benefits. Men were responded to as workers, with concern fixated on preventing adult males from choosing welfare rather than paid employment. These concerns are still evident today, in anxiety to prevent "welfare cheating," and they still have their gendered subtext, with the sole mother and the unemployed adult male most often the focus of such anxiety.

Male welfare states historically were constructed around a male-headed family despite the reality that many women have always headed families. In the absence of a male provider, however, the state reinforced the legitimacy of women's dependent status by stepping into the role of economic provider for sole mothers and widows. Widows' and sole parents' pensions, however, were not usually introduced at the earliest stages of welfare state development. As the

465

modern welfare state developed, age, invalidity, and work injury were generally first to be recognized as the bases for state entitlements by all male national legislatures influenced mainly by class politics. In Australia, for example, age and disability pensions were introduced at the national level in 1908 for poor people, though indigenous people were excluded. Women were mainly covered as spouses and were entitled to the age pension five years earlier than men. Nonetheless, women of European origin without spouses, who were otherwise ineligible, received the pensions on the same basis as men, though at 60 rather than 65 years. Just over 30 years later, pensions for civilian widows (including de facto and deserted wives) were introduced, at the same time as national unemployment benefits. War widows, by virtue of their husbands' highly valued contribution to the military effort, had received pensions from World War I. This entitlement attests to the centrality of the male role in the historic construction of women's welfare states.

Women's Welfare State and Relative Poverty

When we consider the characteristics of contemporary women's welfare states, we find that while all originally incorporated a traditional patriarchal construction of family, this family ideology has since been modified to varying degrees. For some of the twentieth century, in Sweden, for example, this male breadwinner ideology has been only weakly reflected in policy. In many countries, including France and Australia, the male breadwinner focus had been moderated, while in some, such as the United Kingdom, Germany, and the Netherlands, it remained strong (Hobson, 1994). The strength of the breadwinner ideology in social policy does not, on its own, however, indicate how securely a welfare state provides support for women, though it does indicate the basis of gendered citizenship. In Sweden there is a consonance between a high level of state support and a lack of focus on the male breadwinner, but this is not the case everywhere. For example, in the Netherlands, state support for sole mothers is of an adequate standard, whereas in the United Kingdom, with a similarly strong male breadwinner ideology, sole mothers are not provided for and are likely to be poor (Hobson, 1994).

Sole parent families are overwhelmingly likely to be headed by mothers. In fact, in the 1990s in the western welfare states, between 80 and 90 percent of sole parent families were female headed. Moreover, these families are likely to have high rates of poverty. Their position provides something of a litmus test for understanding the nature of women's welfare states, because it is not mediated by a male partner (Hobson, 1994). Of nine European countries that Sandra Kamerman (1984) studied in the 1980s, only Swe-

den, and to a lesser extent France (both with well-developed family support policies), came close to having the income of unemployed single mothers equal the average weekly earnings of a production worker.

The legacy of traditional family ideology also affects women with male partners, as was shown by research using data from 10 welfare states collected in the mid-1980s, for the Luxembourg Income Study (Hobson, 1990). It was found that Swedish women were more likely than others to have achieved financial independence, defined as earnings within 10 percent of the earnings of their male partner. Even so, the proportion of financially independent Swedish women was only 11.2 percent. Next was the United States, with 9.6 percent, even though that country lacks a particularly well developed welfare state. Switzerland and the Netherlands, predictably, had the lowest rates. Both welfare states have a strong male breadwinner focus, and only 2.6 percent and 3.4 percent of women, respectively, had reached financial independence (Hobson, 1990: 240).

Women's Welfare State and the Labor Market

Inferior access to the labor market is typical of women's welfare states. Historically, there have been a range of restrictions on women entering occupations and work environments, such as mining, the military, and a range of skilled and unskilled work. Access to certain professions and educational qualifications was restricted, and a bar to the employment of married women was common. In several countries there is still a lack of formal access to some jobs, and in all countries there are many informal barriers.

Even when there is formal equality of access, women's employment position is routinely inferior to that of men. This is particularly critical where benefits from the welfare state are linked to employment through contributions to social insurance systems. Most welfare states have some entitlements linked to prior earnings. Men are therefore systematically advantaged over women because they are likely to be in higher-paying jobs, and they are less likely to have interrupted work histories.

Where income support programs are linked to employment records, welfare states also provide income support that is directly state funded for those such as young unemployed people or sole mothers who are stranded without the necessary employment history to claim social insurance benefits. Such social assistance, however, tends to be viewed less positively and as less of a right than the benefits from contributory social insurance schemes. Benefits tend to be less generous, means tested, and to involve more social control.

Men's welfare state is more focused on work-related benefits and women's on social assistance, with the United

States providing a striking example of such a system. Those who draw benefits via "masculine" social insurance are seen as exercising their rights and are recognized as consumers of services. Those within the "feminine" social assistance system are seen as dependent clients; women of color are particularly highly represented (Fraser, 1989; O'Connor, Orloff, and Shaver, 1999). Social assistance benefits in the United States are far meaner than in other countries and are likely to be identified as charity and to subject their recipients to severe controls. Furthermore, the provisions are often subject to the vagaries of the political climate. Social insurance entitlements, on the other hand, are protected by the electoral strength of the contributors.

Even in countries such as Australia and New Zealand, where historically income replacement pensions were not based on work records, those in the best position in the labor market reap greater welfare state benefits. This is because additional benefits are linked to the occupational system, which effectively acts as a form of welfare, though it is not popularly defined as such. Richard Titmuss (1974), a much quoted British commentator on the welfare state in the post–World War II era, pointed to the importance of actually defining welfare to encompass the occupational context. He identified three main forms of welfare: social welfare, which is the traditionally recognized form and the one that plays a prominent role within women's welfare state, and fiscal and occupational welfare, which are disproportionately male preserves.

Fiscal welfare is made up of money saved through taxation exemptions or subsidies. These include a range of items, such as profits of varying kinds and business or work-related costs such as those for education and career training, travel, or work-related expenses. These taxation benefits can be achieved only by those who pay taxes and are therefore denied to those, such as sole parent pensioners, who pay little or no taxes. Moreover, the exemptions amount to more for those with higher incomes, because the rate of taxation is likely to be higher. Also, those with high incomes are in a better position to have expert accountants to maximize their benefits from the usually complex taxation system. Occupational welfare is also more likely to be associated with high status and higher-paying occupations and is more typical of men's than women's welfare states. Occupational benefits include allowances for entertainment, dress, equipment, meals, cars, accommodation, trips, and the like and usually involve the additional advantage of avoiding the taxation that would be due were these items and services purchased directly by a worker.

Titmuss (1974) likened social welfare to the visible tip of an iceberg, with the other two forms of welfare the equivalent of the very large part hidden below the waterline. He pointed out that even though fiscal welfare and occupational welfare represent only other methods of making state transfers to individuals, through the state forgoing taxes, they are perceived differently from and more positively than social welfare transfers. Women's welfare state does not encompass a fair share of fiscal or occupational welfare. However, because of their longevity and relative poverty, women are usually well represented in social welfare systems, the most stigmatized of Titmuss's three forms of welfare.

Women's Welfare State as Facilitator of Employment

The most significant changes within women's welfare states over the last quarter of the twentieth century were associated with employment. The demands for women's labor, combined with women's own claims for gender justice, resulted in increasing rates of employment among married women, and in most countries some attempt was made to promote more equal employment opportunity. Measures taken included improved access to education, efforts to stop direct and indirect discrimination in the workforce, and attempts to increase women's pay rates. There were also efforts to facilitate the combination of paid and family work through provisions such as child care, maternity leave, and parental leave for the care of young or sick children. In some countries there was a reduction of the hours of employment for those with caring responsibilities. The Scandinavian welfare states are, however, the only countries to have a reasonably comprehensive approach to the issue of the combination of work and family roles. A sign of the global recognition of the importance of such policies is found in the International Labour Organization's Convention 156, "Equal Opportunity and Equal Treatment for Men and Women Workers: Workers with Family Responsibilities."

The public sector, particularly those areas providing caring services, has become an important source of employment opportunities for some women as welfare states have expanded, though less so for those with the least advantages. These jobs are important for two reasons. First, state employment has traditionally provided better working conditions and been more directly responsible for equal employment policy measures. Second, services providing care for children, the aged, and the sick, and those with disabilities potentially free women from at least some of their traditional family obligations, thus facilitating their independence from family and their access to the advantage of the public sphere of paid employment. The centrality of the public sector for women's employment means that late twentieth-century global trends to cut expenditure on the welfare state had particularly serious implications.

Conclusion

The most important changes in the nature of women's welfare state in the course of the twentieth century were associated with more equal access to the market economy through paid employment, though this has failed to deliver equal citizenship. The shadow of woman's traditional family role and her relationship to a patriarchal husband still hangs over women's welfare state. This is reflected in women's poorer economic circumstances, in their overrepresentation within welfare entitlements based on their family status as wife or mother, and in their distinctive and largely secondary relationship to the economy. Women's unpaid family labor still acts as a gatekeeper to financial independence and can be identified as a tax that women are required to pay (Bakker, 1994: 5) before they move into income-producing work in the public sphere, which would both keep them out of poverty and give them access to social and political resources equivalent to those enjoyed on the basis of men's welfare state.

See Also

CHILD CARE; EQUAL OPPORTUNITIES; POVERTY; PRIVATIZATION

References and Further Reading

Bakker, Isabella, ed. 1994. *The strategic silence: Gender and economic policy.* London: Zed.

Bryson, Lois. 1992. *Welfare and the state: Who benefits?* London: Macmillan.

European Commission. 1999. 1999 employment report. *Equal Opportunity Magazine* 7: 5.

Fraser, Nancy. 1989. Women, welfare, and the politics of need interpretation. In Nancy Fraser, *Unruly practices: Power, discourse, and gender in contemporary social theory,* 144–160. Cambridge: Polity.

Hernes, Helga. 1987. *Welfare state and woman power.* Oslo: Norwegian University Press.

Hobson, Barbara. 1990. No exit, no voice: Women's economic dependency and the welfare state. *Acta Sociologica* 33(3): 235–250.

———. 1994. Solo mothers, social policy regimes, and the logics of gender. In Diane Sainsbury, ed., *Gendering welfare states.* London: Sage.

Kamerman, Sandra. 1984. Women, children, and poverty: Public policies and female-headed families in industrialized countries. *Signs* 10(2): 249–271.

O'Connor, Julia S., Ann Shola Orloff, and Sheila Shaver. 1999. *States, markets, families: Gender liberalism and social policy in Australia, Canada, Britain, and the United States.* Cambridge: Cambridge University Press.

Sainsbury, Diane. 1996. *Gender, equality, and welfare states.* Cambridge: Cambridge University Press.

Titmuss, Richard. 1974. The social division of welfare: Some reflections on the search for equity. In *Essays on "the welfare state."* London: Allen and Unwin.

Lois Bryson

ECOSYSTEM

Ecosystem refers to a unit of the environment. In contrast with many other entities in the natural world, which are defined by a rigid set of characteristics (for example, molecules, species, quasars), ecosystems are defined by their dominant structures or functions (for example, wetland ecosystems, tundra ecosystems). Nevertheless, ecosystems share a number of features (see box). An observer might look out across a wetland and see only the community of plants there, or she might be interested in how birds use the different plants for food and nesting habitat. However, the ecosystem scientist would specifically consider the interactions of the plants, animals, and microorganisms (the biota) with the nonliving (abiotic) elements of that area: the chemical compounds, including major and minor nutrients as well as toxic compounds, geology, climate, weather, and other elements. The interactions are defined as occurring *within* the system boundaries (defined by the observer to fit the scientific question at hand) or as *passing across* the boundaries. Using the wetland example again: the system boundaries might include the extent of saturated soils across the landscape or the areal limits of water-tolerant plant species.

Ecosystems are studied in various ways, but in general the emphasis is on holistic measures that integrate beyond the level of individual organisms or populations. One such approach is to study the structure of food webs—the interactions of all the biota characterized by feeding relationships (who eats whom?). Often these interactions are characterized by the energy flow (joules or calories) within the system. Another, more refined approach is to consider biogeochemical transformations by both the biotic and abiotic components of the system. Typically an element (for example, nitrogen or carbon) or chemical compound (for example, a specific nutrient like ammonia, NH_3; or a toxicant like PCB) is traced through the system, and the inves-

Principles of Ecosystem Science

1. Ecosystems are open to flows of energy, elements, and biota.
2. Ecosystems are continuously changing; yet the present bears the legacies of the past.
3. Ecosystems are spatially heterogeneous on a range of scales, and ecosystem structure and function depend on that heterogeneity.
4. Indirect effects are the rule, rather than the exception, in most ecosystems.
5. The function of an ecosystem depends on its biological structure; species do not have equal effects on an ecosystem; and an organism's size is not a good indicator of its importance to ecosystem function.
6. There is redundancy within functional groups in ecosystems; this reduces variation in ecosystem function when environmental conditions change.
7. Humans are now part of *all* ecosystems. (Meyer, 1997)

tigator learns of the fate (where does it accumulate?) or transformation of the element or compound. Ecosystem ecologists are concerned about not only ultimate fate and transformations but also the rates of transformations (fluxes), the degree of interactions of the element or compound (the scale of interaction), and, often, how human activities alter these fluxes.

Ecosystem ecology is a relatively young science. The term *ecosystem* was coined by Arthur Tansley, a British ecologist, in 1935, to give form and substance to ideas that were developing at the time. Few women were involved in the early development of ecosystem concepts and studies because of the general prejudice against women in the sciences. Among the early women scientists whose work influenced the field, either directly or indirectly (often by influencing their husbands!), were Ellen Swallow Richards (1842–1911), who in the late nineteenth century drew attention to industrial pollution effects in the United States, and Edith Schwartz Clements (1877–1971), who received a doctorate in 1904 and, with her husband, Frederic, developed seminal concepts of plant community interactions. Rachel Carson (1907–1964) provoked public and scientific awareness of the impact of humans on ecosystems with her many writings, particularly *Silent Spring,* published in 1962. Since 1950, the number of women influencing the field has increased exponentially. Many of the important contributions arose in aquatic ecosystems, because it is easier to

conceptualize their boundaries and biotic-abiotic interactions.

Ecosystems are vital for conservation of biodiversity and for the preservation of the "ecological goods and services" on which civilizations depend, including not only food resources but also fertile soils, clean water and air, and a climate within the limits of biological tolerance.

See Also

EARTH; ENVIRONMENT: OVERVIEW; GAIA; MOTHER EARTH

References and Further Reading

Carson, Rachel. 1962. *Silent spring.* Boston: Houghton Mifflin.
Golley, F. B. 1993. *A history of the ecosystem concept in ecology: More than the sum of the parts.* New Haven, Conn.: Yale University Press.
Hagen, Joel B. 1992. *An entangled bank: The origins of ecosystem ecology.* New Brunswick, N.J.: Rutgers University Press.
McIntosh, R. P. 1985. *The background of ecology: Concept and theory.* Cambridge: Cambridge University Press.
Meyer, Judy L. 1997. Conserving ecosystem function. In S. T. A. Pickett et al., eds., *Enhancing the ecological basis of conservation: Heterogeneity, ecosystem function, and biodiveristy,* 126–145. New York: Chapman and Hall.

Karin Limburg

ÉCRITURE FÉMININE

Écriture féminine—or feminine writing—is a concept that derives primarily from the work of the French feminist critic and writer Hélène Cixous (b. 1938). Sometimes glossed as "a writing of the other," it refers to a mode of writing that refuses appropriation and destruction and consequently challenges the premises of patriarchal rule.

Hélène Cixous

In an influential essay, "Sorties" (1975), Cixous outlines some of the features of feminine writing, arguing that it is a practice that is impossible to define. Its importance, she stresses, lies in its capacity to circumvent the binary structures embedded in our current "masculine" system of thinking, whereby whatever is designated as different or "other" is devalued, made use of, or destroyed. Cixous understands the terms *masculine* and *feminine* as behavioral "economies" rather than as adjectives linked to biological sex. On the one hand, there is the masculine position of obedience with its concomitant fear and desire for control; on the other, there is the feminine position of risk, characterized by openness, generosity, and a refusal to destroy. Although Cixous believes that both these positions are open to men as well as women and are in constant flux, she suggests that for cultural and biological reasons women are more likely to adopt a feminine practice than men. As a result, her discussions of feminine writers include both male and female authors.

For Cixous, most writers struggle to "master" their material, annihilating complexity and entirety in their endeavor for order and self-glorification. She argues that feminine writing by contrast begins with the "other," relinquishing the demands of the self and the dictates of convention and faithfully inscribing "life as it is." In thus circumventing the prevailing hegemony, it posits new models for self-other relations and envisions corresponding changes in perception, representation, and ideology.

In *Le Livre de Promethea* (1983, The book of Promethea) Cixous offers a possible model for a writing directed not by the self but by the "other." The book is of Promethea not only because it is about her but also because it is Promethea who produces and directs what it says. This alters the writer's role from author to scribe. The writer's endeavor to convey Promethea involves relinquishing all her previous techniques and tools. Her task of "listening" and faithfully rendering Promethea requires vigilance to prevent her own needs and desires from sabotaging this process. Even her skill as a writer must be continually examined so that it too does not eclipse the truth. Cixous is dismissive of the notion of a work of art and stresses that the feminine writer's mission is a "work of being."

The phrase "write your body" has become a rallying cry for *écriture féminine*. For Cixous, this has three main components. First, she believes that women's bodies—including women's self-perceptions and sexual experiences—have been appropriated and determined by men. Consequently, she urges women to break with these restrictive definitions and to record their discoveries in writing. This inscription, she argues, will detonate the partitions and codes of the masculine schema by opening this up to other possibilities. Second, Cixous insists that language is itself an activity of the body. She believes that repression of the physiological source of writing, together with ongoing body functions such as breathing, pulse, drives, and the influence of stress, is a falsification of the nature of the writing process embarked on in a quest for control. Third, Cixous suggests that our bodies link us back to the period in early childhood before socialization and its imposition of law and that this memory of freedom is an important ally in the feminine writer's undertaking to work against restriction and closure. Cixous here is drawing in part on the work of the Austrian psychoana-

lyst Sigmund Freud (1856–1939) and his description of infant socialization in terms of castration and the Oedipus complex. Cixous stresses that women's experience of the father's intervention into the symbiotic union with the mother is different from men's and that women's bodies figure this capacity for union in a way that potentially challenges the otherwise omnipotent stratification of the masculine "symbolic," exploding its constitution and definitions, and with it the individual's relationship to *him*self, the "other," and the world.

Among the other features of *écriture féminine* that Cixous outlines is inclusivity. Cixous argues that feminine writing must refuse to prioritize and select from the range of possible meanings and work, instead, to include everything. She stresses that this is especially true of those significations that threaten or contradict the design the writer hopes to achieve and wishes to impose on the reader. For Cixous, feminine writing spans the unexpected possibilities generated by the writer's attention to herself—including the motivations of the body and the unconscious—language, the promptings of the writing's subject, and those meanings marginalized or distorted by the masculine. In the bilingual *Vivre l'orange/To Live the Orange* (1979) Cixous shows how her attempt to write about the magnificence of an orange must also embrace the reality of torture and murder.

"Writing the other" demands the inscription of that which is repressed by history and culture. In an important essay entitled "La Venue à l'écriture" (1977, Coming to writing), Cixous insists that this must include death, which has become almost completely taboo in western culture. She suggests that recognition of human mortality is vital in enabling us to live and write in a feminine way. In a series of reflections on her own writing for the theater, *Indiade ou l'Inde de leurs rêves* (1987, Indiada or the India of their dreams), Cixous describes how the confrontation with death on stage returns us to what is essential and forces us to reconsider our own lives, attitudes, and actions.

The task of writing the "other" also requires attention to the process of writing. Cixous believes that the masculine desire to limit and control meaning both is reductive and corroborates the status quo, and she urges writers to actively incorporate the myriad rhythms, sound patterns, and signifying possibilities generated by writing itself. Numerous examples of this play can be found in Cixous's own work, such as the deliberate evocation of the two meanings of *voler* as "stealing" and "flying" in "Sorties."

Cixous's insistence that *écriture féminine* attend to the multifarious possibilities generated by writing and refuse to shy away from difficult or painful subject matter has implications for genre. Conventional characters and plot are dispensed with as the writer engages in the complex task of rendering life. The pages of Cixous's *Le Livre de Promethea,* for example, are presented in the disorder of their composition as the author overcomes her desire to rewrite; other texts, such as the early *Neurtre* (1972, Neutral), involve a radical reworking of syntax, page layout, and even typography to convey a rich polysemy. This has led some critics to question the effectiveness of feminine writing, on the grounds that it is difficult to read and consequently elitist (see Sellers, 1996).

Cixous's extensive criticism details numerous instances of *écriture féminine.* Her work covers male writers as various as William Shakespeare (1564–1616), Heinrich von Kleist (1777–1811), Franz Kafka (1883–1924), Jean Genet (1910–1986), and James Joyce (1882–1941), as well as female writers such as the Russian poet Marina Tsvetayeva (1892–1941) and the Brazilian novelist Clarice Lispector (1925–1977). The latter remains perhaps the outstanding illustration for Cixous of feminine writing.

Luce Irigaray

Though neither uses the phrase directly in her work, Luce Irigaray (b. 1930) and Julia Kristeva (b. 1941) can also be linked to the concept of *écriture féminine.* In an essay entitled "Pouvoir du discours, subordination du féminin" (1977, Power of discourse, subordination of the feminine), the French philosopher Luce Irigaray suggests that inscription of the proximity, fluidity, and multiplicity characteristic of exchanges between women will undermine the destructive forms of conventional discourse. In another essay, "La Mystérique" (1974), she reviews those languages traditionally associated with women and sees in the visions and writings of the mystics the model for a language attempting to express what is repressed by doctrine. Many of the features of what Irigaray terms the *new femininity* parallel those delineated by Cixous. For Irigaray the new femininity will be grounded in an "economy of spending," involving an expansion and dissolution of the self and a subsequent refiguring of relationships with others.

Julia Kristeva

In an important book, *La Révolution du langage poétique* (1974, Revolution in poetic language), the Bulgarian-born linguist and psychoanalyst Julia Kristeva argues that writing has the capacity to transform the symbolic order. She distinguishes between a pre-Oedipal or "semiotic" stage in human development in which body drives predominate and the subsequent repression of these as the child becomes socialized. Kristeva suggests that these energies are expressed in infants' babblings as they attempt to copy sounds and in their body movements. Although the constraints imposed on body drives are the necessary precondition for subjectivity and language, Kristeva stresses that drive energies continue to exert pressure on the individual, affecting socialization and hence the status quo. She believes that poetry, because of its comparative freedom from the rules that govern language, enables the fullest expression of the maternal semiotic and thus has the maximum potential for disruption. In a poem, for instance, rhythmic patterns might take precedence over the conventions of syntax, and these patterns unsettle our expectations and beliefs, preparing the way for change. Although Kristeva discusses male authors, such as the French poet Stéphane Mallarmé (1842–1898), among her list of examples, in essays such as "Stabat Mater" (1983) she draws on her own experience of motherhood and analyzes communication between women to envisage a language that would not depend on individual subject positions with their implicit annexing of the "other" but would involve, instead, a contextualized, multifarious, and fluid form of exchange.

The preoccupations and styles of a number of other French women writers, such as Marie Cardinal (b. 1929), Chantal Chawaf (b. 1948), Jeanne Hyvrard (b. 1945), Annie Leclerc (b. 1940), and Monique Wittig (b. 1935), have also been productively linked to the notion of an *écriture féminine* (see Sellers, 1991).

See Also

DIFFERENCE, *I and II*; FEMININITY; LITERARY THEORY AND CRITICISM

References and Further Reading

Cixous, Hélène. 1972. *Neurtre.* Paris: Grasset.

———. 1975. Sorties. In *La jeune née* (The newly born woman) with Catherine Clément. Paris: Union Générale d'Editions. Trans. Betsy Wing, 1986. Minneapolis: University of Minnesota Press.

———, with Madeleine Gagnon and Annie Leclerc. 1977. *La Venue à l'écriture* (Coming to writing). Paris: Union Générale d'Editions. In *"Coming to writing" and other essays.* Trans. Sarah Cornell, Deborah Jensen, Ann Liddle, and Susan Sellers, 1991. Cambridge, Mass.: Harvard University Press.

———. 1979. *Vivre l'orange/To live the orange.* Trans. Sarah Cornell, Ann Liddle, and Hélène Cixous. Paris: Des Femmes.

———. 1983. *Le livre de Promethea* (The book of Promethea). Paris: Gallimard. Trans. Betsy Wing, 1991. Lincoln: University of Nebraska Press.

———. 1987. *Indiade ou l'Inde de leurs rêves.* Paris: Théâtre du Soleil.

———. 1994. *The Hélène Cixous reader.* Ed. Susan Sellers. London: Routledge.

Irigaray, Luce. 1974. La mystérique. In *Speculum de l'autre femme* (Speculum of the other woman). Paris: Minuit. Trans. Gillian C. Gill, 1985. Ithaca, N.Y.: Cornell University Press.

———. 1977. Pouvoir du discours, subordination du féminin. In *Ce sexe qui n'en est pas un* (This sex which is not one). Paris: Minuit. Trans. Catherine Porter, 1985. Ithaca, N.Y.: Cornell University Press.

———. 1991. *The Irigaray reader.* Ed. Margaret Whitford. Oxford: Blackwell.

Kristeva, Julia. 1974. *La révolution du langage poétique* (Revolution in poetic language). Paris: Seuil. Trans. Margaret Waller, 1984. New York: Columbia University Press.

———. 1983. Stabat mater. In *Histoires d'amour* (Tales of love). Paris: Denoël. Trans. Leon S. Roudiez, 1987. New York: Columbia University Press.

———. 1986. *The Kristeva reader.* Ed. Toril Moi. Oxford: Blackwell.

Sellers, Susan. 1991. *Language and sexual difference: Feminist writing in France.* Basingstoke, U.K.: Macmillan.

———. 1996. *Hélène Cixous: Authorship, autobiography, and love.* Cambridge: Polity.

Susan Sellers

EDUCATION: Achievement

Education allows people to reach their full potential within the value system of their culture. Some feminists define educational achievement in terms of personal development and success, often linked to qualifications that lead to well-paid work. Other feminists see educational achievement in terms of the individual's contribution to the advancement of family and community. Feminist research focuses on issues of race, class, and gender that limit women's educational success worldwide and takes into account the national socioeconomic context in which women live. Depending on this context, if women are not enrolled in school, if they fail to complete a stage of education, or if they do not appear in sufficient numbers in higher education to influence policy, then they are not achieving educational success.

Theoretical Positions

Feminist theorists have various understandings of women's educational achievement and offer various strategies for improving it. Between the 1970s and the 1980s, the discipline of the sociology of women's education was established in Australia, Britain, New Zealand, and the United States. This discipline is characterized by several overlapping and interactive perspectives on educational achievement. Liberal feminists aim to alter women's educational status and opportunities within existing social and educational frameworks. They focus on the negative effects of sexual discrimination and on sexual stereotyping within socialization practices, within the home, and at school. Liberal feminists emphasize the role of formal legal rights and the provision of equal opportunities practices in the advancement of women's educational achievement. Although liberal feminism has been criticized by feminists who think it neglects the causes of socialization practices or who reject its individualistic approach, it has made a positive contribution to the educational life chances of many women. These liberal strategies have secured government funding in many countries. Scandinavian countries, in particular, see formal equality as a reality that has benefited the majority of Nordic women.

Radical and socialist feminists have argued that the liberal program does not address the underlying issues that affect the educational achievement of women. Radical feminists focus on the effects of patriarchy that marginalize women's experience and knowledge while prioritizing men within the educational system. Patriarchal values are reinforced by the content of basic literacy programs in most political systems. Even in countries where schooling is universal, schools can define and reinforce gender roles and identity through the curriculum, teachers' attitudes, and physical and verbal sexual harassment, all of which reinforce girls' low self-esteem.

Socialist feminists emphasize that these gender issues work in combination with social and economic conditions. In parts of Asia, Africa, and Latin America high female illiteracy often is linked to rural poverty. Fees for primary school may be limited to boys while girls work at home. Similarly, in the developed world, parents may subsidize sons but not daughters in higher education. Cultural values interconnect with gender and economic considerations. In some cultural contexts the "marriageability" of girls may require their seclusion, thereby reducing school attendance and hence achievement. Parents also may be involved in discussions about dowry that will directly influence girls' educational aspirations. These limited aspirations may reflect social reality: if working-class girls in urban industrialized societies see that they have little chance of obtaining paid employment, then they may lose the motivation to succeed in education. In contrast, upper- and middle-class girls, particularly white girls, often achieve high levels of education, although they still may suffer from socialization factors, as will be discussed later.

Black Feminism and Educational Achievement

Black feminists have been at the forefront of research that shows how "race" intersects with class and gender to determine the educational achievement of many black women. This is particularly true for women who are members of a minority (in a historical context) whose cultural uniqueness has been undermined or violated. The educational repercussions of a colonialist or imperialist past are far-reaching. Negative experiences ranging from extreme exploitation of labor, impoverishment, and denial of rights and privileges to underfunded education and marginalization have formed the consciousness of many black women. For many Latina women, African-American women, and Maori women, "cultural assault," the ridicule of their culture and language, has been a severe challenge to their self-esteem and educational prospects. This can lead to ambivalence about educational achievement, because success might involve identification with the dominant culture and separation from their own community. In this context, education has frequently become a symbol of empowerment for the whole community. Gaining literacy for black American women has often been seen not just as personal achievement but as "the practice of freedom," helping to liberate the community. Linda Tuhiwai Smith (1993) has described how the establishment of a Maori cultural complex promoted the development of alternative pedagogic practices that validated Maori forms of knowledge, including collective identity. In Britain, feminist subcultural research has investigated the experiences of black women. A "culture of resistance" to the dominant society might involve women using academic success to gain a sense of personal control that also reinforces the power of the family and community.

Socialization, Identity, and Achievement

The varied experiences of women from different races and cultures both between and within countries suggest that achievement in education must be considered in very specific ways. This becomes clear in such a key area as socialization and education. Anglo-American feminist sociologists and psychologists have investigated why (usually white) girls in systems of almost universal schooling seem to "avoid" educational success. They found evidence that families and schools seemed to encourage girls to develop characteristics that were incompatible with academic achievement. It was suggested that the sexual identity and self-image of these girls were connected to a particular model of femininity.

Girls were socialized into this model through strong identification with female patterns in the family and through patriarchal practices both at home and at school. Identification with this vision of passive femininity led many girls to choose an educational path that did not conflict with a domestic role. Feminist research in Britain on the "culture of femininity" among working-class girls, and in the United States on the "culture of romance" among college girls, showed how education might begin to be seen as asexual or as an alternative to a fulfilling personal life.

The impact of socialization has been identified in other countries. Karuna Chanana (1988) has suggested that a rapid increase in female educational success in postindependence India drew to a halt because of socialization factors. She concludes that the internalization of values and identity formation in socialization processes have an overarching influence on the educational achievement of Indian women. Similarly, Bouthaina Shaaban (1988) argues that many Arab women who have benefited from educational development schemes and who have gained public confidence through participation in struggles for national identity are still locked into a model of docile femininity that restricts their success.

Postmodern Feminism and Achievement

Postmodern feminists suggest that what it means to be a woman—to develop feminine subjectivities—might differ significantly in different contexts. A female may receive confusing messages—to achieve academically (as a male's equal) while staying "feminine" (not competing with men). Also, some subjectivities may be unavailable to girls. High-achieving girls are often seen as "mediocre" because an understanding, or discourse, about "brilliant feminine subjects" is not available. Postmodern feminists, however, recognize that it is impossible to abstract a distinct and universal model of feminine behavior. Black feminists point out that different interpretations of femininity instigate different attitudes toward educational achievement.

Female Achievement

Many feminists seek to increase the range of discourses within which female achievement may be conceptualized. Poor achievement may stem from poor motivation or poor teaching, but it also may imply a different cultural or gender construction of such terms as *schoolwork* or *academic success.* Female "fear" of success may be, in fact, a rejection of conventional male definitions of knowledge or success. Feminists have sought to bring a female perspective into academic institutions. Women's studies courses and publications have

473

drawn attention to female achievement and "ways of knowing" worldwide.

See Also

CHILD DEVELOPMENT; EDUCATION: CURRICULUM IN SCHOOLS; EDUCATION: GENDERED SUBJECT CHOICE; EDUCATION: MATHMATICS; FEMININITY; GIRLS' SUBCULTURES; KNOWLEDGE; LANGUAGE

References and Further Reading

Arnot, Madeleine, Miriam David, and Gaby Weiner. 1999. *Closing the gender gap: Postwar education and social change.* Cambridge: Polity.

Chanana, Karuna, ed. 1988. *Socialization, education, and women.* New Delhi: Orient Longman.

Fogelberg, Paul, Jeff Hearn, Liisa Husu, and Teija Mankkinen, eds. 1999. *Hard work in the academy: Research and interventions on gender inequalities in higher education.* Helsinki: Helsinki University Press.

hooks, bell. 1989. *Talking back.* Boston: South End.

Jones, Alison. 1993. Becoming a "girl": Post-structuralist suggestions for educational research. *Gender and Education* 5(2): 157–166.

Luttrell, Wendy. 1997. *School-smart and mother-wise.* New York: Routledge.

Shaaban, Bouthaina. 1988. *Both right- and left-handed.* London: Women's Press.

Smith Linda, Tuhiwai. 1993. Getting out from down under. In Madeleine Arnot and Kathleen Weiler, eds., *Feminism and social justice in education: International perspectives.* London: Falmer.

Spender, Dale. 1980. *Learning to lose.* London: Women's Press.

Stromquist, Nelly. 1989. Determinants of educational participation. *Review of Educational Research* 59(2): 43–83.

Walkerdine, Valerie. 1994. Femininity as performance. In Lynda Stone, ed., *The education feminism reader,* 57–69. New York: Routledge.

Chris Mann

EDUCATION: Adult and Continuing

Adult education is a broad term that encompasses a vast array of learning and training activities for adults, including continuing education. *Continuing education* refers to a type of adult education that focuses on improvements of work skills and career development. Both terms have numerous aliases, including academic education, nonformal education, recurrent education, lifelong learning, distance learning, and literacy campaigns. Variations in these concepts and their meanings differ from country to country. Adult education is a significant component in the efforts of many developing and highly industrialized countries to raise employment levels and retrain workers. Complexities arise when women are added to considerations of adult and continuing education throughout the world.

Throughout the world, adult education has been an unstructured institution, even as it becomes more complex and globalized. Differing terminology makes international comparison difficult. Countries vary in their definition and age of adulthood, for instance. Many societies regard age 15 (Latin America) or 18 (United States) as adulthood; others place the age much younger or older. Developing and rural areas provide the most problematic situations in determining access to adult education because of their lack of available resources. Interconnections among politics, economy, religion, and culture influence the type of services and access to those services. Throughout the world, adult education is voluntary, but has often excluded women. Adult education, however, is closely linked to community demands, and communities around the world are beginning to recognize the needs of women.

Adult education occurs in a variety of settings that have not always included women. The formal sector includes such institutions as employers, labor unions, schools, churches, professional organizations, the military, and nonprofit organizations. Adult programs also exist among social circles, libraries, museums, church groups, community centers, and personal development seminars. These settings have been crucial to women learning practical skills like reading, sewing, cooking, and health care. Co-workers provide an opportunity for professional socialization concerning the work environment and expected duties (Jarvis, 1985) that are not part of the initial work orientation or written in formal guides, such as the culture of the company, acceptable shortcuts, or the dos and don'ts. Advances in technology, especially in computerization, continue to extend adult education throughout the world and into the home. Women may historically have used other educational locations that have yet to be discovered because of a lack of interest in women's experiences.

Adult education is typically financed by private organizations such as religious groups, social and political organizations, and businesses. The state typically plays a minor role as a sponsor of adult education. The United States was the first industrialized society to legislate the Adult Education Act (1966) to provide financial support for adult education. Sweden followed in 1967. Financing for adult education is affected by politics, population needs, economics, and technology, factors that vary widely among countries.

Throughout history, many organizations have conducted international comparisons of adult and continuing education. In the nineteenth century, adult education became an international phenomenon. The United Nations Educational, Scientific, and Cultural Organization (UNESCO) has associated itself with the development of adult education worldwide since 1945. This organization's central emphasis is to bring attention to women's participation in these programs. The Continuing Education Unit is an international organization that sets the standards for continuing education and training for corporations, colleges and universities, health-related organizations, and many other institutions. Women were added to the agenda of adult education during the United Nations International Women's Year in 1975 and the Decade of Women in 1976. The International Council of Adult Education, headquartered in Toronto, Canada, developed a plan of action in 1973 to increase women's participation in adult educational programs worldwide. Throughout the 1980s many countries experienced economic recession, famine, and international debt that put a hold on women's issues in adult programs, but the 1990s brought the emphasis back to women's education because of demographic trends in family planning, globalizing economy, and cross-cultural influences.

Women participate in adult education for a variety of reasons. A central feature of adult education is its power to build self-esteem and self-confidence in women. These programs often provide women with empowerment, identity, and purpose and a network of friends and resources. Many women attend programs to complete their formal education or to start anew; other women enter adult programs to assist in the economic needs of the family. Many participate in continuing education classes to enter or re-enter the labor market after an absence, typically resulting from childbirth, child rearing, or caring for elderly family members. Some women want to better themselves and further their personal development. Some married women who define themselves as housewives enter adult programs to help their children with schoolwork.

Adult education encompasses a variety of fields for women, including civic, political, arts, language, and recreational topics. Programs tailored toward vocational realms interest women who want to enter the labor market. Other classes provide information concerning women's traditional domestic roles, including child rearing, cooking, and housekeeping. For women in the poorest countries of the world, adult education often involves family planning, literacy, and health-related concerns. Rural women of Africa find their main source of work is in food production and preparation, which can become problematic when they are not adequately trained in these areas (Harrison, 1997). Professional associations found in almost every country provide women with a form of adult education. Most adult programs for women tend to focus on the worldwide issue of literacy.

Over half the world's women are illiterate. Throughout the world, many organizations work toward eradicating illiteracy as part of adult education. International comparisons acknowledge that illiteracy is a problem for third world countries, as well as for industrialized countries. Illiteracy is more prevalent among women in rural populations than among women in urban areas, but neither is immune to the problem. Illiteracy rates are highest among women in developing countries because of poor environmental conditions, malnutrition, short life expectancy, and lack of basic human needs. Women's illiteracy can negatively affect family well-being, children's educational performance, and economic prospects in the labor market. Literacy programs often assist women with issues of family planning and self-reflection. Educating women has been a major factor in changing the pattern of world fertility; fertility rates tend to be higher in those countries where women are poorly educated, so many adult programs have focused on this critical problem.

Countries vary in their responses to the problem of women's access to adult educational programs. In Afghanistan, for instance, educating females is officially prohibited. Females are therefore often educated in secret shelters and private homes (Bearak, 2000). Western European countries tend to be more concerned with equal access to education and employment for women and men. Central and eastern Europe view adult education as a way of preparing women for new forms of government and new economic growth. In some of the poorest countries, educating women includes exposure to family planning information, sanitation, and nutrition, all necessary for survival. In many countries, obstacles such as cultural attitudes, the social position of women, economics, and political structures interfere with women's access to adult education. Other countries are expanding their educational connections into rural and urban areas to increase access for those who are in lower socioeconomic positions.

Many adult educational outlets have been unsuccessful in maintaining women's completion of their programs. Most programs are not designed by women, nor do they reflect women's needs. Some women lack financial resources to access or complete educational programs. Family responsibilities, like child rearing and domestic chores, may inhibit women from completing training programs. A significant number of adult educational programs do not provide women with day care centers, transportation, or domestic assistance, which would help many women to complete these programs. Many women do not feel a certificate of completion is much reward if they cannot find employment (UNESCO, 1999). The International Adult Literacy Survey found the number of hours that an individual spends in training is based on her level of educational attainment. Higher levels of educational attainment are associated with greater numbers of training hours. Women who obtain higher levels of education typically have greater financial and family resources that allow them to complete trainings that further their careers. In all countries, those with less than an upper secondary education receive substantially less training on average than those who have completed upper secondary education or more (OECD, 1999). Limited education skills can inhibit women from completing educational programs. Those with a limited education usually are not employed outside the home or work in positions that require minimum skills, where training programs do not better their economic or family position. Overall, women, in all countries, typically receive less hours of training than men at all educational levels, which greatly affects their economic position in society.

Increases in women's participation in adult education, which can positively affect their jobs and continuity in the labor market, have done little to affect the wages women earn. Women's educational levels also strongly affect the occupations they choose. The right of females to receive an education at any age has its political origins in basic human rights. Adult education provides women with a way of discussing and processing information about themselves and others. Although access to adult education is still denied to many women throughout the world, change is occurring, albeit slowly. Women worldwide are finding that adult and continuing education provides the needed skills, access to available resources, and an avenue to raise their status in a globalizing economy.

See Also

EDUCATION: DISTANCE EDUCATION; EDUCATION: HIGHER EDUCATION; EDUCATION: ON-LINE; EDUCATION: VOCATIONAL; LITERACY

References and Further Reading

Bearak, Barry. 2000. Afghanistan's girls fight to read and write. *New York Times,* 9 March.

Harrison, Kelsey. 1997. The importance of the educated healthy women in Africa. *Lancet* 349: 644–648.

Jarvis, Peter. 1985. *The sociology of adult and continuing education.* London: Croom Helm.

Organization for Economic Cooperation and Development (OECD). 1999. *Education policy analysis 1999.* Paris: Centre for Educational Research and Innovation.

UNESCO. 1999. Questioning the ABC's of women's literacy. *UNESCO Courier,* Oct.: 14–19.

Jennifer L. Gossett

EDUCATION: Antiracist

Multicultural education as a concept and a set of practices emerged in the West in the 1960s in response to the demands of minority ethnic groups for better educational opportunities for their children and for equal representation in educational structures and in school curricula. This challenge led to various curriculum reform initiatives that reflected different national concerns and political priorities. The postwar period of global migrations led to dynamic changes in the demographics of western countries, and the types of policies and practices that emerged reflected the specific histories of colonial settlement and the different relations between dominant and subordinate groups within the society.

Although there was no single definition or practice of multicultural education, a common feature of multiculturalism lay in the basic theoretical assumptions about culture and society and the place of different groups within it. Minority ethnic group cultures were represented in dominant discourses as distinctive, homogeneous, internally stable and therefore without different male and female agendas or internal inequalities. Whereas for these groups differences such as gender and class, were rendered invisible, white dominant groups were presented as "nonethnic," unproblematic, and self-evident—the norm against which "others" were measured.

From an official or state perspective, the increasing cultural pluralism of western societies and the supposed cultural distinctiveness of groups were potential threats to social cohesion. With the failure of assimilationist policies, it was deemed necessary to devise strategies that recognized and promoted cultural pluralism and supported the stability of the nation. In Britain part of the threat to national stability was seen to be posed by a growing population of young people (mainly male) from minority ethnic groups, who were said to be failing in the education system and becoming disaffected and alienated.

However, much of the research into the experiences of minorities was itself contained within a simplistic culturalist framework, and policies and practices generally reflected this. Theories about the educational underachievement of minority-group pupils, for example, rarely took into account the different experiences of girls (Mirza, 1992). The tendency was to make comparisons of the academic success or otherwise of supposedly discrete ethnic groups, so that class and gender differences were overlooked and the interactions of class, gender, and ethnicity were excluded from the analysis. A major assumption behind the notion of educational failure among minority-group pupils was that these pupils suffered from low self-esteem, which was said to result partly from white prejudices and also from the experience of cultural exclusion (Bullivant, 1981). Theories of low self-esteem among minority-group pupils, and in particular among black girls, were strongly disputed (Fuller, 1980; Stone, 1981). Multicultural education nevertheless emerged as the panacea for the educational disadvantages experienced by pupils from minority ethnic groups (Swann Report, 1985).

In Britain the strategies adopted by multiculturalists largely consisted of celebrations of superficial aspects of cultural and religious differences. These strategies were criticized by antiracists for being blind to the structural inequalities of groups in the society. As Sarup stated, multicultural education "was associated with . . . thought and consciousness, beliefs and customs—the curries people cook, the music they make, the dances they perform" (1986: 13). Antiracists rejected the idea that the problem lay in minority groups themselves or in the individual prejudices of white children. They underlined the significance of the unequal power relations that existed in the structures and institutions of society, which included unequal gender relations. The strategy for antiracists was to raise awareness of different forms of inequality through training. However, official funding mechanisms generally forced a separation of issues, so that different interest groups dealing with issues of sexuality, gender, disability, or "race" vied with one another for priority or recognition. The antiracist focus on racism led to accusations that antiracists reduced all disadvantages experienced by minority groups to the effects of racism and ignored experiences of class and gender (Gilroy, 1990). Antiracist feminists, however, not only continued to raise gender and class issues (see Bryan et al., 1985) but also remained critical of policies and practices that failed to

acknowledge the different interests and different positions of women within groups. Yuval-Davis (1992), for example, questions the role of predominantly male "community leaders" in deciding the interests of diverse sections within communities. She sees multiculturalism and antiracism as major ideological weapons of religious fundamentalism and of political expediency. By defining culture in primarily religious terms, she argues, multiculturalism helped to legitimate attempts by religious fundamentalists to define and control women's behavior and to attack and undermine women's autonomous mobilizing. Equally, leftist politicians were able to jump on the antiracist bandwagon in order to gain the support of "community leaders," thereby ignoring the concerns and interests of women. On the other hand, the focus on minority-group religions masked the gendered inequalities inherent within Christian religions, so that fundamentalism became associated in the popular mind with Islam and all Muslims came to be defined as fundamentalists.

The prioritization of culture exposed particular tensions and dilemmas for multiculturalists and antiracists around the issue of single-sex schools. Although such schools are said to be generally of benefit to girls' education, single-sex religious schools are viewed by *anti*fundamentalists as a means of ensuring that girls are educated for roles as good wives and mothers. In their support of such schools, multiculturalists were thus said to collude in the oppression of women. Moreover, multiculturalists were seen as the allies of right-wing separatist groups whose support of the notion of freedom of parental choice included a belief in the right of white parents to remove their children from schools attended by minority-ethnic-group children. On the other hand, parents who preferred that their children attend single-sex religious schools argued for the right to send their children to schools that best reflected their own value systems and freed them from the tensions and contradictions inherent in their relations and interactions with mainstream education. Some of these tensions and contradictions arose for Muslim parents, for example, in a range of situations, from negotiating the dietary requirements of their children, to the curricular issue of sex education, to participation in sports. They argued that there was as much variety and diversity of response to girls' education among Muslim parents as there was in other groups (Wade and Souter, 1992). The essentialist nature of many forms of multicultural education, however, largely overlooked this diversity.

Minority women and girls were thus rendered invisible by the multiculturalist neglect of the specifically gendered and classed forms of racism and discrimination in the education system.

See Also

ANTIRACIST AND CIVIL RIGHTS MOVEMENTS; EDUCATION: ACHIEVEMENT; EDUCATION: CURRICULUM IN SCHOOLS; EDUCATION: RELIGIOUS STUDIES; EDUCATION: SINGLE-SEX AND COEDUCATION; ETHNICITY; FUNDAMENTALISM: RELIGIOUS; MULTICULTURALISM; RACISM AND XENOPHOBIA

References and Further Reading

Bryan, Beverley, Stella Dadzie, and Suzanne Scafe. 1985. *The heart of the race: Black women's lives in Britain*. London: Virago.

Bullivant, Brian. 1981. *The pluralist dilemma in education*. Sydney: Allen and Unwin.

Fuller, Mary. 1980. Black girls in a London comprehensive school. In Rosemary Deem, ed., *Schooling for women's work*. London: Routledge and Kegan Paul.

Gilroy, Paul. 1990. The end of anti-racism. In Wendy Ball and John Solomos, eds., *Race and local politics*. London: Macmillan.

Mirza, Heidi. 1992. *Young, female, and black*. London: Routledge.

Sarup, Madan. 1986. *The politics of multiracial education*. London: Routledge and Kegan Paul.

Stone, Maureen. 1981. *The education of the black child*. London: Fontana.

Swann Report. 1985. *Education for all*. London: HMSO.

Wade, Barrie, and Pamela Souter. 1992. *Continuing to think: The British Asian girl*. Clevedon, U.K.: Multilingual Matters.

Yuval-Davis, Nira. 1992. Fundamentalism, multiculturalism, and women in Britain. In James Donald and Ali Rattansi, eds., *"Race," culture, and difference*. London: Sage.

Maud Blair

EDUCATION: Assessment

See EXAMINATIONS AND ASSESSMENT.

EDUCATION: Central Pacific and South Pacific Islands

This article provides an overview of general trends in the educational status of women and girls in Oceania. However, there is enormous variation between and within nations in this region. Oceania includes those countries that are scattered in the southern region of the Pacific Ocean and covers what is commonly known as the Pacific Islands, New Zealand, and Australia. This article deals mainly with the education of women in the Pacific Islands, traditionally categorized into three main groups: Melanesia (for example, Papua New Guinea, Fiji, Vanuatu), Polynesia (for example, Samoa, Tonga, Cook Islands), and Micronesia (for example, Kiribati, Nauru, Tuvalu). It specifically discusses illiteracy rates of women in these nations as well as their access to and participation in formal schooling, including postsecondary and distance education.

Female Illiteracy

Generally speaking, illiteracy in females is significantly higher than in males, because women's access to and participation in education are not priorities in some areas of Oceania. For instance, from a table provided by Fairbairn-Dunlop (1994), we learn that the illiteracy rate was 82 percent for women in Papua New Guinea in 1980, 83 percent for women in the Solomon Islands in 1991, and 40.2 percent for women in Vanuatu in 1989. These figures demonstrate that more girls will need to be educated in the formal schooling system before some progress is made in terms of the future participation of women in national life in these countries. In comparison, the illiteracy rate for women in some Pacific nations is significantly lower than these three Melanesian nations. For instance, in 1986 Fiji had a 15.8 percent illiteracy rate, the Cook Islands 4.0 percent, and Samoa 1.7 percent. Nonetheless, women's illiteracy rates are significantly higher than those of males in most Pacific nations.

Access to and Participation in Formal Schooling

In most Pacific nations, education is not free, nationally available, or compulsory. As with illiteracy rates, women's participation in formal schooling is markedly less than that of males in most of the nations in Oceania. Pacific women's participation in formal schooling is similar to that of women in developed nations (Fairbairn-Dunlop, 1994: 56). This is reflected in the following: fewer females compared with males enter the school system; the attrition rate for women is higher than for males, so the higher the level, the lower the female participation; and there is a concentration of women in social sciences, as opposed to the male predominance in basic sciences.

Women face some critical problems in attaining formal education in many countries in Oceania. First, they need to enter primary school. Girls' access to first grade in many Melanesian countries has improved considerably. For instance, female enrollment in first grade in Papua New Guinea rose from 47.3 percent in 1971 to 68.8 percent in 1981 (Fairbairn-Dunlop, 1994). Similarly, in Fiji, 47 percent of the total first-grade enrollment in 1992 were girls, and 49 percent of the total primary enrollment in 1992 were female.

The next major hurdle facing females is access to and continued enrollment in secondary schools. Female enrollment in secondary and higher education in Papua New Guinea is estimated as one-third that of males; in Vanuatu, secondary-school enrollment figures have been calculated at 24 percent males and 21 percent females; in the Solomon Islands the female population in secondary schools increased from 30 percent in 1980 to 36 percent in 1986 and 1991 (Fairbairn-Dunlop, 1994: 58–59). Some countries are moving toward gender equity at the higher secondary level. For instance, in Fiji 47 percent of form 6 (12th grade) enrollment in 1992 were girls, and 49 percent were enrolled in form 7, the preparatory year for higher education.

In subject disciplines at the postsecondary level females tend to concentrate in the humanities (education, psychology, literature, and language). At the University of the South Pacific (USP), which serves 12 island nations—namely, the Cook Islands, Fiji, Kiribati, Marshall Islands, Nauru, Niue, Solomon Islands, Tokelau, Tonga, Tuvalu, Vanuatu, and Western Samoa—males predominate in the pure and applied sciences (63 percent) and agriculture (81 percent), and females dominate in the humanities (53 percent). In 1995, 43.5 percent of the total full-time enrollment at USP was female.

Distance Education

Although females generally are slowly approaching gender equity in full-time enrollment at primary, secondary, and postsecondary levels in many Oceanic nations, they are still heavily underrepresented in distance education. Women in Melanesian countries do not appear to benefit from the opportunities provided by USP's distance-education programs. In these countries, women's enrollments are low, and they have a high attrition rate (Bolabola and Wah, 1995). On the other hand, women from Polynesian and Micronesian nations generally have high enrollment figures but high attrition rates. The high dropout rate of women from all areas of the South Pacific highlights the problems that women have when they undertake distance education on a part-time basis. Reasons consistently provided by women who withdrew from distance-education courses were heavy workload and family commitments.

Conclusion

Generally, women continue to be disadvantaged and underrepresented at all levels of the educational system. A continued focus on women's issues is necessary, for, on the basis of their gender, women continue to exceed males in all measurable categories of disadvantage.

See Also

EDUCATION: DISTANCE EDUCATION

References and Further Reading

Bolabola, Cema, and Richard Wah, eds. 1995. *South Pacific women in distance education: Studies from countries of the South Pacific*. Suva, Fiji: University of the South Pacific Extension and the Commonwealth of Learning.

Dé Ishtar, Zohl. 1994. *Daughters of the Pacific*. Victoria, Australia: Spinifex.

Fairbairn-Dunlop, Peggy. 1994. Women's education: Pacific overview 1994. *Directions 30, Journal of Educational Studies* 16(1): 55–68.

Flaherty, Teresa A. 1998. *The women's voice in education: Identity and participation in a changing Papua New Guinea*. Goroka, Papua New Guinea: Melanesian Institute.

Government of Federated States of Micronesia and UNICEF. 1996. *A situational analysis of children and women in the federated states of Micronesia*. Suva, Fiji: UNICEF.

Government of Fiji, Ministry of Women and Culture. 1998. *The women's plan of action, 1999–2008*. Suva, Fiji: Ministry of Women and Culture.

Hughes, Helen, et al. 1985. Women in development in the South Pacific: Barriers and opportunities. Paper presented at a conference held in Vanuatu, 11–14 Aug. 1984. Canberra: Australian National University, Development Studies Centre.

Matthewson, Claire, and Ruby Va'a. 1999. The South Pacific: Kakai mei tahi. In Keith Harry, ed., *Higher education through open and distance learning*, 277–291. New York: Routledge.

University of the South Pacific. 1994. *Report of the Pacific workshop for women managers in higher education*. Suva, Fiji: University of the South Pacific.

Priscilla Qolisaya Puamau

EDUCATION: Central and South America and the Caribbean

Adequate educational opportunities are limited for all residents of Latin America. Although there are few disparities in access to education between men and women at all levels in Latin America and the Caribbean, the curriculum is inadequate to meet the needs of young girls for an education free of limiting gender role expectations. Classroom practices often do not encourage girls to further their careers. Furthermore, women are often educated in preparation for teaching or other "feminine" jobs, which pay less than men's jobs. At the university level, women's studies and gender studies programs have been growing. This may have long-term positive results for women's educational experiences.

Preschool education has been recognized as a potential mechanism for stimulating early intellectual development. The trend toward an increasing presence of women in the workplace has led to more children in Latin America and the Caribbean attending preschool and is the area within education that shows the highest growth. The availability and quality, however, of preschool programs vary widely. Government support for preschool education is increasing but is at generally low levels. Typical is Jamaica, where 2.5 percent of the education budget supports preschools. The United Nations Educational, Scientific and Cultural Organization (UNESCO) yearbook for 1999 reports that the percentage of girls enrolled in preschool is about half of all enrolled. Thus the preschool stage of education, although not adequate for all the children in the region, does not appear to be widely discriminatory in its availability to young girls. Of course, the poor and those in rural regions have the most limited access to preschool education.

Access to elementary and secondary education in Latin America varies widely. Guatemala and Bolivia have much lower enrollment rates than Argentina, Chile, or Costa Rica. Within nations, the enrollment rates are much lower among poor, rural, and indigenous people. Furthermore, girls from rural areas and indigenous families are less likely to receive an education than are boys from similar backgrounds. Latin America has one of the lowest educational completion rates. According to the Inter-American Development Bank, only 54 percent of those who enter primary school reach fourth grade, and only four Latin American countries have primary completion rates higher than 75 percent. The gap in enrollment between boys and girls is small. Girls slightly outnumber boys in secondary school. This results in boys entering the workforce more easily.

In some countries, women outnumber men at the university level. This has been attributed to the large numbers of women enrolled in university programs for training as teachers or secretaries. A 1995 study by the Economic Commission for Latin America and the Caribbean (ECLAC) found that women need to have four more years of education in order to compete for salaries similar to those of men. Careers to which women are channeled—teaching and other sex-segregated jobs—do not pay as well as male occupations.

Despite the UNESCO and ECLAC statistics that show little problem with *access* to education based on gender, women still are subordinate to men in types of jobs and wages, in field of study choices, and in occupational segregation. Furthermore, women in Latin America are underrepresented at all political office levels. This suggests that despite women's access to education, the educational process is not resulting in changes in their societal status. Because of the disparate results, a closer study of the educational process is warranted.

Studies have shown that textbooks used in Colombia, Peru, Chile, Argentina, and Mexico depict women as passive, subordinate, and fatalistic. Gender roles prevail and are justified by "natural" differences between the sexes (Wainerman and Raijman, 1984). Studies of classroom practices reveal that teachers (mostly women) transmit traditional views of gender roles. Often these teachers are viewed not as professionals but as poorly paid caretakers (Anderson and Herencia, 1983).

At the university level, there has been a rapid growth of women's studies and gender studies programs. Argentina, Barbados, Bolivia, Brazil, Chile, Costa Rica, Dominican Republic, Mexico, Peru, Puerto Rico, Uruguay, and Venezuela all have programs focusing on gender studies. Women in these programs have formed feminist and women's nongovernmental organizations to challenge sexism and oppressive gender roles. Their impact in society may be transformative in the long run. This is evidenced by increased participation of Latin American and Caribbean women in international women's organizing projects. As women from this region pursue more educational opportunities, their quest for self-determination will be closer to becoming a reality.

See Also

References and Further Reading

Anderson, Jeanine, and Christina Herencia. 1983. *La imagen de la mujer y del hombre en los libros de texto escolares peruanos.* Paris: UNESCO.

ECLAC and UNIFEM. 1995. *Regional programme of action for the women of Latin America and the Caribbean, 1995–2001.* Santiago, Chile: United Nations (CEPAL).

Facio Montejo, Alda. 1992. *Cuando el género suena cambios trae: Una metodología para el análisis de género del fenómeno legal.* San José, C.R.: Ilanud.

Inter-American Development Bank (IDB). 1995. *Social dimensions in the agenda of the IDB.* Copenhagen: World Summit for Social Development. 6–12 March.

Meyers, R. 1992. *Investing in early childhood development programs: Toward definition of a World Bank strategy.* Washington, D.C.: World Bank.

Puryear, Jeffrey, and José Joaquín Brunner, eds. 1999. *Education, equity, and economic competitiveness in the Americas: An inter-American dialogue project.* Washington, D.C.: Organization of American States.

Stromquist, Nelly P., ed. 1992. *Women and education in Latin American countries: Knowledge, power, and change.* Boulder, Colo.: Lynne Rienner.

UNESCO Statistical Yearbook. 1992 Paris: UNESCO. http://unescostate.unesco.org

United Nations Economic Commission for Latin America and the Caribbean: http://searcher.eclacpos.org/

Valverdo, Gilbert A. 1999. Democracy, human rights, and development assistance for education: The USAID and World Bank in Latin America and the Caribbean. *Economic Development and Cultural Change* 47(2: Jan.): 401.

Wainerman, Catalina, and Rebeca Barck de Raijman. 1984. *La division sexual del trabajo en los libros de lectura de la escuela primaria Argentina: Un caso de inmutabilidad secular.* Buenos Aires: CENEP.

World Bank, Mexico. 1992. *The initial educational strategy.* Washington, D.C.: World Bank.

Antoinette Sedillo Lopez

EDUCATION:
Chilly Climate in the Classroom

The term *chilly climate* was developed by Bernice R. Sandler and Roberta M. Hall in 1982 in the first comprehensive report detailing the numerous, subtle ways in which males and females are often treated differently in the classroom, even by the best-intentioned teachers. Although most of the research about classroom behavior has been done in the United States, there is much anecdotal information that confirms that these behaviors are universal.

Women as well as men engage in these behaviors, which may also be directed at men of color, disabled persons, those of lower class, and others viewed as being different or "on the margins." Over time, these small, seemingly insignificant behaviors create a chilly climate, which lessens girls' and women's class participation, dampens their vocational and academic aspirations, and diminishes their self-esteem and confidence. A chilly climate is characterized by the following:

- Girls and women typically get less attention, less eye contact, and less encouragement.
- Females are more likely to be praised for their attractiveness or neatness, whereas males are more likely to be praised for their work and creativity.
- When males speak, teachers often engage in a dialogue with them, whereas girls and women are more likely to receive the ubiquitous "uh-huh."
- Female students may be interrupted more often and be called on less often in many classes.
- Teachers are more likely to call on males, even when females raise their hands.
- Men and boys are more likely to be called by their name than females.
- Teachers are more likely to ask males the harder, higher-order "thinking" questions, such as "Why did the Revolution occur?" By contrast, females are more likely to be asked factual, lower-order questions, such as "When did the Revolution occur?"

These and other subtle behaviors are often unnoticed by faculty members who engage in them or by the persons affected by them.

Why should these behaviors occur, especially when almost all teachers want to be fair? Stereotypes play a role, as does devaluation. In numerous studies, when male and female names are switched on résumés, articles, pictures of works of art, or other items, those with a male name are rated higher by both men and women. Thus female accomplishments are often attributed to "working hard" or to "good luck" rather than to intelligence and talent.

Many of these behaviors are also directed at women faculty members (and other employees) at staff meetings and in their relationships with students, colleagues, and administrators.

See Also

EDUCATION: ACHIEVEMENT; EDUCATION: GENDER EQUITY; EDUCATION: GENDERED SUBJECT CHOICE; EDUCATION: NONSEXIST; EDUCATION: SINGLE-SEX AND COEDUCATION

References and Further Reading

Cohee, Gail E., Elizabeth Daumer, Theresa D. Kemp, Paul M. Krebs, Sue Lafky, and Sandra Runzo, eds. 1998. *The feminist teacher anthology: Pedagogies and classroom strategies.* New York: Teachers College Press.

Sadker, Myra, and David Sadker. 1994. *Failing at fairness: How America's schools cheat girls.* New York: Charles Scribner's Sons.

Sandler, Bernice Resnick, Lisa A. Silverberg, and Roberta M. Hall. 1996. *The chilly classroom climate: A guide to improve the education of women.* Washington, D.C.: National Association for Women in Education.

Bernice R. Sandler

EDUCATION:
Commonwealth of Independent States

The specificity of girls' education in the Commonwealth of Independent States is associated with the political history of the region, as is the case with all countries in the former Soviet bloc. Real educational gains were made early on, although these did not translate into full parity with men in the labor market. The social position of women, whether in education or the labor market, has not in the past been the subject of feminist theorizing or campaigning. That is because, in the absence of liberal civil society, neither educational nor labor market inequalities can be translated into the "political exclusion: of women" (Watson, 1996). Current levels of female educational participation, which are in the main still high, are nevertheless threatened by political and economic changes in the region.

The table indicates the representation of girls and young women in primary, secondary, and higher education in the countries of the Commonwealth of Independent States and the central Asian republics in 1992.

Girls as a percentage of all students in primary, secondary, and higher education in Commonwealth of Independent States and central Asian republics, 1992

	Primary	Secondary			Higher
		Total	General	Vocational	
Belarus	49	–	51	–	–
Moldova	49	–	51	–	–
Russian Federation	49	51	53	42	50
Ukraine	49	–	52	–	50
Azerbaijan	–	–	49	–	38
Kazakhstan*	49	–	52	–	–
Tajikistan*	49	47	–	–	–

*1993
Source: UNESCO, *Statistical Yearbook 1994.*

Women reached levels of educational attainment in the U.S.S.R. far earlier than in the West, although some eastern republics lagged behind somewhat. The educational progress of women during the twentieth century was dramatic. At the time of the Russian Revolution, illiteracy had been a significant problem, with 14 million out of a total of 17 million illiterate people being female (Stites, 1976). But between 1926 and 1939, the proportion of women who could read rose from just over 42 percent to just over 83 percent (Stites, 1976). Coeducation and equal admission conditions and uniform curricula for girls and boys were enforced by early postrevolutionary laws (Stites, 1976). "Equality of the sexes in real life," as N. K. Krupskaya pointed out in 1921, "had to be anchored in educational equality from the very earliest years. Thus, the belief in the omnicompetence of women, long nourished by the female intelligentsia of the nineteenth century, was institutionalized in the Soviet educational system" (Stites, 1976: 397). In 1950 women were 53 percent of the total number of students enrolled in higher education in the U.S.S.R. (Ratliff, 1991). This fell to 43 percent in 1960 but rose again to 49 percent in 1970 and to 55 percent in 1985 (Ratliff, 1991).

The Soviet education system did not develop in an altogether linear fashion, being subject to periodic reform and counterreform. Stalin abolished coeducation in 1943, and until 1954 boys and girls in urban areas were taught separately from the seventh class onward (Matthews, 1982). The system was and continues to be based on the 10-year (now 11-year) general school, which was the main route to higher education. The last three years of this general school provide a standardized curriculum that stresses math and science, where girls usually take the same courses and perform at least as well as boys (Matthews, 1982).

In addition, there is the possibility of vocational training in the lower-level "vocational-technical school" or in the higher-level *teknikum*. With the restructuring of the economy in the Commonwealth of Independent States, the future of vocational training was under question. Young women have been underrepresented in the lower-level vocational schools but have typically constituted more than half of the *teknikum* pupils and more than half of the pupils in the final three years of the general school, since boys have tended to leave school earlier to take up employment.

Traditional ideas of gender identity, paradoxically reinforced under communism (Watson, 1993), have continued to influence subject choice at the *teknikum*, where girl tend to choose courses that lead to feminized sectors of the economy (Ratliff, 1991). The introduction of more subject choice into the secondary curriculum, given these traditional preferences, may lead to a split in the subjects followed within the general school, with boys tending toward math and science and girls toward humanities and languages (Ratliff, 1991). In higher education, women have favored the fields of medicine, teaching, and research in applied and pure sciences and are underrepresented in courses leading to jobs in agriculture, manufacturing, construction, and transportation (Ratliff, 1991). Similarly gendered patterns of preference persist today in the countries of the Commonwealth of Independent States (see UNICEF, 1994). Given the large proportion of women seeking entry to higher education, there is evidence that the informal equal quota systems have sometimes acted against rather than in favor of women. Ratliff (1991) notes two early studies where, although four times as many women applied for admission to certain institutions of higher education, they represented one-half of all students gaining admission to these institutions.

Political and economic change in the region has important implications for education, particularly for the education of girls and young women. Far from being viewed as a universal instrument of social change (cf. Lapidus, 1982), democratization has transformed education into a secondary issue, starved of public funding and dependent on the (future) successful restructuring of the economy. This has been associated with the ascendancy of neoliberal reasoning during the first few years of transformation in the former Soviet bloc. More specific problems arise where transformation has involved violence. Azerbaijan, for example, has seen many schools abandoned as a result of the occupation of some of its territory by Armenian armed forces (UNICEF, 1994).

Moreover, the political and economic changes under way have specific implications for women. These are most striking in the labor market (see Human Rights Watch, 1995), but they also impinge on education. Charges for preschool education in Georgia, the Russian Federation, Moldova, and elsewhere have risen, and the number of places available has generally decreased (UNICEF, 1994). Morozova (1994) notes that since the end of the 1980s, the rates of enrollment of women students in Russia have fallen. Whereas women represented more than 54 percent of undergraduates at the Moscow State University in 1985, they constituted only 45 percent of students at the university in 1991 (Morozova, 1994). She points out that some institutes and departments have strict quotas for women and that in higher military schools and certain elite departments teaching diplomacy, international law, and journalism, women are not admitted at all. The renewed public emphasis on women's "natural domesticity" during perestroika, which was associated with an expected fall in the demand for labor,

produced a school textbook that denounced "the engagement of girls in academic excellence as producing a specific illness of excellence." "These girls are deprived of childhood," the text says, "they spend all day reading books . . . As a result, when they get married, their body is not ready to pass the main exam of life, to give birth to a child" (Posadskaya, 1994: 168).

Educational policy with respect to women in the Commonwealth of Independent States has not been associated with feminist campaigning or theorizing. Indeed, the high rates of female education in most countries of the region, as elsewhere in the former Soviet bloc, have been accompanied by a widely noted antifeminist sentiment. Such attitudes toward feminism are likely to change with the installation of liberal civil society, which brings a new, politically divisive force to gender relations (Watson, 1996).

See Also

COMMUNISM; EDUCATION: SINGLE-SEX AND COEDUCATION; EDUCATION: VOCATIONAL; LABOR MARKET; POLITICS AND THE STATE: COMMONWEALTH OF INDEPENDENT STATES; SOCIALISM

References and Further Reading

Human Rights Watch. 1995. *Neither jobs nor justice*. New York: Human Rights Watch.

Lapidus, Gail. 1982. Sexual equality through educational reform: The case of the USSR. In P. G. Altbach, R. F. Arnove, and G. P. Kelly, eds., *Comparative education*. New York: Macmillan.

Matthews, Mervyn. 1982. *Education in the Soviet Union*. London: Allen and Unwin.

Morozova, Marina Y. 1994. Gender stratification in Russian higher education: The *matrioshka* image. In Suzanne Stiver Lie et al., eds., *The gender gap in higher education*. London: Kogan Page.

Posadskaya, Anastasia. 1994. Women's studies in Russia: Prospects for a feminist agenda. *Women's Studies Quarterly*, nos. 3 and 4: 157–170.

Ratliff, Patricia. 1991. Women's education in the USSR: 1950–1985. In G. P. Kelly and S. Slaughter, eds., *Women's higher education in comparative perspective*. Boston: Kluwer Academic.

Stites, R. 1976. *The women's liberation movement in Russia: Feminism, nihilism, and Bolshevism, 1860–1930*. Princeton, N.J.: Princeton University Press.

UNICEF. 1994. *Women and gender in countries in transition: A UNICEF perspective*. New York: UNICEF.

Watson, Peggy. 1993. Eastern Europe's silent revolution: Gender. *Sociology* 27(3): 471–487.

———. 1996. Civil society and the politicisation of difference in eastern Europe. In Joan Scott and Cora Kaplan, eds., *Transitions, environments, translations: The meanings of feminism in contemporary politics*. New York: Routledge.

Peggy Watson

EDUCATION: Curriculum in Schools

This article first considers definitions of the term *curriculum* before examining how this term has developed historically and the different ways in which feminists have conceptualized its meaning.

Curriculum is a much contested term, although definitions tend to be broad based, incorporating both syllabus and pedagogy. For example, Pring (1989: 2), emphasizing deliberation and intentionality, argues for a simple definition of curriculum as "the learning experiences that are planned within the school."

However, feminists have tended to see the curriculum more as a site of struggle and contestation, suffused with implicit sexist assumptions about the needs and potential of individuals. Late twentieth-century conceptualizations suggested that the curriculum was gender-biased and undervalued "the social contributions and cultural experiences of girls and women generally and working-class and minority racial and ethnic women in particular" (Kenway and Modra, 1992: 141).

Viewing the Curriculum Historically

Before the Enlightenment at the end of the eighteenth century, western conceptions of the curriculum and schooling were principally concerned with promoting spiritual deliverance, whereby Bible study formed the basis of all worthwhile knowledge. Later, teaching and learning became more secular as contemporary developments in the growth of scientific and social knowledge began to infiltrate post-Enlightenment curriculum thinking. These developments were paralleled by the rise of feminism in western Europe, associated with the emergence of liberal Protestantism and religious individualism, together with ideas about natural rights, justice, and political democracy (Banks, 1981).

In the nineteenth century, two opposing themes of *order and control* and *rights and freedom* began to infuse (and clash within) curriculum thinking in western education systems. Whereas male-as-norm curricula focused on boys' public roles for the labor force and as citizens, the female curriculum was invariably linked to girls' biology and their eventual domestic destinies within the family. Parallel female curricula emerged, relating to gender and class, based on Victorian middle-class assumptions concerning "the perfect lady" and her hardworking proletarian sister "the good woman." The curriculum was framed according to the skills, knowledge, and accomplishments thought necessary for women's lives; for example, household management was reserved for the future "lady" of the house, laundry skills for the future working "woman."

Two perspectives on female education predominated during this period (and, some might argue, to the present day). The first and most popular view was that women were *different* from (and inferior to) men, not only biologically but also socially, intellectually, and psychologically. Girls therefore needed an education different from that of boys, relating specifically to their inferior roles in society. A recurrent theme was the fear that the working of the female mind was at odds with the working of the female body and that doing any academic work would destroy women's fertility (Delamont and Duffin, 1978).

The second view (held by most feminists of the period) was that if girls and women were educated equally with boys and men and studied identical curricula, women would be more able to assume their rightful place in society as the social and intellectual *equals* of men.

In the first half of the twentieth century, influenced by the work of Sigmund Freud in Europe and John Dewey in the United States, perceptions of the importance of the framework of the *learner* started to displace previous conceptualizations of the curriculum based exclusively on realms of knowledge. This led to the development of "child-centered" curricula relating to the perceived unfolding nature of the child. Simultaneously, shifts in the school curriculum were being forced by the new work opportunities open to women, such as typewriting, clerical, and telephonic work. However, despite such shifts, the outcomes of "progressive" curriculum changes for female education were fundamentally conservative (Walkerdine, 1990) in that the main purpose of female education was still for motherhood and domesticity.

The early post–World War II period brought new curriculum discourses concerning the role of schooling in the creation of a more highly skilled labor force for the advanced modern industrial state. Official documents stressed the unity of purpose of the school curriculum, and the need was identified for a wider choice of courses to meet the requirements of different levels of student ability, interest, and aptitude. Nevertheless, the outcome for female education remained as before, despite the more liberal tone set by western governments immediately after the war. For example, even during the height of socialist policy making of the

1945–1951 Labour administration in Britain, conventional vocational destinations for men (the workplace) and women (the home) were extensively endorsed (Dean, 1991).

It was only with the foregrounding of equality issues toward the end of the boom years of the 1960s and early 1970s—when there was, possibly uniquely in the history of western schooling, a high level of public investment in curriculum change *and* a commitment to educational equality—that gender was placed nearer the top of the curriculum agenda. Solutions to gender inequalities in the curriculum depended, however, on the various feminist perspectives taken up by educators.

Feminisms and the Curriculum

Four feminist perspectives will be discussed here, although a variety of others have emerged and will be likely to emerge in the future (Weiner, 1994).

Liberal feminists asserted that individual women should be as free as men to determine their social, political, and educational roles and that any laws, traditions, and activities that inhibit equal rights and opportunities should be abolished. Access to the curriculum is thus fundamental, by providing equal education experiences for both sexes. Research from this perspective has tended to focus on girls' "failure" or underachievement in certain curriculum areas such as mathematics, science, and technological subjects.

In contrast, *radical feminists* attributed inequalities in the curriculum to patriarchal forces and male-dominated power relationships in which (hetero) sexuality and hierarchy combine to create the dominant male and subordinate female. Neither the responsibility for nor the solution to sexual inequality can be placed entirely on the shoulders of educators. Rather, educators must be encouraged to develop an "inclusive" curriculum in which female achievements and experiences assume their rightful place. Here, research tends to focus on critiquing "male" school subjects and the patriarchal domination of knowledge more generally.

Marxist and socialist feminists have taken a slightly different perspective, viewing the curriculum as one of the terrains on which both sex and class struggles are played out and in which patterns of social domination and subordination are reproduced and sustained. They argue that working-class girls are doubly disadvantaged by the middle-class, male curriculum: they undergo experiences of invisibility and inequality similar to those of their male, working-class peers, while additionally being cast as inferior to them. In the feminist socialist view, the solution to educational inequality is limited by the perceived structural nature of sexual inequality within capitalism. Research from this perspective has focused on how gender and power relations are continually reproduced within and through the school curriculum such that working-class girls are "schooled" to limit their aspirations to jobs and domestic situations thought appropriate to their class.

Black feminists also have been skeptical about the extent to which education, by itself, can overturn or transform inequalities in society: the law has been more important than education in eradicating some of the most overt forms of racial and sexual discrimination. However, black activists have pointed out the invisibility and lack of representation of black and minority cultures within the curriculum in an effort to reeducate teachers and educationists into more consciously egalitarian practices. Black feminists have also argued that when gender and "race" issues are distinguished in the curriculum (rather than fused), black girls are likely to be rendered invisible in both discourses. Rather than focusing on the "clash of cultures" explanations given by many white teachers for the general underperformance of black girls and young women, black feminists have thus tended to concentrate on exposing how black family culture is viewed as pathological and on fracturing the widely held stereotypes of black femininity—for example, by exploring how the *actual* experience of black girls and young women can be represented in the curriculum and how the sexism and racism of teachers can be eradicated (Mirza, 1992).

For all feminist perspectives, including those described here, the curriculum's central role in defining school knowledge and how it is taught makes it an important vehicle for challenge and for promoting change.

See Also

EDUCATION: ACHIEVEMENT; EDUCATION: GENDER EQUITY; EDUCATION: HIGHER EDUCATION; EDUCATION: MATHEMATICS; EDUCATION: SCIENCE

References and Further Reading

Banks, Olive. 1981. *Faces of feminism*. Oxford: Martin Robertson.

Dean, Denis. 1991. Education for moral improvement, domesticity, and social cohesion: Expectations and fears of the Labor government. *Oxford Review of Education* 17(3): 269–285.

Delamont, Sara, and Lorna Duffin, eds. 1978. *The nineteenth-century woman: Her cultural and physical world*. London: Croom Helm.

Kenway, Jane, and Helen Modra. 1992. Feminist pedagogy and emancipatory possibilities. In C. Luke and J. Gore, eds., *Feminisms and critical pedagogy*. New York: Routledge.

Mirza, Heidi. 1992. *Young, female, and black*. London: Routledge.

Pring, Richard. 1989. *The new curriculum*. London: Cassell.
Walkerdine, Valerie. 1990. *School girl fictions*. London: Verso.
Weiner, Gaby. 1994. *Feminisms in education: An introduction*. Buckingham, U.K.: Open University Press.

Gaby Weiner

EDUCATION: Distance Education

Distance education, also known as open and distance learning (ODL), is a form of structured education in which curriculum is delivered through media other than face-to-face communication—for example, print, audiotapes, broadcast media, and telecommunications of various kinds. Teaching and assessment are also mediated in this way. ODL students are at a geographic and often a temporal distance from their "teacher." The expansion of education globally has produced a corresponding expansion of ODL, because it is seen to offer economies of scale. New institutions have been formed that are dedicated to distance learning—for example, the Indira Gandhi University in India and many other institutions that have become "dual-mode," using both face-to-face and ODL methods.

Historically ODL has provided the only chance for many women to learn when other educational institutions were not open to them. When in 1840 Isaac Pitman offered the first "modern" distance-learning course (in shorthand writing), it was open to women when no women in Europe or the United States had access to university education and many had no schooling at all. In 1873 Anna Ticknor created the Society to Encourage Studies at Home, which provided distance education to adult women of all classes on the east coast of the United States. This organization provided instruction for up to 10,000 women and flourished for 24 years. It influenced the development of U.S. correspondence education for both genders (Watkins, 1991).

Women were also often the mediators of ODL for others. In rural areas of North America they were involved as the unpaid supervisors and tutors of their own children, using "home study" materials (Faith, 1988). In countries where women, even at the turn of the twenty-first century, were still seen as belonging to the private sphere of the home and family, distance education offered the only educational opportunity.

Feminist Critiques of ODL

In 1988, Karlene Faith edited and published the first international collection of essays about gender issues in ODL.

Many contributors to this collection were members of the International Council for Distance Education (ICDE), the largest international network of distance educators. They had become angry about the invisibility of gender in research and publications by members of the council. Until 1988 the total number of published articles in *Teaching at a Distance* and *Distance Education* (the main ODL journals) that took gender as a substantive issue for ODL was six (Burge, 1988). Faith's collection reviewed the participation of women in ODL in a variety of developed and developing countries, demonstrating that gender equality had not been achieved with respect to access, performance, or curriculum provision in most countries. It gave examples of initiatives to improve access for women, some of which were based on a liberal equality model, others on more radical views, such as a critique of the curriculum as gendered. At the same time, an informal grouping of women in the ICDE was formed that called itself the Women's International Network (WIN). This network tries to ensure that every ICDE conference contains some presentations on gender issues.

Since 1988 there has been a steady but small flow of publications about the nature of gender issues in ODL (Burge and Lenskyj, 1990; McLiver and Kruger, 1993). In 1993 the University of Umea in Sweden held the first international conference dedicated to gender and ODL: "Feminist Pedagogy and Women-Friendly Perspectives in Distance Education." An issue of *Open Praxis* in 1994 gave space to reviewing the situation of women staff and students in the years since the publication of the Faith book (see, for example, Taylor and Kirkup, 1994). Many of the authors who have written in the area (Kirkup and von Prümmer, 1990; Burge, 1990), use Carol Gilligan (1982) and Mary Belenky et al. (1986) to theorize the learning needs of women students.

In 1994 Patricia Lunneborg published *OU Women: Undoing Educational Obstacles*, the first "experiential" collection of life histories of women studying at the British Open University. In 1995 Asha Kanwar and Neela Jagannathan edited a collection of essays about the situation of women in distance education in India: *Speaking for Ourselves*. Christine von Prümmer (2000) has looked at the lives and in particular the social mobility of German ODL women students. Before Faith's book there had been a commonly accepted view that ODL was a type of education particularly suited to women. This view was reasonably founded in the knowledge that adult women have many more restrictions on their time and mobility than adult men, as well as on their access to disposable income, which made ODL the most practical option for postschool education. However, there is often an implicit presumption among ODL practitioners that, apart from these material factors, women are the same as men with respect to their motivations to study and their intellectual styles, as well as their domestic circumstances.

Gill Kirkup and Christine von Prümmer (1990) carried out a large-scale survey of European ODL students and identified differences in the preferred learning styles of men and women that made them respond differently to different ODL methods. Women were more likely to be frequent attendees at study centers, despite having more obstacles to getting there, such as less access to transportation and more domestic responsibility. Women valued the opportunity to meet other students and were more likely than men to involve others, such as family and friends, in their learning. Most significant, although roughly the same proportions of men and women reported feeling isolated as ODL students, this was a problem for 24 percent of the men, compared with 40 percent of the women. The work of Gilligan (1982) suggests that this discomfort with isolation emerges from a desire for connection with others.

New Technologies and ODL

The development and convergence of telecommunications and computing are producing sophisticated "telematics" systems, which educational policy makers see as providing the possibility for all students to have access to extensive knowledge/learning resources that can be restructured to specific learning needs. These systems also offer the possibility of fast pedagogic interactions transcending place and time. "Traditional" (that is, face-to-face) institutions are now incorporating ODL—as distributed learning—into their methods. But so far research on information and communication technologies (ICTs) in ODL has only confirmed that these technologies are gendered. Adult women ODL students have much less access to personal computers than do men, and the quality of access when it exists is lower (Kirkup, 1993; Kirkup and von Prümmer, 1996). In addition, women who do get involved with using a personal computer to study with the British Open University, for example, seem to have motivations and interests quite different from those of their male colleagues.

Probably the most important ICT development in ODL is computer-mediated communication through the Internet, which provides the possibility for the connection with others that some women look for in their learning (Burge, 1990). However, Susan Herring (1993) demonstrated that computer-mediated-communication interac-tions often reproduce the gendered aspects of language and power typical of "real world" interactions. Kirkup (1996) has critically examined cyborg theory (Haraway, 1985) to discuss the potential of ICTs for women in distance education. H. Jeanie Taylor, Cheris Kramarae, and Maureen Ebben (1993) have demonstrated that women not only can become silenced in this medium; they also can be pursued and frightened. The Internet does not embody the kinds of values that educational institutions do. At the same time as education has developed strong institutional policies to restrict pornography and sexual harassment, these have become problems on the Internet. Along with a variety of dubious services, messages, and graphics, the atmosphere of much of the Internet is marked by a form of masculinity that is rarely on display in other public arenas. At the turn of the twenty-first century, the atmosphere was more reminiscent of the 1960s (Myburgh, 1999) than the 1990s and would provide an unfriendly learning environment for women ODL students. The question remains: Can computers be incorporated into ODL systems in a more women-friendly fashion?

Around the world, these new media are a real possibility only for rich countries and in many cases not for the poor in these countries. In developing countries, ODL continued to rely on printed texts and public broadcasting in the early twenty-first century, but it was a major tool of development, and here some of the most exciting educational projects for women were being initiated.

See Also

CYBERSPACE AND VIRTUAL REALITY; EDUCATION: ADULT AND CONTINUING; EDUCATION: ON-LINE; INFORMATION TECHNOLOGY; NETWORKS, ELECTRONIC; TELEVISION; TELEWORKING

References and Further Reading.

Belenky, Mary F., Blythe M. Clichy, Nancy R. Golberger, and Jill M. Tarule. 1986. *Women's ways of knowing: The development of self, voice, and mind.* New York: Basic Books.

Burge, Elizabeth. 1988. Foreword to Karlene Faith, ed., *Toward new horizons for women in distance education: International perspectives.* London: Routledge.

———. 1990. Women as learners: Issues for visual and virtual reality classrooms. *Canadian Journal for the Study of Adult Education/Revue canadienne pour l'éducation des adultes* 4(2): 1–24.

——— and Helen Lenskyj. 1990. Women studying in distance education: Issues and principles. *Journal of Distance Education/Revue de l'enseignement à distance* 5(1): 20–37.

Faith, Karlene, ed. 1988. *Toward new horizons for women in distance education: International perspectives.* London: Routledge.

Gilligan, Carol. 1982. *In a different voice: Psychological theory and women's development.* Cambridge, Mass.: Harvard University Press.

Haraway, Donna. 1985. A manifesto for cyborgs: Science, technology, and socialist feminism in the 1980s. *Socialist Review* 15(80): 65–107.

Herring, Susan. 1993. Gender and democracy in computer-mediated communication. *Electronic Journal of Communications/Revue Electronique de Communication* 3(2)

Kanwar, Asha S., and Neela Jagannathan, eds. 1995. *Speaking for ourselves: Women in distance education in India.* New Delhi: Manohar.

Kirkup, Gill. 1993. Equal opportunities and computing at the Open University. In Alan Tait, ed., *Key issues in open learning.* Harlow, U.K.: Longman.

———. 1996. The importance of gender. In Roger Mills and Alan Tait, eds., *Supporting the learner in open and distance learning.* Washington, D.C.: Pitman.

——— and Christine von Prümmer. 1990. Support and connectedness: The needs of women distance education students. *Journal of Distance Education* 5(2): 9–31.

———. 1996. How can distance education address the particular needs of European women? In G. Fandel, R. Bartz, and F. Nickolmann, eds., *University level distance education in Europe.* Weinheim: Deutscher Studien Verlag.

———. 1997. Distance education for European women: The threats and opportunities of new educational forms and media. *European Journal of Women's Studies* 4(1): 39–62.

Lunneborg, Patricia W. 1994. *OU women: Undoing educational obstacles.* London: Cassell.

McLiver, Rhonda, and Kerry Kruger. 1993. Women in distance education. *Open Forum* 3(2): 25–37.

Myburgh, Sue. 1999. The needle in the haystack or using the spade: Women's information-seeking behaviour on the Internet. In Dinah Cohen et al., eds., *Winds of change: Women and the culture of universities, conference proceedings.* Vol 2, 767–778. Sydney: University of Technology.

Open Praxis: Bulletin of the International Council for Distance Education. 1994. (1.)

Prümmer, Christine von. 1993. Women-friendly perspectives in distance education. Keynote address in *Feminist pedagogy and women-friendly perspectives in distance education.* Papers presented at the International WIN Working Conference, 10–13 June 1993, Umea, Sweden. Available from the Women's Studies Center of Umea, Report no. 4.

———. 2000. *Women and distance education: Challenges and opportunities.* London: Routledge.

Taylor, H. Jeanie, Cheris Kramarae, and Maureen Ebben. 1993. *Women, information technology, and scholarship.* Urbana, Ill.: Center for Advanced Study.

Taylor, Lee, and Gill Kirkup. 1994. From the local to the global: Wanting to see women's participation and progress at the OUUK in a wider context. *Open Praxis.*

Watkins, Barbara L. 1991. A quite radical idea: The invention and elaboration of collegiate correspondence study. In Barbara L. Watkins and Stephen J. Wright, eds., *The foundations of American distance education.* Dubuque, Iowa: Kendall Hunt.

Women's Studies Centre of Umea. 1993. *Feminist pedagogy and women-friendly perspectives in distance education.* Papers presented at the International WIN Working Conference, 10–13 June 1993, Umea, Sweden.

Gill Kirkup

EDUCATION: Domestic Science and Home Economics

Many terms have been used for the subject of home economics, particularly in the United Kingdom, including *domestic economy, housecraft, home management, cookery,* and *domestic science.* However, the central themes have remained constant: teaching practical and management skills to improve the quality of life for individuals and families. The term *home economics* was consistently used in the United States, where it originated, though it was not until the 1970s that this term became widely used in the United Kingdom. Changes in subject content aimed at improving the image of the subject have led to this term being replaced, particularly for higher education courses, by *family and consumer science, applied consumer studies,* and *food technology.* In this article the terms *domestic subjects, domestic science,* and *home economics* are used.

Origins

The rationale for the teaching of domestic subjects to girls was promoted by domestic reformers in the 1870s in England. Their efforts between 1870 and 1900 were responsible for setting up national training schools of cookery, the first in England being established in 1873. The teaching of domestic subjects to older girls was made compulsory following the recommendations set out by the Board of Education in the Code of 1900, and the introduction of the payment of grants from 1905 consolidated the position of the subject in schools (Sillitoe, 1933). The Association of Teachers of Domestic Subjects was established in 1896 by the Principals of Training Schools and drew its membership from the growing numbers of domestic subjects teachers. This association continues to support teachers of home economics today using a new name, the National Association of Teachers of Home Economics and Technology.

A similar movement developed in North America when promoters of the subject, such as Melvil Dewey and Ellen Richards, launched the subject of home economics. Between 1899 and 1907 the Lake Placid conferences, held annually for professional home economists and their supporters, discussed and debated the value of home economics and its content (Ehrenreich and English, 1979). A professional association established in the United States in 1908 continues today under the name the American Association of Family and Consumer Sciences.

Schooling for Girls

The schooling of girls has been influenced by ideas about the role of women in the wider society. At the turn of the twentieth century, it was believed that growing up and learning to be "feminine" meant socialization into a future ideal of wifehood and motherhood (David, 1980). Teaching domestic subjects in schools aimed to produce competent wives and mothers. A vocational advantage of the subject was that it offered working-class girls training for employment as domestic servants (Powers, 1992). The importance of home life for the survival and economic success of the nation was reinforced in numerous Board of Education reports during the early twentieth century in England. Domestic subjects (cookery, needlework, and laundry work) taught girls the skills and practices necessary to establish and maintain the home. Thus educational provision for girls was different from that of boys and was based on clearly defined and accepted roles of women and girls within the family, home, and workplace.

The specific and deliberate orientation of the subject to girls has been debated by feminist critics of the subject (for example, Attar, 1990). Middle-class parents were also hostile to the subject, because it was equated with training for domestic service and considered a socially inferior pursuit for their daughters. The low status attributed to home economics continued into the twentieth century despite attempts by home economists to promote the values of the subject and its teaching. Patricia Thompson (1992) maintains that both boys and girls should be educated for domestic life and questions assumptions that give greater value to Hermean (public) knowledge than to Hestian (domestic) knowledge. Home economists in general regard the low status of the subject as a reflection of the low priority afforded to domestic work and child care by policy makers. Around the world women take greater responsibility for these activities, and Marilyn Waring (1988) proposes that fundamental changes in attitudes and fiscal policy are required to ensure that women are justly rewarded for this work. The status of home economics will be raised only when domestic work and caring are given greater importance within society and, more important, are shared more equally by men and women (Barrett and McIntosh, 1991).

Shifts in Focus

The constantly changing names and content of the subject reflect societal values and attitudes toward women, the family, and domestic work. Initially, domestic subjects in the late nineteenth and early twentieth centuries in England and the United States were concerned with developing practical skills. The main method of teaching used was teacher demonstration followed by class practicals (Sillitoe, 1933). Housewifery, laundry work, cookery, and needlework were treated as distinct and separate aspects of the subject. Published education reports and classroom texts provided specific instructions about the content to be taught in each. Textbooks gave both practical instruction and "scientific" explanations, reflecting the debate between 1906 and 1913 about teaching science to girls through domestic subjects, which gave rise to the term *domestic science* (Sillitoe, 1933).

The content of domestic science courses changed after World War II in England and the United States, reflecting advances in technological and scientific knowledge that led to greater automation in the home and new methods of food processing, preparation, and marketing. Course content concentrated on the immediate needs of the family, child care, shopping, and the use of laborsaving domestic equipment, which was becoming more widely available in industrially developed countries. The consumer boom and the expansion in advertising in the 1950s and 1960s stressed domestic life and the role of women in the home as consumers (Friedan, 1963).

Consumerism, caring, relationships, good grooming, budgeting, and the companion role of women were aspects of domestic science teaching in the later 1960s and 1970s. The emphasis in teaching had shifted from cookery to the care and nurturing of family members and their relationships. Understanding people in relation to family and community required that a sociological perspective be introduced. The increasingly interdisciplinary nature of the subject required teachers to have a more generalist knowledge, and domestic science teachers became concerned that the lack of specialist knowledge would lead to teachers of other subjects taking over. The identity of the subject and the need for a definition were hotly debated (Hutchinson, 1993). Attempts were made to identify a core of knowledge covering the concepts central to the subject, irrespective of the influences of technological change and shifting cultural values. Clarifying the boundaries of the subject also resulted in the term *home economics* being more widely used in the United Kingdom, though the term had always been applied in the United States.

Knowledge of food, clothing, and shelter applied to people, and the home became the accepted focus of home economics in the 1980s. The use of the word *home* confined the subject but also reconfirmed its domestic and private identity, despite clear areas of employment in industry for home economists; hence, differences between how the subject was taught in schools and the jobs home economists performed in industry were adopted as a subject of research in the early 1980s by the Institute of Home Economics in the United Kingdom. That the majority of home economics teachers had no industrial experience was considered a factor perpetuating the stereotypical image of the subject as women's work. This image of the subject was, in turn, held partly responsible for the fact that the entry of males into the profession was rare.

Recent Trends

Home economics, how it is perceived, its nomenclature, and the content of courses in different countries reflect cultural and economic circumstances. The interpretation and teaching of home economics in the United Kingdom and the United States have, over time, influenced the development of the subject in other countries. Often teachers in other countries will themselves have received home economics degrees and higher degrees in the United Kingdom or the United States. Former British colonies have traditionally adopted courses and syllabi similar to or the same as those taught in Britain. In countries where the home remains at the center of production, and people depend on the sound management of scant resources, home economics courses emphasize basic nutrition, hygiene, health care, and budgeting. In contrast, in more developed countries where the center of production has moved away from the home, where many women with children are in paid employment, and where the structure of families has changed, interdisciplinary approaches and an emphasis on social issues predominate.

Additionally, in these countries academic and professional home economists have developed a theoretical rationale for the subject, furthered research in the field, and established higher education courses at degree and postgraduate levels (Hutchinson, 1994).

The Education Reform Act in England, Wales, and Northern Ireland in 1988 signaled the end of interdisciplinary home economics teaching in schools in these countries. A new field, design and technology, introduced in 1990, includes content exclusively related to the design and making of food products for the marketplace. The removal of home economics as a distinctive area of study in schools and the shift in the application of subject content from the home to industrial contexts in higher education courses has thus fundamentally changed home economics education in the United Kingdom.

At degree level, home economics courses have a number of guises: applied consumer science, consumer studies, human ecology, applied resource management, consumer product management, and design and technology (Council for National Academic Awards, 1992). Home economics degree courses began to emphasize the management focus within the subject, both of people and of resources. In part, this acknowledges the wider range of jobs available for home economists in public and commercial sectors, and, having learned these skills, home economics graduates are able to compete with other graduates for marketing and managerial positions. The inclusion of a "sandwich," or work placement, year in courses has further improved job opportunities for home economists. Such shifts are made because changes to the names and content of courses will attract more men into the profession and thus reduce the historically overwhelming gender imbalance in favor of women.

See Also

EDUCATION: CURRICULUM IN SCHOOLS; EDUCATION: GENDERED SUBJECT CHOICE

References and Further Reading

Attar, Dena. 1990. *Wasting girls' time: The history and politics of home economics*. London: Virago Education Series.

Barrett, Michèle, and Mary McIntosh. 1991. *The anti-social family*, 2nd ed. London: Verso.

Council for National Academic Awards. 1992. *Review of consumer studies and home economics degree courses*. Council for National Academic Awards.

David, Miriam E. 1980. *The state, the family, and education*. London: Routledge and Kegan Paul.

Ehrenreich, Barbara, and Deirdre English. 1979. *For her own good: 150 years of experts' advice to women.* London: Pluto.

Friedan, Betty. 1963. *The feminine mystique.* London: Penguin.

Hutchinson, Geraldine. 1993. The title debate. *Home Economist: Journal of the Institute of Home Economics* 12(6): 2–4.

———. 1994. Empowering home economists: Career development in focus. *Home Economist: Journal of the Institute of Home Economics* 13(5): 8–9.

Powers, Jane Bernard. 1992. *The "girl question" in education: Vocational education for young women in the progressive era.* London: Falmer.

Sillitoe, Helen. 1933. *A history of the teaching of domestic subjects.* London: Methuen.

Thompson, Patricia. 1992. Home economics: Feminism in a Hestian voice. In Cheris Kramarae and Dale Spender, eds., *Knowledge explosion: Generations of feminist scholarship,* 270–280. New York: Teachers College Press.

Waring, Marilyn. 1988. *Counting for nothing: What men value and what women are worth.* Sydney: Allen and Unwin.

Geraldine Hutchinson

EDUCATION: East Asia

"Three Obediences and Four Virtues"

When Confucius extended education from social elites to common people with a broader scope of private education, women were not benefited. It was Ban Zhao, a female Confucian and historian in the Han dynasty (206 B.C.–A.D. 220), with a solid background of literary education, who applied Confucian values to women's education and thus included women in the realm of Confucian education. In her *Nü jie* (Lessons for Women), the classic instructional manuals for women in east Asian countries before the nineteenth century, Ban asked, "Why should it not be that girls are educated as well as boys?" (Ban, 1997: 34). She enriched the content of the "three obediences and four virtues" in Confucian classics by setting up specific guidelines for women's behavior in everyday life. A woman, Ban believed, will have a harmonious family and a graceful life if she follows these maxims that honor obedience, sacrifice, and modesty.

Instructional manuals on moral education in accordance with Confucian ethics, such as *Nü si shu (Four Books for Women)* in China, *Onna daigaku (Great Learning for Women)* in Japan, and *Naehun (A Guidebook for Womanhood)* in Korea, made up the core texts for generations of east Asian women till the mid-nineteenth century. Although a handful of exceptions from elite families had a better chance to receive literary education from their parents or brothers, education, for the majority of women, meant moral education plus domestic skills practice, taught by mothers, relatives, or female teachers at home.

"Good Wives and Wise Mothers"

As a result of a series of defeats in wars with western countries as well as Japan in the nineteenth and early twentieth centuries, China lost its glory as an educational model for Japan and Korea. Whereas Chinese reformers were seeking ways of strengthening the country, Japan had already strategically reformed its educational system, since the Meiji Restoration (1868), by incorporating the advanced elements in various western models. The successful synthesis of Asian values with western knowledge made Japan a viable model for China as well as Korea.

As early as 1872, Japan had established a system of compulsory education, which made primary education accessible to both boys and girls. A series of laws promulgated between 1880 and 1899 advanced women's education to secondary schools and paved the way to higher education for Japanese women. In 1910, less than 10 percent of the women in China were literate, whereas 97.3 percent of the school-age girls in Japan were enrolled in primary schools.

Chinese reformers of the late Qing dynasty, after examining the situation of their eastern neighbors and of western countries, concluded that the neglect of formal education for women was one major cause behind the weakness of China. In his *Chang she nüxuetang qi (Proposal for Opening Girls' Schools)* 1897, Liang Qichao, an early initiator of female education, argued, "After three generations of women's education, how can China still be inferior to America and Japan?" (Liang, 1999). In 1898, Liang Qichao, Kang Guangren, Jin Yuanshan, and Sheng Xuanhuai established the Chinese Girls' School in Shanghai, the first private girls' school set up by Chinese (Wang, 1995). In 1907, when the Qing government started officially to establish girls' schools modeled on the Japanese educational system, there were already 428 private girls' schools with more than fifteen thousand students in China (Liu, 1989). Women's education at the time, however, was generally confined to segregated primary schools at a lower level than that of their male counterparts. In 1912, the government eradicated gender segregation in primary schools and started to promote secondary education for women. But it was not until 1922, when the national government promulgated the act of school system reform based on the 6-3-3 system in the United States, that this dual system of education came to an end (Liu, 1989).

In 1884, Pak Yong-hyo, a political exile from Korea to Japan, wrote to the king of Korea pressing for a wide range of reforms, including equal education for school-age boys and girls (Y.C. Kim, 1986). Influenced by some enlightened men, a group of elite Korean women founded the first public girls' school, Sunsong, in 1898 (Choi, 1986). During the period of Japanese colonization (1910–1945), in response to the "Japanizing" policy in education, more than one thousand private schools, including some girls' schools—such as Chinmyong, Yangjong, Sukmyong, and Tongdok—were established. But most of these private girls' schools, like the Chinese private schools, suffered from financial difficulty and closed (Y.C. Kim, 1986). Ewha Hakdang, a female mission school, was just about the only place for Korean women to receive formal education till 1945.

It is worth noting that western missionaries played an important role in initiating and promoting formal education for women in east Asia from the early nineteenth century to the 1930s. In 1836, Henrietta Shuck, a Baptist, established the first American school for Chinese girls in Macao (Graham, 1995); in 1886, the Methodist missionary Mary Scranton founded Ewha Hakdang in Korea. The scope of the early mission school was rather modest. For example, there was only one student when Scranton opened Ewha. In 1910, however, Ewha became the first institute of higher education for Korean women (Y.C. Kim, 1986). And in southern China, by 1907 the number of Catholic girls' schools had climbed to 697 with 15,300 students (Wang, 1995). The function of mission schools, thus, had gone beyond propagating Christianity to reshaping the gender beliefs in educational practices in east Asia.

The dominant idea behind women's education in this period in east Asia was to prepare refined and civilized wives and mothers for the citizens of the country. Western knowledge and Confucian values coexisted in the curriculum. In the Chinese Girls' School, for instance, traditional instructional manuals such as *Nü si shu* were still used. There existed, however, a voice that countered this modern version of the traditional Confucian values. The Japanese educator Jinzo Naruse, for example, proposed "a three-pronged approach to instruction for females, first, as human beings, second, as women, and, third, as citizens" (Judge, 1999). Cai Yuanpei, Chen Yiyi, and Ye Shaojun argued in China that the goal of female education should rest on the cultivation of a whole personality of women (Cai, 1999; Wang, 1995).

In parallel with these views and practices, the political and national crisis in China and Korea blended women's education with revolutionary or patriotic movements. One objective of the early Patriotic Girls' School founded in 1902, for example, was to prepare women assassins as part of the anti-Qing revolution (Cai, 1999). Chen Duxiu, the leader of the youth during the May Fourth Movement in 1919, claimed that it was unnecessary to discuss women's problems as educational problems, occupational problems, and so on, for the only way to solve women's problem was to practice socialism (Liu, 1989). The combination of education with politics in Mao's educational policy after the establishment of the People's Republic of China in 1949 became so important that political education was almost the only content of education.

"Modern Traditional Women"

Great progress in the quantity and quality of women's education—though not without reverses—occurred in east Asian countries in the five decades following World War II.

With efforts by the United States, a democratic educational system modeled on the 6-3-3 school system was established both in Japan and in Korea. A series of laws reflecting democratic values guaranteed women's equal rights to education (Beauchamp and Vardaman, 1994). In Japan, compulsory education for both boys and girls was extended to nine years and in Korea to six years. Although both countries experienced the shifts between the Confucian tradition and the U.S. model, a synthesized model came into being in the 1980s.

In China, Mao's revolutionary model extended education from the urban elites to rural people. But his replacing the academic model of education, an imitation of the Russian model in the 1950s, with the revolutionary model during the Cultural Revolution almost paralyzed formal education—especially higher education in China. The scope of higher education shrank to such a degree that the total number of Chinese university students in 1970 dropped to 47,815, which was only 2.6 percent of that in Japan and 24 percent of that in South Korea in the same year (Education and Literacy, 2000). It was not until the late 1970s that the economic impetus boosted a reconstruction of formal education.

After five decades of development, from the 1950s to the 1990s, the gender difference in basic education had diminished, and the gender gap in higher education was narrowing. In China, the most notable progress was the expansion of basic education. From less than 20 percent before the establishment of the People's Republic of China, the enrollment rate of school-age girls soared to 98.8 percent in 1997, and the proportion of female students in secondary schools rose from 25.6 percent in 1951 to 45.7 percent in 1998 (Chen, 1999). In the meantime, the percentage of illiterates aged 15 and above in the female population decreased from 90 percent in 1949 to 23.24 percent in 1997 (*Zhongguo*, 1999). In Japan, with a solid foundation of basic education established prior to World War II, the most striking development in women's education was in higher education. In contrast with 5 percent in 1955, the rate of female high school graduates advancing to higher education climbed to 49.4 percent in 1998 (Office for Gender Equity, 1999). In the Republic of Korea (South Korea), as in China, the proportion of male and female students in basic education is almost equal (Education and Literacy, 2000).

A closer look at the above statistics, however, will reveal the other side of the picture. In China, behind the high enrollment rate was a high dropout rate—four million per year on average (including primary and secondary schools), of which 70 percent were girls from poor areas (P. Zhang, 1995). In Japan, although the rate of female high school graduates advancing to higher education has surpassed that of male students since 1994, with 21.5 percent of female students enrolled at two-year junior colleges, only 27.5 percent went to four-year universities in 1998, whereas 38.9 percent of male graduates went to universities in 1994 (Office for Gender Equity, 1999). In South Korea, 89.4 percent of girls and 90.3 percent of boys were enrolled in high schools in 1995. Only 38.6 percent of girls, however, compared with 69.7 percent of boys, were enrolled in universities in the same year (Y.O. Kim, 1998).

The above figures suggest that equal rights to education, as prescribed in the constitutions and educational laws in all the countries covered in this article, did not necessarily lead to gender equity in education. Among various causes behind the current situation, a more covert factor, according to some studies in the 1990s, came from the educational practice itself. As researchers from all these countries pointed out, traditional gender biases still exist in textbooks in primary and secondary schools (O.Y. Kim, 1996; Yang, 1998). Although equal opportunities to schooling were no longer a dream to most women in east Asia, the old question of what to teach and how to teach kept surfacing in the agenda of educational reformers at the millennium. The cultivation of a whole personality, as some pioneers advocated in the early twentieth century, might still prove significant to reformers in the twenty-first century.

See Also

COMMUNISM; CONFUCIANISM; EQUAL OPPORTUNITIES: EDUCATION; FEMINISM: CHINA; FEMINISM: JAPAN; FEMINISM: KOREA; GLOBALIZATION OF EDUCATION; POLITICS AND THE STATE: EAST ASIA; WOMEN'S STUDIES: EAST ASIA

References and Further Reading

Ban Zhao. 1997. *Nü jie* (Lessons for women). In W. B. Wang, ed., *Zhongguo ertong qimeng mingzhu tonglan* (Chinese classics of enlightenment for children), 31–38. Chinese Children Press.

Beauchamp, E. R., and J. M. Vardaman, eds. 1994. *Japanese education since 1945: A documentary study*. New York: Sharpe.

Cai Yuanpei. 1999. *Jiemin zishu* (Autobiography of Cai Yuanpei). Jiangsu People's Press.

Chen, Z. L. 1999. The development of women's education. *Women of China* (Dec.): 6–7.

Choi, S. K. 1986. Formation of women's movements in Korea. In S. W. Chung, ed., *Challenges for women: Women's studies in Korea*, 103–126, trans. C. H. Shin et al. Seoul: Ewha Woman's University Press.

Education and literacy (2000). [Database.] UNESCO Institute of Statistics. Retrieved 20 Jan. 2000 from the World Wide Web: <http://unescostat.unesco.org/en/stats/stats0.htm>

Graham, G. 1995. *Gender, culture, and Christianity: American protestant mission schools in China, 1880–1930*. New York: Peter Lang.

Judge, J. 1999. Knowledge for the nation or of the nation: Meiji Japan and the changing meaning of female literacy in the late Qing. Retrieved 27 Jan. 2000 from the World Wide Web: <http://www.isop.ucla.edu/ccs/judge.htm>

Kim, O. Y. 1996. Korean women today and toward 2000. In *Asian women*, vol. 1, 1–29. Retrieved 20 Jan. 2000 from the World Wide Web: <http://apwinc.sookmyung. ac.kr/eapwinc/aw/pub/awscan/asi/1/asi-1.html>

Kim, Y. C. 1986. Women's movement in modern Korea. In S. W. Chung, ed., *Challenges for women: Women's studies in Korea*, 75–102, trans. C. H. Shin et al. Seoul: Ewha Woman's University Press.

Kim, Y. O. 1998. Data on gender and science and technology in the work place: Korean case. [APEC document.] Retrieved 25 Jan. 2000 from the World Wide Web: <http://strategis.ic.gc.ca/cgi-bin/basic/ftgetdoc?table>

Liang Qichao. 1999. Chang she nüxuetang qi (Proposal for opening girls' schools). In S. H. Ding, ed., *Zhongguo jindai qimeng sichao* (Enlightenment movement in modern China), 205–206. Shehui kexue wenxian chubanshe (Social Science Literature Press).

Liu, J. C. 1989. *Zhongguo jindai funü yundong shi* (History of contemporary women's movement in China). Chinese Women's Press.

Office for Gender Equity, Japan Prime Minister's Office. 1999. The present status of gender equality and measures: Third report on the plan for gender equality 2000. [White paper.] Retrieved 20 Jan. 2000 from the World Wide Web: <http://www.sorifu.go.jp/danjyo/index2.html.>

Wang, B. Z., and G. H. Yan, eds. 1994. *Zhongguo jiaoyu sixiang tongshi* (General history of Chinese educational ideology). Vol. 5. Hunan Educational Press.

Wang, Q. S. 1995. *Zhongguo chuantong xisu zhong de xingbie qishi* (Gender discrimination in traditional Chinese customs). Peking University Press.

Yang, X. 1998. Zhongguo nuxing jiaoyu de xingli zu'ai ji duice (Psychological obstacles and strategies in women's education in China). *Journal of Shannxi Normal University* 1: 152–159.

Zhang, D. W. 1999. *Riben jiaoyu tezhi de wenhuaxue yanjiu* (A study of the characteristic of Japanese education from the cultural perspective). Northeast Normal University Press.

Zhang, P., ed. 1995. *Zhongguo funü de xianzhuang* (The current situation of Chinese women), chap. 2. Hongqi Press.

Zhongguo tongji nianjian 1999 (China statistical yearbook 1999). China Statistical Press.

Zhang Wei

EDUCATION: Eastern Europe

The educational experience of girls and young women in eastern Europe under communism and postcommunism has differed in a number of important ways from that in the developed democracies. First, parity of educational attainment was achieved in most eastern European countries by the first half of the 1970s, substantially earlier than in the West. Second, the educational gains made by women during the communist period were not in the main the result of gender-specific interventions designed to promote the education of women, nor of feminist campaigning. Rather, women gained disproportionately as a result of the universal character of educational and employment policies. Third, the social-subjective meaning of education was specific insofar as educational differences were less linked to income level than in the West, and, further, since there was no civil society under communism, educational, employment, and income advan-

tage/disadvantage could not be associated with "second-class citizenship" in a given political community (see Watson, 1996).

After the end of communism, women remained well represented at all levels of education in most eastern European countries, despite their experiencing severe problems in the new competitive labor markets in practically all these countries. The table shows that young women and girls represent about half of all pupils/students in primary, secondary, and higher education in most of eastern Europe and in the Baltic States.

In most countries of eastern Europe, where the educational system is still largely based on the pre-1989 model, primary education lasts eight years. (The exceptions are the former German Democratic Republic, Slovakia, Romania, the Federal Republic of Yugoslavia, and Slovenia, where primary education lasts four years and secondary schooling takes correspondingly longer.) Secondary education includes three types of schools: the four-year *lyceum*, which provides a general academic education and is the main route to higher education; the four- to five-year *technikum*, which provides

Level of Education

Girls as a percentage of all pupils/students in primary, secondary, and higher education in eastern Europe and the Baltic states in 1992

	Primary	Secondary	Higher	General	Vocational
Albania	48	45	55	39	52
Bulgaria	48	50	68	38	51
Croatia	49	51	65	47	48
Czech Republic	50	50	57	41	46
EX-GDR	49	48	50	40	52[b]
Hungary[a]	49	49	66	43	51
Poland	49	50	72	42	56
Romania	49	49	52	41	47
Slovakia	49	50	51	47	48
Slovenia	49	49	62	44	54
Macedonia	48	49	62	44	52
Federal Republic of Yugoslavia	49	49	51	45	53
Estonia	49	51	53	43	51
Latvia	49	51	52	44	53
Lithuania	48	50	52	39	55[c]

[a]1991;   [b]1988;   [c]1993–1994

Source: UNESCO, 1994; Lithuanian Department of Statistics, 1994.

a more specialized technical education, a technical qualification for employment, and the possibility of entry to higher education; and the two- to three-year vocational school, which gives a lower work qualification but allows later transfer to the *technikum*. Higher education is a relatively homogeneous category and lasts between four and five years. The table shows that in secondary education, girls tend to be concentrated in the general academic schools and underrepresented in the technical vocational schools. Subject specialization begins at age 15, either with choice of vocational training school or, to a lesser extent, with choice of subject at the *lyceum* (see Watson, 1992). Young women tend to be concentrated in subject areas such as the humanities, health, education, and economics. The process of educational segregation is continued into higher education, with women typically representing more than half of students enrolled in education, medicine, and stomatology but substantially underrepresented in the technical universities. After higher education, the levels of educational participation of women decline; in Poland, for example, women represented about 28 percent of all those completing a doctoral degree in 1993–1994.

The gender patterning of educational attainment in eastern Europe cannot, in the main, be explained in terms of specific educational policies geared toward improving the social position of women. The exception is the German Democratic Republic, where special policy measures were introduced in the 1970s to raise the educational qualifications of older women through the provision of special university courses and sabbaticals (Grimm and Meier, 1994; Quack and Maier, 1994). By way of contrast, in Poland it was the overrepresentation of women, particularly in the prestigious occupation of medicine, that was seen to be a social problem, and until 1987, men in Poland were awarded extra points in the entrance examinations to medical school in order to reduce the proportion of women medical students (see Watson, 1992). In Bulgaria, following the Soviet pattern, a men's and a women's quota (usually a ratio of 50:50) operates in selecting students for higher education (Sretenova, 1994). In some technical institutes the men:women ratio is 60:40, and in dramatic arts it is 70:30 (Sretenova, 1994). But in the main, the gains women have made relative to men—particularly in higher education—are a result of the mobilization of a female labor force, on the one hand, and the provision of a universal and unitary system of public education, on the other. These gains have coexisted with and been influenced by traditional ideas of gender difference. Research has shown that in Poland women attach more importance than men to education per

se as the means to higher social status, whereas men see an improved social position in terms of a combination of education, job, power, and income (Siemien′ska, 1990: 76). Thus, Siemien′ska (1990: 69) sees Polish men as being less interested in higher education and prolonged studies than women, because under communism, in contrast with the prewar period, these were not necessarily routes to higher earnings. Qualifications for the nonmanual work favored by women are obtained at the *lyceum* or at university (Siemien′ska, 1990: 69).

Neither the high rates of female participation in education nor the continuing gendered nature of educational achievement has until now been associated with feminist campaigning in eastern Europe. That is because feminism was itself absent under communism, and despite increasing activism—often with the financial support of the West—the idea of feminism continues to be largely rejected during the period of social transformation in eastern Europe. This lack of receptivity to feminism has to do with the fact that, in the absence of competitive democracy, gender difference has not been felt to be a source of inequality. With the installation of the market, liberal democracy, and liberal civil society, this is likely to change. Liberal civil society is not yet in place in Poland, the country that leads the way as far as "transition" is concerned, but economic liberalism has brought with it the decay of the state educational system and the introduction of a private schooling sector that is likely to favor men—as it did before the war, when parents were less inclined to pay for daughters' than sons' education. There is also a proliferation of new management courses where men predominate. At the turn of the twenty-first century, however, the labor market and the economy itself, rather than the education system, were the major sites for the structuring of a new disadvantage for women. Thus, for example, although girls represented 70 percent of general academic secondary school pupils in 1993–1994 in Poland, they constituted more than 81 percent of unemployed school leavers from this type of school in July 1994. In the case of vocational schools, they represented 43 percent of pupils but 52 percent of unemployed school leavers, and in the case of higher education, 53 percent of students but 63 percent of unemployed graduates (data from Polish Ministry of Labor Statistics).

See Also

DEVELOPMENT: CENTRAL AND EASTERN EUROPE; COMMUNISM; EDUCATION: ACHIEVEMENT; EDUCATION: CURRICULUM IN SCHOOLS; POLITICS AND THE STATE: EASTERN EUROPE; UNEMPLOYMENT

References and Further Reading

Grimm, Susanne, and Uta Meier. 1994. On the disparity of the sexes in German universities. In *World yearbook of education: The gender gap in higher education,* 70–83. London: Kogan Page.

Lithuanian Department of Statistics. 1994. *Lithuanian women.* Vilnius: Lithuanian Department of Statistics.

Polish Ministry of Labor Statistics. 1994. *Polish statistical yearbook.*

Quack, S., and F. Maier. 1994. From state socialism to market economy: Women's employment in East Germany. *Environment and Planning A* 26: 1257–1276.

Siemien´ska, Renata. 1990. *Plec´, Zawo´d, Polityka: Kobiety w z´yciu publicznym w Polsce.* Warsaw: Uniwersytet Warszawski Instytut Socjologii.

Sretenova, Nicolina. 1994. The nation's showcase: Bulgarian academic women between the Scylla of totalitarianism and the Charybdis of change. *World yearbook of education: The gender gap in higher education.* London: Kogan Page.

UNESCO. 1994. *Statistical yearbook 1994.* Paris: UNESCO.

Watson, Peggy. 1992. Gender relations, education, and social change in Poland. *Gender and Education* 4(1–2): 127–147.

———. 1996. Civil society and the politicization of difference in eastern Europe. In Joan Scott and Cora Caplan, eds., *Transitions, environments, translations: The meanings of feminism in contemporary politics.* New York: Routledge.

Peggy Watson

EDUCATION: Equal Opportunities

SEE EQUAL OPPORTUNITIES: EDUCATION.

EDUCATION: Gender Equity

Historically, the education of girls and boys was explicitly different, based on supposed "natural" differences and futures. The formal education of girls was seen as less important than that of boys and was limited and narrowly defined. Students were placed in different schools or rigidly separated where the same building was used, and this division was reflected in the different subjects they were taught. During the 1970s, with the growth of the women's movement in many western countries, these traditional ideas about "women's place" were increasingly challenged, and feminist activists pressured for gender inequalities in education to be addressed.

The terms associated with equity and social justice have no absolute meanings; rather, they are constituted historically and politically and have different meanings in different cultural contexts. The major changes in the framing of gender equity since the 1970s have reflected developments in feminist theory, leading to more sophisticated explanations of the relationship between education and gender inequalities in society. At the same time as these understandings have informed policy developments, the complexities of the issues and the difficulties of making changes in this area have become apparent.

Australia is known internationally for its strong national policy activity and research in the area. However, similar trends have occurred in other parts of the world where gender equity policies have been developed (ten Dam and Volman, 1995).

The initial struggle to achieve gender equity followed research in the late 1960s that documented sex differences in participation and achievement in education. The education of girls first became a policy issue in the early 1970s, and the focus at this time was on increasing participation and retention rates and improving outcomes for girls. Policies drew on liberal feminism and sex-role theory and were underpinned by an equality-of-opportunity approach. During this phase, sexism in education was documented in numerous research studies, and policies focused on "non-sexist education." A significant feature was that the existing structure of schooling was accepted as given—the main challenge was making sure that girls had equal access to educational opportunities. Even where there was a stronger approach—focusing on equal participation and outcomes—the structure and experience of schooling tended to be unquestioned. A good deal of attention at this time was given to issues such as sex differences in subject choices—especially the unequal participation of girls in mathematics and science—and strategies aimed to encourage girls to go into nontraditional areas, such as the trades. By and large these policies operated using a "let's fix up the girls" approach—often referred to as a "deficit approach." Some of the initiatives did help middle-class girls, but gradually feminist educators began to see the curriculum and school organization as the problem rather than the girls themselves.

It became apparent that the "equity and access" approaches failed to challenge patriarchal power relations and that different strategies were needed. Thus followed a stage of reform that was influenced by radical feminism, where there was an attempt to value women's knowledge and experiences and to integrate them into the curriculum. Schooling was seen as "malestream" knowledge, and one important policy focus was the notion of the gender-inclusive curriculum. Policy initiatives during this stage included the introduction of women's studies into the school curriculum, with more attention being given to the use of resources that reflected women's experience. Terminology focused explicitly on "the education of girls," and this focus made it possible to address issues such as sexual harassment—which is addressed through one of the objectives in the *National Policy for the Education of Girls in Australian Schools* (Commonwealth Schools Commission, 1987): the provision of a supportive school environment.

Socialist feminism also became a significant influence, leading to an emphasis on structural aspects of inequality—for instance, on the ways in which the relations of schooling replicated the gender inequalities of the labor market. Socialist feminism was also influential in raising significant questions concerning class and race issues.

In the 1990s, developments built on increasing concerns about sexual harassment and violence, related to a theoretical emphasis on the "construction of gender," influenced by a number of different strands of feminism, including poststructuralist approaches. Feminists began to problematize masculinity and to argue that attempting to deal with the education of girls without also considering boys' issues was misguided and that a relational theoretical approach was necessary. These developments coincided with the "What about the boys?" debates that emerged in response to the increasing educational success of some groups of girls. In this context, the idea that boys had become a disadvantaged group and that the education of girls had "gone too far" gained some currency. A general policy shift toward the use of the term *gender equity* occurred, reflecting both the theoretical move to a "construction of gender" framework and the more strategic move to "hold the line" in the face of a challenge to the policy focus on the education of girls. This shift has resulted in considerable attention to masculinity issues (Gilbert and Gilbert, 1998).

The developments outlined have been broadly chronological because each stage of policy development built on previous understandings (Gilbert, 1996). However, although these broad trends have occurred widely, in no sense has each phase replaced the previous one; rather, vestiges of earlier phases can be found in later policy developments. Indeed, liberal feminist goals, such as equal access to resources, are relevant in debates at the school level over policies to ensure that girls have access to computer laboratories or sporting equipment. And the need for curriculum that takes account of girls' and women's knowledge and experiences, as well as

for an examination of the construction of gender by students themselves, persisted into the twenty-first century.

Finally, there is the important issue of how differences between groups of girls have been acknowledged and addressed in gender equity policies. Although initially policies dealt with girls as if they were a homogeneous group, there has been a growing recognition of the need to take account of difference (Fraser, 1997; Young, 1990). Theoretical work in the late 1990s highlighted the complex ways in which class, gender, and ethnicity, for example, intersect in shaping girls' experience, and policies attempted to address the needs of particular groups of girls. Much of this work also has strategic implications: gender inequalities may have socioeconomic as well as cultural components, demanding a redistributive approach and a recognition of difference (Fraser, 1997). For example, feminist educators may argue for equal access and participation for women in engineering courses, a strategy that plays down gender differences, but they may also argue for special support programs for women going into such courses as an affirmative action strategy, thereby highlighting gender differences. These dilemmas are difficult to resolve: "The best we can do is try to soften the dilemma by finding approaches that minimize conflicts between redistribution and recognition in cases where both must be pursued simultaneously" (Fraser, 1997: 31).

See Also

CURRICULUM TRANSFORMATION MOVEMENT; DIFFERENCE *I and II*; EDUCATION: CURRICULUM IN SCHOOLS; EQUAL OPPORTUNITIES: EDUCATION; FEMINISM: LIBERAL; FEMINISM: RADICAL; FEMINISM: SOCIALIST; SEXUAL HARASSMENT; WOMEN'S STUDIES: OVERVIEW

References and Further Reading

Arnot, Madeleine, and Gaby Weiner, eds. 1993. *Feminism and social justice in education: International perspectives*. London: Falmer.

Commonwealth Schools Commission. 1987. *National policy for the education of girls in Australian schools*. Canberra: Australian Government Publishing Service.

Dam, Geert T. M. ten, and Monique L. L. Volman. 1995. Feminist research and educational policy. *Journal of Education Policy* 10(2): 209–220.

Fraser, N. 1997. *Justice interruptus*. London: Routledge.

Gilbert, Pam. 1996. *Talking about gender: Terminology used in the education of girls policy area and implications for policy priorities and programs*. A Women's Employment, Education, and Training Advisory Group Project. Canberra: Australian Government Publishing Service.

———— and Rob Gilbert. 1998. *Masculinity goes to school.* Sydney: Allen and Unwin.

Kenway, Jane, Sue Willis, Jill Blackmore, and Leonie Rennie. 1997. *Answering back: Girls, boys, and feminism in schools.* Sydney: Allen and Unwin.

Young, Iris Marion. 1990. *Justice and the politics of difference.* Princeton, N.J.: Princeton University Press.

Sandra Taylor

EDUCATION: Gendered Subject Choice

The fact that males and females take different courses in schools is an often concealed but critical part of the organization of education. Male and female students are thereby prepared for different kinds of participation in the adult world, and gender divisions and hierarchies are perpetuated. School becomes gender segregated for most students at key moments, even in coeducational institutions, which promise equal educational opportunity.

Although girls and boys in coeducational schools usually begin their schooling in the same classrooms and studying the same curriculum, as they get older, and as options become available in the school system, they move into different curriculum "tracks" or "streams" or "programs." The closer female students are to the end of their schooling, the more likely they are to be in classrooms where most of the other students are female.

The particular patterns that this segregation takes vary from country to country, reflecting local patterns of allocating work by gender and school systems with various subject traditions. In general, women are enrolled less often in mathematics, science, and technical areas and more often in subjects like languages, the humanities, and domestic science. Vocational subjects like carpentry, engineering, computing, welding, and mechanics tend to be dominated by males. Social service areas like child care, nursing, education, and family studies, as well as clerical and secretarial areas, are dominated by females. The better-paid professional programs like medicine, business, and law have been dominated by men, whereas university programs leading to jobs in social work, teaching, and rehabilitation medicine, for example, are dominated by women. The hierarchies of work are also reflected in the sexual segregation of school programs, with females dominating in programs leading to less well paid areas of work at every level of education.

The reasons for such patterns can be examined in several different ways. One can look to the students themselves and the reasons they give for their choices. One can also look to the educational system, to the social forces that shape the subjects, and their linkages to a gendered labor market.

Research on student choice finds that young women and young men choose courses to prepare for different kinds of work, to find classrooms where they feel confident, interested, and successful, and, often, to be with their friends (Gaskell, 1992). The impact of aspirations for work is clear: students quite sensibly want the courses that will prepare them for and provide the credentials for the jobs they want or expect. Although young women are now aspiring to more participation in the labor force, and in more diverse areas, there are still large differences between the aspirations of young women and young men. Young women gravitate toward a traditionally female labor market, where they think they can find jobs, will not be discriminated against, and will feel comfortable. While believing in equal opportunity, they try to be realistic about what the world offers, and this leads them to a fairly conservative assessment of their chances, especially if they are not academic or from privileged families.

Some of students' choice of subjects is not so future directed, however. The social relations of the school itself affect how likely students are to enroll in courses across traditional gender barriers. Some female students avoid courses that are overwhelmingly male because of the unwelcoming feel (sometimes labeled "chilly climate") of courses that are taught by male teachers to mostly male students (AAUW, 1992; Culley and Portuges, 1985). The courses often assume knowledge that is taken for granted by males but not by females. Assuming students can use tools without instruction, working from analogies with which girls have little familiarity, and speaking only of male contributions to knowledge are three examples of the kinds of curriculum processes that can make female students feel out of place and convince them that such courses are not "interesting" and that they are incompetent. Some research has suggested that girls prefer teaching that is interactive, that relates course content to social issues, and that provides more discussion of context and meaning (Belenky et al., 1990; Gilligan, 1982). This kind of teaching is more frequent in the humanities than in mathematics and science.

Students also choose courses that their friends take. Young women fear the sexual harassment and stigma that can be associated with their enrollment in overwhelmingly male courses. School is as much a social as an academic setting for young people, and social support from peers is key for success.

The notion that students "choose" a program of studies ignores the historical and social context that determines the structure and organization of what is available to be chosen. Schools have required female students to take certain courses, particularly courses related to domestic work, and required male students to take others. Language instruction remains compulsory longer than mathematics and science, which prevents males from "choosing" to avoid instruction in reading or writing, whereas females can avoid math. A schedule that forces students to choose either cooking or technology courses will encourage gender segregation, whereas a schedule that requires all students to take some of each diminishes gender differences. Subject enrollments change as the labor market changes (Rury, 1991).

The organization and content of the school curriculum reflect shared and historically specific notions of what public schooling should teach. The Japanese system emphasizes the same academic courses for all students, whereas the German system has a more differentiated and vocational curriculum that becomes quite differentiated by gender (Bash and Green, 1995). In North America, employers have historically been reluctant to invest in the education of women, so vocational preparation for female-dominated sectors of the labor market like teaching and clerical work has often been vested in the schools, whereas preparation for male areas like business and apprenticeship has been done on the job. In some places in the Middle East and in the former Soviet Union, women filled jobs in engineering and medicine, and school enrollments reflected labor market opportunities.

Making the gendered nature of enrollment in school subjects an issue that concerns educators and policy makers has been a struggle. The statistics on enrollments are not often reported publicly, making the problem relatively easy to conceal. In many countries, equal opportunity legislation has been used to end requirements that males and females take different courses, but attacking the underlying social processes that continue to result in girls "choosing" different courses from boys is more difficult. In third world countries, increased attention to the role of women in economic development by key players like the World Bank has led, on the one hand, to more public discussion of encouraging women in math and science and, on the other hand, to more emphasis on specific vocational education that reflects the different roles men and women play. In North America, women's enrollments in previously male-dominated fields at universities have dramatically increased, but change in clerical and blue-collar vocational areas has been minimal. However, school-based strategies to encourage girls in science have increased in many school districts.

There is some evidence that gender differences in subject choice are beginning to decrease among more educated women and in wealthier countries, but the problem remains a significant one that eludes simple large-scale solutions. Attracting women into traditionally male areas must be accompanied by attempts to desegregate labor markets, create inclusive classrooms, and revalue those areas of the curriculum, like child care, nursing, clerical work, and teaching, where women have predominated and men show few signs of moving.

See Also

EDUCATION: CHILLY CLIMATE IN THE CLASSROOM; EDUCATION: CURRICULUM IN SCHOOLS; EDUCATION: DOMESTIC SCIENCE AND HOME ECONOMICS; EDUCATION: MATHEMATICS; EDUCATION: SCIENCE; EQUAL OPPORTUNITIES: EDUCATION; WORK: OCCUPATIONAL SEGREGATION

References and Further Reading

American Association of University Women (AAUW). 1992. *How schools shortchange girls: A study of major findings on girls and education.* Washington, D.C.: AAUW and the National Education Association.

Bash, Leslie, and Andy Green. 1995. *Youth, education, and work: World yearbook of education.* London: Kogan Page.

Belenky, Mary, Beverly Clinchy, Nancy Goldberger, and Jane Tarule. 1990. *Women's ways of knowing.* New York: Basic.

Cockburn, Cynthia. 1987. *Two track training.* London: Macmillan.

Culley, Margo, and Catherine Portuges. 1985. *Gendered subjects.* London: Routledge and Kegan Paul.

Gaskell, Jane. 1992. *Gender matters from school to work.* Milton Keynes, U.K.: Open University Press.

Gilligan, Carol. 1982. *In a different voice.* Cambridge, Mass.: Harvard University Press.

Harlan, Sharon, and Ronnie Steinberg. 1989. *Job training for women.* Philadelphia: Temple University Press.

Rury, John. 1991. *Education and women's work: Female schooling and the division of labor in urban America, 1870–1930.* Albany: State University of New York Press.

Jane Gaskell

EDUCATION: Globalization

See GLOBALIZATION OF EDUCATION.